Selected Data for the United States

Year	Population (thousands)	Civilian Unemployment Rate (%)	Civilian Employment Rate (%)	Median Family Income (1987 dollars)	Consumer Price Index (1982–84 = 100)	Change in Consumer Price Index (%)	Change in M2 Money Supply (%)
1929	121,767	3.2					
1933	125,579	24.9					
1939	130,880	17.2					
1940	132,122	14.6	47.6				
1941	133,402	9.9	50.4				
1942	134,860	4.7	54.5				
1943	136,739	1.9	57.6				
1944	138,397	1.2	57.9				
1945	139,928	1.9	56.1				
1946	141,389	3.9	53.6		19.5		
1947	144,126	3.9	56.0		22.3	14.4	
1948	146,631	3.8	56.6		24.1	8.1	
1949	149,188	5.9	55.4		23.8	−1.2	
1950	152,271	5.3	56.1		24.1	1.3	
1951	154,878	3.3	57.3		26.0	7.9	
1952	157,553	3.0	57.3		26.5	1.9	
1953	160,184	2.9	57.1		26.7	0.9	
1954	163,026	5.5	55.5		26.9	0.7	
1955	165,931	4.4	56.7		26.8	−0.4	
1956	168,903	4.1	57.5		27.2	1.5	
1957	171,984	4.3	57.1		28.1	3.3	
1958	174,882	6.8	55.4		28.9	2.8	
1959	177,830	5.5	56.0		29.1	0.7	
1960	180,671	5.5	56.1		29.6	1.7	4.9
1961	183,691	6.7	55.4		29.9	1.0	7.4
1962	186,538	5.5	55.5		30.2	1.0	8.1
1963	189,242	5.7	55.4		30.6	1.3	8.4
1964	191,889	5.2	55.7		31.0	1.3	8.0
1965	194,303	4.5	56.2	25,060	31.5	1.6	8.1
1966	196,560	3.8	56.9	26,377	32.4	2.9	4.5
1967	198,712	3.8	57.3	27,004	33.4	3.1	9.2
1968	200,706	3.6	57.5	28,199	34.8	4.2	8.0
1969	202,677	3.5	58.0	29,244	36.7	5.5	4.1
1970	205,052	4.9	57.4	28,880	38.8	5.7	6.5
1971	207,661	5.9	56.6	28,862	40.5	4.4	13.5
1972	209,896	5.6	57.0	30,199	41.8	3.2	13.0
1973	211,909	4.9	57.8	30,820	44.4	6.2	6.9
1974	213,854	5.6	57.8	29,735	49.3	11.0	5.5
1975	215,973	8.5	56.1	28,970	53.8	9.1	12.6
1976	218,035	7.7	56.8	29,863	56.9	5.8	13.7
1977	220,239	7.1	57.9	30,025	60.6	6.5	10.6
1978	222,585	6.1	59.3	30,730	65.2	7.6	8.0
1979	225,055	5.8	59.9	30,669	72.6	11.3	8.0
1980	227,757	7.1	59.2	28,996	82.4	13.5	8.9
1981	230,138	7.6	59.0	27,977	90.9	10.3	9.9
1982	232,520	9.7	57.8	27,591	96.5	6.2	8.8
1983	234,799	9.6	57.9	28,147	99.6	3.2	11.8
1984	237,001	7.5	59.5	28,923	103.9	4.3	8.2
1985	239,279	7.2	60.1	29,302	107.6	3.6	8.4
1986	241,613	7.0	60.7	30,534	109.6	1.9	9.6
1987	243,915	6.2	61.5	30,853	113.6	3.6	3.3
1988	246,113	5.5	62.3		118.3	4.1	5.1

Source: *Economic Report of the President,* 1989, Tables B-30, B-31, B-32, B-33, B-58, B-61, B-67; and *Survey of Current Business,* May 1989, pp. S-5, S-9, S-10, S-15.

ECONOMICS

Third Edition

Martin Bronfenbrenner

Aoyama Gakuin University, Japan
Professor Emeritus, Duke University

Werner Sichel

Western Michigan University

Wayland Gardner

Western Michigan University

HOUGHTON MIFFLIN COMPANY   BOSTON
Dallas   Geneva, Illinois   Palo Alto   Princeton, New Jersey

We dedicate our efforts on this third edition to our colleagues who prescribe our text and ancillary package to their students as the most efficacious and painless remedy for the common ailment of economic ignorance.

MB WS WG

CREDITS

Cover painting by Glenn R. Bradshaw.
Photograph by David Caras.

We gratefully acknowledge the following sources for providing photographs used in this book: Part I essay—Brown Brothers; Culver Pictures. Part II essay—Wide World. Part III essay—Bettmann Archive. Part IV essay—Bettmann Archive; Photo Researchers. Part V essay—UPI/Bettmann Newsphotos; Patricia Evans/University of Chicago; The Hoover Institution/Stanford University. Part VI essay—Wide World. Part VII essay—Historical Pictures Service. Part VIII essay—Wide World; Jeff Albertson/Stock Boston; Daniel Brody/Stock Boston. Part IX essay—UPI/Bettmann Newsphotos; Wide World. Part X essay—Wide World. Part XI essay—Brown Brothers; Bettmann Archive; Wide World.

Preface

As in the first two editions, our goal in this third edition was to write a textbook that will fulfill the needs of students and instructors concerned with the well-established as well as the controversial topics in economics. We believe that a beginning text should (1) be open-minded and strive to present the best in all schools of thought especially where there is disagreement, (2) be thorough and realistic in the presentation of material that is generally accepted, (3) be flexible and be oriented to a broad view in matters such as international trade, economic development, and comparative economic systems, and (4) above all, be as accessible to introductory economics students as possible.

We believe that the characteristics of our book are as appropriate in the 1990s as they were in the 1980s. We also believe that they form the foundation for the type of "economic literacy" that will allow students to understand the *applicability* of economic principles beyond the specific applications in any one topic or any one period of time.

We feel this edition is a substantial enhancement of the previous edition. The changes are not minor, cosmetic, tune-ups of a few parts. In some key areas—particularly in macroeconomics—the changes amount to a significant overhaul. Some of the more important improvements are noted as follows.

MACROECONOMICS

We have made major improvements in our sections on macroeconomics. There is a significant amount of new material and much of the old material has been revised. The new material includes a substantially expanded treatment of rational expectations, new classical economics, neo-Keynesian economics, and post-Keynesian economics, as well as several up-to-date applications of monetary economics. Here is a list of some of the new macro features of our third edition, in the order of their appearance.

1. The first chapter of the macro section now contains the circular-flow model which previously we introduced in a later chapter. Our experience with the first and second editions shows that students find our circular-flow illustration—which includes both government and international trade—to be an extremely useful overview of macroeconomics. In the third edition, we use this illustration to introduce the subject and to provide students with a way to maintain their perspective as they work through specific macro models.

2. The basic aggregate-demand and aggregate-supply format for macroeconomics is also

introduced in the first chapter of the macro section. Our introductory explanation of the *AD-AS* model includes effective illustrations of macroeconomic equilibrium and disequilibrium, but is nevertheless simple enough for presentation at the start of the macro course. This thoroughly reliable but no-frills approach to the *AD-AS* system is repeated in the chapter on economic fluctuations and in introducing both the Keynesian and the monetarist models when they appear. In this way, the *AD-AS* system provides continuity throughout the macro section and the Keynesian and monetarist models are developed according to their roles in a full modern macro system.

3. The subject of economic fluctuations (cast in the aggregate-demand and aggregate-supply framework) is now the fourth chapter in the initial macro part, following chapters on the *AD-AS* model, national income accounting, and inflation and unemployment. This substantially revised fluctuations chapter provides a lead-in for the Keynesian and monetarist models of income determination. Fluctuations are explained as movements along and shifts of aggregate-demand and aggregate-supply curves, thus providing useful practice in the *AD-AS* way of thinking.

4. We have streamlined our presentation of the basic Keynesian model. It now requires only two, easily teachable chapters. This has been accomplished by moving the fluctuations material forward to the earlier section (as noted) and by placing our discussion of deficits and the national debt in an appendix.

5. In our chapter on the Federal Reserve System, we have added new material on interest-rate and borrowed-reserves targeting in the operation of monetary policy and a discussion of the problems of deposit insurance, nonbank banks, and interstate banking, all topics that receive a great deal of attention in the media.

6. Our chapter on monetary economics has been substantially revised and strengthened. It now includes an aggregate-demand and aggregate-supply illustration of the quantity-of-money theory. We also have added emphasis on anticipated, as contrasted with unanticipated, inflation and have strengthened (with graphic illustration) our explanation of inflationary expectations.

7. The first chapter of the final part in the macro section uses the Keynesian and monetarist models that have just been covered to develop the aggregate-demand and aggregate-supply model in greater detail than was possible earlier in the course. The *AD-AS* model is then applied (in the following chapter) to the subject of inflation, starting with the Phillips curve and proceeding through the adaptive-expectations (Friedman-Phelps) model. This chapter focuses on policy alternatives for an economy in which inflationary expectations are a problem.

8. An integrated treatment of rational expectations, new classical economics, neo-Keynesian economics, post-Keynesian economics, and supply-side economics is presented in the next-to-last chapter in the macro section. This chapter, most of which is new to this edition, provides students with a way to further recognize, analyze, and synthesize modern schools of macroeconomic thought. It includes an explanation of the Lucas supply curve as well as an elementary *IS-LM* model which may be omitted without loss of continuity.

9. The final macro chapter, ''Macroeconomics as a Branch of Knowledge,'' is a brand new chapter. It begins with the question: ''Is macroeconomics a science?'' We suggest that the answer to this question is ''yes,'' but that macroeconomics is a relatively immature science, likely to experience significant revision in its future development. It is, however, a science worthy of serious study. By recognizing the scientific aspects of macroeconomics, students can begin to understand the economist's role, albeit a difficult one, in forecasting future trends in the economy. This chapter also considers public choice viewpoints on the federal government's deficit and poses questions concerning debt policy in the event of a serious recession.

Two additional points should be noted about improvements in the macro section of our third edition. First, we have used appendices to chapters more than in the previous editions—one for the leakages-and-injections presentation of the basic Keynesian system, one for the national debt, and one for the history of monetary policy. We have learned from colleagues around the country that they appreciate the flexibility that this system offers. Second, and most important, though this edition contains considerably more material than the second edition, we are confident in saying—and our many reviewers agree—that the reorganization and revisions add so much to clarify and apply the content that students will find the material considerably *easier* to comprehend and enjoy.

MICROECONOMICS

Our material on microeconomics continues to be thorough, interesting, and timely. In this edition we have added some important new material. We have increased our focus on transactions costs, uncertainty, and the role of information in our discussion of business firm choice. In addition, in analyzing oligopoly, we have added new material on leveraged buy-outs that have gained so much attention in recent years.

Several new topics appear in our section on applied microeconomics. Homelessness, panhandling, gender discrimination, and the issues surrounding compulsory labor as a condition for receipt of government assistance have been added to our discussion of poverty and income redistribution. Similarly, our chapter on "International Microeconomics: Free Trade versus Protection" now includes material on administrative protection ("dirty tricks") and market-opening strategies that countries use to combat such actions. These market-opening strategies are called "protection against protection." Our chapter on agriculture goes into greater detail than before on the farm debt crisis. In that chapter, we also have added a discussion of the implications of a drought, such as the one experienced in 1988, and of the "greenhouse effect."

INTERNATIONAL ECONOMICS

We have received much praise for our innovative international coverage and, if emulation is a form of flattery, we have been amply flattered. Our treatment of international economics is even stronger in our third edition. Perhaps the most important feature of our treatment of international economics is that it is an integral part of our chapters on basic macroeconomics. Since international trade and finance are part of the macro model from the very beginning, students do not have to "unlearn" later the model that they were taught earlier. Furthermore, the chapters that focus directly on international economics are not tucked away at the end of the book (as they are in most texts) where they can easily fall victim to the end-of-the-semester rush or appear to be an afterthought. Instead, they appear along with the regular macro and micro chapters.

We have added new material on both the macro and the micro dimensions of international economics. We present a set of macroeconomic identities that show the inherent relationships between the U.S. trade deficit, government budget deficits, and the relatively low saving rate in the U.S. economy. In the microeconomics context, we show that the U.S. trade deficit extends to most of our trading partners and cannot be blamed solely on Japanese "dirty tricks."

ECONOMIC GROWTH AND DEVELOPMENT

In our third edition, economic growth and economic development each has its own chapter, rather than sharing a single chapter as in our earlier editions. Both chapters include significant amounts of new material. The growth chapter explores the consequences of aging populations and examines, more deeply than before, the impact of growth on the environment. In the development chapter, we have added a section on the history and problems of Third-World debt.

COMPARATIVE-SYSTEMS COVERAGE

Gorbachev and *perestroika* provide new material for our chapter on comparative economic systems. We also have new material on "Taking Japan Seriously," showing the Japanese economic system as a modern version of a *corporate society* described as "in the neighborhood of capitalism." In our chapter on radical economics, we have added new material on the present status and future prospects of the New Left.

TOPICAL ESSAYS

We continue to offer thought-provoking essays at the close of each of the eleven parts of the book. Six (*) of the eleven are new or substantially revised for the third edition:

- Classical Economics: The Dismal Science?
- * The Gross Anatomy of Gross Unemployment
- John Maynard Keynes and the Great Depression
- * Economics of Inflation
- * Macroeconomic Policy: The New Frontier and After
- * Japanese-American Economic Warfare?
- Neoclassical Economics: The Complacent Science
- Living with Oligopoly
- * "Fairness" in Industrial Relations—and Beyond
- * Regulation, Deregulation, Reregulation: The S&L Case
- From Karl Marx to the New Left

These essays lead the student beyond the regular text material and show a broader perspective to the subject covered.

"ECONOMICS IN FOCUS" APPLICATIONS OF ECONOMIC PRINCIPLES

As an entirely new feature of our third edition, we close each chapter with a brief, real-world application of some topic covered in the chapter. For example, at the close of our chapter on the Federal Reserve System, our *Economics in Focus* application

is called "The FED Divided" and describes differences of opinion concerning monetary policy among members of the Board of Governors and other members of the Federal Open Market Committee. Following our initial chapter on "What Economics Is" the *Economics in Focus* application compares contrasting contemporary reports on the question "Is Socialism Dying?" In the "Government and Taxation" chapter, the *Economics in Focus* application describes the 1986 tax reforms and questions the achievement of a simplified tax code. These new additions to our text put economics "in focus." They are designed to help the student bridge the gap between textbook explanations and real-world applications of economic models.

INSTRUCTIONAL USE OF COLOR

With a virtually unlimited array of colors available for our third edition, we have carefully developed a consistent color-coding system for our art program. Rather than using color, as do most economics books, as a decorative or highlighting tool, our color system promotes the understanding of economic concepts and relationships. This is true for both our graphs and tables.

First, the consistent color-coding system helps students recognize economic relationships in the graphs and follow the logic of the analysis. For example, a particular curve—such as supply, demand, marginal cost, marginal revenue, average cost, average revenue, aggregate demand, aggregate supply, and so on—is printed in the same color every time it appears. When a curve is shifted, it retains its original color, but with less intensity.

Second, to further clarify the underlying economic meaning, tables are consistently color-coded to appropriate graphs. For example, in the total planned expenditure and macroeconomic equilibrium table, the numerical values below the equilibrium level are shaded to correspond to the same shading of values in the macroeconomic equilibrium graph. Values above the equilibrium level in the table are shaded in a different color; the shading is repeated appropriately in the graph. The equilibrium values are not shaded.

We believe that our efforts result in a dramatic improvement over the art in other texts because our colors are purposeful. Color mobilizes an additional dimension of the human senses and puts it to work in the learning process.

INNOVATIVE LEARNING AIDS

We, and the people at Houghton Mifflin, have made concerted efforts to make our text material ultimately accessible to students. We have retained the well-received glossary, index, end-of-chapter summaries, and end-of-chapter discussion questions (some of them new) from the earlier editions. We have added two innovative learning aids—easy reference text notes and key terms at chapter ends. Therefore, we now offer:

1. **Glossary** A very thorough glossary that is both conceptual and descriptive. These definitions are useful reference tools in that they are more comprehensively written than the key terms.

2. **Index** Our index is considered the most comprehensive listing in the market. As with previous editions, we have included both conceptual and descriptive entries with much cross-referencing.

3. **Discussion Questions at Chapter Ends** Each chapter concludes with a list of questions that are useful for classroom discussion or a student's individual study. We have purposefully chosen questions that will generate interesting analysis and commentary.

4. **Summary at Chapter Ends** Summary statements are listed at the end of each chapter and are page-referenced to the body of the text. These statements allow students to quickly review the most important topics and concepts in each chapter.

5. **Easy Reference Text Notes** Throughout the text, bold-faced "text notes" concisely state the fundamental ideas of the material just covered. They provide instant reinforcement for the student as he or she studies the text.

The text notes assure that the preceding material is well understood before the student goes on to the next topic.

6. **Key Terms at Chapter Ends** Key terms, carefully defined in the context of the material of the particular chapter, are listed alphabetically at the end of each chapter so that the student can build his or her economics vocabulary as he or she proceeds through the course. Each key term is page-referenced to where the topic is defined and discussed in the body of the text. For reference purposes, the key terms are repeated with more general definitions in the glossary at the back of the book.

COMPLETE ANCILLARY PACKAGE

Our ancillaries are better than ever. They were developed to make the myriad of economic concepts more accessible to both instructors and students. Our computer-assisted interactive learning system is new. We have multicolor transparencies (some with overlays) and many new questions in our revised test bank, plus an altogether new test bank. Here is a list of the ancillaries.

1. **Instructor's Manual** Prepared by the text authors, the instructor's manual provides, for each chapter, a schematic outline, teaching tips about especially important or difficult points, and condensed answers to the end-of-chapter discussion questions. The manual also includes transparency masters for all the figures and all the tables in the text.

2. **Study Guide** Prepared by Dr. Rose Pfefferbaum, Mesa Community College, our study guide is recognized as one of the best in the industry. For each chapter, it contains a summary, a list of learning objectives, review terms, new terms, completion exercises, problems and applications, sample true-false questions, sample multiple-choice questions, and discussion questions.

3. **Test Banks** With this edition we publish two complete test banks: SERIES 1 (Chapters 1–40) and SERIES II (Chapters 1–40). In to-

tal, our test banks offer over 5,000 multiple-choice questions with a significant percentage of items requiring graphical analysis. Questions are coded for level of difficulty and type.

4. **Overhead Transparencies** We provide our adopters with over 150 multicolored overhead transparencies. Fifteen percent of these overheads are produced as overlays, allowing instructors to visually demonstrate the dynamic nature of economics.

For the Computer

5. **PC Test Bank Plus** All of our test questions are available free of charge to our adopters, on computer disk in IBM PC, PS/2 and compatibles, and Apple Macintosh format. PC Test Bank Plus is an innovative test assembly program that saves time and assures accuracy. The program renders precise, pre-programmed graphs on the computer which eliminates the need to draw graphs or paste them in place.

   In addition to this offering, adopters can use Houghton Mifflin's Call-in Test Service for test generation.

6. **Computerized Macroeconomics and Microeconomics Tutorial Package** New to this edition is an exciting tutorial program consisting of over 15 modules. Providing students with a highly interactive environment that fully utilizes the dynamic capabilities of the computer, each module reviews the major concepts in a single chapter and then asks questions that allow students to change variables to interact with appropriate graphs. Students are scored at the end of each module. For questions that they did not answer correctly, students are referred back to the text discussion via actual page numbers. Available to adopters for IBM PC, PS/2, and compatible computers.

7. **Computerized Macroeconomics and Microeconomics Simulation** New to this edition is a highly dynamic simulation program consisting of over 15 modules. Each module asks students to apply their chapter knowledge to a real-world situation. By assuming various jobs that require economic un-

derstanding, students must make economic decisions and evaluate the consequences. Unlike most simulation packages, ours is highly graphical, thereby furthering analytical education. In addition, when a student has problems with a particular decision, they are referred back to both the text and appropriate tutorial module. Available to adopters for IBM PC, PS/2, and compatible computers.

8. **Computerized Study Guide** With this edition we offer a brand new computerized version of the printed Study Guide. When questions are answered incorrectly, explanations are offered to guide the students to the correct answer. Available to adopters for IBM PC, PS/2, and compatible computers.

9. **Computerized Instructor's Handbook** This ancillary includes lecture outlines for each chapter. Instructors can modify these lecture files using any commercial word processor to produce personalized lecture notes, course syllabi, or handouts for use in the classroom. Available to adopters for IBM PC, PS/2, and Apple Macintosh computers.

SEQUENCE ALTERNATIVES

Macro-Micro Sequence

In this book, macroeconomics appears before microeconomics because this is the sequence used somewhat more often than the reverse in two-semester principles of economics programs. However, we have planned the book to serve equally well with a micro-first sequence. Chapters 1 through 5 come at the start of the first semester under either sequence. In a micro-first sequence, these chapters are followed by the micro material beginning with Chapter 22. The chapters on comparative economic systems (Chapters 39 and 40) can be included in either the macro or the micro semester of a two-semester sequence.

International Economics

We have also designed the book for maximum flexibility in presenting the chapters on international economics. Chapter 36 ("International Microeconomics: Free Trade versus Protection") can be inserted immediately following Chapter 19 ("Exchange Rates, International Balances, and International Finance") in order to obtain a single section on international economics. Moreover, that section (consisting of Chapters 19, 20, 21, and 36) can be covered in either the macroeconomics or the microeconomics portion of a two-semester course sequence.

THE AUTHORS

Each of us has instructed thousands of students in elementary economics. We have used many different texts, and each of us has taught many parts of the subject—micro, macro, international, comparative systems, and points between and beyond. Each of us has his areas of special interest. Also, we have learned a lot from each other and from the experience of writing and revising our first two editions. Therefore, the final product is far less the work of three individuals than it is the combined efforts of a team. Each chapter is the result of the cooperative efforts of all the authors. The result, we believe, is far superior to what any one of us could have accomplished alone.

ACKNOWLEDGMENTS

It is a pleasure to acknowledge the help we have received in writing this book and preparing it for publication. Since Martin Bronfenbrenner was a visiting professor at Western Michigan University in 1989, all three of us are able to express our gratitude to our colleagues who shared generously their knowledge of economics and their teaching insights. Especially helpful were Sisay Asefa, Phillip Caruso, Kevin Collins, Bassam Harik, Salim Harik, Wei Chiao Huang, William Kern, Jon Neill, Susan Pozo, Theo Sypris, and Raymond Zelder. Also, we benefited from conversations with a former colleague, Barry Krissoff, now with the United States Department of Agriculture, and with a long-time friend, Harry Trebing, professor of economics at Michigan State University. All three of us are grateful for the typing services of Bonnie Guminski and Becky Ryder.

Especially helpful reviews were provided by Professor David Colander of Wesleyan University and by Professor Nancy Jianakoplos of Michigan State University; also Ira Gang of Rutgers University, Harry Holzer of Michigan State University, Pradeep Kotamraju of the University of Minnesota, Harry Landreth of Centre College, Lester Manderschied of Michigan State University, Emlyn Norman of Texas Southern University, Susan Pozo of Western Michigan University, Gerald Sazama of the University of Connecticut, Robert Stuart of Rutgers University, and Jay Sultan of Arizona State University. Rose Pfefferbaum provided especially thoughtful comments as she studied the manuscript in preparing the Study Guide. Insights and inspiration were received from six Nobel Laureate economists (Kenneth Arrow, James Buchanan, Lawrence Klein, Herbert Simon, Robert Solow, and James Tobin) who lectured on "The State of Economic Science" at Western Michigan University during the 1988–1989 academic year.

In the previous two editions, we received expert advice from many reviewers. We are very grateful for their comments which resulted in two very successful editions and the foundation for what promises to be the best edition yet.

David Abel
Mankato State University

Jack Adams
University of Arkansas

Richard Agnello
University of Delaware

J. Barry
Fordham University

Philip Bartholomew
University of Michigan

Paul T. Bechtol
Ohio State University

Klaus Becker
University of Kansas

Carolyn Shaw Bell
Wellesley College

Robert E. Berry
Miami University, Ohio

Calvin Blair
Wilson College

Paul Blume
Hanover College

Joe Brum
Fayetteville Technical Institute

E. Buchholz
Santa Monica College

J. Alvin Carter
Catawba College

Phillip Caruso
Western Michigan University

J. Cavallo
College of Mt. St. Vincent

Ming Chow
Kansas State University

K. Chu
California State University

Charles Cole
California State University

Robert Collier
Western Washington University

Michael T. Cook
William Jewell College

Eleanor Craig
University of Delaware

James M. Cypher
California State University, Fresno

Michael T. Doyle
University of Nebraska, Omaha

Peter Eelkema
University of Kansas

William Field
Depauw University

Max E. Fletcher
University of Idaho

Carroll Foster
University of Michigan

R. Freed
*California State University,
  Dominguez Hills*

Mark Gardner
Emory & Henry College

Ann Garrison
University of Northern Colorado

Kathie Gilbert
Mississippi State University

Otis W. Gilley
University of Texas, Austin

Constantine Glezakos
*California State University,
  Long Beach*

Douglas Gordon
Arapahoe Community College

A. Grow
Mesa Community College

Nicholas D. Grunt
Tarrant County Junior College

George Hartley
Northwestern State University

Curtis Harvey
University of Kentucky

Frank Hefner
Washburn University

Ali Hekmat
Western Washington University

Robert E. Herman
Nassau Community College

C. A. Hofmann
Idaho State University

Donald Holley
Boise State University

Estelle Horowitz
Pratt Institute

Brooks Hull
University of Michigan

Paul C. Huszar
Colorado State University

Harry Hutchinson
University of Delaware

Eric Jacobson
University of Delaware

Jack L. Jeppesen
Cerritos College

Stanley R. Keil
Ball State University

Larry Kendra
Cuyahoga Community College

Dan Knighton
Moorhead State University

A. Kohen
James Madison University

R. Kolinski
University of Michigan

B. Lanciaux
Hobart & William Smith College

John Larson
University of Oregon

Soyen Lee
Illinois Benedictine College

E. Liebhafsky
University of Houston, Clear Lake

M. London
Butte College

Alan B. Mandelstamm
*Virginia Polytechnic Institute &
  State University*

Gabriel Manrique
Quincy College

Wolfgang Mayer
University of Cincinnati

Michelle McAlpin
Tufts University

Roger McCain
*City University of New York,
  Brooklyn College*

Norris McClain
Old Dominion University

Joan M. McCrea
University of Texas, Arlington

Jesse Mercer
College of the Albemarle

Ellen Miller
University of North Carolina

Jack Minkoff
Pratt Institute

Eric Mitchell
University of New Hampshire

Gary Mongiovi
St. John's University

R. B. Moore
U.S. Naval Academy

W. Morrison
Mesa Community College

Joseph Murray
Community College of Philadelphia

P. J. Nickless
University of North Carolina

T. Lee Norman
Idaho State University

James O'Neill
University of Delaware

Carl D. Parker
Ft. Hayes State University

Peter Penndorf
Quinsigamond Community College

R. D. Peterson
Colorado State University

Rose Pfefferbaum
Mesa Community College

John Pisciotta
University of Southern Colorado

Dean Popp
San Diego State University

John A. Powers
University of Cincinnati

Myron Re
Gogebic Community College

Mike Reed
University of Nevada

Terry Riddle
Central Virginia Community College

Richard Roehl
University of Michigan

G. Roth
Hofstra University

Lars G. Sandberg
Ohio State University

Paul J. Schmitt
St. Clair County Community College

Carole Scott
West Georgia College

William Shingleton
Ball State University

Arlene Silvers
Drexel University

Nat Simons
Ohio State University

Gordon Skinner
University of Cincinnati

Charles Skoro
Boise State University

Russell E. Smith
Washburn University

J. Ronald Stanfield
Colorado State University

M. Dudley Stewart, Jr.
Stephen F. Austin State University

Barry Stregeusky
Ball State University

Emily Sun
Manhattan College

Gilbert Suzawa
University of Rhode Island

W. Swift
Hofstra University

K. Taylor
University of Southern California

Tom Till
St. Andrew's Presbyterian College

Ralph Townsend
University of Maine

John F. Walker
Portland State University

Harold L. Wattel
Hofstra University

Charles Weber
University of Michigan

James Wible
University of New Hampshire

Jeffrey J. Wright
Bryant College

William Wood
University of Virginia

Werner Sichel wishes especially to thank Peter Eckstein, his co-author of a previous book, *Basic Economic Concepts,* for his efforts on that volume, which have surely carried over and benefited this one. While Werner Sichel was very careful to use only examples and other material that he had initially contributed, he is indebted to Peter Eckstein for helping him to develop his ideas and materials for the earlier book.

All three of us acknowledge the help of students who, over the years, have plied us with questions that remained in our minds long after the answer was given. And, most importantly, each of us wants to acknowledge the help and support from family members who did without our company, sacrificed vacations, and in many ways were essential to the completion of the project. We trust that they understand the depth of our appreciation.

We also want to thank the many people at Houghton Mifflin who worked hard and well to create an attractive finished product.

M.B.   W.S.   W.G.

Contents in Brief

The Complete Teaching/Learning System

- *Economics*, the hardcover text
- *Macroeconomics* and *Microeconomics*, paperbacks. International trade, comparative economic systems, and radical economics chapters included in both volumes.
- *Instructor's Manual*, prepared by the text authors. Provides for each chapter:

  Schematic Outline

  Teaching Notes

  Suggested answers to all discussion questions in the text

  The Instructor's Manual also provides transparency masters for all figures and tables in the text; and instructions for using the computerized Test Bank.

- *Study Guide*, by Rose Pfefferbaum, Mesa Community College. Provides for each chapter:

  Summary

  List of Objectives

  Review Terms

  New Terms

  Completion Exercises

  Problems and Applications

  True-False Questions

  Multiple-Choice Questions

  Discussion Questions

- *Test Banks*, Series I: Chapters 1–40, prepared by the text authors with Rose Pfefferbaum, Mesa Community College; Series II: Chapters 1–40, prepared by the text authors and Ronald Cipcic of Kalamazoo Community College and Western Michigan University.
- *Overhead Transparencies*, over 150 including overlays.

For the Computer

- *PC Test Bank Plus*, computerized Test Bank in IBM PC, PS/2 and compatibles, and Apple Macintosh formats.
- *Computerized Macro and Micro Tutorial Package*, over 15 modules available for IBM PC, PS/2, and compatible computers.
- *Computerized Study Guide*, available for IBM PC, PS/2, and compatible computers.
- *Computerized Instructor's Handbook*, available for IBM PC, PS/2, and Apple Macintosh computers.

Contents

V INFLATION, EXPECTATIONS, AND CONTEMPORARY MACROECONOMIC THOUGHT

PART I
INTRODUCTION
TO ECONOMICS

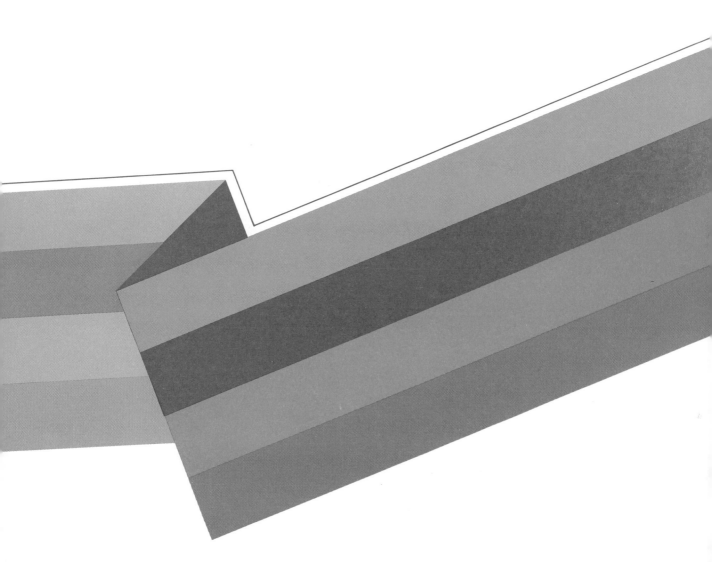

1

What Economics Is

Preview Surely you have heard at least one of the following opinions: "Economists know the price of everything and the value of nothing." "Economists have an irrational passion for dispassionate rationality." "Supply and demand—that's all there is to economics. The rest is nonsense." "If economics were a science, the economists would have all the money, and the rest of us would be broke." "Economics is about what everyone knows in language nobody understands." "Economists are a bunch of do-gooders who want to create a welfare state." "Economists are stooges and mouthpieces of Wall Street; they are for sale to the highest bidder." "If you stretched all the economists end to end, it would be a good thing, but they would reach no conclusion." Notice that some of these criticisms are inconsistent with others. Any of them may be true of one or more particular economists, but they cannot *all* be true of *all* economists (or of economics) at the same time.

This chapter gives an overview of what economics is. After some formal definitions of the subject, we consider its two main divisions, microeconomics and macroeconomics. Microeconomics focuses on individual decision makers, like consumers and business firms, whereas macroeconomics deals with the overall performance of the economy. We also examine economic growth and development, which consider how economies may change over time.

After surveying the basic content of economics, we explore how economic systems are organized to deal with economic problems. Some are organized around systems of markets; others are based on planning. Similarly, some are based on private property ownership and others have collectivist agencies that own the tools of production.

We close by listing a set of criteria that might be used to decide which type of economic system works best. We stress, however, that each person must use his or her own values in answering that sort of question. Our list can only start you thinking about this subject.

WHAT IS ECONOMICS?

Many definitions have been offered for **economics**. Most focus on either (a) the problems that economists usually deal with or (b) the methods that economists use in dealing with these problems. An example of the "problem" type of definition is the following, taken from a widely used textbook:

> Economics can be defined as the social science concerned with the problem of using or administering scarce resources (the means of producing) so as to attain the greatest or maximum fulfillment of society's unlimited wants (the goal of producing).[1]

An example of the "methods" type of definition comes from the famous economist John Maynard Keynes (1883–1946), who said,

> It [economics] is a method rather than a doctrine, an apparatus of the mind, a technique of thinking which helps its possessor to draw correct conclusions.[2]

Most definitions of economics focus on either the problems that economists deal with or the methods that economists use in dealing with these problems.

Most of the "problems" definitions, such as the first one given above, focus on situations that arise as a result of **scarcity**—defined as a situation in which the amount of something actually available would not be sufficient to satisfy the desire for it if it were provided "free of charge." Because of

1. Campbell McConnell, *Economics*, 10th ed. (New York: McGraw-Hill, 1987), p. 21.
2. J. M. Keynes, in introducing each of a series of *Cambridge Economic Handbooks* in the 1920s.

scarcity, people find it necessary to give up some things they enjoy so they can obtain other things they want more urgently. In other words, they have to make choices.

Scarcity is a situation in which the amount of something actually available would not be sufficient to satisfy the desire for it if it were provided free.

The "methods" definitions focus on how economists deal with problems rather than on the problems themselves. They see economics as a tool kit or "apparatus of the mind" that enables the economist to draw correct conclusions not only about subjects ordinarily considered economic but about human actions quite generally. For example, the "new home economics" of Professor Gary Becker and his disciples applies the technical apparatus of economics to the analysis of such problems as whether or not to marry, to have children, to engage in criminal activity, or to make a contribution to a charitable organization.

By combining both approaches, we offer the following definition: **Economics** is (a) the study of how individuals and societies deal with scarcity and (b) the development of methodologies for analyzing such problems.

Now it is time for you to make an economic decision—that is, whether or not to memorize one or more definitions of economics. Memorizing a definition will take some time, and that time could be used by you to do other things. The "problems" approach focuses on the fact that you do not have enough time to do everything that you would like to do. The "methods" approach suggests comparing the benefits of memorizing a definition with the benefits that would come from the best alternative use of your time. Memorizing can be a useful method of learning. But understanding that economics is about scarcity and practicing the processes of economic reasoning will probably do you more good than memorizing a definition. You must make your own evaluation of benefits when comparing one alternative with another. Economic training can sharpen the ability to do this, but each person's own values must be used in actual decisions.

MICROECONOMICS AND MACROECONOMICS

The study of economics is generally divided into two main parts, one called microeconomics and the other called macroeconomics. These two divisions make up the main body of economic analysis. However, there are many special areas of application, such as international trade, government finance, industrial organization, and labor economics, that are important extensions of both parts of this main body.

Microeconomics: Three Basic Choices

Microeconomics focuses on the behavior of decision makers in the economy. A person in his or her role as a consumer or a worker is a decision maker. Business firms and governments are decision makers too. Microeconomics centers on how these decision makers choose among alternatives and what the results of these choices are.

Microeconomics is built around three basic types of choice that must be made in any economy: (1) What goods and services shall be produced, and how much of each per time period? (2) How shall they be produced, with what proportions of labor to machinery (including robots), or of machinery to natural resources, or of natural resources to labor—and within the work force, with what proportions of more-skilled to less-skilled workers? (3) To whom shall the final products be distributed? How much should go to the suppliers of labor, how much to the suppliers of natural resources, and how much to the suppliers of machinery and equipment? Or if we look at the distribution question through personal glasses, how much should go to the poor, how much to the middle classes, and how much to the rich? All these problems are interrelated.

What to Produce Every economic system must establish some way of deciding what to produce. Each must make this decision because of scarcity. Consider, for example, the question of what to produce with certain land resources available to an economy. Shall dairy cattle be grazed so that milk can be produced? Shall beef cattle be grazed so that meat can be produced? Shall corn be grown so that breakfast cereal (or bacon) can be produced? Shall the land be used for a baseball playing field so that recreational services can be produced? Shall a factory be built on it so that manufactured goods can be produced? Shall residential houses be built on it? The possibilities are almost unlimited, but some decision must be made.

How to Produce The question of how to produce is quite different from the question of what to produce. Ice cream can be made in a small shop with a hand-cranked or motor-driven ice cream maker, or it can be produced in a large automated factory in quantities large enough to serve all the people in a great city or a large region. Corn can be grown intensively, with much fertilizer and irrigation, or it can be grown extensively, with more land and less fertilizer or irrigation. Roads can be built with thousands of pick-and-shovel laborers moving soil in woven baskets, or they can be built with huge earth-moving machines and fewer workers. Every economic system must provide some method of choosing among the different available technologies of production.

For Whom to Produce Microeconomic decisions must also be made about which individuals or groups of people will enjoy the goods and services that are produced. Should all persons who are part of the economy share equally in the results of its productive undertakings? Should inequality be permitted in the distribution of the finished goods and services? How much inequality can be justified? If some are to receive more than others, how shall the lucky ones be chosen? This is the "for whom" aspect of microeconomics. It often is called "distribution of income," although income should be understood as goods and services rather than money. Every economic system must establish ways of answering this question.

Microeconomics focuses on the behavior of decision makers in the economy. Every economic system must answer the microeconomic questions of what to produce, how to produce, and for whom to produce.

Macroeconomics: Analysis of Aggregate Economic Activity

Macroeconomics is the part of economic analysis that deals with aggregate, or grand total, economic activity. The actions of the separate decision makers that are analyzed in microeconomics are added together in macroeconomics in order to focus on things that affect the economy as a whole. The two main topics of macroeconomics are inflation and unemployment, although there are important macroeconomics aspects to international trade and economic growth as well.

Macroeconomics deals with aggregate, or grand total, economic activity. Its two main topics of analysis are inflation and unemployment.

Inflation is a sustained increase in the general level of prices. Figure 1 illustrates inflation in the United States since 1969. The price level today is more than three times as high as it was in 1969, which means that a dollar today buys less than one-third as much as one did in 1969. Inflation can put great strains on an economy and on the social arrangements supporting it.

Inflation is a sustained increase in the general level of prices.

FIGURE 1
Inflation in the United States

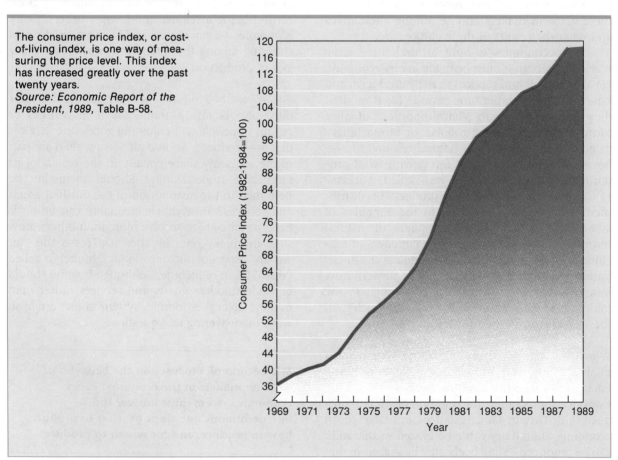

The consumer price index, or cost-of-living index, is one way of measuring the price level. This index has increased greatly over the past twenty years.
Source: Economic Report of the President, 1989, Table B-58.

Unemployment, the second main topic of macroeconomics, means that some people who are qualified and would like to work at the going wage rates are not able to find a job. Unemployment in the United States over the past twenty years, as measured by official statistics, is shown in Figure 2.

Unemployment means that some people who are qualified and willing to work at the going wage rates are not able to find a job.

Unemployment actually is a topic that fits into both macroeconomics and microeconomics—in other words, there are two general types of unemployment as far as economic analysis is concerned.

Unemployment is a microeconomic matter if a person's failure to find a job can be traced to decisions about what to produce or how to produce. For example, if people decide to stop playing golf and start playing tennis, there is likely to be unemployment among people who are trained to work as golf pros and are trying to find such jobs. This would be **microeconomic unemployment** because the reason can be traced to decisions about what to produce. Similarly, if banks switch to electronic teller machines operated by bank customers, people who are trained as bank tellers may fail to find jobs in that line of work. This kind of unemployment can be traced to a decision about how to produce, so it also can be called microeconomic unemployment. In most economies, changes are taking place almost continually in matters of what

FIGURE 2
Unemployment in the United States

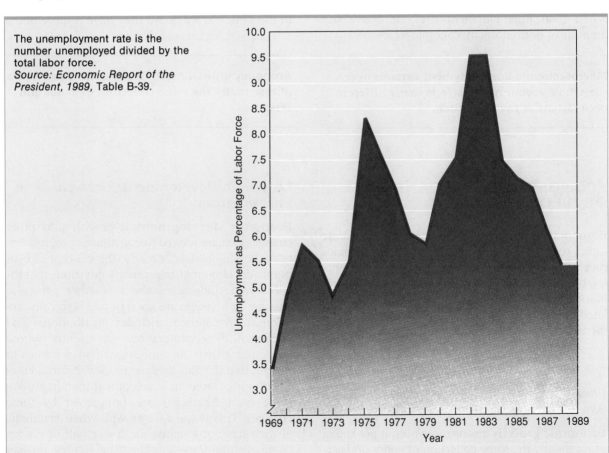

The unemployment rate is the number unemployed divided by the total labor force.
Source: Economic Report of the President, 1989, Table B-39.

and how to produce. Therefore, some amount of microeconomic unemployment usually exists. But this unemployment will be concentrated in certain industries or areas and will be more or less short-term.

Microeconomic unemployment occurs because of changes in the types of goods and services produced or in the ways of producing them.

Macroeconomic unemployment is the kind that exists throughout the whole economy (or at least affects many parts of the economy at the same time) and that is not related to particular decisions about what or how to produce. Golf pros, bank tellers, tennis pros, and many others are out of work at the same time, and their job searches are all unsuccessful. Macroeconomic unemployment sometimes is called ''cyclical'' unemployment because it comes during bad times or recessions, when total unemployment rises far above the amount of normal microeconomic joblessness.

Macroeconomic unemployment extends over the whole economy and affects many different occupations at the same time.

ECONOMIC GROWTH AND DEVELOPMENT

Economic growth and development are economic topics that are considered sometimes part of macroeconomics and sometimes part of microeconomics, but they could, perhaps, be considered separate branches of economics in themselves. Though related, economic growth and economic development are not the same thing.

Economic Growth: More of the Same Output

Economic growth means more output per capita of essentially the same collection of goods and ser-

vices. Development, on the other hand, means ''progress,'' usually represented by some different and presumably ''better'' lifestyle or collection of goods. We can illustrate the difference between them with the aid of the well-known story of Robinson Crusoe and his Man Friday, catching fish and raising vegetables on their Pacific island. Imagine a female Crusoe and a female Friday somehow added to the party, so that the Crusoes and Fridays increase and multiply. Imagine too that every Crusoe, as well as every Friday, becomes a successful practitioner of fishing, farming, boat making, or net making by the original Crusoe-Friday methods. The amount of boats and nets, total and per capita, increases steadily, along with the income to the island population. Does this fanciful tale represent economic growth? Yes, it does. After a generation or two the Crusoes and the Fridays are economically better off than before. Is it economic development? Probably not. The islanders are still consuming the same old products produced and distributed in the same old ways. All they have is more of the same, piled higher and deeper.

Economic growth means more output per capita of essentially the same collection of goods and services.

Economic Development: Growth Plus Progress

Economic development is growth plus other changes that are judged to constitute ''progress'' or to make life ''better.'' Clearly, the concept of economic development raises many questions that involve value judgments about whether particular changes or lifestyles are good or bad. Typically, economic development includes distributional and quality-of-life considerations. A country whose measured growth is concentrated in a particular region, like the Rio de Janeiro–São Paulo area of Brazil, ranks lower in development than in growth since most Brazilians are untouched by these changes. This is the case as well when economic growth has not touched the lower half of the income distribution—so that ''the figures prosper while the people suffer," to quote Premier George Papandreou of Greece.

What are some of the indexes used to measure economic development? Some that have to do with health, education, and welfare are a rising life expectancy at birth, a rising literacy rate, equalizing trends in the distributions of income and wealth, rising numbers of educational and health service personnel per thousand people, falling death and illness rates from contagious and deficiency diseases, and falling dependence on subsistence agriculture. Other kinds of indexes are the rising consumption of steel and electricity per capita, rising ratios of saving and investment to total income, and rising proportions of the representative family budget available for purchases other than food. Each measure has its bias, and no one index tells the whole story. Even so, it is fairly clear what all these indexes are driving at. Figure 3 below and Figure 4 (on page 8) show how some countries compare according to two indexes of development, infant mortality and illiteracy.

Economic development means economic growth plus improvements in the quality of life and distribution of goods and services.

FIGURE 3
Infant Mortality (Selected Countries), 1988

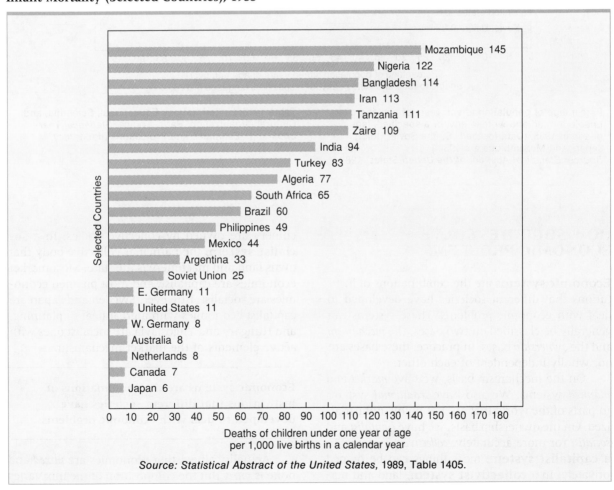

Source: *Statistical Abstract of the United States*, 1989, Table 1405.

FIGURE 4
Illiteracy (Selected Countries), Recent Years

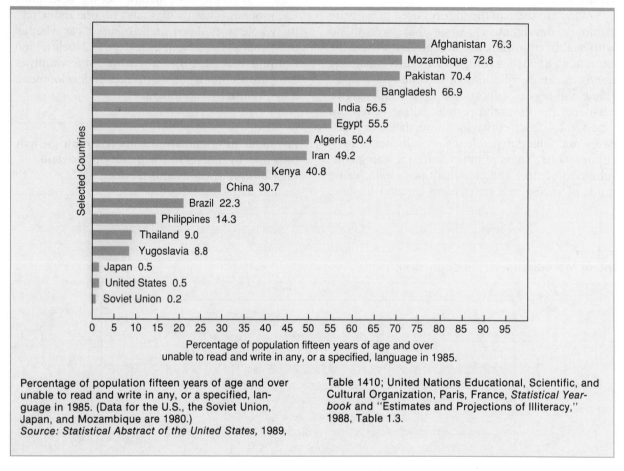

Percentage of population fifteen years of age and over
unable to read and write in any, or a specified, language in 1985.

Percentage of population fifteen years of age and over unable to read and write in any, or a specified, language in 1985. (Data for the U.S., the Soviet Union, Japan, and Mozambique are 1980.)
Source: Statistical Abstract of the United States, 1989, Table 1410; United Nations Educational, Scientific, and Cultural Organization, Paris, France, *Statistical Yearbook* and "Estimates and Projections of Illiteracy," 1988, Table 1.3.

HOW SOCIETIES SOLVE ECONOMIC PROBLEMS

Economic systems are the combinations of institutions that different societies have developed to deal with economic problems. These systems can generally be classified on two bases, the *mechanism* and the *ownership* bases. In practice, these bases are not wholly independent of each other.

On the mechanism basis, we have *market* and *planned* systems. We also have *traditional* systems in parts of the world that are not highly industrialized. On the ownership basis, we have *capitalist* and *socialist* (or more accurately, *collectivist*) systems. In a **capitalist system,** most things can be owned privately. In a **collectivist system,** land and ma- chinery are owned by collective bodies. In a **socialist system,** the particular collective body that owns land and machinery is the state. Most market economies are capitalist, and most planned economies are socialist. However, Sweden and Japan are capitalist economies with a great deal of planning, and Hungary and Yugoslavia are socialist ones with active elements of the market mechanism.

Economic systems are the combinations of institutions that different societies have developed to deal with economic problems.

Actually, all existing economies are *mixed* and none is *pure*. But the composition of the mix varies so greatly that they can be treated as different in kind. We shall call the United States a *market capitalist economy*, despite important elements of planning and/or socialism, ranging from the defense establishment to your city's water-purification plant. And we shall call the Soviet Union a *planned socialist economy*, despite important elements of capitalism and the market mechanism, such as peasants growing and selling products from their private plots within the collective farms. We do not call the Soviet Union a communist economic system, however. A **communist** is a socialist who believes that, after a few generations of near-worldwide socialism, socialist economies will reach a state of communism where most or all important goods will become free, scarcity will have been eliminated, and economics will have no excuse for existence. The Soviet leaders profess to believe that someday the U.S.S.R. will approach a communist economy, but that this utopia has not yet been attained.

Economic systems can be classified on a mechanism basis—market, planned, or traditional—or on an ownership basis—capitalist or collectivist (socialist).

Which Mechanism— Market or Planned?

Every economic system devises, or more often inherits, *mechanisms* that it uses to make the three basic microeconomic decisions of *what* goods and services (and how much of each) to produce, *how* to combine inputs to produce these things, and *for whom* among the population these goods and services are being produced. In modern economies, these decisions are made more or less impersonally and automatically by market mechanisms, or more or less deliberately and personally by planning mechanisms, or by some combination of the two.

Market Economies   Figure 5 presents a simple picture of how these decisions are organized in a **market economy**—an economy in which the interaction of buyers and sellers is the main mechanism for making choices. In this figure, each of the cir-

FIGURE 5
Microeconomic Decisions in a Market Economy

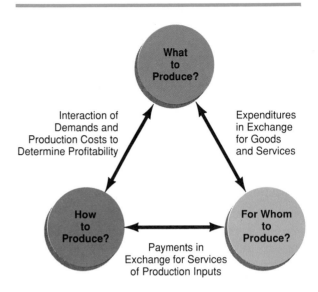

The three circles identify the three microeconomic questions that must be answered in any economic system. The double-headed arrows suggest that, in market systems, the answer to each question both requires information from and provides information for the answer to each of the other questions.

cles stands for one of the basic decisions that must be made in an economic system. Each of these circles is connected to each of the other circles. If we put ourselves inside the "for whom" circle, we are members of households that (under the capitalist system) own productive inputs such as labor, machinery, and natural resources and buy goods and services to consume. We are connected to the "how" circle because we provide inputs for and receive income from the production of goods and services. We are connected to the "what" circle because we spend our income and receive goods and services in exchange.

Business firms occupy both the "what" and the "how" circles. In the "what" circle, they are deciding what goods and services (and how much of each) to produce. They do this by interpreting the dollar votes that come from the "for whom" circle when households purchase goods and services and by combining this with information from the "how" circle about the costs of using alternative technologies for producing goods and services.

In the "how" circle, firms are deciding what mixtures of productive inputs to use in producing goods and services. Information is received from the "what" circle about which goods and services are demanded and from the "for whom" circle about the costs of the different productive inputs that can be used to produce them.

Our tour of the connected circles shows that the market mechanism is actually an integrated process, not just pure chance or "jungle law."

A market economy is an economy in which the interaction of buyers and sellers is the main mechanism for making choices.

Planned Economies The planning mechanism answers the same three microeconomic questions, but does so in a different way. The Soviet revolutionary leader Vladimir Ilich Lenin (1870–1924) thought this way was so simple that it could be explained in adequate detail to any semiliterate Russian worker or peasant. However, he seems to have been too optimistic.

The three microeconomic decisions for a **planned economy** are again shown by three circles in Figure 6. In addition, there is a fourth circle, representing the government in its planning function; in the U.S.S.R., it is an institution called Gosplan. The government (Gosplan) coordinates decisions in the three areas of microeconomics. In a pure planned system, there are no direct links between "what," "how," and "for whom." Each of the three microeconomic decisions depends upon the priorities set by government in the central circle.

Not being fools and having lived through failures, the bureaucrats of Gosplan (as well as the party politicians and military people looking over their shoulders) realize that a plan is not a magic wand. They know that the three types of decisions must be consistent with each other. Writing numbers down on paper will not produce the "shoes and ships and sealing wax" represented by these quantities. So the planners use elaborate statistical techniques to replace the market in integrating their several decisions. Not only is the detail of these techniques beyond the understanding of the Soviet worker or peasant whom Lenin hoped to draw into the planning process, but it is beyond the

FIGURE 6
Microeconomic Decisions in a Planned Economy

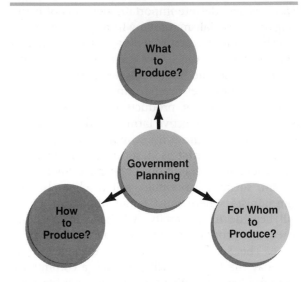

The three circles identify the three microeconomic questions that must be answered in any economic system. The single-headed arrows suggest that, in a planned economy, the answers to the three questions are worked out and coordinated through government planning in the central circle.

level of this book. The plans seldom work out perfectly. Neither, however, does "the obvious and simple system of natural liberty" of the market mechanism as described by Adam Smith, the eighteenth-century scholar who wrote the *Wealth of Nations* and who is credited with launching the modern study of how markets operate.

A planned economy is one in which the government coordinates decisions in the three microeconomic areas of what to produce, how to produce, and for whom to produce.

Traditional Economies It is, of course, much harder to generalize about **traditional economies,** but certain features are common to a good many of them. A great deal of property, particularly in land, is often held by a clan or tribe in common; Karl Marx spoke of this as "primitive communism." At the same time, there is much barter trade (exchanging goods for goods without the use of money) both within tribes and across tribal lines; the anthropologist Sol Tax calls this "penny capitalism." As for the major economic decisions, they are generally made by rulers (priests, kings and queens, chiefs, feudal barons, medicine men) either singly or in conference. They tend to be made on the basis of ethical ideas like "just" prices for goods and "fair" wages for labor, or the "duty" of at least the eldest child to follow the family's occupation of farming or fishing or pottery making. Rather than attempting economic planning or trusting any abstract market mechanism, primitive economies count on divine help, achieved through magic, prayers, and sacrifices, to solve any problems that may result from droughts or floods or earthquakes. The Islamic Republic of Iran under the late Ayatollah Khomeini can be regarded as a revival of a traditional kind of economy. The guiding principles are religious or ethical in nature, with little concern for efficiency or progress in the modern sense.

A traditional economy is characterized by common ownership of property, bartering, centralization of decision-making authority in the rulers, and reliance on divine help.

Ownership—Capitalism or Socialism?

Let us now turn to the *ownership* basis for classifying economic systems. In a *capitalist economy*, which usually relies upon the market mechanism, natural resources and machinery may be privately owned just like food, clothing, or other consumption goods. Not only is private ownership legal, either by individuals or by those "legal persons" called corporations, but it is the dominant form of ownership. In capitalist countries, people engage in the economic game routinely and automatically. They do so as decision makers, as property owners, as workers, and as consumers. The most important motives for engaging in economic activities are, of course, the increase in income and wealth and the satisfaction derived from income and wealth.

In a capitalist economy, natural resources and machinery may be privately owned, just like

consumption goods. Private ownership is the dominant form of ownership.

In a *collectivist economy*, natural resources and machinery are owned only by collective groups. Individuals, however, may own consumption goods privately. The main appeal of socialism and all other collectivist systems is greater equality. These systems strive for a higher standard of living for the poor and an end to poverty, at the expense of the rich rather than of the people in general. Socialists believe that property in productive inputs should belong predominantly to the political state as trustee for the community as a whole.

In a collectivist economy, natural resources and machinery are owned only by collective groups, although individuals may own consumption goods. In a socialist system, the collective body that owns the natural resources and machines is the state.

EVALUATING ECONOMIC SYSTEMS

When Nikita Khrushchev banged his shoe on a United Nations table in the early 1960s and roared, "We shall bury you!" we can only guess what the head of the Soviet state may have meant. The meaning for some is that Khrushchev expected a few more years of competitive coexistence—the period 1960–1980 was often mentioned—to prove the superiority of planned socialism over market capitalism. Other leaders, who favored capitalism, were making exactly the opposite forecasts for the same period, without (to our knowledge) emphasizing their arguments with their shoes.

Six Criteria

What do we mean, anyhow, when we say that one economic system outperforms another? This is basically a subjective value judgment. It may be bas on a great many criteria weighted in a great r different ways, not all of them conscio suggest here six criteria, or bases of judgment, with no weighting system at all. (Other economists use somewhat different criteria, and some try to rank them by importance.) On some of our criteria, some would say that the United States performs better than the Soviet Union; on others, they would argue that the Soviet Union comes out on top.

1. Current Standard of Living   Nearly all of us believe that, other things being equal, a high standard of living here and now is better than a lower one. As the famous singer Sophie Tucker put it, "I been rich and I been poor, but believe me, rich is better." It can be said, however, that even our present living standard may be too high for our own good, because some of us "dig our graves with our teeth," not to mention our lack of exercise. To quote Oliver Goldsmith's *The Deserted Village,*

> Ill fares the land, to hast'ning ills a prey,
> Where wealth accumulates, and men decay.

The **standard of living** is a measure of the material well-being of a person or a community. It is usually expressed in terms of current income or consumption per person, but the results differ when other measures are used. Not enough attention is paid to per capita *wealth.* Also, this criterion allows an economic system to claim credit for what may be due to a favorable location, rich natural resources, or a large population of working age.

The standard of living is a measure of the material well-being of a person or a community.

---

2. Economic Growth—Future Standard of Living   Nearly all of us believe that living standards, at least for "the poor," should improve over time, and also that overall economic growth will make this more likely to happen. People are generally happier when they expect progress than when "Tomorrow, and tomorrow, and tomorrow,/ Creeps in this petty pace from day to day." The prospect of progress is also an incentive for people ut forth the extra effort to make it a reality. At ne time, there may be limits to growth set by rgy, raw materials, pollution, and sheer tropy, so that the same growth that

12

raises economic prospects for our children may only make things worse for our grandchildren.

3. Equity of Distribution   Everyone is in favor of "equity" and "fairness," but nobody knows what they consist of, or how important they are. **Equity** may, but need not, mean "equality" in consumption, income, or wealth. Without economic incentives for risk taking and the development of their economic potentials, the gifted and talented may complain of unfair treatment. Some balance— called by economists a tradeoff—must be achieved between what socialists call the "freedom to exploit" and the ethical judgments of ordinary people who feel that some limits should be placed on inequality. Different economies have consciously or unconsciously hit upon different compromises. Socialist distributions, incidentally, are *not* automatically closer to being equal than capitalist ones. Peter J.D. Wiles, in *Distribution of Income: East and West,* for example, argues that the capitalist United Kingdom is more egalitarian in practice than either the capitalist United States or the socialist Soviet Union. The same argument might be made for capitalist Holland or the Scandinavian countries. On the other hand, he finds socialist Poland more egalitarian than Britain.[3]

Intergroup income distributions within a society are also important. Japanese critics, among others, fault the income position of blacks, Hispanics, and American Indians in the United States, charging quite reasonably that it is due to racial discrimination. But if Japan's own minorities were as large as the American ones, Japanese discrimination and racism problems would probably be about as serious as those in the United States.

Equity may, but need not, mean equality in consumption, income, or wealth. True equity may not be attainable in either a socialist or a capitalist system.

---

4. Security of the Living Standard   People want to be sure that they will not wake up tomorrow morning to find that their jobs have disappeared

3. Peter J.D. Wiles, *Distribution of Income: East and West* (Amsterdam: North Holland Publishing Co., 1974).

without warning in a business cycle downturn, and that they have no other way to maintain their standard of living. Neither do they want to lose their living standards more gradually but just as hopelessly because of technological changes, such as when railroad trains are replaced by trucks and airplanes, or unskilled labor is made idle by robots. This goal suggests an advantage of the large country over the small one, given the difficulties of international migration. It also suggests that an economy, particularly a small one, should not be tied to a single industry. Finally, it suggests the desirability of defenses against these cyclical and technological changes.

5. *Compatibility with Human Rights* Without going into detail as to precisely what human rights are or by what actions they should be protected, we may safely say that an economy that depends on conscripts and prisoners for a major part of its labor force can be faulted on these grounds. This is what Solzhenitsyn says about the Soviet Union in *The Gulag Archipelago.* So, obviously, may be faulted a slave economy like the American South for about two hundred years before the Civil War—and in some states for several generations afterward. Both China under Mao Zedong and the Soviet Union ever since the Russian Revolution have been accused of working people to death in and out of prison camps to speed up their economic development. In the nineteenth century, similar accusations were made against the Central Pacific Railroad in the United States, where the workers concerned were Chinese contract laborers.

6. *Compatibility with Physical and Mental Health* A high "standard of living" is not synonymous with a high "quality of life." A particular economic system may enhance one while making the other more difficult to achieve. In the United States today, some argue that the competitive "rat race" of the capitalist struggle to get ahead drives people to mental hospitals in large numbers.[4] Ac-

cording to some psychologists and psychiatrists, any economy that encourages "keeping up with the Joneses" and conspicuous consumption, while making inadequate provision for the poor, is incompatible with physical and mental health. In such an economy, there are many sources of harmful stress: too heavy a workload, impossible deadlines, the loss of a job, and all sorts of financial worries. It should not be inferred, however, that similar problems are unknown in collectivist societies. Unrealistic expectations and work quotas, the possible loss of a job, and other economic ills are part of the worker's lot in the Soviet Union too.

Six criteria can be used for evaluating the performance of different economic systems: (1) current standard of living; (2) economic growth; (3) equity of distribution; (4) security of the living standard; (5) compatibility with human rights; and (6) compatibility with physical and mental health.

Policy Tradeoffs

Conflicts often arise among accepted social goals, so that choices and tradeoffs are necessary at the most general policy levels. We have noted already what the late economist Arthur Okun called "the big tradeoff" between the common desire to maintain incentives for work and risk taking and the common desire to limit inequality in income and wealth. Another example is the experience of the United Nations in promoting economic growth and development between 1950 and 1970. Measured *economic growth,* our second criterion, appeared to be going quite well. In fact, the less-developed countries grew more rapidly as a group than did the more-developed (industrialized) countries, narrowing the measured gap between them. But *economic development,* which is generally defined to include most or all of our last four criteria, was disappointing. Conditions in rural areas and for the urban poor remained largely unaffected and unimproved in many countries with the highest growth rates. So development specialists, including economists, rejected as "growthmanship" the focus on measured national income and its rate of change per capita. They offered instead a plan based on

---

4. It cannot be doubted that the statistical probability of spending part of one's life in a mental institution is unusually high in the United States; it has been estimated as high as one out of eight. But this figure reflects greater availability of such institutions in the United States and also the greater life expectancy of the adult American, which increases the likelihood of senility.

providing every family in every developing country, rural as well as urban, with **basic human needs.** These needs were defined as minimal amounts of food, clothing, shelter, education, health care, and sometimes also "access" to public decision making. Only after these needs are met, runs the argument, should attention be paid to attaining economic growth. The conflict continues in the developing countries, in the aid-giving industrial countries, and in the international agencies, with no solution or compromise presently in sight.

Conflicts often arise among accepted social goals; mere economic growth without an accompanying improvement in the delivery of such basic human needs as food, clothing, shelter, education, and health care may be a hollow victory.

WHY SO HARD?

Why is economics supposed to be so hard—harder for many students than history or the other social sciences? There are three reasons; if you are prepared, you will have less to worry about.

The first reason is that economics and economists are likely to challenge some of your previous half-formed ideas. You may temporarily find yourself unlearning more than you learn, or operating in a fog of confusion.

The second reason is that economics, like Switzerland, talks three languages at once. There is the language of words, which for us is English. There is the language of diagrams and graphs. And there is also the language of mathematics, which is used more and more extensively as the student goes on to advanced work. Just as the educated Swiss is translator and interpreter between and among the three languages of his or her country, the good economist should be a translator and interpreter among the three languages of this discipline. This is not, for many people, an easy task to accomplish.

A third reason is that economics makes extensive use of theories and models involving more assumptions and higher levels of abstraction than many students have yet encountered. These theories and models are a fundamental part of the "methods," or "way of thinking," view of economics. Since one theory often builds on another, it is important to get a solid grasp of each one before going on to the next. So careful learning, step by step, is important in economics.

Is Socialism Dying?

As recently as the 1960s, many observers thought that socialism or communism was the wave of the future. Dozens of new countries in Africa and Asia, freed from their former colonial masters, adopted systems that combined centralized economic planning with state ownership of crucial industries. Socialist parties of one brand or another played leading roles throughout Europe and Latin America. Old American allies such as Britain—not to mention close neighbors like Cuba—were governed by parties at least loosely committed to socialism. In the United States itself, supposedly the bastion of capitalism, the federal government with its social and economic planners increasingly dominated the economy.

But in the 1980s the pattern began to change. In Britain, West Germany, Belgium, the Netherlands, France, and a number of other European countries, conservative, capitalist-oriented governments pushed aside the socialists. Even Eastern Bloc nations such as Poland and Hungary began to experiment with capitalism. In the United States the Reagan administration, with an old-fashioned appeal to the self-help ethic, tried to reduce the federal role in citizens' everyday lives and liberate the free-market economy.

Most important, the twin giants of socialism, the U.S.S.R. and China, began to adopt capitalist reforms. In the Soviet Union, under the banner of *perestroika* (restructuring), Mikhail Gorbachev struggled to introduce competition and decentralization to the stagnant socialist system. In China similar reforms allowed a flourishing of entrepreneurial centers in the coastal provinces. By the end of the 1980s Gorbachev faced strong opposition, and China was in political turmoil.

From 1980 to 1987 more than 56 state-owned corporations around the world were sold to private shareholders. Small and emerging countries now had a new model to look to. Tanzania, for example, described by *U.S. News & World Report* as "an economic basket case" in the 1970s, abandoned its collective-farm system and introduced free-market capitalism. The result was a startling resurgence for Tanzania's economy.

All in all, the transition toward capitalism has been dramatic enough for magazine headlines to trumpet "the death of socialism." Some observers say that socialism simply cannot compete in an increasingly diverse and high-tech world economy, because central bureaucracies do not adapt as quickly as free-wheeling entrepreneurs. But if socialism is indeed dying, its death rattles will continue for some time, and no one is suggesting that its legacy will disappear. The economies of the twenty-first century will evolve new forms that we cannot yet predict, and capitalism and socialism as we know them will both be important influences.

Sources: Richard I. Kirkland, Jr., "The Death of Socialism," *Fortune*, January 4, 1988, pp. 64–72; "Communism in Turmoil," Special Report, *Business Week*, June 5, 1989, pp. 34–87; John Barnes, "Africa Makes a Hard Choice," *U.S. News & World Report*, June 27, 1988, pp. 28–32 (quotation at p. 28); Louise Lief, "The West's Recipe: Try Again," *U.S. News & World Report*, June 27, 1988, pp. 30–31; Zbigniew Brzezinski, "Will the Soviet Empire Self-Destruct?" *New York Times Magazine*, February 26, 1989, pp. 38–41; Ronald Bailey, "The World Turns," *Forbes*, May 15, 1989, pp. 43–44; Timothy Garton Ash, "Revolution: The Springtime of Two Nations," *New York Review of Books*, June 15, 1989, pp. 3–10.

SUMMARY

1. Some definitions of economics stress subject matter—how scarcity is dealt with and how people's wants are satisfied. Another type of definition stresses the methods and techniques used by economists. (See page 2.)

2. The two main branches of economics are microeconomics and macroeconomics. Microeconomics is the part that focuses on the behavior of decision makers who are inside or part of a larger economic system. Every economic system must provide ways of answering the microeconomic questions of what to produce, how to produce, and for whom to produce. (See page 3.)

3. Macroeconomics is the branch of economics that deals with aggregate, or "grand total," economic activity. It examines how the whole economic system operates and focuses mainly on the topics of inflation and unemployment. (See page 4.)

4. Inflation is a sustained increase in the general price level. Unemployment may be either microeconomic or macroeconomic, depending on the reason why a person is unable to find work. Microeconomic unemployment arises because of changes in the types of goods and services produced or in the ways of producing them—the what and how decisions in microeconomics. Macroeconomic unemployment extends over the whole economy and affects many different occupations at the same time. (See pages 4–6 and Figures 1 and 2, pages 4 and 5.)

5. Economic growth and development are two other important economic subjects. Economic growth is a measured percentage rise each year or each decade in production, either total or per capita. Economic development means economic growth as well as some improvements in the "quality of life" and in the distribution of income. (See pages 6–7.)

6. Economic systems are the combinations of institutions that societies have set up to deal with economic problems. On a mechanism basis, they can be classified as market economies or planned economies. Market economies integrate the various economic questions through the institutions of free exchange in markets. Planned economies use governments and other agencies to accomplish this integration. All existing economies are mixed, with elements of both market and planning systems. (See pages 8–10.)

7. Economic systems can also be classified on the basis of ownership. In capitalist systems, private property rights extend from ordinary consumption goods to productive inputs. In collectivist systems, productive inputs (except for labor) are collectively owned. If the agency owning these goods is the political state or an agency of the state, we have socialism, which is the most important form of collectivism. (See page 11.)

8. In traditional economies, custom and religion play major parts. Much property is usually held in common, and occupations tend to remain in families. There is much stress on "justice" in price and wage fixing, and often we find resort to prayer, magic, and the supernatural. In these economies, the important decisions are made by kings and queens, chiefs, priests, or feudal lords. (See pages 10–11.)

9. A capitalist economy is more apt to rely on the market mechanism than is a collectivist one. Collectivist (including socialist) economies are more likely to be planned than are capitalist ones. Conversely, a market economy is apt to be capitalistic, and a planned economy socialistic, but there are important exceptions to this generalization. (See page 11.)

10. Six criteria are suggested for evaluating economic systems: (a) a high current living standard; (b) economic growth, pointing to a high future living standard; (c) "equitable" distributions of income and wealth; (d) security of the living standard against downward shocks; (e) compatibility with human rights; and (f) compatibility with physical and mental health. (See pages 11–13.)

KEY TERMS

basic human needs: minimal amounts of food, clothing, shelter, education, health care, and access to public decision making (page 14)

capitalist system: an economic system in which natural resources and machinery can be privately owned (page 8).

collectivist system: an economic system in which natural resources and machinery are owned by collective bodies (page 8).

communist: a socialist who believes that socialist economies will eventually reach a state of communism, in which most or all important goods will be free, scarcity will no longer exist, and there will be no need for economics (page 9).

economic development: economic growth plus improvements in the quality of life and distribution of goods and services (page 16).

economic growth: more output per capita of essentially the same collection of goods and services (page 6).

economics: the study of how individuals and societies deal with the problems of scarcity and the methodologies that have been developed for analyzing such problems (page 2).

economic systems: the combinations of institutions that different societies have developed to deal with economic problems (page 8).

equity: fairness in the distribution of consumption, income, or wealth (page 12).

inflation: a sustained increase in the general level of prices (page 4).

macroeconomics: the part of economic analysis that deals with aggregate economic activity; its two main topics are inflation and unemployment (page 4).

macroeconomic unemployment: unemployment that exists throughout the whole economy and that is not related to particular decisions about what or how to produce (page 6).

market economy: an economy in which the interaction of buyers and sellers is the main mechanism for making choices (page 9).

microeconomics: the part of economic analysis that deals with the behavior of decision makers in the economy (page 3).

microeconomic unemployment: unemployment that is due to decisions about what or how to produce (page 5).

planned economy: an economy in which the government coordinates decisions in the three microeconomic areas of what to produce, how to produce, and for whom to produce (page 10).

scarcity: a situation in which the amount of something actually available would not be sufficient to satisfy the desire for it if it were provided free (page 2).

socialist system: an economic system in which the state owns the natural resources and machinery (page 8).

standard of living: a measure of the material wellbeing of a person or a community (page 12).

traditional economy: an economic system characterized by common ownership of property, bartering, centralization of decision making authority in the rulers, and reliance on divine help (page 10).

unemployment: when some people who are qualified and willing to work at going wage rates are not able to find a job (page 5).

DISCUSSION QUESTIONS

1. The famous economist Alfred Marshall defined economics as "a study of mankind in the ordinary business of life; it examines that part of individual and social action which is most closely connected to the attainment and with the use of the material requisites of wellbeing."[5] Is this closer to the problems type of definition or the methodology type of definition? Explain your answer.

2. In market economies, the what, how, and for whom decisions are linked to one another. In fact, many events have roots in all three of these economic decisions. Consider the increase in the quantity of computers produced in our society. Explain how the what, how, and for whom decisions each played a part in this outcome.

3. Market economies use profits and losses to stimulate the search for better production methods. What nonmoney rewards for success exist in capitalist market systems? Is the money or the honor more important for Nobel Prize winners? Is a gold watch better than money for a retirement gift?

4. Do you believe the present distribution of income in the United States is unfair or unjust in any way? If so, how should it be different? What changes would you expect in the way the economy operates if your desired reforms were actually to take place?

5. Alfred Marshall, *Principles of Economics,* 8th ed. (London: Macmillan, 1920), p. 1.

5. The figures in this chapter showing the relations of what, how, and for whom in market and planned economies are great simplifications of reality. Most actual systems are mixed. Explain how the U.S. economy would be better illustrated by putting a government planning circle in the center of Figure 5. Explain how the Soviet Union's economy would be better illustrated by adding arrows between the three outer circles in Figure 6.

6. The distinction between microeconomic and macroeconomic unemployment is helpful in theorizing about the economy. But the unemployed worker may not know (or really care) which has put him or her out of work. Consider an unemployed auto worker in Flint, Michigan, in the early 1980s. Remember that car sales are especially sensitive to general economic conditions and that the economy was in recession during those years. Also, the U.S. auto firms faced severe competition from imported Japanese and German automobiles. Discuss the unemployment in Flint in terms of microeconomic and macroeconomic determinants.

7. As you learned in this chapter, economic development means economic growth plus some qualitative changes in the conditions of life. Growth is a part of development. What arguments can you think of against growth itself? In your opinion, is the United States experiencing economic development today? Explain your answer.

8. Our list of ways to evaluate economic systems may not be the same as a list you would make. If you could add one item to the list, what would it be? Do you believe that people in China or the Soviet Union would want a different set of goals? Explain your answers.

9. President Warren Harding once said, "There is more happiness in the American small town than anywhere else on earth." Do you think he was correct then—in the 1920s? Do you think his statement is true today? Explain.

10. Do you think that human happiness has the best chance of being realized under capitalism, socialism, or a traditional economy? Explain your answer to this question.

2

The Actors on the Economic Stage

Preview   Understanding how an economic system works requires economists to identify the major actors on the economic stage and the roles they play in the operation of the system. We introduce them in this chapter.

We shall look first at households. In a capitalist economic system, households actually contain *two* decision-making entities—consumers and resource owners.[1] Imagine that each member of the household wears two hats, one marked "consumer" and the other marked "resource owner." As consumers, household members help to make the "what to produce" decisions in the economy. As resource owners, they are involved with both the "how" and the "for whom" decisions.

Next we will look at business firms, which are the economic units concerned with production. In the capitalist system, business firms help make all three microeconomic decisions. Business firms obtain resources from households and combine them to produce goods and services. Household members place their resources in the hands of business firms because they expect to be rewarded with income. The firm, if successful, is able to make a profit from its operations.

The third major element in the economy is government. We will describe the major functions and responsibilities that economists say properly fall upon government in a market-capitalist system. These responsibilities involve (1) financing certain goods and services (which contributes to the "what to produce" decision), (2) redistributing income (which influences the "for whom" decision), and (3) moderating business cycles (which is a macroeconomic activity).

1. See pages 44–46 for a discussion of rational economic decision makers.

Households, business firms, and governments in foreign countries are the fourth major element influencing an economy. Foreigners buy goods and services produced in the United States, thus adding to the demand for products from U.S. firms and the demand for U.S. resources. But foreigners also are producers of goods and services bought by Americans, thus competing with U.S. resource owners and firms.

The interactions among the actors on the economic stage—households, business firms, government, and foreigners—will be examined in detail in later chapters.

HOUSEHOLDS

For statistical purposes, a **household** may be defined either as a family group living together or as one or more persons living together in the same dwelling unit. There are about 92 million households in the United States today. Households are made up of individuals who, in capitalist-market economic systems, are the owners of resources as well as consumers of goods and services. Each individual, of course, is the owner of his or her own labor resource. But in capitalist economic systems, nonhuman resources, too, are owned by individuals, either directly or indirectly. Land and buildings can be owned directly by individuals. Indirect ownership, on the other hand, occurs when corporations hold title to resources. This is indirect ownership by individuals, since corporations themselves are owned by shareholders, who are individuals. As resource owners, individuals receive the income generated in the production activities of the economy.

When household members spend the income they have earned as resource owners, they are functioning in their economic capacity as consumers. They are casting "dollar votes" for the goods and services that they want. In this way, they help make the "what to produce" decisions.

A household is a family group (or one or more unrelated persons) living together in the same dwelling unit.

Households are made up of individuals who are the owners of resources as well as consumers of goods and services.

As resource owners, individuals receive the income generated in the production activities of the economy. When they spend the income as consumers, they help determine what goods and services get produced.

Population and Age Groups

The size and age distribution of the population are facts of great importance to economics because they affect production and spending. Will people, or households, demand baby food, rock concerts and sports cars, or retirement homes? What proportion of the population will be of working age, and how many nonworkers will there be for every worker? Will the typical person make decisions with the aggressiveness and flexibility of youth or with the caution and stability of older age?

Figure 1 shows the age distribution of the United States population from 1960 to 2000, based on both actual data and estimates. The total population is expected to increase by almost 50 percent over this forty-year span. The numbers in this figure show the effects of the "baby boom" of the 1950s and 1960s and of the sharp drop in the birthrate during the 1970s. Though the percentage of the population 17 years and under declined greatly during the 1970s, it is expected to decline only moderately through the end of the century as the people born in the 1950s and 1960s produce their own children. The younger working-age group, from age 18 through 44, continued to increase during the 1980s but will decline in the 1990s. The older working-age group, from 45 through 64 years, is expected to begin its growth spurt in the decade of the 1990s. The over-65 age group probably will grow moderately through the end of the century but then experience a major expansion.

This population "ripple" may be one of the most significant economic events in the lives of college students today. Students graduating during the mid-1990s will be entering a labor force that will include a much larger percentage of the popu-

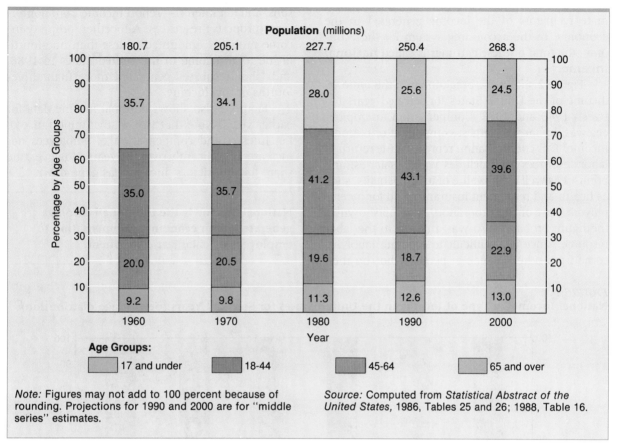

Population (millions)

Age Groups:
17 and under | 18-44 | 45-64 | 65 and over

Note: Figures may not add to 100 percent because of rounding. Projections for 1990 and 2000 are for "middle series" estimates.

Source: Computed from *Statistical Abstract of the United States*, 1986, Tables 25 and 26; 1988, Table 16.

lation than was the case for students graduating in the 1960s and early 1970s. Competition for jobs will probably be vigorous, but living standards may be high because the percentage of nonworkers will be relatively low. These graduates will face different challenges when they will be entering the 45–64 "older-worker" category. The expanding proportion of people over age 65 then will place increasing pressures on those still working, who will be expected to support a larger and larger nonworking population.

The political effect of the "ripple" may also be important. Many believe that people tend to be "liberal" when they are young and "conservative" when they are old. In fact, there is persuasive economic logic behind this observation, since older people have more at stake in the status quo than do younger people. The young people of the 1960s and 1970s were influential in bringing about many changes in the United States through their political activity. Civil rights, women's liberation, antiwar, and antinuclear movements relied heavily on the support of young people. As these same people grow older, they will continue to leave their mark on political history—this time as an older generation.

The size and age distribution of the population are facts of great importance to economics because they affect production and spending. The U.S. population is characterized by the "baby boom" of the 1950s and 1960s, followed by a sharp drop in the birthrate in the 1970s.

Sources of Income

As owners of resources, individuals are the ultimate recipients of the income generated in the economy. In the accounting system for the economy, the total of these earnings is called **national income.**

Figure 2 shows the breakdown of the national income of the United States for selected years between 1940 and 1988. Compensation to employees was, by far, the largest component of national income. This compensation represents the return to labor resources and includes wages, salaries, and bonuses as well as the value of fringe benefits, such as health and retirement insurance paid for by employers. Part of the proprietors' income shown in the figure probably also was a return to the labor resource, since it is difficult to separate labor income from other income of people who run their own businesses. The other components of national income—corporate profits, rental income of persons, and net interest—report income from nonhuman (property) resources. Altogether, property income probably amounted to less than one-fourth of the total income in the United States in 1988, and labor resources generated more than three-fourths of this income.

Figure 2 also shows national income data for earlier years. Note that the relative importance of net interest and compensation of employees has increased significantly over the years. However, the share for proprietors' income has gone down.

National income is the total of all earnings generated in an economy. Compensation to employees is its largest component.

FIGURE 2

National Income by Type of Income in the United States for Selected Years (percentage distribution)

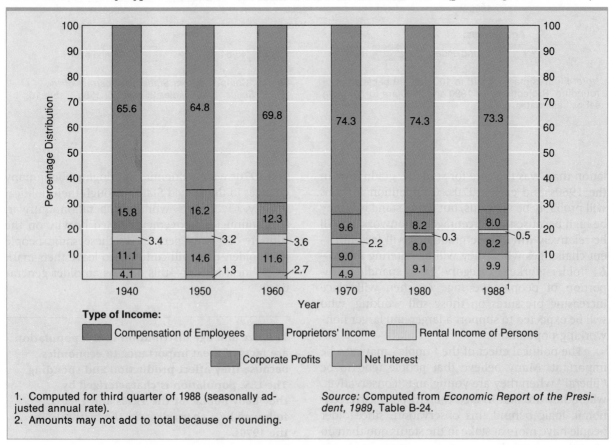

1. Computed for third quarter of 1988 (seasonally adjusted annual rate).
2. Amounts may not add to total because of rounding.

Source: Computed from *Economic Report of the President, 1989*, Table B-24.

FIGURE 3
Median Money Income of U.S. Families in Constant (1986) Dollars, 1960–1986

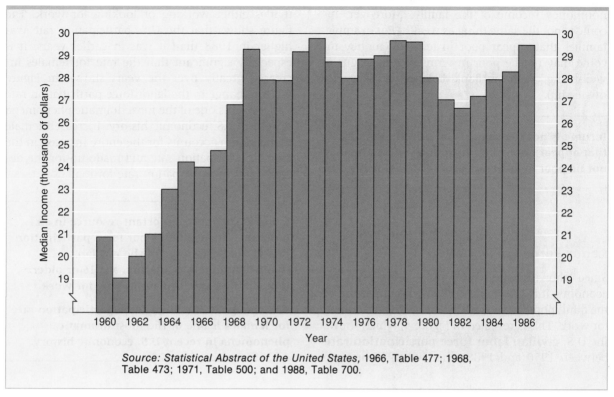

Source: Statistical Abstract of the United States, 1966, Table 477; 1968, Table 473; 1971, Table 500; and 1988, Table 700.

Median Family Income

Figure 3 shows the median family income in the United States from 1960 through 1986. The "median" means that half the families in the country had incomes higher than the one shown for each year and that half had incomes lower than this amount. Also, the income figures have been adjusted so as to remove changes in the cost of living that arose from changes in the price level. All the figures are in dollars of the purchasing power that prevailed in 1986. Therefore, they are useful in showing what has happened to the standard of living of U.S. families over this twenty-seven-year period.

At first you may notice that the median family income was much higher in 1986 than it was in 1960—41.6 percent higher, in fact. A closer examination, however, shows that the highest median family income shown in Figure 3 is for 1973. In the thirteen years from 1960 to 1973, the median fam-

ily income in the United States increased by almost 43 percent, but the median family income fell in 1974 and 1975 and in the years from 1978 through 1982. Although the median family income increased after 1982, as of 1986 it had not yet regained the level of 1973.

Economists are, of course, very interested in the forces that may cause changes in the levels of family income. Even a casual reflection on the numbers in Figure 3 suggest that the shocks to the economy that were caused by large changes in the price of crude oil in 1973 and 1978 may have been at least partly responsible for the lack of growth in U.S. median family income in the late 1970s and early 1980s.

Several words of caution are appropriate even at this early stage in our exploration of economics. Money income tells only part of the story about the economic well-being of a family. Nonmoney incomes, such as subsidized food, housing, and health care, also are important. "Do-it-yourself" home building and repair, as well as back-yard vegetable gardens, are other ways of adding to the nonmoney income of the family. Moreover, income is not the same thing as wealth. For example, families that appear poor in terms of money income may not be poor in terms of other signs of well-being, such as bank balances or property ownership.

Income is not the same as wealth. Households that appear poor in terms of money income may not be poor by other measures of well-being.

Labor Force Participation

Since labor is the most important resource in the economy, it is interesting to know what portion of the adult population actually is working or looking for work. This is revealed in Figure 4, which shows the U.S. **civilian labor force participation rate** between 1950 and 1988. The civilian labor force

participation rate is the percentage of the civilian noninstitutional population, age sixteen or older, that is either working or looking for work. The figure shows that the U.S. participation rate was higher in 1988 than it was in earlier years. It is especially significant that the rate for females increased greatly over the years shown in Figure 4. This change in the labor force participation rate for females is one of the most dramatic phenomena in recent U.S. economic history. Increased female participation accounts for the entire increase in the overall participation rate and made up for the decrease in the participation rate for males.

Labor is the most important resource in an economy. The civilian labor force participation rate is the percentage of the civilian noninstitutional population, age 16 or older, that is either working or looking for work.

The change in the labor force participation rate for females is one of the most dramatic phenomena in recent U.S. economic history.

FIGURE 4
Civilian Labor Force Participation Rate (percent)

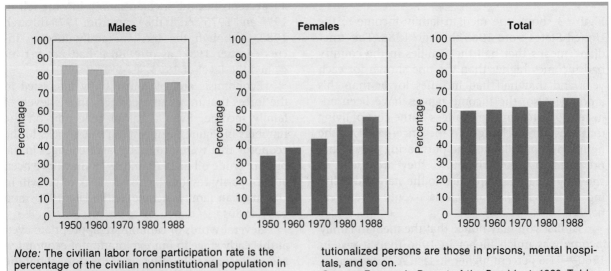

Note: The civilian labor force participation rate is the percentage of the civilian noninstitutional population in the group specified. Data relate to persons sixteen years of age or over. A person is in the labor force if he or she is either working or looking for work. Insti-

tutionalized persons are those in prisons, mental hospitals, and so on.
Source: Economic Report of the President, 1989, Table B-36.

FIGURE 5

Disposition of Personal Income in the United States for Selected Years (percentage distribution)

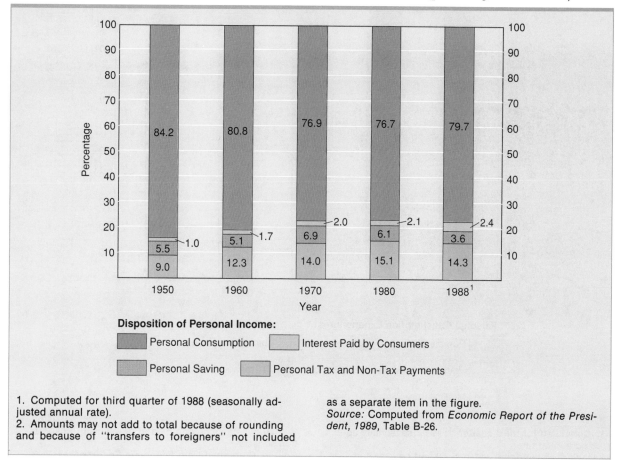

Disposition of Personal Income:

- Personal Consumption
- Interest Paid by Consumers
- Personal Saving
- Personal Tax and Non-Tax Payments

1. Computed for third quarter of 1988 (seasonally adjusted annual rate).
2. Amounts may not add to total because of rounding and because of "transfers to foreigners" not included as a separate item in the figure.

Source: Computed from *Economic Report of the President, 1989,* Table B-26.

Uses of Income

As we have said, household members are helping make the "what to produce" decision when they purchase goods and services. Figure 5 shows how households disposed of their income. In 1988, 79.7 percent went for consumption goods and services, 14.3 percent for taxes, 2.4 percent for interest payments, and 3.6 percent was saved. As you continue to study economics, you will see that each of these dispositions of household income is carefully analyzed by economists in their efforts to understand the economy. The figure shows that the percentage of income used for consumption goods and services has dropped since 1950, while the percentage paid in taxes and interest has increased. Even the money that is saved plays a role in the "what to produce" decision. This happens when savings are placed in banks or other financial institutions and then borrowed by a person or a business firm that wants to buy something.

The percentage of income used for consumption goods and services has dropped since 1950, while the percentage paid in taxes and interest has increased.

Figure 6 gives a breakdown of the consumption expenditures of households. As you can see, housing and household operation now account for

FIGURE 6
Personal Consumption Expenditures in the United States for Selected Years (percentage distribution)

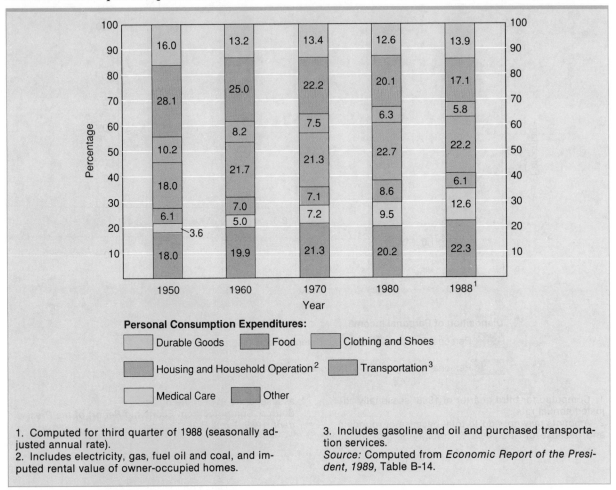

Personal Consumption Expenditures:

Durable Goods   Food   Clothing and Shoes

Housing and Household Operation[2]   Transportation[3]

Medical Care   Other

1. Computed for third quarter of 1988 (seasonally adjusted annual rate).
2. Includes electricity, gas, fuel oil and coal, and imputed rental value of owner-occupied homes.

3. Includes gasoline and oil and purchased transportation services.
Source: Computed from *Economic Report of the President, 1989*, Table B-14.

almost one-fourth of consumption expenditure, while food claims less than 20 percent. The famous trio of "food, clothing, and shelter" add up to considerably less than half of all consumption. The percentages spent for food and clothing decreased significantly while the percentage spent for medical care showed a spectacular increase.

BUSINESS FIRMS

The business firm is the second actor on the economic stage to be examined in this chapter. Business firms purchase resources or resource services and combine them to produce goods and services.

In this sense, business brings resource owners and consumers together.

Business firms purchase resources from households and combine them to produce goods and services.

Forms of Business Organization

The three basic forms of business organization are the proprietorship, the partnership, and the corporation. Each form has special features, which we shall describe briefly.

The Proprietorship A **proprietorship** exists simply because some person decides to start his or her own business. No legal papers have to be filled out, and no formal declaration about being in business is necessary unless there are laws that relate to the particular work to be done, such as the necessity of obtaining a license to practice medicine or permission from a health department to operate a restaurant. The owner, or proprietor, is responsible for financing and managing the business. Assuming the risks of possible losses, the proprietor has the right to whatever profits may come after all outside debts have been paid. A large percentage of small retail stores, small farms, and very small manufacturing companies in the United States are proprietorships.

Proprietorships are businesses owned by one person.

The Partnership A **partnership** exists when two or more people agree to share the financial and managerial responsibilities of a business firm as well as its profits and losses. A partnership agreement is necessary because partners must set the terms and conditions of their participation in the business. The agreement does not have to be in writing, but experience suggests that written agreements will cause much less trouble than oral agreements. In the agreement, the partners can set up almost any methods of financing, managing, and profit sharing that they choose.

A partnership exists when two or more people agree to share the financial and managerial responsibilities of a business firm as well as its profits and losses.

There are two very important legal requirements that apply to *both* proprietorships and partnerships but pose special problems for partnerships. These are unlimited liability and limited life.

Each partner must accept **unlimited liability** (complete responsibility) for all the debts of the business. The partnership agreement may specify how debts are to be paid in most cases, but if any partners fail to meet their obligations, the other partners must make sure that the partnership meets all its commitments to outsiders. Because each partner is liable for the obligations of the whole business, outsiders have extra assurance that any promises made by the partnership will be kept. Of course, before joining a partnership, individuals must be sure that they trust and share the business goals of other members of the partnership.

Unlimited liability means that partners and proprietors bear complete responsibility for all the debts of the business.

Proprietorships and partnerships have **limited life.** A partnership lasts only as long as the partnership agreement is in force. Many events can put an end to the agreement and thus to the life of the partnership. If a partner dies or leaves the business, the other partners must make a new agreement in order to continue together in business. To add a new partner also means making a new agreement. The limited life of the partnership gives the partners the necessary flexibility to deal with changes but at the same time makes it a very fragile form of business organization.

Proprietorships and partnerships have limited life. A proprietorship lasts only as long as the proprietor is in business; a partnership lasts only as long as the partnership agreement is in force.

Creating partnerships and adding partners with special talents or training can give financial power and technical specialization to a business such as a law firm or a medical practice. However, the problems connected with limited life and unlimited liability make many people hesitate to join a partnership.

The Corporation A **corporation** comes into being when the government issues a charter. In the United States, corporate charters are issued by state governments. Obtaining a charter is simple and inexpensive, and the charter itself places very few restrictions on the operations of corporations. The charter authorizes the corporation to issue and sell shares of stock. The people who own these shares, the stockholders, are the owners of the corporation. Also, the charter establishes the corporation as a "legal person," separate from the "real persons" who are the owners and the managers of the corporation.

A corporation is a "legal person" separate from the "real persons" who own and manage it. Corporations are authorized by government charter. They have the right to issue and sell shares of stock that confer ownership rights on those who buy them.

As a legal person, the corporation can enter into contracts and make commitments in its own name. Under the law, the corporation itself is responsible for these obligations. Neither the owners nor the managers are individually liable for its debts and obligations. If the corporation does well, the stockholders reap the profits, but if corporate operations are not successful, a stockholder's loss is limited to the value of the shares owned. This **limited liability** feature of corporations greatly increases their ability to accumulate large sums of money for the enterprise. Because stockholders can share the profits and face only limited liability for losses, they are generally willing to let other people carry out the day-to-day management of the corporation.

The legal person created by the corporate charter has perpetual or **unlimited life,** which means that the corporation itself does not have to be reorganized every time individual persons enter or leave the ownership or management of the corporation. This stability is attractive to shareholders, who need not fear that their wealth will be tied up in endless legal battles, as may happen in partnerships. Also, customers, banks, and other firms can enter into long-term contracts with the corporation, knowing that its existence does not hinge on the lives of mortal human beings.

Thus the corporate form of business overcomes the problems of unlimited liability and limited life to which both proprietorships and partnerships are subject. The corporate form opens up vast possibilities for business firms to bring together financial power and technical expertise. Even though U.S.

proprietorships far outnumber U.S. corporations, it is no wonder that the great majority of business assets in the United States are held by corporations. The corporate share of manufacturing output in the United States is about 98 percent.

Corporations have limited liability— stockholders are not liable for their debts— and unlimited life—their existence is not dependent on a single person or a partnership agreement.

The great majority of business assets in the United States are held by corporations.

The chief disadvantage of the corporate form of business is that the net income of corporations is subject to taxation by the U.S. federal government and also by many state governments. These taxes are in addition to the individual income tax paid by stockholders on the profits they receive from corporations as dividends. Thus, corporation dividends are taxed twice, once when the money is earned by the corporation and again when it is received by the stockholder. From the point of view of the individual decision maker, taxation cancels some of the advantages of the corporate form of business.

The chief disadvantage of the corporate form of business organization is that corporation dividends are taxed twice, once when the money is earned by the corporation and again when it is received by the stockholder.

The Stock Market

The outstanding feature of the corporate form of business is that corporations obtain funds by selling securities that convey ownership rights to the buyers of the securities. These securities are called **shares**, or **stock**, in the corporation. Those who purchase shares or stock obtain, among other things, specified rights to vote on certain matters of corporate policy and in elections for the corporation's board of directors, which is the overall policy-making body. Stockholders also have specified rights to receive **dividends**, which are distributions of money (or additional stock) from the corporation. However, stockholders do not necessarily receive dividends equal to all the profits of the corporation in any particular period of time. The corporation's board of directors decides how much of the profit will be paid out as dividends and how much retained to finance future corporate operations.

Stockholders obtain specified rights to vote on matters of corporate policy and in elections for the corporation's board of directors; they also may receive dividends.

One of the reasons why corporations are able to obtain huge amounts of money to finance their operations is that stockholders can sell some or all of their stock whenever they want to reduce or terminate their association with the corporation. Most buying and selling of shares or stock in corporations is carried out in a stock exchange, where those who want to sell stock carry out transactions with those who want to buy it. There are stock exchanges in major cities all over the world and they are linked by a very effective communication network. Only those individuals or firms that are members of a stock exchange— that is, who own a "seat" on the exchange—are allowed to do business on the "floor" of the exchange. Therefore, a person who wants to buy or sell stock usually works through a **stockbroker**, who can have the transaction carried out on behalf of the buyer or seller. The broker, or brokerage firm, either owns a seat on an exchange or works through someone who does own one. The broker has the transaction carried out on a stock exchange and charges a fee, or **commission**, for the service. Stock exchange memberships are limited in number and are themselves bought and sold.

A person who wants to buy or sell stock in a stock exchange usually works through a stockbroker, who earns a commission for his or her service.

Figure 7 reproduces a portion of a newspaper report of stock market transactions on Tuesday, March 7, 1989.[2] To learn how to read the stock exchange report, look at the line reporting that day's transactions in the common stock of American Express (abbreviated AmExpress and with the symbol of AXP). The numbers in the first two columns report the highest and lowest prices per share paid for this stock over the past 52 weeks; in this example, the highest price was $31.875 a share (31⅞) and the lowest price was $22.875 a share (22⅞). The first number following the symbol of the stock shows that the annual amount of dividend paid per share is 84¢, which is a yield of 2.8 percent (shown in the next column) on its current price. The next number, which is 13, shows the price/earnings (P-E) ratio. This means that the current price of the stock is 13 times the amount of the annual profits per share of the corporation. The last five numbers report this particular day's transactions for this stock. On that day, 16,722 "blocks" (of 100 shares each) were traded. The highest-priced block traded at $30.75 per share (30¾), the lowest-priced block at $30.00 per share (30), and the last block sold that day went at $30.375 per share (30⅜). The price in this "closing" transaction was the same as the price of the closing transaction on the preceding business day.

As you can see, a huge amount of information is contained in the stock exchange reports. Investors and brokerage firms study this information carefully in deciding whether and what to buy or sell. Since stock market prices reflect expectations about future profitability, they provide useful information for guiding resources among alternative uses in capitalist-market economies.

Business Accounting

Keeping records is extremely important in business operations. Thus it is not surprising that some of the earliest known writing and calculating techniques were developed to keep business records. Information provided through business records can improve management's ability to make wise decisions. It also helps others, such as stockholders, banks, and investors, to judge the profitability of the business. Economists study these records to

2. *The Wall Street Journal,* March 8, 1989, p. C3.

FIGURE 7
Newspaper Report of Stock Exchange Transactions

NEW YORK STOCK EXCHANGE COMPOSITE TRANSACTIONS

WEDNESDAY, MARCH 8, 1989
Quotations as of 4:30 p.m. Eastern Time
Tuesday, March 7, 1989

52 Weeks Hi	Lo	Stock	Sym	Div	Yld %	PE	Vol 100s	Hi	Lo	Close	Net Chg
38¼	28	AlbertoCl	ACV	.36	1.0	18	78	35⅝	35⅛	35⅛	- ½
29¾	21	AlbertoCl A	ACVA	.36	1.3	15	236	28¼	28¼	28¼	- ¼
43	28	Albertsons	ABS	.80	2.0	18	1657	41¾	40¾	41	- ½
s 36⅛	26¼	Alcan	AL	1.68	5.3	6	7512	32½	32	32	- ⅜
28	22	AlcoStd	ASN	.76	2.9	11	769	26¼	25¾	26	...
28⅛	21¼	Alex&Alex	AAL	1.00	4.1	14	581	24⅜	24¼	24⅛	...
77	49¾	Alexanders	ALX		...	88	8	63½	63¼	63¼	- ⅜
85½	69⅛	AlleghanyCp	Y		...	11	18	82½	82	82⅜	+1
4½	1¼	vjAllegInt	AG		...	...	122	1¾	1½	1⅝	+ ⅛
27⅛	7½	vjAllegInt pf			...	...	2	12¾	12¾	12¾	- ¼
↑ 38	21⅝	AllegLud	ALS	1.00a	2.6	8	558	38½	37¾	38½	+ ⅝
x 40⅜	35⅞	AllegPwr	AYP	3.08	8.4	9	x692	36⅞	36⅝	36⅞	+ ¼
15¾	9¼	AllenGp	ALN		...	77	88	15½	15	15⅜	+ ⅜
18⅞	13	AllenGp pf		1.75	9.6	...	41	18¾	18⅛	18¼	+ ½
n 12½	9⅝	AllncCapMgt	AC	1.33	11.0	24	103	12¼	12	12⅛	- ⅛
21	13¾	AlliedPdts	ADP		...	18	16¾	16½	16¾	+ ⅛	
36⅞	30¾	AlliedSgnl	ALD	1.80	5.3	11	1924	34⅜	34	34	- ¼
10¾	9⅝	AllstMuniTr	ALM	.78a	7.5	...	199	10⅜	10¼	10⅜	+ ⅛
n 10	9⅜	AllstMunPrem	ALI	.04e	.4	...	133	9⅝	9½	9½	- ⅛
n 10¼	9¼	AllstMunInIl	ALT	.50e	5.1	...	418	9¾	9¾	9¾	...
n 10½	9⅞	AllstMunInTr	AMO	.24e	2.4	...	284	10⅛	10	10	...
↑ 41	29⅞	ALLTEL	AT	1.72	4.3	14	2312	41¾	39⅞	40	+ ⅝
65⅝	41½	Alcoa	AA	1.60a	2.6	6	5046	61¼	60⅝	61⅛	+ ¼
15¼	10	Amcastind	AIZ	.48	4.0	9	83	11⅞	11¾	11⅞	...
14⅝	7½	Amdura	ADU		...	22	797	14½	13⅞	14¼	+ ¼
25¼	19½	Amdura pf		1.95	7.7	...	262	25¼	25	25¼	+ ¼
↑x 36	25¾	AmerHess	AHC	.60	1.7	24	x9669	36⅜	36	36	+ ¼
23	14¾	AmBarrick	ABX	.10e	.4	...	1716	22⅞	22¾	22⅜	- ¼
71¾	42¼	AmBrand	AMB	2.44	3.8	11	3817	65½	63⅞	64½	+ ¼
30⅝	26⅝	AmBrand pf		2.75	10.1	...	27	27⅛	26⅞	27⅛	+ ⅜
134½	85½	AmBrand pf		2.67	2.0	...	3	131	129½	131	+2½
29⅞	20⅝	AmBldgMaint	ABM	.92	3.2	16	12	29⅛	29	29	- ⅛
29	23¼	AmBusnPdts	ABP	.96	3.3	13	22	28¾	28⅜	28¾	+ ⅜
↓ 22¼	19¾	AmCapBdFd	ACB	2.20e	11.1	...	96	19⅞	19⅝	19¾	...
24⅝	19¼	AmCapCvSec	ACS	3.03e	14.2	...	21	21¾	21⅜	21⅜	- ⅛
n 10⅛	8⅞	AmCapIncTr	ACD	1.10a	12.1	...	121	9¼	9	9⅛	...
14	8¼	AmCapMgt	ACA	1.00	9.2	11	23	10⅞	10¾	10⅞	...
55⅛	44	AmCyanmd	ACY	1.20	2.4	14	3574	49⅝	49	49¼	- ⅝
29¼	25⅞	AmElecPwr	AEP	2.32a	8.7	8	1537	26⅝	26¾	26⅝	- ⅛
31⅛	22⅞	AmExpress	AXP	.84	2.8	13	16722	30¾	30	30⅜	...
17	11½	AmFamily	AFL	.28	1.8	12	1215	16	15¾	15¾	...
36⅞	27¾	AmGenerl	AGC	1.50	4.4	10	2059	34	33½	33¾	- ½
n 8½	7½	AmGvIncFd	AGF	.84a	10.8	...	146	7¾	7½	7¾	...
n 10⅛	9⅛	AmGvIncoP	AAF	1.06a	11.6	...	111	9¾	9⅜	9¾	- ¼
19½	17	AmHlthProp	AHE	2.16	11.4	12	261	19⅛	19	19	...
x 27	24¼	AmHeritgLf	AHL	1.08	4.1	11	x1	26½	26½	26½	+ ⅛
88¾	70⅜	AmHomePdts	AHP	3.90	4.6	13	1278	86	85¼	85⅜	- ⅛
s 52¾	42¼	Ameritech	AIT	2.92	5.7	11	2520	51½	51¼	51¼	- ¾
↑ 75½	49	AmIntGroup	AIG	.40	.5	10	3803	75⅞	75	75⅛	+ ⅛
18¾	13⅞	AMI	AMI	.72	3.9	19	2854	18¾	18½	18½	...
36¾	24¼	AmPresidnt	APS	.50	1.4	10	178	35⅝	35	35⅝	+ ⅜
62⅜	53½	AmPresidnt pf		3.50	5.9	...	6	59½	59½	59½	+ ¼
16⅞	14¾	AmRE Ptnrs	ACP	2.00	12.8	8	80	15⅞	15⅝	15⅝	...
5⅛	3⅞	AmRltyTr	ARB	.72	16.9	3	403	4⅜	4¼	4¼	- ⅛
18⅝	11¾	AmSvgBk	ASB	.80	4.8	4	242	16⅞	16¾	16¾	...
s 20⅛	9⅝	BannerInd	BNR		...	13	167	19⅞	19⅝	19⅝	+ ⅛
x 33⅜	21	Barclays	BCS	1.85e	6.0	16	x125	30⅞	30¾	30¾	+ ¾
s 24⅝	18⅛	Bard CR	BCR	.32	1.5	15	2074	21½	20¾	21	- ½
37¼	32⅜	BarnesGp	B	1.40	4.1	11	15	34¼	34	34	...
37⅜	29⅛	BarnettBks	BBI	1.04	3.2	9	606	33⅜	32½	32⅞	- ⅜
n 6½	4⅜	BaroidCp	BRC	.05e	.8	38	2202	6⅜	6⅛	6⅜	+ ¼
9	4¼	BarryWrgt	BAR		...	34	83	4¾	4⅝	4¾	+ ⅛
1¼	⅛	vjBasix	BAS		...		4	13/32	13/32	13/32	...
19½	13⅛	BattleMtn	BMG	.10	.6	17	1706	15⅝	15¼	15⅝	+ ⅛
x 48	39⅞	BauschLomb	BOL	1.16	2.5	14	x864	46⅞	45⅛	46¼	+ ⅝
26⅛	16¼	BaxterInt	BAX	.56	2.8	15	18564	20⅛	19⅝	20	+ ½
47¾	37⅛	BaxterInt pf		3.65e	9.2	...	58	39⅞	39¾	39⅞	...
83	56¾	BaxterInt pf		3.50	5.3	...	225	66	64¾	66	+1⅜
19¾	9⅞	BayFnl	BAY		...		100	10⅜	10⅛	10¾	- ⅛
27	21	BayStGas	BGC	1.68	6.3	10	29	26⅞	26½	26⅝	- ⅛
15½	11⅛	BearStearns	BSC	.56	3.7	10	3634	15¼	15	15¼	+ ⅛
41⅞	30⅞	BearingsInc	BER	.80a	2.1	12	65	38⅜	38	38⅛	+ ⅛
15⅞	10¾	Beazer	BZR	.52e	3.4	9	3	15⅛	15⅛	15⅛	+ ¼
n 19½	17⅛	Beckmaninstr	BEC	.07e	.4	13	12	18⅞	18⅞	18⅞	+ ⅛
62⅛	46½	BectonDksn	BDX	1.00	1.9	13	953	52½	52	52	- ⅞
40	24	BeldenHem	BHY	.52	1.9	11	52	27¼	26⅞	27¼	+ ⅜
75¾	64⅛	BellAtlantic	BEL	4.08	5.5	11	3224	74½	73¼	74⅛	+ ⅛
16⅛	13½	BellIndus	BI	.28	1.8	15	3	15⅜	15⅜	15⅜	...
53¾	41⅝	Beneficial	BNL	2.20	4.9	11	523	44¾	44⅝	44½	- ⅜
26½	23¼	Beneficial pf		2.50	10.0	...	z30	25	25	25	- ¼
4⅝	3⅛	Benguet B	BE	.19r	4.8	6	125	4	3⅞	4	+ ⅛
4¼	11/64	vjBerkey	BKY		...	...	210	11/16	5/32	11/16	...
5050	3075	BerkHathwy	BRK		...	17	z104825	4825	4825	+25	
15⅜	6⅞	BestBuy	BBY		...	21	60	10⅛	9⅞	9⅞	- ⅛
28½	18	BethSteel	BS		...	5	2085	25⅞	25½	25⅝	- ¼
56¼	46¼	BethSteel pf		5.00	9.5	...	106	52⅞	52¾	52⅞	- ⅜
27⅝	22½	BethSteel pf		2.50	9.6	...	106	26	25⅞	26	- ⅛
9¼	3¾	BeverlyEnt	BEV		...		3839	9	8⅝	9	+ ¼
20¼	9¾	BeverlyInv	BIP	1.79e	14.2	10	9	12⅜	12½	12⅝	...
21⅜	7½	BiocraftLabs	BCL		...	18	69	10⅛	9⅞	9⅞	- ¼
s 29⅞	16⅝	BirmghamStl	BIR	.50	1.9	8	126	27	26⅜	26⅜	- ½
25¼	17⅛	BlackDeck	BDK	.40	1.7	13	911	23⅞	23½	23¾	+ ⅛
28¼	24½	BlackHills	BKH	1.52	5.8	11	51	26½	26⅜	26⅜	...
n 10⅛	9¼	BlackstnIncTr	BKT	1.10	12.1	...	733	9¼	9⅛	9⅛	- ⅛
n 10⅛	9⅜	BlackstnTgt	BTT	1.00	10.3	...	1369	9¾	9⅝	9¾	...
x 33	22¾	BlockHR	HRB	1.04	3.7	16	x1425	28⅜	27⅝	28	+ ⅜
n 22¾	14⅝	BlueArrow	BAW	.39e	2.5	...	1259	16⅛	15⅞	15⅞	- ¼
6⅝	5½	BlueChipFd	BLU	.34e	5.3	...	135	6½	6¼	6⅜	- ⅛
67⅜	44½	Boeing	BA	1.60	2.4	16	5323	65¾	65	65	...
50	39¼	BoiseCasc	BCC	1.40	3.3	7	2767	42⅛	41¾	42	+ ¼
19¾	9	BoltBerNew	BBN	.06	.6	31	142	9⅞	9¾	9¾	...
n 11¾	6¾	BondIntGold	BIG		...		594	7⅜	7¼	7¼	...
4⅛	1⅛	BondIntGold wt			...		12	1½	1½	1½	+ ⅛
23½	13⅛	BordChm un	BCP	3.02e	13.1	7	1462	23	22¾	23	...
n 23	17	BordChm	BCU	3.02e	13.4	7	814	22⅝	22¾	22½	- ⅛
61⅛	48¾	BordenInc	BN	1.56	2.7	14	1060	58	57⅛	57⅜	-1
15¾	12¼	BostCelts	BOS	1.60e	11.3	8	22	14¼	14	14⅛	...
17¼	12½	BostEdsn	BSE	1.82	11.4	10	337	16⅛	15⅞	16	...
91¼	82	BostEdsn pf		8.88	10.6	...	z1090	84	84	84	+1
36⅞	25¼	Bowater	BOW	1.12	4.1	6	2590	27½	27¼	27⅜	+ ⅛

TABLE 1
Precision Printing Company, Balance Sheet, December 31, 1990

Assets		Liabilities	
Current Assets		**Current Liabilities**	
Cash	$ 30,000	Accounts Payable	$ 40,000
Inventory	210,000	Notes Payable	70,000
Fixed Assets		**Long-Term Liabilities**	
Equipment	420,000	Bonds	380,000
Buildings	160,000	Total Liabilities	$490,000
		Net Worth	
		Preferred Stock	$ 30,000
		Common Stock	220,000
		Retained Earnings	80,000
		Total Net Worth	$330,000
		Total Liabilities and	
Total Assets	$820,000	Net Worth	$820,000

discover trends and changes in the economy. The two basic financial statements of a firm are the balance sheet and the income statement.

The Balance Sheet   The **balance sheet** is an accountant's report on the condition of a business firm as of the close of business on a particular date. It is like a snapshot or still photograph that shows the firm's financial condition at some instant in time. The balance sheet has three elements, called assets, liabilities, and net worth (or owners' equity). **Assets** represent all the things that the firm owns. **Liabilities** are the claims that outsiders have for payments from the firm. The amount that is left over for the owners of the firm is called **net worth**. These three elements make up the balance-sheet equation:

$$\text{assets} = \text{liabilities} + \text{net worth}$$

Accountants make the best estimates they can of the actual values for assets and liabilities. Then, to satisfy the balance-sheet equation, the net worth of the business (the value that belongs to the owners) must be adjusted upward or downward until the equality is established. But first the accountant will need to evaluate both assets and liabilities as objectively as possible. Because legitimate accounting must stick to the facts in evaluating assets and

liabilities, the value of the owners' equity (net worth) is the only item that can be adjusted to achieve the necessary balance.

The balance sheet shows assets (all the things the firm owns), liabilities (all the claims outsiders have for payments from the firm), and net worth (the amount left over for the owners of the firm) as of the close of business on a particular date.

A hypothetical balance sheet is illustrated in Table 1. Assets are listed on the left side of the account, and liabilities and net worth are listed on the right side. The total on one side must equal the total on the other side; that is, the balance sheet must "balance." Though the specific items that will be listed on a balance sheet depend on the nature of the business itself, there are some general rules or guidelines that accountants follow in presenting balance sheets. On the asset side, items are listed according to how quickly they can be converted into cash. In the illustrated balance sheet, cash itself comes first, of course, followed by inventory (goods on hand), equipment, and buildings. The assets that ordinarily would be converted to cash in the course of a normal year's business are called current assets. Items that would not be converted to cash during a normal year's operation are called fixed, or long-term, assets. The order of the liabilities (on the right side of the balance sheet) follows a similar pattern. Current liabilities are obligations that normally are payable during a year's business operations. Long-term liabilities are obligations that will be payable at some more distant time.

On the asset side of the balance sheet, items are listed according to how quickly they can be converted into cash. Items that would not be converted to cash in the course of a normal year's business are called fixed assets.

Current liabilities are obligations that normally are payable during a year's business operations. Long-term liabilities are obligations that will be payable at some more distant time.

Of special interest to the owners or potential owners of a company, of course, is the net worth section of the balance sheet. The entries in this section will vary depending on whether the firm is organized as a proprietorship, a partnership, or a corporation. The net worth section for a partnership will show the ownership interests of the different partners, and the net worth section for a corporation will show the interests of the various classes of stockholders. Also, a distinction is usually made between amounts paid in by owners and amounts of earnings that have been retained by the firm.

The Income Statement   The **income statement,** or **profit and loss statement,** is an accountant's report of the operations of a business firm over some specified period of time. In a sense, it is like a movie, or part of one, because it reports the firm's activities over a finite period. It is different from the balance sheet, which, as we said, is like a still picture or snapshot and describes the condition of the firm at some fixed point in time.

The income (profit and loss) statement is an accountant's report of the operations of a business firm over some specified period of time.

Table 2 illustrates a hypothetical income statement. There is no balancing feature in this statement. Instead, it starts at the top with a report of the net amount of money received from sales during the time period. Then it shows how various items are subtracted from these receipts. At the bottom is the amount left over or remaining with the business. The specific items that appear on the income statement will differ greatly among firms, but certain general categories appear in almost all statements. For example, businesses usually want to separate manufacturing costs, selling and administrative costs, interest costs, and taxes. Cost-accounting and tax-accounting techniques are used to determine these various amounts. After costs and taxes have been subtracted, the statement shows the amount of income left. This is the amount available to be paid to the owners (as dividends in the corporate form of business) or to be retained for use by the company. The income statement will report the disposition that was made of these earnings.

Balance sheets and income statements can be fitted together to give a full and continuous account of the financial life of a firm. Balance sheets report the condition of a business firm at specific points in time, and income statements report its operations over periods of time. The difference between the balance sheet picture on one date and the balance sheet picture on another date is "explained" by the income statements that cover the period of time between the balance sheets.

Balance sheets report the condition of a business firm at specific points in time, and income statements report its operation over periods of time. Income statements and balance sheets can be fitted together to give a full and continuous account of the financial life of a firm.

GOVERNMENTS

Government is the third actor on the economic stage. The economic role of government depends a great deal upon the type of economic system in a

TABLE 2
Income Statement for Precision Printing Company for the Year Ended December 31, 1990

Net Sales		$380,000
Manufacturing Cost		
Materials	$ 40,000	
Labor	90,000	
Depreciation	75,000	
Subtotal	$205,000	
Plus Beginning Inventory	$245,000	
Less Closing Inventory	−210,000	
Subtotal	35,000	
Total Manufacturing Cost		240,000
Gross Profit from Sales		$140,000
Selling and Administrative Costs		40,000
Fixed Interest Charges and State and Local Taxes		15,000
Net Income Before Income Taxes		$ 85,000
Corporation Income Taxes		35,000
Net Income After Taxes		$ 50,000
Dividends Paid on Preferred Stock		2,000
Net Income After Preferred Stock Dividends		$ 48,000
Dividends Paid on Common Stock		26,000
Addition to Retained Earnings		$ 22,000

country. For example, you learned in Chapter 1 that socialist governments own many natural and capital resources and may develop detailed plans for the economy. On the other hand, government typically plays a much smaller role in capitalist-market economies. In this chapter, we shall limit our discussion to the main functions of government in capitalist-market economies. In these economic systems, there are three basic economic responsibilities or functions of government—the allocation function, the distribution function, and the stabilization function.

The Allocation Function

The **allocation function** refers to the allocation of resources among alternative uses. Specifically, the allocation responsibility of government is to take appropriate corrective action in circumstances where private markets fail to provide the combination of goods and services desired by the people. Such **market failures** occur when the markets, left to themselves, produce too much of certain goods and services and not enough of others. In other words, without government action, resources would be misallocated.

The allocation responsibility of government is to take appropriate corrective action in circumstances where private markets fail to provide the combination of goods and services desired by the people.

There are several reasons why markets may give wrong answers to the "what to produce" question and thus misallocate resources. One is that monopolistic firms (*inadequate competition*) may restrict output, thereby causing the prices of their products to rise and distorting the choices available to consumers. A second source of allocational market failure lies with **externalities,** which arise when the production or consumption of a good or service affects people who have no way, through the markets, to influence the decision about how much of the good or service should be produced. Pollution is a common example of a harmful ("negative") externality. Smoke in the air can damage the lungs of people who have no way, through markets, to cause factories to install filters on their smokestacks. In this case, there may be overproduction of the good manufactured in the smoke-producing factory. Beneficial ("positive") externalities also can arise, as when people other than parents, students, and teachers benefit from the education of children in the community. In this situation, the market system might provide too small a quantity of education service.

Third, markets typically fail to provide efficient quantities of **collective goods**. Collective goods are those which, by their nature, must be consumed in common by all the people in an area, that is, all must consume the same quality and quantity of the good or service. Examples of collective goods include national defense, police, and judicial services.

Collective goods are those which, by their nature, must be consumed in common by all the people in an area.

The Distribution Function

Under the **distribution function**, government has the responsibility to adjust the distribution of income among individuals. This responsibility relates directly to the "for whom" decision that must be made in every economic system. The distribution responsibility arises because the normal operation of the market system results in some amount of inequality in the distribution of income among individuals. If the markets fail to generate the degree of inequality that is considered desirable, the government may redistribute incomes to achieve a better distribution.

Government has the responsibility to adjust the distribution of income among individuals to achieve an appropriate degree of equality.

There are many causes of inequality in a market-capitalist system. If the system is operating effectively, people who have great talent, are skillful, work hard, and are lucky will be rewarded with high incomes. Others can gain income if they have rich parents or obtain monopoly power. But the market system generates very little income for people who lack these advantages. Therefore, market-capitalist (as well as most collectivist-planned) economic systems are likely to generate more inequality than the people, speaking through the political system, say ought to exist. Of course, people do not agree on exactly what is a "fair" or "just" or "equitable" distribution of income, and there is no scientific way to prove that one distribution is necessarily better than another. Nevertheless, voters do let their governments know what kind of distribution they want. Their instructions may be vague, since they are filtered through political candidates who may campaign on confusing and complicated sets of promises. They may often be self-serving too, since most people apparently feel that fairness means more income for themselves. But the fact is that citizens do expect their government to take steps to ensure that the distribution of income is not unreasonable. Government programs aimed, in part at least, at income redistribution include progressive income taxes, welfare programs, and a complicated set of taxes and subsidies for particular goods and services that are intended to improve the income position of certain groups. Minimum wage laws and farm subsidies illustrate this last redistributive approach.

One aspect of income distribution must be emphasized now, before you go further in your study of economics. The demand curves that you will study in this book reflect both the willingness and the ability of people to purchase products. The ability to purchase goods and services reflects the income distribution. How much caviar and how much corn flakes we produce depends in part on the distribution of income. Demand-and-supply analysis will work equally well under any income distribution, but whether the choice of goods and services that comes out of the market process fits what you believe is right depends in part on whether you approve of the income distribution influencing demand throughout the economy.

The Stabilization Function

The **stabilization function**, or responsibility, of government is to achieve price stability, a high level of employment, and a reasonable rate of economic growth for the economy. It is a function that focuses heavily on macroeconomics, although microeconomic instruments also are involved. The stabilization responsibility arises because the market system of economic organization has a record of business cycles, or fluctuations, bringing unemployment, inflation, or both. Before the 1930s, most economists (Karl Marx and his followers excepted) believed that fluctuations in the capitalist system were fairly minor and self-correcting so that there was no need for government to step in. But the experience of the Great Depression and the economic theories of the famous British economist John Maynard Keynes (1883–1946) brought a great change in economic thought about this aspect of government activity. Since Keynes, macroeconomics has been important in influencing government policy.

You probably have heard about the major instruments of government stabilization policy, since they often make headlines in newspapers and television news reports. For example, government may try to control the size of the nation's money supply in the belief that the amount of money in the economy has a lot to do with inflation or other changes in the price level. Similarly, a lot of attention is paid to whether or not the government's budget is balanced because deficits are thought to stimulate the economy, whereas surpluses are thought to slow down economic activity.

THE REST OF THE WORLD

The fourth actor on the economic stage for any particular economy is "the rest of the world"—that is, the exporting, importing, and financial transactions that take place with households, business firms, and governments in other countries. In 1988, U.S. business firms sold $536.1 billion of goods and services to foreigners, which amounted to 10.9 percent of the total production in the U.S. economy. In that same year, Americans bought $616 billion of goods and services from foreigners, so that the United States had a trade deficit of some $79.9 billion.[3] Clearly, these transactions are important in the operation of the U.S. economy. Many American workers have jobs producing goods for export, and American consumers enjoy the products that they buy from foreigners. But other American workers feel that their jobs are threatened by foreign competitors.

Figure 8 shows that the dollar value of U.S. exports as a percent of gross national product (the value of total production) has increased substantially since World War II. This means that "the rest of the world" is much more important to the U.S. economy today than it was in earlier times. Important as "the rest of the world" is for the United States, it is much more important for many other countries in the world. A country that allows relatively unrestricted trade across its borders is called an **open economy**; if such an economy is small, it is likely that transactions with foreigners will be extremely important. On the other hand, large countries that have a great variety of resources have to depend less on obtaining goods from foreigners, and for them "the rest of the world" is less important. Of course, **closed economies**, which severely restrict trade across their borders, are more insulated from outside forces. China and the Soviet

3. *Economic Report of the President, 1989,* Table B-1. The import and export numbers that we reported as 1988 are actually third quarter of 1988 data that have been seasonally adjusted and annualized.

FIGURE 8
U.S. Exports as a Percentage of Gross National Product for Selected Years

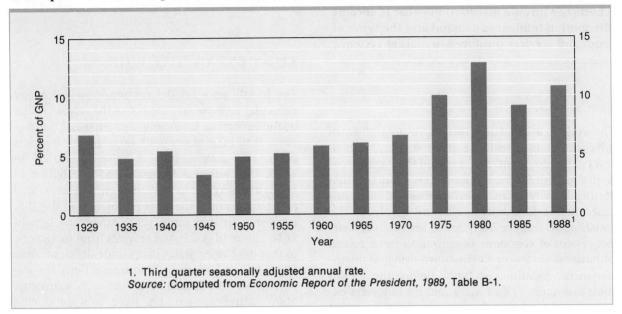

1. Third quarter seasonally adjusted annual rate.
Source: Computed from *Economic Report of the President, 1989,* Table B-1.

Union are relatively closed economies, although China is becoming more and more involved in international transactions.

The dollar value of U.S. exports as a percent of gross national product has increased substantially since World War II.

The importing, exporting, and financial transactions that take place with households, business firms, and governments in other countries are much more important to the U.S. economy today than in earlier times.

A country that allows relatively unrestricted trade across its borders is called an open economy. Closed economies severely restrict trade across their borders.

Exports and imports are not the only reasons why "the rest of the world" is an important actor on a country's economic stage. Money also flows from country to country in search of the best returns in interest on bonds and bank accounts or dividends from corporate stocks. These financial, or "capital account," transactions have important effects on economic conditions in the countries involved, since they influence economic growth by affecting the funds available to finance new capital goods. Business firms, governments, the United Nations, and major banking houses are active in international lending and finance.

THE ACTORS IN ACTION

The economic actors that you have met in this chapter—households, business firms, governments, and "the rest of the world"—will appear again and again in your study of economics. In microeconomics, you will learn about decision-making criteria and processes and how the actors interact with each other. In macroeconomics, you will find that the four actors provide the organizing scheme for the model of how the macroeconomy works and how the national income accounting system keeps track of total income and production in the economy.

Economics in Focus

Women in the Labor Force

The change has been so rapid and fundamental that economists have called it a revolution in the U.S. labor force. A generation ago the "typical" American woman, with or without children, was not employed outside the household. By the late 1980s, however, well over 50 percent of all American women worked outside the home; in the key age group of 25 to 44, the labor-force participation rate was over 70 percent.

Not only do more women have jobs, but they work longer hours, and motherhood is not as much of a deterrent as it used to be. Sixty percent of school-age children have mothers in the labor force, compared to 39 percent in 1970. Moreover, the fastest-growing segment of the labor force consists of women with children under six years old.

The revolution is expected to continue. Now that the baby-boom generation has begun to reach middle age, the pool of young workers is shrinking. As companies cast their nets ever wider to find qualified new employees, the proportion of jobs held by women will continue rising, so that by the year 2000 the total number of working women will nearly equal the number of working men.

This revolution has had—and will continue to have—profound social and economic consequences. Day care, for example, has become a burning issue. Some women are dissuaded from working because of a lack of acceptable day care for their children; others lose valuable productivity when they have to deal with such problems as the babysitter quitting or Johnny catching the flu. Although both the federal and state governments are getting involved, businesses themselves will provide part of the solution. More and more, large companies are realizing that one way to attract and keep women workers is to offer help with day care. As late as 1988 only about 300 corporations sponsored their own day-care facilities, but the number should grow rapidly as companies compete for female employees. Flexible schedules, family leaves, alternative work styles—these are other corporate accommodations that allow women to balance the demands of home and work.

Overall, the feminization of the work force has proceeded smoothly—perhaps surprisingly so for a "revolution." But many sensitive issues remain to be dealt with in the 1990s and beyond. Should companies have a "mommy track," and is this an aid for female employees or a new form of discrimination? Is sexual harassment on the job increasing, and are companies doing enough to prevent it? Should special executive-training or mentoring programs be established to offer women a better chance of advancement?

Sources: Sharon Nelton, "Meet Your New Work Force," *Nation's Business,* July 1988, pp. 14–21; Thomas W. Merrick and Stephen J. Tordella, "Demographics: People and Markets," *Population Bulletin,* vol. 43 (February 1988), pp. 17–19; Elizabeth Ehrlich with Susan B. Garland, "For American Business, a New World of Workers," *Business Week,* September 19, 1988, pp. 112–120; Susan E. Shank, "Women and the Labor Market: The Link Grows Stronger," *Monthly Labor Review,* March 1988, pp. 3–8; Elizabeth Ehrlich, "Is the Mommy Track a Blessing—or a Betrayal?" *Business Week,* May 15, 1989, pp. 98–99; Gretchen Morgenson, "Watch That Leer, Stifle That Joke," *Forbes,* May 15, 1989, pp. 69–72.

SUMMARY

1. To understand how economic systems operate, economists consider four actors on the economic stage—households, business firms, governments, and "the rest of the world." (See pages 19–21.)

2. Households are made up of individuals, who, in capitalist economic systems, are the owners of resources. As the owners of resources in capitalist systems, individuals are the ultimate recipients of the income generated by production. (See page 20.)

3. Household members also are the ultimate consumers of the goods and services produced in an economy. When individuals spend the income earned as owners of resources, that is, when they function in their role as consumers, they are helping to make the "what to produce" decision. (See page 20.)

4. Business firms are the decision-making units concerned with production. They purchase resources and resource services from households and combine them to produce goods and services. Thus, their role is to make the "how to produce" decisions in the economy. (See page 26.)

5. Proprietorships, partnerships, and corporations are the three major kinds of business organizations. Corporations have become large and powerful because their charters grant limited liability and unlimited life, which allow them to accumulate large quantities of money and technical expertise. (See pages 27–29.)

6. Corporations obtain funds by selling shares, or stock, which convey to the buyer certain ownership rights in the corporation. The shareholders may receive dividends and normally may vote in electing the board of directors and in deciding corporate policy. (See page 28.)

7. The sale and purchase of corporate stock usually is carried out in stock exchanges located in major cities. An individual wishing to buy or sell stock works through a stockbroker, who carries out the transaction and charges a commission for the service. Reports of stock exchange transactions are published regularly in major newspapers. (See pages 28–29 and Figure 7, page 30.)

8. Balance sheets and income statements are accounting reports about the condition and the operation, respectively, of firms. Together these two reports give a continuing record of a company's financial life. (See pages 31–32.)

9. Most economists recognize three basic responsibilities, or "functions," of government in capitalist-market economic systems—the allocation function, the distribution function, and the stabilization function. In its allocation function, government is viewed as correcting for market failures in deciding "what to produce." In its distribution function, government is expected to promote a desirable distribution of income among individuals. The stabilization function involves moderating business cycles while maintaining high-level employment and stability in the general price level. (See pages 32–35.)

10. Households, business firms, and governments in "the rest of the world" make up the fourth actor on the economic stage of any given country. This actor has become increasingly important for the U.S. economy. (See pages 35–36.)

KEY TERMS

allocation function: the responsibility of government to take appropriate corrective action in circumstances where private markets fail to provide the combination of goods and services desired by the people (page 33).

assets: the value of all the things a business firm owns (page 31).

balance sheet: an accountant's report on the condition of a business firm as of the close of business on a particular date (page 31).

civilian labor force participation rate: the percentage of the civilian noninstitutional population, age sixteen or older, that is either working or looking for work (page 24).

closed economy: a country that severely restricts trade across its borders (page 35).

collective goods: goods that must be consumed in common by all the people in an area (page 34).

commission: the fee earned by a stockbroker for carrying out a transaction for a buyer or seller on a stock exchange (page 29).

corporation: a business firm that is granted "legal person" status by government charter; it has limited liability, unlimited life, and the ability to issue and sell shares of stock (page 27).

distribution function: the responsibility of government to adjust the distribution of income among individuals (page 34).

dividends: distributions of money (or additional stock) from a corporation to its owners (page 29).

externalities: a source of allocational market failure that arises when the production or consumption of a good or service affects people who have no way, through markets, to influence decisions about how much of the good or service should be produced (page 33).

household: a family group (or one or more persons) living together in the same dwelling unit (page 20).

income (profit and loss) statement: an accountant's report of the operations of a business firm over some specified period of time (page 32).

liabilities: the claims that outsiders have for payments from a business firm (page 31).

limited liability: a feature of corporations whereby stockholders are not responsible for the corporation's debts (page 28).

limited life: a characteristic of proprietorships and partnerships; a proprietorship lasts only as long as the proprietor is in business, and a partnership lasts only as long as the partnership agreement is in force (page 27).

market failure: when markets, left to themselves, produce too much of certain goods and services and not enough of others (page 33).

national income: the total of all earnings generated in an economy (page 24).

net worth: the amount that is left over for the owners of a business firm after total liabilities have been subtracted from total assets (page 31).

open economy: a country that allows relatively unrestricted trade across its borders (page 35).

partnership: a business that is formed when two or more people agree to share the financial and managerial responsibilities of a firm as well as its profits and losses (page 27).

profit and loss statement: *see* **income statement.**

proprietorship: a business owned by one person (page 27).

shares (stock): securities sold by a corporation that convey ownership rights to the buyers (page 28).

stabilization function: the responsibility of government to achieve price stability, a high level of employment, and a reasonable rate of economic growth for the economy (page 35).

stock: *see* **shares.**

stockbroker: a person who buys or sells stock on a stock exchange on behalf of another (page 29).

unlimited liability: a characteristic of proprietorships and partnerships whereby the proprietor or each partner must accept complete responsibility for all the debts of the business (page 27).

unlimited life: a characteristic of a corporation whereby the corporation does not have to be reorganized every time individual persons enter or leave the ownership or management of the firm (page 28).

DISCUSSION QUESTIONS

1. It is often observed that, in political action dealing with legislation, consumer-interest lobbies are unable to prevail against lobbies promoting the interests of producers and resource owners. But each individual involved is a consumer as well as an owner of resources. Why, in your opinion, do people tend to place their interests as resource owners ahead of their interests as consumers?

2. The population ripple is one of the causes of problems in financing the Social Security retirement program. In view of these population changes, some experts estimate that Social Security taxes as high as 25 percent may be necessary to support the large retired population. You may be asked to pay this tax to help those ten or fifteen years older than yourself. Will you vote for such a tax on your paycheck? What effects might such a tax have on the economy?

3. Adding together the percentages in Figure 2 for compensation of employees and proprietors' income yields a sum that is fairly constant over a forty-five-year period. But compensation has increased significantly while proprietors' income has decreased as a percentage of national income. What trends in the society might, in your opinion, tend to produce this result?

4. Although the distribution of income receives a great deal of attention in the media and in government debate, many economists believe that the distribution of wealth is equally (or perhaps more) important. Describe a set of circumstances in which a person would have low income but a significant quantity of wealth. Describe the circumstances in which a person would have high income but little wealth.

5. Many forces have combined to increase the percentage of the female population in the labor force. Identify two such forces and explain how you believe they have led to greater female labor force participation. What changes do you expect in the future?

6. Explain how both unlimited liability and limited life can cause problems for firms organized under the proprietorship or the partnership form. Explain how the corporate form of business organization resolves these problems.

7. Suppose that you believe that the future profitability of corporation A will be better than the future profitability of corporation B, in which you now own some stock. Therefore, you sell your shares of B and purchase shares of A. How would the prices of these stocks be affected if many people behave the same as you?

8. Using the following information, construct a simple balance sheet for a business firm: accounts payable, $15,000; equipment owned, $120,000; stock outstanding, $70,000; notes payable, $40,000; cash on hand, $10,000; retained earnings, $15,000; inventory, $50,000; bonds outstanding, $100,000; buildings, $60,000. Explain how a balance sheet is different from an income statement.

9. Name the three functions of government that are described in this chapter. Which do you believe will be the most important to voters in the next election? Under which function would you place a responsibility to promote economic growth? Why?

10. The increasing importance of "the rest of the world" in the economy of the United States has been accompanied, lately, by great political pressure for laws that would restrict entry of foreign goods into the United States. Discuss how this is related to the differing interests of individuals as consumers and as resource owners.

3

How Economists
Approach Problems

Preview We human beings are curious creatures who want to know what makes things "tick." More important, we have problems to be solved. Very often we do not have enough of the things we would like to have, yet sometimes we may even have too much. These are the problems that economists try to solve, or at least try to describe clearly, using economic theories and mathematical models of functional relationships.

In this chapter we look at the methods used in economics—how economists deal with economic problems. Most of what will be described and explained applies to all fields that use scientific analysis. A few terms and concepts may be unique to economics.

We begin with a discussion of economic theory and the difficulties inherent in testing these theories. We describe how the analysis of economic theories rests on assumptions, and the role played by the central assumption of economic rationality. Then we explain how economists show the relationships among variables in terms of functions, and we give a short review of how functions are shown in graphs. Next we introduce marginal analysis and equilibrium, two very important ideas often used in economics.

The rest of the chapter points out some difficulties that often beset beginning students of economics (and sometimes careless veterans as well). One such problem is that fairly common terms may take on entirely different meanings in economics. Other difficulties lie in assuming that when one event follows another in time, there is necessarily a cause-and-effect relationship, and in assuming that what is true for a part is also going to be true for the whole. Two final problems result from not paying enough attention to time lags and to expectations.

ECONOMIC THEORY

The discipline of economics consists of a large number of theories. A reasonable, if not precise, definition of an economist is one who knows the major economic theories and is engaged in testing and modifying some of them.

A **theory** is a systematically organized body of knowledge that can be applied in a fairly wide range of circumstances. It provides a set of rules or assumptions for analyzing information, for studying cause-and-effect relationships, and for solving real-life problems by enabling us to better explain economic happenings and/or to improve our ability to predict future events. In fact, theory guides research.

Economic theories are often called models. A **model** is a formal statement of a theory—a simplified view of how some part of the economy is assumed to operate. For example, a simple model of total consumption might describe it as dependent only on current income, whereas a more sophisticated model might describe other influences, like wealth or expected future income. Economic models are often expressed mathematically, but we shall minimize our dependence on mathematics in this elementary textbook.

A theory is a systematically organized body of knowledge that provides a set of rules for analyzing information, studying cause-and-effect relationships, and predicting future events. A model is a formal statement of a theory.

The study of economics is a search for relationships that occur between different economic variables. A **variable** is a quantity that can assume any of a set of values. For example, the price of a good is a variable, and the quantity of this good that is demanded is another variable. We may be interested in the relationship between them. That is, we want to know how a change in the price will affect the amount people will buy. Theory, however, is more than just a description of particular relationships. It is an effort to generalize about relationships that occur regularly, not about coincidental happenings. The observation that a certain rela-

tionship between two variables occurs very often leads to the prediction that it will occur again in the future.

A variable is a quantity that can assume any of a set of values.

The most important requirement of a theory is that it be useful. Most economists are not interested in theorizing for its own sake. They want to learn how to solve economic problems, and the answers lie in the use of present theories or of theories not yet devised.

Testing Economic Theory

Economics is a social science. In general, the social sciences are less exact than the natural or physical sciences. For this reason the social scientist must often be satisfied with predicting the direction of change rather than the amount. The natural scientist deals with molecules and cells and is concerned with people in an anatomical or physiological sense; the social scientist is interested in people's behavior. Therefore, the social scientist is usually not able to use the "laboratory method," or the controlled experiment, as effectively as can the natural scientist. If a chemist wants to discover the color reaction of chemical A with chemical B, he or she can place in two identical and sterile test tubes the same measured amount of chemical B and then add a certain amount of chemical A to one of the two test tubes. If the chemist now sees a color change in the test tube to which chemical A was added but observes no color change in the other test tube, the color change may clearly be attributed to the reaction between chemicals A and B. If this experiment were performed hundreds of times, we would expect the same results to occur each time.

Economics is a social science and, as such, is concerned with people's behavior. The controlled experiments that characterize the natural and physical sciences are usually not feasible in economics.

How would a simple experiment in economics be performed? Suppose that we want to find out by means of a controlled experiment what effect a one-shot $1,000 increase in income will have on people's spending and saving patterns. We choose 100 people for group A and another 100 people for group B. These people are not chosen at random. They are selected because they have certain similar characteristics: all have annual incomes of $25,000, all have about the same wealth, all are thirty years of age, all have three dependents, and all live in the same section of the same city. After giving $1,000 to each person in group A but nothing to the people in group B, we note the difference in spending patterns of the two groups. Let us assume we find that group A spends more than group B; specifically, that group A members spend an average of $738.50 more per person than do members of group B. How much faith do you have in this experiment? Would you expect that if the $1,000 had been given to the people in group B instead of group A, they, too, would have spent $738.50 more per person than those of group A? The chances are that the figure would be at least slightly different—perhaps quite different. Why? The reason is that we are dealing with people, who do not all behave in the same way. Though this experiment may allow us to predict that a one-shot increase in income will cause people to spend more, it does not allow us to predict confidently that they will spend 73.85 percent of their additional income.

From this example it is clear that the social scientist must make use of "experiments" that come from everyday experiences. Irrelevant variables must be filtered out by using statistical methods. How do we do this? First, we develop a theory predicting that, if one event occurs, another event will follow. Next, we devise a way of measuring exactly when and where the two events actually took place. Then we use statistical techniques to find out whether the time and place of the first event are associated, or correlated, with the time and place of the second event, as predicted by the theory. This correlation procedure can measure the probability, or likelihood, that the relationship between the two events could have arisen purely by chance. If we find the relationship too strong to be attributed to chance, the statistical technique has

given us some evidence that the theory being tested has a foundation in fact or in the real world. Of course, many more tests would have to be run to convince social scientists that a theory is valid and useful. Perhaps the two events were really the common outcome of some third event. This possibility would have to be tested through the development of another theory, which, in turn, would be tested against actual experience.

Social scientists must make use of data that come from everyday experience. They use statistical techniques to find out whether events are related to one another as predicted by theory.

Clearly, the approach to truth and understanding in economics and the other social sciences is a continuing process. New evidence may arise that casts doubt on long-established theories, and new theories can offer fresh approaches to understanding that may make older theories obsolete. But knowledge builds on knowledge, and new theories, when tested and supported by evidence, should be better than the old knowledge that is displaced. Economics is an optimistic science.

The Role of Assumptions

A theory need not fit all the facts. This statement often bothers beginning students of economics. It should not. Nor does ignoring certain real-world happenings mean that the theory is naive. Reality is often too complex to be grasped all at once. Sometimes we must simplify and isolate facts in order to see and understand relationships between particular variables. This is the role of **assumptions**—to set forth the limits of the variables in a theory and to state which of the variables are to be omitted.

An especially useful assumption in economics is expressed by the Latin phrase **ceteris paribus**, which means "other things being equal," that is, all other variables are held constant. For example, in order to analyze the effect of a change in the price of fuel oil on the quantity of fuel oil that is consumed, it may be helpful, at least initially, to disregard such other relevant variables as consumer incomes, the prices of competitive energy sources, and the severity of the weather. Thus, we might say, "When the price of a good such as fuel oil changes in one direction, the amount consumed changes in the opposite direction, *ceteris paribus*." This may be a valid and useful theory that can yield reliable and meaningful predictions about things or events that we may not yet have observed.

Assumptions set the limits of the variables in a theory and state which of the variables are to be omitted. The assumption of *ceteris paribus* means that all other variables are held constant.

However, this simple theory may not be sufficient for predicting events in the real world. During a very mild winter or just after a big price change in a substitute fuel, we would certainly not want to predict on the assumption that these variables had not changed. Theories that take into account these important variables must be brought into the total analysis before any predictions are made and real-world policy conclusions are drawn.

Ceteris paribus is, of course, an example of only one simplifying assumption. Countless others may be made. For example, we shall next discuss "economic rationality," which assumes that people behave in a particular way. Some other frequently used assumptions are those about the degree of certainty of a particular outcome, about the level of information that people have, about the degree of competition that exists, and about the role that government does or does not play.

Economic Rationality

How would you describe human behavior in a word? Puzzling? Unpredictable? Because it is so complex, economists must make certain assumptions about the way people are likely to act. Thus, most economic theories contain a key assumption—that people act rationally. Economically rational behavior, or **economic rationality**, is any action that people take to make them better off or to prevent them from becoming worse off. The assumption of economic rationality allows economists to predict on the basis that people are motivated by self-interest. It is assumed that individuals

appraise alternative courses of action and then choose that one that promises the greatest net gains.

The assumption of economic rationality means that economic predictions are based on the belief that people are motivated by self-interest.

Rational behavior need not be totally selfish. "Good things" come in many different packages. Though it is rational for Sally to prefer two new pairs of jeans to only one new pair, it may also be rational for her to prefer to buy her brother a shirt for his birthday rather than buy herself the second pair of jeans. If a rich old uncle wishes to be well remembered after he leaves this world and feels a sense of responsibility to his relatives, it is rational for him to leave $500,000 to his favorite niece. Furthermore, it is rational to give to one's favorite charity. Self-interest, then, has a broader meaning in economics than it does in common usage. People not only consider themselves better off when they add to their stock of material goods but also feel better off when they believe that they have done the right thing.

Actually, most individuals base decisions on social, political, and ethical considerations as well as on personal gain. Also, what people do may be strongly affected by habit, custom, and tradition. Every society weaves a fabric of institutions that guide economic behavior. Whether self-interest is institutionally determined or whether it is just part of human nature is a question that few economists feel qualified to explore. Instead, they merely recognize that theories using this assumption have been tested time and again and found to be good predictors. Self-interest is a powerful economic insight.

In studying economic rationality, we shall examine four decision-making groups: (1) consumers; (2) business decision makers; (3) owners of capital, natural resources, and labor; and (4) government. Let us see what economic rationality means for each of these groups.

The Rational Consumer The rational consumer is one who seeks to gain the greatest possible satisfaction from purchases. To get the best value from income, the consumer chooses to buy a set of goods and services that is more attractive than any other set that he or she can afford. This means that the rational consumer is consistent and can calculate. If this person prefers corn to beans and beans to peas, then he or she must prefer corn to peas. The consumer need not be maximizing satisfaction under perfect conditions, but doing so in an uncertain environment and with the limited information available at the time. Therefore the consumer who is disappointed after a purchase will buy different things on the next shopping trip because he or she now has more or better information.

The rational consumer is one who seeks to gain the greatest possible satisfaction from purchases.

The Rational Business Decision Maker   The rational *entrepreneur*—the business decision maker—is defined as one who seeks maximum profits. Therefore, an entrepreneur will be willing to produce more goods only as long as expected additional revenue (income) is greater than expected additional cost. Likewise, he or she will be willing to limit output if such action is expected to result in lowering cost more than revenue. In this way profits can be increased—or losses reduced.

The rational entrepreneur seeks maximum profits.

The Rational Owner of Capital, Natural Resources, and Labor   The rational owner of capital, natural resources, and labor tries to get the greatest possible return. In much the same way as the rational entrepreneur, the rational owner of capital (such as machines and factory buildings) seeks the maximum interest payment, the rational owner of natural resources (such as land and minerals) seeks maximum rent payment, and the rational owner of labor (the laborer) seeks the maximum wage. Suppose, for example, that someone is offered a job as a nurse at the XYZ hospital at a wage of $11.00 per hour. This person would not be a rational laborer if he or she would accept what appears to that person to be the same job for the same number of hours

and under similar working conditions at the ABC hospital at a wage rate of only $10.00 per hour.

The rational owner of capital seeks maximum interest payment, the rational owner of natural resources seeks maximum rent payment, and the rational owner of labor seeks maximum wage payment.

Rational Government   The groups discussed so far are all concerned primarily with maximizing their own incomes or satisfactions. Clearly, however, this is not the function that governments are supposed to perform. We shall briefly describe several approaches to the concept of rational government.

One approach is for the economist to recognize that government is made up of individuals who have their own personal motives. Here the economist tries to predict government behavior on the assumption that government workers, just like other workers, will direct their behavior toward ends that will serve their self-interest. Specifically, government workers are expected to try to maximize their own job security, income, and glory. In the case of elected officials, job security—or being re-elected—is of major importance. This goal may lead them to advocate "popular" policies or at least to offer whatever they believe the majority of their constituents favor. But all government workers, including those whose jobs do not depend on the voting public, are concerned with keeping their jobs, being promoted, and enjoying good working conditions. In this view, rational government action is that which brings government workers closer to these goals, however useless it may be to the public.[1]

Quite a different approach is to define rational government in terms of the functions and services that government should perform, such as the allocation, distribution, and stabilization responsibilities outlined in Chapter 2. Economists might define a rational government as one that can most accurately reflect what its citizens want government to do in these areas. Other economists define a rational government as one that will maximize social

1. In terms of maximization, it has been suggested that each government bureau or department tries to maximize its own appropriation, or budget, year in and year out.

welfare (if they can define social welfare), even if the policies to be followed are not always popular. For example, suppose that a policymaker decides on the basis of a value judgment that the elderly widows of World War I veterans are more deserving of additional income than are wheat growers. Then it is rational to cut price supports for wheat and use the money to increase pensions for the widows, even though the wheat growers may represent many more votes than the widows. In this view, rational government is judged in the light of its own goals, rather than those of the majority of its citizens.

According to one view, rational government action is driven by government workers acting in a manner that maximizes their personal goals such as high income, keeping their jobs, being promoted, and enjoying good working conditions. Rational government can also be defined in terms of the functions and services that government should perform, as a government that accurately reflects what its citizens want, or as a government that maximizes social welfare.

Positive and Normative Economics

Economics plays an important role in our lives. It is therefore not surprising that people have strong feelings concerning many economic issues, such as inflation, unemployment, nationalization of industry, unionization, minimum wages, energy, and environmental pollution. So that we are not misled by those who hope to have us side with them, a distinction is made between positive and normative approaches in economics.

Positive economics deals with what is. It tries to be objective and to stay away from value judgments or opinions. **Normative economics** concerns itself with what ought to be. It is subjective and expresses a person's or a group's opinion. One example of positive economics would be a front-page newspaper article on the facts and figures of inflation. Another would be an article presenting various economic theories that try to explain inflation. By contrast, the same newspa-

per's editorial stating that inflation is the country's most serious problem and calling for certain courses of action is an example of normative economics.

Positive economics deals with what is; normative economics concerns itself with what ought to be.

One approach is not necessarily better than the other—as long as it is clear to the reader which is being employed. People can easily be fooled, however, when normative economics is disguised in positive clothes.

Of course, the positive-normative separation can become quite fuzzy when normative ideas enter the choice of subjects to be studied positively. Some suggest that for a long time black-white and male-female wage differences were not approved subjects for detailed study, because the results might provide ammunition to "radicals."

FUNCTIONAL RELATIONSHIPS

In discussing economic theory, we pointed out that economists look for relationships that occur between different economic variables. Such a relationship is often expressed in terms of a **function**—a statement of how one variable depends on one or more other variables. For example, one variable—the weekly earnings of coal miners in West Virginia—may be a function of such variables as the number of hours worked per week and the wage rate per hour. This relationship may be written as

$$E = f(H, W)$$

where E is the weekly earnings of the coal miners, f is a symbol for function and can be read as "depends on," H is the number of hours worked per week, and W is the hourly wage rate.

A function is a statement of how one variable depends on one or more other variables.

Dependent and Independent Variables

When one variable is being described as a function of other variables, it is called the **dependent variable**, and the variables upon which it depends are called the **independent variables**. Thus, in our example, the dependent variable is the weekly earnings of West Virginia coal miners, and the independent variables are the number of hours that they work per week and the hourly wage rate that they receive. If we were considering another functional relationship, however, the classification of variables might change. For example, the hourly wage rate of the miners might be treated as a function of such variables as the desirability of the particular task performed on the job (that is, how clean, safe, and pleasurable it is), the number of years worked on the job, and the level of skill that the job requires. If these were the independent variables, the hourly wage rate of the miners would then be the dependent variable in this functional relationship.

The dependent variable is a function of one or more other variables. An independent variable is one upon which another variable depends.

Direct and Inverse Relationships

The relationship between the dependent and independent variables in a function may be either direct or inverse. A **direct relationship** is one where the dependent and the independent variables change in the same direction. The relationship $E = f(H, W)$ is a direct one between earnings and hours worked and between earnings and the wage rate. Coal miners' earnings go up when they work more hours or when their hourly wages are higher, *ceteris paribus*. Likewise, their earnings go down when they work fewer hours or when their wage rates are lower, *ceteris paribus*. An **inverse relationship** is one in which the dependent and independent variables change in opposite directions. An example is the case where we related the hourly wage rate of miners to the desirability of the task per-

formed. This relationship may be expressed as

$$W = f(T)$$

where the symbols W and f are as before and T is the degree of desirability of the task. The more desirable the task is for the miners, the lower the wage rate would be; the less desirable they find the task, the higher the wage rate would be, other things being equal.

In a direct relationship, the dependent and the independent variables change in the same direction. In an inverse relationship, the dependent and independent variables change in opposite directions.

Graphs

Functional relationships are often expressed algebraically or geometrically. The geometrical expression, by means of graphs, is usually simpler for most students than the algebraic one. There is an old saying that "a picture is worth a thousand words." In economics that is often the case. The "thousand words," or even a hundred words, are not as easy to grasp as a simple "picture"—a graph. Learning to read graphs will help you to understand a functional relationship at a glance.

Quadrants and Scales A review of the basics of graphing will be helpful. Figure 1 shows the four sections, or **quadrants**, that are formed when a horizontal axis is placed on a vertical axis. The point of intersection is at zero and is called the **origin**. Each axis is marked off with numbers, or **scaled**, to show the different values for the variable being measured along that axis. In the upper right part of the graph is quadrant I, showing values that are positive on both axes. To the left, quadrant II is for values that are negative on the horizontal axis and positive on the vertical axis. Just below, quadrant III provides for values that are negative on both axes. In the lower right, quadrant IV takes care of values that are positive on the horizontal axis and negative on the vertical axis. Most graphs in this book will be in quadrant I, where both axes show positive values.

FIGURE 1
Axes and Quadrants for Graphing

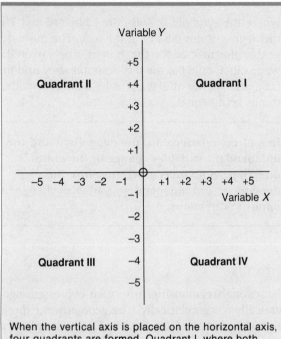

Variable Y

+5

Quadrant II   +4   Quadrant I

+3

+2

+1

−5 −4 −3 −2 −1   +1 +2 +3 +4 +5
                   −1
                                    Variable X
                   −2

                   −3

Quadrant III   −4   Quadrant IV

                   −5

When the vertical axis is placed on the horizontal axis, four quadrants are formed. Quadrant I, where both axes show positive values, is the one most often used in this book.

TABLE 1
Relation of Coal Miners' Earnings to Hours Worked (Hypothetical Numbers)

Coal Miners' Weekly Earnings (in dollars)	Number of Hours Worked per Week
50	5
100	10
200	20
350	35

establishes the other three points (B, C, and D in Figure 2). The plotted points may then be joined by drawing a line through them, and additional information can be obtained from this line. Though Table 1 did not contain information about coal miners' earnings when they work 15 hours or when they work 23½ hours a week, the line or curve provides good estimates of such intermediate values. Just draw a perpendicular from the horizontal axis at 23½ hours to the curve and then read off the earnings ($235) for that point on the vertical axis. The graph, then, is a quick way of summarizing information about the relationship between coal miners' earnings and the number of hours they work.

The intersection of the horizontal axis and the vertical axis is called the origin. Four quadrants are formed by the intersection.

Data are plotted on a graph through the use of perpendiculars drawn to the appropriate values on the axes of the graph.

Plotting Recall the functional relationship $E = f(H, W)$, where coal miners' earnings are a function of the number of hours they work and of their hourly wage rate. Table 1 shows a hypothetical relationship between the weekly earnings of coal miners and the number of hours they work per week. The wage rate is held constant at $10 per hour.

In Figure 2 the information from Table 1 has been plotted on a graph. Each point is located by drawing two straight lines, called **perpendiculars**, from the values along the axes. For example, the perpendicular drawn at $100 of earnings meets the perpendicular drawn at 10 hours to determine point A. The information in Table 1 also

Slope When dealing with functional relationships, economists are often very much interested in knowing the size of the change in one variable that is associated with a one-unit change in the size of the other variable. The term used to express this relation is **slope**.

Slope is stated in the following form:

$$\text{slope} = \frac{\text{change in variable on vertical axis}}{\text{change in variable on horizontal axis}}$$

Slope may be positive, negative, zero, or undefined. A direct relationship between the variables indicates a **positive slope**, and an inverse relationship a **negative slope.** The slope of a horizontal straight line is zero. The slope of a vertical

FIGURE 2
Relation of Coal Miners' Earnings to Hours Worked

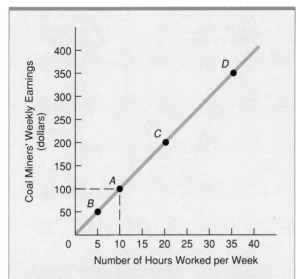

The curve pictures the function $E = f(H)$, where E is the weekly earnings of coal miners and H is the number of hours per week that they work. Their hourly wage rate is fixed at $10.

The numbers plotted from Table 1 establish the points B, A, C, and D. The line or curve that is drawn to join these points gives you good estimates of intermediate values.

straight line is undefined since we can not divide by zero.

Slope is the magnitude of the change in the variable on the vertical axis that is associated with a one unit change in the magnitude of the variable on the horizontal axis. A direct relationship between the variables indicates a positive slope; an inverse relationship indicates a negative slope.

The example that was pictured in Figure 2 illustrated positive slope, since when a coal miner works an additional hour, earnings increase by $10, and when the miner works an hour less, earnings decrease by $10. The slope in this example is therefore 10/1, or 10. Clearly, the slope of a line depends on the scaling values that were used in constructing the graph. If earnings were scaled in pennies, the slope would be 1,000/1, or 1,000.

The case of the inverse relationship between hourly wage rates received by coal miners and the desirability of the task performed offers an example of a negative slope. This is graphed in Figure 3, where the curve goes down from left to right, indicating that the slope is negative. (This is in contrast to the curve in Figure 2, which goes up from left to right, showing that the slope is positive.)

The curves drawn in Figures 2 and 3 are straight lines and represent **linear relationships**. This means that for the range of values shown, the dependent variable is uniformly responsive to changes in the independent variable. In other words, the slope is constant throughout the length of the curve.

Many relationships between economic variables are **nonlinear**, which means that equal changes in the independent variable do not always bring about the same response in the dependent variable. Simple nonlinear curves fall into four

FIGURE 3
Relation of Coal Miners' Wage Rates to Desirability of Tasks

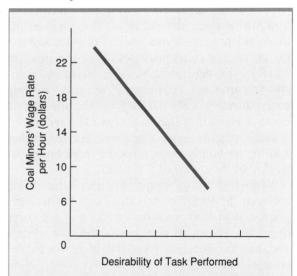

The curve pictures the function $W = f(T)$, where W is the hourly wage rate received by coal miners for performing different tasks and T is the desirability of the task performed (how clean, safe, and pleasurable it is). It shows an inverse relationship between these variables and therefore has a negative slope.

FIGURE 4
Nonlinear Curves

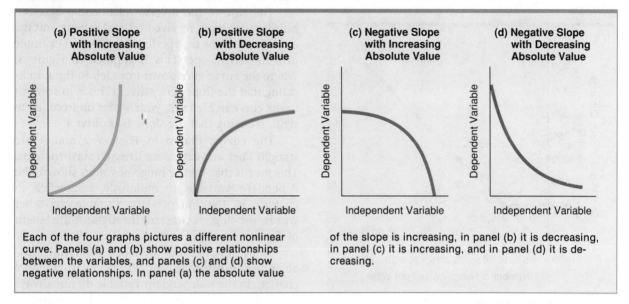

(a) Positive Slope with Increasing Absolute Value

Dependent Variable

Independent Variable

(b) Positive Slope with Decreasing Absolute Value

Dependent Variable

Independent Variable

(c) Negative Slope with Increasing Absolute Value

Dependent Variable

Independent Variable

(d) Negative Slope with Decreasing Absolute Value

Dependent Variable

Independent Variable

Each of the four graphs pictures a different nonlinear curve. Panels (a) and (b) show positive relationships between the variables, and panels (c) and (d) show negative relationships. In panel (a) the absolute value of the slope is increasing, in panel (b) it is decreasing, in panel (c) it is increasing, and in panel (d) it is decreasing.

categories, which are graphed in Figure 4. In describing slopes as increasing or decreasing, we use *absolute values* (values without reference to sign) to avoid confusion when dealing with curves that have negative slopes. Panel (a) shows a direct relationship between the variables. However, as the independent variable increases, so does the slope of the curve. For equal increases of the independent variable, the dependent variable increases by increasing amounts. For example, the curve relating coal miners' weekly earnings to the number of hours a week that they work would have an increasing positive slope if miners received higher and higher hourly wage rates the more hours per week that they worked.

Panel (b) also shows a direct relationship between the variables, but this time, as the independent variable increases, the slope of the curve decreases. For equal increases of the independent variable, the dependent variable increases by decreasing amounts.

Panels (c) and (d) illustrate nonlinear inverse relationships. In (c), as the independent variable increases, the dependent variable decreases at an increasing rate—the curve becomes steeper, showing that the absolute value of the slope becomes greater. In (d), as the independent variable in-

creases, the dependent variable decreases at a decreasing rate—the curve becomes flatter, showing that the absolute value of the slope becomes smaller.[2]

Linear relationships (shown on graphs by a straight line) have a constant slope. Nonlinear relationships have increasing or decreasing slopes.

In Figure 4, the dependent variable appears on the vertical axes and the independent variable appears on the horizontal axes of the graphs. This is convenient for our explanation of slope. In illustrating actual economic theories, the dependent variable is *not* always on the vertical axis and the independent variable is *not* always on the horizontal axis. In each economic graph, the theory itself

2. *Percentage* changes present us with special problems in graphing. For example, a quantity rising at a constant percentage rate is rising by increasing amounts. Therefore, it would be shown in our diagrams as a curve that is concave upward. If you have studied logarithms, you will remember that a linear *logarithmic* function represents a constant *percentage* rise or fall. Curvature on a logarithmic function represents rising or falling percentage changes. The slope of a logarithmic function is therefore a percentage change.

must be consulted to determine which variable is dependent and which is independent. However, slope is always measured as the change on the vertical axis divided by the change on the horizontal axis.

MARGINAL ANALYSIS

Economists often use **marginal analysis** to predict or evaluate the outcome of economic decisions. **Marginal** means "extra" or "additional." It refers to either the last unit that has been added or the next unit that may be added. For an individual thinking about how much of a product to buy, the marginal unit is the last one bought, or the next one that might be bought. Being "on the margin" means being in the process of deciding between alternatives. The child standing in front of a candy counter with 40¢ in hand is on the margin for various kinds of candy. The youngster may buy one more Hershey bar, one more roll of Lifesavers, or one more Milky Way.

Marginal means "extra" or "additional"—either the last unit that has been added or the next unit that may be added.

Marginal analysis recognizes that economic decisions are only rarely of an all-or-nothing nature. Business firms are not usually trying to decide whether to produce or not to produce. Rather, they are more often concerned with how much of certain goods to produce this week or this year. Individuals, likewise, rarely ask whether they should purchase food, clothing, or shelter, but instead ask what combination of these things they should purchase. Should they buy a little more food and a little less clothing, or more of both at the expense of renting a somewhat less attractive apartment? Individuals also face marginal decisions in regard to the amount of work they wish to do. Students typically do not think in terms of studying versus not studying at all. Rather they decide how much time to devote to study and therefore how much to leisure activities or to outside jobs. Should a third hour be devoted to studying for an exam, or should that hour be spent resting?

Marginal Analysis in Functional Relationships

Marginal analysis can be joined with the earlier discussion of functional relationships. Economists are often concerned with how much one variable changes as another variable changes. How much will an individual miner's weekly earnings increase if the hourly wage rate increases by a certain amount? The miner may receive an increase in hourly wage rate from $10 to $12, so that the marginal change in the hourly wage rate is $2. If the miner works 40 hours a week, then the weekly earnings will increase from $400 to $480, or a marginal increase of $80.

Relationship Between Marginal, Average, and Total Amount

Many theories in economics make use of marginal, average, and total measures. Thus, it is important to recognize how they differ and how they are related. The *total* is the whole of whatever variable is being measured. What is added to the total or subtracted from it in any one step is the *marginal* amount. The *average* is the total divided by the number of units. For example, a student may have gone to the movies 25 times this year and paid $4 each time. The total amount spent on movies is $100, the average expense is $4 ($100/25), and the marginal expense is also $4 (the price of the last movie). The total amount is always the sum of all the marginal amounts—25 movies at $4 per movie add up to $100. Suppose that the student were to go once more to the movies and find that the price had suddenly increased to $5. In this case, the marginal expense (on the 26th movie) is $5, the new total expense is $105, and the new average expense is about $4.04 ($105/26 = $4.04). Note that the increased marginal expenditure caused an increase in the average expense. Whenever a marginal amount is higher than an average amount, the average amount must be increasing over that range of values. Likewise, whenever a marginal amount is below an average amount, the average amount must be decreasing. Therefore, only when the marginal amount is equal to the average amount— as in our case before the price of movies increased—is the average amount neither increasing nor decreasing. This relationship will always hold because the marginal amount causes the average amount to rise or fall or remain the same.

The total is the whole of whatever variable is being measured. What is added to the total or subtracted from it in any one step is the marginal amount. The total amount is always the sum of all the marginal amounts.

The average is the total divided by the number of units.

Marginal Cost and Marginal Benefit

Many economic theories predict by comparing **marginal cost** with **marginal benefit.**[3] People are expected to act so as to maximize their well-being, and they will normally do so by equating their marginal cost with their marginal benefit.

Many important economic theories predict by assuming that people generally maximize their well-being by equating their marginal cost with their marginal benefit.

The idea of equating marginal cost and marginal benefit is best explained in terms of an example. Suppose you are out hiking in the woods and come across an area where wild blueberries are growing. You reach down and pick a handful growing at your feet. Since you were hungry, the blueberries give you a good deal of benefit in return for very little cost in terms of effort. You see more berries growing nearby and walk over and pick those as well. The satisfaction of eating fresh blueberries is still well worth a little bit of extra effort. After you have spent twenty minutes or so eating blueberries, you are no longer as hungry as you were, but still you derive some satisfaction from eating additional blueberries. The longer you pick

---

3. This is an important example of an "apparatus of the mind" and why we introduced a methods definition of economics at the beginning of Chapter 1.

and eat, however, the harder it is to find berries that are conveniently located. Some of them are up on a hill, others are guarded by thistles, and still others are perilously close to what looks like poison ivy. So as you continue picking blueberries, the cost of picking them becomes greater, since it is harder to get to them. At the same time, the longer you continue eating blueberries, the less enjoyment the next handful provides. After half an hour or so, you reach the point where the benefit to you from eating another handful of blueberries is just equal to the cost (in inconvenience) of picking another handful. At this point, you stop picking blueberries and continue with your hike. Any additional berries you might pick at this time would be more trouble than they would be worth. Thus, consciously or not, you used marginal analysis to reach an optimal—best—level of blueberry picking and eating. You continued up to the point at which the marginal benefit of eating blueberries was equal to

FIGURE 5
The Marginal Benefit and Marginal Cost of Picking and Eating Blueberries

Well-being is maximized by picking and eating 25 handfuls of blueberries. If you eat any less than that amount, the marginal benefit of eating blueberries is greater than the marginal cost of picking them, and so you have not taken full advantage. Any more than 25 handfuls finds the marginal cost greater than the marginal benefit, so that well-being has been reduced.

the marginal cost of picking blueberries, and after that you stopped.

This example is clearly illustrated through the use of a diagram. Figure 5 includes a positively sloped curve, showing the marginal cost of picking blueberries, and a negatively sloped curve, showing the marginal benefit from eating blueberries. On the far left part of the diagram, the marginal benefit is far greater than the marginal cost (you're very hungry and the blueberries are very easy to reach). On the far right part, the marginal cost is much greater than the marginal benefit (your hunger is pretty well satisfied and the blueberries are quite hard to reach). Anywhere to the left of the intersection of the two curves (less than 25 handfuls of blueberries), the marginal benefit exceeds the marginal cost, and it pays to continue picking. Anywhere to the right of the intersection of the two curves (more than 25 handfuls of blueberries), the marginal cost exceeds the marginal benefit, and it is not economically rational to pick and eat blueberries. Therefore, during this particular stop on your hike you pick and eat exactly 25 handfuls of blueberries, your optimal level of picking and eating.

This simple story illustrates a technique that can be applied to a great many economic problems. When marginal benefits are high but declining and marginal costs are low but rising, it generally is true that an individual or an organization will reach an optimum point by equating marginal cost and marginal benefit. A worker may use this technique in deciding how many hours of overtime to put in. Sometimes a family uses it in deciding how big a car to buy. It can also be used by a company in deciding how much of a good to produce or how many workers to hire. And a government may use it in deciding how many tax dodgers to prosecute. Equating marginal benefit and marginal cost, then, is the basis upon which economists predict the outcomes of decisions made by individuals and organizations.

When marginal benefits are declining and marginal costs are rising, it generally is true that an individual or organization will reach an optimum point by equating marginal cost and marginal benefit.

Criticism of Marginal Analysis

The marginal technique is not every economist's "cup of tea." The institutionalist school of American economists argues that economic choice can be understood only in the framework of history and contemporary economic laws, customs, and attitudes. Radical political economists take particular issue with marginalism. They argue that marginalism deliberately ignores history and present institutions and is too narrowly concerned with the mechanics of choice. Furthermore, they believe that marginalism diverts the economist's attention from other issues, such as income distribution, freedom of consumer choice, economic growth and the environment, that are of greater importance. The question is whether the usefulness of marginal analysis as a tool can be separated from normative questions about the issues themselves. The majority of American economists believe that it can, and therefore that marginalism is equally consistent with both changing institutions and constant ones.

EQUILIBRIUM

Equilibrium is a state of balance. In a state of equilibrium, forces for change within a system offset each other so that there is no net tendency for the system to change.

Equilibrium is a state of balance—forces for change offset each other, so there is no net tendency for the system to change.

An example will help to make the meaning of equilibrium clearer. Imagine a line of three adjoining rooms, connected by two doors. These doors are closed. The room on the right is heated to, say, 90°. The room on the left is air-conditioned, say, at 30°. There is neither heating nor air-conditioning in the middle room. If the doors are opened, both hot air and cold air will rush into the middle room. After a while the temperature in the middle room will reach an equilibrium position—that is, a state of balance.

Stable and Unstable Equilibrium

Equilibrium may be stable or unstable. In our example it is likely that the temperature of the middle room will go to about 60° and stay there. This would be a **stable equilibrium**—one that tends to restore itself following disturbances. For example, if a large cake of ice were placed in the middle room, it would cause the temperature to drop, say, to 50°. However, after a while the ice will melt and the temperature in the room will return to 60°—the stable equilibrium.

Unstable equilibrium may also be observed. Suppose that you are attempting to balance an egg on its end. Small shifts in direction that you make with your hand allow you to bring it to an equilibrium position and leave it there. However, one small gust of wind or a gentle push will cause it to fall over. There will be no tendency for it to bounce back up and regain its unstable (upright) equilibrium position.

Stable equilibrium tends to restore itself following disturbances. Unstable equilibrium, once disturbed, does not tend to return to its state of equilibrium.

Equilibrium is an important idea in economic analysis because it is a basic tool that economists use to predict future situations. Knowing the requirements for an equilibrium enables economists to identify events that might cause a change, the direction of that change, and what the new equilibrium will be. If an event upsets an existing equilibrium, economists try to find out whether a new equilibrium has been established or whether the initial equilibrium will tend to be restored. If the initial equilibrium is considered to be a stable one, economists can predict on that basis. If a new equilibrium has been established, a different set of predictions will be needed. Disturbances to equilibrium happen almost continuously, so that most of the time situations are moving from one equilibrium to another. In our earlier example involving the three adjoining rooms, the thermostats controlling the temperature in the heated room and in the air-conditioned room may be changed from time to time, altering the equilibrium temperature in the

middle room. But disturbances do not make the equilibrium concept any less useful as a tool for predicting what will happen as a result of disturbances. In fact, the idea of economics as a useful guide for carrying out economic policy is based on this ability to predict consequences of disturbances. If the consequences of a certain disturbance are judged to be desirable by policymakers, the disturbance itself may be created as an instrument of policy.

Equilibrium is a basic tool that economists use to predict future situations.

Partial Equilibrium versus General Equilibrium

Equilibrium analysis may be partial or general. **Partial equilibrium analysis** deals with the effects of a disturbance on one set of economic variables, assuming that all other variables are unaffected. **General equilibrium analysis** takes into account the disturbance's effects on all variables.

Widely used in economics, partial equilibrium analysis can be justified by the need to simplify and handle as few variables as possible at one time. This approach is proper for a wide range of economic problems. For example, in the automobile industry—one of the largest and most influential industries in the United States—partial equilibrium analysis is appropriate in some cases, but in other cases general equilibrium analysis is necessary. A rise in the hourly wage rate for auto workers will raise the cost of producing cars. Partial equilibrium analysis would examine this immediate effect, which may be all that is of concern. However, several other effects could be examined if a general equilibrium framework were used. The increase in the income of auto workers will increase their ability to buy automobiles. But if the increase in the cost of producing automobiles leads to higher prices of automobiles, it may change the percentage of consumers' incomes spent on automobiles and therefore affect how much they buy of other goods and services. These effects could, in turn, feed back on the automobile market and thus influence the price and quantity of automobiles sold as well. Partial equilibrium analysis does not take all these factors into account, but general equilibrium analysis tries to take account of them. In the automobile industry, where a wage hike may have a great impact on the demand for both automobiles and other goods, the use of partial equilibrium will sometimes be insufficient. However, in smaller and less economically important industries, such as those producing watchbands or golf carts, a wage hike would have fairly mild effects, and the use of partial equilibrium would usually be sufficient.

Partial equilibrium analysis deals with the effects of a disturbance on one set of economic variables. General equilibrium analysis takes into account the disturbance's effects on all variables.

Statics, Comparative Statics, and Dynamics

The description of an equilibrium state is called **static analysis.** No element of time is introduced. Since there is no action or change in static analysis, it is of limited usefulness in analyzing the impact of events or in developing policies designed to bring about new situations. When chance is brought into the picture, some variable in the initial static equilibrium situation is altered and a new equilibrium situation arises. The procedure of comparing the initial static equilibrium situation with the new static equilibrium situation is called the method of **comparative statics.** Comparative statics analysis is used widely by practicing economists and is the method most often relied upon in this book.

Another economic methodology is called **dynamic analysis,** which deals with time as a variable. It concerns itself with the process of adjustment that takes place between equilibrium situations. Dynamic analysis usually is reserved for relatively advanced courses in economics.

Comparative statics compares different equilibrium situations. It is the most widely used method of economic analysis.

A WORD TO THE WISE . . .

So far we have described some essential tools for understanding and using economics. A few warnings are needed now to identify some of the problems that can lead to wrong conclusions.

Terms

When students enter a new field, they usually expect to encounter some unfamiliar terms. What they may not expect, however, is that familiar words can take on quite different meanings. An important example is **capital.** In everyday language, particularly in a business context, the word refers to money. A person who is thinking of starting a neighborhood restaurant may wonder how much "capital" is required to make a go of it— $150,000 or $200,000? In economics, however, *capital* refers to real goods, such as machinery and factory buildings, which are used in a production process.

A related term, **investment**, is another good example of a word that has a particular meaning in economics. In everyday language, a person is said to "invest" when he or she buys financial securities such as stocks and bonds, or real estate, or works of art. In economics, investment refers to the creation of capital. Business people invest when they purchase goods that enable them to produce yet other goods.

In economics, *capital* refers to real goods, such as machinery and factory buildings, which are used in a production process. *Investment* refers to the creation of capital.

Cause and Effect

Mistaken causation is another danger in economic reasoning. The fact that one event precedes another does not necessarily mean that the first causes the second to occur. Just after more and more college students began to wear jeans to school, they got higher and higher grades in their courses. Would the rise in grades have occurred if jeans had not become so popular? It probably would have. There is no apparent cause-and-effect logic showing that the increased wearing of jeans led to students' higher course grades.

It has been suggested that union-imposed wage increases cause inflation and that the massive stock market crash of 1929 caused the Great Depression of the 1930s. More careful analysis leads us to regard these ideas with great skepticism. Though facts are important, they cannot be relied upon alone to explain relationships. Theory based on logical analysis must serve as the real foundation of the search for truth.

The fact that one event precedes another does not necessarily mean that the first caused the second. Facts alone cannot be relied upon to explain relationships.

Fallacy of Composition

The **fallacy of composition** is another pitfall to watch out for in economics. We can avoid the difficulty by understanding that what is true for one part is not necessarily true for the whole. A person watching a soccer match in a crowded stadium may be better able to see an exciting play when she stands up. But if the whole crowd stands up to see the play, no one will be able to see any better than when all were seated. Similarly in economics, what is advantageous behavior for a single individual may be quite harmful if engaged in by many individuals or an entire economy. Consider a wheat farmer who produces more wheat in order to increase his income. If he were the only one, or one of a few, to do so, he might achieve his objective. But if all or most of the wheat farmers in the country increased output, the much greater amount of wheat produced would lower the price of wheat so much that each individual farmer's income might actually be reduced.

The fallacy of composition is another pitfall to watch out for in economics. We can avoid the difficulty by understanding that what is true for one part is not necessarily true for the whole.

Time Lags

Yet another difficulty often faced in economics is the matter of **time lags**—the amount of time it takes for a change in an economic variable to have an effect. For example, consider the effect that a tuition increase will have on enrollment at a certain college or university. The immediate effect may be very minor, since most students will already have paid tuition for the present semester or term and are not affected until the next one begins. In the new term some students will drop out or transfer to other schools, but probably most will grudgingly pay the higher tuition rather than leave their friends, lose credits in transfer, and go through the hassle of making a move. Just the same, the effect of the tuition hike may still be substantial on new enrollment. Students who would have enrolled for the next and subsequent terms may decide that the higher tuition is too much. There are a number of time lags in this example, and the more time that passes, the greater the effect. In order to make a useful prediction about the effect on enrollment of the tuition increase, valid information about the length of the time lags must be examined.

A time lag refers to the amount of time it takes for a change in an economic variable to take effect. Time lags should not be ignored in economic analysis.

Uncertainty and Expectations

We live in a world of **uncertainty;** that is, we can never predict with absolute accuracy what will happen next. We have to rely on the past as a guide to the future. We usually react to events according to our past experience, tempered by any additional information that we might have. In other words, we form certain *expectations* and react to what we expect will happen rather than to what actually is happening. The more sure we are of a particular outcome, the more willing we are to react to our expectations. For example, a large increase in the price of a good usually discourages people from buying it. However, there are cases where we find the opposite result. The price rise may make people think that the price will go up even more—in other words, it changes their expectations concerning future prices. If the good is storable, purchasers hurry to buy it in order to avoid the still higher price yet to come.

What is the explanation for the fact that at one time the price of General Motors stock goes up after the company reports higher earnings and at another time the stock price goes down after just as glowing a report? The answer may be expectations. In the first instance, the earnings increase may have been a pleasant surprise since people had expected poorer earnings. The second time, it may have been a disappointment because people expected even higher earnings. Likewise, a government action such as a tax cut may at one time cause people to spend the extra money, but at another time have no such effect. The explanation may be that in the second case the tax cut had been anticipated for months so that people were spending according to the amount of money they expected to receive long before the tax cut actually took place.

It is important to be aware of the effect that a change in a variable has on expectations. Changes in expectations depend upon a great many different variables, which extend well beyond the realm of economics and are very difficult to predict.

Often people react to what they expect will happen rather than to what actually is happening.

Pervasive Errors

The major problems of amateur economic thinking lie, we think, not so much in errors of logic as in *nonrational ways of knowing* and in *temporal limitations*.

The main nonrational ways of knowing are intuition, faith, and slogan thinking. Do you believe an economic argument or policy is right or wrong simply because it is "radical" or "progressive" or "conservative" or "reactionary" or "hard-headed" or "compassionate" or "probusiness" or "prolabor" or "socialistic" or "fascistic" or "old-fashioned" or "un-American"? (The list is endless.) If you do, you are indulging in some combination of these nonrational ways of knowing, as indeed everyone does some of the time.

One temporal limitation—a most common one among politicians—is a refusal to consider ideas or policies that are not likely to win votes in the next election—for example, the possibility that problems can ever be caused by any wage rate being too high. Another mistake—more common among professional economists—is to consider only policies that will work too slowly to help in emergencies—like doing nothing in a depression while waiting for wages and prices to fall.

In addition to errors of logic, students should be wary of nonrational forms of knowing, such as intuition, faith, and slogan thinking, and of temporal limitations.

Economics in Focus

Economic Experiments

Traditionally economics has not been a laboratory science. For the most part economists study patterns created by actual economies, not simulations in a lab. But during the last three decades a number of economists have changed the traditional approach, turning to experimentation in order to test prevailing economic theories.

In a typical experiment a group of volunteers (usually students) will create a miniature version of a particular kind of market. Students assigned to be "sellers" might receive a list of possible sale prices for an imaginary commodity. Other students, playing the role of "buyers," would work from a separate list of possible purchase prices. Then a trading session would start; the buyers would try to buy at the lowest prices, the sellers to sell at the highest prices. Of course the students would need some motivation to play their roles with enthusiasm; normally the students earn cash or other rewards based on their success in the game.

Experiments have been especially useful in analyzing auctions—sales in which the goods are sold to the highest bidder. In some auction experiments economists were surprised at how well the results matched theoretical expectations. For instance, in double oral auctions (auctions in which buyers are free to announce their offers and sellers to announce their prices) the participants tend to reach an equilibrium level of prices, and that level is just what supply and demand curves might have predicted. Because auctions of one type or another can be found in many real-life situations (the stock market being an obvious example), the insights gained from auction experiments help researchers extend and refine their theories.

Experiments can shed light on the *why* of economic behavior as well as the *how*. Why do people buy at certain prices or at certain times? What reasoning or impulses are they following? In a carefully designed experiment the participants can indicate their motives and thoughts much more clearly than people in a real-life situation would do. According to Vernon L. Smith, one of the pioneers of experimental economics, people start out with "homegrown beliefs" about economic markets—beliefs that often reflect a notion of "fairness." Their original behavior reflects these beliefs, but they adjust that behavior over time as they see how a certain market actually functions.

Critics of the experimental approach say that studies of a few people in controlled conditions have little bearing on the real world. Experimentalists retort that theories need to be tested, and experiments offer the most direct testing method available to economists. Gradually the experimental approach has won more converts, and its best contributions probably still lie ahead.

Sources: Vernon L. Smith, "Theory, Experiment and Economics," *Journal of Economic Perspectives,* vol. 3 (Winter 1989), pp. 151–168; Edgar K. Browning and Jacquelene M. Browning, *Microeconomic Theory and Applications,* third edition (Glenview, Ill.: Scott, Foresman, 1989), pp. 422–425.

SUMMARY

1. Economic theory is used for logically analyzing information, studying cause and effect, and solving real problems in economics. (See page 42.)

2. Because economics is a social science, it must often be satisfied with predicting the direction of change instead of the exact amount of change. (See pages 42–43.)

3. In order to keep theories as simple as possible and to isolate extraneous, or less important, variables, economists often use assumptions such as *ceteris paribus* and economic rationality. (See pages 43–44.)

4. Economically rational behavior is any action that people take to make them better off or to keep them from becoming worse off. Economists predict on the basis that all economic units—consumers; businesses; owners of natural resources, capital, and labor; and government—act in a rational way. (See pages 44–45.)

5. Positive economics deals with what is—with facts. Normative economics concerns itself with what ought to be—with opinions. It is important to be aware of this difference. (See page 46.)

6. Functional relationships between dependent and independent variables may be direct or inverse. Economists find it useful to present these functions by means of graphs or diagrams. On these graphs, direct relationships are shown as a positive slope, and inverse relationships are shown as a negative slope. If the slope of a curve is constant throughout its length, it will be linear (appear as a straight line), and if the slope increases or decreases, the curve will be nonlinear. (See pages 46–51.)

7. Marginal means extra or additional—one more or one less. Marginal analysis recognizes that most economic decisions are made ''on the margin'' and are not of an all-or-nothing type. (See page 51.)

8. When the marginal cost of an activity is increasing and marginal benefit from the same activity is decreasing, a person will maximize his or her well-being gained from the activity by equating marginal cost and marginal benefit. (See pages 52–53.)

9. Equilibrium is a state of balance. Though the economy may only rarely be at equilibrium, this is an important concept. It allows economists to focus on the effects of particular disturbances and to predict future events. (See pages 53–55.)

10. It is important to watch out for several problems in the study of economics:

a. Some familiar terms, such as *capital* and *investment*, take on quite different meanings in economics from those in common usage.

b. The fact that one event precedes another does not necessarily indicate a cause-and-effect relationship between them.

c. What is true for a part is not necessarily true for the whole.

d. It is important to consider time lags—how long it takes for a change in an economic variable to have an effect.

e. Living in a world of uncertainty, people often react to what they expect will happen, rather than to what is actually occurring. (See pages 55–57.)

KEY TERMS

assumptions: statements that set forth the limits of the variables in a theory and identify which of the variables are to be omitted (page 43).

capital: real goods, such as machines and factory buildings, which are used in a production process (page 55).

ceteris paribus: Latin for ''other things being equal''; it is an assumption that states that all other variables are held constant (page 43).

comparative statics: the technique of studying variations in equilibrium positions that result from changes in the underlying variables (page 55).

dependent variable: a variable that is a function of one or more other variables (page 47).

direct relationship: one where the dependent and the independent variables change in the same direction (page 47).

dynamic analysis: the description of the process of adjustment between equilibrium positions (page 55).

economic rationality: the assumption that people act to make themselves better off or to prevent themselves from becoming worse off (page 44).

equilibrium: a state of balance wherein forces for change within a system offset each other so that there is no net tendency for the system to change (page 53).

fallacy of composition: a type of faulty reasoning that assumes that what is true for one part is true for the whole (page 56).

function: a statement of how one variable depends on one or more other variables (page 46).

general equilibrium analysis: analysis of a state of equilibrium that takes into account all the effects related to the specific economic disturbance that is being studied (page 54).

independent variable: a variable upon which one or more other variables depend (page 47).

inverse relationship: one in which the dependent and independent variables change in opposite directions (page 47).

investment: the creation of goods that are used to produce other goods (page 55).

linear relationship: a relationship that has a constant slope (page 49).

marginal: extra; additional; incremental (page 51).

marginal analysis: a type of analysis that predicts or evaluates the outcome by comparing incremental values (page 51).

marginal benefit: the additional advantage gained when one more unit of a good is consumed or produced (page 52).

marginal cost: the addition to total cost when one more unit of output is produced (page 52).

model: a formal statement of a theory (page 42).

negative slope: an inverse relationship between variables as shown in a graph (page 48).

nonlinear relationship: a relationship between variables in which equal changes in the independent variable do not always bring about the same response in the dependent variable (page 49).

normative economics: an economic approach that concerns itself with what ought to be (page 46).

origin: the intersection of the horizontal and vertical axes of a graph (page 47).

partial equilibrium analysis: analysis of a state of equilibrium that deals with the effects of a disturbance on one set of economic variables, assuming that all other variables are unaffected (page 54).

perpendiculars: straight lines drawn from values along the horizontal or vertical axes of a graph (page 48).

positive economics: an economic approach that deals with what is. It tries to be objective and avoid value judgments (page 46).

positive slope: a direct relationship between variables, as shown in a graph (page 48).

quadrants: the four sections that are formed when a horizontal axis is placed on a vertical axis (page 47).

scale: to mark value-intervals on the axes of a graph (page 47).

slope: the change in the variable read on the vertical axis of a graph divided by the associated change in the variable read on the horizontal axis of that graph (page 48).

stable equilibrium: an equilibrium that tends to restore itself following disturbances (page 55).

static analysis: the description of an equilibrium state (page 55).

theory: a systematically organized body of knowledge that can be applied in a fairly wide range of circumstances (page 42).

time lags: the amount of time it takes for an economic variable to have an effect (page 56).

uncertainty: the condition of not knowing the probability of the outcome of an event (page 56).

unstable equilibrium: an equilibrium that does not tend to restore itself following a disturbance (page 54).

variable: a quantity that can assume any of a set of values (page 42).

DISCUSSION QUESTIONS

1. Marcia and Jim are having a discussion concerning a certain theory of inflation. Jim explains the theory, including the variables involved, the relationships among the variables, and the assumptions that the theory sets forth. Marcia responds that she considers the theory to be quite meaningless because it seems to be based on several quite unrealistic assumptions. Putting yourself in the place of Jim, how would you defend yourself?

2. Experimentation ought to be left to physical scientists. Since economics is a social science, economists should stick to describing human behavior. Do you agree? Explain.

3. Using the economist's assumption that human beings act rationally in their economic decision making, describe how:

a. a consumer will shop
b. an entrepreneur will decide what and how many inputs to use and outputs to produce
c. a worker will choose among job alternatives

4. Why is it so much more difficult to describe rational government than to describe rational consumers, entrepreneurs, and the owners of capital, natural resources, and labor?

5. Differentiate between positive and normative economics. Give three examples of positive statements and three examples of normative statements in the field of economics. Would a positively or a normatively oriented economist be of greater value to a politician?

6. How is the demand for public transportation related to the price of gasoline? Tell what type of variable each is and how they interact.

7. The Greasy Spoon is open daily from 4 P.M. to 4 A.M.. The employees (primarily college students) may choose the number of hours they wish to work. Their daily earnings, then, depend on the number of hours worked and the hourly wage, which is $5.00. On weekends they choose to work fewer hours than on weekdays. Write the function for this relationship. Using the following information, graph the relationship and show the slope:

Daily Earnings	Hours Worked
$15.00	3 (Friday)
15.00	3 (Saturday)
20.00	4 (Sunday)

Daily Earnings	Hours Worked
25.00	5 (Monday)
30.00	6 (Tuesday)
35.00	7 (Wednesday)
40.00	8 (Thursday)

8. The Miller Brewing Company buys barley from a group of farmers in Iowa. The more Miller buys, the greater is its total expenditure on barley. However, the more Miller buys, the lower is the price per bushel that it has to pay. What is the sign of the relationship between the amount of barley purchased and the total expenditure on barley? Is this a linear relationship? Draw a graph that shows the relationship between the amount of barley purchased and the total amount paid for barley.

9. During a certain month John buys a pound of hamburger every third day (ten pounds in all). He pays $1.50 for each of the first five pounds, $1.60 for each of the next four pounds, and $1.70 for the tenth pound. Calculate John's total cost, average cost, and marginal cost for hamburger for that month.

10. Suppose that you have an economics exam tomorrow and decide to study for it tonight. Suppose further that your negatively sloped marginal-benefit curve for studying intersects your positively sloped marginal-cost curve for studying at four hours of studying. (You may now want to draw these two curves on a set of axes, scaling marginal benefit and marginal cost along the vertical axis and the number of study hours along the horizontal axis.)

Using marginal benefit–marginal cost analysis, explain why you would not want to stop studying after only three hours.

Using marginal benefit–marginal cost analysis, explain why you would not want to study as much as five hours.

11. Why are economists so concerned with equilibrium when, in fact, it is very seldom reached?

12. Under what conditions might an economist prefer to use partial rather than general equilibrium analysis?

4

Scarcity: The Economic Problem

Preview   This chapter returns to the concept of *scarcity*, which you briefly met at the beginning of Chapter 1. Most economists assume, despite the doubts of the communists, that scarcity is unavoidable and that there is no such thing as an economy of abundance.

Scarcity is the central problem of economics. All our everyday economic problems can be traced back to it. Furthermore, goods and services are scarce because they are produced by combining resources, which are themselves scarce. These resources are divided into labor, natural resources, and capital (further divided into physical and human capital), and we shall discuss each in turn. The special function of combining these resources—particularly in the production of new goods or services and in the application of new ways to produce standard goods and services, all under conditions of uncertainty—we call enterprise or entrepreneurship, an important form of the labor resource.

A major theme running through this chapter is that the existence of scarcity necessitates choice. In other words, we must answer the basic questions raised in Chapter 1: what to produce, how to produce it, and to whom it should go. Also because of scarcity we must consider opportunity cost, the idea that the real cost of something is what is given up to obtain it. Opportunity cost applies to both consumption and production decisions. The chapter is thus an introduction to the important topics of consumer choice, to the production decisions of firms, and to the concepts of supply and demand.

SCARCITY

There are many economic problems. We have them, our neighbors have them, business firms have them, and government agencies have them— not just in this country, but around the whole world. You would like to have a new car but cannot afford it. You want to go to a party on Thursday night; however, there is an economics exam Friday morning and you need time to study for it. Your family wants to live in a better house, but it costs too much. The farmer wants a new tractor, but the bank is unwilling to provide a loan. Though the Pentagon desires a new-generation bomber, Congress refuses to pass the enabling legislation. The family in rural Bangladesh wishes to have enough to eat but does not have the means to grow or buy the food. These and trillions of other economic problems are common. Though they vary greatly in type and in urgency, they are all just examples of a single problem—scarcity, *the* economic problem.

Scarcity means that the amount of something actually available is not sufficient to meet some requirement. The critical word in this definition is *requirement*, since a given amount of something may or may not constitute scarcity, depending on how this amount compares with the requirement. In the illustrations given in the preceding paragraph, the requirement appeared in such terms as "would like to have," "wishes," "wants," or "desires." The things discussed were scarce because the amount actually available was less than the amount wanted or desired. Thus, economics specifies a very distinctive meaning for the term *scarcity*. It is an important term to remember.

Scarcity means that the amount of something actually available is not sufficient to meet some requirement. Scarcity is the central problem of economics.

Scarce Goods and Services

We warned you in the previous chapter that economists use some words in ways that differ from ordinary usage. *Scarcity* is such a word. In everyday language a good or a service is "scarce" when the demand for it is greater than the supply available.

Economists agree *only* if the terms *demand* and *supply* are understood to refer to amounts demanded and supplied at a price of zero. (Price also does not have to take the form of money. So the "price of zero" can mean that a demander does not have to give up goods or time and that a supplier does not receive goods or anything else in the exchange.) Whenever people want more of a good or service than is available free of charge, economists refer to that good or service as scarce. Suppose that a clothing manufacturer decides to introduce a new line of designer socks and after doing some market research offers 1,000 pairs per day for sale at a price of $8 per pair. If only 400 pairs are sold per day, these socks would not be considered scarce in everyday language. However, economists would want to withhold judgment until they had information about the quantity demanded at prices below $8. If, indeed, 1,000 pairs per day are sold at $3 per pair and if consumers would buy more than 1,000 pairs at some even lower price, then economists would consider these socks to be scarce. At a price of zero, the quantity of pairs of socks demanded would far exceed the quantity offered by suppliers. Economists reason that the good (in this case, socks) is the same whether sold for $8, $3, or 10¢. No matter what the price is, scarce resources are used to produce them, and some other goods are not produced with those resources. Indeed, if these socks are defined as scarce at a price of 10¢, they are also scarce at a price of $8.

Whenever people want more of a good or service than is available free of charge, economists refer to that good or service as scarce.

A good or service becomes scarce over time if the difference between the quantities demanded and supplied at a price of zero increases. Similarly, a good or service becomes less scarce over time if the difference between the quantities demanded and supplied at a price of zero decreases.

A good or service becomes more scarce over time if the difference between the quantities demanded and supplied at a price of zero increases.

Scarce Resources

Why do most goods and services command a positive price? Why are most goods and services scarce? The answer can be found by examining how goods and services are produced.

Production involves bringing together certain inputs—called **factors of production** or **resources**—to create goods and services, that is, the output. Resources are the ingredients necessary for producing goods and services. Just as you cannot bake a cake without the ingredients of flour, eggs, sugar, and so on, you cannot produce goods and services without resources. It is these resources that are scarce and, in turn, cause goods and services that are produced with them to be scarce.

Goods and services are scarce because the resources, or factors of production, needed to create them are scarce.

It is useful to separate resources into three broad classes:

1. **Labor resources** are all kinds of human work efforts that are or can be directed at production or at enterprise, which is the organizing of production.

2. **Natural resources** are all things provided by nature that can be used in production, such as land and minerals.

3. **Capital resources** are goods or tools or skills that are produced for use in further production.

These three kinds of resources—labor, natural, and capital—are defined broadly enough to cover everything that goes into production.

There are three kinds of resources: labor, natural, and capital.

Labor Resources Labor includes all forms of human work, blue-collar and white-collar alike, from the most menial and routine to the most intellectual and managerial.

It is easy to recognize the labor of the machine operator, the ditch digger, the assembly-line worker, and the fruit picker. But other types of labor are included in the concept of the labor resource. The accountant, the secretary, and the company president are all examples here. Also classified as labor are **enterprisers**, or **entrepreneurs**—those who seek the best opportunities for production and take risks when making such decisions.

Labor resources include all kinds of human work, from manual laborers to office laborers to entrepreneurial labor.

Enterprise differs from administrative and managerial labor in that it is less routine. The labor done by the entrepreneur is to make the basic choices and decisions within a company, particularly those decisions that involve taking chances. The entrepreneur must judge the merits of past and present ways of producing goods or services and must decide how to apply new production methods or how to produce new goods. Thus an enterpriser, or entrepreneur, is often an innovator, but only rarely an inventor.

The distinction between innovator and inventor is worth clarifying. It is the **inventor** who discovers or devises a new or improved process or product. The **innovator** is the one who brings the invention out of the laboratory, makes it practical, and applies it to actual production. The physicist Enrico Fermi was an inventor of the fission process of releasing atomic energy, but he was not an important innovator in either the civilian or the military applications of atomic energy. Henry Ford was the innovator who applied assembly-line techniques to automobile production, and Alfred Sloan, Jr., was the innovator who introduced the annual model change in automobile marketing. So far as we know, neither invented anything of importance. Many of us are surprised that the innovators of new products and processes so often make higher incomes and amass greater wealth than the inventors do. Both Ford and Sloan made more money from their innovations than Fermi did from his invention. (Of course, Fermi won a Nobel Prize—something that Ford and Sloan never did.)

Quantity and Quality of Labor The quantity of labor available to a society is determined by the size of its population, the age distribution, and the prevailing attitudes about who should work, over what periods of their lives, and for how long each year. Countries with large populations and with small percentages of very young (below working age) and very old (above working age) people have large amounts of labor. Societies that deny work to certain groups of people or support a leisure class possess less labor. Those that offer many years of schooling to young people and provide retirement income to older people have less labor. Finally, the amount of labor that a country has will depend on the length of the workday and the workweek, and the amount of holiday and vacation time that workers receive.

The quantity of labor available to a society is determined by the size of its population, the age distribution, and prevailing institutions.

There is also a qualitative aspect of the labor resource. Certainly, production is more than simply expending energy. The workers' attitude toward the job, for example, is important to production. When that attitude is wholesome and constructive and when the workers enjoy what they are doing and take pride in the results, there will be more production from the work effort than when the attitude is negative.

Combination with Other Resources Because the labor resource is usually employed in combination with other resources, it is sometimes difficult in practice to recognize these resources separately. For example, the skills that people use in combination with their labor effort are a kind of capital, called **human capital**. These skills are the results of production efforts (education or training) carried out sometime in the past and used for future production. A long period of schooling, then, lowers the society's quantity of labor resource, but the lost working time is offset by the greater amount of human capital that results from the knowledge and skill gained from the education. Even the strength, health, and vigor that are displayed along with the work effort can be distinguished from the work effort itself, but it is hard to decide whether these should be considered natural resources or capital. Does health come from the "natural resource" of

being born healthy or from capital that previously provided health care?

Human capital consists of the skills that people use in combination with their labor effort.

Actually, none of the resource categories can be fully understood if examined in a vacuum. The quantity and quality of natural resources and capital will affect labor's ability to produce, just as the productivity of capital depends on the quantity and quality of the labor and natural resources that can be combined with it. A worker with a bulldozer can produce more than the same worker with a shovel. Should the whole difference be attributed to the bulldozer? A bulldozer with a worker can produce a lot, but the bulldozer could produce nothing without the worker. Should the entire difference be attributed to the worker?

Natural Resources Natural resources are things that are provided by nature and that are used or usable in production. These "gifts of nature" include the land in its natural state, the sea, the minerals in the ground, the vegetation that grows without anyone planting it, and all the living creatures that are found in the wild.

To be usable, natural resources must often be combined with labor resources and capital resources. Crude oil in a pool deep under the surface of the earth is a natural resource, but bringing it to the surface requires labor and machines (capital). So when the crude oil becomes available for use in production, it has already been mixed with labor and capital. Land in its natural state is a pure natural resource, but land with an irrigation system or with contour plowing is more than a natural resource, since it has been combined with labor and capital.

The idea that a natural resource is something that is "usable" in production brings up still another interesting aspect of the relationships among the resources of labor, natural resources, and capital. For many hundreds of years, crude oil seeped to the surface of the earth. However, it had no value as a natural resource until knowledge and skills were developed to allow this crude oil to be used in production. Future advances in knowledge may bring to light some natural resources that exist today but are as yet unrecognized. Are natural resources being used up in production, or is the development of knowledge expanding the quantity of recognized natural resources?

Natural resources are things provided by nature that are usable in production. To be usable, natural resources must often be combined with labor resources and capital resources.

Capital Resources Capital resources are goods, tools, and skills that are meant for use in further production. Factory buildings as well as many machines and tools are produced, not for consumers or households to enjoy, but for the entrepreneur to combine with labor and natural resources to produce consumer goods.

Capital goods are "derived" rather than "original" resources because they are produced from other resources. They are made by people and/or other capital goods. An old-fashioned textbook definition was "Capital is wealth used to produce other wealth," and economists spoke of production that makes use of capital as a "roundabout" way of using labor and natural resources in production. Karl Marx wrote that capital was "dead labor that, vampire-like, lives by sucking living labor." Most modern economists do not resent capital, but instead give it credit for providing billions of people with a much higher standard of living than would otherwise be possible. Public and private capital resources are used to educate and train labor. In the form of tools and human skills, capital is also used to explore for coal, iron, or oil, which increases the amount of known natural resources. Various combinations of capital resources are used to raise or maintain the fertility of farmland, as well as to produce the land in Boston's Back Bay, Tokyo's Marunouchi, or half of Holland by filling in and desalinating sea bottoms, river bottoms, or swamps.

Capital resources are goods, tools, and skills that are meant for use in further production. They

---

are made from other resources including other capital goods.

Capital is a very important resource for production. The quantity and quality of capital in a country depend upon decisions made concerning the use of its scarce resources. The more a nation chooses to employ its resources in the production of consumer goods and services, the less will be available for the production of capital (and vice versa). Consider the case of a poor nation that is endowed with few and low-grade natural and labor resources. Its people are probably living near the subsistence level, with barely enough consumption goods and services to sustain their lives. It is unlikely that much capital would be produced under such conditions, since almost all of this country's resources would be used to produce consumer goods.

The quantity and quality of capital in a country depend upon decisions made concerning the use of its scarce resources. The more a nation uses its resources in the production of consumer goods and services, the less is available for the production of capital.

The definition of capital offered at the beginning of this section included human skills. Skill, or **technological know-how**, is the ability to combine resources in producing the goods and services that a society wants. It is a kind of capital because skills are developed through experience, that is, through the use of resources in some sort of an educational process.

Technological know-how is an especially important kind of capital because it helps to determine how much a society will be able to produce with its limited amounts of other resources. A society with a substantial stock of technological know-how will be able to produce a great many more goods and services with its other resources than it could produce if it had less. No level of technological excellence will "solve" the economic problem of scarcity, but gains in "know-how" can go a long way toward easing the burden of scarcity.

One form of capital resources is skill or technological know-how—the ability to combine resources to produce the goods and services a society wants.

Choice

The economic problem—the existence of scarcity—necessitates choice. Since we cannot all have as much of everything as we would like, choices, or economic decisions, have to be made. Chapter 1 introduced the three major decisions that face all societies: what to produce, how to produce, and who shall receive the finished goods and services. It also explored some of the economic arrangements that societies have made to answer these questions. Now, these three questions can be applied directly to the problems of scarcity and choice.

The question of what to produce is based on the realization that choices have to be made between alternative uses of scarce resources. How many telephones shall be produced? How much toothpaste? How many factories? How many machines? How much conservation? How much research? Clearly, the "what to produce" question not only divides resources among alternative consumer goods but also allocates resources to the creation of capital, which will open the way for more and better consumer goods in the future.

In deciding what to produce, choices have to be made between alternative uses of scarce resources.

The question of how to produce involves the choice of which resources to use in production. It is almost always possible to substitute one resource for another, such as a machine (capital) for some labor, or a more elaborate machine for two less elaborate ones. Certainly, in the case of an economy that finds itself with a large amount of labor and a small amount of capital, this question would be answered differently than it would be in an economy in the opposite situation.

In deciding how to produce, choices also have to be made about which resources to use.

The question of for whom to produce also shows the existence of scarcity in the real world. If there were enough resources for us all to have as much of everything as we wanted, there would be little need to make the hard choices of providing more to some people and less to other people. The fact that societies have to make this choice is the "bottom line" of the economic problem. Because receiving goods and services is a powerful incentive, the way goods and services are distributed has a lot to do with the labor, natural resources, and capital resources that will be available in the future.

In deciding for whom to produce, choices have to be made about the distribution of goods and services.

OPPORTUNITY COST

Since resources are scarce, the decision to use them for one thing means that something else will be given up. Suppose that a company could manufacture either 100 chairs or 30 tables using the same resources. The opportunity cost of using its resources to produce 100 chairs is the benefit that could have been obtained from producing 30 tables (the best alternative) with the same resources. Thus, **opportunity cost** is the true cost of choosing one alternative over another. With limited resources, people cannot "have their cake and eat it too." Opportunity cost recognizes the fact that when resources are employed in a certain way, there is a simultaneous choice made not to use those resources in some other way. That which is given up, then, is the opportunity cost of what is actually chosen. If, instead of producing one case of beer, we might have produced three dresses or five taxi rides or seven hours of leisure, the opportunity cost of one case of beer is whichever of these would yield the most benefit. It is certainly *not* the sum of all three.

Opportunity cost is the true cost of choosing one alternative over another. That which is given up is the opportunity cost of what is actually chosen.

Opportunity Cost in Consumption

Opportunity cost applies to both consumption and production. In discussing consumption, we consider how consumers spend their income, wealth, and time and how governments spend the resources that they have at their disposal.

The Individual   Since people have only so much income and hold a limited amount of wealth, they are continually faced with buying decisions. When consumers decide to spend their dollars for one item, those dollars are not available to them for some other item. The opportunity cost of buying a blue sweater may be the green sweater that was therefore not bought. Taking a trip to the Caribbean might mean forgoing, or giving up, a new car.

To get a better understanding of the opportunity cost involved in consumer choice, consider the following example. Suppose that you are having dinner in a seafood restaurant and that you select the combination shrimp and scallop plate shown on the menu for $10. This restaurant allows you to choose the particular mix of shrimps and scallops that you want. Shrimps, however, are twice as expensive ($1 each) as scallops (50¢ each). Thus, the opportunity cost of each shrimp is two scallops, and the opportunity cost of each scallop is one-half shrimp.

Your eleven possible combinations are listed in Table 1 and are plotted graphically in Figure 1. Since shrimps are on one axis and scallops on the other, any point on the diagram represents some combination of shrimps and scallops. Your $10 plate will not allow you, however, to choose a point in the blue area (like *X* with 8 shrimps plus 10 scallops). You would not want to order a combination in the purple area (like *Z* with 4 shrimps plus 4 scallops), since you can have more shrimps and/or scallops for your $10. Depending upon your

TABLE 1
Alternative Combinations of Shrimps and Scallops (Hypothetical Example))

Combination	Number of Shrimps	Number of Scallops
1	10	0
2	9	2
3	8	4
4	7	6
5	6	8
6	5	10
7	4	12
8	3	14
9	2	16
10	1	18
11	0	20

taste, your order might be all shrimps (point *A*) or all scallops (point *B*), but most likely it will be some combination like *C* (6 shrimps plus 8 scallops) because it offers some variety.

The graph in Figure 1 helps you to visualize opportunity cost. The slope of the line (ignoring the sign) measures opportunity cost of scallops because it shows how many shrimp must be sacrificed to obtain one more scallop. In this illustration, the curve is actually a straight line, which means that the slope is the same all along the line, because opportunity cost neither increases nor decreases from one combination on the line to another.

People also face opportunity costs in allocating their time and their effort. This choice may be between work and leisure, between one kind of work and another kind of work, or between one leisure activity and another leisure activity. If a particular Saturday night offers a college student both a movie show and a basketball game, and if these are the best alternatives available, the event that the student doesn't attend is the opportunity cost of the one that he or she does decide to attend. A student who decides to attend a summer session may experience three kinds of opportunity costs. The first cost is the goods and services that the student forgoes so that he or she can pay for tuition and books. A second includes the goods and services that the student could have bought with the money he or she would have earned on a summer job. The

FIGURE 1
Alternative Combinations of Shrimps and Scallops (Hypothetical Example)

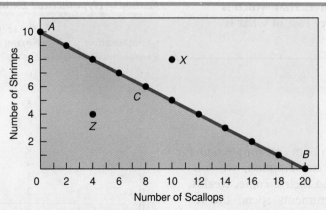

The numbers plotted from Table 1 establish the points along the curve *AB*. These eleven possible combinations of shrimps and scallops are available to a person ordering the $10 shrimp and scallop plate in the restaurant. The opportunity cost of each shrimp is two scallops, and the opportunity cost of each scallop is one-half shrimp.

Any combination that lies in the blue area above *AB* (such as *X*) is not available on the $10 plate. Any combination that lies in the purple area below *AB* (such as *Z*) is available but offers fewer shrimps and/or scallops than the restaurant is willing to provide on the $10 plate.

third is the extra leisure time that the student would have enjoyed, since school is more time-consuming than a job would have been.

People continually face opportunity-cost decisions when allocating their income, time, and effort.

The Government Government also is faced with opportunity costs. At first, it may seem that government is exempted because it can tax people, borrow money, or even print money if it wishes to undertake more programs. On closer examination, however, we discover that when government draws additional resources from private individuals or businesses, private goods must be forgone. This is the opportunity cost of the expanded government operation. For example, if a country became fearful of its neighbors, it might raise taxes to buy more military equipment. The opportunity cost of the defense buildup would be the private goods, such as clothing and vacations, that the taxpayers could no longer afford to buy.

If a total dollar budget has already been set, the opportunity cost of one government program is an-

other program that must be given up. A state legislature may have to decide between funding mass transportation or the prison system. If you are told the amount of the total budget and the prices of mass transportation and prison facilities, this opportunity-cost calculation can be illustrated just like the consumer-choice case involving shrimps and scallops.

Government is also faced with opportunity costs. If government operations expand, some private goods must be forgone. If only one government program can be funded, the opportunity cost is another government program that must be given up.

Opportunity Cost in Production

The concept of opportunity cost can be applied to production choices in a way similar to consumption choices. Opportunity cost in production is also a **tradeoff**—how much of one good or service must be given up to gain a certain quantity of another good or service. Extending opportunity cost further leads us to the concept of **production possibility**, which describes the limits to the quantities of goods and services that can be produced with a given supply of resources including technological knowledge during any given time period. We shall consider production possibilities both for an individual firm and for an entire nation.

Production choices made by firms involve opportunity costs—how much of one good or service must be given up to gain a certain quantity of another good or service.

Production possibilities are the limits to the quantities of goods and services that can be produced during any given time period with a given supply of resources including technological knowledge.

The Firm Suppose that a firm is set up to manufacture only two products: ice cream and sherbet. Suppose further that its factory building contains machinery that can be used equally well to produce ice cream or sherbet and that its workers can produce either product equally well. The capacity of the factory building and the machinery is 500,000 gallons of ice cream and/or sherbet per month.

Figure 2 illustrates this case. The amount of ice cream is on one axis and the amount of sherbet is on the other. Any point on the diagram represents some combination of the production of ice cream and sherbet. If the company chooses to produce all the ice cream that it can (and therefore no sherbet), it can produce 500,000 gallons (point *A*). Alternatively, if it chooses to produce all the sherbet that it can (and therefore no ice cream), it can produce 500,000 gallons of sherbet (point *B*). All the remaining maximum production possibilities are combinations of positive amounts of both ice cream and sherbet and fall along the curve drawn between *A* and *B*. (It is actually a straight line because all the resources in this example are able to produce either good equally well.) We call *AB* a **production possibilities boundary**—a curve that represents all the alternative maximum combinations that can be produced during a given time period with a given supply of resources including technological knowledge.

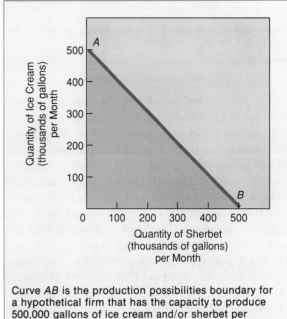

Curve *AB* is the production possibilities boundary for a hypothetical firm that has the capacity to produce 500,000 gallons of ice cream and/or sherbet per month. Its fixed supply of resources is equally well able to produce either good. The opportunity cost of a gallon of ice cream is a gallon of sherbet, and vice versa.

A production possibilities boundary is a curve that represents all the alternative maximum combinations that can be produced during a given time period with a given supply of resources including technological knowledge.

The Whole Economy Let's see how opportunity cost in production may now be applied to an entire economy. No matter what economic system prevails—whether private business firms like the ice cream–sherbet company exist or not—each nation is limited in what it can produce by its resources, including its technological know-how. Of course, the actual production possibilities of a nation are too diverse to be expressed in tabular form or to be represented in a diagram. But for illustrative purposes all the different goods and services that a nation produces can be lumped together in two categories, such as "consumption goods" and "capital goods," or "guns" and "butter," or "goods" and "services."

Each nation is limited in what it can produce by its resources including its technological know-how.

A Production Possibilities Schedule Table 2 represents a production possibilities table or schedule for the fictitious nation of Yano. All possible production has been divided into the two categories of goods and services, and there is a common unit of measure for each category. For example, a haircut may be 1 service unit, and an examination by a physician may be 10 service units. A potholder may be 1 goods unit, and a pound of hamburger 3 goods units. Imagine that during a particular year (1990) Yano's production possibilities have been tabulated in this fashion. The numbers are based on the amount of resources including technological know-how available for use in Yano's production during 1990. The numbers in Table 2 show that there is no way for Yano to produce more than 10,000 billion units of goods or to produce more than 4,000 billion units of services. In fact, the only way to produce such a high level of either category is to produce none of the other.

Between these all-of-one-and-none-of-the-other choices are many possible combinations of goods and services for Yano to produce. The schedule gives seven examples (such as 9,800 billion units of goods plus 500 billion units of services, or 7,000 billion units of goods plus 2,500 billion units of services), but there are countless others. It follows from the data that if Yano decides, for example, to produce 2,000 billion units of services in 1990, then no more than 8,000 billion units of goods can be produced. Alternatively, if Yano decides to produce 9,400 billion units of goods, it can produce no more than 1,000 billion units of services.

Increasing Marginal Opportunity Costs The tradeoff between goods and services is different in different parts of the table. At the top is the combination of 10,000 billion units of goods and no services. By giving up 200 billion units of these goods, Yano can gain 500 billion units of services.

TABLE 2
Production Possibilities for the Nation of Yano in 1990

Goods (in billions of units)	Services (in billions of units)
10,000	0
9,800	500
9,400	1,000
8,800	1,500
8,000	2,000
7,000	2,500
5,800	3,000
4,400	3,500
0	4,000

This table, or schedule, shows nine of the countless alternative combinations of goods and services that the fictitious nation of Yano is able to produce in 1990. The alternatives range from 10,000 billion units of goods plus no services to no goods plus 4,000 billion units of services. It is most likely that the people of Yano will want a mix of goods and services, and so they might choose a combination such as 8,000 billion units of goods plus 2,000 billion units of services.

Thus the opportunity cost of 500 billion units of services is 200 billion units of goods. However, Yano must give up 400 billion units of goods to get the next 500 billion units of services. The marginal opportunity cost of 500 billion units of services has increased from 200 billion units of goods to 400 billion units of goods. Note that this pattern continues. As you move down Table 2, larger and larger amounts of goods must be given up in order to gain additional blocks of 500 billion units of services. If you compare the last two lines in the table, you will see that the opportunity cost of the last 500 billion units of services is 4,400 billion units of goods.

Likewise, the marginal opportunity cost of goods in terms of services increases as you move up Table 2. Going from the combination of no goods and 4,000 billion units of services to the next higher combination, you will see that the opportunity cost of 4,400 billion units of goods is only 500 billion units of services. Finally, when you compare the top two lines in the table, you will observe that the opportunity cost of only 200 billion units of goods is 500 billion units of services.

Why should increasing marginal opportunity costs be expected? Why is it that the more goods or the more services that Yano has, the higher the opportunity cost of gaining even more units? The answer is that not all of Yano's resources are equally suited to producing both goods and services. Some are much more capable of producing goods, and others are much better at producing services. Workers skilled in performing appendectomies may be unsuited for producing cars. Land that is just right for growing wheat may be a poor location for a barbershop. And a factory building designed for manufacturing steel may be poorly suited as a dental clinic.

It is reasonable to expect that, at some combination around the middle of Table 2, most resources are being used in the way that suits them reasonably well. Perhaps this combination would be 8,000 billion units of goods plus 2,000 billion units of services. At other combinations—either up or down the table—resources are shifted to tasks for which they are less well suited. Toward the very top of the table, only the resources best fitted to the production of services will be producing services. At the same time, it is necessary to use less-suitable resources for producing goods, making it very expensive to produce any more goods by giving up more services. Likewise, toward the very bottom of the table, only the resources best suited to the production of goods will be producing goods and those resources less capable of producing services will be doing so, making it very expensive in terms of goods forgone to produce any more services.

A Production Possibilities Boundary Just as a production possibilities boundary was drawn for the ice cream–sherbet firm in Figure 2, a production possibilities boundary may be drawn for the nation of Yano. Figure 3 (page 74) plots the data from Table 2 on a set of axes and joins the points to obtain a production possibilities boundary. The curve is bowed out, reflecting increasing marginal opportunity costs because Yano's resources are not all equally good at producing both goods and services. In contrast, the straight-line production possibilities boundary for the ice cream–sherbet firm reflected a constant marginal opportunity cost, since all its resources were equally good at producing ice cream and sherbet.

The production possibilities boundary in Figure 3 represents the maximum amounts that Yano can produce in 1990. Production levels in the blue area (such as X, a combination of 9,500 billion

units of goods plus 3,000 billion units of services, or Z, a combination of 8,500 billion units of goods plus 3,500 billion units of services) are impossible for Yano to achieve. However, the entire purple area is made up of combinations of goods and services that are attainable. For example, point A (a combination of 6,500 billion units of goods plus 1,500 billion units of services) is an attainable combination for Yano. But, given its resources including technological know-how, Yano can do better than point A by producing more goods, or more services, or more of both. Instead of 6,500 billion units of goods, it could produce 8,800 billion (which would place it at point B), with no reduction in the services produced. Or, instead of 1,500 billion units of services, it could produce 2,700 billion (which would place it at point C), with no reduction in the amount of goods produced. Finally, it could produce more of both and move to a point such as D (7,500 billion units of goods plus 2,250 billion units of services).

Suppose that Yano is producing at point A in the purple area of Figure 3. What does this fact tell us about the Yano economy? One possible cause of the relatively low production indicated by point A may be that some resources are idle—that is, unemployed. For example, certain workers may not be able to find jobs, some mineral deposits may not be mined, or machines to stamp out automobile bodies may not be in operation. The other possibility that gives rise to producing below the production possibilities boundary is the inefficient use of resources. This could be due to outright waste, for example, not allowing qualified and healthy people over the age of sixty-five to hold jobs. Or it could be due to combining resources in a less than optimal way. For instance, if each individual Chevrolet fender were cut out by hand instead of stamped out by a press, the cost of production would be greatly increased. Whenever goods or services are produced at higher cost than could be achieved by using another combination of resources, production is not efficient.

Whenever goods and services are produced at higher cost than could be achieved by using another combination of resources, production is not efficient.

FIGURE 3
Production Possibilities for the Nation of Yano, 1990

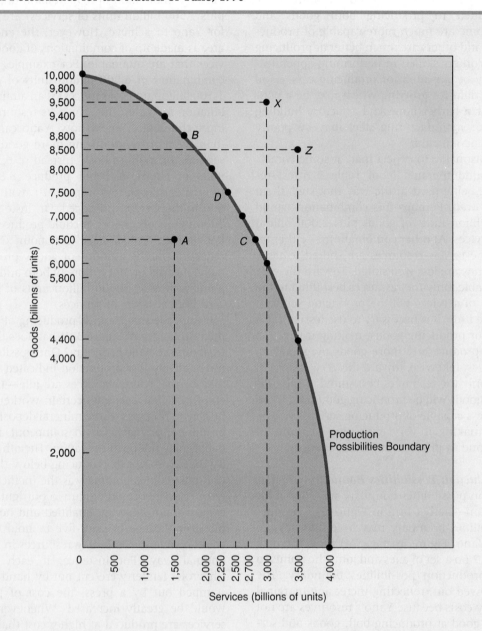

The curve pictures the production possibilities boundary for the fictitious country of Yano. It is established by joining the points plotted from Table 2. All points on the curve (such as B, C, and D) represent alternative maximum combinations of goods and/or services that Yano can produce in 1990.

Any combinations that lie in the blue area above the curve (such as X and Z) are not attainable. Any combinations that lie in the purple area below the curve (such as A) are attainable, but indicate some level of unemployment of resources and/or inefficient use of resources.

Point A production, or some other point in the purple area below the production possibilities boundary, is a very likely combination for Yano. In fact, Yano would be a very rare nation if it did not experience some unemployment of resources and some production inefficiencies. It is important to understand, however, that a country producing below its production possibilities boundary can increase output without an expansion of its resource base which takes time to achieve. In Yano's case, the nation could produce more goods or more services, or more of both, with its present resources.[1] But if Yano were producing on its production possibilities boundary, it could increase its production of goods at this time only by decreasing its production of services. Alternatively, Yano could increase its production of services only by decreasing its production of goods.

A country producing below its production possibilities boundary can increase output without an expansion of its resource base. A country producing on its production possibilities boundary can increase its production of something only by decreasing its production of something else.

Shifts in Production Possibilities Boundaries
What might the production possibilities boundary for Yano be expected to look like in 1995? Since the 1990 boundary was limited by Yano's resource base including technological knowledge, it would be very surprising if the boundary had not shifted by 1995. Figure 4 illustrates an outward shift. The 1995 production possibilities boundary is everywhere above the 1990 boundary because Yano has increased its resources related to both goods and services during those five years. Resources may have increased because the population has grown (more working-age people), the amount of physical capital has increased, or more new natural resources have been discovered than have been used up. Probably the technological knowledge, or the

1. Such improvement may be made through better management by Yano's private businesses and through more enlightened policy by the government of Yano.

FIGURE 4
Shift of Production Possibilities Boundary for the Nation of Yano, 1990 to 1995

The production possibilities boundary of Yano has shifted outward over the period 1990 to 1995. In 1995, Yano can produce greater amounts of goods and services than it could in 1990.

"state of the art," in many industries has also improved, so that by 1995 more goods and services could be produced even with no additional physical resources.

Figure 4 shows the output points B, D, and C—maximum output combinations in 1990—to be less than maximum output combinations in 1995. Point Z, which was impossible to reach in 1990, is on the new production possibilities boundary and therefore attainable in 1995. But point X, which was impossible to reach in 1990, is still unattainable, though not by nearly so much.

Alternative shifts are shown in Figure 5. Panel (a) shows a situation in which the 1995 production possibilities boundary has expanded for goods, but not for services. This might have been the result of

FIGURE 5

Alternative Production Possibilities Shifts for the Nation of Yano, 1990 to 1995

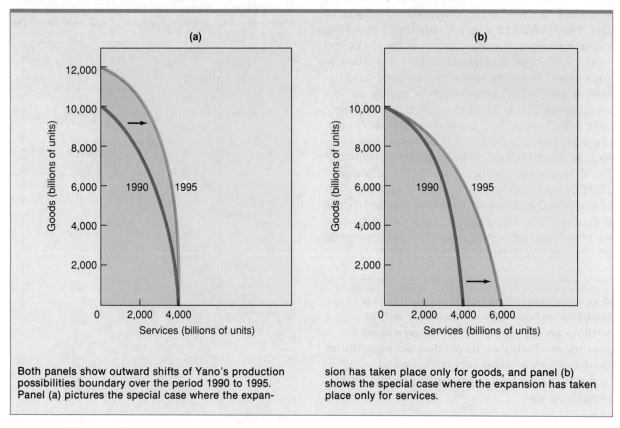

Both panels show outward shifts of Yano's production possibilities boundary over the period 1990 to 1995. Panel (a) pictures the special case where the expansion has taken place only for goods, and panel (b) shows the special case where the expansion has taken place only for services.

a gain in some resources including technological knowledge that can only produce goods. In 1995, Yano can produce as much as 2,000 billion additional units of goods, but still no more than 4,000 billion units of services. Note, however, that in 1995 compared with 1990, with the exception of the "all-services" output choice, Yano is able to produce combinations of output with more goods and the same amount of services, with more services and the same amount of goods, or with more goods and more services.

Panel (b) shows an alternative situation—the production possibilities boundary has expanded for services, but not for goods. This might have occurred because of a gain in resources including technological knowledge that can only produce services.

Production possibilities boundaries are expected to shift outward over time, but there is no guarantee that they will. They could remain the same or actually shift inward. Population—especially of working age—could drop. A decrease in capital goods could take place if saving and investment do not keep up with the replacement of capital goods as they wear out. And natural resources may be used up faster than new discoveries are made.

Production possibilities boundaries are expected to shift outward over time, but they could remain the same or even shift inward.

Economics in Focus

Opportunity Costs in Health Care

Sometimes opportunity-cost decisions can be difficult to make. This is particularly true in the health care field where choices can literally involve life and death. In 1987 the Oregon legislature voted to cut off Medicaid funds for expensive transplants that benefited only a few patients and use the money instead to expand health care for poor women who were pregnant. On the face of it, this seemed a reasonable decision, but soon the media reported the case of Coby Howard, seven years old and suffering from leukemia, whose family could not pay for the bone-marrow transplant he needed. Without Medicaid funds for the transplant, Coby died. With Medicaid support, he might have lived. Thus his life was one small fraction of the opportunity cost problem in the legislature's decision.

Cases like Coby Howard's are receiving increased attention because of a recent move to "ration" health care. Costs for health care services have been spiraling out of control—reaching nearly 12 percent of U.S. GNP by 1988—and many experts argue that the nation does not have the resources to offer the best medical care to everyone who may want it. Therefore, the critics say, we ought to make sensible decisions about the ways in which health care is allocated. To determine whether a particular kind of procedure should be offered or withheld (or funded or not funded), we should consider its life-saving potential, its effect on quality of life, and its relative cost. Some analysts have even suggested that very elderly people should not be given expensive life-prolonging treatments, such as open-heart surgery and liver transplants, because the resources could be better used for other patients.

Arguments such as these often bring an angry response. *Omni* magazine envisioned the following scary scenario: Two Medicare patients, both having severe heart attacks, appear in an emergency room. One is 79, the other 80. The 79-year-old is given an expensive drug that saves his life. But the 80-year-old is past the maximum age for Medicare sponsorship of such treatments. Because there are no family members on hand to promise to pay for the drug, the doctors let the patient die.

If the decisions in a rationing plan are made intelligently, the overall benefits should be greater than the opportunity costs. But many people believe it is unethical to deny medical care for any reason related to economics or budgets. They point out that each human life is priceless, at least to the person who owns it, and often to others as well. Could we tell an aged Picasso that he was too old for government-funded surgery?

In practice, of course, the health care system rations scarce resources every day. Nurses run to the patient who needs them most; hospitals choose whether to spend money on a new dialysis unit or a larger staff; states decide who qualifies for Medicaid and who does not. But the debate on rationing has raised public awareness of the opportunity costs involved in all health care decisions.

Sources: Susan B. Garland with Barbara Buell, "Health Care for All or an Excuse for Cutbacks?" *Business Week,* July 26, 1989, p. 68; Michael D. Reagan, "Health Care Rationing: What Does It Mean?" *New England Journal of Medicine,* vol. 319 (October 27, 1988), pp. 1149–1151; Bill Lawren, "We're Sorry, Your Time Is Up," *Omni,* May 1988, p. 31; Eli Ginzberg, "US Health Policy—Expectations and Realities," *Journal of the American Medical Association,* vol. 260 (December 23, 1988), pp. 3647–3650.

SUMMARY

1. Scarcity refers to the limitations on obtaining all the goods and services that people want. Scarcity is considered *the* economic problem since it gives rise to the trillions of economic problems experienced by people everywhere. Most economists believe that scarcity of the goods and services that people want is unavoidable. (See page 64.)

2. Goods and services are considered scarce whenever people want more of a good or service than is available to them at a price of zero. They are scarce because the ingredients necessary to produce them, called resources, or factors of production, are scarce. (See page 64.)

3. Resources, or factors of production, are divided into three broad categories: (a) labor resources, (b) natural resources, and (c) capital resources. On closer examination, it becomes clear that the productive ability of any one of these resources depends very much on the quantity and quality of the other resources. (See pages 65–68.)

4. Whenever resources are scarce, the decision to produce or consume something involves an opportunity cost. Opportunity cost—that which is given up—can be seen as the true cost of choosing a particular alternative. (See pages 68–69.)

5. People face an opportunity cost in allocating their limited incomes as well as their time and effort. Government, too, must make choices; the opportunity cost of certain programs may be other programs, or it may be private sector spending. (See pages 69–70.)

6. Opportunity cost in production may be applied to a single firm or to an entire economy. In both cases it can be incorporated into a production possibilities boundary—a curve that shows all the alternative maximum combinations that can be produced with a given supply of resources including technological knowledge. (See pages 70–72.)

7. Production possibilities are expected to reflect increasing marginal opportunity costs. This means that the more units of a good or service that are produced, the higher the opportunity cost of producing even more units. The reason is that resources are generally not equally well suited for producing all kinds of goods or services. (See pages 72–73.)

8. A business firm or a country cannot produce amounts that are beyond its production possibilities boundary. It may, however, produce below the boundary. When it does so, it is either not using all of its resources or using them in an inefficient way. (See pages 73–75.)

9. Over time, production possibilities boundaries may shift outward or inward. It is more likely that the shift will be outward, reflecting an increase in resources including technological know-how. There will be an inward shift when fewer resources are available for production. (See pages 75–76.)

KEY TERMS

capital resources: goods, tools, or skills that are produced for use in further production (page 65).

enterpriser (entrepreneur): one who seeks the best opportunities for production and takes risks when making such decisions (page 65).

entrepreneur: see **enterpriser.**

factors of production: see **resources.**

human capital: the skills that people use in combination with their labor effort (page 66).

innovator: one who brings an invention out of the laboratory, makes it practical, and applies it to actual production (page 65).

inventor: one who discovers or devises a new or improved process or product (page 65).

labor resources: all kinds of human work efforts that are or can be directed at production or enterprise (page 65).

natural resources: all things provided by nature that can be used in production (page 65).

opportunity cost: the true cost of choosing one alternative over another; the best alternative forgone when a choice is made (page 68).

production possibility: the limits to the quantities of goods and services that can be produced during any given time period with a given supply of resources including technological knowledge (page 71).

production possibilities boundary: a curve that represents all the alternative maximum combinations that can be produced during a given time period with a given supply of resources including technological knowledge (page 71).

resources (factors of production): input; the ingredients necessary for producing goods and services (output) (page 65).

scarcity: a condition that exists when the amount of something actually available and free of charge would not be sufficient to meet some requirement (page 64).

technological know-how: the ability to combine resources in producing the goods and services that a society wants (page 67).

tradeoff: when one good or service must be given up to gain a certain quantity of another good or service (page 70).

DISCUSSION QUESTIONS

1. Alex, who has just studied this chapter, tells his friend Beth that new cars are scarce in this country even though there are many unsold cars sitting around in new-car dealer show rooms and lots. Beth disagrees. She argues that these cars are not scarce goods, since there are plenty around waiting to be sold. Putting yourself in Alex's place, convince Beth that these cars are indeed scarce goods according to the definition of scarcity in economics.

2. Explain the relationship between the scarcity of goods and services and the factors of production, or resources, available in an economy.

3. The three classes of resources—labor, natural resources, and capital—are defined so broadly that all ingredients of production can be included. Classify each of the following and justify your answer:
 a. an automatic fruit picker
 b. a brain surgeon
 c. a wild horse
 d. an inventor
 e. an irrigated piece of land

4. Suppose you were the ruler of the country of Tava. Because you would like to increase the productive output of Tava, you decide to do whatever you can to increase the quantity of labor available for production. List ten different actions that you might take.

5. Joe says to Mary, "I just bought a beautiful blue cardigan sweater. It cost me $29.95." Mary responds, "It did? I thought it cost you those $29.95 slacks that you also wanted but now can't afford to buy." Who is right? Explain.

6. Government has the power to tax, borrow money, and even print money if it wishes to provide more goods and services. Therefore, government is *not* subject to opportunity cost. True or false? Explain.

7. Suppose that the nation of Doodag can produce only doods and dags and that its production possibilities schedule is the following:

Doods	Dags
0	1,000
200	800
350	600
425	400
500	200
550	0

 a. Construct a graph showing Doodag's production possibilities curve.
 b. Pick a point on the diagram that shows a combination of doods and dags that Doodag cannot now produce.
 c. Pick another point on the diagram that shows a combination of doods and dags consistent with some idle resources.
 d. Pick a third point at which no more doods can be produced, no matter how many or how few dags are being produced.

8. The production possibilities curve that you drew in the previous question was bowed out.
 a. What does that tell you about the marginal opportunity cost of doods in terms of dags and dags in terms of doods?
 b. Set up a new production possibilities schedule for Doodag, using output levels of doods and dags that result in a straight-line production possibilities curve.
 c. What does that tell you about the marginal opportunity cost of doods in terms of dags and dags in terms of doods?
 d. Set up yet another production possibilities schedule for Doodag, using output levels of doods and dags that result in a bowed-in production possibilities curve.

e. What does that tell you about the marginal opportunity cost of doods in terms of dags and dags in terms of doods?

9. What are the public policy implications for a nation that is producing on its production possibilities curve compared with those for one that is producing below (to the left of) its production possibilities curve?

10. Suppose that you know the production possibilities curve for a particular nation. What would you expect this nation's production possibilities curve to look like ten years later? Why?

11. Describe a set of specific circumstances that you believe would result in an inward (to the left) shift of a nation's production possibilities boundary.

5

Demand and Supply— or Supply and Demand

Preview Ask the man or woman on the street what economics is about. The answer is apt to be either "supply and demand" or "demand and supply." If you ask a few more questions, you may hear about an "economic law" of supply and demand, which says that demand and supply determine prices and employment and the standard of living. You may also hear about the dangers that come from tampering with this "law." But if you go still further and inquire how we can tell what demand or supply *is* without already knowing the price, you can expect a blank stare, or hostility, or some less-than-flattering comment about economics and economists.

There is a problem here, which we must face at once. *Demand* and *supply* are used in two meanings. The person on the street uses them in the sense of *quantity*—amounts actually demanded or supplied, usually per week, month, or year. In this sense, the "economic law" of demand and supply means nothing more than that the amount bought must also be the amount sold. But most economists most of the time use *demand* and *supply* in the sense of a *schedule*, involving planned amounts demanded or supplied over a range of different prices. As will become clear in this chapter, no more than one point on a demand schedule, or on a demand curve graphed from a demand schedule, represents demand in the quantity sense. The same is true for supply.

This chapter introduces demand and supply in a schedule sense on two levels: (1) the individual consumer and individual firm, and (2) consumers and firms in markets. Let us take a quick look at these.

Individual consumer demand stems from each consumer's decisions. A consumer who has the money to spend will decide just what and how much to buy. Likewise, individual firm supply stems from decisions made by each business firm. A company that can attract labor resources, natural resources, and capital will decide what and how much to offer for sale.

Market demand is the sum of all the individual consumers' demands for a particular good or service in a certain location. Market supply is the sum of all the individual firms' supplies of that good or service in that same location. The interaction of market demand and market supply determines the market price used in buying and selling and the amount that is bought and sold in the quantity sense.

INDIVIDUAL CONSUMER DEMAND DECISIONS

Individual consumer demand refers to the quantity of a good or service that an individual consumer is willing and able to purchase at a particular moment at each possible price that might be charged for that good or service.

The term *demand* should not be confused with words such as *want, desire,* or *need.* A college student may very much want or desire to purchase an expensive sports car, but that does not constitute demand unless he or she is also able to buy it. The same college student may even be convinced that he or she really needs that sports car. But, once again, if the student cannot afford to buy the car, it is not considered demand. On the other hand, a very wealthy person may be able to afford to buy five such sports cars, but if that person decides to keep the money in the bank, there is also no demand. Demand requires both willingness and ability to buy a product.

The definition at the start of this section indicated that economists view demand "at a particular moment at each possible price." How is it possible for a consumer actually to be faced with different prices for the same good at the same time? It isn't, of course. The point is that the economist conceives of the individual's demand as his or her *plan* about how much to buy at different possible prices. The "at a particular moment" part of the definition simply means that we do not have to consider at the same time any variables other than the price and the quantity demanded of the good being studied. It is thus a simplifying assumption—a somewhat disguised use of the *ceteris paribus* assumption, which was introduced in Chapter 3.

Individual consumer demand is the quantity of a good or service that an individual consumer is willing and able to purchase at a particular moment at each possible price that might be charged for that good or service.

To illustrate the relationship between price and quantity demanded by an individual consumer, let's take the case of Alex, who buys and wears jeans. Economists might express his demand function for jeans as follows:

$$QD_j^A = f(P_j), \textit{ ceteris paribus}$$

In this functional relationship, QD_j^A is the quantity demanded of good j (jeans) by person A (Alex), f is the symbol for function (which may be read "depends on"), P_j is the price of jeans, and *ceteris paribus* means that all other variables are held constant. That is, we assume that there are no changes in such influential variables as Alex's tastes, his income, and the prices of other goods that he could or does buy. (Later in this chapter we shall discuss the effects of changes in these other variables.)

The relationship between price and quantity demanded of a good or service may be expressed in the form of a functional relationship such as: $QD_j = f(P_j)$, *ceteris paribus*.

Think of Alex being interviewed as part of a market survey that seeks to discover consumers' demand for jeans at various prices. During a period of a minute or so, the interviewer may ask Alex how many pairs of jeans he would buy over the next twelve months at five different prices. The interview is not long enough for Alex's tastes to have changed, nor does Alex receive any new information about his income or the prices of other goods that he could or does buy. Thus the interview setting comes close to meeting economists' requirements for defining demand: at alternative prices, different quantities of a good are demanded, provided other influential variables are held constant.

The Demand Schedule and Curve

Information such as that obtained from interviewing Alex may be recorded in a **demand schedule**—a table showing different prices for a good and the quantity of that good demanded at each of these prices.

Table 1 illustrates a demand schedule that is based on the interview with Alex. His answers are not surprising, since he said that he would demand fewer pairs of jeans at higher prices and more pairs at lower prices.

The information given in the demand schedule may be plotted on a graph. It is customary in eco-

TABLE 1
Alex's Demand Schedule for Jeans,
September 24, 1990

Price per Pair of Jeans (in dollars)	Quantity of Jeans Demanded (over next 12 months)
50	0
40	1
30	2
20	4
10	7

nomics to put the price on the vertical axis and quantity demanded on the horizontal axis. Price is the independent variable, and the quantity demanded is the dependent variable. Panel (a) of Figure 1 includes exactly the same information as is

FIGURE 1
Alex's Demand for Jeans, September 24, 1990

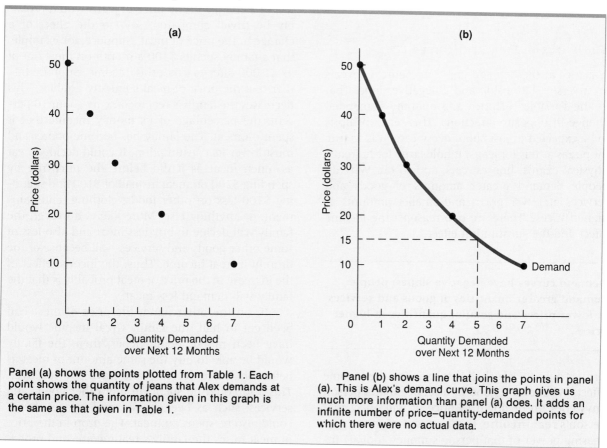

Panel (a) shows the points plotted from Table 1. Each point shows the quantity of jeans that Alex demands at a certain price. The information given in this graph is the same as that given in Table 1.

Panel (b) shows a line that joins the points in panel (a). This is Alex's demand curve. This graph gives us much more information than panel (a) does. It adds an infinite number of price–quantity-demanded points for which there were no actual data.

given in the demand schedule in Table 1. In panel (b) of Figure 1, a line has been drawn through these five plotted points to join them. This line adds an infinite number of price–quantity-demanded points. For example, you can read from the graph that, at a price of $15, Alex will demand five pairs of jeans. However, since the interviewer did not ask Alex how many jeans he would demand at $15, it is only an assumption that his answer would have been five pairs. All the points along the demand curve, except those few that come from actual data, are based on the assumption that the connecting line accurately describes the consumer's demand.

A demand schedule is a table that shows different prices for a good and the quantity of that good demanded at each of these prices. A demand curve is a graphic representation of the relation of quantity demanded and price.

Slope of the Demand Curve

A glance at the demand curve in Figure 1 reveals an inverse relationship and a negative slope. That is, the variables of price and quantity demanded change in opposite directions. This relationship is to be expected in just about every case. It is as true for pizzas as it is for jeans. It holds true for haircuts, physical exams, houses, cars, and so on. Why do people demand greater amounts of goods and services at lower prices and smaller amounts at higher prices? There are two reasons: the income effect and the substitution effect.

Demand curves have negative slopes: people demand greater quantities of goods and services at lower prices and smaller quantities at higher prices.

Income Effect   We shall first examine the income effect. Whenever a good or a service that a person buys goes up or down in price, it will affect that person's **real income**, that is, it will affect the purchasing power of that person's money (dollar) income. If the good or service goes up in price, the

person's real income will go down (other things being equal). Alternatively, if it goes down in price, the person's real income will go up. Alex is somewhat "richer" when jeans are $10 per pair than when they are $30 per pair because he can buy more with his money income. The **income effect** is the influence that a change in a person's real income (resulting from a change in the price of a good or service that this person buys) has on the quantity that this person demands of that good or service.

Whenever a good or service that a person buys goes up or down in price, it affects the purchasing power of that person's money income and therefore changes his or her real income.

For a typical American family, the income effect of a change in the price of jeans would probably be trivial compared, say, to the effect of a change in the price of meat. Suppose, for example, that a family spends $100 a month on meat out of its $1,000 after-tax monthly income. Suppose further that the price of meat suddenly doubles. This decreases the family's real income by about 10 percent, the percentage of its money income that it spent on meat. The family has become poorer and must lower its consumption. It could decide to eat as much meat as it did before the price rise by spending $200 on meat instead of $100 and spending $100 less on other foods, clothing, entertainment, or anything else. More likely, however, the family will decide to buy less meat and also less of some other goods and services—all because of the drop in its real income. Thus, the income effect of the increase in the price of meat probably is that the family will demand less meat.

If, on the other hand, the price of meat had been cut in half, the family's real income would have been raised. Being richer, then, the family would be able to buy the same amount of meat as before the price decrease and have $50 left over. This $50 could be spent on any other goods and services, such as beer, books, and movies, but it could also be spent on meat. The drop in the price of meat raises the family's real income and probably increases the quantity of meat it will demand.

The income effect is the influence that a change in a person's real income has on the quantity of a specific good or service this person demands.

Substitution Effect The second reason why the demand curve is expected to be negatively sloped is the **substitution effect**. This is the effect that a change in *relative* prices of substitute goods or services (resulting from a change in the price of a good or service) has on the quantity that a person demands of that good or service. Whenever the price of any one good or service changes while other prices stay constant, relative prices are altered. People will wish to substitute goods that became relatively cheaper for those that became relatively higher priced. At higher prices for jeans, Alex will find that other types of pants, such as cotton casuals, will be relatively cheaper. He will probably substitute some cotton casuals for some jeans. On the other hand, at lower prices for jeans, cotton casuals are relatively higher priced, and Alex will most likely buy more jeans and fewer cotton casuals. Thus, because of the substitution effect, the quantity demanded of a good will be higher at lower prices of that good and lower at higher prices of that good.

The substitution effect is the effect that a change in relative prices of substitute goods or services has on the quantity that a person demands of a good or service.

The preceding discussion has treated the income effect and the substitution effect separately; in fact, they occur together. Alex is quite typical in that he finds that at higher prices of jeans his real income is lower *and* he will substitute other types of pants for jeans. Thus the income effect and the substitution effect work together to explain the negative slope of the demand curve.

The income effect and the substitution effect occur together; higher prices cause lower real incomes and lead people to substitute other goods and services.

Changes in the Quantity Demanded and Changes in Demand

Economists usually mean something different when they talk about a "change in the quantity demanded" than when they talk about a "change in demand." The quantity demanded of a good is expected to be different at different prices of that good. A *change in the quantity demanded* is reflected in a **movement along a demand curve**. It is important to keep in mind that while this movement along the demand curve is taking place, tastes, income, and prices of other goods are being held constant through the *ceteris paribus* assumption. As you will recall, Alex said that he would demand four pairs of jeans at a price of $20 per pair, but only two pairs at a price of $30 per pair. A glance back at panel (b) of Figure 1 reveals several such changes in the quantity demanded—movements from one plotted point to another along Alex's demand curve for jeans.

A "change in demand," on the other hand, is not caused by a change in the price of that good. A *change in demand* is reflected in a **shift of the demand curve**—a displacement of the entire curve to the right or to the left. But this can happen only when the *ceteris paribus* assumption is relaxed or removed. If time is allowed to enter the model (another interview takes place at a different time), tastes, income, and prices of other goods may change. This means that at any given price of the good, either more or less may be demanded. Figure 2 illustrates two alternative demand shifts. Curve D_1—the original demand curve—is the same demand curve as that derived for Alex in Figure 1. Curve D_2 is the result of a demand shift to the right, which shows that Alex will demand more jeans at any given price. Curve D_3 is the result of a demand shift to the left, which shows that Alex will demand fewer jeans at any given price. For example, Figure 2 shows that Alex originally demanded four pairs of jeans at $20 a pair. When Alex demands seven pairs at $20 a pair, it shows that the demand curve has shifted to the right (to D_2). When he demands only two pairs of jeans at the same $20 price, the demand curve has shifted to the left (to D_3).

A change in quantity demanded is reflected in a movement along a demand curve. A change in

FIGURE 2
Alex's Demand for Jeans: Two Alternative Demand Shifts

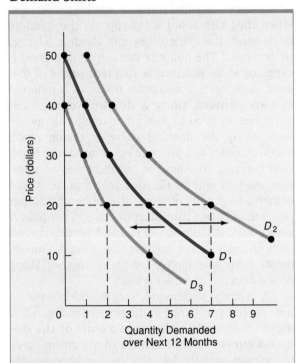

Curve D_1 is the original demand curve that was derived for Alex in Figure 1. When time is allowed to enter the model so that Alex's taste, his income, or the prices that he pays for other goods may change, his demand curve may shift to D_2 or D_3. A shift to D_2 shows that Alex will demand more jeans at any given price. A shift to D_3 shows that Alex will demand fewer jeans at any given price.

right, and a decrease in taste will bring about a shift to the left, other things being equal. If Alex, who has been wearing dress pants to work, suddenly decides that jeans are more comfortable and just as appropriate, his demand curve for jeans will shift to the right. On the other hand, if Alex has been wearing jeans to work and his boss "suggests" that dress pants are more correct, his demand curve for jeans will probably shift to the left.

An increase in a consumer's *income* will usually cause his or her demand curve to shift to the right, and a decrease in income usually brings about a shift to the left. Alex can afford to buy more jeans when his income is higher and fewer when it is lower. Only in rare cases will higher income cause people to demand less and lower income cause them to demand more. It is possible, however, that at very much higher income levels some people will demand fewer hamburgers since they will have switched to steak.[1]

Shifts in demand for a good also result from *price changes of other goods*, especially closely related goods. Such "other" goods may be grouped into two categories: substitutes and complements.

Shift variables, related to demand, are variables, such as taste, income, and price changes of other goods, that may cause an individual's demand curve to shift (be relocated on a graph).

Substitutes **Substitutes** are goods that may be used instead of one another. Examples of good substitutes are beer and ale, Coca-Cola and Pepsi-Cola, and vinyl kitchen flooring and kitchen carpeting. An increase in the price of a substitute will cause the demand curve for the other good to shift to the right, and a decrease in the price of a substitute brings about a shift to the left. If Alex finds that jeans and cotton casuals are fairly good substitutes, and if cotton casuals go up in price, he will buy more jeans and fewer cotton casuals. In this case, Alex's *quantity demanded* for cotton casuals goes down and his *demand* for jeans goes up. Similarly, a decrease in the price of cotton casuals will cause Alex to demand fewer jeans and more cotton casuals. This time Alex's *quantity demanded* for cotton

1. When the demand for a product is negatively related to a person's income (such as the hamburgers in our example), economists refer to that product as *inferior*.

demand is reflected in a shift of the whole demand curve.

Shift Variables Economists use the term *shift variables* to refer to variables that cause a curve to be relocated—to "shift"—on a graph. Clearly, there can be a great many shift variables for any function or curve, since there is no limit to the number of variables that are covered by the *ceteris paribus* assumption. There are three especially important shift variables for an individual's demand curve.

An increase in a consumer's *taste* for a good or service will cause the demand curve to shift to the casuals goes up and his *demand* for jeans goes down.

Complements **Complements** are goods that are used with each other. Examples are automobiles and gasoline, ski boots and ski poles, and kites and string. Alex will demand fewer jeans if the type of belt that he wears with jeans, but not with other pants, goes up in price. That is, if the package, made up of a pair of jeans and one of these belts, has gone up in price, he will demand fewer jeans. Also, if the price of these belts decreases, Alex may demand more jeans.

Substitutes are goods that may be used instead of one another; complements are goods that are used with each other.

When goods have several uses, they may be complementary in some cases and substitutable in others. It is then a complicated problem in economic statistics (econometrics) to discover which relation dominates at any particular time or place. And, of course, the answer may vary from time to time or from place to place. At a time or place where soft drinks like Coca-Cola or Seven-Up are never used as mixers for alcoholic drinks, soft drinks will be substitutes for alcoholic ones. At a time or place where soft drinks are used almost entirely as mixers and almost never consumed by themselves, the dominant relation will be complementary.

This discussion of complementary and substitute goods has been limited to the demand side of the market. As you will see, there are similar relationships on the supply side, and it will be useful to distinguish between the effects of complementarity and substitutability in demand (as here) and the effects of complementarity and substitutability in supply.

INDIVIDUAL FIRM SUPPLY DECISIONS

Individual firm supply refers to the amount of a good or service that an individual business firm is willing and able to sell at a particular moment at

each possible price. Notice that this definition is quite similar to the one offered for demand on page 82. The only real difference is that the word *sell* is substituted for the word *purchase*.

More than just the willingness to supply a good is needed in order to supply it. A firm must be able to attract the resources, or factors of production, that are necessary to produce the good or service. A company that manufactures jeans may wish to produce 10,000 pairs per week, but it will not supply that many if it lacks the right machinery or enough employees to do the work.

As was true of demand, economists use the *ceteris paribus* assumption when viewing supply. Thus they avoid having to consider at the same time any variables other than the price and the quantity supplied of the good being studied.

Individual firm supply is the quantity of a good or service that an individual business firm is willing and able to sell at a particular moment at each possible price.

To illustrate the functional relationship between price and quantity supplied by an individual firm, we shall use the hypothetical Cohen Clothing Corporation, which manufactures jeans, as an example. In economics, we might express the relationship as follows:

$$QS_j^C = f(P_j), \text{ } ceteris \text{ } paribus$$

Here QS_j^C is the quantity supplied of good j (jeans) by firm C (Cohen Clothing Corporation), f is the symbol for function (and may be read as "depends on"), P_j is the price of jeans, and *ceteris paribus* means that all other variables are held constant.

Specifically, *ceteris paribus* holds constant a number of influential variables. Most important among them are the prices of inputs needed for production, the state of the technology, the company's expectations about the prices of other goods that it does or could produce, and its goals. (As you will see, these are *shift variables* in respect to the firm's supply curve.)

Imagine that Mr. Cohen, the president of Cohen Clothing Corporation, is being interviewed as part of a survey trying to discover the quantity of jeans supplied by companies at various prices. During a very short interview, the interviewer may ask Mr. Cohen how many pairs of jeans his firm would supply over the next twelve months at each of five alternative prices. The interview is not long enough for Mr. Cohen's goals to change, nor does he receive any new information on the prices of inputs, the state of jean technology, or the prices of other goods that his firm is or could be producing. Thus, this interview setting, like that used in defining demand, closely meets economists' needs for defining supply: at alternative prices, different quantities of a good are supplied, as long as other influential variables are held constant.

The Supply Schedule and Curve

Information such as that obtained from interviewing Mr. Cohen may be placed on a **supply schedule**—a table showing different prices for a good and the quantity of that good supplied at each of these prices.

Table 2 illustrates the supply schedule based on the interview with Mr. Cohen. Economists are not surprised to learn that his firm would supply more jeans at higher prices and fewer jeans at lower prices.

A supply schedule is a table showing different prices for a good and the quantity of that good supplied at each of these prices.

The information in the supply schedule is plotted on the graphs in Figure 3. As we pointed out earlier, the economist customarily places price on

TABLE 2
Cohen Clothing Corporation's Supply Schedule for Jeans, September 24, 1990

Price per Pair of Jeans (in dollars)	Quantity of Jeans Supplied (over next 12 months)
50	80,000
40	70,000
30	50,000
20	30,000
10	0

the vertical axis and the quantity variable—quantity supplied in this case—on the horizontal axis. Price is the independent variable, and quantity supplied is the dependent variable. Panel (a) of Figure 3 shows the plotted points from Table 2. Panel (b) of Figure 3 has a line drawn through the plotted points to show all the price–quantity-supplied points, whether plotted from actual interview data or only assumed, which make up the supply curve.

Slope of the Supply Curve

The supply curve in Figure 3 shows a direct relationship and a positive slope—the variables of price and quantity supplied change in the same direction. This relationship can be expected in just about every instance as long as we stick to the conditions existing for the interview with Mr. Cohen. Under these conditions, which hold other influential variables constant, what is true for jeans will be true for almost any good or service that a firm might produce. Why, under these circumstances, do firms supply greater amounts at higher prices and smaller amounts at lower prices? In a word, the reason is *profit*. The supply curve for an individual firm is expected to be positively sloped because profits are an important goal for businesses. Under the *ceteris paribus* assumption used in deriving the supply curve, supplying jeans will be more profitable when their price is $30 than when their price is $20. Therefore, the company will naturally want to put more resources into the production of jeans when their price is $30 than it would when the price is only $20.

The company might find that it pays to use some of its older equipment (despite a higher production cost) to produce more jeans when their price reaches a certain higher level. It is likely that the Cohen Clothing Corporation produces other clothing besides jeans—that it is a multiproduct firm. It may also produce shirts, skirts, and socks. If, indeed, the Cohen Clothing Corporation is a multiproduct firm, it will probably find that, at a high price of jeans, it pays to alter its product mix. Thus it will commit more of its production facilities and its employees to the production of jeans and less to the production of shirts, skirts, and socks. Taken together, these various explanations make it quite clear why firms find it profitable to supply

FIGURE 3
Cohen Clothing Corporation's Supply of Jeans, September 24, 1990

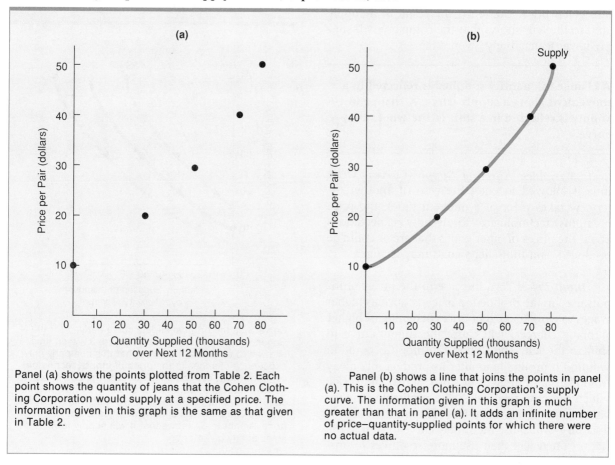

Panel (a) shows the points plotted from Table 2. Each point shows the quantity of jeans that the Cohen Clothing Corporation would supply at a specified price. The information given in this graph is the same as that given in Table 2.

Panel (b) shows a line that joins the points in panel (a). This is the Cohen Clothing Corporation's supply curve. The information given in this graph is much greater than that in panel (a). It adds an infinite number of price–quantity-supplied points for which there were no actual data.

more of a good when they can sell it at a higher price and less of a good when its price is lower.

Supply curves have positive slopes; firms find it profitable to commit more resources to the production of a good or service when its price is higher and less when its price is lower, *ceteris paribus.*

Changes in the Quantity Supplied and Changes in Supply

Now it is time to make a distinction between a "change in the quantity supplied" and a "change in supply," which is similar to the distinction made between a "change in the quantity demanded" and

a "change in demand." The *quantity supplied* of a good is expected to be different at different prices of that good (shown as a **movement along a supply curve**). A *change in supply* is expected to take place when the variables held constant by the *ceteris paribus* assumption, which we can call "shift variables," are allowed to change (shown as a **shift of the supply curve**).

Panel (b) of Figure 3 showed several changes in the quantity supplied—movements from one plotted point to another—along the Cohen Clothing Corporation's supply curve for jeans. Figure 4 shows changes in supply—two possible shifts of Cohen's supply curve that result from relaxing or removing the *ceteris paribus* assumption. Curve S_1, the original supply curve, is the same as that derived for the Cohen Clothing Corporation in Figure

3. Curve S_2, the result of a supply shift to the right, shows that the company will supply more jeans at any given price. Curve S_3, the result of a supply shift to the left, shows that the company will supply fewer jeans at any given price.

A change in quantity supplied is reflected in a movement along a supply curve. A change in supply is reflected in a shift of the whole supply curve.

Shift Variables Affecting Supply Curves Once time is allowed to enter the case (if another interview takes place at a different time), the price of inputs, technological know-how, expectations about the prices of other goods that are or could be produced, and the seller's goals may change.

Input Prices An increase in the prices of inputs used in the production of jeans, such as higher wages to workers, higher prices of denim, or higher shipping charges, will cause the supply curve to shift to the left. The Cohen Clothing Corporation will find it profitable to alter its product mix away from jeans and in favor or shirts, skirts, and socks, which are now relatively more profitable. The reverse case—decreasing prices of inputs used in production—will cause the supply curve to shift to the right. Cohen will then use more resources to produce more jeans at each price.

Technological Know-How An advance in technological know-how related to producing jeans, such as new and more efficient sewing machines or a better managerial technique, results in decreased costs. The Cohen Clothing Corporation would not be expected to adopt a new method of producing jeans unless it lowered costs and increased profits. In such cases, the supply curve shifts to the right.

Expected Prices of Other Goods The supply curve may also shift because of a change in the expected prices of other goods that the supplying firm does or can produce. At any given price of jeans, the Cohen Clothing Corporation will alter its product mix in favor of more jeans if it expects

FIGURE 4
Cohen Clothing Corporation's Supply of Jeans: Two Alternative Shifts

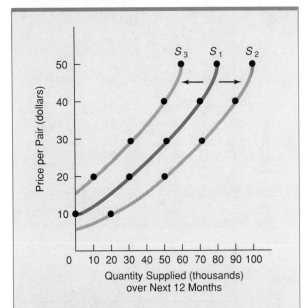

Curve S_1 is the original supply curve derived for the Cohen Clothing Corporation in Figure 3. When time is allowed to enter the model so that this company may experience changes in the price of inputs, technological know-how, expectations about the prices of other goods that it is or could be producing, or its goals, its supply curve may shift to S_2 or S_3. A shift to S_2 shows that the company will supply more jeans at any given price. A shift to S_3 shows that it will supply fewer jeans at any given price.

lower prices for shirts, skirts, and socks. Likewise, it will produce fewer jeans and more shirts, skirts, and socks if its price expectations for these other goods are raised. Hence, a firm's supply curve for one product tends to shift to the right when expected prices of its other products fall and to shift to the left when expected prices of its other products rise.

Goals of Sellers Finally, supply curves shift because of changes in the goals or motives of sellers. Throughout this discussion it has been assumed that the sellers were in business to make profits. If firms did not care about profits, the theory of supply would break down, since they would just as soon sell more as less when the price is low.

However, the assumption that firms prefer more rather than less profit does not mean that no other motives can play a role.

The desire to *do good* may be a strong motive. Part of Cohen's desire to sell more jeans may be that they last well and give people good value for their money. *Security*, or a concern about survival, may be another motive for firms. Perhaps the Cohen Clothing Corporation wants to sell more jeans because it expects *"bigness"* will give greater long-term security, and not because it expects larger profits. Firms may wish to avoid large risks—even if there is a chance that they will pay off handsomely—and decide not to commit themselves to produce certain goods whose prices have temporarily gone up.

Individual managers' goals—as distinct from the firm's goals—may also affect supply. The president of the Cohen Clothing Corporation may seek the *prestige* and *salary* that go with being the head of a very large firm. Thus the supply curve would shift to the right, as he would be willing to supply more at any given price. Of course, another firm's president may be motivated to act in exactly the opposite way. That president may wish to decrease the size of the firm so that he or she can have a hand in every part of the business. In that case, the supply curve would shift to the left, as the firm would supply less at any given price.

Shift variables that affect supply curves include changes in input prices, advances in technological know-how, changes in the expected price of other goods the firm can or does produce, and changes in the goals or motives of sellers.

"Increases" and "Decreases" in Supply   When is a supply shift an increase in supply, and when is it a decrease? Because supply curves usually slope upward, there sometimes is confusion on this important point. (Because demand curves normally slope downward, there is no similar problem on the demand side.) To illustrate the problem, we shall return to Figure 4. The shift from S_1 to S_2 is an increase in supply, since for any given price, quantity supplied is greater on curve S_2 than on curve S_1. The shift from S_1 to S_3 is a decrease in supply, since for any given price, quantity supplied is less on curve S_3 than on curve S_1. The direction of the arrows tells us which is which, but notice that S_3 lies vertically *above* S_1, which lies vertically above S_2. When reading supply and demand curves, then, we should remember to concentrate on horizontal rather than vertical comparisons.

MARKET DEMAND AND SUPPLY

A **market** is the organized action between potential buyers (market demand) and potential sellers (market supply) that enables them to carry on exchange or trade. In a free market, demand and supply determine the terms of trade, or the price at which a purchase or sale is made.

A market is the organized action between potential buyers and potential sellers that enables them to carry on exchange or trade.

Market demand is the sum of all of the individual consumers' demands (the information found in their demand schedules) for a particular good or service in a certain place over some period of time. Recall Alex, whose demand schedule for jeans was shown in Table 1. Suppose that Alex lives in Chicago and that everyone in that city also gives us his or her demand schedule for jeans. All the quantities demanded at each possible price can then be added together to determine the market demand for jeans in Chicago over the same twelve-month period. Table 3 presents some hypothetical numbers, and Figure 5 illustrates that market-demand curve.

Market supply is the sum of all of the individual firms' supplies (the information found in their supply schedules) of a particular good or service in a certain place over some period of time. One such schedule, the Cohen Clothing Corporation's supply schedule for jeans, was given in Table 2. Suppose that the Cohen Clothing Corporation supplies jeans only to the Chicago area and that all the other clothing firms that also serve Chicago

TABLE 3
*Market-Demand Schedule for Jeans in Chicago,
September 24, 1990*

Price per Pair of Jeans (in dollars)	Quantity of Jeans Demanded (over next 12 months)
50	50,000
40	500,000
30	2,000,000
20	5,000,000
10	9,000,000

provide us with their Chicago supply schedules for jeans as well. The quantities supplied at each possible price can then be added up to determine the market supply for jeans in Chicago over the same twelve-month period. Table 4 provides some hypothetical numbers, and Figure 6 pictures that market-supply curve.

FIGURE 5
**Market Demand for Jeans in Chicago,
September 24, 1990**

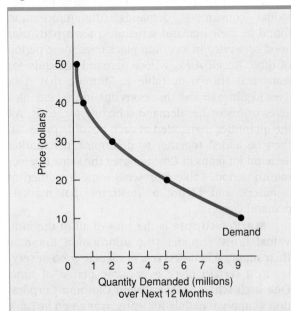

The numbers plotted from Table 3 establish the points along this market-demand curve. It combines all of the individual consumers' demands for jeans over the next 12 months in Chicago.

Market demand is the sum of all the individual consumers' demands for a particular good or service in a certain place over some period of time. Market supply is the sum of all the individual firms' supplies of a particular good or service in a certain place over some time period.

Equilibrium Price and Quantity

Up to this point, demand and supply have been treated separately but in a similar way. In real life, of course, demand and supply actions take place at the same time. Only when they are examined together, therefore, can it be seen how market demand and market supply determine the price of a product and the quantity that is bought and sold.

Both market demand and market supply limit the quantity of a product that is traded. The amount of a product that is sold at a certain price cannot exceed the demand for it at that price. Nor can more of a product be bought at a particular price than firms are willing to supply at that price. Therefore, the price tends to change whenever it does not equate the quantities of market demand and market supply.

Market demand and market supply determine the price of a product and the quantity that is bought and sold.

The price that does equate quantity demanded with quantity supplied in the market is called the **equilibrium price**, and the accompanying quantity is called the **equilibrium quantity**. As you will recall, equilibrium means that a state of balance has been achieved and that there is no longer a tendency for change.

The price that equates quantity demanded with quantity supplied in the market is called the equilibrium price; the accompanying quantity is called the equilibrium quantity.

TABLE 4
Market-Supply Schedule for Jeans in Chicago, September 24, 1990

Price per Pair of Jeans (in dollars)	Quantity of Jeans Supplied (over next 12 months)
50	8,000,000
40	7,000,000
30	5,000,000
20	3,000,000
10	0

To illustrate equilibrium price and quantity, let us return to our example involving the market demand and market supply of jeans in Chicago. Figure 7 combines the market-demand curve shown in Figure 5 and the market-supply curve shown in Figure 6 in a single diagram. At any price above $23.50, more jeans will be supplied than are demanded. For example, Figure 7 shows that at a

FIGURE 6
Market Supply of Jeans in Chicago, September 24, 1990

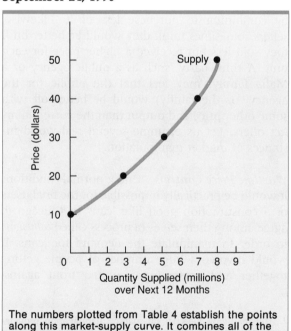

The numbers plotted from Table 4 establish the points along this market-supply curve. It combines all of the individual firms' supplies of jeans over the next 12 months in Chicago.

FIGURE 7
Market Demand and Market Supply for Jeans in Chicago, September 24, 1990

The market-demand curve shown in Figure 5 is combined with the market-supply curve in Figure 6. Their intersection marks the equilibrium price ($23.50) and equilibrium quantity (3.8 million pairs of jeans) in this market. At prices above $23.50 there is excess supply, and at prices below $23.50 there is excess demand.

price of $30 a pair, only 2 million would be demanded but 5 million would be offered by suppliers. (These numbers can also be taken from the market-demand and market-supply schedules shown in Tables 3 and 4.) Such **excess supply**—quantity supplied exceeding quantity demanded—will cause supplier firms to compete with one another in an attempt to sell their jeans, thereby driving down the price. Alternatively, at any price below $23.50, more jeans will be demanded than firms are willing to supply. Figure 7 shows, for example, that at a price of $20 per pair of jeans, 3 million would be supplied, but 5 million would be demanded. Such **excess demand**—quantity demanded exceeding quantity supplied—will cause buyers to compete with one another in an attempt to buy jeans, thereby driving up the price.

When there is excess supply (the quantity supplied exceeding the quantity demanded), supplier firms compete with one another and drive down the price. When there is excess demand (quantity demanded exceeding quantity supplied), buyers compete with one another and drive up the price.

Only at a price of $23.50, where the market demand of 3.8 million jeans is exactly equal to the market supply of 3.8 million jeans, will excess demand and excess supply be eliminated. In a **free market**—one in which the forces of demand and supply have the opportunity to alter the price—a market equilibrium will tend to appear.

In real-world markets, equilibria are rather elusive—that is, they are moving targets rather than points that will be reached and then remain. Changing demand and/or supply conditions cause changes in the equilibrium price and/or quantity. In our discussion of demand shifts and supply shifts, we offered several reasons why such shifts may occur. For example, demand may shift to the right if consumers' incomes increase, if their taste for the good gets stronger, if prices of substitute goods increase, or if prices of complementary goods go down. Supply may shift as a result of changes in input costs, technological knowledge, prices of other goods that firms are or could be producing, or the motives to which sellers respond. We expect fairly frequent changes in some of these variables. Every such change will bring about a shift, except for the coincidental case in which changes exactly offset each other—as, for example, where income goes up at the same time as there is a compensating decrease in the price of a substitute good. Every shift will bring with it a new equilibrium price and/or quantity. But supply and demand curves usually shift so often that there is not enough time to adjust to any one equilibrium before a new one appears. Thus, market equilibria are seen as moving targets that may never be reached.

In a free market—one in which the forces of demand and supply have the opportunity to

alter the price—a market equilibrium tends to appear, although shifts in demand and/or supply cause the equilibrium state to be a moving target.

Market Manipulation[2]

Markets can be manipulated, or controlled, by buyers, sellers, or outsiders (regulators). These manipulators can try either to change the equilibrium position or to preserve a disequilibrium position. Equilibrium and disequilibrium cases should be distinguished carefully. As you know, equilibrium in a market is a state of balance between quantity demanded and quantity supplied. When the two are unequal, there is **disequilibrium**.

When quantity demanded and quantity supplied do not balance in a market, disequilibrium exists.

Buyers sometimes think that they would be better off if they forced the price of a product down by combining to purchase less of it. Likewise, sellers sometimes think they would be better off if they sold less but received a higher price for each unit. A third party, such as a public agency or a Mafia family, may feel that the public (or the agency, or the family) would be better off with some other price and output than the current market offers. Let us examine several real-world instances of market manipulation.

Wartime Price Controls Under normal conditions it would be practically impossible for the final users of a consumption good like jeans in Chicago to agree among themselves (a process called *collusion*) in order to manipulate the demand for jeans. It would involve a huge number of people getting together and presenting a united front against

2. The following material on market manipulation provides useful exercises with the concepts of market demand, market supply, and market equilibrium. However, instructors who wish to move more quickly to later portions of the text may skip this section.

those who broke their agreement, often called "chiselers." But consider the market for a civilian good—jeans will do—in a war economy, after productive capacity has been diverted to the production of a military good—uniforms. Look at Figure 8, which again shows the supply (S_1) and demand (D_1) curves found in Figure 7. Think of these curves as describing the prewar situation—the equilibrium quantity is 3.8 million pairs of jeans, and the equilibrium price is $23.50. Next, consider how diverting production from jeans to military uniforms will affect the supply of jeans. Because of the war, supply has fallen (shifted to the left) from S_1 to S_2 and the free-market price has risen from $23.50 to $30.

Now suppose that the government proposes to hold the price at $23.50 without restraining civilian demand in general by some means such as higher taxes. Government can try to hold the price of jeans at $23.50 by either an equilibrium or a disequilibrium method. Since the disequilibrium method is simpler, at least on the diagram, we will examine it first. The government may establish a **ceiling price**—a maximum price at which a product may legally be sold—at $23.50. This is called a *disequilibrium method* because, since the new supply curve (S_2) shows that only 1.1 million pairs of jeans will be supplied at $23.50, an excess demand, or a **shortage**, of 2.7 million pairs is created (3.8 million demanded minus 1.1 million supplied equals the 2.7 million shortage). The legal price can be enforced reasonably well for a time, especially if the war is a popular one like World War II in the United States between 1942 and 1945. (No such method was tried during the unpopular Vietnam War between 1963 and 1973.)

The disequilibrium method of market manipulation involves creating shortages or surpluses of goods and services.

The *equilibrium method* of market manipulation involves shifting the demand curve or the supply curve for a good or service. For example, the demand curve may be shifted through "formal" rationing. (Shortages usually also give rise to "informal rationing," through individual merchants reserving supplies for their best customers, and so

FIGURE 8
Market Manipulation: Disequilibrium Method with a Ceiling (Maximum) Price in the Market for Jeans

In this diagram, S_1 is the supply curve and D_1 is the demand curve before the war, when 3.8 million pairs of jeans are bought and sold at a price of $23.50. In wartime the supply falls from S_1 to S_2, which would cause the price to increase to $30 and the sales to drop to 2 million. If the government dislikes this free-market solution and decides to hold the price at $23.50 (a ceiling price), only 1.1 million pairs of jeans will be supplied, and a disequilibrium situation (a shortage of 2.7 million pairs) is created.

on.) Formal **rationing** calls for a detailed and often complicated plan involving the issuance by government of special coupons, or tokens, that act as a second form of money.[3] For example, it might take $23.50 plus a special ration coupon to buy a pair of jeans. If successful, a formal rationing sys-

---

3. Consider gasoline rationing. The plan would need to take into account many different factors. For example, some families have more cars and some more drivers than others. Some people live much closer to work than others. Access to public transportation and to car pooling also varies greatly. Some people use automobiles in their jobs more than others, especially in emergencies. And a few also use gasoline for tractors, trucks, and other vehicles.

tem will cut demand. This is shown in Figure 9, which is identical to Figure 8 except that it shows a shift of the demand curve from D_1 to D_2. The new demand curve is shown to be vertical at 1.1 million pairs of jeans, since the government issues only 1.1 million ration coupons. The shortage at the $23.50 price is eliminated.

The equilibrium method of market manipulation involves shifting the demand curve or the supply curve for a good or service. A successful formal rationing system will shift the relevant portion of the demand curve to the left.

In the real world, things seldom work out quite so neatly. With either the disequilibrium or the equilibrium method, a problem arises when quantities of the goods—jeans in our example—are diverted to a "black market," in which goods are sold at illegally high prices. This makes the situation worse by shifting S_2 in the legal market further to the left and increasing the shortage at the $23.50 price. History suggests that neither a formal nor an informal rationing system can satisfy all consumers as "equitable." It also suggests that strong measures (perhaps even death for large-scale black-marketing) would be necessary to maintain an equilibrium or a disequilibrium system in the long run. In the United States, rationing and price controls practically collapsed within a year after the end of World War II.

Both the disequilibrium and the equilibrium methods of market manipulation can be stymied by the development of black markets, in which goods are sold at illegally high prices.

Farm Price Supports and OPEC Manipulations that set minimum prices, or floor prices, for certain products can also be analyzed and explained with our supply and demand curves. We shall describe the American farm price supports as a case of disequilibrium and the OPEC (Organization of Petro-

FIGURE 9
Market Manipulation: Equilibrium Method with Rationing in the Market for Jeans

In this diagram, S_1 is the supply curve and D_1 is the demand curve before the war, when 3.8 million pairs of jeans are bought and sold at a price of $23.50. In wartime the supply falls from S_1 to S_2, which would cause the price to increase to $30 and the sales to drop to 2 million. If the government dislikes this free-market solution, it may wish to hold the $23.50 price through rationing, shown as lowering the demand to D_2. A new equilibrium situation is created as 1.1 million pairs of jeans are bought and sold at $23.50.

leum Exporting Countries) system as a case of equilibrium.

Agricultural price supports have been in use in the United States for over fifty years. They are applied on a product-by-product basis. Figure 10 illustrates a hypothetical case involving wheat. Let's say that if a free market were allowed to determine equilibrium price and quantity, the price would settle at $4.50 a bushel, and the quantity bought and sold would be 1.2 billion bushels. If, instead, a **floor price**, or **support price**—a minimum price that is legally set for a product—of $5.25 were established by the government, a surplus would be

FIGURE 10
Market Manipulation with a Floor (Minimum) Price: Price Support in the Wheat Market

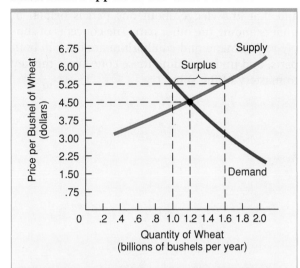

Pictured are the market-demand and market-supply curves for wheat. The equilibrium price is $4.50 per bushel of wheat, and the equilibrium quantity is 1.2 billion bushels per year. The government decides to impose a support price of $5.25. At this disequilibrium price, the quantity supplied is 1.6 billion bushels per year, and the quantity demanded is only 1.0 billion bushels. The result is a surplus of 0.6 billion bushels per year.

created. A **surplus** is the amount of excess supply that stems from a disequilibrium situation. The amount of the surplus in this example is 0.6 billion bushels. At the support price of $5.25, consumers would demand 0.2 billion bushels less and farmers would supply 0.4 billion bushels more than they would have at the free-market price of $4.50. Government can maintain the floor price by purchasing the surplus.[4]

A floor price (support price) is a minimum price that is legally set for a product. Government can maintain a floor price by purchasing the surplus, or excess supply, of a product.

---

4. In practice, a system of production controls is used along with government purchase of the surplus.

The OPEC experience illustrates an equilibrium variety of market manipulation aimed at achieving a higher price. Formed in 1960, OPEC became an effective international petroleum force in the early 1970s. Through market manipulation it was successful in raising the price of crude oil about forty-fold in less than a decade. Figure 11 is a simplified illustration of how this system operates. The market-supply and market-demand curves are labeled S_1 and D, respectively. If a free market were allowed to determine equilibrium price and quantity, the price would be $13 per barrel, and the quantity bought and sold would be 39 million barrels per day. But OPEC has the authority to reduce supply to 17 million barrels per day, as shown by the vertical line labeled S_2. The new price of $28 per barrel of crude oil is an equilibrium one that leaves no surplus.

FIGURE 11
Market Manipulation with a Floor (Minimum) Price: OPEC Price in the Crude Petroleum Market

In this diagram, S_1 is the market-supply curve and D is the market-demand curve. In a free market, 39 million barrels of crude oil per day are bought and sold at $13 per barrel. When OPEC reduces the supply to 17 million barrels, as shown by the new vertical supply segment S_2, the resulting equilibrium price increases to $28 per barrel.

WHICH SEQUENCE: MACRO-MICRO OR MICRO-MACRO?

You may study macroeconomics before you study microeconomics, or you may study microeconomics first and then study macroeconomics. The sequence depends in part on the plans made by your own college or university. Whichever sequence you use, it is important to remember that each is simply a portion of the total subject of economics and that knowledge about one part is helpful in understanding the other part. The concepts of supply and demand and equilibrium are basic in both parts, and understanding these concepts is the key to mastery of the subject.

Economics in Focus

Drought and Food Prices *or* No Rain—A Lot of Pain

The price of eggs jumped 9.6 percent in one month. Fruit and vegetable prices rose 4.7 percent, poultry prices 7.4 percent. The month was July 1988, and shoppers across the nation felt the pinch. A severe drought was damaging U.S. farm crops, causing food prices to surge upward. Newspapers, magazines, and TV news programs offered pictures of dying corn stalks and dry, cracked earth.

The drought of 1988 provides a dramatic illustration of how changes in supply affect everyday life. As dry weather continued throughout the summer, grain crops withered in the field. The reduction in crops shifted the grain supply curve to the left; this meant that for any given price of grain, the quantity reaching the market would be less than before. By August corn prices stood at $2.89 per bushel, up from $1.60 in July 1987—an increase of over 80 percent. In the same period the price of wheat rose 49 percent.

The rise in grain prices soon affected others foods as well. Since farmers fed grain to their livestock, their costs shot up, and these higher costs reached the consumer as increased prices for eggs and milk products. Meat supplies increased temporarily as many farmers slaughtered their stock to avoid large feed bills; but after a while meat prices tended to follow the general upward trend.

The U.S. market was also influenced by foreign supply and demand. By late 1988 farmers in Argentina, attracted by the high price of soybeans in the United States, were planting more of that crop. This might have been good news for consumers of soybean products, but the situation was complicated by several other factors: (1) In planting more soybeans, the Argentinians reduced their acreage devoted to corn; (2) Argentina was a major supplier of corn to the Soviet Union, which also bought corn from the United States; and (3) Argentina too was suffering from a drought. The overall outcome, some analysts feared, would be a tiny corn crop in Argentina and a resulting increase in Soviet purchases from the United States; then the price of U.S. corn would be forced up even further.

The 1988 rise in grain prices did not cause any substantial drop in the quantity demanded. As prices start up, buyers do not curtail their buying by very much. One paradoxical effect is that many U.S. farmers do well in drought years such as 1988. Although harvests are reduced, prices rise so quickly that farmers often make a greater profit on their small crop than they would in a normal year on a large crop. This is not true, of course, for farmers whose fields are entirely devastated by the lack of rain. They can only hope that the next year will bring better weather for themselves and bad weather for other farmers who grow the same crops.

Sources: "Heatstroke," *Time,* September 5, 1988, p. 51; Timothy Tregarthen, "Drought Sends Farm Prices Soaring," *The Margin,* January–February 1989, pp. 22–23; Theodore Young, "The Drought Will Boost Food Prices—and Farmers' Incomes," *Fortune,* September 12, 1988, pp. 19–22.

SUMMARY

1. The economic meaning of *demand* is that a consumer is both willing and able to purchase a good or a service, and not that he or she merely wants, desires, or needs that good or service. Likewise, the term *supply* means that a firm is both willing and able to produce a good or a service. (See pages 81–82.)

2. Individual consumer demand and individual firm supply are defined at a particular moment in time. This method of definition holds all variables constant except for the quantity and price of the good or service being studied. The functional relationships of demand and supply relate the respective quantities to the respective prices, while all other variables are held constant. (See pages 82–83.)

3. Demand curves have negative slopes, which means that the variables of price and quantity demanded change in opposite directions. The first reason for this relationship is the income effect, or the effect that a change in a person's real income (brought on by a change in the price of a good) has on the quantity that he or she demands of that good. The second is the substitution effect, or the effect that a change in relative prices of substitute goods (brought on by a change in the price of a good) has on the quantity demanded of that good. (See pages 84–87.)

4. Supply curves have positive slopes, which means that the variables of price and quantity supplied change in the same direction. The reason is that firms find it profitable to commit more resources to the production of a good or a service when its price is higher and less when its price is lower, other things being equal. (See pages 88–89.)

5. Changes in the quantity demanded and in the quantity supplied are reflected as movements along their respective curves, whereas changes in demand and supply are reflected as shifts of the curves. A movement along a curve is caused by a change in the price of the good or service being studied. A shift of a curve occurs when the *ceteris paribus* assumption is relaxed. Demand curves shift when tastes, income, or prices of other goods change. Supply curves shift when input prices, technological know-how, expectations about the prices of other goods that the firm is or could be producing, or a seller's goals change. (See pages 89–91.)

6. Market demand and market supply are derived by adding up, at each possible price, individual consumer demands and individual firm supplies of a particular good or service in a certain place over some period of time. (See pages 91–92.)

7. When market supply is greater than market demand, there is excess supply, causing supplier firms to compete with one another and thereby driving down the price. When market demand is greater than market supply, there is excess demand, causing buyers to compete with one another and thus driving up the price. In a market, when quantity demanded is equal to quantity supplied, there is a state of balance—the equilibrium price and the equilibrium quantity have been reached. (See pages 92–94.)

8. Markets are sometimes manipulated by buyers or by sellers. This manipulation may result from a collusive agreement. Buyers may shift the market-demand curve to the left, thereby achieving a lower equilibrium price. Sellers may shift the market-supply curve to the left, thereby achieving a higher equilibrium price. (See pages 94–96.)

9. Disequilibrium in a market is the condition in which quantity demanded is not equal to quantity supplied. It may arise as a temporary situation, or it may be maintained by government action. Government may impose a higher-than-equilibrium price, which will be marked by excess supply, or a surplus. Or the government may impose a lower-than-equilibrium price, which will be marked by excess demand, or a shortage. (See pages 96–97.)

KEY TERMS

ceiling price: a maximum price at which a product may legally be sold (page 95).

complements: goods that are used with each other (page 87).

demand schedule: a table showing different prices for a good and the quantity of that good demanded at each of these prices (page 83).

disequilibrium: a market state in which the

quantity demanded does not equal the quantity supplied (page 94).

equilibrium price: the price that equates quantity demanded with quantity supplied in a market (page 92).

equilibrium quantity: a quantity of a good or service that equates the quantity supplied and the quantity demanded at a particular price in a market (page 92).

excess demand: the extent to which the quantity demanded exceeds the quantity supplied (page 93).

excess supply: the extent to which the quantity supplied exceeds the quantity demanded (page 93).

floor price (support price): a minimum price that is legally set for a product (page 96).

free market: a market in which the forces of demand and supply determine the price (page 94).

income effect: the influence that a change in a person's real income (resulting from a change in the price of a good or service that this person buys) has on the quantity that this person demands of that good or service (page 84).

individual consumer demand: the quantity of a good or service that an individual consumer is willing and able to purchase at a particular moment at each possible price that might be charged for that good or service (page 82).

individual firm supply: the quantity of a good or service that an individual business firm is willing and able to sell at a particular moment at each possible price that might be charged for that good or service (page 87).

market: the organized action between potential buyers and potential sellers that enables them to carry on exchange or trade (page 91).

market demand: the sum of all of the individual consumers' demands for a particular good or service in a certain place over some period of time (page 91).

market supply: the sum of all the individual firms' supplies of a particular good or service in a certain place over some period of time (page 91).

movement along a demand curve: a change from one point on a demand curve to another point on the same curve due to a change in the price of the product (page 85).

movement along a supply curve: a change from one point on a supply curve to another point on the same curve due to a change in the price of the product (page 88).

rationing: any method of restricting the demand for a good or service. Government may formally invoke a system of rationing in order to deal "fairly" with what would otherwise be an excess demand situation (page 95).

real income: the purchasing power of a person's money income (page 84).

shift of the demand curve: a displacement of an entire demand curve to the right or left showing a change in demand (page 85).

shift of the supply curve: a displacement of an entire supply curve to the right or left showing a change in supply (page 88).

shortage: the extent to which the quantity supplied of a good or service is less than the quantity demanded for it (page 95).

substitutes: goods that may be used instead of one another (page 86).

substitution effect: the effect that a change in relative prices of substitute goods or services (resulting from a change in the price of a good or service) has on the quantity that a person demands of that good or service (page 85).

supply schedule: a table showing different prices for a good and the quantity of that good supplied at each of these prices (page 88).

support price: see **floor price.**

surplus: the amount of excess supply that stems from a disequilibrium situation (page 96).

DISCUSSION QUESTIONS

1. Dave says, "I need three pairs of shoes this year." Will this information help you in constructing Dave's demand curve for shoes? Explain your answer.

2. Carefully describe what is meant by an income effect and a substitution effect. Then explain how the income effect and the substitution effect of a price change normally cause the demand curve for a good or service to be negatively sloped.

3. Construct a graph showing a demand curve for automobiles as you would expect it to look. On this diagram show a "change in the quantity demanded" and a "change in demand" that exactly compensate for each other. (The quantity of automobiles shown on the horizontal axis should be the same before and after these two changes occur.) What do you suppose happened to bring about these two changes?

4. Give five examples of pairs of goods and/or services that are viewed as substitutes by some consumers and as complements by others. For each pair, tell what conditions cause them to be both substitutes and complements.

5. A company's supply curve for micro-computers has shifted to the right. Give four reasons why this may have occurred.

6. Becky Ryder buys one pound of Jarlsberg cheese for $5.60, but when the price rises to $6.00, she buys only three-fourths of a pound. Draw a demand curve that shows her purchases. Is this a shift or a movement along a curve? Becky's favorite cheese is Brie, the price of which has just dropped to $4.00 a pound. Show the effect of this change on her demand curve for Jarlsberg. Is this a shift or a movement along a curve?

7. If faced with a serious excess supply in a particular market, what would you advise the government to do? Explain the basis for your recommendation.

8. During an emergency period a government may impose a ceiling price on a certain good in order to slow down the flow of an important resource into the production of that good. This ceiling price may go along with either an equilibrium or a disequilibrium situation. How might the government bring about each of these situations? Why might it choose one over the other?

9. In New York City certain apartments have been "rent controlled" for the last several decades. (Rent control is a form of ceiling price.) How does this help you to explain each of the following?

    a. Poor maintenance of these apartment houses

    b. Apartment shortages

    c. Well-to-do rental agents (often superintendents)

Classical Economics: The Dismal Science?

Two unflattering terms, "dismal science" and "pig philosophy," were attached to political economy, as economics was called, in mid-Victorian Britain. They both come from the pen of the great Scottish historian and social critic Thomas Carlyle (1795–1881). The term "dismal science" has survived, though "pig philosophy" has not. Which economic doctrines of Carlyle's day inspired the term "dismal science"?

Adam Smith, who died before Carlyle was born, could hardly be called a dismal scientist, for his doctrine was quite upbeat. In an essay on development, written in 1755, Smith said,

> Little else is requisite, to carry a state to the highest level of opulence from the lowest barbarism, but peace, easy taxes, and a tolerable administration of justice, all the rest being brought about by the natural course of things.

FIVE DISMAL IDEAS

It was with the two following generations of economists, writing under the influence of the French Revolution, the Napoleonic Wars, and the Industrial Revolution, that the "dismal" ideas—some indeed implied by other passages in Smith's work—achieved their prominence. We stress five of these doctrines:

1. The Malthusian principle of population
2. The subsistence theory of wages
3. The principle of diminishing returns (to both labor and capital)
4. The tendency of profits to a minimum
5. Economic stagnation in the stationary state

Adam Smith (1723–1790)

The first of these ideas is due primarily to Thomas Robert Malthus (1766–1834) and the others mainly to David Ricardo (1772–1823). These doctrines are all related to each other in what is called "the English classical system." Even though they refer only to a pure market economy, their proponents are sure that no other economic organization can do better than what Adam Smith described as "the obvious and simple system of natural liberty."

The first two doctrines (of the above five) are dismal in their implication that the ordinary worker gains little or nothing from economic progress. The

David Ricardo (1772–1823)

Thomas Robert Malthus (1766–1834)

second pair imply that the ordinary capitalist may also lose as capital is accumulated in a growing economy, so that the major beneficiary of economic growth is a passive and unproductive class of landowners. The fifth and last of these ideas predicts that economic progress itself will be short lived, and will eventually peter out in a dull and gloomy stagnation.

It is interesting to note, however, that the most popular "classical" economics textbook, John Stuart Mill's *Principles of Political Economy* (1848), was far from dismal as to either the future of the working class or the nature of the stationary state. Mill thought wages might rise gradually to meet the basic needs of the workers. And he imagined the stationary state as a pleasant period of economic inactivity, when people might turn their attention from money grubbing and materialism to plain living, high thinking, and the higher culture generally.

But let us return to the five dismal ideas themselves.

Malthusian Principle of Population Malthus believed he observed, mainly from what happened in the American colonies, a natural tendency for population to grow faster than the means of subsistence (the food supply). As the population grew at a geometric rate (2, 4, 8, . . .), the food supply would rise only at an arithmetical one (1, 2, 3, 4, . . .). Only the "positive checks" of famine, war, and disease would hold the population within bounds, unless of course human nature could be changed to accept such "preventive checks" as later marriage and sexual continence within marriage.[1]

Subsistence Theory of Wages From Malthusian demography to a subsistence theory of wages is only a short step. If wage rates, set by supply and demand, remain higher than the workers' customary level of subsistence, workers will marry earlier and more of their children will live, until the rising supply of workers pushes wage rates down again. On the

1. Malthus, an ordained clergyman of the Church of England, regarded contraception, abortion, infanticide, and homosexuality as forms of "vice," and did not include them in his "preventive checks."

other hand, if wage rates fall below the subsistence level, later marriage, infant mortality, and emigration will after a time lower the supply of workers and raise wages again. There is a complication, however, because the classical economists all knew that English wages and subsistence levels were higher than those of Ireland or of Continental Europe. They reasoned that this could happen if wages remained high or low for long enough to improve or lower workers' levels of living in general—raising the staple diet from potatoes to wheat, or lowering it from wheat to potatoes. But this important complication was often overlooked in the simpler statements of classical wage theory.

Principle of Diminishing Returns "With every mouth," said Benjamin Franklin, "God sends a pair of hands." And so, especially if more machinery is accumulated along with the extra hands, why should food ever run short? Because, according to the dismal scientists, the principle of diminishing returns is operating. The extra hands, even with extra equipment, yield lesser amounts of additional output from a constant stock of agricultural land and other natural resources. It follows, then, that a doubling of the population, even if accompanied by a doubling of the capital supply, does not double the total output. For this reason, output per person falls off. (This argument ignores any qualitative improvements in either physical or human capital—as when a tractor replaces a team of oxen or a literate peasant steps into the shoes of his or her illiterate parent.)

Tendency of Profits to a Minimum Classical economists used the term "profits" to refer to the returns to capital. As physical capital in particular is accumulated and becomes subject to diminishing returns, new investment will only be demanded at a real rate of interest that tends to fall over time.[2] And as the return on their savings falls, capitalists will save less. These processes of falling real interest rates and falling saving rates will continue until the rate of return to capital is so low, and capitalists'

savings are so small, that there is no longer any net increase in the capital stock. In other words, capitalists' savings will just balance the depreciation and obsolescence of the existing stock.

Economic Stagnation With wages approximately constant and return on capital falling to a minimum, which some economists suspect is near zero, the principal gainer from economic progress becomes the landlord. Landlords win out because both increasing population and increasing capital raise the demand for land, both good and bad. Much land that is infertile or remote and that commands no rent in "the early and rude state of society" comes to earn substantial rent as society grows—in the American case as the frontier moved west. The gain comes with minimum effort on the part of the landowning family, which may be descended from a successful capitalist of a few generations back.

ARE THE IDEAS STILL ALIVE TODAY?

Some combination of the five gloomy ideas that gave economics the name of "the dismal science" has outlived the English classical school itself. The depressing ideas live on today in such statements as "American agriculture is a losing proposition, subsidized by returns from land speculation," and in assurances that no other system could do better than the free market.[3] Perhaps the name itself persists also because so many students are required to take economics when they would rather study an easier or more immediately appealing subject.

Strange as it may seem, there are more than a few economists today who, calling themselves "new-classicals" or "neo-Ricardians," propose to bring back these ideas about the working of a market economy. However, they would substitute the gloomy ideas for the pleasanter "neoclassical" ideas that succeeded them and to some extent de-dismalized the subject!

2. A real rate of interest is one that has been adjusted to correct for inflation.

3. The argument here is that every individual is a better judge of his or her own interest than is any government bureau, and that every individual will work harder in his or her own interest than in carrying out the orders of superiors.

The Circular Flow, Aggregate Demand, and Aggregate Supply

National Income Accounting

Inflation and Unemployment

Economic Fluctuations

PART II
THE MACROECONOMY

6

The Circular Flow, Aggregate Demand, and Aggregate Supply

Preview You cannot see, touch, hear, smell, or taste a macroeconomy. You are not likely to meet one on the street or be introduced to one at a party. What *is* a macroeconomy, then? This chapter answers that question by providing a way of visualizing a macroeconomy as a *circular flow* of economic activity. It emphasizes interactions among the various actors on the economic stage and shows that one person's expenditures or expenses become another person's income. In a sense, we support ourselves by "taking in each other's laundry." This circular flow of income and expenditures through the economy shows how the different actors depend on each other and how they experience together the ups and downs of the macroeconomy.

The circular flow also provides an introductory explanation of the concepts of equilibrium and disequilibrium in the macroeconomy. It illustrates how business firms make production plans based on forecasts of future sales receipts. It shows how the macroeconomy changes when actual sales receipts turn out to be different than planned.

The last part of the chapter introduces the concepts of aggregate demand and aggregate supply—the macroeconomic counterparts of the microeconomic demand and supply concepts presented in Chapter 5. The aggregate demand and aggregate supply concepts not only illustrate macroeconomic equilibrium but they also provide the analytical framework that will integrate the various theories examined in later chapters.

THE CIRCULAR FLOW OF ECONOMIC ACTIVITY

Macroeconomics is the part of economics that is concerned with aggregate, or *grand total*, economic activity.[1] In contrast to **microeconomics,** which studies the activities of individuals and business firms, macroeconomics examines the functioning of the entire economy—the aggregate supply of goods and services and the aggregate demand for them.

Macroeconomics examines the functioning of the entire economy—the aggregate supply of goods and services and the aggregate demand for them.

In order to provide a visual representation of the macroeconomy, economists have developed various illustrations of the **circular flow** of aggregate economic activity. Like satellite pictures on television weather shows, these illustrations help viewers see patterns that are too vast to be recognized easily from ground level. From the perspective of the circular-flow model, it is easier to understand relationships among the various parts of the macroeconomy and to appreciate the internal consistencies needed for its continued operation. The circular flow provides an introduction to the macroeconomy.

A circular-flow representation of the macroeconomy is shown in Figure 1. All the households in the economy are represented by the red box on the left side of the figure. Inside this box, the functions of households as consumers and resource owners are noted. All the firms in the economy are represented by the purple box on the right side of the figure. The functions of firms as buyers of resources and producers of final goods and services are noted inside this box. The circular flow itself is shown by the arrows going in a clockwise direction around the circle. These arrows represent flows of income and expenditures. Although they are not shown in Figure 1, you may imagine another set of arrows, running opposite to those shown. These imagined arrows would represent flows of goods and services moving counterclockwise around the

circle. The flows represented by the arrows are payments made in exchange for goods and services. We will first give a quick survey of these flows, without interruption for definitions and discussion. Then we will follow each path in detail.

A circular-flow diagram can be used to represent the working of the macroeconomy. The arrows show the flow of income and expenditures.

The flow across the bottom of the figure represents payments by firms to households in exchange for the use of resources that, in a capitalist economy, are owned by household members. These payments consist of wages (and benefits), rents, interest, and profits. These payments are the income of the factors of production—labor, natural resources, capital, and entrepreneurship. Because entrepreneurs are members of households, profits are included in this flow. We assume that this income amounts to $1,000 billion per year.

In the upper half of the circle, the flow of expenditures is divided into four streams.

1. Consumption purchases, where expenditures are made directly to firms. This is the largest use of funds by households. In our illustration, we assume that $700 billion is spent for consumption purchases.

2. Saving, which flows to financial markets and then, if borrowed to finance purchases of capital goods, goes on to the firms as investment purchases. We assume that saving amounts to $50 billion, which is 5 percent of income.

3. Net taxes, which flow to the government and then, if spent for government purchases, go on to the firms. We assume net taxes of $150 billion, or 15 percent of income.

4. Purchases of imports, which flow through international markets and, if spent by foreigners to buy products from the country whose flows are illustrated, go on to the firms as purchases by foreigners (exports). We assume $100 billion spent for imports.

The arrow across the bottom of the circular-flow diagram represents income to

---

1. See Chapter 1, page 6.

FIGURE 1
The Circular Flow of Economic Activity

Purchases from Foreigners (Imports) ($100)

International Markets

Purchases by Foreigners (Exports)

Net Taxes ($150)

Government

Government Purchases

Saving ($50)

Financial Markets

Investment Purchases

Consumption Purchases ($700)

Households Consumers Resource Owners

Firms Producers Resource Purchasers

Wages, Rents, Interest, and Profits ($1,000)

Firms are producers of goods and services and also purchasers of resource services. They pay wages, rents, and interest to owners of resources and expect to earn profits for entrepreneurs. These payments flow through the stream at the bottom of the circle. Households, which are consumers and resource owners, receive payments from firms and divide this income among consumption purchases, saving, net taxes, and purchases from foreigners (imports), as shown by arrows on the top left part of the circle. Saving, net taxes, and import payments pass through financial markets, governments, and international markets, respectively, and flow on to firms as investment purchases, government purchases, and purchases by foreigners (exports). Circular-flow equilibrium exists if the amount received by firms through the top streams of the circle matches the amount paid out in the lower stream, including expected profits. (The illustrative amounts in parentheses are in billions of dollars.)

households. The arrows across the top represent expenditures.

To get a taste of how a macroeconomy operates, we will now follow the flow of income and expenditure around the circle, from the payments of income by firms to hire resources until the money returns to the firms in receipts from the sale of goods and services.

Payments for Resources

As you know, firms are the "actors on the economic stage" responsible for production.[2] In the

2. See Chapter 2, page 28.

circular flow, this means that, inside the purple box representing firms, entrepreneurs make forecasts about the prices and quantities of goods and services they expect to sell in the coming time period. If we think of the circle as representing the flows that take place in a year, entrepreneurs are planning production for the year ahead. We assume that the firms forecast a grand total sales volume of $1,000 billion for the coming year. To obtain the resources needed to produce these goods and services, firms expect to pay $1,000 billion for labor compensation, rent, interest, and profits. Except for profits, these payments are assumed to be contractual obligations during the period. As we will see, profits may turn out to be larger or smaller than expected but, if actual sales match the forecast, $1,000 billion will flow through the lower part of the circle. As noted earlier, entrepreneurs are members of households and expect to receive the planned amount of profit.

Household Uses of Funds

In the circular flow, households (in the red box at the left side of Figure 1) receive, or expect to receive, $1,000 billion from firms. Let us examine alternative uses for these funds and how they flow back to the firms across the upper portion of the diagram.

Consumption Purchases **Consumption purchases (C)** are expenditures by households to acquire the goods and services used during the period. If Figure 1 is for the United States economy, the arrow labeled "consumption purchases" shows income spent by U.S. households to buy goods and services produced by U.S. domestic firms during that accounting period. These expenditures flow directly to the firms and are used to finance labor, natural resources, capital, and profits in the production plans of the firms. We assume that $700 billion flows in this stream during the accounting period.

Saving and Investment Purchases **Saving (S)** means setting aside current income in order to increase wealth. Households may wish to prepare for consumption purchases or other expenditures they plan to make in the future, or they may wish to transfer wealth to others, through gifts or bequests,

at some future time. In the circular flow, the arrow labeled "saving" represents the income that households save during the year. The funds flow to banks, credit unions, savings and loan associations, stock and bond brokers, etc., which are located in the blue financial markets box in the diagram. These **financial intermediaries** accept deposits of income saved and offer to loan these funds, in return for interest payments, to those who wish to borrow.

Our simple circular flow does not contain an arrow to represent saving carried out by firms. But firms do set aside funds for future use and therefore do contribute to the aggregate flow of saving. They do this when some or all of their profits are not actually paid as dividends to stockholders and when funds are put into depreciation reserves to prepare for the eventual replacement of capital goods. Instead of drawing another arrow on the diagram and making it more complicated, imagine that household saving includes saving from firms and that the firms are saving on behalf of the stockholders, who are members of households.

In the circular-flow diagram, the **investment purchases (I)** arrow that emerges from the financial markets box represents expenditures on domestically produced **capital goods** (buildings, machines, and human capital) during the period. We assume that those who want to acquire capital goods borrow the needed funds in the financial markets. Firms do this explicitly when they borrow from financial institutions or sell stocks or bonds in financial markets. Even funds from "in-house" saving such as undistributed profits and funds put into depreciation reserves (which we include in household saving) usually are placed in financial institutions until the firms actually acquire the capital goods.

Does the amount of domestic investment (I) exactly match the amount of saving (S)—$50 billion a year in our illustration? Not necessarily. As we will see, some of the $50 billion saved may be diverted to government or to international markets so that domestic investment could be less than the amount saved. On the other hand, it is possible for the financial markets to draw funds *from* government or international markets so that domestic investment could exceed the amount saved. We will examine these possibilities later.

FIGURE 2
Government Borrowing in Financial Markets

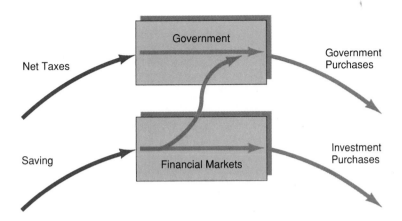

The green arrow represents funds borrowed by governments to finance deficits in their income and product budgets. In this way, funds that have been saved may pay for government purchases rather than for investment purchases. Investment purchases are *crowded out* by the government purchases financed with the borrowed funds.

Net Taxes and Government Purchases The money that flows from the household box to the government as **net taxes (Tn)** consists of the total amount of tax paid by households and firms minus **transfer payments,** such as checks sent from the government to welfare recipients, veterans, unemployed workers, and social security retirees. Transfer payments do not arise from any service rendered or product sold during the accounting period. Instead they are negative taxes—payments that are the opposite of taxes and go *from* government *to* households. In our illustration, we assume net taxes (taxes minus transfer payments) of $150 billion.

Inside the blue government box, net taxes constitute receipts for federal, state, and local governments, calculated to match the macroeconomist's treatment of transfer payments as negative taxes. Subtracting these transfer payments from total government expenditures leaves **government purchases (G)** of currently produced goods and services from domestic firms. These purchases provide a way for income paid in taxes to find its way back to the firms that hire resources to produce goods and services. Government budgets that treat transfer payments as negative taxes rather than as expenditures are called **income and product budgets.**

Does the amount received by firms through government purchases exactly equal the amount of net taxes? If the government income and product budgets are balanced, the answer is "yes." But if these budgets show a **deficit** (government purchases greater than net taxes), expenditures from governments to firms are greater than the amount of net taxes. Where do governments get the funds to cover their deficits? They borrow in the financial markets. This is illustrated in Figure 2, which focuses on the portion of the circular flow showing the government box and the financial markets box. The green arrow from the financial markets box to the government box represents funds borrowed by governments when their budgets are in deficit. In the United States, it is the responsibility of the U.S. Treasury to finance federal government purchases. So the arrow between the boxes in Figure 2 includes funds used to purchase U.S. Treasury securities. The securities become part of the national debt of the United States. This means that some of the saving flowing through the financial markets is used to pay for government purchases rather than to finance investment purchases. It is said that the

FIGURE 3
Government Budget Surplus Funds Flowing into Financial Markets

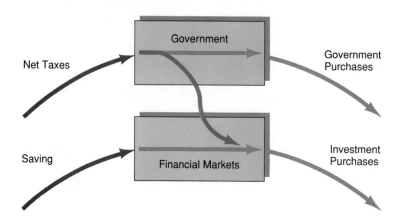

The green arrow represents funds from a government income and product budget surplus flowing into financial markets to retire government securities. In this way, income paid in taxes may finance private purchases of capital goods (investment).

government deficit is **crowding out** potential private uses of these funds.

In a *deficit* budget, government purchases are greater than net taxes. Government borrowing from financial markets in response to a deficit budget tends to *crowd out* private investment purchases.

If government purchases are less than net taxes paid, budgets are in **surplus.** In this situation, some tax receipts can be used to retire some of the securities that make up the national debt. Figure 3 shows funds flowing from the government into the financial markets. This is the reverse of crowding out, because some tax receipts are used to retire government debt securities and then may go on to firms to be used to finance private investment purchases.

If government purchases are less than net taxes paid, budgets are in surplus. In the case of a budget surplus, government can channel funds into financial markets. In this way, some tax

receipts can be used to retire government debt securities and then become available to finance private investment purchases.

Imports and Exports The top stream of the circular-flow diagram in Figure 1 shows income flowing to international markets as households use some of their income to purchase goods and services produced abroad—to pay for **imports (Im).** We may imagine that this channel also includes payments for foreign-made capital goods, semifinished goods, and raw materials purchased by government or firms acting on behalf of those members of households who are stockholders. We assume that $100 billion is used to pay for imports.

Income that reaches international markets through payments for imports may emerge from those markets as purchases by foreigners, that is, as payments for **exports (X)** from the country whose circular flow is illustrated. The exports arrow represents payments by foreigners for goods and services produced by domestic firms. If the value of exports exactly equals the value of imports, the amount received by firms from export sales exactly matches the amount paid for imports. The country's **balance of trade** is in balance.

Imports **are purchases of goods and services produced abroad.** *Exports* **are domestically produced items purchased by foreigners.**

Although exports and imports the world over must balance, individual nations rarely achieve a perfect balance of trade. If a country has a deficit in its trade with the rest of the world, the amount of income flowing into the international markets box is greater than the expenditures flowing from that box to firms in that country. Foreigners have received more income from the importing country than they wish to spend on goods and services produced in that country. What do they do with this extra income? The answer is that they probably use it to earn interest and dividends by purchasing securities in the financial markets of the importing country. This is illustrated in Figure 4, which focuses on relationships between international markets and financial markets. The green arrow represents funds that flow from the international markets to the financial markets and become available to finance capital goods purchases (invest-

ment) or, if the government budget is in deficit, securities purchases by foreigners may help finance this deficit. A substantial amount of funds actually did follow this route in the U.S. macroeconomy in the 1980s, when the country had sizable deficits both in international trade and in its government budget. The United States went heavily into debt to foreigners.

If a country has a deficit in international trade, foreigners are receiving more income from the importing country than they wish to spend on goods and services produced in that country. In this instance, international markets may channel funds into domestic financial markets.

When a country has a surplus in international trade, the value of goods and services that foreigners are buying (exports of the country whose circular flow is illustrated) exceeds the value of goods and services that foreigners are selling to households and firms in that country (imports of

FIGURE 4
Inflow of Funds from International Markets

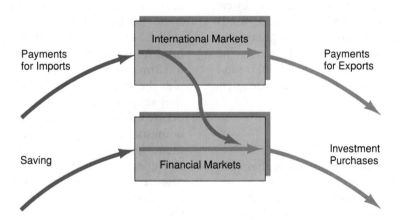

The green arrow represents funds flowing into domestic financial markets from international markets. This may happen when a country has a deficit in its trade with foreigners and the foreigners find attractive investment opportunities in the importing coun-

try. In this situation, purchases from foreigners (imports) are financed by going into debt to or selling assets to foreigners. The income paid for imports returns to the circular flow as foreigners finance investment in the importing country.

FIGURE 5
Outflow of Funds Due to an International Trade Surplus

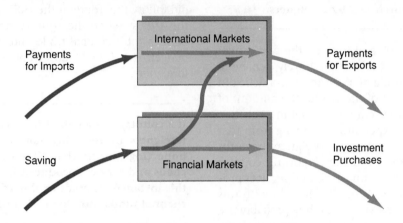

The green arrow represents funds flowing from domestic financial markets into international markets as foreigners borrow to help pay for goods and services they have purchased. In this way, some domestic saving returns to firms through the payments-for-exports channel.

that country). In this situation, foreigners may finance their extra purchases by borrowing in the financial markets of the country that has the trade surplus. This is illustrated in Figure 5, where the green arrow between the boxes represents funds flowing from the financial markets box to the international markets box. In this case, some funds saved by households and firms pay for goods and services purchased by foreigners. Of course, the foreigners have to promise to repay the loan (and also to pay interest), which means that foreigners are going into debt.

A surplus in international trade means that the value of goods and services foreigners are buying from a country exceeds the value of goods and services that foreigners are selling to that country. In this case, household savings and government budget surplus funds may flow into international markets.

MACROECONOMIC EQUILIBRIUM AND DISEQUILIBRIUM

Recall from Chapter 3 that **equilibrium** is a state of balance among opposing forces such that there is no tendency for change. In the circular-flow model, this requires that payments received by firms from sales of their products equal the amount the firms planned to pay out to purchase resources, plus the amount of profit that they expected when they set production plans. In other words, **macroeconomic equilibrium** exists when the sum of domestic consumption, investment and government purchases, plus exports (purchases by foreigners) equals the amount paid out by firms for resources used in production plus expected profits.

Circular-flow equilibrium can be expressed in the equation

$$C + I + G + (X - Im) = Y$$

where Y is income (the total earnings of resources, including expected profits), C is total purchases (including imports) of consumption goods by households, I is total purchases (including imports) of investment (capital) goods, G is total purchases (including imports) by governments, X is exports (total purchases by foreigners), and Im is imports (total purchases from foreigners). We have placed $X - Im$ in parentheses because it sometimes is convenient to refer to the terms together as *net exports*. The letter Y represents the amount of income flowing through the bottom stream of the circular flow in Figure 1, while the streams in the upper-right part of the circle represent total expenditures: consumption purchases, investment purchases, government purchases, and exports.[3]

When equilibrium exists, the plans firms made when they undertook production are fulfilled, so there is no reason (*ceteris paribus*) for them to plan any different level of production in the next round of the circle. In other words, given the level of prices expected when the plans were made, the output demanded by consumers, investors, governments, and foreigners equals the output supplied by firms. The firms find that inventories at the end of the process are exactly as they had planned.

Macroeconomic equilibrium exists (*ceteris paribus*) when payments received by firms from sales of their products equal the amount they planned to pay out to purchase resources, plus the amount of profit they expected when they set production plans.

Disequilibrium means that there is an imbalance among opposing forces such that there is some tendency for change. In the circular-flow model, disequilibrium exists when the total of purchases by consumers, investors, governments, and foreigners does not equal payments firms have made to employ resources plus their planned profit. Disequilibrium may be either *expansionary* or *contractionary*.

Expansionary Disequilibrium

Expansionary disequilibrium exists when the value of purchases by consumers, investors, governments, and foreigners is *greater than* the amount firms have paid for resources used in production plus their planned profits. That is,

$$C + I + G + (X - Im) > Y$$

Disequilibrium often originates in one of the three blue boxes at the top of the circular-flow diagram in Figure 1. Money may be created by financial institutions or by government or may flow into an economy from abroad. If the new money finances added investment purchases, added government purchases, or exports, it may cause expansionary disequilibrium.

Because profits are greater than planned, firms usually are delighted with this situation. However, the total quantity of output supplied according to the firms' plans has not been sufficient to meet the greater demand. Inventories have been depleted to satisfy the greater than expected demand for output. At the close of the path around the circle, the firms' inventories are smaller than desired.

Economists predict that, when inventories are smaller than desired, firms will increase production and/or prices for the coming round of the circle.[4] The increase in planned output may arise because estimates for the previous round had been too low. But even if the entrepreneurs stick with the sales estimates of the previous round, restoring inventories to desired levels will require a production increase. Prices will be increased in order to increase profits and slow the depletion of inventories.

Expansionary disequilibrium **exists when the value of purchases by consumers, investors, governments, and foreigners is *greater than* the amount firms have paid for resources used in production plus their planned profits.**

---

3. The letter Y is the symbol customarily used by economists to represent total production or total income in an economy.

4. Actually, firms may increase prices *during* the round of the circular flow. To simplify the description, we assume that prices do not change until the next round of the circular flow.

Contractionary Disequilibrium

Contractionary disequilibrium exists when the value of purchases by consumers, investors, governments, and foreigners is *less than* the amount paid for resources used in production plus the firms' expected profits. That is,

$$C + I + G + (X - Im) < Y$$

Again, the cause of the disequilibrium often lies in the blue boxes at the top of the circular-flow diagram. It may be that the supply of money has been reduced by the banking system, by the government, or by international transactions, so that investment purchases, government purchases, or exports are reduced, causing payments received by firms to decrease. Firms are unhappy with this situation because profits are less than expected. At the prices expected when the plans were made, the quantity of output demanded is less than the quantity supplied. The output that is not sold is added to business inventories. At the close of the round, inventories are greater than desired.

Economists predict that, when inventories are larger than desired, firms will reduce production and/or prices for the coming round of the circle.[5] Planned output may be reduced because estimates in the previous round proved to be too high. But even if firms make the same estimate of sales for the next round, some reduction in output will be needed to bring inventories down to desired levels. Firms also may reduce the prices of their products

---

Contractionary disequilibrium exists when the value of purchases by consumers, investors, governments, and foreigners is *less than* the amount paid for resources used in production plus the firms' expected profits.

When inventories are smaller than desired, firms tend to increase production and/or prices; when inventories are larger than desired, firms tend to reduce production and/or prices.

---

5. Again, for simplicity, we assume that prices are not changed *during* the round of the circular flow.

in order to help reduce inventories, especially if there is vigorous competition for customers.

AGGREGATE DEMAND AND AGGREGATE SUPPLY

The circular flow and the idea of equilibrium that you have just studied can now be used to introduce the macroeconomic concepts of aggregate demand and aggregate supply—concepts that provide the basic organizing scheme for modern macroeconomics. We will introduce these concepts now, in an elementary way. As we develop specific macroeconomic models, we will refer back to these basic organizing concepts to show how the specific models fit into the full picture. In Chapter 15, we will return to the aggregate demand and aggregate supply concepts and develop them in greater analytical and theoretical detail.

Aggregate Demand

The concept of demand was introduced in Chapter 5. In that chapter, the concept was applied to a specific good—jeans. At any specified price, consumers would be willing and able to purchase a given quantity of jeans per week or per year. This is the concept of *quantity demanded*. At different possible prices, different quantities of jeans would be demanded, *ceteris paribus*. The entire set of possible prices along with the quantity demanded at each price made up a *demand schedule*. The demand schedule, in turn, was represented on a graph as a *demand curve*. Applying the demand concept to jeans (or to any specified good or service) is an exercise in microeconomics. Let us now see how the concept of demand can be applied at the macroeconomic level of analysis.

Aggregate Quantity Demanded In macroeconomics, the quantity demanded cannot relate to a specific good or service, but must relate, instead, to the total of all goods and services that consumers (households), investors (business firms), governments, and foreigners are willing and able to buy during some time period (such as a year) and at some specified price level (average of all prices). In our circular-flow diagram, the sum of total purchases, $C + I + G + X - Im$ (the flows across the top half of the circle), constitute the **aggregate quantity demanded** at the prices prevailing at the time. If the economy illustrated in Figure 1 were at equilibrium so that all of the $1,000 billion of household income actually completed the route across the top of the circle and was received by the firms, the aggregate quantity demanded would be $1,000 billion of goods and services, valued at prevailing prices. Thus, the concept of aggregate quantity demanded is a simple extension of the demand concept introduced in Chapter 5.

The aggregate quantity demanded in an economy is the sum of total purchases made, $C + I + G + X - Im$, during a specified time period at a certain price level.

The Aggregate-Demand Curve   In macroeconomics, other things remaining unchanged, a change in the price level (the average of all prices) leads to a change in the aggregate quantity demanded—that is, it leads to a change in the quantities purchased by households (C), business firms (I), governments (G), and foreigners ($X - Im$). If prices rise, smaller quantities of goods and services will be demanded and if prices go down, larger quantities will be demanded. This negative (inverse) relationship between the price level and the aggregate quantity demanded is the same pattern that is expected for microeconomic demand schedules and curves. But we must note, even in this introductory explanation, that the logic behind the aggregate-demand relationship is different from the logic behind the price to quantity-demanded relationship in microeconomics.[6] The logic of the aggregate-demand relationship requires knowledge about interest rates and about how people respond to changes in wealth. Since you have not yet studied these matters, the theoretical derivation of aggregate demand

---

6. Recall from Chapter 5 that the microeconomic price to quantity-demanded relationship depends on changes in relative prices (*substitution effects*) and on changes in real incomes (*income effects*).

FIGURE 6
An Aggregate-Demand Curve

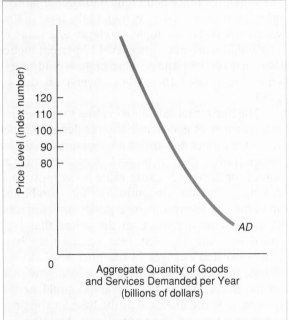

The aggregate-demand curve illustrates how the aggregate quantity of goods and services demanded depends on the price level. The price level is an average of all prices and is expressed as an index number based on the average prices in a selected base year. The aggregate quantity demanded is expressed in dollar values using the prices that prevailed in some selected base year.

schedules and curves must come later in your study of macroeconomics (see Chapter 15).

An **aggregate-demand curve** is the graphic representation of the relationship between changes in the price level and the resulting changes in the aggregate quantity demanded, *ceteris paribus*. Since several leading theories of macroeconomics direct special attention to aggregate demand, it will be useful to know what an aggregate-demand curve looks like. An aggregate-demand curve is illustrated in Figure 6. As with any new graph, we first must examine the labels on the axes. They identify the variables whose relationship is represented by the curve.

The variable on the vertical axis is the **price level,** showing averages for the prices of all goods and services in the economy. The numbers on this axis are **index numbers,** computed with the prices that prevailed in a selected base year (such as 1989) as a reference point (equal to 100) and other price levels expressed in relation to the level of that selected year. For example, in Figure 6, a value of 110 would represent a price level 10 percent higher than that of 1989 and a value of 90 would represent a price level 10 percent lower than that of 1989.[7]

The horizontal axis shows values for the aggregate quantity of goods and services demanded per year.[8] Quantities demanded are measured in dollar values (rather than in physical measures such as pounds or dozens) because value is the most convenient common denominator for combining quantities of many different goods and services. Measurements are made in the prices that prevailed in some specified year—called the "base year"—so that changes in the price level do not change the measuring system. The base year used on the horizontal axis of the graph could be the same year as the one used as the base for the price index numbers on the vertical axis, but it is not necessary that they be the same year.

The aggregate-demand curve (*AD*) illustrates a functional relationship showing quantities demanded at various possible price levels. In algebraic form, the aggregate demand relationship is

$$QD = f(P), \text{ceteris paribus,}$$

which states that the aggregate quantity demanded (*QD*) depends on or "is a function of" the price level (*P*), assuming that other variables remain unchanged. The price level is the independent variable that causes changes in the quantity of goods and services demanded, which is the dependent variable. As you see in Figure 6, the aggregate-demand curve shows a negative relationship between changes in the price level and the resulting changes in quantity demanded. Increases in the price level lead to reductions in aggregate quantities demanded and decreases in the price level lead

to increases in aggregate quantities demanded (*ceteris paribus*).

An aggregate-demand curve shows the negative relationship between the price level (the independent variable) and the aggregate quantity of goods and services demanded (the dependent variable) for an economy.

Shifts of the Aggregate-Demand Curve   In Chapter 5 you learned that the demand curve for jeans may shift—change its location—due to changes in variables *other than* the price of jeans. Similarly, in macroeconomics, the aggregate-demand curve may shift due to changes in variables other than the price level. The blue boxes in the upper half of the circular flow diagram in Figure 1 suggest some of the variables that may shift the aggregate-demand curve. For example, changed economic conditions in foreign countries can easily increase or decrease the willingness and ability of people and governments of those countries to purchase goods and services from the United States. If foreigners buy more from the U.S., net exports (*X − Im*) would increase and the aggregate-demand curve would shift to the right, *ceteris paribus*. If they buy less from the U.S., net exports (*X − Im*) would decrease and the aggregate-demand curve would shift to the left, *ceteris paribus*. Shifts in aggregate demand can also come from changes that take place in the government box of the circular-flow diagram. For example, a national emergency may arise or policies may change and lead to increases in government purchases (*G*) which, *ceteris paribus*, would shift the curve to the right. Conversely, decreases in government purchases would shift aggregate demand to the left, *ceteris paribus*.

Shifts of the aggregate-demand curve are especially likely to come from changes that take place in the financial markets box of the circular-flow diagram. As we will learn in Chapter 13, financial institutions and the country's central bank are able to increase or decrease the quantity of money in the economy. Providing additional money can easily increase investment purchases (*I*) if the new money is loaned to firms which desire to purchase more capital goods. The new money also may

---

7. Index numbers and the calculation of other price level measures are explained on pages 142–145.

8. Gross National Product (GNP) is a familiar measure of total production in an economy in a year and could be the variable on this axis. The measurement of Gross National Product is explained on pages 126–130.

come into the hands of governments, or consumers, or even of foreigners and lead these groups to increase the quantity of goods and services they would be willing and able to buy at any given price level. So the aggregate-demand curve would shift to the right, *ceteris paribus.* Of course, if financial institutions reduce the money supply, the quantities of goods and services demanded may fall and the aggregate-demand curve shift to the left.

Shifts of the aggregate-demand curve are very important in macroeconomics. Sometimes such shifts are the intended results of official policies and sometimes they arise from random events. In your study of economics, you will find that the "action" often starts with a shift of the aggregate-demand curve.

The aggregate-demand curve for an economy may shift due to changes in variables other than the price level.

Aggregate Supply

You studied the microeconomic concept of supply in Chapter 5. As you recall, the Cohen Clothing Corporation had to make a decision about the quantity of jeans it would be willing and able to offer for sale at various possible prices. In order to maximize profit, the quantity supplied by the Cohen Corporation would be greater at higher prices for jeans than at lower prices for jeans, *ceteris paribus.* The entire set of possible prices along with the quantity supplied at each price made up a supply schedule, which, when represented on a graph was the Cohen Company's supply curve for jeans. With the help of the circular-flow model, we can now offer an introductory explanation of aggregate supply.

Aggregate Quantity Supplied At the macroeconomic level of analysis, the Cohen Corporation is just one of the many firms in the purple box on the right-hand side of the circular-flow diagram in Figure 1. Each of these firms must select the quantities of its particular products or services to produce and offer for sale in the forthcoming round of the circular flow. The price that a firm expects to receive for its product is one of the variables it must consider

in making the production decision. However, since macroeconomic analysis deals with many firms and many different goods and services, the aggregate supply concept uses the price level (the average of all prices) as the variable on which the **aggregate quantity supplied** depends. In the circular-flow diagram in Figure 1, the $1,000 billion amount shown as wages, interest, rents, and expected profit flowing through the bottom half of the circle indicates that, on the basis of the prices that firms expect will prevail, they have decided to supply $1,000 billion worth of goods and services.

The aggregate quantity supplied in an economy is the value of the sum of all the goods and services that firms will produce and offer for sale in that economy during a specified time period at a certain price level.

The Aggregate-Supply Curve The **aggregate-supply curve** is the graphic representation of the relationship between changes in the price level and the resulting changes in the aggregate quantity of goods and services supplied in an economy during some specified period of time and assuming that no other variables change. In algebraic terms, this can be expressed as

$$QS = f(P), \textit{ ceteris paribus}$$

where QS is the aggregate quantity supplied, f means "depends on" or "is a function of," P stands for the price level, and *ceteris paribus* states the assumption that no other variables change.

In Chapter 5, you learned that supply curves for specific goods or services typically slope upward and to the right, that is, that changes in quantities supplied are directly related to changes in price. The Cohen Corporation, for example, was expected to supply a greater quantity of jeans at higher prices than at lower prices, *ceteris paribus.* In macroeconomics, most economists agree that, at least in most circumstances, changes in the aggregate quantity supplied also have a direct or positive relationship with changes in the price level. However, we must offer a word of caution: *the slope of the aggregate-supply curve is hotly debated among macro-economists.* In some circumstances, they see the curve as horizontal, with quantities supplied determined by variables other than the price level. In other circumstances, they see the curve as vertical so that changes in the price level have no effect on quantities supplied. Between these two extremes are circumstances in which changes in the aggregate quantity supplied vary directly with changes in the price level—a relationship similar to the typical microeconomic supply curve.[9]

An aggregate-supply curve with a middle-range positive slope is illustrated in Figure 7. As in Figure 6, where the aggregate-demand curve was illustrated, the label on the vertical axis is the price level. The horizontal axis shows the aggregate value of goods and services supplied in the economy in a year.

The aggregate-supply curve (*AS*) shown in Figure 7 states that an increase in the price level leads to an increase in the aggregate quantity of goods and services supplied. In terms of the circular-flow diagram in Figure 1, it suggests that the firms in the purple box on the right-hand side of the diagram will decide to supply larger quantities of goods and services when the price level goes up and smaller quantities when it goes down.

An aggregate-supply curve shows the relationship between the price level (the independent variable) and the aggregate quantity of goods and services supplied (the dependent variable) for an economy.

Shifts of the Aggregate-Supply Curve Shifts of the aggregate-supply curve are the result of changes in variables other than the price level. It is too early in your study of macroeconomics to go into much detail about the causes of such shifts. Basically, these shifts come from changes (other than price-level changes) that alter the profitability of producing goods and services. For example, if

---

9. Lest you conclude that macroeconomics is unreasonably complicated about the aggregate-supply curve, we must note that microeconomic analysis more advanced than that in Chapter 5 recognizes all the supply-curve possibilities noted above and, in addition, finds circumstances in which microeconomic supply curves can have *negative* slopes!

FIGURE 7
An Aggregate-Supply Curve

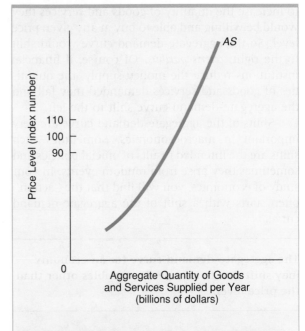

The aggregate-supply curve illustrates how the aggregate quantity of goods and services supplied depends on the price level. The price level is an average of all prices and is expressed as an index number based on the average prices in a selected base year. The aggregate quantity supplied is expressed in dollar values using the prices that prevailed in some base year.

the relationship between production costs and final-product prices changes so that profit margins are squeezed, firms may react by reducing quantities supplied, thereby shifting the curve to the left. In the reverse situation, if the relationship between final product prices and production costs changes to offer opportunities for larger profit margins, firms may increase quantities supplied in order to obtain more profits. This shifts the aggregate-supply curve to the right.

Shifts of the *AS* curve are important in macroeconomics. Sometimes shifts come from official policies, such as those designed to strengthen profitability and work incentives. Sometimes shifts come from random events that increase or decrease available resources. Sometimes shifts come from subtle changes in attitudes of workers or business firms and their expectations about the future course of the economy.

The aggregate-supply curve for an economy may shift due to changes in variables other than the price level. When such variables affect firms' profit margins, they may shift an economy's aggregate-supply curve.

Macroeconomic Equilibrium

In the circular-flow model, macroeconomic equilibrium exists when the amount received by firms from sales of their products (the total of the spending flows through the top half of the circle) equals the amount that they had planned to receive from these sales. In the equilibrium situation, firms can pay the planned amounts for wages, rents, and interest and enjoy the level of profits they had built into these plans. The total flow through the top half of the circle represents aggregate quantity demanded and the flow through the bottom half represents aggregate quantity supplied, including planned profits.

In the aggregate-demand and aggregate-supply model, the macroeconomic equilibrium situation is illustrated by the intersection of the aggregate-demand curve and the aggregate-supply curve. In Figure 8, the aggregate-demand curve from Figure 6 is combined with the aggregate-supply curve from Figure 7. At one particular price level, shown as the price index value of 100, the aggregate quantity demanded of $1,000 billion equals the aggregate quantity supplied, also $1,000 billion. The plans of business firms are fulfilled and there is no reason to expect, *ceteris paribus*, that firms will make different plans for the next round of the circle.

Macroeconomic equilibrium exists when an economy's aggregate quantity demanded is equal to its aggregate quantity supplied.

Macroeconomic Disequilibrium

Macroeconomic disequilibrium exists when the aggregate quantity supplied at a given price level does *not* equal the aggregate quantity de-

FIGURE 8
Macroeconomic Equilibrium

Macroeconomic equilibrium exists at the intersection of the aggregate-demand curve and the aggregate-supply curve. In the illustration above, when the price level has a value of 100, both the aggregate quantity demanded and the aggregate quantity supplied are $1,000 billion of goods and services.

manded at that price level. In terms of the circular-flow model, a contractionary disequilibrium arises when receipts from sales (aggregate quantity demanded as shown in the top half of the circle) are less than the firms had planned. After paying wages, interest, and rents, the firms' profits are lower than planned and the firms have undesirably large inventories of unsold merchandise. Economists expect that they will reduce output and lower prices in the next round of the circle.

In the aggregate demand and aggregate supply graph of Figure 8, the contractionary disequilibrium situation suggests a price level such as 110, that is, one higher than the one that would balance aggregate quantities demanded and supplied. There is excess aggregate supply. As firms cut back production and lower prices, the economy moves toward the equilibrium illustrated by the intersection of the curves in Figure 8.

Expansionary disequilibrium exists when aggregate quantities demanded (the upper flows in the circular-flow diagram) bring to the firms a greater amount of income than they anticipated when they made their production plans. After paying planned amounts for wages, interest, and rent, the firms' profits are larger than expected and their inventories have been sold down to undesirably low levels. The expected response is to increase production and to raise prices, that is, to expand.

In the aggregate-demand and aggregate-supply graph of Figure 8, expansionary disequilibrium suggests a price level such as 90, that is, one *below* the one that would provide equilibrium between quantities demanded and supplied. There is excess aggregate demand. As firms increase production and raise prices, the economy moves toward equilibrium.

Macroeconomic disequilibrium may be either contractionary because the economy's aggregate quantity supplied is greater than its aggregate quantity demanded or expansionary because its aggregate quantity demanded is greater than its aggregate quantity supplied.

A LOOK AHEAD

This chapter has explained the concept of macroeconomic equilibrium. But it is only a first step in macroeconomic analysis. It merely opens the door to many questions that economists try to answer. What events or behavior changes are most likely to shift aggregate-demand or aggregate-supply curves and thereby affect the economy? Can these events or behavior changes be anticipated, controlled, or counteracted? What can be done to help reestablish equilibrium once disequilibrium has set in? Does equilibrium represent the best the economy can do? Let us look briefly at some examples of the types of questions examined in macroeconomics.

Changes in Buying Behavior

Many economists believe that the Great Depression of the 1930s was brought on by events that caused

households, investors, governments, and foreigners to greatly reduce their purchases of currently produced goods and services. The stock market crash of 1929 was said to have weakened the confidence investors needed to justify purchases of new capital goods. International trade restrictions reduced purchases by foreigners. Consumers, fearful of unemployment, reduced purchases and hoarded cash. Bank failures reduced the money supply and governments, determined to balance their budgets in the face of falling tax receipts, reduced purchases of public goods. Each of these changes tended to shift the aggregate-demand curve to the left, leaving firms with unsold inventories and leading to reductions in employment and output. Economists desperately looked for ways to bring about the economy's recovery. But, because of the unprecedented seriousness of the depression and because of uncertainty about how to deal with it, the economy did not recover until purchases associated with World War II shifted the aggregate-demand curve to the right.

The Great Depression in the United States may be seen as a period of time during which circumstances caused a significant leftward shift of the economy's aggregate demand curve.

Oil Shocks and the Great Stagflation

Twice during the 1970s, many industrialized economies in the world experienced leftward shifts of aggregate supply caused by cuts in the production of crude oil by members of the Organization of Petroleum Exporting Countries (OPEC). These supply shocks caused unemployment, higher price levels, and reductions in production and living standards in economies not benefiting from the higher prices of crude oil. This combination of faltering production and increasing prices is called **stagflation,** a word created by combining the words *stagnation* and *inflation*.

Once again, economists desperately tried to find ways to ease the burdens of inflation and unemployment but no comfortable solutions could be found. Compromise policies attempted to divide the hardships more or less equitably among different groups in the society and to help workers and other resources transfer their activities into occupations less dependent on low priced petroleum. Both unemployment rates and inflation rates remained high for extended periods of time while these adjustments were made. As oil consuming countries accomplished the transitions and as crude oil sources were found in countries not members of OPEC, the scarcity of petroleum diminished and its price stabilized. Eventually, OPEC countries themselves increased oil production, shifting aggregate-supply curves to the right in most industrialized economies and bringing production increases, higher living standards, and a slackening of inflation in many economies.

The stagflation period in the United States during the 1970s may be seen as a time during which two major oil shocks caused a significant leftward shift of the economy's aggregate-supply curve.

Government Monetary and Fiscal Policy

Shifting the aggregate demand curve is one of the key elements in government macroeconomic policy. Suppose, for example, that the economy is suffering from a recession caused by a leftward shift in aggregate demand—the situation described above in connection with the Great Depression of the 1930s. Government policy makers undoubtedly want to shift the aggregate-demand curve to the right to recover from the recession. **Monetary policy** offers one method of increasing aggregate demand. In the context of the *AD-AS* model, increasing the money supply increases purchases of currently produced goods and services. The aggregate-demand curve shifts to the right and a greater quantity of output is demanded at any given price level. The rightward shift of the *AD* curve reverses the process that caused the recession or depression, returning prices and output to their original levels.

Government policy makers also may use **fiscal policy** to shift the aggregate-demand curve. In fiscal policy, government purchases are increased in order to increase aggregate demand or taxes are reduced so that households and business firms will increase purchases.

Government monetary and fiscal policies also can be used to shift the aggregate-demand curve to the left. This may be done if policy makers want to "cool off" the economy and reduce inflationary pressures. The money supply can be reduced, or its rate of growth slowed, leading to a reduction in the demand for goods and services. Or government purchases can be reduced and/or taxes increased, if policy makers choose to use fiscal instruments to shift the aggregate-demand curve.

An economy's aggregate demand curve may be shifted by its government's use of fiscal policy (changes in the amount that it taxes or spends) and monetary policy (changes in the amount of money that it supplies).

We will have much more to say about government fiscal policies in Part IV and about government monetary policies in Part V.

Economics in Focus

Econometric Models

The circular flow is an elementary, intuitive model of the operation of the macroeconomy. In recent years, aided by the computer, economists have produced many new and powerful econometric models. *Econometrics* is the area of economics that uses a combination of theory, mathematics, and statistics to analyze economic questions. Econometric models are especially useful in forecasting what the economy is likely to do.

When Federal Reserve officials responsible for the nation's money supply contemplate a change in monetary policy, econometric models help them predict the new policy's effect on interest rates and money reserves. Researchers have used econometric models to analyze patterns in tax receipts, government expenditures, wage-price relationships, unemployment, and so on. But perhaps the most widespread use of econometrics is in forecasting for business firms.

One of the early leaders in the business-forecasting field was Wharton Econometric Associates, now The WEFA Group. Founded by Nobel Prize-winner Lawrence Klein, the firm has based its forecasts on a variety of econometric models: for example, a quarterly model for short-term cycles, a long-term model with a heavier emphasis on industrial trends and demographics, and specialized models for predicting prices, wages, and productivity for specific industries. To keep such models useful, economists must continually reevaluate not only the input data and assumptions but also the performance of the basic equations.

Many firms use their own computer programs to help them predict business trends. Even small firms can do econometric modeling with the aid of software packages for microcomputers. Packages already on the market can simulate macroeconomic forces, perform fairly complex statistical manipulations, and print out the results in an easy-to-read format. Economists themselves often find such ready-made packages helpful for research purposes. Recently a number of scholars have also used econometric modeling to investigate some very untraditional approaches to economics. For instance, some economists have questioned the basic notion of equilibrium, arguing that economic fluctuations are more irregular than equilibrium theories suggest. Along with computer scientists and experts from such remote disciplines as physics, these untraditional economists have developed computer models of nonlinear systems that produce variable patterns much like the ones of a real economy.

As software continues to grow better and more sophisticated, econometric modeling should increase in vigor and usefulness. Of course, no model, no matter how fine-tuned, can predict all the changes in our world, but computerized econometric modeling is a powerful tool that has already changed the discipline and will continue to change it in years to come.

Sources: John R. Connelly, ''Econometric Modeling,'' *PC Magazine,* March 14, 1989, pp. 203–220; Howard J. Howe and Gene D. Guill, ''The Wharton Model,'' in A. Migliaro and C. L. Jain, *An Executive's Guide to Econometric Forecasting* (Flushing, N.Y.: Graceway, 1983), pp. 44–49; Elizabeth Corcoran, ''Disequilibrium,'' *Scientific American,* December 1988, pp. 108–110; Everette S. Gardner, Jr., ''How to Monitor Your Forecasts,'' *Lotus,* April 1989, pp. 54–57.

SUMMARY

1. The circular-flow model provides a visual representation of the macroeconomy and illustrates how income flows from firms to households as resources are hired to engage in production. It also illustrates household uses of income for consumption purchases, saving, net taxes, and purchases from foreigners. Finally, the circular flow illustrates how income dispensed by households flows to firms, through purchases of consumption goods, investment purchases of capital goods, government purchases of public goods, and foreign purchases of exported goods. (See pages 104–110 and Figure 1, page 105.)

2. Governments borrow from financial markets when their budgets are in deficit. Therefore, governments obtain funds that came to financial markets either from household saving or from foreigners who had sold goods to domestic households (imports) and did not care to use these funds to purchase exports from the domestic economy. In this manner, government borrowing can crowd out private investment purchases. (See pages 107–108 and Figure 2, page 107.)

3. Governments can channel funds into financial markets if they have budget surpluses, and use the extra net tax collections to retire debt securities. In this way, income paid in net taxes becomes available for lending to investors to finance capital goods purchases or to foreigners to finance their purchases of exports from the domestic economy. (See page 108 and Figure 3, page 108.)

4. International markets may channel funds into domestic financial markets. If the economy represented by the circle has a deficit in its international trade, leaving more income in the hands of foreigners than they wish to use to pay for goods and services purchases from that country, these funds may flow into domestic financial markets. In this situation, the domestic economy goes into debt or sells assets to foreigners, and funds from foreigners become available for lending to investors to finance capital goods purchases. (See page 109 and Figure 4, page 109.)

5. Household saving or government income and product budget surpluses may flow from financial markets into international markets when the economy has a surplus in its international trade.

Foreigners borrow funds to help finance their purchases of goods and services exported by firms of the domestic economy. (See pages 109–110 and Figure 5, page 110.)

6. Circular-flow equilibrium exists when the total of consumption purchases, investment purchases, government purchases, and purchases by foreigners (exports) *equals* income, the total earnings of resource owners plus expected profits—that is, when $C + I + G + (X - Im) = Y$. (See page 110.)

7. Expansionary disequilibrium exists when the total of consumption purchases, investment purchases, government purchases, and purchases by foreigners (exports) is *greater than* the total earnings of resource owners plus expected profits—when $C + I + G + (X - Im) > Y$. (See page 111.)

8. Contractionary disequilibrium exists when the total of consumption purchases, investment purchases, government purchases, and purchases by foreigners (exports) is *less than* the total earnings of resource owners plus expected profits—that is, when $C + I + G + (X - Im) < Y$. (See page 112.)

9. Aggregate quantity demanded is represented by the spending streams in the top half of the circular-flow diagram. In the aggregate-demand and aggregate-supply model, aggregate demand is represented by the equation $QD = f(P)$, *ceteris paribus*, where QD is the value of goods and services demanded in an economy and P is the price level. The relationship is negative (inverse), showing that increases in the price level result in reductions in aggregate quantity demanded and vice versa, *ceteris paribus*. The aggregate-demand curve illustrates this function graphically. (See pages 112–115.)

10. Aggregate quantity supplied is decided by business firms represented by the purple box at the right-hand side of the circular-flow diagram. In the aggregate-demand and aggregate-supply model, aggregate supply is represented by the equation $QS = f(P)$, *ceteris paribus*, where QS is the value of goods and services supplied in an economy and P is the price level. Although economists disagree about the magnitude of the slope of the AS curve, a positive relationship suggests that increases in the price level result in increases in aggregate quantity supplied and vice versa, *ceteris paribus*. The aggregate-supply curve illustrates this function graphically. (See pages 115–117.)

11. Macroeconomic equilibrium exists at the price level that equates aggregate quantity demanded with aggregate quantity supplied, that is, at the intersection of the aggregate-demand curve and the aggregate-supply curve. (See page 117.)

12. Expansionary disequilibrium exists when, at the existing price level, aggregate quantity demanded exceeds aggregate quantity supplied. In the circular-flow model, firms have sold more goods and services than they planned. Inventories are depleted below desired levels and production and/or prices will be increased in the next round of the circle, *ceteris paribus*. (See page 118.)

13. Contractionary disequilibrium exists when, at the existing price level, aggregate quantity demanded is less than aggregate quantity supplied. In the circular-flow model, firms have sold less goods and services than they planned. Inventories are above desired levels and production and/or prices will be decreased in the next round of the circle, *ceteris paribus*. (See page 117.)

14. Macroeconomists devote a great amount of time and energy to forecasting events or behavior changes that will shift aggregate-demand or aggregate-supply curves. They also attempt to find ways to restore macroeconomic equilibrium after disequilibrium conditions have set in. The Great Depression of the 1930s illustrates problems associated with disequilibrium caused by shifts in aggregate demand. The Great Stagflation of the 1970s illustrates problems associated with disequilibrium caused by shifts in aggregate supply. (See pages 118–119.)

15. Monetary policies and fiscal policies are government actions commonly used in dealing with macroeconomic disequilibrium situations. Monetary policy emphasizes changes in the money supply. Fiscal policy emphasizes changes in government spending and taxation. (See page 119.)

KEY TERMS

aggregate-demand curve: the graphic representation of the relationship between changes in the price level prevailing in an economy and the resulting changes in the aggregate quantity demanded in that economy, *ceteris paribus* (page 113).

aggregate quantity demanded: the sum of total purchases, $C + I + G + X - Im$, of an economy during a specified time period at a certain price level (page 113).

aggregate quantity supplied: the sum of all the goods and services that firms will produce and offer for sale in an economy during a specified time period at a certain price level (page 115).

aggregate-supply curve: the graphic representation of the relationship between changes in the price level prevailing in an economy and the resulting changes in the aggregate quantity of goods and services supplied in that economy, *ceteris paribus* (page 115).

balance of trade: when the value of exports equals the value of imports (page 108).

capital goods: buildings, machines, and human capital (page 106).

circular-flow equilibrium: when the sum of consumption purchases, investment purchases, government purchases, and net exports equals the amount paid out by firms for resources used in production plus expected profits: $C + I + G + (X - Im) = Y$ (page 104).

consumption purchases (C): expenditures by households to acquire goods and services for use during the accounting period (page 106).

contractionary disequilibrium: when the aggregate quantity supplied is greater than the aggregate quantity demanded so that output will be reduced and/or prices lowered (page 112).

crowding out: when some of the saving flowing through the financial markets is used to pay for government purchases rather than to finance investment purchases (page 108).

deficit: the extent to which government purchases are greater than net taxes (page 107).

disequilibrium: an imbalance among opposing forces such that there is some tendency for change (page 111).

equilibrium: a state of balance among opposing forces such that there is no tendency for change (page 110).

expansionary disequilibrium: when the aggregate quantity demanded is greater than the aggregate quantity supplied so that output will be increased and/or prices raised (page 111).

exports: goods and services produced by domestic firms and purchased by foreigners (page 108).

financial intermediaries: banks, credit unions, saving and loan associations, stock and bond brokers and other institutions that accept deposits of income saved and offer to loan these funds, in return for interest payments, to those who wish to borrow (page 106).

fiscal policy: a government's attempt to influence macroeconomic variables by changing the amount that it taxes or spends (page 119).

government purchases (G): purchases by government of currently produced goods and services (page 107).

imports: goods and services, produced abroad and purchased for use by domestic firms, governments and households (page 108).

income and product budgets: budgets that treat government transfer payments as negative taxes rather than as expenditures (page 107).

index number: a number that expresses a particular value in relation to some other value that has been specified as a base or reference value (page 114).

investment purchases (I): expenditures for newly produced capital goods (page 106).

macroeconomic equilibrium: when the aggregate quantity demanded is equal to the aggregate quantity supplied in an economy. The intersection of an economy's aggregate demand and aggregate supply curves (page 110).

macroeconomics: the part of economics concerned with aggregate economic activity—the functioning of the entire economy (page 104).

microeconomics: the part of economics that studies the activities of individual persons and business firms (page 104).

monetary policy: a government's attempt to influence macroeconomic variables by changing the economy's money supply (page 119).

net taxes (Tn): the total amount of tax paid by households and firms minus transfer payments received (page 107).

price level: an average of all prices prevailing in an economy that is expressed as an index number based on the average prices that prevailed in a selected base year (page 113).

saving (S): setting aside current income in order to increase wealth (page 106).

stagflation: the prolonged combination of inflation, substantial unemployment, and sluggish growth (page 106).

surplus: the extent to which government purchases are less than net taxes received (page 118).

transfer payments: funds paid by government to welfare recipients, veterans, unemployed workers, social security retirees, etc.; considered to be negative taxes (page 117).

DISCUSSION QUESTIONS

1. Without looking at Figure 1, construct the circular-flow diagram showing the four streams of household uses of funds. Compare your drawing with Figure 1 to be sure you have it right. Assuming that financial institutions can expand or reduce the quantity of money in the economy, discuss how disequilibrium can arise in the circular flow.

2. Net taxes differ from total tax collections by government. Explain why. Government purchases differ from the total budget expenditure of government. Explain why. How do transfer payments provide the key to the differences? How does income conveyed through transfer payments enter into the circular flow?

3. Since government has the power to control both its inflows and its outflows, why should a disequilibrium condition ever arise in the net taxes-government purchases flow? Is government's control complete? Explain. Is disequilibrium undesirable? Explain.

4. Carefully explain the connections between the government box and the financial-markets box in the circular flow. Explain the concept of crowding out and discuss when it may be desirable and when it may be undesirable.

5. Explain how dollars spent by U.S. households to purchase foreign goods and services can be used by foreigners to purchase investment goods in the United States or U.S. national debt securities. The "twin deficits" (international trade and governmental budget) problem experienced by the U.S. economy in the middle 1980s was said to set the stage for lower U.S. living standards in the future. Discuss why that could happen.

6. Draw a graph illustrating an aggregate-demand curve, taking special care to label the axes correctly. Compare your drawing with Figure 6. Write the algebraic expression for the aggregate-demand curve and discuss the roles played by dependent and independent variables in this equation. Also discuss why it is essential to add the *ceteris paribus* condition to the equation.

7. On the graph that you have drawn for question 6, add an aggregate-supply curve. Then shift *one* of the curves to illustrate the effect of an increase in quantity of money circulating in the economy. As a result of the increased spending, will firms have inventories that are too large or too small? Illustrate the inventory imbalance on the graph.

7

National Income Accounting

Preview Since macroeconomics is concerned with aggregate, or "grand total," economic activity, it is essential to have a way to measure total production and income in the economy.[1]

In this chapter, we explore the system of national income and product accounting that is used to measure the overall performance of the U.S. economy. This system is made up of five different measures of economic activity, each used for its own purpose. The best known is called the gross national product, which measures the market value of all the goods and services produced in the economy in a given year. The other measures break down this grand total to focus on particular parts that are useful in understanding how the economy works.

We also describe some of the shortcomings of the American national accounting system. For example, it does not count the work that people do at home, such as caring for their children and keeping house. Nor does it take into account the damage done to the environment that is an undesired by-product of certain kinds of production. In some areas, it may overstate income by counting intermediate products as final products.

Of course, no accounting system can be perfect in the sense that it provides all the information that anyone might want about the economy. What matters is that there is a consistent set of definitions and measures to help economists in their efforts to understand how the economy operates and what it is likely to do in the future.

1. See Chapter 1, page 6.

NATIONAL INCOME AND PRODUCT ACCOUNTS

The **national income and product accounts** are a set of reports on the volume and composition of economic activity in the United States over a specified time period. This accounting system was developed during the 1920s at a private research agency, the National Bureau of Economic Research. One of its principal developers, Simon Kuznets, later received a Nobel Prize in Economics for his work. Today, the tasks of collecting data and preparing the accounts are carried on by the Department of Commerce. The major components of the accounts are published regularly in *The Survey of Current Business*. Macroeconomic forecasts usually are made in terms of these accounts. Also, one of the best-known parts of the accounts—the gross national product—is the measure usually presented on the horizontal axis of the aggregate-demand and aggregate-supply graph.

The national income and product accounts are a set of reports of the volume and composition of economic activity in the United States over a specified time period. Macroeconomics forecasts are usually made in terms of these accounts.

Table 1 presents the essentials of the U.S. national income and product accounts for the calendar year 1988. This table shows the three major sections of the system: the national product section, the national income section, and the personal income section. The *national product* section, on the upper left in the table, shows the value of total production in the economy, as measured by the market value of all goods and services produced in the economy during the year. The best-known entry in this section is for the gross national product, which we shall discuss in detail later. The classification of gross national product as consumer spending, investment spending, government spending on goods and services, and net exports corresponds with the spending paths illustrated in the upper half of the circular-flow diagram in Chapter 6.

The national income and product accounting system has three major sections: the national product section, the national income section, and the personal income section.

The *national income* section, on the upper right in Table 1, shows the total amount earned by owners of resources used in producing goods and services during the year.[2] Note that the bottom-line entry in the national income section equals the bottom-line entry in the national product section. This relationship shows the kind of double-entry bookkeeping used in the national accounts. The idea behind this double-entry system is that the amount spent for goods and services (national product) should equal the amount earned by owners of the resources used in producing these goods and services (national income). The national income section contains amounts for the flows of income represented by the lower half of the circular-flow diagram in Chapter 6.

There are some complications in making the double-entry system actually work in the national accounting system. These are resolved through the specific entries in the lower portion of the national product section in Table 1. These adjustments (capital consumption allowance, indirect business taxes and subsidies, and statistical discrepancy) will be explained later.

The third major part of the national accounting system is the *personal income* section, at the bottom in Table 1. This section breaks down the total national income into special categories that are useful in economic forecasting. The most useful entry in this section is for disposable personal income. This figure shows the amount that people can divide between consumption spending and saving. It is widely used in forecasting.

---

2. It is interesting to note that the United States includes all services performed by lawyers, doctors, barbers, civil servants, etc., as part of its national income and product. Marxist countries, particularly the Soviet Union and the People's Republic of China, include services only insofar as they contribute directly to the production of *physical* goods.

TABLE 1
National Income and Product in the United States, 1988 (billions of dollars)

National Product Section		National Income Section	
Consumption spending	$3,227.5	Compensation of employees	$2,904.7
Investment spending	766.5		
Government spending on goods and services	964.9	Proprietor's income	324.5
Net exports	− 94.6		
Gross national product	**$4,864.3**	Rental income of persons	19.3
Capital consumption allowance (subtract)	− 506.4	Corporate profits	328.1
Net national product	**$4,357.9**		
Indirect business taxes and subsidies	− 375.6	Net interest	391.5
Statistical discrepancy	− 14.1		
National income	**$3,968.2**	**National income**	**$3,968.2**

Personal Income Section

National income (from above)	$3,968.2
Earnings not received (subtract)	−492.1
Receipts not earned (add)	586.0
Personal income	**$4,062.1**
Personal tax and nontax payments (subtract)	−590.3
Disposable personal income	**$3,471.8**
Disposition:	
Personal consumption	$3,227.5
Personal saving	144.3
Interest paid to business	98.9
Transfers to foreigners	1.0
	$3,471.8

The national product section records the value of goods and services produced during the year. The national income section records amounts earned by owners of resources used in producing goods and services. This is a double-entry bookkeeping system, and the same total appears at the bottom of each section. The personal income section records certain additions and subtractions that are necessary to show amounts actually received by people and available to use for consumption and saving.

Note: Items may not add to total because of rounding.

Source: U.S. Department of Commerce, Bureau of Economic Analysis, *Survey of Current Business*, Vol. 69, No. 3 (March 1989). Tables 1.1, 1.9, and 2.1.

The national product section of the national income and product accounts records the market value of goods and services produced during the year. The national income section records amounts earned by owners of resources used in producing goods and services. The personal income section breaks down the total national income into special categories used to make economic forecasts.

The National Product Section

The national product section shows the market value of goods and services produced during the year. In other words, it records the "value" of the year's production.

Two basic requirements govern the Commerce Department's system for estimating national production. First, it must include only current-year production and must not include transactions that merely transfer title to goods produced in earlier years. Thus, exchanges of old houses or used cars are not recorded, although the services of the realtor and the used-car salesperson—that is, their salaries and commissions—are included as currently produced services.

The second requirement is that the values assigned are those applicable to the final sale of the good or service during the accounting period. In most instances, this is a sale of a final good or service to a consumer, a firm, a government, or a foreigner. However, at the close of the year, some of the year's production is in inventory, either as a semifinished good or as a good not yet sold to its final purchaser. In the accounts, the value of the year's beginning inventory is subtracted from the value of the year's closing inventory and the difference is included as an investment purchase (positive or negative) during the year.

It is not possible, of course, actually to record each of the billions of final-sales transactions that occur in the economy each year. Instead, the calculation of GNP and its components is done by the Department of Commerce with information from tax returns, surveys, and other data sources. Their results are estimates based on statistical samples rather than exact figures.

The procedure used estimates the value of the goods and services sold by firms and then subtracts an estimate of the value of the inputs, or "intermediate goods," that firms purchase from each other. What remains is an estimate of the **value added** by firms and reflects the production from resources employed directly by them. The value-added method estimates the value of current production, avoids multiple-counting, and gives the same results as a summation of final sales.

The market value of a firm's final sales minus the amounts paid by the firm to purchase intermediate goods from other firms equals the value added by the resources employed by the firm.

Table 2 illustrates how the value-added calculation accounts for the full final-sale value of a good or service. As shown in the sales-value column, a loaf of bread sells for 70 cents at retail. In the value-added column, the contributions from all the resource owners who helped to produce the bread also add up to 70 cents. For simplicity, we have assumed that the farmer does not purchase any intermediate goods, such as seed or fertilizer. We avoid double-counting because we do not count any of the payments made for intermediate goods. As you will see, the U.S. system is not entirely successful in excluding payments for intermediate goods. However, many countries, including the Soviet Union, use a measure called **value of output**, which makes no attempt to avoid double-counting.

Gross National Product In the national product section, spending is divided into four categories: consumption, investment, government, and net exports. In general, *consumption spending* refers to goods and services purchased by households, including durable goods such as autos and appliances. *Investment spending* includes purchases of buildings and equipment for use in future production and net additions to inventories of raw materials, goods in process, and unsold final products. (It does not refer to purchases of stocks and bonds, which are titles to goods already in existence or claims against future goods and services. Such pur-

TABLE 2
Value Added and Final Sales

	Sales Value	Cost of Intermediate Goods	Value Added
Farmer sells wheat	.15	− .00	= .15
Miller sells flour	.35	→ .15	= .20
Baker sells bread (wholesale)	.60	→ .35	= .25
Grocer sells bread (retail)	.70	→ .60	= .10
Totals	$1.80	− 1.10	= $.70

The sales value of the final product (bread at retail) is equal to the sum of the values added by the firms that have processed raw materials and intermediate goods into this final product.

chases, of course, are what the person in the street means by "investment.") The investment category also includes new residential structures. Included in *government spending* are purchases of goods and services by federal, state, and local governments, as well as by public companies like the postal service.[3] It does not include cash **transfer payments**, which is money paid to people even though these people did not provide a good or service to earn this money during the accounting period. Welfare, Social Security, and veterans' benefit checks are examples of cash transfer payments. They are not counted in the government purchases category of the national product section but are counted (in the consumption section) when the recipients spend the money received from the government. Governments also can transfer actual goods and services, such as food or hospital care, directly to individual recipients. Since the government must purchase these goods and services, their value is counted in the government entry in the accounts.

The consumption spending category of the GNP refers to goods and services purchased by households.

3. The United States treats all government purchases as public consumption; there is no separate "public investment" account. In the United Nations system, however, this distinction is made and investment has a public component. An example of public investment would be highway construction.

The investment spending category of the GNP includes purchases of buildings and equipment for use in future production and net additions to inventories of raw materials, goods in process, and unsold final products.

The government spending part of the GNP includes purchases of goods and services by federal, state, and local governments.

Net exports represent the value of American goods and services purchased by foreigners less the value of foreign goods and services purchased by Americans. Often it is a negative quantity. That is, the value of U.S. exports may be less than the value of imports from other countries. The **gross national product (GNP)**, perhaps the most familiar measure of aggregate economic activity, is the total of all purchases—by consumers, by investors, by governments, and (net) by foreigners—of currently produced goods and services.

The net exports part of the GNP represents the value of American goods and services purchased by foreigners minus the value of foreign goods and services purchased by Americans.

The gross national product (GNP) is the total of all purchases—by consumers, by investors, by

governments, and by foreigners—of currently produced goods and services.

Net National Product The only difference between the gross and the net national product is the treatment of depreciation and obsolescence. Some of the new buildings and equipment included as investment in GNP were needed to replace buildings and equipment that had worn out, become obsolete, or suffered accidental damage during the year. We say that some capital goods (production equipment) were "consumed" in the process of producing other goods. Therefore, a **capital consumption allowance** is estimated and subtracted from the gross national product to obtain a figure for the **net national product (NNP)**. In other words, GNP is gross of capital consumption allowances, whereas NNP is net of them. (It is a good idea, when using the terms *gross* and *net* in economics, to be able to answer the question "gross (or net) of *what?*")

Net national product (NNP) is GNP minus a capital consumption allowance (replacement costs for worn-out or obsolete buildings and equipment).

Since the capital consumption allowance relates to buildings and equipment, it is really an adjustment to the investment component of GNP. This means that the only difference between GNP and NNP is the difference between investment before the subtraction of the capital consumption allowance ("gross" investment) and investment after this subtraction ("net" investment). So we may write

$$GNP = C + I_g + G + X - Im$$

and

$$NNP = C + I_n + G + X - Im$$

where C is consumption, I_g is gross investment, I_n is net investment, G is government purchases, X is exports, Im is imports, GNP is gross national product, and NNP is net national product. Expressing net exports as $X - Im$ will be useful later when we explain what determines these amounts. Also, it

will be helpful to remember these equations. As we will see, many macroeconomic theories are built around the summation of consumption, investment, government purchases, and net exports.

National Product Section Adjustments Net national product is a figure that estimates the actual (net) gain from all production during the year. It would equal the total income earned by all persons and companies engaged in production, except for two problems that arise in our double-entry accounting system.

The first problem arises because taxes and government subsidies drive a wedge between amounts paid by purchasers of goods and services and amounts received by the resources used in producing them. In the double-entry system, the national product section is computed at market prices, which are higher because of taxes on these products and lower because of subsidies given to them. But the national income section is computed according to the earnings of the factors of production and adds up to an estimate of what the market prices would have been without any sales taxes, excise taxes, property taxes, or subsidies. Therefore, a major adjustment is needed in the national product section to adjust for the tax and subsidy components of market prices. This is the **indirect business taxes and subsidies** entry in Table 1.

A handy way to understand the necessity of this adjustment for indirect taxes and subsidies is as follows. Think about the federal tax on gasoline, which increases the price that you pay for gasoline at the pump. The tax part of this price is counted (along with your purchase of gasoline) as a consumption purchase (C) in estimating gross and net national product. The tax revenue is used by the government to pay for construction and repair of the highway system, and this spending is counted as part of the government purchases (G) component of GNP and NNP. In other words, the tax revenue is counted twice in the national product calculations of the accounting system. But in the national income section of the accounts, it is counted only once—as the payment to the resources (labor, capital, natural) used in the highway work. Therefore, the indirect tax must be subtracted to remove the double-counting and to secure a balance with the earnings reported in the national income section of the accounts. Government subsidies to business work the other way—they reduce the prices paid for final goods, but do finance the earnings of factors of production. Therefore, these subsidies are an added item in the adjustments section.

The indirect business taxes and subsidies entry in the national product section is an adjustment that adjusts for the tax and subsidy component of market prices.

The second problem in securing a balance between net national product and national income arises because, in figuring both national product and national income, estimating procedures are used rather than full and complete tabulations of all production and all incomes. Also, national product is estimated separately from national income. The **statistical discrepancy** entry in the national product section in Table 1 simply reports the extent to which the two estimates were not equal to each other, or the difference between them. Because the national income estimates are usually more accurate than the national product estimates, the statistical discrepancy entry is placed in the national product section.

The statistical discrepancy entry in the national product section reflects the fact that the Department of Commerce makes separate estimates for the national product and the national income sections of the accounts.

The National Income Section

National income (NI) is the total amount that is earned in producing the national product. The five parts of national income are listed in Table 1. They are compensation of employees, proprietors' income, rental income of persons, corporate profits, and net interest. *Compensation of employees* covers both money wages and the amounts that are spent by employers for such things as Social Security and fringe benefits (paid vacation, sick and holiday pay, and so on). *Proprietors' income* records the incomes

of all unincorporated businesses and in fact combines profits, rental income, and the labor income of the partners and proprietors in these businesses. The rents received on properties owned by businesses are included in the income or profit for these businesses, so that only the *rental income of persons* is stated as a separate item in the accounts. Capital consumption allowances are subtracted in calculating the rental income of persons and the incomes of proprietorships, partnerships, and corporations. Inventory-value adjustments are made for price-level changes that occur during the year. *Corporate profits* are recorded before the payment of dividends. *Net interest* is the total interest income of persons, minus interest paid by consumers to businesses and net interest paid by government, which are considered transfer payments (and not production) in the accounting system. Adding these five components together gives the amount of national income, which is equal to the net national product after the adjustments noted earlier (indirect business taxes and subsidies, statistical discrepancy) have been made.

National income (NI) is the total amount that is earned in producing the national product. National income is equal to net national product after certain adjustments are made.

A half-whimsical illustration of all this is as follows. Consider a super-stereo sound system selling for $4,864—an amount about one-billionth of the 1988 GNP. You buy it. Where does your money go? Part ($506) goes into a fund to replace machines that were worn out in producing this glorious stereo system, and part ($376) goes for sales, excise, and property taxes (net of subsidies) and a $14 statistical discrepancy in adding up the sales slip! The remainder ($3,968) is the total earned by the people who worked to produce the stereo or who owned other resources that were used in its production. Most ($2,905) goes to workers, salaried managers, etc. Smaller amounts go to others in the production process—$325 as profits to proprietors or partners (perhaps subcontractors for component parts of the stereo), $19 to pay rent for land under some factory building, $328 as profits to the corporation that was the prime producer of the stereo, and $391 as interest to people who loaned money to the prime producing company or to the subcontractors. You enjoy listening to the stereo. Other people enjoy having the money you spent. The next step is to see what they do with it.

The Personal Income Section

The personal income section of the accounting system starts with the amount of national income. It then shows amounts that must be added or subtracted in order to arrive at the amount of income that was actually available to people for spending and saving decisions.[4] Two steps are used in this process. The first reports personal income and the second reports disposable personal income.

Personal Income The adjustment process begins by recognizing that some of the income that was earned in a given year was not actually received by the people who earned it. In Table 1, this is called *earnings not received*. The biggest part of the earnings not received is contributions for social insurance, or Social Security taxes. This category also includes corporate profits that were not paid out in dividends. The gap between profits and dividends includes both corporate income taxes paid to the government and earnings retained for reinvestment by the corporation. All these items are subtracted from national income as ''earnings not received.''

Receipts not earned is a companion item to earnings not received. In other words, some income that people received during a year was not earned by them in that year. The largest item under this heading is government transfer payments, which include Social Security benefits and welfare checks. It also includes interest that the government pays to people (as for savings bonds). Adjusting national income by adding receipts not earned and by subtracting earnings not received, we derive the amount of **personal income (PI)**.

Personal income (PI) is calculated by adjusting national income by adding receipts not earned and by subtracting earnings not received.

---

4. *People* refers primarily to households, but nonprofit institutions are also included.

Disposable Personal Income The last step in the adjustment process recognizes that people have certain obligations that must be subtracted from personal income to discover how much income is left for spending or saving. We subtract payments of *personal taxes* (individual income, estate, and inheritance taxes) and then certain other small *nontax items*, such as traffic fines, penalties, and charges for government services. The amount that remains after these obligations are subtracted is called **disposable personal income (DPI)**.

Disposable personal income is that amount of personal income actually available to people for spending or saving.

Finally, the accounting system reports on the disposition of DPI—how disposable personal income was actually used in a given year. It comes as no surprise that *personal consumption* spending claims most of disposable personal income. *Personal saving* is another very important item here. Finally, personal transfer payments, including *interest paid to businesses* and *transfers to foreigners*, must also be recorded in accounting for disposable personal income.

Why Five Series?

The accounting system gives us five data series to estimate the volume of economic activity. In their usual order of size, these are GNP, NNP, NI, PI, and DPI. Just what, you may ask, *is* the national income or product anyway? Why bother with five separate series? What kind of dodge-ball game are the statisticians playing with us?

Economists believe that the five series, even though they are correlated closely with one another, have different meanings and can be used for different purposes. Of the five series, gross national product is the most closely related to measured *employment* and *unemployment*. Net national product, which is GNP minus capital consumption allowances, comes close to defining the economist's all-purpose symbol Y as a measure of national income and product. When stated on a per capita basis, national income is a rough but useful measure of *long-run economic welfare*, though the whole welfare idea is really much more complicated than this estimate. Personal income, on the other hand, is often used as a rough measure of *short-run economic welfare*. In the short run, it is a gain for persons to have their incomes raised when transfer payments increase or business maintains dividend rates even when profits fall. However, the long-run effects may be unfavorable if savings are neglected or debts pile up. Finally, disposable personal income is closely connected to *consumption expenditures*, which play an important part in macroeconomic theories.

The public has not objected to the duplication and "mystification" involved in having five national series to deal with all at once. On the contrary, private bodies have gone beyond the government and have come up with estimates of their own. Some private economic and statistical consulting firms deduct "necessary consumption" (defined in different ways) from DPI to obtain what they call "discretionary" or "supernumerary" income, which they say is correlated closely with consumption spending for durable goods such as stoves, radios, and washing machines. Another innovation is "final buying income," which eliminates rises and falls in inventories—stocks of unsold goods either finished or in the process of production. Because "final buying income" smooths out a good part of the short-term fluctuations in economic activity, administration politicians are especially fond of it when recessions seem to be getting under way.

SHORTCOMINGS OF THE SYSTEM

No social accounting system is perfect for all purposes. It may omit production and income that some people think should be counted. To this extent, it understates actual income and production. For example, Americans criticize the Soviet system for omitting services, except those directly related to the production of goods. Or the system may include certain items that some people think should not be counted at all. To this extent, the system overstates national income and product. The Soviets criticize the American system for including meaningless and artificial consumer frills as items of national income. We shall mention some of the more controversial points in the American system.

"Do-It-Yourself" Production

"Do-it-yourself" production is not counted in the national income accounting system, except for estimates of farmers' home-produced food and the imputed rent on owner-occupied housing (what the cost would be to a nonowner). The problem is that it is impossible to estimate the value of most "do-it-yourself" production with much accuracy.

Housekeeping and child rearing illustrate the importance of do-it-yourself production and the seriousness of its omission from the national accounts. If both husband and wife are employed in wage-paying jobs, both of their earnings will be recorded as part of the national income. If they hire help with housekeeping and child rearing (domestic servants, baby sitters, nursery schools, TV dinners), the earnings of those who produce these goods and services will also be counted. If one spouse chooses to be a housewife or househusband, the value of these services is not included. The national income declines not only by the wages of the one who keeps house but also by those of the housekeeper or baby sitter who is not hired. There is an old saw in national income statistics: "When you marry your cook, you lower the national income of the country."

Important as do-it-yourself production is in the United States, it is much more important in less-developed countries (LDCs). Thus, the comparison between income per head in the United States, or in any other more-developed country (MDC), and income per head in the typical LDC is apt to be biased and misleading. The MDC standard of living is not as much higher than the LDC standard of living as the national income figures would suggest. And by the same token, the present U.S. standard of living is probably not so much higher than the standard of living in pioneer days, when women made the family's clothes and families built their own cabins. Their replacement by frame houses built by specialized building contractors and hired labor represented a smaller rise in the true national income than in the recorded one.

The Underground Economy

Allied to the do-it-yourself economy is the **underground economy**. Much income and production is not included in the national accounts because no records are kept of transactions that take place in terms of **barter** (direct exchange of one good or service for another), or even in terms of cash transfers between unlicensed business units. Rough estimates can be made of the volume of such unrecorded transactions if conditions are stable. But in periods of rapid change, serious errors in the estimate are likely. Some have estimated that the underground economy amounts to over 20 percent of the measured American GNP.

In the United States as well as in many other countries, both capitalist and socialist, there seems to be a movement away from recorded market transactions toward unrecorded barter deals and other nonmarket and off-the-books transactions. Thus we have come to speak of an "underground," "parallel," "second," or "black" economy.

Services are generally better fitted to the underground economy than is the production of physical goods. A house painter may paint a house for his garage proprietor neighbor in exchange for an engine overhaul, an auto paint job, and body work done by the neighbor. A lawyer may draw up a will or a contract in exchange for carpentry or cabinet work in her home. The tax laws are quite clear: all such earnings should be reported at their money values. But when they are not in fact reported, the national accounts may underestimate the national income at the same time that taxes are evaded.

Other motives besides tax evasion inspire the underground economy. Sometimes people wish to evade certification and licensing rules, as when bureaucrats or law clerks sell advice on legal matters without a license to practice law. Others want to get around certain trade-union rules, as when union plumbers work on their own below the union scale, or do the electrical or painting or carpentry work associated with a plumbing job. At times the motive is to evade labor and welfare laws. So an "unemployed" worker will operate his or her own business while continuing to receive unemployment benefits and/or welfare payments. (In Italy, the term *lavoro nero*, or "black labor," refers not to the labor of blacks but to work done below the minimum wage and without deductions for Social Security.) Also, workers who use their employers' tools, truck, or premises for work on their own during or after working hours will, of course, not report income received from the job. Nor will those involved in criminal activities like prostitution, gambling, and the narcotics trade report their profits.

Intermediate Products

An **intermediate product**, such as a ton of steel girders, is something that is produced as an input to further production. The national accounts, by using the "value-added" system, try to avoid the double-counting that would result if they included both the intermediate products used in producing a good or service *and* the final good or service as well. (If the accounts were to include a gross "value of output" series, as the Soviet ones do, there would be no problem.)

An intermediate product is one that is produced as an input to further production.

The distinction between intermediate products and final products, however, is often hard to apply in practice. Consider gasoline that a suburbanite buys and uses mainly for commuting to and from a job in the city. Is this gasoline a final product (a consumption good) or an intermediate product (an input to the production generated at the city job)? Or should it be an intermediate good on the morning trip to the job but a final good on the way from the job to home "consumption"? Would the problem be different if the commuter took a train or bus instead of his or her own car? What if the employer were to provide a special bus?

The problem is that many goods and services are used both for consumption and for further production. The two sorts of uses are separated in the accounts by a set of rules of thumb, which probably lead on balance to an overestimate of the national income.

Relations with the Environment

The relations between people and their environment give rise to more problems in social accounting. To understand the problem, consider the following illustration.

To control or modify my immediate small environment, I purchase a furnace, fuel, insulation, sweaters, and gloves in the winter. In the summer, I buy air-conditioning equipment, fuel, fans, and sunglasses. Producing these things generates income, which is recorded in the national income and product accounts, even though we may think they are overcoming "bads" rather than providing "goods" in themselves.

Complications for the accounting system arise when we recognize that millions of other people also are doing the same things that I am doing. On this large scale, human behavior burdens the ecosystem, making the air around us less pure than it once was. So I equip my heating and cooling systems with filters to keep out the polluted air, after doing my share to cause the pollution. Should the production of these filters be counted as part of the GNP, without offsetting (or negative) entries somewhere in the accounts to record the environmental damage that made the filters necessary? The accounts do record the filters, but they use no negative entry to record the harm done. For this reason, the accounting system may overstate the actual amount of income and production, if we mean by "income and production" truly positive contributions to welfare and living standards.

The problem has many illustrations in the U.S. economy. In addition to air purification filters, there are devices to lessen automobile emissions, to dispose of radioactive wastes, and to purify drinking water. Should the treatment of lung cancer be a positive entry in the accounts if the air pollution that helps to cause the cancer is not a negative entry?

The problem of environmental degradation has applications in the economies of many LDCs as well, since primitive farming methods can harm the environment. The "slash-and-burn" technique, which calls for cutting and burning trees to clear land, leads to air pollution, soil erosion, floods, and fouled water supplies. There is no nega-tive entry in the accounts to record the reduced value of the environment.

Consider the opposite case, too, when nature destroys the works of human beings. The capital consumption allowance, with which you are familiar, includes certain estimates of the results of nature's violent side. But the capital consumption allowance for nature's violence is spread evenly over the years, while the violence itself is not. How, then, would national income be affected if we suffered a major disaster like the destruction of Pompeii and Herculaneum by volcanic eruption, or of Tokyo and Yokohama by earthquake and fire? Such a disaster would result in an increase in national income, as people would earn incomes repairing the damage caused by nature and replacing what was beyond repair.

War and Violence

Preparing for war and waging war are recorded as parts of national income and production. People earn incomes for producing weapons of destruction and for serving in the armed forces. In fact, durable military goods like tanks are treated as consumption goods like loaves of bread rather than as investment goods like farm tractors. So total tank production is included in NNP as well as in GNP, even when the new tanks simply replace older ones, which wear out or become obsolete. (Loaves of bread are treated in this way for obvious reasons, but tractors are subject to capital consumption allowances.)

The issues involved in national accounting for war goods are both subtle and controversial. Does production of nuclear weapons deter war in the same way that riot police on duty at sports events deter rioting? If so, nuclear weapons production and riot-police training are legitimate entries in the social accounts, like the production of dikes as insurance against flood damage. But if weapons invite wars and police incite riots,[5] a case can be made to exclude these activities from production and income. (Criminal activity is not counted as

5. Consider the remark by the late Richard J. Daley, long-time mayor of Chicago: "The police are not there to create disorder. They are there to preserve disorder."

part of national income, though crime prevention is counted.)

The U.S. national income accounting system is not perfect; its flaws include its inability to take into account "do-it-yourself" production and the underground economy, the difficulty of distinguishing between intermediate and final products, and serious problems in measuring the effects of environmental damage and war.

Usefulness of the Accounts

As you can see, no accounting system provides completely acceptable measures of production or income in terms of welfare and living standards. Over the years, many ideas have been offered for making the system a better measure of "genuine" production in the sense of contributions to the standard of living. In the early 1970s, experimental systems called the measure of economic welfare (MEW) and net national welfare (NNW) were worked out for the United States and Japan, respectively. They attempted to subtract estimated environmental damage and wartime destruction.

Though they have been compared and criticized, they have not been continued on a permanent basis by any government.

The faults in our own and other national accounting systems, however, should not dim their usefulness. As a tool for the study of macroeconomics, the system offers information on changes in the volume of economic activity over time.

Changes over time are very important to the understanding of how an economy operates in the aggregate (macro) sense. Macroeconomics studies both the short-term changes and the long-term growth trends in the aggregate performance of an economy. When we focus on movements of uniformly defined measures over time, many of the problems concerning the absolute values used in the accounting system disappear. For example, the difference between one year and the next may be measured with reasonable accuracy even by questionable methods when the same rules for measurement have been used for each year.

Although the national income accounting system has flaws, it still serves a valuable purpose as a means of understanding the macroeconomy.

Economics in Focus

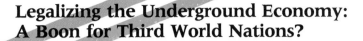

Legalizing the Underground Economy: A Boon for Third World Nations?

Food retailing in Lima, Peru, is dominated by 90,000 street vendors who sell their goods illegally. Most of the taxis and buses also are unlicensed. But none of this "informal" or "black market" activity seems unusual to the city residents, almost half of whom, according to one estimate, live in housing that was built illegally.

Lima offers a good example of the kind of underground economy that flourishes in many less-developed countries. Legalize the underground, some economists argue, and less-developed nations can reduce their debts, raise their standards of living, and compete on more equal terms with developed countries. The idea has been forcefully advanced in *The Other Path: The Invisible Revolution in the Third World*, a book by Peruvian Hernando de Soto.

But why are ordinary citizens like food vendors "underground" in the first place? The answer, in many countries in Latin America and Africa, lies in government regulations and bureaucratic tangles that make it impossible for a small entrepreneur to get legal approval. Those who apply for the proper permit or license may wait years while the bureaucracy fiddles; worse, bribes are often necessary. Wealthy business owners may use their political influence to keep out the small-time competition.

In Peru de Soto estimates that the underground economy adds an extra 29 percent to the nation's official GNP. In Argentina, where most of the managers and professionals participate in the underground economy, the unofficial GNP has been calculated at almost three-quarters the size of the official GNP. In the view of de Soto and his allies, legalizing underground economies would greatly increase their contribution to national welfare. Freed of the need to evade official scrutiny, small entrepreneurs could expand their businesses. They would have the security of legal title to their property, and access to the courts would help them enforce their contracts. They could borrow money more easily and at better rates.

Some economists disagree with these predictions, contending that underground businesses are less important than de Soto thinks. Nevertheless, a number of steps have been taken in the direction de Soto and his supporters advocate. The U.S. Agency for International Development (AID) helped to sponsor a 1988 conference on underground economies. AID and other international agencies have also assisted "microbanks" such as Ademi, an organization that supplies small-scale loans to unofficial businesses in the Dominican Republic. Research institutes in several Third World countries have begun to study underground economies and pressure governments for reform. Endorsing some of the new ideas, Malcolm Forbes declared that less-developed nations have "entrepreneurial energy of almost volcanic proportions waiting for release"—if they can be freed from the strangleholds their governments impose.

Sources: Jeremy Main, "How to Make Poor Countries Rich," *Fortune*, January 16, 1989, pp. 101–106; Robert McGough, "Let a Thousand Flowers Bloom," *Forbes*, April 28, 1986, pp. 57–60; Ronald Bailey, "The Right Path," *Forbes*, January 23, 1989, pp. 80–81; quotation from Malcolm S. Forbes, Jr., "Self-Made Crisis," *Forbes*, February 20, 1989, p. 27. See also Hernando de Soto, *The Other Path: The Invisible Revolution in the Third World* (New York: Harper & Row, 1989).

SUMMARY

1. Measuring the amount of economic activity is an important first step in understanding short- and long-term changes in the economy. (See page 125.)

2. The national income and product system has three main parts, one for measuring current production, one for measuring current income earned, and one for measuring amounts received as personal income. (See page 126 and Table 1, page 127.)

3. Gross national product is broken down into different kinds of spending: consumption, investment, government purchases, and net exports. The spending classification parallels the spending streams illustrated in the top half of the circular-flow diagram in Chapter 6. GNP records only currently produced goods and services. (See page 128.)

4. Net national product is smaller than gross national product by the amount of the capital consumption allowance, which takes into account the depreciation of capital goods. After certain adjustments are made, NNP becomes equal to national income. (See page 130.)

5. National income records the total earnings of factors of production during the accounting year. It corresponds with the income flows represented by the bottom half of the circular-flow diagram in Chapter 6. It is broken down into compensation of employees, proprietors' income, rental income of persons, corporate profits, and net interest. National income is equal to net national product after adjustments have been made for indirect business taxes, subsidies, and the statistical discrepancy. (See page 131.)

6. Personal income is the sum that remains after "earnings not received" have been subtracted and "receipts not earned" have been added to national income. When personal tax and nontax payments have been subtracted from personal income, the amount left is called disposable personal income. (See page 132.)

7. Attempts to explain national income and product in terms of human welfare face difficulties because of such matters as "do-it-yourself" production, the underground economy, intermediate goods and services, cleaning up the environ-

ment, and producing goods for war. (See page 133.)

8. Even though there is disagreement about how the national income and product accounting system should record certain activities, the system still is very useful for understanding the economy and making predictions. This is because changes in national production may be reliably reported if the same accounting methods are used consistently throughout the period. (See page 136.)

KEY TERMS

barter: the direct exchange of one good or service for another (page 134).

capital consumption allowance: estimated replacement costs for buildings and equipment that wear out or become obsolete during the accounting period (page 130).

disposable personal income (DPI): the amount of personal income actually available to people for spending or saving (page 132).

gross national product (GNP): the total market value of all currently produced goods and services (page 129).

indirect business taxes and subsidies: an entry in the national product section that removes the tax and subsidy components of market prices (page 130).

intermediate product: something that is produced as an input to further production (page 134).

national income (NI): the total amount that is earned in producing the national product (page 131).

national income and product accounts: a set of reports on the volume and composition of economic activity in the United States over a specified time period; it consists of three major parts: the national product section, the national income section, and the personal income section (page 126).

net national product (NNP): GNP minus the capital consumption allowance (page 130).

personal income (PI): an amount calculated by adjusting national income by adding receipts not earned and subtracting earnings not received (page 132).

statistical discrepancy: an entry in the national product section that reports the extent to which the estimate of net national product differs from the estimate of national income (page 131).

transfer payments: money paid to people even though they did not provide a good or service to earn this money during the accounting period (page 129).

underground economy: unrecorded barter or cash transactions (page 134).

value added: the market value of a firm's final sales minus the amounts paid by the firm to purchase intermediate goods from other firms (page 128).

DISCUSSION QUESTIONS

1. Name the three major parts of the national income and product accounting system. Which two are related through a double-entry bookkeeping system? Explain the adjustments that must be made to assure that these two sections balance with each other.

2. Suppose that the values added in producing a pair of shoes are $14 by the cattle raiser, $7 by the processing plant and tannery, $12 by the shoe manufacturer, $2 by the truck lines, and $11 by the retailer. Assuming no intermediate goods were purchased by the cattle raiser, what would the shoes sell for as a final product? How much double-counting would arise if intermediate goods were not excluded in evaluating this product?

3. List the five major components in the national income section of the U.S. income and product accounts. In which entry would you record fringe benefits received by workers? Where would you put the rent payment for land owned by a corporation? Where would you record interest on the national debt?

4. Suppose that national income is $100 billion. Calculate the amount of personal income if Social Security taxes are $10 billion, undistributed corporate profits are $1 billion, Social Security benefit checks are $11 billion, corporation profits taxes are $2 billion, government transfer payments are $2 billion, and interest on government bonds and consumer credit is $1 billion. (Assume that these are all the entries that are needed in this section.)

5. A good way to summarize the national income and product accounting system is to list the "big five" data entries in the system and to explain how each differs from those closest to it. Try this exercise. Then note for each entry the particular use that economists make of it.

6. The national income and product accounting system uses estimates of the rental value of owner-occupied homes but does not use estimates of the wage value of do-it-yourself housekeeping services. Why are estimates used in the one case and not in the other? List three other types of do-it-yourself income that are not included in the national income and product statistics.

7. The chapter discusses how gasoline cannot be easily classified as either a final good or an intermediate good. Identify two other products that in some uses are intermediate products and in other uses are final products. How do you believe these items should be treated in the accounting system?

8. Many states have bottle-deposit laws that encourage people to return empty beer and soft-drink containers to the store to recover their deposit. The store must hire people to handle this transaction and to return the empties to the bottler. Should the wages of these workers be counted as part of national income? What difference, if any, do you see between producing a "good" and preventing a "bad"?

8

Inflation and Unemployment

Preview   In this chapter, we examine the two problems that are of greatest concern to macroeconomists—inflation and unemployment. The economists' concern with inflation is two-fold. First, inflation upsets social relationships and adds uncertainty to economic decision making. Second, since the price level is the independent variable in aggregate-demand and aggregate-supply analyses, inflation (an increase in the price level) plays a key role in explaining the causes of economic fluctuations. Economists are concerned about employment because of the personal hardship of unemployed persons and because of the lost production that results from it.

The first part of the chapter discusses inflation, explaining the economists' concept of inflation and the index numbers used to measure it. The choices made by all the actors on the economic stage are affected by inflation and by expectations of future inflation. Also, unanticipated inflation redistributes income and wealth in ways that many people believe to be unfair. The effects of inflation on economic, social, and political life are profound.

The second part of the chapter deals with unemployment. Economists have a well-defined concept of unemployment, but measuring the actual amount of unemployment in the economy is difficult. After examining the economists' concept of unemployment and the methods used for measuring the amount of unemployment, we note how unemployment affects different groups in the society. If allowed to go too far, either inflation or unemployment can disrupt an economy and a society.

INFLATION AND THE PRICE LEVEL

Inflation is a significant and sustained increase in the general price level. We start our study of inflation by learning about index numbers and how they are used to compare different prices. Then we examine two methods of applying the index-number technique to the average of all prices in the economy. These will give us actual measurements of the changes in the general price level that occur with inflation and deflation. We will look at the record of price-level changes in the United States. Finally, we will consider some of the economic and social consequences of inflation.

Inflation is a significant and sustained increase in the general price level.

Price-Index Numbers

Statisticians, economists, and others use index numbers as a method of comparing one value with another. We can define an **index number** as a way of stating a value by expressing it in terms of some other reference, or "base" value. For example, if the number 25 were the base value, the number 20 would have an index-number value of 0.80, because 20/25 equals 0.80.

An index number is a way of stating a value by expressing it in terms of some other reference value. Price-index numbers provide a standardized system for measuring price-level changes.

Since an index number expresses values in terms of some reference point, the first step is to select this reference point. To apply the index-number method to prices, the prices that prevailed in some specified year are chosen as the base, or reference point, for constructing the index. Then the prices prevailing in other years are expressed in relation to these base-year prices. For example, if the price of apples increases from 50 cents a pound in year 1 to 60 cents a pound in year 2 and then to $1.00 a pound in year 3, and if we select year 1 as the base, we can construct price-index numbers for apples by dividing each year's apple price by the base-year apple price, as follows.

Year	Apple Price ($)	Base-Period Apple Price ($)	Index Number
1	0.50	0.50	1.00
2	0.60	0.50	1.20
3	1.00	0.50	2.00

As you can see, the index numbers provide a standardized system for measuring the change that has taken place in apple prices. In our illustration, in year 2, the price of apples was 20 percent above the base-period price, as shown by the 1.20 value of the index number. In year 3, the apple price was twice what it was in the base period, and the index number was 2.0.

Price-index numbers are useful because they provide a way to adjust for changes in prices. In order to find the base-year equivalent of any price in the series, all we have to do is divide by its index number. For example, the price of a pound of apples in year 2 was 60 cents. If we divide 60 by 1.2 (the index number for year 2), the answer is 50. So 60 cents worth of apples in year 2 is equivalent to 50 cents worth of apples in year 1, assuming that apple quality is the same in both years. In year 3, the price of a pound of apples is $1.00. If we divide $1.00 by 2.0 (the index number for year 3), the answer is $0.50. So one dollar's worth of apples in year 3 is equivalent to $0.50 worth of apples in year 1, again assuming the quality of apples has not changed. Price-index numbers also can be used to compare any pair of prices in the series. This is done by dividing one index number by the other. For example, by dividing the index number for year 3 (2.00) by the index number for year 2 (1.20), we obtain a value of 1.67, which indicates that the price of a pound of apples had risen by 67 percent between the two years. In this way, index numbers can be used to measure price changes.

TABLE 1
Computing a Consumer Price Index

Item	Market-Basket Quantity	Base-Year Price	Base-Year Cost	Current-Year Price	Current-Year Cost
Hamburger	100 lbs.	$0.80	$ 80.00	$1.80	$ 180.00
Gasoline	500 gals.	0.40	200.00	1.60	800.00
Movies	40 shows	3.00	120.00	3.50	140.00
Total			$400.00		$1,120.00

$$\text{consumer price index} = \frac{\text{current-year cost}}{\text{base-year cost}} \times 100 = \frac{\$1,120}{\$400} \times 100 = 280$$

The index number is based on the cost of a specified collection of goods and services in the base year. The cost of purchasing this "market basket" of goods is calculated both in base-year prices and in current-year prices. The index number is the ratio of current-year cost to base-year cost, multiplied by 100.

Sometimes it is desirable to change the base period in a series of index numbers. To accomplish this, all we have to do is divide each index number in the series by the index number for the year we want to establish as the base period. With year 3 as the base period, the index number for year 1 becomes 0.50 (1.00/2.00) and the index number for year 2 becomes 0.60 (1.20/2.00). It often is convenient to adjust the base period of a series of index numbers to the most recent time possible, since it is easier for most people to relate to recent prices.

It is common practice to move the decimal point two places to the right in published price-index numbers so that the index number for the base period is 100. Thus, our basic formula for a price-index number becomes

$$\frac{\text{current price}}{\text{base-period price}} \times 100 = \text{index number}$$

With this system, the published index number for year 3 in our illustration would be calculated as

$$\frac{1.00}{0.50} \times 100 = 200$$

Now that you know what a price-index number is and how it can be used, we proceed to the next step, which is computing a measure of the general price level—an average of all the prices in the economy. Two different systems are widely used to compute these averages. One is used with the gross national product (GNP), and the other is used in estimating the cost of living with the consumer price index.

The Consumer Price Index

The **consumer price index (CPI)**, often called the "cost-of-living index," is an index number used to measure changes in the cost of purchasing a specific group, or "market basket," of consumer goods and services. This collection of consumer goods and services is determined from studying actual purchases by families chosen because they represent important types of spending units in the economy.

Table 1 shows how to calculate a consumer price-index number. We assume that the selected market basket consists of 100 pounds of hamburger, 500 gallons of gasoline, and 40 movie tickets a year. In the prices of the base year, this market basket of goods and services cost $400.00. In the current year, the prices of these goods and services are higher, and the cost of purchasing the market basket is $1,120.00. To calculate the index number, divide the current-year cost of the market basket by its base-year cost and multiply the result by 100, as follows: ($1,120/$400) × 100 = 280. In this case, the index number is 280, meaning that the cost of the market basket in the current year is 2.8 times its cost in the base year. Thus, the "cost of living" increased by 180 percent.

Table 2 shows the consumer price index for the United States for the years 1960 to 1988. The base period for these data is the average of prices for the three years 1982, 1983, and 1984. By dividing the index number for 1988 (118.3) by the index number for 1960 (29.6), we find that the "cost of living" measured by this method had increased by 300 percent. In other words, by this measure, the price level was four times higher in 1988 than in 1960. The table also shows the **purchasing power of the dollar**, which is the reciprocal of the consumer price-index number, that is, it is 1 divided by the index number. Compared to the base period of 1982 to 1984 the dollar's purchasing power had fallen to 85.0 cents by 1988. By dividing the index number for 1960 (29.6) by the index number for 1988 (118.3), we find that the dollar's purchasing power had fallen from $1.00 in 1960 to 25.0 cents in 1988.

The consumer price index (CPI), also called the cost-of-living index, is an index number used to measure changes in the cost of purchasing a specific group of consumer goods and services. It is calculated by dividing the current-year cost of the goods and services by the base-year cost and multiplying the result by 100.

The purchasing power of the dollar is the value of goods and services that can be bought with a dollar compared with the value of goods and services that could have been bought with a dollar in a selected reference (base) period. It can be computed as the reciprocal of the consumer price-index number.

The consumer price index is the most widely publicized price-index number in the United States. It often is used in **cost-of-living adjustment (COLA)** clauses in contracts between labor and management. When agreed to in a contract, a COLA clause specifically connects changes in wage rates to changes in the consumer price index. For example, a COLA clause may state that the wage rate will be increased by a specified amount an hour as a result of some specified increase in the CPI. COLA clauses offer a way to build future price-level changes into a contract.

A cost-of-living adjustment (COLA) clause in a contract connects changes in wage rates to changes in the CPI.

The Weighting Bias of the CPI   As a measure of the cost of living, the consumer price index suffers from several biases. One of the most serious of these involves the weighting system used to establish the relative importance of the different goods and services in the market basket. In computing the CPI, the relative importance, or "weight," of each good or service in the market basket is set according to the quantity purchased by representative households in some past year. The **weighting bias of the CPI** arises because this system fails to recognize that consumer buying patterns—and therefore the relative importance of the different goods and services in the market basket—their "weights"—tend to change when the price level changes. For example, consider the index number calculated in Table 1. The price of gasoline increased very substantially relative to the prices of the other goods and services. In the base year, a gallon of gasoline cost half as much as a pound of hamburger and less than one-seventh as much as a movie ticket. But in the "current" year, a gallon of gasoline cost almost as much as a whole pound of hamburger and was almost half the cost of a movie ticket. The CPI implies that people buy the same quantities of gasoline, hamburger, and movie tickets after the change in relative prices as they did before. Actually, when gasoline becomes more expensive in relation to other goods and services, it is likely that some consumers will switch some of their buying from gasoline to other things. People will go to the movies instead of driving to the Rockies. The CPI does not recognize these switches. Since consumers do change their buying habits to escape the higher prices, the CPI tends to overstate the rise in the cost of living. We may say that the CPI shows the change in the cost of the base-year "way of living" but that most families probably don't live that way any more.

TABLE 2
The Consumer Price Index and the Purchasing Power of the Consumer Dollar (1982–1984 = 100)

Year	Consumer Price Index	Purchasing Power of the Dollar	Year	Consumer Price Index	Purchasing Power of the Dollar
1960	29.6	3.38	1975	53.8	1.86
1961	29.9	3.34	1976	56.9	1.76
1962	30.2	3.31	1977	60.6	1.65
1963	30.6	3.27	1978	65.2	1.53
1964	31.0	3.23	1979	72.6	1.38
1965	31.5	3.17	1980	82.4	1.21
1966	32.4	3.09	1981	90.9	1.10
1967	33.4	2.99	1982	96.5	1.04
1968	34.8	2.87	1983	99.6	1.01
1969	36.7	2.72	1984	103.9	0.96
1970	38.8	2.57	1985	107.6	0.93
1971	40.5	2.47	1986	109.6	0.91
1972	41.8	2.39	1987	113.6	0.88
1973	44.4	2.25	1988[a]	118.3	0.85
1974	49.3	2.03			

The consumer price index shows the cost of purchasing a "market basket" of goods, which represents actual purchases by families. The base year for this series is 1982–1984. The purchasing power of the consumer dollar is computed as the reciprocal of the CPI—that is, 1/CPI.

[a] Estimated.

Source: Economic Report of the President, 1989, Table B-58, p. 373.

One weakness of the CPI as a measure of changes in the cost of living is its weighting bias: this system fails to recognize that consumer buying patterns tend to change when the price level changes.

The Quality Bias of the CPI   The consumer price index implies that the quality of goods and services stays the same over the years. However, this is surely not the case. In fact, there is a **quality bias**. Because new products are invented and improvements are made in existing products, the goods produced in the current year are generally of higher quality, per dollar of constant value, than were their counterparts in the base year. If quality is generally improving, the "cost of living" has not risen as much as the CPI implies. People are living "better" because products have improved.

Students sometimes find it hard to believe that quality is generally improving, when we all know of cases where it seems to be getting worse. Ask yourself, however, what would happen if someone invented a new type of television set that was inferior in picture quality to those already on the market. Would anyone buy it? That would depend on its relative price. If its price were equal to (or higher than) the price of the earlier model, the new set would not survive in a competitive market. The market would "weed out" such products and would assure that product quality, adjusted for price changes, would not go down. To test whether quality has actually gone up, you might think about exchanging today's television set for the equivalent model of several years ago, assuming, of course, that the old-style set was new and unused. If the exchange were even, with no money changing hands, would you be willing to make the exchange? If your answer is "no," then quality has gone up.

The hypothetical exchange of today's product for the product of past times illustrates an inescapable problem in comparing quality over time. Often it is not possible to find a truly equivalent product. For example, videocassette recorders (VCRs) were not on the market twenty years ago but are popular products today. Also, one kind of quality sometimes is exchanged for another kind of quality. Automobiles today offer poorer "performance" (that is, acceleration) than those of twenty years ago, but they also create less air pollution. It is still technically possible to produce the old-style cars. The fact that we choose (in this case through various government regulations) not to produce them is some indication that we prefer the new type of quality to the old type of quality in automobiles. In this sense, quality is higher and the cost of living has not increased as much as implied by the consumer price index. The CPI has overstated the increase in the cost of living.

Another weakness of the CPI is its quality bias: it assumes that the quality of goods and services stays the same, whereas in reality, the quality of goods and services generally improves over time.

Biases That Understate Inflation   In some cases, the CPI fails to reveal the full impact of price increases on the actual cost of living. For example, if official price controls are in effect, along with their predictable shortages, consumers may buy products at higher (illegal) prices in **black markets**— markets that operate outside the law and sell at illegal prices. In this case, the CPI reported at official prices understates the actual cost of living. Moreover, the quality of goods and services may decline in these circumstances.

The CPI also may fail to reflect accurately changes in the cost of living for specific groups in the population when there are large changes in relative prices of important goods or services. For example, during the 1970s and early 1980s, the prices of certain necessities—food, housing, medical care, and fuel—increased more than did the CPI as a whole. Large families and low-income families, including retirees, tend to spend much of their incomes on these goods and services. For them, the official consumer price index understated the actual increase in the cost of living.[1]

1. For further information on how inflation affects different groups in the society, see Robert T. Michael, "Variations Across Households in the Rate of Inflation," *Journal of Money, Credit and Banking* (February 1979): 32–46.

The CPI may also fail to reveal the full impact of price increases on the actual cost of living or may fail to reflect changes in the cost of living for specific groups in the population.

The GNP Implicit Price Deflator

As you learned in Chapter 7, the **gross national product** is a measure of the value of a year's total production in the economy. In estimating GNP for the United States, the U.S. Department of Commerce evaluates production at the prices that actually prevail during the year in question. The result is gross national product measured in **current dollars** or **nominal values**. But the use of current dollars or nominal values leads to a problem in comparing one year's GNP with another year's GNP when the price level changes. What part of the change in nominal or current-dollar GNP is due to changes in production and what part is due to the change in the price level? When the current-dollar GNP has been adjusted to remove the influence of price level changes it is called the **constant-dollar GNP** or the GNP in **real values**. Separating these components is the job of a special type of index number, called the **GNP implicit price deflator**.

Table 3 illustrates how the GNP implicit price deflator is determined. In this very simple illustration, we assume that the entire GNP consists of the stated quantities of apples, oranges, and bananas, valued at the prices indicated for the current year. As you can see, the nominal, or current-dollar, value of the GNP is $250.00. But when these quantities are valued in the prices that prevailed in the year chosen as the base year, the GNP is only $167.50. With this information, we can calculate an index number to compare the average of prices in these two years. We simply apply the basic index-number formula to these two GNP values as follows:

$$\frac{\text{current-year value GNP}}{\text{base-year value GNP}} \times 100 = \text{index number}$$

which is equal to

$$\frac{\$250.00}{\$167.50} \times 100 = 149.25$$

TABLE 3
Computing a Price Deflator

Item	Current-Year Quantity	Current-Year Price	Current-Year Value	Base-Year Price	Base-Year Equivalent Value
Apples	100 lbs.	$1.00	$100.00	$0.60	$ 60.00
Oranges	75	1.50	112.50	0.90	67.50
Bananas	50	0.75	37.50	0.80	40.00
GNP			$250.00		$167.50

$$\text{implicit GNP deflator} = \frac{\text{current-year-value GNP}}{\text{base-year-equivalent-value GNP}} \times 100$$

$$= \frac{\$250.00}{\$167.50} \times 100 = 149.25$$

Values for goods in the current year are compared with the amounts that would have been needed to purchase the same goods at the base-year prices. The deflator index number is equal to 100 times current-year GNP divided by base-year equivalent GNP.

By dividing the current, or nominal value, GNP by the implicit GNP deflator, we find the amount of money that would have been needed to purchase the same goods and services at the prices that prevailed in the base year. Table 4 shows the results of applying this deflation procedure to the U.S. GNP from 1960 through 1988. In this table, 1982 is the base year (that is, the 1982 prices are the common denominator). So current-dollar GNP for 1982 is exactly the same as the constant-dollar (1982) GNP, and the implicit price deflator for 1982 is 100.0. The current-dollar columns show nominal values and the constant-dollar (1982) columns show real values, that is, values adjusted for changes in the price level. Note how much the real economic growth rates (measured as the percentage change in GNP from the preceding year) differ from the growth rates measured in nominal values. In real terms, economic growth was negative in five years (1970, 1974, 1975, 1980, and 1982) and reached a high point of 6.8 percent in 1984.

Special-Purpose Index Numbers

Index numbers can be used for many purposes other than measuring changes in the cost of living or in real GNP. Dozens of special-purpose index

numbers are published monthly in the *Survey of Current Business*.[2] Indexes of producer prices for farm products, chemicals, fuels, and so forth, are computed regularly. These are widely used to predict future changes in consumer prices, since price changes at the producer's level will probably be passed on soon to the consumer. Price-index numbers and deflators also are regularly published for many specific producer goods, such as agricultural chemicals, lumber, iron, and steel. These data are useful in anticipating changes in relative prices for food, housing, automobiles, and so forth. Still another special-purpose index number is maintained for purchases by governments. This index can be used to translate government budget figures from nominal to real values in order to compare real budget amounts for different time periods. Over the past decade, the prices for goods and services purchased by governments have risen more rapidly than the general price level.

Index numbers and deflators must be used carefully. The prices of goods that some consumers

2. Price indexes and deflators for many components of national income and product and for many different industrial inputs and outputs are published regularly in the *Survey of Current Business*. Cost-of-living index numbers for different cities and countries are published every year in almanacs and in *The Statistical Abstract of the United States*.

TABLE 4
U.S. GNP in Current and Constant (1982) Dollars, 1960–1988

	Current Dollars		Constant (1982) Dollars		
Year	GNP ($ Billions)	% Change	Implicit GNP Deflator	GNP ($ Billions)	% Change
1960	515.3	3.9	30.9	1,665.3	2.2
1961	533.8	3.6	31.2	1,708.7	2.6
1962	574.6	7.6	31.9	1,799.4	5.3
1963	606.9	5.6	32.4	1,873.3	4.1
1964	649.8	7.1	32.9	1,973.3	5.3
1965	705.1	8.5	33.8	2,087.6	5.8
1966	772.0	9.5	35.0	2,208.3	5.8
1967	816.4	5.8	35.9	2,271.4	2.9
1968	892.7	9.3	37.7	2,365.6	4.1
1969	963.9	8.0	39.8	2,423.3	2.4
1970	1,015.5	5.4	42.0	2,416.2	−.3
1971	1,102.7	8.6	44.4	2,484.8	2.8
1972	1,212.8	10.0	46.5	2,608.5	5.0
1973	1,359.3	12.1	49.5	2,744.1	5.2
1974	1,472.8	8.3	54.0	2,729.3	−.5
1975	1,598.4	8.5	59.3	2,695.0	−1.3
1976	1,782.8	11.5	63.1	2,826.7	4.9
1977	1,990.5	11.7	67.3	2,958.6	4.7
1978	2,249.7	13.0	72.2	3,115.2	5.3
1979	2,508.2	11.5	78.6	3,192.4	2.5
1980	2,732.0	8.9	85.7	3,187.1	−.2
1981	3,052.6	11.7	94.0	3,248.8	1.9
1982	3,166.0	3.7	100.0	3,166.0	−2.5
1983	3,405.7	7.6	103.9	3,279.1	3.6
1984	3,772.2	10.8	107.7	3,501.4	6.8
1985	4,014.9	6.4	110.9	3,618.7	3.4
1986	4,240.3	5.6	113.9	3,721.7	2.8
1987	4,526.7	6.8	117.7	3,847.0	3.4
1988[a]	4,866.4	7.5	121.7	3,997.3	3.9

Current values have been adjusted to their equivalent in prices that prevailed in 1982. Growth rates are shown as the percentage change from the preceding year.

[a] Estimated.

Source: Economic Report of the President, 1989, Tables B-1, B-2, and B-3.

buy may not change in the same way as prices for goods that other consumers buy. There are at least two reasons for this difference. First, prices themselves are not the same at all locations. For example, prices may be higher in urban areas than in rural areas. Second, different people (old and young, rich and poor) buy different goods and so face different situations when prices change. There-fore, those who use price indexes should be sure that both the price data and their choice of goods are suited to the way in which they are using the index.

Price-index numbers and deflators are useful but they must be used carefully, since the prices

---

of goods that some consumers buy may not change in the same way as prices for goods that other consumers buy.

Inflation in the United States

Figure 1 shows recent U.S. price-level history. Panel (a) shows the GNP implicit price deflator for 1960 through 1988, plotted from the values in Table 4. As you can see, the price level, as measured by the GNP deflator, rose gradually during the 1960s, climbed rapidly during the 1970s, and resumed a more gradual rate of increase during the 1980s.

Panel (b) in Figure 1 plots the percentage change in the GNP implicit price deflator from one year to the next, calculated by dividing the GNP deflator value for each year by the GNP deflator value for the previous year, subtracting 1.0, and multiplying the result by 100. The resulting figure is the annual **inflation rate**. For example, the GNP deflator (1982 = 100) was 121.7 for 1988 and 117.7 for 1987, which means that the price level in the United States increased by 3.4 percent during 1988 (121.7/117.7 = 1.034). The rate of inflation was 3.4 percent.

Panel (b) in Figure 1 provides a picture of inflation in the United States over those years. In the first half of the 1960s, the inflation rate hovered around 1½ percent a year. This was called inflation at the time, since it was a sustained increase in the general price level, but might not now be called inflation as compared with other periods. Price-level increases in this modest range can quite possibly be offset against normal increases in the quality of the goods and services that make up the GNP.

Inflation clearly existed after 1965. If we accept the early 1960s as a benchmark, or point of reference, the years after 1965 brought the longest period of sustained significant price-level increases in the nation's history. The rate of increase in the price level remained above the benchmark throughout the entire period, and the 1988 price level was 3.6 times the 1965 price level (121.7/33.8 = 3.6). Prices had more than tripled. For comparison, the inflationary period in the United States

from 1940 through 1948, during and after World War II, lasted for nine years, and the price level did not even double (52.98/29.06 = 1.82).

The annual inflation rate is calculated by dividing the GNP deflator value for each year by the GNP deflator value for the previous year, subtracting 1.0, and multiplying by 100.

Figure 1(b) also shows that the rate of inflation decreased greatly after 1981. Economists use the term **disinflation** to refer to a falling inflation rate. During periods of disinflation, the price level is still rising and inflation is taking place, but the rate of increase in the price level is becoming less and less.

Disinflation means that the inflation rate is falling—the rate of increase in the price level is becoming less and less.

Economic Consequences of Inflation

As you learned in Chapter 6, changes in the general price level—inflation, disinflation, and deflation—play a key role in aggregate-demand and aggregate-supply analyses. Changes in the price level are expected to cause changes in the aggregate quantity demanded and in the aggregate quantity supplied. This is why an index number representing the price level (usually the GNP implicit price deflator) is used on the vertical axes of aggregate-demand and aggregate-supply graphs. Therefore, your understanding of price index numbers is a useful preparation for your study of modern macroeconomic theories in later chapters.

It is important to understand, however, that there is nothing sacred about any particular price level. The price level in 1990 is no better or worse than the price level in 1980 or 1970. An economy can function satisfactorily at any price level. Even changes in the price level can take place without seriously upsetting economic systems, if these changes are small and reasonably predictable. But fairly substantial and unanticipated inflation can cause serious problems. The consequences of infla-

FIGURE 1
General Price-Level Changes in the United States, 1960 through 1988

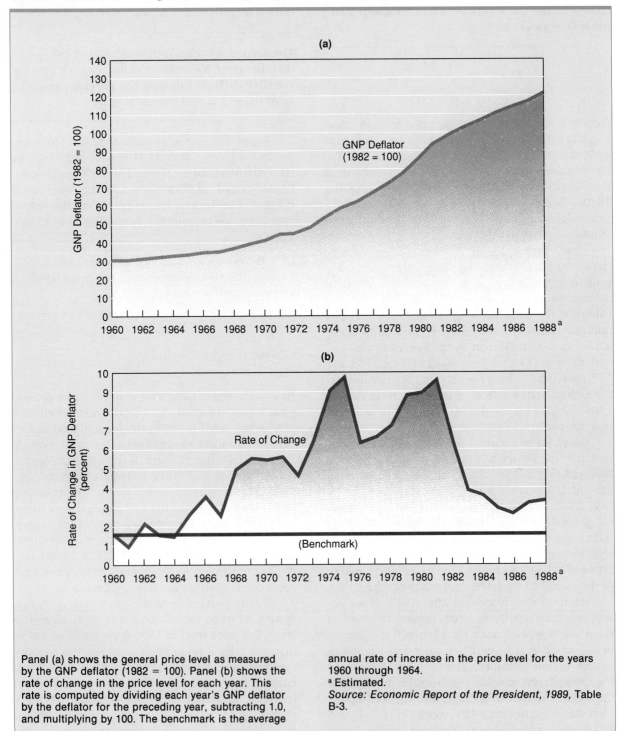

Panel (a) shows the general price level as measured by the GNP deflator (1982 = 100). Panel (b) shows the rate of change in the price level for each year. This rate is computed by dividing each year's GNP deflator by the deflator for the preceding year, subtracting 1.0, and multiplying by 100. The benchmark is the average annual rate of increase in the price level for the years 1960 through 1964.

[a] Estimated.

Source: Economic Report of the President, 1989, Table B-3.

tion differ importantly depending on how well people have been able to forecast or anticipate the change in the price level.

Imperfectly Anticipated Inflation The most serious consequences of inflation arise because a price-level-change factor must be included in the day-to-day decisions that guide the operation of the economy. Labor must predict the price-level change when it bargains for wages. Firms must predict price-level changes when they plan new investments and estimate depreciation allowances. Individuals must consider price-level changes when deciding about consumption spending and saving. To estimate the costs of services, governments must take account of price-level changes. If price-level changes are not correctly anticipated, it will lead to mistakes concerning all of these important decisions. Of course, mistakes are made even when the price level does not change, but more mistakes are likely to be made in periods of unanticipated inflation. Unanticipated inflation can change aggregate quantities demanded and supplied and distort the operation of the macroeconomy.

American farmers are painfully aware of the hardships that arise from failure to correctly forecast the rate of inflation. During the 1970s, many farmers borrowed large sums to expand production. Because the rate of inflation was high and was expected to continue at a high rate, lenders insisted on relatively high interest rates on loans. Farmers also expected rapid inflation to continue, so they agreed to these relatively high rates and pledged their farmlands as security for the loans. There seemed little cause for concern, since the price of farmland was rising even more rapidly than the general price level. Hardship came because farmers failed to correctly foresee the great disinflation of the early 1980s. The inflation rate fell to approximately half its earlier rate. As a result, interest rates and the prices of farmland went down, and the prices of farm crops were not as high as expected. Many farmers could not earn enough to meet the interest payments required on their loans. Because of the unexpected low prices for farmland, many farmers lost their farms when lenders foreclosed on mortgages. Had the disinflation been accurately forecast, farmers would have been more cautious about borrowing, interest rates would have been lower, and there would have been fewer farms lost as a result of mortgage foreclosures.

Imperfectly anticipated inflation also can cause changes in the distribution of wealth among groups in a society. Imperfectly anticipated changes in the price level redistribute wealth by changing the real purchasing power of the monetary unit—the dollar in the United States, the yen in Japan, the mark in Germany. Wealth that is held in cash, savings accounts, bonds, insurance policies, and other forms of "paper wealth" specified in dollar amounts, drops in *real* value when the price level rises and rises in *real* value when the price level falls. If their holders did not expect the inflation and insist on adjustments such as a lower purchase price or a higher interest rate, they will be victims of inflation. Their wealth will be redistributed to those who transferred the cash or who sold the paper wealth to them or who made better decisions about inflation. The winners from inflation may have been wiser and anticipated that inflation was coming. Perhaps they borrowed money to purchase land, "collectibles" such as art, stamps or coins, precious metals such as gold or silver, or precious gems such as diamonds or emeralds—all goods whose nominal values would increase along with the inflation. As often as not, however, their gains may have been "just luck."

Luck may be randomly distributed, but this cannot be said for knowledge or for the possession of the kinds of wealth that are most vulnerable to inflation. Inflation tends to be especially damaging to those people in a society who have a large portion of their wealth in savings accounts and insurance policies, which are most vulnerable to inflation. Unexpected inflation drains wealth from this group. Since these people generally have a moderating and stabilizing effect on the social and political system, their loss of wealth can lead to radical shifts in political positions, either to the left or to the right. After World War I, groups hurt by inflation showed a greater tendency to move to the right than to the left.

Even though redistribution of wealth due to past inflation is "water over the dam," it may leave its mark on the society's future.

Perfectly Anticipated Inflation The problems of wealth redistribution and decision errors would not arise if everyone in the economy made accurate forecasts of the future price level, that is, if inflation were perfectly anticipated. It is, of course, virtually impossible that price-level changes could be perfectly anticipated by all economic decision makers, but it is equally true that inflation is seldom entirely unexpected. It is not likely to come as a complete surprise to everyone in the economy. Since the real world includes some accurate inflation forecasting and since experience with inflation may lead to still better forecasts, it is useful to ask whether price-level changes would cause any difficulty if they were perfectly anticipated.

Even if it were perfectly anticipated, inflation would cause some problems. For example, firms would have to update price lists frequently or else work out ways to communicate prices without using published price lists. These are called **menu costs** of inflation, because the costs are illustrated by restaurants having the expense of printing new menus oftener than in noninflationary times. Another drain on resources would arise because people would have to go to the trouble of transferring assets from one form to another whenever they anticipated a change in the inflation rate. For example, real estate may be a good wealth form when prices are rising, while bonds may be better when prices are falling or when the rate of inflation is decreasing, that is, in times of disinflation. The costs of switching ownership rights back and forth are called **shoe-leather costs** of inflation. Finally, even if perfectly anticipated, inflation imposes losses on firms and individuals who must use currency in their day-to-day activities. This is because the purchasing power of a unit of currency (one dollar, for example) goes down when the price level goes up. So economic activities that must use currency, such as fast-food restaurants and vending machine operations, would be hurt by inflation because the currency they must hold loses value while in their possession. Making currency less useful and desirable reduces the efficiency of the economy.

The menu costs of inflation are those costs entailed by frequent updating of price lists.

Shoe-leather costs of inflation are those costs incurred when assets are transferred from one form to another.

Political Consequences of Inflation

History offers many examples of political changes both from sustained periods of rising prices (inflations) and from sustained periods of falling prices (deflations). In Europe, price levels rose in the 1500s and 1600s after the Spanish discovered the gold and silver mines of Mexico and South America and began taking their riches back home. Feudal lords who had converted the obligations of their serfs from services to fixed money rents grew poorer as prices rose. For support they turned to the rising group of national monarchs who could collect money from growing trade and business activities. These events hastened the decline of feudalism and the rise of nation-states in Europe.

In the United States, price levels dropped greatly from the end of the Civil War until the close of the 1800s. Farmers and small business people who depended on debt financing were hurt as prices fell and they had to repay loans in money of a higher value than the money they had borrowed. The resulting political agitation led to reform movements that had lasting effects on government in the United States.[3] Resentment against big business and banking, believed to be gainers from the falling price level, was widespread around the turn of the century and still colors political and economic thought in the United States.

In Germany after World-War I, inflation wiped out the savings of many middle-income people. The resulting frustrations provided a fertile seedbed for the rise of Hitler's National Socialist (actually fascist) party. The following is quoted from the reminiscences of a German woman about her experiences in 1923:

> ". . . workers had discovered the 'trick of inflation,' which was to figure the value of money in gold. Time and again the workers struck for the

---

3. Douglass C. North, *Structure and Change in Economic History* (New York: W. W. Norton & Co., 1982).

'adjustment of their wages.' After their strikes, their wages had been adjusted—to the actual price increases. But the price increases went on and so the workers had to strike again for new adjustments. What they asked for now was wages paid daily.

"While this struggle went on, chaos increased. The Middle Ages came back. Communities printed their own money, based on goods, on a certain amount of potatoes, of rye, for instance. Shoe factories paid their workers in bonds for shoes which they could exchange at the bakery for bread or the meat market for meat.

"At this stage, the Communists believed that their time had come. They attempted an uprising. . . ."[4]

In the United States, the inflation of the 1970s played a prominent role in political affairs. Taxpayer revolts flared because citizens blamed the government for the inflation and because both property-tax and income-tax bills were pushed upward by inflation. Popular reaction against inflation contributed to the defeat of President Ford in 1976 and to the defeat of his successor, President Carter, in 1980.

EMPLOYMENT

Along with inflation, employment and unemployment are major concerns in macroeconomics. Both employment and unemployment are closely related to the standard of living and to the volume of real GNP in the economy. Therefore, policy makers and macroeconomists pay close attention to changes in employment and unemployment and have developed detailed theories about the causes of these changes. Real GNP—the total output of the economy adjusted for price-level changes—varies directly with the level of employment and inversely with the level of unemployment. Therefore, understanding changes in employment and unemployment help economists understand changes in the level of real GNP.

The horizontal axis on the aggregate-demand and aggregate-supply graph shows real GNP.

4. Pearl S. Buck, *How It Happens,* as cited in Fritz K. Ringer (ed.), *The German Inflation of 1923* (New York: Oxford University Press, 1969), pp. 144–145.

Movements to the right along that axis indicate increases in production, and movements to the left indicate decreases in production. Such changes in the volume of production come from changes in quantities of resources (labor, natural resources, and capital) used in production and from changes in technology—the application of science to the production process. If we assume that technology is fixed (a not-too-unreasonable assumption for short intervals of time), we can say that movements to the right along the horizontal axis of an aggregate-demand and aggregate-supply graph correspond with increases in the quantities of resources employed and that movements to the left correspond with decreases in the quantity of resources employed.

Macroeconomists are concerned about the employment of all resources, but they are particularly interested in the labor resource because it receives such a large portion (about three-fourths) of total income and because it affects human beings so directly. Therefore, in economics, the term **employment** usually is used in reference to the labor resource and is defined as "labor engaged in regular work for pay." Movements to the right on the horizontal axis of the aggregate-demand and aggregate-supply graph reflect increasing employment of labor, and movements to the left reflect decreasing labor employment. As you can imagine, measuring the precise connection between changes in real GNP and changes in the number of workers employed is an important focus of research by statisticians and economists.

In economics, the term *employment* means "labor engaged in regular work for pay."

The Civilian Employment Rate

The **civilian employment rate** is the percentage of the civilian noninstitutional population, age 16 and over, that is regularly working for pay. To estimate this rate, the Bureau of Labor Statistics of the United States Department of Labor conducts surveys of representative samples of the U.S. population, excluding those in active military service and in institutions such as mental hospitals and prisons. One of the questions on the survey asks whether the individual is currently working for pay or has been employed during the past month. Part-time work on a regular basis is counted—a person who works regularly as little as one hour a week for pay is classified as employed. Using this method, the Department of Labor reported that there were 115,976,000 people employed in the United States in November 1988. To compute the civilian employment rate, this figure is divided by the total U.S. civilian noninstitutional population, age 16 and over, which, on that date, was 185,244,000. Thus, the civilian employment rate for November 1988 was 62.6 percent.

Figure 2 shows the civilian employment rate for the United States from 1970 to 1988. Low points were reported for 1971, 1975, and 1982. High points for the civilian employment rate were reported for 1973 and 1974, 1979, and 1988.

The civilian employment rate is the percentage of the civilian noninstitutional population, age 16 and over, that is regularly working for pay.

The Civilian Labor Force Participation Rate

Figure 2 shows not only fluctuations in the employment rate but also a general upward trend. Successive high points and low points tend to be somewhat higher than their predecessors, and a line fitted to represent the long-term trend of the employment rate would slope upward from left to right. Why might this happen? Is an increasingly larger percentage of the civilian noninstitutional population interested in regular employment for pay?

It is true that a larger percentage of the civilian noninstitutional population is either working or actively looking for work now than in 1970. This fact is illustrated in Figure 4 (on page 24 in Chapter 2), which displays the **civilian labor force participation rate**—the percent of the civilian noninstitutional population that is sixteen years of age or older and either working or actively looking for work. The latter conditions—sixteen years of age or older and either working or looking for work—are the official requirements for a person to be

counted in the **civilian labor force**. Therefore, the civilian labor force participation rate is equal to the number of people in the civilian labor force divided by the number in the civilian noninstitutional population, age 16 and over. In November 1988, there were 122,572,000 persons in the civilian labor force in the United States and 185,244,000 persons in the comparable civilian noninstitutional population. Therefore, the civilian labor force participation rate was 66.2 percent.

Between 1960 and 1988 the civilian labor force participation rate increased partly because a much larger percentage of the female population held paying jobs or was looking for paid employment. Another reason was that, as a result of the "baby boom" of the 1950s, an especially large portion of the population was between ages sixteen and sixty-five. Many economists believe that the U.S. economy did well in providing jobs for this large increase in the civilian labor force, especially in view of the problems often encountered by people entering the labor force for the first time.

The civilian labor force consists of those members of the civilian noninstitutional population who are sixteen years of age or older who are either working or looking for work. The civilian labor force participation rate is the percentage of the noninstitutional civilian population, sixteen years of age or older, that is either working or looking for work.

UNEMPLOYMENT

To understand economic theories about unemployment, it is important to distinguish between the economic concept of unemployment and the definition of unemployment used in official statistics. We shall examine the economic concept first and then look at the statistical definition.

The Economic Concept of Unemployment

The economic concept of **unemployment** is that a person is spending more time for leisure and less

FIGURE 2
Civilian Employment Rate, United States, 1970–1988

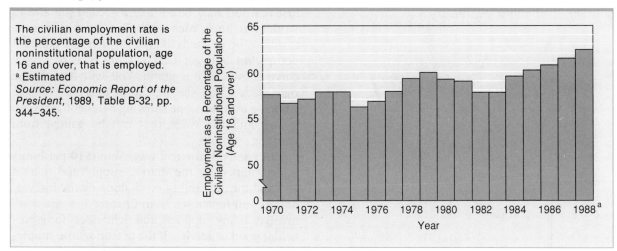

The civilian employment rate is the percentage of the civilian noninstitutional population, age 16 and over, that is employed.
[a] Estimated
Source: Economic Report of the President, 1989, Table B-32, pp. 344–345.

time for wage earning than he or she desires at the going wage rate for his or her occupation. To understand this concept of unemployment, we use the demand and supply concepts you learned in Chapter 5 and examine the supply of labor from the point of view of an individual worker. Then we broaden this concept and look at labor demand and supply for the entire economy.

In economics, the term *unemployment* means that a person is spending more time for leisure and less time for wage earning than he or she desires at the going wage rate for his or her occupation.

An Individual's Supply-of-Labor Curve Figure 3 shows an individual's supply-of-labor curve. On the vertical axis are different possible wage rates, which we specify to be **real wage rates**—that is, wage rates adjusted for expected price-level changes so that they represent the goods and services the individual expects to be able to purchase with the earnings. We use real wage rates because we believe workers and employers use the real wage rate, or what they believe is the real wage rate, in making work decisions.

Real wage rates are wage rates adjusted for expected price-level changes so that they

represent the goods and services the individual expects to be able to purchase.

The horizontal axis shows quantities of work the individual will supply. The curve on the graph shows the number of hours of work per week that the individual is willing and able to supply at various possible real wage rates. To understand this curve, remember that when a person is working, he or she is exchanging leisure-time activities for wage income. The supply-of-labor curve shows his or her willingness to make this exchange. The curve slopes upward, suggesting that a person is willing to give up more leisure activity when real wage rates are high than when they are low, *ceteris paribus.*

A useful way to view an individual's supply-of-labor curve is to think of the wage rate as the opportunity cost of leisure-time activities. In other words, when a person takes time off to enjoy leisure activities, he or she is giving up the wage income that otherwise would have been earned during that time. At low wage rates, leisure activities are inexpensive and people use more of their time for them. But at higher wage rates, the trade-off is more favorable for wage income and less favorable for leisure. This is another way of saying that the quantity of labor an individual supplies is

FIGURE 3
An Individual's Supply-of-Labor Curve and the Concept of Unemployment

The supply-of-labor curve shows the number of hours per week that a person would like to work at various possible wage rates. When the wage rate is $10.00 per hour, a person is underemployed if he or she is working 32 hours per week (point A), fully employed if working 40 hours per week (point B), and overemployed if working 48 hours per week (point C).

positively related to the wage rate.[5]

An individual's supply-of-labor curve shows a person's willingness to exchange leisure for wage income.

Before you go on, take a moment to think through this concept of the individual's supply-of-labor curve. Be sure you understand the reasoning behind the idea that people want to work more hours when the real wage rate is high than when it is low. Of course, we realize that low-wage earners sometimes work more hours per week than high-wage earners, but since that proposition compares different people, it does not match the specifica-

5. In microeconomics you learn that some part of the individual's supply-of-labor curve may have a negative slope—the so-called backward bending supply curve of labor. In dealing with macroeconomics and aggregate data, this possibility can be ignored.

tions of our graph in Figure 3. Also, we realize that, when a worker experiences a wage cut, his or her first reaction may be to take a second job and to work more hours each week. But, given more time to adjust, he or she is likely to switch to a different occupation and get back on the type of supply curve shown in our graph. You will stay on the right track if you see the supply-of-labor curve as having a positive slope showing a tradeoff between leisure and the wage that can be gained from working.

In Figure 3, the real wage rate ($10 per hour) is determined by the market supply and market demand for the kind of work done by the individual. As you remember from Chapter 5, a "market" involves many suppliers and demanders for a particular good or service. If the person whose supply-of-labor curve is shown is working forty hours per week at this wage rate (point *B*), he or she is fully employed—working exactly the desired number of hours per week. But if that person is working only thirty-two hours per week (point *A*), he or she is underemployed—working fewer hours per week than desired at $10.00 per hour. At point *C*, the person is overemployed, since, at forty-eight hours of work per week, he or she is giving up more hours of leisure than desired at that wage rate. Neither point *A* nor point *C* is an equilibrium situation for this individual.

A person who is working exactly the desired number of hours at the going real wage rate for a particular occupation is considered to be fully employed. If that person is working fewer hours per week than desired at that wage rate, he or she is underemployed. If the person is giving up more hours of leisure than desired at that wage rate, he or she is overemployed.

Macroeconomic Unemployment Figure 3 illustrated overemployment, full employment, and underemployment from the perspective of an individual worker. We now broaden the scope to consider all workers in an economy. Figure 4 represents the labor market for the entire economy. The vertical axis shows average real wage rates, and the horizontal axis records the aggregate quantities of labor supplied by individuals at various possible

FIGURE 4
The Labor Market for an Entire Economy

The supply curve shows the tradeoff between wage income and leisure from the point of view of workers. The demand curve represents the aggregate quantities of labor demanded at various possible wage rates. The equilibrium wage rate is *W*, and the equilibrium quantity of labor demanded and supplied is 50 million hours per week.

real wage rates, *ceteris paribus*. The supply curve shows the tradeoff between wage income and leisure from the point of view of workers, and the demand curve represents the aggregate quantities of labor demanded by firms in the economy at various possible average real wage rates.[6] The intersection of the demand curve, *D*, and the supply curve, *S*, identifies the equilibrium average real wage rate—the rate at which the quantity of labor supplied equals the quantity demanded. In Figure 4, the equilibrium average real wage rate is *W*. At *W* the equilibrium quantity of labor demanded and supplied is 50 million hours per week.

Figure 5 illustrates how unemployment may arise in the macroeconomy. In this graph, point *A*

6. The demand for labor is derived from the demand for the goods and services that labor produces. When other inputs are held constant, the marginal product of labor declines as more labor is used so employers are willing to pay less for successive units of labor input. This accounts for the downward slope of the labor-demand curve.

represents the equilibrium illustrated in Figure 4. To illustrate how unemployment can arise, suppose that the labor-demand curve shifts unexpectedly to the left, from D_1 to D_2. The equilibrium real wage rate falls from $10.00 to $9.50, and the equilibrium quantity of labor falls from 50 million hours per week to 45 million hours per week. However, actual wage rates usually are slow in moving to the new equilibrium. Some wages are set by contracts that last for a year or more and even when they are not set by contract they have a tendency to be quite sticky. They lag behind changes in other prices. As long as the *actual* wage rate stays above the new *equilibrium* rate ($9.50 an hour in Figure 5), the quantity of labor demanded will be less than the new equilibrium quantity. This is because, in nonequilibrium situations, actual employment is determined by the *lesser* of the

FIGURE 5
Macroeconomic Unemployment as
Disequilibrium in the Labor Market

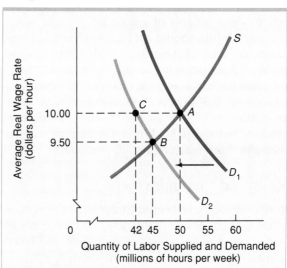

The initial equilibrium is at point *A* with a real wage rate of $10.00 an hour and 50 million hours of work per week demanded and supplied. If the demand curve shifts from D_1 to D_2, the new equilibrium is at point *B*, with a real wage rate of $9.50 an hour and 45 million hours of work demanded and supplied per week. Point *C* illustrates a case of disequilibrium with 42 million hours of work per week demanded, 3 million hours per week of macroeconomic unemployment, and 8 million hours a week of measured unemployment.

quantity demanded and the quantity supplied. When the actual wage rate is above the equilibrium wage rate, **macroeconomic unemployment** exists. In Figure 5, if the actual wage rate were to remain at $10.00 an hour, actual employment would be 42 million hours per week and macroeconomic unemployment would amount to 8 million hours per week.

Macroeconomic unemployment exists when the actual wage rate is above the equilibrium wage rate.

Does the Labor Market "Clear" at Equilibrium? Is the economy at full employment when equilibrium is achieved in the labor market? According to the logic of the aggregate-demand and aggregate-supply model, if the demand curve and the supply curve have been stable long enough for workers and firms to adjust fully to the equilibrium real wage rate, the answer is "yes." Realistically, however, this equilibrium is never achieved, and several modern schools of economic thought argue that equilibrium should *not* be considered full employment. Part of the reason is that changes are always taking place in specific *microeconomic* markets, and the effects of these changes are never fully worked out before new changes occur. Also, there are problems of discrimination, lack of information, and barriers to labor mobility that prevent the economy from reaching its full potential.[7]

Measured Unemployment

Now that you have been introduced to the economists' concept of unemployment, you are ready to learn how unemployment is measured in official statistics. In this section, you will discover why it is so hard to devise measurements that correspond to the economists' concept of unemployment.

Economists define unemployment by comparing actual work time with a person's desired work time. Many difficulties arise in finding a measuring system consistent with the theory. Take, for example, the forty-hour workweek, which is more or less standard in the United States today. At the

current wage rate, do you feel that this workweek provides the best combination of leisure time and wage income? You may know some people who prefer part-time work (less than forty hours a week) and others who want to work overtime or hold two jobs at the same time (moonlighters). If all these people actually work forty hours a week, economists would call the first group "overemployed" and the second "underemployed." This may sound like a strange conclusion, but thinking about it will help you understand the economists' concept of unemployment and will suggest some of the problems in measuring unemployment with statistics.

In official U.S. government statistics, each of the people in the preceding example is called "employed." Thus it is clear that the official statistics are only an approximate measure of unemployment, in the economists' view. But since decisions that affect all of us are based on official statistics, they are very important in policy making.

The Civilian Unemployment Rate The published **civilian unemployment rate** is the percentage of the civilian labor force that is unemployed. As noted earlier, the civilian labor force consists of the civilian noninstitutional population, age sixteen and over, who are working or looking for work. The civilian unemployment rate is calculated by dividing the number of unemployed people by the number of people in the civilian labor force. In other words,

$$\frac{\text{civilian}}{\text{unemployment rate}} = \frac{\text{unemployed persons}}{\text{civilian labor force}}$$

In November 1988 there were 6,595,000 people unemployed and the civilian labor force totaled 122,572,000 people. Therefore the civilian unemployment rate was .054. It is customary, however, to move the decimal point two places to the right by multiplying by 100, so as to give the rate as a percentage. The published civilian unemployment rate in our illustration was 5.4 percent.

The civilian unemployment rate is the percentage of the civilian labor force that is unemployed. It is calculated by dividing the

---

7. These views are discussed further in Chapter 17.

number of unemployed people by the number of people in the civilian labor force.

The civilian unemployment rate is computed monthly by the Bureau of Labor Statistics of the Department of Labor. As stated earlier in the chapter, a representative sample of people is selected for interview. If a person is not working, the interviewer asks whether he or she is searching for work. If the answer is "yes," the person is classified as unemployed.

The question about the job search is important because it helps establish the size of the civilian labor force, which is the denominator of the fraction used in computing the civilian unemployment rate. A person who is neither holding a job nor searching for one is not part of the civilian labor force according to the official statistics. In this group are retired people as well as students, homemakers, and others who have chosen nonmarket activities. Some may be **discouraged workers**—labor force dropouts who have stopped searching for work because they believe there is little chance of ever finding a job. Others may claim to be looking for work but really are not because they prefer unemployment compensation to the best job they expect to find.

Drawing the line at the sixteenth birthday may be somewhat arbitrary, but you will agree that some cutoff is needed for a meaningful definition of the civilian labor force. There are proposals to raise the cutoff line to seventeen or eighteen. If these changes were made, they would lead to important changes in the civilian unemployment rate because sixteen- and seventeen-year-old job seekers, who are often high school dropouts, have great difficulty in finding work. Not counting people in this age group would lower the official civilian unemployment rate. On the other hand, including the "discouraged worker" would raise the rate.

The Unemployment Record Figure 6 shows the official civilian unemployment rate for the United States from 1970 through 1988. The lowest rate during this period was 4.9 percent. This point was reached in 1970 and again in 1973. The highest rate for any full year during the period was 9.7

percent, reached in 1982. Compared with the 1950s and 1960s, unemployment was relatively high all through the 1970s and 1980s. In the 1950s, annual civilian unemployment rates averaged 4.5 percent and never exceeded 6.8 percent. In the 1960s, civilian unemployment rates averaged 4.8 percent and never exceeded 6.7 percent. For 1933, during the Great Depression, measured civilian unemployment was 24.9 percent. For 1944, during World War II, it was 1.2 percent.

Types of Unemployment

In Chapter 1 you learned to classify unemployment as either microeconomic or macroeconomic. Now it is time to refine the classification still further. In common usage, economists generally classify unemployment as seasonal, frictional, structural, or cyclical.

Seasonal Unemployment **Seasonal unemployment** arises because some occupations require workers during only part of each year. Many seasonal occupations, such as picking and processing fruits and vegetables, depend on the growing seasons for various crops. Some, like tourism and resorts, depend on annual climatic conditions. Some, like the post office or retail sales, arise from the Christmas rush or other special annual events. People who work in occupations such as these often are unemployed part of the time each year.

Seasonal unemployment explains why some people have low money incomes, but for others it is an opportunity to earn extra income. Because this type of unemployment follows a pattern that is more or less regular each year, it can be predicted with reasonable accuracy. To avoid misleading numbers, most published statistics on unemployment are "seasonally adjusted," meaning that the seasonal component has been smoothed out or averaged so that direct month-to-month and year-to-year comparisons can be made for other types of unemployment.

Seasonal unemployment occurs because some occupations require workers during only part of each year.

FIGURE 6
Unemployment in the United States, 1970 through 1988

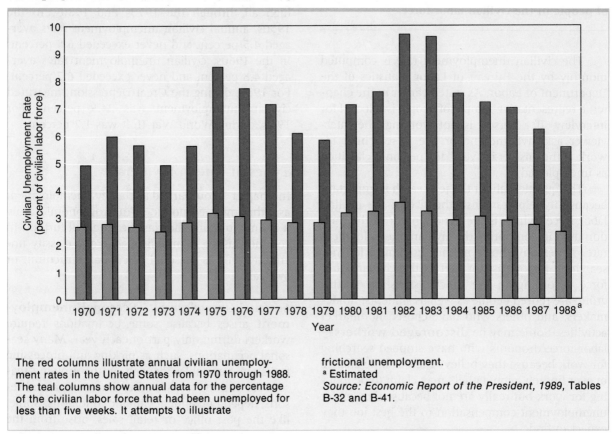

The red columns illustrate annual civilian unemployment rates in the United States from 1970 through 1988. The teal columns show annual data for the percentage of the civilian labor force that had been unemployed for less than five weeks. It attempts to illustrate

frictional unemployment.
[a] Estimated
Source: Economic Report of the President, 1989, Tables B-32 and B-41.

Frictional Unemployment **Frictional unemployment** arises because it takes time to move from one job to another. Because people do not have perfect information about alternative jobs, they must take time to search and to make decisions among jobs. They may need to learn a new skill as they move from their old jobs to ones that pay better or that they expect to like better. Delays arise, too, in gaining entry to a new line of work. All of these facts of life suggest that some frictional unemployment will always exist in a society in which people are free to move from place to place and job to job.

Barriers to the freedom of movement that increase frictional unemployment are of course not desirable. Some barriers are particularly unfair to groups or individuals, such as discrimination based on age, race, or sex, unnecessary apprenticeship requirements, or union membership limitations. However, frictional unemployment is not consid-

ered a serious problem in itself. Continuous movement among jobs and locations is the way in which an economy refines and tunes its operations to the preferences of people.

Actual measurements of frictional unemployment are not exact. One way to estimate its size is to look at very short-term unemployment. Looking back to Figure 6, we see the percentage of the civilian labor force for whom the current spell of unemployment had lasted less than five weeks. This percentage changed only a little each year (though it increased slightly over this period). It is like a "background noise" regularly picked up by government unemployment statistics.[8]

8. Many labor economists prefer to estimate frictional unemployment by using the percentage unemployed for up to fourteen weeks. For this reason, Figure 6 may understate the amount of frictional unemployment, but it illustrates the idea that frictional unemployment almost always exists in the economy.

Figure 7 shows another way to distinguish frictional from other kinds of unemployment. This chart shows not only the civilian unemployment rate but also the unemployment rate for people who left their last job voluntarily or who were entering the civilian labor force either for the first time or after being out of the civilian labor force for a while. The unemployment rate for this group is quite similar to that in Figure 6 for people out of work for less than five weeks.

Frictional unemployment arises because it takes time to move from one job to another. Some frictional unemployment will always exist in a society in which people are free to move from job to job.

Even though these illustrations of frictional unemployment are helpful, a precise measure of this kind of joblessness is impossible. The barriers to movement between jobs that lead to frictional unemployment are hard to separate from the more serious problems that define structural unemployment.

Structural Unemployment **Structural unemployment** involves a mismatch between worker qualifications and job requirements. It often arises when changes take place in production methods (how to produce) and in the types of goods and services produced (what to produce). It corresponds to our definition of microeconomic unemployment. As we noted in Chapter 1, new automatic banking machines may mean unemployment for bank tellers and bookkeepers, and a switch in consumer preference from golf to tennis might mean unemployment for golf pros and golf-ball makers. Structural unemployment also comes

FIGURE 7
Reasons for Unemployment in the United States, 1970 through 1988

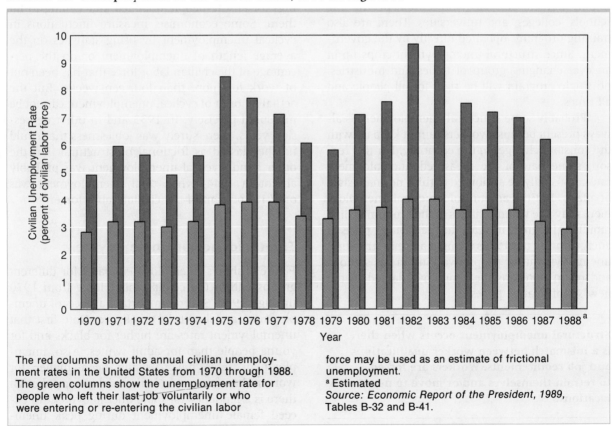

The red columns show the annual civilian unemployment rates in the United States from 1970 through 1988. The green columns show the unemployment rate for people who left their last job voluntarily or who were entering or re-entering the civilian labor force may be used as an estimate of frictional unemployment.
[a] Estimated
Source: Economic Report of the President, 1989, Tables B-32 and B-41.

from job discrimination and other barriers in the job market.

Structural unemployment is more serious than frictional unemployment because workers are not leaving their old jobs voluntarily in order to search for better ones. Their old jobs have disappeared owing to circumstances beyond their control, so they are forced to retrain themselves and move their families to wherever new jobs are opening up. Moreover, the new job often will not pay as well as the old one, and some time may pass before the worker recognizes the reality of his or her lower real wage and living standard. This can cause delay in accepting the new job.

Dealing with structural unemployment requires programs that not only retrain people but also help them discover and move to where new jobs are available. However, it is hard to design and operate these retraining and relocation programs. An approach that sometimes succeeds is on-the-job training, in which employers receive government subsidies to help pay the workers who are being trained for new jobs. Another program provides tuition aid to persons who enroll in training schools, colleges, and universities. There are also training programs operated directly by the government. Since structural unemployment crops up in an ever-changing group of trades and industries, no single program will be right for all people and all times.

Probably some structural unemployment is always present because workers cannot keep up with the constant changes in the economy. For this reason, some part of the measured unemployment rate can usually be attributed to this "normal" state of affairs. But the amount of structural unemployment may rise when changes in the economy come rapidly. The great increase in the relative price of energy during the 1970s brought a rise in structural unemployment for people working in gas stations and resort hotels as the economy adapted to the new set of relative prices.

Structural unemployment occurs when there is a mismatch between worker qualifications and job requirements. Workers are forced to retrain themselves and/or move to new locations.

The rate of unemployment that combines seasonal, frictional, and structural unemployment is sometimes called the **natural rate of unemployment** for an economy. This is the unemployment rate measured by official statistics when the economy's labor market is at equilibrium (as illustrated in Figure 3). Many economists contend that the economy has reached full employment when the official unemployment rate equals this natural rate of unemployment. If measured unemployment falls below the natural rate, they fear that inflation pressures will arise in the economy.

The rate of unemployment that combines seasonal, frictional, and structural unemployment is called the natural rate of unemployment.

Cyclical Unemployment **Cyclical unemployment** shows alternating ups and downs, and affects the whole economy rather than particular industries. There are simply not enough job openings for all the people qualified and willing to fill them. Some economists measure fluctuations in cyclical unemployment by using statistics on the average length of unemployment or on the percentage of the civilian labor force that has been out of work for more than fourteen weeks. But the actual amount of cyclical unemployment cannot be measured precisely. In 1933 and in other depression years, there surely was joblessness that could not be classed as frictional or structural. On the other hand, cyclical unemployment was probably absent in 1944, when total unemployment was only 1.2 percent of the civilian labor force.

The Incidence of Unemployment

Figure 8 shows unemployment rates for different groups within the civilian labor force from 1970 through 1988. Several important aspects of unemployment are shown in this figure. Note first that unemployment rates are higher for blacks and for young people than for adult whites. Also, unemployment rates have usually been higher for women than for men in both racial groups, though there is a tendency for male unemployment to exceed female unemployment during peak unem-

FIGURE 8

The Incidence of Unemployment in the United States, 1970 through 1988

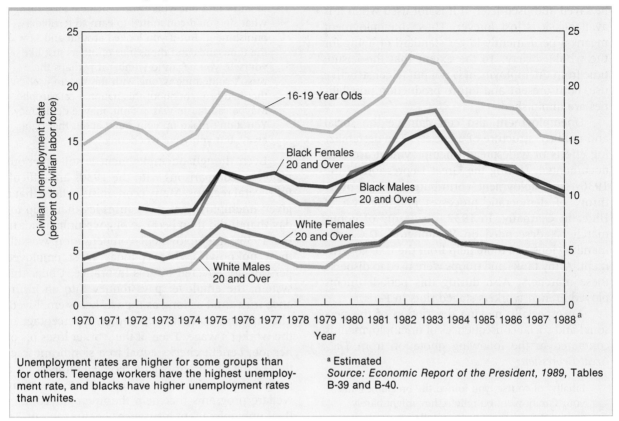

Unemployment rates are higher for some groups than for others. Teenage workers have the highest unemployment rate, and blacks have higher unemployment rates than whites.

[a] Estimated
Source: Economic Report of the President, 1989, Tables B-39 and B-40.

ployment periods. Unemployment rates for young people, age sixteen through nineteen, are much higher than for any of the other groups shown in the chart. The figure does not show male–female or racial distinctions within the sixteen- to nineteen-year-old group, but important differences do exist. Unemployment rates are much higher for black teenagers than for whites in this age group. These facts show that unemployment does not affect different groups in the society equally. Some are much more vulnerable to unemployment than others.

There is also another message in the data shown in Figure 8. All the unemployment rates move up and down together. This fact suggests that all groups share a common experience of fluctuating good and bad times. The range between peaks and troughs is greater for sixteen- to nineteen-year-olds and for black males than it is for others, so these people gain more from prosperity and lose

more from recession than others do. But effective policies on unemployment are important to all segments of the labor force.

Some groups in society, such as blacks and young people, are more vulnerable to unemployment than others.

The Social Consequences of Unemployment

Unemployment is more than a statistic and more than just a topic in economic theory. Anyone who has lost his or her job or has been laid off recognizes the shock, the frustrations, and the fears of unemployment. Few events in life are more devastating both to individuals and to families. For the society as a whole, unemployment is a loss of production that can never be replaced. No factor of production is more perishable than labor. It cannot be saved and used later. If it is not used when it is available, it is lost forever. Thus, unemployment means a permanently lower standard of living for the whole society. To the extent that the leisure time from unemployment is not put to constructive use, both present and future production possibilities are diminished.

Unemployment also can damage the social and political structure of a society. The destabilizing effects of widespread unemployment are well documented. During the Great Depression of the 1930s, unemployment contributed to the overthrow of democratic processes and the rise of Hitler in Germany. In 1932, an "army of bonus marchers" descended on Washington, D.C., demanding jobs and more help from the U.S. government. Army tanks and troops were used to disperse these marchers. Also during this period, unemployed French workers staged riots in Paris.

An especially moving description of the personal and social consequences of unemployment is contained in the following quotation from *The Great Depression*:

> Finally, of course, you joined the breadlines and your family went on relief. They might barely survive on the three or four dollars a week that local relief agencies could afford. Or they might break up. You might go to the local poorhouse, your children to an orphanage. Or the family might scatter to stay with more fortunate relatives in the country, where food, at least, could be grown for consumption. If your children were over the age of eight or nine, they might start wandering over the countryside, looking for handouts at farmhouse doors. In the end, it would seem to you that you had never known any other life than that of a beggar. Even humiliation would be too exhausting an emotion for you; only numb hopelessness and sick despair could

find room in your emaciated body. And you wondered what you'd done wrong. You wracked your brain to find out where you'd made a false turn, what sin you'd committed to earn so terrible a punishment. But if you looked around and saw the thousands and thousands of others just like yourself, you began to wonder if perhaps there wasn't something wrong with the system itself that had brought about this national catastrophe. Maybe capitalism was at fault, maybe democracy. You didn't make up your mind about that right away, but you were wondering.[9]

Even though unemployment is still a serious problem, comparisons with the 1930s are difficult for several reasons. Many economists believe that a given unemployment rate causes less hardship today than it did then because of government aid. In the 1930s unemployment compensation was almost unknown, whereas today most employed persons are covered by this insurance. Under this system, the employer pays money into an insurance trust fund as long as the worker is employed. The amounts paid in are based on a percentage of the worker's wage. Then, if the worker loses his or her job, benefit checks equal to a significant fraction of the old wage will be received, at least for a period of time. In addition, today there are many welfare programs that help the unemployed after their unemployment insurance benefits run out. To a large extent, it was the suffering of the 1930s that brought the introduction of many of these programs.

Another important difference between now and the Great Depression years is the increase in the number of women in the labor force. During the 1930s, few women worked outside the home, so when a man lost his job, there were usually devastating economic effects on the family and psychological effects on the family "breadwinner." Today, with a second income often available to the family, unemployment is less damaging.

9. Robert Goldston, *The Great Depression* (New York: Bobbs-Merrill, 1968), pp. 48–49.

Economics in Focus

Can the Unemployment Rate Fall Too Low?

Can the unemployment rate fall too low? Is it possible for too few people to be jobless? According to many economists, it is indeed possible. They believe that whenever unemployment drops below the natural unemployment rate, there is a strong tendency for inflation to accelerate. Since inflation is generally undesirable, an unemployment rate lower than the natural rate is considered too low.

When the natural rate of unemployment prevails, the only members of the labor force who are out of work are those between jobs or those who require retraining or relocation to qualify for jobs. When unemployment dips below this level, employers often struggle to fill their job vacancies. They have to entice applicants and they may be forced to raise wage rates. Most analysts believe that under these conditions wage rates do in fact go up, forcing an upward trend in prices.

This theory prompted a good deal of discussion in late 1988 and 1989, after monthly figures for the unemployment rate actually fell to 5 percent, the lowest point in fourteen years. Many economists, believing that the natural rate was about 6 percent, worried that the drop in unemployment heralded a surge in inflation. They urged the government (Federal Reserve Board) to pursue anti-inflationary policies. Other economists disagreed. Some thought the natural unemployment rate might be lower than 6 percent. Others feared that excessive economic restraint would plunge the nation into recession. Some unconventional economists even dismissed the entire theory, arguing that low unemployment rates would not affect inflation.

It was also suggested that changing demographics may have altered the way the system works. Largely because of the baby boom from the late 1940s to the early 1960s, the percentage of persons in their prime working years (ages 25 to 54) increased from the late 1960s to the early 1980s. The baby boom also caused changes in the ranks of the unemployed. In the late 1960s and 1970s, only 40 to 45 percent of the jobless were in their prime years; by the late 1980s that figure exceeded 55 percent. Consequently, some economists reason, the unemployed are more likely to have families to support and more likely to accept job offers quickly; hence, they exert less pressure on employers to boost wage rates.

According to this analysis, a very low unemployment rate no longer means that inflation must accelerate—or, at least, the link is weaker than it used to be. As the 1990s unfold, economists will continue to debate the complex association between the natural rate of unemployment and inflation.

Sources: Alan S. Blinder, "Right Now, an Ounce of Prevention Is All Inflation Needs," *Business Week*, March 20, 1989, p. 22; Gene Koretz, "Age vs. Wage: How Baby Boomers May Cool Inflation," *Business Week*, February 6, 1989, p. 26; Randall W. Forsyth, "Jobs Jump Brings Market Back to Earth," *Barron's*, November 7, 1988, pp. 120–121; Henry F. Myers "Talk of Stagflation: Hot Issue or Hot Air?" *Wall Street Journal*, April 24, 1989, p. A1; James C. Cooper and Kathleen Madigan, "A Feast of Jobs Is Setting the Table for Inflation," *Business Week*, November 21, 1988, pp. 29–30.

SUMMARY

1. Inflation is a sustained and significant increase in the general price level. The rate of inflation is the percentage change, from one year to the next, in whatever index number is chosen to measure the price level. (See page 142.)

2. A price-index number is calculated by dividing the price existing in a given year by the price for the equivalent item (or items) in the year selected as the base year. The price in a given year can be converted to its base-year equivalent by dividing it by the index number for that given year. (See page 142.)

3. The consumer price index is used to compare the cost of a selected "market basket" of goods and services in the current year with the cost of the same market basket of goods in the base year. It is often called the "cost-of-living" index. However, it may overstate the increase in the cost of living because it fails to recognize quality improvements and changes in the composition of family purchases. Similarly, it may understate inflation in the cost of living if prices of necessities increase more than the cost of other goods and services. (See pages 143–144.)

4. The implicit price deflator for the gross national product (GNP) shows the ratio between GNP measured at current prices and the amount that would have been required to purchase the same goods in a base year. It is used to convert GNP in "nominal" values to GNP in "real" values. (See page 146.)

5. Index numbers are used for many purposes in economic statistics. For example, index numbers for producers' goods help to predict future changes in the prices of goods and services to consumers. (See page 147.)

6. Inflation has serious economic effects because a price-level-change factor must be included in decisions that guide the operation of the economy. To many of these decisions, inflation adds uncertainty and can cause the economy to operate less efficiently. (See pages 149–150.)

7. History suggests that the social and political consequences of inflation can be serious. Some of these problems arise because unanticipated inflation redistributes wealth and tends to impoverish the groups in society that contribute stability and moderation to the social and political order. (See pages 152–153.)

8. Employment is related directly and unemployment is related inversely to changes in real GNP, which is the variable on the horizontal axis of the aggregate-demand and aggregate-supply graph. (See page 153.)

9. A commonly used measure of employment is the civilian employment rate, which is the percentage of the civilian noninstitutional population, age 16 and over, that is actually working. This rate has increased significantly in the United States over the past 50 years. (See page 153.)

10. The civilian labor force participation rate is the percentage of the civilian noninstitutional population, age 16 and over, that is in the civilian labor force. In order to be counted in the civilian labor force a person must be sixteen years of age or older, working or looking for work, and neither institutionalized nor in military service. (See page 154.)

11. The economic concept of unemployment is that people are consuming unwanted quantities of leisure time and devoting less time to wage earning than desired at the going wage rate. The individual's supply-of-labor curve, which shows a person's willingness to exchange leisure for money, is a key to understanding this concept of unemployment. A person is unemployed or underemployed if he or she is operating under a wage and hour combination to the left of his or her supply-of-labor curve. (See pages 154–155.)

12. The measured civilian unemployment rate is the percentage of the civilian labor force that is out of work. Included in the civilian labor force are only those noninstitutionalized civilians who are either working or looking for work and who are over sixteen years of age. Not included are retirees, persons in institutions or active military service, and people under age sixteen. A person is counted as employed even if working only part time if the work is on a regular basis. (See page 158.)

13. Seasonal unemployment is joblessness that arises because the person is engaged in an occupation that does not require workers all year round. For some, this is a cause of low income. For others, it is a source of extra income. In most published statistics, adjustments are made for seasonal unemployment to avoid confusion in comparing month-to-month or year-to-year changes in unemployment. (See page 159.)

14. Frictional unemployment is joblessness that arises because of the time needed to move from one job to another. Some amount of this kind of unemployment is always present in an economy where people are free to move from one job to another. It is not considered a serious problem for an economy. (See page 160.)

15. Structural unemployment arises when changes take place in production methods and in the kinds of goods and services produced in the economy. People must be retrained and relocated to match the requirements of different jobs. Training programs are helpful in dealing with structural unemployment. (See pages 161–162.)

16. The rate that combines seasonal, frictional, and structural unemployment is sometimes called the natural rate of unemployment. (See page 162.)

17. Measured cyclical unemployment affects most parts of the economy at the same time and arises because jobs are not available for all who want to work at the going wage rate. Though the actual amount of cyclical unemployment cannot be measured exactly, it can clearly cause serious problems for an economy. (See page 162.)

18. Unemployment rates are higher for some groups in the civilian labor force than for others. Blacks experience a higher unemployment rate than whites, and teenagers have especially high unemployment rates. (See pages 162–163.)

19. Serious consequences follow from widespread cyclical unemployment. Potential production is irretrievably lost. Moreover, an economic system is flawed if it fails to provide employment for persons willing and able to work at prevailing wage rates. Unemployed persons suffer economic and emotional hardships. (See pages 163–164.)

KEY TERMS

black market: a market that operates outside the law and sells goods at illegal prices (page 146).

civilian employment rate: the percentage of the civilian noninstitutional population, age 16 or over, that is regularly working for pay (page 153).

civilian labor force: noninstitutional civilians who are age 16 or over and either working or actively looking for work (page 154).

civilian labor force participation rate: the percent of the civilian noninstitutional population that is age 16 or over and either working or actively looking for work (page 154).

civilian unemployment rate: the percentage of the civilian labor force that is unemployed (page 158).

constant-dollar GNP: GNP measured in dollars that have been adjusted for price level changes (page 146).

consumer price index (CPI): an index number used to measure changes in the cost of purchasing a specific group of consumer goods and services; also called the cost-of-living index (page 143).

cost-of-living adjustment (COLA): a clause in a labor contract that connects changes in wage rates to changes in the consumer price index (page 144).

current dollars: the purchasing power of the dollar reflecting the price level prevailing at the time of a transaction (page 146).

cyclical unemployment: unemployment that occurs when there are not enough job openings in the economy for all the people qualified and willing to fill them at the prevailing wage rate (page 162).

discouraged workers: labor force dropouts who have stopped searching for work (page 159).

disinflation: a period when the rate of increase in the price level is becoming less and less (page 149).

employment: labor engaged in regular work for pay (page 153).

frictional unemployment: the unemployment that occurs as workers move from one job to another (page 160).

GNP implicit price deflator: an index number that shows the ratio between GNP measured at current prices and the amount that would have been required to purchase the same goods and services in a base year (page 146).

gross national product (GNP): a measure of the value of a year's total production in the economy (page 146).

index number: a way of stating a value by expressing it in terms of some other reference value (page 142).

inflation: a significant and sustained increase in the general price level (page 142).

inflation rate: a measurement of the change in the price level calculated by dividing the GNP deflator value for each year by the GNP deflator value for the previous year, subtracting 1.0, and multiplying the result by 100 (page 149).

macroeconomic unemployment: unemployment that exists throughout the whole economy or affects many parts of the economy at the same time and is not related to particular decisions about what or how to produce (see page 158).

menu costs: costs entailed during a period of inflation by the need for frequent updating of price lists (page 152).

natural rate of unemployment: the rate of unemployment that combines seasonal, frictional, and structural unemployment; believed by many economists to approximate full employment (page 162).

nominal values: values expressed in current dollars; values not adjusted for changes in the price level (page 146).

purchasing power of the dollar: a measure of the value of the dollar in terms of its purchasing power of goods and services. It can be computed as the reciprocal of the consumer price-index number (page 144).

quality bias: a flaw of the consumer price index arising from its implication that the quality of goods and services stays the same over time (page 145).

real values: values adjusted for changes in the price level (page 146).

real wage rates: wage rates adjusted for price-level changes so that they represent the goods and services the individual expects to be able to purchase with his or her earnings (page 155).

seasonal unemployment: unemployment that occurs because some occupations require workers for only part of each year (page 159).

shoe-leather costs: costs entailed during a period of inflation by the switching of assets from one form to another (page 162).

structural unemployment: unemployment that occurs when there is a mismatch between worker qualifications and job requirements; it often arises when changes occur in production methods and in the types of goods and services produced (page 161).

unemployment: the economic concept of unemployment refers to a person who is spending more time for leisure and less time for wage earning than he or she desires at the going wage rate for his or her occupation (page 154).

weighting bias: the failure of the CPI to recognize that consumer buying patterns tend to change when the price level changes (page 144).

DISCUSSION QUESTIONS

1. Index numbers are illustrated in this chapter with a set of prices for apples. But the index-number principle appears in many places, such as the use of IQ values for comparing intellectual capabilities. Describe three other examples of the use of the index-number principle of stating one value by reference to some other "standard" value. (Hint: consider baseball players.)

2. The CPI is based on a selection of commodities purchased by urban households and the prices paid by them. If you live in a nonurban area, discuss how your selection of commodities and the prices you pay may differ from those used in the CPI. Would you gain or lose if the CPI were used to adjust your wage rate for inflation? Explain.

3. Try this exercise about the quality bias in index numbers. Think of a product that you believe has gone down in quality over the past ten years. Use the CPI (or some other) index number to find out whether the product has increased or decreased in price after the inflation effect has been removed. If its real price has fallen, lower quality may have been exchanged for lower price. If its real price has risen, you may have a genuine case of falling quality. Try to explain why this has happened.

4. In Table 4, the base year is 1982, and all the numbers in the constant-dollar column are expressed in terms of 1982 dollars. How could we adjust the numbers in this column to express them in dollars valued for some other base year, say, 1977? There is a simple method for doing this.

5. From the *Survey of Current Business* or the *Economic Report of the President* or from recent issues of news magazines, look up the GNP deflator or the consumer price index for last year and for the year before. From these data, calculate the rate of inflation for that year. How does this rate compare with those shown in Figure 1? How can it be that the price level itself may not matter but that changes in the price level can cause problems in the economy? Discuss.

6. Construct an individual's supply-of-labor curve using the real wage rate on the vertical axis and the hours of work supplied per week on the horizontal axis. With reference to this graph, explain the economic concepts of underemployment and overemployment. Why can unemployment not be measured (to the economist's satisfaction) unless the wage rate is specified?

7. Suppose you are working a forty-hour week and receiving the going wage rate for that kind of work. Are you "employed" in terms of official statistics? If you would prefer to work only thirty-two hours at this wage rate, are you, in the economist's theoretical view, overemployed, underemployed, or fully employed? Explain your reasoning.

8. From memory, write down the formulas for computing the civilian unemployment rate, the civilian employment rate, and the civilian labor force participation rate. Check to be sure you have them right. Explain how both the unemployment rate and the employment rate can increase at the same time. Explain how the participation rate is involved in this situation. Do you believe that the civilian labor force participation rate will grow or decrease over your lifetime? Does it matter?

9. Explain how each of the following is counted in computing the official civilian unemployment rate: a full-time student who has no paying job, a person working regularly but only part time, a retired person, a fifteen-year-old with a paper route, a person in military service, a person who is out of a job and has given up looking for another because no jobs appear to be available.

10. Explain the difference between seasonal and frictional unemployment. Discuss whether seasonal unemployment is a problem in the economy. Why is seasonal unemployment usually removed (by a statistical adjustment) from most published unemployment statistics? Why is frictional unemployment usually not considered to be a serious problem in the United States? Describe two causes of frictional unemployment that you believe *are* damaging to the economy. Explain your reasons for finding them damaging.

11. Why is structural unemployment likely to be higher during periods when rapid technological change is taking place in the economy? Do you believe that government help should be given to people who are unemployed because of structural changes in the economy? If so, what type of help should be given? Explain the basis for your answer.

12. "Although unemployment still is a serious economic problem, the human and social consequences of unemployment are less today than they were in the Great Depression." Do you believe that this is a correct statement? Explain your answer. What are some changes since the Great Depression that have affected the human and social aspects of unemployment?

9

Economic Fluctuations

Preview   Fluctuations in the level of economic activity are familiar aspects of capitalist-market economies. Periods of rising production are followed by periods of falling production in a seemingly endless sequence of economic ups and downs. Price levels also have risen and fallen over the years. Even if these fluctuations were harmless to human welfare, curiosity undoubtedly would lead economists to try to understand them. But the fact is that economic fluctuations are not harmless. Declines in output mean declines also in employment, causing workers to lose their jobs and forcing lower living standards upon them and their families. Even periods of rising production can generate harmful consequences. Economies that expand too far or too fast may suffer inflationary price-level increases. Changes in price levels, either upward or downward, redistribute income and wealth among individuals and families in ways that may be quite unjust.

This chapter uses the aggregate-demand and aggregate-supply model introduced in Chapter 6 to provide an explanation of what happens during economic fluctuations. After a brief review of this model and a short summary of the history of economic fluctuations, we describe two types of fluctuations—one brought on by an increase in aggregate demand and one brought on by a decrease. These illustrations show the workings of the aggregate-demand and aggregate-supply model and explain why one phase of a fluctuation leads to later phases. They also provide an introduction to one of the most important questions debated by macroeconomists: "What is the best way to help the economy recover from recession and severe unemployment?" Most of the remaining chapters on macroeconomics are devoted to explaining alternative answers to this question.

Finally we offer a brief description of how shocks from the supply side can cause an economy either to enjoy prosperity or to be plunged into recession. This is followed by a look ahead at the specific theories and models that economists use to prescribe policies for moderating economic fluctuations.

FLUCTUATION THEORIES AND PATTERNS

Economic fluctuations are alternating expansions and contractions in the volume of real GNP in an economy. These alternating expansions and contractions suggest that the equilibrium level of GNP changes through time with periods of increasing equilibrium GNP followed by periods of decreasing equilibrium GNP, and so on. It makes sense, therefore, to begin our analysis of economic fluctuations by reviewing the aggregate-demand and aggregate-supply (*AD-AS*) model.

To refresh your understanding of the *AD-AS* model, look at Figure 1, which illustrates an aggregate-demand curve (*AD*) and an aggregate-supply curve (*AS*). In this graph, equilibrium is at *A*, with price level 100 and real GNP demanded and supplied of $1,000 billion per year.[1]

As explained in Chapter 6, the aggregate-demand curve can shift either to the left or to the right as a result of the events that increase or decrease, at any given price level, the total spending by consumers, investors, governments, or foreigners—that is, by events that increase or decrease $C + I + G + X - Im$. At any given price level, the aggregate quantity demanded in the economy can increase or decrease. Look at Figure 1 and imagine the *AD* curve shifting either to the right or to the left. If the *AS* curve remains unchanged, a shift to the right of the *AD* curve causes the equilibrium point (the intersection of the curves) to move upward and to the right along the *AS* curve. The equi-

---

1. In the aggregate-demand and aggregate-supply graphs in Chapter 6, the horizontal-axis label was "Value of Goods and Services Demanded and Supplied Per Year (in billions of dollars)." Now that you have studied the national income accounts, we can simplify this to "Real GNP (billions of dollars per year)."

FIGURE 1
Aggregate Demand and Aggregate Supply

Point *A* represents macroeconomic equilibrium, because it is the intersection of the aggregate-demand curve (*AD*) and the aggregate-supply curve (*AS*). Macroeconomic equilibrium will change when there is a shift of either the *AD* curve or the *AS* curve.

librium real GNP increases, meaning that the economy expands while the equilibrium price level increases. If the *AD* curve shifts to the left, the equilibrium point (the intersection of the curves) moves downward and to the left along the *AS* curve. The equilibrium real GNP decreases, meaning that the economy contracts while the equilibrium price level falls.

If you now look again at Figure 1 and imagine shifts of the aggregate-supply curve to the left or to the right, it is evident that aggregate-supply shifts also can cause expansions and contractions in equilibrium real GNP. A shift of the *AS* curve to the right, *ceteris paribus*, causes an economic expansion and a shift of the *AS* curve to the left, *ceteris paribus*, causes an economic contraction.

As we proceed in our analysis, we will find that alternating expansions and contractions in real GNP (economic fluctuations) can be understood as sequences or patterns through time of shifts in aggregate-demand and aggregate-supply curves. For example, an increase in equilibrium real GNP (an expansion) followed by a decrease in equilibrium real GNP (a contraction) can result from a rightward shift of the *AD* curve followed by a leftward shift of the *AS* curve. Or, the fluctuation may be seen in the alternative sequence, with the contraction coming first, probably from a leftward shift of the *AD* curve, followed by the expansion as the *AS* curve shifts to the right.

Essentially, modern macroeconomic theory suggests that a fluctuation begins with a shift of one of the curves (usually the *AD* curve) and that the fluctuation is completed when the other curve (usually the *AS* curve) shifts in the opposite direction—an *AD* shift to the right followed by an *AS* shift to the left or an *AD* shift to the left followed by an *AS* shift to the right. Although demand shifts are most likely to start fluctuations, a supply shift sometimes is the initiating event.

Shifts of the aggregate-demand curve or the aggregate-supply curve result in changes in employment and real GNP.

The Historical Record

Figure 2 gives a picture of economic fluctuations in the United States from 1881 to 1987. The vertical axis is scaled with an index number for some measure of aggregate economic performance. Real GNP could be used for this axis. Both positive and negative values appear on the vertical axis because the index measures deviations above and below the growth trend of the economy. In unadjusted data, the trend line would slope upward toward the right because the economy tends to grow larger year by year. However, in order to make it easier to see the fluctuations of the economy, the trend line has been made horizontal by statistical manipulations that remove the growth component from the data. As you can see, the economy has fluctuated both above and below this line. Sometimes the economy has been above the line and enjoyed "prosperity," and sometimes it has been below the line and suffered "panics" and "depressions." Closer examination reveals that fluctuations, up and down, also have occurred *during* prosperity or depression periods. It appears that the economy changes direction from downward to upward and vice versa every

few years—sometimes entirely above the line, sometimes entirely below it, and sometimes pushing across the line and moving all the way from prosperity to depression or from depression to prosperity.

Several points should be made regarding Figure 2. The first is a matter of terminology. Should we refer to *fluctuations* or should we use the word *cycles* to characterize the experience of the economy? **Cycle theories** imply that a regular pattern exists, that the causes for an upswing lie in the preceding downswing and that the causes for a downswing lie in the preceding upswing. Cycle theories have long-standing prominence in economic and business literature. However, some economists argue that the word *cycle* implies more regularity than actually exists. They contend that cycle theories are too mechanical, that they divert attention from events outside the economy, and that they leave too little room for policy initiatives to direct the course of the economy. In this chapter, we will examine some theories that follow the cycle idea, but our main focus will be on happenings and policies that cause fluctuations—movements in real GNP that may be unique to particular policies or events.

Cycle theories imply that a regular, predictable pattern exists to explain changes in the economy. The term *fluctuations* is preferred by those who find the cycle concept too narrow and too mechanical.

A second point to note from Figure 2 is the enormous magnitude and length of the depression during the 1930s and the large size of the World War II prosperity. This helps explain the great interest in macroeconomics around the world since those times. Also, note the relatively minor magnitude of fluctuations since 1945. Does this mean that macroeconomic policy has been successful in smoothing the course of the economy? Periods of prosperity have been longer than periods of depression. Some economists are concerned, however, because recessions were sharper and deeper in the 1970s and 1980s than at any time since the immediate post–World War II period. Does this suggest

FIGURE 2
Historical Record of U.S. Economic Fluctuations, 1881–1987

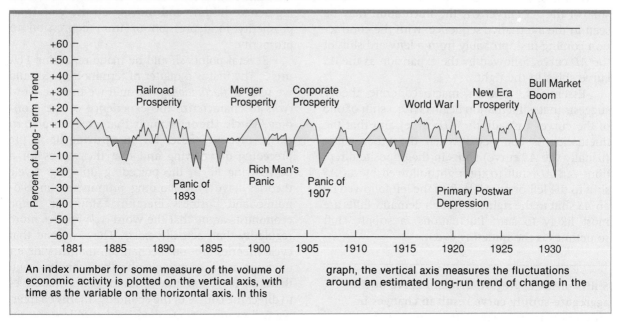

An index number for some measure of the volume of economic activity is plotted on the vertical axis, with time as the variable on the horizontal axis. In this graph, the vertical axis measures the fluctuations around an estimated long-run trend of change in the

that there will be more serious depressions in the future?

The U.S. economy fluctuates both above and below its long-run trend of economic growth. Major fluctuations occurred during the Great Depression and World War II.

Measuring Fluctuations

The first step in analyzing economic fluctuations is to identify and name their recurring features. These features and names are shown in Figure 3. Note first the upward-sloping black line called the **trend line**. It represents growth that is taking place in the economy because of increases in the size and quality of the labor force (labor), the quantity of machinery, equipment, and human skills (capital), and better technology. This trend expresses essentially the same concept as the horizontal line in the historical record chart of Figure 2. Deviations from this trend line provide the statistical measures of fluctuations.

The trend line represents growth that is taking place in the economy because of increases in labor and capital and improvements in technology.

Next note the sequence of terms describing the fluctuations themselves—lower turning point, expansion, upper turning point, and contraction. Expansions and contractions sometimes are called *cumulative* phases of the fluctuation because they describe periods or intervals during which the economy's course proceeds in a given direction—either upward or downward. The **upper turning points** sometimes are called *peaks*, representing high points in the volume of economic activity. Similarly, **lower turning points** sometimes are called *troughs* because they represent low points of economic activity.

Expansion and contraction are called *cumulative* phases of the fluctuations because they describe periods during which the economy's course

Figure 2 (*cont.*)

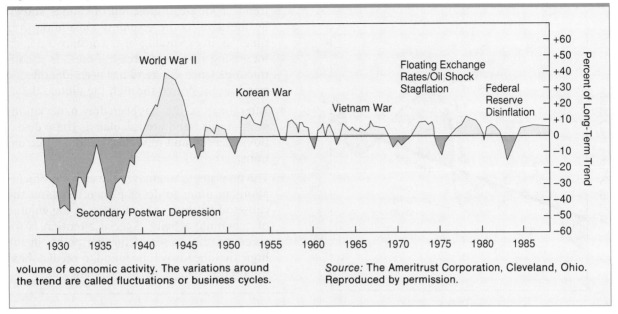

volume of economic activity. The variations around the trend are called fluctuations or business cycles.

Source: The Ameritrust Corporation, Cleveland, Ohio. Reproduced by permission.

proceeds in a given direction—either upward or downward.

Upper turning points are called *peaks;* lower turning points are called *troughs*.

The length, or period, of a complete fluctuation or cycle is the time between either a pair of upper turning points or a pair of lower turning points. The length of an expansion is the time between a lower turning point and the next upper turning point. Similarly, the length of a contraction is the time from an upper turning point to the next lower turning point. Since fluctuations often are not symmetrical, different measuring systems may give different answers even using the same data. The amplitude of an expansion or a contraction is measured by the change in the volume of economic activity between one turning point and the next. Here also there are great differences among fluctuations. Some expansions are weak and peaks occur *below* the trend line, and some contractions are minor and troughs occur *above* the trend line. Each fluctuation is, to some extent, unique.

The length, or period, of a complete fluctuation or cycle is the time between either a pair of upper turning points or a pair of lower turning points.

Statistical measurements of economic fluctuations use index numbers. You have already learned how index numbers can be developed for prices, production, and many other series of data. The following five steps describe how index-number data are used to measure economic fluctuations.

1. A series of index numbers (or a composite of several series) is selected to show GNP, industrial production, or some other measure of economic activity. This is an important step because different data series perform differently in relation to the economy as a whole. Some, like stock market prices or the average hours worked per week, are **leading indicators** and tend to anticipate or "lead" changes in the total economy. Others, like wage rates, are **lagging indicators** and tend to change direction after changes in the volume of total

FIGURE 3
Characteristics of Economic Fluctuations

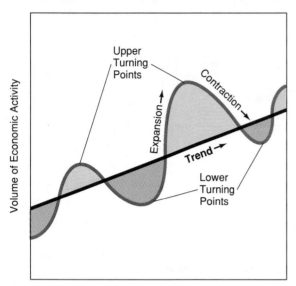

The vertical axis records some measure of the volume of economic activity. Time is recorded on the horizontal axis. Each fluctuation consists of an expansion phase and a contraction phase, an upper turning point and a lower turning point. The period, or length, of a fluctuation is measured from one upper turning point to the next or from one lower turning point to the next.

economic activity. **Coincident indicators** that move along with the total economy should be chosen to measure fluctuations.

Fluctuations should be measured by *coincident indicators*—**index numbers that move along with the total economy**—**rather than by** *leading indicators* **(which tend to anticipate changes) or by** *lagging indicators* **(which tend to change direction after changes in total economic activity).**

---

2. Statistical adjustments are made to remove seasonal variations from the selected data series. Seasonal variations arise due to growing seasons, holiday shopping patterns, the school year, and so on. Removing seasonal variations simplifies the data and makes it easier to spot actual fluctuations.

3. Next, the adjusted data series is plotted on a time-series chart, and the analyst looks for any trend or long-run direction of change shown by the data. Is the economy expanding over time? Is it expanding at a constant rate, an increasing rate, or decreasing rate? Is it contracting? Once the trend has been identified, a trend line is drawn through the plotted data.

4. After the trend line has been drawn, deviations around this trend are calculated. These deviations identify and measure economic fluctuations.

5. The final step is to analyze the cycles or fluctuations in order to develop theories about the causes of patterns or regularities in the volume of economic activity. Special attention is focused on the causes of turning points in the hope that means will be found to predict these important changes in the economy.

Statistical measurement of fluctuations involves selecting index numbers, adjusting them to remove seasonal variations, plotting them on a time-series chart, calculating deviations from the trend, and analyzing the fluctuations in the hope of learning how to predict them in the future.

Cycle Patterns

Analysts believe that they have identified several clear cyclical patterns for the U.S. economy. These are distinguished from one another by their length, by their causes, and by their names—since each has been named for the economist who is credited with discovering and explaining the particular pattern.

The shortest one, named the **Kitchin cycle**, has a length of some three to five years between turning points. Because it is believed to be connected with the alternate buildup and depletion of business inventories, it is sometimes called the **inventory cycle**. You may recall from the circular-flow model introduced in Chapter 6 that the build-up of excess inventory leads to a subsequent reduction in output and employment.

Next in length is the **Juglar cycle**, which has a period of some seven to ten years. Though this is a major pattern in U.S. economic history, economists have not agreed on specific causes for it. The Great Depression of the 1930s came between the upper turning points on either side of one of these cycles.

The statistical record reveals a cycle that appears to last between fifteen and twenty-five years and to run from the construction of buildings and transportation facilities until the time when they wear out and must be replaced. This is called the **building** (or **Kuznets**) **cycle**. Since its length corresponds roughly to the length of a generation, one theory is that it may be related to population waves set in motion by birthrate changes following wars.

Finally, some theories assume a long wave, or **Kondratieff cycle**, of economic activity with a length of thirty to fifty years. Reliable records have not been kept over a long enough time for economists to agree on these very long cycles. Some theories suggest that they may be associated with major technological innovations, such as railroads and automobiles.

All of these cycles (Kitchin, Juglar, Kuznets, and Kondratieff) are occurring at the same time and interact with one another. The shorter cycles that come during the expansion phases of the long cycles display long and vigorous expansion phases of their own with short and mild contraction phases. The short cycles that occur during the contraction phases of long cycles show the opposite pattern.

Some common cyclical patterns in the U.S. economy are the Kitchin cycle (three to five years), the Juglar cycle (seven to ten years), the Kuznets cycle (fifteen to twenty-five years), and the Kondratieff cycle (thirty to fifty years).

Cycles and Capitalism

Over the years, the persistence of cyclical patterns in the volume of economic activity in capitalist-market economies has prompted scholars, reformers, and revolutionaries to see these fluctuations as fundamental characteristics of these systems. Some have prophesied far-reaching consequences from cycles. We shall describe two theories that, we think, deserve attention.

Karl Marx on Cycles   Cycle theory plays an important part in the teachings of Karl Marx (1818–1883), who believed in the inevitable collapse of capitalism and rise of socialism. According to Marx, capitalists have an insatiable drive to earn profits and to invest in machinery and equipment to expand production capacity. Indeed, the capitalist is a necessary part of the evolution from an agricultural economy to an industrial economy. The capitalist's profits, which, according to Marx, come from the exploitation of workers, pay for these machines. The "contradiction" in capitalism is that these machines reduce the chances to exploit current labor and so lower the rate of profit—driving the capitalist to more frantic efforts at exploitation and capital accumulation.

The falling rate of profit that comes from the capitalist's drive to accumulate is very important to Marx's theory. Capitalists use machines to gain the capacity to produce more goods and services than the workers, with their low incomes, are able to buy. Because there is not enough demand to buy the output of the added capital capacity, the economy contracts and a depression follows. The depression does not end until the excess capacity has been worn out. Then the process starts all over again. Marx believed that depressions would become worse and worse and would in time cause the overthrow of the capitalist system by the ever-growing and ever more exploited working class. In the 1930s, many people saw the Great Depression as the fulfillment of Marx's prophecies.

Marx believed that economic depression would be the occasion for the overthrow of capitalism.

Joseph Schumpeter and Innovations   Joseph Schumpeter (1883–1950) offered an explanation of business cycles based on the timing of major innovations in a capitalist system. Under this system, great, though temporary, rewards often come to the successful innovator. Major breakthroughs, such as railroads, automobiles, and electricity, bring bursts of expanding economic activity. Eventually these booms run their course and give way to relative declines in business activity as the economy waits for the next burst of innovation. "Long waves," or cycles, of economic activity may be traced (after the fact) to major innovations. Shorter cycles, such as those described earlier in this chapter, may occur along with these longer waves.

Schumpeter also predicted that capitalism would someday be replaced by a different economic system. In Schumpeter's model, business cycles were simply part of the capitalist system and could not be eliminated, but cycles themselves would not be the reason or occasion (as in Marx) for replacing that system. Instead, the very success of capitalist innovation in raising living standards and in generating wealth would help to draw attention away from production itself and toward matters of distribution of income and welfare and toward less purely "economic" values. So, in Schumpeter's view, capitalism's success in solving economic problems would someday lead to its replacement by planning, by socialism, and, he feared, by a dictatorship. He did not want to live under such a regime.

Schumpeter believed that business cycles were related to major technological innovations.

EXPANSIONARY DEMAND-SHOCK FLUCTUATIONS

Let us see how the aggregate-demand and aggregate-supply model of the economy describes a fluctuation that starts with an increase in aggregate demand, such as might arise from preparation for war.

The Expansion Phase

In Figure 4 point *A* represents the equilibrium situation at the start of the fluctuation. The expansionary demand shock is represented by a shift of the aggregate-demand curve to the right, from AD_1 to AD_2 (shown by arrow number 1), causing real GNP to expand to $1,100 billion as equilibrium moves

FIGURE 4
An Expansionary Demand-Shock Fluctuation

An expansionary demand-shock fluctuation is started by an increase in aggregate demand, which shifts AD_1 to the right to AD_2, shown by arrow number 1. During the expansion phase, macroeconomic equilibrium moves from its initial position at point *A* up and to the right along the AS_1 curve to point *B*. As wage rates and other resource costs eventually start to rise, the aggregate-supply curve shifts from AS_1 to AS_2, shown by arrow number 2. Thus, the upper turning point of the fluctuation occurs at point *B* and the contraction phase occurs while equilibrium moves from point *B* to point *C*.

up and to the right along the AS_1 curve to point *B*. Before the end of the expansion is reached, it is likely that the economy will be operating with unemployment below the natural rate.

An expansionary demand shock is an increase in aggregate demand.

As the economy expands, production and employment increase month by month. Times are "good," and both households and firms are optimistic about the future. In terms of the circular flow, higher incomes earned in each round of the circle provide funds to finance increased purchases in the next round so that each round builds on the previous one. Thus the expansion has a cumulative character.[2]

During the expansion, the rate of increase in production is greater than the rate of increase in production capacity—the economy is expanding faster than its long-run trend in production capacity. The price level is driven upward. As the expansion proceeds, purchases through the consumption, saving-investment, and net tax-government purchases channels increase, fueling continuation of the expansion. The import-export channel, however, is likely to play a moderating or dampening role in the expansion. Higher household income increases import purchases, sending some of the expansion's force into foreign economies. The rising price level is expected to reduce exports so that a deficit in the economy's international trade will develop.

During the expansion, the rate of increase in production is greater than the rate of increase in production capacity; the price level is driven upward.

The Upper Turning Point

Why can't the expansion continue? The main reason is that expansion in the fluctuation means a rate of increase in output and employment that is greater than the long-run trend of growth of the economy itself. In other words, an upper turning point may be reached simply because the expansion has bumped into "capacity," or resource limits. During the expansion, the use of natural resources, labor, and capital has been rising. New capital goods can still be produced, but labor and natural resources are limited. At some point, shortages or bottlenecks in these inputs will bring a slowdown in the expansion of total output.

Eventually the expansion reaches the upper turning point as the limits of labor and natural resources are reached.

---

2. The Keynesian concept of the multiplier, discussed in Chapter 11, pages 223–231, deals further with this cumulative effect.

The Accelerator The slowing down in the *rate* of economic expansion can lead to an *absolute* contraction in production and employment in industries that produce machines and other capital goods. This is called an **accelerator effect**. In capital goods industries, production schedules have been geared to provide equipment for the expanding economy and to replace machines that wear out. The slackening of the expansion brings an absolute drop in demand for new capital goods. So capital goods producers cut down production schedules and lay off some workers. This decline is a key factor in turning the expansion into a contraction. Lower earnings by labor and other resources in the capital goods industries lead to decreases in consumption, which bring reductions elsewhere in the economy and further cuts in spending. The economy will turn around and move into the contraction phase.

The slowing down in the rate of economic expansion can lead to an absolute contraction in production and employment in industries that produce machines and other capital goods. This is called the accelerator effect. This decline is a key factor in turning the expansion into a contraction.

Smaller Profit Margins In the aggregate-demand and aggregate-supply model, the upper turning point comes as tighter labor and resource markets cause wage rates and other input prices to rise, squeezing business firm profit margins. Layoffs occur and some businesses fail. In Figure 4, the upper turning point comes at point B, when the AS_1 curve starts to shift to AS_2 (shown by arrow number 2). Thus, after expansions have gone on for some time, analysts fear that an upper turning point is near and are on the watch for signs of tightness in labor and other resource markets. When prices in these markets start to rise, they predict that the turning point will arrive soon.

The upper turning point comes as wage rates and other input prices start to rise and reduce profit margins.

Circumstances and Events Nearly all expansions *top out*, or reach their upper turning points, long before actual capacity has been reached. Why? Part of the answer is that bottlenecks may arise in some sectors of the economy while idle capacity still exists in other sectors. Resources are not fully interchangeable. For this reason, the pattern of the fluctuation may depend on which industries or parts of the economy are leading the expansion. Sometimes external events, such as the "oil shock" following the embargo by OPEC (Organization of Petroleum Exporting Countries) in 1973, can bring an end to expansion. At other times, the ending of a war may put a stop to spending on war-related items. Upper turning points also may be triggered by subtle changes in business psychology, by decreases in demand from foreign customers, or by disappointing outcomes from business ventures that were begun in the enthusiasm of the expansion.

One of the aims of economic policy is to moderate the economy's expansion rate to bring it into line with the rate of growth of the economy's capacity. If the two rates could be brought together, expansion might continue as long as no external shocks occurred. Unfortunately, bringing the two expansion rates together is even harder than linking up two spacecraft in flight. In short, the idea that the economy might be sustained for very long at a high rate of economic activity implies a delicate balancing of many forces.

One of the aims of economic policy is to moderate the economy's expansion rate to bring it into line with the rate of growth of the economy's capacity.

Those who favor planning contend that planned economies can control business fluctuations because decision making is more highly concentrated in a central planning agency, and also because they can cut themselves off from changes elsewhere in the world. Even if these claims could be proved, there may be a tradeoff between the slope of the trend line and fluctuations around it. Planned economies may sacrifice some growth in favor of greater stability.

The Contraction Phase

In fluctuations initiated by increases in aggregate demand, the contraction phase takes place as wage rates and resource prices rise and reduce profit margins, causing the aggregate-supply curve to shift to the left. In Figure 4, the contraction takes place as equilibrium moves along the AD_2 curve from B to C. Profit margins are squeezed, and production and employment decrease month by month. Times are "bad," and firms and households are likely to be pessimistic. Falling average real income leads to reductions in consumption purchases by households and investment purchases by firms. Unsold inventories bring declines in output, which reduce real income and production in each successive round of the circular flow so that the contraction feeds upon itself and has a cumulative character. The contraction continues as long as wage rates and other costs continue to force smaller profit margins on firms. Since layoffs are taking place and new jobs are not being created, unemployment increases. The combination of a rising price level along with increasing unemployment is called **stagflation**.

The contraction phase takes place as rising wage rates and resource prices reduce profit margins.

The combination of a rising price level and increasing unemployment is called stagflation.

The Lower Turning Point

What about the bottoming out of the economy after a contraction? Why doesn't the contraction in the flow of income and production continue indefinitely? Part of the explanation is that there is a *floor*, which at some point will end the decline in expenditure and production. Some consumption spending is needed simply for survival. Households will borrow money, sell assets, or dip into savings to pay for this minimum. Even though net investment may be negative in severe contractions, gross investment (except for inventory) cannot be negative. Government purchases will not fall to zero and, in fact, may be made specifically to reverse the direction of the economy. As we shall see later in the book, a major thrust of macroeconomics is that the worst-case scenario need not be played out in the contraction. In other words, the experience of the 1930s Great Depression need not be repeated.

At some point in a contraction phase, a floor will be reached that will end the decline in expenditure and production.

The Accelerator, Again The **lower turning point** of a fluctuation requires not only the leveling off of a contraction but also the upturn into a new expansion. Once again, the accelerator concept can help us understand how the economy operates. As the economy experiences the contraction of business activity, idle capacity has been increasing. Labor, capital, and natural resources are not being fully used. According to the accelerator concept, capital equipment producers help to bring the upturn, just as they helped to bring the downturn earlier in the fluctuation. Some machines and equipment will wear out even at the relatively low rates of use that characterize the economy during the contraction. At first, idle machines can be put into service when other machines wear out. But at some point, the reserves of idle machinery will be gone, and some expansion of capital equipment production will be needed to meet the demand for replacement. This rise in capital equipment production starts a new expansion of the economy. Rising output, employment, and income in these industries will lead to increases in expenditure, and the economy will be back on the expansion path of economic activity.

Random Events Must the timing of the upturn wait until all reserves of capital equipment have been used up? Not necessarily. The upturn may come from a particularly successful innovation, which can create investor optimism in some important line of business. Foreign demand may rise, or government spending may stimulate the economy. With the start of World War II in 1939, increases in spending helped the country recover from the Great Depression. The point is that the exact timing of the upturn may depend on particu-

lar events. But reliable forecasting of such events is almost impossible.

The upturn into a new expansion can be caused by the accelerator effect, random events, or government policy.

Wage Rate and Input Price Adjustments The aggregate-demand and aggregate-supply model in Figure 4 suggests that the fluctuation ends at point C, when wage rates and other production costs have ceased to rise and price-level increases have brought profit margins back to normal. However, a more complex version of this model (which will be explained in Chapter 15) suggests that the leftward-shifting AS curve could overshoot the long-run equilibrium point at C and push the economy into further contraction. The model says that since the price level has been rising more or less continuously since the expansion started (at point A), labor and other resource owners may believe that it will continue to rise. If they build these **inflationary expectations** into their contract demands from firms, profit margins may be squeezed even further, and the contraction could continue to an output level of less than $1,000 billion—until rising unemployment and increasing resistance from firms force reductions in costs. The contraction could continue until wage rates and other costs were forced down or until some event or government policy shifted aggregate demand to the right thereby launching another demand-driven expansion.

CONTRACTIONARY DEMAND-SHOCK FLUCTUATIONS

A contractionary demand shock is some event that causes a drop in purchases by consumers or investors or governments or foreigners or by several or all of these groups. For example, the stock market crash of 1929 was an event that many analysts believe cast a cloud of fear and uncertainty over consumers and investors, causing them to cut back on purchasing. This demand shock led, they say, to the Great Depression of the 1930s.[3] Contractionary demand shocks often come at the end of major wars, when government purchases drop abruptly. For economies that depend heavily on international trade, a drop in purchases by foreigners can be a demand shock.

The theory for contractionary demand-shock fluctuations is generally similar to the one just explained for expansionary demand shocks, but there are some important differences. For one thing, the story of the cycle starts with its contractionary phase. More important, the price level tends to fall. This deflationary aspect is important because of its consequences for international trade and for financial institutions, and because it opens the way for government to play a more active role in bringing about the lower turning point.

The Contraction Phase

Figure 5 is an aggregate-demand and aggregate-supply graph illustrating a contractionary demand-shock fluctuation. When the aggregate-demand curve shifts to the left, from AD_1 to AD_2 (shown by arrow number 1), equilibrium moves downward and to the left along the aggregate-supply curve, AS_1, from point A to point B. The drop in production from \$1,000 billion to \$900 billion shows the magnitude of the contraction of output and employment. The contraction feeds on itself as lower production and income (the lower half of the circular flow) lead to lower purchases (the upper half of the circular flow) and still lower production and income in each successive round of the circle. According to the theory of the aggregate-supply curve, wage rates and input prices do not decline as quickly as prices of final goods so that the declining price level reduces profit margins, causing some firms to go out of business and others to cut production.

A contractionary demand shock is some event that causes a drop in purchases by consumers, investors, governments, and/or foreigners—that is, there is a decrease in aggregate demand.

FIGURE 5
A Contractionary Demand-Shock Fluctuation

A contractionary demand-shock fluctuation is started by a decrease in aggregate demand, which shifts AD_1 to the left to AD_2, shown by arrow number 1. During the contraction phase, macroeconomic equilibrium moves from its initial position at point A down and to the left along the AS_1 curve to point B. As wage rates and other resource costs begin to fall, the aggregate-supply curve shifts from AS_1 to AS_2, shown by arrow number 2. The lower turning point of the fluctuation occurs at point B and the expansion phase occurs while equilibrium moves from point B to point C or returns from point B to point A if government policy shifts AD_2 back to AD_1.

The declining price level is the major difference between the contractionary demand-shock model and the expansionary demand-shock model presented earlier. Two consequences of the declining price level merit special attention. They relate to breakdowns in international trade and in financial markets.

The difference between the contractionary demand-shock model and the expansionary demand-shock model is the declining price level.

Restriction of International Trade For an economy experiencing a demand-shock contraction, declining prices for goods it produces reduce household and business purchases from foreigners (imports) and increase purchases by foreigners (exports), thereby moderating the severity of the contraction. However, this moderating effect comes at the expense of the foreign economies, which experience the opposite set of effects—increasing imports and decreasing exports. Their economies are then in danger of suffering a contractionary demand shock. Rather than allowing this to happen, they are likely to impose tariffs, quotas, and other restrictions on international trade to reduce their imports. During the Great Depression of the 1930s, international trade was severely restricted.

Collapse of Financial Institutions A second important consequence of a declining price level is the danger that it will bring collapse and bankruptcy for firms in the financial sector of the economy—firms that carry out transactions in the financial markets box of the circular-flow diagram. This is because a substantial portion of the assets of banks, insurance companies, and other financial institutions consists of loans made to business firms. A falling price level makes it very difficult for business firms and other borrowers to repay loans, since the real value of the repayment is going up at the very time that business profits are falling. When business firms fail, banks and other financial institutions suffer declines in the value of their assets and may themselves be forced into bankruptcy. When financial institutions fail, depositors—including many financially sound households and firms—may lose the savings and reserves they had on deposit and may themselves be forced into bankruptcy.[4] Moreover, when financial institutions have failed, firms that want to borrow to finance continued or expanded production may be unable to obtain credit. Thus, falling prices can greatly increase the severity of the contraction.

There are two major consequences of a declining price level: the breakdown of international trade and the danger of bankruptcy for firms in the financial sector.

---

4. Since the financial disaster of the Great Depression, government-sponsored insurance systems such as the Federal Deposit Insurance Corporation and the Federal Savings and Loan Insurance Corporation have been set up to protect deposits in financial institutions.

The Lower Turning Point

It is generally agreed that some of the causes of lower turning points, such as floors on economic activity and the accelerator effect, apply as well to contractionary demand-shock fluctuations as to expansionary demand-shock fluctuations. But, for reasons that will become clear as we trace the lower-turning-point logic of the aggregate-demand and aggregate-supply model, debate among economists and government policymakers goes far beyond these generally accepted phenomena.

In contractionary demand-shock fluctuations, as illustrated in Figure 5, the lower turning point comes at point B, when wage rates and other resource prices begin to fall fast enough to ease the pressures on profit margins, that is, when the aggregate-supply curve starts to shift to the right, from AS_1 to AS_2 (shown by arrow number 2). This shift comes when contracts for labor and other inputs are renegotiated and when the pressures of unemployment have become great enough so that lower wage rates and resource prices are accepted. According to the aggregate-demand and aggregate-supply model, when the AS_1 curve starts to shift toward AS_2, profit margins improve, leading to increased production.

How severe must the contraction be and how long must it last before the AS curve will start to shift to the right? This is a crucial question for economic policymakers. If prices—especially wage rates—respond quickly (are "flexible"), the contraction may be brief and only a modest amount of unemployment need arise. But if prices—especially wage rates—do not respond quickly (are "inflexible"), the contraction may go on for a long time, and unemployment may become so severe that the society's political and social structure are threatened. In such cases the government may step in and bring about the lower turning point by boosting aggregate demand back toward its original level of AD_1. On the other hand, wages could prove flexible enough so that government intervention would not be necessary. These views, and their supporting theories and arguments, will be examined at length in later chapters.[5]

5. The original Keynesian versus classical debate arose during the Great Depression of the 1930s. Today, there are modern versions of these positions, called "Neo Keynesian" and "new classical." These are examined in Chapter 17, pages 373–383.

The Expansion Phase

In contractionary demand-shock fluctuations, the character of the expansion, or recovery, phase depends on whether or not the government intervention has been responsible for the lower turning point. If the government has been able to shift the aggregate-demand curve to the right, the expansion is essentially the same as the expansion phase of the expansionary demand-shock fluctuation described earlier. The profit margins of firms improve because the added demand boosts final-product prices ahead of wage rates and other resource costs. Equilibrium moves upward and to the right along the AS_1 curve from point B to point A. Unemployment decreases, and workers are not required to accept the wage-rate cuts that appeared imminent at point B.

If the aggregate-demand curve has not been shifted to the right, the expansion phase of the fluctuation is characterized by declines in the wage rates and other resource prices. If wage rates and resource prices are flexible downward, the adjustment occurs quickly. Unemployment is reduced dramatically and real GNP increases.

Extremely divisive social pressures are expected to develop if the recovery from the demand-shock contraction is accomplished through deflation—the route from B to C in Figure 5. For one thing, the declining price level means an increase in the real (purchasing power) value of bonds and other fixed-dollar denominated assets. Many of these are held by the wealthy segment of the population. Therefore, the wealth of the wealthy increases at the same time that nominal and real wage rates are falling. It is easy to charge that the wealthy are using the recovery and the hardships of workers to increase their already comfortable economic situation. The retired segment of the population, together with those who own insurance policies, also gain from the declining price level, since the real value of their insurance policies and pension checks increases. Thus, the older and relatively better-off segments of the population benefit relative to younger and less well-off segments, where unemployment has been widespread and where real and nominal wage rates are falling. Finally, there is a rift between workers who are employed and those who are unemployed. Falling real wage rates may be resented by those fortunate enough and skilled enough to have held their jobs during the preceding contraction. The re-employment of workers who had lost jobs earlier may offer little consolation.

In the absence of increases in aggregate demand, the recovery phase of a contractionary demand-shock fluctuation is characterized by divisive social pressures.

The Upper Turning Point

The aggregate-demand and aggregate-supply graph (Figure 5) implies that the upper turning point of the contractionary demand-shock fluctuation comes either at point A or point C, depending on whether the recovery from point B has come through a shift of aggregate demand or a shift in aggregate supply. It is conceivable, however, that the economy could overshoot this level of output ($1,000 billion of real GNP in Figure 5) if both labor and business firms develop expectations that the expansion will continue. As we will see, political pressures may build for still further rightward shifts of either the aggregate-demand curve or the aggregate-supply curve.

SUPPLY SHOCKS

In 1973 and again in 1978, the Organization of Petroleum Exporting Countries (OPEC) abruptly reduced supplies of crude petroleum available to the world markets. In each instance, in international crude-petroleum markets, equilibrium prices increased and equilibrium quantities demanded and supplied decreased. The economies of industrialized countries around the world experienced contractionary supply shocks, that is, their aggregate-supply curves shifted to the left, as illustrated in Figure 6. At any given price level, the aggregate quantity of output supplied was less than before the shock. The shift of the AS curve forced equilibrium up and to the left along the aggregate-demand curve, from point A to point B. Output and

FIGURE 6
A Contractionary Supply Shock

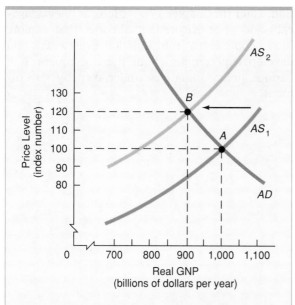

A contractionary supply shock shifts the aggregate-supply curve to the left, from AS_1 to AS_2, since, at any given price level, less will be supplied than before the shock. Macroeconomic equilibrium moves from its initial position at point A upward and to the left along the aggregate-demand curve (AD) to point B. Stagflation occurs as unemployment increases, real GNP decreases, and the price level rises.

employment decreased. These economies suffered stagflation, since their price levels rose at the same time that employment and production decreased.

Twice during the 1970s, the economies of industralized countries experienced contractionary supply shocks when OPEC suddenly reduced supplies of crude petroleum available to world markets.

As equilibrium moved toward point B, economic policymakers confronted a dilemma. Shifting aggregate demand to the right in order to restore employment to its earlier level would push the price level still higher.[6] But shifting aggregate

6. OPEC leaders complained of such inflationist policies and threatened further supply cuts.

demand to the left to fight inflation would increase the severity of the contraction, cutting output and employment still more. Thus, demand-side policies had little to offer beyond allocating the hardships of the supply shock among different segments of population.

Since demand-side remedies were unattractive, policy focused on attempts to shift aggregate-supply curves back to the right. Crude-oil production from non-OPEC countries was encouraged, as were new technologies designed to use less energy from petroleum. Considerable time was required for these efforts to bear fruit. By the mid 1980s, however, the world had become less dependent on OPEC petroleum, partly because of new supplies from non-OPEC countries and partly from success in developing new, petroleum-conserving technologies. OPEC failed in its efforts to continue restrictions on crude-petroleum output. The collapse of OPEC's output restrictions increased supplies of petroleum, lowered its price, and shifted aggregate-supply curves to the right in countries around the world. This expansionary supply shock increased output and employment in industrialized countries and helped stamp out inflationary expectations that had become established during the 1970s. Although price levels did not fall in absolute terms, there was substantial **disinflation**. In the United States, the political careers of Presidents Ford and Carter suffered from the contractionary supply shocks of the 1970s, while that of President Reagan benefited from the expansionary shock of the 1980s.

A LOOK AHEAD

Economic fluctuations impose hardships. During contractions, output is lost that can never be regained, and workers, especially the unskilled, suffer unemployment. Hardships also are imposed by price-level changes, which usually accompany economic fluctuations. Unanticipated price-level changes redistribute income and wealth, and those least skilled in financial management are likely to suffer most. Large changes in either employment or the price level can destabilize the social and political order.

The chapters ahead explore theories about how economic fluctuations can be moderated. We start (in Chapters 10 and 11) with Keynesian theories, which grew out of the experience of the Great Depression of the 1930s and proposed government policies to speed recovery after a contractionary demand-shock. Next (in Chapters 12, 13, and 14), we examine money, banks, and monetarist economic theories, which focus on control of the money supply and place special emphasis on preventing inflation. Later (in Chapter 17), we look at "new classical" and "Neo-Keynesian" theories that explore how people learn from inflation experiences and develop expectations about the consequences of various policy initiatives undertaken by government.

Economics in Focus

Baby Booms and Economic Cycles

Much has been written about the baby boom following World War II and its effect on American society and culture. But economist Richard Easterlin has taken the analysis one step further, contending that population changes are responsible for fluctuations in our degree of social and economic contentment. He identifies what he calls a "new Kuznets cycle," a fluctuation caused not by changes in demand for goods or labor but rather by shifts in the supply of one basic commodity: babies.

Simplified, Easterlin's argument goes like this: In the economic boom following World War II, there were plenty of new jobs available. Because of low birth rates in the late 1920s and 1930s and federal laws restricting immigration, young American workers faced little competition in the postwar job market, and prospects for advancement looked good. With no fear of hard times to come, young people were quick to marry and produce offspring, causing the famous baby boom that lasted into the early 1960s. But as these children began to enter the labor force, their sheer numbers changed the economic outlook. There was much more competition for the available jobs. The average young worker had more difficulty finding appropriate work, advanced more slowly, saw fewer golden prospects ahead. In order to maintain a standard of living similar to their parents', the baby boomers had to marry later, find jobs for both spouses, and ultimately have fewer children.

In this way Easterlin uses population data to account for some well-known changes in American social behavior. He also argues that many disturbing trends of the 1960s and 1970s—increasing alienation among the young, as well as violence, crime, divorce, illegitimacy, and suicide—can be linked to the mass of young baby boomers and the stress caused by their difficulty in realizing their economic expectations.

Turning this analysis on its head, Easterlin then supposes that the generation now maturing will reverse the pattern. The children of the baby boomers are a relatively small group. Finding less competition for jobs and status, they will be less alienated, more willing and able to resume traditional husband-wife roles, and more prolific. Thus there may be a recurring cycle of roughly two generations in length, with baby booms producing economic tribulations and baby busts, which in turn produce times of greater opportunity and baby booms.

Because Easterlin's argument is extrapolated from a single instance of the supposed cycle, it is too early to judge its accuracy. Moreover, as he himself recognizes, many other factors may intervene; surges in immigration, for example, may disrupt the pattern. Clearly, too, demographic fluctuations by themselves cannot explain changes in marriage age, childbearing, and women's participation in the labor force. Still, economists and policymakers may want to ponder the means of interrupting the cycle or softening its effect on the unfortunate "boom" generations.

Source: Richard A. Easterlin, *Birth and Fortune: The Impact of Numbers on Personal Welfare,* 2nd edition (Chicago: University of Chicago Press, 1987).

SUMMARY

1. In the aggregate-demand and aggregate-supply model, shifts of either the aggregate-demand curve or the aggregate-supply curve result in changes in employment and real GNP. Fluctuations begin as the shift of one of these curves relocates the equilibrium intersection of the aggregate-demand curve and the aggregate-supply curve. (See pages 172–173 and Figure 1, page 172.)

2. The historical record shows that the U.S. economy fluctuates considerably around its long-run trend rate of growth. This historical picture is dominated by the Great Depression of the 1930s and the World War II economic boom. Since 1945, fluctuations have been relatively moderate. (See pages 174–175 and Figure 2, page 173.)

3. The period of a cycle or fluctuation is the time between a successive pair of upper turning points or a successive pair of lower turning points. The cumulative phases of fluctuations—the expansion phase and the contraction phase—occur between successive turning points. (See page 175 and Figure 3, page 176.)

4. Statistical identification and measurement of fluctuations involves selecting relevant data series, removing seasonal variations, plotting the trend, and calculating deviations from this trend. Identification and measurement is followed by theorizing about causes. (See page 176.)

5. Four cyclical patterns have been identified: the Kitchin (inventory) cycle of three to five years, the Juglar cycle of seven to ten years, the Kuznets (building) cycle of fifteen to twenty-five years, and the Kondratieff cycle of thirty to fifty years. (See pages 176–177.)

6. Both Karl Marx and Joseph Schumpeter believed that economic fluctuations reveal fundamental characteristics of capitalism. Marx argued that depressions would become worse and worse and would finally occasion the overthrow of capitalism. Schumpeter contended that fluctuations accompany economic growth, which would eventually shift attention from production to income redistribution and lead to a welfare state. (See pages 177–178.)

7. Expansionary demand-shock fluctuations are caused by shifts to the right of the aggregate-demand curve. The resulting expansion reaches its limit through the accelerator effect, increases of wage rates and other input prices, and/or from outside events. The contraction phase takes place while wage rates and other resource prices continue to squeeze profit margins. The lower turning point is reached through a floor to economic activity, the accelerator effect, random events, or government policy. (See pages 178–179 and Figure 4, page 178.)

8. Contractionary demand-shock fluctuations are caused by shifts to the left of the aggregate-demand curve. The model for these fluctuations parallels that for expansionary demand-shock fluctuations except that prices tend to fall rather than rise. Falling prices may make the contraction worse by leading to restrictions on international trade and causing collapse of financial institutions. (See pages 181–182 and Figure 5, page 182.)

9. Economic policy debates focus on how quickly wage rates and other resource prices adjust during contractions in the economy. If resource prices are flexible and can adjust rapidly, little or no government intervention is needed. If resource prices are inflexible, government intervention may be needed to speed recovery. (See page 183.)

10. The deflation remedy for a contraction caused by a demand shock exposes the social order to severe stress. Real values of bonds and insurance policies rise at the same time that real and nominal wage rates are falling. (See page 184.)

11. Contractionary supply shocks cause the aggregate-supply curve to shift to the left, leading to stagflation, that is, to increases in the price level and reductions in employment and output. Policies using shifts of the aggregate-demand curve face unattractive alternatives. Policies attempting to shift aggregate-supply curves to the right usually require a long time to be effective. (See pages 184–185 and Figure 6, page 185.)

KEY TERMS

accelerator effect: increases or decreases of capital goods production that tend to cause lower and upper turning points of economic fluctuations (page 179).

coincident indicators: index numbers that move along with the total economy; they should be used to measure fluctuations (page 176).

cycle theories: theories that imply that a regular, predictable pattern exists to explain changes in the economy (page 173).

disinflation: a period of decreasing inflation rates (page 185).

economic fluctuations: alternating expansions and contractions in the volume of real GNP in an economy (see page 172).

inflationary expectations: a belief that the price level will continue to rise (page 181).

Juglar cycle: a business cycle of seven to ten years (page 176).

Kitchin (inventory) cycle: a business cycle of three to five years that is believed to be connected to the alternate buildup and depletion of business inventories (page 176).

Kondratieff cycle: a business cycle of thirty to fifty years (page 177).

Kuznets (building) cycle: a business cycle of fifteen to twenty-five years that runs from the construction of buildings and transportation facilities until the time when they wear out and must be replaced (page 177).

lagging indicators: index numbers that tend to change direction after changes in the volume of total economic activity (page 175).

leading indicators: index numbers that tend to anticipate changes in the total economy (page 175).

lower turning points: also called *troughs,* they represent low points of economic activity (page 174).

stagflation: a period of a rising price level and increasing unemployment (page 180).

trend line of economic activity: a pattern of growth taking place in the economy because of increases in the size and quality of labor, the quantity of capital, and better technology (page 174).

upper turning points: also called *peaks,* they represent high points in the volume of economic activity (page 174).

DISCUSSION QUESTIONS

1. Draw a graph including a trend line and a complete economic cycle. Identify the parts of the cycle. How is the trend line related to the growth rate of the economy?

2. Explain the difference between the term *cycles* and the term *fluctuations* as applied to periodic changes in the volume of economic activity. Why is there some validity to each term? Why does neither tell the whole story?

3. Write down the names that have been given to the four major cycle patterns described in this chapter. After each, note its usual length and some of the causes that have been suggested for it. At what stage of each of these cycles do you believe the economy is operating at the present time? Discuss.

4. Both Karl Marx and Joseph Schumpeter placed great emphasis on business fluctuations. However, one saw them as signs of health and the other saw them as signs of sickness in capitalist economies. Explain their points of view. Both saw capitalism giving way to socialism, but for different reasons and by different processes. Explain.

5. Draw an aggregate-demand and aggregate-supply graph and explain the axis labels carefully. Then explain and illustrate on the graph how an event that increases aggregate demand launches a chain of responses that constitute an economic fluctuation. Which groups in a society are most likely to benefit from this process? Which are most likely to suffer?

6. Explain the concept of bottlenecks and how it helps in understanding the upper turning points of fluctuations. How does the accelerator effect operate when the rate of expansion in the economy slackens?

7. How might a sharp fall in prices on the stock market lead to a contraction of the economy? Illustrate such a contraction with an aggregate-demand and aggregate-supply graph. Discuss how falling prices may bring international trade restrictions and the collapse of financial institutions.

8. What are some of the factors that place a floor or lower limit on downswings of economic activity? Does the economy have to go all the way to the floor before it can start to recover? How may the accelerator process contribute to a lower turning point?

9. How is the flexibility or inflexibility of wage rates and other resource prices related to the length of a demand-shock contraction? Discuss the arguments for and against government intervention to bring about the lower turning point and recovery from a demand-shock contraction.

10. Think of some happening (other than another OPEC petroleum supply cut) that could bring a contractionary supply shock to an economy. Discuss whether shifts in aggregate demand could help resolve the stagflation problem. What other things might be done?

The Gross Anatomy of Gross Unemployment

Some are so immunized to numbers, especially to statistics, that unemployment rates of 50 percent in "Faroffistan" mean absolutely nothing. "Figures," it is said, "do not bleed." But most of us wonder, at least momentarily, how a society can survive with such rates and what these rates mean in human terms. Will these unemployed masses die of starvation next week or next month? Will they emigrate or revolt? Does Faroffistan have unemployment compensation or poor relief? Are employed family members obligated by Faroffistani custom to support their jobless relatives, even those cousins "whom they number by the dozens"? Are the numbers perhaps artifacts of some special Faroffistani form of statistical malpractice? Do these people really want to work, or are they waiting for venison on gold spoons, as Messrs. Gradgrind and Bounderby described their "hands" as doing in Charles Dickens's *Hard Times*?

The present discussion, however, concentrates on "the figures" rather than "the facts." At first glance, unemployment statistics seem simple enough for comparability over time and between countries. A community, which may be an entire country or a smaller unit, has a *labor force*, most of whose members are usually *employed*, while a minority are *unemployed*. The unemployed are subdivided further into the *involuntarily* unemployed, who are actively seeking work at going wages in occupations for which they are qualified, and the *voluntarily* unemployed, who insist on lower qualifications or rate their qualifications higher than the market seems to do.[1] Economic analysis and social criticism

are concerned only with the involuntarily unemployed, but published statistics cannot in practice distinguish between them.[2]

Many countries also classify the unemployed by the length of time they have been unemployed and by whether or not they have ever been employed. The long-term unemployed are usually the more serious social problem. Together with the long-term "never worked," they comprise a large part of the economic underclass. If there is a waiting period between the loss of a job, or from entry into the labor force, and eligibility for unemployment benefits, some countries register jobless workers as unemployed only after this period ends. Much frictional unemployment is thus not reported at all, and the published unemployment rates are low by comparison with those of other countries.

Only after a quick look at the "bugs" and "gremlins" of the published figures can we be sure that Country A has a more or less serious unemployment problem than Country B, or that Country A's unemployment problem is more or less serious now than it was when the present administration came to power.

---

1. People who need not work, cannot work, or refuse to work are not included in the labor force, and therefore are not considered voluntarily unemployed—a statistical paradox.

2. Another statistical breakdown of unemployment is into the categories introduced in Chapter 8—*frictional, seasonal, cyclical,* and *structural* unemployment. A person briefly unemployed between jobs as a free-lance actor or carpenter is frictionally unemployed. A teacher with a nine-month contract may be seasonally unemployed during the summer vacation. A steelworker laid off because "business is bad" is ordinarily cyclically unemployed. But if his plant is closed for good, or his employer has moved his operations to another town (or out of the country), the steelworker is structurally unemployed, especially if there is no other steel mill in that particular metropolitan area. Here again, the statistician cannot keep pace with the analyst, except that employment and unemployment series can be adjusted more or less accurately for normal seasonal fluctuations associated with Christmas, Easter, or the crops. In our voluntary-involuntary classification system, the structurally unemployed fall in the involuntary category, since they are actively seeking work at the going wage. During the off-season, seasonally employed people are not in the labor force because they either need not work, they cannot work, or they refuse work.

Let us therefore sample a few of the bugs—a dozen or so—as an exercise in statistical entomology. (Almost nobody is proposing that the figures be thrown out, or that we should stop collecting them.)

UNEMPLOYMENT AND POVERTY

In the first place, we should remember to distinguish unemployment from poverty, and poverty from unemployment. Other things being equal—many other things—the unemployed are poorer than the employed. But many of the unemployed, especially the voluntarily unemployed, are far from poverty, even though the "wealthy playboys" hold no-work jobs or drop out of the labor force. Also, many if not most of the poor are employed at least part time, or are members of large families whose breadwinners are in low-paid jobs. Nor should it be forgotten that the representative unemployed person in a rich country—Canada or the United States, Sweden or Switzerland—is better off than the typical employed person in a poor country—Bangladesh or Haiti, Ethiopia or Somaliland.

TEMPORARILY NOT WORKING

A worker who is sick or injured, who is on strike, on vacation, or on leave of absence is not considered unemployed as long as he or she believes that there is a job to return to and intends to return to it. This is in most cases nothing more than common sense, but problems arise even here. A striker may have every intention to return to work after the strike is settled, but his or her employer may propose instead to replace the striker with a strikebreaker, or possibly with a machine. A woman on extended maternity leave may intend to resume work on the assumption that she can have her old job back, while her employer has vacancies only in inferior jobs. A worker on vacation, having quarreled with the boss or the supervisor, may spend this vacation job hunting and have no intention of ever going back—may even be reported as unemployed while still on the payroll, whether or not the former employer expects him or her back.

GROSS OR NET UNEMPLOYMENT?

Suppose a full-employment economy. For all sorts of jobs in such an economy, some people are seeking work and there are some job vacancies. The numbers are in balance, and so there is no *net* unemployment (net of job vacancies). There is, however, *gross* unemployment, which is reported as "unemployment" in all countries. (Job-vacancy statistics are less complete than unemployment statistics.) The differential between gross and net unemployment is estimated under American conditions as between 3 and 4 percent of the labor force. The reported unemployment statistics therefore have an upward bias when used as indicators of shortfalls from full employment.

THE MILITARY LABOR FORCE

A country's labor force excludes persons not seeking work, children below the school-leaving age, and the institutional population of prisoners, hospital patients, etc., some of whom may actually be at hard labor. The *civilian* labor force also excludes the uniformed military, naval, and air forces.[3] A country with large defense forces, whether volunteer or conscript, can sweeten its published unemployment statistics and exaggerate its statistical prosperity by relating unemployment to the total rather than to the civilian labor force, which is the more common procedure.[4]

MADE WORK

This term is chiefly used for public projects undertaken primarily as unemployment relief. Workers on such projects are an important part of the so-called *disguised unemployed*—persons who appear to be employed *only* because work was "made" for them. Also, no statistical account is taken of featherbedding, or excessive workers on other projects, either public or private. During the New Deal—the first two administrations of President Franklin Roosevelt (1933–1941)—employees of Civilian Conservation Corps (CCC) and Works Progress Administration (WPA) projects were counted as unemployed. In later periods, and in most other countries, such workers are counted as employed. Because of this change in American statistical practice, contemporary writers using contemporary concepts may unknowingly exaggerate the magnitude of unemployment during the Great Depression and also the magnitude of subsequent improvement.

3. Civilian employees of defense departments are not excluded from the civilian labor force. Neither are policemen, firemen, or members of such "private armies" as the Nazis' Storm Troopers or Peru's Shining Path guerrillas.

4. A hypothetical example: a country has a total labor force of 2 million, including 100 thousand members of the armed forces and 150 thousand unemployed. Its unemployment rates are 7.5 percent of the total labor force and 7.9 percent of the civilian labor force.

EXCESS WORKERS AND DISCOURAGED WORKERS

If a family breadwinner loses his or her job, other family members—housewives, househusbands, students, retirees—may join him or her in looking for work. In doing so, they enter or re-enter the labor force. Until they find jobs, their (temporary) presence in the labor markets exaggerates the extent of genuine unemployment. When one or more family members find jobs, and especially if the principal breadwinner does so, the others leave the labor market. Statistical "unemployment" is reduced unduly, and the statistical "recovery" is exaggerated.

A larger and therefore more important category is composed of the *discouraged unemployed*. This is another important component of disguised unemployment. A discouraged worker is one who is sure that no jobs fitting his or her skills are open in the community and who is unable or unwilling to move, to acquire new skills, or to seek unskilled work. This worker therefore stops looking for work in any regular or systematic way. Such behavior removes this worker from the statistical labor force. When prosperity returns, or when new firms enter the community, previously discouraged workers become an important source of new hires. For example, during World War II, the availability of discouraged workers seems to have been important in the acceleration of American war production in the critical period from 1940 to 1943.

HOUSEWIVES, STUDENTS, PENSIONERS

When not actively seeking work, people such as housewives, househusbands, students, and pensioners are not included in the labor force, although many of them swell the ranks of the discouraged workers and disguised unemployed. When they are employed, either full or part time, they are employed members of the labor force, even when they are part-timers actively seeking full-time jobs.

When these so-called *secondary workers* are seeking work but cannot find it, their statistical treatment varies across countries. American practice classifies them as unemployed. In Japan, however, they are not included in the labor force unless they are employed.[5] This is another reason why Japanese unemployment ratios are so low.

5. In Japanese practice, a person is first classified as working or not working. If he or she is not working, his or her

THE SELF-EMPLOYED

A physician, attorney, or accountant in independent professional practice is of course treated as employed, even without a formal employer. Problems arise when such a worker's income is insufficient for self-support or for the support of the worker's family. In an extreme case the worker is not a street vendor, musician, or artist but a beggar or panhandler, or the worker's earnings are supplemented by relatives, private charity, public relief, or criminal activities. In these gray areas, the worker's own classification of his or her status is usually accepted by the busy statistician or survey researcher. When street people,[6] for example, claim to be unemployed and seeking work, or to be discouraged unemployed, they are so classified, but if instead they claim to be self-employed, they are included in the employed population. This statistical liberalism also reduces comparability of employment statistics across countries. The Japanese word for an unemployed person, translated literally, is "a person who has lost a job," with undesirable connotations of dishonesty, incompetence, or laziness. A Japanese, then, is apt to call himself or herself self-employed in circumstances where an American would admit himself or herself to be unemployed. In the immediate postwar demobilization crisis of 1945–46, official Japanese unemployment remained low. Unemployment benefits were almost nonexistent, and people could not "afford" to be unemployed.

UNDEREMPLOYMENT AND SUBEMPLOYMENT

The underemployed and the subemployed are also included at times in the broad category of disguised unemployment. They are sometimes pointed to by critics who argue that a nation is really not doing as well as its low unemployment figures may suggest. Many of the underemployed are also subemployed, so that separate estimates of these two categories should not be added together.

The *underemployed* are of two sorts, quantitative and qualitative. The quantitatively underemployed work part time, but would prefer full-time jobs and may be actively seeking them. (A full-time worker seeking a moonlighting second job should not be included under this head.) The qualitatively underemployed are, by ordinary standards, over-qualified for their present jobs. They would prefer, and may be actively seeking, jobs that use their skills at a higher level. Examples include the electrical engineer working as an electrician or TV repair person and the immigrant doctor or surgeon working as a hospital orderly because his or her foreign degree is not recognized in the United States.

The term *subemployment* refers to the level of the worker's pay. The subemployed are the lower levels of the so-called *working poor*. Their compensation falls below some standard, which most commonly is a poverty line but may be considerably higher. For example, for a construction worker, it may be anything below the union scale for the worker's trade in the worker's community. Or a feminist may consider secretarial work as subemployment until secretaries, mostly female, earn as much as workers in primarily male jobs of comparable worth, such as truck driving. A standard wage in a poor country in Black Africa or Central America may, of course, be a subemployment one in North America or Western Europe.

SEARCH UNEMPLOYMENT

In distinguishing between voluntary and involuntary unemployment, we tacitly assume that for each type of labor there are in each community well-known and recognized standards of wages, working conditions, and the qualifications required for employment. This is seldom if ever completely true. The actual situation is an imperfect market with considerable ranges of difference and ignorance about all these matters. Sometimes a single employer may use a tiering system with wages and working conditions better for the tier of workers hired in periods of labor shortage than for the tier hired in periods of unemployment.

Suppose a worker gets a job offer fairly close to his specialty in his home labor market area of Houston, Texas. He rejects this offer, thinking, rightly or wrongly, that he can do better, either in the Houston labor market or by broadening his search to other areas. He may have friends or relatives in Los Angeles. Is his continued unemployment, after his

dependency status is next ascertained. If he or she is found to be a dependent of a family, or of the state, the question whether or not he or she is seeking work is generally left unasked, since such dependents are usually ineligible for unemployment compensation.

6. Street people live or work on the public streets. They may but need not also be homeless; they may or may not also be unemployed.

rejection of the Houston offer, voluntary or involuntary?

Such consequences of labor-market imperfection are generally put in an intermediate category called *search unemployment*; neither strictly voluntary nor strictly involuntary. Some economists who prefer to deny the importance of involuntary unemployment do not consider search unemployment to be unemployment at all.[7] They describe job search rather as a form of employment, whose "wage" is the worker's unemployment compensation plus any assistance in cash or in kind that he or she may get from family, friends, or private charity.

NATURAL RATE AND NAIRU

We have noted that unemployment is recorded gross of unfilled vacancies. This implies that if there are more unfilled vacancies in most branches of labor than there are workers seeking jobs, there will be upward pressure on wages even in the presence of considerable gross unemployment as statistically recorded.

At what level of reported unemployment does such pressure begin? Is there, perhaps, a level of reported unemployment below which we cannot in practice lower the unemployment rate, because increased labor demand only accelerates wage inflation?

The belief that some such rate exists, and that it can be estimated with reasonable accuracy at any point in time, is more common among conservative labor economists and employment statisticians than among their reformist or radical colleagues. In the United States, such a rate (when presumed to exist) is called a *natural rate* of unemployment and used as an indicator of full employment. In Great Britain such a rate is called NAIRU, an acronym for the mouth-filling "nonaccelerating-inflation-rate-of-unemployment." Such a rate may of course vary over time. More generous unemployment compensation will increase it by subsidizing job search, and so will a higher velocity of circulation between jobs. The heterogeneity of both workers and jobs detracts from the usefulness of such estimates, as does the size or the openness of the labor market one has in mind. A shortage of computer programmers in California's Silicon Valley cannot be filled by a surplus of migrant labor in Florida's citrus groves. And free immigration from cheap-labor countries overseas or across a political border can lower natural rates and NAIRUs for jobs that immigrants can fill.

FINAL NOTE

Financial pages and financial journals may tell us that the published unemployment rate, adjusted or unadjusted for seasonal variation, has risen or fallen by one- or two-tenths of 1 percent, and they may go on to forecast what this change may imply for the economy as a whole. All that may have happened is statistical sampling error, and the forecasting may be entirely off base. It is often a mistake to put too much weight on minor changes, and likewise to ignore the failures of statistical comparability over time and space.

7. This is an aspect of *rational expectations* macroeconomics, which we will take up in Chapter 17. One can get the same results by considering search unemployment to be entirely voluntary.

The Keynesian Model of Income Determination

Fiscal Policy

PART III
KEYNESIAN ECONOMICS AND FISCAL POLICY

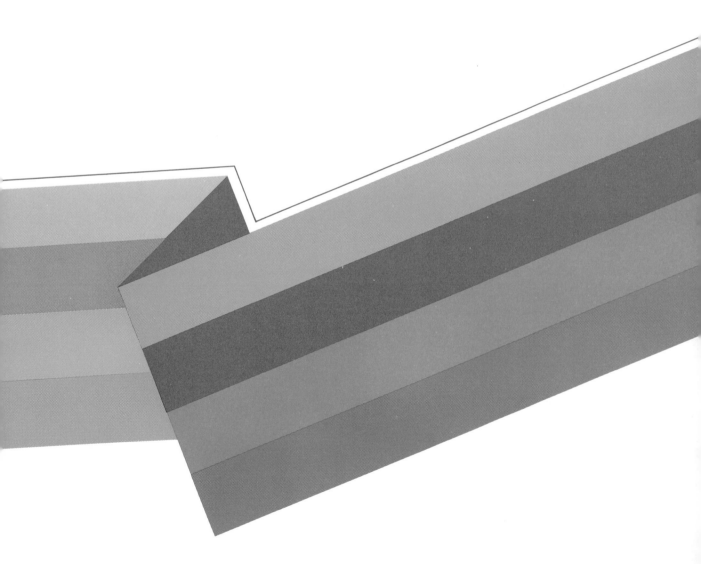

10
The Keynesian Model of Income Determination

Preview This chapter presents the basic Keynesian model of the macroeconomy. It begins with a brief description of how Keynes disagreed with the macroeconomic model of his time. It explains that Keynes was skeptical of models that suggest that market-capitalist economies necessarily and automatically generate "ideal" outcomes, such as full employment. Instead, Keynes argued that government may be able to improve macroeconomic outcomes.

The chapter explains the basic Keynesian model by referring to the four expenditure pathways (consumption, saving and investment, net taxes and government purchases, and imports and exports) of the circular-flow model. It shows how the Keynesian approach adds these expenditure flows together to develop the concept of total planned expenditure and to predict the equilibrium level of national income and product. The concept of macroeconomic equilibrium generated by the Keynesian model differs sharply from that held by mainstream economists and business people prior to Keynes's time. Most important, in the Keynesian model equilibrium need not correspond with full employment in the economy.

The appendix to this chapter explains how the Keynesian model can identify macroeconomic equilibrium by focusing on funds that are injected into the circular flow and on funds that leak out of that system. The leakage-and-injection procedure results in the same equilibrium conclusions as found through the total-planned-expenditure procedure.

KEYNESIAN ECONOMICS

Keynesian economics is a body of knowledge and a set of principles and procedures that have their roots in the work of the British economist John Maynard Keynes (pronounced "cains"), whose most famous work, *The General Theory of Employment, Interest, and Money*, appeared in 1936.[1] The theory presented in his book explained how government initiatives could bring recovery from the Great Depression that gripped industrialized capitalist countries at that time. Keynesian theory dominated macroeconomic thinking in the 1950s and 1960s, but encountered strong criticism for its inability to deal effectively with the simultaneous problems of inflation and rising unemployment that occurred during the 1970s. Today, the Keynesian school of economic thought faces several competing schools, most notably the monetarist, the new classical, and the supply-side schools. The competing schools, along with the modern Neo-Keynesian school, are explained in later chapters.[2] In this chapter, we explore the original and still basic Keynesian model of the macroeconomy.

Keynesian economics, developed in the 1930s by British economist John Maynard Keynes, has its roots in the inability of the then prevailing theories to adequately explain long periods of serious unemployment in market economies.

Two aspects of the basic Keynesian model are important at this stage of learning macroeconomics. First is the criticism that Keynes directed at the macroeconomic theories that prevailed before the Great Depression. Second is the macroeconomic model that Keynes offered as an alternative explanation of the determination of macroeconomic equilibrium. Keynesians believe that their model is more realistic and therefore more effective than the models offered by the competing schools of macroeconomic thought.

Rejection of Say's Identity

At the time Keynes wrote the *General Theory*, most non-Marxist economists were of the neoclassical school of economic thought. **Neoclassical** economists placed great emphasis on the role of suppliers in determining macroeconomic equilibrium and made special use of a proposition known as **Say's Identity,** named after Jean Baptiste Say (1767–1832), a French economist whose *Treatise on Political Economy* appeared in 1803.

The idea behind Say's Identity is that "supply creates its own demand." To understand this proposition, think back to the lower half of the circular-flow diagram—the flow made up of all wages, salaries, rents, interest, and profits in the economy. According to Say's Identity, the sum of all these payments must, by definition, provide enough purchasing power to allow the households to pay for all the goods and services produced at whatever price level was in effect when they were produced. This balance would be true at any given price level.

Of course, neoclassical economists recognized that households would use some of their income for purposes other than consumption and that the proportion so diverted might change from time to time. But they argued that prices, wage rates, and interest rates would move up or down in accordance with market forces so that all funds would complete the circle. For example, if households spent less on consumption, the prices of consumption goods would fall, so that unsold goods would not accumulate. At the same time, the additional funds flowing through the saving, net tax, or import stream would automatically lead to responses that would ensure that they also would complete the circle. Greater saving would lower interest rates in the financial markets, so that businesses would plan to spend more on investment and households would plan to save less. Increased funds in the foreign markets would drive up the relative price of foreign goods, so that there would be fewer imports and more exports. Government budgets, which were expected to balance, would not keep funds from completing the circle. Of course, because of time lags in price changes and in responding to

---

1. John M. Keynes, *The General Theory of Employment, Interest, and Money* (New York: Harcourt, Brace and Co., Inc., 1936).

2. The monetarist model is examined in Chapters 12, 13, and 14. New classical, the supply-side, and Neo-Keynesian economics are explained in Chapter 17.

them, there could be temporary changes in economic activity. However, these time lags would be relatively short, so that problems would soon disappear.

According to Say's Identity, the sum of all the wages, salaries, rents, interest, and profits in the economy must provide enough purchasing power to allow households to pay for all the goods and services produced at whatever price level was in effect when they were produced.

Say's Identity led to the conclusion that full employment would be the equilibrium condition in an economy. Flexible wage rates were the basis for this conclusion. If people lost their jobs, they would offer to work for wages a little below the rate currently being paid. They would surely find work, since the wages paid would (by Say's Identity) be just enough to ensure demand for their goods or services at the lower price level that would result. The only people who could remain unemployed would be those refusing to work for a wage that matched the value of the goods or services that they could produce.[3]

Say's Identity led to the conclusion that full employment is the equilibrium condition in an economy.

Keynes rejected the argument that changes in product prices, wage rates, and interest rates will accomplish the tasks assigned to them by Say's identity and the neoclassical economists. There were two dimensions to Keynes's criticism of the neoclassical model. First, he argued that consumer goods prices, interest rates, wage rates, and foreign exchange rates are not flexible enough to assure that all the money received by households will find its way across the top of the circular flow and be

3. This wage theory led to several doctrines with powerful social and political overtones. The so-called "iron law of wages" suggested that if population growth followed its "natural" course, wages would move toward subsistence levels. From ideas such as this, economics earned the "dismal science" label.

received by firms. This position is based on the view that modern economies do not follow competitive pricing practices. Business firms are not strongly pushed by rivals to lower prices when sales volume drops, preferring to lay off workers while unplanned inventories are used up. Also, powerful labor unions are unwilling to lower wage rates even when unemployment is widespread. Without flexibility of prices and wage rates, there is no assurance that "supply will create its own demand" and that full employment will exist at equilibrium.

Keynes also argued that changes in prices and wage rates, when and if they do come, may not bring economic recovery from a serious recession. This is because a drastic lowering of the price level will impoverish firms and individuals who incurred debt when the price level was high. If debts cannot be repaid, financial institutions may become bankrupt or unwilling to provide the financing needed to restore production and return the economy to prosperity. Firms that want to launch new products may not be able to borrow the funds needed to get started.

Keynes rejected Say's Identity and neoclassical economics because he believed that prices, interest rates, wage rates, and foreign exchange rates were not flexible enough to maintain the economy at full employment and that even if prices and wage rates were to change, they would not be able to effect economic recovery from a recession.

Aggregate Demand Is Crucial

Although Keynes raised important questions about competing models, his greatest influence came from the theory that aggregate-demand is the crucial determinant of GNP. Figure 1 shows how the aggregate-demand and aggregate-supply graph might be modified to illustrate the Keynesian view that aggregate demand is crucial in determining macroeconomic equilibrium. In this graph, the aggregate-demand curve appears the same as that illustrated in previous chapters, but the aggregate-supply curve is a horizontal line. Making the aggregate-supply curve horizontal is an exaggeration of the Keynesian view, since Keynesians do recognize that the supply side of the economy matters and that increases in aggregate-demand can result in inflation. The horizontal aggregate-supply curve simply reflects the view that an increase in aggregate demand *can*, in an economy with widespread unemployment, result in an increase in the aggregate quantity supplied without a *significant* increase in the price level.

What might explain a horizontal (or near-horizontal) aggregate-supply curve? Part of the Keynesian argument is that business firms choose to let demand changes have their first impact on the volume of sales rather than on prices. Prices, Keynesians say, are "sticky." Another reason for a horizontal (or almost horizontal) aggregate-supply curve is that the Keynesian model focuses on an economy in which there is a significant pool of unemployed resources, as typically is the case in a recession. In a situation with widespread unemployment, output can increase without bidding up input prices and forcing firms to increase product prices.

Keynes believed that aggregate demand is the crucial determinant of macroeconomic equilibrium: in an economy with widespread unemployment, an increase in aggregate demand can result in an increase in aggregate quantity supplied without a significant change in price level.

Focusing on the demand side of the economy, the Keynesian theory provides a detailed explanation of aggregate demand. It provides a system for estimating the flows in each of the four pathways in the upper portion of the circular flow—planned consumption, planned saving and investment, net taxes and government purchases, and imports and exports. According to the Keynesian model, the sum of the planned spending components of these pathways, called **total planned expenditure**, determines equilibrium GNP. Since the price level is not expected to change significantly, the change in equilibrium GNP is both nominal and real.

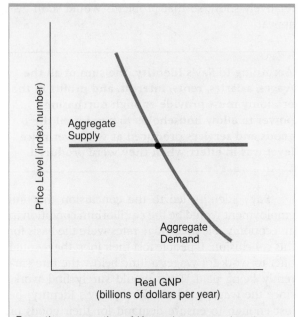

FIGURE 1
A Keynesian View of Aggregate Supply

Price Level (index number)

Aggregate Supply

Aggregate Demand

Real GNP
(billions of dollars per year)

From the perspective of Keynesian economics, the aggregate-supply curve is drawn as a horizontal line. This reflects the Keynesian view that firms respond to increases or decreases in demand by changing quantities supplied rather than by changing prices. Also, the Keynesian approach focuses on situations where significant amounts of unemployed resources are available so that production can be increased without driving resource prices upward.

In the Keynesian model of the macroeconomy, the sum of planned consumption, planned saving and investment, government purchases, and net exports (total planned expenditure) determines equilibrium GNP.

PLANNED CONSUMPTION EXPENDITURE

The planned or intended behavior of consumers is at the heart of the Keynesian model. Consumption expenditure amounts to a large part of national product. It is clear, therefore, that relatively small changes in consumer spending can cause large proportional changes in the funds flowing through the other pathways of the circular flow. If households decide to spend a larger part of their income for consumption goods and services, the proportional impact of this change on the other pathways can be great. It is no surprise that Keynes focused great attention on consumption spending.

The key to the Keynesian model of the macroeconomy is the behavior of consumers. Relatively small changes in consumer spending can cause large proportional changes in the funds flowing through the other pathways of the circular flow.

The Consumption Function

The key idea in the theory of consumer behavior is the **consumption function,** which is the relationship between the amount that households plan to spend to buy consumption goods and services and the level of disposable personal income. More specifically, economists say that the amount of planned consumption purchases (*C*) *depends on* the amount of disposable personal income (DPI), *ceteris paribus*. Thus, the consumption function can be written

$$C = f(\text{DPI}), \textit{ceteris paribus}$$

For economists using the Keynesian system, the task is to determine precisely the nature of this relationship.

To illustrate how the Keynesian model works, let us specify some values for the consumption function equation and trace through the model. For example, suppose that the consumption function is

$$C = \$100 \text{ billion} + 0.75(\text{DPI})$$

where *C* is the annual dollar flow for planned consumption purchases and DPI is disposable personal income. We will assume that there is no inflation either taking place or expected, so that the consumption behavior of households is not distorted by misunderstandings (illusions) about real in-

comes or about the real prices of the things they buy. With these assumptions, we can state that the values for planned consumption expenditure and disposable personal income are *real* values. The importance of these assumptions will be clear later in the book, when we study the theory of inflationary expectations.

Table 1 illustrates how the consumption function in our example provides a set of planned consumption and disposable personal income combinations for an economy. Reading the table, we see that if disposable personal income is zero, planned consumption expenditure is $100 billion. Households are obtaining the funds for their consumption purchases by reducing their savings accounts or by going into debt. These sources of funds are negative saving. So, when disposable personal income is zero, planned saving is −$100 billion.

If disposable personal income rises to $100 billion, the second term in our consumption function shows that planned consumption expenditure will rise by $75 billion to a total of $175 billion. But even at this higher level of income, households must fund part ($75 billion) of their planned consumption spending from past saving. According to our consumption function, planned consumption expenditure will equal disposable personal income when DPI has reached $400 billion a year. If DPI is higher than $400 billion, planned consumption can be funded entirely from current income and there will be positive amounts of planned saving.

The consumption function is the relationship between the amount that households plan to spend to buy consumption goods and services and the level of disposable personal income: $C = f(\text{DPI})$.

Marginal Propensities to Consume and Save

Keynesian theory has special names for the two numerical values that appear in the consumption function equation. The first value (the 100 in our illustration) is called **autonomous consumption**

TABLE 1
The Marginal Propensity to Consume (MPC) and the Marginal Propensity to Save (MPS) Based on Disposable Personal Income (DPI)

Disposable Personal Income (DPI) [in billions of dollars]	Planned Consumption Expenditure (C) [in billions of dollars]	Change in Planned Consumption (ΔC) [in billions of dollars]	MPC	Planned Saving (S) [in billions of dollars]	Change in Planned Saving (ΔS) [in billions of dollars]	MPS
$ 0	$100			$−100		
		$75	0.75		$25	0.25
100	175			− 75		
		$75	0.75		$25	0.25
200	250			− 50		
		$75	0.75		$25	0.25
300	325			− 25		
		$75	0.75		$25	0.25
400	400			0		
		$75	0.75		$25	0.25
500	475			25		
		$75	0.75		$25	0.25
600	550			50		
		$75	0.75		$25	0.25
700	625			75		
		$75	0.75		$25	0.25
800	700			100		
		$75	0.75		$25	0.25
900	775			125		
		$75	0.75		$25	0.25
1,000	850			150		

These hypothetical schedules show planned consumption spending and planned savings at different levels of disposable personal income. The illustrated intervals of DPI are $100 billion. Over each interval, planned consumption spending increases by $75 billion and planned saving increases by $25 billion. Therefore, $MPC = 0.75$ and $MPS = 0.25$.

expenditure, meaning that this amount of planned consumption expenditure (*C*) is independent of the level of disposable personal income (DPI). In Table 1, autonomous consumption expenditure amounts to $100 billion—the amount that would be spent if disposable personal income (DPI) were zero. The amount of autonomous consumption expenditure is determined by variables not included in the equation.

Autonomous consumption expenditure is the amount of planned consumption spending that would take place if disposable personal income were zero; that is, this amount of planned consumption expenditure is independent of the level of DPI.

The second value in the equation (the 0.75 in our illustration) is called the **marginal propensity to consume (*MPC*)** because it shows how much planned consumption expenditure will be induced by a change in disposable personal in-

come. The *MPC* is expressed as a percentage of any change in the level of disposable personal income. In our equation, when disposable personal income increases by $100 billion, planned consumption expenditure increases by $75 billion, that is, by 75 percent of the change in DPI. Of course, the marginal propensity to consume (*MPC*) works in the opposite direction as well—when disposable personal income falls by $100 billion, planned consumption expenditure falls by $75 billion. Thus, on the basis of the consumption function in our example, the marginal propensity to consume value in Table 1 is calculated as follows:

$$MPC = \frac{\text{change in planned consumption}}{\text{change in disposable personal income}}$$

$$= \frac{\$75 \text{ billion}}{\$100 \text{ billion}} = 0.75$$

The marginal propensity to consume (*MPC*) expresses a relationship between changes in disposable personal income and changes in

---

planned consumption expenditure. The *MPC* is equal to the change in planned consumption spending divided by the change in disposable personal income that induced it.

In Keynesian theory, the companion to the marginal propensity to consume is the **marginal propensity to save (*MPS*),** which is the change in planned saving induced by a change in disposable personal income expressed as a percentage of the accompanying change in disposable personal income. If we assume that consumption and saving are the only uses for disposable personal income, $MPC + MPS = 1.0$. The marginal propensity to save value in Table 1 is calculated as follows:

$$MPS = \frac{\text{change in planned saving}}{\text{change in disposable personal income}}$$

$$= \frac{\$25 \text{ billion}}{\$100 \text{ billion}} = 0.25$$

The marginal propensity to save (*MPS*) is the change in planned saving expressed as a percentage of the change in disposable personal income that induced it.

We have set up the illustration in Table 1 so that *MPC* is 0.75 and *MPS* is 0.25 throughout the whole range of incomes shown. It is not essential to the theory that these values be constant over the whole range of incomes. It is a simplifying assumption for an introductory explanation of the Keynesian model.

Average Propensities to Consume and Save

Average propensities to consume and save should be clearly distinguished from the marginal propensities discussed above. The **average propensity to consume (*APC*)** is simply the amount of planned consumption expenditure (*C*) divided by the amount of disposable personal income (DPI). Similarly, the **average propensity to save (*APS*)**

is the amount of planned saving (*S*) divided by the amount of disposable personal income (DPI).

Table 2 illustrates the calculation of *APC* and *APS*, using the data from the same hypothetical consumption function used to illustrate the marginal propensities. Note that the average propensity to consume decreases as disposable personal income increases while the average propensity to save follows the opposite course, increasing as disposable personal income increases. These patterns in the data in Table 2 conform with the widely held belief that consumption absorbs a larger portion of lower incomes than it does of higher incomes. The point here, however, is not whether this widely held belief is true or false. There are, in fact, certain concepts of income—discussed later—where it may be false. At this stage in the explanation of the Keynesian model, the point is to underline the distinction between marginal values and average values in the consumption function. Marginal values, such as *MPC* and *MPS*, focus on what happens at the "growing edge" of changing levels of income. This is the focus that is basic in the Keynesian model. Average propensities also are important but are less critical to an initial understanding of the model. The important thing is to remember the difference between the marginal values and average values.

The average propensity to consume (*APC*) is the amount of planned consumption expenditure (*C*) divided by the amount of disposable personal income (DPI). The average propensity to save (*APS*) is the amount of planned saving (*S*) divided by the amount of disposable personal income (DPI).

The Keynesian-Cross Graph

Figure 2(a) illustrates the consumption function as the red line on a Keynesian-cross graph.[4] Instead of

4. The term *cross* in the name of this graph comes from the technique of showing equilibrium as the intersection of lines plotted on the graph. The technique is best known from the supply-and-demand graph of Chapter 5. That graph is often called a Marshallian cross, after the great English neoclassical economist Alfred Marshall (1842–1924).

TABLE 2
The Average Propensity to Consume (APC) and the Average Propensity to Save (APS) Based on Disposable Personal Income (DPI)

Disposable Personal Income (DPI) [in billions of dollars]	Planned Consumption Expenditure (C) [in billions of dollars]	Average Propensity to Consume (APC)	Planned Saving (S) [in billions of dollars]	Average Propensity to Save (APS)
0	100	——	−100	——
100	175	1.75	− 75	− .75
200	250	1.25	− 50	− .25
300	325	1.08	− 25	− .08
400	400	1.00	0	.0
500	475	.95	25	.05
600	550	.92	50	.08
700	625	.89	75	.11
800	700	.88	100	.12
900	775	.86	125	.14
1000	850	.85	150	.15

These hypothetical schedules show planned consumption spending and planned saving at different levels of disposable personal income. The average propensity to consume is the amount of planned consumption expenditure divided by the amount of disposable personal income. The average propensity to save is the amount of planned saving divided by the amount of disposable personal income.

price and quantity on the axes, the **Keynesian cross** measures dollar quantities on each of its axes. In Figure 2(a) the vertical axis measures dollars of planned consumption spending, and the horizontal axis measures dollars of disposable personal income. When disposable personal income is zero (at the origin of the graph), planned consumption spending is $100 billion (on the vertical axis). This shows the amount of autonomous consumption expenditure. When disposable personal income rises to $100 billion, planned consumption rises to $175 billion, and so on. The slope of the consumption line shows the marginal propensity to consume. (See Chapter 3 for measuring slope.) The marginal propensity to consume (MPC) here is 0.75 over the whole range of disposable personal income (DPI). For this reason, a straight line describes the functional relationship. Thus, our consumption function uses the algebraic equation $C = a + b$ (DPI) where a is autonomous consumption and b is the marginal propensity to consume.

The Keynesian-cross graph displays some measure of income on its horizontal axis and some measure of expenditure on its vertical axis.

On this graph, we also have drawn a straight line from the origin at a 45-degree angle. This **45-degree line** is very helpful because if the units of measure are the same on both axes (as is true here), the line will connect all points at which the value on one axis is equal to the value on the other axis. The 45-degree line is helpful in another way as well. The vertical distance to the 45-degree line from any specified point on the horizontal axis is equal to the horizontal distance from the origin of the graph to that same point on the horizontal axis. So values measured horizontally from the origin can also be measured vertically by referring to the 45-degree line. In effect, both variables can be compared in the vertical dimension on the graph. The geometry of isosceles right triangles explains why this is so.

In Figure 2(a) the red consumption line crosses this 45-degree line at a DPI of $400 billion. This is the **breakeven point**, since there is neither planned saving nor planned **dissaving** (negative saving, or financing current consumption by draw-ing on past savings) at this income level. With the 45-degree line, we can show planned saving and dissaving on the same graph with the consumption function. The red wedge-shaped gap between the consumption line and the 45-degree line, to the left of the intersection point, shows planned dissaving. The red wedge-shaped gap to the right of the inter-section shows positive planned saving.

FIGURE 2
Consumption Function and Saving Function Based on Disposable Personal Income

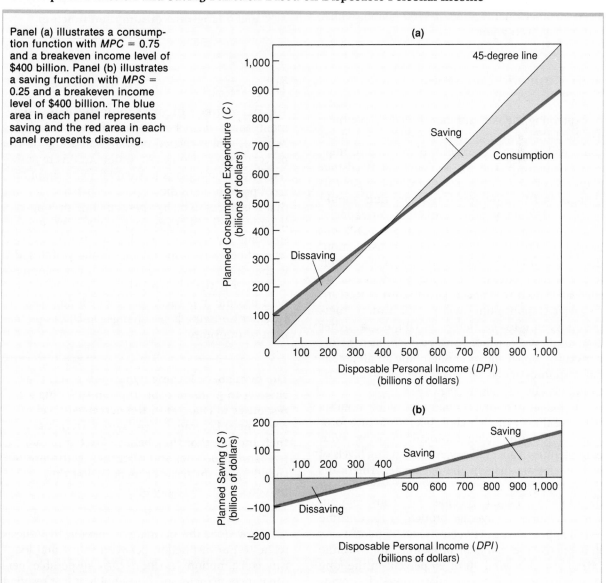

Panel (a) illustrates a consumption function with *MPC* = 0.75 and a breakeven income level of $400 billion. Panel (b) illustrates a saving function with *MPS* = 0.25 and a breakeven income level of $400 billion. The blue area in each panel represents saving and the red area in each panel represents dissaving.

Figure 2(b) illustrates the saving function, drawn from the same hypothetical data. It is the blue line on this graph. When disposable personal income is zero, planned saving is −$100 billion (dissaving). The slope of the saving line shows the marginal propensity to save (equal to 0.25 in this figure), and the planned amount saved is zero at disposable personal income of $400 billion, which is the breakeven point.

Short-Run and Long-Run Consumption Functions

In explaining the consumption function, we have assumed that a change in disposable personal income will lead to a change in planned consumption expenditure. That is, we have theorized that planned consumption expenditure will *respond* to changes in DPI. How much response time should be allowed? Clearly, time is an important variable. If very little time is allowed, a change in DPI will bring very little change in planned consumption, the *MPC* will be very small, and the consumption line will have only a little slope. In this case, we shall have a **short-run consumption function**. A longer response time will permit a more complete response to the change in DPI and a higher *MPC* until we reach a **long-run consumption function**, which allows enough time for all potential responses to be realized. The long-run consumption line will be steeper.

It is clear that time is important for economists who use the Keynesian concepts for making forecasts or for prescribing economic policies. With enough time to adapt lifestyles to changing levels of DPI, it appears that, in the aggregate, Americans choose to spend about 90 to 95 percent of their disposable personal income for consumption. Thus, the long-run average propensity to consume (*APC*) appears to be between 90 and 95 percent. As it happens, the *marginal* propensity to consume (*MPC*) also is around 90 or 95 percent in the long run. However, in the Keynesian approach, unemployment and inflation are seen as problems that

must be treated with short-run remedies. Therefore we shall, in our exposition of the basic Keynesian theory, use *MPC* values much lower than 90 or 95 percent.

The Permanent Income Hypothesis

The **permanent income hypothesis** is a statement about household consumption and saving behavior that is related to short-run and long-run perceptions of income. According to this hypothesis, a household plans to spend for consumption a fixed proportion of the disposable personal income that it believes to be its "permanent," or long-run, income level. Changes in planned consumption spending are responses to changes in the perceived level of permanent income. A corollary of this idea is that income that is perceived as temporary—called **transitory income**—is saved. The permanent income hypothesis places great emphasis on whether households see changes in DPI as permanent or transitory.

How does the permanent income hypothesis relate to our distinction between short- and long-run consumption functions? As disposable personal income increases, households at first respond as if they believe that the increase in the flow of income is transitory. So, in the short run, the *MPC* is low and the *MPS* is high. However, as time passes, a greater part of the increased income flow is perceived to be permanent. The *MPC* rises and the *MPS* falls. In the long run, the consumption function reflects basic attitudes about spending and thrift that are deeply embedded in the society itself.

In the short run, after a change in DPI the *MPC* is low and the *MPS* is high; in the long run, the *MPC* rises and the *MPS* falls.

Even though we shall be using short-run perspectives in explaining the Keynesian model for equilibrium national income, the permanent income hypothesis is a useful reminder that "perceptions" and "consumer psychology" are important in economics. For example, the question of whether a reduction in taxes would significantly increase consumer spending may depend on whether consumers expect that the reduction will continue year after year or whether they expect that it will be only temporary. So changes in the basic tax structure would be more likely to affect the economy than a one-year cut or hike in taxes.

Taxes and the Consumption Function

The consumption and saving functions illustrated in Table 1 and Figure 2 were calculated on the basis of disposable personal income. However, the problems of inflation and unemployment are more directly related to the concepts of net national product (NNP) and national income (NI) than to disposable personal income (DPI). Therefore, it will be helpful to adjust our consumption function so that it is based on national income and product rather than on disposable personal income. To make this adjustment, recall two points from the explanation of the national income and product accounts discussed in Chapter 7. First, national income and net national product are equal to each other conceptually, even though the accounting system shows a difference due to indirect business taxes and subsidies and the statistical discrepancy. In explaining the Keynesian theory, we will ignore these differences and treat NNP and NI as identical.

We will refer simply to national income or to national income and product and use the symbol Y to denote this value. Second, taxes and transfer payments account for the difference between national income (Y) and disposable personal income (DPI). If we lump taxes and transfer payments together in the concept of "net taxes" (as the term was used in the circular-flow model), we can simply add a value for net taxes to our assumed values for disposable personal income to arrive at values for national income and product.

In the United States, many different types of taxes are used—payroll taxes, individual income taxes, corporation income taxes, sales taxes, and property taxes. The combined effect of all these taxes may be roughly equivalent to a flat-rate tax on all income. However, calculating net tax as a percentage of income adds complications that are not necessary in an elementary explanation of the Keynesian model. Therefore, in adjusting our consumption function from a disposable personal income base to a national income and product base, we will assume that the government collects a "lump-sum tax" of $100 billion, regardless of the level of national income and product.

Table 3 illustrates how the assumed $100 billion lump-sum tax enables us to change the consumption function shown in Table 1 from a disposable personal income base to a national income and product base. All the columns in Table 3, except those in the box on the left side, are the same as in Table 1. The numbers in the box show that national income and product (Y) is higher than disposable personal income (DPI) by the amount of net tax, which we have assumed to be $100 billion at every level of national income and product.

To adjust the consumption function so that it is based on national income and product rather than on disposable personal income, a value for net taxes is added to the value for disposable personal income.

Figure 3 illustrates these consumption and saving functions based on national income and product. Because we have assumed that the amount of net tax is unchanged by changes in the level of

TABLE 3
Marginal Propensity to Consume (MPC) and Marginal Propensity to Save (MPS) Based on National Income and Product (Y)

National Income and Product (Y) [in billions of dollars]	Net Tax [in billions of dollars]	Disposable Personal Income (DPI) [in billions of dollars]	Planned Consumption Expenditure (C) [in billions of dollars]	Change in Planned Consumption (ΔC) [in billions of dollars]	MPC	Planned Saving (S) [in billions of dollars]	Change in Planned Saving (ΔS) [in billions of dollars]	MPS
$ 100	$100	$ 0	$100			$−100		
				$75	0.75		$25	0.25
200	100	100	175			− 75		
				$75	0.75		$25	0.25
300	100	200	250			− 50		
				$75	0.75		$25	0.25
400	100	300	325			− 25		
				$75	0.75		$25	0.25
500	100	400	400			0		
				$75	0.75		$25	0.25
600	100	500	475			25		
				$75	0.75		$25	0.25
700	100	600	550			50		
				$75	0.75		$25	0.25
800	100	700	625			75		
				$75	0.75		$25	0.25
900	100	800	700			100		
				$75	0.75		$25	0.25
1,000	100	900	775			125		
				$75	0.75		$25	0.25
1,100	100	1,000	850			150		

All of the columns except those in the box at the left side are the same as in Table 1. The box at the left shows an amount of net tax ($100 billion) that does not change as a result of changes in the level of national income and product. Therefore, national income and product is uniformly $100 billion larger than disposable personal income.

national income and product, the consumption line in panel (a) and the saving line in panel (b) have the same slopes as they did in Figure 2. Any given amount of planned consumption expenditure and any given amount of planned saving correspond with a level of national income and product that is $100 billion greater than the equivalent level of disposable personal income. In panel (a) of Figure 3, the wedge-shaped gap between the 45-degree line and the consumption line includes both savings and net taxes. The saving line, illustrated in panel (b) intersects the horizontal axis— indicating zero net saving—at $500 billion of national income and product which is made up of $400 billion of consumption expenditure and $100 billion of net taxes.

Shifting the Consumption Function

On the Keynesian-cross graph, planned consumption expenditure (C) is the *dependent* variable and national income and product (Y) is the *inde-*

pendent variable. Changes in the national income and product will cause *movements along* the consumption function line. But the consequences of changes in any other variable will be represented by a relocation, or *shift*, of the line itself. Thus, all nonincome variables are shift variables in the Keynesian-cross graph. Changes in these variables change the *average* propensity to consume, but they need not change the *marginal* propensity to consume.

Clearly, there are many variables that influence consumption and saving—variables that are held unchanged by the *ceteris paribus* assumption attached to the formal statement of the consumption function. For example, if households are stocking up on durable goods (cars, appliances, and the like) after a period of shortages or hard times, planned consumption may be an especially large fraction of income. Also, when financial wealth increases because of a rise in stock market prices, planned consumption may claim a higher fraction of income simply because households feel that they need not set aside as much of their current income as insurance against future financial problems. Expectations play an important role, too. When the outlook is promising, households may spend their incomes more freely than when they are fearful of bad times to come.

The list of nonincome variables that may influence planned consumption expenditure is very long. In the next chapter, we shall consider these matters in greater detail. For the moment, however, it is helpful to note that changes in these variables, indeed changes in *any* variable other than national income and product, may cause *shifts* in the consumption function as illustrated in the Keynesian-cross graph.

FIGURE 3

The Consumption Function and the Saving Function Based on National Income and Product

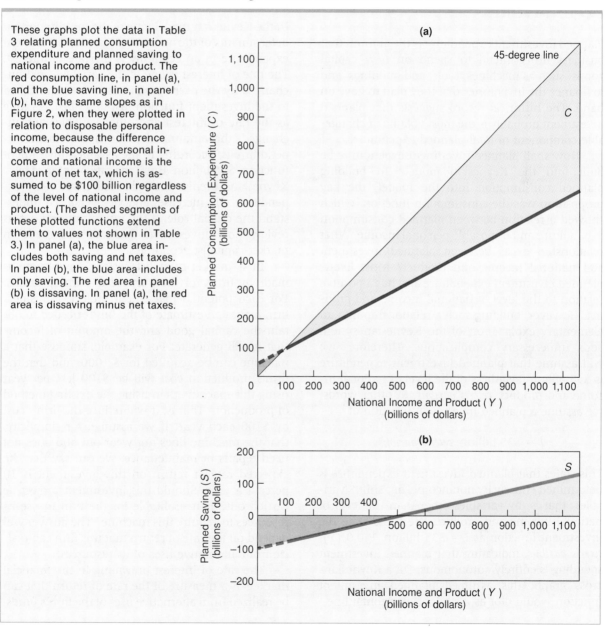

These graphs plot the data in Table 3 relating planned consumption expenditure and planned saving to national income and product. The red consumption line, in panel (a), and the blue saving line, in panel (b), have the same slopes as in Figure 2, when they were plotted in relation to disposable personal income, because the difference between disposable personal income and national income is the amount of net tax, which is assumed to be $100 billion regardless of the level of national income and product. (The dashed segments of these plotted functions extend them to values not shown in Table 3.) In panel (a), the blue area includes both saving and net taxes. In panel (b), the blue area includes only saving. The red area in panel (b) is dissaving. In panel (a), the red area is dissaving minus net taxes.

> Shifts in the consumption function can be caused by changes in other variables but not by changes in the amount of national income and product.

> Planned investment expenditure—the amount that business firms intend to spend on new capital goods and to finance inventories they expect to have on hand—is an important part of Keynesian theory.

PLANNED INVESTMENT EXPENDITURE

Planned investment expenditure is the amount that business firms intend to spend on new capital goods, such as machines, tools, and buildings, and to finance the inventories that they plan to have on hand. The historical record suggests that planned investment probably is the most volatile or changeable component of total planned expenditure.

How shall planned investment expenditure be built into the Keynesian model? In building planned consumption into the model, the key proposition was the consumption function, which showed a relation between planned consumption expenditure and disposable personal income. What relationship exists between planned investment and national income and product? Most likely, planned investment expenditure also has a positive relation to the level of national income and product. However, building such a relationship into an elementary explanation of the Keynesian system adds unnecessary complications. Therefore, we will assume that planned investment expenditure is $35 billion regardless of the level of national income and product, *ceteris paribus*. In other words, we assume a planned investment function of

$$I = \$35 \text{ billion, } ceteris \ paribus$$

This states that planned investment expenditure is determined entirely by nonincome, or "shift," variables, that is, by variables other than the level of national income and product. We could state the investment function as $I = \$35$ billion $+ 0.0 \ (Y)$, *ceteris paribus*, indicating that planned investment spending is entirely autonomous. On a Keynesian-cross graph, this assumed planned investment function would plot as a straight, horizontal line.

Planned Investment and the Rate of Interest

In the Keynesian model, one of the most important determinants of the amount of planned investment expenditure in an economy is the rate of interest. The rate of interest is one of the variables held unchanged by the *ceteris paribus* assumption attached to the investment function just described. As long as the rate of interest and other variables are unchanged, the amount of planned investment expenditure is, according to the assumed investment function, $35 billion. But if the rate of interest falls, Keynesians predict that planned investment expenditure will increase, and vice versa. To understand the crucial role of the rate of interest, let us review how investment decisions are made in market-capitalist economies.

In a market-capitalist system, investment is made by firms for the purpose of earning profits. For each potential investment project, a business firm makes an estimate of the funds needed to obtain the capital good and the amount of income that it will generate. For example, suppose that a machine can be acquired for $1,000, and that the firm's production cost will be $100 less per year using this machine than using the existing method of production. That is, it will reduce the firm's cost by $100 each year. If we assume, for simplicity, that the machine does not wear out and does not need repairs or maintenance, we can say that the expected rate of return on this investment is 10 percent a year. Should this investment project be carried out? Is it profitable for the firm to use its resources to acquire this machine? The answer will depend on the rate of return that this firm can realize from alternative uses of its resources.

The rate of interest prevailing in the financial markets is a measure of the rate of return that can be realized from alternative uses of the firm's funds.

Therefore, the rate of interest plays a key role in the decision about whether the new machine should be acquired. If the rate of interest is, say, 8 percent, the company in the example just given could borrow $1,000 to acquire the machine and would pay $80 each year in interest to the lender. After the interest is paid, the firm would have $20 more profit each year because of the $100 cut in production cost. If the firm feels sure of this estimate, it will make the investment. If the interest rate had been 12 percent, so that annual interest payments would have been $120, the firm would not make the investment. Profits would be $20 less with the machine than without it.

Let us see how this illustration can be expanded to show a demand curve for planned investment for the whole economy. Instead of just one project with a rate of return of 10 percent, suppose that there are thousands of investment projects, some with rates of return greater than 10 percent and some with rates below 10 percent. Table 4 and Figure 4 show how these thousands of possible investment projects can be displayed as a planned-investment-demand curve. In this hypothetical illustration, $10 billion of possible investments are expected to yield rates of return of more than 14 percent. If the interest rate were 14 per-

FIGURE 4
Demand Curve for Planned Investment

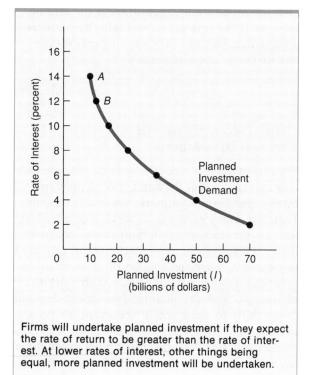

Firms will undertake planned investment if they expect the rate of return to be greater than the rate of interest. At lower rates of interest, other things being equal, more planned investment will be undertaken.

TABLE 4
Demand Schedule for Planned Investment

Rate of Interest (percent)	Planned Investment (in billions of dollars)
14	$10
12	12
10	17
8	25
6	35
4	48
2	70

Planned investment will be undertaken when the rate of return from the investment is expected to be greater than the rate of interest. In this hypothetical illustration, the planned-investment column shows the amount of investment that is expected to have a rate of return greater than the interest rate shown.

cent, all of these projects could be carried out profitably, and the amount of planned investment would be $10 billion (point A in Figure 4). An additional $2 billion of potential investment has an expected rate of return between 12 and 14 percent. If the interest rate were 12 percent, all of these projects, plus the $10 billion of investment yielding more than 14 percent, would be undertaken, so that total planned investment expenditure would be $12 billion. (See point B in Figure 4.) The demand curve for planned investment suggests that the rate of interest is one of the determinants of the volume of planned investment.

In the planned-investment-demand graph, the rate of interest is the *independent* variable that causes changes in the amount of planned investment expenditure—the *dependent* variable. The curve has a negative slope, meaning that falling interest rates bring increased planned investment expenditure and vice versa, *ceteris paribus*.

One of the key determinants of the amount of planned investment expenditure is the rate of interest. If the rate of interest falls, Keynesians predict that planned investment expenditure will increase, and vice versa.

Other nonincome variables that can affect the amount of planned investment expenditure include expected business conditions, changes in operating costs, government policies, and technological changes.

Other Determinants of Planned Investment

The rate of interest is not the only nonincome variable that can change the amount of planned investment expenditure in a market-capitalist economy. There are many events that can change a business firm's expectation of profit from a proposed investment. If the event causes expectations of increased profitability, a greater volume of planned investment expenditure will take place at any given rate of interest, and the planned-investment-demand curve shifts to the right. If the event lowers expected profitability, the curve shifts to the left and a smaller volume of planned investment expenditure takes place at any given rate of interest. Let us look at a few events that can have important influence on the planned-investment-demand curve.

Expected business conditions can be very important. If firms expect sales to increase, the expected rate of return on investments will probably be higher than if they expect sales to drop. The curve will shift to the right as optimism rises and to the left as pessimism grows. When a firm expects changes in the *cost of operating* some of its machines or equipment, the expected rates of return for different investment projects will be rearranged and may cause the curve to shift. *Government policies* relating to taxation or regulation also are important. For example, if Congress enacts a major tax cut, the demand curve for planned investment may shift to the right. On the other hand, laws calling for strict regulation of a major industry may shift the curve to the left. Also of great importance to the location of the planned-investment-demand curve are *technological changes*. A fast rate of technological change may offer substantial profit possibilities and shift the curve to the right, whereas a slowing rate of technological change may move the curve to the left.

GOVERNMENT PURCHASES

Fitting government purchases into the Keynesian model raises many of the same questions considered in our explanation of planned investment expenditure. Once again it is customary and convenient to assume a government-purchases function in which the amount of these purchases is independent of the level of national income and product. We will assume a government-purchases function of

$$G = \$100 \text{ billion}, \textit{ceteris paribus}$$

In other words, we assume a government purchases function $G = \$100$ billion $+ 0.0(Y)$, *ceteris paribus*.

As with our assumed investment function, it probably is unrealistic to assume that the annual volume of government purchases is unrelated to the level of national income and product. In practice, government purchases probably are positively related to the level of national income and product. Nevertheless, in this introduction to the Keynesian system, we will assume that government purchases do not vary as a direct result of changes in the level of national income and product.

There are, of course, many nonincome variables that can influence the volume of government purchases and that are very important in the Keynesian system. These include government policies, domestic and world conditions, the attitudes of voters and taxpayers, and so on. In the Keynesian approach, the policy position taken by the government to deal with macroeconomic unemployment is especially important. As you recall, the neoclassical approach argued against active government intervention in the economy. Keynesians, on the other hand, suggest that government should take forceful action to bring the economy out of recession.

Many nonincome variables, such as government policies, domestic and world conditions, the attitude of voters, etc., can influence the volume of government purchases. Keynesians believe that government should intervene actively in the economy to combat recession.

IMPORTS AND EXPORTS

The import-export path in the circular flow remains to be studied. Again, building this pathway into the Keynesian model raises the question of how the volume of imports and exports (or "net exports") will respond to changes in the level of national income and product.

American purchases from foreigners (imports), like purchases of domestic goods, can be expected to increase as income rises. The reasoning is the same as that offered for planned consumption, planned investment, and for government purchases. Imported goods are probably "normal" in their relation to income, that is, increases in income bring increases in quantities demanded. However, purchases by foreigners from Americans (exports) are less likely to show a predictable response to changes in the U.S. national income and product. Instead, they respond to income changes in the foreign countries themselves, or to changes in foreign exchange rates (which we cover in Chapter 19).

When we combine imports and exports and then seek to find the relationship between "net exports" and national income and product, the normal goods assumption suggests that net exports are a declining function of national income and product. That is, net exports grow smaller as national income and product rises, because *gross* exports will remain the same while *gross* imports grow larger as U.S. national income rises. Americans *will* be buying more from foreign countries, but foreigners will *not* necessarily be buying more from the United States.

In our explanation of the Keynesian model, we assume a net export function of

$$X - Im = \$15 \text{ billion, } ceteris \ paribus$$

meaning that the volume of net exports is unrelated to the level of U.S. national income and product and that changes in net exports are determined by nonincome variables. This is a net export function of $X - Im = \$15$ billion $+ 0.0(Y)$, *ceteris paribus*. This is the same approach used for incorporating planned investment and government purchases into the Keynesian system. Although reality suggests a more complicated functional relationship, these complications can be left to more advanced courses in economics.

We assume that net exports do not change when national income and product changes, although in fact net exports grow smaller as national income and product rises because gross exports remain the same while gross imports grow larger.

EQUILIBRIUM NATIONAL INCOME

We now have studied the four spending streams that make up total planned expenditure. We have given them numerical values so that we can show a functional relationship between national income and product and total planned expenditure. In doing so, we shall, in turn, discover the equilibrium level for national income and product according to the Keynesian model.

Table 5 brings together all four components of planned expenditure. The columns for national income and product and for planned consumption expenditure are the same as those in Table 3. The next three columns—planned investment, government purchases, and net exports—illustrate our assumptions that these spending streams are not altered by changes in national income and product. We assume $35 billion of planned investment, $100 billion of government purchases, and $15 billion of net exports regardless of the level of national income and product. The last column shows

TABLE 5
Total Planned Expenditure and Macroeconomic Equilibrium (in billions of dollars)

(1) National Income and Product (Y)	(2) Planned Consumption Expenditure (C)	(3) Planned Investment Expenditure (I)	(4) Government Purchases (G)	(5) Net Exports (X − Im)	(6) Total Planned Expenditure (C + I + G + X − Im)
$ 100	$100	$35	$100	$15	$ 250
200	175	35	100	15	325
300	250	35	100	15	400
400	325	35	100	15	475
500	400	35	100	15	550
600	475	35	100	15	625
700	550	35	100	15	700
800	625	35	100	15	775
900	700	35	100	15	850
1,000	775	35	100	15	925
1,100	850	35	100	15	1,000

Columns 1 and 2 repeat data from Table 3. Columns 3, 4, and 5 illustrate our assumptions that the planned investment, government purchases, and net export spending streams are not altered by changes in national income and product. Column 6 shows the total of columns 2 through 5. Equilibrium exists when total planned expenditure equals national income and product ($700 billion).

the total planned expenditure corresponding to each level of national income and product, that is, $C + I + G + X - Im$. Macroeconomists devote a great deal of effort to finding accurate values for the components of total planned expenditure. However, for the purpose of introducing you to the theory, these hypothetical numbers are convenient.

The values in Table 5 indicate that the conditions for equilibrium exist when national income and product is $700 billion. This is shown by the row of numbers with the white background. For income levels of *less* than $700 billion, total planned expenditure is greater than production, so that inventories go down. As you learned from the circular flow, this is a case in which pressures arise for greater production and/or higher prices in the next production period. On the other hand, for all income levels *greater* than $700 billion, total planned expenditure is less than production. So unplanned inventory piles up, and there are pressures to lower production and/or prices in the next period. Only at a national income and product level of $700 billion are production and total planned expenditure equal. Here we have the condition for equilibrium national income and product. If we let the symbol

Y^* represent the equilibrium level of national income and product, we can state this equilibrium condition as

$$Y^* = C + I + G + X - Im$$

This equation states that the equilibrium level of national income and product is determined by total planned expenditure.

Figure 5 shows this relationship on a Keynesian-cross graph. National income and product appears on the horizontal axis and planned expenditure on the vertical axis. The red consumption-function line (C) is the same as in Figure 3. Total planned expenditure is represented by the purple line labeled $C + I + G + X - Im$. This line lies above the consumption-function line by the amount of the other expenditure streams—planned investment (I), government purchases (G), and net exports (X − Im). The total-planned-expenditure line ($C + I + G + X - Im$) is parallel with the consumption-function line because we have assumed that each expenditure stream other than planned consumption is independent of the level of national income and product.

FIGURE 5
Macroeconomic Equilibrium Illustrated on a Keynesian-Cross Graph

Planned consumption expenditure (C) is the same as in Figure 3. Planned investment expenditure (I), government purchases (G), and net exports (X − Im) are added on top of the red planned-consumption-expenditure line to show the purple total-planned-expenditure line C + I + G + X − Im. Macroeconomic equilibrium is at E, where total planned expenditure of $700 billion equals national income and product of $700 billion. At lower levels of national income and product, total planned expenditure exceeds production (as shown by the red area) so that inventories are drawn down, generating pressures for expansion. At national income and product levels above $700 billion, production exceeds total planned expenditure (as shown by the purple area) so that excess inventories accumulate, generating pressures for contraction of the economy. (The dashed lines extend to include data not shown in tables.)

The total-planned-expenditure line (C + I + G + X − Im) crosses the 45-degree line at the $700 billion level of national income and product. This intersection point identifies the equilibrium condition (E). To the left of this intersection, total planned expenditure is greater than production, as shown by the red space between the C + I + G + X − Im line and the 45-degree line. So inventories are driven down, and pressures for expansion are generated. To the right of the intersection point, total planned expenditure is less than production by amounts shown by the purple space. Unplanned inventory begins to pile up, and there are pressures to lower production and/or prices in the next period. Only at a national income and product level of $700 billion is there a balance among the opposing forces such that there is no tendency for change—that is, equilibrium.

It is important to remember that, in the Keynesian model, equilibrium is not necessarily a desirable situation for the economy. Serious unemployment may exist, or the economy may be plagued by inflation. All the model shows is that the economy will tend to move toward its equilibrium situation. Whether that situation is good or bad and whether something should be done to change the equilibrium point are matters of public policy.

Macroeconomic equilibrium exists when total planned expenditure equals national income and product: Y* = C + I + G + X − Im. In the Keynesian model, equilibrium can exist despite serious unemployment.

KEYNESIAN VERSUS NEOCLASSICAL EQUILIBRIUM

The idea of equilibrium national income and product is at the heart of both the neoclassical and the Keynesian models. Each views equilibrium as a state of balance among opposing forces such that there is no tendency for change. Also, both suggest that the economy tends to move toward equilibrium from any nonequilibrium situation. In the Keynesian model, inventories that are too large or too small cause firms to change production levels and thereby move the economy toward equilibrium. In the neoclassical model, disequilibrium conditions lead to changes in wage rates, prices of goods, interest rates, and foreign-exchange rates, and these move the economy toward equilibrium.

A basic difference between the Keynesian and the neoclassical models is the latter's prediction that, in the long run, equilibrium will bring full employment. The Keynesian model offers no such prediction. In the Keynesian model, the equilibrium level of national income and product need *not* correspond to full employment.

Economics in Focus

Consumer Psychology: Exploring the Mysteries of the Consumption Function

In late 1988, while economists and financial analysts worried about inflation, American consumers continued to spend freely. Although the Federal Reserve had acted to raise interest rates and cool the economy, consumers seemed to be paying little attention. In fact, the Index of Consumer Confidence, a measure of the optimism with which consumers view the economic future, jumped to its highest point in twenty years.

How could consumers remain so confident, and so free with their dollars, while economists were issuing dire warnings and short-term interest rates had risen 2.5 to 3 percentage points in the previous twelve months? First, the short-term interest rates did not greatly affect most consumers; their VISA and MasterCard rates might go up, but only after a fairly substantial lag. Also, if they paid off their balances quickly, the total interest costs increased only a small amount. Even for a relatively large purchase, such as a new car, the monthly payments did not rise enough to discourage most people. Second, and probably more important, disposable personal income (DPI) had continued to grow, partly because of the rise in employment. Consumers simply had more money available than they had the year before. According to some estimates, the percentage jump in consumer spending from the fourth quarter of 1987 to the fourth quarter of 1988 almost exactly matched the percentage growth in DPI. This parallel illustrates the close connection between DPI and consumer spending predicted by the Keynesian model.

But the continual shifts in consumer psychology are difficult to anticipate. A few months after the 1988 buying binge, car sales slowed, as did house sales and general retail sales. The growth in consumer spending eroded considerably in the first quarter of 1989. Consumer confidence had dropped. But—and this was the puzzling part—personal-income growth continued to accelerate, and disposable income was increasing much faster than spending. Thus the money was still available, but now it was being used to swell savings accounts and other financial assets.

Why did consumers, after speeding through the early stop signs, become suddenly cautious? The rise in interest rates must finally have produced its predicted effect. But this was a delayed reaction at best, and no one knew whether the downturn in consumer spending would continue or reverse itself. Although most economists believe in certain general principles of consumer psychology, accurately predicting which way the public will turn at a given moment can be difficult or impossible. Many factors, such as political news, overseas events, even the weather can have unforeseen impacts. Some say that such unpredictability makes economics an inexact science; but it also makes the field continually surprising and challenging.

Sources: Gene Koretz, "Why the Fed Can't Seem to Brake the Buying Binge," *Business Week*, January 23, 1989, p. 26; James C. Cooper and Kathleen Madigan, "Slower Growth? The Jury Still Can't Reach a Verdict," *Business Week*, May 15, 1989, pp. 27–28; Henry F. Myers, "Talk of Stagflation: Hot Issue or Hot Air?" *Wall Street Journal*, April, 24, 1989, p. A1; "The Fed Can't Lick Inflation Single-Handed," *Business Week*, April 10, 1989, p. 104; Jeffrey M. Laderman, "Is It Inflation? Recession? Or Just Spring Fever?" *Business Week*, April 10, 1989, pp. 70–71.

SUMMARY

1. The Keynesian approach to macroeconomic equilibrium was presented by the British economist John Maynard Keynes in his book, *The General Theory of Employment, Interest, and Money,* which appeared in 1936. (See page 192.)

2. Keynesian economists reject models, such as the neoclassical model and Say's Identity, that rely on flexible prices, wage rates, interest rates, and foreign-exchange rates to maintain the economy at equilibrium and to assure that full employment is the normal equilibrium situation. They believe that prices are not in fact flexible enough to assure this and that, even if prices were to fall drastically in a recession, the resulting distress among debtors and financial institutions would prevent the economy from recovering promptly. (See pages 192–193.)

3. An aggregate-supply curve representing the Keynesian approach in macroeconomics would be almost horizontal. This is because Keynesian economists believe that firms prefer to permit the initial impact of demand changes to fall on output rather than on prices and because Keynesians often concentrate on situations in which significant quantities of unemployed resources are available. For these reasons, prices are "sticky." In the Keynesian model, aggregate demand is the primary determinant of real GNP. (See pages 193–194 and Figure 1, page 194.)

4. The Keynesian theory uses the concept of the consumption function, which is a relationship between the level of disposable personal income and the amount of planned consumption expenditure in the economy. The marginal propensity to consume (*MPC*) expresses a relationship between changes in disposable personal income and changes in planned consumption expenditure. Autonomous consumption expenditure is the amount of planned consumption spending that would take place if disposable personal income were zero. (See pages 195–196.)

5. Saving is also a function of disposable personal income. The marginal propensity to save (*MPS*) is the relation between changes in disposable personal income and changes in planned saving. (See page 197.)

6. The value of the marginal propensity to consume is smaller when only a little time is allowed for households to respond to income changes than when more time is allowed to respond. The permanent income hypothesis states that people save increments to their income that they believe to be temporary or "transitory." As more time passes after a change in level of income, a larger part of the change is seen as "permanent" and available for expenditure on consumption. (See page 197.)

7. The Keynesian cross is a graph that displays national income and product on its horizontal axis and planned expenditure on its vertical axis. A 45-degree reference line is drawn from the origin of the Keynesian-cross graph. (See pages 197–200 and Figure 2, page 199.)

8. Adjustments for taxes allow consumption and saving functions to be calculated on a basis of national income and product rather than on a basis of disposable personal income. (See pages 201–202 and Table 3, page 202.)

9. Planned investment expenditure is an important component of the Keynesian theory. The rate of interest is a determinant of planned investment expenditure, as are also other considerations that affect business expectations about the profitability of investments. Government purchases and net exports also are important components of the Keynesian theory. (See pages 204–207.)

10. Total planned expenditure combines all streams of planned spending. In the Keynesian model, macroeconomic equilibrium exists when total planned expenditure equals national income and product, as indicated by the equation $Y^* = C + I + G + X - Im$. According to the Keynesian theory, this equilibrium need not correspond with full employment. (See pages 207–209 and Table 5, page 208.)

11. If national income and product is greater than total planned expenditure, inventories become larger than desired by business firms, leading them to reduce prices and/or output, thus lowering the level of national income and product. If national income and product is less than total planned expenditure, inventories will fall below the levels desired by business firms, leading them to increase prices and/or output, thus causing national income and product to rise. (See pages 207–209 and Figure 5, page 209.)

KEY TERMS

autonomous consumption expenditure: in the consumption function equation, it is the amount of planned consumption expenditure (C) that is independent of the level of disposable personal income (DPI) (page 195).

average propensity to consume (APC): the amount of planned consumption expenditure (C) divided by the amount of disposable personal income (DPI) (page 197).

average propensity to save (APS): the amount of planned saving (S) divided by the amount of disposable personal income (DPI) (page 197).

breakeven point: the income level at which there is neither net planned saving nor net planned dissaving (page 199).

consumption function: the relationship between the amount that households plan to spend to buy consumption goods and services and the level of disposable personal income (page 195).

dissaving: negative saving, or financing current consumption by drawing on past savings (page 199).

45-degree line: a straight line drawn at a 45-degree angle from the origin of a diagram, such as the Keynesian cross. If the units of measure are the same on both axes, the line will connect all points at which the value on one axis is equal to the value on the other axis (page 198).

injections: planned expenditures other than consumption purchases, that is, planned investment (I), government purchases (G), and exports (X) (page 215).

Keynesian cross: a graph that measures dollar amounts of spending on the vertical axis and dollar amounts of income on the horizontal axis (page 198).

Keynesian economics: an approach to macroeconomics developed by John Maynard Keynes in the 1930s that emphasizes the importance of demand in determining the equilibrium level of national income and product (page 192).

leakages: household uses of funds for other than consumption purchases, that is, saving (S), net taxes (T_n), and imports (Im) (page 215).

long-run consumption function: the relationship between a change in disposable personal income and the resulting change in planned consumption expenditure after enough time has elapsed for all potential responses to occur (page 200).

marginal propensity to consume (MPC): the value in the consumption function equation that shows how much planned consumption expenditure will change as a percentage of the associated change in the level of disposable personal income (page 196).

marginal propensity to save (MPS): the change in planned saving expressed as a percentage of the associated change in disposable personal income (page 197).

neoclassical: a school of economic thought that concludes that the macroeconomy tends toward equilibrium at full employment (page 192).

permanent income hypothesis: a hypothesis that states that a household plans to spend for consumption a fixed proportion of the disposable personal income that it believes to be its permanent, or long-run, income level (page 200).

Say's Identity: a proposition that states that the sum of all the wages, salaries, rents, interest, and profits in the economy must provide enough purchasing power to allow households to pay for all the goods and services produced at whatever price level was in effect when they were produced (page 192).

short-run consumption function: the relationship between a change in disposable personal income and the resulting change in planned consumption expenditure before enough time has elapsed for all the potential responses to be achieved (page 200).

total planned expenditure: the sum of planned consumption, planned investment, government purchases, and net exports (page 194).

transitory income: income that is perceived as temporary as distinguished from income that is perceived as permanent (page 200).

DISCUSSION QUESTIONS

1. Explain how Say's Identity provides a basis for arguing that an economy will tend to operate at full employment. If planned saving temporarily exceeds planned investment, how, according to this theory, would interest rates change? What would be the effect of this change?

2. Keynes challenged neoclassical macroeconomic theory by claiming that prices, wage rates, and interest rates actually do not change as quickly as the neoclassical economists believed. Describe one current government policy or program that relates to these adjustments. Does this policy or program strengthen or weaken the neoclassical adjustment mechanism?

3. If planned consumption spending increases by $80 billion whenever disposable personal income increases by $100 billion, what is the value of the marginal propensity to consume? What is the value of the marginal propensity to save? Given these values, what will be the breakeven level of disposable personal income if planned consumption spending is $50 billion when disposable personal income is zero?

4. If real disposable personal income in the United States goes up by $100 billion and enough time passes so that the long-run consumption function can be effective, by about how much would planned consumption spending increase? How would this increase differ if a shorter time period were being used? Give reasons for your answer.

5. According to the permanent income hypothesis, what do people do with an increase in income that they view as only temporary? If you were to win a large amount of money in a lottery, how much of your winnings would go to a higher day-to-day level of living and how much would go into your savings account or to purchase something special that you had wanted for a long time? How much of that something special would be used up during the first year?

6. Without looking at Figure 4, draw the demand curve for planned investment, carefully labeling the variables shown on each axis. Now compare your graph with Figure 4 to be sure you have it right. How does the rate of return on a particular investment project determine its position along this demand curve? Name one change that would shift this curve to the left and one that would shift it to the right.

7. The assumption that in the short run government purchases do not change in response to changes in national income and product is useful to simplify the presentation of the Keynesian theory. The assumption *does* allow government purchases to change in response to policy actions. Explain whether this change should be shown as a shift or as a movement along a government-purchases curve graphed on a Keynesian-cross diagram.

8. In this chapter, total planned expenditure was $175 billion when national income and product was zero and the marginal propensity to consume was 0.75. Under these conditions, equilibrium national income and product was $700 billion. If equilibrium national income and product is Y^*, we can say that $Y^* = 175 + 0.75Y^*$. Solve this equation for Y^* to assure yourself that it works. Then test your understanding by assuming that the marginal propensity to consume is 0.80. What would the equilibrium national income and product be in that case?

9. The Keynesian equilibrium described at the end of this chapter differs sharply from the neoclassical theory on the matter of unemployment. Explain the nature of this difference.

Appendix:
The Leakage-and-Injection
Version of
the Keynesian Model

As an alternative to the concept of total planned expenditure, the Keynesian model can explain the equilibrium level of national income and product by using the concepts of **leakages** and **injections.** Leakages are household uses of funds for other than consumption purchases. That is, leakages consist of saving (S), net taxes (T_n), and imports (Im). Injections are planned expenditures other than consumption purchases, that is, planned investment (I), government purchases (G), and exports (X). Because imports are separated from exports in this analysis, investment and government purchases include only purchases of domestic (home) outputs. Thus, our notation for injections is that government purchases are G_d and planned investment expenditure is I_d, where the subscript stands for "domestic." With these definitions, macroeconomic equilibrium exists when planned injections equal planned leakages, that is, when

$$I_d + G_d + X = S + T_n + Im$$

Table 6 provides hypothetical values for injections and leakages related to various levels of national income and product. The values are the same as those used to explain the total-planned-expenditure method. This means that we assume that the investment and government purchases discussed there were all from domestic producers and that all imports were household purchases of consumption goods and services.

In Table 6, the injections columns for planned domestic investment (I_d) and for government domestic purchases (G_d) are taken directly from Table 5. For the other injection, exports (X), we use a constant value of $25 billion. In the leakages section, the numbers for planned saving and net taxes

are taken directly from Table 3, which showed the saving function and net taxes equal to $100. For imports (Im), we use a constant $10 billion in our example. We realize that it is unrealistic to assume that changes in national income and product do not change imports, but we make this assumption to simplify our explanation of the Keynesian system. Of course, exports of $25 billion minus imports of $10 billion equal the net export figure of $15 billion used in the explanation of total planned expenditure.

Leakages are household uses of funds for other than consumption purposes. Injections are planned expenditures other than consumption purchases.

Macroeconomic equilibrium exists when total leakages equal total injections, so that they offset each other. This occurs when they are both equal to $160 billion, when national income and product is $700 billion (the row of numbers with the white background in Table 6). This equilibrium point is shown at E in Figure 6, where the purple line for injections $(I_d + G_d + X)$ and the blue line for leakages $(S + T_n + Im)$ cross. At national income and product levels of less than $700 billion, total injections are greater than total leakages. So inventories are driven down below the desired levels, and there are pressures to raise production and/or prices in the next period. But when national income and product levels are higher than $700 billion, total leakages are greater than total injections, inventories become larger than desired, and pressures grow to lower production and/or prices. Note

TABLE 6
Injections and Leakages (in billions of dollars)

National Income and Product (Y)	Injections				Leakages			
	I_d +	G_d +	X =	Total	S +	T_n +	Im =	Total
$ 100	$35	$100	$25	$160	$-100	$100	$10	$ 10
200	35	100	25	160	- 75	100	10	35
300	35	100	25	160	- 50	100	10	60
400	35	100	25	160	- 25	100	10	85
500	35	100	25	160	0	100	10	110
600	35	100	25	160	25	100	10	135
700	35	100	25	160	50	100	10	160
800	35	100	25	160	75	100	10	185
900	35	100	25	160	100	100	10	210
1,000	35	100	25	160	125	100	10	235
1,100	35	100	25	160	150	100	10	260

The hypothetical values for planned domestic investment (I_d) and government domestic purchases (G_d) are taken from Table 5. Exports (X) are assumed to be constant at $25 billion. Values for planned saving (S) and net taxes (T_n) are taken directly from Table 3. Imports (Im) are assumed to be constant at $10 billion. Equilibrium exists when total injections equal total leakages so that they offset each other. Equilibrium is illustrated by the row of numbers with a white background. Notice that equilibrium does not require a balance in each separate stream of the circular flow. In this illustration, planned saving exceeds planned domestic investment at equilibrium, but there is an excess of exports over imports.

that it is *not* necessary to have a balance in each separate stream of the circular flow. In our illustration of equilibrium, saving exceeds domestic investment, but exports exceed imports.

Macroeconomic equilibrium exists when planned injections equal planned leakages: $I_d + G_d + X = S + T_n + Im$.

You should be warned of possible confusion in comparing the injection–leakage approach with the planned-expenditure approach. The problem arises because of the different ways of treating imports. Using the injection–leakage approach, we record imports as a leakage and exports as an injection. However, when we use the planned-expenditure approach, we combine the two as "net exports." Therefore, in terms of our graphs, the wedges shown for total planned expenditure in Figure 5 are *not* the same as the wedges for injec-

tions and leakages in Figure 6. Since we believe it is easier to understand and more directly related to policy making, we shall depend on the total-planned-expenditure method rather than on injections and leakages.

DISCUSSION QUESTIONS

1. Write an algebraic statement showing that leakages are equal to injections when the economy is at equilibrium. Explain what would be wrong with this statement if investment and government purchases were not limited to domestic purchases.

2. Without looking at Figure 6, draw the graphic illustration of the leakages and injections model of equilibrium. Check to be sure you have it right. Why does the leakages line slope upward? Does each leakage component contribute to this slope? Discuss whether it is realistic to draw the injections line as horizontal.

FIGURE 6
Macroeconomic Equilibrium Illustrated on a Leakages-and-Injections Graph

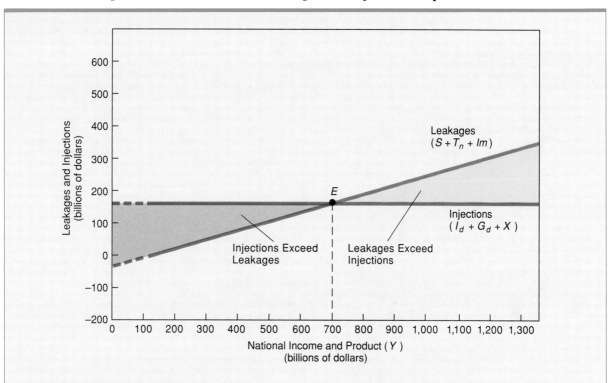

Values from Table 6 are plotted on this graph. The purple injections line ($I_d + G_d + X$) is horizontal, reflecting the assumption that none of these values changes because of a change in national income and product. The blue leakage line ($S + T_n + Im$) has a positive slope equal to the marginal propensity to save, since net taxes (T_n) and imports (Im) are assumed to be unchanged by changes in the level of national income and product. Equilibrium is at E, where injections are equal to leakages, and national income and product is $700 billion. To the left of E, the wedge-shaped red area shows injections exceeding leakages, reducing inventories below desired levels and generating pressures for expansion of the economy. To the right of E, the wedge-shaped blue area shows leakages exceeding injections so that inventories become larger than desired, generating pressures for contraction of the economy. (The dashed lines extend to include data not shown in Table 6.)

11
Fiscal Policy

Preview   What good is all this analysis? Can it tell us anything about what caused the Great Depression of the 1930s or about the possibility of it happening again? According to the Keynesian system, what tools can the government use to deal with inflation and unemployment? What can it do to prevent or to control these problems?

In this chapter we begin our study of the instruments or tools that a government can use to influence the aggregate performance of the economy. Here we consider the fiscal instruments, which make use of the taxing and spending powers of the government and which affect the government's budget.

We begin by discussing the target levels of national income and product. These are the levels that are thought to have the most desirable effects on employment, prices, and growth rates, as well as on other elements of the national economy. Congress, the president, and officials in various government agencies all take part in setting these targets.

Next we describe gaps between the target level of national income and product and the level that will prevail if the government takes no special action. An expansionary gap means that, if left to itself, the economy will expand beyond the target. A contractionary gap means that, if the economy is left to itself, national income and product will be less than the target.

The third part of the chapter explains the *multiplier* relationship that connects a change in total planned expenditure with the resulting change in equilibrium national income and product.

In the final part of the chapter, we describe the fiscal instruments that the government can use to alter total planned expenditure and move the economy to the target level of national income and product. These instruments include changes in planned government purchases, changes in planned tax collections, and changes in both at the same time. We show how the multiplier process operates in response to the use of the different fiscal instruments. We also describe how certain government programs work automatically to stabilize the economy.

The appendix to the chapter describes how the national debt is created and discusses the impact of the debt on the economy.

TARGET LEVELS OF NATIONAL INCOME AND PRODUCT

As noted in Chapter 10, Keynesians argue that the economy, left to its own adjustment mechanisms, may operate for long periods of time at levels of national income and product far lower than the level seen as desirable. During such lengthy recessions, a great amount of potential production can be lost and living standards can be depressed for large segments of the society. According to Keynesians, appropriate policy initiatives can shorten periods of recession, reduce the amount of lost production, and stabilize living standards.

According to the Keynesian model, public policies can influence the volume of total planned expenditure ($C + I + G + X - Im$) and thereby change the equilibrium level of national income and product in the economy. Therefore, the first step in putting the Keynesian model into practical operation is to identify a desired **target level of national income and product.** This is the level chosen through political processes as a goal for macroeconomic policy. It may include a target for real production and for the inflation rate as well.

Keynesian economists believe that public policies can influence the volume of total planned expenditure and thereby change the equilibrium level of national income and product. Before government policies can be put in place, government officials must identify a desired target level of national income and product.

Setting appropriate targets requires forecasts of the production capability of the economy. Several

agencies of the United States government are engaged in this task. In the executive branch of the government, the **Council of Economic Advisers (CEA),** which was established by the **Employment Act of 1946,** is particularly involved in this forecasting, since the council is responsible for advising the president on economic policy. For the legislative branch, similar work is done by the staff of the **Joint Economic Committee (JEC)** of Congress. Both use data provided by other agencies, such as the departments of commerce, labor, agriculture, and treasury. The CEA and the JEC receive reports on the amount of production in recent years and the labor, capital, and natural resource inputs used. Productivity data are calculated, showing output per hour of labor and per unit of capital. To make the forecast of production capability for a future time period, these agencies estimate the amounts of labor, capital and natural resources that will be available and multiply by their estimates of productivity.

There are many crucial judgments that must be made in setting the target level for national income and product the nation should try to achieve. The basic judgment is about the level of employment to seek. There is no iron-clad number that represents full employment as there is divided opinion as to the magnitude of the natural rate of unemployment. If the target is set too high—at an output and employment level that cannot be reached—attempts to reach the target may result in inflation. On the other hand, setting the target too low can result in failure to make full use of the nation's resources and impose hardships on the unemployed.

Choosing a target level involves making many crucial judgments, especially about the level of employment to seek.

In the United States, targets for national income and product usually are not formally spelled out in legislation.[1] Instead, they are considered when taxing and spending proposals are drafted

---

1. An exception is the **Humphrey-Hawkins Act of 1978,** which set specific goals for both price stability and employment but provided no enforcement mechanism to assure that these goals would be achieved.

and presented to Congress. The targets and the desirability of achieving them are used in arguments seeking legislative and citizen support. Different interest groups and political parties are likely to promote different targets as desirable and achievable. For our purpose of explaining government fiscal policies and instruments, it is the concept of a target level of national income and product that is important.

CONTRACTIONARY AND EXPANSIONARY GAPS

Contractionary or expansionary gaps exist when forecasts indicate that the performance of the economy will not match the target, or desired level, of national income and product. In other words, economists with the Council of Economic Advisers and the Joint Economic Committee forecast the volume of total planned expenditure and the corresponding equilibrium level of national income and product for some coming time period on the assumption that present economic programs remain in effect. Then they compare their forecasts with the target levels that have been set by policymakers to find out whether the economy will hit the target or whether a contractionary or an expansionary gap will exist. A **contractionary gap** exists if the predicted equilibrium level of national income and product is less than the target. An **expansionary gap** exists if the predicted equilibrium level of national income and product exceeds the target.

A contractionary gap exists if the predicted equilibrium level of national income and product is less than the target. An expansionary gap exists if the predicted equilibrium level of national income and product exceeds the target.

Contractionary Gaps

When a contractionary gap exists, Keynesian economists expect macroeconomic unemployment and idle production capacity in the economy. Figure 1 pictures such a gap. The $C + I + G + X - Im$ curve

FIGURE 1
A Contractionary Gap

The $C + I + G + X - Im$ curve represents the levels of total planned expenditure that are forecast for various levels of national income and product on the assumption that present economic programs remain in effect. Macroeconomic equilibrium is at Y^*, as indicated by the intersection of the total-planned-expenditure curve and the 45-degree line at point a. If the target level of national income and product is Y_T, the amount of the contractionary gap is the amount of lost national income and product indicted by $Y_T - Y^*$. At the target level of national income and product (Y_T), total planned expenditure is less than the target level of national income and product by the distance from point b to point c.

represents the volume of total planned expenditure that is expected at various levels of national income and product if there are no changes in existing programs. So the equilibrium condition will be at point a, where this curve crosses the 45-degree line. The equilibrium level of national income and product is Y^*, but the target level is Y_T. Because the equilibrium is less than the target, there is a contractionary gap. The implication is that, if left alone, the economy will operate below the desired level, Y_T, that macroeconomic unemployment will exist, and that production of some goods and services will be lost. The size of the contractionary gap is equal to $Y_T - Y^*$. Total planned expenditure is too small to enable the economy to reach the target level of national income and product.

The basic Keynesian remedy for dealing with a contractionary gap is illustrated in Figure 2, which shows a predicted macroeconomic equilibrium level of Y^* and a target level of Y_T, so that a contractionary gap exists. The Keynesian model indicates that this contractionary gap can be closed by shifting the total-planned-expenditure curve upward, from $(C + I + G + X - Im)_1$ to $(C + I + G + X - Im)_2$. Equilibrium will move from E_1 to E_2 and the equilibrium level of national income and product will match the target level. The upward shift of the curve will move the intersection point upward along the 45-degree line.

When a contractionary gap exists, Keynesian economists expect macroeconomic unemployment and idle production capacity in the economy. Closing a contractionary gap calls for an upward shift in the total-planned-expenditure curve.

Expansionary Gaps

Expansionary gaps arise when total planned expenditure is greater than the value of the output the economy can provide at the target level of national income and product. These gaps are generally associated with shortages and inflationary pressures on the economy. Figure 3 pictures this situation. Here the forecast equilibrium level of economic activity, Y^*, is greater than the target, Y_T. If the target has been set at full employment or capacity production, the expansionary gap means that planned spending will be greater than production as measured at the existing price level.

In the Keynesian approach, closing an expansionary gap calls for a downward shift in the total-planned-expenditure curve. This is illustrated in Figure 4. The inflationary pressures being generated at equilibrium E_1 can be relieved by shifting the total-planned-expenditure curve downward, from $(C + I + G + X - Im)_1$ to $(C + I + G + X - Im)_2$. This will move the equilibrium from point E_1 to point E_2, so that macroeconomic equilibrium

FIGURE 2
Closing a Contractionary Gap

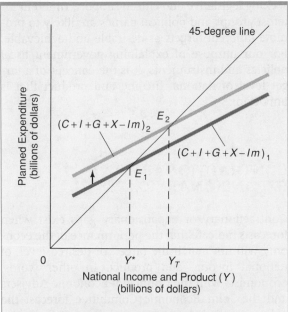

The predicted equilibrium for the economy is Y^*, where the total-planned-expenditure curve $(C + I + G + X - Im)_1$ intersects the 45-degree line at E_1. The target level of national income and product is Y_T. The contractionary gap can be closed by shifting the total-planned-expenditure curve upward to $(C + I + G + X - Im)_2$. After this shift, equilibrium is indicated by the intersection of $(C + I + G + X - Im)_2$ with the 45-degree line at E_2, and the contractionary gap has been closed.

will correspond with the target level of national income and product.

When an expansionary gap exists, Keynesian economists expect shortages and pressure for inflation. Closing an expansionary gap calls for a downward shift in the total-planned-expenditure curve.

Although the Keynesian prescription for dealing with an expansionary gap is clear, the Keynesian system was designed for recession situations—not for situations in which the equilibrium GNP (Y^*) exceeds the target GNP (Y_T). For real GNP levels greater than the target level, Keynesians do not see the aggregate-supply curve as horizontal, that is, they do *not* see the *AS* curve as in the illustration of the Keynesian view in Figure 1 of Chapter 10. Instead, they expect the *AS* curve to slope upward so that an expansionary gap generates pressure for inflation. In this connection, it is important to note that many of the causes of the inflationary pressures of the 1970s can be traced to expansionary gaps arising from forces at work on the supply side of the economy. Problems arose owing to restrictions on the supply of petroleum imposed by the Organization of Petroleum Exporting Countries (OPEC). Also, supply-side effects arose as delayed reactions to price-level increases that had taken place during the 1960s. Difficulty in dealing with expansionary gaps caused by supply-side

FIGURE 3
An Expansionary Gap

The $C + I + G + X - Im$ curve represents the levels of total planned expenditure that are forecast for various levels of national income and product on the assumption that present economic programs remain in effect. Macroeconomic equilibrium is at Y^*, as indicated by the intersection of the total-planned-expenditure curve and the 45-degree line at point *a*. At the target level of national income and product of Y_T, there is an excessive amount of planned expenditure, indicated by the distance from *b* to *c*. This extra expenditure may generate inflationary pressures.

FIGURE 4
Closing an Expansionary Gap

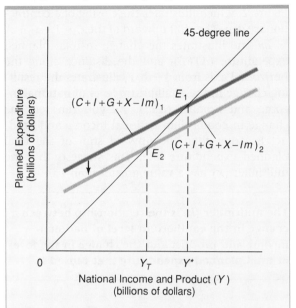

The forecast equilibrium for the economy is Y^*, where the total-planned-expenditure curve $(C + I + G + X - Im)_1$ intersects the 45-degree line at E_1. The target level of national income and product is Y_T. The expansionary gap can be closed by shifting the total-planned-expenditure curve downward to $(C + I + G + X - Im)_2$. After this shift, equilibrium is indicated by the intersection of $(C + I + G + X - Im)_2$ with the 45-degree line at E_2, and the expansionary gap has been closed.

events is one of the reasons the Keynesian model did not fare well during the Great Stagflation of the 1970s.

THE MULTIPLIER

The **multiplier** is the relationship between a change in the equilibrium level of national income and product and the change in the level of total planned expenditure that caused it. If we let the triangle "delta" (Δ) stand for "the change in," the multiplier is $\Delta Y^*/\Delta TPE$, where *TPE* stands for the volume of total planned expenditure. Expressed as a functional relationship,

$$\Delta Y^* = k(\Delta TPE), \textit{ceteris paribus}$$

where k represents the multiplier. The multiplier relationship can be visualized by looking back to Figure 2, which illustrates the closing of a contractionary gap. The shift upward of the $C + I + G + X - Im$ line illustrates the change in total planned expenditure (ΔTPE), and the distance along the horizontal axis from Y^* to Y_T illustrates the resulting change in the equilibrium level of national income and product (ΔY^*). As you can see, the change in equilibrium national income and product is larger than the upward shift of the total planned expenditure line. This suggests that the multiplier (k) has a value greater than 1.0.

The multiplier (k) is the relationship between a change in the equilibrium level of national income and product and the change in the level of total planned expenditure that caused it.

Shifting the Total-Planned-Expenditure Curve

Since the multiplier and the resulting change in equilibrium national income and product start from a shift of the total-planned-expenditure line, it is helpful to examine some of the variables that can cause such a shift. Because we are dealing with a *shift* (and not a *movement along*) the total-planned-expenditure line, the only variable *not* eligible for consideration is a change in national income and product itself, since the effects of changes in this variable are already accounted for in the slope of the total-planned-expenditure line. But there are many variables that can cause a shift in this curve. For example, planned consumption expenditure can be affected by changes in stocks of durable goods already owned, by changes in financial wealth (stocks, bonds, savings accounts, etc.), and by changes in expectations about whether good times or bad times are in store. If any of these variables change, planned consumption expenditure at any specified level of national income and product may change and thus shift the total-planned-expenditure line.

Variables that can change the planned investment expenditure component of total planned expenditure include changes in the rate of interest

and all forces that bear upon estimates of the rate of return that will come from investment projects. Among these are anticipated business conditions, expected operating costs (especially wages), taxes and government regulations, new technologies, and a host of other matters.

The government purchases component can change when government policies change, when a national emergency arises, or when there is a change in voter attitudes toward government spending.

Finally, the net-export component of planned expenditure may change because of changes in the relative prices of foreign goods and in foreign exchange rates. It may also be affected by changes in economic conditions in the foreign countries themselves.

Many variables can cause a shift in the total-planned-expenditure curve, such as changes in stocks of durable goods already owned, changes in financial wealth, and changes in expectations which affect planned consumption expenditure. Other variables can cause changes in the planned investment component, the government purchases component, and the net-export component of planned expenditure.

Changing Equilibrium

To illustrate how the multiplier works, let us assume that one of the nonincome variables affecting planned investment expenditure (I) changes and brings about a shift in the $C + I + G + X - Im$ curve. How will this shift affect the equilibrium level of national income and product?

The multiplier process is started by a change in some nonincome determinant of planned spending, which alters the amount of planned spending and changes the equilibrium level of national income and product.

Suppose that someone discovers a new process to lower the cost of extracting fuel from a type of

TABLE 1
Increased Planned Expenditure and Equilibrium National Income and Product (in billions of dollars)

(1) National Income and Product (Y)	(2) Planned Consumption Expenditure (C)	(3) Planned Investment Expenditure (I)		(4) Government Purchases (G)	(5) Net Exports (X − Im)	(6) Total Planned Expenditure (C + I + G + X − Im)		
		Original	New			Original		New
$ 100	$100	$35	→ $85	$100	$15	$ 250	→	$ 300
200	175	35	→ 85	100	15	325	→	375
300	250	35	→ 85	100	15	400	→	450
400	325	35	→ 85	100	15	475	→	525
500	400	35	→ 85	100	15	550	→	600
600	475	35	→ 85	100	15	625	→	675
700	550	35	→ 85	100	15	700	→	750
800	625	35	→ 85	100	15	775	→	825
900	700	35	→ 85	100	15	850	→	900
1,000	775	35	→ 85	100	15	925	→	975
1,100	850	35	→ 85	100	15	1,000	→	1,050

At the original level of total planned expenditure, equilibrium occurs when both total planned expenditure and national income and product are $700 billion as shown by the row of red numbers. A $50 billion increase in planned investment increases total planned expenditure by $50 billion at all levels of national income and product. The new equilibrium is at a national income and product of $900 billion as shown by the row of blue numbers. Thus, a $50 billion increase in planned expenditure increases equilibrium national income and product by $200 billion in this illustration.

rock called oil shale. Let us imagine that this discovery convinces business firms to increase the flow of planned investment expenditure by $50 billion each year at all levels of national income and product. (We realize that this is an extremely large increase compared with the other values in our hypothetical illustration but the large size will make it easier to show changes in graphic form.) Because the discovery gives business people great hopes for profits, the demand curve for planned investment spending, such as the curve in Figure 4 on page 205, shifts to the right by $50 billion. At any specified rate of interest, planned investment is $50 billion greater than it was before the change in business outlook brought about by the discovery. To keep things simple, assume that this is the only change that takes place.[2] Let us see how this

change alters the equilibrium level of national income and product according to the Keynesian model.

In Table 1, we reproduce Table 5 of Chapter 10 (page 208) but increase every entry in the planned-investment-expenditure column by $50 billion, since we assume that, for every level of national income and product, every year, planned investment will be $50 billion greater than before the new production process began. Of course, we must also increase every entry for total planned expenditure by $50 billion. From this table we note that the conditions for macroeconomic equilibrium, which require an equality between total planned expenditure and national income and product, now exist when national income and product is $900 billion as shown by the row of numbers printed in blue. The equilibrium level of national income and product has increased from $700 billion to $900 billion.

The same information is presented in Figure 5, which illustrates the upward shift of the $C + I + G + X − Im$ curve on a Keynesian-cross diagram. The $C + I_1 + G + X − Im$ line shows total planned

2. Of course, we realize that a rise in the demand for investments may change the rate of interest and that many other related changes will take place. If we were presenting a *general equilibrium* model, we could not allow ourselves the simplifying assumption that planned investment is the only thing that changes. However, at this stage, we shall use *partial* analysis for simplicity.

Shifting the Total-Planned-Expenditure Curve Produces a Change in the Equilibrium Level of National Income and Product

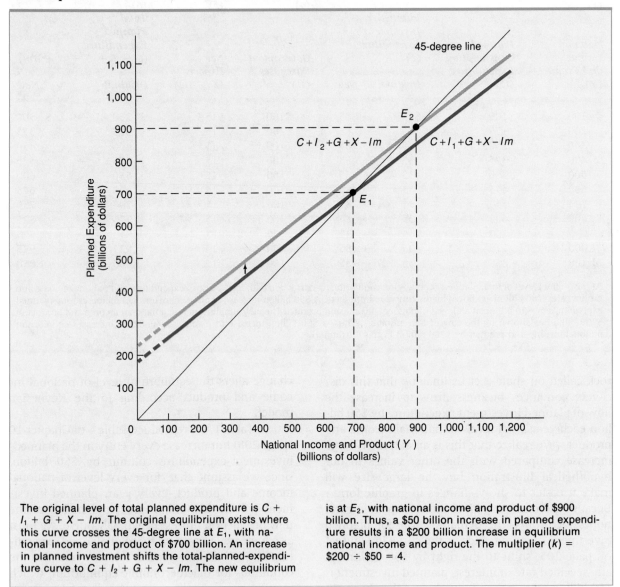

The original level of total planned expenditure is $C + I_1 + G + X - Im$. The original equilibrium exists where this curve crosses the 45-degree line at E_1, with national income and product of $700 billion. An increase in planned investment shifts the total-planned-expenditure curve to $C + I_2 + G + X - Im$. The new equilibrium is at E_2, with national income and product of $900 billion. Thus, a $50 billion increase in planned expenditure results in a $200 billion increase in equilibrium national income and product. The multiplier (k) = $200 ÷ $50 = 4.

expenditure before the assumed increase in planned investment, and the $C + I_2 + G + X - Im$ line shows total planned expenditure after this increase. The conditions for equilibrium exist where the total-planned-expenditure curve crosses the 45-degree line. Before the rise in planned expenditure, this happened at a national income and product of $700 billion. After the rise, the inter-section is at national income and product of $900 billion.

The multiplier shows the size of the change in the equilibrium level of national income and product as a multiple of the shift in total planned expenditure that began the process.

TABLE 2
The Multiplier (in billions of dollars)

Time Period ("round")	This Period's Addition to Flow of National Income and Product	Additional Planned Expenditure Induced in This Period	Total Addition to National Income and Product Flow
1	$ 50	$ 37.5	$ 50
2	37.5	28.1	87.5
3	28.1	21.1	115.6
4	21.1	15.8	136.7
5	15.8	11.9	152.5
.	↓	↓	
.	(total of $47.5)	(total of $35.6)	(total of $47.5)
.	↓	↓	
nth	_____	_____	200.0
Sum total	$200.0	$150.0	—

We assume a $50 billion increase in planned expenditure caused by a change in some nonincome variable. This results in a $50 billion increase in the flow of national income and product in round 1. This added income *induces*, or brings about, a $37.5 billion increase in planned expenditure, which in round 2 generates a further increase in the flow of income and product. The process repeats itself. When induced planned spending is 0.75 of the national income and product change that caused it, the multiplier value will be 4. In the nth round (or limit), the income and product flows will have expanded by $200 billion as a result of an initial shift of $50 billion. This is shown in the right-hand column, which shows the total addition to the flow of national income and product.

The Multiplier Process

In this illustration, an increase in the annual volume of planned investment expenditure has resulted in an increase in equilibrium national income and product that shows the multiplier effect. The upward shift of the $C + I + G + X - Im$ curve in Figure 5 was $50 billion, but the equilibrium level of national income and product rose by $200 billion—four times as much as the increase in planned spending that brought it about. The multiplier implies that the average dollar of the initiating change in planned spending is multiplied several times (in this case, four times) in the process of reaching the new equilibrium level. In our illustration, dividing $200 billion by $50 billion, we get a multiplier of 4. Measuring the size of the multiplier in this way, however, is "after the fact" and of little use in forecasting changes in equilibrium national income and product. Let us see, then, how the multiplier comes about and what determines its size.

The multiplier process is illustrated in Table 2.

The initiating increase in planned investment expenditure takes place in round 1. At that time, income is paid to workers and the owners of other resources that are employed in producing the machinery and equipment involved in the new shale investment.[3] A $50 billion per year addition to the flow of income starts during this time period as shown in the right-hand column of the table. But this is not the final result of the increased rate of planned expenditure. The people who receive the additional $50 billion of income will spend some of it to buy things they want and save some of it. Our assumption about marginal propensities (see Chapter 10) was that 75 cents of each additional national income dollar would move around the circular flow as planned expenditure *induced*, or caused, by the increase in income. The planned

3. We shall assume that money to finance this new investment is available to companies without taking funds away from other planned expenditure. We shall have more to say about this assumption when we describe how the banking system operates and how the stock of money in the economy changes.

expenditure induced in round 1 is $37.5 billion ($50 billion × 0.75). This induced expenditure brings about new production and income in round 2, that is, the expenditure of $37.5 billion provides income for the resources used in producing these goods and services. During round 2, the flow of income and production includes both the $50 billion flow per period that started in round 1 and the $37.5 billion flow that started in round 2. So income and production flow at the rate of $87.5 billion more than before the multiplier process started, as shown in the "total addition" column. But the expansion has not ended. Equilibrium has not yet been reached.

The multiplier process continues in round after round. Each time, the flow of income and production increases (in our illustration) by an amount equal to 75 percent of the increase experienced in the preceding round—$37.5 billion in round 2, $28.1 billion in round 3, $21.1 billion in round 4, and so on. The total flow of national income and product is larger than its premultiplier level by $50 billion in round 1, $87.5 billion in round 2, $115.6 billion in round 3, $136.7 billion in round 4, and so on.

With each round of the multiplier process, the addition to national income and product becomes smaller. Mathematically, a progression of this kind approaches a limit. In this case, the total additions to the flow of income and production (the sum of the numbers in the second column in Table 2) will approach $200 billion. This total is made up of the initiating $50 billion increase in planned expenditure plus $150 billion in planned-expenditure increases induced by the expanded production and income (the sum of the numbers in the third column of the table). In the right-hand column, the entry for the total addition to the flow of national income and product in the nth round (the limit) is $200 billion. Equilibrium is reached when the flow of national income and product is $200 billion a year greater than it was before the upward shift in planned expenditure. At that point, the multiplier process has run its course.

The multiplier process operates through successive rounds of the circular flow.

Time Lags in the Multiplier Process   There is a time dimension in the operation of the multiplier. First of all, a certain amount of time will pass before the increased rate of spending brings about increases in incomes. Second, it will take time for these increases in incomes to induce still further increases in spending. It may be roughly accurate to assume that about three months are needed for each round of the multiplier process. In one year, then, about four rounds might be completed. In our example, these first four rounds expand the total flow of national income and product by $136.7 billion—from $700 billion to $836.7 billion. Though the whole multiplier effect is never fully realized, a great part of it comes fairly early in the process.

About three months are needed for each round of the multiplier process—for increases (or decreases) in incomes to induce further increases (or decreases) in spending.

The multiplier may operate in either an upward or a downward direction. The preceding example showed how an increase in planned expenditure would increase equilibrium national income and product. But, in a similar way, when total planned expenditure falls, the multiplier will have a downward effect on the economy.

An Algebraic Calculation of the Multiplier   The values shown in Table 2 involve a numerical process that is familiar to mathematicians. It is a geometric progression in which each number in a series is a constant proportion of the number before it. In this case, each addition to national income and product is 75 percent of the preceding one. If we let 1 represent the first value in the series, we can write a generalized description of the process as follows:

$$1 + (0.75) + (0.75)(0.75) + (0.75)(0.75)(0.75)$$
$$+ (0.75)(0.75)(0.75)(0.75) \text{ plus on and on}$$

Or we can write it in a more usual way:

$$1 + (0.75) + (0.75)^2 + (0.75)^3 + \cdots + (0.75)^n$$

where n is the final round of the process. Mathematicians demonstrate that the sum of this series will approach a predictable limit. In our illustration, this sum approaches a value of

$$\frac{1}{1-0.75} \quad \text{or} \quad \frac{1}{0.25} \quad \text{or} \quad 4$$

In Table 2, we started with a $50 billion increase in planned expenditure and ended with a $200 billion increase in the equilibrium level of national income and product. The multiplier had a value of 4.

The Multiplier Formula

We may now give a formula for the multiplier by recognizing that the value (0.75) in the case just given was the value of the slope of the $C + I + G + X - Im$ lines in Figure 5. The numerical value of this slope is equal to the amount of total planned expenditure induced by a change in national income and product divided by the size of that change in national income and product. The same idea appeared in Chapter 10, when we discussed the marginal propensity to consume. In that discussion, it was easy to understand how an increase in income could induce households to raise planned consumption expenditure. Now we simply apply this concept to total planned expenditure for the whole economy. If we assume that net taxes and all the other expenditure streams (planned investment, government purchases, and net exports) are not altered by changes in national income and product, we can put MPC into our multiplier calculation in place of the 0.75 value used in Table 2.[4] We can then say that the value of the multiplier is

$$\frac{1}{1-MPC}$$

If the MPC is 0.75 (as in our case), the multiplier

---

4. A more realistic model of equilibrium and of the multiplier could not make the assumption that the marginal propensities for net taxes, planned investment, government purchases, and net exports all are zero. Instead, it would have to recognize that changes in national income and product induce changes in each of these streams, just as our model has recognized that planned consumption spending is induced by income changes. The marginal propensities for planned investment and for government purchases probably would be positive, but the marginal propensity for net exports probably would be negative. In the more realistic model, the multiplier would be based on the increase in total planned expenditure that is induced by changes in national income and product.

will have a value of 4. So a $50 billion initial rise in total planned expenditure leads eventually to a $200 billion rise in national income and product. If the MPC were 0.60, the multiplier would have a value of 2½. In this case, a $50 billion initial increase in planned expenditure would result in a $125 billion change in the level of equilibrium national income and product. If the MPC were 0.8, the multiplier would have a value of 5, and so forth.

The equation given above for the multiplier can also be expressed by using the marginal propensity to save (MPS) rather than the marginal propensity to consume (MPC). If we assume that consumption and saving account for all disposable personal income, it follows that $MPS = 1 - MPC$. By substituting in the multiplier formula given above, we find that it also can be stated as

$$\frac{1}{MPS}$$

With our value for MPS of 0.25, this formula also gives a multiplier value of 4, since $1/0.25 = 4$.

If we assume that net taxes and all expenditure streams other than consumption are not altered by changes in national income and product, the formulas for the multiplier are

$$\frac{1}{1-MPC} \quad \text{and} \quad \frac{1}{MPS}$$

A Summary of the Multiplier

The multiplier is not a complicated concept, but is an important one for understanding the application of the Keynesian model to achieve a target level of national income and product. In this process, a basic distinction is made between events that *initiate* the process (shifts the $C + I + G + X - Im$ curve) and responses that are *induced* by the resulting income changes (movements along the relocated curve). The multiplier process is launched by some externally caused change in planned expenditure. Feeding upon itself, it then generates changes in income and product until it finally dwindles to insignificance.

FIGURE 6
The Multiplier Process

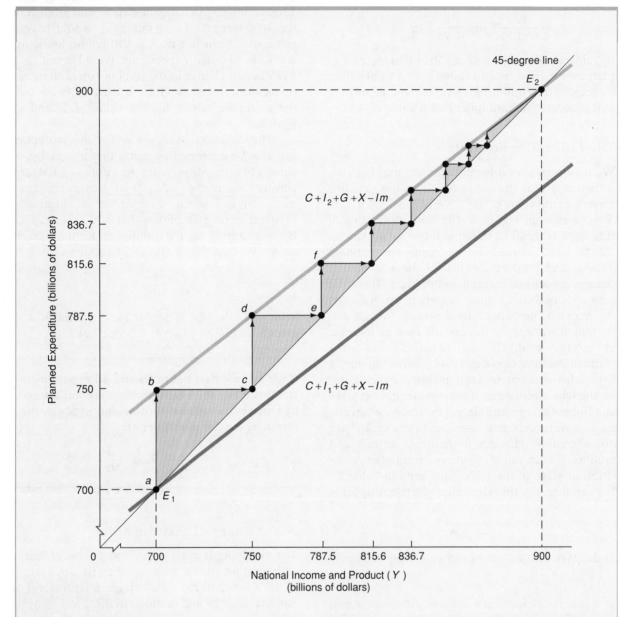

The initial equilibrium is at point E_1, with national income and product and total planned expenditure balanced at $700 billion. A $50 billion increase in planned expenditure shifts the $C + I_1 + G + X - Im$ curve upward to $C + I_2 + G + X - Im$. Planned expenditure increases from a to b and generates increased national income and product from b to c. This increase in income induces a $37.5 billion increase in planned expenditure, from c to d, which, in turn, generates increased national income and product from d to e. This process continues until the multiplier exhausts itself at the new equilibrium, E_2.

Figure 6 is a graphic illustration of the multiplier process. It is an enlargement of the part of Figure 5 that showed the area between the original equilibrium of $700 billion ($E_1$) and the new equilibrium of $900 billion ($E_2$). The process begins with an upward shift of the total-planned-expenditure curve, which we assumed to be $50 billion. In the figure, this is the distance from a to b. This spending generates an equal amount of national income and product ($50 billion), shown by the distance from b to c. The increase in national income and product *induces* a $37.5 billion increase in planned expenditure, shown by the distance from c to d. Then this increase generates additional income and product of $37.5 billion, shown as the distance from d to e. The multiplier process repeats itself in smaller and smaller steps, which dwindle to insignificance as the new equilibrium national income and product of $900 billion ($E_2$) is approached.

FISCAL INSTRUMENTS

The Keynesian model suggests that macroeconomic equilibrium need not correspond with full employment in the economy. Equally important, it suggests that government is able to alter the level of total planned expenditure and thus change the equilibrium level of national income and product. The actions that government can take to change total planned expenditure by altering its budget (revenues and expenditures) are called **fiscal instruments.**[5] Specifically, fiscal instruments include changes in government purchases, changes in net tax collections, and features of taxing and spending legislation that encourage households and firms to change their consumption, saving, and investing behaviors.

In the Keynesian model, government can change the equilibrium level of national income and

---

5. Other instruments also are available. Chief among these are **monetary instruments,** which change the amount of money in the economy.

product by using fiscal instruments—changes in government purchases, net tax collections, and taxing and spending legislation.

Changing Government Purchases

Change in the annual flow of government purchases of goods and services is a basic Keynesian fiscal instrument. As you remember from the circular-flow diagram in Chapter 6 and the model in Chapter 10, government purchases (G) consist of currently produced goods and services. They do not include transfer payments, such as veterans', welfare, or Social Security benefits, which are treated as negative taxes in calculating net taxes.

To begin our study of the government-purchases instrument, we assume that other things remain unchanged. Thus, in describing the effects of changes in the yearly volume of government purchases, we assume that no changes are made in the tax laws and that interest rates and the availability of money for private investment are not affected by the change in government purchases.

In the Keynesian approach, the purpose of changing the amount of government purchases is to shift the total-planned-expenditure curve and thereby to close contractionary or expansionary gaps. Increases in the volume of government purchases (G) will, other things being equal, shift the $C + I + G + X - Im$ curve upward and help to close a contractionary gap, as was illustrated in Figure 2. Conversely, decreases in the volume of government purchases will, other things being equal, shift the $C + I + G + X - Im$ curve downward, helping to close an expansionary gap, as was illustrated in Figure 4.

In each of these changes, the multiplier operates just as described previously. For example, if the *MPC* is 0.75, a $50 billion increase in the annual volume of government purchases will lead eventually to a $200 billion increase in the equilibrium level of national income and product. The multiplier will have a value of 4. Similarly, a $50 billion decrease will lead to a $200 billion decrease in this equilibrium level. The change in government purchases shifts the $C + I + G + X - Im$ curve, which then intersects the 45-degree line on a Keynesian-cross graph at a different equilibrium level of national income and product.

In the Keynesian model, increasing the volume of government purchases will shift the total-planned-expenditure curve upward; decreases in the volume of government purchases will shift the curve downward.

In real life, the government-purchases instrument does not always operate as smoothly as in our hypothetical cases. For one thing the multiplier is not as sure and precise as our illustration suggests. Much depends on the mood of the economy at the time. Also, sometimes a **displacement effect** will arise, that is, a change in one component of total planned expenditure causes an opposite change in some other component. For example, suppose that the expanded flow of goods and services provided by greater government purchases is a substitute for things that households ordinarily buy with their own income. What would happen if government expanded its purchases of medical services and delivered these services free to the public? Wouldn't household spending on health care go down as the government's spending on these services went up? Then wouldn't the decrease in household spending offset, to some degree, the increase in government purchases? If the goods and services involved in the increased government purchases are substitutes for things that consumers are already buying, then a downward shift in the consumption function (consumer purchases) may partly or fully offset the increase in government purchases. In such a case, the $C + I + G + X - Im$ curve does not shift by the full amount of the change in government purchases.

What happens when government decreases its purchases in order to close an expansionary gap? If consumers purchase more to make up for the things that are no longer provided by government, the shift in the $C + I + G + X - Im$ curve will again be less than the change in government purchases, and the government-purchases instrument will be less effective in closing the gap.

A displacement effect occurs when a change in one component of total planned expenditure causes an opposite change in some other component.

Changes in Taxes

Changing the amount of taxes collected is another fiscal instrument in government's macroeconomic tool kit. Changing tax collections, like changing the amount of government purchases, can shift the total-planned-expenditure curve and change the equilibrium level of national income and product. Let us examine how these changes operate in the Keynesian model.

Tax Increases What happens when the government increases the amount of net tax that it collects, while keeping government purchases unchanged? In terms of the circular-flow model, an increase in net tax forces households to reduce the amounts that they use for other purposes. Let us first consider two extremes of possible household reaction to a tax increase and then look at a more realistic response.

If *all* of the added tax payments were obtained from reductions in planned saving, there would be no shift of the $C + I + G + X - Im$ curve, if we assume that planned investment (I), government purchases (G), and net exports ($X - Im$) are unchanged. The tax increase would be completely ineffective in changing the equilibrium level of national income and product.

If, on the other hand, *all* of the increase in net tax were taken from planned consumption expenditure, the $C + I + G + X - Im$ curve would shift downward by the full amount of the added tax, again assuming that the other spending streams remain unchanged. Since the total-planned-expenditure curve would shift by the full amount of the tax change, the multiplier effect of the tax change would be just as large as the multiplier effect of changes in government purchases, as explained earlier.

But neither of these cases is likely to fit the real world. In practice, the money for the additional tax bill is likely to be paid partly from consumption and partly from saving, so that the outcome of a change in net tax is likely to lie somewhere between the extremes just outlined. In the Keynesian model, the marginal propensities to consume and to save indicate how households will respond to changes in net taxes. For example, if the *MPC* is 0.75 and the *MPS* is 0.25, an application of the Keynesian model suggests that a $50 billion tax increase will cut planned consumption expenditure by $37.5 billion and planned saving by $12.5 billion. If the other spending streams continue as before, the total-planned-expenditure curve will shift downward by $37.5 billion. Since the multiplier [$1/(1 - MPC)$ or $1/MPS$] would have a value of 4, this shift would lower the equilibrium level of national income and product by $150 billion ($37.5 \times 4$).

Tax Decreases In the Keynesian model, a tax decrease is a fiscal instrument that can shift the total-planned-expenditure curve upward, raising the equilibrium level of national income and product and helping to close a contractionary gap. In other words, tax decreases operate in the same manner, but in the opposite direction, as tax increases.

When net taxes are cut, households have additional income that can be used to increase planned consumption expenditure and planned saving. The power or multiplier effect of a tax cut depends on how taxpayers use the income retained from the tax cut. In the Keynesian model, the marginal propensity to consume (*MPC*) gives an answer to this question. If the marginal propensity to consume is 0.75, a $50 billion cut in net taxes will lead to a $37.5 billion increase in planned consumption expenditure, *ceteris paribus*. The total-planned-expenditure curve will shift upward by this amount. Since the multiplier would again have a value of 4, the equilibrium level of national income and product would rise by $150 billion ($37.5 \times 4$). The logic is simply that some of the expansionary power of the tax cut is lost because households use some of the income to increase planned saving. The total-planned-expenditure curve does not shift by the total amount of the net tax change.

In the Keynesian model, a tax increase can shift the total-planned-expenditure curve downward;

a tax decrease can shift the curve upward. Changing the net tax causes changes in consumption expenditure.

The Tax-Change Multiplier In the Keynesian system, the power of changes in net taxes to alter the equilibrium level of national income and product is summarized in the concept of a **tax-change multiplier,** which is equal to the change in equilibrium national income and product divided by the change in net taxes that causes it. If we use a triangle (Δ) to mean "the change in," the tax-change multiplier is $\Delta Y^*/\Delta T_n$. In the illustrations given previously, the tax-change multiplier had a value of -3, since equilibrium national income and product changed by $150 billion (in the opposite direction) as a result of a change in net taxes of $50 billion.

The tax-change multiplier is smaller, by one unit in absolute terms, than the multiplier for investment changes or changes in government purchases. This relationship arises from the assumption that the *MPS* shows the percentage of a change in tax liability that comes out of saving in the case of a tax increase or goes into saving in the case of a tax reduction. This means that the change in total planned expenditure that arises is in the opposite direction from the tax change, and is smaller than the tax change by the percentage indicated by the *MPS*. When the regular multiplier process comes into play, it starts with only the part of the tax change that actually appears as a change in planned expenditure. For example, if the *MPS* is 0.25, the multiplier starts with a change in planned expenditure 25 percent smaller (and in the opposite direction) than the change in net tax. This shrinkage of the initial change in planned expenditure is itself multiplied as the multiplier process proceeds to the ultimate change in equilibrium national income and product. The multiplier values work in such a way that the shrinkage of the ultimate change in equilibrium national income and product equals (with the opposite sign) the initial change in net tax. For example, if the *MPS* is 0.25, the initial change in planned expenditure is 25 percent smaller than the amount of the tax change, but, since the multiplier value is 4 when the MPS is

0.25, the 25 percent shrinkage at the start leads to a reduction of the end result equal to 100 percent of the initial tax change. If the MPS were 0.20, an initial 20 percent shrinkage would be multiplied five times, and again equal 100 percent of the initial tax change, and so on.[6]

The tax-change multiplier is equal to the change in equilibrium national income and product divided by the change in net taxes that causes it. Tax changes have a smaller multiplier value than changes in planned investment expenditure.

The Balanced-Budget Multiplier

In practice, it is not necessary that either the government-purchases or the tax-change instrument be used by itself in closing a contractionary or expansionary gap. Usually, these instruments are combined (along with other instruments) so that several policy goals can be pursued at the same time. For example, contractionary gaps might be closed primarily with increases in government purchases if policy goals called for more public services, or with tax cuts if the goals called for more private services. The choice or the mixture of the two instruments would depend on how policymakers wanted to divide the hoped-for expansion of the economy.

---

6. The proposition that the tax-change multiplier value is (in absolute terms) smaller by one than the investment or government-purchases multiplier can be illustrated by a series of equations. We start with the multiplier that applies to changes in planned consumption expenditure, with ΔY^* representing a change in the equilibrium level of national income and product and ΔC representing a change in planned consumption expenditure. The regular multiplier calculation gives us

$$\Delta Y^* = \Delta C(1/MPS)$$

Next, we assume that a change in net tax affects planned consumption as follows:

$$\Delta C = -\Delta T_n(MPC)$$

where ΔT_n represents a tax change. By substituting the second equation into the first equation, we have

$$\Delta Y^* = -\Delta T_n(MPC)(1/MPS)$$

In this equation, we see that the tax-change multiplier is represented by $(MPC)(1/MPS)$. If we let $-K_{T_n}$ represent the tax-change multiplier, it can be written as

---

Government purchases and tax changes can be used together to alter the equilibrium level of national income and product.

Could the government-purchases and the tax-change instruments be used together to alter the equilibrium level of national income and product while also keeping the government's budget in balance? Yes. For example, a contractionary gap could be closed with just the right combination of increases in both government purchases and tax collections to maintain a balanced budget. The combination would be expansionary. This is because the upward shift of the $C + I + G + X - Im$ curve that comes from $50 billion of added government purchases, for example, is greater than the downward shift that comes from a $50 billion addition to tax collections each year. With an MPC of 0.75, this downward shift would be only $37.5 billion (75 percent of $50 billion), leaving a $12.5 billion net upward shift in the curve. Since the multiplier factor is 4, this $12.5 billion shift would bring a $50 billion rise in the equilibrium level of national income and product. This gives us what is sometimes called the **balanced-budget multiplier,** with a value of 1, or unity (the change in equilibrium national income and product is the same as the change in the size of the budget). Balanced changes in government purchases and tax collections could also close an expansionary gap. In this case, both

$$-K_{T_n} = (MPC)(1/MPS) = MPC/MPS$$

But we know that $MPS = 1 - MPC$. Therefore, we can express the tax-change multiplier as

$$-K_{T_n} = MPC/(1 - MPC)$$

which reduces to

$$-K_{T_n} = [1/(1 - MPC)] - 1$$

Since the term in the brackets $[1/(1 - MPC)]$ is the regular multiplier, the -1 in the equation indicates that the tax-change multiplier in absolute value is smaller, by one, than the regular multiplier.

A demonstration of the last step is as follows:

$$\begin{aligned} -K_{T_n} &= MPC/(1 - MPC) \\ &= [1 - (1 - MPC)]/(1 - MPC) \\ &= [1/(1 - MPC)] - (1 - MPC)/(1 - MPC) \\ &= [1/(1 - MPC)] - 1 \end{aligned}$$

government purchases and tax collections would be cut.

Combining the government-purchases multiplier with the tax-change multiplier gives a numerical value for the balanced-budget multiplier that is equal to the arithmetic difference between the two. If the government-purchases multiplier is 4 and the tax-change multiplier is −3, then the balanced-budget multiplier is 1. If the *MPC* were 0.80, so that the government-purchases multiplier would be 5, the tax-change multiplier would be −4, so that the balanced-budget multiplier would still be 1. In this way, the balanced-budget multiplier is 1, regardless of the size of the *MPC*.

The balanced budget multiplier is 1: the change in equilibrium national income and product is the same as the change in the size of the budget.

As a tool for closing expansionary or contractionary gaps, balanced changes in government purchases and tax collections make the balanced budget the determining consideration in the choice of fiscal instruments. However, other goals may be more important. Also, the great changes in the size of government required by the balanced-budget system could easily make the package less attractive.

Automatic or Built-in Stabilizers

Automatic or **built-in stabilizers** are specific provisions in the tax and spending laws that work automatically—without the need to take any action—to moderate economic fluctuations. Progressive income taxes are one of these stabilizers. When national income rises, taxpayers on the average move into a higher tax-rate bracket and pay more taxes in proportion to their income. Other things being equal, the increase in taxes leaves less of the households' additional income to use for consumption spending and puts a downward pressure on the $C + I + G + X − Im$ curve, limiting the expansion of national income and product. In times of inflation, this same "tax-bracket push" would put some people into a higher bracket even though they are no better off in real terms. "Index-ing" income taxes by automatically lowering tax rates or widening tax brackets in step with inflation reduces the automatic stabilization effect of progressive taxes in inflationary times. Of course, the stabilizing effect of automatic tax changes assumes that the government does not spend the extra tax revenues collected during economic expansions or cut its purchases when taxes fall automatically during economic contractions.

The built-in stabilizing effect of progressive tax rates can also be explained as a change in the power of the multiplier factor. In Chapter 10, our discussion of taxes and the marginal propensity to consume used a lump-sum tax. This tax produced a constant marginal propensity to consume based on national income and product. With progressive income tax rates, the total-planned-expenditure curve would become flatter and flatter as national income and product rose—and the multiplier effect would become smaller as well.

The progressive individual income tax is not the only built-in stabilizer that operates from the tax side of the budget. Corporation profits fluctuate disproportionately with the total economy so that tax collections based on these profits are unusually high in good times and unusually low in bad times. For this reason, they have an automatic stabilizing effect. Social Security taxes and unemployment taxes also behave in this way.

Automatic stabilizers can also be built into the expenditure side of the government budget. But since most of these government expenditures are for transfer payments, rather than for goods and services, we would call them changes in net taxes. Welfare, unemployment, and Social Security expenditures all tend to rise during a recession at the same time that payments into these funds become less. This combination of more benefit checks and fewer tax payments helps support consumer spending and moderates the contractionary gap. We have the opposite pattern during inflationary times, when expansionary gaps are moderated.

The existence of automatic stabilizers has led some economists to propose a policy called the **full-employment balanced budget.** Under this plan, the amount of government purchases and transfer payments would be based on how much the voters would want, and could afford, when the economy was operating at full employment. Tax rates would be set to balance this amount of spending when there was full employment. During economic contractions, the automatic stabilizers would lower net taxes. During expansions, the automatic stabilizers would raise net taxes. No legislative action is needed under this plan, since economic fluctuations are automatically moderated.

Automatic stabilizers have not been powerful enough to stop all fluctuations in the economy. Other policy matters put a limit on how progressive the tax rates can be, as well as on the level of corporation profit taxes and the size of transfer payments. So there is a ceiling on the amount of automatic stabilization that can be built into the fiscal system.

Automatic or built-in stabilizers are provisions in the tax and spending laws that work automatically to moderate economic fluctuations.

In a growing economy, the moderating effect of automatic stabilizers is sometimes called **fiscal drag**, since the automatic increase in net tax collections dampens the rate of growth of the economy. Of course, under the full-employment-balanced-budget policy, economic growth calls for a reevaluation of spending and tax legislation—meaning that the voters and their representatives must decide whether the benefits of growth are to be taken through more public goods and services or through tax reductions which allow more private goods and services. Thus, fiscal drag need not happen.

The operation of automatic stabilizers in the context of economic growth is called fiscal drag.

Influencing Economic Behavior Through Fiscal Instruments

So far we have looked only at the financial aspect of fiscal instruments. But the tax and expenditure system is also one of the most powerful instruments available to influence the economic behavior of important actors on the economic stage. Changing these behaviors may change planned expenditure and the performance of the economy. To illustrate the importance of these fiscal instruments, we shall briefly note how depreciation allowances and capital gains taxes can affect planned investment expenditure.

Depreciation is defined as the decline in the market value of a capital good as it wears out or becomes obsolete. On income tax returns, it is a deductible cost of doing business. The tax laws specify how quickly or how early in the life of a machine these deductions can be taken. Deductions that are taken earlier mean less tax payment and encourage businesses to invest in machines and equipment. Therefore, changing the schedules or timetables for depreciation is one of the favorite fiscal instruments for changing planned investment expenditure.

Depreciation is the decline in the market value of a capital good as it wears out or becomes obsolete. Changing depreciation schedules in income tax returns is a fiscal instrument for changing planned investment expenditure.

A **capital gain (or loss)** is the change in the market value of an asset that takes place while it is owned by the taxpayer. Many people buy stocks, hoping that the company will prosper and that the market value of the stock will rise, providing a capital gain. In a capitalist system, this is an important means of channeling resources into promising growth industries. In the United States, capital gains are taxable as income, but tax laws have changed over the years in specifying the fraction of such gains that must be listed for taxation. The 1986 law required full taxation of capital gains, but controversy continues about how heavily they should be taxed. Lowering tax rates on capital gains could increase the flow of funds into growth industries. So changing the capital gains tax rates is another fiscal instrument for influencing planned investment expenditure.

The list of the regulatory features of tax and expenditure laws could go on and on. There have even been proposals for using taxes to reward or punish people and companies for cooperating or not cooperating with nonfiscal regulations.

A capital gain (or loss) is the change in the market value of an asset that takes place while it is owned by a taxpayer. Changing the capital gains tax rate is a fiscal instrument for influencing planned investment expenditure.

Economics in Focus

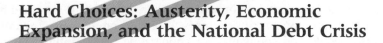

Hard Choices: Austerity, Economic Expansion, and the National Debt Crisis

During the Reagan administration the national debt more than doubled, reaching a staggering $2.6 trillion by the end of 1988. Everyone agreed that something should be done or the massive burden would be passed on to future generations. William Simon, a former secretary of the treasury, stated the peril bluntly and dramatically: "If the next Administration does not mount an immediate, decisive and effective attack against those twin towers of debt—our budget deficit and our trade deficit—the United States cannot continue as leader of the free world."

Two basic choices emerged, loosely labeled "austerity" and "growth." Those who believed in austerity said that the budget deficit should be reduced at once, even if many Americans suffered. Simon, for example, favored strong cuts in government spending. "Nothing is sacrosanct," he declared, even Social Security. Others focused in particular on entitlement programs—Social Security being a prime example. These government outlays amounted to 11 percent of GNP, and some benefited the wealthy as well as the poor; thus many economists urged policymakers to bite the political bullet and cut entitlements—an action that, in the Keynesian model, would be an increase in net taxes.

Advocates of austerity often presumed that the consequence would be an economic slowdown, at least in the short term. This was an ill they were willing to accept. The alternative, they warned, would be spiraling inflation, instability, and an economy so out of control that the next downswing could be a disaster. The advocates of economic expansion, in contrast, argued that the austerity program would itself court a disaster—a severe recession or, at worst, complete financial collapse. They argued that the economy should be allowed to expand in a modest fashion, with a small continuing deficit, controlled inflation, intelligent investment, and a concentration on overcoming trade deficits. The supporters of these policies seemed less fearful of debt than their opponents; they pointed out that the current national debt actually represented no greater a proportion of GNP than the debt during the Kennedy administration—and a far smaller proportion than in the years following World War II.

For many champions of expansion, however, the key issue in austerity programs was the question of *whose* belt would be tightened. According to some statistical analyses, the Reagan years had increased the disparity between the rich and the poor, and the talk of austerity often implied a willingness to let the poor bear the brunt of the cutbacks. A short, sharp recession might cure the ills of the economy, but at what price?

Clearly this is a political debate which will be decided in the political arena. Debt-reduction policies established by the president, the Congress, and other economic policymakers will affect the lives of Americans throughout the 1990s and for many decades to come.

Sources: William Greider and William E. Simon, "Which Way Out of Debt: Growth or Austerity?" *New Perspectives Quarterly,* Spring 1988, pp. 8–15 (Simon quotations at pp. 12, 14); Robert Kuttner, "Against Austerity," *The New Republic,* December 28, 1987, pp. 16–18; "Get the Rich Off the Dole," an interview with Peter Peterson, *Time,* October 31, 1988, pp. 66–68; Peter Brimelow with Lisa Scheer, "Is the Reagan Prosperity for Real?" *Forbes,* October 31, 1988, pp. 85–90.

SUMMARY

1. Target levels of national income and product are chosen as goals of macroeconomic policy. Choosing a target for national income and product involves value judgments and tradeoffs among different goals. (See page 220.)

2. A contractionary or an expansionary gap is the difference between the chosen target and the equilibrium level of national income and product that is expected if no new initiatives are taken. A contractionary gap means that equilibrium will be below the target, and an expansionary gap means that equilibrium will be above the target. (See pages 221–223.)

3. The multiplier process is started by a shift in the $C + I + G + X - Im$ curve, that is, by a change in some nonincome determinant of planned spending. This change alters the amount of planned spending and changes the equilibrium level of national income and product. (See page 224.)

4. The multiplier shows the size of the change in the equilibrium level of national income and product as a multiple of the shift in total planned expenditure that launched the process. Equilibrium national income and product changes by several times as much as the initial spending change because further expenditure changes are induced by the income changes themselves. (See pages 225–226.)

5. The multiplier operates through successive "rounds" of the circular flow. Time is needed for these rounds of activity to take place. The full multiplier effect is never realized, but most of its potential will be felt within a year following the shift in total planned expenditure. (See pages 227–229.)

6. The value of the multiplier is determined by the propensity of income changes to induce changes in planned expenditure. If we assume zero marginal propensities for planned investment, government purchases, and net exports, the value of the multiplier is $1/(1 - MPC)$ or $1/MPS$, with MPC and MPS based on national income and product. (See page 229.)

7. Changing the yearly flow of government purchases of goods and services is a fiscal instrument that can shift the total-planned-expenditure curve up or down and so change the equilibrium level of national income and product. This tool be-

comes less effective if other components of total planned expenditure, such as household purchases, are displaced by a change in government purchases. (See pages 231–232.)

8. Changing the yearly flow of tax collections is another fiscal tool that can shift the total-planned-expenditure curve. Part of the change in net tax results in a change in consumption expenditure. (See pages 232–234.)

9. In the elementary Keynesian model, changes in government purchases have the same multiplier value as changes in planned investment expenditure. But, tax changes have a multiplier value that is smaller because some of the tax change goes into or comes out of planned saving. Combining changes in government purchases with changes in net tax results in a balanced-budget multiplier with a value of 1. (See page 234.)

10. Automatic, or built-in, stabilizers are provisions in the tax and spending laws, such as progressive income taxes, corporation profit taxes, and transfer payment systems, that work automatically to moderate economic fluctuations. The full-employment balanced budget is a policy that relies on built-in stabilizers. In the context of economic growth, automatic stabilizers are sometimes said to cause fiscal drag. (See page 235.)

11. Fiscal instruments can be used to regulate the economy by changing specific rules in the tax law. The tax treatment of capital gains and the allowances for depreciation are examples of the regulatory aspects of fiscal tools. (See page 236.)

KEY TERMS

automatic (built-in) stabilizers: provisions in the tax and spending laws that work automatically to moderate economic fluctuations (page 235).

balanced-budget multiplier: the change in equilibrium national income and product divided by the change in the size of the budget that caused it. It's value is 1 (page 234).

bankruptcy: a state of insolvency; the inability to repay creditors (page 236).

capital gain (or loss): the change in the market value of an asset that takes place while it is owned by the taxpayer (page 236).

contractionary gap: a gap between the equilibrium level and the target level of the national income and product that exists when the equilibrium level is less than the target level (page 221).

Council of Economic Advisers (CEA): part of the executive branch of the government; its main purpose is to advise the president on economic policy (page 220).

crowding out: the replacement of private investment expenditure by government purchases in a budget deficit situation (page 243).

cyclical deficit: the amount of government budget deficit that arises because the economy is operating below its target level of national income and product (page 242).

depreciation: the decline in the market value of a capital good as it wears out or becomes obsolete (page 236).

displacement effect: a change in one component of planned expenditure that causes an opposite change in some other component (page 232).

Employment Act of 1946: the law that established the Council of Economic Advisers and stated the responsibility of the United States government to promote high level employment, price stability, and economic growth (page 220).

expansionary gap: a gap between the equilibrium and the target level of national income and product that exists when the equilibrium level is higher than the target level (page 221).

fiscal instruments: the actions that government can take to change total planned expenditure by altering its laws relating to taxation and expenditure (page 231).

full-employment balanced budget: a plan to moderate economic fluctuations by basing the amount of government purchases and transfer payments on how much the citizens desire and are willing to pay for when the economy is operating at full employment and by setting tax rates to balance this budget when the economy is operating at full employment (page 235).

Humphrey-Hawkins Act of 1978: a law that set specific goals for both price stability and employment (page 220).

Joint Economic Committee (JEC): a congressional committee that is responsible for advising the legislative branch on economic policy (page 220).

monetary instruments: actions that the government can take to change the amount of money in the economy (page 231).

multiplier (k): the relationship between a change in the equilibrium level of national income and product and the change in the level of total planned expenditure that caused it (page 223).

structural deficit: the total government budget deficit minus that portion arising because the economy is operating below its target level of national income and product (page 242).

target level of national income and product: the level chosen through political processes as a goal for macroeconomic policy (page 218).

tax-change multiplier: a value that is equal to the change in equilibrium national income and product divided by the change in net taxes that causes it (page 233).

DISCUSSION QUESTIONS

1. Why was the setting of target levels for national income and product considered unnecessary and inappropriate in the neoclassical theory but important and necessary in the Keynesian theory?

2. Without looking at Figures 1 and 3, draw the Keynesian-cross diagrams that illustrate a contractionary gap and an expansionary gap. Then check to make sure you have them right. What is the standard Keynesian strategy for dealing with a contractionary gap?

3. Suppose that a new and much better type of home computer is developed. Would this development shift the planned-investment curve on a Keynesian-cross diagram? If so, in which direction? Explain. Might the development of this product shift any of the other components of total planned expenditure? Which one(s)? Why?

4. This chapter illustrated a multiplier started by a change in planned investment. Could the process be started by a change in some other component of total planned expenditure? Why or why not? What would the value of the multiplier be if the *MPC* were 0.9, based on national income and product? Would stable economic conditions exist if the *MPC* were greater than 1.0? Explain.

5. Without looking at Figure 6, draw an illustration of the multiplier process on a Keynesian-cross diagram. Be sure to label all axes and lines. Check your illustration with Figure 6 to be sure you have it right. How would your illustration be different if the *MPC* were smaller? If it were larger?

6. The multiplier illustration in this chapter is based on the assumption of a permanent increase in the annual flow of some spending stream. How would the multiplier be different if the initiating change were only a one-shot expenditure, which was not repeated in the next time period? Explain.

7. How large a contractionary gap would be closed by a $100 billion change in the annual amount of government purchases if the *MPC* is 0.80 and if other variables are held constant? Explain how you got your answer. If displacement effects are present, should your answer be larger or smaller? Explain.

8. If the *MPC* is 0.80, you know that the multiplier for government purchases is 5. What would the numerical value of the multiplier be for a tax cut, given this *MPC?* Why would it be different?

9. The choice between changes in government purchases and changes in tax collections involves microeconomic questions about the mix between public and private goods in the economy. How does this factor influence your preference between them as macroeconomic instruments? Do you have a different preference between purchases changes and tax changes when promoting economic expansion than when promoting economic restraint? Explain.

10. By combining the purchases multiplier and the tax-change multiplier, explain why the balanced-budget multiplier always has a value of 1. Compare the advantages and disadvantages of making the balanced budget a basic guideline for macroeconomic policy.

11. Explain why progressive taxes, corporation taxes, and transfer payments automatically tend to stabilize the economy. Under a progressive tax system, would a 10 percent change in national income and product bring about a change in tax collections of 10 percent, or more, or less? How does the answer to this question help you to understand the automatic stabilizers in the government budget? Explain. How would the full-employment balanced-budget policy operate?

Appendix: Deficits and The National Debt

In the Keynesian system for using fiscal instruments, deficits or surpluses in the government budget are almost inevitable. For example, in explaining the government-purchases instrument, we assumed no change in tax laws. Given the lump-sum tax that was assumed in that explanation, the government would continue to collect the same amount of net tax. If the government increased its purchases in order to close a contractionary gap, the increase in government purchases would move the government budget toward a deficit. Similarly, if government purchases were reduced in an effort to close an expansionary gap, the government's budget would move toward surplus.

These same conclusions hold even under more realistic assumptions about tax rates. For example, if the government uses a percentage income tax of 20 percent, a $50 billion increase in government purchases adds only $10 billion to government tax collections in the first round of the circular flow. Of course, annual tax collections would grow in future time periods, but, since the government would also continue its higher level of purchases, it would be a long time before a budget balance could be restored.[7]

It is even more apparent that the government's budget would move toward deficit or surplus with the use of the tax-change instrument. If government purchases remain unchanged while net taxes are reduced, the budget will move toward deficit. If net taxes are increased in an effort to close an expansionary gap, the budget will move toward surplus.

STRUCTURAL AND CYCLICAL DEFICITS

Government budget deficits are not always—and probably not usually—the result of purposeful attempts to engage in fiscal policy. Since the federal budget usually is in deficit, how can we estimate the part that can be related to fiscal policy? The answer is found by estimating how much more net-tax revenue would be collected under existing tax laws if the economy were operating at the target (or full employment) level of national income and product. A deficit equal to this amount—the revenue lost because the economy is operating below its target—is the **cyclical deficit.** In a sense, it is caused by the below-target level of economic activity.

If the actual deficit exceeds the revenue shortfall caused by the failure of the economy to reach the target level of national income and product, the additional part of the deficit is called the **structural deficit.** The structural deficit reflects an inability or unwillingness of the government to impose taxes sufficient to balance its budget in the context of a fully employed economy. Many observers believe that most of the federal budget deficits in the late 1980s were structural rather than cyclical, since, in those times, the economy was operating with approximately its natural rate of unemployment, that is, it was close to full employment. These observers concluded that the deficits in those years reflected not fiscal policy but an unwillingness of Congress to reduce expenditures and/or increase taxes.

The *cyclical deficit* is the tax revenue shortfall due to the economy operating below the target level of national income and product. The remainder of any actual deficit is the *structural deficit.*

---

7. You may wish to use the "Total Addition to National Income and Product Flow" column in Table 2 to estimate when the government budget would regain a balance if a percentage income tax were used.

DEFICITS AND CROWDING OUT

As you remember from the circular-flow model introduced in Chapter 6, budget deficits and surpluses activate connections between the government box and the financial-markets box. A government deficit takes funds out of the financial markets—funds that might otherwise flow on as planned investment in the circular flow. This is called **crowding out**. It means that some private investment expenditure is replaced ("crowded out") by government purchases. The reverse situation exists when the government's budget moves to surplus. Surplus funds are channeled to the financial markets and flow onward as increases in planned investment expenditure.

The process by which crowding out takes place is quite simple. The government sells bonds to finance its budget deficit. These bond sales increase the demand for funds available for borrowing in the financial markets. Other things being equal, this increase in demand for loans drives interest rates upward. These higher rates, in turn, mean that some private investment projects, which would have appeared profitable at the lower interest rates, will no longer appear to be so. These private investments are crowded out by the budget deficit.

In our explanation of the Keynesian use of fiscal instruments, we assumed that interest rates were unaffected by government deficits and surpluses. Although this may be the case in periods of extreme depression (as when Keynes wrote in the 1930s), it is not likely to be true in more normal times. If crowding out takes place, fiscal instruments that move the government budget toward a deficit will not be as effective in closing a contractionary gap as our simple model indicates. Similarly, fiscal instruments that move the budget toward a surplus will be less effective in closing an expansionary gap than the simple model indicates. Fiscal instruments may still have significant effects, but the connection between the government budget and the financial markets suggests that we must not make any final judgment about them until we have studied financial markets and government's monetary instruments. Also, it is important to remember that funds may enter the financial-markets box from the foreign-markets box. Inflows of funds from abroad can reduce the crowding-out effects of government budget deficits.

In a deficit situation, some private investment expenditure is replaced ("crowded out") by government purchases. In a surplus situation, there may be an increase in private planned investment.

HOW PUBLIC DEBT IS CREATED

When a deficit arises in the U.S. government budget, the Treasury Department, which is responsible for financing government operations, issues bonds and other securities and offers them for sale in securities markets. Private persons, depository institutions, insurance companies, business firms, and others purchase these securities just as they might buy other kinds of securities.[8] The Treasury uses the funds received from sales to finance the deficit in the government budget. These funds flow between the financial markets and the government as pictured in the circular flow.

When a deficit occurs in the U.S. government budget, the Treasury Department issues bonds and other securities and offers them for sale in securities markets.

It is not true that the government literally "prints money" to cover its deficits as is sometimes alleged. In the past, as during the "Greenback Era" of the Civil War, currency was issued directly by the Treasury Department, but this is not the case today. The currency now in circulation is issued by the Federal Reserve Banks. In Chapters 12 and 13, we shall explain how money is created.

HOW LARGE IS THE NATIONAL DEBT?

The national debt has not always been very large in the United States. In the 1830s, the debt had been completely eliminated, and excess federal revenues

8. Some national debt securities are issued to agencies of the federal government itself. These are "special issues" and are not bought and sold in the open market.

were turned over to the states. In 1917, before the United States entered World War I, the debt was $12.36 per capita. Today the debt is over $3 trillion, around $12,400 for every man, woman, and child in the country. Even when inflation and the vast growth in the economy are allowed for, it is evident that the national debt has increased significantly.

Table 3 shows the dollar amount of the gross federal debt from 1970 through 1990. In dollar amount, the debt grew continuously during these years. The dollar amount of public debt is a simple (and simplistic) way of stating the size of the debt. It is simply a monument to net budget deficits accumulated over the years.

A more interesting picture appears, however, when the debt is expressed as a percentage of GNP. As shown in Table 3, this percentage went down between 1970 and 1981, and then increased significantly. Expressing the debt as a percentage of GNP is better than focusing on the dollar amount because a large economy probably can support a larger debt than a small economy, other things being equal. But recording debt as a percentage of

GNP also brings price-level changes into the calculation, since GNP is expressed in current dollars. When we bring price-level changes into our measurement of the debt, we run into great controversy. When inflation occurs, the GNP (in current dollars) goes up. But the face value of bonds that were bought before the inflation does not increase in dollar value along with the price level, unless they have been indexed to change in face value automatically with changes in the price level. Since U.S. bonds are not indexed, inflation automatically reduces the national debt as a percentage of GNP. In fact, some people believe that inflation amounts to partial default on the debt. The inflation rate was much higher during the 1970s than during the 1980s. The high inflation rate of the 1970s helped to hold down the debt-to-GNP percentage. The lower inflation rate of the 1980s contributed to the more rapid rise in this percentage.

Debt as a percentage of GNP has increased significantly since 1981.

TABLE 3
The Gross Federal Debt, 1970–1990

End of Year	Gross Federal Debt (billions of dollars)	Percentage of GNP	End of Year	Gross Federal Debt (billions of dollars)	Percentage of GNP
1970	380.9	38.5	1981	994.3	33.3
1971	408.2	38.7	1982	1,136.8	36.2
1972	435.9	37.8	1983	1,371.2	41.3
1973	466.3	36.4	1984	1,564.1	42.4
1974	483.9	34.2	1985	1,817.0	46.0
1975	541.9	35.6	1986	2,120.1	50.6
1976	629.0	37.0	1987	2,345.6	52.9
1977	706.4	36.5	1988	2,600.8	54.4
1978	776.6	35.8	1989[a]	2,868.8	56.0
1979	828.9	33.9	1990[a]	3,107.2	56.7
1980	908.5	34.0			

The gross federal debt grew continually between 1970 and 1990. When these amounts are expressed as a percentage of GNP, the percentage declined through 1974, fluctuated within fairly narrow bounds through 1981, and then increased significantly.

[a] Estimated

Source: *Economic Report of the President, 1989,* Table B-76.

CAN DEBT LEAD TO NATIONAL BANKRUPTCY?

Bankruptcy is a legal concept used to indicate a state of insolvency—of being unable to repay creditors. Could the national debt ever become so large that the federal government would become bankrupt? The standard answer to this question is that it depends on the taxing power of the government, the strength of the economy, and the wealth of the citizens. If the government is firmly established, if the economy is strong, and if valuable properties exist in the country, bankruptcy is unlikely. Certainly, the U.S. government is not likely to become bankrupt.

But governments that have borrowed heavily sometimes repudiate their debts or try to renegotiate their obligations. Also, when one government is replaced by another (as by revolution), the debts of the fallen government may or may not be assumed by the new government. Even the assumption of colonial debts by the new United States government was a controversial action. Several states refused to pay their debts for construction of canals and roadways in the 1830s, and the U.S. government repudiated the Confederate debt after the Civil War. After the 1917 revolution, the Soviets refused to pay the czarist debts. What about deliberate inflation as a means of eliminating the debt in real terms? In a sense, this would be another kind of repudiation, since debts would be paid back in money that was less valuable than the money originally borrowed.

DO DEFICITS BURDEN FUTURE GENERATIONS?

In private finance, debt financing is a way to postpone final payment for a good or service. Funds are borrowed and used to purchase something. The borrower uses the funds to acquire an asset and also has a liability—the obligation to pay off the loan. The burden of payment is put off while funds are "rented" and interest is paid. A future generation becomes involved because the heirs of a debtor inherit whatever remains of the assets purchased with the borrowed funds, and they inherit less of something else, since the debt will have to be paid off when the estate is settled. The debt itself (the "less of something else") is a burden. In this illustration, it is not obvious that the future generation is, on balance, worse off or better off, since this depends on the value of the assets bought with the borrowed funds.

What about the debt of the national government? Reasoning by analogy is, we agree, a dangerous procedure. However, analogy may point to some important issues. For example, if we consider only the debt and ignore whatever benefits may have been gained in exchange, it is easy to conclude that debt is a burden to future generations. The government of the future generation must pay interest on a debt that would not exist if the transaction had not been carried out or if the government expenditure had been financed by taxes. But this just introduces the main question.

If we consider both sides of the matter and penetrate the "money veil" to examine real goods and services and real resources, the question becomes very complex. U.S. government debt is not incurred on a project-by-project basis. For this reason, it is not possible to point to any specific government goods and services as being debt financed. Nor can the opportunity cost (the private goods and services that were given up in exchange) be clearly identified. In our circular-flow figure, the connections between the government box and the financial-markets box suggest that government debt financing may be at the expense of private capital goods investments (machines and equipment) that could have raised both productivity and the living standard of future generations. This may be as close as we can come to finding the opportunity cost to the future generation.

But we must record some reservations even here. A depression-period argument points out that the resources used by the debt-financed government operations might otherwise have been idle, so that there might have been no real burden to the future. When there is no depression, debt financing may be at the expense of private investment. But tax financing can also impinge on investment spending, though perhaps not quite so much.

Thus we cannot accept a strict "yes" or "no"

answer to the question of whether debt financing is a burden to future generations. Much depends on the wisdom of political decision makers and on the time horizons and incentive systems operating in the political processes. If political decisions are dominated by short-run considerations and if public funds are spent foolishly, debt financing may, on balance, result in a net burden on future generations.

government, its taxing power, the size of the economy, and the wealth of the citizens suggest that debt is not likely to mean bankruptcy for the U.S. government.

4. The effect of deficit financing on future generations depends on decisions made at the time when the debt is incurred. In some cases, deficit financing will be a burden on future generations, but in other cases, it will not be a real burden.

SUMMARY

1. Movements toward deficit or surplus in the government budget typically arise from the use of fiscal instruments in the Keynesian model. Deficits extract funds from financial markets, and surpluses put funds into these markets. Thus, deficit financing may "crowd out" private investments and budget surpluses may lead to increases in private planned investment.

2. The U.S. national debt has grown continually in dollar amount. Debt as a percentage of GNP has increased significantly in recent years. The debt comes into being when the Treasury sells bonds to finance a budget deficit.

3. Bankruptcy is a state of insolvency—of not being able to repay creditors. The strength of the

DISCUSSION QUESTIONS

1. Why is it overly simple to express the size of the national debt in total dollar figures? Why is it better to express its size as a percentage of GNP? But why does the latter method run into trouble when the economy has experienced inflation?

2. If the government borrowed a million dollars, used the funds to construct a highway, and paid off the debt (with interest) through taxes on people using the highway, would the debt have been a burden on the future generation? Explain your answer. Some of the U.S. debt arose in World War II. Do you suppose that the war would have been lost if taxation had been use instead of borrowing? If so, is today's generation burdened in net effect by this debt? Explain.

John Maynard Keynes and the Great Depression

The Great Depression of the 1930s, which began much earlier in Great Britain than in the United States, was no ordinary business-cycle downturn. It was the worst such depression of at least the preceding half century. In most countries complete recovery came only after the start of World War II. The depression itself confounded many mainstream economists, particularly in the United States, who believed or hoped in 1929 that they had entered a depression-proof "New Era."[1]

CAUSES AND CURES

When the Wall Street stock market crash of October 1929 was followed by depression, and when the depression showed signs of hanging on, many suggestions were made to bring about recovery. These suggestions ranged from doing nothing at all to what would later be called "voodoo economics." They also included business-dominated "economic plans." It is certainly not true that nobody had any ideas about the causes and cure of the Great Depression. The problem was rather that so few of the would-be saviors were able to convince anyone else that they knew what they were talking about.

Some of the more or less seriously considered ideas about depression control, dating from the early 1930s, are listed below. Their order is largely arbitrary:

1. Prosperity was "just around the corner," since the country's physical plant had not been damaged. Nothing need be done but wait patiently for prosperity to return.

2. The depression was the punishment by the Almighty for the sins of "flaming youth" during the "jazz age." The remedies were moral reform and prayers to the Almighty for forgiveness.

3. The depression had been foisted on the people by certain other wicked people, such as "the international bankers" or "the elders of Zion." The economic power of such groups should be broken, and all would be well.

4. Capitalism should be scrapped in favor of a system close to Soviet communism, since the U.S.S.R. had been able to maintain full employment.

5. A national plan should be devised primarily by the leaders of big business, with the government in a secondary role, to eliminate overproduction and assure profitable prices for output.

6. The supply of money and credit should be increased by going off the gold standard, raising the price of gold, or printing inconvertible paper money. This action would "reflate" the levels of prices, wages, and profits. A more extreme form of this proposal would introduce an entirely new monetary system based on an hour of labor or an erg (small unit) of physical energy.

7. Unemployment should be exported abroad, primarily by raising tariffs and otherwise decreasing imports, and secondarily by subsidizing exports of goods and services.

8. Unemployment should be reduced by keeping the young, the elderly, and married women out of the labor force and reserving jobs for heads of families.

9. Idle plants should be taken over and run by unemployed workers at minimum cost, with the products distributed as far as possible to the poor and the unemployed.

---

1. Most cyclical booms had been accompanied by substantial price inflation. What was different about the 1920s boom was precisely its accompaniment by price-level stability, which led most economists to assume that prosperity might continue indefinitely.

10. Income and wealth should be redistributed by taxation or confiscation from the rich to the poor (or from property to labor income) so as to increase purchasing power.

11. The government budget should be balanced as an aid to business confidence, preferably by cutting public expenditures but if necessary also by raising taxes.

12. The cause of the depression was that prices and wages had not yet fallen to their "natural" (pre-1914) levels. Therefore the cure was to force them down by drastic deflation, or "liquidation."

13. The government budget should be unbalanced deliberately to increase spending for public projects to employ the unemployed. These projects should be mainly in public works and construction, civil or military. The resulting deficit should be financed either by selling public securities or by expanding the money supply as in 6 above.

KEYNES AND HIS *GENERAL THEORY*

The contribution of John Maynard Keynes, later Lord Keynes (1883–1946), was to formalize, more fully and effectively than anyone else, the approach we have numbered 13. Indeed, this was the method that was used a decade later to ward off any renewed depression after World War II. However, many of the individual building blocks of Keynes's *General Theory*—particularly the consumption function and the multiplier—had already been devised by less well-known members of the "economic underworld" years before the *General Theory* itself appeared in 1936. Also, some policies now called "Keynesian" had already been advocated and even enacted before 1936 in Britain, in Sweden, and in the United States under the New Deal.[2] On a larger scale and for military purposes, they had also been adopted by Nazi Germany and expansionist Japan as the "economics of rearmament."

AN ECONOMIC HERETIC

Who was this man, and how did he become so influential? The son of a well-known Cambridge University economist, Keynes received the best conventional education of his day. However, he was to become best known as an economic heretic.

As a young man, he wrote widely on both economic theory and policy for the intelligent general reader as well as for the scholarly professional. He

Depression soup kitchen

also taught at Cambridge University and achieved early prominence in the British Civil Service. In the world of economics he was noted for changing or at least modifying his views to suit changing conditions, and for placing small value on consistency over time. His most famous early work was *The Economic Consequences of the Peace* (1920), in which he concluded that the excessive burden of German monetary reparations would, if enforced, prevent the recovery of Germany and all of Europe after World War I. Many of Keynes's writings after 1920 were on monetary policy. In a period of low gold production, he was a leader among those economists who felt that the traditional gold standard (with circulating currency convertible to a fixed amount of gold) was a deflationary drag on the domestic economy.

The *General Theory* broke even more sharply with generally accepted ideas, as you know from reading Chapter 10, by attacking Say's Identity and calling for budgetary deficits to counter depression conditions.

KEYNESIAN AND POST-KEYNESIAN ECONOMICS

Keynes viewed his doctrines as a general theory, which is to say, as something more than "depression economics." He applied the same system to check inflation, when it threatened to become a problem during World War II, mainly by raising taxes.[3]

After the war, organized labor, business, and agriculture in Britain and elsewhere used the Keynesian doctrine as a means of guaranteeing "full employment and full production at whatever cost" despite inflationary wage, price, and profit increases. Keynes responded by turning his back on his own disciples, speaking of "modern stuff gone silly and sour." Not long afterward, in April 1946, he died.

Today the self-styled "post-Keynesians" are still important at Cambridge University and elsewhere. They go beyond Keynes and "generalize the *General*

John Maynard Keynes

Theory" in ways that Keynes himself might not have welcomed. They support wage controls, price controls, and capital rationing as necessary features of the peacetime high-employment economy, in the interests of inflation control, income redistribution, and accelerated economic growth. Occasionally they even claim that Keynes "never really understood the *General Theory*." What they mean is that in his haste to publish a tract for his time, he never developed what the post-Keynesians consider to be its full implications in a world of imperfect competition, simultaneous inflation and unemployment, and maldistribution that aims at high growth as well as full employment.[4] What Keynes would himself have said of all these ideas we cannot guess.

2. Keynes came to the United States, met President Franklin Roosevelt, and tried unsuccessfully to persuade Roosevelt to increase sharply the volume of New Deal spending and the size of the government budget deficits. Roosevelt apparently distrusted Keynes, believing him to be "more mathematician than economist."

3. Foreseeing postwar depression, however, Keynes proposed to "sweeten" wartime taxes by making them compulsory loans, to be repaid when depression conditions returned.

4. Post-Keynesian views are explained further in Chapter 17.

Money and Depository Institutions

The Federal Reserve System and Monetary Instruments

Monetary Economics

PART IV

MONEY, BANKING, AND MONETARY POLICY

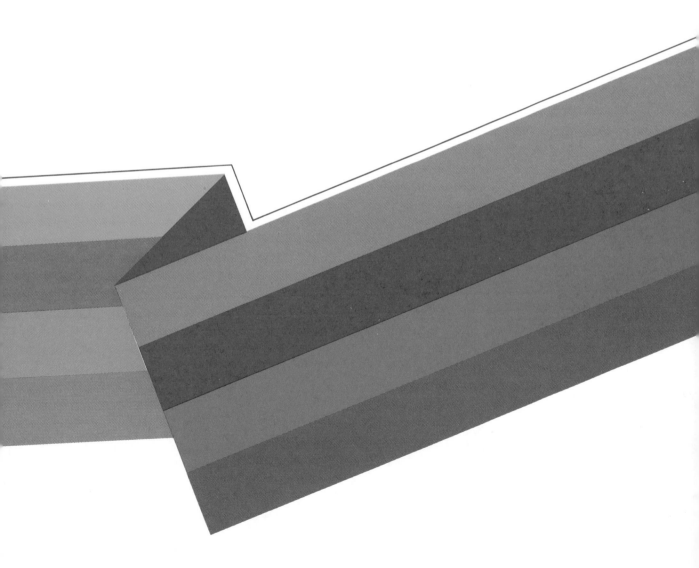

12

Money and Depository Institutions

Preview   You may have some coins and some currency in your pocket or wallet at this moment. Perhaps you examined this money and discovered the year that the coin was minted (manufactured) and even the location of the mint itself. Did you notice that the currency is a Federal Reserve Note? Was it issued by a bank in Boston, Chicago, San Francisco, Dallas, or somewhere else? These bits of information may satisfy your curiosity, as long as you are sure that the coins and currency will buy your lunch or a ticket to the movie this evening. But economists want to know a lot more about what money is and what it does in the economy.

With this chapter we begin the study of the role of money in the economy and in the determination of equilibrium national income and product. We devote three chapters to this important topic. This chapter examines the nature of money itself and how depository institutions are able to expand and contract the amount of money in an economy. Chapter 13 explains how the Federal Reserve System (the "central" bank in the United States) controls the money supply. The final chapter in the trio, Chapter 14, develops the economic theory of how money may affect the equilibrium level of national income and product, both in real terms and in terms of inflation or deflation of the price level. Just as you learned about fiscal instruments and theory in Part III, you will come to understand monetary instruments and theory in Chapters 13 and 14.

This chapter, on money and depository institutions, starts with a brief discussion of the importance of money in the economy and why economists must understand money. After explaining the functions of money, we describe the things that actually serve as money in the United States.

In order to understand money, you will need to have some

information about depository institutions and how they operate. The second half of the chapter describes how depository institutions are organized as profit-seeking business enterprises that are usually able to operate successfully on partial reserves. That is, their obligations to depositors can be greatly in excess of their cash and readily available assets. Finally, you will learn how depository institutions influence the money supply in the economy as a by-product of their partial reserve operation.

MONEY

The economics that you have already learned will give you some clues about the importance of money. Business firms and governments keep track of their economic activities with accounts recorded in money amounts. In a similar way, the national income accounting system measures the volume of economic activity in money terms.

What would happen if the quantity of money itself were expanded or contracted? Could such expansions and contractions in the quantity of money affect the volume of economic activity in the economy? Could such changes make any real difference in production, jobs, and living standards? Or would they simply change the price level and bring inflation or deflation but leave real production unchanged? Can changes in the money supply be controlled so that money can be used as an instrument of policy?

Economists find that the answer to each of these questions is "yes." The speed, or velocity, of the circulation of money through the economy does change from time to time. It is also true that the amount of money itself changes. The resulting changes in the quantity and velocity of money can bring further changes, not only in the real volume of production and jobs but also in the general price level. We shall consider these questions in detail in Chapter 14. However, before we can do that, it is important to understand what money is and what determines the amount of money in the economy.

Changes in the amount of money in the economy and in the speed of its circulation

through the economy can affect the real volume of production and jobs and also the general price level.

The Functions of Money

Before you can understand what money is in terms of economics, you need to know the functions of money. The reason for this "function first" approach is that, in various times and places, many different things have served as money. For certain people, seashells or distinctively colored or shaped stones have been money. For others, cigarettes or the bark from particular trees have served as money. Livestock or even human slaves have been "money." Today, specially printed pieces of paper or specially minted pieces of metal (and other things as well, as you will see) serve as money. So it is clear that economists cannot define money in terms of its composition. Instead, they first specify certain "functions of money" and then define money itself as that which is generally used in carrying out these functions. If this way of defining money seems a little backwards at first, remember that you cannot define a "split end" or a "defensive linebacker" without first specifying their functions in the game of football. The position itself is defined by the functions it performs. In economics, we usually list four functions of money: medium of exchange, unit of account, store of purchasing power, and standard for deferred payment.

Medium of Exchange The easiest way to understand the **medium of exchange** function of money is to compare a direct, or **barter,** exchange in which one item is traded directly for another with an exchange that takes place through an intermediate transaction, that is, through the "medium" of money. Consider the teacher-student exchange, for example. The famous painter and recorder of birds and animals, John James Audubon, agreed to tutor the children of a Mississippi family in exchange for room and board and half days free to roam the plantation and paint. This was a barter exchange. As you can see, there was no "medium," or intermediate step. It was a unique transaction because it required a specific combination of wants: Audubon wanted to be supported while painting, and the family wanted instruction for its children. These special conditions lasted for only one year. Then Audubon moved on. Today, the typical teacher-student exchange takes place through the medium of money. Instead of providing the teacher with room and board, students pay tuition in money. The teacher receives money, which he or she can use to pay for room and board, among other things.

Using money as a medium of exchange greatly extends the range of feasible exchanges. No longer do people need to match their specific wants with those of other people. The medium of exchange lubricates the economic machinery. Whenever the medium of exchange is eliminated, as has sometimes happened because of war or runaway inflation, the living standard falls rapidly as the system reverts to barter exchange. We can now see part of the definition of money: money must be generally accepted as a medium of exchange, that is, it must be used for the intermediate step in exchange.

The medium of exchange function is basic to the economist's definition of money. The other functions that we shall explain are closely related to this one, but they are to some degree subsidiary to it. That is, if something is not customarily used as a medium of exchange, it is not likely to be accepted for the other functions.

Unit of Account   The **unit of account** function of money is the "common denominator" function—a way of comparing the values of different items. It is simply easier to remember, for example, that the price of a loaf of bread is $0.80 or that the price of a gallon of milk is $2.40 than it is to remember that one gallon equals three loaves. Without the unit of account function of money, people would have to remember millions of continually changing exchange ratios, one for each pair of commodities. A common denominator, or unit of account, simplifies things by selecting one item, *money*, and expressing all other values in terms of that one item.

It is almost inevitable that the item that has been accepted as the medium of exchange will also be selected as the unit of account. The unit of account function is virtually a by-product of the medium of exchange function.

What happens when the two functions are different? If you travel in France, you expect price tags to be in francs. If you are carrying francs and

have gotten used to them, there is no problem. But if you are accustomed to thinking in dollars, the mental gymnastics of converting from one unit to the other can be troublesome, especially if prices are subject to bargaining. You may have the same type of problem in converting from yards to meters, or from gallons to liters, or from semesters to quarters. Conversion itself is the problem. When the same money is used for both a unit of account and a medium of exchange, no conversion is needed.

Store of Purchasing Power   The third commonly listed function of money is the **store of purchasing power** function. This simply means that people who have units of the medium of exchange want to have the option of saving some for use at some later time. Surely a medium of exchange that was good "today only" would be less than ideal for most people. Each day people who wished to save would want to exchange some of today's money for money stamped with tomorrow's (or some later) date. Even though we could expect special moneychangers to set up shop soon to help people manage their money over time, the whole process of dated money would be quite a waste of time and talent. Up to a point at least, what is used as the medium of exchange and the unit of account will probably be used as a store of purchasing power as well.

The store of purchasing power function adds a time dimension to the unit of account function of money. No longer is money comparable to yards and meters or to liters and gallons. In these physical measures, we expect tomorrow's liter to contain as much liquid as today's liter and tomorrow's meter to be the same as today's. Inflation and deflation don't affect these measures. Printing more meter sticks does not threaten the size of the meter. But money is different. Price levels do change (as we noted in discussing index numbers), and when this happens, we move part way back to having dated money—"today's money" can be different from "tomorrow's money." In inflationary times, holding money until tomorrow means converting it automatically into "tomorrow's money," which is less valuable. Thus, inflation threatens the store of purchasing power function of money. Because people become less and less willing to hold it for this purpose, moneychangers, banks, and dealers in money substitutes (such as securities, gold, and precious gems) do big business. Also, as you will see, interest rates may be pushed up as people insist on extra compensation for holding notes, bonds, and other IOUs that have fixed dollar amounts.

Standard for Deferred Payment The fourth function that people expect of their money is that it should serve as a **standard for deferred payment.** When people make an agreement that involves payments to be made at some time in the future, it is convenient to have some standard way to specify the amount of such payment. Of course, whatever is used as a medium of exchange and a unit of account is most likely to be used as the standard of deferred payment as well. A substantial portion of the transactions that take place in a modern economy involve contracts that extend over a period of time.

Changing price levels bring up some of the same problems for money as a standard for deferred payment as they did for money as a store of purchasing power. Inflation means that the money value of the deferred payment will overstate its future purchasing power equivalent measured at today's prices. Conversely, deflation means that the money value of the deferred payment will understate its future purchasing power equivalent in terms of today's prices. Of course, if the parties to the contract expect prices to change during the term of the agreement, their expectations can be built into the deferred payment amounts that are written into the contract.

Money has four functions: as a medium of exchange (used as the intermediate step in exchange), as a unit of account (a way of comparing the values of different items), as a store of purchasing power (can be saved for use at a later time), and as a standard for deferred payment (for payments due at some time in the future.)

Forms of Money in the United States

Having described the basic functions that money is expected to perform, we can now define **money.**

Money is anything generally accepted in an economy as a medium of exchange, a unit of account, a store of purchasing power, and a standard for deferred payment. A careful look at this definition, however, reveals that we still have to deal with some obscure concepts. The word *anything* places no limit on the composition of money. As you will see, money may be metal, paper, entries in an account book, or even electronic impulses on magnetic tape. Also, the term *generally accepted* is difficult to pin down. *Accepted* means that people routinely use the substance in exchanges, but, as we shall explain shortly, acceptance must sometimes be enforced by law. How general must acceptance be in order for something to be money? Again, the definition is loose. In the United States today, coins, currency, and checkable account balances (account balances against which checks can be written) are the basic forms of money. Let us take a brief look at each of these forms.

In the United States, coins, currency, and checkable account balances are the basic forms of money.

Coins The medium of exchange function goes a long way toward helping us understand why coins are a component of most money systems. People want a form of money that is durable, portable, and uniform because they want to carry money with them to make "convenience transactions," such as operating automatic vending machines. The absence of many of these characteristics helps explain why livestock, slaves, wampum, and tree bark did not fare well as money. But because cigarettes came quite close to having these qualities, they served reasonably well as money in prisoner-of-war camps during World War II. Of course, convenience, durability, portability, and uniformity do not guarantee success as money. The Susan B. Anthony dollar coin still does not circulate well in the United States, perhaps because people fear it will be mistaken for a twenty-five-cent piece.

Coins have the advantage of durability, portability, uniformity, and convenience.

The uniformity feature is especially important in making coins generally accepted. Long ago, gold dust or nuggets in a pouch had to be weighed when a transaction was made. But by minting the gold into a coin, it was possible to achieve uniformity. Sometimes, in an effort to gain a certain edge in the transaction, people would rub or chip away some of the coin. Though even kings and princes did this, they soon found that the official mint itself was the best place to cheat on the money system. To make more money with a given amount of gold, they could add *base* (less-valuable) metal before the coins were minted. This practice led to one of the earliest economic theories about money, called **Gresham's Law,** which states that base money always drives the *dear* (more-valuable) money out of circulation. Of two coins with the same face value, the one containing base metal circulates, while the one containing dear metal is hoarded or perhaps melted down to recover the metal. This law still operates today, it seems. The real silver coins in the United States are almost all in hoards or have been melted down.

Gresham's Law states that base money always drives more valuable or dear money out of circulation.

Currency Printed paper money is easy to carry, reasonably durable, and can be printed in whatever denominations are wanted and even in different colors to aid in recognition. Clipping and rubbing won't erode the value of the paper money. For larger transactions, paper money clearly has advantages over coin. In fact, paper currency evolved from coins and precious metal partly because of its extra convenience. Coins or, more likely, gold would be deposited with a bank or other institution of recognized reliability in exchange for deposit receipts, that is, for promises to return the coins or the gold when the receipt was presented. The certificate might read "Pay to the bearer on demand the sum of _____." This warehouse receipt payable to the bearer was, in fact, paper currency and was called a **bank note** when it was issued by a bank. Its acceptability depended on the integrity of the issuing bank or commercial establishment since it was backed by a promise to exchange coin or precious metal for the certificate.

Paper currency, which originated as bank notes, is more convenient than coins for large transactions.

The early days of paper money were confusing times because many different institutions would issue these notes, and some were more reliable than others. People could never be sure that their notes were really worth the amount printed on them. The reason for this confusion was that banks and others who issued notes had discovered that, in normal times, new deposits of gold or coins would just about balance withdrawals of these precious metals. So why not issue a few extra notes and lend them, charging interest, to people who want to borrow? As you will see, this was the beginning of modern partial reserve banking. However, our immediate point is that some banks would push their luck in issuing bank notes, and a bank failure would occur, shaking confidence in all bank notes, even those from banks that were not overextended. U.S. history is filled with accounts of bank panics triggered by the inability of some banks to redeem their notes. In an attempt to reduce this danger, a system of national banks was set up in 1863 to issue paper currency, and a tax was imposed on the circulation of bank notes issued by banks chartered by states. The tax drove the bank notes out of existence, but, as we shall see, the banks responded with something even better—the checkable account.

The history of government-sponsored currency is at least as fascinating as that of private bank notes. Governments also can yield to the temptation to issue too much currency. Government currency has often been issued without any (or very much) "backing" with precious metal. The official U.S. currency today, called the Federal Reserve Note, is not backed by any promise to exchange it for gold or silver or anything else. However, the particular advantage of government-issued currency is that an official government decree, or "fiat," usually states that the currency is **legal tender.** Your Federal Reserve Note, for example, bears the statement "This note is legal tender for all debts, public and private." This means that a person who is offered this currency but refuses to accept it in settling a debt cannot continue to collect interest on the debt or go to court to claim that the debtor had refused to pay. This goes a long way toward making the official currency generally acceptable, but it does not guarantee this result. In times of actual or prospective inflation, private contractors may try to force payment in real goods or precious metal rather than legal tender money. So even legal tender money can become worthless if people refuse to exchange goods and services for it. During the American Revolution, General Washington's troops at Valley Forge often went cold and hungry because of the difficulties the Continental Army had in buying supplies with continental currency. Similarly, during the Civil War, foreign money and gold became the most valuable part of the Confederacy's treasury. One of the last acts of the Confederacy was the attempt to get its gold and foreign money to Cuba for safe-keeping.

The official U.S. currency today is the Federal Reserve Note, which is backed by a government decree, or fiat, stating that it is legal tender.

Checkable Account Balances   In the United States today, balances in accounts against which checks can be written also serve as money. Although personal checks are not always accepted, a huge volume of obligations regularly are paid by check. Note that our description of this money refers to the balances in **checkable accounts**, not to the checks themselves. Under this definition, checks that are not backed by sufficient balances are not money.

Checkable account balances come into being partly as a result of deposits of coins or currency but mostly as a result of loans made by **depository institutions**—organizations such as banks, savings and loan associations, and credit unions that accept deposits of funds and offer checking services. When a person negotiates a loan, he or she may ask for and receive currency and coin, but most likely both the borrower and the lending institution will prefer the simple procedure of adding the borrowed sum to the balance in the borrower's checkable account. Through this simple operation, the borrower's promise to repay the loan (the borrower's debt) is "monetized." That is, it becomes

actual money. For this reason, many people say that most of our money supply is simply **monetized debt.** In the context of U.S. history, it is interesting that checkable account money expanded as bank note currency was eliminated. When taxes were imposed on the bank notes, bank lending switched to checkable account balances. Checks replaced the bank notes and had the extra convenience of being written for the exact amount needed to discharge an obligation. Instead of promises to pay issued by the bank, a check is a payment order to a depository institution signed by the person or business with rights to the checkable account. Bad checks are written, but they do not compromise the institution itself or invite a panic.

Depository institutions are profit-seeking business enterprises such as banks, savings and loan associations, and credit unions that accept deposits of funds and offer checking services on these accounts.

Balances in accounts against which checks can be written also serve as money. Most of the U.S. money supply today is monetized debt—loans by depository institutions that borrowers promise to repay.

The U.S. Money Supply

As you might expect from the phrase "anything that is generally accepted" in our definition of money, the actual measurement of the money supply can be somewhat complicated. Moreover, the things that are money may change from time to time as new technologies bring better ways to carry out exchanges. Four different measures of the U.S. money supply are illustrated in Figure 1. These are alternative definitions that are used in measuring the actual U.S. money supply. The definitions have been established by the Federal Reserve System, which we describe in Chapter 13. In Figure 1, we encounter broader and broader definitions of money as we move down the column.

M1   Coins and currency are listed at the very top of the money column in Figure 1 because these

FIGURE 1
Official Measures of the U.S. Money Supply, October 1988 (in billions of dollars)

At the top of the money column are the most liquid, or spendable, types of money. The most widely used measure of the money supply (M1)—in the darkest shade of green—includes coins, currency, and checkable account balances. More inclusive measures of the money supply extend—in lighter shades of green—further down the column. Cumulative totals at the right show the larger and larger size of the money supply as more inclusive definitions are used.

a. Overnight repurchase agreements, Eurodollars, money market mutual fund shares.

b. Term repurchase agreements, term Eurodollars, institution-only money market mutual fund balances.

Source: Economic Report of the President, 1989, Table B-67.

items are extremely liquid—that is, they are easily used as a medium of exchange. Next in line come checkable account balances, which are also very liquid. Checkable account balances include not only the traditional demand deposits (on which the depository institution pays no interest) but also interest-bearing accounts such as NOW (negotiable orders of withdrawal) accounts, ATS (automatic transfer service) accounts, share-draft accounts in credit unions, and other accounts that offer check-writing services. Such interest-bearing checkable accounts expanded rapidly during the 1970s and have remained very popular ever since. Their advantage is that interest is earned during the period before checks are written against the account. The **M1 money supply concept**—shown in the darkest shade of green in Figure 1—is the one that is used most by economists and is the one we refer to when we discuss the money supply in later chapters.

The M1 measure of money includes coins, currency, and checkable account balances (including interest-bearing NOW, ATS, and share-draft accounts as well as the non-interest-bearing demand deposit accounts).

M2, M3, and L As we proceed down the money supply column in Figure 1, we encounter assets that are less and less liquid. Small time deposits (such as certificates of deposit), money market deposit accounts, and (noncheckable) savings accounts are not spendable in their present form, but can usually be exchanged for directly spendable forms without delay or cost. These deposit balances generally are accessible on demand. A bit less liquid are "other" types of assets such as repurchase agreements (RPs)—arrangements with banks or with securities dealers that give the owner the chance to convert back to spendable money without great delay or cost. Also included in this "other" category are Eurodollars, which are dollar-denominated accounts outside the United States. Even though they appear in the accounts of American banks, the lending business on these accounts is done mainly in Europe. The **M2 money supply concept** consists of M1—the darker green area in

Figure 1—plus these less liquid accounts, which have a slightly lighter green background in the figure.

The **M3 money supply concept** includes, in addition to M2, large time deposits, fairly long-term repurchase agreements, and certain other assets, shown with a still lighter green background in Figure 1. All of these are somewhat harder to convert into spendable money. Finally, money watchers also keep track of U.S. Savings Bonds, several relatively liquid kinds of U.S. government securities, payment promises by large corporations, and other items that are potentially convertible into spendable money. The **L money supply** is M3 plus these forms of wealth, which are sometimes called **near money.**

M1, M2, M3, and L are definitions of the money supply established by the Federal Reserve System. They are used to measure the actual U.S. money supply. Their liquidity becomes less and less as we move from M1 to M2 to M3 and to L.

M2, M3, and L include assets that are less liquid than M1 assets.

Some observers contend that economists, bankers, government officials, and other money watchers have gone too far in developing so many different measures of the money supply. They argue that confusion results from such a variety of money measures. The problem is that there are many ways of holding wealth and that very gradual changes in liquidity occur as assets are moved from one form to another. Usually there is a trade-off between liquidity, which has its advantages, and interest earnings, which are desired for obvious reasons. The many asset forms simply give people a large number of options. In fact, the liquidity column could be extended still farther into such other less liquid assets as jewelry, stamp collections, and works of art. Even credit cards have some moneylike features, though they simply give a person an easy way to borrow money.

Sometimes the rate of change in the money supply according to one measure is different from its rate of change according to another measure.

Therefore, when economists use money supply changes to make predictions about the economy, it may make a difference which measure they use.

DEPOSITORY INSTITUTIONS

From the economist's definition of money, we know that balances in checkable accounts are money. Also, we know that these checkable account balances are part of the official M1, M2, M3, and L measures of the U.S. money supply. Our next step in understanding money is to examine the institutions in which these checkable account balances are kept.

In a modern economy, there are many types of firms that provide financial services. In studying the money supply, we concentrate on *depository institutions,* which include both commercial banks and thrift institutions. **Commercial banks** accept deposits and make all kinds of loans, including loans to business firms. **Thrift institutions**, such as savings and loan associations, mutual savings banks, and credit unions, accept deposits and make primarily consumer and mortgage loans. As we shall see, these institutions play an important role in determining the actual quantity of money in the economy.

Depository institutions include commercial banks, which accept deposits and make all kinds of loans, and thrift institutions, which accept deposits and make primarily consumer and mortgage loans.

Depository Institutions and Partial Reserves

Depository institutions are profit-seeking business enterprises. With money from depositors and shareholders, they earn income by lending money and by purchasing and holding interest-bearing securities. Some of the income that they obtain is used to pay interest to depositors. Some is used for other expenses, such as wages for employees. What is left are earnings that may be paid to shareholders if the firm is organized as a private corporation, or may be credited to the accounts of shareholder-depositor members of credit unions, mutual savings banks, or some savings and loan associations.

Depository institutions earn income by lending money and by purchasing and holding interest-bearing securities.

In many ways, starting a depository institution is similar to starting any new business. But what makes it somewhat different is that state and federal laws require that a charter must be obtained before the depository institution can do business. The **charter** is the legal authority to accept deposits and make loans, much as the corporate charter is the legal authority to do business as a corporation or a medical license is the legal authority to practice medicine.

In the United States, charters are issued both by the federal government and by state governments. Often, the institution's name will tell where its charter came from. The First National Bank has a federal charter, and the Home Town State Bank has a state charter, for example. Although federal and state charters have similar provisions specifying permissible operations, state charters are frequently more generous. Along with general legislation, the charter sets the rules that must be followed in doing business. Violating these rules may mean the withdrawal of the charter and the end of business. Once the charter is in hand, the depository institution can sell stock and/or otherwise gather the money needed to launch its operations.

Depository institutions must obtain charters (the legal authority to accept deposits and make loans) from either the federal government or a state government.

A key idea in understanding the operation of depository institutions is the concept of partial, or fractional, reserves. In their simplest form, **partial, or fractional, reserves** mean that the amount of cash or immediately available funds on hand is less than the total of the obligations to the people who have deposited money in the institution. If all depositors appeared at the same time and wanted their money, the institution would not be able to keep its promise of repayment. This would be a "run" on the institution and could be disastrous for the depositors, for the depository institution, and for those planning to borrow from it.

The partial reserve system under which depository institutions operate means that the amount of cash immediately available is less than the total of the institution's obligations to all who have deposited money in it.

Why do depository institutions operate on a partial reserve basis and run some risk of this disaster? Why are depositors willing to place their money in these institutions? The answers to these questions are not as difficult as you might imagine. Depository institutions engage in partial reserve operations because it is profitable to do so. Depositors place their funds in these institutions because they can receive checking and other services and can earn interest on their deposits. To understand how this system works, let's view it through the eyes of the management of the depository institution. If a wide variety of depositors can be persuaded to deposit their money, it will soon become apparent that day-after-day new deposits will just about equal withdrawals from these accounts. Some customers will be writing checks to others who hold deposits in the same institution. No change in net deposits will occur. Also, checks written to outsiders will approximately match checks from outsiders. Suppose that over a long period of time, the difference between withdrawals and new deposits fluctuates within a range of, say, 5 percent of the average amount on deposit. With this knowledge, the management recognizes that 95 percent of the deposited money (or perhaps only 90 percent, to leave a margin for safety) could be loaned out at interest. The interest earned from the loans enables the institution to pay interest to the depositors, and the spread between the interest charged to borrowers and the interest paid to depositors leaves money for expenses and for dividends to the owners and members.

There are also advantages from the point of view of the depositors. These people have wealth and can choose among many alternative ways to hold it. To obtain quick spendability (liquidity), they might hold cash but will earn no interest. To obtain dividend or interest earnings, they might purchase stocks or bonds, but their risk will be greater, and their wealth will have less liquidity. However, the depositor today can have both liquidity and interest earnings by placing funds in a depository institution.[1] As long as the danger of loss of deposits is minimal, there is little reason to forgo the advantages of earning interest. In a well-run depository institution, the stockholders and members, the depositors, and also those who borrow can all find the arrangement beneficial.

Depository institutions use the partial reserve system because it is profitable to do so. Depositors are willing to place their funds in these institutions because they receive checking and other services and can earn interest on their deposits.

The partial reserve feature clearly implies that money put into a depository institution, either by shareholders or by depositors, can be used as a reserve for a considerably greater quantity of money circulating in the economy. In times past, this money took the form of bank notes. Today, it takes the form of checkable account balances. We shall carefully explain this process of monetary expansion later in the chapter. But first it is important to understand how partial reserve banking can also be safe banking.

Regulation and Deposit Insurance

Government regulation of depository institutions has its roots in the attractiveness of the fractional,

or partial, reserve system and in the temptations that go along with it. For example, if operating with a 50 percent reserve is profitable, operating with only a 25 percent reserve is more profitable. Why not only 10 percent reserve, or even 5 percent, if depositors can be persuaded that their funds are safe? At various times in U.S. history, the virtual absence of effective regulation gave rise to the devious and unscrupulous practices generally referred to as **wildcat banking.** Institutions were started with the barest minimum amounts of initial funding from investors. Depositors were persuaded to entrust their savings to these institutions. Loans were made and bank notes were issued until obligations far exceeded readily available assets. In this precarious situation, uncollectible loans or the least hint of a business downturn could force the institution into bankruptcy. Then, one failure would follow another as depositors scrambled to withdraw deposits from surviving institutions. Runs on financial institutions would spread like wildfire until an entire region, or even the whole economy, was engulfed in a financial panic.

There are essentially two lines of defense against the panics and financial disasters that can come from fractional reserve systems. One is regulation of the operations of depository institutions and the other is insurance for deposits in them.

The partial reserve system can lead to financial panic if depositors lose trust and all try to withdraw their money at once. Runs on depository institutions can be averted by regulation and insurance.

Regulatory Agencies Each depository institution is subject to regulation by the government that issued its charter. Since charters are issued by the federal government and by each of the fifty state governments, there are many regulatory agencies. At the federal level, the chief regulatory agencies are the Federal Reserve System for member banks and bank holding companies, the Comptroller of the Currency for nationally chartered banks, the Federal Home Loan Bank Board for federal savings and loan associations, and the National Credit Union Administration for credit unions with federal charters.

---

1. Interest is not paid on demand deposit balances. But NOW accounts, ATS accounts, credit union share drafts, and the like, in effect offer both checking services and interest earnings for depositors. Before the introduction of these accounts, checking service was usually offered without charge—an arrangement that offered a valuable service in place of cash interest earnings.

The primary function of regulatory agencies is to examine the books of the institutions for which they are responsible and to determine whether they should be allowed to continue operation. Examiners from the regulatory agencies come unannounced to depository institutions and examine the records of deposits and withdrawals and of loans that these institutions have made. If the examiners conclude that a particular institution has many outstanding loans that will not be repaid and that it is in danger of bankruptcy, the regulatory agency has the authority to require the closing of the institution, the sale of its assets, and the distribution of the proceeds to satisfy the claims of depositors and other creditors. If the sale of the insolvent institution does not yield enough money to cover obligations to depositors, the deposit insurance system (described next) is called upon to make payments to the depositors to the extent of insurance obligations.

Each depository institution is regulated by an agency of the government that issued its charter. The regulatory agencies examine the records of deposits, withdrawals, and loans at depository institutions to make sure that they are financially sound.

Deposit Insurance The second line of defense against the problems of partial reserve operation is deposit insurance. Deposit insurance guarantees that, should an institution fail, depositors will recover their deposits up to the (current) limit of $100,000 per account. To purchase this insurance, depository institutions pay premiums to the insuring agency. Deposit insurance protects depository institutions against runs by depositors fearful that they might lose their deposits if the institution were to fail. If deposits are protected by insurance, there is no need for depositors to withdraw their funds.

As in the case of regulatory agencies, both federal and state agencies provide deposit insurance. At the federal level, the Federal Deposit Insurance Corporation (FDIC) insures deposits in banks, the Federal Savings and Loan Insurance Corporation (FSLIC) insures deposits in savings and loan associations, and the National Credit Union Share Insurance Funds (NCUSIF) insures accounts in credit unions.

Deposit insurance guarantees that depositors will recover their deposits (up to $100,000 per account) should the institution fail. Deposit insurance is designed to forestall runs on depository institutions.

Deregulation and the Crisis of Thrift Institutions

Despite the protection offered by regulatory agencies and deposit insurance, depository institutions can still face the threat of bankruptcy. Insolvency became a major concern in the 1970s and 1980s, when technological advances brought enormous changes to financial institutions. The combination of telecommunications and computers made it possible to transfer balances instantaneously between types of accounts and between one institution and another around the world. It became easy for depositors to move their balances between accounts and between institutions in their search for high rates of return. Competition among institutions to attract deposits became fierce.

Interest on Checkable Accounts One of the first results of the new technology was the inability of regulatory agencies to prevent the payment of interest on balances in checkable accounts. In their competition to attract deposits, institutions developed various procedures to allow interest to be paid on checkable balances. Basically, these procedures allow balances in interest-bearing accounts to be transferred automatically and instantaneously to a checkable account whenever a check is presented for payment. The various names for these procedures include **automatic transfer service (ATS) accounts** in banks, **negotiable order of withdrawal (NOW) accounts** in savings and loan associations, and **share-draft accounts** in credit unions. These procedures first became widespread in the early 1970s.

Technological advances led to fierce competition among financial institutions in the 1970s and 1980s. Interest payments on checkable balances became widespread as a means of attracting depositors.

Elimination of Interest-Rate Ceilings Record high nominal interest rates existed during the inflationary years of the late 1970s and early 1980s. These high nominal rates greatly increased competitive pressures among financial institutions and caused large losses of deposits from those depository institutions prevented, by government regulation, from paying more than a stated maximum rate of interest to their depositors. Especially hard hit by losses of deposits were savings and loan associations, for which interest-rate ceilings had been set at low levels in order to provide low-priced financing for residential mortgages. Funds were drained away from regulated depository institutions in favor of the more generous returns offered by money-market accounts maintained by stock brokerage firms. In an effort to help threatened savings and loan associations and other depository institutions, the Depository Institutions Deregulation and Monetary Control Act of 1980 mandated a gradual elimination of the interest rate ceiling that was allowed to be paid on deposits.

High nominal interest rates in the 1970s and 1980s greatly increased competitive pressures among financial institutions and led to large losses of deposits from those depository institutions that had to conform to government-set interest-rate ceilings.

Thrift Institution Bankruptcies Allowing thrift institutions to pay higher interest rates to their depositors opened the way for another threat of bankruptcy for these institutions. Although they could attract deposits with the higher interest rates, their earnings on already outstanding loans and mortgages continued at the low interest rates carried over from the era of regulation. Profit margins were squeezed, and an increasing number of thrift institutions faced bankruptcy. Further deregulation attempted to deal with this problem. The Thrift Institutions Restructuring Act of 1982 (Garn-St. Germain) relaxed regulations limiting the types of loans that these institutions might make. The purpose of this legislation was to enable thrift institutions to gain higher rates of return by extending loans in areas of greater yield (and greater risk) than offered by their previous home mortgage and consumer credit lending.

Although the federal government eased its restrictions on interest rates in 1980, depository institutions still faced financial difficulty because their earnings on already outstanding loans and mortgages continued at the low interest rates carried over from the era of regulation.

For most thrift institutions, the opportunity to move into higher-risk lending was not sufficient to overcome their difficulties. Problems were especially common in agricultural areas and in petroleum-producing regions of the southwestern United States. Falling land values and crude oil prices and the collapse of the oil drilling market added to the bad debt problems of thrifts and other financial institutions. Depository institution bankruptcies reached record high levels.

In 1982, the federal government relaxed regulations limiting the types of loans depository institutions may make in a further attempt to prevent widespread bankruptcies, but depository institution bankruptcies reached record high levels in the early and mid-1980s.

The Crisis in Deposit Insurance

What happens when a depository institution faces bankruptcy? First, examiners from regulatory agencies find that the institution is in danger of being unable to meet its obligations to depositors. Then, the regulatory agency must decide whether the institution should be closed, its assets sold, and its deposits returned to their owners. If the sale proceeds do not generate enough money to cover obligations to depositors, the deposit insurance agency is called upon to make good on its insurance commitment to these institutions.

In 1986, the Federal Savings and Loan Insurance Corporation did not have enough reserves to meet its insurance obligations to all the thrift institutions that were, at that time, believed to be insolvent. In other words, the crisis in the thrift industry had become so serious that it was a crisis for the insurance system as well. Since the FSLIC did not have enough reserve funds to close the insolvent institutions, "creative accounting" devices, including certificates provided by the FSLIC that could be counted as assets, were used so that the institutions could appear solvent and could continue to operate while the FSLIC looked for funds and strategies to bolster its ability to meet its insurance obligations. Nevertheless, by 1989, five hundred U.S. savings and loan associations were insolvent.

What were the FSLIC's options at this point? Should it raise insurance premiums on still-solvent thrifts and risk pushing them into bankruptcy also? Should it scale back its coverage to less than the promised $100,000 per account? Should it adjust its insurance premium schedules so that thrifts taking greater risks would have to pay more for their insurance? Should it deny insurance to thrifts that fail to follow prudent lending strategies?

The two strategies mentioned last—risk-based insurance premiums and denial of insurance to imprudent thrift institutions—point specifically to additional problems connected with the deposit insurance system. From the viewpoint of some thrift institution managers, the availability of deposit insurance and the relaxation of limitations on deposit interest payments opened up "heads I win, tails you lose" opportunities. Loans could be made at terms favorable to the borrower and at high risk to the lending institution. If the venture succeeded, the loan would be repaid and the lender would prosper. If the venture failed, the loans would default, the thrift institution would become insolvent, and the insurance system would be called upon to pay off the depositors. As more and more thrift managers, in desperation or for personal gain, took this path, more and more thrift institutions failed, and the insurance system fell further and further behind in its ability to fulfill its obligations to depositors.

In 1986, bankruptcies in the thrift industry reached such proportions that the FSLIC did not have enough reserves to meet its obligations to all the depository institutions that were insolvent. By 1989 five hundred savings and loan associations were insolvent.

Where will it end? At the time of this writing, it appears increasingly likely that U.S. taxpayers will eventually be required to make good the deficit in the deposit insurance system.

Interstate Banking and Nonbank Banks

The revolution in computer technology and telecommunications has made financial institutions more competitive and has broken through barriers that previously separated financial institutions from other business firms. Two areas of particular interest are interstate banking and nonbank banks.

Interstate Banking In the United States, the business of **banking**—accepting deposits and making commercial (business) loans—has, for the most part, been confined within the boundaries of the separate states. Federal charters for banks were authorized by the National Banking Act of 1863, and a few of these national banks were allowed to open branches in states other than the one in which their head offices were located, but the McFadden Act of 1927 put a stop to this as it specifically prohibited bank extension across state lines.

During the past two decades, as the rapid transfer of account balances became more and more feasible through advancing technology, there arose new interest in permitting banks to extend branches across state lines. Part of the pressure for these extensions came from possible economies of scale in banking—a larger bank might experience lower unit cost and therefore offer more and better services. Another part came from the desire of financial interests in one state to take advantage of profit opportunities in other states.

The Douglas Amendment of 1970 to the Bank Holding Company Act of 1956 permitted bank holding companies (corporations that own one or more banks) to engage in **interstate banking**— to own banks in several states. However, holding companies could purchase banks only in those states passing laws permitting this type of activity. Starting with Maine in 1975, state after state changed its laws to allow interstate banking. By now interstate banking has become widespread, and many banks are owned by bank holding companies headquartered in other states.

Nonbank Banks The legal definition of a bank, according to the Bank Holding Company Act, is that it is an institution that accepts deposits and makes commercial loans. But what is the status of an institution that provides one of these services but not the other—for example, one that accepts deposits but does not make commercial loans? Is it a bank or isn't it? The answer is that it is a "nonbank bank"!

Nonbank banking began after 1970 when bank holding companies were authorized to acquire nonbanking subsidiaries. The question that arises with respect to mixing banking and nonbanking operations is whether firms that are not primarily in the banking business should be allowed to provide banking services. Should firms such as General Motors, Sears, American Express, or Merrill Lynch be allowed to mix banking with their other lines of business? Can it lead to undesirable financial practices or excessive concentrations of economic power? Or will it just be healthy competition in the financial industry? These questions have arisen time and again in recent discussions concerning bank legislation and regulation.

Interstate banking and nonbank banking (allowing firms not primarily in the banking business to provide banking services) became widespread in the 1980s.

DEPOSIT EXPANSION AND CONTRACTION

The fractional, or partial, reserve system described earlier in the chapter opens the way for depository institutions to expand or contract the money supply. This capability is a by-product of the fractional reserve system. There is nothing illegal or magical about financial institutions "creating" or "destroying" money. The process is not difficult to understand.

The partial reserve system allows depository institutions to expand or contract the money supply.

The Balance Sheet of a Depository Institution

In order to understand the deposit expansion process, it is necessary to have some acquaintance with the balance sheet of a depository institution. In Table 1, we present a simplified balance sheet for commercial banking institutions in the United States. The types of assets and liabilities on this balance sheet are representative of those for depository institutions in general. Assets are listed on the left side, and liabilities and net worth on the right.

Assets Let us briefly explain each entry on the left side first.

Reserves and Cash Items. **Reserves** consist mainly of deposits that depository institutions are required by law to maintain with the Federal Reserve System. In the next chapter, we shall describe the Federal Reserve System and how reserve requirements are set. This item on the balance sheet is very important in the deposit expansion process. Cash items consist of all cash in the vault and in the tellers' cages, along with other miscellaneous items.

A depository institution's reserves consist primarily of the deposits that it is required by law to maintain with the Federal Reserve System.

Loans. These are the IOUs from individuals and/or businesses who have borrowed from the institution. They are the main source of interest earnings for the depository institution. Interest earnings from these loans and from securities provide funds to pay interest to depositors, to cover operating expenses, and to pay dividends to shareholders or members.

Loans are the main source of interest earnings for depository institutions.

Securities. These are mainly government bonds that depository institutions buy and hold in order to generate interest income while at the same time retaining fairly quick access to funds.

Other Assets. These consist of buildings, furni-

TABLE 1
Balance Sheet of Commercial Banking Institutions in the United States, February 28, 1989 (in billions of dollars)

Assets		Liabilities and Net Worth	
Reserves and cash items	226.0	Checkable deposits	601.4
Loans	2,057.9	Savings deposits	528.7
Securities	535.5	Time deposits	991.7
Other assets	211.4	Borrowings	500.9
		Other liabilities	212.3
		Total liabilities	2,835.0
		Net worth	195.8
	3,030.8		3,030.8

Source: Federal Reserve Bulletin, May 1989, Table 1.25.

ture, and equipment needed to carry on the institution's operations. This category also includes minor items not conveniently listed elsewhere.

Liabilities and Net Worth Now let's take a look at the entries on the right side of the balance sheet.

Checkable Deposits. These are amounts owed to holders of accounts against which checks can be written. When a depositor writes a check, he or she is placing a demand on the institution to transfer money to someone. These accounts are payable on demand and therefore sometimes called **demand deposits,** or **transaction deposits.**

Savings Deposits. These are amounts owed to holders of savings accounts. Checks cannot be written against these balances. Technically, they are not payable on demand. Some waiting period or advance notice may be required.

Checkable deposit (sometimes called demand or transaction deposit) accounts are payable upon demand—that is, whenever a depositor writes a check. Savings deposits are technically not payable upon demand, since checks cannot be written against them.

Time Deposits: Time deposits are obligations to the holders of accounts that have stated dates when they will have to be paid—that is, they have fixed maturity dates. Certificates of deposit are examples of this type of account. Depository institutions can pay somewhat higher rates of interest on these deposits since they are committed to remain in the institution for a longer period of time. This kind of account gives greater flexibility in lending out this money.

Borrowings: These are IOUs given by depository institutions when they borrow from other financial institutions. If an institution can borrow at a low rate of interest and lend the money out at a higher rate, there is every reason to expect that it will do so.

Other Liabilities: These are obligations that depository institutions, like any other business, have but which do not fit into other categories.

Net Worth: Assets minus liabilities equal net worth—that is, the book value of the business to its owners. The net worth of a business includes the money that was paid in by original stockholders minus losses that have been suffered plus profits that have been earned but not paid out as dividends.

The Reserve Ratio

The **reserve ratio** is a key term in understanding how depository institutions expand and contract the money supply. This ratio is the institution's total of cash and official (government-approved) reserves divided by the amount of its checkable account liabilities. Suppose that a depository institution has $20 in cash and official reserves and $100 in checkable deposit liabilities. Its reserve ratio would be 20 percent. Official reserves must be held in the form of deposits with the Federal Reserve System or vault cash, except that sometimes institutions can arrange to hold these reserves with other financial institutions, which, in turn, maintain reserve deposits with the Federal Reserve System.

Another term that is important to understand is the **reserve requirement**—the amount of official reserves that depository institutions must maintain in order to avoid penalties. The reserve requirement is generally expressed as a minimum required reserve ratio. In our example, if the reserve requirement were 20 percent, the institution in our illustration would be exactly in conformity with the law. It would not have too few reserves, and it would have no **excess reserves.** This is another key idea in the expansion process. Excess reserves are official reserves over and above the reserve requirements.

A depository institution's reserve ratio is the total of cash and official reserves divided by the amount of its checkable account liabilities. The reserve requirement is the amount of official reserves that depository institutions must maintain in order to avoid penalties.

Excess reserves are those over and above the official reserve requirements.

The Deposit-Expansion Process

Depository institutions are able to expand and contract the nation's money supply because they operate with partial reserves. This means that, when a new deposit is received, only part must be held as reserve for the deposit itself and the rest can be loaned out. The money loaned out is, in effect, new money, because the original depositor still has full command over the whole amount of the initial deposit.

When a new deposit is received in a depository institution, only part must be held as reserve for the deposit itself, and the rest can be loaned

---

out. This process expands the money supply because the money loaned out is, in effect, new money.

We will illustrate the deposit-expansion process with a series of balance sheets starting with those in Table 2. These balance sheets are simplified to show only the entries needed to explain the expansion process and by showing zero balances initially (top panel) for each account. We shall assume that the reserve requirement for checkable accounts is 20 percent. We shall ignore the fact that depository institutions must also maintain reserves for other types of accounts.

The **deposit-expansion process** starts when a new deposit is made in a depository institution. This is shown in the middle panel of Table 2. To use the simplest illustration, we assume that Bill Brown deposits $100 of currency that previously had been circulating as hand-to-hand money.[2] He deposits the $100 in his checkable account, which is a liability entered on the right side of the balance sheet for Depository Institution A. On the asset side, the $100 is recorded in the "reserves and cash" category. In parentheses below this entry, you will note that these reserves consist of $20 that is required and $80 of excess reserves. No expansion of the money supply has yet taken place. Even though Bill Brown's checkable account balance is counted as money, only coins and currency *outside* depository institutions are included in the official definition of the money supply. Therefore, Bill's checkable account balance simply replaces the currency that he deposited.

The stage is set, however, for an expansion of the money supply. Depository Institution A has excess reserves in the amount of $80, given our assumed 20 percent reserve requirement for checkable accounts. If Ron Black wants to borrow $80 and if the institution is willing to lend it to him, an expansion of the money supply will take place. This step is shown in the bottom panel in Table 2. Mr. Black signs a note to the depository institution, which it lists as an asset in the loans category, and

---

2. You will learn in the next chapter that the central bank is the most likely originating source of new deposits into the banking system.

TABLE 2
Deposit-Expansion Process: Depository Institution A (amounts in dollars)

Start		
Assets		**Liabilities**
Reserves and cash	0	Checkable deposits	0
(Required: 0)			
(Excess: 0)			
Loans	0		
Securities	0		
	0		0

New Deposit Step		
Assets		**Liabilities**
Reserves and cash	100	Checkable deposits	
(Required: 20)		Bill Brown	100
(Excess: 80)			
Loans	0		
Securities	0		
	100		100

Loan Step		
Assets		**Liabilities**
Reserves and cash	20	Checkable deposits	
(Required: 20)		Bill Brown	100
(Excess: 0)			
Loans			
Ron Black	80		
Securities	0		
	100		100

The process begins in the "new-deposit step" when Bill Brown deposits $100 in his checkable account. The depository institution then has excess reserves of $80, which are loaned to Ron Black in the "loan step."

Mr. Black takes the proceeds of his loan in currency. The reserves and cash account is reduced to $20, all of which is required, and both Ron Black and Bill Brown have money to spend.

Since Mr. Black did not borrow the money for the sheer pleasure of paying interest, we assume that he soon spends it to buy something, say, electronic equipment from the Green Radio Company. Green Radio deposits the currency in its checkable account in Depository Institution B (top panel in Table 3). After this institution places the money in its reserves and cash account, it is ready (even eager) to lend out the $64, which is in excess of the prevailing 20 percent reserve requirement. The story continues. Sue Blue, who keeps her checkable account with Depository Institution B, has a good credit rating and wants to borrow $64 to pay for a repair on her car. So she signs a note to Depository Institution B, which lists it as an asset in the loans category (bottom panel in Table 3). For

TABLE 3

Deposit-Expansion Process: Depository Institution B (amounts in dollars)

New Deposit Step			
Assets		**Liabilities**	
Reserves and cash (Required: <u>16</u>)	80	Checkable deposits Green Radio Co.	80
(Excess: <u>64</u>)			
Loans	0		
Securities	<u>0</u>		—
	80		80

Loan Step			
Assets		**Liabilities**	
Reserves and cash (Required: <u>16</u>)	16	Checkable deposits Green Radio Co.	80
(Excess: <u>0</u>)			
Loans			
Sue Blue	64		
Securities	<u>0</u>		—
	80		80

When cash loaned by a depository institution returns to the system as a new deposit, the stage is set for a second round of deposit expansion. In this stage, Green Radio Company deposits the $80 spent by Ron Black. Depository Institution B now has excess reserves of $64, which it loans to Sue Blue.

convenience, Ms. Blue takes her loan in the form of a $64 addition to the balance in her checkable account and writes a check for $64 to the White Motor Company to pay for the auto repair. Since we expect borrowers (Ron Black and Sue Blue) to spend their money promptly, it does not matter whether they accept the loan in cash or as an entry in their checkable accounts. The depository institution expects the prompt departure of the borrowed money, either in cash or as soon as the White Motor Company or someone else presents Sue's check for payment.

As you probably expect, the deposit-expansion process is far from over. As soon as White Motor deposits the $64 in Depository Institution C (see top panel in Table 4), that institution finds that it has excess reserves in the amount of $51.20—the $64 deposit minus the $12.80 of required reserves. Depository Institution C decides to put these excess reserves to work by purchasing bonds in the bond

market. Bonds of the Yellow Cab Company appear to be a good buy, and on that day Grace Gray happens to be selling her holdings of these bonds. The institution buys the bonds, which it lists as an asset in the securities category on its balance sheet (see the bottom panel of Table 4), and, through the system of markets and brokers, Grace Gray receives a check for $51.20. She deposits the check in her checking account in Depository Institution D, and the expansion process continues.

The deposit-expansion process is summarized in Table 5. It started in our example when Bill Brown put $100 of currency into a checkable account. Once this money was in the system of depository institutions, the expansion process went into operation as new checkable account balances were created for the Green Radio Company, the White Motor Company, Grace Gray, and others. The cumulative-totals column in Table 5 emphasizes that all of these balances exist at the same

TABLE 4
Deposit-Expansion Process: Depository Institution C (amounts in dollars)

New Deposit Step			
Assets		**Liabilities**	
Reserves and cash	64	Checkable deposits	
(Required: 12.80)		White Motor Co.	64
(Excess: 51.20)			
Loans	0		
Securities	0		
	64		64

Loan Step			
Assets		**Liabilities**	
Reserves and cash	12.80	Checkable deposits	
(Required: 12.80)		White Motor Co.	64
(Excess: 0)			
Loans	0		
Securities			
Yellow Cab Co.	51.20		
	64.00		64

In the third round of the deposit-expansion process, White Motor Company deposits the check written by Sue Blue, and Depository Institution C has excess reserves of $51.20. The institution purchases $51.20 of Yellow Cab Company securities from Grace Gray.

time and that all of them are money according to the prevailing definition. Our example assumed that money loaned out was then deposited in a different depository institution. However, the process would work in the same way if the money came back to the same institution that made the loan.

The **deposit-contraction process** follows the same sequence, except that it starts with a withdrawal instead of a deposit. If the depository institutions are in exact conformity with the reserve requirement when the withdrawal occurs, securities will be sold, and loans will be called in or not renewed. As a result, checkable deposits will shrink.

The deposit-contraction process follows the same sequence as the deposit-expansion process, except it begins with a withdrawal instead of a deposit.

The Deposit-Expansion Factor

You undoubtedly recognize that the arithmetic in Table 5 is like that used in the Keynesian model to explain the multiplier effect of changes in total planned expenditure on equilibrium national income and product. In other words, we have a geometric progression, in which each successive round generates new deposits equal to a fixed percentage of those created in the preceding round. The reserve ratio operates in the same way that $(1 - MPC)$ did in the formula for the multiplier. In terms of the reserve ratio actually operating in the depository institutions, the **deposit-expansion factor**

TABLE 5
Summary of Deposit-Expansion Process

	Checkable Deposit Balances	
	Individual Accounts	*Cumulative Totals*
Bill Brown (Depository Institution A)	$100.00	$100.00
Green Radio (Depository Institution B)	80.00	180.00
White Motor (Depository Institution C)	64.00	244.00
Grace Gray (Depository Institution D)	51.20	295.20
etc. (Depository Institution E)	40.96	336.16
etc. (Depository Institution F)	32.76	368.92
etc. (Depository Institution G)	26.21	395.13
.	.	.
.	.	.
.	.	.
(*n*th Depository Institution)	.	$500.00
	$500.00	

Bill Brown's initial deposit is expanded by deposits for Green Radio, White Motor, Grace Gray, and others. All of these demand deposits exist at the same time, and all count as money. With a 20 percent reserve ratio, total deposits may be five times the initial deposit.

is

$$\frac{1}{\text{reserve ratio}}$$

In our example, we assumed that the depository institutions were always in exact conformity with the legal reserve requirement, so that the reserve ratio was 20 percent at all times. In this case, the deposit-expansion factor was $1/0.2$, which works out to a value of 5.[3] The first deposit of $100 was expanded to support an added $400 in checkable deposits, so that the total of checkable deposits was $500. If the reserve ratio had been kept at 25 percent, the expansion factor would have been 4. If the reserve ratio had been kept at 10 percent, the expansion factor would have been 10, and so on.

The deposit-expansion effect, like the multiplier effect, is a geometric progression, in which each

---

3. We arrive at the answer in the following way:

$$1 + (0.8) + (0.8)^2 + (0.8)^3 + \cdots$$

$$+ (0.8)^n = \frac{1}{1 - 0.8} = \frac{1}{0.2} = 5$$

successive round generates new deposits equal to a fixed percentage of those created in the preceding round.

Controlling the Expansion Factor

The reserve ratio, and therefore the expansion factor, is controlled through the Federal Reserve System's authority to set the official minimum reserve requirement. This is stated as a percentage of the amount on deposit in accounts that offer check-writing services. As of May 1989, the required reserve was 12 percent of such balances. We shall explain in the next chapter just how this official minimum ratio is set. The profit motive will encourage depository institutions to keep the actual reserve ratio fairly close to the official ratio, since excess reserves earn no interest and a deficiency in reserves will force the institution to borrow and pay interest. So the Federal Reserve System can control the deposit-expansion factor by setting the official reserve ratio.

Depository institutions may not always remain in exact conformity with the official reserve requirement, and therefore the Federal Reserve System's control of the expansion factor is less than perfect. Institutions may keep some excess reserves on hand to avoid problems from unexpected withdrawals or so that they will be ready to accommodate especially good customers when they ask for loans. These are called **desired excess reserves.** There also is a second reason why the control of the expansion factor is not exact. Our expansion process assumed that borrowers (Ron Black and Sue Blue) quickly spent every cent that they borrowed. However, if some of the funds borrowed are kept as pocket money or simply allowed to circulate from hand to hand in the economy, the deposit expansion will stop short of its full potential. The actual expansion, therefore, is not as exact as the deposit-expansion factor and our example imply.

The Federal Reserve System controls the expansion factor through its ability to set the

---

---

official minimum reserve requirement. However, its control is not perfect, because depository institutions may not always remain in exact conformity with the official reserve requirement and also because not all borrowed funds are quickly spent.

Controlling the Money Supply

In the United States, the money supply is regulated by (a) controlling the deposit-expansion factor and (b) by controlling the actual amount of reserves in the depository institution system, as will be described in the next chapter. You will learn about the Federal Reserve System, which is the "central bank" in the United States and is responsible, under legislation from Congress, for administering both of these steps in controlling the money supply.

Economics in Focus

The S&L Crisis

The 1980s brought a heady expansion in the savings and loan industry, then a resounding crash. By 1989 five hundred savings and loan institutions, commonly called S&Ls, were insolvent. Losses throughout the industry were climbing at a rate of a billion dollars a month. The Federal Savings and Loan Insurance Corporation (FSLIC), the agency that insures customers' deposits, was itself essentially bankrupt.

How did this happen? Before 1980 the S&L industry was a staid, conservative one. The federal government limited the interest rates that S&Ls could pay, and industry analysts joked about the 3-6-3 rule: pay 3 percent on deposits, make home mortgage loans at 6 percent, and leave for the golf course at 3 o'clock. But because S&Ls had trouble competing in the inflationary period of the late 1970s, Congress began to deregulate the industry. Soon S&LS were allowed to pay whatever interest they liked, compete with each other recklessly for "brokered" deposits (money deposited by such large money-management companies as Merrill Lynch), and enter such risky fields as development and construction.

The new rules attracted some unscrupulous players, especially in states such as Texas where real estate boomed in the early 1980s. Potential profits were huge, and the FSLIC was there to back up large mistakes. The situation was summed up "Heads I win, tails FSLIC loses."

But the mid-1980s brought a collapse in real estate values in the large oil cities of Texas. S&Ls began to slide, and some spectacular failures occurred. A too-late attempt by government regulators to curb the industry's excesses only made matters worse, and soon it became clear that the FSLIC could not possibly support all the failing institutions. The Federal Home Loan Bank Board, the FSLIC's parent agency, tried to bypass the problem by arranging mergers of weak S&Ls into stronger ones, but a massive government bailout program was still required.

Critics have charged that the federal government itself is responsible for much of the disaster. Government regulators, the critics say, had too cozy a relationship with S&L executives, lobbyists, and politicians. Lenient practices allowed S&Ls to conceal their losses and overstate their profits. Some aggressive S&Ls even made single loans greater than their net worth, with no objection from examiners. A few regulators who issued warnings were ignored. In the hastily arranged mergers certain rules were bent; takeover artists seemed to profit unduly; and some of the new "superthrifts" looked hardly less shaky than their predecessors.

In the end the public will foot the bill, and estimates of the long-run cost range as high as $230 billion. One lesson seems clear: However many safeguards are established by law, the banking system needs sensible and trustworthy supervision by the appropriate government agencies.

Sources: Thomas Moore, "The Bust of '89," *U.S. News & World Report,* January 23, 1989, pp. 36–43; Kathleen Day, "When Hell Sleazes Over," *The New Republic,* March 20, 1989, pp. 26–30; Catherine Yang and Frederic A. Miller, "Can Bush's Thrift Doctors Find a Treatment That Will Take?" *Business Week,* February 13, 1989, pp. 80–81; Robert E. Norton, "When You're in a Hole, Stop Digging," *U.S. News & World Report,* January 23, 1989, p. 46; Terry Bivens and Richard Burke, "A Look Inside Perelman's S&L Deal," *Philadelphia Inquirer,* May 7, 1989, pp. 1-A, 19-A; Rich Thomas, "How Taxpayers Lost the S&L Numbers Game," *Newsweek,* February 20, 1989, pp. 32–33.

SUMMARY

1. Most economists believe that changes in the amount of money in the economy and in the speed of its circulation can cause changes in the general price level and can also cause changes in real levels of production and employment. (See page 248.)

2. Economists define money as anything that is generally accepted as a medium of exchange, a unit of account, a store of purchasing power, and a standard for deferred payment. At various times and places, many different things have served as money. (See pages 250–251.)

3. According to the definition most widely used in the United States—called M1—the money supply consists of coins, currency, and checkable account balances. Checkable account balances are the largest component. The currency is "fiat money"; that is, the government specifies it to be legal tender. (See pages 252–253.)

4. Broader definitions of the money supply— M2, M3, and L—include forms of wealth that are somewhat less liquid than coins, currency, and checkable account balances. (See pages 253–254 and Figure 1, page 253.)

5. Depository institutions include banks, savings and loan associations, credit unions, and mutual savings banks. They earn their incomes by obtaining money from investors and depositors and lending money to individuals and businesses. The difference between interest charged and interest paid provides money to cover expenses and to pay dividends to shareholders. (See pages 254–255.)

6. Depository institutions operate with partial, or fractional, reserves, which means that money deposited can be used to support new checkable account balances that are created when the institution makes loans to customers. (See page 255.)

7. The partial reserve system involves risks of bank failure. These risks are reduced by officially designated examiners and by deposit insurance. Nevertheless, many thrift institutions became insolvent in the mid-1980s when interest rate ceilings were eliminated. In 1986, the Federal Savings and Loan Insurance Corporation did not have enough money to meet its insurance obligations to thrift institutions that were insolvent and by 1989 about five hundred were considered to be insolvent. (See pages 255–259.)

8. A depository institution's reserve ratio is its total of official reserves divided by its total checkable account liabilities. The reserve requirement is the official reserve ratio that must be kept in order to avoid penalties. Excess reserves are those over and above the official reserve requirement. (See pages 260–262.)

9. Because depository institutions operate with partial, or fractional, reserves, a new deposit gives rise to excess reserves. There is a deposit expansion when these excess reserves are loaned out or used to buy stocks and bonds. When the new loan or the payment for the securities is itself deposited in a depository institution, the expansion can be repeated. The deposit-expansion factor is 1 divided by the reserve ratio actually in use. (See pages 262–266 and Tables 2–5, pages 263–266.)

10. The Federal Reserve System's authority to set minimum reserve requirements allows it to regulate the size of the deposit-expansion factor. This regulation is not precise, however, because some depository institutions may not be in exact conformity with the official reserve requirement and because some of the money brought about through new loans may not be returned to the system. (See pages 266–267.)

11. The deposit-contraction factor operates to reduce the money supply. Deposit contraction is begun when deposits are withdrawn and not deposited again. In this case, depository institutions must sell some of their securities, call in loans, or refuse to renew loans when they fall due. (See page 265.)

12. The Federal Reserve System's control of the money supply is carried out in two ways: it can control both the deposit-expansion factor and the amount of reserves in depository institutions. (See page 267.)

KEY TERMS

automatic transfer service (ATS) account: a checkable account that permits the payment of interest (page 257).

banking: the business of accepting deposits and making loans including commercial loans (page 259).

bank note: a certificate issued by a bank which promises to pay a specified sum to the bearer of the certificate (page 251).

barter: a direct exchange of one good or service for another (page 248).

charter: the legal authority, issued by either the federal government or a state government, to operate a depository institution, that is, to accept deposits and accept loans (page 255).

checkable accounts: accounts in depository institutions against which checks can be written. Balances in these accounts are sometimes called demand deposits or transaction deposits (page 252).

commercial banks: banks that accept deposits and make all kinds of loans, including loans to business firms (page 254).

demand deposits: *see* **checkable accounts.**

deposit-contraction process: the process by which depository institutions are able to contract the nation's money supply (page 265).

deposit-expansion factor: 1 divided by the reserve ratio maintained by depository institutions (page 265).

deposit-expansion process: the process by which depository institutions are able to expand the nation's money supply by holding only part of a new deposit as reserve for the deposit and loaning the rest out (page 262).

depository institution: an organization such as a bank, a savings and loan association, or a credit union that accepts deposits of funds and offers checking services (page 252).

desired excess reserves: reserves held by depository institutions that are over and above those required by law so that they can avoid problems from unexpected withdrawals or be ready to accommodate customers who ask for loans (page 267).

excess reserves: reserves held by depository institutions that are over and above those required by law (page 262).

fractional reserves: *see* **partial reserves.**

Gresham's Law: the proposition that coins made with base (less-valuable) metal drives the more-valuable money out of circulation (page 251).

interstate banking: when holding companies own banks in more than one state (page 259).

L money supply: M3 money supply plus near money (U.S. Savings Bonds, certain kinds of U.S. government securities, payment promises by large corporations, and other items that are potentially convertible into spendable money) (page 254).

legal tender: government-issued currency that legally must be recognized as a valid offer of payment for a debt (page 251).

M1 money supply concept: coins, currency, and checkable account balances (page 252).

M2 money supply concept: M1 plus such less liquid assets as small time deposits, money market mutual fund balances, noncheckable savings balances, repurchase agreements, and Eurodollars (page 254).

M3 money supply concept: M1 and M2 plus large time deposit balances, long-term repurchase agreements, and certain other assets that are somewhat harder to convert into spendable money (page 254).

medium of exchange: something used for the intermediate step in exchange (page 248).

monetized debt: money created on the basis of debt obligations (page 253).

money: anything generally accepted in an economy as a medium of exchange, a unit of account, a store of purchasing power, and a standard for deferred payment (page 250).

near money: items such as U.S. Savings Bonds and several relatively liquid kinds of U.S. government securities, and payment promises by large corporations that are potentially convertible into spendable money (page 254).

negotiable order of withdrawal (NOW) account: a checkable account in a savings and loan association that permits the payment of interest (page 257).

partial (fractional) reserves: the situation in which cash or immediately available funds kept on hand by depository institutions are less than the total of the obligations to the people who have deposited money in the institutions (page 255).

reserve ratio: a depository institution's total of cash and official (government-approved) reserves divided by the amount of its checkable account liabilities (page 261).

reserve requirement: the amount of official reserves that depository institutions must maintain to avoid penalties (page 262).

reserves: cash on hand plus deposits that depository institutions maintain with the Federal Reserve System (page 260).

share-draft account: a checkable account in a credit union that permits the payment of interest (page 257).

standard for deferred payment: a standard way to specify the amount of a payment that is to be made some time in the future (page 250).

store of purchasing power: the ability to save some of the medium of exchange for use at a later date (page 249).

transactions deposits: *see* **checkable accounts.**

thrift institutions: depository institutions such as savings and loan associations, mutual savings banks, and credit unions that accept deposits and make primarily consumer and mortgage loans (page 254).

unit of account: a function of money that allows it to be used to compare the values of different items (page 249).

wildcat banking: banking practices in which depositors were persuaded to entrust their savings to institutions that then made loans and issued bank notes until their obligations far exceeded their readily available assets (page 256).

DISCUSSION QUESTIONS

1. Why is it not possible to define money in terms of its composition? Identify the four functions of money that are specified in economics. Which of them is the most basic? Why? Which is (are) most affected by inflation?

2. Write down the definition of money given in this chapter. Then explain why the words "generally accepted" are basic to this definition. What is Gresham's Law? Explain why it still works.

3. Explain how a bank note is an ancestor of modern paper currency. Does today's U.S. currency have more or less backing than did the early bank notes? Explain your answer. What does *legal tender* mean?

4. Describe two different ways in which you can add to the balance in your checkable account. Why is much of our money actually "monetized debt"? Explain.

5. Explain the term *liquidity*. Why do slight differences among assets in their liquidity create problems in measuring the money supply? Briefly summarize the types of assets included in the M1 category of the U.S. money supply.

6. What is a "run" on a depository institution? Since runs are always possible under the partial reserve system, why are depositors willing to expose their money to this risk? Explain how the partial reserve system operates to the advantage of all people involved.

7. Discuss the roles of examiners and deposit insurance in improving the safety of deposits under the partial reserve system. Why does a reserve requirement not guarantee safety? What is the reason for the legal reserve requirement in the U.S. depository institution system?

8. How did ceilings on interest rates payable by thrift institutions cause problems for these institutions during the 1970s? Why is it important to have premium payments on deposit insurance bear reasonably close relationships to the risks taken when deposited money is loaned out?

9. Without looking at Table 1, prepare a simplified balance sheet for a depository institution and record its major entries. Then check to make sure you have it right. Explain how electronic technology led regulators to allow interest to be paid on checkable account balances.

10. Carefully distinguish between the actual reserve ratio and the official required reserve ratio. What happens if the actual ratio is less than the requirement? What happens if the actual ratio is more than the requirement? Explain what is meant by "excess" reserves and why they are important in the economy.

11. Trace the process by which the depository institution system expands the amount of money when excess reserves appear. How does the official reserve requirement control the amount of this expansion? Write the formula for the deposit-expansion factor. Describe two situations that may cause the actual expansion not to follow exactly the formula for money expansion.

13

The Federal Reserve System and Monetary Instruments

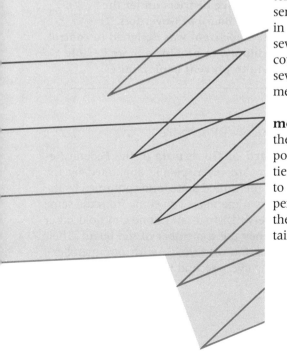

Preview As you have learned, depository institutions operate on partial reserves and are able to expand and contract the money supply. This chapter will explain how the Federal Reserve System, the central bank of the United States, regulates the money supply. Regulating the money supply is a key ingredient in the *monetarist* approach to macroeconomic policy, just as regulating taxes and government purchases are key ingredients in the *fiscalist* approach. In this chapter, we examine monetary instruments for macroeconomic policy.

We start by describing the beginnings of the Federal Reserve System—how it was set up after many years of dissatisfaction with an earlier system. Then we explain how the Federal Reserve System is organized through twelve district banks and describe the services that it offers. The Board of Governors of the system meets in Washington, D.C., to set policy. Many people believe these seven governors to be the most powerful nonelected officials in the country. The Federal Open Market Committee, which includes the seven members of the Board of Governors, buys and sells government securities to affect the money supply.

The second part of this chapter describes **monetary instruments,** or the tools used to regulate the money supply. Among the monetary tools are the setting of reserve requirements for depository institutions, the buying and selling of government securities (open market operations), the setting of interest rates on loans to depository institutions (called discount rates), and attempts to persuade them to cooperate with central bank policy. We explain the money multiplier concept to show how difficult it is to maintain exact control of the money supply.

We review the various guidelines or target variables that have been used in the operation of monetary policy. These discussions set the stage for the following chapter, which will explain the relation of the money supply to inflation and to the level of equilibrium real national income and product. Finally, in an appendix, we review the record of actions taken by the Federal Reserve in its job of controlling the money supply.

THE FEDERAL RESERVE SYSTEM

Most industrial countries have a centralized monetary authority, generally called a central bank, which is an arm of the Treasury or the finance ministry. The central bank of the United States, called the **Federal Reserve System,** is different from most central banks because of its relative independence from the Treasury and the other offices of the administration.

The Federal Reserve System is the central bank of the United States. Created in 1913, it is relatively independent of the Treasury Department and White House.

The Federal Reserve System, often called the "Fed," was begun by an Act of Congress in 1913 because Americans had come to dislike the earlier system. The National Banking System, which dated from the Civil War, operated without a central bank. It had developed two major problems. These were the seasonal "money shortages" in farming areas when crops had to be financed and a susceptibility to nationwide panics because of the "pyramiding" of reserves. The seasonal money shortages arose because the amount of currency that could be issued did not respond to seasonal changes in the demand for cash.

The system's susceptibility to nationwide panics was a more serious problem. This happened because a large part of the reserves of small banks could be held as deposits in banks in larger cities and because these banks, in turn, could hold a large part of their reserves as deposits in banks in a few major cities. So, as small banks called for funds from the larger city banks and as these larger banks called for funds from the major city banks, cash demands and reserve problems arising in isolated areas would build up and create a panic. This **pyramiding of reserves** set the stage for repeated nationwide bank panics. One such panic in 1907 led to the passage of the Federal Reserve Act in 1913.

Many Americans favored a strong European type of central bank, but those in the agricultural parts of the country were suspicious of the East and "Wall Street" and wanted as much control as possible over regional monetary conditions. Because they did not really trust bankers, they wanted farmers and business people to share control of the system. Under the Federal Reserve Act, the country was divided into twelve districts, a Federal Reserve Bank was set up in each district, and a Board of Governors was charged with supervising the operation of the whole system. The new system was designed to control the money supply, to provide a more flexible currency (the Federal Reserve Note), and to be a lender of last resort that could prevent bank failures by making loans to banks when trouble arose, thus forestalling panics. Though modified by experience and additional legislation, the structure set up in 1913 is much the same today.

To ensure regional rather than central control over monetary conditions, the country was divided into twelve districts under the supervision of a Board of Governors. The Federal Reserve System was designed to control the money supply, to provide a more flexible currency, and to prevent bank failures.

The Board of Governors

On the **Board of Governors** of the Federal Reserve System are seven people appointed by the president of the United States and confirmed by the Senate. No two members can come from the same Federal Reserve District, and none can hold other jobs while they are a member of the board. Their terms are for fourteen years, with one member's term expiring every second year. Part of the reason for this long term of office is to protect the Board from short-run political pressures and so to give the Federal Reserve a degree of independence from the executive and legislative branches of the government.

The Board is responsible for directing the nation's monetary policy, which can be used either to counteract or to reinforce the fiscal policy undertaken by the president and Congress. Thus, the independence of the Board is one of the checks and balances that have been built into the U.S. system of government.

As a practical matter, however, we should not overstate the independence of the Board of Governors. Members sometimes resign before the end of their fourteen-year terms, so that appointments must usually be made oftener than every two years. Also, every four years the president can choose a member of the Board to serve as chairperson.

Over the years, the monetary policy followed by the Board has generally been consistent with the fiscal policy of the president and the Congress, but on important occasions conflict has arisen.

The seven members of the Board of Governors are appointed by the president to fourteen-year terms. These long terms are intended to give the Federal Reserve a degree of independence from political pressure.

The Federal Open Market Committee

The **Federal Open Market Committee (FOMC)** has twelve members, seven of whom are the members of the Board of Governors. The other five members come, one each, from five of the Federal Reserve District Banks. The Federal Reserve Bank of New York always provides one of these five committee members, and the other four positions are filled, on a rotating basis, from the other Federal Reserve Banks.

The Federal Open Market Committee was not a part of the original (1913) structure of the Federal Reserve System, but experience during the 1920s showed that the purchase and sale of securities by the Federal Reserve Banks could have important effects on the economy. When the FOMC became an official agency of the Federal Reserve System in the 1930s, informal cooperation among the banks was replaced by direct control by the Board of Governors. Buying and selling government securities in the open market is one of the most powerful tools of monetary policy, and most of the major decisions for the system are made at the regular meetings of the FOMC.

The Federal Open Market Committee has twelve members, the seven members of the Board of Governors plus five members from the Federal Reserve District Banks. The FOMC controls the buying and selling of government securities on the open market.

The Thrift Institutions Advisory Council

The Depository Institutions Deregulation and Monetary Control Act of 1980 extended the authority of the Federal Reserve System to all depository institutions, including savings and loan associations, mutual savings banks, and credit unions. The **Thrift Institutions Advisory Council** was set up in 1983 to provide a channel through which these newly covered institutions could present their views. The council has ten members, seven from savings and loan associations, two from mutual savings banks, and one from credit unions. Although it has no voting power, the council meets with the Board of Governors four times each year to present the views of thrift institutions.

Federal Reserve District Banks

The map in Figure 1 shows the locations of the twelve **Federal Reserve Banks** and the boundaries of their districts. This geographic distribution recognized the diverse interests of the various parts of the country and countered the fears of centralized banking and eastern domination that had plagued the earlier attempts to set up a central bank. Each district bank is expected to serve the banking and commercial interests of its district

FIGURE 1
The Federal Reserve System

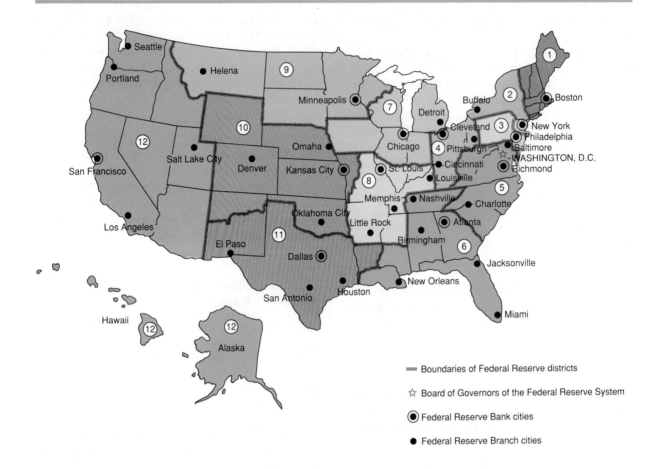

Note: Alaska is in the Seattle Branch Territory and Hawaii in that served by the Head Office of the Federal Reserve Bank of San Francisco. Both are in the Twelfth District.
Source: Federal Reserve Bulletin, May 1989.

with appropriate expertise, such as ranching in Kansas City, oil and gas in Dallas, agriculture in Chicago, and trade and finance in New York. Each Federal Reserve Bank is owned by the banks in its district which become members of the system by purchasing stock in their district bank. All **national banks** (those chartered by the federal government) must be members of the system. If state banks choose to join, they may do so. The Federal Reserve Banks generate profits from interest on the securities they own and pay dividends to their shareholding member banks. However, federal law

limits the amount of dividends that can be paid. Any "excess" profits must be turned over to the U.S. Treasury.

There are twelve Federal Reserve Banks; each district bank is owned by banks in its district and is expected to serve the banking and commercial interests of its district.

Each Federal Reserve Bank receives deposits and handles checks for the federal government and provides many services to depository institutions. Among their main services are check clearing and making loans. A detailed description of most of these services is best left to specialized courses in money and banking. However, their service of making loans is directly related to the Federal Reserve's regulation of the money supply, which is our focus in this chapter.

The Depository Institutions Deregulation and Monetary Control Act of 1980, which extended Federal Reserve authority to cover thrift institutions as well as banks, specified that Federal Reserve District banks could make loans to savings and loan associations, mutual savings banks, and credit unions in their districts. Making loans to depository institutions is a way to meet one of the major goals in setting up the Federal Reserve System in 1913—assuring the soundness of the financial system and preventing panics. To achieve this goal, each Federal Reserve Bank is expected to understand the economic needs of its district. If a depository institution has temporary difficulty, a loan from the Federal Reserve Bank can be arranged. This **lender of last resort** service ranked high among the objectives in setting up the system. Loans are carried out through a process called **discounting,** because originally securities or prom-

ises from a borrower were purchased by a Federal Reserve Bank at less than their value at maturity. Today, direct loans are made instead of the more complicated procedure of discounting. The **discount rate** is the rate of interest charged on these loans. Discounting not only can help depository institutions but also can be an instrument for controlling the money supply.

The Federal Reserve Banks clear checks for and make loans to depository institutions. The Federal Reserve System is able to influence the country's money supply by means of this loan-making service.

Federal Reserve Bank Balance Sheet

A simplified balance sheet for the twelve district banks of the Federal Reserve System is presented in Table 1. On the asset side, the most important item is U.S. government securities. These are debt instruments that have been issued by the U.S. Treasury. They make up part of the national debt. Even though most of the national debt is held by private

TABLE 1
Balance Sheet for Federal Reserve Banks, February 28, 1989 (in billions of dollars)

Assets		Liabilities	
U.S. Government securities	229.5	Federal Reserve Notes	222.8
Other securities	8.4	Deposits	
Other assets	46.7	Reserve accounts[a]	37.0
		U.S. Treasury	6.3
		Other	0.8
		Other liabilities	12.6
			279.5
		Capital Account	
		Paid in	2.1
		Other	3.0
Total	284.6	Total	284.6

a. These are deposits from depository institutions.
Source: Federal Reserve Bulletin, May 1989, Table 1.18.

citizens and firms (including depository institutions), the part held by the Federal Reserve Banks is very important. Most of this part consists of short-term securities (ninety-day Treasury bills) that have been acquired by the Federal Reserve Banks in carrying out open market operations, which are described later in this chapter.

On the liability side of the balance sheet, the major item is the Federal Reserve Notes circulating in the economy. These notes are the legal tender currency of the United States. Two other entries on the liabilities side also are important. One of these is the reserve accounts. In describing reserve requirements in Chapter 12, we noted that official reserves must be held as vault cash or as deposits in the Federal Reserve Banks. This is the balance sheet entry that records these reserve deposits. The other important entry on the liability side of the balance sheet is the deposit of the U.S. Treasury. One of the tasks of the Federal Reserve System is to handle the checking account of the federal government.

INSTRUMENTS OF MONETARY POLICY

Now that you know the structure of the Federal Reserve System and the services it provides, we can examine how it seeks to control the U.S. money supply. As you learned in the last chapter, checkable account balances are the major component of the money supply. You also know that the ability of banks to create checkable account balances depends on the amount of reserves in these banks and on their reserve ratios. Federal Reserve influences on the reserve ratio and the amount of reserves are the main elements of monetary policy in the United States.

Reserve Requirements

Cash and regular required reserves deposited with Federal Reserve District Banks earn no interest. Therefore, depository institutions try to keep the lowest possible reserve ratio that is safe and in keeping with the official reserve requirements. By setting minimum required reserve ratios, the Fed-

eral Reserve Board can strongly influence actual reserve ratios.

Federal Reserve influences on the reserve ratio and the amount of reserves are the main instruments of monetary policy in the United States. By setting minimum required reserve ratios, the Board can strongly influence actual reserve ratios and thus affect the deposit-expansion factor.

The deposit-expansion process described in Chapter 12 shows the importance of the Federal Reserve Board's power to raise or lower official reserve requirements. Raising the official reserve requirement will most likely raise the actual reserve ratio maintained by depository institutions and so will lower the deposit-expansion factor. Suppose that the actual reserve ratio is 12 percent. In this case, the depository institution system can support $833.33 of checkable deposits when the amount of reserves in the system is $100 ($100/0.12 = $833.33). But if the Board raises the reserve requirement so that the actual reserve ratio becomes 14 percent, this same $100 of reserves will support only $714.29 in checkable deposits ($100/0.14 = $714.29). The Board's action could force a great reduction in the money supply. On the other hand, lowering the reserve requirement so that the actual reserve ratio becomes 10 percent would allow these reserves to support $1,000 of checkable deposits ($100/0.10 = $1,000). The Board would have invited a large expansion in the money supply.

Raising the reserve requirement forces a reduction in the money supply. Lowering the reserve requirement invites an expansion in the money supply.

The Depository Institutions Deregulation and Monetary Control Act of 1980, which broadened the Federal Reserve System's authority to include all checkable and time accounts in all depository institutions, also specified ranges within which the Board of Governors could set official reserve requirements. For the first $31.7 million of checkable accounts in each institution, the law requires only a 3 percent reserve.[1] Above \$31.7 million, the Board can set the reserve requirement anywhere it chooses between 8 percent and 14 percent. As of this writing, this required reserve ratio is 12 percent. For time deposits, the required reserve is 3 percent.

Before the 1980 law, the Federal Reserve System had had difficulty in regulating the money supply. There were different reserve requirements for different kinds of financial institutions. For this reason, the amount of required reserves would change when money was moved from one institution to another. These problems caused great trouble during the 1970s with the combination of very high interest rates and the vast changes taking place in the banking industry as computers and electronic bookkeeping systems were introduced. Operational distinctions between different types of accounts faded, as did the difference between banks and other kinds of depository institutions. In this atmosphere, the Depository Institutions Deregulation and Monetary Control Act of 1980 was seen as a necessary step to help the Federal Reserve System keep up with changing times.

Raising or lowering the official reserve requirement is a powerful instrument, but it is quite sparingly used. The main problem with the reserve-requirement instrument is that changes in reserve requirements can cause embarrassing problems for depository institutions as they try to serve their customers. Increases can cause the most trouble. If an institution is operating close to the official ratio in order to serve its stockholders or members, it may find that an increase in this ratio forces it to deny loans to customers or to borrow funds from a Federal Reserve Bank. For this reason, changing the reserve requirement is a heavy-handed and somewhat crude tool for adjusting the money supply. As you will see, there is another instrument that can perform more smoothly.

Open Market Operations

Open market operations consist of the buying and selling of government securities by the Federal Reserve Banks. These operations allow the Federal

1. This "break point" is determined by a formula. It stood at \$31.7 million in 1988.

Reserve System to control the *quantity* of reserves in depository institutions, just as control of the reserve ratio makes it possible to control the deposit-expansion factor. Together, these two tools give the Federal Reserve System great power over the money supply in the United States.

Open market operations consist of the buying and selling of government securities by the Federal Reserve Banks. They enable the Fed to control the quantity of reserves in depository institutions.

Open market operations are directed by the Federal Open Market Committee (FOMC), which was described earlier. These operations are called "open market" because they are carried out in the same securities markets as those open to ordinary citizens and businesses. When the FOMC decides to buy securities, it pays the existing market price, and when it sells, it accepts the existing market price. The securities bought by the FOMC come from the holdings of private persons, depository institutions, or business firms, and those that are sold move into these private holdings. Even though the FOMC deals only in short-term government securities, the effects of its buying and selling are quickly felt in the prices of other securities in the open market.

Open market operations are directed by the FOMC.

Open Market Purchases   A good way of illustrating open market operations is to describe the effects of a \$100 purchase of government securities by the Federal Reserve System. The person, business, or depository institution that sells the securities receives a check from a Federal Reserve Bank in payment for the securities. When this check is deposited in a depository institution and cleared through the check-clearing system, the reserve account of the depository institution will be larger by \$100. The Federal Reserve System has *created* \$100 of reserves where nothing existed before. If the reserve ratio is 20 percent, only \$20 of these new reserves will be required for the new deposit. The

TABLE 2
Open Market Purchase (amounts in dollars)

Federal Reserve Banks				The Depository Institution System				
Securities	+100	Reserve deposits	+100	Reserves	+100	Demand deposits		
						Seller of security	+100	
				New loans	+400	New loans	+400	
					+500		+500	

When the Federal Reserve System purchases $100 of securities, its securities assets account expands by $100. When the check in payment for these securities is cleared, reserve deposits of depository institutions increase by $100. These accounts are liabilities to the Federal Reserve System and assets to individual depository institutions. If the reserve ratio is 20 percent, new loans can be made, so that the money supply may increase by as much as $500. The entries in the area with the white background represent new money created by the open market purchase.

remaining $80 is excess reserve, which the depository institution can use for lending. Because of the deposit-expansion process, which you studied earlier, the $100 open market purchase can expand the money supply by as much as $500.

Our hypothetical open market transaction is summarized in Table 2. On the balance sheet of the Federal Reserve Banks, the $100 expansion of the securities assets account is balanced by the $100 expansion of the liabilities account for reserve deposits. On the balance sheet for the depository institutions, the area with the white background shows that the $100 of new reserves supports $500 of new demand deposits, $100 of which came from the initial deposit and $400 from new loans made by the depository institutions. The effect on the money supply would have been the same if the security had been sold by a depository institution itself. New reserves would at first have come from a reduction in securities holdings, and all of these new reserves would have been "excess." The system could then generate up to $500 of new loans and demand deposits from these new reserves.

Open Market Sales   Open market sales by the Federal Reserve System have the opposite effects from open market purchases; that is, sales contract the money supply. When the Federal Reserve sells a security, its asset account for securities shrinks. Then, when the purchaser sends his or her check to pay for it, clearing the check reduces the balance in the reserve accounts of the depository institution system. The $100 of reserves has been destroyed

and ceases to exist. If a 20 percent reserve ratio is being maintained, a $100 sale of securities by the Federal Reserve will bring as much as a $500 reduction in checkable account balances.

The Importance of Open Market Operations   The great advantage of the open market instrument is its flexibility. Since the Federal Reserve Banks are trading most of the time in the open market, they can carry out policy in a subtle and gradual way. The net purchases or net sales position of the Federal Reserve can be adjusted day by day to meet seasonal or short-run needs for money and, at the same time, can lean in either an expansionary or a contractionary direction as long-term policy may require. Changes in policy need not subject individual depository institutions to untimely pressures, as is the case with changing reserve requirements. Through open market operations, changes in the money supply can be brought about without upsetting the routine operations of depository institutions.

The important part that could be played by open market operations was not recognized when the Federal Reserve System was set up in 1913. However, coordination of securities buying and selling among the Federal Reserve Banks began during the financially active 1920s. Then, in the 1930s, the FOMC was established, providing an orderly procedure for open market operations. Since that time, open market operations have become the most important instrument of monetary policy.

The Discount Rate

The third basic instrument of monetary policy is the **discount rate,** which is the rate of interest that Federal Reserve Banks charge on loans to depository institutions. Loans to member banks and the discount rate were expected to be major monetary control tools when the Federal Reserve was set up in 1913. The loans would supplement reserves and allow the needed expansion of the money supply during prosperous times. Then, during recessions, the Federal Reserve Banks would be lenders of last resort to prevent bank failures and forestall bank panics. History was unkind to both of these expectations. As a money-supply regulator, the discount rate was largely displaced by open market operations. As a lender of last resort, the Federal Reserve System failed miserably to prevent bank failures in 1932 and 1933.

Changes in the discount rate have little *direct* impact on depository institutions unless they need to borrow from the Federal Reserve System. If a depository institution has excess reserves, it will not need to borrow, nor will borrowing be necessary if it holds government securities that can be sold on the open market to obtain reserves. For these reasons, most depository institutions are not directly affected by changes in the discount rate. However, these changes can have important *indirect* effects on lending and the money supply. A decision by the Board of Governors to raise the discount rate, for example, may be a signal that the Board plans to restrict the money supply, perhaps through future open market sales. Such action most likely will raise interest rates. In this case, the discount rate signal may suggest that depository institutions can earn a higher rate of interest by putting off lending until the higher rates really appear in the market. This can be a self-fulfilling prophecy, since lending restraint by depository institutions may, in fact, bring the higher interest rates that were expected. Of course, the signal can also operate in the other direction. Lowering the discount rate may lead to more aggressive lending operations in anticipation of expansionary open market policies from the Federal Reserve.

The Federal Funds Rate

Borrowing by depository institutions through the discounting procedure is, according to Federal Reserve policy, a privilege rather than a right. Federal Reserve policy is that these loans should be made only when the institution's shortage of reserves is temporary and due to circumstances that could not reasonably have been anticipated by the borrowing institution. Thus, depository institutions are encouraged to look elsewhere for money before asking for a loan from the Federal Reserve. The logical place to look, of course, is to institutions that have excess reserves in their accounts in the Federal Reserve Bank. Balances in these accounts are called **federal funds.**

In the United States, there is a well-developed federal funds market. In this market, funds that are excess reserves for some depository institutions are loaned to others that need more reserves. The rate of interest charged on these loans is called the **federal funds rate.** This rate will generally rise when economic activity and lending are expanding rapidly.

If the federal funds rate is lower than the discount rate set by the Federal Reserve System, depository institutions will clearly prefer to borrow in the federal funds market and will not come to their district Federal Reserve Bank for loans. But when the money supply is tightening, the federal funds rate may rise above the discount rate, and loans from the Federal Reserve Bank can ease the problems of individual depository institutions in adjusting to the tighter money situation. Thus, the "discount window" is a safety valve for individual depository institutions during a time when open market operations are restrictive. In these times, of course, the Federal Reserve Banks must carefully examine requests for loans and must ration this bank credit to prevent lending operations from canceling the effects of restrictive open market operations. The federal funds rate has also served as a guide for the implementation of Federal Reserve monetary policy. As will be described shortly, monetary policy has, at times, been "targeted" on the federal funds rate.

Other Instruments

Several other instruments are available to the Board of Governors besides the three that we have already mentioned. Even though reserve requirements, open market operations, and discounting are by far the most important, the other instruments do have their special uses.

Margin Requirements   The Board may set **margin requirements** for stock market trading. In the language of the stock market, trading "on margin" means that money from the purchaser of a stock covers only a fraction of the price of the stock being bought, while the rest of the cost is borrowed from the stockbroker. The money put in by the purchaser is called the *margin*. The broker collects interest on the money loaned to the purchaser and is also protected by receiving the power to sell the stock to recover the amount loaned if the price of the stock falls far enough to wipe out the buyer's margin. The experience in 1929 showed that this arrangement could turn a stock market decline into a stock market disaster, since sales by brokers would force stock prices still farther down. Since the 1930s, the Board has had the power to set margin requirements in a range between 25 and 100 percent of the value of the stock. In the late 1960s, for example, the margin requirement was set at 80

percent, but since 1974 the margin requirement has been 50 percent.

Moral Suasion   The Federal Reserve System can publicize the actions that it wants depository institutions to take. Using what is often called **moral suasion,** the Fed urges "cooperation" in promoting certain policy goals. Sometimes this approach is called jaw-boning. When there is danger of inflation, for example, the Fed may urge "restraint" in granting new loans. Moral suasion, like the other minor instruments of monetary control, may have some limited effect on the money supply and the behavior of depository institutions. However, the most important of the monetary instruments are the reserve requirements, open market buying and selling, and the discount rate for loans to depository institutions.

The three most important instruments of monetary policy used by the Federal Reserve System to control the money supply are reserve requirements, open market operations, and discounting. There are other instruments in addition to these, however, such as margin requirements on the purchase of stocks and moral suasion.

MONETARY POLICY

So far, we know that the Federal Reserve System is responsible for determining and implementing monetary policy. We also have examined the instruments available for implementing this policy. We now look at the goals that have been established for monetary policy and at the specific targets that are used in pursuit of these goals.

The Goals of Monetary Policy

Full employment, price stability, and economic growth are the accepted goals of national economic policy and therefore also of the monetary policy set by the Federal Reserve System. There is no generally agreed priority order among these goals. In times of slack economic activity, full employment is the top goal. When inflation threatens, priority is given to price stability. In the late 1970s and early 1980s, when the U.S. dollar rose and then fell greatly in relation to the monies of other countries and the U.S. trade deficit widened, "a reasonable balance in transactions with other nations" was included among the stated goals of monetary policy. Essentially, the Federal Reserve System examines the current economic scene, determines what it believes to be the most pressing problem facing the macroeconomy, and sets monetary policy to meet this problem.

Conflicts can arise among the goals of monetary policy. For example, in 1987 the U.S. dollar had fallen to low levels relative to major foreign monies. As a result, foreign goods sold in U.S. markets or used in U.S. factories had risen in price in terms of the dollar, raising fears of inflationary increases in the U.S. price level. Tightening the money supply and raising interest rates would strengthen the dollar and reduce the danger of inflation but could also slow economic growth, dampen economic activity, and cause unemployment. In early 1987, the Federal Reserve System saw inflation as the immediate threat and restricted money-supply growth.

The situation changed abruptly in October 1987, when the stock market experienced its most severe decline since the historic "crash" of 1929. Now, the Federal Reserve feared that economic uncertainty might stifle consumption and investment spending and plunge the economy into recession. A conflict existed between the price-stability goal and the goal of avoiding recession and unemployment. Stability in financial markets and in the economy became the priority goals of monetary policy. Fear of recession replaced fear of inflation, and money supply increases were permitted in spite of the effect they might have on the exchange value of the dollar and on the prices of imported goods.

The monetary policy goals set by the Federal Reserve System are full employment, price stability, and economic growth. The Fed sets monetary policy to solve what it feels are the most pressing economic problems at any given time.

Operating "Targets" for Monetary Policy

Once the "ultimate" goal has been selected, the Federal Reserve System must develop an effective procedure to carry out its policy. To do this, some variable that is important in the economy and readily available to money managers is selected and those who actually implement monetary policy—typically those in the New York Federal Reserve Bank who buy and sell on the open market—are directed to keep this **monetary-policy-target variable** within some range of values.

To carry out a monetary policy, the Federal Reserve System selects some variable that is important to the economy and directs those who actually implement monetary policy to keep this target variable within some range of values.

Interest-Rate Targeting A specific interest rate, such as the federal funds rate, may be selected as an operating target used for monetary policy. If the FOMC wanted to fight inflation by restricting growth of the money supply, it could raise the target level of the federal funds rate. In order to bring the federal funds rate to this target level, open market purchases would be scaled back, causing depository institutions to experience less than their usual growth in reserves. Some institutions would then be forced to borrow federal funds and, at the same time, the supply of these funds would be diminished, causing the federal funds rate to rise to the target level. Conversely, an easier, more expansionary monetary policy could be indicated by lowering the target for the federal funds rate. In this case, increased open market purchases would provide depository institutions with more reserves, reducing demand and increasing supply in the federal funds market and bringing the rate down to the target level.

Interest-rate targeting, such as stabilizing the federal funds rate, is called a policy of **accommodation.** It can be illustrated as follows. First, suppose an increase in demand for loans by businesses or consumers results in increased lending by depository institutions. This puts pressure on reserves and brings an increase in the federal funds rate as demand increases and supply decreases in that market. However, if the monetary target is to stabilize the federal funds rate, open market purchases would be increased, providing additional reserves and reducing the need for depository institutions to borrow in the federal funds market. In this way, the increased demand for loans (money) would be "accommodated" by an increase in the money supply.

Money Supply (Nonborrowed Reserves) Targeting
Inflation rates reached unprecedented levels during the 1970s, and fighting inflation was an important goal of macroeconomic policy. Although inflationary pressures came from several directions, including government deficits and petroleum price increases orchestrated by the Organization of Petroleum Exporting Countries, the Federal Reserve System was criticized for not being more effective in stopping it. Some of the blame fell on interest-rate targeting and the policy of accommodation. In 1975, Congress mandated that the Federal Reserve System establish targets expressed as rates of increase in standard (M1, M2, and M3) measures of the money supply itself. In its annual reports to Congress and after its regular meetings every two months, the FOMC was to announce ranges for the percentage growth rates of M1, M2, and M3. Ranges rather than specific percentage rates were used partly because the FOMC recognized that its control of the money supply was not perfect and partly because the ranges left room for the exercise of judgment during the intervals between meetings of the FOMC.

In the 1970s, fighting inflation became an important goal of macroeconomic policy. In 1975, Congress directed the Federal Reserve System to establish target ranges for the percentage growth rates of the money supply.

Under the money-supply targeting system, those directly carrying out open market operations were instructed to base their actions on changes in the amount of **nonborrowed reserves** on hand in depository institutions—that is, on total reserves minus amounts borrowed through discounting

from Federal Reserve Banks. This was different from the federal-funds-rate target and the accommodation system used earlier. Specifically, increased demand for loans from depository institutions would not automatically be accommodated by open market purchases to increase the reserves of these institutions. Instead, when the FOMC specified stability or some limited rate of increase in nonborrowed reserves, institutions that wanted to expand lending would have to seek reserves either in the federal funds market or through loans from the discount window of their district Federal Reserve Bank. If the Federal Reserve System held firm against expanded lending through the discount window, expanded lending by depository institutions would cause higher interest rates and impose a moderating pressure on the economic expansion. Interest rates fluctuate more when money-supply targets are used than they do under an accommodation monetary policy regime.

To control money supply growth, the target ranges for percentage growth rates were based on the amount of nonborrowed reserves in depository institutions, that is, on total reserves minus amounts borrowed through discounting from Federal Reserve Banks.

Borrowed-Reserves Targeting In 1982, the operational guideline was changed from nonborrowed reserves to **borrowed reserves**—reserves borrowed at the discount window from district Federal Reserve Banks. Open market operations continued as the basic instrument of monetary policy, but day-to-day operations focused on borrowed reserves. Under the borrowed-reserves-targeting system, those in charge of open market operations are guided by the volume of borrowing through the discount windows of the Federal Reserve Banks. Low borrowed-reserve targets are used for expansionary monetary policy and high borrowed-reserve targets are used for restrictive monetary policy. This is because an expansionary monetary policy of open market purchases gives depository institutions more *nonborrowed* reserves and reduces their need to borrow at the discount window. A restrictive policy, on the other hand, reduces the *nonborrowed* reserves of depository institutions and increases borrowing at the discount windows.

In effect, borrowed-reserves targeting parallels interest-rate targeting, since lower levels of borrowed reserves typically are reflected in lower federal funds rates and higher levels of borrowed reserves typically involve higher federal funds rates. Thus, the use of borrowed-reserves targeting in the 1980s suggested an emphasis on stabilizing interest rates—a move part-way in the direction of accommodation.

In 1982, the Federal Reserve changed the operational guidelines for monetary policy from nonborrowed reserves to borrowed reserves—reserves borrowed at the discount window from district Federal Reserve Banks.

Problems in Targeting Monetary Aggregates

Three problems arise for monetary policy targeted on money supply aggregates such as M1, M2, and M3. They involve the monetary base, the money multiplier, and the velocity of circulation of money.

The Monetary Base   The **monetary base** is made up of reserves in depository institutions along with the coins and currency circulating in the economy. The Federal Reserve System can influence the size of the monetary base through open market operations and lending to depository institutions. But there are forces outside the Federal Reserve System that can also change the monetary base. For example, many U.S. dollars are held in foreign countries and are used in overseas operations. Changes in interest rates or in investment opportunities can bring funds into the U.S. economy or drain them out and so affect the U.S. monetary base. Similarly, U.S. Treasury operations influence the monetary base when there are changes in the flows of tax collections and transfer payments and when national debt securities are issued or retired. Therefore, when the Federal Reserve System uses its open market and lending ("discounting") instruments to regulate reserves, it must anticipate

changes that may come from these outside influences.

The monetary base consists of reserves in depository institutions plus the coins and currency circulating in the economy. Several forces can influence the size of the monetary base, including flows of funds to and from foreign economies, and changes in the flows of tax collections and transfer payments.

The Money Multiplier   The **money multiplier** is the ratio between the amount of money (such as M1) in the economy and the size of the monetary base. For the money managers of the Federal Reserve System, the money multiplier is another variable that must be taken into account in doing their job of controlling the money supply. If the money multiplier is stable, their job is easier because they can be reasonably sure that a given change in the monetary base—achieved perhaps through open market operations—will result in a predictable change in the money supply. But if the money multiplier is not stable, it is difficult to predict accurately the effects of changes in the monetary base.

The money multiplier is the ratio between the amount of money in the economy and the size of the monetary base. If the money multiplier is not stable, it is difficult to predict accurately the effects of changes in the monetary base.

At least two forces can cause the money multiplier ratio to move up or down. One is that the reserve ratio actually maintained by depository institutions can fluctuate somewhat above the legal minimum reserve ratio set by the Board if these institutions maintain "desired" excess reserves. Therefore, the deposit-expansion factor may fluctuate. A second reason is that there is an ebb and flow of currency and coin between depository institution reserves and hand-to-hand circulation in the economy. When currency and coin are in hand-to-hand circulation, they count as money, but they are not official reserves. When they are deposited in depository institutions, they are not counted as money, but they become official reserves that can support several times their own worth in checkable account money. In other words, reserves themselves move up and down as currency and coin flow into and out of depository institutions.

Since the money multiplier equals the money supply divided by the monetary base, a different money multiplier is calculated for each of the three money supply concepts—M1, M2, and M3. When deposit holders shift their balances among different types of accounts, changes take place in the totals for the different money supply concepts and therefore also in the values of these different money multipliers. During the 1970s, when interest rates rose, depositors transferred funds out of M1-type (checkable) accounts, M1 became smaller relative to other asset categories, and the M1 multiplier fell. The trend reversed in the 1980s. Interest rates fell, depositors returned funds to M1-type accounts, and the M1 multiplier rose. Although their patterns were not so dramatic, the M2 and M3 multipliers also changed considerably over this period. Federal Reserve instruments influence the monetary base, but if the linkage to the money supply—the money multiplier—is unreliable, it is difficult to predict the ultimate effect on the money supply. Money supply management was difficult during the 1970s and 1980s.

Velocity of Money   The velocity of money is the third problem in carrying out monetary policy targeted on measures of the money supply. **Velocity** is the speed with which the average dollar circulates through the economy. For example, if the average dollar of the M1 money supply is used four times a year in purchasing currently produced goods and services, M1 velocity has a value of 4. In other words, M1 velocity is gross national product (GNP) divided by M1, M2 velocity is GNP divided by M2, and M3 velocity is GNP divided by M3. Velocity tells how hard the average dollar of the measured money supply works in the operation of the economy. Since the ultimate goals of monetary policy deal with the operation of the aggregate economy, velocity is important. Stable or reliably predictable velocity would greatly simplify the task of regulating macroeconomic activity through changes in the money supply. A given change in

the money supply would be expected to have a given effect on the economy, other things equal. But if velocity is not stable or reliably predictable, it is difficult to predict the effect of money-supply changes.

Velocity is the speed with which the average dollar circulates through the economy. If velocity is not stable, it is difficult to predict the effect of money-supply changes.

Computer technology and deregulation have led to great fluctuations in the velocity of money. Because of these innovations, account balances can be moved swiftly in response to changes in interest rates. If interest rates rise, balances are quickly withdrawn from M1 accounts, which offer relatively low interest rates, and redeposited in M2 or M3 accounts or used to purchase assets not included in the array of official measures of the money supply. The measured money supply shrinks and the measured velocity of money goes up. Conversely, when interest rates fall, the opposite movements take place. The measured money supply grows and measured velocity decreases. Obvious problems arise for monetary policy targeted on money supply data alone. For example, increased economic activity could cause higher interest rates and a consequent reduction in the measured M1 money supply. But a policy target of stable growth in M1 would lead Federal Reserve monetary operations to expand open market purchases, thus in effect accommodating the expansion of economic activity. In this way, a policy of stable growth in the measured money supply would have destabilizing effects on the macroeconomy.[2]

When interest rates rise, the measured money supply shrinks and the measured velocity of money goes up. When interest rates fall, the measured money supply grows and measured velocity decreases.

---

2. In October 1982, the Federal Reserve suspended the targeting of M1 because it believed that this measure of the money supply had become too volatile and was not a useful guide for implementing monetary policy.

Economics in Focus

The Fed Divided

Since its founding in 1913, there have been some dramatic disagreements between the Federal Reserve and the incumbent administration. Although the Fed does not have to follow administration dictates, the board usually tries to reach common ground on basic strategy with the White House. But what happens when the Fed cannot agree with itself?

Lately a strong division has developed between the seven-member Board of Governors and the presidents of the twelve regional banks. As of 1989, all seven governors were appointees of the Reagan administration; all, in fact, had joined the board between 1984 and 1988. As Reagan appointees, they tended to share the supply-side outlook that dominated the Reagan years. For example, Manuel H. Johnson, vice chairman of the board, was a former economics professor and Treasury official who had backed the Reagan tax cut of 1981. Martha Seger, the first woman appointed to serve a full term on the board, was a Michigan economist and professor who clearly remembered the damage done to Michigan's economy by the 1982 recession. Given their backgrounds and opinions, most of the board would be wary of continually forcing up interest rates to cool inflation; instead, they would tend to favor a somewhat looser monetary policy with more stimulus to the economy and less risk of recession.

Some of the twelve regional bank presidents, on the other hand, were holdovers from another era. By 1989 the Richmond bank's president, Robert P. Black, had been in his post for fifteen years; at the Philadelphia bank Edward G. Boehne had served for eight years. As a group, the regional presidents took a harder line against inflation.

A few years earlier, the differences of opinion would have had little impact because the Board of Governors, led by the chairman, dominated central policymaking. But by the end of the 1980s the balance of power had shifted somewhat, and the regional presidents—"the most articulate, most analytic group in modern history," according to one ex-board member—began to make their voices heard. Since the Fed's actions on the open market are determined by the Federal Open Market Committee (FOMC), on which regional presidents hold five of the twelve positions, the presidents do at least have a strong minority position. Moreover, their personal and intellectual clout has been greater than their number of votes would suggest.

Federal Reserve Chairman Alan Greenspan, appointed as the Fed's leader in 1987, seems to hold an intermediate view about the relative dangers of inflation and recession, and his general strategy has been to hammer out a compromise between the "hawks" (strongly anti-inflation) and the "doves" (afraid of recession). The approach appears to have worked well, at least in the short run. However, some veteran analysts have suggested that Greenspan's balancing act will not succeed indefinitely and there may at some point be a decisive showdown.

Sources: Mike McNamee, "Now the Inflation Battle Is Inside the Fed," *Business Week,* March 13, 1989, pp. 124–126 (quotation at p. 126); Louis Uchitelle, "Alan Greenspan: Caution at the Fed," *New York Times Magazine,* January 15, 1989, p. 18ff.; Mike McNamee, "The Group of Seven Is Acting More Like the Seven Dwarfs," *Business Week,* June 5, 1989, p. 90.

SUMMARY

1. The Federal Reserve System was established by an act of Congress in 1913 to provide a means for controlling the money supply, to assure a flexible national currency, and to be a lender of last resort to forestall financial panics. (See page 274.)

2. The Board of Governors of the Federal Reserve System is made up of seven persons appointed by the president and confirmed by the Senate. The Board sets policy for the Federal Reserve System. The independence of the Federal Reserve System from the elected officials of the government is an important issue, since the Fed wields great power in the economy. (See pages 274–275.)

3. The Federal Open Market Committee consists of the seven members of the Board of Governors plus five members from the Federal Reserve Banks. This committee directs and coordinates the purchase and sale of securities by the Federal Reserve System in the open market. (See page 275.)

4. There are twelve Federal Reserve Districts, and a Federal Reserve Bank is located in each district. These banks, which are owned by member banks in the district, provide services to the depository institutions and commercial interests of the district. Federal Reserve banks provide bank examiners, make loans to depository institutions, operate a check-clearing system, and serve as fiscal agent for the federal government. (See pages 275–276.)

5. From the beginnings of the Federal Reserve System, the Board had the power to set minimum required reserve ratios for banks that were members of the system. The Depository Institutions Deregulation and Monetary Control Act of 1980 broadened this power by giving the Board authority to set minimum reserve requirements for all checkable accounts in all depository institutions. By setting minimum required reserve ratios, the Board can strongly influence the deposit-expansion factor that relates depository institution reserves to the money supply. (See pages 275–279.)

6. Open market operations consist of the buying and selling of government securities by the Federal Reserve Banks in the general, or open, market. When securities are purchased by the system, reserves held by depository institutions are increased, inviting an expansion of the money supply. When

securities are sold by the system, reserves held by depository institutions are reduced, and the money supply is restricted. Open market operations are the most actively used of all the monetary instruments of the Federal Reserve System. (See pages 279–280.)

7. The discount rate is the rate of interest charged by a Federal Reserve Bank on a loan to a depository institution. Since these loans are intended only as temporary aid to institutions that face unexpected reserve problems, the discount rate does not directly affect most depository institutions. However, the discount rate may be read as a signal of upcoming Federal Reserve policy. A higher discount rate may suggest a tightening of the money supply, and a lower discount rate may suggest an easing of the money supply. (See page 281.)

8. Federal funds are depository institution reserve deposits in Federal Reserve Banks. Depository institutions may borrow federal funds from one another as an alternative to borrowing through the discounting procedure with the Federal Reserve System. The federal funds rate is the rate of interest charged on these loans. A rising federal funds rate indicates a tightening of the money markets, and a falling federal funds rate indicates an easing of the money markets. (See pages 281–282.)

9. The Board of Governors has the authority to set margin requirements for stock market trading. These requirements specify the minimum percentage of the purchase price of stock that must be paid in by the purchaser himself or herself—the remainder of the purchase price being borrowed from the broker. Experience in 1929 showed that stocks owned on small margins could be "dumped" on the market, turning a modest decline into a stock market disaster. (See page 282.)

10. The goals of monetary policy are full employment, price stability, and economic growth in the economy. Conflicts can arise among these goals. Based on its evaluation of current situations, the Federal Reserve System determines which has top priority at any given time. (See pages 282–283.)

11. In order to achieve the goals of monetary policy, the Federal Reserve establishes operating targets, such as a selected interest rate, nonborrowed reserves, or borrowed reserves. Efforts to target monetary aggregates such as M1, M2, and M3 have encountered problems, including (a) inability to fully control the monetary base, (b) instability of the money multiplier, and (c) changes in the velocity of circulation of money. (See pages 283–284.)

12. The monetary base consists of reserves in depository institutions plus coins and currency circulating from hand to hand in the economy. The Federal Reserve System can influence the monetary base by open market operations and by loans to depository institutions (discounting). The money multiplier is the relationship between the monetary base and a specified monetary aggregate, such as M1, M2, or M3. (See pages 285–286.)

13. The velocity of circulation of money is the number of times per year the average dollar of the money supply is used to purchase newly produced goods and services. It is equal to GNP divided by the chosen measure of the money supply. Changes in the velocity of circulation of money increase the difficulty of estimating the relationship between the money supply and the level of aggregate economic activity in the economy. (See page 286.)

KEY TERMS

accommodation: the practice of increasing or decreasing the money supply as the demand for loans increases or decreases, thus tending to stabilize interest rates (page 283).

Board of Governors: a group of seven people who supervise the Federal Reserve System and thus direct the nation's monetary policy (page 274).

borrowed reserves: reserves borrowed by depository institutions at the discount window from district Federal Reserve Banks (page 284).

discounting: a loan process through which securities or promises from a borrower were purchased by a Federal Reserve Bank at less than their value at maturity (page 277).

discount rate: the rate of interest that Federal Reserve Banks charge on loans to depository institutions (page 281).

disintermediation: when people take funds out of financial institutions in order to get higher interest elsewhere (page 293).

federal funds: depository institution reserve deposits in Federal Reserve Banks (page 281).

federal funds rate: the rate of interest charged on loans of federal funds (page 281).

Federal Open Market Committee (FOMC): a twelve-member committee that controls Federal Reserve buying and selling of government securities on the open market (page 275).

Federal Reserve Banks: the twelve banks of the Federal Reserve System that control the money supply, provide a flexible currency (the Federal Reserve Note), and serve as lenders of last resort to prevent bank failures (page 275).

Federal Reserve System: the central bank of the United States (page 274).

gold standard: a promise by a government to exchange a fixed amount of gold for its currency (page 292).

lender of last resort: a function of the Federal Reserve System: if depository institutions have temporary difficulty, a loan from a Federal Reserve Bank can be arranged (page 277).

margin requirement: the percentage of the value of a stock which the purchaser must finance from his or her own resources (page 282).

monetary base: the reserves in depository institutions along with the coins and currency circulating in the economy (page 285).

monetary instruments: the tools used to regulate the money supply (page 273).

monetary-policy-target variable: a variable used by the Federal Reserve System as a guide in implementing monetary policy (page 283).

money multiplier: the ratio between the amount of money in the economy and the size of the monetary base (page 285).

moral suasion: the approach used by the Federal Reserve System when it urges cooperation in promoting certain policy goals (page 282).

national banks: banks chartered by the federal government (page 276).

nonborrowed reserves: total reserves in depository institutions minus amounts borrowed through discounting from Federal Reserve Banks (page 284).

open market operations: the buying and selling of government securities by the Federal

Reserve Banks (page 279).

pyramiding of reserves: when small banks keep their reserves on deposit in banks in larger cities, which, in turn, keep a large part of their reserves as deposits in banks in a few major cities (page 274).

stagflation: a combination of inflation, rising unemployment, and sluggish economic growth (page 294).

Thrift Institutions Advisory Council: a council set up in 1983 to provide a channel through which savings and loan associations, mutual savings banks, and credit unions can present their views to the Federal Reserve Board of Governors (page 275).

velocity of money: the speed with which the average dollar circulates through the economy (page 286).

DISCUSSION QUESTIONS

1. How are Federal Reserve Board members selected? What systems have been set up to insulate, to some degree, the Board of Governors of the Federal Reserve System from control by the president or the Congress? Do you believe that the Federal Reserve Board should be more closely or less closely tied to the president and the Congress? Explain your position.

2. How are members of the Federal Open Market Committee selected? Describe the operations carried out by this committee. Explain how these operations affect the money supply.

3. Explain how, under the pyramiding of reserves system, a relatively minor problem of a few banks not having enough reserves to cover withdrawal requests might build up to a nationwide crisis. How does the system today provide help for a depository institution that is short on reserves?

4. How is the help that a Federal Reserve Bank gives to depository institutions in its district related to the discount rate? Explain the conflict that sometimes arises between contracting the money supply in the economy and helping out troubled depository institutions.

5. Construct a balance sheet for the Federal Reserve Banks, showing the main entries on both the assets and the liabilities sides. Then compare your work with Table 1. Explain how the U.S. Government securities entry is related to the national debt. Explain how the reserve accounts entry is related to the laws that control individual depository institutions.

6. Explain how the profit motivation of depository institutions helps to assure that actual reserve ratios will stay close to legal reserve ratio requirements. If the Federal Reserve lowers the legal reserve requirement, how is the amount of checkable account money likely to be affected? Explain the process that leads to this result.

7. The Depository Institutions Deregulation and Monetary Control Act of 1980 broadened the Federal Reserve's authority over checkable accounts in two ways. What were they? How did technological changes create the need for these broader Federal Reserve powers?

8. By drawing a pair of balance sheets, one for the Federal Reserve Banks and one for the entire system of depository institutions, show how a Federal Open Market Committee purchase of securities can expand the money supply. Compare your balance sheets with Table 2. Select a different legal reserve requirement and rework your balance sheets to show a different change in the money supply.

9. What are federal funds? If an individual depository institution needs to borrow money, why might it wish to borrow federal funds rather than to borrow from its Federal Reserve Bank? In terms of the money supply and the demand for loans, what is usually happening in the economy when the federal funds rate is rising?

10. Two minor powers of the Federal Reserve are margin requirements and moral suasion. Briefly describe how they may have some influence on economic activity.

11. What did the Depository Institutions Deregulation and Monetary Control Act of 1980 do with respect to interest rate limits? Do you believe that deregulation will increase or decrease competition in financial markets? Explain.

12. What happens to the U.S. monetary base when dollars move to other countries to take advantage of investment opportunities? How does the money multiplier show the effect of a change such as this on the money supply in the United States? If you were trying to manage the U.S. money supply, would you want the money multiplier to be high, or low, or just stable? Explain.

Appendix:
A Brief History of
Federal Reserve Policies

Over the years that the Federal Reserve System has operated, there have been quiet intervals of "normalcy," but there also have been times when conditions changed quickly and the System faced choices that were controversial, important, and shrouded in uncertainty. We shall begin by describing the first real test of the System's ability to stabilize the economy.

THE RECESSION OF 1921

The Federal Reserve System was launched, in 1913, onto financial waters that soon would be stirred to great turbulence by World War I. As people tried to find a safe haven for their wealth, gold, which then was part of the money supply and could be used as reserves for loans, flowed into the United States and added to bank reserves.[3] Businesses borrowed large sums to build factories for war production, and the government sold Liberty Bonds to finance the war effort. When the war ended, some gold flowed back to Europe, foreign demand for U.S. products slackened, and the U.S. economy slipped into a severe, though short, recession in 1921. Somewhat belatedly, the Federal Reserve lowered the discount rate, which of course was an expansionary move, but otherwise did very little to stop the economic decline. Supporters of the Federal Reserve contend that its members were worried that expansionary policies might speed the outflow of gold. Critics say that the Federal Reserve was too timid and failed to ease the shock of the postwar recession.

THE STOCK MARKET CRASH: 1929

Rapid expansion in the automobile and other markets made the decade of the 1920s a period of prosperity for the United States, except for farmers, who had not recovered from the loss of wartime markets. In Europe, the aftermath of the war and the Versailles peace treaty were causing problems.[4] As people again began to seek safety and profitable investment, gold flowed back into the United States, bolstering the money supply. At the same time, the national debt, which had grown during the war, provided bonds and other securities that were well suited to bank holdings and open market dealings. The Federal Reserve Banks learned that open market operations could affect the economy. Even though the economy appeared to be running smoothly, the Federal Reserve worried about increased speculation in the stock market. Since it did not yet have the authority to regulate margin requirements, the Federal Reserve tried in early 1929 to reduce stock market speculation by putting modest restraints on the growth of the money supply. Economists do not agree about the causes of the crash. However, when the stock market crashed later that year, the Federal Reserve quickly reversed itself, lowering discount rates and buying government securities in the open market. The blow from the stock market crash in the United States was soon followed by further problems, as conditions kept growing worse in world financial markets. In Europe, declining economic conditions led, in 1931, to the failure of the leading banking house in Austria, the Credit Anstalt. Runs on European banks began as people withdrew gold and

---

3. Legislation in effect at this time and on through the 1970s authorized only banks to provide checking account services. Therefore, the term *bank* can be used rather than the term *depository institution*.

4. In one of the more remarkable exhibitions of economic forecasting, the British economist John Maynard Keynes in 1919 predicted that the Versailles peace treaty would mean economic misfortune for Europe. See Keynes, *The Economic Consequences of the Peace* (1920).

currencies in fear of further bank failures. First Austria, then Germany, and then Great Britain had to go back on their promises to exchange a fixed amount of gold for their paper currencies (in other words, they went off the **gold standard**). Fear spread that the United States might soon follow suit. As gold and currency started flowing out of U.S. banks, the stage was set for one of the most controversial and critical decisions yet faced by the Federal Reserve System.

The gold standard is a promise by the government to exchange a fixed amount of gold for its paper currency.

At this time (1931), the quantity of Federal Reserve Notes that could be issued was limited by the amount of gold and commercial paper (business IOUs obtained by the Federal Reserve Banks when loans were made to commercial banks) held by the Federal Reserve. The Federal Reserve Banks' holdings of both gold and commercial paper (the IOUs) were declining in 1931, and this decline threatened to force a drop in the Federal Reserve Note money supply. The Fed decided not to use open market purchases to expand the money supply because that would reduce the need for local banks to borrow from the Federal Reserve, thus further reducing the central bank's holding of business IOU backing for Federal Reserve Notes. Instead, the Federal Reserve Banks *raised* discount rates and allowed further tightening of the money supply, an act that would be unthinkable to today's understanding of appropriate monetary policy.

When a major bank in Detroit failed in early 1933, the governor of Michigan closed all the banks in the state to prevent runs on other banks. Soon all the other states followed with bank closings. One of the first acts of incoming President Franklin D. Roosevelt was to declare a nationwide ''bank holiday.'' The money supply had fallen drastically, and the Federal Reserve System had again failed to stabilize the economy.

REPAIRING THE MONETARY SYSTEM

Repair of the monetary system started even before the collapse in 1933, though too late to prevent it.

In 1932, new legislation (the Glass–Steagall Act) allowed the Federal Reserve System to use government bonds for backing Federal Reserve Notes, thus clearing away the obstacle that had kept it from using open market operations vigorously. Under the Banking Act of 1935, the Federal Open Market Committee was officially established, further improving the ability to use open market operations.

In 1933, as panic spread and gold was withdrawn from the banks, the United States went off the gold standard, as Great Britain and others had done earlier. Thus, the government was no longer obligated to give up its gold holdings in exchange for currency. The United States remained off the gold standard for almost two years. In 1934, when conditions were more stable, a modified gold standard was established and a higher price for gold was offered. Gold flowed back into the U.S. banking system, strengthening the reserve position of the Federal Reserve System. Excess reserves in banks climbed to high levels. Strangely enough, the stage was now set for another Federal Reserve act that history has called a mistake.

In 1936, the large and growing excess reserves in the banking system led the Federal Reserve to fear the coming of inflation, which might get out of control. For this reason, it doubled reserve requirements over a short period of time and used open market sales to counteract the effect of gold imports. Within a year, the economy plunged into even deeper recession. Criticism was heaped on the Federal Reserve for once again having made the wrong move.

In fairness, however, it must be added that certain fiscal events were taking place at about the same time. The Social Security system had started collecting taxes but few could yet collect benefits. Also, through a legislative mistake, taxes on corporations were increased significantly.

MONEY GOES TO WAR: 1941–1945

After the disastrous experience of the 1937–1938 recession, the chastened Federal Reserve reversed itself and began to follow an expansionary, or easy-money, policy. In 1939, World War II started in Europe, and the U.S. economy expanded to produce war goods. After the attack on Pearl Harbor in December 1941, the U.S. economy went all out for war production. The Federal Reserve promised that open market operations would support the bond market to make sure that the massive sales of war bonds would not force interest rates upward. This meant huge and continuing open market purchases and a great expansion of the money supply. The money supply grew and grew during the war, while civilian production was cut back. To hold down inflation, the government used price and wage controls as well as rationing. Congress authorized and the Federal Reserve applied controls over lending and borrowing. Banks were permitted to play favorites among customers to favor war production and essential civilian needs. Money and prices had gone to war.

When the war ended, price controls were removed. Even though inflation was beginning in earnest, fear was widespread that the economy soon would fall back into recession, since this had happened in the past when wartime pressures subsided. At this time, the Federal Reserve again faced important and controversial questions. If open market purchases stopped supporting bond prices, would the bond market collapse and trigger financial chaos and bank failures? The Fed had been criticized for its restrictive policies in 1931 and in 1936. Should it risk another recession? The Treasury, wanting interest costs to stay low on the greatly expanded national debt, put strong pressures on the Federal Reserve to follow an easy-money policy. Under all this pressure, the Federal Reserve decided to continue open market purchasing to support the bond market and to limit its inflation fight to maintaining higher discount rates and reserve requirements. Inflation spread, reaching a peak in 1948.

THE "ACCORD" OF 1951

War-related problems and inflationary conditions arose again in 1950 as the United States became involved in the Korean War. Again the Treasury wanted more open market purchases to support the bond market, but this time the Federal Reserve chose to fight for its independence. After a great political struggle, open market operations were freed from the commitment to support the bond market. The "accord" was announced on March 4, 1951. The Federal Reserve was again independent of the Treasury.

In the period after the accord of 1951, the Federal Reserve System generally followed a policy of "leaning against the wind." This meant using open market purchases and sales, as well as small adjustments in reserve requirements and discount rates, to moderate expansions and contractions of the economy. The Fed was neither swept along by the winds of war nor overcome by forces it wished to oppose.

DISINTERMEDIATION

The economy's performance was sluggish in the last half of the 1950s, but picked up speed in the early 1960s. Taxes were reduced in 1964 in a clear application of fiscal instruments and Keynesian economic theory. By 1966, the Federal Reserve detected inflationary dangers. As the "war on poverty" was waged and as hostilities increased in Vietnam, the federal budget moved deeper and deeper into deficit. Restrictive open market operations were applied, and almost no increase in the money supply was permitted. But because the demand for loans kept on growing while the money supply was stabilized, interest rates climbed. When market interest rates rose above the legal ceiling rates that banks and other regulated financial institutions were allowed to pay, many people took their deposits out of these institutions in order to get higher interest on their savings elsewhere. This process is called **disintermediation.** Thrift institutions and the home-building industry, which depends heavily on loans from them, suffered greatly from a shortage of available funds in 1967. Unfortunately, the inflationary danger that the Fed was trying to combat was only partly defused.

Disintermediation occurred in the 1960s when market interest rates rose above the legal ceiling rates that banks and other regulated financial institutions were permitted to pay, and people took their money out of these institutions to get higher interest on their savings elsewhere.

In 1968, the Federal Reserve System started using monetary tools in an expansionary direction. The reason was that the economy was beginning to contract. Gold and financial capital were flowing out of the country as the United States' competitive position in world trade grew weaker. Also, Congress raised taxes by 10 percent. To counter the economic overkill that it thought would come from the combined effect of these events, the Fed expanded open market buying. By this time, the U.S. economy was starting to show signs that were contradictory according to the prevailing economic theories. Growth was lagging, unemployment was increasing, and inflation continued. In other words, the economy was beginning to suffer from *stagflation*. At the end of the 1960s, the Federal Reserve tightened the money supply in an effort to slow the inflation. Interest rates rose, and disintermediation took place once again.

THE GREAT STAGFLATION

The combination of inflation, rising unemployment, and sluggish economic growth is called **stagflation.** As the stagflation problem grew in the early 1970s, the Nixon administration decided to use both fiscal and monetary tools to aid production and reduce unemployment. Taxes were cut, government spending was increased, the FOMC bought securities, and discount rates were lowered. To hold down inflation, President Nixon announced a freeze on prices and wage rates and a suspension of U.S. gold payments in international transactions. However, during the control period, the money supply was expanded. When the controls were lifted, inflation burst forth with new vigor. President Ford, who replaced President Nixon after the Watergate scandal, undertook a program called "Whip Inflation Now" (abbreviated "WIN"). Money supply growth was restricted and unemployment increased.

Stagflation is a combination of inflation, rising unemployment, and sluggish economic growth.

The election victory of President Carter in 1976 brought confrontation between the Federal Reserve on the one hand and the president and the Congress on the other. Armed with the election mandate to expand the economy, President Carter refused to name Board member Arthur Burns (who was associated with a "tight" money policy) to another term as chairman. Burns retired, and the Federal Reserve, under new leadership, expanded the money supply. Over the four years of the Carter administration, the M1 money supply grew at a yearly rate of 7.7 percent, and the inflation rate rose to around 9 percent a year, sometimes reaching a double-digit figure. Alarmed by these high inflation rates, President Carter installed a new Federal Reserve Board Chairman, Paul Volcker, and backed a tighter monetary policy.

The election of President Reagan in 1980 gave a further mandate for a strong anti-inflation policy. Restrictive monetary measures continued throughout 1981 and into 1982. Interest rates and unemployment remained high, but the inflation rate came down dramatically. Monetary instruments can claim some, but not all, of the credit for the very significant slackening of the inflation rate in the first half of the 1980s. The sluggish economy weakened the demand for funds. In addition, restrictive monetary policy was powerfully assisted by decreases in petroleum prices, as the Organization of Petroleum Exporting Countries (OPEC) encountered increased difficulty in limiting petroleum output. Although money supply increases were allowed, real interest rates—interest rates adjusted for the now much lower inflation rate—were very high by historical standards. Some argued that fear of future inflation prevented a sufficient downward movement of real interest rates. Whatever the cause, high interest rates caused great trouble for some financial institutions and for farmers, who faced the problem of lower prices for their crops along with extremely high interest costs on their indebtedness.

Through the middle and later 1980s, the economy enjoyed a long period of economic expansion. Following the stock market crash in late 1987, the Federal Reserve sharply increased the money supply in order to prevent the crash from pushing the economy into recession. No recession occurred and, by 1989, the economy was operating near to what many economists believed was the natural rate of unemployment. Price-level increases in 1989 led the Federal Reserve to adopt moderately restrictive monetary policies, hoping to prevent inflation while not leading the economy into recession.

AN OVERVIEW

As our brief history has suggested, the monetary policies of the Federal Reserve System have often been controversial. With 20–20 hindsight, it is clear that mistakes were made in 1921, 1931, and 1936, though it would be unfair to place all the blame for these hard times on monetary policy. The Fed's support for the war effort during World War II can hardly be faulted, and its fight for independence from the Treasury and its noninflationary financing of the Korean War merit praise. During the 1950s and the early 1960s, monetary policies operated smoothly most of the time.

Monetary policies, like most other demand-side approaches, were not able to solve the complicated riddle of stagflation in the 1970s, and, as in the Great Depression of the 1930s, the Federal Reserve was often blamed for unemployment. However, in 1980 and 1981, monetary instruments proved their power to bring down the inflation rate.

The relative independence of the Federal Reserve from control by the elected officials of the government continues to be a focus of debate. When monetary policies are unpopular, calls are heard to place monetary policy under the control of the Treasury or, by some other means, to give the president or Congress greater power over the Federal Reserve. So far, independent monetary policy has survived these attempts, providing another aspect of our checks-and-balances system.

DISCUSSION QUESTIONS

1. The Glass–Steagall Act of 1932 allowed the Federal Reserve System to use government bonds for backing the Federal Reserve Notes. What had the system been required to use before this law was passed? How could higher discount rates bring in more of the pre-1932 legal backing to the Federal Reserve?

2. Federal Reserve policy during and after World War II was to support the price of government bonds and to keep interest rates low. Explain how the Federal Open Market Committee was involved in these operations. How did these operations affect the money supply? What was the "accord" reached in 1951?

3. What is disintermediation? Why did disintermediation happen in 1967 when the Federal Reserve engaged in restrictive monetary policy? Would disintermediation have happened then if the Depository Institutions Deregulation and Monetary Control Act had been in effect? Explain.

14
Monetary Economics

Preview In the last chapter you learned how the Federal Reserve System (the central bank) uses various monetary instruments to influence the supply of money in the economy. Now it is time to see how changes in the money supply affect the equilibrium level of national income and product.

We start our study by examining the quantity-of-money theory, a model based on what is called the equation of exchange. We illustrate this theory in terms of aggregate demand and aggregate supply and discuss the long-run monetary policy implications of that theory.

We next examine how monetary policy is able to exert a short-run effect on interest rates and the equilibrium level of national income and product. This involves a study of the money market in which monetary actions are carried out. Our analysis is based on a model of how interest rates affect investment. We discuss the factors that make monetary instruments more or less able to influence employment and output. We include a discussion of the importance of the velocity of money and of alternative approaches to the day-to-day direction of monetary policy.

Price-level (inflation) effects are important in all theories relating to monetary policy. In the final portion of the chapter, we examine what happens if increases in the money supply lead people to expect the price level to increase. In a context of inflationary expectations, money supply increases are less able to promote expansion in real national income and product.

THE QUANTITY-OF-MONEY THEORY

The quantity-of-money theory has been famous in economics for a long time. It is based on a simple relationship called the **equation of exchange.** The equation is $MV = PQ$, where M stands for the quantity of money in the economy, V stands for its **velocity of circulation** (the average number of times each dollar is used per year to buy newly produced goods and services), P stands for the price level, and Q stands for the quantity of real output for the year.[1]

The equation of exchange states that the quantity of money in the economy multiplied by the number of times the average dollar is used each year to purchase newly produced final products must be equal to the quantity of these final products multiplied by their average price. It is called the equation of exchange because the left side, MV, represents total money spent by purchasers, and the right side, PQ, represents total money received by sellers. Because the two sides of the equation must be equal by definition, the equation is more properly called an *identity*.

Since a relationship that is true by definition cannot be used to prove a cause-and-effect relation, the equation of exchange does not establish any necessary connection between the quantity of money, as a cause, and the equilibrium level of national income and product, as an effect. But it does provide a framework for a great deal of debate about the importance of money in the economy.

The equation of exchange, $MV = PQ$, states that the quantity of money in the economy multiplied by the number of times the average dollar is used each year to purchase newly produced final goods and services must be equal to the quantity of these final goods and services multiplied by their average price.

---

1. In its original form, developed in 1911 by the American economist Irving Fisher, the equation was $MV = PT$, where T represented all transactions in the economy and V was defined as the number of times a year the average dollar was used in any type of transaction.

The equation of exchange is used in the **quantity-of-money theory,** which asserts that the velocity of money circulation is constant in the long run, so that changes in the quantity of money provide a good way to predict changes in gross national product (GNP), since the PQ part of the equation corresponds with the definition of GNP. In other words, if the V in the equation of exchange is constant, a 10 percent increase in the quantity of money (M) would mean a 10 percent increase in gross national product (PQ).

The quantity-of-money theory states that the velocity of money circulation is constant in the long run, so changes in the quantity of money provide a good way to predict changes in GNP.

An "Aggregate-Demand" View of the Quantity Theory

The equation of exchange can be rearranged to become a statement about the aggregate quantity of goods and services demanded in an economy. If we let Q in the equation represent the aggregate quantity of goods and services demanded, the equation of exchange says that $Q = MV/P$. In this arrangement, Q and P are inversely related, that is, a decrease in P (the price level) is associated with an increase in Q (real national income and product demanded) provided that there is no change in either M (the money supply) or V (the velocity of circulation of money). This inverse relationship is illustrated in Figure 1. In this figure, we have put quotation marks around the references to aggregate demand in the title and in the label on the curve because the line on the graph is merely a derivation from the equation of exchange and is not a true aggregate-demand curve. As you remember from Chapter 6, a true aggregate-demand curve is a statement of cause and effect—that the aggregate quantity or real GNP demanded *depends on* the price level, *ceteris paribus*, or $QD = f(P)$, *ceteris paribus*. Since the equation of exchange is an identity, it cannot be used to establish a cause-and-effect relationship.

FIGURE 1
An "Aggregate-Demand" Relationship Derived from the Equation of Exchange

The curve "AD" is derived from the equation of exchange ($MV = PQ$), assuming that M and V are constant and therefore that the product of M and V also is constant. The curve is a rectangular hyperbola because each point on it represents a product of P and Q (price level times real GNP) that is constant. If the variable on the horizontal axis (real GNP) is understood to be the aggregate quantity of goods and services demanded, the curve illustrates the concept of "aggregate demand" implicit in the quantity theory.

The equation of exchange can be rearranged to become a statement about the aggregate quantity of goods and services demanded in an economy: $Q = MV/P$.

Although the "AD" curve in Figure 1 is not a true aggregate-demand curve, it is helpful in understanding the economics of the quantity-of-money theory. In drawing the curve in Figure 1, the money supply (M) and the velocity of money (V) are held constant. Changes in either of these variables, therefore, will shift the curve. Increasing the value of these variables shifts the curve to the right and decreasing their values shifts it to the left.

The Classical Aggregate-Supply Curve

According to the quantity-of-money theory, the velocity of money circulation is constant and there is a one-to-one relationship between percentage changes in the money supply and percentage changes in the price level—a 10 percent increase in M causes a 10 percent increase in the price level, and so on. What does this say about the aggregate quantity supplied? It says that the aggregate quantity supplied does not change when the price level changes. This is illustrated in Figure 2, where the "AD" curve is reproduced from Figure 1 and labeled "AD_1" and an "AD_2" curve is added to illustrate a 10 percent increase in the quantity of

FIGURE 2
"Aggregate Demand" and "Aggregate Supply" Derived from the Quantity-of-Money Theory

The "AD_1" curve shows the relationship between aggregate quantity or real GNP demanded and the price level according to the equation of exchange, assuming the money supply and the velocity of its circulation are constant. The "AD_2" curve illustrates a 10 percent increase in the money supply, with velocity remaining constant. Since the quantity-of-money theory states that a 10 percent increase in the money supply is associated with a 10 percent increase in the price level, the implicit aggregate supply curve is a vertical line, labeled "AS."

money. The original macroeconomic equilibrium is at *A*, with real GNP of $1,000 billion and a price level index of 100. The 10 percent increase in the money supply (illustrated by the distance from *A* to *C*) results in a 10 percent price level increase from *A* to *B*. The vertical line labeled "*AS*" is the aggregate supply curve implicit in the quantity theory argument.

According to the quantity-of-money theory, the velocity of money circulation is constant, and there is a one-to-one relationship between percentage changes in the money supply and percentage changes in the price level.

According to the quantity-of-money theory, the vertical "aggregate-supply" curve represents the full employment level of output for the economy and incorporates the view that this level of output is the same regardless of the price level. In other words, changes in the money supply affect only the price level and do not affect real output.

According to classical economics, changes in the money supply affect only the price level and do not affect real output.

Is there any truth in the classical view that changes in the money supply affect only the price level? Time and again throughout history, when governments have printed large amounts of money or when large quantities of gold or silver have been discovered, the resulting increases in the money supply have been followed by increases in prices. As a result, it is widely accepted that there is some truth in the quantity theory, although many believe that money-supply increases affect more than just the price level. Milton Friedman, the economist recognized as intellectual spokesman for monetarism, states that although there are significant and variable time lags between a change in the money supply and a resulting change in the price level, inflation "always and everywhere" is a monetary phenomenon.

The Steady-Money-Growth Policy

What guidelines does the quantity-of-money theory offer for monetary policy? Basically, the theory suggests that, in order to stabilize the price level, money-supply growth should be keyed to growth in production capacity. Following Friedman, the school of economic thought known as **monetarism** proposes that monetary policy should make no attempt to deal with short-term fluctuations in economic activity but instead should establish a fixed rate of increase for the money supply and stay with this rate year in and year out. The goal of the policy is long-term price stability.

Monetarism is a school of economic thought that proposes that monetary policy should not attempt to deal with short-term fluctuations in economic activity but should instead establish a fixed rate of increase for the money supply and stay with this rate.

The stable-money-growth policy suggests that the first task of the Federal Reserve is to estimate the growth rate in production capacity for the economy due to improvements in technology and increases in the labor force and the stock of physical and human capital. If the real growth in production capacity is expected to be 2½ percent a year, for example, and if the velocity of money is expected to be constant, monetary policy should aim at a steady 2½ percent a year increase in the money supply. In Figure 3 the rate of increase in the money supply shifts the aggregate-demand curve to the right each year by the same distance as that year's shift in the aggregate-supply curve, and the price level remains unchanged. Real GNP increases 2½ percent, from $1,000 billion to $1,025 billion, and the price level remains stable at an index number of 100.

The stable-money-growth policy suggests that the Federal Reserve should estimate the growth

---

FIGURE 3
The Steady-Money-Growth Policy

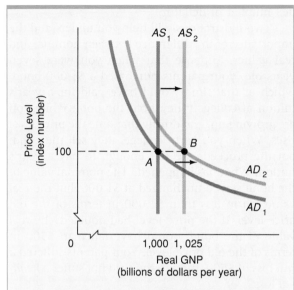

Initial macroeconomic equilibrium is at point *A*, with real GNP of $1,000 billion and a price level of 100. Growth in the production capacity of the economy shifts aggregate supply from *AS*₁ to *AS*₂, an increase of 2½ percent. The policy of steady money growth calls for a 2½ percent increase in aggregate demand, illustrated by the shift of the *AD*₁ curve to *AD*₂. If velocity is constant, this increase in aggregate demand is accomplished through a 2½ percent increase in the money supply. Macroeconomic equilibrium moves from point *A* to point *B*.

rate in production capacity for the economy and increase the money supply at the same rate.

The word *steady* is the key feature of the steady-money-growth policy. In other words, the rate of growth of the money supply should be the same, year in and year out, regardless of temporary fluctuations in actual output or the actual price level. According to its supporters, stabilizing the rate of money growth removes one source of uncertainty faced by participants in the economy's credit markets. In their view, the economy will operate more smoothly with the steady-money-

growth policy than with a monetary policy subject to change from day to day or month to month. They say that adjustments to temporary changes in real output and/or prices would take place quickly so that monetary changes would not be necessary.

According to its supporters, the economy operates more smoothly with a steady-money-growth policy than with a monetary policy subject to change from day to day or month to month.

The steady-money-growth policy does not require the rate of increase in the money supply to exactly match the rate of growth of real production capacity. In fact, the rate of money growth might be set slightly higher than the expected rate of growth of production capacity so that the measured price level would rise gradually. Advocates of the policy assert that this would cause no serious problems. All sectors of the economy soon would adapt to a steady and modest upward drift of the price level. Moreover, if price index numbers contain biases that ignore quality improvements, a modest upward drift of the measured price level might not be an actual increase in the quality-adjusted cost of living.

THE ROLE OF INTEREST RATES

The equation of exchange ($MV = PQ$) does not offer any guideline about what determines changes in the volume of production (Q) in the economy. It simply states that changes in MV must involve also changes in PQ. It is clear, therefore, that the quantity-of-money theory cannot tell us all we want to know about the relation of money to equilibrium national income and product. To gain an understanding of how the quantity of money affects real production, we must explore the **interest rate**—the annual payment for the use of funds, expressed as a percentage of the funds used. We must examine how interest rates are determined and how they affect production.

The interest rate is the annual payment for the use of funds, expressed as a percentage of the funds used.

You already have some understanding of how the rate of interest affects production. In Chapter 10, in the Keynesian model of income determination, the real interest rate appeared as a variable influencing the quantity of planned-investment purchases in the economy. As you recall, at lower real interest rates, the volume of planned-investment purchases was greater than at higher interest rates, *ceteris paribus*. So monetary policy can affect production in the economy (the Q in the equation of exchange) if it can change real interest rates.

Real and Nominal Values

In studying the relation between money, interest rates, and national income and product, it is essential to distinguish between real and nominal values. The distinction is especially important in connection with interest rates, since they are used in contracts that extend over considerable periods of time. With the passage of time, the price level may change so that, dollar for dollar, funds repaid may have a different purchasing power than the funds originally borrowed. Both lenders and borrowers are very concerned about such changes in the purchasing power of funds. They will surely want to distinguish between nominal values and real values. Therefore, in studying money and interest rates, we must also be clear about this distinction.

Nominal values are values that are stated or measured in terms of some monetary unit. In the United States, the monetary unit is the dollar. Thus, the nominal value of an item is the number of dollars that would be exchanged for it. Nominal values have *not* been adjusted for price-level changes by dividing them by an index number or deflator.

Real values are values that are stated or measured in terms of goods and services. The real value of an item is the quantity of goods and services that would be exchanged for it. A real value *has* been adjusted for price-level changes by applying an index number or deflator.

Two illustrations will help you understand the importance of the difference between nominal and real values. Suppose that when you were seven years old, your parents purchased a $1,000 bond, which at that time would have paid for a year's tuition at college. They hold the bond while you are growing up, and during that time the price level rises. When you go to college, they sell the bond, but the proceeds are not enough to pay a year's tuition. What has happened? The nominal value of the bond stayed unchanged at $1,000, but the real value fell to less than $1,000 in terms of the old price level. If the price level had doubled, the real value of the bond would have fallen to $500 in terms of the old price level. Your parents suffered a *real* loss of $500, though they did not suffer a *nominal* loss.

As another illustration, suppose you borrow $1,000 and promise to pay it back on some future date. The nominal value of the promise is clearly stated in terms of money. But the real (goods and services) value of the promise depends on the price level that will exist when you must pay the money. Since that time has not come yet, neither you nor the person to whom you make the promise can be entirely sure about its real value. If the price level rises, the real value will fall, and vice versa.

Nominal values are values that are stated or measured in terms of some monetary unit. Real values are values that are stated or measured in terms of goods and services; they are always adjusted for price-level changes.

Real and Nominal Interest Rates

There is a simple rule about the relation between real and nominal interest rates. This rule states that the difference is equal to the rate of change in the price level.[2] Here is an illustration. If the price level

---

2. When both inflation rates and interest rates are extremely high, some modification of this simple rule is needed. This refinement will be left for more advanced courses.

is *rising* by 5 percent annually, a nominal 12 percent interest rate is a real 7 percent interest rate and a nominal 9 percent interest rate is a real 4 percent interest rate. We simply subtract the inflation rate from the nominal interest rate to determine the real interest rate. Conversely, if the price level is *falling*, the real interest rate will be above the nominal interest rate. If the price level is falling by 2 percent a year, a nominal interest rate of 5 percent is a real interest rate of 7 percent. The logic behind these adjustments is that the dollars used to pay back a loan will have a different purchasing power from the dollars that were borrowed. If the price level is rising, the loan will be paid back in dollars that are worth less than those initially borrowed, thus reducing the real cost of borrowing and the real return to the lender. The real interest rate is below the nominal interest rate. If the price level is falling, the loan will be paid back in dollars that are worth more than those that were borrowed, thus increasing the real cost of borrowing and the real return to the lender. Here, the real interest rate is higher than the nominal interest rate.

When the lender-borrower agreement is negotiated, neither side can be certain about the price-level change that may actually take place during the term of the loan. Each must make a best guess. In other words, it is the *expected* rate of price-level change (inflation) that each party uses to determine the difference between the nominal and the real interest rate. Of course, the two parties may not, in their own minds, be using the same expected rate of price-level change. One or the other, or both, may prove to have been mistaken, with consequent unexpected gains or losses.

As we proceed now to examine how interest rates are determined, we will use the *real rate of interest* in explaining the demand and the supply of money. It is important to remember that this is not necessarily the same as the *nominal* rate of interest that would get written into contracts and reported in the press.

The difference between real and nominal interest rates is equal to the rate of change in the price level.

Loanable-Funds Markets

In the quantity-of-money approach to monetary policy, changes in the money supply are not used to influence interest rates in the economy. Instead, interest rates are determined solely by the interaction of borrowers and lenders in **loanable-funds markets,** which bring together those who wish to lend and those who wish to borrow funds. If monetary policy follows the steady-growth rule and money-supply changes keep pace with changes in production capacity of the economy, the interest rates determined in these markets are **real interest rates**—rates that reflect actual purchasing-power values.

Real interest rates are determined by the interaction of borrowers and lenders in loanable-funds markets.

Figure 4 illustrates a loanable-funds market. The horizontal axis shows the real (adjusted for price-level change) quantities of money demanded and supplied for loans. The vertical axis shows the real rate of interest. The supply curve represents the behavior of people who are willing to let others use part of their wealth in exchange for the payment of interest. It comes from both households and financial institutions. It reflects **time preferences** between using wealth for current consumption or saving it for future uses. The supply curve has a positive slope because, other things being equal, suppliers are willing to loan more money when real interest rates are high than when they are low.

The demand curve in the loanable-funds market illustrates the behavior of borrowers, including households, governments, and business firms. It shows the amounts that they are willing to borrow at various possible real interest rates, *ceteris paribus*. In the loanable-funds model, one of the main reasons for borrowing is to finance capital, such as plant and equipment to be used in production. The quantity of funds that firms are willing to borrow, at any given interest rate, depends on the expected profitability of using capital in production. The location of the demand curve is determined by forces that influence the expected profitability of capital

FIGURE 4
The Loanable-Funds Market

In the loanable-funds market, the supply curve represents the relationship between the real rate of interest and the amounts of money that households and financial institutions are willing to lend. Its location reflects the money supply and preferences between present use and future use of these funds. The demand curve represents the relationship between the real rate of interest and the amounts that borrowers are willing and able to borrow. Its location depends, among other things, on the expected profitability of capital goods. Governments, households, and business firms participate in the demand for loanable funds. At equilibrium, the real rate of interest balances the amount that lenders are willing to lend with the amount that borrowers are willing to borrow.

itself. Inventions, favorable government policies, and promising economic conditions shift this curve to the right. Conversely, forces that reduce expected profitability shift the curve to the left. The demand curve also reflects borrowing by consumers and governments that wish to purchase goods and services today but want to postpone payment until some future time.

The supply curve of the loanable-funds market has a positive slope because suppliers are willing to loan more money when real interest rates are high than when they are low. The demand curve shows the amounts borrowers are willing to borrow at various real interest rates.

Most economists agree that, in the long run, real interest rates are determined in the loanable-funds markets and that monetary policies have little long-term impact on these rates. The policies that do affect real interest rates in the long run are those that shift the demand or the supply curves in these markets. For example, policies that encourage saving and a preference for future consumption rather than present consumption shift the supply curve of loanable funds to the right, and, other things unchanged, lower real interest rates and increase the volume of saving and investment. Policies that increase the profitability of capital goods shift the demand curve for loanable funds to the right and, *ceteris paribus,* raise real interest rates and the volume of saving and investment.[3]

THE MONEY MARKET

The loanable-funds market just described presents a great amount of important information about lending and borrowing and the determination of real interest rates. It illustrates, for example, how the time preferences of wealth holders and the profit expectations of investors affect real interest rates and the quantity of borrowing and lending. Monetary variables, such as changes in the money supply, are among the factors affecting the supply curve in that market. Increases in the money supply may, at least for a time, shift the loanable-funds supply curve to the right, and decreases may shift it, at least for a time, to the left. However, to provide a clearer and more direct illustration of the interest-rate effects of monetary policy, it is useful to examine another market—the **money market.** The money market illustrates the concepts of demand and supply for money itself.

The economic concept of the money market is illustrated in Figure 5. The vertical axis shows the

3. A more complete explanation of the loanable-funds market is presented in microeconomics.

real rate of interest—the rate after adjustments for expected changes in the price level. The horizontal axis shows the real quantity of money demanded or supplied *as of any given point in time.* Thus, this axis is different from the horizontal axes on graphs showing demand and supply for ordinary goods and services, where the values reflect flows *over a period of time.* The horizontal axis shows the real quantity of money according to some accepted measure such as the quantity of M1 dollars divided by a price-level index number, such as the GNP deflator. Amounts on this axis represent the real quantities of money that are demanded as an asset to be held as a form of wealth. The notion of money as an asset is important in understanding the money market.

The money market treats money itself as a commodity subject to the concepts of supply and demand.

The Demand-for-Money Curve

The demand-for-money curve is the graphic representation of the statement that the quantity of money demanded as an asset *depends on* the rate of interest, that is $QD = f(i)$, *ceteris paribus,* where QD is the quantity of money demanded as an asset and i is the rate of interest. In explaining the demand-for-money curve, economists consider the speculative demand, the transactions demand, and the precautionary demand for holding money. We shall describe each of these and explain how they help in understanding the slope and the location of the demand-for-money curve.

The quantity of money demanded as an asset depends on the rate of interest: $QD = f(i)$.

Speculative Demand Speculative demand is mainly responsible for the slope of the demand-for-money curve. To understand this point, you must understand what speculation is and how money can be used for this purpose.

FIGURE 5
The Money Market

The vertical axis shows the real rate of interest—the rate *after* adjustment for changes in the price level. The horizontal axis shows the *real* quantity of money—the nominal quantity of money divided by a price-index number such as the GNP deflator. This axis shows quantities of money demanded and supplied at a given time as an asset, or form of wealth. The money-supply curve (*MS*) has a positive slope and its location may be influenced by monetary policy. The demand-for-money curve (*MD*) has a negative slope and its location may be shifted by changes in the level of income and wealth in the economy.

Most people think of speculation as the holding of risky assets like oil wells or uranium mines. Actually, **speculation** means taking actions based on expectations of *future changes* in the market values of assets. Imagine that you are wealthy (not an unpleasant thought) and that you want to manage your wealth to make it grow as much as you can. Managing your wealth means that you are placing it in money, stocks, bonds, real estate, and so on, depending on which forms promise you the best return.

For speculative purposes, the most important type of return on your wealth is not the rate of interest you can obtain but the gain that you can make from changes in the market value of whatever types of assets you have chosen as wealth forms. For example, if you expect the market value of bonds, stocks, or real estate to rise in the future, you will place your wealth in these promising forms and demand very little, if any, money for speculative purposes. On the other hand, if you expect the market value of bonds, stocks, or real estate to fall in the future, you will sell these assets and hold cash. In this case, you have a **speculative demand for money.**

Speculation means taking actions based on expectations of future changes in the market values of assets.

The next step in understanding the demand-for-money curve is to see how anticipated gains or losses on nonmoney assets are related to the real rate of interest, which is the variable on the vertical axis of the money-market graph. An inverse relationship exists between the rate of interest prevailing at a given time and the likelihood that the values of stocks, bonds, and other nonmoney assets will rise or fall in the future. This relationship is derived from the formula that converts a stream of expected future income into a present value. The standard formula for calculating the *present value* (*PV*) of income to be received in some future year is

$$PV = \frac{\text{expected income}_t}{(1 + i)^t}$$

where i is the rate of interest, and t is the number of years before the income is received. If we assume that the same amount of income is expected each year and that the stream of income will continue indefinitely, the present value formula reduces to

$$\text{present value} = \frac{\text{expected annual income flow}}{\text{rate of interest}}$$

Consider, for example, a nonmoney asset that will pay net income of $100 a year indefinitely. If the rate of interest that can be earned on similar wealth forms is 10 percent a year, the present value of this nonmoney asset will be $1,000—that is, $100/0.10. A person would not pay more than $1,000 because he or she would then earn a rate of return of less than the going rate of 10 percent. Some other form of wealth would be more attrac-

tive. Similarly, the seller would not accept less than $1,000.

According to the present value formula, when interest rates are low, the present value of any given expected annual income flow is high.

Let us apply this idea to our demand-for-money curve. The real quantity of money demanded for speculation will be large when real interest rates are considered "low." According to the present value formula, when interest rates are low, the present value of any given expected annual income flow is high, other things being equal. For example, if the interest rate were 3 percent, our hypothetical nonmoney asset earning $100 per year would have a present value of $3,333, that is $100/0.03. When the interest rate is "low" and the present value of nonmoney assets therefore are "high," speculators will sell the nonmoney assets because they expect their prices (present values) to fall as interest rates return to higher levels. In other words, speculators will hold money, speculating on the coming price decrease of nonmoney assets. On the other hand, the quantity of money demanded as a speculative asset will be small when interest rates are considered high because the present value of nonmoney assets then will be considered low. At an interest rate of 15 percent, for example, the asset bringing a net $100 a year will have a present value of only $667, that is $100/0.15. Speculators will hold nonmoney assets, expecting to profit when interest rates fall and the present values of these assets rise. In this way, the speculative demand for money assets provides a strong reason for the demand-for-money curve having a negative slope.

There is an inverse relationship between the real rate of interest prevailing at a given time and the likelihood that the real values of stocks, bonds, and other nonmoney assets will rise or fall in the future.

The speculative demand for money is sometimes called the **liquidity** demand for money. It is the "spendability" of an asset—that is, the ease with which it can be used in exchange or converted into a form that can be used in exchange. Cash and checkable accounts are fully liquid. They can be used directly in exchange for anything a person wants to buy. The liquidity demand for money simply means that people want to hold it so that they will be in a position to take advantage of opportunities to purchase other assets when favorable terms arise. When people hold money because they expect the prices of nonmoney assets to be lower in the future, their demand for liquidity is speculative.

The speculative demand for money is sometimes called the liquidity demand for money.
Liquidity is the ease with which an asset can be used in exchange or converted into a form that can be used in exchange.

Transactions and Precautionary Demands The **transactions demand for money** arises because people want to hold some of their wealth in a form that is convenient for day-to-day buying and selling of goods and services. The **precautionary demand for money** arises because people want to be prepared for unexpected changes in the pattern of their receipts and expenditures.

The transactions demand for money arises because people want to hold some of their wealth in a form that is convenient for day-to-day buying and selling of goods and services.

The precautionary demand for money arises because people want to be prepared for unexpected changes in the pattern of their receipts and expenditures.

The role of the interest rate in determining the quantity of money demanded for these purposes can be understood by using the concept of *opportunity cost*. The basic point is that people who hold money receive relatively little interest return on this portion of their wealth. Cash earns no interest at all and checkable accounts earn relatively low rates of interest. The amount of interest earning that is given up is the opportunity cost of holding money instead of nonmoney assets. It follows that the opportunity cost of holding money is greater when the rate of interest is high than when the rate of interest is low.

Economists expect that less money will be demanded for transactions and precautionary purposes when real interest rates are high and that more money will be demanded when real interest rates are low, other things being equal. In other words, the transactions and the precautionary demands for money impart a negative slope to the demand-for-money curve, just as the speculative motive did. In fact, opportunity cost reasoning also applies to the speculative demand for money, giving further support for the negative slope of the demand-for-money curve.

The opportunity cost of holding money is greater when the real rate of interest is high than when it is low. Less money will be demanded for transactions and precautionary purposes when real interest rates are high; more money will be demanded when real interest rates are low.

Shifting the Demand-for-Money Curve The demand-for-money curve may shift when there is a change in some variable other than the real rate of interest. There are many variables that might do this. Changes in the amount of wealth, for example, are expected to affect all three of the demands for money assets. When wealth increases, these demands for money are expected to increase, and when wealth decreases, these demands are expected to decrease. In macroeconomic analysis, one of the most important shift variables for the demand-for-money curve is the level of national income and product itself. When national income and product increases, the curve is expected to shift to the right and when it decreases, the curve is expected to shift to the left.

Changes in national income and product affect all of the demands for money, but their effects on the transactions demand is especially apparent. For most people, the transactions demand for money arises because receipts and expenditures are not perfectly timed with each other. For example, suppose that you receive $700 every two weeks and that you spend $50 every day. When you receive your pay, you have $700 in money. At the end of the first day you have $650, at the end of the next day you have $600, and at the end of the fourteenth day you have no money. On the average, your money holding is equal to half of your pay, that is, $350. Now suppose that your productivity improves and you get a 10 percent raise to $770 every two weeks and that you increase your spending also by 10 percent to $55 per day. At the end of the first day after you receive your pay, you have $715 ($770 − $55 = $715) and at the end of the fourteenth day you again have no money. In this case, your average money holding is $385 (half of $770), which is 10 percent greater than in the previous case. The 10 percent change in income has led to a 10 percent change in the transactions demand for money. In Figure 5, this change would appear as a shift (change in the location) of the demand-for-money curve because it was not the result of a change in the real rate of interest but was due to a change in some other variable—in this case, income. We conclude that income changes will shift the demand-for-money curve in the same direction as the change in income—that is, to the right when income increases and to the left when income decreases.

This example of the transactions demand shows no precautionary demand for money because we assume that you allow your money holding to fall all the way to nothing just before the next payday. It is more reasonable to expect that you would keep some "back-up" money on hand just in case the paycheck was late or some unusual expense, such as an illness, or buying opportunity, such as a sale, should come along. In our illustration, if you keep a $100 backup, your average money holding would have been $450 when your income was $700, and $485 when your income was $770. In each case, you would have had a $100 cash balance on hand just before you received your next pay. However, it seems reasonable that an increase in your income and in the volume of your routine transactions would also lead you to keep a larger backup of money. In this

way, changing the level of income is a shift variable for the precautionary demand for money as well.

Variables other than the real rate of interest, such as changes in the amount of wealth and changes in national income and product, can shift the demand-for-money curve.

The Money-Supply Curve

The money-supply curve (*MS*) in Figure 5 shows the relationship between the real rate of interest and the real quantity of M1 money in the economy. The curve is drawn with a positive slope because, in the deposit-expansion process, banks will work more eagerly to expand the money supply when real interest rates are high than when they are low. This is because the profitability of loaning money will be greater when real interest rates are high, other things being equal, and banks will hold smaller amounts of "desired" excess reserves. Therefore, with a given monetary base and reserve requirement, the amount of money that is supplied will be greater when real interest rates are high.

Banks will work more eagerly to expand the money supply when real interest rates are high because the profitability of loaning money will be greater.

The location of the money-supply curve is very important to the theory of interest-rate determination. The monetary instruments of the Federal Reserve (open market buying and selling, reserve requirements, and discount rates) shift this curve either to the left by restrictive policies or to the right by expansionary policies.

Equilibrium in the Money Market

In Figure 5, the point where the *MD* curve crosses the *MS* curve identifies the equilibrium condition. At the equilibrium real interest rate, *i*, the amount of money actually supplied is equal to the amount demanded. Given the location of these curves, no other real interest rate could bring about that balance.

At the equilibrium real interest rate (i in Figure 5) the quantity of money actually supplied equals the quantity demanded.

The equilibrating action of the interest rate becomes clear when we examine what would happen at interest rates above or below the equilibrium rate. Let us assume that i in Figure 5 represents a real interest rate of 5 percent. Consider a non-money asset that pays $100 a year to its owner. At the 5 percent rate of interest, the present value of this asset is $2,000 (that is, $100/0.05). Now think about what would happen at a real interest rate of 7 percent. At this higher interest rate, the quantity of money supplied is greater than the quantity demanded. Speculators use the extra money to bid for

the nonmoney asset, which has a value of $1,428.57 (that is, $100/0.07) when the interest rate is 7 percent. These bids push the price of the nonmoney asset upward. But when the price rises above $1,428.57, the yield, or rate of return, on the asset falls to less than 7 percent, since the asset still promises to pay only $100 per year to its owner. What this means is that no interest rate other than i (5 percent in our numerical illustration) can be sustained, given the locations of the MS and MD curves in the money market assumed for this illustration. In order for equilibrium to exist, the rate of interest in the money market must correspond with the yield, or rate of return, of the nonmoney assets that are alternative assets for holding wealth.

In order for equilibrium to exist, the rate of interest in the money market must correspond with the yield, or rate of return, of the nonmoney assets that are alternative assets for holding wealth.

MONETARY INSTRUMENTS IN ACTION: A NO-INFLATION SCENARIO

We will now examine how the Federal Reserve System can influence real interest rates by shifting the MS curve in the money market. Figure 6 illustrates an expansionary central bank action. We begin with equilibrium at the intersection of the MD curve with the MS_1 curve, with real interest rate i_1 and the real quantity of money M_1. Next, we assume that the central bank takes some expansionary action, such as might be carried out through open market purchases, lower reserve requirements, and/or lower discount rates. If this leads to no expectation of any change in the price level, the money-supply curve will shift to the right (from MS_1 to MS_2). *The assumption that no price-level change is expected is critical in shifting this curve.* If no price-level rise is expected, each dollar of the M1 money recorded on the horizontal axis keeps its original purchasing power. So an increase in the

FIGURE 6
Expansionary Monetary Policy (a No-Inflation Scenario)

If people do not expect any change in the price level, expansionary Federal Reserve action can shift the MS curve to the right from MS_1 to MS_2 as illustrated by the arrow. This will cause real interest rates to fall from i_1 to i_2. Contractionary action would shift the MS curve to the left and raise real interest rates.

number of these dollars is an increase in the real money supply. As a result, the real interest rate falls from i_1 to i_2. If, instead, the Federal Reserve Board wanted to raise real interest rates, the money supply would be reduced, shifting the MS curve to the left.

The Federal Reserve System can influence real interest rates by shifting the MS curve in the money market. The curve can be shifted to the right by expansionary actions (assuming no price-level changes are anticipated) and to the left by contractionary actions.

The process of moving to the new equilibrium is as follows. When the money supply is increased, people find that they have more money assets (and less nonmoney assets) than they want at the i_1 rate of interest. To adjust to this new situation, people

bid on such nonmoney assets as stocks, bonds, or real estate. Their bids push up the market prices of these assets, and, according to the present value formula, the rise in their prices leads to a drop in the rate of interest. On the other hand, if the money supply is reduced, shifting the MS curve to the left, wealth holders will find themselves with less money than they desire at the initial interest rate. In order to hold more wealth in the form of money, they will offer to sell stocks, bonds, real estate, and so forth. These sale offers will lower market prices for these assets and cause interest rates to rise.

Indirect Transmission

When monetary instruments shift the real money-supply curve and lower the real interest rate, as shown in Figure 6, how are the effects transmitted to the equilibrium level of real national income and product?

FIGURE 7
Transmission from Change in Real Money Supply to Change in Equilibrium Real National Income and Product

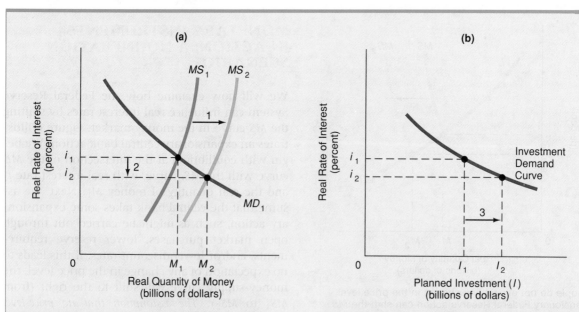

Panel (a) shows how an increase in the real money supply shifts the MS curve to the right (step 1) and causes a reduction in the real rate of interest (step 2). Panel (b) shows how this decrease in the real interest rate causes an increase in the volume of planned

investment (step 3). Panel (c) shows how an increase in planned investment, other things being equal, causes an upward shift in the $C + I + G + X - Im$ curve (step 4). This shift in planned expenditure brings an increase in equilibrium real national income and

The **indirect transmission mechanism** uses the Keynesian model and stresses the importance of planned investment. It is illustrated in Figure 7, which combines the interest-rate-determination model (which you have just studied) with the planned-investment and the Keynesian-cross models. Here is how the connections work. The Federal Reserve undertakes expansionary action by buying bonds in the open market, by reducing reserve requirements, or by reducing discount rates. This, according to the "no-inflation scenario," shifts the real money-supply curve in panel (a) from MS_1 to MS_2 (step 1). The real rate of interest falls from i_1 to i_2 (step 2). These lower real interest rates affect the volume of planned investment, as shown in panel (b). The original volume of planned investment was I_1, corresponding to the original rate of interest of i_1. When interest rates fall to i_2, the volume of planned investment rises to I_2 (step 3). Planned investment is part of total planned expenditure $(C + I + G + X - Im)$. Panel (c) shows the effect of the change in planned investment on the equilibrium level of real national income and product. When the volume of planned investment rises, other things being equal, the total planned-expenditure curve shifts from $C + I_1 + G + X - Im$ to $C + I_2 + G + X - Im$ (step 4), and the equilibrium level of real national income and product rises from Y_1 to Y_2 through the operation of the multiplier process (step 5).

In the indirect transmission mechanism, an increase in the real money supply leads to lower real interest rates and a larger flow of planned investment which raises the equilibrium level of real national income and product.

The "no inflation" assumption is very important in the transmission displayed in Figure 7. This is because the variable displayed on the horizontal axis of the money-market graph, panel (a), is the *real* quantity of money, that is, the *nominal* quantity divided by a price-level index number. If the price-level rises, this index number becomes larger with the result that the *real* quantity of money shrinks. Therefore, if inflation takes place, the real money-supply curve shifts to the left. In panel (a), the MS_2 curve would shift back toward the MS_1 curve. Real interest rates would not fall as much as shown in panel (a), and all of the subsequent effects on planned investment and on the equilibrium level of real national income and product would be correspondingly reduced. The effectiveness of the expansionary monetary policy would be reduced. In an extreme case, inflation could cancel the entire impact of the expansionary monetary policy on real interest rates and real national income and product. Its only effect would be on the price level. If expansionary monetary policy triggers an *expectation* that the price level will rise, nominal interest rates will rise immediately, and little or no reduction in real interest rates will take place.

(c)

product from Y_1 to Y_2 (step 5). The three panels together illustrate a transmission mechanism linking monetary changes to changes in equilibrium real national income and product.

If expansionary monetary policy triggers an expectation that the price level will rise,

---

nominal interest rates will rise immediately, and little or no reduction in real interest rates will take place.

Direct Transmission

Many economists say that monetary instruments do not have to work through the complicated process of interest-rate changes, followed by planned-investment changes, and finally by changes in national income and product. They contend that changes in the money supply also work directly through household budgets and consumption expenditure. For example, if Federal Reserve Banks purchase securities in the open market, the households that sell the securities receive money, which they spend directly for consumption goods and services. The economy can expand without going through the step of an interest-rate change. This is called the **direct transmission mechanism.**

Monetary instruments can also work through the direct transmission mechanism: money-supply changes can directly affect household spending without going through the complicated process of interest-rate changes followed by planned-investment changes, followed by changes in national income and product.

Feedback to the Demand for Money

The transmission mechanism shown in Figure 7 does not tell the complete story of the effects of monetary actions. When the level of national income and product changes, as it did in step 5, there will be a feedback effect in the money market. This feedback will counteract some of the initial effects of the monetary action. It operates through *shifts* in the demand-for-money curve.

When you studied the speculative, transactions, and precautionary demands for money, you learned that changes in income and wealth shift

the demand-for-money curve. Therefore the rise in national income and product from Y_1 to Y_2 (step 5 in Figure 7) leads to a shift in the demand-for-money curve. With higher incomes, people want more money because they are engaging in more transactions. This feedback shifts the demand-for-money curve to the right and increases the rate of interest to some level higher than i_2 in Figure 7. This rise partly offsets the drop in interest rates from the original policy action of the Federal Reserve. The rise in the interest rate carries over to panel (b) and partly offsets the rise in planned investment from the first round of the process. Finally, in panel (c), the reduction in the volume of planned investment caused by the feedback effect brings a downward shift in the total-planned-expenditure curve, from $C + I_2 + G + X - Im$, and a drop in the equilibrium level of national income and product. What happens is that some of the new money that pushed interest rates down initially is now being used in hand-to-hand circulation and is no longer being used in bidding for securities and other assets.

The feedback process repeats itself, in ever-weakening rounds, until the national income and product reaches a new equilibrium, which will lie somewhere between Y_1 and Y_2 in Figure 7.

When the level of national income and product changes, there will be a feedback effect in the money market that will counteract some of the initial effects of the monetary action.

Are Monetary Instruments Strong or Weak?

According to the model illustrated in Figure 7, which assumes that money supply changes do not trigger inflationary expectations, the power of monetary policy—its ability to change the volume of national income and product—depends on the importance of the interest rate in changing the quantity of money demanded and the volume of planned-investment expenditure. In other words, the power of monetary instruments depends on the responsiveness of the quantity of money demanded and the quantity of planned investment demanded to changes in the rate of interest.[4]

The power of monetary instruments depends on the responsiveness of the quantity of money demanded and of the quantity of planned investment demanded to changes in the rate of interest.

The Responsiveness of the Quantity of Money Demanded   Figure 8 illustrates a shift of the money-supply curve from MS_1 to MS_2. It has two demand-for-money curves, one called "more responsive" and the other called "less responsive." To understand the issue, start at point A, where equilibrium would exist between money-supply curve MS_1 and either of the two demand-for-money curves. Next, shift the money-supply curve to the right, from MS_1 to MS_2, to represent an expansionary application of monetary instruments. How great a change will take place in the rate of interest? The "less responsive" demand-for-money curve suggests a substantial drop in the interest rate, from i_1 to i_3, as shown at point B. But the "more responsive" demand-for-money curve suggests a smaller interest-rate decrease, from i_1 to only i_2, as shown at point C.

The lower the degree of responsiveness of the quantity of money demanded to changes in the interest rate, the more powerful is monetary policy, *ceteris paribus*. Shifts in the money-supply curve bring great changes in interest rates. But if the quantity of money demanded is highly responsive to changes in interest rates, shifts in the money-supply curve will have less influence on interest rates. Increases in the quantity of money are simply absorbed into greater money holdings. A flat demand-for-money curve illustrates what is called a **liquidity trap.** This is a problem mainly at very low interest rates (and very high asset prices) when people hold large amounts of money waiting for these asset prices to fall (and for interest rates to

4. Students who have studied microeconomics will recognize that the responsiveness of the quantity demanded to a change in price is the economic concept of *elasticity*. We use the term "responsiveness" here because many students study macroeconomics before they study microeconomics.

FIGURE 8
The Responsiveness of the Quantity of Money Demanded to Changes in the Rate of Interest

From an initial equilibrium at A, a shift in the money-supply curve from MS_1 to MS_2 lowers the equilibrium real interest rate to i_3 if the quantity of money demanded is "less responsive" to real interest rate changes (see point B), but only to real interest rate i_2 if the quantity of money demanded is "more responsive" to interest rate changes (see point C).

rise). Economists disagree about how important it has been in the past or may be in the future.

The less responsive the quantity of money demanded to changes in the rate of interest, the more effective monetary instruments will be.

The Responsiveness of Planned Investment Expenditure   The second issue about the strength or weakness of monetary instruments relates to the planned-investment-demand curve. To understand this question, look at Figure 9. This figure shows two planned-investment-demand curves, one labeled "more responsive" and the other labeled "less responsive." Consider what happens as a result of a fall in the rate of interest from i_1 to i_2. According to the more responsive demand curve, many potential investments become profitable at

FIGURE 9

The Responsiveness of Planned-Investment Expenditure to Changes in the Rate of Interest

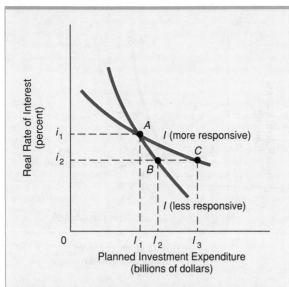

From an initial equilibrium at point *A*, with real interest rate i_1 and planned-investment expenditure of I_1 a fall in the rate of interest to i_2 results in a small increase in planned-investment expenditure (from I_1 to I_2) to point *B*. Planned-investment expenditure is relatively unresponsive ("less responsive"). But the same drop in the interest rate results in a large increase in planned-investment expenditure (from I_1 to I_3) to point *C* if the planned-investment expenditure is more responsive.

Monetary instruments are more powerful the greater the responsiveness of planned-investment expenditure to changes in the interest rate.

this lower interest rate, and the quantity of planned investment will increase from I_1 to I_3, as indicated by point *C*. But the less responsive demand curve shows a smaller increase in planned investment, from I_1 only to I_2, as indicated by point *B*.

The actual degrees of responsiveness of planned-investment expenditure depends on conditions in the economy. If interest costs are only a small part of the total costs of investment projects or if only a small backlog of such projects exists, the quantity demanded will be relatively unresponsive to interest rate changes. This may be true in the short term. A longer-term point of view usually sees a larger backlog of investment projects and finds interest costs to be a significant part of their costs. This view expects a more responsive demand for planned-investment expenditure.

SHORT-RUN MONETARY POLICY

In spite of the prescriptions of Milton Friedman and other monetarist economists, monetary instruments are, in practice, used in efforts to moderate short-term fluctuations in the economy. These "activist" monetary policies are based on the proposition that monetary policy does influence real interest rates, at least temporarily, and can be used to stabilize the economy. In these applications, policymakers must consider changes in money velocity and must decide whether to counteract or accommodate short-run fluctuations in economic activity.

Changes in Money Velocity

The long-run velocity of money is determined by the basic institutional structures of the economy, such as how frequently people receive paychecks. When pay is received frequently, a given stock of money works harder and circulates faster, so velocity goes up. If people are paid less frequently, velocity is lower. However, changes in these institutional patterns take place slowly and are not critical for short-run monetary policy.

Short-run changes in the velocity of money also occur and are important for short-run monetary policy. When velocity increases, a given stock of money works harder, and the result is like an increase in the quantity of money. Similarly, a decrease in money velocity has the same effect as decreasing the quantity of money. If the goal is to have a steady rate of change in the product of M and V, increases in V must be offset by decreases in M, and vice versa. Therefore, monetary policymakers must recognize and respond to short-run changes in velocity.

> **When the velocity of money increases, a given stock of money works harder, and the result is like an increase in the quantity of money. A decrease in money velocity has the same effect as decreasing the quantity of money.**

What variables influence short-run velocity? One important variable is the optimism or pessimism of the public about their economic future. When people are optimistic, they tend to spend money freely and velocity rises. When they are pessimistic, they tend to hold money longer and velocity falls. These attitudinal changes tend to average out over longer time periods, but short-run monetary policy attempts to compensate for them. For example, fear of impending recession typically reduces money velocity and reduces the effective money combination of M times V. In effect, this is equivalent to a restrictive monetary policy and increases the danger of recession. Therefore, short-run monetary policymakers attempt to counteract such short-run reductions in velocity by increasing, temporarily, the rate of money growth.

The opposite situation arises when velocity increases because of public optimism or perhaps because of fear of impending inflation. Rising velocity, other things unchanged, parallels an expansionary monetary policy and can increase the likelihood of inflation. Again, short-run monetary policymakers attempt to compensate by lowering the rate of growth in the money supply.

> **Short-run velocity is affected by the optimism or pessimism of the public about their economic future. Fear of impending recession reduces money velocity, while optimism increases it.**

Changes in the operating procedures of the economy's financial institutions affect velocity and are especially troublesome for monetary policy. For example, computers and telecommunications technology dramatically increase the speed with which balances can be transferred from one account to another. Speedier handling of financial transactions increases velocity. But, more critical for monetary policy, rapid transfers of balances from one type of account to another cause changes in *measured* velocity even if no change in *actual* velocity is taking place. If interest rates increase and balances counted as part of M2 experience larger interest-rate increases than balances counted only in M1, account owners respond by transferring funds out of M1 and into M2 balances. Measured M1 velocity rises and measured M2 velocity decreases, *ceteris paribus*. Moreover, if balances are shifted to wealth forms not in any of the various money supply measures, all measured velocities increase. In the 1980s, computer and telecommunications innovations, along with deregulation of financial institutions, greatly complicated the practical application of monetary policy. Money managers, trying to adjust the money supply for changes in velocity, could not be sure that they had accurate measures of velocity.

> **Advances in computer and telecommunications technology have greatly complicated the practical application of monetary policy by making it difficult to measure money velocity accurately.**

Figure 10 shows the velocity of money in the United States from 1960 through 1988 as measured by dividing nominal GNP by the M1 and the M2 quantities of money for each year. M1 velocity increased substantially over this period, and M2 velocity, although reasonably stable in the long run, showed important fluctuations from year to year.

A Policy of Accommodation

The monetary policy of **accommodation** attempts to shift the money-supply curve back and forth in order to offset shifts in the demand for money, thereby stabilizing the rate of interest. Accommodation is illustrated in Figure 11, which shows the money market. In this figure, the demand-for-money curve shifts to the right from MD_1 to MD_2 (arrow 1) due, for example, to an expansion in the volume of economic activity in the economy. Without an increase in the money supply, the equilibrium rate of interest rises from i_1 at point A to i_2 at point B and moderates the economic

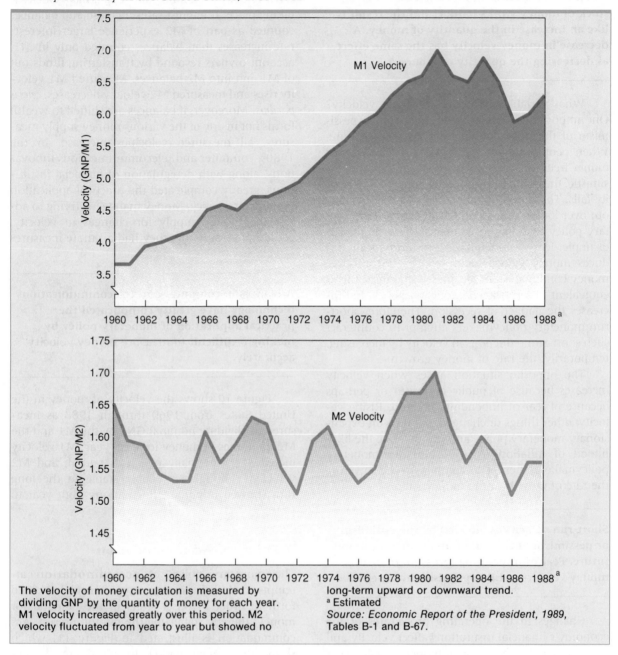

FIGURE 10
Velocity of Money in the United States, 1960–1988

M1 Velocity

M2 Velocity

The velocity of money circulation is measured by dividing GNP by the quantity of money for each year. M1 velocity increased greatly over this period. M2 velocity fluctuated from year to year but showed no long-term upward or downward trend.
[a] Estimated
Source: Economic Report of the President, 1989, Tables B-1 and B-67.

expansion, since higher interest rates reduce the volume of planned business investment and household purchases. The policy of accommodation is represented by the shift of the money-supply curve from MS_1 to MS_2 (arrow 2). With this accommodating increase in the money supply, the new equilibrium is at point C and the interest rate is prevented from rising and exerting its moderating pressure on the economic expansion. In other words, the monetary policy of accommodation stabilizes interest rates rather than the volume of economic activity in the economy.

An important aspect of the policy of accommodation involves the government's sales of securities to finance its budget deficit. Other things being equal, these sales drive up interest rates and crowd out private investment. By purchasing government securities in the open market, the Federal Reserve System can reduce this upward pressure on interest rates. In this way, monetary policy accommodates not only economic expansion but also the sale of government securities.

The policy of accommodation attempts to shift the money-supply curve back and forth to offset shifts in the demand for money.

Accommodation stabilizes interest rates rather than the volume of economic activity in the economy. Accommodation may be used to help the government's sales of securities to finance its budget deficit.

The question of whether or not to follow a policy of accommodation can lead to conflict between the monetary authorities of the Federal Reserve System and the fiscal authorities of the White House and Congress, where budget decisions are made. Expansionary fiscal policy can be defeated or greatly weakened if the monetary authorities refuse to accommodate it by increasing the money supply. In the same way, restrictive fiscal policies can be defeated or weakened if the monetary authorities refuse to accommodate by reducing the growth rate of the money supply. Heated discussions arise about whether the Board of Governors, whose members are appointed rather than elected and who are or have been closely connected with banking, should have such great power. On the other hand, the tension between fiscal and monetary authorities can be viewed as another of the checks and balances that are part of the U.S. government system. Each side holds something of a veto power over the other.

Judgment-Based Monetary Policy

William McChesney Martin, Jr., who served as chairman of the Board of Governors from 1951 to 1970 (the longest tenure in the history of the

Board), once characterized Federal Reserve policy during his term as "leaning against the wind," meaning that monetary policy occupied a middle ground between a steady-money-growth policy and a policy of accommodation. When the economy was in the expansion phase of an economic fluctuation, the expansion would be only partially accommodated. Interest rates would be allowed to rise some, but partial accommodation would moderate the increase in an effort to extend the expansion of the economy. On the other hand, in the contraction phase of a fluctuation, the growth of the money supply would be accelerated, pushing interest rates downward in order to stimulate the economy and moderate the contraction of economic activity.

FIGURE 11
Accommodation

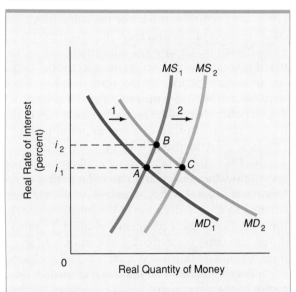

Accommodation means shifting the money-supply curve so that shifts in the demand-for-money curve do not cause changes in the rate of interest. In this diagram, we assume that the demand-for-money curve has shifted to the right, from MD_1 to MD_2 (arrow 1), perhaps because of an increase in national income and product. Without accommodation, equilibrium would move from point A to point B, and the rate of interest would rise from i_1 to i_2. However, accommodation, accomplished by shifting the money-supply curve to the right, from MS_1 to MS_2 (arrow 2), moves equilibrium to point C and prevents a rise in the rate of interest.

When Chairman Martin assumed his post the Federal Reserve System had freed itself of the obligation to follow the strict policy of accommodation adopted in the emergency period of World War II. He left the Board in 1970 after it had pursued severely restrictive policies attempting to limit inflationary pressures unleashed by the combination of war in Vietnam and domestic government spending under the Great Society program of President Johnson's administration.

During the 1970s, contractionary supply shocks caused both inflationary pressures and high levels of unemployment. Monetary policy partially accommodated ("validated") the higher price level by increasing the rate of growth in the money supply in an attempt to moderate the unemployment consequences of the shocks. Nominal interest rates (which include an upward adjustment for anticipated inflation) were used as an operational target for monetary policy. Rising price levels pushed nominal interest rates upward, and the accommodation policy then called for further increases in the money supply. Instead of lowering nominal interest rates, these increases led to further inflation.

In 1979, the Federal Reserve abandoned the accommodation policy and entered a period of restrictive monetary policy. This policy change contributed to a rapid decrease in the inflation rate. In the mid-1980s the Fed again modified its procedures, directing open market operations to target their actions on borrowed reserves. Many observers believed that monetary policy had turned, once again, in the direction of accommodation, because increases in borrowing through the discount procedure usually go along with higher nominal interest rates. Both borrowed-reserve targeting and interest-rate targeting lend themselves to a policy of accommodation, since stabilizing borrowed reserves tends also to stabilize interest rates.

MONETARY POLICY AND INFLATIONARY EXPECTATIONS

Economic models of **inflationary expectations** attempt to explain how anticipated changes in the price level affect decisions. Such expectations are especially important for transactions that involve commitments that extend over a period of time. For example, when higher prices are anticipated, consumers tend to make planned durable goods purchases sooner than they otherwise would in order to obtain desired goods before their prices go up. Similarly, business firms acquire capital equipment sooner, other things equal, in an atmosphere of anticipated price increases than in a stable price atmosphere.

To explain how inflationary expectations are related to monetary policy, we begin by assuming that the Federal Reserve System has carried out an expansion of the money supply in an effort to lower real interest rates and thereby increase planned-investment expenditure and the equilibrium level of national income and product. (This procedure was illustrated in Figures 6 and 7). We also assume, however, that this expansionary monetary policy triggers inflationary expectations, that is, people conclude that the money supply increase will drive the price level upward. What effect will these expectations have on nominal and real interest rates, on the volume of planned-investment expenditure, and on the equilibrium level of national income and product?

Inflationary Expectations and the Loanable-Funds Market

Figure 12 illustrates a loanable-funds market. In order to illustrate inflationary expectations, the vertical axis shows *nominal* interest rates, that is, the interest rates actually written into borrowing and lending contracts. In the absence of inflationary expectations, there is no difference between the

FIGURE 12
Inflationary Expectations in the Loanable-Funds Market

The quantities of loanable funds supplied and demanded are recorded on the horizontal axis, and the nominal (not the real) interest rate appears on the vertical axis. Point A represents the equilibrium before inflationary expectations arise. The nominal rate of interest is 6 percent and, since there is no inflation expected, the real interest rate also is 6 percent. Inflationary expectations cause the supply curve to shift to the left, from S_1 to S_2, as lenders require a higher nominal interest rate in order to be compensated for the loss in real value of their funds during the term of the loans. Inflationary expectations also cause the demand curve to shift to the right, from D_1 to D_2, because lenders expect to repay loans in dollars with less purchasing power than those originally borrowed. Thus, with inflationary expectations, equilibrium is at point B, the nominal rate of interest has risen by the appropriate percentage point rate of the expected price level increase (from 6 percent to slightly more than 9 percent if the expected rate of inflation is 3 percent), and the real interest rate has remained unchanged.

nominal and the real interest rate, and Figure 12 would be equivalent to Figure 4, which used real interest rates on its vertical axis. But, as we shall see, when inflationary expectations arise, nominal interest rates are no longer equal to real interest rates. Let us see why.

We begin with equilibrium at point A, with a nominal interest rate of 6 percent and $1,000 million of loanable funds demanded and supplied. We now inject an expectation that the price level is going to increase at the rate of 3 percent a year. Consider first a lender deciding whether or not to loan $100 at the nominal interest rate of 6 percent. At this interest rate, at the end of the first year of the loan, this lender would have $106. However, if the price level rises by 3 percent, this $106 will have a *real* value of only $102.91, calculated by dividing $106 by the price index number of 1.03, which reflects the 3 percent increase in the price level. Therefore, in *real* terms, the lender will have earned slightly less than 3 percent interest, rather than the 6 percent indicated by the nominal interest rate. The *real* rate of interest has turned out to be lower than the *nominal* rate by approximately 3 percentage points, which is the anticipated rate of inflation.

If the lender desires to obtain a *real* rate of return of 6 percent—the rate obtainable before inflationary expectations arose—he or she must insist on a higher *nominal* rate of interest. How much higher must this rate be? In order to have a *real* $106 at the end of one year, the lender must, at that time, have a *nominal* $109.18, determined by multiplying $106 times 1.03, reflecting the increase in the price level. Therefore, in order to receive a *real* return of 6 percent, the lender must obtain a *nominal* rate of interest of slightly over 9 percent. In other words, from the viewpoint of the lender, inflationary expectations drive the required *nominal* interest rate upward by a number of percentage points approximately equal to the expected rate of inflation. In Figure 12, the expectation of inflation causes the supply curve of loanable funds to shift to the left, from S_1 to S_2, to adjust for the expected rate of inflation.

The logic of inflationary expectations applies similarly to the borrowers of loanable funds and to the demand curve in Figure 12. Since the borrower expects to repay the loan with dollars whose real purchasing power will be smaller by 3 percent due to the higher price level, he or she is willing to pay the higher nominal interest rate in order to obtain the desired funds. Other things being equal, an investment project that appeared profitable at a *real* interest rate of 6 percent will, in the presence of an anticipated 3 percent increase in the price level, appear equivalently profitable at a *nominal* interest rate of slightly over 9 percent. Therefore, with a 3 percent anticipated rate of inflation, the demand curve in Figure 12 shifts to the right, from D_1 to D_2, and the new equilibrium is at point *B*, with a *nominal* interest rate of approximately 9 percent. The *nominal* interest rate has increased by approximately the amount of the expected rate of inflation, but the *real* interest rate is unchanged.

Inflationary expectations drive nominal interest rates upward by a number of percentage points approximately equal to the expected rate of inflation.

Inflationary Expectations and Monetary Policy

If expansionary monetary policies trigger inflationary expectations, the power of these policies to lower real interest rates, increase planned investment, and bring about a larger real national income and product is weakened. If a 3 percent increase in the money supply triggers the expectation of a 3 percent increase in the price level, expansionary monetary policy merely increases nominal

interest rates by approximately 3 percentage points and leaves real interest rates unchanged. In turn, if real interest rates are unchanged, planned investment and real national income and product also are unchanged. Expansionary monetary policy is helpless to affect real economic activity.

If expansionary monetary policies trigger inflationary expectations, their power to affect real economic activity is weakened.

How likely is it that expansionary monetary policies will trigger inflationary expectations? Will such expectations fully cancel the real effects of monetary policy? If the economy's experience with inflation is recent and vivid, as it was in the late 1970s, inflationary expectations are easily ignited. Monetary policies are weakened and the Federal Reserve must exercise caution. But if the price level has been stable for a long time, it is less likely that expansionary monetary policy will bring inflationary expectations. In such times, monetary policy may succeed, temporarily at least, in lowering real interest rates and promoting economic expansion.

Economics in Focus

Money Supply and the Crash of 1987

For a dramatic example of the Federal Reserve's manipulation of the money supply, we can look back to the days following October 19, 1987, the date the stock market suffered a record-breaking crash. On that Monday the Dow Jones industrial average lost 508 points, or 22.6 percent of its value—the worst such plunge in history. Overall, the market value of U.S. securities declined by an astounding $500 billion. Although the stock market recovered slightly in the following week, the next Monday brought another drop of 8 percent.

Stock-market experts and ordinary citizens alike feared that the crash would bring on a recession and subsequently reduce spending and money velocity throughout the economy. More immediately, brokerage houses might fail, possibly followed by important investment banks. To prevent these occurrences, a massive increase of credit was needed.

Into the breach stepped the Federal Reserve, led by its new chairman, Alan Greenspan. Until then, Greenspan had made his mark as an inflation fighter. In fact, in the inevitable analysis after the crash, his anti-inflation policies were blamed for helping to trigger the stock market's decline. In early September the Fed had raised the discount rate for the first time in over three years. In the ten weeks between the date Greenspan took office and the morning of the crash, the yield on 30-year Treasury bonds had risen from 8.8 percent to 10.5 percent, and the federal funds rate had jumped from 6.5 percent to 7.6 percent. The critics declared that these moves had been made at exactly the wrong time, when the stock market was already showing signs of shakiness.

But on the morning of October 20, the day after the market's disaster, Greenspan began to redeem himself. He issued a one-sentence statement to reassure brokerage houses, banks, and investors: "The Federal Reserve, consistent with its responsibilities as the nation's central bank, affirmed today its readiness to serve as a source of liquidity to support the economic and financial system." Under Greenspan's guidance the Fed then reversed its restrictive policy, pumping money into the economy by buying up Treasury securities on the open market. As a result, the M1 measure of the money supply increased $8.9 billion in one week. The prime rate correspondingly fell a quarter of a percentage point. The federal funds rate dropped by over 2 percent and the yield on 30-year Treasury bonds by over 1 percent.

Nearly everyone applauded the Fed's quick reaction. Credit crises were averted; and when no recession loomed around the corner, many believed that the Fed's short-term increase in the money supply had helped the economy escape a serious danger.

Sources: Larry Martz et al., "After the Meltdown of '87," *Newsweek*, November 2, 1987, pp. 14–20; George J. Church, "Panic Grips the Globe," *Time*, November 2, 1987, pp. 22–33; Jeffrey M. Laderman, "How the Bull Crashed into Reality," *Business Week*, November 2, 1987, pp. 48–50; Jeffrey M. Laderman with David Zigas and Michael E. Kreca, "Better Keep Those Seat Belts Fastened," *Business Week*, November 9, 1987, pp. 38–39; Ann Reilly Dowd, "Where Does the U.S. Go from Here?" *Fortune*, November 23, 1987, pp. 50–58; Gene Koretz, "Is the Fed Playing It Too Close to the Vest?" *Business Week*, December 14, 1987, p. 24; Seymour Zucker, "Is Alan Greenspan Really Such a Hero?" *Business Week*, December 14, 1987, p. 35; Vince Valvano, "The Morning After: Can the Fed Save the Economy?" *Dollars & Sense*, December 1987, pp. 6–8, 22.

SUMMARY

1. The quantity-of-money theory is based on the equation of exchange, $MV = PQ$. Assuming that the velocity of money circulation is constant, the theory states that changes in the quantity of money (M) will result in an equal proportional change in nominal gross national product, PQ. An aggregate-demand and aggregate-supply interpretation of the quantity-of-money theory postulates a vertical aggregate-supply curve. (See pages 298–299.)

2. A monetary policy prescription based on the quantity-of-money theory calls for a steady growth of the money supply at a rate approximately equal to the expected growth in the economy's capacity to produce goods and services. A goal of this policy is a stable price level. The policy does not propose changes in the money supply aimed at responding to short-run economic fluctuations. (See pages 300–301.)

3. Real interest rates are determined in markets for loanable funds. In these markets, the money supply and preferences of lenders between present and future uses of funds are represented by the supply curve. The demand curve represents the willingness and ability to borrow funds of households, governments, and business firms. The expected profitability of investments is reflected in this curve. (See pages 303–304.)

4. Monetary policy seeks to influence the supply of money in the money market, which illustrates the demand and supply of money held as an asset. In this market, the demand for money arises from transactions, precautionary, and speculative motivations for holding cash balances. The equilibrium interest rate balances the quantity of money supplied with the quantity demanded. (See pages 304–309.)

5. If inflation is not anticipated, increases in the money supply lower real interest rates, and decreases in the money supply raise real interest rates. In a noninflationary atmosphere, monetary policy can influence real interest rates, which, in turn, change the volume of planned investment and the equilibrium level of real national income and product. (See pages 309–310.)

6. In the indirect transmission mechanism, the strength of monetary policy depends on the responsiveness of the quantity of money demanded in the money market and on the responsiveness of the quantity of investment expenditure demanded to changes in the rate of interest. According to the direct transmission view, money-supply changes operate directly on household spending and do not rely on interest-rate changes to have their effect. (See pages 310–312.)

7. Short-run monetary policy must adjust for changes in the velocity of money circulation in order to regulate the effective money supply, measured as M times V. Changes in financial institution technology and deregulation of these institutions have speeded the transfer of balances among different types of accounts. Velocity changes according to one money-supply concept may then differ from velocity changes according to other money-supply concepts, increasing the difficulty of short-run monetary policy. (See pages 314–315.)

8. A monetary policy of accommodation calls for changes in the money supply to match changes in the demand for money. The result is stabilization of nominal interest rates. Under this approach, monetary policy does not exert an independent force for moderating economic fluctuations or limiting inflation. Accommodation also assists Treasury sales of national debt securities by preventing such sales from increasing nominal rates of interest. Accommodation is associated with policy operations guided by interest-rate targeting or borrowed-reserve targeting. (See pages 315–317.)

9. Except for emergency periods, the Federal Reserve generally has taken a flexible approach in the direction of short-run monetary policy. This judgment-based approach authorizes only partial accommodation to changes in the demand for money. It permits some stabilizing changes in interest rates and attempts to moderate fluctuations in the volume of economic activity. (See pages 317–318.)

10. Inflationary expectations push nominal interest rates upward to levels higher than real interest rates. In loanable-funds markets, both demanders and suppliers respond to these expectations. To the extent that money-supply increases trigger inflationary expectations, monetary policy is weakened because it is not able to affect real interest rates. (See pages 318–320.)

KEY TERMS

accommodation: a monetary policy that attempts to shift the money-supply curve back and forth in order to offset shifts in the demand for money, thereby stabilizing the rate of interest (page 315).

direct transmission mechanism: the process whereby real national income and product changes, in response to money-supply changes, without going through the step of an interest-rate change (page 312).

equation of exchange: an identity that states that the quantity of money in the economy multiplied by the number of times the average dollar is used each year to purchase newly produced final products must be equal to the quantity of these final products multiplied by their average price: $MV = PQ$ (page 298).

indirect transmission mechanism: a process whereby the effects of a shift of the real money-supply curve are transmitted to the equilibrium level of real national income and product by affecting interest rates and the volume of planned investment (page 311).

inflationary expectations: expectations that the price level will rise (page 318).

interest rate: the annual payment for the use of funds, expressed as a percentage of the funds used (page 301).

liquidity: the ease with which an asset can be used in exchange or converted into a form that can be used in exchange (page 306).

liquidity trap: when people hold large amounts of money waiting for high asset prices to fall and for low interest rates to rise (page 313).

loanable-funds market: the market that brings together those who wish to lend and those who wish to borrow funds (page 303).

monetarism: a school of economic thought that proposes that monetary policy make no attempt to deal with short-term fluctuations in economic activity but should instead establish a fixed rate of increase for the money supply and stay with this rate year in and year out (page 300).

money market: the market in which money itself is treated as a commodity subject to the concepts of supply and demand (page 304).

nominal values: values that are stated or measured in terms of some monetary unit; they are not adjusted for price-level changes (page 302).

precautionary demand for money: the demand that arises because people want to be prepared for unexpected changes in the pattern of their receipts and expenditures (page 307).

quantity-of-money theory: a theory that states that the velocity of money circulation is constant in the long run, so changes in the quantity of money provide a good way to predict changes in GNP (page 298).

real interest rates: interest rates that reflect actual purchasing-power values (page 303).

real values: values that are stated or measured in terms of goods and services; they are adjusted for price-level changes (page 302).

speculation: taking actions based on expectations of future changes in the market values of assets (page 305).

speculative demand for money: the demand that arises when people seek to gain from declines in the market value of nonmoney assets (page 306).

time preferences: the relative attractiveness of consumption at the present time compared to consumption at some future time (page 303).

transactions demand for money: the demand that arises because people want to hold some of their wealth in a form that is convenient for day-to-day buying and selling of goods and services (page 307).

velocity of circulation: the average number of times each dollar is used per year to buy newly produced goods and services (page 298).

DISCUSSION QUESTIONS

1. Write down the equation of exchange and define each of its terms. Which side of the equation is actually GNP as usually measured in the national accounting system? Explain the reasoning contained in the equation, noting why this is properly an identity rather than an equation that can be used for predictions.

2. Assume that the current GNP is $1,000 billion and the stock of money averages $250 billion during the year. What is the velocity of money circulation? If this velocity is unchanged, how many dollars of added money would be needed to support a 2 percent growth in output if the price level is to remain unchanged? If the actual increase in the money supply is twice as great as your answer to the preceding question, what will be the nominal GNP after one year? If the price level in the first year was 100, what will it be in the second year?

3. Suppose that a machine costs $1,000 and, for simplicity, that it never wears out or requires any operating cost. Suppose also that using this machine will increase returns to the firm by $60 a year. Would it be profitable to purchase and use this machine if the interest rate were 5 percent? How about 10 percent? Discuss how the real rate of interest influences the amount of planned investment. Explain how a change in the productivity of machines would affect the real rate of interest if lenders kept their preferences unchanged between present and future consumption.

4. Write down, from memory, the definition of speculation, and then check in the chapter (or the Key Terms) to be sure it is correct. Under what expectations about future asset prices would a speculator decide to hold cash? When would this speculator decide to hold nonmoney assets instead of cash? Carefully explain how this reasoning suggests that a demand-for-money curve, drawn with the real interest rate on the vertical axis, would have a negative slope.

5. Explain the transactions demand for money. Suppose that there is an economic boom in your hometown, perhaps because the price of its main product has risen on the national market. The incomes of many local people have gone up. Since your hometown is a small part of the total economy, its prosperity has not influenced the interest rate. What will happen to the quantity of money demanded for transactions in the town? Explain why this is a shift and not a movement along the demand-for-money curve.

6. Assume that the monetary authorities increase the amount of M1 money in the economy

and that no one expects this to cause any increase in the price level. What will happen to the demand for stocks and bonds and other nonmoney assets? How will this affect the prices of these assets? How will this, in turn, affect the equilibrium rate of interest as determined in the market for money? Trace this same sequence for a reduction in the amount of money in the economy.

7. Without looking at Figure 7, construct the set of three graphs that illustrate the transmission of a change in the money supply to a change in equilibrium real national income and product. Trace through the transmission system, starting with an increase in the money supply. Check to be sure you have it right, and then write a brief description of the system. Include a discussion of the feedback effect.

8. If the nominal GNP is $1,200 billion and the quantity of M1 money averaged $300 billion during the year, what is the implicit velocity of money circulation? In Germany during the inflation after World War I, people wanted to be paid every day instead of only once each week. What would a change like that do to the velocity of circulation of money? Discuss the effect of electronic banking machines on the velocity of circulation of money in the United States since they were introduced in the 1970s.

9. In some circumstances, an increase in the money supply may bring a rise in nominal interest rates but no change in real interest rates. Describe the circumstances and the viewpoints of lenders and borrowers that can bring about this situation.

10. If the money-supply curve is drawn on a graph with real values on both axes, a change in the price level could cause a shift in this curve. Which way will the money-supply curve shift if the price level increases? Why? Which way will it shift if the price level decreases? Why?

11. Suppose you sign an agreement to borrow money and to pay a nominal interest rate of 10 percent. If you expect the price level to rise by 6 percent a year, what real interest rate do you expect to pay? If the lender expects the price level to rise by 5 percent a year, what real interest rate does he or she expect to receive? If the price level actually rises by only 4 percent a year, is the lender pleased with the outcome of the transaction? Are you pleased with the outcome? Explain.

Economics of Inflation

People dislike inflation—a general rise in the prices they pay. The faster the inflation, the more they dislike it. The German hyperinflation of the early 1920s is blamed for the rise of Nazism, the decline of the Weimar Republic, and the elevation of Hitler to power. Although people dislike inflation, a general rise in their incomes—which are part of the *costs* of the things they buy—looks like something quite different. It is "belated recognition of merit" or "catching up with inflation already under way." Both of these are highly popular. Failure on the part of the general public to recognize the connection between their incomes and the prices they must pay makes inflation a difficult problem for the policymaker.

Another problem is that inflation is almost entirely a redistribution of real incomes and real assets, whereas the alternatives to inflation either risk or require recession and unemployment. Inflationary redistributions are (1) from receivers of incomes that are largely fixed in monetary terms to receivers of incomes that are more flexible in those terms (from pensioners to farmers, for example), and (2) from people who hold monetary assets or are creditors on monetary contracts to holders of nonmonetary assets or debtors on monetary contracts (from savings-bank depositors to real estate speculators, or from holders of domestic government bonds to the domestic government that issued them). The redistribution need not, and usually does not, reduce either the flow of current *real* income or the total value of *real* assets. The problem is that the standard preventives and cures for inflation (restrictive monetary or fiscal policies) involve at least the risk of recession, depression, and bankruptcy. Thus, inflation and its acceleration may be considered a "least worst" alternative.

"Inflation," Milton Friedman has said, "is always and everywhere a monetary phenomenon." This sentence is the greatest half-truth in inflationary theory. Its correct implication is that inflation requires some sort of monetary fuel if it is not to be stalled or reversed. Its misleading implication is that the monetary expansion must come first in time and the price-level rise only thereafter. We shall discuss the relations between money and inflation, but an initial warning is in order: the key question of the division of a monetary stimulus between changes in the price level and changes in the volume of output has, as yet, been solved only for the polar cases of full employment on the one hand and the ultra-Keynesian "liquidity trap" on the other.

We shall now discuss nine secondary problems of inflationary theory:

1. When is inflation? (supply shocks and their monetary aftermaths)

2. When is inflation? (rationing, controls, and suppressed inflation)

3. Do budget deficits cause inflation?

4. Does inflation keep interest rates down?

5. Does inflation break the "death grip" of debt?

6. Would a restored gold standard cure inflation?

7. "Cost-pushes": should they be validated?

8. Inflation, democracy, and the separation of powers.

9. Is inflation inevitable?

WHEN IS INFLATION? (SUPPLY SHOCKS AND MONETARY AFTERMATHS)

We know from the history of supply shocks, notably the two OPEC oil shocks of the 1970s, that supply shocks run up the prices of a few key commodities, that monetary systems "accommodate" by increased money supplies, and that inflation spreads to the entire economy. But should we date the inflation from the supply shock or from the monetary accommodation? Did OPEC cause inflation in oil-importing countries or did these countries bring it on themselves?

This is more than a terminological quibble. To see this, imagine a monetary system that did not (or could not) increase the money supply to accommodate to an oil shock. What would happen? In the short run, the result would surely be recession and inflation. The prices of crude oil and oil-intensive commodities like petrochemicals would rise. No other price would fall. The measured price level would rise. There would be a money shortage with tight credit and high interest rates. There would surely be political-economic pressure to change the monetary system and accommodate the new and higher price level.

But if the authorities could resist this pressure, the non-oil commodity prices (and wages) would eventually fall. The price level would return to approximately its preshock level.[1] The permanent change would be confined to *relative* prices—those of oil and oil-intensive commodities would rise relative to the general price level, and the prices of non-oil commodities would fall.

This counterfactual scenario is not a policy prescription. (In America, the slowness and reluctance of monetary accommodation to the first oil shock is blamed for a recession in 1974–75 and the failure of President Gerald Ford's bid for re-election in 1976.) It indicates only why many, if not most, economists date supply-shock inflations not from the shocks themselves but from the monetary accommodations to them.

WHEN IS INFLATION? (RATIONING, CONTROLS, AND SUPPRESSED INFLATION)

Imagine now a popular war, either a resistance to foreign aggression (as in World War II) or a "War on Poverty" at home, financed by monetary expansion. There are popular and well-enforced systems of price controls, wage and profit-margin controls, rationing and allocations, "incomes policies," or whatever one chooses to call them.[2] The measured price

level does not rise. There is no measured inflation. People merely accumulate "undesired" hoards of cash, bank deposits, or government securities. These situations are called "suppressed" or "repressed" inflation, in contrast to the "open" inflation reflected in published price statistics.

The scenario continues. The war is won, or at any rate ended. The controls are lifted, or enforcement is curtailed. The price level rises. The suppressed inflation comes out of the closet and there is open inflation. Many economists (although not the general public) would include "suppressed inflation" as a form of inflation and date the inflation from the original resort to controls.

In a famous pamphlet called *How to Pay for the War,* Lord Keynes, the most famous economist of the twentieth century, anticipated in 1939 that the wartime expansion might be followed by a resumption of the Great Depression of the 1930s, which could itself be relieved (without inflation) by postwar spending of the balances accumulated in wartime. Had he been right, we might speak of suppressed inflation being followed by suppressed deflation or disinflation. But he was wrong, and no appropriate terminology ever developed.

DO BUDGET DEFICITS CAUSE INFLATION?

A budget deficit must be financed, but the financing need not be inflationary. Whether it is inflationary or not is a matter of political-economic decision.

The inflationary case is simple. The deficit is financed by monetary expansion, either openly or covertly.[3] The inflation will originate not with the deficit, but with its financing method.

But a deficit need not be inflationary. There are at least two alternative financing methods that do not have inflationary consequences, either singly or in combination. The more common of these, and the more consistent with the market economy, is the sale of securities to the general public without the accompaniment of expanded bank reserves. The problems here are high interest rates, both real and nominal, and the "crowding out" of some private

---

1. If some international "monetary base" like the world gold supply were redistributed in favor of the OPEC countries, the price level of the non-oil countries would have to fall, and OPEC policies would have *deflated* the rest of the world!

2. These controls also could be enforced harshly by an authoritarian government, perhaps with death penalties for "economic crimes" like large-scale black-marketing.

3. In a typical covert monetary expansion, a central bank buys government securities and creates new government deposits against them. When the government deposits are spent for the goods and services supplied by customers of depository institutions, deposits and reserves of these institutions are increased by equal amounts. These increased reserves form the basis for loan expansion in a fractional-reserve banking system.

investment (or consumer credit). These effects may be exported by attracting capital from abroad and keeping at home domestic capital that might otherwise go abroad. In this case, foreign interest rates come under upward pressure and overseas investors are crowded out.

A less common form of noninflationary finance is the official or unofficial requirement that financial institutions—depository institutions, savings and loan associations, insurance companies, investment houses—purchase the government's debt at below-market interest rates. This method, in (Japanese) practice,[4] produces a credit squeeze on small business and agriculture, which are forced to save more, and in some cases to borrow at unrecorded and usurious interest rates from the criminal underworld.

DOES INFLATION KEEP INTEREST RATES DOWN?

We have mentioned that noninflationary financing methods raise interest rates. By the same token, the "easy money" of inflationary finance might be expected to lower them—whether the expansion is directed at financing a government deficit, business investment, or consumer credit. Yet we also know that in rapid inflation, long-term credit (if available at all!) commands astronomical interest rates. (The American prime rate reached over 20 percent in the Carter inflation of the late 1970s, and home mortgage rates went to about 17 percent.) How can we explain this paradox?

Economists' explanations involve the distinction between real and nominal interest rates, and also a "snapback" theory of the nominal rate.

The nominal rate of interest (i) is the rate directly observed in the marketplace. Let it be the sum of two elements: the real annual rate (r) that would prevail in a regime of long-term price-level stability and an added compensation (j) to the lender for the inflation rate expected during the year. (The money that is lent has higher purchasing power than that which is received in return.) In the simplest algebraic terms, we have

$$i = r + j$$

where j is zero in a stable-price regime and negative in a deflationary one.[5]

The snapback theory says that, at least in the early stage of an accelerating inflation, the expected inflation rate (j) lags behind the actual rate and is "too low." Monetary expansion can temporarily lower both (r) and (j), only to have them rise again, usually above their initial values, when "the market" (borrowers along with lenders) realizes what is going on.

DOES INFLATION BREAK THE "DEATH GRIP" OF DEBT?

A dollar invested at 6 percent compounded interest will grow according to the following table, with the end-value depending on the time period and the frequency of compounding.

5. More precisely, we compute the total real return $(1 + r)$ as follows:

$$(1 + r) = (1 + i)(1 - j) = 1 + i - j - ij$$

so that, solving for (i):

$$i = \frac{r + j}{1 - j}$$

The $(1 - j)$ term may be important when (j) is large.

4. The method is more effective in Japan than elsewhere because a principal Japanese savings institution is a postal savings system whose investments are limited to public securities.

Time Period	Annual Compounding	Semi-annual Compounding	Continuous Compounding
10 years	1.791	1.806	1.822
20 years	3.207	3.262	3.320
50 years	18.420	19.219	20.086
2000 years	4.090×10^{50}	2.233×10^{51}	1.304×10^{52}

According to this table, a dollar invested at the time of the Prophet Mohammed (let alone Jesus, Moses, the Buddha, or Adam and Eve) could now buy the entire real and personal wealth of "Spaceship Earth"! This is an extreme case of what has been called the dead hand of the creditor, rentier, or coupon-clipping class. Why do not people take more advantage of the vast economic bonanzas indicated by our little table? (A pocket calculator would suffice to flesh it out much further.) An obvious reason is the length of human life. The Biblical patriarch Methuselah of the Book of Genesis and the immortal Struldbruggs of *Gulliver's Travels* would surely have been more impressed than ourselves by such a table. In addition, preferences that various interest theorists have called time preference, agio, impatience, etc., have kept saving rates down.

One cannot help feeling, however, that fear of and experience with inflation are important factors that have kept the creditor class small—and the dead hand of its power normally weak. The early Soviet economist Yevgeny Preobrazhensky compared the printing press of "War Communism" (1917–18) to machine guns mowing down the coupon-clippers of the leisure or rentier class, by expropriating their wealth and incomes and forcing them to go to work. Nearly seventy years later, Northwestern University economist Robert Eisner suggested that in thinking about American budget deficits one should also consider the effect of inflationary financing on the real value of the national debt (and the economic power of individual and institutional bondholders).

WOULD A RESTORED GOLD STANDARD CURE INFLATION?

The standard yardstick or meterstick itself has length. The standard pound weight or kilogram weight itself has weight. But what about the unit of monetary value? Should it not itself have value apart from its monetary use—as a dollar bill, for example, does not?

Such analogical thinking has been strong throughout the ages. The monetary reformer Irving Fisher warned in his *Purchasing Power of Money* that experiments with no-value "fiat" money always ended in runaway inflation. (The same argument also applied to paper money based on land values or tobacco or coonskins. As prices rose the prices of land or tobacco or coonskins rose too, offering bases for further monetary issues, and so proceeded *ad infinitum.*)

Because of its durability, uniformity, portability, and the limitation of its supply, "commodity" or "full-bodied" money has come to mean gold, or paper fully convertible with gold at some fixed price. The main thing wrong with the wampum of the American Indians was the ease with which enterprising British and Dutch colonists could augment its supply by counterfeiting. All over the world, the major defect of cattle, goats, and other livestock—our words *pecuniary, impecunious,* and *peculation* derive from the Latin word for cattle—was the lack of uniformity. Smart tradesmen try to palm off inferior specimens as standard "money," while retaining superior ones for food, hides, wool, breeding, etc.

In major inflations, a popular sport is to compute prices in terms of gold (or some foreign money convertible into gold). The arithmetic is simple. For example:

$$\frac{\text{"gold" price of a}}{\text{pound of fish}} = \frac{\text{paper price of a pound of fish}}{\text{paper price of an ounce of gold}}$$

During the period 1864–1879, during and after the American Civil War, such computation was unnecessary, as prices were quoted in both gold and "greenbacks." Much of the painful deflation of the 1870s was confined to greenback prices. As the probability of "resumption" (convertibility) increased, gold prices were largely immune to this deflation. During inflationary times, it is not unusual to find that the gold prices of many commodities have not risen above their preinflationary values. In many cases they will have fallen, as gold is a favorite inflation hedge. This naturally adds to the nostalgia or mystique of the gold standard.

It is sometimes inferred that a system that uses gold as money would not have inflation. In actual history, however, inflation has by no means been eliminated under gold standards (or other metallic standards). Counterfeiting, usually involving adulteration with heavy base metals (most often lead), was one inflation cause. It was engaged in by chancellors of the exchequer as well as by ordinary citizens and by alchemists professing to transmute lead into gold. (Had transmutation been successful, it could have been the end of the gold standard.) More common devices were "clipping" and "sweating"; the first involved shaving the edge off a coin's circumference, the second, shaking coins together vigorously to reduce their weight and give off gold dust, which constituted the revenue of the operation. If you look at contemporary American coins, you will see that the quarter and dime have milled edges (defenses against clipping) while the nickel and penny do not. Presumably it was decided at some past time that it was worth protecting the first two against clipping, but that nobody would bother to clip nickels or pennies. As defenses against sweating, pure gold and silver were replaced by alloys that were harder and more resistant to sweating. The two main sources of "gold inflation" have been:

1. Increases in the gold stocks of the Western world, either through conquest, as in Mexico and Peru, or through discovery, as in California, Australia, the Yukon, and the Transvaal.

2. Economies in the use of gold, through technological improvements in financing and banking. These permitted gold reserves to be reduced and increased the rapidity with which money could circulate. The use of bank checks and credit cards are examples.

The world's most massive gold inflation followed the conquest of Mexico and Peru by Spain in the sixteenth and seventeenth centuries. It was slow by contemporary standards—2 or 3 percent per year on average—but long-continued. It might have been much greater than it was but for (a) the European recovery after the Black Death and (b) the European taste for such luxuries as tea, coffee, sugar, spices, silk, porcelain, and cotton textiles. The Black Death (a succession of epidemics of bubonic plague during the fourteenth century) reduced the population of Western Europe by a quarter or a third, raising

real wages as a result. Subsequent increases in the population and labor force seem to have kept wages down and thus reduced the inflation rate during the period of the gold inflow. At the same time, the European taste for Oriental luxuries, probably traceable to the earlier Crusades, caused a movement of monetary gold to India and China, where much of it was hoarded in nonmonetary forms like jewelry and ornamentation, thus disappearing from the money supply.

COST-PUSHES: SHOULD THEY BE VALIDATED?

In the first section of this essay, supply shocks were mentioned as possible causes of inflation. Such shocks were treated as *exogenous* to the domestic economy, having been brought on by foreign forces (OPEC) or natural events (drought, earthquake). The term *cost-push* refers to *endogenous* supply shocks—usually rises in money wages, profit margins, or interest rates. The successive rounds of wage and price increases following World War II in the United States were centered around "key bargains" in autos, steel, and other major industries. In these bargains, money wage gains were sandwiched between previous and subsequent profit-margin increases in a wage-price spiral that defied objective disentangling in terms of cause and effect, stimulus and response, or any similar formula.

Economists try to distinguish cost-push inflation (sometimes called "new inflation" or "administered inflation") from the "demand-pull inflation" of early Keynesian theory. In terms of aggregate supply and demand, cost-push inflation results from a leftward shift in the aggregate-supply curve, while demand-pull inflation results from a rightward shift in the aggregate-demand curve. Both shifts not only can but often do occur together.

When we discussed supply shocks, we said that the macroeconomic policy problem they present is one of accommodation versus resistance (refusal to accommodate). Accommodation, especially increases in the money-supply growth rate was, we said, the true cause of domestic inflation—not the supply shock itself. Resistance would balance the supply shock with downward demand pressures in the unshocked sectors of the economy and eliminate overall inflation in the long run at the cost, or at least the risk, of depression, stagflation, or recession, with no guarantee that it would end before the next election.

Let us imagine an epidemic of money-wage increases and/or higher profit margins over and above rises in productivity.[6] The wage increases are overtly inflationary. Profit-margin increases are disguisable as "new and improved models" or in the quiet discontinuance of standard, budget, or economy items. (As Henry Ford said, "Small cars mean small profits.") Prices rise, but will the increases stick? Our contention is that they will not, unless they are *validated* by macroeconomic accommodation—primarily an acceleration of monetary growth. In that case, the general inflation should be blamed on the macroeconomic validation and accommodation of the cost-pushes rather than on the cost-pushes themselves.

We should not forget that resistance (refusal to accommodate) has its costs in the risks of recession and social unrest, especially if organized pressure groups counterattack to force a policy reversal. For a slogan sparking such a counterattack, we quote Lane Kirkland of the United Auto Workers in the early 1970s: "We will not let Mr. Nixon's depression rob us of our wage increases!"

INFLATION, DEMOCRACY, AND THE SEPARATION OF POWERS

The political economy of inflation can be separated from the pure economics of the subject. Its basic questions are: Why do governments insist, despite the advice of financial experts, both on large-scale deficit financing and on financing their deficits increasingly by monetary expansion? If they know what to do, why don't they—why can't they—do it?

Historically, much of the blame has been put on democratic institutions, particularly on the extension of the suffrage to the propertyless, the debtors, and the recipients of public largesse. Mark Twain's recipe for political success in America was never voting for a tax or against an appropriation. (He might have added, never voting for tight money or against low interest rates.) This is supposedly an aspect of what some pessimistic political scientists have called "the increasing ungovernability" of populations under democratic regimes. It is supported by the success of armies of occupation in checking postwar inflations in the late 1940s, either by imposing financial stringency themselves (as in Japan) or

by shielding disinflationary politicians from political reprisals (as in West Germany).

At first glance, of course, such pessimism makes little historical sense. The rise of parliamentary democracy in Western Europe and North America may be said to cover the century and a quarter between the French Revolution and World War I. But the great inflation of the recent past began a generation later, with the persistence of the "wartime" inflation of World War II into the peacetime generation that has followed it. (Mark Twain's denunciations of American congressmen and state legislators actually came from a *deflationary* period.)

There is, however, a pessimistic explanation of the delay. The rise of democracy was accompanied by what has been called a religion, or perhaps a superstition, of "sound money" backed primarily by gold and secondarily by silver. Inflationist movements—in America, the Greenbackers and the Populists—were reactions to deflations allegedly engineered on Wall Street. They faded as the deflation was reversed. As late as 1932, Franklin D. Roosevelt devoted an entire radio address to denying vile rumors that he was an enemy of the gold standard or that his election would endanger sound money. But within a year both Roosevelt and the American people had changed their minds. (The British, possibly influenced by Keynes, had already changed theirs!) The "religion of money" was no more. Inflation followed from the resulting iconoclasm, godlessness, or agnosticism of the continued populist democracy of America and Europe.

Another political economy argument, leading to similar conclusions, is about the separation of governmental powers into the executive (and administrative), the legislative, and the judicial branches. This application of eighteenth-century liberal political thought—Locke in England, Montesquieu in France, the American *Federalist* papers—allocated "the power of the purse" (increasing basic fiscal and financial control) to the legislative branch, Parliament or Congress. This was a natural reaction to the expensive dynastic warfare and courtly luxuries of such absolute monarchs as Louis XIV of France and Frederick the Great of Prussia. But after "one man (or woman), one vote" and the passing of the gold standard, a mixed bag of compassion, the pork barrel, log-rolling, and the welfare state supplemented (but did not replace) warfare and bureaucratic perquisites as sources of public deficits and inflationary financing. It now has led to calls for the curtailment of legislative fiscal and financial powers.

Specimen proposals are easy to find: increased independence and de-politicizing of central banks;

---

6. The case of increased interest rates is more complex. The higher rates induce their own offsets or remedies by decreasing the growth rates of money and credit.

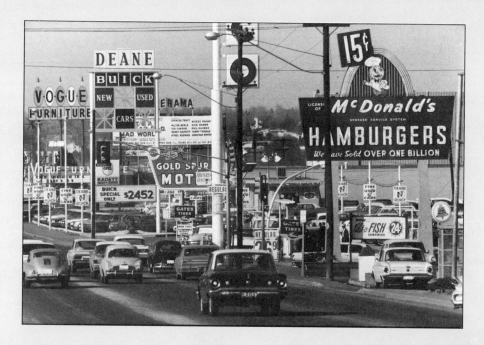

the "monetary rule" proposals of Milton Friedman and other monetarist economists to forestall excessive money creation; an "item veto" for the executive on appropriation bills—already in force in many American states; authorization of "impoundment powers" for the executive to interpret some or all appropriations as *permissions* rather than *requirements* to spend money.[7] In 1985 the U.S. Congress enacted the Gramm-Rudman Act to force automatic cuts in certain expenditure categories when budgetary deficits threatened, while exempting other categories. All these can be looked on as anti-inflationary measures or proposals.

IS INFLATION INEVITABLE?

The secular trend of the price level has undoubtedly been upward. The imaginary dollar invested (in our little table) two thousand years ago would actually be worth not 1.304×10^{52} or 4.090×10^{50} or even $1 today. Inflation (and war), like "drink and the devil" in *Treasure Island,* would have "done for the rest," meaning the whole thing. (The value today would almost certainly be zero anywhere in the world!)

7. Impoundment powers seem to have been exercised freely if infrequently by early American presidents, but fell into disuse during the nineteenth century. President Nixon attempted to revive them in 1973–74. This action was ruled unconstitutional by the Supreme Court, unless congressional consent could be obtained.

This historical record has convinced many economists that inflation control is a lost cause, or at least, that any effective cure is necessarily worse than the disease. In this view it is enough to prevent runaway inflation.

But let us take a closer look at this strange, eventful history of inflation. A long series of price indices for southern England from 1300 to the 1980s has been compiled by Ivor Pearce of the University of Southampton. He concluded that for the first five hundred years and more the level of prices showed no upward trend.[8] There were ups and downs, sometimes quite violent, but the recent U.S. experience of the doubling of prices in four to six years has only one precedent. This was a single great orgy toward the end of Henry VIII's reign. (Henry's experiments in monetary economics seem to have been no more successful than his better-known experiments in serial polygamy and domestic discipline.)

From this section and the last section of this essay, it is hard to avoid the conclusion that some combination of political democracy (including frequent elections), the current model of the separation of powers, and the abandonment of the old-time "religion of money" for the contemporary religion of the welfare-warfare state has made inflation endemic, with occasional epidemics checked but never reversed.

8. Similarly, Sherman Maisel of the University of California at Berkeley has estimated that the 1939 level of wholesale prices in the United States was approximately the same as that at the close of the American Revolution in 1780.

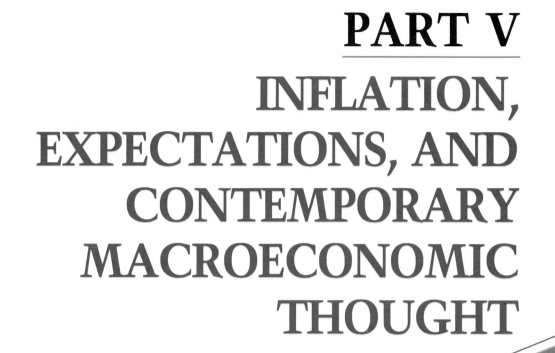

PART V

INFLATION, EXPECTATIONS, AND CONTEMPORARY MACROECONOMIC THOUGHT

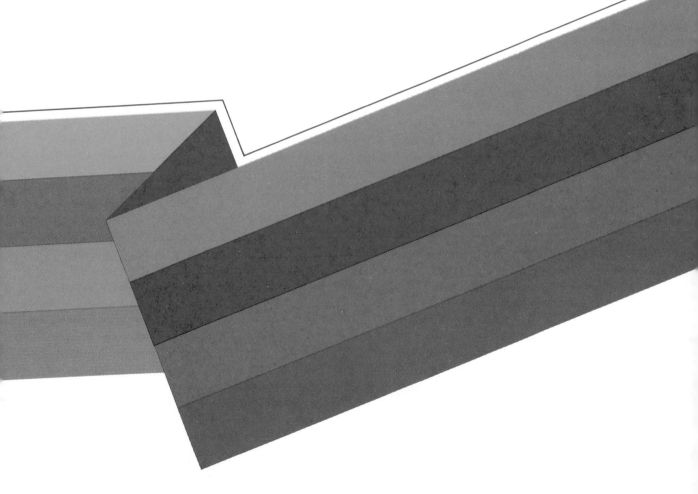

15

Aggregate Demand, Aggregate Supply, and Potential GNP

Preview This chapter brings together almost everything that you have learned so far about macroeconomics and focuses this knowledge on two important matters: the price level and the volume of real GNP that the economy can provide in its long-run equilibrium situation.

We start with an expanded explanation of the concepts of aggregate demand and aggregate supply, which were first examined in Chapter 6. Now that you have studied the Keynesian and monetarist theories, it is possible to give a much more complete explanation of the slope of the aggregate-demand curve and of ways in which this curve may be shifted in response to public policy decisions. We are also able to give a more complete explanation of the aggregate-supply curve. The aggregate-supply curve reflects production decisions of firms and the availability of resources that can be used in production. We show how wage-cost lags and money illusion explain both the slope and shifts of the aggregate-supply curve.

To help you understand the effects of shifts of aggregate-demand and aggregate-supply curves, we use them first to describe an expansionary and then a contractionary situation in the economy. In each case, we show how a shift of the aggregate-supply curve returns the economy to its long-run equilibrium position. This long-run equilibrium position is sometimes called the economy's potential GNP.

AGGREGATE DEMAND

You were introduced to the concepts of aggregate demand and aggregate supply in Chapter 6. To refresh your memory, the graph illustrating the aggregate-demand and aggregate-supply model is reproduced here in Figure 1. This is the same graph as in Figure 8 of Chapter 6, except that the label on the horizontal axis now is Real GNP instead of the more cumbersome phrase "Aggregate Quantity of Goods and Services Demanded and Supplied."

In Chapter 6 the explanations of aggregate demand and aggregate supply were elementary and nonanalytical because at that point you had not studied the Keynesian model of planned expenditure or the monetarist model of interest rate determination. Now that you have studied these theories, a more complete explanation of aggregate demand can be given. In this chapter our intent is to show how fiscal and monetary instruments can be used together to implement macroeconomic policies.

Keynesian and monetarist theories help explain the slope and shifts of the aggregate-demand curve.

The aggregate-demand curve in Figure 1 shows an inverse relationship between changes in the price level and the resulting changes in real GNP demanded—that is, the *AD* curve has a negative slope. The theory behind this negative slope was not explained in Chapter 6 because, at that stage in your study of macroeconomics, you had not learned about interest rates or the price level or about how these can be changed by increases or decreases in the money supply. We now can explain the slope of this curve.

In explaining the slope of any curve in economics, the only variables that are allowed to change are the ones shown on the axes of the graph. In this case, these are the price level (on the vertical axis) and real GNP (on the horizontal axis). Our reasoning is that the quantity of real GNP demanded depends on the price level, other things being equal. Thus, the price level is our independent variable, and the real GNP is our dependent variable. We do not reason in the opposite direc-

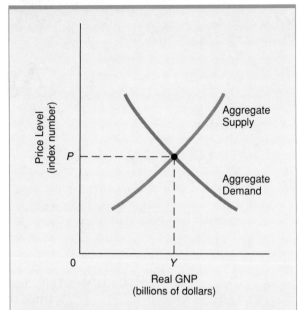

FIGURE 1
Aggregate Demand and Aggregate Supply

The aggregate-demand curve illustrates how the quantity of real GNP demanded depends on the price level. The aggregate-supply curve illustrates how the quantity of real GNP supplied depends on the price level. The intersection of the aggregate-demand and the aggregate-supply curves signifies macroeconomic equilibrium—the price level at which equality exists between real GNP demanded and supplied.

tion, that the price level depends on the quantity of real GNP demanded, because our theory is that the price level depends on the combination of both aggregate demand and aggregate supply, and not on either one individually. This is the same type of reasoning that is used in demand-and-supply models for particular products.[1] We present two theories that offer explanations for the slope of this curve. One is the interest rate theory and the other is the real cash balances theory.

In explaining the slope of any curve in economics, the only variables that are allowed to change are those shown on the axes of the graph.

---

1. See Chapter 5.

In aggregate-demand and aggregate-supply analysis, the price level is determined by the interaction of aggregate demand and aggregate supply and not by either of them by itself.

The Interest Rate Theory

The **interest rate theory** is based on the fact that a rise in the price level shrinks the *real* quantity of money in the economy, if other things remain unchanged. This was explained in Chapter 14. In real terms, each dollar has less purchasing power than before the rise in prices. The way this theory explains the slope of the aggregate-demand curve is shown in Figure 2, which repeats the transmission mechanism illustrated in Figure 7 in Chapter 14, but with the steps represented by the arrows running in the opposite direction. Panel (a) shows what happens to the real money supply when the price level increases. The money-supply curve shifts to the left, from MS_1 to MS_2 (step 1). This leads to a rise in the real interest rate from i_1 to i_2 (step 2). Panel (b) shows how this rise in the real interest rate reduces the volume of planned-investment expenditure from I_1 to I_2 (step 3). This reduction in planned-investment expenditure lowers the total-planned-expenditure curve in panel (c) from $C + I_1 + G + X - Im$ to $C + I_2 + G + X - Im$ (step 4). According to this demand-side reasoning, the equilibrium level of real GNP falls from Y_1 to Y_2 (step 5), as indicated by the movement of the intersection with the 45-degree line from E_1 to E_2. Panel (d) shows how all these responses are summarized in the slope of the aggregate-demand curve. At the initial price level of P_1, the real GNP demanded was Y_1, as shown by point A on the aggregate-demand curve. At the new price level of P_2, the real GNP demanded is Y_2, as shown by point B on the aggregate-demand curve. Therefore, working through the demand side of the economy, the rise in the price level has brought a reduction in real GNP. Our aggregate-demand curve therefore has a negative slope. Because this theory uses the basic Keynesian technique of linking interest rates to planned investment and real GNP, it sometimes is called the Keynes effect.

A step-by-step summary of how the interest rate theory explains the negative slope of the aggre-gate-demand curve is as follows:

1. A rise in the price level (P) leads to

2. an increase in the quantity of money demanded to carry on any given level of buying and selling activity in the economy. Since the *ceteris paribus* assumption specifies that the quantity of money in existence in the economy is not changed, it follows that

3. interest rates (the cost of credit which is the price for the use of money over time) will be driven upward as households and firms compete for the limited amount of money available. Because of higher interest rates

4. firms find capital goods more costly and less profitable and households find the financing of durable goods purchases more expensive. As a result

5. quantities demanded of capital goods and consumer durable goods are reduced, which means a smaller aggregate quantity demanded (QD).

There are some qualifications to this model. A lot may depend on how steep or how flat the demand-for-money curve and the planned-investment-demand curve are. There also is debate about whether the demand-for-money curve, in real terms, would shift as a result of a change in the price level. Even in view of these qualifications, however, it still seems reasonable to draw the aggregate-demand curve with a negative slope.

The interest rate theory states that the aggregate-demand curve has a negative slope because increases in the price level, *ceteris paribus*, lead to higher real interest rates and less planned investment expenditure (and vice versa).

The Real Balances Theory

The **real balances theory**[2] reasons that a rise in the price level will mean reductions in real wealth for the people who hold money or certain assets

2. This theory is sometimes called the Pigou effect, after the British economist A. C. Pigou, who analyzed how changes in wealth influence spending and saving.

whose value is given in monetary terms, such as government bonds. The real goods and services equivalent of these assets is reduced by the increase in prices. This is a familiar result of inflation. As you learned in Chapters 10 and 11, reductions in wealth can cause a downward shift in the consumption function, which is part of the $C + I + G + X - Im$ curve in the Keynesian-cross diagram, just as lower investment shifted the curve in panel (c) of Figure 2 (step 4). This shift will lower the equilibrium level of real GNP (step 5). In this way, the real balances theory also concludes that a rise in the price level will bring a drop in real GNP and that the aggregate-demand curve has a negative slope.

The net strength of the real balances effect may be quite small. Often one person's loss from inflation is another person's gain. Only a small part of the total wealth in the economy, such as cash itself, is free of this counterbalancing effect.

A step-by-step summary of how the real balances theory explains the negative slope of the aggregate-demand curve is as follows:

1. An increase in the price level (P) leads to

2. a reduction in the buying power (real value) of assets held in cash or government bonds.

Therefore,

FIGURE 2
How Changes in the Price Level Can Change Real GNP

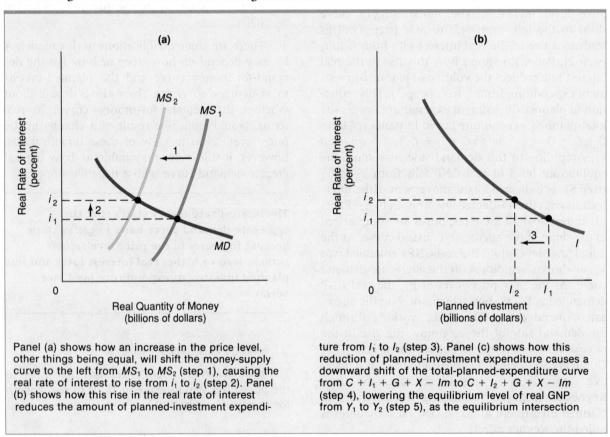

Panel (a) shows how an increase in the price level, other things being equal, will shift the money-supply curve to the left from MS_1 to MS_2 (step 1), causing the real rate of interest to rise from i_1 to i_2 (step 2). Panel (b) shows how this rise in the real rate of interest reduces the amount of planned-investment expendi-

ture from I_1 to I_2 (step 3). Panel (c) shows how this reduction of planned-investment expenditure causes a downward shift of the total-planned-expenditure curve from $C + I_1 + G + X - Im$ to $C + I_2 + G + X - Im$ (step 4), lowering the equilibrium level of real GNP from Y_1 to Y_2 (step 5), as the equilibrium intersection

Figure 2 (continued)

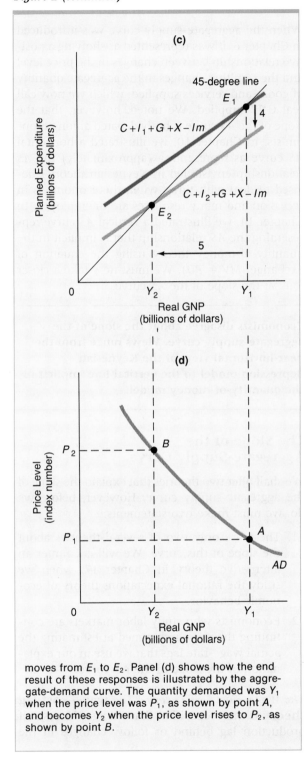

moves from E_1 to E_2. Panel (d) shows how the end result of these responses is illustrated by the aggregate-demand curve. The quantity demanded was Y_1 when the price level was P_1, as shown by point A, and becomes Y_2 when the price level rises to P_2, as shown by point B.

3. the real wealth of the holders of these assets is reduced. This reduction in real wealth leads to

4. reduced consumption expenditure and lower total planned expenditure ($C + I + G + X - Im$), which leads to

5. a reduction in the quantity of real GNP demanded.

Both the interest rate theory and the real balances theory suggest that it is reasonable to draw the aggregate-demand curve with a negative slope. We cannot say whether the aggregate-demand curve should be relatively steep or relatively flat but, for convenience, our graphs show a substantial negative slope for this curve.

The real balances theory states that the aggregate-demand curve has a negative slope because increases in the price level reduce the real wealth of those holding money-denominated assets, leading to reduced planned expenditure (and vice versa).

Shifting the Aggregate-Demand Curve

In order for the aggregate-demand curve to shift, there must be a change in some variable other than the ones shown on the axes of the graph. Since the price level *does* appear on the graph showing the *AD* curve, shifts of this curve must come from a change in some variable *other than* the price level. Now that you have studied the Keynesian and the monetarist theories, you know that many variables can alter total-planned expenditure ($C + I + G + X - Im$).

For example, when you studied the Keynesian theory, you learned (in Chapter 11) that government fiscal policy can change government purchases (G) and—by changing net taxes—change consumption expenditure (C). Fiscal policies that increase total-planned expenditure shift the *AD* curve to the right—that is, at any given price level the quantity of real GNP demanded will be greater than before the expansionary fiscal action, other things unchanged. Contractionary fiscal policies—like reductions in government purchases or increases in net taxes—shift the *AD* curve to the left, *ceteris paribus*.

Monetary policy also can shift the *AD* curve. You learned in Chapter 14 that increases in the money supply can, at least temporarily, lower real interest rates. These lower real interest rates, in turn, can increase total planned expenditure by increasing investment (I). With more planned investment, the quantity of real GNP demanded will be greater, at any given price level, than before the expansionary monetary policy. In other words, expansionary monetary policy shifts the *AD* curve to the right. On the other hand, if the money supply is reduced, the resulting higher interest rates will reduce planned investment, lower total planned expenditure, and lead to a smaller quantity of real GNP demanded at any given price level. Contractionary monetary policy shifts the *AD* curve to the left.

Fiscal and monetary policies that increase total-planned expenditure ($C + I + G + X - Im$) shift the aggregate-demand curve to the right, *ceteris paribus*. Fiscal and monetary policies that reduce total planned expenditure shift the aggregate-demand curve to the left.

It is important for you to recognize that in describing shifts of the *AD* curve, we have stated that the real GNP demanded would be greater or smaller *at any given price level*. Most students of economics realize that increased government purchases or increases in the money supply may, in fact, lead to increases in the price level. However, whether or not that is true, or the extent to which it is true, depends on aggregate supply as well as on aggregate demand. Therefore, we must examine aggregate supply before we can determine whether shifts of the *AD* curve will lead to changes in the price level.

AGGREGATE SUPPLY

When the aggregate-supply curve was introduced in Chapter 6, it was represented as showing a positive relationship between changes in the price level and the resulting changes in the aggregate quantity of goods and services supplied, which we now call real GNP supplied. We noted, however, that the slope of the *AS* curve is hotly debated among economists. In Chapter 10, we illustrated a horizontal *AS* curve as representing (approximately) the *AS* relationship envisioned in Keynesian theories devised to deal with times when the economy is in recession and many resources are unemployed. In Chapter 14, we illustrated a vertical *AS* curve representing the *AS* relationship that is implicit in the quantity-of-money theory using the equation of exchange ($MV = PQ$). We must now take a closer look at the slope of the *AS* curve.

Economists disagree about the slope of the aggregate-supply curve. Views range from the near-horizontal view of the Keynesian depression model to the vertical line implicit in the quantity-of-money model.

The Slope of the Aggregate-Supply Curve

We shall offer two theories that explain the slope of the aggregate-supply curve. However, before we do, we must make two statements:

1. These are only two of several theories about the slope of this curve. We will encounter an alternative theory in Chapter 17, when we study the rational expectations theory of economic behavior.

2. Economists who study labor markets are continuing their research aimed at estimating the actual wage-rate lags that we use in our explanation of the slope of the AS curve.

The Wage–Cost Lag Theory   The **wage–cost lag theory** is the proposition that changes in costs of production lag behind or follow changes in the general price level. Consider labor costs, for example. Many workers in the economy are employed under contracts that run for one or more years into the future. When the prices of finished goods change, it may be some time before the wages of these workers catch up with the new cost of living. Even for workers not under contract, wage-rate adjustments usually are not made as frequently as are adjustments in the prices of final goods and services. Therefore, if a stable condition in the economy is upset by a change in the price level, it is likely that the prices of products sold by firms will change more than wage rates and labor costs of production. When the price level increases, the lag of labor costs increases profit margins and encourages firms to expand output, in order to get as much profit as possible while the favorable conditions last. When the price level falls, the lag will squeeze profit margins and firms will cut back on production so as not to suffer too much. Applying these ideas to the *AS* curve suggests that a rise in the price level will lead to an increase in the quantity of real GNP supplied and that a fall in the price level will lead to a reduction in real GNP supplied. Thus, the aggregate-supply curve will have a positive slope.

It is not only labor costs that may lag behind finished product prices when the price level changes. It is not unusual for firms to have contracts or understandings that govern the prices they pay for raw materials and intermediate products used in production. Just as for labor costs, there may be some time lag after a change in the price level before these costs of production are fully adjusted. When the price level rises, the lag will cause profit margins to increase and encourage greater output, and when the price level falls, the lag will shrink profit margins and encourage firms to reduce output. Thus, these cost lags also suggest a positive slope for the aggregate-supply curve.

When the price level starts to rise, increases in wage rates and other costs of production lag behind so that profit margins are temporarily increased. When the price level starts to fall, the

---

lag in wage rates and other costs makes profit margins smaller. Firms react to these changes in profit margins by increasing or decreasing their levels of output.

The wage–cost lag theory is not difficult to understand, but a cautionary note is necessary at this point. As we shall see, there are circumstances when changes in wages and other costs of production can be the *cause* rather than the *effect* of changes in the general price level. We will have more to say about wage-push and cost-push theories of inflation. Those theories involve *shifts* of the *AS* curve rather than *movements along* this curve. Those theories do not concern us now because we are limiting our explanation to the slope as distinguished from the location of the *AS* curve.

A summary of the wage–cost lag explanation of the slope of the aggregate-supply curve is as follows:

1. An increase in the price level means that there has been an increase, on average, in the prices of goods and services sold in the economy. However,

2. labor and raw materials often are purchased by firms under contracts that set prices for a period of time, with the result that changes in costs of production lag behind changes in the prices firms receive from sales of final products. Therefore,

3. profit margins tend to expand when the price level starts to rise and tend to fall when the price level starts to fall. In response to these changing profit margins,

4. firms increase the quantity of goods and services supplied when the price level starts to rise and reduce the quantity of goods and services supplied when the price level starts to fall.

The wage–cost lag theory suggests that changes in real GNP supplied are positively related to changes in price level.

The Money-Illusion Theory **Money illusion** is the belief that changes in nominal values are the same as changes in real values. This belief can have an important influence on the economy when the price level is changing. For example, if all prices were to increase by 10 percent, there would be no change in relative prices among different goods and services and their real values would not have changed from what they were before the price-level increase. Of course, the real value (purchasing power) of money would have changed. A person under money illusion would believe, however, that the purchasing power of money had stayed the same and that the real value of goods and services had changed.

Money illusion is the mistaken belief that a change in a nominal value is a change in a real value.

Here is how the money-illusion theory explains the positive slope of the aggregate-supply curve. Suppose that there is an increase in the price level and that everyone in the economy operates under complete money illusion. Since wages, interest, rent, and profit are rewards for production-related (supply-side) activities, everyone who now receives greater money-rewards from these supply-side activities is apt to believe that the real tradeoff between work and leisure has changed in favor of more work. So everyone works harder, and real GNP increases. In this way, behavior based on money illusion suggests a positive slope for the aggregate-supply curve.

The money-illusion theory and the wage–cost lag theory work together to suggest a positive slope for the *AS* curve. This is because, when the general price level starts to increase, nominal wage, rent, interest, and profit rates also may increase to some extent, even though other prices are rising faster. In this situation, a worker under money illusion may believe that his or her *real* wage rate has risen, even though in fact it has fallen. Under the mistaken belief that the real wage rate has risen, the worker may be quite willing to work more hours per week, as may be requested by firms as they expand output.

Money illusion can operate also if the general price level starts to fall. If nominal wage, rent, interest, and profit rates also fall—but fall less than the prices of final goods—workers and other resource owners may mistakenly believe that their *real* rates of compensation have fallen, even though, in fact, they have risen. Under money illusion, resource owners may refuse to accept reductions in nominal rates of compensation so that strikes, layoffs, and business failures result.

A step-by-step summary of the money illusion explanation for a positively-sloped aggregate-supply curve is as follows:

1. Nominal wage rates may increase when the general price level starts to increase, even though their increases are smaller than the increases in the prices of final goods. In this situation,

2. workers under money illusion mistakenly believe that their real wage rate has increased, even though it actually has decreased. Under the illusion that their real wage rate has increased,

3. workers are willing to work more hours per week as requested by firms which, in these circumstances, are increasing their level of output.

Wage–cost lag and money illusion can work together to support the view that the aggregate-supply curve is positively sloped.

Shifting the Aggregate-Supply Curve

Any particular aggregate-supply curve is drawn on the assumption that all variables other than the price level and the real GNP are held constant. When there is a change in any other variable, a shift (change in location) of the aggregate-supply curve may occur.

In examining shifts of the aggregate-supply curve, we are interested in the two phenomena that we have already discussed in connection with the slope of this curve, that is, the wage–cost lag and the money illusion. According to our theory, with the passage of time, changes can take place in each of these variables. Specifically, both wage–cost lag and money illusion are expected to melt away with the passage of time. Such time-related changes in these variables will shift (relocate) the *AS* curve.

With the passage of time, changes can take place in the degree of wage–cost lag and money illusion. These changes can shift the aggregate-supply curve.

Wage Rates and Costs "Catch Up" The lag in wage rates and other costs of production after a price-level change will not continue indefinitely. As time passes, wage rates and other costs will start to catch up with the prices of final goods and the lag will disappear. For example, after a price-level increase, labor will demand extra wage increases as soon as possible. As these adjustments are made, the profit margins of firms shrink. Firms respond by reducing the quantity of output that will be supplied at any given price level, shifting the *AS* curve to the left.

If the price level has recently fallen, the initiative to eliminate the wage–cost lag will come from firms, which then will want to lower wage rates and other costs. As their efforts bear fruit, profit margins become larger, the quantity of output that will be supplied at any given price level is increased, and the *AS* curve shifts to the right.

When wage rates start to catch up with changes in the prices of final goods, profit margins change and the aggregate-supply curve shifts.

It is worth noting, in addition, that after the shift the *AS* curve may have a steeper slope than it had before the shift. The reason for this is that the strength of the wage–cost lag depends on the laws and customary patterns of behavior in relations between firms and workers and between firms and their suppliers. Consider, for example, the average length or time period of a labor–management contract governing wage rates and working conditions. If price levels have been stable for some time, it may have been convenient for both labor and management to have relatively long-term contracts. But

changing price levels will prompt one side or the other to want to shorten contracts in order to reduce the wage-rate lag from future price-level changes. For example, after an experience with inflation, labor will want shorter contracts and "reopener" provisions to shorten future wage-rate lags. Automatic cost-of-living adjustment (COLA) provisions may be added to contracts. On the other hand, if the recent experience has been with price-level declines, it is likely that firms, rather than their workers or their suppliers, will want to shorten contracts and to include reopener provisions. This also will make the new *AS* curve steeper than the old one. We will return to this matter when we consider theories of rational expectations in Chapter 17.

The aggregate-supply curve tends to be steeper if there has been recent experience with price-level changes.

Changes in Money Illusion The passage of time after a price-level change will also cause money illusion to melt away. Consider what happens when people finally come to realize that *all* prices, including the prices of consumption goods that they buy, have gone up? Now they begin to realize that the changes in nominal wage rates, which had led them to work harder, were not actually changes in real wage rates. Their real wage, interest, rent, or profit had not gone up but actually had gone down. When this realization dawns on them, money illusion starts to evaporate, and the tradeoff between work and leisure is re-examined. In the light of their now clearer understanding of real wage, interest, rent, and profit rates, people move back toward their old work habits. As this happens, the aggregate-supply curve shifts to the left.

How long does it take for people to recognize that changes in nominal values are not also changes in real values? The answer depends on many things. How long was the price level stable before the inflation or deflation occurred? How large is the change in the price level? How rapidly is the price level changing? In actual policy making, these questions are very important, and economists spend much time discussing and researching them. For our purposes, however, it is the concept of money illusion and the concept of shifting the aggregate-supply curve that are important.

The aggregate-supply curve shifts as the degree of money illusion changes with the passage of time, after a price-level increase.

Now that we have examined the forces that determine the slope and the location of the aggregate-supply curve, we can offer the following definition: *the aggregate-supply curve represents the relationship between changes in the price level and changes in real GNP supplied when wage-rate and cost changes lag behind changes in the price level and while money illusion due to that price-level change distorts choices between work and leisure.*

Macroeconomic Equilibrium

The intersection of the aggregate-demand and the aggregate-supply curves shows the price level at which the quantities of real GNP demanded and supplied are equal to one another. This is **macroeconomic equilibrium.** At any price level above equilibrium, there will be excess supply in the economy. Production will be reduced and prices will be lowered as firms attempt to dispose of excess inventories. Conversely, at any price level lower than equilibrium, there will be excess demand in the economy. Firms find that inventories have been reduced to below desired levels and will increase production and prices in order to regain their desired position.

Macroeconomic equilibrium exists when the price level is such as to secure an equality between real GNP demanded and supplied.

Is macroeconomic equilibrium a desirable situation for the economy? Does it represent full employment? Economists disagree on the answers to these important questions. We will explore their differing views in Chapters 16 and 17. However, to prepare for those chapters, we shall review how contractions (recessions) and expansions take place in the macroeconomy.[3] The aggregate-

demand and aggregate-supply model provides a useful framework for understanding the causes and alternative policies for dealing with changes in macroeconomic equilibrium.

RECESSION

Our first illustration is a model of recession. In Figure 3 we start at point *A*—an equilibrium condition at the intersection of aggregate-demand curve AD_1 and aggregate-supply curve AS_1. We assume that this equilibrium has lasted for a long enough time that people have become well adjusted to it. This assumption is important because it means that wage rates and other costs are in step with product prices and that people have adjusted their economic behavior to the price level, P_1.

In this illustration the recession begins with a shift of the aggregate-demand curve to the left from AD_1 to AD_2 (arrow 1 in Figure 3). Such a shift may have brought about the Great Depression of the 1930s. Keynesians find that it was caused by falling planned investment due to poor business prospects after the stock market crash. Monetarists believe that the cause was a reduced money stock due to widespread bank failures. In each view, however, there was a demand-side shock to the economy, which tended to reduce the equilibrium level of real GNP. Unplanned inventories accumulate because of the fall in aggregate demand and, in order to rid themselves of this unwanted inventory, firms lay off workers and cut production and prices. As the aggregate-demand curve shifts to the left, the equilibrium point moves down and to the left along the AS_1 curve from point *A* to point *B*. Unemployment rises and both output and prices decline to Y_2 and P_2, respectively.

The seriousness of the move from *A* to *B* depends on the slope of the aggregate-supply curve and on how far the aggregate-demand curve shifts to the left. If the aggregate-supply curve is steep, few people will lose their jobs. If it is flat, many jobs will be lost. If the recession is severe enough, the pessimism caused by rising unemployment and

---

3. See Chapter 9 for an introduction to this subject.

falling prices may bring further leftward shifts in the aggregate-demand curve. In other words, the recession may feed on itself in a pattern called **hyperdeflation**. Probably this really did happen in the Great Depression of the 1930s. For simplicity, we do not illustrate this extra shift of the aggregate-demand curve in Figure 3.

Starting from an equilibrium situation, a shift to the left of the aggregate-demand curve will cause recession, with falling real GNP and increasing unemployment.

Recovery by Deflation

Point B in Figure 3 is not a stable or long-run equilibrium position because the changes in economic conditions have set in motion forces that will shift the aggregate-supply curve. The shift comes as the wage–cost lag disappears and as the money illusion breaks down, causing the AS curve to shift to the right, from AS_1 to AS_2 (arrow 2). Wage rates and prices of other input are reduced as resource owners realize that *real* rates of compensation have not fallen. Moreover, the hard facts of the recession have sapped the financial reserves of many people. Therefore, they decide not to hold out any longer for higher wages for labor, higher interest on bonds, higher rent on natural resources, or higher profits.

The rightward shift of the aggregate-supply curve illustrates a **"deflationist"** solution for the problem of economic recession. The squeeze on profits, which motivated firms to reduce output and employment in the recession, is to be relieved by lowering wage rates and the prices of other inputs. According to the deflationist prescription, the fading money illusion will make these reductions acceptable to workers and other resource owners. As the AS curve shifts to the right, the equilibrium condition slides down the AD_2 curve, bringing lower prices and greater output. Our model shows real GNP at the new equilibrium (point C) to be exactly the same as at point A before the initial shift in aggregate demand. However, some economists doubt that the AS curve will shift far enough to bring the economy all the way back to its original level.

FIGURE 3
Recession Caused by a Decrease in Aggregate Demand

The initial macroeconomic equilibrium is at A. In this illustration, recession is caused by a reduction in aggregate demand, shifting AD_1 to the left to AD_2 (arrow 1). Macroeconomic equilibrium moves from point A to point B, the price level falls from P_1 to P_2, and real GNP falls from Y_1 to Y_2.

The "deflationist" remedy for the recession is to allow the AS curve to shift to the right (arrow 2) as the wage–cost lag and money illusion disappear. In this way, equilibrium moves from point B to point C, real GNP increases from Y_2 to Y_1 in the recovery, and the price level falls to P_3.

The "reflationist" remedy for the recession is to use expansionary monetary and fiscal policies to return aggregate demand to its original level, shifting the aggregate-demand curve from AD_2 to AD_1. Real GNP returns to Y_1 and the price level returns to P_1.

Recovery from a recession may come through reductions in wage rates and prices of other inputs. These reductions enlarge profit margins and invite increases in output.

Recovery by Reflation

In the situation that existed in the Great Depression, many people felt that solving the problem with the "deflation" solution would take too long, cause too much suffering, and endanger the political stability of the country. Over the early years of the 1930s, prices had fallen by almost 25 percent and about 25 percent of the labor force was unemployed.

Shifting the aggregate-demand curve back to its original position offers an alternative way out of a recession caused by a demand-side shock. This is recovery by **reflation,** that is, by causing the price level to return upward to a level that prevailed earlier. The "reflationist" prescription can be illustrated with the same graph that showed the "'deflationist" approach. Starting from point B in Figure 3, expansionary fiscal and monetary actions can be undertaken in order to shift the aggregate-demand curve to the right, from AD_2 back to AD_1. This was the route that the Keynesian model indicated as a way out of the depression of the 1930s. By using expansionary fiscal and monetary policies (see Chapters 11 and 14), aggregate demand can be increased, reversing the decline that had caused the recession. Both employment and prices return to their earlier levels as the equilibrium condition moves upward and to the right along the original aggregate-supply curve, AS_1.

Shifting the aggregate-demand curve to the right by monetary and fiscal policies is a reflationist proposal to obtain recovery from recession.

In retrospect, the reflationist prescription for the problems of the Great Depression appears clearly preferable to the deflationist prescription. At the time, however, the prospect of large and intentional government deficits was upsetting to many people and especially to business and financial leaders. They feared unrestrained government spending and the taxes that they believed would eventually be required. The expansionary moves undertaken by the New Deal administration were timid by later standards and produced disappointing results.[4]

4. See "John Meynard Keynes and the Great Depression" following p. 246.

EXPANSION

Our second illustration of aggregate demand–aggregate supply analysis is something like the one just studied, except that it pictures the process of **expansion.** As in the recession model, the initiating event comes from the demand side. However, this time the aggregate-demand curve shifts to the right rather than to the left. This occurred in the 1960s when fiscal and monetary instruments of government generally worked in an expansionary direction to stimulate the economy and to carry on a "War on Poverty" at home and a war in Vietnam without large rises in taxes. Another example was in the first half of the 1980s when expansion was fueled by reductions in taxes and increases in defense purchases. These expansionary policies shifted the aggregate-demand curve to the right.

Figure 4 illustrates the model of economic expansion. We begin at point A, the intersection of the initial aggregate-demand curve, AD_1, and the initial aggregate-supply curve, AS_1. Again we assume that this situation has lasted long enough for people to have adjusted their behavior to this price level and to this level of real GNP.

After the shift to the right of the aggregate-demand curve, the new equilibrium is at B, where the new aggregate-demand curve, AD_2, intersects aggregate-supply curve, AS_1. The rise in demand causes inventories to fall below planned levels, and companies respond with higher prices (to keep inventory from being used up too quickly and to make higher profits) and with increased production to restore inventories to desired levels.

Expansion may be started by monetary and fiscal policies that shift the aggregate-demand curve to the right.

Higher Output and Prices

Along the path from A to B, the economy is experiencing good times. Wages and other costs of production are lagging behind increases in prices of finished goods so profit margins are attractive. Employment is increasing. Even though wage rates are lagging behind increases in the general price level,

FIGURE 4
Expansion Caused by an Increase in Aggregate Demand

The initial macroeconomic equilibrium is at *A*. In this illustration, expansion is caused by an increase in aggregate demand, shifting AD_1 to AD_2 (arrow 1). Macroeconomic equilibrium moves from point *A* to point *B*, the price level rises to P_2, and real GNP increases to Y_2.

The expansion of real GNP ceases at point *B* when the wage–cost lag and money illusion fade away, causing AS_1 to shift to the left to AS_2 (arrow 2). While this shift is taking place—during the move from *B* to *C*—the economy suffers stagflation. At the new equilibrium, point *C*, real GNP has returned to Y_1 and the price level has risen to P_3.

faster until money becomes virtually worthless and economic collapse is threatened.[5]

In an expansion, the mixture between output increases and price-level increases depends on the slope of the aggregate-supply curve.

In hyperinflation situations, the rising price level causes people to speed up purchasing, shifting the aggregate-demand curve to the right and causing more inflation.

Stagflation

Point *B* does not represent a stable or long-run equilibrium for reasons that are parallel to those in the recession case. In the movement from *A* to *B* along the AS_1 curve in Figure 4, some people mistakenly believe that the increases in nominal wage (and profit, interest, and rent) rates represent equivalent increases in real rates. They believe that these increases in nominal wage (and profit, interest, and rent) rates have changed the real tradeoff between work and leisure in favor of working more. Because of the supposedly higher rewards, more jobs and overtime are accepted and more business ventures undertaken. However, as time passes, these people realize that some of the increases in nominal wage (and profit, interest, and rent) rates have been lost to increases in the general price level and the rising cost of living. Real wages have not increased as they thought they had.

As people gain a more accurate understanding of the relative prices of work and leisure, the money illusion evaporates. Workers start to play "catch-up" in wage negotiations, asking for wage-rate increases in excess of productivity increases so that they can make up for the purchasing power losses they have suffered from inflation. Strikes are more frequent as wages and other costs catch up from the wage–cost lag and close the gap that had existed during the expansion. Profit margins become smaller. Through these actions, reflecting the closing of the wage–cost lag and the fading of

workers are working longer hours and taking home larger paychecks. Because of money illusion, they overestimate their increase in real income and the attractiveness of work compared with leisure.

The mixture between price increases and output increases depends on the slope of the *AS* curve. If the curve is quite flat, prices will rise little and output will expand significantly. But if the *AS* curve is steep, as may be the case if there has been recent experience with inflation, prices may rise rapidly with only modest increases in output. In extreme situations, called **hyperinflation,** the rising prices induce further shifts of the aggregate-demand curve as people hurry to spend their income before it loses its buying power. Prices rise

5. See the discussion of inflation in Germany, pp. 152–153.

money illusion, the AS curve in Figure 4 shifts to the left, from AS_1 to AS_2 and the equilibrium condition moves along the AD_2 curve from point B to point C.

The move from B to C involves falling output, rising unemployment, and continuing increases in the price level—a combination that economists have labeled **stagflation.** Stagflation offers the "worst of both worlds" in macroeconomics. The U.S. economy and many others in the world suffered from stagflation during the 1970s, partly as a result of earlier aggregate-demand increases and partly from supply-side shocks, which we will discuss shortly. Our illustration in Figure 4 suggests that equilibrium will be established at point C, when profit margins have returned to normal and people have adapted to the new price level of P_3, so that money illusion and "catching up" no longer influence behavior.

As wage rates and other input prices catch up with earlier increases in the prices of final goods and as money illusion fades, the aggregate-supply curve shifts to the left and the economy experiences stagflation.

Monetary and fiscal policy alternatives for dealing with stagflation are unattractive. Shifting the aggregate-demand curve to the right promises still more inflation, whereas shifting it to the left threatens still greater unemployment.

LONG-RUN AGGREGATE SUPPLY AND POTENTIAL GNP

In each of the exercises just completed, the consequences of a shift of the aggregate-demand curve were, first, a movement along the aggregate-supply curve, while money illusion and wage–cost lags operated, and then a shift of the AS curve as money illusion faded and as wage rates and costs caught up with other prices. Now we must ask about the relation between the price level and real GNP supplied in the long run, after the shift of the AS curve has been completed.

To keep our discussion conceptually clear, suppose that no change takes place in physical production capabilities (level of technology, size and skill of the labor force, size and quantity of the stock of capital, and so on) during the time it takes for wage and cost gaps and money illusion effects to disappear. Then we can define **long-run aggregate supply** as follows: *the relationship between changes in the price level and changes in real GNP supplied that prevails as long as there is no change in production capability but when enough time has passed for people to adapt completely to the existing price level.*

The concept that we have defined above as long-run aggregate supply is sometimes referred to as **potential GNP**—the real GNP produced when all resources, except those idle for seasonal, frictional, or structural reasons, are fully employed. As defined in Chapter 8, they are fully employed when working exactly the amount of time that they wish at their going real rates of compensation. In terms of our present discussion, it means that there are no wage–cost lags and no money illusion.

Long-run aggregate supply (also called potential GNP) is equal to the level of real GNP that the economy will produce when wage–cost lags and money illusion are not distorting choices. All resources (except those seasonally, frictionally, or structurally out of work) are working for exactly the number of hours per week that they wish to work at the going real wage rates.

Does the Price Level Affect Long-Run Aggregate Supply and Potential GNP?

Figure 5 shows long-run aggregate supply and the potential GNP suggested in the recession and expansion models studied earlier. Let the intersection of AD_1 and AS_1 (point A) show the beginning equilibrium point for both of these models. The recession process is shown by the shift of the aggregate-demand curve from AD_1 to AD_2, followed by the shift of the aggregate-supply curve from AS_1 to AS_2 as wage–cost lags and the money illusion wear off. Equilibrium is finally restored at the intersection of AD_2 and AS_2 (point B). The expansion process is

FIGURE 5
Long-Run Aggregate Supply and Potential GNP

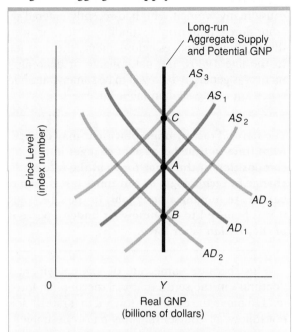

This graph combines Figures 3 and 4 to suggest that the economy eventually returns to its long-run aggregate supply or potential GNP after disturbances caused by changes in aggregate demand. The recession model starts at point A and eventually returns the economy to point B. The expansion model also starts at point A, but eventually returns the economy to point C. Long-run aggregate supply and potential GNP are represented by real GNP of Y and by the vertical line passing through points A, B, and C.

slope—that in the long-run, real GNP is greater at high price levels than at low price levels, other things being equal. These economists say that, even without wage–cost lags and money illusion, the price level can influence production behavior. It is the choice between work and leisure that is involved. Their argument parallels the real balances theory, which we explained earlier in connection with the aggregate-demand curve. It goes like this. At high price levels, assets whose values are given in fixed nominal amounts (such as money and government bonds) have low real purchasing power value. The low real wealth of people holding these assets persuades them to work harder and longer than they would at a lower price level. At low price levels, however, these assets have high real purchasing power, and their holders have greater real wealth, so they consume more leisure and do less work than at high price levels. These economists conclude, therefore, that the long-run aggregate-supply curve is not a vertical line but has some positive slope.

Although some argue that long-run aggregate supply or potential GNP is positively related to the price level, most believe that the price level has no effect on its value.

---

shown by the shift of the aggregate-demand curve from AD_1 to AD_3, followed by the shift of the aggregate-supply curve from AS_1 to AS_3, again as wage–cost lags and the money illusion wear off. Here, equilibrium is finally restored at the intersection of AD_3 and AS_3 (point C). In each case, we have assumed that the final equilibrium is at exactly the same real GNP as the starting equilibrium, so that the long-run aggregate-supply curve is a vertical line. In other words, we suppose that, in each case, the aggregate-supply curve shifts far enough to return the economy to its potential GNP.

Some economists believe that the vertical long-run aggregate-supply curve is a special case and that more often the curve has a positive

The Natural Rate of Unemployment

In Chapter 8 when we introduced the concept of the **natural rate of unemployment**—it was defined in the context of official government statistics—the rate that is limited to seasonal, frictional, and structural unemployment. It is also the rate of unemployment that corresponds with long-run aggregate supply and potential GNP. If the *microeconomy* were functioning perfectly, each person would be on his or her own labor-supply curve. As explained in Chapter 8, this means that each person would be working exactly the number of hours per week or per month or per year that he or she wished to work at the prevailing real wage rate. The balance between work and leisure would exactly match his or her preferences at this wage rate.

> **The natural rate of unemployment is the measured rate of unemployment that exists when the economy is operating at its potential GNP.**

In both the recession and the expansion exercises in this chapter, we assumed that the initial price level had existed long enough so that everyone had fully adjusted to it. Thus, there were no distortions due to wage–cost lags or money illusion. In other words, the natural rate of unemployment existed at the start of each exercise (at points *A* in Figures 3 and 4). Similarly, the natural rate of unemployment existed at the close of each of these exercises (at points *C* in these figures), since wáge–cost gaps and money illusion faded out as the aggregate-supply curve shifted. What happened during these exercises was that *actual* unemployment rose above the natural rate during the recession exercise and fell below the natural rate during the expansion exercise.

> **During recessions, the actual rate of unemployment is greater than the natural rate of unemployment.**

What will the official or "measured" rate of unemployment be when the economy is at potential GNP? There will be some structural, some frictional, and some seasonal unemployment. The structural unemployment exists because some industries are growing and others are contracting, so that workers must retrain and move around to qualify for different job openings. Frictional unemployment exists as people seek jobs that pay better or are more satisfying. In addition, measurement problems arise because people falsely claim to be unemployed in order to collect unemployment compensation payments. There is no macroeconomic or cyclical unemployment when the economy is at potential GNP.

The natural rate of unemployment itself may change from time to time because of changes in the composition of the labor force, in consumer tastes, in the rate of change of technology, and in barriers to moving from one job to another. For example, it is likely that the natural rate of unemployment rose during the 1970s because of the great changes in relative prices caused by oil-price increases and because many women who had recently entered the labor force had trouble finding a job or went through several moves before finding the right job. In the late 1980s, the natural rate of unemployment was generally believed to be somewhat under 6 percent of the civilian labor force.

> **The natural rate of unemployment may change from time to time because of changes in the composition of the labor force, in the rate of change in technology, in consumer tastes, and in barriers to moving among jobs. In the late 1980s, it was believed to be somewhat under 6 percent of the civilian labor force.**

Just because some rate of unemployment is "natural" in the sense that macroeconomic forces tend to move the economy toward that rate, it does not follow, of course, that this rate is desirable or that nothing can be done to lower it. *Microeconomic* tools may be able to lower the natural rate of unemployment and so raise the real living standard of the society. Among these microeconomic tools are measures to improve mobility and reduce discrimination in job markets, ways to make more information available to workers, and so on.

Changes in Long-Run Aggregate Supply and Potential GNP

In our definition of long-run aggregate supply, we assume that there is no change in physical production capabilities, such as might come from changes in the level of technology, the size and skill of the labor force, and the size and quality of the stock of capital equipment. Now we ask what will happen if a change in physical production capability does take place.

The answer is that long-run aggregate supply and potential GNP change along with the size and productivity of the economy's labor force, the size and quality of its stock of capital goods, and its level of technology. It is ordinarily presumed that these determinants increase from year to year and nourish economic growth.

Cultural and institutional matters are important in determining long-run aggregate supply and potential GNP. Cultural factors may influence the way in which people divide their time between work and leisure, say, between enjoying a new car and watching the sunset. Institutional factors, such as whether the economy is organized through free markets or through central planning, may also be important.

SUPPLY SHOCKS

The recession and the expansion models in this chapter both began with a shift in the aggregate-demand curve. That is, they originated in demand-side events or shocks. Expansions and contractions can also be caused by shifts in the aggregate-supply curve, that is, by **supply shocks.** An expansionary

shock might be an important technological break-through, the discovery of a great new natural resource, or a rise in labor force participation. Such shocks would shift the aggregate-supply curve to the right and increase long-run aggregate supply and potential GNP. Contractionary supply shocks can result from the destruction of productive capacity through wars or other disasters. They can also be artificially created, as when the Organization of Petroleum Exporting Countries (OPEC) cut the output of oil in the 1970s. These shocks can shift the aggregate-supply curve to the left.

Supply shocks are events that shift an economy's aggregate-supply curve.

Figure 6 shows the two forms of supply shocks. In the contractionary supply-shock case in

FIGURE 6
Supply Shocks

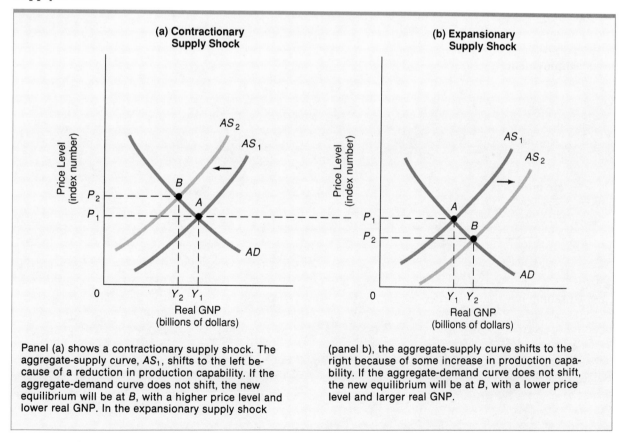

Panel (a) shows a contractionary supply shock. The aggregate-supply curve, AS_1, shifts to the left because of a reduction in production capability. If the aggregate-demand curve does not shift, the new equilibrium will be at B, with a higher price level and lower real GNP. In the expansionary supply shock

(panel b), the aggregate-supply curve shifts to the right because of some increase in production capability. If the aggregate-demand curve does not shift, the new equilibrium will be at B, with a lower price level and larger real GNP.

panel (a), the initial equilibrium is at A. A shift to the left in the aggregate-supply curve leads to a new equilibrium at B, a higher price level, P_2, and a lower level of real GNP, Y_2. These changes follow as long as the aggregate-demand curve does not shift, because a given money supply (implied in the aggregate-demand curve) is being used to purchase a smaller amount of output.

In the expansionary supply-shock case in panel (b), the initial equilibrium is at A, and the aggregate-supply curve shifts to the right. If the aggregate-demand curve does not shift, the new equilibrium will be at B, with a lower price level, P_2, and greater real GNP, Y_2. The given money supply (implied in the aggregate-demand curve) is being used to buy more goods and services.

An important assumption in each of these cases is that there is no shift in the aggregate-demand curve. But you know that the aggregate-demand curve can be shifted by means of the mon-etary and fiscal instruments of government policy. So it is quite possible that the government will decide that shifts in the aggregate-supply curve should be met with shifts in the aggregate-demand curve. The aggregate-demand policy choice in the face of an expansionary supply shock undoubtedly would be to increase aggregate demand. However, aggregate-demand policy faces a dilemma in the contractionary supply-shock case. Increasing aggregate demand will push the price level further upward while decreasing aggregate demand will reduce real GNP and increase unemployment.

Monetary and fiscal policy poses a dilemma in the face of contractionary supply shocks, since expansionary policy will increase inflation while contractionary policy will increase unemployment.

Economics in Focus

Raising Employee Productivity

Productivity is an important force causing changes in aggregate supply from year to year. Faced with increasingly stiff international competition, U.S. executives have tried various ways to raise productivity: computerizing, automating, restructuring, merging, and so on. Quite naturally, one major trend involves a focus on the largest component of the total production—the workers. Through profit sharing and employee stock-ownership plans (ESOPs), more and more firms are boosting their employees' stake in the business.

In a profit-sharing system, employees' compensation varies according to the firm's profits. In good times the employees earn more, in bad times less. The rewards can be distributed as extra cash in the paychecks or (more often) as contributions to a retirement package. In ESOPs (frequently considered a variant of profit sharing), employees receive company stock, generally as part of the pension arrangement.

Both of these methods have a number of short-term benefits for the company and may shorten lags between price-level changes and changes in wage costs. Profit sharing offers a financial cushion during hard times, and it also helps the company avoid automatic annual salary increases. ESOPs bring tax breaks, discourage corporate raiders, and often reduce the cash the company must lay out for retirement benefits. But in both cases the principal benefit may be the effect on productivity.

The A&P supermarket chain was foundering in the early 1980s when it negotiated a profit-sharing agreement with the workers at some of its stores. In exchange for a 25 percent cut in base pay, the company agreed to pay bonuses linked to productivity at each participating market. When the employees kept a store's labor costs at 10 percent of the sales total (below the industry average), A&P paid a cash bonus of 1 percent of sales. As a result, per-store sales climbed by 24 percent in two years.

An example of success with ESOPs is the Brunswick Corporation, which introduced an employee stock plan in 1983. In the next five years, sales per employee rose by almost 50 percent. Other major companies with ESOPs include Procter & Gamble, Polaroid, Texaco, and US West. In 1987 Avis became 100 percent employee-owned and was quick to proclaim that fact in advertising. By 1989 *Business Week* was able to declare that American businesses were "rushing headlong" into ESOPs.

But giving employees a stake in the company seems to work best when they also have a strong voice in operations, and this is a power many managers are reluctant to yield. Some critics say it is unfair to base compensation on profits, since poor profits may not be the workers' fault; others worry that ESOPs leave retiring employees at the mercy of stock market fluctuations. Nevertheless, profit sharing and ESOPs may well offer at least a partial remedy for ailing American productivity.

Sources: David R. Altany, "Profit-Sharing Plans Work," *Industry Week,* May 2, 1988, p. 19f.; Christopher Farrell and John Hoerr, "ESOPs: Are They Good for You?" *Business Week,* May 15, 1989, pp. 116–123 (quotation at p. 116); Christopher S. Eklund, "How A&P Fattens Profits by Sharing Them," *Business Week,* December 22, 1986, p. 44; Karen Pennar, "The Productivity Paradox," *Business Week,* June 6, 1988, pp. 100–102.

SUMMARY

1. Aggregate-demand curves and aggregate-supply curves show relationships between changes in the price level, as measured by some index number, and changes in real GNP. These concepts are helpful in understanding the economics of inflation and unemployment. (See page 326.)

2. Two theories help to explain the negative slope of the aggregate-demand curve. The interest rate theory is that higher price levels, if other things are equal, reduce the *real* money supply and cause higher real rates of interest, which reduce planned investment spending and thereby lower real GNP demanded. The real balances theory is that higher price levels lower the real value of wealth held as money or assets denominated in terms of money. These wealth reductions may reduce planned consumption spending, thus lowering the level of real GNP demanded. (See pages 327–329.)

3. A shift in the aggregate-demand curve means a change in the quantity of real GNP demanded at any given price level. Many variables may shift this curve. Monetary and fiscal policies are important because they permit governments to influence variables that change the location of this curve. (See pages 329–330.)

4. The aggregate-supply curve shows how changes in the price level affect the quantity of real GNP supplied in the economy. It has a positive slope because wage rates and other costs of production tend to lag behind changes in the price level and because, when the price level changes, the behavior of many people in the economy is affected by money illusion—the belief that changes in nominal values are the same as changes in real values. (See pages 330–331.)

5. Money illusion and lags of wage rates and costs do not continue indefinitely after a change in the price level. As wage rates and costs catch up to the change in the prices of final goods, and as money illusion fades away, the aggregate-supply curve shifts in such a way as to move the quantity supplied in the direction of the initial volume of real GNP. (See pages 331–334.)

6. In macroeconomic equilibrium, the price level exactly balances the quantity of real GNP demanded with the quantity supplied. This condition exists at the intersection of the aggregate-demand curve and the aggregate-supply curve. (See page 334.)

7. The recession model describes how an economy may experience a period of high unemployment and declining price levels due to a leftward shift in aggregate demand. But as the *AS* curve shifts to the right, the economy expands toward its original level of real GNP. (See pages 334–336.)

8. The expansion model describes how an economy may experience a period of low unemployment and rising price levels due to a rightward shift in aggregate demand. But as the *AS* curve shifts to the left, the economy contracts toward its original level of real GNP. (See pages 336–338.)

9. A situation with sluggish growth, inflation, and increasing unemployment is called stagflation. This combination of problems arises as a result of a leftward shift of the aggregate-supply curve. Demand-side remedies are unattractive in this situation. (See page 338.)

10. Long-run macroeconomic equilibrium—the economy's potential GNP—is achieved when a given price level has existed long enough so that neither wage–cost lag nor money illusion is distorting decisions in the economy. The long-run relationship between the price level and the quantity of real GNP supplied may appear as a vertical line on an aggregate-demand and aggregate-supply graph, although some economists believe that it has a positive slope. (See pages 338–339.)

11. Long-run aggregate supply and potential GNP can be changed by changes in production capabilities. Expansions in production capability increase long-run aggregate supply and potential GNP. Reductions in production capability reduce long-run aggregate supply and potential GNP. Cultural and institutional variables also are important. (See pages 338–340.)

12. The natural rate of unemployment is the rate of measured unemployment that corresponds with potential GNP. It includes seasonal, frictional, and structural unemployment, but not macroeconomic (or cylical) unemployment. This natural rate may change over time if changes take place in the labor force or in the pace of other changes in the economy. (See pages 339–340.)

13. Economic disturbances can arise from supply-side shocks, which shift the aggregate-supply curve. Shocks that reduce production shift the curve to the left, and shocks that increase production shift the curve to the right. (See pages 341–342.)

KEY TERMS

aggregate demand: the relationship between a change in the price level and the resulting change in the quantity of real GNP demanded (page 326).

aggregate supply: the relationship between a change in the price level and the resulting change in the quantity of real GNP supplied (page 326).

aggregate-supply curve: the graphic representation of the relationship between changes in the price level and changes in real GNP supplied (page 330).

cost of living adjustment (COLA): an agreement under which wage rates are changed automatically on the basis of specified changes in the price level (page 333).

deflationist policy: the plan to recover from a recession by allowing wage rates and other input prices to fall so that profit margins will expand and invite increases in output (page 335).

expansion: a situation in the economy when real GNP is increasing and unemployment is falling (page 336).

hyperdeflation: a situation in which the pessimism engendered by recession induces shifts to the left of the aggregate-demand curve, increasing the severity of the recession (page 335).

hyperinflation: a situation in which a rising price level induces shifts to the right of the aggregate-demand curve, increasing the rate of inflation (page 337).

interest-rate theory: the proposition that an increase in the price level, *ceteris paribus*, reduces the real money supply, increases the real rate of interest, and thereby reduces planned investment and the quantity of real GNP demanded. The theory works in the opposite direction for decreases in the price level; also called Keynes effect (page 327).

long-run aggregate supply: the relationship between changes in the price level and changes in

real GNP supplied that prevails as long as there is no change in production capability but when enough time has passed for people to adapt completely to the existing price level; also called, potential GNP (page 338).

macroeconomic equilibrium: the situation in which the price level is such as to secure an equality between real GNP demanded and supplied (page 334).

money illusion: the mistaken belief that changes in nominal values are changes in real values. The theory suggests a positive slope for the aggregate-supply curve (page 332).

natural rate of unemployment: the measured rate of unemployment when the economy is operating at its potential GNP. (Only seasonal, frictional, and structural unemployment exists) (page 339).

potential GNP: the quantity of real GNP indicated by an economy's long-run aggregate supply curve (page 338).

rate of economic growth: the percentage change per year in an economy's potential GNP (page 338).

real balances theory: the proposition that an increase in the price level, *ceteris paribus*, reduces the real wealth of those holding assets denominated in money terms and that this reduction in wealth leads to reduced planned expenditure and a smaller quantity of real GNP demanded. The theory works in the opposite direction for decreases in the price level; also called Pigou effect (page 327).

recession: a situation in the economy when real GNP is falling and unemployment is increasing (page 334).

reflation: an increase in the price level that returns it to a level that had existed previously (page 336).

stagflation: a situation in the economy when the price-level is rising while unemployment is increasing (page 338).

supply shock: an event which causes a shift in an economy's aggregate-supply curve (page 341).

wage–cost lag theory: the proposition that changes in wage rates and the prices of other inputs to production lag behind changes in the prices of final goods (page 330).

wage-rate and cost "catch up": the process through which wage rates and other input prices cease to lag behind the prices of final goods (page 333).

DISCUSSION QUESTIONS

1. Draw an aggregate-demand and aggregate-supply graph, being careful to label correctly each axis. Then compare your curve with Figure 1. Why is it *not* correct to refer to the $C + I + G + X - Im$ curve as a demand curve?

2. The interest rate theory (or Keynes effect) about the slope of the aggregate-demand curve uses the transmission system that you learned in Chapter 14. Without looking at Figure 2, draw the four graphs in this transmission system and then check to be sure you are right. If the investment-demand curve is steep, will the aggregate-demand curve be steep or flat? Explain.

3. What will happen to the real value of your life insurance policies when the price level rises? Will this change cause you to divide your current disposable income between consumption and saving in a different way? Explain how your answers to these questions can lead to an understanding of the real balances theory about the slope of the aggregate-demand curve.

4. Average gross hourly earnings in private nonagricultural employment were $4.53 in 1975, and $9.32 in 1988. Assuming a complete money illusion, explain how this change would affect worker behavior according to an aggregate-supply curve. After adjustment for price-level change, real wages in 1988 were almost the same as in 1975. Explain how elimination of money illusion places the economy at its long-run aggregate-supply or potential GNP level of output.

5. Without looking at Figure 3, construct the graph illustrating a recession process. Then check to be sure you have it right. Using the concepts of wage–cost lag and money illusion, explain why the first phase of the process involves rising unemployment while the second phase involves falling unemployment.

6. Hyperdeflation involves a leftward shift of the aggregate-demand curve, which is induced by the hard times resulting from some ongoing contraction of the economy. Explain hyperdeflation in terms of the graph that you drew for Question 5.

7. Thinking now about the expansion process, illustrate on a graph how a rightward shift of the aggregate-demand curve brings a higher price level and a temporary increase in real GNP. Check with Figure 4 to be sure you are correct. Explain the process in words, again stressing the role of wage–cost lag and money illusion.

8. Construct a pair of aggregate demand–aggregate supply graphs, one to illustrate a contractionary supply shock and the other to illustrate an expansionary supply shock. Compare your graphs with Figure 6. How did the drought in 1988 in U.S. agricultural areas affect the aggregate-supply curve?

9. Write down from memory our definition of long-run aggregate supply and potential GNP. Check to be sure you have it right. Explain how the wage–cost lag and money-illusion concepts relate to these values. Discuss two forces (one of them social and the other environmental) that could change long-run aggregate supply and potential GNP.

10. Explain the reasoning that concludes that macroeconomic equilibrium tends to establish the natural rate of unemployment. Why can this rate also be called full employment? How does racial discrimination or sex discrimination in labor markets affect the natural rate of unemployment? How would elimination of such discrimination change the real level of potential GNP? Explain.

16

The Phillips Curve, Adaptive Expectations, and Inflation Economics

Preview For more than half a century—ever since the Great Depression—the U.S. economy has experienced continuous increases in its price level. From the late 1960s through the early 1980s, the U.S. economy experienced almost continuous significant rates of increase in its price level. Some of the pressures for inflation during that time came from war expenditures for the Vietnam conflict, some were thrust upon the economy by supply shocks coming from increased world petroleum prices, and some arose from domestic policies such as the War on Poverty and Great Society programs. Whatever the causes, inflation became a focus of attention in economic analysis. This chapter examines several important aspects of the economic analysis of inflation.

The first section of the chapter examines the Phillips curve, which achieved wide acceptance in the early 1960s as a guide for macroeconomic policy. Although the Phillips-curve model appeared to work in the early and middle 1960s, it failed as a policy guide in the late 1960s and throughout the 1970s. We proceed, therefore, by exploring theories that contend that the Phillips-curve model failed because it requires that inflation be unanticipated when, in fact, the extended experience with inflation nourished inflationary expectation.

The second part of the chapter looks at the phenomenon of stagflation—simultaneous increases in both the unemployment rate and the inflation rate. We examine several alternative macroeconomic policies that may be adopted in the face of stagflation driven by inflationary expectations. Choosing among these alternatives was the focus of macroeconomic policy during the 1970s and early 1980s.

The last part of the chapter deals with wage and price controls, such as typically are imposed in emergency times, when large increases in aggregate demand are expected to bring inflationary pressures. We examine not only the theoretical basis for believing that controls can help fight inflation, but also the real-world difficulties in effectively sustaining these controls.

THE PHILLIPS CURVE AND ADAPTIVE EXPECTATIONS

Toward the close of the 1950s, a number of events set the stage for active macroeconomic policy. In 1957, the Soviet Union beat the United States into space by launching *Sputnik,* an orbiting space vehicle the size of a basketball. In 1958, the U.S. economy experienced its worst recession (up to that point) since World War II. The recession and the Soviet success in space contributed to the success of John F. Kennedy's 1960 campaign slogan, "Let's Get This Country Moving Again." When President Kennedy took office in 1961, Keynesian economics, which had been taught in classrooms for a generation, became the vehicle for active macroeconomic policy. Also, in 1958 an article written by A.W.H. Phillips appeared in *Economica.*[1] It described a relationship between unemployment and wage rates in Great Britain from 1861 to 1957. This relationship provided the basis for what became known as the Phillips curve, which played an important part in macroeconomic policy during the 1960s and 1970s.

A **Phillips curve** is illustrated in Figure 1. The horizontal axis shows the unemployment rate, and the vertical axis shows the inflation rate, that is, the annual percentage change in the price level. The curve is derived by plotting the actual experience of the economy for a number of years. For example, in Figure 1, in year 1 the inflation rate was 1 percent and the unemployment rate was 5 percent. In year 2, the inflation rate was 3 percent and the unemployment rate was also 3 percent. In year 3,

1. A.W.H. Phillips, "The Relationship Between Unemployment and the Rate of Change of Money Wage Rates in the United Kingdom, 1861–1957," *Economica,* November 1958.

FIGURE 1
A Phillips Curve

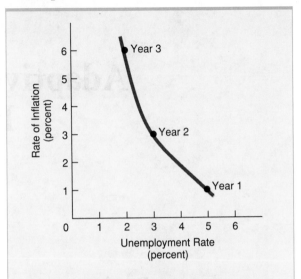

A Phillips curve is constructed by plotting the unemployment-rate and inflation-rate experience over a number of years and by constructing a line representing the pattern determined by the location of these plotted points. In the figure, year 1 had 5 percent unemployment and a 1 percent inflation rate, year 2 had 3 percent unemployment and a 3 percent inflation rate, and year 3 had 2 percent unemployment and a 6 percent inflation rate. As applied in the 1960s, the Phillips curve suggested that policymakers could choose their preferred combination of unemployment and inflation from among those located on the curve.

the inflation rate was 6 percent and the unemployment rate was 2 percent. The curve itself is generated by connecting the plotted points with a smooth line. In actual practice, points are plotted for many years, and a curve is fitted by statistical procedures.

The Phillips curve displays the relationship between the unemployment rate and the inflation rate over a number of years.

The Phillips Curve and Macroeconomic Policy

As a guide for macroeconomic policy, the Phillips curve suggests not a cause-and-effect relationship but a tradeoff between inflation and unemployment. It implies that a reduction in the unemployment rate can be "bought" by accepting an increase in the rate of inflation. On the other hand, a reduction in the rate of inflation can be "bought" by accepting a rise in the rate of unemployment. In the context of policy formulation, the curve suggests that political parties and candidates can key their economic policy platforms to particular points along the Phillips curve. Parties looking for votes from workers who feel threatened by unemployment will most likely choose points toward the upper end of the curve, accepting inflation in order to save jobs. On the other hand, parties seeking votes from people who see inflation as their more serious problem will choose points toward the lower end of the curve, accepting higher unemployment (for others) in exchange for less inflation. Election results would, in a democracy, establish the general outline for macroeconomic policy according to the Phillips-curve model.

The Phillips curve implies that a reduction in the unemployment rate can be achieved by accepting a higher rate of inflation, and a reduction in the rate of inflation can be achieved by accepting a rise in the rate of unemployment.

Aside from determining its precise location, the economist's concern with the Phillips curve is to discover ways to shift the curve in order to improve the combinations available to decision makers. A shift of the Phillips curve downward and to the left offers an improved set of choices, since the economy could then have less unemployment, or less inflation, or some combination involving less of both, compared with any point on the original curve. On the other hand, a shift of the Phillips curve upward and to the right clearly worsens the choices available, since decision makers then would have to accept either more inflation, or more unemployment, or some combination involving more of both, compared with any point on the original curve.

The economist's concern with the Phillips curve is to discover ways to shift the curve in order to

improve the combinations available to decision makers.

Phillips-Curve Experience

Figure 2 shows the inflation-unemployment combinations that actually developed from 1961 through 1969. Most of the time during these years, fiscal and monetary actions were expansionary. The economy responded with higher and higher rates of inflation (from less than 2 percent a year in the early 1960s to almost 6 percent a year by 1969) and with reduced rates of unemployment (from almost 7 percent in 1961 to around $3\frac{1}{2}$ percent in 1968). The Phillips curve appeared to work as a guide for economic policy.

FIGURE 2
Unemployment and Inflation in the United States, 1961 through 1969

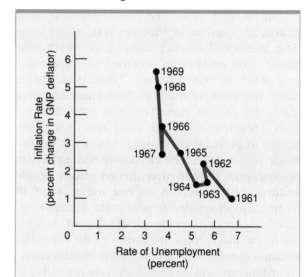

Each dot on the graph represents the combination of unemployment and inflation that existed in that year. Experience during the 1960s appeared to confirm the Phillips-curve relationship between these variables. Monetary and fiscal actions were generally expansionary, and the economy appeared to move upward along the Phillips curve. In the early part of the decade, reductions in unemployment dominated the moves. In the later years, increases in the inflation rate dominated.
Source: *Economic Report of the President, 1989,* Tables B-3 and B-39.

The Phillips-curve relationship was extremely favorable to expansionary macroeconomic policy in the early 1960s. The unemployment rate fell and the inflation rate remained at what today would be seen as very low levels. In a policy initiative inspired by the Keynesian model, President Kennedy's economic advisers recommended tax reduction as a means of increasing total planned expenditure and raising the equilibrium level of real GNP. Under President Johnson, individual income taxes were reduced substantially. True to the Keynesian model, economic expansion followed, and true to the Phillips-curve model, the rate of inflation increased as the unemployment rate fell.

In the 1960s, the Phillips curve appeared to work as a guide for economic policy. Under an expansionary macroeconomic policy, the rate of inflation increased as the unemployment rate fell.

In the mid-1960s, the United States became heavily involved in the Vietnam War. At the same time, President Johnson pushed forward with a domestic "War on Poverty" and the building of what was called the "Great Society." Deficits increased, and a rising rate of inflation dominated the move along the Phillips curve. Antiwar protests along with discontent about the rising rate of inflation helped to persuade President Johnson not to seek re-election in 1968. The election of Richard Nixon in that year showed that the American people wanted to be rid of both the war and inflation. In terms of macroeconomic policy, the election signaled a desire to lower the rate of inflation. According to the macroeconomic theory of the time, this meant a move downward along the Phillips curve.

Monetary and fiscal policies were restrictive in the first part of the Nixon administration (1969 and 1970). According to the Phillips-curve model, these restrictive policies should have produced a movement downward and to the right along the Phillips curve, that is, they should have resulted in a lower inflation rate and a somewhat higher rate of unemployment. Instead, the unemployment rate increased dramatically, and the inflation rate was higher rather than lower. In short, the results did *not* follow the Phillips-curve model.

In the late 1960s, Americans grew discontented with the rising rate of inflation. President Nixon's attempt to lower inflation by using restrictive monetary and fiscal policies failed, however, and both unemployment and inflation rose.

Figure 3 shows Phillips-curve plots for the years 1961 through 1988, with the years connected in chronological order. Clearly, the pattern is not as simple as it appeared in the 1960s. Some intervals show northwestward movement such as prevailed in the 1960s. These periods of falling unemployment and increasing inflation occurred for 1973, 1977, 1978, 1979, 1984, 1987, and 1988. There also were periods of rising unemployment and falling inflation rates, that is, when the movement was southeastward. These occurred for 1971, 1975, 1981, and 1982—the latter being part of the **Great Disinflation,** which eventually brought the inflation rate to below 2 percent. Both northwesterly and southeasterly moves are consistent with the Phillips-curve model.

There were, however, several years when the moves were different from the tradeoff relationship of the Phillips-curve model. The "worst of both worlds" situation appears in Phillips-curve graphs as a northeastward move. This shows stagflation, the combination of a rising unemployment rate along with a rising inflation rate. In Figure 3, the symptoms of stagflation appear in 1970, 1974, and 1980. The second and third of these bouts with stagflation were caused, in large measure, by supply shocks originating with increases in the price of crude petroleum imposed by the Organization of Petroleum Exporting Countries (OPEC) in 1973 and 1978. But oil shocks cannot explain the stagflation move for 1970, when the Philips-curve relationship did not work for President Nixon.

Southwesterly moves identify the "best of both worlds" situations, with reductions in both the inflation rate and the unemployment rate. These good times appeared in 1972, 1976, 1985, and 1986. The 1972 record is artificial because wage and price controls were in effect. But such controls were not in effect in the other years showing a southwesterly move on the chart. Thus, the record

FIGURE 3
Phillips-Curve Experience in the United States, 1961 through 1988

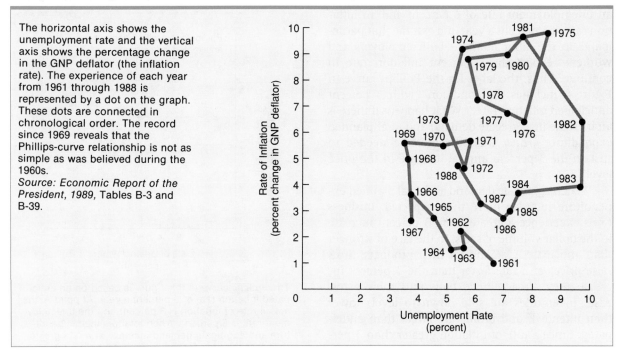

The horizontal axis shows the unemployment rate and the vertical axis shows the percentage change in the GNP deflator (the inflation rate). The experience of each year from 1961 through 1988 is represented by a dot on the graph. These dots are connected in chronological order. The record since 1969 reveals that the Phillips-curve relationship is not as simple as was believed during the 1960s.

Source: Economic Report of the President, 1989, Tables B-3 and B-39.

makes it clear that the relation between unemployment rates and inflation rates is more complex than suggested by the original Phillips-curve model.

The economy did not follow the Phillips-curve model in the 1970s and 1980s. The relationship between unemployment rates and inflation rates is more complex than suggested by the original Phillips curve.

Because experience failed to confirm predictions based on the Phillips curve, economists set to work to re-examine that model and to search for other factors affecting the inflation-unemployment relation. As explained in Chapter 15, supply shocks offered one explanation. Drastic increases in the price of a basic resource, such as petroleum, could easily force simultaneous increases in the unemployment rate and the inflation rate. But supply shocks were not the only force at work during the 1970s and 1980s. In studying the Phillips-curve model, economists concluded that expectations about coming price-level changes significantly in-

fluence the relationship between the unemployment rate and the inflation rate.

One of the factors affecting the inflation-unemployment relation is expectations about coming price-level changes.

Unanticipated Inflation

In examining the theoretical foundations of the Phillips curve, economists Milton Friedman and Edmund Phelps concluded that it contains the implicit assumption that people do not anticipate changes in the rate of inflation.[2] Friedman and Phelps reasoned that the negative relationship between the unemployment rate and the inflation rate arises because the change in the inflation rate is *not anticipated.*

2. Milton Friedman, "The Role of Monetary Policy," *American Economic Review,* March 1968, pp. 1–17; Edmund S. Phelps, "Money Wage Dynamics and Labor Market Equilibrium," *Journal of Political Economy,* July-August 1967, pp. 678–711.

Figure 4 illustrates the role of anticipation in the Phillips-curve model. We begin at point *A*, with an unemployment rate of 6 percent and an inflation rate of 3 percent a year and assume that participants in the labor market—both employers and workers—expect the 3 percent inflation rate to continue. Thus, the label for the Phillips curve in Figure 4 includes the condition "with 3 percent anticipated inflation rate." What happens if there is an increase in aggregate demand and total planned expenditure *greater* than the increase needed to sustain the 3 percent annual increase in the price level?

When aggregate demand and total planned expenditure increase more than expected, business firms experience a greater than 3 percent increase in the dollar volume of sales. In the face of stronger than anticipated demand for their products, firms raise prices at a rate faster than the 3 percent increase they already have built into their plans. Also, inventories are sold down to levels lower than intended, and profits are larger than anticipated. Since a rate of inflation greater than 3 percent is not anticipated, money illusion exists, firms believe that their *real* profit rates have increased, and, therefore, set about to expand production to earn maximum profits during the good times. To do this, they enter the resource markets to employ more labor and other production inputs.

In the labor and other resource markets, both demanders and suppliers, by assumption, expect a 3 percent increase in the price level and have built this increase into their demands and offers. If both the demand curves and the supply curves in these markets shift upward by 3 percent in nominal values, no change takes place in the equilibrium quantities demanded and supplied. However, since firms have experienced depleted inventories and profitability has increased, the demand curves for resources increase by *more* than the 3 percent built into the anticipated 3 percent inflation rate.

According to Friedman and Phelps, the negative relationship between the unemployment rate and the inflation rate arises because the change in the inflation rate is not anticipated.

FIGURE 4
The Phillips Curve and Unanticipated Inflation

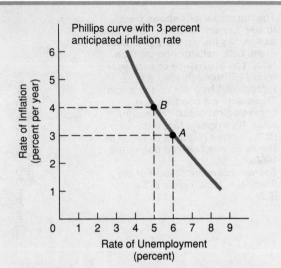

The Phillips curve in this figure is based on an anticipated inflation rate of 3 percent a year. At point *A*, the actual rate of inflation is 3 percent and the unemployment rate is 6 percent. When total planned expenditure and aggregate demand increase at a rate *greater* than that required for the 3 percent inflation rate, the unemployment rate decreases because unemployed workers receive acceptable wage offers sooner than under the previous rate of increase in aggregate demand. Therefore, as the actual rate of inflation rises above the anticipated rate, the unemployment rate decreases. Point *B* illustrates the relationship between the unemployment rate and an actual 4 percent inflation rate when the anticipated rate of inflation is 3 percent.

How does this increase in demand affect the potential workers who make up the 6 percent of the labor force that is unemployed when the economy is at point *A* in Figure 4? Labor-market theory suggests that these people are engaged in a search for jobs and that each of them has in mind a **reservation wage rate**—a desired wage rate that must be found before a contract of employment is agreed to. According to this theory, at the start of a spell of unemployment, each unemployed worker's reservation wage rate is optimistically high. After all, why not aim high and hope for the best job? Job offers at wage rates below the reservation wage are rejected. Some workers find work soon at acceptable wage rates, but others, as time passes and the job search lengthens, revise their reservation wage rates downward toward what they conclude are more realistic levels.

A reservation wage rate is a wage rate that a worker desires to find before he or she will agree to a contract of employment.

In the environment of greater than anticipated increases in aggregate demand and planned expenditure, the quantities of resources demanded increase as firms increase production to restore inventories to desired levels. Workers also suffer money illusion. Job offers at or above the unemployed worker's reservation wage rate are received after a shorter than normal period of job search. Both the average duration of unemployment and the unemployment rate in the economy fall. In Figure 4, this new situation is illustrated at point B. The unemployment rate has fallen to 5 percent and the inflation rate has risen to 4 percent a year, driven mainly by increases in the price charged by firms for their products. The Phillips-curve relation prevails, but only because the actual rate of inflation (4 percent) is greater than the anticipated rate of inflation (3 percent).

Adaptive Expectations

Will employers, workers, and other resource owners continue to anticipate inflation at the rate of 3 percent when the actual inflation rate is 4 percent? Of course not. Money illusion will eventually fade away. Before very long, workers and job seekers are sure to recognize that the actual inflation rate is 4 percent, not 3 percent. They will then re-examine their expectations about future rates of inflation. What change will be made in expectations about inflation? According to the **adaptive expectations** model, the inflation rate that is being experienced during the present time period becomes the inflation rate that is anticipated for the future. In our illustration, after the economy has operated at point B for a while, business firms, workers, and other resource owners will anticipate inflation at 4 percent a year rather than at 3 percent a year.

According to the adaptive-expectations model, the inflation rate being experienced during the present time period becomes the inflation rate that is anticipated for the future.

In labor markets, the change to a 4 percent anticipated inflation rate means that reservation wage rates are boosted to reflect a 4 percent annual rate of increase. Job offers that would have been accepted under the old 3 percent inflation expectation are declined under the revised 4 percent expectation. Also, workers already on the job at pay rates negotiated under the old set of expectations demand higher pay rates as soon as their contracts permit adjustments. They demand pay boosts to compensate them for the reduced *real* pay rate under the 3 percent contract. From the point of view of employers, the revised expectation not only forces higher resource costs but also forces them to revise downward their forecasts about their profitability. Production and employment are scaled back.

Figure 5 illustrates how expectations adapted to actual experience show a new aspect of the Phillips-curve model. Points A and B and the "Phillips curve with 3 percent anticipated inflation" are the same as in Figure 4. But Figure 5 includes a new Phillips curve reflecting a 4 percent anticipated inflation rate. Point C illustrates the equilibrium suggested by the Friedman-Phelps analysis. Unemployment has returned to the 6 percent rate. According to Friedman and Phelps, when the rate of inflation is correctly anticipated, the economy operates at its natural rate of unemployment—the 6 percent rate in this illustration. The negative slope of the Phillips curve arises, according to their analysis, from the failure to anticipate correctly the rate of inflation. The unemployment rate is less than the natural rate when the actual inflation rate is greater than the anticipated inflation rate and, conversely, the unemployment rate rises above the natural rate when the actual inflation rate is less than anticipated.

In Figure 5, a line connecting points A and C would be vertical and would represent a "long-run" Phillips curve, the relationship between the rate of inflation and the rate of unemployment when the actual rate of inflation is equal to the anticipated rate of inflation, that is, when inflation is correctly anticipated.

According to Friedman and Phelps, when the rate of inflation is correctly anticipated, the economy operates at its natural rate of unemployment. The negative slope of the Phillips curve arises from the failure to anticipate correctly the rate of inflation.

The Phillips Curve and the Aggregate-Supply Curve

There is a strong parallel between the theory of the shifting Phillips curve, as illustrated in Figure 5, and the theory of the shifting aggregate-supply curve explained in Chapter 15. Since modern macroeconomics most often uses the aggregate-demand and aggregate-supply format rather than the Phillips-curve format, let us transfer what we have learned about the shifting Phillips curve into the aggregate-demand and aggregate-supply framework.

Figure 6 shows aggregate demand and aggregate supply. It essentially reproduces Figure 4 in Chapter 15 (page 337). Note first the label on the horizontal axis of the *AD-AS* graph. Real GNP increases as we move to the right on this axis. The Phillips-curve graph, in contrast, shows the rate of unemployment increasing as we move to the right on this axis. Clearly, the two axes report approximately the same information, but a move to the right on the horizontal axis of the Phillips-curve graph (increasing the unemployment rate) appears as a move to the left on the *AD-AS* graph (decreasing real GNP).

Now look at the vertical axes of these graphs. The *AD-AS* graph shows the price level on this axis, expressed as an index number. Inflation is shown as a movement upward on this axis and deflation by a movement downward. On the Phillips-curve graph, the vertical axis shows the *rate* of inflation,

FIGURE 5
The Phillips Curve Shifted by Adaptive Expectations

This graph continues the analysis started in Figure 4. At point *B*, actual inflation is at a rate of 4 percent a year, but the anticipated rate of inflation is only 3 percent a year. According to the theory of adaptive expectations, expectations will soon be adjusted to match the inflation rate currently being experienced. When the anticipated inflation rate becomes 4 percent a year, the Phillips curve will have shifted upward and unemployment will have risen to 6 percent. The natural rate of unemployment prevails, other things being equal, when the anticipated rate of inflation is the same as the actual rate of inflation.

that is, the annual percentage change in the price level. Again, the vertical axes of the graphs present similar information but in different ways. A given point on the vertical axis of the Phillips curve graph, such as a 3 percent inflation rate, must be represented on the *AD-AS* graph as a series of successively higher price levels if the price level rises by 3 percent each year.

Let us now examine the logic of the Phillips curve to see how it parallels the logic of the *AS* curve in the *AD-AS* framework. According to the Friedman-Phelps analysis, the negative slope of the Phillips curve arises because higher rates of inflation are not anticipated, particularly by participants in labor and resource markets. Increases in total planned expenditure and aggregate demand cause inventories of final goods and services to be reduced below intended levels and cause the prices of these goods and services to rise. But wage rates lag behind the increases in final good and service prices because workers anticipate no change in the rate of inflation. Therefore, the rate of unemployment falls as workers quickly find jobs at wage rates equal to or greater than their reservation wage rates set according to out-of-date expectations. In the *AD-AS* framework, the increase in total planned expenditure and aggregate demand appears explicitly on the graph as a shift to the right of the aggregate-demand curve, from AD_1 to AD_2 in Figure 6 (arrow 1). Because of the lag in the prices of labor inputs behind the rise in the general price level, profit rates rise and firms increase production. At the same time, the prices of final goods and services rise. Thus macroeconomic equilibrium moves from point *A* to point *B*. This parallels the movement that appears from *A* to *B* in the Phillips curve in Figure 5. There is some difference, however. The Phillips-curve graph suggests that the full inflationary effect of the expanded aggregate demand has already been realized at point *B*. The *AD-AS* format reserves some of this inflationary effect for the second stage of the process.

The second stage in the Friedman-Phelps analysis of the Phillips curve is based on the theory of adaptive expectations, that is, that workers and other resource suppliers adapt their expectations to the new, higher, inflation rate and that the Phillips curve shifts upward when this happens. In the *AD-AS* framework, this step takes place as contracts expire and other institutional barriers are overcome so that wage rates and other input prices catch up with the higher price level. As wage rates and other resource prices catch up, the aggregate-supply curve shifts to the left, from AS_1 to AS_2 in Figure 6 (arrow 2). In the *AD-AS* framework, equilibrium moves from point *B* to point *C*, with output returning to potential GNP and unemployment returning to its natural rate. This parallels the movement from *B* to *C* on the Phillips curve graph in Figure 5. In the *AD-AS* framework, this move has an upward slope because the vertical axis of the graph shows the price *level* rather than the inflation *rate*. The price level of 104—equivalent to the 4 percent inflation rate of the Phillips-curve model—is reached at point *C* in the *AD-AS* system. Thus, in the *AD-AS* framework, the second, or "catch-up," phase of the process displays the characteristic stagflation combination of both increasing unemployment and a rising price level.

FIGURE 6
Shifts of the Aggregate-Supply Curve

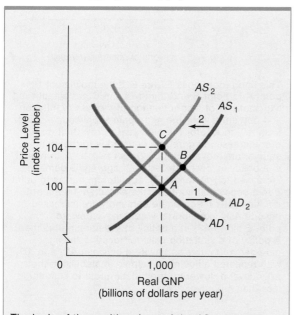

The logic of the positive slope of the *AS* curve parallels the logic of the negative slope of the Phillips curve. Starting at point *A*, an increase in aggregate demand, from AD_1 to AD_2 (arrow 1), leads to equilibrium at point *B*, with lower unemployment and a higher price level. Wage costs lag behind increases in the prices of final goods because the higher price level was not anticipated. When expectations adapt to anticipate a continuation of the existing inflation rate, the aggregate-supply curve shifts from AS_1 to AS_2 (arrow 2) and equilibrium moves to point *C*. At point *C*, real GNP and unemployment with it have returned to the same rate that prevailed at point *A*.

The Phillips-curve model can be transferred into an aggregate-demand and aggregate-supply framework.

STAGFLATION AND POLICY ALTERNATIVES

Are the inflation and output consequences of a boost in total planned expenditure and aggregate demand really completed when the economy has returned to potential GNP and when unemployment has returned to its natural rate? In the context of the adaptive expectations theory, the answer is "no." In Figure 6, when the economy has moved from point A to point B and then to point C, the society has experienced a 4 percent rise in the price level. If this has taken place over the period of one year, the rate of inflation has been 4 percent. According to the theory of adaptive expectations, both firms and suppliers of labor and other resources build this experience into their expectations about *forthcoming* changes in the price level. In bargaining for new contracts, workers add an *extra* 4 percent to their wage demands to reflect their expectation that the prices of final goods and services and the cost of living will rise by 4 percent per year during the term of the contract being negotiated. Employers, who share the same inflationary expectation, build the anticipated 4 percent increase in the price level into their sales forecasts and, other things being equal, grant the increases demanded by labor and other resource suppliers. They anticipate that the price level one year in the future will be 4 percent higher than the current price level.

Expectations of a continuing 4 percent increase in the price level are incorporated into the *AD-AS* model by shifting the aggregate-supply curve still farther to the left. Figure 7 reproduces Figure 6 and adds a new aggregate-supply curve, AS_3, with prices 4 percent higher than curve AS_2 (arrow 3). This curve incorporates the inflationary expectations adapted from the earlier experience of the price level having risen at a 4 percent rate. Business firms and workers expect the price level to be 108.16 a year in the future (104 times 1.04 equals 108.16).

The *AD-AS* model makes it clear that macroeconomic policymakers must face up to the implications of the AS_3 curve. What alternatives are available to them?

FIGURE 7

Adaptive Expectations and the Aggregate-Supply Curve

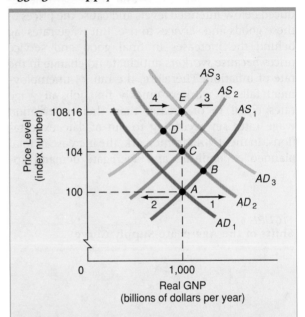

This figure continues Figure 6. If the movement from point A to point B and then to point C has established expectations of a continuation of the rate of inflation at 4 percent a year, the aggregate-supply curve shifts from AS_2 to AS_3 for the next year (arrow 3). If no further increase in aggregate demand is forthcoming, equilibrium moves to point D, but falls back to point C in a policy involving deflation. If aggregate demand is increased to AD_3 (arrow 4), equilibrium moves to point E in a policy that confirms the expected 4 percent inflation rate. If aggregate demand were increased beyond AD_3, equilibrium would move upward from point E along AS_3 in a policy of accelerating inflation. A policy of disinflation calls for locating the aggregate-demand curve somewhere between AD_2 and AD_3 with repeated adjustments aimed at stabilizing the price level or lowering the inflation rate to something less than 4 percent a year.

Deflation as a Policy Option

If macroeconomic policymakers make no adjustment in aggregate demand, that is, if they take no action to increase the money supply and initiate no expansionary fiscal policies, the aggregate-demand curve will, other things being equal, remain as shown by AD_2 in Figure 7. According to the *AD-AS* model, if no demand change is made, equilibrium moves first to point D. The movement to point D is accompanied by increasing unemployment, higher prices, and reductions in real GNP—a combination sure to be unpopular. But point D is only a temporary equilibrium. The price level will not have risen by the 4 percent anticipated by firms, workers, and other resource owners. With expectations not confirmed, with unemployment higher than the natural rate, and with output below potential GNP, employers and workers are forced to re-examine their expectations. If policymakers hold firm in their refusal to increase aggregate demand, wage rates and other prices eventually must fall, *deflation* will take place, and the economy will return to equilibrium at point C. The price level will stabilize at the 104 index number.

Is a deflation policy reasonable? The deflation policy forces the society to endure unemployment and reduced output in exchange for a lower price level. Since the economy, economists believe, can function as well at one price level as at another, there is little support for a deflation policy.

A policy of deflation—causing a reduction in the price level—forces the society to endure unemployment and reduced output in exchange for a lower price level.

Confirming Inflationary Expectations

The easiest policy to follow when the economy is at point C in Figure 7 is to increase total planned expenditure and aggregate demand, shifting the aggregate-demand curve to the right, to AD_3 (arrow 4). Under this policy, equilibrium moves upward from point C to point E. Output remains at potential GNP, unemployment is at its natural rate, and the anticipations of firms and resource suppliers that the price level will rise by 4 percent are confirmed.

Are there problems associated with a policy of confirming inflationary expectations and maintaining a constant rate of inflation, such as the 4 percent rate in the illustration? Some difficulties would undoubtedly arise in the early stages of such a policy, before all participants in the economy become aware of it and learn how to adjust their economic affairs to meet the constantly increasing price level. But if all buyers and sellers correctly anticipate price-level changes, appropriate adjustments can be built into contracts so that neither of the parties need gain or lose from the changing price level. Even anticipated inflation, however, is a burden on activities that must hold cash balances or must publish price lists.

If policymakers choose to confirm the expected price level of 108.16 for the time period during which the economy operates at point E, they must understand that the aggregate-supply curve will continue shifting, anticipating inflation at the rate of 4 percent a year. For the following year, buyers and sellers in both product and resource markets will anticipate a price level of 112.49 (that is 108.16 times 1.04), and policymakers will have to increase aggregate demand appropriately to confirm this expectation. If the 4 percent inflation-rate policy is successfully implemented for an extended period of time, the shifts of the AS curve and the AD curve adjustments could occur smoothly and automatically with virtually no fluctuations in real GNP either above or below potential GNP.

Another approach to dealing with inflationary expectations is simply to confirm them by maintaining a constant rate of inflation. This is the easiest policy to follow, but it is a burden on those enterprises that must hold cash balances or publish price lists.

A Policy of Accelerating Inflation

Still another policy option is available to an economy at point C in Figure 7. If expansionary monetary and fiscal measures are implemented that shift the aggregate-demand curve *beyond* the level of AD_3, macroeconomic equilibrium is pushed upward and to the right of point E, that is, the price level rises *more* than expected, wage rates and other input prices again lag behind the prices of final goods and services, profits are greater than anticipated, output exceeds potential GNP, and unemployment is below its natural rate. In short, the situation parallels that at point B, when the economy experienced expansion from the initial shift of aggregate demand.

Can the economy continue for long with unemployment below the natural rate and output exceeding potential GNP? That depends on future macroeconomic policy and on how the society reacts to the now higher rate of inflation. The adaptive-expectations model suggests that the higher inflation rate soon will be built into labor and input contracts so that the aggregate-supply curve will shift to the left from the AS_3 location. Then policymakers must again decide how far to shift the aggregate-demand curve. It is conceivable that they might, once again, choose to increase aggregate demand by more than the amount needed to confirm inflationary expectations. The economy could have another period of unemployment below the natural rate and output above potential GNP.

How long could this process of accelerating inflation be sustained? According to the adaptive-expectations model, in order for the accelerating inflation policy to be effective, each year's inflation rate must be greater than the rate in the preceding year, thereby always being greater than the anticipated rate of inflation. Can policymakers deceive the economy year after year? Or will people sooner or later anticipate the higher and higher inflation rate and thus cause the accelerating inflation policy to become ineffective? It appears inevitable that a sustained policy of accelerating inflation would end with runaway inflation and an eventual breakdown of the economy in hyperinflation.[3]

Still another policy option in dealing with inflationary expectations is to accelerate the rate of inflation. This approach can lead to runaway inflation and the eventual breakdown of the economy in hyperinflation.

---

3. In hyperinflation, the rising price level persuades people to spend their incomes more quickly, increasing the velocity of money circulation and inducing a shift to the right of the aggregate-demand curve.

A Policy of Disinflation

There remains another policy alternative for an economy that has arrived at point C in Figure 7, where there has been established the anticipation of a 4 percent annual rise in the price level. This is the policy of **disinflation**, that is, the policy of gradually lowering the rate of inflation to a more acceptable level, perhaps to a zero rate (price stability). The disinflation policy calls for some increase in aggregate demand, but not enough of an increase to confirm fully the expectation that the price level will rise by 4 percent (to 108.16). Imagine, for example, an aggregate-demand curve roughly halfway between AD_2 and AD_3 in Figure 7. The new macroeconomic equilibrium occurs along the AS_3 curve, upward and to the right of point D. Output will fall from the level enjoyed at point C, and unemployment will increase. However, the expectation of a 4 percent inflation rate will *not* be confirmed and, in due time, the AS_3 curve will shift to the right, as inflationary expectations are scaled back to less than the 4 percent rate. With successive replays of this "less than full confirmation" policy, inflationary expectations can gradually be squeezed out of the economy, and equilibrium at potential GNP and the natural rate of unemployment can be achieved at whatever price level or rate of inflation is considered appropriate.

Viewed graphically, as in Figure 7, the disinflation procedure appears in a cold and analytical light. In the real world of economic policy, such a policy is anything but cold. How long can the government force the economy to operate below its potential GNP and how long can it permit unemployment to continue above its natural rate? Since disinflation requires sacrifices from the public, the ability of a government to carry out a policy of disinflation depends on the strength and determination of that government. Can the disinflation be accomplished quickly, with a sharp but short-lived period of high unemployment and depressed output? Will expectations change (shifting the AS curve) quickly enough so that the suffering will have subsided and been forgotten before the next election? Or is it better strategy to pursue the disinflation policy gradually, imposing unemployment rates only moderately higher than the natural rate but sustaining the pressure for an extended period of time?

Another policy alternative is disinflation, that is, gradually lowering the rate of inflation to a more acceptable level. This policy requires the society to endure high employment and depressed output for some period of time.

The most successful recent disinflation experience in the United States occurred in the early to middle 1980s during the administrations of President Reagan. Although fiscal policy was expansionary, the Federal Reserve maintained a restrictive monetary policy. Hardships were severe, and the Reagan administration was accused of causing, or at least increasing the severity of, the recession in the early 1980s. But the Reagan administration enjoyed a strong anti-inflation mandate carried over from the record-setting inflations of the late 1970s. Also, the disinflation policy was greatly aided by significant decreases in energy prices, as the Organization of Petroleum Exporting Countries (OPEC) failed in its efforts to restrict world petroleum production. The result was that the disinflation process advanced much farther and much faster than planned. The U.S. dollar reached new highs in international currency markets, favoring foreign travel by Americans but causing great difficulty for American exporters. Farmers were hit from all sides, with high interest rates, depressed sales, and huge indebtedness carried over from debt incurred in the 1970s.

The United States experienced a period of disinflation in the early to middle 1980s under President Reagan. Hardships were severe, especially for American exporters and farmers.

Indexing

Indexing is a procedure that automatically adjusts wage rates, savings accounts, taxes, interest rates, bond values, and all other contracts for changes in the price level. It has important applications in an economy beset by fears of inflation, by actual inflation, or by inflation arising from macroeconomic policy. The appeal of indexing is evidenced by the fact that it often is included in labor-management contracts as an **escalator clause** or a **cost-of-living adjustment (COLA)** provision. In these contracts, the parties agree to use some generally accepted measure of inflation, such as the consumer price index, as a basis for automatic changes in wage rates. For example, it might be agreed that wage rates would be increased by, say, 3 percent, whenever the consumer price index for the preceding six-month period increased by 4 percent. Automatic adjustments in wage rates need not exactly match changes in the chosen price-index number. The precise relationship is a matter for negotiation. The appeal of the escalator, or cost-of-living adjustment, is that it eases the problem of forecasting future inflation rates. Workers do not need to press for wage increases to cover anticipated increases in the cost of living, since the escalator, or COLA clause, will provide the needed adjustment should inflation actually occur.

Indexing is a procedure for automatically adjusting wage rates, savings account balances, taxes, interest rates, bond values, and all other contracts for changes in the price level. It is often included in labor-management contracts.

Indexing *as a public policy* would not be negotiated on a contract-by-contract basis but would be incorporated in rules and regulations governing all contracts and agreements in the economy. To see how indexing would work for savings accounts, suppose you have an account balance of $1,000 at the start of a year and that the interest rate on the account is specified as 6 percent per year. In the absence of inflation, your account balance at the end of the year would be $1,060, assuming you made no deposits or withdrawals. What would happen to this account if inflation, as measured by the index number specified in the indexing regulations, took place at the rate of 10 percent? In order to protect the depositor from any loss in real purchasing power, the balance in the account would be adjusted, automatically, to $1,166, which is equal to $1,060 times an inflation adjustment of 1.1. In effect, this indexing procedure increases both your initial balance and the contracted rate of interest by 10 percent—the rate of inflation indicated by the approved index number.

If indexing were established by law for all agreements, arrangements similar to the one described above would be required for all wage and salary contracts, savings accounts, checking accounts, stocks, bonds, mortgages, tuition, room and board, and so on throughout the entire economy. As it stands, however, indexing is not required by law but can be written into contracts if desired by those involved. Indexing is in effect for the U.S. Individual Income Tax. During the 1970s and early 1980s, before the tax was indexed and when inflation rates were high, taxpayers justly complained of **bracket push** because, as their incomes rose along with the price level, the unindexed tax system forced them into higher tax-rate brackets. Average tax rates paid went up even when real incomes and real standards of living did not. The government was accused of profiting from inflation and of increasing actual tax rates without passing tax legislation. Starting with the 1986 tax year, the size of personal exemptions, tax-rate brackets, and certain other features of the tax were indexed. As a result, increases in the price level no longer force taxpayers into higher rate brackets and require them to pay a higher average rate of tax on their income.

Indexing is not required by law but can be written into contracts by those involved. It is used for the U.S. Individual Income Tax.

What does indexing have to do with inflation economics and inflationary expectations? Probably the greatest appeal of indexing is the protection it offers to important groups, such as retirees, savings-account owners, and persons on fixed pension or annuity incomes. Since these groups are often committed to long-term agreements, they can easily be hurt by unanticipated inflation. But indexing also has appeal at theoretical and policy levels for an economy driven by inflationary expectations, as illustrated at point *C* of Figure 7. If indexing were in place, people would no longer need to build inflation expectations into their wage and other negotiated agreements. Negotiators could put inflation expectations out of their minds because each side could be sure that it would receive an appropriate adjustment for any inflation that actually arose. Overestimates of coming inflation would not drive the economy to higher inflation rates or cause hardship if such overestimates proved unfounded. So *expectations* of inflation would no longer drive the economy to higher price levels by shifting the aggregate-supply curve. In this sense, those who favor indexing claim that it would help fight inflation.

The appeal of indexing is that if it were used as a policy tool, people would no longer need to build inflation expectations into their contract agreements.

If indexing is such a great idea, why don't we have it? The basic problem is that many doubt that indexing could, in practice, be done fairly and effectively. It is hard to image a truly general and complete indexing system that would not leave out some people. Moreover, there are serious problems in finding index numbers that are unbiased and have broad applicability throughout the economy. Since inflation usually involves relative price changes as well as changes in the average of all prices, any given index number will favor some groups and disfavor other groups. For example, when food prices change, the cost-of-living impact differs between urban dwellers and rural dwellers, between large families and small families, and between high-income families and low-income families. When energy prices change, the cost-of-living impact depends on heating and cooling requirements in different parts of the country and on whether energy is provided from coal, electricity, fuel oil, or natural gas. In effect, indexing proposals are easily bogged down in disagreements over which index numbers should be used.

Indexing also encounters opposition of a more general nature. Many say that indexing amounts to giving up the fight to stop inflation. If all were protected from it, who would step forward to try to stop it? Interest in indexing was great during the 1970s, when the inflation rate was high. This interest proved strong enough to achieve the indexing for social security benefits and the individual income tax. However, interest in indexing subsided with success on the income-tax and social security fronts and with the Great Disinflation of the early and middle 1980s. Even interest in escalator and cost-of-living adjustment clauses lost appeal when inflation rates fell.

WAGE AND PRICE CONTROLS

Wage and price controls are limits imposed by law on increases in wage rates and prices. Sometimes the controls are very precise and rigid, as when all prices and wage rates are "frozen"—that is, when they are not allowed to change at all. At other times they are more flexible, as when an official agency is given the power to approve or disapprove proposed changes in wage rates and prices. Sometimes the controls are mandatory, meaning that persons who violate the laws may be fined or put in prison or both. When violators cannot be officially punished, the controls are said to be voluntary (sometimes called **wage and price guidelines**). When controls are used throughout the whole economy and attempts are made to coordinate wages and prices to reach a certain set of goals, the controls are part of an **incomes policy**. Incomes policies are related to government planning for the economy. Political decisions replace market decisions in determining what, how, and for whom to produce.

Wage and price controls have been used at one time or another in most organized economies of the world. They are a standard feature of planned economies, where the major sectors of the economy normally operate under controls. In market economies, direct controls over wage rates, prices, profits, and outputs are usually used in times of war, when massive increases in government spending are expected. The United States imposed a full set of controls during World War II and less-comprehensive controls during the Korean War. Wage and price guidelines were used during the 1960s and 1970s, by both Republican and Democratic administrations. In 1971, President Nixon, faced with inflationary pressures and serious international payments problems, placed a ninety-day freeze on all wages and prices. This was followed by a comprehensive system of controls that were applied to the economy with varying degrees of stringency until they were removed in April 1974. After these controls were removed, the price level leaped upward, leading most observers to conclude that the controls had only suppressed inflation but had not prevented it. In fact, many believed that the controls disrupted the economy so much that production was lower and the price level higher than they would have been had the controls never been used.

Changing the Aggregate-Supply Curve

Wage and price controls aim to change the shape of the aggregate-supply curve. This is illustrated in Figure 8. Suppose that equilibrium exists at point A, with price level P_1 and real GNP of Y_1. Now let the aggregate-demand curve shift to the right, from AD_1 to AD_2, perhaps from wartime spending or perhaps as a policy initiative to reduce unemployment. In this situation, the theories that you have studied lead economists to predict that macroeconomic equilibrium will move to point B, with a larger real GNP (Y_2) and a higher price level (P_2). These theories also suggest that the inflation will set the stage for a leftward shift of the AS curve and a period of stagflation when wage–cost lags fade away. Moreover, inflationary expectations that could lead to still further leftward shifts of the aggregate-supply curve may be built up.

If a national emergency is felt to exist, as is likely in these circumstances, strong sentiment may arise in favor of wage and price controls to hold prices at the original level (P_1). In terms of Figure 8, the aim of these controls is to make the AS curve horizontal at this price level. If the controls are effective and if patriotic enthusiasm encourages people to work hard, macroeconomic equilibrium might be reached at point C on the horizontal part of the AS curve, with price level P_1 and real GNP at Y_3. Under these ideal assumptions about the effectiveness of wage and price controls, aggregate demand could be increased with no increase in the price level. Having prevented inflation, the controls might also prevent subsequent leftward shifts of the AS curve and the stagflation that would result.

Wage and price controls attempt to change the shape of the aggregate-supply curve.

Problems with Wage and Price Controls

Experience indicates that wage and price controls do not in practice achieve the ideal results illustrated in Figure 8. Part of the problem is that controls inevitably lead to rationing and other enforcement problems. In addition, the social, political, and economic compromises built into the control program sooner or later break down.

Rationing Rationing of goods and services is likely to be used along with wage and price controls, especially if these controls are expected to remain in effect for very long. The reason for ra-

FIGURE 8
Wage and Price Controls and the Aggregate-Supply Curve

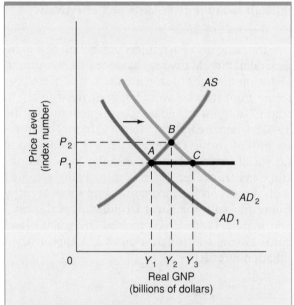

Wage and price controls can be used in an attempt to make the aggregate-supply curve horizontal at the existing price level. Starting from equilibrium at A, a shift of aggregate demand from AD_1 to AD_2 would, in the absence of wage and price controls, produce a new equilibrium at B, with price level P_2 and real GNP of Y_2. However, if wage and price controls work perfectly, the AS curve would become horizontal at price level P_1 and the shift in aggregate demand would produce equilibrium at C, with real GNP of Y_3 and no change in the price level.

tioning is easily understood from the supply and demand curves shown in Figure 9. These curves represent market demand and supply for a good or a service and *include* the inflationary pressures that price and wage controls are trying to combat. For this reason, the equilibrium price P_1 shown by the intersection of these curves is above the price set by the controls, which is shown as P_2. At the controlled price, the quantity demanded (Q_d) is greater than the quantity supplied (Q_s), and there is a shortage.

Rationing systems are intended to divide up the limited quantities of goods and services actually supplied under wage and price controls and thereby to relieve some of the upward pressure on prices. Ration coupons are issued to each individual or household for each of the various goods or services subject to rationing. Then, when a purchase is made, the buyer must give the merchant the required number of ration coupons along with the money price of the item bought.

Aside from the complexity of the system itself, a major problem is that illegal ("black") markets arise that do not require coupons and that sell rationed items at illegally high prices. Moreover, since rationing cannot cover all the goods and services that people want to buy, spending power not usable for rationed items may spill over and increase demand for nonrationed items, putting extra upward pressure on their prices. During wartime emergencies, patriotic appeals encourage cooperation with price controls and rationing, but problems increase the longer the system is in operation. Shortages become more severe and black markets more widespread. Only totalitarian systems can make rationing work over extended periods.

FIGURE 9
Rationing and Price Controls

The supply curve and the demand curve include inflationary pressures that wage and price controls are designed to combat. Without controls, the equilibrium price is P_1. The controlled price for this good or service is illustrated by P_2. At this price, the quantity demanded is Q_d, where this controlled price meets the demand curve. The quantity supplied is Q_s, where the controlled price meets the supply curve. A shortage is shown by the distance between Q_d and Q_s. Rationing is used to divide up the available supply (Q_s) and to hold down pressures for prices to rise above P_2.

> Rationing systems are intended to divide up the limited quantities of goods and services actually supplied under wage and price controls.
> Rationing tends to lead to black markets, which sell rationed items at illegally high prices.

Changes in Relative Prices The second type of problem encountered by wage and price controls involves changes in relative prices and the complicated set of compromises and assurances needed to gain the political support needed to adopt and maintain controls. Besides rationing, the plan is likely to call for subsidies to industries that are asked to operate at a loss under the controlled prices and deficits for government operations that buy or import food or other goods for the public. In countries where public payrolls are a large part of total labor income, civil service wage rates are often frozen, leading to corruption, absenteeism, and poor performance on the job.

Ultimately the major problems with wage and price controls spring from hard facts of both life and arithmetic. The arithmetic fact is that it is impossible to fix the prices of two goods without automatically fixing the ratio between them. But flexibility of relative prices is essential in any economy as conditions change. The relative prices of some goods must rise, and the relative prices of other goods must fall. If these changes do not occur, shortages will appear in some markets and surpluses in others.

The facts of life are that no set of price or wage ratios can satisfy all the parties concerned even after their leaders have accepted it. For this reason, after the controls have been in place for a few months or years and the original "emergency" has somewhat subsided, they may begin to break down. Sometimes black markets expand into second economies, militants appear among the pressure groups, and there are wildcat strikes, slowdowns, and shutdowns in protest against one or another part of the system. There may be a breakdown of the controls, as in the United States after World War II and after the Nixon controls of 1971–1973 and in Britain from 1976 to 1979. At other times the country may resort to martial law or similar dictatorial methods to reinforce the system, as in Poland in 1956, 1970, and 1980–1982.

Economics in Focus

Inflationary Expectations: Actions and Reactions in Europe

Like the United States, European economies experienced some very good years in the late 1980s. Fueled by high consumer spending and solid investment, national income and product grew impressively. By the end of the decade, however, there were signs—as in the United States—that inflation would once again be a problem. Across Europe the overall inflation rate reached 5 percent by early 1989, up two points from the year before. German industrialists, worried that inflation would bring rising costs, began to push up their prices. BMW, for instance, raised its car prices an average of 2.5 percent in one jump.

In Britain the most unsettling reactions came from labor unions, which began to demand large wage increases to compensate for the anticipated rise in the cost of living. Some of these demands amounted to double-digit raises, and by early 1989 wage costs were climbing at an average annual rate of 9 percent. Analysts feared that Britain was entering an upward wage-price spiral that might damage the economy for years to come.

Among the Common Market countries, Britain and West Germany took particularly strong steps to counter the trend. British policymakers expected inflation to be severe, and their policies were equally so. When the inflation rate headed over 7 percent in Britain, Chancellor of the Exchequer Nigel Lawson prompted nine separate rises in prime-lending rates in the course of a year, so that prime rates reached 13 percent by the end of 1988. This was an uncompromising attempt to slow down the economy and cool inflationary expectations.

In West Germany the policies were similar. The Bundesbank, West Germany's central bank, boosted its discount rate three times in less than a year, and the government also raised consumer taxes and added a new withholding tax on interest income. What was remarkable about these strong measures was that German prices had risen *only 1.2 percent* in 1988. There were other reasons besides inflation for the stern policies (for example, excess growth in the money supply and a "softness" of the German mark), but some U.S. analysts complained that the Germans were overreacting. Since a slowdown in European economies would hurt efforts to curb the U.S. trade deficit, *Forbes* magazine accused the Bundesbank of "inflation paranoia."

These examples illustrate some of the ways in which inflation is linked to attitudes and expectations. A particular inflation rate—whether it be 2.5 percent of 6.9 percent—is often less important than the way people perceive it and react to it.

Sources: Bianca Riemer with Mark Maremont and John Templeman, "In Europe, Inflation Is No Longer Distant Thunder," *Business Week,* March 20, 1989, pp. 54–55; Peter Fuhrman with William Heuslein, "The Bundesbank Brakes," *Forbes,* January 9, 1989, pp. 56–58; "Other G-7 Nations Optimistic About Their Economies," *Wall Street Journal,* April 7, 1989, p. A2f.; Mike McNamee, "The Group of Seven is Acting More Like the Seven Dwarfs," *Business Week,* June 5, 1989, p. 90; "Inflation Rises in Europe," *New York Times,* April 18, 1989, p. D19; "Inflationary Flap" (editorial), *Christian Science Monitor,* April 25, 1989, p. 20.

SUMMARY

1. A Phillips curve displays a relationship between the rate of unemployment during a given year and the percentage increase in the price level that took place during that year. Rather than a cause-and-effect relationship, the curve is interpreted as identifying combinations of inflation and unemployment that can be selected as goals for macroeconomic policy. (See pages 348–349 and Figure 1, page 348.)

2. The economy appeared to follow the Phillips curve during the 1960s. However, President Nixon's attempt, at the end of the decade, to move back down the curve failed. Instead, the economy experienced a higher inflation rate and a higher unemployment rate simultaneously. A great variety of inflation-rate and unemployment-rate combinations appeared during the 1970s and 1980s. The apparent breakdown of the Phillips-curve model prompted economists to search for other variables affecting unemployment and inflation. (See pages 349–351 and Figures 2 and 3, pages 349 and 351.)

3. Economists Milton Friedman and Edmund Phelps concluded that the negative (Phillips-curve) relationship between the unemployment rate and the inflation rate arises when changes in the inflation rate are not anticipated by workers and firms in the economy. When inflation is not anticipated, increases in total planned expenditure and aggregate demand lead to depleted inventories and increased hiring by firms. When inflation is not anticipated, money illusion exists, the reservation wage rates of unemployed workers are not adjusted upward, and increased demand for labor results in shorter job searches and a lower unemployment rate. (See pages 351–353 and Figure 4, page 352.)

4. The theory of adaptive expectations states that the rate of inflation experienced by workers and employers during the present time period becomes the rate of inflation anticipated for the next time period. Changes in the anticipated rate of inflation cause the Phillips curve to shift. According to the adaptive-expectations model, unemployment is at its natural rate when the inflation rate is correctly anticipated. Unemployment is less than the natural rate when inflation is greater than anticipated and higher than the natural rate when

inflation is less than anticipated. (See pages 353–354.)

5. The logic of the slope and shifts of the Phillips curve parallels the logic of the slope and shifts of the aggregate-supply curve. The *AD-AS* format shows how shifts of the aggregate-demand curve can initiate expansion or contraction processes and how leftward shifts of the *AS* curve result in stagflation—the combination of inflation along with increasing unemployment. (See pages 354–355 and Figure 6, page 355.)

6. Once inflationary expectations are built into the plans of workers and employers, policymakers may choose among several alternative policies: a deflation policy, a policy of confirming inflationary expectations, a policy of accelerating inflation, or a policy of disinflation. (See pages 356–359.)

7. Indexing automatically adjusts wage rates, savings account balances, taxes, interest rates, bond values, and all other contracts for changes in the price level. It frequently is negotiated into labor-management contracts as cost-of-living or escalator clauses. If required of all contracts, it could weaken the power of inflationary expectations to shift the *AS* curve. (See pages 359–361.)

8. Wage and price controls are limits imposed by law on increases in wage rates and prices. These controls attempt to change the shape of the *AS* curve so that expansionary increases in aggregate demand will not lead to price-level increases and ultimately to inflationary expectations becoming built into the economy. (See pages 361–362 and Figure 8, page 362.)

9. Rationing usually is needed to go along with wage and price controls. This is because shortages arise when the legal price is below the free-market equilibrium price for a good or service. Rationing tries to divide up the available quantity of the product and to reduce pressures for price increases. Illegal (''black'') markets tend to arise and erode the effectiveness of rationing and wage and price controls. (See pages 362–363.)

10. Price controls have often been used, but they typically postpone, rather than prevent, inflation when pressures for inflation persist in the economy. The main problem with controls is that they are not able to respond to needed changes in relative prices. (See pages 362–363.)

KEY TERMS

adaptive expectations: a proposition that states that the inflation rate that is being experienced during the present time period becomes the inflation rate that is anticipated for the future (page 353).

bracket push: a term that describes what happens to taxpayers during times of high inflation rates if a progressive income tax is not indexed; taxpayers are pushed into higher tax-rate brackets as their incomes rise along with the price level (page 360).

cost-of-living adjustment (COLA) (escalator clause): a provision in a labor-management contract that grants workers automatic increases in wage rates as the price level increases (page 359).

disinflation: a lowering of the rate of inflation (page 358).

escalator clause: *see* **cost-of-living adjustment.**

Great Disinflation: the period of time in the early and middle 1980s when the rate of inflation was greatly reduced (page 350).

incomes policy: a coordinated program of wage and price controls designed to implement government planning of the economy (page 361).

indexing: a process that automatically adjusts wage rates, savings accounts, taxes, interest rates, bond values, and all other contracts for changes in the price level (page 359).

Phillips curve: a graphic representation of the relationship between the unemployment rate and the inflation rate (page 348).

reservation wage rate: the wage rate that a worker feels he or she must be offered before signing a contract of employment (page 352).

wage and price controls: limits imposed by law on increases in wage rates and prices of goods and/or services (page 361).

wage and price guidelines: officially recommended limits on increases in wage rates and prices of goods and/or services (page 361).

DISCUSSION QUESTIONS

1. Construct a graph of the Phillips curve as it appeared according to U.S. data for the 1960s. How might political parties use the Phillips-curve relationship in developing their campaign platforms? Discuss how the election of Richard Nixon in 1968 involved issues related to the Phillips curve.

2. Assume that unemployed workers expect no change in the price level and that the average spell of unemployment lasts four weeks. If an inflationary increase in aggregate demand takes place, will the length of the average spell of unemployment increase, decrease, or remain unchanged? Explain your answer using the concepts of reservation wage rates and job search.

3. Assume that one of the unemployed workers from the previous question had a reservation wage rate of $12.00 an hour when he or she expected no inflation. According to the theory of adaptive expectations, what will this reservation wage become if an actual inflation rate of 3 percent is experienced? What if the actual inflation rate in the next time period turns out to be 4 percent? How do adaptive expectations affect the Phillips curve?

4. In terms of the relation between the anticipated inflation rate and the actual inflation rate, when is the natural rate of unemployment realized? When will the unemployment rate be above the natural rate? When will it be below the natural rate? How will the Phillips curve shift in these situations? Discuss what you believe the relationship is at the present time.

5. Compare the adaptive-expectations explanation for a shifting Phillips curve with the wages catch-up explanation for the shifting aggregate-supply curve. If the two curves reflect similar models of labor-market behavior, why does one have a positive slope and the other a negative slope?

6. What is the difference between a shift of the aggregate-supply curve that comes from the elimination of wage lags from past inflation and a shift of that curve that comes from inflationary expectations? List four policy alternatives available when inflationary expectations have been established in the economy. Which of these alternatives do you recommend? Why?

7. Assume that inflation is led by increases in food prices. Identify two consumer groups that would favor indexing based on the consumer price index and two groups that would oppose indexing on that basis. Do the same for an inflation led by increases in energy prices. Do you believe that indexing would be popular if the price level were to fall?

8. Draw an *AD-AS* graph, shift the aggregate-demand curve to the right, and then change the shape of the aggregate-supply curve to illustrate how wage and price controls try to prevent inflation in emergency spending periods. Do you believe wage and price controls are justified in wartime? Are they justified in peacetime? Explain. If you answer "yes" in one case and "no" in the other, explain the basis for the difference.

9. Why do wage and price controls invariably require rationing as well? If price controls and rationing are effective, discuss alternative uses for consumer spending power that cannot be utilized in purchasing controlled goods and services. Where does saving rank among these alternatives?

17

Rational Expectations and Contemporary Schools of Macroeconomic Thought

Preview   The stagflation and supply shocks of the 1970s sent a good many economists halfway back to their drawing boards in efforts to refine old models and devise new ones. In microeconomics the response was a certain amount of deregulation. In macroeconomics, the response was a broad array of new models and revisions of old ones. In this chapter we look at the macroeconomist's arsenal of theories to be used and tested in the 1990s. We begin by explaining an important new theory called rational expectations, which is sometimes called the "new classical" economics. It replaces or expands the theory of adaptive expectations explained in the preceding chapter.

Keynesian economists did not sit idle while their models were under attack. The second part of the chapter describes two dimensions of the Keynesian response to the problems of the 1970s. First, traditional Keynesian models were broadened to include the money supply and monetary variables. Secondly, Keynesian economists counterattacked, criticizing the assumptions of the new classical model and, at the same time, revising their own model to utilize the aggregate-demand and aggregate-supply technique of analysis. What emerged is called the "neo-Keynesian" school of macroeconomic thought. There arose also a so-called "post-Keynesian" economics, contending that the competing models fail to penetrate to the basic problems facing capitalist economic systems. Post-Keynesian models propose basic institutional changes in the capitalist system, mainly in a Marxian direction.

The last portion of the chapter outlines supply-side economics, which achieved prominence in the first Reagan administration and still influences macroeconomic policy. Supply-side economists focus on the production side of the economy and offer their own formula for economic expansion.

RATIONAL EXPECTATIONS

As explained in Chapter 16, economists Milton Friedman and Edmund Phelps used adaptive expectations in their explanation of the Phillips curve and its shifts. Their theory—that deviations from the natural rate of unemployment and potential GNP arise because firms and resource owners are surprised by changes in the price level—raised the question of how people actually arrive at their forecasts of future price levels. The **theory of rational expectations** is an alternative to the theory of adaptive expectations. Instead of forecasts being projections of recent experience, the rational-expectations theory proposes that people learn from their mistakes and use conventional economic principles to make their forecasts, following a rational reasoning process about how one thing leads to another in economics.

An analogy will clarify the distinction between adaptive and rational expectations. Suppose that a television weather forecaster always forecasts that the weather tomorrow is going to be the same as the weather today. This would be an adaptive expectation, since it anticipates continuation of the current situation. The forecast would be accurate much of the time, but would fail to forecast *changes* in the weather. Now consider a meteorologist, with his or her carefully plotted data and maps of the jet stream and storm systems moving around the world. This meteorologist's forecast of tomorrow's weather is based on scientific principles. It is "rational," rather than "adaptive." Although the adaptive forecaster may have a high average accuracy in forecasting, the rational forecaster should do a better (but still imperfect) job of predicting changes in the weather. In our analogy, changes in the weather correspond with changes in an economic variable, such as an unemployment rate or an inflation rate. If changes in the inflation rate

cause deviations from potential GNP and the natural rate of unemployment, then forecasting such changes becomes crucial. Forecasters using rational expectations and people who follow their forecasts should fare better economically.

The theory of rational expectations proposes that people learn from their mistakes and use economic principles to make their forecasts.

Rational Expectations in the *AD-AS* Framework

How does the aggregate-demand and aggregate-supply model of macroeconomic equilibrium change when expectations are assumed to be formed rationally rather than by adaptation to current and recent past price-level experience? Figure 1 reproduces Figure 6 in Chapter 16. Starting from equilibrium at point *A*, suppose that expansionary fiscal and monetary policies shift the aggregate-demand curve from AD_1 to AD_2 (arrow 1). In the adaptive-expectations model, equilibrium moves from point *A* to point *B* because wage rates and other input prices lag behind the increase in the general price level. But in the rational-expectations model, no lag can be counted on. Workers, other resource owners, and business firms (or their economic forecasters) have studied the principles of economics and recognize that the increase in aggregate demand will lead to an increase in the price level. Assuming that prices adjust quickly, workers and resource owners do not permit production costs to lag behind increases in the price of final goods and services. Also, business firms do not expect or experience increases in their rates of profit and, consequently, do not expand production. Therefore, *at the same time* that the aggregate-demand curve shifts to the right, from AD_1 to AD_2, the aggregate-supply curve shifts upward and to the left, from AS_1 to AS_2 (arrow 2). Macroeconomic equilibrium moves directly from point *A* to point *C* (as illustrated by the vertical black arrow in Figure 1), with no systematic change in real GNP. In effect, to the extent that wages and prices adjust quickly, the rational-expectations model says that the aggregate-supply curve is vertical. In Figure 1,

FIGURE 1
The Rational-Expectations Model of Response to a Policy-Induced Increase in Aggregate Demand

Starting from macroeconomic equilibrium at point *A*, the aggregate-demand curve shifts from *AD*₁ to *AD*₂ (arrow 1) as a result of government policy initiatives. However, because price-level expectations are assumed to be formed rationally, the price-level consequences of this initiative are recognized immediately and, if prices adjust quickly, the aggregate-supply curve shifts quickly from *AS*₁ to *AS*₂ (arrow 2). Macroeconomic equilibrium does not occur at point *B*, as in adaptive-expectations models. Instead, equilibrium moves directly from *A* to *C* as shown by the vertical black arrow. There is no systematic fluctuation in real GNP and the only effect of the policy is an increase in the price level.

we show the new equilibrium level of real GNP (at point *C*) as exactly the same as the original equilibrium level (at point *A*). This is an extreme case. According to the rational-expectations theory, point *C* is equally likely to be either to the left or to the right of point *A*.

The theory of rational expectations changes the *AD-AS* model of macroeconomic equilibrium by predicting that no systematic change in real GNP arises in response to fiscal and monetary policies.

Discretionary Fiscal and Monetary Policies Are Useless

What are the policy implications of the rational-expectations theory? The most striking is that, with rapidly adjusting wages and prices, it is useless for discretionary fiscal and monetary policies to try to push unemployment below its natural rate, that is, to try to raise real GNP above potential GNP. According to the rational-expectations model, workers, other resource owners, and business firms use the same economic models as government policymakers and are as well informed about conditions in the economy. They quickly predict outcomes of policy changes. If prices and wage rates can be adjusted, the aggregate-supply curve shifts so quickly in response to policy-induced changes in aggregate demand that no changes in "real" variables—output and employment—take place. As long as policy actions do not surprise firms and resource owners, government monetary and fiscal initiatives cause changes in the price level, but they do not change real GNP.

The conclusion that demand-side macroeconomic policy is useless is a stunning implication of the combination of flexible prices and rational expectations. It wipes away the theoretical foundation for Keynesian and monetarist policy initiatives. The only demand-side policy initiatives that are systematically or predictably effective are those that come as surprises. In order to be effective, policymakers must engage in deception and concealment. Since such procedures are not compatible with democratic processes in a free society, the model suggests that democratic governments cannot take effective aggregate-demand initiatives in macroeconomic policy. Moreover, deception and concealment increase the risks involved in doing business, thus increasing costs.

The key policy implication of the rational-expectations theory is that it is useless to use discretionary fiscal and monetary policies to try to raise real GNP above potential GNP. Their only effect is to cause changes in the price level.

Deficits Don't Matter

According to some economists another implication of the rational-expectations theory is that government deficits don't matter. Those who hold this view are called **neo-Ricardians** in recognition of the early nineteenth century British economist, David Ricardo, who first pointed out the possibility. This is in sharp contrast to the traditional Keynesian view that budget deficits, if financed by money creation, increase total planned expenditure and raise the equilibrium level of real GNP. It also contradicts the view that if the central bank does not accommodate deficits by increasing the money supply, deficits are financed from private saving and crowd out private investment, cutting back the increase in total planned expenditure and dampening economic growth. According to neo-Ricardians, the rational-expectations theory suggests that the method used to finance government expenditure does not matter. It doesn't matter, they say, whether government expenditures are financed by taxation or by bond sales. In the neo-Ricardian view, taxpayers believe that budget deficits require higher taxes in the future and that they set aside (save) funds in order to prepare for the higher taxes they believe are coming. These added savings are channeled into financial markets, where they become available to purchase the new securities issued by the government to finance the deficit. Therefore, real rates of interest do not change and deficits do not crowd out private investment any more than would taxes of the same amount. Private investment is crowded out by government expenditure, regardless of how the expenditure is financed.

The theory of rational expectations can also be applied to challenge the traditional view that voters are less resistant to expenditures financed by debt than to expenditures financed by taxes. The traditional public finance view is that tax increases are unpopular with voters, so the opportunity to finance by debt biases the political process in favor of deficit finance. But, if voters behave according to the neo-Ricardian application of rational expectations, this proposition may be questioned. Voters are not biased in favor of debt finance. Government expenditure is not greater because of debt finance, and there is little need for a constitutional amendment prohibiting deficits in government budgets.

Neo-Ricardian applications of the rational-expectations theory suggest that it doesn't matter whether government expenditures are financed by taxation or by bond sales. Private investment is crowded out by government expenditure, no matter how that expenditure is financed.

Surprises Cause Fluctuations

Does the combination of rational expectations and price flexibility suggest that the economy always operates at potential GNP? The answer is no,'' since sudden or unpredicted events (surprises) have real effects on the economy. According to the rational-expectations model, unexpected changes in aggregate demand lead to fluctuations in employment and real GNP because firms do not correctly interpret information about these unexpected changes. Suppose, for example, that aggregate demand increases due to an increase in exports caused by unexpected events abroad, a sudden rise in consumer optimism, investor reactions to stock market gains or new technologies, or emergency government purchases. If the demand-changing events are unexpected, their price effects appear to firms to be increases in the *relative* prices of their products rather than increases in the *general* price level. They respond by increasing production. Conversely, if the price level declines unexpectedly, firms believe they are experiencing declines in the relative prices of their products and reduce output. Therefore, when unexpected changes take place in aggregate demand, the economy rises above or falls below potential GNP.

According to the rational-expectations model, unexpected changes in aggregate demand lead to fluctuations in employment and real GNP because firms do not correctly interpret information about these unexpected changes. When unexpected changes take place in aggregate demand, the economy rises above or falls below potential GNP.

The view that unexpected changes in the price level (price-level surprises) lead to changes in the quantity of real GNP supplied is illustrated graphically in Figure 2. The curve on this graph is called a **Lucas supply curve,** after Professor Robert Lucas of the University of Chicago, one of the pioneers in developing the theory of rational expectations. Note that the vertical axis on this graph shows *unexpected* changes in the price level—price "surprises." Point *A* on the curve identifies the quantity supplied when there is no unexpected change in the price level. This corresponds with the value of zero (0) on the vertical axis. The curve has a positive slope, indicating that unexpected price-level increases (the independent variable in this model) result in increases in the quantity of real GNP supplied (the dependent variable) and vice versa. The quantity supplied changes because firms misinterpret unexpected price-level changes, believing them to be changes in the relative prices of their products rather than changes in the general price level. The profit-maximizing position that the firms expect because of their misinterpretation of price changes moves up and to the right from point *A* along the Lucas supply curve when there are unexpected increases in the price level and downward to the left from point *A* along the curve when there are unexpected decreases in the price level. When the surprise wears off and firms realize that their products have not actually experienced changes in relative prices, firms retrace their route along the curve back to point *A*, and production returns to its initial (normal) volume. The prevailing price no longer is a surprise.

The Lucas supply curve illustrates graphically that price-level surprises lead to changes in the quantity of real GNP supplied. The quantity supplied changes because firms misinterpret unexpected price-level changes, believing them to be changes in the relative prices of their products rather than changes in the general price level.

The Lucas supply curve expresses much the same reaction process as the aggregate-supply curve in an aggregate-supply and aggregate-demand graph, except that the Lucas curve relates

FIGURE 2
The Lucas Supply Curve

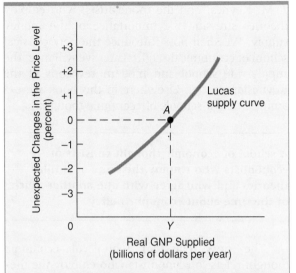

Unexpected changes in the price level are interpreted by firms as changes in the relative prices of their products. Firms respond by increasing production when they believe the relative prices of their products have increased and by reducing production when they believe that the relative prices of their products have decreased. The altered volume of real GNP continues as long as firms believe that relative prices have changed.

only to "surprises" and not to price-level changes in general. As surprises wear off, movements *along* the Lucas supply curve back to point *A* are represented by *shifts* of the aggregate-supply curve. For the Lucas supply curve itself, shifts arise from changes in the production capacity of the economy. This is the concept represented by changes in long-run aggregate-supply and potential GNP.

THE NEW CLASSICAL SCHOOL OF ECONOMIC THOUGHT

A **school of economic thought** is made up of economists who employ the same or similar theories and who agree with one another much of the time about economic policy. We have already met several such schools—the neoclassicals, who dominated economic thinking before the Great Depression and who employed concepts such as Say's Identity; the Keynesians, who accept the models of J. M. Keynes; and the monetarists, who employ theories stressing the importance of the money supply. We shall now introduce the new classical school of economic thought. Later we will meet the supply-side school and modern revisions of the Keynesian school. Elsewhere in this book we examine Marxist schools of economic thought.

A school of economic thought consists of economists who employ the same or similar theories and who agree with one another much of the time about economic policy.

The **new classical** school of economic thought refers to economists who employ the theory of rational expectations and who, in building their macroeconomic models, stress the importance of **microfoundations**—the microeconomic behavior of individuals and firms. Two propositions that have attracted considerable attention to the new classical school are that (a) market prices adjust so quickly to changing situations that fluctuations are brief and mild and (b) markets operate so effectively to equate quantities demanded with quantities supplied that high levels of welfare are achieved.

The new classical school of economic thought refers to economists who use the theory of rational expectations and who stress the importance of microfoundations—the microeconomic behavior of individuals and firms. Two propositions associated with the new classical school are that prices are very flexible and that markets are very effective in equating quantities demanded and supplied.

Price Flexibility

The price-flexibility assumption is that prices adjust so quickly to changes in supply and/or demand that very little time is required for markets to move from one equilibrium to another. In the new classi-

cal model, a shift of a demand curve or a supply curve is recognized immediately by all traders in a market. Since traders the world over are linked by computer technology and satellite communications, prices move promptly to each new equilibrium. Also, and very importantly, it is suggested that institutional barriers, such as long-term contracts or legal requirements for advance notice of proposed actions, do not interfere significantly with price adjustments.[1]

According to the new classical school, prices adjust so quickly to changes in supply and demand that very little time is required for markets to move from one equilibrium to another.

Combining the propositions that (1) only demand or supply shifts that come as surprises affect the equilibrium level of real GNP, and (2) prices adjust quickly to changes in demand and supply, new classical economists conclude that fluctuations in employment and output from sudden or surprise changes in an economic variable are both moderate and of short duration. When surprises occur, firms and resource owners mistake price-level changes for changes in relative prices so that output and employment change. But surprise evaporates quickly, shifting the *AS* curve and returning equilibrium quickly to potential GNP. In the view of new classical economists, most economic fluctuations will be brief and moderate unless government intervenes or unless there is a deliberate attempt to force government to change its macroeconomic policies. In their view, government intervention is likely to do more harm than good, since political uncertainties inherent in government intervention delay needed adjustments in the economy itself.[2]

---

1. This assumption in particular is challenged by Keynesians.

2. The argument that shocks trigger economic fluctuations and that these fluctuations will be moderate and brief does not explain business cycles—the sequence of fluctuations in which each fluctuation has its origins in the previous fluctuation. The assumptions of rational expectations and price flexibility cast doubt on traditional explanations for cycles. To fill this gap, new classical economists have developed **real business cycle theories,** built upon patterns of changing labor productivity or labor supply.

> **New classical economists believe that fluctuations in employment and output from surprise changes in an economic variable are both moderate and brief unless government intervenes.**

Market Clearing

A second proposition of the new classical school is that, at equilibrium, markets are "cleared." **Market clearing** means that, at the equilibrium price, no potential sellers who are willing and able to sell at that price are unable to carry out their desired transaction, and no buyers who are willing and able to buy at that price are unable to carry out their desired transaction. For example, in a labor market for some specified skill level and occupation, market clearing means that if the equilibrium wage rate is $12.85 per hour, every worker willing and able to work for this wage will be employed. There will be no excess supply or demand at equilibrium. At equilibrium, unemployment does not exist and neither does any labor shortage.[3]

> **Market clearing means that, at the equilibrium price, no potential sellers or buyers are unable to carry out their desired transactions. There will be no excess supply or demand at equilibrium; neither unemployment nor labor shortages exist.**

Market clearing has powerful welfare implications. It means that, given existing demand and supply curves, the equilibrium price maximizes the quantity of the good or service demanded and supplied. At any above-equilibrium price, less would be exchanged because demanders are unwilling or unable to buy as much as they would at the equilibrium price. Similarly, a smaller quantity would be exchanged at any below-equilibrium price, because, in this case, suppliers are unwilling or unable to supply as much as they would at the equilibrium price. These conclusions follow because, in a free market, each party—the buyer as well as the

seller—has the power to veto the transaction. With the market-clearing assumption, when equilibrium exists, buyers are "on their demand curves" and sellers are "on their supply curves," meaning that the plans of each group are being fulfilled. Potential GNP is the best that can be achieved, given the microeconomic properties (competition, monopoly, etc.) of the individual markets that make up the economy. Lower volumes of real GNP are inferior because resources are wasted through unemployment. Higher volumes of real GNP are also inferior, because the extra employment is not worth its cost in forgone leisure activities. New classical economists conclude that, at equilibrium, resources are fully employed and welfare is maximized.

> **New classical economists conclude that, at equilibrium, resources are fully employed and welfare is maximized.**

The two propositions—that prices adjust quickly to their equilibrium levels and that markets clear at equilibrium—combine to generate very powerful conclusions from the new classical model. The price-flexibility proposition suggests that deviations from potential GNP will be moderate and brief and that government intervention is not needed to achieve and maintain that level of economic activity. The market-clearing proposition suggests that potential GNP is a very satisfactory condition in terms of economic welfare. The policy implications of the new classical school are similar to those of the neoclassical school dominant prior to the Great Depression of the 1930s—that the economy tends normally to full employment and that there is no need of government intervention. All that is needed is to follow fixed rules that everyone understands.

> **The policy implications of the new classical model are similar to those of the neoclassical model dominant prior to the Great Depression—that the economy tends normally to full employment and that there is no need of government intervention.**

Would new classical economists refuse to make use of monetary and fiscal instruments

3. We assume that supply and demand curves do not appear as horizontal lines on a graph.

should an emergency arise? This question has not, as yet, been put to the test. After the stock market crash of 1929, the economy actually suffered a severe and lengthy departure from potential GNP. But the stock market crash of 1987 was not followed by such problems. The question of emergencies to one side, the basic thrust of the new classical argument is simply that, in normal times, the economy can right itself quickly from minor disturbances and that government need not preside over day-to-day operation of the economy.

NEO-KEYNESIAN ECONOMICS

Chapters 10 and 11 presented certain basic features of Keynesian economics—the consumption function, the investment function, total planned expenditure, the Keynesian cross, and so on. That model dominated macroeconomic policymaking from 1945 into the 1960s, although it was persistently criticized by monetarist economists for its failure to recognize the importance of monetary variables in determining the equilibrium level of real GNP. Extended debates took place between Keynesian and monetarist economists during the 1960s. From these debates came more sophisticated Keynesian models, preserving the basic approach but giving greater importance to monetary variables. This expanded and more sophisticated model is call **neo-Keynesian economics.** Its primary difference from the original Keynesian model is that the "monetary" dimensions of the economy—the money supply and financial variables—are added to the original consumption, investment, government, and net export variables. In the macroeconomic turmoil of the 1970s and 1980s, it was not the original Keynesian model that contested with the new classical model of the macroeconomy. Instead it was the more powerful and sophisticated neo-Keynesian model.[4]

Neo-Keynesian economics preserves the basic approach of Keynesian economics but gives greater importance to monetary variables.

---

4. Many of Keynes's direct disciples call this sort of thing "bastard" Keynesianism.

The *IS-LM* System

Modern Keynesian economics is built around the **IS-LM system,** in which *I* stands for investment, *S* stands for saving, *L* stands for liquidity (the demand for money), and *M* stands for the money supply, that is, the quantity of money existing in the economy. The hyphen in *IS-LM* signifies the division of the model into two components, the *IS* component and the *LM* component. The *IS* portion incorporates the requirement that saving must equal investment at macroeconomic equilibrium. This is the "real goods" aspect of the economy. The *LM* portion brings in the demand and supply of money and the financial aspect of the economy. We shall first explain the *IS* component, then the *LM* component, and then bring the two together to show how the modern Keynesian model explains macroeconomic equilibrium in the economy.

Modern Keynesian economics is built around the IS-LM model. The IS portion of the model incorporates saving and investment as determinants of equilibrium GNP; the LM component incorporates the financial aspect of the economy.

The IS Curve The investment-saving, or real goods and services component of the economy is represented by the *IS* curve in panel (b) of Figure 3. The horizontal axis of this graph shows real GNP. The vertical axis shows the real rate of interest. The *IS* curve is not a cause-and-effect relationship between these variables but shows, instead, combinations that are mutually consistent and necessary for equilibrium to exist. In other words, *ceteris paribus,* for any specified level of real GNP, there is one and only one real interest rate that is consistent with equilibrium in the real goods and services ($C + I + G + X - Im$) component of the economy. The statement can also be made in reverse. *Ceteris paribus,* for any specified real rate of interest, there is one and only one level of real GNP that is consistent with equilibrium in the real goods and services component ($C + I + G + X - Im$) of the economy.

The two panels of Figure 3 illustrate how the *IS* curve is derived from the basic Keynesian-cross model presented in Chapter 10. The illustration begins at point *A* in panel (a), which represents mac-

FIGURE 3
Derivation of the *IS* Curve

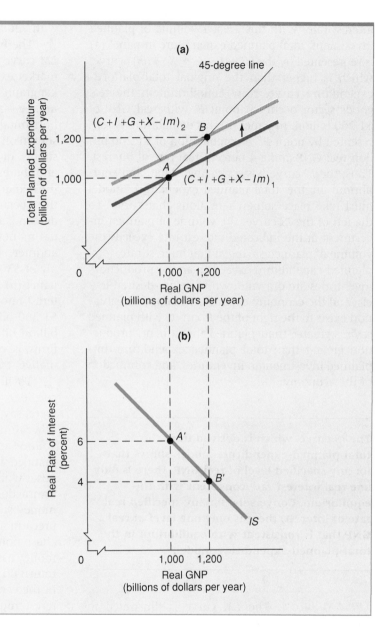

In panel (a), point A represents equilibrium in the real component of the economy because total planned expenditure ($C + I + G + X - Im$)$_1$ and the value of real GNP are equal at $1,000 billion. Assuming that the real interest rate is 6 percent, this equilibrium is represented in panel (b) by point A'. At an interest rate lower than 6 percent, total planned expenditure would be greater, *ceteris paribus*, mainly because planned investment would be greater. Therefore, in panel (a), total planned expenditure with a 4 percent real rate of interest is represented by the ($C + I + G + X - Im$)$_2$ curve. Equilibrium in the real component now is at point B in panel (a), with real GNP of $1,200 billion. In panel (b), this new equilibrium is represented by point B'. Points A' and B' lie on the *IS* curve.

roeconomic equilibrium, according to the total-planned-expenditure model, at $1,000 billion of real GNP. At point A, total planned expenditure—($C + I + G + X - Im$)$_1$—equals $1,000 billion, as shown on the vertical axis of the Keynesian-cross graph. With real GNP also at $1,000 billion, inventories are exactly at the levels planned by firms so, *ceteris paribus*, there is no reason for firms to change planned production in the next time period. In

panel (b), this equilibrium is represented at point A'. Point A' states that when real GNP is in equilibrium at $1,000 billion, there is some real rate of interest—6 percent in Figure 3—that prevails in the economy and balances planned saving and planned investment.

To identify a second point on the *IS* curve, consider what the situation would be if the interest rate were lower, say at 4 percent instead of 6 percent.

Other things being unchanged, the volume of planned investment would be greater at the lower interest rate. With this greater volume of planned investment, total planned expenditure in panel (a) is represented by the $(C + I + G + X - Im)_2$ curve, which is higher than the original total-planned-expenditure curve. Now equilibrium in the real goods sector occurs at point B, with real GNP of $1,200 billion. In panel (b) this equilibrium is represented by point B', a combination of $1,200 billion real GNP and a 4 percent real rate of interest. Thus, the IS curve has a negative slope, and equilibrium in the total-planned-expenditure model must take place somewhere along that curve. To the left of the IS curve, the volume of planned investment at the indicated interest rate exceeds the volume of planned saving at that interest rate, total planned expenditure exceeds planned production, inventories are drawn down to below-desired levels, and the economy expands. The opposite situation exists to the right of the IS curve, with planned saving greater than planned investment, production greater than total planned expenditure, unplanned investment in inventories, and contraction of the economy.

The IS curve, which is derived from the total-planned-expenditure model, shows that for any specified level of real GNP, there is only one real interest rate consistent with the equilibrium. Conversely, for any specified real rate of interest, there is only one level of real GNP that is consistent with equilibrium in the total-planned-expenditure model.

The LM Curve The LM curve is illustrated in panel (b) of Figure 4. As with the IS curve, the LM curve does not represent a cause-and-effect relationship between the real interest rate and the level of real GNP. Instead, it shows the combinations of the two variables that are consistent or necessary for equality between the quantity of money demanded and the quantity of money supplied. *Ceteris paribus*, for any given level of real GNP, there is one and only one real interest rate that is consistent with equilibrium in the money market. Con-

versely, for any given real interest rate, there is one and only one level of real GNP that is consistent with equilibrium in this market, *ceteris paribus*.

The two panels of Figure 4 illustrate how the LM curve is derived from the graph of the money market explained in Chapter 14. The money-market graph appears in panel (a). The real quantity of money—as measured by M1—is shown on the horizontal axis, and the real rate of interest is shown on the vertical axis. The MS curve shows the supply of money created by the Federal Reserve and the banking system, and the MD curve shows the demand for money as an asset as determined by the speculative, transactions, and precautionary demands for money balances. In panel (a) the initial money-market equilibrium is at point A, with an interest rate of 8 percent and a real money supply of $300 billion. This situation is represented in panel (b) at point A', where the 8 percent real interest rate is shown as consistent with real GNP of $1,200 billion. In this illustration, all of the $300 billion of money is willingly held by households, firms, governments, and foreigners for either speculative, transactions, or precautionary purposes.

To illustrate the derivation of the LM curve, consider what the situation would be if real GNP were, say, $1,000 billion instead of $1,200 billion, other things remaining unchanged. With a smaller volume of real GNP, the quantity of money demanded for transactions and precautionary purposes would be smaller as well, since the volume of transactions is smaller. The part of the existing money supply not demanded for transactions and precautionary purposes will be used instead to purchase nonmoney assets, driving the prices of nonmoney assets upward and lowering both the rate of return on nonmoney assets and the rate of interest in the economy. In our illustration, the rate of interest must fall from 8 percent to 6 percent to achieve equilibrium, *ceteris paribus*, when real GNP is $1,000 billion. This is illustrated by point B' in panel (b). What has happened is that the lower volume of real GNP has shifted the MD curve in panel (a) to the left (as shown by the arrow) enough to lower the real rate of interest to 6 percent. Otherwise, equilibrium would not have been achieved in the money market. The lower interest rate is necessary in order for the demand for money to match the $290 billion quantity of money now

FIGURE 4
Derivation of the *LM* Curve

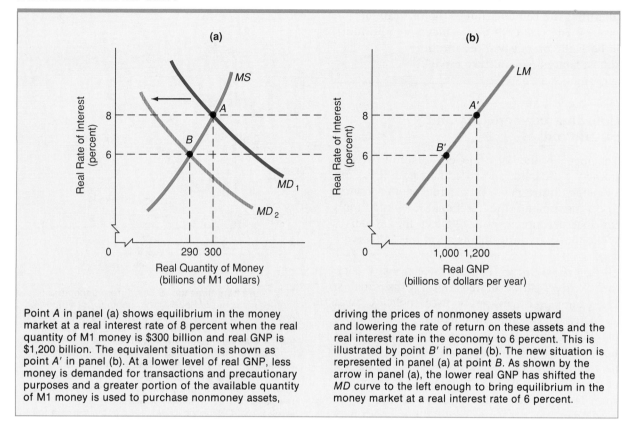

Point *A* in panel (a) shows equilibrium in the money market at a real interest rate of 8 percent when the real quantity of M1 money is $300 billion and real GNP is $1,200 billion. The equivalent situation is shown as point *A'* in panel (b). At a lower level of real GNP, less money is demanded for transactions and precautionary purposes and a greater portion of the available quantity of M1 money is used to purchase nonmoney assets,

driving the prices of nonmoney assets upward and lowering the rate of return on these assets and the real interest rate in the economy to 6 percent. This is illustrated by point *B'* in panel (b). The new situation is represented in panel (a) at point *B*. As shown by the arrow in panel (a), the lower real GNP has shifted the *MD* curve to the left enough to bring equilibrium in the money market at a real interest rate of 6 percent.

available in the economy. In this way, the *LM* curve displays all equilibrium combinations of the real rate of interest and real GNP. To the left of the *LM* curve, the real GNP is so low that, at the indicated rate of interest, the quantity of money demanded (*L*) is less than the quantity supplied (*M*), forcing real interest rates downward. To the right of the curve, real GNP is so large that the demand for money exceeds its supply, forcing real interest rates upward.

The *LM* curve shows the combinations of the real rate of interest and real GNP that equate the demand for money with the supply of money. For any given level of real GNP, there is only one real interest rate that will equate the demand and the supply of money. Conversely,

---

for any given real interest rate, there is only one level of real GNP that will provide this equality.

IS and LM Combined Figure 5 brings together the *IS* and the *LM* curves developed in the preceding illustrations. The two curves intersect with real GNP of $1,000 billion and a real interest rate of 6 percent. According to the *IS-LM* system, this represents "full" equilibrium in the macroeconomy. The "real" economy (represented by the total-planned-expenditure model) is in equilibrium according to the *IS* curve, and the "financial" economy (represented by the money market) is in equilibrium according to the *LM* curve. No other rate of interest is consistent with equilibrium simultaneously in both dimensions of the economy.

The intersection of the *IS* and *LM* curves identifies the combination of the real rate of interest and real GNP that achieves equilibrium in both the money market and in the total-planned-expenditure model.

Coordinated Monetary and Fiscal Policies

The appeal of the *IS-LM* model is that it provides a framework to guide and coordinate both fiscal and monetary instruments of macroeconomic policy. Fiscal instruments, the traditional Keynesian tools for macroeconomic policy, affect the *IS* curve, while monetary instruments affect the *LM* curve.[5]

Shifting the IS Curve   In the neo-Keynesian model, the *IS* curve can be shifted by fiscal instruments. For example, expansionary fiscal policies, such as increased government purchases, lower taxes, or changes in tax laws that improve the after-tax profitability of investments, shift the *IS* curve to the right. With expansionary fiscal policies, at any given real rate of interest, the equilibrium level of real GNP is greater. If there is no accompanying ("accommodating") expansionary monetary policy, the *LM* curve remains stationary, and an expansionary fiscal policy results in macroeconomic equilibrium moving upward and to the right along the *LM* curve. The result is higher real rates of interest and some increase in real GNP. The precise mixture of these two consequences depends on the slopes of the curves. Thus, the *IS-LM* system recognizes that the financial dimension of the economy can limit the real effects of expansionary fiscal policy.

Fiscal instruments shift the *IS* curve. The real effects of fiscal policy actions depend upon the slopes of the *IS* and *LM* curves.

Shifting the LM Curve   The *LM* curve can be shifted by monetary instruments, that is, by central

5. More advanced courses take up the questions of whether changes in *IS* can avoid also changing *LM,* and vice versa.

FIGURE 5
The *IS* and *LM* Curves Combined

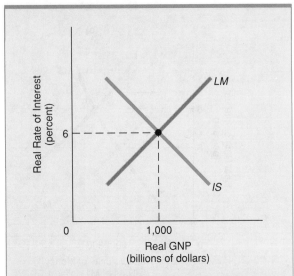

This figure combines the *IS* curve from panel (b) of Figure 3 and the *LM* curve from panel (b) of Figure 4. According to the neo-Keynesian model, at equilibrium in the total-planned-expenditure model, the combination of the real interest rate and the level of real GNP must be somewhere along the *IS* curve. Similarly, at equilibrium in the money market, the combination must be somewhere along the *LM* curve. Therefore, the intersection of the *IS* and the *LM* curves identifies the particular combination of real interest rate and level of real GNP necessary for full equilibrium in the macoeconomy.

bank policies affecting the real money supply. If the real money supply is increased, as the neo-Keynesians claim is possible through open market purchases, lower reserve requirements, and lower discount rates, the *LM* curve shifts to the right. A greater amount of money will be available, at any given real interest rate, for speculative, transactions, and precautionary purposes in the economy. If such an expansionary monetary policy is undertaken without any accompanying change in fiscal policy, macroeconomic equilibrium moves downward and to the right along the *IS* curve, resulting in lower real rates of interest and an expansion of real GNP. The precise mixture between these two outcomes depends on the slope of the *IS* and *LM* curves, that is, on the sensitivity of the economy to changes in real interest rates.

Monetary instruments shift the *LM* curve. The real effects of monetary policy actions depend upon the slopes of the *IS* and *LM* curves.

Shifting Both IS and LM The most powerful implication of the *IS-LM* model points to simultaneous expansionary applications of *both* fiscal and monetary policies. If both curves are shifted to the right, the *IS-LM* model suggests that real GNP can be increased without an accompanying increase in real interest rates. In other words, the effectiveness of fiscal instruments would not be limited by the financial elements in the economy, nor would the effectiveness of monetary instruments be limited by unsupportive fiscal policies.

If the *IS* and *LM* curves can be shifted separately, the neo-Keynesian model suggests that it is possible to adjust the locations of the two curves to achieve some ideal combination of the real rate of interest and the real GNP. For example, real GNP could be tuned to achieve potential GNP as determined by macroeconomic policymakers. At the same time, the real rate of interest could be made consistent with the profitability of investments and the preferences of suppliers in loanable-funds markets.

If the *IS* and *LM* curves can be shifted independently, macroeconomic policy can pursue both output and interest-rate goals.

Neo-Keynesian Economics and the Price Level

Our explanation of the *IS-LM* model was carried out under the assumption of a constant price level. This enabled us to use "real" interest rates on the vertical axes of *IS-LM* graphs and "real" GNP on their horizontal axes. But the price level cannot be ignored in macroeconomics, just as individual prices cannot be ignored in microeconomics.

As you remember, the price level is an important variable in the aggregate-demand and aggregate-supply approach to macroeconomic equilibrium. But the *IS-LM* model does not use the price level as an independent variable. Instead, price levels usually are policy variables in the neo-Keynesian system. If the goal is a stable price level, the *IS-LM* model must adapt the target GNP to match the economy's potential real GNP. Target levels of *nominal* GNP may be selected by policymakers. Such nominal targets incorporate inflation-rate considerations as well as real employment and output considerations and must consider the slope of the economy's aggregate-supply curve.

NEO-KEYNESIAN VERSUS NEW CLASSICAL ECONOMICS

During the 1970s and 1980s, both neo-Keynesian and new classical economists focused attention on the supply side of the economy. Both made use of aggregate-demand and aggregate-supply formulations. The basic differences between these two schools of modern macroeconomic thought revolve around three propositions: (1) how important are rational expectations? (2) how flexible are prices? and (3) do markets always clear?

How Important Are Rational Expectations?

Neo-Keynesian economists contend that rational expectations cannot completely eliminate the systematic effectiveness of government demand-side intervention in the economy. They grant that the society may be more knowledgeable about the price-level consequences of demand-side initiatives than it was in earlier times. They also grant that large corporations and labor unions employ competent economists who forecast the effects of economic events and government policy actions. Nevertheless, neo-Keynesian economists argue that economics is not an exact science and that these forecasts are subject to large variations. Therefore, neo-Keynesians conclude that expectations are significantly less "rational" than supposed by new classical economists. Furthermore, they conclude that the aggregate-supply curve does have a significant positive slope, and that shifts of this curve do *not* take place as quickly as supposed by the new classicals.

Because the *AS* curve has significant positive slope and does not shift quickly, neo-Keynesian economists contend that systematic government demand-side initiatives are effective and are not immediately counteracted by shifts of the aggregate-supply curve. In the neo-Keynesian view, policy-induced shifts of the aggregate-demand curve result in changes in real GNP and the volume of employment.

Neo-Keynesian economists contend that actual economic behavior is not as "rational" as the new classical economists claim and that systematic government demand-side policy initiatives are effective.

How Flexible are Prices?

Neo-Keynesian economists are emphatic in their criticism of the new classical view that markets adjust quickly to changes in demand and/or supply, that is, to the proposition that prices are flexible. They believe that rigidities and barriers to rapid price changes are significant in many parts of the economy. Rigidities and barriers are especially important, they say, in resource markets, where firms have long-term contracts and understandings for labor services and where established practices, or institutions, delay price adjustments. They argue that employers postpone layoffs and wage-rate reductions in recessions because of a sense of obligation to their employees, with whom they wish to maintain good relations, and because of concern for public opinion. Also, since firms do not want the expense of recruiting and training new employees when the recession ends, they hold on to their employees even when current sales are low. In good times, overtime work is done and wage-rate increases or expansions in employment are delayed until firms are sure that the expansion will continue long enough to justify long-term commitments to higher wage rates and additional employees. Retirement programs, unemployment insurance, and fringe benefit packages add to the costs of hiring and firing and are additional discouragements to layoffs and hirings.[6]

Keynesian economists criticize the new classical belief in price flexibility. They believe that rigidities and barriers to rapid price changes are significant in many parts of the economy.

From your study of aggregate demand and aggregate supply, you know that price flexibility is an important determinant of both the slope and the shifts of the aggregate-supply curve. The less flexible the prices, especially in resource markets, the flatter the aggregate-supply curve, since lags in resource prices contribute to large changes in profit margins and encourage increases or decreases in production. Thus, in the neo-Keynesian view, aggregate-demand shifts cause large fluctuations in employment and real GNP. Also, price inflexibility causes fluctuations to last longer. More time elapses before the aggregate-supply curve completes its "catch-up" shift. Neo-Keynesians argue that price inflexibility means that serious fluctuations take place and that large amounts of GNP are lost if government does not intervene to moderate the consequences of shocks to the economy. Moreover, since Keynesians discount the impact of rational expectations, they believe that such intervention is effective.

Neo-Keynesians argue that price inflexibility means that serious fluctuations take place and that large amounts of GNP are lost if government does not intervene to moderate the consequences of shocks to the economy.

Do Markets Always Clear?

Neo-Keynesians believe that markets do not clear as completely as claimed by the new classicals, Their doubt about market clearing is based on bar-

---

6. Price inflexibility may also arise from the expectation that government policy will bail out depressed sectors of the economy or that political pressure can force government to do so.

riers and restrictions to mobility which, they say, exist in most markets. All economists recognize that excess demand or excess supply exist when markets are in disequilibrium and prices are on the move toward their equilibrium levels. In these situations, some willing and able buyers or sellers are unable to complete transactions at the going price. All agree also that frequent shifts of demand and supply take place so that equilibrium is a "moving target." Barriers and restrictions on resource mobility slow the approach to equilibrium and cause losses in potential GNP. Neo-Keynesians believe that new classicals underestimate the seriousness of barriers and restrictions to mobility and expect equilibrium to be approached more quickly and with less lost output than in fact is the case.

A slow approach to equilibrium is not the only problem that arises from barriers and institutional arrangements, including monopoly and monopsony, that limit resource mobility. Discrimination, lack of information, and immobility contribute to serious market failures. Restrictions that deny resources access to markets that would best utilize their capabilities force these resources into other markets, where their presence creates further distortion.

Neo-Keynesians believe that because of barriers and restrictions to mobility, markets do not clear as completely as the new classical economists claim.

The notion that markets do an imperfect job even at equilibrium is not seriously open to doubt. Perfect knowledge and perfect mobility are difficult to envision. The real questions, therefore, cannot be answered simply "yes" or "no," and one cannot find a yes-or-no dividing line between new classicals and neo-Keynesians on this point. Instead, the issues are "How serious are imperfections in the market system?" "To what extent should market processes be supplemented by government intervention?" "How can markets be made to work better?" "To what extent should the market system be altered by planning?" Neo-Keynesians differ from new classicals on the answers to these questions. They tend to favor more government intervention

than do members of the new classical school. But economists working in the Keynesian tradition also disagree among themselves on the seriousness of market imperfections and on the desirability of government intervention. Intervention through traditional fiscal and monetary policy is needed, according to neo-Keynesians, but most do not argue that large increases of government involvement in specific markets or major extensions of central economic planning are also needed. Most neo-Keynesians agree that excessive government intervention can do more harm than good.

According to neo-Keynesians, intervention through traditional fiscal and monetary policy is needed, but not large increases of government involvement in specific markets or major extensions of central economic planning.

POST-KEYNESIAN ECONOMICS

Among modern Keynesians, a small but occasionally vocal group of economists called **post-Keynesians** are strongly in favor of permanent government direction of both the macro- and the microeconomy, taking positions close to Marxian socialism. They believe that market failures are frequent and serious and that government intervention is therefore desirable. Post-Keynesians believe that the basic message of J. M. Keynes in the 1930s should not have been the model that he offered to resolve the short-run crisis of the Great Depression, but rather his diagnosis of the structural problems that cause crises in market economies. These include the monopolization of product and labor markets, which brings price rigidities, as well as the highly concentrated and panic-prone collection of financial institutions that collapse in hard times and turn recessions into deep and long depressions. Post-Keynesians contend that monetary and fiscal policies deal only with the symptoms of a sick economic system and fail to attack the underlying causes of the sickness. They claim that Keynes himself "did not understand the *General Theory*"—by which they mean that he did not understand its longer-term implications. Prominent post-Keynesians include Joan Robinson (1901–1983) in England and John Kenneth Galbraith (1908-   ) in the United States.

Post-Keynesians propose greatly expanded government intervention in the economy, including detailed regulation of major industries, comprehensive systems of incentives and penalties imposed through tax laws and government expenditure programs, **incomes policies** (comprehensive wage, price, and profit controls), and a substantial amount of economic planning by the government. Post-Keynesians operate within the context of a capitalist-market economic system substantially modified by government regulations, income redistribution, and welfare-state measures.

Post-Keynesian economists take positions close to Marxian socialism in that they favor permanent government direction of both the macro- and the microeconomy.

SUPPLY-SIDE ECONOMICS

So far in this chapter, government intervention (supported in varying degrees by neo-Keynesian economists and generally disapproved of by new classical economists) has been limited to the demand side of economic activity. Now we examine **supply-side economics,** which argues that government actions affecting the aggregate-supply curve are at least as important as government actions affecting the aggregate-demand curve— and probably more. Supply-side economists were prominent in the first Reagan administration (1981–1985), when they actively promoted reductions in tax rates intended to stimulate investment and work incentives. On that basis they claimed substantial credit for the strong performance of the economy during the second Reagan administration (1985–1989).

FIGURE 6
Supply-Side Economics

At point A, the economy is in macroeconomic equilibrium, producing its potential GNP of $1,000 billion a year at a price level of 100. Supply-side policies increase production capabilities and shift the aggregate-supply curve from AS_1 to AS_2 (shown by arrow 1). A policy of low interest rates requires some increase in the price level in order to increase potential GNP. Tax cuts and low interest rates shift the aggregate-demand curve from AD_1 to AD_2 (shown by arrow 2), bringing macroeconomic equilibrium at point B, with real output of $1,200 billion and a price level of 110.

Supply-side economists argue that government actions affecting the aggregate-supply curve are at least as important as government actions affecting the aggregate-demand curve.

Figure 6 illustrates the basic propositions of supply-side economics. Point A represents an equilibrium situation for an economy producing its potential GNP but operating without the advantages of supply-side economic policies. The price-level index number is 100, and $1,000 billion of real GNP is produced per year. Supply-side economists contend that the economy can do better than $1,000 billion of real GNP. They argue that properly conceived and executed government policies can shift both the aggregate-demand curve and the aggregate-supply curve to the right, moving macroeconomic equilibrium from point *A* to point *B*.

How are these results to be obtained? First, they say that government regulations and taxes on business have, for years, restricted the free exercise of entrepreneurship and profit seeking. To correct for this, supply-siders advocate deregulation, freeing producers from the red tape of government bureaucracy, and reductions in tax rates under the corporation income tax. These moves would give a green light to business investment and innovations. Second, supply-side economists advocate lower tax rates under the individual income tax to increase the after-tax returns to both working and saving. They especially favor lowering *marginal* tax rates—the rates payable on the *next* dollar that a person might earn. By lowering marginal tax rates on the returns on savings—and by going even further and offering tax shelters for saving—supply-siders expect to increase the amount of saving, thus providing funds to finance increased investment by firms. Some would exempt saving altogether by allowing it full deductibility in calculating income taxes. By lowering marginal tax rates on income from work, they expect to increase work incentives. Third, supply-side economists favor monetary policies that keep interest rates low in order to encourage investment and modern production facilities.

Supply-siders advocate deregulation, reductions in corporate and individual income-tax rates, and low interest rates.

The combination of these programs, they say, will increase potential GNP and shift the aggregate-supply curve to the right, as illustrated in Figure 6 by the shift from AS_1 to AS_2 (arrow 1). They grant that the easy-money policies used to keep interest rates low may cause an increase in the price level, but this, they say, is a fair price to pay for greater output.

Although supply-side economists emphasize shifts of aggregate-supply curves, they do not ignore aggregate demand. In their models, the aggregate-demand curve shifts to the right at the same time that the aggregate-supply curve shifts in that direction. They expect tax cuts and low interest rates to increase aggregate demand. In Figure 6, arrow 2 shows aggregate demand shifting from AD_1 to AD_2—just enough to produce macroeconomic equilibrium at the new potential GNP of $1,200 billion.

This "best-case" scenario usually is not achieved in the real world, of course. The tax reductions of the early Reagan years were implemented piecemeal rather than all at once, and supply-siders contend that this weakened their impact on incentives. Furthermore, supply-siders complain that restrictive monetary policies, carried out in the early 1980s to fight inflationary pressures in the economy, denied demand-side support for their programs aimed at shifting aggregate supply. The economy suffered a severe recession in the early 1980s, and supply-siders argued that their programs were not given a fair test. When the economy recovered, starting in 1982, it was not clear whether credit should go to delayed reactions from the earlier supply-side initiatives, to the stimulative effects of large government deficits arising from the combination of tax cuts and increases in military spending, or to both.

Say's Identity Again?

Doubters of the supply-side approach say that by shifting aggregate demand just enough to hit their target, supply-siders come close to reasserting **Say's Identity,** that supply creates its own demand. These critics say that there is no reason to expect that the expansion of production and the fiscal measures that brought it about will necessarily lead to just the right amount of aggregate demand.

The supply-siders' answer is much like that of physicians about "normal" body temperatures or the normal values of any other life sign. That is, they say that any failure to hit the target is a symptom of something that is wrong with the working of the economy—such as overly high tax rates or excessive regulation. So if aggregate demand doesn't shift to the proper level, it is not the policy but "something else" in the economy that must be corrected. When that "something else" is corrected, then Say's Identity will return, just as body temperature returns to 98.6 degrees when measles or pneumonia has been cured.

The Laffer Curve

A second problem for supply-side economics has to do with the possibility that tax cuts will cause large government deficits and that financing these deficits will raise interest rates, crowding out the private investment that supply-siders hope to increase through their tax cuts.

The supply-side counterargument is based on the **Laffer curve,** pictured in Figure 7. The vertical axis shows the net tax revenues of government, and the horizontal axis shows the average net tax rate. The curve itself displays Arthur Laffer's idea of how net tax revenues respond to changes in average tax rates.[7] No revenue would be collected if the tax rate were zero. But neither would any be collected at a tax rate of 100 percent, since no one would find it worthwhile to work if government took all the earnings. In between, the Laffer curve suggests that tax revenues will rise as average tax rates rise, but only up to a point. If tax rates rise above a certain level, the level corresponding to the peak of the curve, the work-discouraging effects of rate increases more than offset their revenue-raising effects, and total revenue falls.

The Laffer curve shows how net tax revenues respond to changes in average tax rates. The curve suggests that if tax rates rise above a certain level, the work-discouraging effects of rate increases more than offset their revenue-raising effects.

Many supply-side economists, among them Arthur Laffer himself, claim that the United States

FIGURE 7
The Laffer Curve

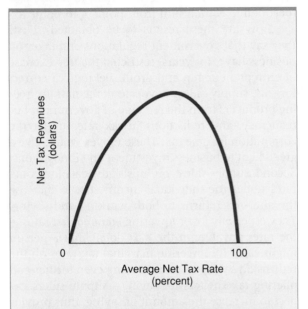

The Laffer curve illustrates the proposition that net tax revenues increase as average net tax rates increase, but only up to a point. If net tax rates go too high, net revenues actually collected by the government may fall. This is shown on the right side of the curve, where it has a negative slope. Some supply-siders suggest that the United States is on the right side of the curve so that reductions in tax rates would actually increase net tax revenues.

and many other countries are on the right-hand side of the curve. If this is true, supply-side policies can avoid large deficits, and there need be no crowding out of private investment. Lower tax rates could in fact increase tax revenues. Many economists, however, are not persuaded that the United States really is on the right-hand side of the curve.

7. Arthur Laffer, formerly professor of economics at the University of Southern California, is at this writing an economic consultant.

Economics in Focus

Reagan and the Supply Side: Success or Failure?

Although the policies of Ronald Reagan's two administrations were not a pure exercise in supply-side economics, they were the closest the United States has come to direct application of supply-side principles. For that reason the successes and failures of "Reaganomics" sparked an economic debate that has continued to simmer since Reagan left office.

Supporters of Reagan and his supply-side advisers have pointed, first of all, to the long expansionary period beginning in late 1982—the longest such period in U.S. history. They note that 19 million new jobs were created between 1982 and 1989; that domestic investment increased remarkably; that, in the words of the 1989 *Economic Report of the President*, there was "an explosion of small business growth"; and that manufacturing productivity rose at an average annual rate of 4.4 percent, compared to 2.3 percent in the 1970s. Just as important, inflation was kept under control despite the expansion. And, it was flattering to Reagan when all of the major industrial nations known as the Group of Seven followed his lead in reducing tax rates.

But critics have been quick to point out the downside of Reaganomics. There was a sharp recession in 1982. The nation continued to borrow heavily from foreigners, though less so than during the Carter years. There were large, continuing budget deficits, which failed to disappear despite the administration's rosy projections. Ultimately the national debt reached astounding proportions—over two and a half trillion dollars by the time Reagan left office. Many analysts claim that the United States is now the largest debtor nation in the world, although the validity of that label is hotly disputed by the supply-siders. Perhaps most important, President Reagan's economic theories were partly responsible for his decision to slash social and educational programs. The number of homeless swelled across the country; cities increasingly struggled to maintain basic services with reduced federal support; and educators painted a picture of school systems in grave danger because of federal funding cuts and government indifference. Some of Reagan's most intense critics charged him simply with befriending the rich and abandoning the poor.

A few analysts have tried to reach a balanced assessment of Reagan's policies. They note that the national debt, huge as it may be, does not seem so threatening when it is seen as a percentage of GNP; in those terms, in fact, it is no worse than during the Kennedy administration, and far better than during World War II. Of course, there was no world war during the Reagan years. His war was against the stagflation of the 1970s—and he clearly emerged the winner. Whether he paid too high a price is the issue that still confronts us.

Sources: Paul Craig Roberts, "It's Time to Face Facts: Supply-Side Was a Smash," *Business Week,* February 6, 1989, p. 14; Paul Craig Roberts, "While Critics Carp, the Supply-Side Revolution Sweeps On," *Business Week,* April 25, 1988, p. 15; Peter Brimelow with Lisa Scheer, "Is the Reagan Prosperity for Real?" *Forbes,* October 31, 1988, pp. 85–90.

SUMMARY

1. The assumption of rational expectations is that people form their expectations about future price levels through the use of economic analysis. When applied to an aggregate-demand and aggregate-supply model, the rational-expectations assumption suggests that the aggregate-supply curve shifts as a direct result of policy-initiated shifts of the aggregate-demand curve. An alternative statement of this result is that the aggregate-supply curve is vertical. (See pages 370–371 and Figure 1, page 371.)

2. When combined with assumptions that prices and wage rates are flexible, the theory of rational expectations suggests that discretionary fiscal and monetary policies of government do not change real variables, such as output and employment, but result only in changes in the price level. (See page 371.)

3. The neo-Ricardian application of the rational-expectations theory suggests that taxpayers interpret government budget deficits as promising higher taxes in the future and respond by increasing current saving and reducing current consumption. Therefore, tax finance and deficit finance have equivalent macroeconomic effects. Crowding out comes from government expenditure, no matter how financed. The theory also suggests that the availability of deficit finance does not bias government-expenditure decisions. (See page 372.)

4. The Lucas supply curve illustrates a positive relationship between unexpected changes in the price level and the quantity of real GNP supplied per year. This relationship is based on the proposition that firms interpret unexpected changes in the price level as changes in the relative prices of their products and expand or contract output accordingly. (See page 373 and Figure 2, page 373.)

5. A school of economic thought consists of economists who employ the same or similar theories and who agree with one another much of the time about economic policy. New classical economists make extensive use of the theory of rational expectations and stress the microeconomic foundations of their macroeconomic models. They contend that prices are flexible and that markets clear so that markets operate effectively in equating quantities demanded and quantities supplied. At equilibrium, unemployment does not exist. (See pages 373–374.)

6. The assumption of price flexibility suggests that fluctuations in output and employment are moderate and brief, provided that no deliberate attempt is made to force government to change its policies, thereby increasing uncertainty and delaying needed adjustments. (See page 374.)

7. The assumption of market clearing leads to the conclusion that, at equilibrium, the quantities exchanged in markets maximize economic welfare, given the degrees of monopoly or competition present in individual markets. Market clearing suggests that full employment is achieved at potential GNP. (See page 375.)

8. Neo-Keynesian economics extends the traditional Keynesian analysis of total-planned-expenditure to include, as well, the monetary dimension of the economy. In the *IS-LM* model, the *IS* component deals with total-planned-expenditure ($C + I + G + X - Im$) and the *LM* portion deals with the money market. (See page 376.)

9. The intersection of the *IS* and the *LM* curves identifies the real rate of interest and the level of real GNP that provide simultaneous equilibrium in both the real and the financial components of the economy. (See pages 376–380 and Figures 3, 4, and 5, pages 377, 379, and 380.)

10. Neo-Keynesian economists contend that the theory of rational expectations overstates the extent to which the consequences of government initiatives are counteracted by shifts of the aggregate-supply curve. They also reject the new classical assumptions of price flexibility and market clearing. Price inflexibility increases the severity of economic fluctuations. Because markets fail to clear, equilibrium does not employ all resources. (See pages 381–383.)

11. There are varying views among modern Keynesians about the seriousness of price inflexibilities and failures of markets to clear and on the extent to which government intervention is desirable. Generally, neo-Keynesians are more favorable to government intervention than new classical economists. (Sees page 382–383.)

12. Post-Keynesian economists believe that fundamental problems in market economies cause fluctuations and magnify recessions into severe depressions. They advocate substantial government

intervention in the economy. (See pages 383–384.)

13. Supply-side economics focuses on shifting the aggregate-supply curve to the right, offering greater real GNP at any given price level. Deregulation and lower marginal tax rates on both corporations and individuals are advocated in order to provide greater incentives for innovation, entrepreneurship, and work. Supply-side economists were prominent in the first Reagan administration and claim that their policies were effective even though not fully implemented. (See pages 384–385 and Figure 6, page 385.)

14. Critics contend that supply-side economics comes close to reasserting Say's Identity. The Laffer curve suggests that tax-rate reductions need not reduce government tax collections. (See pages 385–386 and Figure 7, page 386.)

KEY TERMS

incomes policies: comprehensive wage, price, and profit controls that implement economic planning (page 384).

IS-LM system: a model used in modern Keynesian economics; the *IS* curve incorporates the equilibrium requirements of the Keynesian total-planned-expenditure model, and the *LM* curve incorporates the requirements for equilibrium in the money market (page 376).

Laffer curve: a curve that shows how net tax revenues respond to changes in average tax rates (page 386).

Lucas supply curve: a curve that shows that unexpected changes in the price level lead to changes in the quantity of real GNP supplied (page 373).

market clearing: the proposition that at the equilibrium price, no potential sellers who are willing and able to sell at that price are unable to carry out their desired transaction, and no buyers who are willing and able to buy at that price are unable to carry out their desired transaction (page 375).

microfoundations: the microeconomic behavior of individuals and firms that lie behind macroeconomic models (page 374).

neo-Keynesian economics: a school of economic thought that preserves the basic Keynesian approach but includes monetary variables as well (page 376).

neo-Ricardian: an application of the rational-expectations theory that says that the method used to finance government expenditure does not matter (page 372).

new classical: a school of economic thought that employs the theory of rational expectations and accepts the propositions that prices adjust quickly and that markets clear at equilibrium (page 374).

post-Keynesian: economists who are in favor of permanent government direction of both the macro- and the microeconomy; they take positions close to Marxian socialism (page 383).

real business cycle theories: explanations of economic fluctuations based on patterns of changing labor productivity or labor supply (page 374).

Say's Identity: the view that supply creates its own demand (page 385).

school of economic thought: a group of economists who employ the same or similar theories and who agree with one another much of the time about economic policy (page 373).

supply-side economics: a school of economic thought that states that government actions affecting the aggregate-supply curve are at least as important as government actions affecting the aggregate-demand curve (page 384).

theory of rational expectations: a theory that proposes that people learn from their mistakes and use conventional economic principles to make their forecasts, following a rational reasoning process about how one thing leads to another in economics (page 370).

DISCUSSION QUESTIONS

1. List three forecasts that you might want to make. Examples: the weather for a picnic next Saturday, the score of your next home football game, the grade you will earn on the next exam. Make two forecasts for each subject, one on an adaptive-expectations basis and the other on a rational-expectations basis. What arguments appear in the rational-expectations forecast that do not appear in the adaptive-expectations forecast?

2. Construct an aggregate-demand and aggregate-supply graph, labeling the axes and the curves carefully. Assuming that your indicated equilibrium has prevailed for a long time, discuss and illustrate on the graph what would happen if an election put in office a political party that everyone expects will pursue expansionary macroeconomic policies.

3. Discuss whether a government deficit incurred today will lead to higher taxes on the next generation of taxpayers. Then consider whether that coming generation will actually pay high taxes or whether their government will sell new securities and use the money to pay off the bonds issued today. What does the neo-Ricardian application of rational-expectations theory suggest that taxpayers in each generation do?

4. Construct a Lucas supply curve, carefully labeling the axes. Suppose that prices increase and that you are an entrepreneur and, as such, correctly judge that it is an increase in the general price level. Assuming perfect price flexibility and no lags in resource prices, what change, if any, will you make in the volume of output of your firm? Are you better off or worse off than entrepreneurs who mistake the rise in the price level for a rise in the relative price of their products?

5. Discuss the similarities between the new classical school of economic thought of the 1980s and the neoclassical school of the 1920s. If a contractionary demand shock were to occur today, do you believe that the new classical prescriptions would be the same as those of the neoclassicals early in the Great Depression of the 1930s? Explain.

6. Without looking at Figure 3, construct a Keynesian-cross graph and a companion graph for the *IS* curve. Explain and illustrate what happens if government purchases are increased. Why is it important to consider possible effects of this action on the price level?

7. Without looking at Figure 4, construct a money-market graph and a companion graph for the *LM* curve. Explain and illustrate what happens if there occurs an autonomous shift to the right of the demand-for-money curve. What might cause such a shift of the *MD* curve?

8. List three contemporary schools of macroeconomic thought. Arrange these groups in order of the degree of intervention that they believe appropriate for government in modern market economies. How does this listing relate to the question of market clearing?

9. Consider leftward shifts of the aggregate-supply curve due to (a) external shocks, (b) catch-up from lags in wage rates and resource prices, (c) anticipated results of government policy actions to increase aggregate demand, and (d) realization that what was thought to be a change in relative prices was actually a change in the price level. For each of these, note the theories and/or schools of thought that recognize and deal with that shift.

18
Macroeconomics as a Branch of Knowledge

Preview This chapter concludes our explanation of basic macroeconomics. We try to show that macroeconomics is neither cut and dried nor in shambles but a developing science somewhere between these extremes. The chapter is built around several questions that, we believe, provide useful food for thought about macroeconomics.

We begin by asking if macroeconomics is practical. We suggest that a practical application of macroeconomics lies in the area of public policy and citizenship. Next we discuss what it means for a discipline to be "scientific" and note that disciplines differ in their degrees of maturity in this regard—macroeconomics being neither the least nor the most mature. Since science deals with what "is" rather than with what "ought to be," we proceed to an elementary explanation of how macroeconomists forecast the volume of economic activity for a coming time period.

If macroeconomics is practical and scientific, perhaps it can offer insights about matters that may be important in the 1990s, such as the national debt. Is the debt primarily a burden on the generation that contracted it, or does the debt constitute a burden that one generation of citizens is able to pass on to later generations of citizens? What about deficits? Should the Constitution be amended to prohibit deficits in the federal government budget?

Finally, we offer some thoughts and forecasts about macroeconomic problems that may face President George Bush. What sorts of macroeconomic crises may arise during his term or terms of office? Which would be most difficult to resolve? How would concerted efforts at deficit reduction affect these potential problems? In the world of political reality, how may the president and the Congress deal with the deficit?

IS MACROECONOMICS PRACTICAL?

Over and above idle curiosity, people have two sets of reasons for interest in their economy. One set arises from *direct* participation in the system—as suppliers and consumers of its outputs and as suppliers and demanders of inputs. The other set arises from *indirect* participation in the political economy, as voters in elections both national and local and perhaps as officeholders or civil servants.

The balance between these interests is usually different in macroeconomics than in microeconomics. As a direct participant, one's interest tends to be concentrated on immediately practical issues related to the particular goods and services one principally buys and sells—one's wage or salary, the prices of food and clothing, the sale or rental value of one's house or apartment. These are primarily microeconomic matters. But as an indirect participant in the economy—as a voter, civil servant, or legislator—the macroeconomic side enters more strongly, at least at the national level of policy formulation and administration. Perhaps, by reason of the primacy of our direct interests over our indirect ones, macroeconomics appears less "practical" than microeconomics. "Supply and demand," for example, means more to more people than "saving and investment" or even "unemployment and inflation."

As a direct participant in the economy, one's interest is usually concentrated on microeconomic issues related to the particular goods and services one buys and sells. As an indirect participant, macroeconomic issues assume more importance.

IS MACROECONOMICS SCIENTIFIC?

In this age of science, it is believed important to claim for any subject of study that it is, at least partially, scientific. By this we mean that it has an objective, factual, and systematic basis. Any admis-sion that one's specialty is less than scientific equates it with hocus-pocus and mumbo-jumbo.

What Does It Mean to Be Scientific?

Science is about what *is* rather than what *ought* to be.[1] Also, most sciences, or most branches of science, make major use of the method of controlled experiment, although astronomy can rarely do this, nor can mathematics.

Some sciences are **pure** or theoretical, and others **applied.** One characteristic of applied sciences like medicine—despite its groundwork of chemistry and biology—is that their practices extend well beyond their theoretical bases in pure science. Medical practitioners use devices they cannot yet justify scientifically, under the rubric of "It works, but we don't yet know why." Sometimes later advances justify such practices, and sometimes they repudiate them. Few features of medicine seem less scientific than the doctor's "bedside manner," which nevertheless seems to accelerate (or retard) recovery. Few medical practices, however, seem more ludicrous than the use of leeches—a standard procedure for centuries.

The several branches of science have developed in different places and at different rates of progress. It seems obvious, for example, that physics and astronomy are further advanced in their scientific aspects than are psychology and sociology. (This is not to deny the importance of scientific elements in either of the last two disciplines as currently studied and practiced.) One irritating sign of a science's immaturity is the unsatisfactory nature of any "unified field" theory interrelating its several branches. The division between micro- and macroeconomics is an example of this defect; perhaps your generation can remedy it. But even physics has a similar difficulty; the great Albert Einstein spent much of his later years in a (futile) attempt to unify nuclear physics with the "ordinary" physics of mechanics, electricity, sound, heat and light.

---

1. Life would be easier for many engineers, for example, if all numbers were perfect squares, or if *pi* were 3 instead of 3.14159, or if Planet Earth completed its annual circuit round the sun in precisely 365 days.

But a science need not develop fully to become scientific. An embryonic science following false leads is as scientific as an adult one with all its problems solved and no loose ends for the next generation of scientists. The Ptolemaic cosmology, placing the earth at the center of the universe, was a scientific system—and an impressive one. For centuries, it was useful as a basis for forecasting such phenomena as the phases of the moon, eclipses of the sun, and the positions of stars and planets in the sky as seen from different points on the surface of the earth. The Newtonian (or Copernican) cosmology that displaced it is a *better* scientific system that does a better job of forecasting a wider range of phenomena with a somewhat simpler kit of tools. Quite generally, a theory, *T*, retains its scientific status even after displacement by superior theory *T'*. The fact of displacement does not deprive either a theory (such as Keynesian) or its field (macroeconomics) of scientific status. A more developed science may perhaps expect fewer displacements than a less developed one, but we should not forget the modifications of classical Newtonian physics in the twentieth century.

A scientific theory retains its scientific status even after displacement by a superior theory.

Nonscientific Aspects of Macroeconomics

If, to become a full-fledged science, a discipline must shed all its nonscientific aspects, the scientific status of macroeconomics is less than fully established. Let us see why this may be so by considering the macroeconomic effects of unanticipated demand and supply shocks—a major earthquake (Japan, 1923), a major drought (United States, 1988), the emergence of OPEC (1973), "black Thursday" and "black Monday" on Wall Street (1929 and 1987).

Analysis of the macroeconomic effects of such shocks cannot be confined within the limits of impersonal and automatic economic systems moving along growth paths. That is, analysis cannot be confined to scientific models. It must add estimates of the nature, size, and efficiency of highly personal and individual policy responses of agencies and people all over the world—presidents, kings, dictators, Lords and Commons and Congresses, finance ministers and central bankers and "gray eminences." Who are the authorities, worldwide? Are they wise, mad, or something in between? How much authority can they or will they exercise? Will they act in unison or at cross-purposes? Answering such questions involves us in "economic psychiatry," which (if a science at all) is less developed than macroeconomics. Such are the limitations of macroeconomics as a pure science.

Analysis of the macroeconomic effects of unanticipated supply and demand shocks cannot be confined to scientific models; it must also take into account the highly personal policy responses of agencies and people all over the world.

WHAT ABOUT FORECASTING?

We can look at **quantitative economic forecasting**—predicting the values of economic variables through systematic analysis of empirically estimated relationships—as a rough-and-ready test of the scientific validity of macroeconomics. Astronomy is an advanced and reputable science because astronomers' forecasts of tides, solar eclipses, and the appearance of certain key comets are so accurate. Meteorology has advanced by leaps and bounds in the computer age, because weather forecasts can take more variables into account, becoming more accurate for longer time periods and for smaller areas. Macroeconomic forecasts, however, have lagged in public esteem and may continue to do so indefinitely. Nonetheless, the same private citizens, public agencies, and business firms who make fun of economic forecasts also feel called upon to make them, or even to purchase forecasts made by specialized forecasting companies.

A note of caution is in order when dealing with forecasting. Economic forecasts are useful only insofar as they are known and acted upon, yet reactions to forecasts may either confirm or falsify the forecasts themselves. In the nineteenth century, for example, 1837, 1847, and 1857 were all years of recession or depression, whose ten-year periodicity gave rise to "sunspot" theories of economic fluctuations. Another depression was accordingly forecast for 1867. People appear to have responded to this forecast by cutting investment and perhaps also purchases of durable consumption goods in 1866. The result was that the recession came a year early, in 1866.[2] (One wonders how good our weather forecasts would be if some Weather Demon could adjust the jet stream in response to Weather Bureau forecasts.)

Reactions to economic forecasts may either confirm or falsify the forecasts.

A Primer on Forecasting

Nobody learns **macroeconomic forecasting** in an elementary economics class, but students can get some idea of how macroeconomics is used by some forecasters. Because forecasting is quantitative, mathematics cannot be avoided entirely, but in practice most of the math is done by computer programs. We can pose as forecasters, kindergarten-level ones perhaps, by using a simplified Keynesian model.[3] In this model neither the government nor the international sectors are separated from the private domestic economy, all functions are linear, there are no time lags, and neither taxes nor interest rates affect decisions about either saving or investment. Also, we assume no change in the price level so that the symbol for national income, Y, is the same as real GNP. Our clients are (like most such clients) interested primarily in *changes* from this year's or last year's values of the principal variables rather than in the absolute values of aggregates like GNP.

Our simplified illustrative model is:

$$Y = C + I$$

$$C = C_o + MPC(Y)$$

$$I = I_o$$

C_o is autonomous planned consumption expenditure, MPC is the marginal propensity to consume based on national income, and I_o is autonomous planned investment expenditure. But since we are interested primarily in changes over time, for forecasting purposes we transform (differentiate) these equations with respect to time. If ΔY represents the change in Y over one time period, and similarly for ΔC and ΔI, the model becomes:

$$\Delta Y = \Delta C + \Delta I$$

$$\Delta C = \Delta C_o + MPC(\Delta Y)$$

$$\Delta I = \Delta I_o$$

Just as the original model can be solved for Y, the transformed one can be solved for ΔY.[4]

$$Y = \frac{C_o + I_o}{1 - MPC} \qquad \Delta Y = \frac{\Delta C_o + \Delta I_o}{1 - MPC}$$

Suppose that we believe, perhaps from surveying the intentions of a sample of potential consumers and investors, that our best estimates of ΔC_o and ΔI_o, respectively, are $+10$ and -5, and that the marginal propensity to consume will remain constant at, say, 0.75. Then, using the preceding equations, we can forecast

$$\Delta Y = \frac{10 - 5}{1 - 0.75} = 20$$

In other words, we can forecast that the national income, Y, will be 20 units higher this period than it was in the preceding one.

If our model is larger (contains more equations and more variables), the process becomes more difficult. Also, we or our clients may desire forecasts of ΔC and ΔI—not to mention many other

---

2. This is, of course, an oversimplification of the 1866 downturn. To mention just one other factor, the American Civil War had ended in 1865, and demobilization was under way in the following year.

3. Most commercial forecasters do in fact use Keynesian models in their work. People distrustful of Keynesian macroeconomics sometimes feel an added reason to seek out a non-Keynesian (usually monetarist) forecasting company or to do it themselves.

4. The solution for Y would have been more complex if the consumption function had been nonlinear, or if we had included a possible change in the marginal propensity to consume.

---

changes, along with ΔY. In such an event, the usual trick is to rewrite the "transformed" model in the following way:

$$\Delta Y - \Delta C - \Delta I = 0$$

$$-MPC(\Delta Y) + \Delta C + O = \Delta C_o$$

$$O + O + \Delta I = \Delta I_o$$

Such groups of equations can be solved readily by computer programs. In the numerical case we have just used, the solutions are:

$$\Delta Y = 20 \text{ (as before)}$$

$$\Delta C = 25$$

$$\Delta I = -5$$

These results are consistent with each other; the total change, ΔY, is the sum of its parts, ΔC and ΔI.

Problems in Forecasting

There remain many problems in forecasting, some purely technical and others with broader implications. One's entire model may be wrong or incomplete, with irrelevant variables included and relevant ones omitted. A supply-sider would reject our demand-side Keynesian model at once. Time lags between causes and their effects must often be explored if one is to understand what is going on. But in our model, all figures relate to the same time interval. Functional relations in the real world may be nonlinear, and such important coefficients as the marginal propensity to consume may change without much warning. Supply shocks—we have mentioned the Tokyo earthquake, the rise of OPEC, and the American drought—can invalidate forecasts. So, of course, can changes in public policy. Examples of policy changes include tax reforms, monetary reforms, the socialization or privatization of economic sectors, and changes in tariffs, quotas, and similar regulations of international trade and investment. Moreover, a peacetime model may not work in wartime, and a wartime model may not work if peace breaks out.

Economists of the Austrian school, most notably the late Ludwig von Mises and his disciples, oppose forecasting on philosophical grounds. When we deal with the decisions of free people,

presumably possessed of free wills, the results of their decisions cannot, they claim, be forecast either individually or in the aggregate. If a forecast is reasonably correct, this particular forecaster has merely been lucky—nothing more.

Forecasts can be incorrect because of inaccurate or incomplete models, time lags, supply shocks, and policy changes. Some economists oppose forecasting in general, believing that the results of decisions of free people cannot be forecast with any accuracy at all.

It is often argued that macroeconomic forecasting has passed the market test. Forecasting firms, some affiliated with major universities, have profited by selling their services to clients who have, presumably, profited by using them. Other concerns, mainly financial institutions, have set up their own in-house forecasting ventures, some of which pay for themselves. But the costs of subscribing to forecasting services, or of operating one's own service in-house, are tax-deductible as business expenses and therefore subsidized indirectly by the government. Without this implicit subsidy, the forecasting industry's scale of operations might be smaller. There is, accordingly, some doubt as to whether the whole forecasting enterprise is worthwhile. The same is true, however, of the operations of other for-profit professional services to business—some of the services of attorneys, accountants, consultants, etc.

WHAT ABOUT THE NATIONAL DEBT?

Macroeconomics is mainly about *flows* of economic activity over periods of definite length—this year's GNP, for example, or the level of measured unemployment during that year. Macroeconomists are therefore accused at times of insufficient concern with **stock phenomena,** which are the sums, or cumulatives, of the flows. In particular, Keynesian macroeconomics, in concentrating on annual excesses of government purchases over net taxes (budget deficits)—which are flows—is accused of being entirely too cavalier about **public debt,** which is the accumulation over time of public deficits.

Recall our discussion of deficits and the national debt in the appendix to Chapter 11. At that point in your study of macroeconomics you had only been introduced to Keynesian economics. Now you have a wider perspective from which to view some debt issues. A balanced treatment of macroeconomics should include two issues concerning the public debt. Is it in any sense a burden on the economy, comparable to the burden of an individual's private debt upon his or her private economy? If so, is it a burden primarily on the generation that contracted it or primarily upon future generations of taxpayers, who must pay the interest and other service charges on the debt, including partial or total repayment? Great Britain, we are told, has never paid for the Napoleonic Wars, while Germany and Japan were permitted to inflate away their debts from World War II. Does this help explain why West Germany and Japan have on balance outperformed the United Kingdom economically during the latter third of the twentieth century?

The "We Owe It to Ourselves" View

We can surely agree that a private individual or firm cannot spend his, her, or its way into prosperity by **deficit financing** (going into debt). Were you a plumber with expensive tastes, no significant portion of your expenditures for living beyond your means could be expected to recycle back to you as increased demand for your services as a plumber. The same is almost equally true for a small public body like Gopher Prairie (the locale of Sinclair Lewis's *Main Street*) or even for such real-world sovereign states as Vanuatu and Kiribati in the South Pacific.

The case is, however, quite different for a large country like the United States. Here a popular view has been that "we owe it to ourselves," where "it" is the **national debt** with only a small (but increasing!) portion owed to foreign bondholders. When the national debt is increased, as by continued **deficit spending,** there may be an immediate loss to the private sector of the American economy by the surrender to public use of resources that would otherwise be used privately, although even this loss does not occur in the case of resources otherwise unemployed. But the private sector's loss is the public sector's gain. Advocates of this position make additional points:

1. With deficit financing there is no net loss to the bond purchasers because their giving up of resources for public use is in exchange for an increase in their wealth position, in the form of interest received from public securities.

2. With gains and losses to bondholders balanced out, there remains a net gain to the beneficiaries of the public expenditure. These may be public pensioners, relief clients, defense industries, users of an enlarged highway system—the list is endless.

3. As far as future generations are concerned: debt service is a redistributive matter. The new generation of taxpayers loses; the next generation of bondholders gains.[5]

According to the "we owe it to ourselves" view, public debt is not a burden to the economy, and future generations will not be burdened by it.

"We owe it to ourselves" and the arguments listed above were never convincing to all observers even before foreign capitalists and central bankers began large-scale investments in American public debt securities. Two groups of economists have carried the argument about public debt further. These are often called "neo-Ricardian" (see Chapter 17) and "public-choice" writers. We shall examine their views in that order.

The Neo-Ricardian View

Neo-Ricardians contend that the public debt *is*, in fact, a burden on future generations. First they argue that public debt instruments (government

5. A digression into formal logic. Among the fallacies catalogued by Aristotle and his followers, centuries before the birth of Christ, is the *fallacy of composition,* which is the application to the whole of an argument valid only for a part (or vice versa). Economics abounds in examples, of which this is one. (What is true of an individual's debt may not be true of a society's debt, and vice versa.)

bonds) do *not* add to a society's net wealth. Bond-holders may indeed gain net wealth as compensation for surrendering to the government command over real resources here and now, but their gains are canceled by losses to the rest of society. These gains and losses arise because rational taxpayers, including the bondholders themselves, realize that debt service requires future taxation, either in the overt form of more and higher taxes or in the covert forms of inflation or reduced future public services. Such future liabilities, say the neo-Ricardians, are largely taken into account in the planning of the present generation, and result in slower economic growth. As a result, future generations incur a burden primarily in the form of lower incomes.

The second neo-Ricardian argument is harsher and focuses more directly on the burden on future generations. From the strictly economic point of view, they say, governments do not invest as wisely as the private sector. Public debts represent potential assets dissipated in warfare, much of it misguided and useless. Or they represent potential assets dissipated in raising or maintaining the living standards of people who should have been forced to work in the private sector or left to the mercies of private voluntary charity—which supposedly distinguishes more carefully the "deserving" from the "undeserving" poor. Dissipation of resources on warfare, relief, and public-sector "make work" lowers an economy's real growth rate and therefore the level of living of future generations.[6] This argument writes off as quantitatively unimportant the public-sector contribution to the public works and public services necessary to the social infra-structure of economic growth—except for those which taxpayers are willing to support on a "pay as you go" basis.

Neo-Ricardians contend that public debt *is* a burden on future generations, primarily in the form of lower income after taxes. They also argue that governments do not invest as wisely as the private sector.

---

6. Misguided policies of *panem et circenses*—free bread and free entertainments—for the urban poor allegedly wrecked the great Roman Empire.

The Public-Choice View

Public-choice economists view suppliers and consumers of the public services as collections of special-interest groups and electorates as systematically biased in favor of the present as against the future. So these economists favor constitutional limitations on budget deficits (debt increases) or constitutional requirements of peacetime budgetary balance.

Most voters, and economists, see the public service bureaucracy as, among other functions, an impartial umpire between conflicting special interests—workers versus employers, the city versus the country, etc. Public-choice economists, however, see bureaucrats themselves as a formidable interest group. In their view, each branch of the bureaucracy is trying to maximize its own budgetary appropriation in much the same way that consumers maximize utility or satisfaction, or business firms maximize profits or the market value of their enterprises. When the several bureaucracies—the military services, the diplomatic service, the judicial services, the police and fire departments, the public-agency social workers, the public-school and public-university teachers, and so on—are added together, say public-choice economists, the full-time producer pressures for public spending threaten to overbalance the part-time consumer pressures from taxpayers and bondholders. This is especially true when parallel pressures from private industry, from the military-industrial complex to the highway lobbies, are factored in.

At the level of local government, balance is often provided by constitutional limitations, by concern for a city's credit rating, and especially by prohibitions against the issue of local-government legal-tender money. At the national level in the United States, the basic restraints have been the gold standard and the annual budgetary balance. Public-choice economists claim that these have been weakened by macroeconomic heresies, based primarily on doctrines propounded by—or blamed on—John Maynard Keynes. Public choices, it is alleged, are further biased against future generations by the voters' own time preference for the present.

Economists of all persuasions see public appropriations as providing two streams extending into the future—one a stream of benefits from public services, the other a stream of costs in the form of taxes that pay for these services. Even if the present value of the benefits exceeds the present value of the costs, public-choice theory has it that the stream of benefits tends in practice to be front-loaded and the stream of costs back-loaded so that they concentrate net benefit on the present generation and net cost on the future. To put this matter less abstractly, today's weapons systems and today's highways will generally wear out, become obsolete, or otherwise require replacement before they have been paid for. Our children and grandchildren will be left to deal with the unpaid balances of the bills we contract for ourselves. Nobody believes this must be true, and everyone agrees that under ideal conditions it would not be true. But public-choice economists insist that in this imperfect world it generally *is* true.

The public-choice school has become a major intellectual force behind proposals for one or another balanced-budget amendment to the United States Constitution, although many supporters of such amendments do not associate themselves with this school.[7] In three less extreme forms, public-choice economists have backed (1) the Gramm-Rudman-Hollings plan for phased deficit reduction,[8] (2) the item veto for the president on appropriation bills, and (3) presidential authority, on behalf of taxpayers, to impound appropriated funds rather than being required to spend them.

Public-choice economists favor constitutional limits on budget deficits or constitutional requirements for a balanced budget.

From One Generation to the Next

Your generation is to past generations as future generations are to yours. So public debts surviving

7. Public-choice economists believe that it can be made feasible to outlaw, or at least regulate, such fancy fiscal footwork as evasion of budgetary balance by falsified forecasts, juggling of cash and accrual accounting bases, contingent public liabilities, off-budget expenditures, and similar devices often considered in advanced courses in public finance.

8. Before embarking on a political career, Senator Phil Gramm (R-Tex.) was a prominent public-choice economist as a professor at Texas A&M University.

from the past may in some sense be a burden upon you. But in what sense, precisely?

If the neo-Ricardians and public-choice economists are right, there has been slower economic growth since 1815 (or 1944), and your present living standard is lower than it would have been if the Battle of Waterloo (or the Normandy invasion) had been financed by Great Britain (or the United States) on a more nearly pay-as-you-go basis. You might be paying lower taxes; the price level might be lower; the real interest rate might be lower as well. But since your generation is, even with these burdens, more affluent than that of 1815 (or 1944), it may be thought only fair that you should share with your comparatively poor ancestors the cost of repelling Napoleon Bonaparte (or Adolf Hitler).

WHERE DO WE GO FROM HERE?

As these pages are written (1989), the administration of President George Bush has taken over from that headed for eight years by President Ronald Reagan. Americans, and not only Americans, are asking such deficit-and-debt policy questions as: To what extent was the Reagan Administration responsible for the federal deficits and the national debt? How serious are the country's current deficit and debt positions? How important is it to reduce the deficit and slow down the growth of the debt? What are the probable costs of deficit reduction? Do these benefits and costs depend significantly on the speed of deficit reduction or on the particular devices (revenue enhancement, cost containment) used to bring that reduction about?

Macroeconomics, in its present stage of development, is in a poor position to answer such questions with confidence or to forecast what the administration and Congress will finally decide to do. There is no accepted formula or rule of thumb to govern such decisions. What formula or rule of thumb should be used to tell us what proportion of public expenditure (or what proportion of a *change* in public expenditure) should be financed by taxes (or by a corresponding change in taxes)? Surely the answer, if there is one, depends on many other variables, such as the inflation, unemployment, and growth rates, and on the most desirable relation among them. Accurately predicting these matters is difficult. Most mainstream macroeconomists over thirty years of age will probably admit in their more honest and less pretentious moments that they would have predicted, from the fiscal and debt policies of the Reagan years, substantially higher rates of both interest and price inflation than actually occurred in the 1980s.

The Reagan Experience

Some consider continuous deficits and rising debt to have been Reagan innovations. But we should not forget that when President Reagan took office in 1981, the federal budget had been in deficit for twelve successive years, and the national debt was estimated at the astronomical sum of $1 trillion. On taking office, President Reagan hoped to attain budgetary balance and debt stability by 1984, despite his proposals for tax cuts and increased military expenditures. In fact, deficits increased sharply, and the debt approximately tripled (to $3 trillion) during his two presidential terms. Even so, the debt remained not much more than half of the annual GNP—the equivalent of about seven months' income. By international standards, this is not dangerously large. The debt and deficit records since 1975 are illustrated in Figures 1 and 2.

The federal debt as a percent of GNP (Figure 1) fluctuated during the 1975 to 1982 period and increased significantly during the 1983 to 1990 (estimated) period. Federal deficits as percentages of federal outlays (Figure 2) provide an indication of the federal government's success or failure in bal-

FIGURE 1
Gross U.S. Federal Debt as Percent of GNP

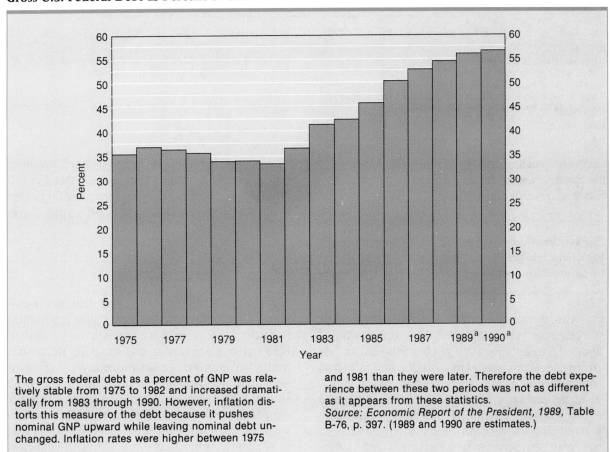

The gross federal debt as a percent of GNP was relatively stable from 1975 to 1982 and increased dramatically from 1983 through 1990. However, inflation distorts this measure of the debt because it pushes nominal GNP upward while leaving nominal debt unchanged. Inflation rates were higher between 1975 and 1981 than they were later. Therefore the debt experience between these two periods was not as different as it appears from these statistics.
Source: Economic Report of the President, 1989, Table B-76, p. 397. (1989 and 1990 are estimates.)

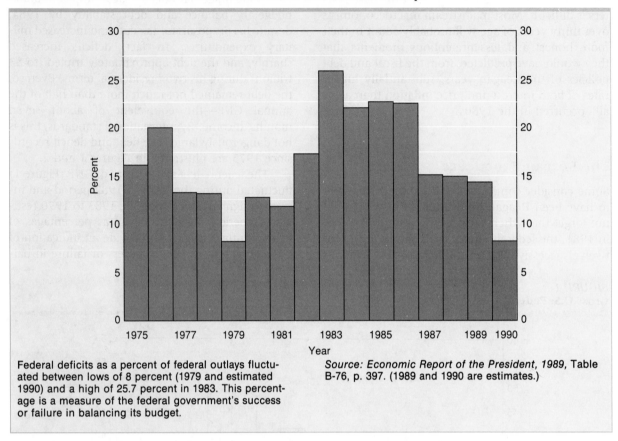

FIGURE 2
Federal Government Deficits as Percent of Federal Government Outlays

Federal deficits as a percent of federal outlays fluctuated between lows of 8 percent (1979 and estimated 1990) and a high of 25.7 percent in 1983. This percentage is a measure of the federal government's success or failure in balancing its budget.

Source: Economic Report of the President, 1989, Table B-76, p. 397. (1989 and 1990 are estimates.)

ancing its budget. During the time period shown in the figure, the highest deficit-to-outlay percentage was 25.7 recorded in 1983.

The national debt tripled (to $3 trillion) under President Reagan, but it is not dangerously large by international standards.

Also, the Reagan deficits and debt increases did not bring the "credit crunch," the "runaway inflation," the international "flight from the dollar," or any of the other varieties of crisis that his critics had anticipated with both apprehension and glee. Instead, general prosperity—at least in the upper and middle classes—continued for a surprisingly long period. One short, sharp downturn in 1981–82 was overcome by monetary expansion and moderating disinflationary pressure. Seven years after

Reagan was first elected president, a serious financial downturn—"Black Monday," October 19, 1987—was absorbed without spreading far beyond Wall Street. In the absence of crisis, why change policy?

Living with Deficits

A rapid move against deficits and debt increases—either a major tax increase or a major expenditure reduction (either military or civilian)—might set off a significant recession on essentially Keynesian-multiplier grounds. Could monetary policy be relied upon to overcome such a recession, while stopping short of accelerated inflation? It seems dangerous and unnecessary to risk the results of such contractionary fiscal policy. The path of least resistance is rather to do little about the deficit or the debt, while taking the politician's customary refuge in rhetoric and oratory. We have learned, it seems, to live with a deficit and a rising-debt economy—perhaps even to manage such an economy. Why not continue? Why take chances of upsetting apple carts? Such, as we see it, is the path of least resistance.

Such is also our tentative guess at the compromise the Republican administration of President Bush and the Democratic Congress may be forced into by the exigencies of the political process and the disinterest of the electorate in economic technicalities. It is a policy of living with, and perhaps even managing, the deficit and the debt, and blaming the other party for failure to do more. Until a crisis develops, macroeconomic thinking will be on hold. Moreover, the American body politic may well consent to continuing deficits and rising debt—not, we repeat, for their own sakes but as paths of least risk and least resistance.

A major policy initiative against deficits and debt increases, such as a tax increase or expenditure reduction, might set off a significant recession. Unless a crisis develops, the best policy may be simply to live with the deficit and rising debt.

Possible Crises

If an economic crisis develops, such as a credit crunch, an accelerating inflation, or a capital flight from dollar assets, the policy response may include cuts in the deficit by tax increases and cuts in public spending. In other countries, it may also include partial or complete debt repudiation or renegotiation, which would free public expenditures for immediately useful purposes and away from debt servicing. We shall encounter this alternative in connection with the problems of developing-country debt, but it is extremely unlikely for the United States.

If the crisis is an underconsumption, underinvestment, or debt-deflation one like the Great Depression of the 1930s, both deficits and the national debt may deliberately be increased again, paralleling the Roosevelt New Deal experience.

Most difficult would be a stagflationary crisis—prices, interest rates, and unemployment all rising, while real consumption, investment, and GNP are stagnant or falling. In such an **inflationary depression,** deficit and debt policy would indeed require rethinking, if we do not yield instead to the Man on Horseback (or in a plane or tank, or at the head of a mindless mob) to impose order by dictatorial methods.

Economics in Focus

Budget Arithmetic

Most detailed discussions of the national debt and budget deficits rely on numerical estimates and projections—numbers that by their very specificity take on the guise of hard-edged facts. But in reality the numbers are often in dispute. Expert fiscal analysts disagree with Congress, which in turn disagrees with the president. For instance, Ronald Reagan's last budget proposal, presented to Congress just as he was leaving office, projected a 1990 deficit of $27 billion above the target set by the Gramm-Rudman-Hollings Act. Congress, however, estimated that the 1990 deficit would run $41 billion above the target. That is quite a difference, and it obviously had great implications for policy decisions.

Budget projections often suffer from two questionable assumptions. One is that the economy will continue to grow at a reasonable rate. Even if the rate chosen is close to the historical average, the assumption leaves no room for a downturn or recession. Historically, of course, recessions do occur. Second, projections often assume that spending for many or most established government programs can be held in check, with little or no growth in real terms. Because of the vast number of programs the U.S. government maintains—as well as the constant pressures for better health care, improved education, drug-abuse prevention, and so on—this assumption frequently proves unrealistic.

A further problem is that politicians and policymakers do not like to be the bearers of bad news. No one wants to cut a popular program or demand an unpopular tax increase, especially if this would involve fudging on a campaign promise. As President Bush tried to reduce the deficit and simultaneously live up to his 1988 promise of no new taxes, *The Economist* put his predicament succinctly: "The political loser in the budget game is the first player to be caught using the word tax."

Squeezed between political pressures on the one hand and the demands of the Gramm-Rudman-Hollings Act on the other, the budget-makers have resorted to complicated fixes. Some expenses are shifted from one fiscal year to another to meet deficit-reduction goals. In other cases, spending can be declared "off-budget" despite the fact that the money will actually be spent. For example, in the 1989 bailout for savings and loan institutions, some of the funds were not counted in the national budget because they would technically be spent by a new quasi-governmental agency rather than by the government itself.

Critics charge that such inventive maneuvers, especially when combined with rosy projections, obscure the problem and make deficits more difficult to overcome. Others counter that the Gramm-Rudman-Hollings Act invited this kind of budget manipulation. Economists, whether they agree or disagree with current policies, must constantly be aware of the quirky nature of budget arithmetic.

Sources: "Curtain Up on the Budget Ballet," *The Economist*, January 14, 1989, pp. 25–28 (quotation at p. 27); Rudolph G. Penner, "What Worries Me Now About Federal Deficits," *Across the Board*, July/August 1989, pp. 50–54; Joseph J. Minarik, "Fiscal Reality and Exploding Myths," *Challenge*, July–August 1988, pp. 4–13.

SUMMARY

1. The practicality of microeconomics arises mainly from its usefulness in guiding direct participation in supplying and demanding inputs and outputs. The practicality of macroeconomics arises from its usefulness in guiding indirect participation in the economy, as voter, legislator, or civil servant. (See page 392.)

2. Science deals with what is. Among the several branches of science, some are more mature than others, but a branch of science can be scientific even if not fully developed. As a less than fully established science, macroeconomics can expect its theories to be displaced as better theories are devised. (See pages 392–393.)

3. One of the problems of macroeconomic forecasting is that outcomes often depend in part on highly individualized responses by agencies and people all over the world. These responses cannot be confined to scientific models. In addition, the forecasts themselves may bring responses that may, in turn, confirm or invalidate the forecasts. (See pages 393–394.)

4. Elementary forecasting can be illustrated using the Keynesian model, in which a change in income (ΔY) equals the sum of a change in planned consumption spending (ΔC) and a change in planned investment spending (ΔI), with $\Delta C = \Delta C_o + MPC(\Delta Y)$. (See pages 394–395.)

5. Although there are many ways in which forecasts can go wrong, it appears that forecasting has passed the market test, testifying to some usefulness in practical affairs. The Austrian school of economic thought, however, argues that the actions of people with free will cannot be forecast reliably. (See page 395.)

6. Among economists, views differ on whether the public debt is a burden on the economy and, if so, whether this burden falls upon the present or a future generation. The "we owe it to ourselves" view concludes that public debt is not a burden on the economy and that future generations are not involved. (See pages 395–396.)

7. The neo-Ricardian view is that taxpayers recognize that public debt requires future taxation and that these future taxes are taken into account by the present generation. As a result, debt falls as a burden on future generations, primarily in the form of lower incomes after taxes. Neo-Ricardians also argue that government uses resources unwisely, thus reducing the economic inheritance of future generations. (See pages 396–397.)

8. The public-choice view is that public debt reflects the present-generation bias of voters, bureaucrats, and legislators who, as interest groups, place their own interests above those of future generations. This view supports constitutional amendments limiting budget deficits. It also supports the item veto and presidential impoundment of appropriated funds. (See pages 397–398.)

9. The national debt was about $1 trillion when President Reagan took office and grew to about $3 trillion over his two terms. At somewhat over one-half of GNP, the U.S. public debt is not dangerously large by international standards. Nor did the Reagan policies result in any of the serious crises that many economists feared would arise. (See page 399.)

10. The U.S. economy appears to have learned how to live with public deficits. Deficit finance, consequently, is likely to be the practice under President Bush, barring serious economic crisis. Among several crises that could arise, a stagflation crisis would call for the most serious reconsideration of national debt policy. (See pages 400–401.)

KEY TERMS

applied science: an objective, factual, and systematic search for knowledge that includes practical utilizations along with theoretical inquiries (page 392).

deficit financing: funding those expenditures that are in excess of current receipts through borrowing, that is, through incurring debt (page 396).

deficit spending: expenditures that are in excess of current receipts (page 396).

inflationary depression: a situation in which an economy experiences a decrease in real GNP and also an increase in its general price level (page 401). See also **stagflation**.

macroeconomic forecasting: predicting the values of economic variables through systematic analysis of empirically estimated relationships (page 394).

national debt: the total value of outstanding securities issued by a nation's government (page 396).

public-choice economists: economists who specialize in the study of the decision making procedures and outcomes of governments (page 397).

public debt: see **national debt**.

pure science: an objective, factual, and systematic search for knowledge utilizing assumptions, principles and rules, but not engaging in practical applications (page 392).

quantitative economic forecasting: the practice of using observed and/or estimated values for the variables in a macroeconomic model in order to predict future values for those variables (page 393).

stock phenomena: the sums or quantities of economic variables as they exist at a specified time, as distinguished from flows of such quantities over a specified period of time (page 395).

DISCUSSION QUESTIONS

1. Many colleges and universities recommend microeconomics in one semester and macroeconomics in another—some in one sequence and some in the other. To what extent is the sequencing choice based on a view that one or the other course is more practical? What other considerations may influence the sequencing choice?

2. Discuss the maturity of macroeconomics as a science, organizing your discussion around the concepts of (a) displacements of one theory by another and (b) a "unified field" for economics. What, if any, displacements have taken place? Is there any progress toward a unified field?

3. As a review of your understanding of forecasting using the Keynesian system, make up a set of values (different from those in the chapter) for the marginal propensity to consume (*MPC*), the

change in autonomous consumption spending (ΔC_O), and the change in investment (ΔI). Calculate the change in income (ΔY). Now retain the ΔY value, remove one of the independent variables, and ask a classmate to solve the equation for the missing variable. The process may continue to other classmates. You may want to continue the exercise by changing one of the independent variables—such as the marginal propensity to consume—and observing the effect on the calculated value of ΔY.

4. Business publications and bank newsletters frequently publish macroeconomic forecasts. Your reference librarian can help you locate one of these. Examine it for forecasts and then discuss how actual GNP might be affected by (a) war in the Middle East that cuts off supplies of crude petroleum, (b) a threat of war and shortages that do not actually happen, and (c) some other event of your own choosing. Is there any sense to the statement "My forecast was good, but reality was wrong?"

5. Suppose the U.S. Treasury offers to sell you a security that would pay you $100 a year but that carries no maturity date, that is, the Treasury promises to pay $100 interest per year forever but makes no promise ever to repay the initial sum borrowed. Would you buy the security? What is the amount of the national debt based on this security? Will this debt burden future generations?

6. Discuss how the U.S. economy "lives with" a deficit in the budget of the federal government. When new issues of Treasury securities are sold, does it matter who buys them? What effect does the sale have on interest rates, *ceteris paribus?* Do Federal Reserve open market operations make any difference? Does the growth rate of the U.S. economy matter?

7. Review the three types of crises noted in the chapter as possibilities during the administration of President Bush. Have any of them actually arisen? Have the consequences been as anticipated in this chapter?

The New Frontier
and After

BACKGROUND

The two Eisenhower administrations (1953–1961) in the United States are known as years of the "American celebration" and of general prosperity—interrupted only briefly by three mild recessions. At the close of the 1950s, however, critics noted that in these recessions the measured unemployment rate rose to increasingly higher points and that in the revivals it fell by increasingly smaller amounts.[1] This small sample of statistical measurements gave rise to worry about economic stagnation and demands to get the economy moving again. These concerns played a considerable part in the presidential election of 1960, in which John F. Kennedy narrowly defeated the sitting vice president, Richard Nixon.

Because of his youth and personal charm, his rhetorical gifts both oral and written, his openness to new ideas, his war record, and his great wealth, President Kennedy (1917–1963) was already a uniquely attractive figure to activist reformers of his generation. The Washington, D.C., of his term and the first years of the Lyndon Johnson administration that followed his death[2] was called the "New Frontier."

Kennedy's main intellectual interests were politics and history, but he had developed a collateral interest in economics as a student at Harvard. Among the activist reformers of his age group—"the best and the brightest" of their generation—were a number of Keynesian economists, interested in putting Lord Keynes's idea into posthumous practice. (Keynes had died in 1946.)

POLICIES OF THE NEW FRONTIER

As things worked out, Keynesian stabilization policy reached its zenith in the United States during a brief five-year period of the Kennedy-Johnson administration (1961–1966). The major economic aspects of their "practical Keynesianism on the New Frontier" can be summarized in a half-dozen propositions.

1. The importance of the maintenance and growth of aggregate demand was emphasized, while aggregate supply was relatively neglected. Some critics have devised a short statement they call *Keynes's Law:* "Aggregate demand creates its own supply in the presence of significant unemployment." This statement, which stands Say's Identity on its head, would surely have been disowned by Keynes himself. Also, the growth path of high-employment GNP was taken as technically given, or at least as independent of changes in macroeconomic policy.

2. Fiscal policy—the management of public receipts, expenditures, surpluses, and deficits—was to bear primary responsibility for maintaining income and employment, with monetary policy relegated to inflation and interest-rate control. However, New Frontier economics did not include any legal obligation for the government to act as employer of last resort in providing jobs for all.[3]

---

1. Many economists now discount these figures as "statistical artifacts." That is, they resulted chiefly from the entry of more married women into the labor force and from the movement of black workers from subsistence-level self-employment in rural southern agriculture to better-paid industrial jobs in urban areas.

2. Johnson was Kennedy's vice president. Many of the Kennedy policies passed into law only under Johnson's leadership. It is doubtful how many could have been enacted at all without Johnson's political skills—he had been majority leader in the Senate—and without the wave of sympathy for Kennedy's ideas after his assassination.

3. This extreme extension of Keynesian employment theory was proposed later in the Humphrey-Hawkins Bill of the 1970s. It was not, however, included in the Humphrey-Hawkins Act as passed in 1978.

To the disappointment of many veterans of the New Deal of the Franklin Roosevelt administrations in the 1930s, the expansive fiscal policy of the New Frontier meant cuts in tax rates rather than expansions of public expenditure. In the atmosphere of the early 1960s, however, these cuts raised federal receipts rather than lowering them. Also, President Kennedy read Michael Harrington's *The Other America,* an intellectual inspiration for the War on Poverty. Before Kennedy's assassination, Walter Heller, chairman of the Council of Economic Advisers, was preparing the groundwork for a bold new expenditure program without waiting for either a recession or a balanced budget.

3. Okun's Law was another basic proposition of New Frontier Keynesian economics, with which Keynes had no connection. This law is a statistical generalization from actual U.S. experience—when a growth rate of 3.75 percent a year had seemed to keep the unemployment rate stable while the labor force grew. Okun's Law stated that the measured unemployment rate would fall by one percentage point for every three percentage points by which the GNP growth rate exceeded 3.75 and rise by one percentage point for every three percentage points of shortfall in this growth target.

4. The Phillips curve was another extension of Keynesian doctrine the New Frontiersmen accepted. The Phillips curve maintains that to lower the unemployment rate, one must also accept some acceleration of wage inflation, which might in turn lead to acceleration of price inflation. Price stability in the United States was estimated by Paul Samuelson and Robert Solow to require a 6 or 7 percent unemployment rate—an unacceptable bargain.

5. New Frontier economists accepted the bland proposition that "money matters"—that Federal Reserve action to increase or decrease the supply of money makes a difference—but only for regulating the inflation rate and the (nominal) interest rate. When these rates could not be held down simultaneously, New Frontier doctrine considered it at least as important to restrain interest rates by easy money (increasing the supply of money) as to restrain inflation by tight money (decreasing the supply of money).

6. The practical Keynesians of the New Frontier cared about income distribution. They sought to increase the worker's share of the national income (which meant reducing the property owner's share) and also to reduce the measured degree of inequality in the personal distribution of income. Accord-ingly, they favored low interest rates over high ones and progressive direct taxation (of incomes and estates) over indirect sales and excise taxes.

CLOSING THE NEW FRONTIER

New Frontier policies are credited today by many economists with keeping the American growth rate high and the American unemployment and inflation rates low during the first half of the 1960s. These policies also gave economics, and especially Keynesian macroeconomics, a prestige and self-confidence that economics had seldom, if ever, possessed previously and that it has not yet regained. At their height—in fact, somewhat thereafter—their success led President Nixon (President Johnson's successor in office) to assure the public that "we are all Keynesians now."

What closed the New Frontier? Not so much the gestation and development of anti-Keynesian economics as a series of external shocks to which the system was prevented from adjusting by political considerations. The first shock was the explosion of the American involvement in Vietnam into a full-scale intervention and undeclared war, which America eventually lost. The second was President Johnson's refusal to finance the war either by raising taxes or by postponing the War on Poverty. The third shock—perhaps an aftershock—was the sudden quadrupling of the world price of oil by OPEC in 1973–74, followed by a further rise after the Iranian revolution of 1979.

SOME NEW FRONTIERSMEN

From among the eminent economists who assisted Lord Keynes (and his ghost) in framing New Frontier economic ideas, we choose a half-dozen for special mention: Walter Heller, Lawrence Klein, Arthur Okun, Paul Samuelson, Robert Solow, and James Tobin. None was over forty-five years old when President Kennedy was inaugurated. All but one were old enough to have lived through the Great Depression in a state of social consciousness. All were partisans of both Keynes and the New Deal. Most came from, and returned to, prestigious academic posts. Four eventually received Nobel Prizes in economics. Most remained active in policy formulation into the 1980s.

Walter Heller (1915–1987, University of Minnesota) was chairman of Kennedy's Council of Economic Advisers (CEA). A specialist in public finance,

Heller was a principal architect of the Kennedy fiscal policies. A superb communicator, he retained a common touch that belied both expertise and eminence.

Lawrence Klein (1920– , University of Pennsylvania), Nobel laureate and author of *The Keynesian Revolution,* became the country's macroeconomic model-builder *par excellence*. An obvious CEA possibility, Klein remained in the background, lest his youthful radicalism embarrass the administration, but the fundamental "numbers" of New Frontier policies were worked out by methods of his devising.

Arthur Okun (1928–1980, Yale University and Brookings Institution) devised Okun's Law during his service with the Kennedy administration. He later served as chairman of President Johnson's CEA. His interest in income distribution is reflected in his book *Equality and Efficiency,* while his interest in labor problems is apparent in *Prices and Quantities,* which presents a theory of implied contracts in labor relations that keep wages impervious to monetary

and fiscal policy until substantial unemployment develops.

Paul Samuelson (1915– , MIT) is a Nobel laureate and leader of his generation of American Keynesians. Samuelson writes at every level, from letters to the editor and columns in weekly magazines to mathematical and philosophical contributions to abstract scholarly journals. He has contributed to almost every branch of economics. As a student, he fitted the first statistical consumption function. Rather than seeking power in the Washington bureaucracy, Samuelson prefers the role of "grey eminence" behind the throne.

Robert Solow (1924– , MIT) is also a Nobel laureate. Solow's principal scholarly contributions have been in the economics of growth, capital, and production functions. We have mentioned his application (with Samuelson) of the Phillips curve to American data. Like Heller, Solow is a celebrated communicator outside as well as within the classroom.

James Tobin (1918– , Yale University) is another Nobel laureate and a specialist on monetary and investment theory, including portfolio balance. Tobin served with Heller on Kennedy's CEA. In the fields we have mentioned, as an econometrician, and in studies of income distribution, the quiet, unpretentious Tobin has retained his Keynesianism through thick and thin, including a preference for inflation, even accelerating inflation, over tolerance of continued unemployment.

POTENTIAL SUCCESSORS

As we shall soon see, the New Frontier has survived. However, as it seemed to close, interest tended to shift to two groups of successors, almost as hostile to each other as each was to the Keynesian "heresy." Some of these potential successors to the New Frontiersmen may be called *monetarists* and others *supply-siders.*[4] Despite their disagreements, they are often confused in the press. Both were important in the Reagan administrations, where Reaganomics represented less a settled body of doctrine than a series of compromises in their competition for the economic "soul" of the president.

The basic tenets of monetarism, as expounded by "Chicago School" economist, Milton Friedman, are as follows:

1. The money supply, defined in any consistent manner, is the principal determinant of aggregate demand and the level of economic activity in nominal terms. In particular, it is more important than the autonomous expenditures I, G, and X in the Keynesian model. This is a generalized restatement of the classical quantity theory of money.

2. The money supply exercises its influence not immediately, but with a long and variable lag that economists do not yet understand well. In general, monetary influences on real income and product appear before their influences on the price level, and the price-level effects often counteract and nullify the real-income ones.

3. The historical record suggests that discretionary monetary policy, or monetary "fine-tuning," has not been successful. Whether exercised by politicians, bureaucrats, bankers, or academic experts, monetary policy has been unable to wait for the lags to work themselves out. Instead, it has accentuated economic fluctuations and increased their amplitude. In short, it has been destabilizing. It would be better to replace such discretion with a monetary rule, requiring some monetary aggregate to grow steadily at a rate approximating the long-term growth rate of real GNP, regardless of resulting fluctuations in interest rates.

Monetarists do not agree among themselves about what the monetary rule should be—whether the indicator should be the monetary base, M1, or M2, whether account should be taken of shifts in *liquidity preference* (the demand for money as an asset), and how, if at all, the demand variables should be factored in.

As a monetarist subgroup, we should mention the rational-expectations school headed by Robert Lucas (University of Chicago) and Thomas Sargent (Stanford University). These economists believe that the responses of commodity, security, and labor markets to policy and policy changes are rational—that they do not include the confusion between nominal and real changes called *money illusion.* They also believe that all markets are therefore in the neighborhood of equilibrium, with Phillips curves nearly vertical at the natural rate of unemployment and with search unemployment treated as voluntary.[5] In such a world, policy exercises important influence only on the price level. It systematically influences output or employment only when the markets have been deceived as to what the policy is or how it will soon change. The best the policymaker can hope to do—purely random fluctuations apart—is to reduce risk (an element in production costs) by announcing and following policy rules, particularly about the money supply and its growth rate.

Monetarists are not Keynesians but, like them, they view macroeconomic policy as largely a matter of influencing aggregate demand. Supply-siders, on the other hand, propose to shift the emphasis back to aggregate supply, where it was before the "repeal" of Say's Identity. Indeed, the supply-siders can be interpreted as implying that Say's Identity holds in a well-run economy. In such an economy, aggregate supply creates its own demand.

---

4. Public-choice economists, whose chief spokesman has been the Nobel laureate James Buchanan (George Mason University) are of somewhat less importance. They insist that budgetary balance be required as a corollary of fiscal policy and blame Keynesian doctrine for the several "great inflations" of World War II and thereafter.

5. Search unemployment is interpreted as a preference for spending time looking for "good" jobs over spending it at work in "bad" jobs—whether or not the good ones in fact exist.

Robert Lucas

Thomas Sargent

What is a well-run economy? How does it differ from the existing one, if indeed it does? Supply-siders see two weaknesses in the existing American economy: excessive taxation and excessive regulation. They are not libertarians or anarchists. They do not propose to dispense with either taxation or public regulation completely. They believe only that excessive taxation and excessive regulation should be cut back sharply. The cuts can be made together, since some of the costs of regulation are borne by taxpayers. Supply-siders believe that income-tax progressivity should not go too far and that corporate income tax rates should not be too high. As for regulation, favorite targets include antimonopoly legislation, delays in technical progress in the name of safety, health, or the environment, and increases in the cost of employing labor. The latter includes minimum wages, encouragements to trade unionism, and high relief standards—which reduce the labor supply.

The Laffer curve, a supply-side artifact, caught the public eye in the early 1980s. Arthur Laffer, then an economist at the University of Southern California, argued that not only GNP but government reve-nues as well could be increased by tax cuts and the deficit reduced. In addition to the well-known Laffer curve, Laffer presented evidence from several episodes in American history—including the New Frontier tax cuts of twenty years before—and from the effects of lowered high-bracket income tax rates on the taxes received from high-bracket taxpayers weaned from tax shelters to more productive investments. The record, however, has not borne out Laffer's optimistic anticipations.[6] *Revolution,* Martin Anderson's account of the Reagan years, denies that short-run "Lafferism" ever dominated the administration's fiscal policy.

6. This apparent failure is explained away by Lafferite supply-siders on two grounds: Federal Reserve disinflationary policy and the timing of the tax cuts. In lowering the inflation rate, the Federal Reserve permitted interest rates to remain high. The high cost of credit, supply-siders believe, offset the effect of lower taxes on economic activity and thus on government receipts. Also, the tax cuts themselves were staggered over three years instead of being made all at once in 1981. Anticipation of further cuts in later years may have reduced the effectiveness of the 1981–82 tax reductions.

KEYNESIAN REVIVAL

During a fifteen- or twenty-year period beginning in the late 1960s, essays and lectures entitled "Is Keynes Dead?" were featured in economists' professional journals and conventions on three important Keynesian anniversaries—Lord Keynes's birth (1883), the publication of the *General Theory* (1936), and his death (1946). While a great many economists argued that Keynesian macroeconomics was dead, others not only defended its worth but by their research and theorizing laid the groundwork for a genuine Keynesian revival. The surviving New Frontiersmen have played important parts in this revival, aided and abetted by such younger disciples as Alan Blinder (Princeton University) and Lester Thurow (MIT).

Survivals and revivals are more common in the social than in the natural sciences and strengthen doubts about the "scientific" character of the "softer" social studies. Seventeenth-century mercantilism never really died in the business community, in contrast to the phlogiston theory, its approximate contemporary in chemistry. Karl Marx, who died the year Keynes was born, survives numerous "autopsies" and remains very much alive, perhaps less so in the capitalist countries than in socialist ones.

In the case of Keynes, the shortcomings of monetarism and the supply side have favored Keynesian revival. The monetarists never solved their difficulties with the definition of money, the specification of the monetary rule, and the ingenuity of the financial community in devising evasions in near-money and money-substitute forms.[7] In addition, monetarists seem to have underestimated the consequences of high nominal interest rates, such as result from the disinflationary tightening of money during the interval before inflation rates actually collapse. Hope, however, springs eternal in the human breast—including hope for the superior acumen of the next generation of monetary experts, now aided by computers and international cooperation.

Supply-side economics was largely an American phenomenon and was blamed in the United States, rightly or wrongly, for both the apparent fiasco of Lafferism and the burgeoning deficits of the Reagan administrations. More important to economists, however, was the anatomy of the accompanying Reagan prosperity. Supply-siders had expected the tax cuts and deregulation of the Reagan years to fuel an expansion primarily of private investment, supported by increased private saving more than proportionate to the rise in GNP. In Keynesian terms, this would have been a rise in both saving and returns on investment. Keynesians expected, instead, a movement along existing functions and a consumption boom with no significant change in either saving or investment as proportions of GNP. The Keynesian anticipations were in fact correct, and influentially so. Private saving ratios actually *fell*,[8] and investment was maintained largely by tapping the savings of foreigners, both European and Japanese, with a smattering of Canadians as well.

7. To Sir Charles Goodhart (Bank of England) we owe "Goodhart's Law" that empirical regularities break down when policy is based on them. Sir Charles surely had in mind the thwarting of British monetarism by the superior ingenuity of the London financial community.

8. Harvard University's Martin Feldstein ascribes this decline in the private saving ratio largely to the expanded Social Security and Medicare systems, which reduce the need to save for old age and its medical accompaniments. Though he was chairman of the CEA during most of the Reagan period, Feldstein became increasingly "out of sync" with the remainder of the administration.

Exchange Rates, International Balances, and International Finance

Economic Growth

Economic Development

PART VI
INTERNATIONAL TRADE, ECONOMIC GROWTH, AND ECONOMIC DEVELOPMENT

19

Exchange Rates, International Balances, and International Finance

Preview When people in one country trade with people in another country, the price levels in the two countries must somehow be related to one another. When people in one country make investments in another country, the interest rates in the two countries must somehow be related to one another. So far, in our economic analysis, we have not explored these relationships. In this chapter, we examine those portions of international economics which do explore them.

It is quite unrealistic to presume that international economic relations do not affect economic behavior. After making this point, we start our analysis by examining how foreign exchange markets determine the value of a country's money in terms of the monies of other countries. From here, we go on to explain how governments sometimes intervene in the operation of these markets and try to control the exchange value of different monies. We discuss the question of whether foreign exchange rates should be fixed or free to find their own relationships, and we briefly review the history of exchange rate fixing schemes, from the gold standard to the present-day "dirty float" arrangement.

The second part of the chapter explains the balance of payments accounting system and what is meant by "favorable" or "unfavorable" balances of trade and payments. We trace the evolution of a country from immature debtor to mature creditor and examine balance-of-payments problems and possible solutions.

The appendix to this chapter explores international macroeconomics. Specifically, it examines (a) exchange rate systems that are consistent with macroeconomic policy autonomy, (b) simultaneous equilibrium for both the domestic economy and the balance of payments, and (c) a set of macroeconomic identities that specify interrelationships between the domestic and the international aspects of a nation's macroeconomy. This appendix is best understood by students who have already studied the principles of macroeconomics.

THE WORLD IS ALWAYS WITH US

Before we plunge into the details of international trade and finance, let us note how important these topics are. In the United States, it is estimated that one out of every six workers owes his or her job to exports, two out of every five acres of farmland produce for export, and about 20 percent of industrial output is exported.

The world's financial markets are more closely interconnected than ever before, thanks to instantaneous international transmission not only of voices but also of documents, statistical data, and computer output. Since time zones remain different, people wonder "When can the Chief Financial Officer sleep?" This question is not always funny. The decisions of a few large Tokyo and Hong Kong companies in 1985 to withdraw their very large (and therefore uninsured) deposits from the Continental Illinois Bank in Chicago were made during East Asian business hours—in the middle of the night, Chicago time. Chicago bankers who had gone to bed under normal conditions were awakened in the small hours of the morning with the news that Continental Illinois, the eighth-largest bank in the United States and the largest in the entire Midwest, was threatened with bankruptcy.

International trade and finance also play large roles in world politics. Early in the Great Depression, both the United States and the British Empire raised their **tariffs** (taxes on imported goods), trying to "export unemployment" to other countries by producing at home goods previously imported. The United States passed the high Hawley-Smoot tariff in 1930 to keep foreign goods out. At about the same time, Britain set up a system of Imperial Preference, or tariffs against non-Empire countries. Later other tariffs were added to protect the British Isles themselves. A major victim of these tariffs was Japan, a resource-poor country that depended upon its exports to pay for its imports of both food and industrial raw materials. Largely in order to

avoid the serious economic effects expected from the Anglo-American blockage of their exports, the Japanese sought for themselves a "co-prosperity" sphere of influence in China and East Asia from which they could import the goods that they needed, and in which they could sell their exports, free from Anglo-American competition. In 1931 they set up a puppet government in Manchuria, as a source of iron ore, coal, soybeans, and salt for fertilizer. They also built up mines and factories in Manchuria. This aggression started Japan on the slippery slope toward Pearl Harbor.

We cannot say how the course of history would have been different if the United States or Great Britain or Japan had behaved differently in their international economic relations. Knowledge about how these international relationships operate will not guarantee the peaceful resolution of problems. But to understand them and search for solutions, we must learn the basics of international trade and finance.

International trade and finance play key roles in world politics.

FOREIGN EXCHANGE MARKETS

Let us start the study of international trade and finance with **foreign exchange markets,** which are markets in which the monies of different countries are exchanged (traded) for one another. In fact, **foreign exchange** simply means the money of other countries. The reason these markets are needed is that the people who produce and sell things want to be paid in the money of their own country. Therefore, if the buyer has only the money of another country, some exchange of monies must take place. It is a convenient simplification to suppose that a German who wishes to buy something from the United States must first buy American dollars and then buy the American good or service, or that an American who wishes to buy something from Japan must first buy Japanese yen and then buy the Japanese product.

Foreign exchange is the money of other countries. Foreign exchange markets are markets in which the monies of different countries are traded for one another.

Foreign exchange markets are needed because the people who produce and sell things want to be paid in the money of their own country.

Two-Country Model

Figure 1 illustrates a foreign exchange market as it might exist between the U.S. dollar and the Japanese yen, assuming for the moment that these are the only monies in the world.[1] The quantity of dollars demanded and supplied in international transactions is shown on the horizontal axis, and the price of these dollars is shown on the vertical axis. The price of the dollar is expressed in terms of foreign exchange, which, in this case, is Japanese yen. In this illustration, the equilibrium value of the dollar is 200 yen, balancing the quantity demanded with the quantity supplied at $5 billion a year. At a higher exchange value, say, 300 yen per dollar, a greater number of dollars would be supplied, but fewer would be demanded, so that the exchange value of the dollar would tend to fall. At a lower exchange value, more dollars would be demanded but fewer supplied, pushing the exchange rate upward.

The foreign exchange value of a country's money tells how much of a foreign country's money can be exchanged for one unit of the domestic money.

In this simple two-country illustration, part of the demand for dollars comes from Japanese who want to buy American goods and services. Some of these buyers are Japanese tourists in the United States. Others are residents of Japan who want to import American goods, such as coal or lumber, or

FIGURE 1
Two-Country Foreign Exchange Market

The horizontal axis shows the quantity of dollars supplied and demanded per year in international transactions. The demand comes from people and firms that wish to acquire dollars in order to complete transactions with Americans. The supply comes from those who wish to acquire foreign money (yen) in order to carry out transactions with Japan. The vertical axis shows the foreign exchange value of the dollar, that is, how many yen can be exchanged for one dollar.

Japanese companies that want to import American machines for their factories. Some of the demand for dollars comes from Japanese investors who want to purchase bonds or shares of stock in U.S. stock and bond markets, and some comes from Japanese who send money to relatives in the United States. A portion of the demand may also come from the Japanese government itself, if it wishes to acquire American dollars to hold as part of Japan's official reserves.[2]

The supply of dollars, on the other hand, comes from Americans who wish to buy Japanese goods or travel in Japan, who want to invest through the Japanese bond and stock markets, or who want to send money to Japanese friends or relatives. The U.S. government may even supply

1. In practice, most foreign exchange transactions involve short-term government securities rather than money. But the explanation is clearer if we assume that money is exchanged.

2. Official reserves will be described later in this chapter in connection with balance of payments accounting.

dollars in order to acquire yen to hold as part of its official reserves.

Multilateral Trade

Our simple model of a two-country world provides the basic idea of the demand and supply of a nation's money in international trade, but it is only of limited use in exploring international trade and finance. In practice, many countries are involved on both the demand side and the supply side of the international exchange market for dollars and other monies. In actual international finance, an American who wants to buy a Japanese product does not have to get yen directly from a Japanese who wants to buy an American product. The American may, just as well, get the yen from a German who got them by selling goods to Japan. Generally he or she buys them from banks and foreign exchange dealers who specialize in handling monies from many countries. We can still draw a graph for the U.S. dollar in the international exchange market, as in Figure 1, but the vertical axis now should be labeled simply as the foreign exchange value of the dollar, rather than as Japanese yen, or West German marks, or British pounds, or some other specific foreign money (see Figure 2). For actual measurements, the units on the vertical axis are an average value of all foreign monies, "trade-weighted" by their importance in trade with the United States, without reference to capital movements involving the dollar. In practice, the units on the vertical axis are index numbers, with the exchange value of the dollar on some chosen date or base year set equal to 100. We shall simply refer to the dollar's exchange value as P so that we can say that the foreign exchange value of the dollar rises or falls, without measuring the rise or fall in any specific money. It is important to do so because the American dollar may possibly rise in its foreign exchange value even while it is falling in its exchange relation with some specific money, if that other money is rising even faster in its foreign exchange value.[3]

3. Of course, it is still possible and useful in many cases to express the international exchange value of the dollar in terms of some specific money. If you plan to travel to Canada, for example, you want to know the exchange rate between the American dollar and the Canadian dollar.

FIGURE 2
Foreign Exchange Market for the Dollar

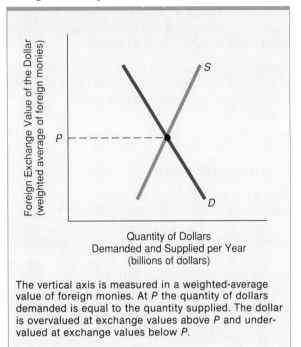

The vertical axis is measured in a weighted-average value of foreign monies. At P the quantity of dollars demanded is equal to the quantity supplied. The dollar is overvalued at exchange values above P and undervalued at exchange values below P.

The Slopes of Demand and Supply Curves

In Figure 2, the demand and supply curves for the American dollar look much the same as demand and supply curves for actual goods and services. But there is an important difference that must be cleared up before we go on to talk about equilibrium in foreign exchange rates. Let us concentrate on the supply curve and suppose that the dollar's exchange value goes up for some reason. Does this mean that the quantity of dollars supplied to the international exchange market will increase? The answer depends on how the change in exchange value affects the behavior of the people and firms that are supplying dollars. Americans who buy foreign goods are one of these supplier groups. The increased exchange value of the dollar means that the dollar price of foreign goods has fallen. As a result, we expect that these Americans will buy more foreign goods, but we do not know how much more they will buy. Suppose that the exchange value of the dollar rises by 10 percent and that, as a result, Americans purchase 10 percent more foreign goods. Is there any change in the number of dollars supplied to the international exchange market? The answer is no, because the effective cut in the unit price of foreign goods exactly cancels the increase in the number of these goods bought. In this situation, the supply curve of dollars in the international exchange market would be a vertical line.

This exercise tells you that when we draw a positively sloping supply curve for dollars, we are assuming that Americans (and others who supply dollars) are quite sensitive to changes in the dollar's exchange value—so sensitive in fact that their response in actual buying and investment and so on is more than proportional to the change in the dollar's exchange value. This is a reasonable assumption that is borne out by experience in normal times. It often does not hold for short time periods or in abnormal times.

The responsiveness conditions that we have just outlined for the supply curve also apply to the demand curve for the dollar. In this case, the reasoning process asks you to put yourself in the place of those who demand dollars and consider how you would respond to changes in its exchange value. More than proportionate responses to exchange value changes give this curve the negative slope shown in Figure 2.[4]

Equilibrium Foreign Exchange Rates

Movements toward equilibrium in foreign exchange markets operate in essentially the same way as in markets for goods and services (see Chapter 5). At any exchange rate above P in Figure 2, the dollar is said to be "overvalued," which means that a dollar will buy more in foreign countries than it will buy at home. An overvalued dollar also means that American goods are overpriced in international trade. In this case, more dollars will be supplied than are demanded, and pressure is exerted for a decrease in the exchange value of the dollar. The exchange value of the dollar will decline if it is free to move in response to market

4. If you have already studied microeconomics, you will recognize that the slopes of foreign exchange market demand and supply curves involve the well-known concept of elasticity.

conditions. In the language of foreign exchange, the dollar will **depreciate**. At any exchange rate below P, on the other hand, the dollar is said to be "undervalued" in the sense that it will buy less in international trade than it will buy at home. An undervalued dollar also means that American goods are underpriced in international trade. Now more dollars will be demanded than supplied, and pressure will be exerted for a rise in its exchange value. If exchange rates are free to move in response to market conditions, the dollar will **appreciate** as its exchange value rises. When equilibrium exists in a free international exchange market, the dollar is neither overvalued nor undervalued.

An overvalued dollar means that American goods are overpriced in international trade. If exchange rates are free to move in response to market conditions, the dollar will depreciate as its exchange value falls.

An undervalued dollar means that American goods are underpriced in international trade. If exchange rates are free to move in response to market conditions, the dollar will appreciate as its exchange value rise.

To extend our understanding of foreign exchange rates and markets, let us think of a foreign exchange market as divided into two separate submarkets. One submarket (which will be called the "capital account" when we study the balance of payments accounting system) is limited to transactions involving stocks, bonds, bank accounts, and other financial assets. In this "capital account" submarket, equilibrium would mean that the dollar rate of return on $1,000 would be the same as the foreign-money rate of return on $1,000 worth of foreign money after conversion to U.S. dollars. This condition is called **rate-of-return parity**.

Rate-of-return parity means that the rate of return on a dollar invested at home is the same as it would be if that dollar were exchanged for foreign money and invested in a foreign country.

The other submarket (which will be called the "current account" when we study the balance of payments accounting system) is limited to transactions in goods and services. In the current account submarket, equilibrium involves a condition known as **purchasing power parity.** This means that, as far as traded goods and services are concerned, a country's money will buy as much in traded goods abroad as it will at home. (Nontraded goods and services, like homes and haircuts, are not really in the picture.)

Purchasing power parity exists when the buying power of a country's money for traded goods and services is the same at home as abroad.

In practice, these two submarkets cannot be separated. The actual common or overall exchange rate is usually somewhere between the purchasing power and the rate-of-return parity values, so that neither parity condition is satisfied. A rate that over- or undervalues a currency in terms of either purchasing power or rate of return may nevertheless be a persistent equilibrium condition. How, for example, are we to explain the steady rise of the dollar against the yen over a six-year period (1979–1985) when the Japanese export balance in bilateral trade was generally rising and the American export balance accordingly falling? There are two major reasons. First, on the U.S. side, increasing public deficits had to be financed by the sale of securities to the public. If the inflation rate was simultaneously to be brought down, high interest rates had to be offered to sell these securities. Second, on the Japanese side, financial internationalization removed the legal and extralegal limitations on investment abroad and increased the demand for the higher-interest-bearing American securities.

FIXED VERSUS FLEXIBLE EXCHANGE RATES

Foreign exchange rates are called **free,** or **floating,** or **flexible,** when they are free to move up or down in response to shifts in demand and supply curves arising from the ordinary operations of international trade and finance. But many countries have been and remain unwilling to allow the international values of their monies to move freely. Politically persuasive arguments have generally led to **fixed exchange rates**—rates maintained through government intervention. We shall first describe how the exchange values may be fixed. Then we shall present both sides of the debate about fixed versus flexible rates.

Foreign exchange rates are called flexible (or floating) when they are free to move up or down in response to shifts in demand and supply curves arising from the ordinary operations of international trade and finance. Fixed exchange rates are rates maintained through government intervention.

Fixing Exchange Rates

Governments generally hold reserves of gold and monies (both their own and those of other countries). The governments of the major trading countries are therefore able to influence exchange rates if they choose to do so. They may be able to raise (or lower) the prices of foreign monies by buying (or selling) them. (Recall that a rise, or fall, in the price of foreign exchange constitutes depreciation, or appreciation, of the domestic money.) A government may choose not to recognize the exchange value set by the market. It may instead choose to set an official value for its money. Changing such an official exchange value is called **revaluation**. Lowering its official value is called **devaluation**.

During the 1960s, the United States held the foreign exchange value of the dollar above its free-market equilibrium rate as it tried to maintain a fixed rate in spite of a decline in the dollar's free-market value. The essentials of how this influence may be applied are easy to see by looking at Figure 3, which shows the international market for dollars. To maintain the dollar's value at, say, P_1, the United States dipped into its reserves of gold and foreign exchange and sold them for dollars. As long as the United States had enough reserves to purchase quantity *AB* of dollars per year, it could support the exchange value of the dollar at P_1. In effect, the demand curve became horizontal at the fixed rate, as shown by D_2, and the equilibrium moved to point *B*. On the other hand, if the United States wants to push the exchange value of the dollar below the free-market equilibrium level, say, to P_2, it can take dollars from its reserves or create more dollars and sell them in the foreign exchange market. If it sells quantity *EF* per year, it will succeed in depreciating the exchange value of the dollar to P_2. In this case, the supply curve becomes horizontal (as shown by S_2) at the fixed exchange rate, and equilibrium moves to *F*. A depreciated dollar would lower the cost of U.S. goods to foreign buyers and promote U.S. exports.[5]

Governments may try to influence exchange rates by buying or selling foreign monies. A rise (or fall) in the price of foreign exchange constitutes depreciation (or appreciation) of the domestic money. Governments may also set official values for their monies. Lowering an official value is called devaluation.

The Case for Flexible Rates

Those who favor flexible rates argue that they are prices like any others. They say that flexible exchange rates are better than fixed or government-controlled rates simply because free markets generally do a better job of setting prices and allocating resources than governments do. They also say that fixed rates are not really as safe and sure and stable as their advocates claim or hope. Governments, they say, often try to fix rates that they cannot maintain with the gold and foreign exchange re-

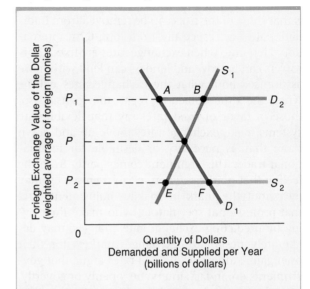

FIGURE 3
Fixing Foreign Exchange Rates

If the United States wants to fix the exchange value of the dollar at P_1, it can use its gold and foreign exchange reserves to demand dollars at that exchange value. The demand curve becomes horizontal at that exchange value (D_2), and equilibrium is at *B*, with the United States purchasing *AB* quantity of dollars per year. To fix the exchange value at P_2, the United States may sell dollars at that value, bringing about the horizontal supply curve S_2, equilibrium *F*, and selling quantity *EF* per year.

serves at their command.[6] When the reserves run out, drastic exchange rate changes can do more harm than the steady and moderate movements that would have come under a free-rate system. Worse yet, governments often resort to tariffs, quotas, and direct controls when their reserves start to fall too low. These direct controls reduce freedom and seriously distort world trade.

Adherents of flexible rates believe that free markets do a better job of setting prices and allocating resources than governments do.

---

5. Some countries, such as Nazi Germany, developed very complex multiple exchange rates. Such systems are usually combined with **exchange controls,** which require licenses to buy foreign money or forbid its use to buy luxury imports, to travel abroad, or to buy foreign securities or other assets abroad. Generally, multiple rate systems involve the central bank selling foreign exchange to importers cheaply for essential imports and selling it dearly for less important uses. An **inconvertible currency** can exist under such control systems. For example, the Soviet ruble is inconvertible because Soviet citizens must have special licenses in order to buy foreign currency legally.

6. This is often a matter of prestige. A falling value of a country's money—rising prices of foreign monies—can, rightly or wrongly, be taken to signify weakness or failure of the government's economic policies.

The Case for Fixed Rates

The main argument of those who favor fixed rates is that some of the risks can be removed from international trade, especially from long-term international lending, when exchange rates are fixed. Borrowers can borrow and lenders can lend with more assurance about what the exchange rates will be when the time comes to repay the loans. Also, those in favor of fixed rates say that flexible-rate systems make exchange rates move up and down more than is necessary or desirable for international trade. This argument comes partly from the feeling that markets, when left to themselves, may overshoot the mark in making adjustments and that professional speculators, who make their living by predicting exchange rate changes, may deliberately destabilize exchange markets for their own gain. Adherents of fixed rates argue that governments do, in fact, intervene, openly or covertly, in exchange markets and that it is better that they do so overtly, under a fixed-rate system, than covertly for reasons that may be unclear. They see no reason why fixed-rate systems should not work if countries, with the assistance of the International Monetary Fund (described on pages 413–414), hold large sufficient reserves and do not impose domestic price and wage rigidity on the international system.

Adherents of fixed rates believe that some of the risks can be removed from international trade, especially from long-term international lending, when exchange rates are fixed. Since governments intervene in exchange markets anyway, it is better that they do so openly, under a fixed-rate system.

A Brief History of Exchange-Rate Systems

Historically, fixed-rate systems have been more common than floating-rate systems. Probably the best-known system for fixing exchange rates is the gold standard, which was used by most major trading countries from the 1870s to the 1930s, except for the World War I period. After World War II, a new rate-fixing system was set up under the Bret-

ton Woods plan and carried out through the International Monetary Fund. We shall take a look at these systems and at why the most recent system broke down in the 1970s. We shall also see how Eurocurrencies fit into this picture.

The best-known system for fixing exchange rates is the gold standard.

The Gold Standard   Under the **gold standard,** countries promised to back their own money with a fixed amount of gold. That is, they promised to buy their own money and pay a stated amount of gold for it. Among the countries that followed this system, exchange rates were fixed, because a money that can be exchanged for twice as much gold as another money could also be exchanged for twice as much of that other money. For this reason, the price levels in gold-standard countries were linked to one another. Except for goods and services not traded and the costs of shipping goods and gold, the price levels in the trading countries would match (inversely) the fixed exchange ratios of their monies. A country whose money had a low gold equivalent would have a high price level, and a country whose money had a high gold equivalent would have a low price level. The price-level change would tend to bring purchasing power parity into international trade.

Under the gold standard, countries promise to back their own money with a fixed amount of gold. Under this system, the price levels of trading countries tend to match inversely the fixed exchange ratios of their monies.

The major problems with the gold standard came in times of rapidly changing economic conditions. For example, if a recession caused prices to fall in one country, its goods would become attractive in international trade compared with the goods of countries whose prices had not fallen. In the country suffering from the recession, exports would grow, helping it to recover. In order to carry out these purchases, foreigners would buy the exporting country's money partially with gold or convertible monies. Under the gold standard, such "gold inflows" or increases in reserves, would expand the exporting country's money supply, causing its price level to rise back toward its original level. But its trading partners would have falling exports and rising imports. They would lose international reserves, including gold, and they might suffer recession. Of course, if price levels and wage rates could change quickly enough, the linkage would not bring much hardship and unemployment, but if wage rates and prices were slow to change, unemployment would grow. The gold-standard linkage could be uncomfortable as economies not suffering recession found themselves vulnerable to the effects of recessions elsewhere in the world. Recession and unemployment afflicting one country could spread to its trading partners.

The major problems with the gold standard come in times of rapidly changing economic conditions. Recession and unemployment affecting one country could spread to its trading partners.

For smooth working of the gold standard, at least one of the major trading countries must be willing to permit its price and employment levels to be affected by events and/or policies originating in other countries. Also, at least one major trading country in the system must "make a market" for "distress goods" exported by countries in recession, despite the resulting damage to its domestic import-competing industries and work forces.

Great Britain satisfied these conditions in the Victorian and Edwardian generations before 1914. It maintained world confidence in the pound sterling, and reduced deflationary and contractionary pressures on its trading partners during depressions, at considerable sacrifice to Great Britain itself.

After World War I, the United States and (after 1925) France, both protectionist countries, took over Great Britain's leading role in the gold-standard system, but did not follow the policies required for smooth working of the gold standard. Therefore, the gold standard took on, for countries suffering recession, a pronounced deflationary bias, while concentrating the burdens of economic ad-

justment on these same countries. Small wonder that, in the first major test of the postwar gold standard—the Great Depression of the 1930—it failed miserably. Country after country, including Great Britain itself in 1931 and the United States in 1933, went "off gold" in the sense that they no longer provided gold to holders of their domestic currencies, even though the price of gold remained fixed.

The mid-Depression abandonment of gold led to a six-year period (1933–1939) of **competitive depreciation** and **exporting unemployment** that lasted until the outbreak of World War II. Countries anxious to increase exports, reduce imports, and reflate their domestic price levels bid up the prices of foreign monies and thereby cheapened their own. The process was accompanied by increased protection all around and, in many countries, by exchange controls as well. The volume of world trade contracted. Resource-poor countries like Japan, and to some extent Germany and Italy, doubting their ability to prosper by trade, turned eagerly to military imperialism as a replacement, with disastrous consequences.

The gold standard was abandoned in the 1930s, leading to a six-year period of competitive depreciation and exporting unemployment.

The International Monetary Fund The **International Monetary Fund (IMF)** was set up shortly before the end of World War II at a meeting of central bankers and finance ministers at Bretton Woods, New Hampshire, and is sometimes called the **Bretton Woods system.** Its major goal was to maintain stable exchange rates and to avoid competitive depreciations and devaluations. Gold and the U.S. dollar were established as joint monetary standards, tied to each other at the ratio of $35 per ounce of gold, and the exchange values of other monies were fixed ("pegged") in relation to the dollar. Thus, a new set of fixed exchange rates was set up. Next, a fund (the IMF) was established from contributions of gold and monies from the major trading countries, roughly in proportion to their trading activity. The IMF directors then could make loans from the fund to help individual countries maintain these fixed exchange rates.

The International Monetary Fund (IMF), or Bretton Woods system, was established at the end of World War II to maintain stable exchange rates and avoid competitive depreciations and devaluations.

To understand how the fund was expected to operate, look again at Figure 3. Suppose that the fixed, or pegged, exchange value of the country's money is P_1, where the IMF believes the demand and supply curves will intersect in normal times. In other words, the IMF directors believe that the demand and supply curves, as shown in Figure 3, represent temporary circumstances and that they eventually will shift to bring equilibrium back to the P_1 exchange value. To maintain the fixed value, gold or foreign exchange in the amount of AB per time period would have to be used to support the demand for the nation's money. If the country did not have enough reserves of gold or foreign exchange to continue to pay out this quantity, an IMF loan could tide it over until demand and supply curves shifted back to "normal" positions and made the equilibrium value match the fixed value. If these shifts were not expected to take place, the IMF could deny the loan and require the country to devalue its money. Or it could set conditions for its assistance, generally in the form of lowered inflation rates and lowered budget deficits. The idea of the fund was that such devaluations would be limited and would not be permitted to lead to competitive devaluations as they had before World War II.

The Breakdown of Fixed Rates How did the Bretton Woods system actually work out? The U.S.S.R. and the Soviet bloc never joined the IMF, and that body itself could impose its wishes mainly on the weaker developing countries, which came to resent IMF-imposed "austerity." Nevertheless, the Bretton Woods system worked reasonably well until the Vietnam War and the War on Poverty combined to put increasing downward pressure on the dollar itself, and fears arose that the United States would not have enough gold or other reserves to maintain the $35 per ounce relationship with gold. The resulting European preference for gold rather than dollars in their reserve holdings added further

to this pressure. After the failure of various compromise solutions, President Nixon "pulled the plug" on the Bretton Woods system in August 1971 by refusing any longer to exchange gold for dollars even with foreign governments and central banks.

Since then, foreign exchange markets have operated under what has become known as a **dirty float.** Many developing countries have pegged their money to the dollar, in practice at least. But individual governments often try to influence the exchange value of their own money by buying or selling large amounts of foreign exchange. The result is a weak imitation of a fixed-rate system.

The Bretton Woods system collapsed in 1971 when the United States refused to continue exchanging gold for dollars. Since then, foreign exchange markets have operated under a dirty float, in which individual governments try to influence the exchange value of their money by buying or or selling large amounts of foreign exchange.

Eurocurrencies

We hear a great deal about Eurodollars today. Why are there no Eurodollar bills? Is a Eurodollar different from a U.S. dollar?. Is a Euromark or Eurofranc different from an ordinary Deutschmark or Swiss franc?

To answer these questions, we turn to history. The **Eurocurrency** system began in the 1950s with the Eurodollar, which in turn seems to have begun with the Soviet Union. The Soviet authorities needed dollar reserves for purchases in the West, but they did not want to hold dollars in the United States, where the government might freeze or confiscate them if the Cold War heated up. It was tempting for them to buy pounds or francs and earn the higher interest rates that then prevailed in western Europe, but the instability of European monies was a problem. The dollar was the world's most stable money and was widely used in contracts between and among citizens of European countries. So the Soviets deposited their dollar funds in special dollar accounts in European banks.

For the European banks, these dollar accounts could serve as reserves for dollar loans at high European interest rates—the best of both worlds, so to speak. The dollar accounts in European banks became known as Eurodollars.

The system spread. Financiers from all countries, the United States included, took advantage of it to increase their interest earnings when U.S. interest rates were low. The dollars that European banks were lending came to include not only their depositors' dollar funds in Europe but other dollar funds purchased or borrowed and then deposited. From an original base in London, the market spread all over Western Europe and beyond. When the dollar weakened in the wake of the Vietnam War, the market expanded from Eurodollars to include the other Eurocurrencies.

The Eurocurrency's main attraction is freedom. A dollar deposit in a London bank, which may be a London branch of a New York or San Francisco bank, is not subject to U.S. laws and regulations about reserve ratios, interest rates, and the quality or its loans, because it is located physically in Britain. But neither is it subject to British law, since the status of the British money and the ordinary British depositor are not involved. (If the British should try to regulate the Eurodollar market too much, it would soon leave London!)[7] So it has grown into a major oasis of freedom in an overregulated world (according to its friends) or a major unguided missile on the world financial scene (according to its enemies).

Eurodollars are dollar accounts in European banks. Eurocurrencies are deposits of a country's money in banks in a foreign country, which are free of the issuing government's laws and regulations about reserve ratios, interest rates, and the quality of loans.

The Eurocurency market has expanded greatly over the years. The principal expansion has been a *Eurobond* market in dollar bonds issued and marketed outside the United States, to avoid U.S. regulations on matters that may include taxes, interest rates, insurance, trading practices, credit rationing, and so on. Similarly, a *Euroyen,* or "Samurai" bond, is a yen bond issued outside Japan to avoid Japanese regulations and "administrative guidance." In addition to markets in Europe itself, there are also offshore markets physically close to a country's financial centers yet still unregulated. These may even be located within the country's territorial waters, like the Isle of Wight in the English Channel. The Bahamas, the Cayman Islands, and the Republic of Panama have been offshore financial markets of the United States.

When regulation increases in severity, and when real interest rates diverge between countries, Eurocurrency, Eurobonds, and similar instruments gain in importance. On the other hand, when deregulation and financial internationalization proceed, and when the world moves closer to uniformity of real interest rates, markets using these instruments decline.[8]

The Eurodollar should not be confused with the **European Currency Unit (ECU),** which is the monetary unit of the European Currency Union. There is no physical distinction between an ordinary dollar and a Eurodollar, but the ECU is a money of account, which does not exist in any physical sense. It is a weighted average of the values of a number of European Community (EC) monies. Although ECUs cannot be circulated, bank accounts may be held in them. The value of the ECU is not fixed relative to the dollar, the yen, or any other "outside" money, but it is hoped that it will fluctuate less violently than the Deutschmark, the Dutch guilder, or other member-country monies.

BALANCE OF PAYMENTS ACCOUNTS

Our next task is to explain the accounting system that countries use to keep track of the international transactions that give rise to the demands for and supplies of their money. The record of transactions affecting the international demand and supply for a

---

7. Much of the Eurodollar "market" is now international, with centers in such places as Tangier, Hong Kong, and Singapore.

8. An excellent brief treatment of this subject is "Euromarkets," *The Economist* (London), May 16, 1987.

nation's money is that nation's **balance of payments account.** In order to introduce you to the idea of international transactions, we first present two hypothetical cases. Then we outline the U.S. balance of payments accounts.

A balance of payments account is the record of transactions affecting the international demand and supply for a nation's money.

We start by limiting our attention to a single pair of international transactions. The two are, we shall suppose, of equal size. Herr Braun, of Hamburg, West Germany, has instructed his broker to buy for him $15,000 worth of International Business Machines (IBM) stock on the New York Stock Exchange on Wall Street. Payment must be made in dollars, but we suppose that Herr Braun and his broker have only German marks. At the same time, Mr. Brown, of Chicago, buys from a local dealer a $15,000 sports car made by the Toyota Company in Nagoya, Japan. Eventually Toyota wants payment in Japanese yen, but both Mr. Brown and the Toyota dealer in Chicago have only American dollars.

What do these two transactions mean in terms of U.S. international balances? Herr Braun's purchase of IBM stock is part of both the demand for American dollars and the supply of German marks in foreign exchange markets. From the American point of view, transactions such as this are usually called positive, active, credit, or favorable because they build up American-owned reserves of foreign currency. On the other hand, Mr. Brown's purchase of the Toyota automobile is part of both the American demand for foreign exchange (in this case the Japanese yen) and the supply of American dollars as seen by foreigners. From the American point of view, transactions such as this are usually called negative, passive, debit, or unfavorable because they draw down American reserves of foreign exchange. Later we shall see how important this distinction is and whether a positive item, leading to the accumulation of foreign exchange, is really any more favorable than a negative item, which draws down such reserves. For the moment, we shall look at the accounting system that keeps track of international transactions.

U.S. International Accounts

Actual international data cover thousands, even millions, of transactions taking place among more than 150 countries. Few of these transactions cancel out quite as neatly as in our hypothetical cases. Also, the number of different types of transactions is much greater.

Table 1 presents the U.S. international account balances at five-year intervals from 1967 to 1987. It summarizes the millions of transactions that took place between Americans and foreigners during those years. Each transaction recorded in the international accounts system must be entered as either a credit (+) or a debit (−) to show its effect on the exchange value of the dollar.

What determines whether any particular transaction is recorded as a credit (positive item) or a debit (negative item) in the account? The general rule is as follows. If a certain kind of transaction normally leads to a demand for domestic (in this case, U.S.) money or a supply of foreign money, it is a positive transaction. If it generally leads to a demand for foreign money or a supply of domestic money, it is a negative transaction. This is clearly shown by the entries in the current account part of Table 1, where exports are positive and imports are negative. Exports of U.S. goods generally mean that foreigners demand dollars and supply their own money in international exchange markets to pay for goods purchased from U.S. citizens. On the other hand, when Americans buy goods from foreigners, they must supply dollars and demand foreign money in order to pay for these imports. It is a bit harder to understand the positive and negative entries in other sections of the accounts, but the general rule holds there as well.

If a certain kind of transaction generally leads to a demand for domestic money or a supply of foreign money, it is a positive transaction (a credit). If it generally leads to a demand for foreign money or a supply of domestic money, it is a negative transaction (a debt).

The next step in understanding the international accounts in Table 1 is to note that the differ-

TABLE 1
U.S. International Account Balances, Five-Year Intervals, 1967–1987 (billions of dollars)

	1967	1972	1977	1982	1987
Current Account					
1. Merchandise Exports	30.7	49.4	120.8	211.2	249.6
2. Merchandise Imports	−26.9	−55.8	−151.9	−247.6	−409.9
3. BALANCE OF TRADE	3.8	−6.4	−31.1	−36.4	−160.3
4. Investment Income Receipts	8.0	14.8	32.2	83.5	103.8
5. Investment Income Payments	−2.7	−6.6	−14.2	−54.9	−83.4
6. BALANCE ON INVESTMENT INCOME	5.3	8.2	18.0	28.7	20.4
7. Balance on Remittances and other Services	−6.5	−7.6	−1.4	−1.0	−14.1
8. CURRENT ACCOUNT BALANCE	2.6	−5.8	−14.5	−8.7	−154.0
Capital Account					
9. Capital Inflow	7.4	21.5	51.3	93.7	211.5
10. Capital Outflow	−9.8	−14.5	−34.4	−116.2	−85.1
11. CAPITAL ACCOUNT BALANCE	−2.4	7.0	16.9	−22.5	126.4
12. Statistical Discrepancy	−0.2	−1.9	−2.0	36.1	18.5
13. U.S. OFFICIAL RESERVES[1]	0.0	0.7	−0.4	−5.0	9.1

[1] Includes allocations of Special Drawing Rights by the International Monetary Fund. This is one concept of the overall balance of payments.

Note: Detail may not add to total because of rounding.

Source: Economic Report of the President, 1989, Table B-102, p. 424f.

ent types of transactions that take place during the year are listed (and numbered) down the left side of the table. To explain how the accounting system works, we will work through the accounts from one concept of balance to the next.

Balance of Trade   The **balance of trade** (line 3 in Table 1) is the most familiar and therefore the easiest to understand. It is the amount by which the value of a country's exports of goods (line 1) exceeds or falls short of the value of its imports of goods (line 2). The U.S. balance of trade has been negative since the mid-1970s, after two generations of positive values. Mr. Brown's purchase of the Toyota automobile would be recorded as an import in this part of the account.

The balance of trade is the amount by which the value of a country's exports of goods exceeds or falls short of the value of its imports of goods

---

Balance on Investment Income   In Table 1, line 4 shows investment income (dividends, interest, and rent) received by Americans from foreigners. This item is a credit in the U.S. international accounts because it represents a demand for dollars and a supply of foreign monies. Line 5 shows the flow of investment income from Americans to foreigners. It is a debit item in the U.S. international accounts. Line 6 shows the balance on investment income. The balance was positive throughout the period shown in Table 1, but the positive balance declined between 1982 and 1987. If the U.S. national debt continues to rise, this balance threatens to turn negative because of interest payments to foreign holders of U.S. government securities.

Current Account Balance   The **balance on current account,** sometimes called simply the **current balance,** is also easy to derive. It adds transactions in services and unilateral transfers such as individual gifts and foreign aid (line 7 in Table 1) to the balance of trade and the balance on investment income. The current account balance is shown on line 8 of Table 1. It became negative between 1967 and 1972. Its negative balance increased enormously between 1982 and 1987 mainly due to the larger negative entry for the trade balance.

The balance on current account, or current balance, adds such items as transactions in services and unilateral transfers to the balance of trade and the balance on investment income.

Capital Account Balance   The figures on lines 9 to 11 of Table 1 show the U.S. capital inflow (line 9), the U.S. capital outflow (line 10), and the *balance on capital account,* or *capital balance,* (line 11) as the difference between them. Both private and public capital movements are included in all of these accounts. We need go into detail only with regard to the capital outflow, or export figures.

The balance on capital account, or capital balance, is the difference between capital inflow (imports) and capital outflow (exports).

Capital exports, or outflows, are purchases of foreign assets and should not be confused with exports of capital goods. The foreign sellers of foreign securities, foreign real estate, or the control of a foreign firm ordinarily demand foreign money in payment; the exporters of trucks or oil-well rigs ordinarily demand domestic money. So a capital export is a debit item, whereas a capital-goods export is a credit item.

Capital outflows (line 10) include private purchases of foreign assets and similar purchases by the government. Capital imports, or inflows (line 9), are presented in the same way. Changes in the government's official reserves of gold, convertible foreign monies, and credits with the International Monetary Fund are treated separately (line 13).

Statistical Discrepancy   When we add a country's balance on current and capital account (Table, 1, lines 8 and 11), including also the change in government official reserves (line 13), the theoretical

result is zero, by the principles of double-entry bookkeeping. The sum is, in practice, never zero, and a special account called "statistical discrepancy" or "errors and omissions" is added to force a balance—*not* an approved accounting practice!

With the rise of illegal traffic in drugs and weapons (on current account) and of illegal capital flight (on capital account), the "statistical discrepancy" account has risen disconcertingly even though there was a significant decrease between 1982 and 1987 (see line 12 of Table 1). In fact, imports of all reporting countries taken together amount to $800 billion more than their exports—a "black hole" of international economics. Since trade with the moon and with outer space remains physically impossible, we ascribe the great bulk of this current-account discrepancy to crime, smuggling, and fraudulent evaluation.

Theoretically, a country's current account balance plus its capital account balance, and the changes in official reserves, should equal zero. In practice, it never does—a balance is forced by using a special "statistical discrepancy" account.

Balances of Payments   After the insertion of the artificial "statistical discrepancy" entry, each country's international accounts for each period are apparently in balance. So what is this thing called the balance of payments? Do not the payments always balance?

In practice, most attention focuses on the balance concepts already described—the trade balance, the investment-income balance, the current account balance, and the capital account balance. Is there any concept that gives an overall view and that could be called *the* balance of payments? One popular approach is to define a country's balance of payments is as the sum of its balance on current account and its balance on whatever capital-account transactions may have been undertaken for their own sakes, rather than merely in settlement for other transactions. Economists, however, are not mind readers, so how can they know the motivations of each and every capital movement?

They do not know, but use various rules of thumb to divide the capital accounts into autonomous items and settlement items.

Another concept of *the* balance of payments is the entry called "U.S. Official Reserves" on line 13 of Table 1. This line indicates small buildups or draw-downs of U.S. government holdings of "official reserve assets" each year. In the special vocabulary of balance-of-payments specialists, this means that the American "official settlements" balance was slightly in surplus or slightly in deficit. But the American government refuses to attach any precise meaning to these figures. It does not take sides among the several varieties of balance-of-payments concepts and does not publish balance-of-payments figures of its own.

A country's balance of payments is sometimes defined as the sum of its balance on current account and its balance on whatever capital-account transactions may have been under taken for their own sakes, rather than merely in settlement for other transactions. The entry for changes in U.S. official reserves also is sometimes used as an indication of the payments situation.

Balance of Payments Stages

A country's balances of trade and capital movements generally go through several stages of balance and imbalance in the course of economic growth and development. Table 2 illustrates one theory about how this happens. Plus signs (+) indicate credit balances, and minus signs (−) indicate debit balances. (Two pluses or two minuses indicate greater magnitude.) According to this view, a country such as the United States moves from the stage of an "immature debtor" to that of a "mature creditor" in the following way.

1. An **immature debtor,** such as the North American colonies in the seventeenth century, imports goods and especially capital goods. The result is a deficit in the goods and services entries of the balance of payments accounts. Payment is through

capital inflow from abroad, which is a positive item in the capital account. There is some return flow as loans are repaid, but the net flow still is positive.

2. A **mature debtor,** such as the American colonies in the eighteenth century and the United States through much of the nineteenth century, has developed agricultural exports (wheat, cotton, and tobacco), which turn its trade balance positive. It continues to import capital, but its return flow of dividends, interest, and loan repayments has become much larger over the years and the net flow is now negative.

An immature debtor imports goods, especially capital goods, resulting in a deficit in the goods and services entries of the balance of payments accounts. A mature debtor has developed agricultural exports, which turn its trade balance positive.

3. There is often an intermediate stage, which was cut short in the United States by World War I. The trade balance remains normally positive, but the country begins a net export of capital, mainly to less developed countries like Canada and Mexico. The return flow of dividends, interest, and loan repayments due to previous European loans and investments in America continues so that the combined return-flow account may go either way. The net flow is generally negative.

4. An **immature creditor,** like the United States from the end of World War I through World War II and until about 1960, exports enough capital to balance both return flows and continuing trade surpluses.

5. From the point of view of the payments balance, a **mature creditor,** like the United States today, tends to live off its income from investments abroad. Repayments from past capital exports exceed its present capital exports. The country's trade balance also turns negative, because some of its natural resources have been depleted and it has become a high-living, high-cost country. It is not unusual for a rich mature creditor country's receipts from repayment of past loans from any particular poor country to exceed its new exports of

TABLE 2
Balance of Payments Stages

Stage No.	Stage Description	Trade in Goods and Services	Capital-related Transactions		
			New Investments	Interest, Dividends, and Loan Repayments	Net Flow
1	Immature debtor	−	+ +	−	+
2	Mature debtor	+	+	− −	−
3	Intermediate	+	−	?	−
4	Immature creditor	+	− −	+	−
5	Mature creditor	−	−	+ +	+

This table lists five international payments stage through which a country may pass in the course of its economic development. Plus signs (+) indicate net credit balances, and minus signs (−) indicate net debit balances. Two pluses (+ +) or two minuses (− −) indicate greater magnitude.

capital to that country, so that money appears to be flowing from the poor country to the rich one. The capital flow between Latin America and the United States is following this pattern insofar as the Latin American countries are servicing their large debts to the United States. This pattern is therefore causing great resentment in Latin America. In the United States itself, the rise of the national debt has reduced the net new investments abroad and the receipts of "interest, dividends, and loan repayments'" entries in Table 2. Therefore, the net flow of capital-related transactions, which combines current and capital account items, is probably less positive than the typical case.

An immature creditor exports enough capital to balance both return flows and continuing trade surpluses. A mature creditor tends to live off its income from investment abroad.

Favorable or Unfavorable Balance?

An active, positive, or surplus balance of trade or payments is often called a **favorable balance.** It is thought to be a good thing. On the other hand, a passive or negative balance is often called a deficit, or **unfavorable balance**—a bad thing. These terms were developed by the mercantilist school of political economy, which dominated Western economic thought for 250 years ending in about 1750 and which is now being revived under the banner of protectionism. According to mercantile theory, which has never died, gaining and keeping positive international balances and accumulating treasure should be among the major goals of a country's trade policy.

A positive, or surplus, balance of trade or payments is called a favorable balance. A negative, or deficit, balance of trade or payments is called an unfavorable balance.

The mercantilist policy makes a good deal of sense when the macroeconomy's main problem is achieving or maintaining high employment, since exports add to aggregate demand and imports often have a negative effect. But when the main problem is inflation, or too little domestic aggregate supply, the reverse of the mercantilist policy makes sense. In order to control inflation, a negative balance is a good thing and a positive balance is a bad thing. Countries may restrict exports to hold down prices at home. For example, in the 1970s the United

States put restrictions on the export of Alaskan oil, building materials such as lumber, and animal feed such as soybeans. When a country is experiencing stagflation, with *both* unemployment and inflation, there is no general answer to the question of whether a positive or a negative balance is better.

A positive balance of trade is good if the economy is trying to achieve high employment, but when the main problem is inflation, a negative balance is good.

Readers may notice that the "favorable-unfavorable" terminology, like the mercantilist and protectionist viewpoints from which it developed, recognizes people's interests as producers but ignores their interests as consumers, which may be radically different. This point is emphasized further in the chapter which deals with free trade versus protection.

BALANCE OF PAYMENTS PROBLEMS

When one speaks of a country as suffering balance-of-payments problems, this usually means that the country is losing international reserves so persistently and rapidly at the current exchange rate that these reserves will soon be exhausted. This is a primary payments problem. An example of a primary balance-of-payments problem is Brazil, which, in the same decade, seemed condemned (in the absence of debt relief) to two large negative capital-related balances, a negative investment balance on debt service and a negative capital balance on the debt itself. These threatened to swallow up so large a portion of Brazil's positive export balance as to leave little for economic growth. To preserve its international reserves, Brazil claims to have sacrificed a decade of development. In ordinary times, primary balance-of-payments problems are now largely limited to developing countries. (This was decidedly untrue during periods of large-scale warfare and postwar reconstruction like 1914–1925 and 1939–1955.)

A balance-of-payments problem means that a country is losing international reserves of gold and convertible foreign monies so persistently and rapidly that these reserves will soon be exhausted.

Secondary payments difficulties arise when either a country's current or capital balance turns sharply negative, even without affecting its international reserve position. A large negative capital balance, however, is usually *not* a payments problem when it represents the accumulation of assets overseas. In the 1980s, the Japanese case is the obvious example. For the first two-thirds of the twentieth century, the obvious example was the United States. Continued *accumulation* of reserve assets may, however, be unwise. Why not buy more foreign goods or other foreign assets instead? Why emulate King Midas, the legendary hoarder of gold?

SOLUTIONS FOR PAYMENTS PROBLEMS

The treatment of payments problems, whether primary or secondary, presents a maze of unsolved problems in both theory and policy. Economists want not only to remedy the difficulties but to do so at minimum cost in terms of income, employment, development, and economic freedom. Although we must leave full analysis to more advanced students in international trade and finance, our introductory discussion in terms of domestic policy can be helpful as a first step.

Consider, for example, what is called the "classical medicine" of **laissez faire**. This policy permits prices and wage rates to fall until the trade and current accounts rise sufficiently not only for their own balance but also to compensate for any negative capital accounts. In macroeconomics this translates into a disinflationary monetary policy with passive fiscal policy.

A laissez-faire policy permits prices and wage rates to fall until the trade and current accounts

---

rise sufficiently to compensate for any negative capital accounts.

Many suggested remedies for balance-of-payments problems, however, go well beyond ordinary macroeconomic policy and introduce additional variables. We shall comment on a half-dozen of these.

Among the most popular, although perhaps less so than formerly, has been currency depreciation, or **devaluation**. It is usually intended to raise current balances by raising the prices of imports at home and lowering the prices of exports overseas. In the practice of the 1980s, it appears to have raised capital account balances instead. For example, in the American and Japanese cases, as the dollar fell and the yen rose, U.S. assets became better bargains than U.S. goods.

International loans—bilateral or multilateral, conditional or unconditional—are additional capital movements. They raise either the present capital balance or the present international reserve position of the receiving country, at the expense of future balances when the loans are serviced or repaid.

International aid is a pure transfer, increasing the receiving country's current account and international reserves. It need not be repaid and makes negative payments balances easier to live with, pending growth or technical change to permit receiving countries to restore their economic health. The Marshall Plan from the United States to western Europe in the late 1940s and early 1950s is the classic example of success here.

Protection of domestic industries that face competition from imports and *subsidy* of export industries increases trade and current balances, at the expense of consumers and taxpayers. They may also attract foreign capital to locate inside the country and thereby avoid the tariff and other trade restrictions. If so, they increase the country's capital balance as well.

Exchange controls can increase a country's current account by disallowing entire classes of foreign-exchange purchases—for foreign travel, for transmission of investment income, etc. Controls can also increase the capital balance by disallowing

both capital export and debt repayment. They are in practice difficult to enforce without major restrictions on fundamental personal liberties.

Countertrade is a modernized version of primitive barter. It is the direct exchange of contracted amounts of goods (or occasionally services) between two or more countries, with (almost) no pressure on the international reserves of any of the trading partners. When one trading partner is a large country like Nazi Germany, on whom a number of economic or political satellites are economically dependent for goods, for markets, or both, the satellites often lose from such arrangements. They may lose by accepting lower terms of trade for their goods than they might have obtained on the world market, by accepting imports they do not want and must re-export, or by exporting goods they need for home consumption.

Countertrade is the dominant trading system of the Comecon (Soviet bloc) countries,[9] many of which would apparently prefer to reduce their dependence on countertrade with the Soviet Union in favor of ordinary trade with the hard-currency countries of the West. Their particular grievance is that they must export goods they need for home consumption.

Much countertrade is not reported to international authorities. Some suggest that as much as a third of all world trade is carried on in this way, but these estimates include "in-house" trading between branches of affiliated multinationals, partners in joint ventures, etc.

Suggested remedies for balance-of-payments problems include currency depreciation, international loans, international aid, protection of income-competing industries and subsidy of export industries, exchange controls, and countertrade.

---

9. The Comecon system is not pure countertrade. Accounts are kept in world prices and, at year's end, outstanding balances are in principle settled in Soviet rubles.

Economics in Focus

Buying and Selling America

Who owns America? Not long ago, such a question would have prompted debate about the roles of big business, government, the average worker and homeowner, and other traditional segments of American society. Now, however, the answer is likely to be a shouted chorus: America is owned by the British! By the Japanese! By all of the foreign investors who are buying up not only American stocks and bonds but also entire corporations and large chunks of real estate.

By 1988 the value of U.S. assets owned by foreigners was estimated at $1.5 trillion. The largest landlord in Manhattan was Canadian, and major portions of other American cities were owned by the Japanese. Firestone Tire was purchased by Bridgestone, a Japanese company. RCA Records went to Bertelsmann, a giant media firm from West Germany. Such familiar American brand names as Endicott Johnson shoes, Ball Park franks, and Inglenook wines belonged to the British. Foreign investment in the United States was setting new records each year—$40.6 billion in 1987 alone—and increasingly it was directed toward "hard" assets, such as land and manufacturing, rather than bonds or stocks.

The reasons for this trend were clear. The continued U.S. trade deficits left foreigners with large quantities of dollars to invest, and the best buy for a dollar was in America. Moreover, because of the stock market crash of 1987, as well as fluctuations in the bond market and in currency exchange rates, foreign investors were wary of paper assets; they preferred tangible property whose value would grow over the long term.

The general public's reaction to the trend has been overwhelmingly negative. In a survey conducted by Smick Medley & Associates, 78 percent of the respondents said they would like to see limits placed on foreign purchases. But many economists have argued that the wave of foreign investment has much to recommend it. First, the foreign money has financed American economic growth. Foreign owners have created jobs for American workers, and they are paying $80 billion in wages each year, not to mention $8 billion in corporate taxes. In addition, they have brought in new technology and production techniques that will benefit American industry for years to come.

As of the late 1980s, U.S. holdings abroad still exceeded the total value of foreign investment in America. Besides, the much-feared foreign assets accounted for only 2 percent of U.S. corporate profits. Thus most economists have seen no immediate reason to panic. On the other hand, they do believe the rapid pace of foreign acquisition should not go on indefinitely. In the long run, if the current trends persist, the U.S. standard of living will decline and foreign investors will control large segments of the American economy. The solution, in the view of many observers, is not to penalize or exclude foreign buyers but to increase the U.S. saving rate and improve the trade deficit.

Sources: Jaclyn Fierman, "The Selling of America (Cont'd)," *Fortune,* May 23, 1988, pp. 54–64; Gene Koretz, "The Buying of America: Should We Be Worried?" *Business Week,* May 9, 1988, p. 36; Peter Brimelow with Lisa Scheer, "Is the Reagan Prosperity for Real?" *Forbes,* October 31, 1988, pp. 85–90.

SUMMARY

1. Open economies cannot conduct economic policies as though they were closed to international trade and capital movements. What the rest of the world does affects the economy of a country. (See page 405.)

2. The money of one country is exchanged for the money of another country in foreign exchange markets. These markets are needed in international trade because people wish to be paid in the money of their own country. (See page 406.)

3. The intersection of the demand curve and the supply curve in the foreign exchange market indicates the equilibrium foreign exchange value of a nation's money. Purchasing power parity exists when the buying power of a country's money for traded goods and services is the same at home as abroad. Transactions on the capital account involve the concept of rate-of-return parity, where the rate of return on a dollar invested at home is the same as it would be if that dollar were exchanged for the foreign money and invested there. (See pages 409–410.)

4. Countries may try to raise the exchange value of their money by using their gold and foreign exchange reserves to supplement the demand for their money. They may lower its exchange value by selling their own money in the foreign exchange market. (See page 410.)

5. The argument for flexible exchange rates is that they do a more efficient job of pricing goods and allocating resources than do government-controlled rates. Moreover, government attempts to control rates often break down and cause serious problems. (See page 411.)

6. The argument for fixed exchange rates is that they reduce uncertainty and thus help international trade and investment. Moreover, since governments usually influence exchange rates anyway, it is better that it be done openly. (See page 412.)

7. Under the gold standard, monies are linked to each other because each is guaranteed to be exchangeable for a stated amount of gold. Under this system, gold and trade flows tend to force the price levels in gold-standard countries into fixed relationships, corresponding inversely to the gold backing of their monies. The gold-standard system

collapsed in the unstable economic conditions following World War I. (See pages 412–413.)

8. The International Monetary Fund was set up near the end of World War II to make loans to countries to help them hold the exchange value of their monies in line with fixed exchange rates approved by the IMF directors. This fixed-exchange-rate system broke down in 1971 when the United States refused to continue to exchange gold for dollars, thus letting the reserve money itself float in foreign exchange value. (See page 413.)

9. Eurocurrencies are deposits of a country's money in banks in a foreign country. These deposits are free from their issuing government's controls over reserve ratios, interest rates, and the quality of loans. The advantages of this freedom from control have led to a great expansion of Eurocurrency accounts. (See pages 414–415.)

10. Balance of payments accounts record transactions that involve demands (credit entries) and supplies (debit entries) for a nation's money in international payments. Widely recognized concepts of balance are (a) the balance of trade, (b) the balance on investment income, (c) the balance on current account, (d) the balance on capital account, and (e) the official settlements balance of payments. (See pages 415–416 and Table 1, page 417.)

11. If the sum of a country's current and capital accounts is positive, the country's balance of payments is in surplus. If the sum is negative, its balance of payments is in deficit. (See pages 418–419.)

12. It is sometimes suggested that countries move through several balance of payments stages in the course of economic development. They start as immature debtors and end as mature creditors, living off dividends and interest from previous investments abroad. (See pages 419–420 and Table 2, page 420.)

13. Following mercantilist views, a positive payments balance usually is considered favorable and a negative balance is unfavorable. However, in terms of macroeconomic policy, these judgments depend on whether the goal is to expand the economy or to fight inflation. (See page 420.)

14. A country has a primary payments problem if its international reserves of gold and convertible foreign monies are low and its balance of payments is usually negative. (See page 420).

15. A country has a secondary payments problem (1) if its current account is in deficit but its payments are balanced by undesired capital imports, or (2) if its capital account deficit, or *capital flight*, is absorbing a large portion of the export surplus the country had hoped to use for other purposes. (See page 420).

16. Remedies for payments problems, either primary or secondary, include price deflation—the so-called "classical medicine" of laissez faire—currency devaluation or depreciation, international aid or lending, trade protection, exchange controls, and countertrade. (See pages 421–422.)

KEY TERMS

appreciation: an increase in the exchange value of a country's money in the foreign exchange market (page 409).

balance of payments account: the record of transactions affecting the international demand and supply for a nation's money (page 416).

balance of trade: the amount by which the value of a country's exports of goods exceeds or falls short of the value of its imports of goods (page 417).

balance on current account (current balance): the balance of trade plus the balance on investment income plus such items as transactions in services and unilateral transfers (page 417).

Bretton Woods system: international financial arrangements that fixed exchange rates and were built around the International Monetary Fund. It was set up just before the end of World War II (page 413).

competitive depreciation: the practice of causing a depreciation of a nation's money for the purpose of achieving an exchange value lower than that of the monies of competing countries (page 413).

current balance: see **balance on current account.**

depreciation: a decrease in the exchange value of a country's money in the foreign exchange market (page 409).

devaluation: lowering the official exchange value of a country's money (page 422).

dirty float: when individual governments try to influence the exchange value of their money by buying or selling large amounts of foreign exchange (page 414).

Eurocurrency: a deposit of a country's money in a foreign bank which is, therefore, free of the issuing government's regulations about reserve ratios, interest rates, and the quality of loans (page 414).

European Currency Unit (ECU): the monetary unit of the European Economic Community (page 415).

exchange controls: a set of regulations governing licenses required to buy foreign money and permission to buy luxury imports, to travel abroad, or to buy foreign securities or other assets (page 422).

exporting unemployment: causing unemployment to decrease at home and increase abroad by restricting the import of foreign-made goods (page 413).

favorable balance: an active, positive, or surplus balance of trade or payments; the value of exports exceeding the value of imports (page 420).

fixed exchange rates: foreign exchange rates maintained through government or international monetary agency intervention (page 410).

foreign exchange: the money of other countries (page 406).

foreign exchange markets: markets in which the monies of different countries are exchanged (traded) for one another (page 406).

free (floating, flexible) exchange rates: foreign exchange rates that are free to move up or down in response to shifts in demand and supply curves arising from the ordinary operations of international trade and finance (page 410).

gold standard: a system for fixing exchange rates through a country's promise to exchange its money for a fixed amount of gold (page 412).

immature creditor: a creditor country that exports enough capital to balance both return flows and continuing trade surpluses (page 419).

immature debtor: a debtor country that imports goods, especially real capital goods (page 419).

inconvertible currency: the money of a country that does not allow it to be freely exchanged for money of other countries (page 411).

International Monetary Fund (IMF): an agency established just before the end of World War II by the major trading countries to maintain stable exchange rates and to avoid competitive depreciations and devaluations (page 413).

laissez faire: a policy of government noninvolvement in economic affairs (page 421).

mature creditor: a creditor country that tends to live off its income from investments abroad (page 419).

mature debtor: a debtor country that has developed agricultural exports, which turn its trade balance positive (page 419).

purchasing power parity: when a country's money will buy as much in traded goods abroad as it will at home (page 410).

rate-of-return parity: when the rate of return on a unit of money invested at home is the same as it would be if that money were converted into the money of a foreign country and invested there (page 409).

revaluation: changing the official exchange value of a country's money (page 422).

tariffs: taxes on imported goods (page 406).

unfavorable balance: a passive or negative balance of trade or payments; an excess of the value of imports over the value of exports (page 420).

DISCUSSION QUESTIONS

1. Construct a graph showing the demand and supply for U.S. dollars in the foreign exchange market. Describe an action that the U.S. government might take or a development in the U.S. economy that would cause the dollar to depreciate in exchange value. Use your graph to illustrate why this would happen.

2. What interests in the American economy benefit when the dollar rises on the international exchange markets? What interests benefit when the dollar falls?

3. What is the difference between fixed and flexible exchange rates? What are the advantages and disadvantages of each for the United States?

4. It is often proposed in conservative circles that the United States return to the gold standard, but not to the pre-1971 gold price of $35 an ounce. How do you think an appropriate gold price might be estimated? What would happen if the estimate were seriously wrong in either direction?

5. What are Eurodollars? Why are they important to an entrepreneur?

6. Explain how it can happen that a country can have a positive balance of trade at the same time that it has a negative balance of payments, or vice versa.

7. Explain why an export of a country's capital and an export of capital goods (such as machinery) have opposite effects on a country's international balances.

8. Analyze the effects of a currency devaluation on a country's balances on current and capital account if both its domestic demand for imported goods and services and foreign demand for its own goods and services are completely unresponsive to price changes.

9. Does the United States have either a primary or a secondary payments problem?

Appendix:
International Macroeconomics*

THE POLICY AUTONOMY ISSUE

Most countries and their governments believe that it is important to protect their freedom to choose and carry out internal fiscal and monetary policies with little thought about the rest of the world. But whether this policy autonomy favors fixed or flexible exchange rates depends on whether fiscal or monetary tools are most important to the country's policy. On the one hand, freedom to use fiscal policy for lowering the measured unemployment level is protected more fully under fixed rates. On the other hand, freedom to use monetary policy for the same purpose is protected more fully under flexible rates. Let us see why this is so.

Expansionary fiscal policy, aimed at reducing measured unemployment, usually raises government budget deficits. These deficits must be financed. If inflation is to be avoided, financing a deficit requires an increase in the supply of government securities. This increase lowers security prices and raises interest rates. In the foreign exchange market, the higher rates shift the demand curve for the country's money to the right, because the opportunity of earning higher returns makes the country a more attractive place for foreigners to invest—and makes foreign countries less attractive places for the country's own citizens to invest. Under floating rates, the resulting inflow of capital causes an appreciation of the country's money. With this higher value of the country's money, its exports may fall and its imports may rise, making the expansionary fiscal policy less effective. Under fixed rates, higher net capital inflows promote the expansionary policy without interfering with international trade. Instead of currency appreciation, there is an accumulation of foreign currency re-

serves, sometimes called a *positive balance of payments*.

Expansionary monetary policy, on the other hand, favors flexible exchange rates. Expanding the money supply would normally lead to lower real interest rates in the short run (see Chapter 14). Fixed exchange rates would increase the flow of capital out of the country and would mean less investment at home. Under floating rates, however, there would be a lower exchange value for the country's money, reducing the capital outflow, encouraging exports, and discouraging imports.

Freedom to use fiscal policy to lower measured unemployment is more fully protected under fixed rates. Freedom to use monetary policy to lower measured unemployment is more fully protected under flexible rates.

For countries wishing to disinflate—reduce their inflation rates—these arguments work in the opposite direction. As witnessed in the early 1980s in the United States, disinflationary *monetary* policy raises interest rates at home and brings capital inflows. Disinflationary *fiscal* policy, by lowering interest rates at home, raises capital outflows. So a country that is trying to lower its inflation rate by monetary means would favor fixed exchange rates to avoid a loss of exports. If such a country stresses fiscal disinflation, it would favor flexible rates to help its exporters. Table 3 sums up each of these cases.

A country that is trying to lower its inflation rate by monetary means would favor fixed exchange rates. A country that stresses fiscal disinflation would favor flexible rates.

---

* The material in this appendix presumes that students have already studied macroeconomics.

TABLE 3
Which Exchange-Rate Regime Maximizes Internal Macroeconomic Policy Autonomy?

| Primary Policy Instrument | Policy Goal | |
	Reducing Unemployment	Disinflation
Fiscal policy	Fixed rates	Flexible rates
Monetary policy	Flexible rates	Fixed rates

PAYMENTS EQUILIBRIA AND DISEQUILIBRIA

In our study of the domestic economy, we have learned that it tends at any time to an equilibrium real income and an equilibrium real interest rate. But these domestic-equilibrium values will not necessarily equilibrate the country's international payments as well. On the contrary, they may leave the country accumulating reserve assets it does not particularly want or facing the prospect of exhausting its reserves altogether.

Changes in a country's income level and interest rates affect its current and capital account balances in the following principal ways:

1. Changes in *income* affect primarily the *current* balance. A rise in income tends to decrease this balance because it brings about a rise in imports of goods and services. A fall in income tends to increase the current balance because it brings about a fall in imports of goods and services.

2. Changes in *interest rates* affect primarily the *capital* balance. A rise in the interest rate tends to increase this balance because it attracts capital from abroad and also reduces capital export by the country's own residents. A fall in the interest rate tends to decrease the capital balance because it repels capital from abroad and increases capital export by the country's own residents.

Changes in a country's income level affect primarily the current balance. Changes in

---

interest rates affect primarily the capital balance.

We also know that in an isolated economy:

1. An easy *fiscal* policy aimed at reducing unemployment tends to raise both income levels and interest rates. A tight fiscal policy aimed at disinflation tends to lower both income levels and interest rates.

2. An easy *monetary* policy aimed at reducing unemployment tends to raise income levels and lower interest rates. A tight monetary policy aimed at disinflation tends to lower income levels and raise interest rates.

An easy fiscal policy tends to raise both income levels and interest rates; an easy monetary policy tends to raise income levels and lower interest rates. A tight fiscal policy tends to lower both income levels and interest rates, while a tight monetary policy tends to lower income levels and raise interest rates.

It follows that an easy *fiscal* policy, taken by itself with monetary policy passive, will tend to reduce the country's *current* account balance and increase its *capital* account balance. An easy *monetary* policy, however, taken by itself with fiscal policy passive, will tend to reduce *both* the current and capital account balances. A tight fiscal policy, with monetary policy passive, will tend to increase the country's current account balance and decrease its capital account balance. A tight monetary policy, with fiscal policy passive, will tend to increase both the current and capital account balances.

For the more interesting cases where fiscal and monetary policy operate together, we combine all the preceding information and derive Table 4. This table summarizes the effects of different policy combinations on both the current and capital accounts of the country concerned. (A zero entry in the table indicates only that the policies counteract each other to some extent, not that they must offset each other completely.)

TABLE 4
Effects of Fiscal-Policy and Monetary-Policy Combinations on Current and Capital Account Balances

			Aim of Fiscal Policy	
			Reduced Unemployment	Disinflation
Aim of Monetary Policy	Reduced Unemployment	Current Account	−	o
		Capital Account	o	−
	Disinflation	Current Account	o	+
		Capital Account	+	o

The primary international effect of fiscal policy acts through changes in income and is on the country's current account. The primary international effect of monetary policy acts through changes in its real interest rate and is on the country's capital account.

(+) and (−) denote increases and decreases, while (o) denotes minimal or offsetting effects.

INTERNATIONAL MACROECONOMIC IDENTITIES

There are many important connections between the macroeconomics of the domestic and the international economies. A great deal of political and journalistic discussion of international trade and finance is flawed by violation of one or more of three fundamental macroeconomic identities that arise from these connections—or by reading particular causal patterns into them.

There are three basic macroeconomic identities that arise from the connections between the macroeconomics of the domestic and the international economies.

The first identity comes from our study of total planned expenditure and the circular flow. It is

$$Y = C + I + G + X - Im$$

where Y represents real GNP, C is consumption expenditure, I is investment expenditure, G is government purchases, X is exports, and Im is imports. Mercantilists read a special pattern of causation

into this identity. They say that net exports ($X - Im$) *determine* real GNP (Y).

Mercantilists say that net exports determine real GNP.

To derive our second identity, we examine the uses of income in the macroeconomics of a closed economy, that is, in an economy with neither exports nor imports. You can recognize these uses of income from the left side of the circular-flow diagram. With no imports, household uses of funds consist of consumption expenditure (C), saving (S), and net tax payments (T_n). Therefore, we have $Y = C + S + T_n$. To derive our second international macroeconomic identity, we subtract this equation from our first identity and get

$$(C + I + G + X - Im) - (C + S + T_n) = 0$$

The consumption terms cancel and the remaining terms can be rearranged into the form that we wish to use for the second identity. This is

$$(I - S) + (G - T_n) + (X - Im) = 0$$

This identity says that the sum of the three balances must be zero so that they cannot all be either positive or negative. The three balances are between private domestic investment and private domestic saving $(I - S)$, between government purchases and net taxes $(G - T_n)$, which is the public deficit,[10] and between exports and imports of goods and services $(X - Im)$, which is the current-account balance.[11]

The sum of three balances, $I - S$, $G - T_n$, and $X - Im$, must be zero.

The third international macroeconomic identity arises from the fact that international economic transactions are not limited to goods and services currently produced. Assets and titles to assets can also be transferred internationally. Therefore, payments for goods and services may take the form of either the creation or the transfer of assets—whether these are government securities or private IOUs. Conversely, payments for foreign assets may take the form of exports of goods and services currently produced.

To develop the third international macroeconomic identity, we will write X_k for capital exports and Im_k for capital imports. From the balance, $X_k - Im_k$, we exclude the change in monetary assets held as official reserves, which we label BP for balance of payments. We must then have, as accounting identities:

$$(X - Im) = (X_k - Im_k) + BP$$

which may be restated as

$$(X - Im) + (Im_k - X_k) - BP = 0$$

These identities state that a *positive* balance on current account $(X - Im)$ is also an acquisition of foreign assets, either in the form of a *negative* balance on capital account $(X_k - Im_k)$ or of a *positive* balance of payments (BP). Similarly, a *negative* balance on current account $(X - Im)$ is a diminution of foreign assets, either in the form of a *positive* balance on capital account $(X_k - Im_k)$ or a *negative* balance of payments (BP).

10. Confusion is easy at this point, because the deficit enters the identity as a *positive* item and a public surplus as a *negative* one.
11. *Not* the balance of trade. Strictly speaking, $(X - Im)$ is the current-account balance abstracting from international transfer payments, which do not enter into Y.

A negative balance on current account is a diminution of foreign assets.

Before we proceed to consider applications of these identities, let us review them and note that they can be expressed in terms of *changes*. The three identities are

$$Y = C + I + G + X - Im$$

$$(I - S) + (G - T_n) + (X - Im) = 0$$

$$(X - Im) + (Im_k - X_k) - BP = 0$$

In applying these identities to actual situations, we will be interested in year-to-year changes in values more than in absolute values. Therefore, it will be helpful to restate the identities in differentiated form, that is, in the form of changes. We use the symbol Δ (*delta*) to mean *change in*. In this form, the identities are

$$\Delta Y = \Delta C + \Delta I + \Delta G + \Delta X - \Delta Im$$

$$(\Delta I - \Delta S) + (\Delta G - \Delta T_n) + (\Delta X - \Delta Im) = 0$$

$$(\Delta X - \Delta Im) + (\Delta Im_k - \Delta X_k) - \Delta BP = 0$$

Illustration: The Trade Act

The omnibus trade act passed by the United States in 1988 provided protection against "unfair" imports and retaliation against "market closing" by America's trading partners to American exports. Debates leading to this legislation indicated that it was expected to raise the American current account balance (ΔX positive and ΔIm negative). These effects, in turn, were expected to raise income and employment (ΔY positive)—all without changes in American habits as reflected in other macroeconomic variables. Thus, the debates leading up to this act stressed the first identity in its differentiated form:

$$\Delta Y = (\Delta C + \Delta I + \Delta G) + (\Delta X - \Delta Im)$$

But when we consider our second identity in differentiated form,

$$(\Delta I - \Delta S) + (\Delta G - \Delta T_n) + (\Delta X - \Delta Im) = 0$$

it becomes clear that all the anticipated benefits of the trade act could occur only to the extent that income and employment increases were shunted into saving net of investment ($\Delta I - \Delta S$) and net tax payments net of government purchases ($\Delta G - \Delta T_n$). Did Congress and the media miss this point in the debate? Or did they ignore it as "too technical" for the average voter to understand? Probably both, but especially the first.

The trade act sought an increase in real GNP, but its supporters often failed to see that this result would also require changes in the other components of the second identity.

Illustration: Trade Shifting

Americans are sometimes urged to shift imports from country A (often East Asian) to country B (often Latin American) because the United States has a large negative bilateral trade balance with country A but not with country B. It should be clear immediately that such a shift would not raise the U.S. current account balance at all. Its effects would only be a cosmetic reduction of the bilateral balance with A, an injury to A's export industries, and perhaps some injury to American consumers.

Shifting trade from one trading partner to another will not raise the total U.S. current account balance.

Illustration: "Twin Towers"

The Reagan administration fiscal policies (such as tax cuts) combined with congressional qualms about cutting social spending and the ever-present local pork barrels, raised American budget deficits and the national debt in the mid-1980s both absolutely and as percentages of the GNP. At the same time, the American current account deficit rose to record levels, again both absolutely and relative to GNP. The budgetary and current-account deficits were called "twin towers" by the president's critics, on the theory that the current-account deficit was a *necessary* consequence of the budgetary one. This criticism involves our second identity which, in differential form and related to income growth

(ΔY) is

$$\left(\frac{\Delta I}{\Delta Y} - \frac{\Delta S}{\Delta Y}\right) + \left(\frac{\Delta G}{\Delta Y} - \frac{\Delta T_n}{\Delta Y}\right) + \left(\frac{\Delta X}{\Delta Y} - \frac{\Delta Im}{\Delta Y}\right) = 0$$

From this, it becomes clear that the rising budget deficit relative to GNP

$$\frac{\Delta G}{\Delta Y} - \frac{\Delta T_n}{\Delta Y}$$

might have been balanced by a fall in the private investment–private saving balance relative to GNP

$$\frac{\Delta I}{\Delta Y} - \frac{\Delta S}{\Delta Y}$$

that is, a rise in the ratio of private saving to GNP greater than the rise in the ratio of private domestic investment to GNP. But the saving ratio fell, and its fall was quantitatively more important than the rise in the deficit. Thus, the trade deficit, in fact, increased relative to GNP. The administration had hoped for and anticipated a higher saving ratio but also a higher investment ratio!

The "twin towers" viewpoint suggested that the trade deficit was an inevitable consequence of the budget deficit—but the identities show that this was not necessarily true.

Illustration: Predatory Foreigner or Prodigal American?

In attempts to explain the difficulties of the international economic position of the United States after approximately 1960, we encounter two rival scenarios, each a causal interpretation of our third international macroeconomic identity: $(\Delta X - \Delta Im) + (\Delta Im_k - \Delta X_k) - \Delta BP = 0$. One is the "predatory foreigner" thesis and the other is the "prodigal American" thesis.

The "predatory foreigner" thesis is as follows: by dumping and subsidizing their exports to the United States, by closing their domestic markets to U.S. exports, and by shifting to the United States the burdens of defense against aggression, foreigners have achieved positive current balances with the United States. These have cheapened the dollar in the world's exchange markets. Next, foreigners use their current surpluses to buy up American assets "on the cheap" (ΔIm_k). They have displaced the United States from its dominant position as the world's creditor and their holdings of both debt and equity securities permit them to influence American political and economic decision making in their own interests. If nothing is done, the United States will become their economic colony, with its workers limited to menial jobs and its government at the mercy of foreign bondholders' threats to refuse or to dump its securities. Thus, the "predatory foreigner" thesis traces causation from the current account balance ($\Delta X - \Delta Im$) to the capital account balance ($\Delta Im_k - \Delta X_k$).

The "prodigal American" thesis accuses America of three economic misdemeanors: (1) unrealistic expectations that its high wages and incomes (relative to foreign ones) were part of the natural order of things and should survive the rest of the world's recovery after World War II; (2) a penchant for fighting undeclared wars and overextending its commitments beyond its borders; and (3) living beyond its means domestically. Americans, it was said, financed their prodigalities by selling securities and other assets, including an increasing fraction of the rising American debt. To make American assets attractive to foreigners, in large amounts, their prices had to fall. So the value of the dollar has fallen, and American interest rates have stayed high. To finance such purchases of American assets, foreigners chose to reduce purchases of U.S. goods below what they would otherwise have been and also to sell aggressively their own goods in U.S. markets. Thus, the "prodigal American" thesis traces causation from the capital account to the current account.

The predatory foreigner thesis traces causation from the current account to the capital account, while the prodigal American thesis traces causation from the capital account to the current account.

The point is that these self-serving causal interpretations are at best half-truths that ignore many other things going on at the same time (such as the demographics of population and its distribution and the development and exhaustion of such resources as fossil fuel and agricultural land). The advantage of an algebraic identity, on the other hand, is that it expresses the result of *all* the forces acting on it—not just the one or two chosen with an eye to propaganda. At the same time, the maintenance of the identity may restrain the variability of each force taken individually, after the fashion of Newton's Third Law about forces generating their own counterforces. Our exercises in macroeconomic identities illustrate, we believe, the usefulness of economic analysis in understanding the complex world of international exchanges.

The advantage of an algebraic identity is that it expresses the result of all the forces acting on it—not just the one or two chosen with an eye to propaganda.

SUMMARY

1. Many countries wish to maintain their freedom to carry out domestic macroeconomic policy without adverse effects from international trade and capital flows. Whether this suggests flexible exchange rates or fixed exchange rates depends on whether the policies are aimed at reducing unemployment or at reducing inflation and on whether they are carried out with fiscal or monetary instruments.

2. An apparent equilibrium in a single country's macroeconomy may actually involve deficits and surpluses in the country's various international accounts.

3. These surpluses or deficits may be in either the country's current or its capital accounts and may be remedied in principle by changes in the country's macroeconomic policies.

4. Changes in a country's real national income and product affect primarily its trade and current account balances. The effects are inverse. Increases in real national income operate primarily to reduce the current-account balance by increasing imports, and vice versa.

5. Changes in a country's real interest rates affect primarily its capital-account balance. The effects are direct. Increases in real interest rates operate primarily to attract foreign capital and discourage capital exports.

6. A looser (tighter) fiscal policy tends to lower (raise) a country's current-account balance and raise (lower) its capital-account balance.

7. A looser (tighter) monetary policy tends to lower (raise) a country's current-account balance and also to lower (raise) its capital-account balance.

8. Three international macroeconomic identities assist in understanding relationships between the international and the domestic dimensions of the economy. These identities are

$$Y = C + I + G + X - Im$$

$$(I - S) + (G - T_n) + (X - Im) = 0$$

$$(X - Im) + (Im_k - X_k) - BP = 0$$

9. Negative U.S. balances on current account have been balanced by positive balances on capital account—the purchase of U.S. assets by foreigners. It has been feared that this may impair U.S. control of its resources and also the autonomy of its macroeconomic policy.

10. Applications of international macroeconomic identities reveal that the effects of legislation, such as trade shifting and the omnibus trade act, depend on accompanying actions taken in the domestic economy.

11. The U.S. budget deficit is associated with its current account deficit only because the U.S. private sector is investing more than it saves.

DISCUSSION QUESTIONS

1. Analyze the effects of a disinflationary monetary policy with fixed exchange rates on a country's balances on current account and capital account.

2. If the U.S. private saving rate rises to 10 percent of disposable personal income, what would happen to the country's international accounts?

3. Explain why a country's balances of private saving and investment, of public expenditures and receipts, and of exports and imports of goods and services, cannot all have the same sign.

4. If the U.S. public sector were to balance its combined budget, the so-called "twin towers" theory implies that the U.S. current-account deficit would also be eliminated. Is this correct?

5. Since the U.S. negative balance on current account is approximately balanced by a positive balance on capital account, why has it caused so much concern?

20
Economic Growth

Preview How have we progressed and whither are we drifting? The key questions of economic change, economic evolution, economic progress, or economic drift are usually treated by economists under two heads. One of these is the economic *growth* of those countries that have apparently progressed sooner and faster than the rest of the world. The other is the economic *development*, or underdevelopment, of the much larger group of countries, with a much larger population, that have developed later and more slowly. These are the so-called *less-developed countries* (LDCs). The two sets of problems are by no means independent of each other. A persistent question is: "Has growth of the rich countries advanced or retarded the development of the poor countries?"

This chapter is about the economic growth of the advanced countries, sometimes called DCs or MDCs (developed countries, more developed countries) in contrast to LDCs. These advanced countries include those in North America, Western Europe, and Australasia, as well as Japan, South Africa, and Israel, with a number of "newly industrializing countries" (NICs) knocking at the gates. Almost all the advanced countries are industrial, and some are postindustrial. This means that their nonagricultural sectors produce large and growing parts of their GNPs and national incomes. The manufacturing, mining, construction, and transport sectors dominate in the industrial countries, and the various service sectors (trade, finance, education, government, etc.) dominate in the postindustrial ones.

Are advanced countries rich because they are industrial, or industrial because they are rich? Or does some third factor (technical progress, perhaps, or human capital) account for both their greater wealth and their greater emancipation from agricultural stoop labor? Many hold strong views on these questions, but we do not know the answers.

The advanced countries might be thought of as the swanky suburbs of a largely underdeveloped world. We shall first consider why they have developed as they have. This is the relatively upbeat part of the chapter. We then discuss their prospects for future growth, assuming that it will take place at approximately the same rates as in the recent past. Here the picture is mixed, partly because of environmental problems and partly because of a mathematical problem. An economy growing at a constant percentage rate, or by constant amounts, must eventually "explode." That is to say, its GNP must eventually exceed any preassigned limit. It will approach infinity, as the mathematicians say. Since this is economically impossible, growth rates and growth amounts must eventually decrease. GNP must approach some upper limit. One international group of distinguished economists, engineers, environmentalists, and other social scientists, called the Club of Rome, expects demographic and environmental limits to growth to begin operating early in the next (twenty-first) century. Most economists, however, are less alarmist.

The general public assumes without question that economic growth is a good thing. This assumption, however, is not necessarily correct. We end the chapter by taking up the dissenting views in regard to the further growth of advanced industrial countries.

WHAT DOES GROWTH MEAN?

In a statistical sense **economic growth** is an increase in the real GNP of a country. Since some notion of improved material welfare is usually intended, an increase in per capita GNP is the most common measure. To put life into the abstraction of economic growth, think of a person born during or soon after the First World War (1914–1918) being asked by a grandchild; "Grandpa, what did people eat when you were a boy?" or "Grandma, when you were a girl, how could you have fun without TV?" The answers to questions like these are what growth "means." If the human life span were longer, answers to the questions of great-great-grandchildren would tell us even more about the meaning of economic growth.

Economic growth is an increase in real GNP, usually measured on a per capita basis.

Let us take for an example the period since World War I. Let us focus on the United States, which may have seen either more or less change than other advanced countries in the period we are considering. What are the principal advantages of "modern" life that the American youngster of, say, 1920, would have known nothing about except perhaps as amazing science fiction? (There was, of course, amazing science fiction well before 1920. Jules Verne in France and H.G. Wells in England were two great names in that field.)

To the grandchild, perhaps most immediately impressive would be electronic news and entertainment—radio, television, VCRs, and all that. The first American radio broadcast transmitted 1920 election returns from station KDKA in Pittsburgh. Boys and girls with technically gifted parents and older brothers or sisters could, soon thereafter, hear the squawks and squeals of stations in Chicago, New York, Montreal, or even Havana, often in the middle of the night. There were (silent) movies. Records could be played on (wind-up) phonographs.

Next came electric appliances—the refrigerator, home laundry, and vacuum cleaner. Some were completely unknown in 1920, while others were highly experimental, not to say temperamental. These, with the aid of frozen food (another newcomer), displaced domestic servants (maids, cooks, laundresses), icemen and, in many families, unmarried or retired relatives. We should also mention air conditioning. In 1920, the British foreign service considered Washington, D.C., a hardship post, due to its summer climate!

The automobile became an adult after 1920. True, the Ford Model T was commonplace nationwide in that year, and Henry Ford himself was many times a millionaire. But an automobile trip from Boston to New York was still a significant adventure. The rural road system alternated between choking dust and impassable mud. The shopping center was unknown. The horse and wagon dominated home deliveries, and the trolley car dominated urban transit as well as short-distance intercity transit—Boston to Worcester, Long Beach to Los Angeles, Chicago to Milwaukee, Hartford to New Haven.

As for the airplane, one was called outside to crane one's neck for a glimpse of a two-seater biplane when it appeared. Air travel was unknown. Intercontinental travel was by sea—a week across the Atlantic by the "monarchs of the seas," and ten days to two weeks across the Pacific in less pretentious vessels. Only the rich and adventurous went. The ordinary John or Joan Q. Public lived his or her entire life in one state, with perhaps a graduation, honeymoon, or retirement trip to one or two neighboring ones.

This listing leaves to the end the developments of nuclear power and electronic computation. To the grandchild, these may mean little more than computer games and shortcuts in homework, but they have revolutionized energy generation and business practice. Neither existed in 1920.

In numerical terms, the U.S. GNP was $482 billion in 1920, compared to $4,030 billion in 1988, both measured in 1982 dollars. The later figure was 8.4 times the earlier one—a rise of 3.2 percent per year on the average over that 68-year period.[1]

THE ECONOMIC GROWTH RECORD

After the Goths sacked Rome (A.D. 476), the various "barbarian" sovereignties of western Europe that succeeded the western Roman Empire had neither

hope nor ambition for what we call economic growth. "The glory that was Greece and the grandeur that was Rome" were apparently gone for good, relics of a vanished paradise of living standards, culture, and civilization. Survival sufficed for the "Dark Ages." The eastern Roman Empire, centered in Byzantium, of Constantinople, was more hopeful, and struggled on for nearly a thousand years before the fall of Constantinople to the Turks in 1453.

We can only guess when and why economic growth became an objective of various western European city-states—initially Venice and Genoa in northern Italy—and of emerging national states like Spain, Portugal, France, and England. Chiefly through the seven medieval Crusades, western Europeans became acquainted quite early with the wealth and power of the Arab and Turkish caliphates and sultanates of the Middle East and with the fading glories of the eastern Roman Empire. Later travels by Marco Polo, Christopher Columbus, Vasco da Gama, and their followers acquainted Europe with the wealth of India and China in the Far East and of the Aztecs and Incas of the New World. Europeans recognized the gains to be made from trade or conquest in these areas. Also, as gunpower replaced the armored knight, and the castle proved susceptible to artillery, the religious, dynastic, and other wars of Europe came to be fought largely with mercenary armies. Mercenaries had to be recruited and paid, not merely dragooned. They had the bad habits of going home, or deserting to the enemy, when the money ran out. Two centuries before Adam Smith's discourse in *The Nature and Causes of the Wealth of the Nations* (1776), monarchs, princes, barons, and republics alike had come to see wealth and income as routes to power as well as to luxury and also as attainable even beyond the levels they associated with the ancient world of Greece and Rome.

The West subsequently surpassed classical antiquity in economic matters and continued to grow. Important changes of economic structure occurred. Economic historians disagree as to what the most important of these changes were. They also disagree on whether change was gradual or "revolutionary." For example, was there any industrial "revolution" in Britain during the long reign of George III (1760–1820), or have we simply gener-

---

1. If a number, Y_o, grows r percent per period over n periods, its value at the end of the growth process, Y_n, is given by the formula:

$$Y_n = Y_o(1 + r)^n \quad \text{or} \quad \log Y_n = \log Y_o + n \log (1 + r)$$

By this formula, a number growing at 1 percent per year will double at the end of 69.7 years (not 100!). To check this result, solve for n when $Y_o = 1$, $Y_n = 2$, and $r = .01$. And if the growth rate is 2 percent, or .02, the number will double in 35.0 years (not 50!).

alized from the experience of a few industries, particularly the cotton textile industry?[2]

Economic growth gradually became an objective of western European countries during the course of the Middle Ages.

Changes in the economies of the West involved more than the development of the modern corporation and mass production. They also involved more than the shift in emphasis from **primary production** (agriculture, forestry, and fisheries) to **secondary production** (manufacturing, mining, construction, and transport) and eventually to **tertiary production** (the service industries of trade, finance, government, education, etc.). These changes are themselves among the things the economic historian needs to explain.

Some of the structural changes in the economies of the West are listed and discussed in the opening chapter of *How the West Grew Rich* by Nathan Rosenberg and L.E. Birdzell, Jr.[3] A slightly modified Rosenberg-Birdzell list of fundamental causes for the economic performance of the West since about 1500 includes:

1. The rise of an autonomous economic sphere and a merchant class with substantial and secure property rights, independent of royal courts, the military, and the established churches.

2. Innovation (invention made practical), plus other changes not usually considered invention at all. Rosenberg and Birdzell list extension of trade, discovery of new resources, introduction of new products, and lowering costs of production.

3. Development of sources of innovative ideas, including educational systems, patent systems, etc.

4. Diversity, uncertainty, and experimentation, as opposed to centralized, continent-wide patterns of doing things sanctioned by governments, by religious bodies, or by economic organizations like guilds and trade associations.

Fundamental causes for the economic performance of the West since 1500 include the rise of a merchant class, innovations and inventions, development of sources of innovative ideas, and diversity, uncertainty, and experimentation.

Equally important is the Rosenberg-Birdzell list of factors often claimed, by detractors of the West, to have largely explained Western economic growth but that Rosenberg and Birdzell downgrade. This list includes:

1. Natural resources

2. "Economistic" psychology

3. Inequalities of wealth and income

4. Slavery

5. Exploitation of less developed countries, including countries with higher degrees of civilization but less developed military arts and sciences

6. Miscellaneous misconduct by modern standards (looting, piracy, etc.)

7. Pure blind luck

Certainly these factors existed or occurred. The unsettled question, however, is just how important were they in the five-hundred-year sweep of modern Western economic history, or in the West as a whole? We shall see some of the more derogatory items on this list again, as explanations for the poverty of the LDCs. Look for them in the next chapter, under the heading "Dependencia Theories of Underdevelopment."

A SUPPLY-SIDE ECONOMIC GROWTH MODEL

We now turn from economic history to economic analysis to explain economic growth after its desir-

---

2. For the skeptical "new view" that change was evolutionary, and also the view that western European development did not follow the British model, see Rondo Cameron, "A New View of European Industrialization," *Economic History Review* (February 1985).

3. Nathan Rosenberg and L.E. Birdzell, *How the West Grew Rich: The Economic Transformation of the Industrial World* (New York: Basic Books, 1986).

---

ability and attainability became recognized by those in power.

To explain growth from the supply side (that is, based on inputs to production), it is natural for an economist to turn to one of his standard tools, a *production function*, such as

$$Y = f(K, N)$$

in which the symbols are defined as follows:

Y an estimate of the annual real GNP of a country.

K an estimate of the **rental value**—roughly, the sale value times the interest rate—of the country's capital (machinery and equipment) and natural resources.

N an estimate of the country's employed labor force—measured in years of labor (person-years), including self-employed and family labor at one end of a scale of liberty and slave labor at the other end.

Production functions such as this one explain economic growth quite well for periods of a generation or so.[4]

A production function shows the relationship between inputs and outputs for short periods—about a generation—but is unsatisfactory for long-term growth estimates.

Expanding their production-function analysis, many economists now break down the supply-side causes of economic growth into five broad groups of factors, with many individual items under each head. Edward F. Denison of the Brookings Institution and the United States Department of Commerce has been an international leader in this sort of work, devising both time series and comparisons between countries. The principal groups of causative factors in economic growth can be classified as:

1. The *quantity of labor* employed.

2. The *quality of labor* employed. This is seen as dependent on such subfactors as the education and age of the labor force and the length of the working week. Education is a plus and the decline of the work week is a minus. Also, a labor force should neither be too young nor too old.

3. The *quantity of capital* (machinery and equipment) and *natural resources* employed, with adjustments for depreciation and obsolescence. Land and natural resources are generally treated separately. Capital and natural resources that are available but not in use are a serious statistical problem, especially in recession or depression years.

4. The *quality of capital* employed, which includes technical change. For example a new-model computer or word processor is of higher quality than one of less recent vintage, because it embodies the most recent improvements, even when the older model is still usable.

5. **Disembodied technical change,** that is, technological change reflected incompletely or not at all in the quality of specific types of labor or machinery. Examples might be an improved road network or long-distance communications system.[5]

According to the supply-side model, the main factors of economic growth are the quantity of labor, the quality of labor, the quantity of capital, the quality of capital, and disembodied technical change.

---

4. But when short-run production functions are extended over longer periods, they significantly underestimate *Y*. The longer the period covered, the greater the underestimate. There is an unexplained residual, sometimes called the Abramovitz residual for the Stanford University economist who focused professional attention on it. Clearly, the ordinary production function is an unsatisfactory long-term growth estimator.

5. Disembodied technical change can be explained this way. Suppose an improved highway system lowers transport costs for both inputs and outputs and therefore shifts supply curves to the right for a wide range of industries in the neighborhood of the improved highway system. Some of these industries are agricultural, some are manufacturers of various kinds, and some may be service industries. The cost reductions and supply increases occur whether or not the highway-construction industry uses modernized equipment or whether any of the beneficiary industries do so. In technical terms, there is no embodied technological change anywhere in the economy.

Some Results from the Supply-Side Model

Let us compare U.S. GNP in 1983 with U.S. GNP fifty years earlier, at the inauguration of Franklin Roosevelt and the beginning of the New Deal in 1933. Both GNPs are expressed in 1982 dollars. The fifty-year growth rate was 3.97 percent per year (see footnote 1), almost precisely 4 percent.[6] Using this elementary and optimistic result for the United States alone as representing the world's advanced industrial countries generally, we can, perhaps, use 4 percent growth for such countries. This does not in the least deny the possibility of much higher growth rates over shorter periods of "miraculous" growth for Japan or Korea or Hong Kong, which were reconstructing after warfare or introducing foreign technology at abnormal speed. Japan, for example, grew at rates of 10.9, 8.7, 9.7, and 12.2 percent in four successive five-year periods, from 1951–1970.[7] For a really long-term trend, however, estimates of 4 percent growth (3 percent per capita if population rises 1 percent a year) are more likely to err on the high side than on the low.

Four percent growth per year, or 3 percent per capita growth, are hardly exciting numbers in themselves, but they accumulate rapidly over the generations, as illustrated in Table 1. The income figures are impressive, although too high to be credible, at least for the third and fourth generations. We offer, also, several other observations on the growth experience of the past half-century.

1. The rate of employment has been falling in the wake of the population growth rate (after adjustments for such shorter-period phenomena as the 1946–1958 baby boom that followed World War II).

2. Labor quality has been rising because of increased education and improved on-the-job training (OJT). This has more than offset a downward drift in the length of the working week, which affects labor productivity statistics in the same way as a quality decline.

3. There is as yet no evidence of a declining growth rate of the quality-adjusted labor force.

4. The growth rate of the capital stock has been greater than that of the labor force, both before and after adjustments for changes in quality.

5. The capital-labor ratio has grown, and at an increasing rate.

6. Measured average productivity per unit of labor and per unit of capital services, both unadjusted for quality change, have risen, especially for labor.

7. General, or multifactor, productivity has risen at an intermediate rate, lower than labor productivity but higher than capital productivity. **Multifactor productivity** is a weighted average of labor and capital productivity. The weights are the labor and property shares in the national income—between two-thirds and three-fourths for labor and between one-third and one-fourth for capital.

8. Productivity growth rates and growth rates of the national income fell below their long-term trends during the 1970s. These slow growth rates were largely caused by environmental concerns, energy supply shocks, and inadequate responses to them. There has been partial but not complete recovery in the 1980s.

Over the past fifty years, the rate of employment has been falling in the wake of the population growth rate, labor quality has been rising, the growth rate of the capital stock has been greater than that of the labor force, the capital-labor ratio has grown, and measured average productivity per unit of labor has risen, as has multifactor productivity.

The Neoclassical Growth Model

Observations and results such as those just cited yield a simple supply-side explanation of economic growth, sometimes called the **neoclassical growth model.** Its main idea is that a country's growth rate is the weighted sum of the changes in the productivities of its productive inputs (such as

6. Our comparison has some upward bias because 1933 was the bottom of the Great Depression and 1983 was a year of high prosperity. Short-term business fluctuations therefore raise the apparent long-term trend.

7. Yutaka Kosai, *The Era of High-Speed Growth*, Table 9-1, p. 4.

TABLE 1
The Power of Sustained Growth in Income

	4% Growth per Capita per Year	3% Growth per Capita per Year
Initial Per Capita Income (index number)	1.00	1.00
One generation later (after 25 years)	2.67	2.09
Two generations later (after 50 years)	7.11	4.38
Three generations later (after 75 years)	18.95	9.18
Four generations later (after 100 years)	50.51	19.22

Because growth in one year becomes part of the base for growth in the next year, sustained rates of growth result in large increases in income from one generation to the next. For example, with a sustained 4% a year per capita growth rate, grandchildren can be more than seven times as affluent as their grandparents.

changes in the output per hour of labor), changes in their qualities, and an additional term reflecting disembodied technical progress. The model involves major statistical problems of practical numerical estimations, some of which have caused professional controversy among statisticians.

According to the neoclassical growth model, a country's growth rate is the weighted sum of the changes in the productivities of its productive inputs plus an additional term reflecting disembodied technical progress.

A sample of the data used in neoclassical growth models for the United States is presented in Table 2. Note the important distinction between the *levels* of productivity in part A of this table and the *rates* of productivity growth in part B. In making sense of the figures, we should recall that "units of capital services" are overestimated in recession periods by the inclusion of machinery and equipment that is available but not actually in use. Also, automation and robotization raise "labor" rather than "capital" productivity because the equipment itself is expensive and because it makes possible increases in output with minimal increases in employment.

Table 3, estimated by John W. Kendrick of George Washington University, deals with the slowing of U.S. private sector growth rates from 1948 to the year 2000. Kendrick estimated that the growth rate of real gross product in the United States was 3.7 percent a year over the quarter century from 1948 to 1973, then fell to 2.1 percent a year from 1973 to 1981, but would recover to 4.0 percent in the decade from 1981 to 1990 and to 3.2 percent in the last decade of the century. Advances in knowledge and changes in labor quality made important contributions to productivity and growth in all periods studied. Other forces estimated by Kendrick seem to be neutral or negative.

The neoclassical growth model is often said to assume continuous full employment. In fact, it merely assumes that microeconomic market adjustments and macroeconomic fiscal and monetary policies work together to keep employment rates fairly steady. When unemployment rates are in fact rising, neoclassical growth projections tend to be overly optimistic. When unemployment rates are falling, neoclassical projections tend to err on the side of pessimism.

A DEMAND-SIDE ECONOMIC GROWTH MODEL

Assuming that a 4 percent real annual growth rate (3 percent per capita) is attainable on the supply side, is there any guarantee of its absorption on the demand side? To deal with this question, the rele-

TABLE 2
Levels and Rates of Change of U.S. Productivity, Selected Years, 1960–1987

A. Levels (index numbers, 1977 = 100)					
	1960	1970	1979	1983	1987
All private business					
Output per hour of all persons	67.3	88.4	99.5	103.0	111.2
Output per unit of capital services	103.7	102.7	99.7	88.3	93.7
Multifactor productivity	78.5	93.1	99.6	97.6	104.7
Manufacturing only					
Output per hour of all persons	66.2	80.8	101.4	112.0	131.9
Output per unit of capital services	103.0	99.1	99.5	86.7	102.0
Multifactor productivity	72.0	85.3	100.9	105.0	123.6

B. Annual Percentage Rates of Growth						
	1982	1983	1984	1985	1986	1987
All private business						
Output per hour of all persons	−0.2	2.7	2.5	2.2	2.2	0.8
Output per unit of capital services	−6.2	2.0	5.0	0.2	0.1	0.7
Multifactor productivity	−2.4	4.3	3.4	1.5	1.5	0.8
Manufacturing only						
Output per hour of all persons	2.0	5.8	5.4	4.6	3.3	3.3
Output per unit of capital services	−8.3	6.3	10.1	1.9	1.1	3.3
Multifactor productivity	−6.1	6.4	6.8	3.8	2.7	3.4

Source: Monthly Labor Review (December 1988), Table 43, p. 98.

vant apparatus comes from macroeconomics. We explore a growth identity devised by a Keynesian economist, Sir Roy Harrod, Keynes's official biographer.[8]

Harrod utilized a **capital coefficient** or **capital-output ratio** representing the amount of additional capital required, under current technology, for a unit increase in the net national product. His

8. Sir Roy argued as early as 1939 that the growth rate of the economy, $(\Delta Y/\Delta t)/Y$, where Y is GNP, t is a time period, and Δ stands for a small incremental change in the value of a variable, should be written, to the first approximation, as:

$$\frac{\Delta Y/\Delta t}{Y} = \frac{\Delta Y/\Delta t}{I} \quad \frac{S}{Y} = \frac{\Delta Y/\Delta t S}{\Delta K/\Delta t Y}$$

using the saving-investment identity in an economy with balanced public budgets and balanced current accounts in international trade. The second step in the derivation equates investment with an incremental change in the capital stock, which is true if investment is *net* of depreciation and obsolescence, in which case Y is no longer GNP but NNP.

incremental capital output ratio is written as $(\Delta K/\Delta t)/(\Delta Y/\Delta t)$, or simply as $\Delta K/\Delta Y$. If we use the symbol K for capital, t for a time period, Y for NNP, v for the incremental capital-output ratio, G for the growth rate, and s for the saving ratio (saving, net of depreciation, as a percentage of NNP), we have the Harrod equation (or identity):

$$Gv = s \quad \text{or} \quad G = s/v$$

The capital coefficient, or incremental capital-output ratio, represents the amount of additional capital required for a unit increase in the net national product. According to Sir Roy Harrod, an economy's growth rate (G) equals its saving ratio (s) divided by its incremental capital-output ratio (v), that is $G = s/v$.

TABLE 3
Sources of Growth in Real Gross Product for the U.S. Domestic Economy, 1948–1981,
with Projections to 2000

Source of Changes in Real Gross Product	1948–73	1973–81	1981–90	1991–2000
Changes in variables influencing productivity				
1. Advances in knowledge	1.4	0.7	1.2	1.0
2. Changes in labor quality[a]	0.5	0.6	0.9	0.9
3. Changes in quality of land	—	−0.2	−0.3	−0.3
4. Resource reallocations	0.4	0.1	—	—
5. Volume changes[b]	0.3	−0.3	0.6	0.4
6. Net government impact[c]	—	−0.2	−0.1	−0.1
7. Other productivity variables[d]	−0.6	−0.6	−0.5	−0.5
Subtotal (total factor productivity)	2.0	0.1	1.8	1.4
Changes in quantity of productive resources	1.7	2.0	2.2	1.8
Total change in real gross product	3.7	2.1	4.0	3.2

Note: Figures are averages of annual percentage rates of change.

a. Includes changes arising from education and training, health, and age-sex composition of labor force.

b. Includes effects of economies of scale and intensity of demand.

c. Includes services to business and the effects of government regulations.

d. Includes the ratio of actual efficiency to potential efficiency and items not elsewhere classified.

Source: John W. Kendrick, "Long-Term Economic Projections: Stronger U.S. Growth Ahead," *Southern Economic Journal* (April 1984), Table 1, p. 953. Used by permission.

The Harrod model can be illustrated with U.S. data. In 1985 the U.S. net national product was $3,192.0 billion, and net domestic private investment was $210.3 billion, both in 1982 dollars. In 1986 net national product (still in 1982 prices) rose to $3,278.5 billion, an increase of $86.5 billion.[9] If we ignore statistical discrepancies in these estimates, the Harrod equation gives us the following figures for 1986:

a growth rate (G) of 2.71%, that is, 86.5/3,192.0

an incremental capital-output ratio (v) of 2.43, that is, 210.3/86.5

a saving rate (s) of 6.59%, that is, 210.3/3,192.0

The year 1986 was prosperous, but not a high-growth year. All the above numbers, which are of course mutually consistent, are somewhat low by long-period standards. For a 4 percent growth rate

9. *Economic Report of the President, 1989*, Tables B-2 and B-17.

with an incremental capital-output ratio of 3, the United States would require a saving rate (combining private saving, any budget surpluses of government, and any international surplus on current account) adding up to 12 percent of the net national product.[10] This was not attained in 1986, and in fact the budget surplus and international current account numbers were negative. Thus, it appears that the check to American growth in the mid-1980s was neither oversaving nor a shortage of demand.

An equilibrium path of economic growth should satisfy both an expanded production function on the supply side and the Harrod equation on the demand side. But what happens if the paths diverge? To deal with this question, let us suppose an advanced economy cruising along at 4 percent

10. The Harrod equation can be adjusted to an international economy with current-account and budgetary imbalances by redefining saving (S) to include surpluses, as follows: $S = S' + [(T_n - G) + (X - Im)]$, where S' is private domestic saving, Tn is net taxes, G is government purchases, X is exports, and Im is imports.

real annual growth and at high employment equilibrium. There is a sudden shock either to the supply side or to the demand side. What is likely to happen? Even if the initial shock comes only from one side, we must consider consequences on both supply and demand.

An equilibrium path of economic growth should satisfy both an expanded production function on the supply side and the Harrod equation on the demand side.

Supply-shock cases are the easier ones to analyze, if not to deal with in practical politics. For example, should energy become scarce, the aggregate-supply curve shifts to the left and upward. In the Harrod equation, the capital-output ratio rises because, to compensate for the increased energy cost, more capital is required per unit of income increase. The growth rate falls. On the other hand, if a technical advance—safer nuclear power or cheaper solar energy—solves our recurrent energy crisis, the aggregate-supply curve shifts to the right. The capital-output ratio falls, and the growth rate rises. In each of these cases, workers may have to move to different jobs as the economy adjusts to different supply conditions, but, once the moves have been made, there is no reason, in economic theory, for total employment to fall.

Analysis of demand-side shocks is more difficult. For our first example, let us suppose a successful thrift campaign that increases the saving ratio with no change in the inducement to invest at any given interest rate.[11] The Harrod equation suggests that the higher saving ratio requires a higher growth rate. But what is there about a higher saving rate that *causes* income to grow faster? If a higher saving ratio means a drop in consumption purchases, a likely short-run effect of a thrift campaign would be a fall in employment. Then with less labor employed, there would be a *decline* in the growth rate. In the Harrod equation, less salable output would be obtained from the same capital

stock. In fact the capital-output ratio may rise by more than the saving ratio, if a lower interest rate encourages capital formation. However, in the absence of offsetting changes, a decline in the income growth rate is an expected outcome.

Now suppose a demand shock of the opposite sort—a successful campaign to increase domestic spending on current output. The saving ratio tends to fall, and interest rates tend to rise. If there is already high employment, and if the incentive to invest is presumed unchanged, the real income growth rate has little if any room to increase. Therefore, there must be a fall in the capital-output ratio approximately parallel to that in the saving ratio. Where does it come from? Primarily, one supposes, from the rise in the interest rate. The higher interest rate is the villain of the piece on the supply side as well, where it restrains the growth of both the quantity and the quality of capital equipment so that the growth rate moves little if at all.

LOOKING AHEAD

Thus far, our analysis of economic growth has been based mainly on economic history and its extrapolation. Its tone has been optimistic, although less so than it would have been at the beginning of this century. At that time, informed opinion was not only optimistic about economic growth but also held that long wars between the world's great powers were economically unprofitable and therefore obsolete. A sad mistake!

As the century draws to its close, following two enormously destructive world wars, it is difficult to remain optimistic about economic growth in advanced countries. In addition to the threat of renewed military spasms and to the difficulties of relationships between the advanced countries and less-developed countries, it is worthwhile to call attention to three problems related to continued economic growth in the advanced countries. These problems are:

1. Resource exhaustion and environmental pollution.

2. Aging of advanced-country populations and the prospect of intergenerational conflict.

---

11. In the loanable-funds market, we are supposing that the supply curve shifts to the right while the demand curve remains in its initial position.

3. Possible contradiction between distributional equity and the encouragement of growth through public finances.

Three principal problems that hinder continued economic growth in advanced countries are: resource exhaustion and environmental pollution, aging of advanced-country populations and the prospect of intergenerational conflict, and the dilemma of growth versus distributional equity.

Resource Exhaustion and Environmental Pollution

Ever since the dawn of civilization, and quite possibly before, mankind has been in the process of running out of exhaustible resources like wood, coal, oil, and metals. In the 1870s, the eminent British economist William Stanley Jevons wrote *The Coal Question*. His thesis was that Britain's industrial empire would fall because of exhaustion of its high-grade coal resources. Jevons was wrong, or at least premature, because non-British coal supplies came to the rescue and because other fuels replaced coal. Thus, technical "fixes," including cheap transport of foreign supplies, intervened to save the day. But can we be sure that technical fixes will always be available? Do we have replacements in the offing for petroleum? For uranium?

Environmental pollution, a great by-product of economic growth, raises two important economic issues that are, and may always remain, unsolved. The first is, whether (and by whom) the basic rules of the market game should be changed to ban "excessive" pollution—treating it like murder, robbery, and fraud. A less drastic action would recognize pollution as a cost of production and would internalize this cost by making producers pay for a "license to pollute."[12] Would such less drastic action suffice?

The second economic issue is how any worldwide scheme of regulating or reducing pollution can, simultaneously, (a) meet the concerns of environmentalists like the several Green parties of Europe, (b) maintain employment in "dirty" industries in advanced countries, and (c) permit industrial development in the LDCs. This is a tradeoff problem, and tradeoffs are conceivable, but how are the terms of the tradeoff to be determined and enforced?

Two questions about pollution are: (1) should the rules of market economies be changed to reduce pollution and (2) how can pollution reduction balance the concerns of environmentalists, workers in "dirty" industries, and the development hopes of LDCs?

As we enter the 1990s, the principal large-scale pollution problems include the following:

1. The gradual heating of the earth's atmosphere under the influence of increased carbon dioxide (CO_2) production. This is the so-called greenhouse effect. It threatens to melt both polar ice caps and to flood important coastal areas.

2. The destruction of the atmosphere's ozone (O_3) layer by hydrofluorocarbons and other emissions. This threatens to admit more carcinogenic ultraviolet rays from outer space.

3. The destruction of forests—in advanced countries by acid rain (sulfur dioxide, or SO_2, and other sulfur compounds)—and in other countries by rapid clearing of tropical rainforests.[13]

4. The killing of rivers, lakes, and even ocean areas with assorted chemical wastes, causing red tides and fish kills and threatening important parts of the food chain.

5. The threats of catastrophic disasters from nuclear-plant accidents —especially in areas sub-

---

12. A variant, which is more complex but which many economists find preferable, would be to subsidize low-pollution methods of production where they exist.

13. Many of the areas affected are in the LDCs. The motivation for the destruction in the LDCs is the export of lumber to the developed countries or the clearing of land for ranching and cash-crop agriculture, also primarily for export.

ject to earthquakes—and the accumulation of radioactive waste products.[14]

These pollution processes may be reversible. Some have already been reversed to some extent. For example, "dead" areas like Lake Erie, the Hudson River, and parts of Japan's Inland Sea have been restored to life. But reversing past pollution is expensive and directly competitive with provision for future growth as well as with various forms of private consumption, private investment, and public service.

Reducing pollution and using resources to undo previous pollution damage is directly competitive with economic growth.

Aging of Advanced-Country Populations

In economic demography, the immediate and direct issue for the world's advanced countries is the aging of their populations. Part of this problem—perhaps only the smaller part—is the anticipated decline of the quantity and quality of their labor forces. Aging enables an increasing proportion of advanced-country populations to leave the labor force to live in retirement. Meanwhile, there has been a tendency for retirement ages to fall while post-retirement second careers have not become popular. Labor-force participation rates for male workers over sixty have fallen. To make matters still worse, an increasing proportion of the active labor force will be rising into what are sometimes unkindly called the "dead wood" years shortly preceding retirement. In these years a worker's attention is supposedly fixed on the prospects for the good life ahead, with neither hope nor ambition for further advancement or recognition on the job. Of at least equal importance is the prospect of intergenerational conflict. It is symbolized by disquieting forecasts of the falling number of prime-age workers available, however unwillingly, to support each member of the elderly population in the style

14. Nor should we forget that the breakdown of uranium, in nature and without human intervention, has among its by-products a carcinogenic gas called radon.

to which the elderly feel entitled. The next step is doubt about the willingness of the young to bear the increasing burden of supporting the old. In the United States, at least, the elderly seem somewhat more inclined than are younger voters to exercise their rights to vote and have become conscious of their power to vote themselves expensive pensions, health care, and other entitlements at public expense.

Such trends need not, of course, lead to intergenerational conflict. A retired parent or grandparent can help a young man or woman begin his or her career in the same way as an employed parent or grandparent, given the same income. The retired parent or grandparent might even afford greater generosity than an employed one, if his or her future income and health-care are insured. But a real intergenerational problem may arise if the falling size of the nuclear family is reflected in a rising proportion of senior citizens with few close relatives who need their aid, or a rising proportion living isolated and alienated from younger family members. The reluctance of retirement communities to support bond issues for public schools may be an indication of a diversion of funds away from provision for growth toward support of the elderly. In his *Constitution of Liberty*, the philosophical economist Friederich Hayek wondered whether disenfranchising the elderly might not be desirable so as to limit the diversion of public funds to the elderly and away from, among other things, financing future growth.

The aging of the populations of advanced countries reduces the labor force and poses the prospect of intergenerational conflict.

Growth versus Equity

Providing for economic growth requires the saving and investment of resources in both the private and the public sector. We have mentioned the possibility, in an aging society, of such resources being drained away to support senior citizens. The poor and the near-poor of preretirement age are another large class of advanced-country populations with claims competing with those of economic growth.

Their claims to guaranteed useful employment, to self respect, and to guaranteed incomes above the conventional poverty line have been forcibly espoused for Americans in a pastoral letter by a group of Roman Catholic bishops (as well as others) under the leadership of Archbishop Rembert Weakland of Milwaukee. Do the costs of eliminating poverty, guaranteeing employment, and assuring distributional equity (in conformity with the moral law as interpreted by the bishops and others) include the slowing down of economic growth? Should we include, in the costs of economic growth, the toleration of "immoral" distributions of income and wealth and "immoral" rates of unemployment, longer than might be necessary in a static society? Economic policies, like economic goods, have their opportunity costs.

Answers to these questions are related to answers to another question that we avoided earlier in this chapter. Has the principal check to long-term growth come from the supply side (production functions) or the demand side (the Harrod equation)? Redistribution of income and wealth toward greater equality aims, after all, at increasing the consumption of necessities at the expense not only of luxuries but also of saving and investment as well. Insofar as the ceiling on growth is a supply-side matter of inadequate capital formation, there is a conflict between growth and distributional equity. But insofar as the ceiling reflects high capital-output ratios (capital coefficients) due to capital used below capacity by reason of inadequate demand, there may be no conflict at all. Rather, the reverse may be true.

Conflict may exist between the promotion of economic growth and the provision of guaranteed employment and distributional equity.

IS GROWTH A GOOD THING?

Most of us would rather be rich than poor, or at least we would like to have some of the comforts of life. Only a few of us really seek plain living, with or without high thinking. Those few become hermits, join communes, vow allegiance to Lady Poverty, and remember the sad emperor of China. (His psychiatrist proposed to cure his depression by having him sleep in the shirt of a happy man. When the happy man was found, he had no shirt!)

Advantages of Growth

The consumption advantages of higher income, and thus of growth, are clear despite the tendencies of MDC people to "'dig their graves with their teeth" and bang each other with automobiles. There are also security advantages if crime and environmental pollution can be controlled and if basic welfare can be assured without too great a cost in individual freedom or the right to privacy. There seems no doubt that the average MDC worker lives better than the medieval lord and lady did in their unheated castle, covered with "ermine and vermin," and expecting death or major illness before the age of fifty.

For society, growth yields a dividend, which can be used to raise the standard of living for those at the lowest levels and even redistribute income and wealth above these lowest levels without absolute loss to the "haves" or the community. The moral of Lester Thurow's *Zero-Sum Society* is that "doing something about poverty" is more costly to the rich and the middle class when the country's per capita income is stagnant than when it is growing.

The same principles hold between countries. MDCs can be expected to offer more aid to LDCs when MDC income per capita is growing than when it is not. And the more that world income growth slows down, the greater the likelihood that the LDCs must give up all ambition for catching up with today's MDCs.

There are personal consumption and security advantages to economic growth, and there are societal advantages as well in that growth yields a dividend that can be used to raise the standard of living for those at the lowest levels.

Antigrowth Arguments

Antigrowth literature is not quite as old (among economists) as progrowth literature, but it too dates back at least to the English classical school. David Ricardo (1772–1823), the greatest economist of his time, feared that growth would end in a "stationary state" as capital accumulated. Since capital was subject to diminishing returns, profits would fall to a low point, and net saving and investment would then fall to zero. This prediction, though less extreme than Marx's, helped to give economics the name of "dismal science."

John Stuart Mill John Stuart Mill (1806–1873) did not agree. His *Principles of Political Economy* (1848) included a *defense* of the stationary state and an attack on what we now call **growthmanship** (an overemphasis on measured economic growth). Here is a quotation:

> I cannot regard the stationary state with . . . unaffected aversion. . . . [It] would be a very considerable improvement on our present condition. I am not charmed with the ideal of life held out by those who think that the normal state of human beings is that of struggling to get on: that the trampling, crushing, elbowing, and treading on each other's heels, which form the existing type of social life, are the most desirable lot of human kind, or anything but the disagreeable symptoms of one of the phases of industrial progress.[15] . . . [The] best state of human nature is that in which, while no one is poor, no one desires to be richer, or has any reason to fear being thrust back by the efforts of others to push themselves forward. It is only in the backward countries of the world that increased production is still an important object; in those most advanced, what is economically needed is a better distribution. . . .
>
> . . . Nor is there much satisfaction in contemplating the world with nothing left to the spontaneous activity of nature; with every rood [unit of measure] of land brought into cultivation, which is capable of growing food; every flowery waste ploughed up, all quadrupeds or birds which are not domesticated for man's use exterminated as his rivals for food, and scarcely a place left where a wild shrub or flower could grow without being eradicated as a weed. If the earth must lose that great portion of its pleasantness which it owes to things that the unlimited increase of wealth and population would extirpate from it, I sincerely hope, for the sake of posterity, that they will be content to be stationary, long before necessity compels them to it.
>
> A stationary condition of capital and population implies no stationary state of human improvement. There would be as much scope as ever for mental culture, and moral and social progress; as much room for improving the Art of Living, and much more likelihood of its being improved, when minds cease to be engrossed by the art of getting on.

Ezra Mishan The twentieth-century equivalent of Mill (in his antigrowth opinions) has been Ezra Mishan, author of *The Costs of Economic Growth* and *The Economic Growth Debate*. Mishan puts Mill's points in today's context. He sees industry, urban sprawl, the automobile, and tourism as great dangers to the environment. And he fears the effects on human life of radio, television, air travel, the computer, herbicides, pesticides, the civilian and military applications of nuclear technology, and other recent inventions.

Erich Schumacher Erich Schumacher wrote *Small Is Beautiful*, subtitled *Economics as if People Mattered*. Economists, incidentally, agree that they do! Schumacher is not against growth but against *growthmanship*. He wants a world in which people live in greater harmony with their natural environment than they do in large cities. In such a world, people will have interesting jobs, which they need not fear losing to machines or to robots. He wants people to know where their work fits into some useful finished product, and to be regarded as something more than faceless numbers on time cards or stations on assembly lines. He believes that excessive concern for higher measured growth has

15. At this point Mill's first edition paid its respects to the United States. "The northern and middle states of America are a specimen of this stage of civilization in very favourable circumstances; the proportion of capital to land is such as to ensure abundance to every able-bodied member of the community who does not forfeit it by misconduct. All that these advantages seem to have done for them is that the life of the whole of one sex is devoted to dollar-hunting, and of the other to breeding dollar-hunters." This passage was later dropped.

pushed the division of labor, the substitution of machinery for human skills, the alienation of the worker, and the pollution of the environment too far. These trends not only should be prevented from spreading to the LDCs but should be reversed in the MDCs. The key to this better world is "appropriate technology," an undefined term in Schumacher's book. It may not always exist. A major task is to develop it when it does not, as well as to apply it when it does exist despite any sacrifice in growth.

Limits to Growth Another strain of antigrowth literature tells us that growth will end in catastrophe. Technical fixes for one problem will give rise to other problems—or make other problems worse. The best-known "model of doom" is *Limits to Growth*, published by the Club of Rome.

The Club-of-Rome analysis of growth begins with an undeniable mathematical fact. Growth of any quantity at any constant rate "explodes," going beyond any finite upper limit. For this reason, it is impossible, in the long run, unless the upper limit is itself growing at the same rate (or at a higher one). But given a finite limit set by the earth's resources growing only slowly or not at all (and they may be falling!), the growth rate must eventually fall toward zero.

The Club-of-Rome pessimism, however, is more immediate than we have suggested so far. If population, especially in the LDCs, continues to explode, and if per capita real income and product levels as a consequence decline, some terrible combination of fatal maladies lies ahead in the short-term future (twenty-first century). There will be starvation, war, and disease if the food supply runs out. If countries return to agricultural production, living standards will fall sharply. There will be a sharp rise in environmental pollution if technical fixes are used to keep total output rising on a limited resource base. *Limits to Growth* spells out these alternatives in the language of computer simulation. However, the underlying statistical proofs for the equations fed into the computers are not always made clear. The Club of Rome sees "hope" only in drastically limiting population in the short-term future.

Arguments against growth include John Stuart Mill and Erich Schumacher's attacks on growthmanship, Ezra Mishan's concerns about the environment and the quality of human life, and fears about the ultimate outcome of continued growth.

Economics in Focus

South Korea: Two Sides of a Miracle

The startling growth in the South Korean economy has been called a miracle, and the statistics look miraculous indeed. Between 1953 and 1988 the real national income in South Korea rose 1,200 percent. Back in 1961 the per capita GNP was less than $100 a year; by 1988 it was nearly $3,000. In some years the economy's growth rate has reached 14 percent, propelled by a population that seems to thrive on a 54-hour work week. As a result, South Korea has become one of the young powerhouses of world trade—the "next Japan," many observers have said.

The spectacular growth began after the coup that installed Park Chung Hee as president in 1961. Park's government borrowed large sums of money, mainly from the United States, to build Korean industry. The concentration was on export industries: steel, autos, ships, and so on. government policies encouraged the rise of the *chaebol,* a handful of huge corporations that have come to dominate the Korean economy. The success of the *chaebol* has been built on broad diversification: Hyundai, for example, makes not only cars and trucks but also ships and computers; Samsung manufactures textiles, ships, military planes, and computers and also sells insurance.

The growth has helped create a solid and prosperous middle class. Education is now excellent: the literacy rate is well over 95 percent, and more than a third of Korean students reach the university level. The material trappings of middle-class life are also prevalent: in 1970 only 2 percent of the households had refrigerators, but now that figure has risen to about 75 percent. Furthermore, South Koreans live almost twenty years longer than they did two generations ago. To round out the miracle, South Korea has been struggling toward a more genuine democracy.

But is the miracle as great as it looks at first glance? Many critics say it is not. They say that the *chaebol* hold too dominant a position and that smaller businesses have been discouraged. They say that housing, welfare, and care of the elderly have been left on the back burner. Many Koreans themselves see an intolerable gap between the rich and the poor. Moreover, there are strong regional disparities. While Seoul has built office towers and expressways, major cities such as Kwangju, a provincial capital in the south, are still dominated by peasants with their handcarts. Finally, in the political arena, the long march toward democracy has been punctuated with student riots, thousands of labor union strikes, and scandals surrounding political leaders.

Seen as a whole, the South Korean economy demonstrates the differences between growth and development. Growth may help to provide the opportunity for development, but it does not automatically resolve problems of income distribution, health and welfare, and the overall quality of life.

Sources: "South Korea," *The Economist,* May 21, 1988, p. 3ff.; Laxmi Nakarmi, Larry Armstrong, and William J. Holstein, "Korea," *Business Week,* September 5, 1988, pp. 44–50; Louis Kraar, "Korea: Tomorrow's Powerhouse," *Fortune,* August 15, 1988, pp. 75–81; Pico Iyer, "The Yin and Yang of Paradoxical, Prosperous Korea," *Smithsonian,* August 1988, pp. 47–58; Peter C. Du Bois, "Olympian View: A Skeptical Look at South Korea," *Barron's,* September 26, 1988, p. 75.

SUMMARY

1. The meaning of economic growth can be illustrated by the impressive changes that have taken place in the United States since World War I. (See pages 436–437.)

2. Economic historians do not agree on the causes of the economic growth of Western countries during the past five hundred years. Rosenberg and Birdzell offer a number of fundamental causes as well as a number of less important explanations. (See pages 437–438.)

3. Production function analysis is helpful in explaining short-period economic growth but significantly underestimates GNP for periods much longer than a single generation. (See page 438.)

4. Supply-side causes of economic growth may be grouped into those involving (1) the quantity of labor, (2) the quality of labor, (3) the quantity of capital, (4) the quality of capital, and (5) disembodied technical change. (See page 439.)

5. Advanced-country growth experience over the past 50 years has been impressive, although the rate of 4 percent per year (3 percent per capita per year) probably cannot be sustained. (See page 440.)

6. When examining the past fifty years of advanced-country growth experience, one should recognize that the rate of employment has been falling, the growth rate of the quality-adjusted labor force has not declined, the capital-labor ratio has grown at an increasing rate, and average productivity per unit of labor and per unit of capital have risen, with the former rising more than the latter. (See page 440.)

7. Neoclassical (supply-side) growth theory focuses on the quantities and qualities of the major inputs to production and also on disembodied technical progress. Its projections are overly optimistic when unemployment rates are rising and overly pessimistic when unemployment rates are falling. (See pages 440–441 and Tables 2 and 3, pages 442 and 443.)

8. Keynesian (demand-side) growth theory is represented by a Harrod model. It shows the growth rate to be the quotient of two ratios: the saving ratio (saving, net of depreciation, as a percent of income) is the numerator, and the capital-output ratio (the net amount of additional capital

required to increase output by one unit) is the denominator. (See pages 442–443.)

9. Demand-side and supply-side shocks can affect both the production function and the Harrod equation. (See page 444.)

10. Resource exhaustion and environmental pollution problems loom before us. We cannot be sure that technical fixes will bail us out, nor can we be sure that we will choose the best methods of protecting ourselves from destructive pollution. Should we change the basic rules of the market mechanism? (See pages 445–446.)

11. Another problem for economic growth in advanced countries stems from the aging of their populations, which may lead to serious intergenerational conflicts. (See page 446.)

12. Economic growth in advanced countries may also be threatened by the diversion of savings and investment from such growth-stimulating functions as research and development and education to equity uses, such as supporting the aged, the poor, and the homeless. (See page 447.)

13. The advantages of economic growth include both material comforts and greater opportunities for society to devote resources to matters of social concern. (See page 447.)

14. Antigrowth arguments range widely over matters related to the welfare of individuals swept along in the dynamics of growth and concerns about environmental damage resulting from it. (See pages 448–449.)

KEY TERMS

capital coefficient (capital-output ratio): the amount of additional capital required for a unit increase in the net national product (page 442).

disembodied technical change: technical change reflected incompletely or not at all in the quality of specific types of labor or machinery (page 439).

economic growth: an increase in the real GNP of an economy, usually stated on a per capita basis (page 436).

growthmanship: an overemphasis on measured economic growth (page 448).

multifactor productivity: a weighted average of labor and capital productivity (page 440).

neoclassical growth model: a model that describes a country's growth rate as the weighted sum of the changes in productivities of its productive inputs plus an additional term reflecting disembodied technical progress (page 440).

primary production: agriculture, forestry, and fisheries (page 438).

rental value: in a production function such as $Y = f(K, N)$, it is the K or roughly the sale value times the interest rate of a nation's capital and natural resources (page 439).

secondary production: manufacturing, mining, construction, and transport (page 438).

tertiary production: trade, finance, government, education—the service industries (page 438).

DISCUSSION QUESTIONS

1. How should we distinguish between economic *growth* and economic *development?*

2. What is the difference between *embodied* and *disembodied* technical change? Between *labor* and *multifactor* productivity?

3. Would the economic development of present-day Central America be easier or more difficult if the United States had not recovered from the Great Depression?

4. What is the difference between neoclassical and Keynesian growth theories?

5. What is the Club of Rome? Is its pessimistic "model of doom" valid?

6. Would you expect the antigrowth arguments of Mill, Schumacher, Mishan, and others to have their greatest appeal in MDCs or in LDCs? Explain your opinion.

21

Economic Development

Preview Poverty has always been the norm of the human economic condition. Economic history and economic geography are stories of almost unrelieved wretchedness. The typical human society permits a humane existence to only a small number, while the great majority lives in abysmal squalor. In part by the grace of poetry, romance, and legend—which celebrate those who live well and forget those who live in the silence of poverty—we forget the misery. Eras and areas of misery have been mythologized and may even be remembered as golden ages of pastoral simplicity. They were not, and are not.[1]

This chapter is about the efforts of the great majority of the world's countries and population to lift themselves out of the morass of poverty. We begin by pointing out that the less-developed countries (LDCs) are not all alike. They differ among themselves in many ways. Also, they are neither jungles nor deserts nor coral islands. Like the more-developed countries (MDCs), they are rapidly becoming urbanized.

Our next topic is development theory. Does standard (MDC) economic analysis apply? Has MDC growth helped or hindered LDC development? Why have some countries developed more rapidly than others? What hope is there for the present-day LDCs? There are as yet no agreed-upon answers to these questions. We examine a number of contrasting views.

Next we introduce the subject of income distribution, comparing the "growth first, distribution later" implications of the work of Simon Kuznets with the "redistribution with growth" stand of

1. Condensed and adapted from Nathan Rosenberg and L.E. Birdzell, Jr., *How the West Grew Rich: The Economic Transformation of the Industrial World* (New York: Basic Books, 1986), p. 3.

the Institute of Development Studies in Britain and with the "basic human needs" approach, which sacrifices measured growth to development.

During the present generation, political-economic relations between the so-called First World of advanced industrial countries ("the North") and the Third World ("the South") have tended to deteriorate. Many LDCs feel that the MDCs have prospered because of cheap raw materials and labor from the LDCs. "The South" has accordingly voiced a set of demands through the United Nations Conference on Trade and Development (UN-CTAD) and other UN agencies. These demands call for a New International Economic Order (NIEO). We list a number of NIEO demands but concentrate on the most acute one, namely, the renegotiation of the debt burdens of Third World countries to First World governments and commercial banks.

WHAT IS ECONOMIC DEVELOPMENT?

Economic development means that progress is taking place in some sense that brings gains in welfare, making life better for the masses. We may look at the process through the eyes of the **basic human needs (BHN)** approach. To its partisans, a country is developing if and only if a steadily increasing percentage of its people has an adequate diet, clean water, decent shelter, basic health care, elementary education, and a means of expressing individual views through petitions, demonstrations, and genuine elections. When attention shifts to BHN, it makes no difference whether economic growth, as measured by changes in per capita GNP, slows down or even turns negative. There can be development without growth, just as (they claim) too much growth is unrelated to development.

According to the basic human needs approach, a country is developing if and only if more and

more of its people are gaining adequate diets, clean water, decent shelter, basic health care and education, and a peaceful means of making their views known to the government.

Clearly, economic development means different things to different people. To many Americans, it means progress toward a goal not very different from an idealized version of the present American economy. To many Russians, one supposes, the developmental goal is an idealized form of the Soviet economy, possibly after a certain measure of reform (*perestroika*). To members of certain countercultures, the development goal is a world of idealized Israeli *kibbutzim*, communes, labor-managed cooperatives, or similar groups, sharing such ideas as "plain living and high thinking" or "respect for nature and the environment."

Many development economists and LDC politicians emphasize more sharply than we the distinction between economic growth and economic development. Situations in which "the numbers prosper while the people suffer"[2] may be growth, but they are not development. What Premier Papandreou, the author of this statement, wanted to avoid was situations of rising GNP, total and per capita, that left the person on the street or behind the plow worse off than before, if not in absolute terms at least by comparison with the rich. Also, a rise in measured GNP may reflect largely the growth of goods and services that critics call "decadent" rather than "civilized"—"bads" rather than "goods." Fidel Castro had this opinion about wide-open Havana—and to a lesser extent the rest of Cuba—before his takeover of the country in 1959.

Economic development can occur without economic growth; similarly, a rise in GNP does not necessarily mean that the lot of the average person has improved.

2. The quotation is from former premier of Greece, George Papandreou.

TABLE 1
Population, Income, and Growth Rate of Countries, 1987

Country or Countries	Population (millions) Mid-1987	GNP per Capita 1987 (U.S. dollars)	Annual Average Growth Rate of GNP per Capita 1965–1987 (%)
42 Low-Income Countries	2,822.9	290	3.1
(China and India)	(1,866.1)	(300)	(3.9)
53 Middle-Income Countries	1,038.5	1,810	2.5
(35 Lower-Middle Income Countries)	(609.6)	(1,200)	(2.2)
(18 Upper-Middle Income Countries)	(432.5)	(2,710)	(2.9)
25 High-Income Countries	777.2	14,430	2.3
(United States)	(243.8)	(18,530)	(1.5)
(Japan)	(122.2)	(15,760)	(4.2)
(Canada)	(25.9)	(15,160)	(2.7)
(United Kingdom)	(56.9)	(10,420)	(1.7)

Note: The U.S.S.R. is among countries not reporting to the World Bank.

Source: The World Bank, *World Development Report*, 1989, Table 1, pp. 164–165. New York: Oxford University Press, 1989. Used with permission.

The Vast and Variegated Majority

Statistics cannot bleed. However, despite their emotional unconcern and their technical flaws, much can be gained by examining them. Table 1 shows per capita incomes (GNPs), measured growth rates, and populations, for somewhat more than two-thirds of the world's 170-odd countries. The omitted countries are nearly all small, poor, and underdeveloped. Although the table is neither accurate nor complete, it does show how the **First World** of industrial-market economies (most of the 25 high-income countries in the table) differs from the **Third World** of 100 or so LDC countries scattered among the low- and middle-income countries.[3] Note the wide range of per capita in-

come among countries. Per capita income in the 42 low-income countries was less than 2 percent of the per capita income in the United States. In the lower and upper middle-income countries, per capita incomes were, respectively, 6.5 percent and 14.6 percent of the U.S. per capita income. Even granting the difficulties of statistical comparison (see Chapter 7), the differences are almost beyond comprehension.

The figures in Table 1 do not confirm the common claim that the gap between the richer and the poorer countries is increasing over time in percentage terms. From 1965 to 1987, for example, the 25 high-income countries of the First World grew at a 2.3 percent rate, compared to 2.5 percent for the middle-income countries and 3.9 percent for the 42 low-income countries of the Third World. The lowest-income LDCs, sometimes called the Fourth World, grew still faster at 3.1 percent. At the same time, the *absolute* gap between rich and poor countries is indeed increasing for the same reason that 2 percent of 100 is less than 1 percent of 500.

---

3. The **Second World** comprises the centrally planned economies, regardless of their degrees of development or industrialization. Most of them, including the Soviet Union, are "nonreporting nonmembers" of the World Bank.

The First World consists of advanced industrial countries, the Second World of centrally planned economies, and the Third World of developing countries. The lowest-income countries are sometimes called the Fourth World.

Table 2 presents basic data (for the LDCs only) on a geographical basis. It uses **gross domestic product (GDP)**—the production and income generated within a country—rather than gross national product (GNP) figures which counts all income of the citizens of a country, even when that income is generated in a foreign country. The most important difference between GDP and GNP figures is their treatment of international payments of property income. For example, rent, interest, and other service charges on the international indebtedness of Mexico and its residents are part of Mexico's GDP because the capital services were presumably carried on in Mexico. But they are counted as part of the U.S. GNP because they were received by residents of the United States. It follows that an international creditor country's GNP may rank somewhat higher than its GDP, and vice versa for an international debtor.

An international creditor country's GNP may be somewhat higher than its GDP, while an international debtor country may have a higher GDP than GNP.

The figures in Table 2 point out the differences between and among the Third World countries more clearly than do the figures in Table 1. East Asia is apparently doing quite well, despite downward drag from the Philippines and the three Indochinese countries. Sub-Saharan Africa is apparently doing very badly, although Kenya is a special case.

We put primary stress on per capita income estimates because the individual welfare of a person or family is connected more closely with per capita than with total income. But if one of the social goals of a nation, a race, or a religious body is to achieve a large population—for reasons ranging from cannon fodder to propagation of the faith—the total income becomes more important. Nor do these figures give the full picture about population and income. There are rich people in the poorest countries, just as there are poor people in the richest ones. Foreign aid, in fact, is sometimes criticized as a process for transferring income from poor people in rich countries to rich people in poor countries. Moreover, a country's position can change both drastically and rapidly. In the mid-1950s Libya was an economic "basket case"—like Bangladesh a generation later. But then oil was discovered in Libya. (Will Bangladesh be equally fortunate?) Finally, the Third World differs from such poverty pockets as the Scottish Highlands or Appalachia because of the number of Third World cities with populations in the millions. Mexico City is a contender for the dubious distinction of being the world's largest city. Bangkok (Thailand), Buenos Aires (Argentina), Cairo (Egypt), Calcutta (India), Ibadan and Lagos (Nigeria), Jakarta (Indonesia), Nairobi (Kenya), São Paulo (Brazil), Seoul (Korea), and Taipei (Taiwan) are not far behind.

Differences in Living Standards

Personal and family income statistics surely exaggerate differences between MDCs and LDCs. Activities like baking bread, making clothes, and building homes commonly involve the market in the First World, and account is therefore taken of them in income statistics. In the Third World, these activities are commonly performed within households and are excluded from the statistics. Even recognizing these statistical problems, however, the difference between First World and Third World per capita income is huge. Here, from Robert Heilbroner's *The Great Ascent*, is a comparison between life in the United States and life in an urban area of some low-income LDC. We have adjusted Heilbroner's numbers for the inflation that has occurred since his book was published (1963). The facts, unfortunately, need no adjustment.

> [Let us imagine] how a typical American family could be transformed into an equally typical family of the under-developed world.
> We begin by invading the house of our American family to strip it of its furniture. Everything goes: beds, chairs, tables, TV set. . . . Each member of the family may keep his oldest suit or

TABLE 2
GDP Annual Growth Rates of Developing Countries by Geographical Area, 1980–1987

Geographical Area	GDP (percent)			GDP per Capita (percent)		
	1980–1987	1986	1987	1980–1987	1986	1987
All Developing Countries	3.3	4.9	4.5	1.2	2.8	2.3
Sub-Saharan Africa	−0.5	2.0	−1.5	−3.6	−0.5	−5.1
East Asia	7.7	7.3	8.6	6.2	5.7	7.0
South Asia	5.4	4.7	2.7	3.1	2.4	0.5
Europe, Middle East, and North Africa	2.9	4.2	3.1	0.6	2.0	1.1
Latin America and the Caribbean	0.2	3.8	2.5	−2.0	1.6	0.4

Source: Reuters Information Services, Inc., New York. Reprinted with permission.

dress, a shirt or blouse. We permit a pair of shoes to the head of the family, but none for the wife or children.

We move into the kitchen. . . . The box of matches may stay, a small bag of flour, some sugar and salt. A few moldy potatoes, already in the garbage can, must be rescued, for they will provide much of tonight's meal. We leave a handful of onions and a dish of dried beans. We take away: the meat, the fresh vegetables, the canned goods. . . .

. . . Next we take away the house. The family can move to the toolshed. It is crowded, but "it is not uncommon for a family of four or more to live in a bedspace, that is, on a bunk bed and the space it occupies—sometimes in two or three tiers—their only privacy provided by curtains."

All the other houses in the neighborhood have also been removed; our suburb has become a shantytown. Our family is fortunate to have a shelter. . . . [In] Cali, Colombia, "on one hillside alone, the slum population is estimated at 40,000—without water, sanitation, or electric light. And not all the poor of Cali are [so] fortunate. Others have built their shacks on land which lies beneath the flood mark. To these people the immediate environment is the open sewer of the city, which flows through their huts when the river rises."

Communication must go next. No more newspapers, magazines, books—not that they are missed, since we take away our family's literacy

as well. Instead, in our shantytown we will allow one radio.

Now government services must go. No more postman, no more fireman. There is a school, but it is three miles away. . . . There are no hospitals or doctors nearby. The nearest clinic is 10 miles away and tended by a midwife. It can be reached by bicycle, provided the family has a bicycle, which is unlikely. Or one can go by bus—not always inside. . . .

. . . We will allow our family a cash hoard of $20. Meanwhile the head of the family must earn his keep. As a peasant cultivator with three acres, he may raise the equivalent of $500 to $1,500 worth of crops a year. If he is a tenant farmer, a third or so will go to his landlord, and probably another 10% to the local moneylender. But there will be enough to eat. Or almost enough. The human body requires an input of 2,000 calories [a day] to replenish the energy consumed by its cells. If our displaced American fares no better than an Indian peasant, he will average no more than 1,700–1,900. His body, like any insufficiently fueled machine, will run down. . . .

This is only an impression of life in the underdeveloped lands. It is not life itself. There are lacking the things that underdevelopment gives as well as those it takes away: the urinals smell of poverty, the disease, the flies, the open sewers. And there is lacking a softening sense of familiarity. A [scene], shocking to American eyes, is less shocking to eyes that have never known any other. . . . When we are told that half the world's population enjoys a standard of living "less than $400 a year," this is what the figures mean.[4]

The difference between First World and Third World per capita income and living conditions is huge.

THEORIES OF DEVELOPMENT AND UNDERDEVELOPMENT

There is as yet no generally accepted theory to explain why some countries have developed while others have not. Historically speaking, of course, there have been a number of different theories. We shall sample a few of the more important ones.

A number of different theories have attempted to explain why some countries have developed and others have not.

The development economist Albert Hirschman, now at the Institute of Advanced Studies at Princeton, suggests classifying these theories in the following ways:

1. According to whether or not the theories assume what Hirschman calls **monoeconomics,** that is, whether they assume that economic analysis methods devised in MDCs to deal with MDC problems work equally well in LDCs, despite differences in religion, culture, and history. For example, suppose we are studying the demand for automobiles in three countries (A, B, and C). In A and B, the quantity demanded depends exclusively on price and income, although price is more important than income in A but less important than income in B. In country C, demand for automo-

4. Robert L. Heilbroner, *The Great Ascent* (New York: Harper, 1963), pp. 23–27. Abridged and adapted from "The Tableau of Under-Development" in *The Great Ascent* by Robert L. Heilbroner. Copyright © 1963 by Robert L. Heilbroner. Reprinted by permission of Harper & Row, Publishers, Inc.; and by permission of William Morris Agency on behalf of the author.

biles depends, in addition, on astrological forecasts about the weather and the crops. Monoeconomics holds between A and B. It does not hold between C and either of the other countries.

Monoeconomic theories assume that methods of economic analysis devised to deal with MDCs work equally well in LDCs.

---

2. According to whether or not the theories claim community of interest between MDCs and LDCs, that is, whether or not the theories claim that a set of policies that helps (or injures) one group of countries will also help (or injure) the others.

We shall soon see that Adam Smith's development theory, for example, is strongly monoeconomic, while *dependencia* theory denies community of interest.

Some theories of economic development claim community of interest between MDCs and LDCs—that a set of policies that help (or injure) one country will help (or injure) the others.

Adam Smith's Development Theory

Oldest in time is the sunny optimism of Adam Smith (1723–1790), as seen in the following words quoted from an essay on development, written in 1755, twenty-one years before his *Wealth of Nations:*

> Little else is requisite to carry a state to the highest degree of opulence, from the lowest barbarism, but peace, easy taxes, and a tolerable administration of justice; all the rest being brought about by the natural course of things.

This is less simple-minded than it sounds, for Smith goes on:

> All governments which thwart this natural course, which force things into another channel or which endeavor to arrest the progress of society at a particular point, are unnatural, and to support themselves are obliged to be oppressive and tyrannical.

How many of today's LDCs, either as colonies or as independent countries, have enjoyed "peace, easy taxes, and a tolerable administration of justice" under governments not "oppressive and tyrannical?" The Chinese case is instructive. For 109 years (1840–1949), the country had one civil or international war after another, from the Opium War to the conquest of power by Mao Zedong's Communists. With peace came development, for which communism claims the credit.

In Book III of *The Wealth of Nations*, Adam Smith spelled out "the natural course of things" mentioned in the quotation. It leads from agriculture to manufacturing, and finally to (foreign) trade. But even so, "Smith on Development" seems to a present-day reader to underestimate the problems and the roadblocks. At the very least, he might have noted the danger of population explosion. It may well be, as suggested in Julian Simon's *Ultimate Resource*, that the world would be better off with a higher population level, which might include the additional inventors and innovators necessary to overcome static diminishing returns to population. But the population-explosion argument is about the *rate* at which the population grows. The growth rate can be "too high" even when the population level is "too low."

Smith might also have noted the need to obtain natural resources that the developing country may not have within its own borders. However, many LDCs have been too quick to claim they have "nothing to export" in exchange for imports. Under free trade, a poor country can become what is called a *processing economy* and export its imports plus the value added by its cheap labor. For example, it can import cotton and export cloth, import leather and export footwear, and so on. Japan, Korea, Hong Kong, and other East Asian countries have done just this in their LDC histories.

Adam Smith optimistically believed that little else was necessary for economic development than peace, low taxes, and just administration of laws. He overlooked, however, the difficulties caused by an ever-increasing population growth rate and the importance of access to natural resources.

Malthusian Pessimism

The name of Thomas Robert Malthus (1766–1834) has come to symbolize pessimism about long-term growth in any economic system whatever. According to Malthus, populations increase faster than the food supply, thus leading ultimately to poverty and hunger. "Products rise by one, two, three, four but people rise by one, two, four, eight," or, as another poet put it:

> Come, Malthus, and with Ciceronian prose
> Show how a rutting population grows,
> Till all the produce of the earth is spent,
> And brats expire from lack of aliment.

Malthus did not envisage invention and innovation as benefits of population growth. Moreover, his limited evidence was drawn largely from what is today the Atlantic seaboard of the United States, where population seemed to be doubling every generation in the eighteenth century—assisted, however, by immigration, including the slave trade. Modern Malthusianism has a certain racist tinge when, after it has proved quite wrong for themselves, it is applied by MDC pessimists to "those people" in the LDCs.

Thomas Malthus pessimistically believed that ever-growing populations meant that no economy could avoid poverty and hunger in the long run.

Marxian Theories

It is no surprise to find Karl Marx (1818–1883) and his followers less cheerful than Adam Smith about development under capitalism. Their conclusions, however, are based on more than the intuitive emotionalism of much Marxist political activism. Let us see how the Marxist answer is derived.

Exploitation and the Falling Rate of Profit The key proposition in Marxian economics is that all value comes from labor and, for that reason, the profits of capitalists arise from the exploitation of labor—that is, by taking from workers some of the fruits of their labor. In Marxian reasoning, capitalist profits are plowed back into production through ever-rising investments in machines. But this increasingly capital-intensive method of production lowers the proportion of new labor input, in this way allowing the capitalist fewer chances for further exploitation. The result is a falling rate of profit, for each dollar invested. The capitalist's responses to this falling rate of profit are the keys to Marxist forecasts of economic suffering, the collapse of capitalism, the rise and fall of imperialism, and the problems of the Third World. Rather than raising their consumption as the classical economists expected, Marxists contend that capitalists will keep on accumulating and simply hoard money or cash balances. The results of this hoarding, as Keynes would agree, are stagnation, unemployment, and misery, ending, Marxists say, in revolution and capitalist downfall.

According to Karl Marx, the profits of capitalists arise from the exploitation of labor. He predicted that when profit rates decreased, capitalists would hoard money, leading to stagnation, unemployment, and—ultimately—revolution and capitalist downfall.

Impact on the Third World After Marx's death, the writings of his followers spelled out what the falling rate of profit would mean for imperialism and the Third World. In the view of Lenin (1870–1924), the great theorist of imperialism, Third World countries will be brought into the capitalist system. As capital accumulates, it will be exported there, and native people will be put to work at lower (more exploitative) wages than are paid in the more developed countries. In this way, stagnation in the MDCs can be slowed down or even reversed, and the capitalist system can continue onward and upward for a while. But the LDCs themselves will neither grow nor develop. The profits from their businesses go mainly to MDC residents.

Other Marxists, especially Rosa Luxemburg (1871–1919), saw imperialism somewhat differently. In "Red Rosa's" view, to keep up employment and get rid of goods that its own consumers could not buy at profitable prices, each capitalist country would take over LDC areas as happy dumping grounds. The poor LDCs would pay for these goods mainly by selling their assets, meaning the control of their land and mineral resources. The final results of "Luxemburg" imperialism were to be no different from those of "Lenin" imperialism.

Both Lenin and Luxemburg predicted that the end will come because the Third World too is limited in size. The rival imperialist powers will clash over colonization or control of the most promising LDCs. Within its LDCs, each imperialist power will face "liberation movements" that are pitted against the mother country and against its allies in the native capitalist class. The United States fought Spain over Cuba, the Philippines, and Puerto Rico. Later the U.S. fighting in Vietnam gave rise to civil disobedience and rioting in the United States itself. The end result of all this warfare and revolution, the Marxists say, will be the downfall of capitalism, for the wars will spread beyond the Third World. As Lenin put it during World War I, "The road to London and Paris leads through Peking and Calcutta."

Dependencia Theories of Underdevelopment

Dependencia (dependency) theories of LDC underdevelopment spring from the Third World, particularly from Latin America. This is why they are known by their Spanish name. They are forms of neo-Marxism, in which MDC protectionists and labor unions play "bad guy" roles alongside MDC capitalists. They go beyond standard Marxism to argue that the prosperity of the First World is *dependent upon* the poverty of the Third—"They are rich because we are poor." And similarly, the poverty of the Third World is *dependent upon* the prosperity of the First.

According to *dependencia* theory, the prosperity of the First World is dependent upon the poverty of the Third World; similarly, the poverty of the Third World is dependent upon the prosperity of the First World.

To understand *dependencia* theory, let us go back in time to Europe of the sixteenth, seventeenth, and eighteenth centuries. The dominant economic thinking of the time was *mercantilism*. In England, France, the Netherlands, Spain, and elsewhere, the mercantile system took different forms, but all agreed that the goal of a state's economic activity was to strengthen its political (military) power in Europe. This is the key to mercantilist doctrine. The aim was to win colonies in faraway lands, first as sources of precious metals and industrial raw materials for the mother country, and second to keep such riches away from that country's rivals. It was believed to be dangerous for colonies, especially for their non-European natives, to develop any kinds of modern industry that would compete with mother-country producers or provide economic bases for revolt and independent political existence.

According to a number of writers, both the present MDCs and the present LDCs were undeveloped at the start of the mercantilist age, but the MDCs had the edge in military technology. This they used to gain control over the rest of the world, profiting from the world's resources and confining "the natives" to low-paid unskilled work. And the gains that resulted from such exploitation financed the subsequent Industrial Revolution and prosperity. To quote the late Premier Jawaharlal Nehru of India, Britain's Industrial Revolution was "financed by the loot of Bengal."

The mercantilist system of the sixteenth, seventeenth, and eighteenth centuries encouraged the acquisition of colonies as sources of raw materials. According to *dependencia* theory, the countries that had the edge in military technology were able to gain colonies and thus develop themselves at the expense of the colonies.

Mercantilism never died. After their American colonies won their freedom, the mother countries and other powers kept on using colonies as raw material sources by putting high tariffs (import taxes) on their manufactures and other finished goods while admitting their food and raw materials tax-free, even though they competed with the mother country's own farmers and landlords. Still mainly for military reasons, MDCs tried for some

time to control the "trade secrets" of the Industrial Revolution against all others, even their old colonies. Students of U.S. economic history may remember Samuel Slater, who memorized the blueprints of advanced British textile machinery whose export was against the law, brought his secret to Rhode Island, and started the New England textile-manufacturing business.

Later in the nineteenth century, as labor movements developed in western Europe and the United States, skilled workers came more and more to support what is called *neomercantilism*. Modern industry offered more skilled jobs than farming had, and these jobs were more highly paid than unskilled ones. Workers and their unions demanded protection against low-wage LDC competition, with the same results for the LDCs as they had known under the older military mercantilism.

Mercantilism survived as neomercantilism—a demand by MDC workers and their unions for protection against low-wage LDC competition, with the same results for the LDCs as under the old brand of mercantilism.

Also, technical progress has had different effects on manufacturers in MDCs and on farm products and raw materials in LDCs. In the LDCs, progress led to higher outputs and lower prices on competitive export markets. But in the MDCs, progress appeared to be used mainly to raise profits and wages while holding prices steady or raising them. In the LDCs, the prices of exports generally seemed to fall as compared to the prices of imports. The opposite seemed to be true for the MDCs. These tendencies have been stressed by *dependencia* writers.

Dependencia thinking is an important basis for LDC pressure for bigger and better OPECs, price supports for their countries' exports of goods, and for what is called "redeployment," or transfer, of a higher percentage of world manufacturing capacity into LDC countries from the MDCs. (Because of the lower wage scales in the LDCs, some redeployment is occurring in textiles, clothing, and shoes, to the great concern and dismay of the U.S. labor movement.)

Rostow's Non-Communist Manifesto

W. W. Rostow's *Stages of Economic Growth* is subtitled *A Non-Communist Manifesto*. It may be regarded as an argument not only against Marxism but also against *dependencia* theory, which was not well known when Rostow was writing (1960). Rostow's work is an example of an institutional stage theory.

The Rostow stages of growth are five in number: (1) traditional society, (2) preconditions for takeoff, (3) takeoff itself (the kernel of the theory), (4) drive to maturity, and (5) high mass consumption.

W. W. Rostow offered a five-part institutional stage theory. His five stages of growth are traditional society, preconditions for takeoff, takeoff, drive to maturity, and high mass consumption.

We need say little about stage 1. Even though economic activity is limited largely to farming and handicrafts and per capita income is low and stationary, life is not always as miserable as that portrayed by Heilbroner earlier in this chapter.

In stage 2, which may last a long time and in which many LDCs now find themselves, there may develop Adam Smith's combination of "peace, easy taxes, and a tolerable administration of justice." In this stage countries often have some accumulation of **social overhead capital** (roads and harbors, schools and public health facilities), and also one or more leading industries (textiles and transportation in Britain and the United States, oil extraction and refining in the OPEC countries).

The takeoff (stage 3) is quite sudden when it comes. It covers just about one generation. Rostow's estimates are 1783–1802 for Britain, 1843–1860 for the United States, 1850–1873 for Germany, 1878–1900 for Japan, 1890–1914 for (czarist) Russia. It is marked by two features. One is the spread of modern methods from the leading sectors to the rest of the economy, which supplies their raw materials and purchases most of their products. The second feature is a sudden sharp rise in saving and investment, often aided by an influx of foreign capital.

The takeoff stage is marked by the spread of modern methods from the leading sector to the rest of the economy and by a sudden sharp rise in saving and investment, often aided by an influx of foreign capital.

After the takeoff, Rostow believes the drive to maturity (stage 4) is a much easier matter because it is aided by reinvestment of the gains from takeoff—or the force of compound interest. However, takeoffs may be followed by crashes, as in Mexico under Porfirio Díaz (due to revolution) and Russia under Nicholas II (due to World War I). Maturity itself is described by Rostow in terms of higher average labor skills, a shift in economic leadership from self-made "robber barons" to professionally trained managers, and a certain "boredom with the miracle of industrialization," leading to moves in other directions. It was supposedly reached in Britain about 1850, in the United States about 1910, in Japan about 1940, and in (Soviet) Russia in about 1950.

Once maturity (stage 5) is achieved, Rostow says, it can be used in some combination of three ways: militarism and imperialism, the welfare state, and high mass consumption. Rostow favors some judicious combination of the last two. He criticizes Germany and Japan for concentrating on the first for as long as they did, and believes that the Soviet Union still has its choice to make. He believes that the United States used too much of the gains from growth to pay for a postwar "baby boom." His advice to the LDCs is to speed up their takeoffs, and he pays little attention to whether MDC policy speeds up or slows down LDC growth. You should also remember that Rostow sees nothing inevitable in this whole evolution.

"Vicious-Circle" Theory

Decidedly less optimistic than Rostow's theory are the "vicious-circle" theories popular in the West during the 1950s. They were developed primarily by the Baltic refugee economist Ragnar Nurkse. Their moral is that, under contemporary conditions, a poor country cannot develop without external aid, simply because it is poor.

Vicious circles are set up on both supply and

demand sides. The supply-side argument is that, because a country is poor, it cannot save. Because it cannot save, it cannot increase its capital stock unless it receives foreign assistance. Without an adequate stock of physical capital, its labor productivity and income level will both remain low. Demand-side arguments are usually put in Keynesian terms to fit more easily into the Harrod-model analysis of the last chapter. Because a country is poor, its consumption level is low. Therefore, investment to supply its home market is not a commercially attractive proposition. Without investment on concessionary terms, productivity and incomes will remain low.

According to the vicious-circle theory, a poor country cannot save and therefore cannot increase its capital stock unless it receives foreign assistance, nor can it attract investment to its home market.

The vicious-circle theory has some drawbacks. For example, it has difficulty explaining Japan, especially Meiji Japan (1868–1912), when that country raised itself from the ranks of the LDCs without significant foreign financial aid. Also, as human-capital theorists point out, the theory ignores both the quantity and the quality of the labor force.

Cultural-Development Theories

The theories we have treated thus far have been essentially economic—even monoeconomic in Hirschman's sense. Cultural-development theories, on the other hand, are espoused widely—mainly by others than economists. These theories emphasize the importance of religion, custom, tradition, and other cultural factors, even in the very long run (over centuries).

The father of such theories may be the great German sociologist and social historian Max Weber, the author of *The Protestant Ethic and the Spirit of Capitalism* (1904). Weber concentrated his attention on the Protestant Reformation, on the breakdown of the authority of the church and canon law in economic matters, and on the probusiness applications of Calvinism in particular. More recently, Japanese economist Michio Morishima's *Why Has*

Japan Succeeded? (1982) ascribes his country's economic performance largely to Confucian doctrine in its specifically Japanese variant. The American social psychologist David McClelland's *Achieving Society* (1961) traces economic development largely to a society's "need for achievement," which is implanted by its methods of child rearing and manifested in the stories children read and listen to. American area specialist Lawrence Harrison, in an attack on *dependencia* theories in *Underdevelopment Is a State of Mind* (1985), claims that Latin American culture, influenced by that of the Spanish and Portuguese *conquistadores*, is "anti-progress, anti-intellectual, and, among the affluent, anti-work." In Harrison's view, this culture, reinforced in some countries by various African-based religious traditions known as voodoo, has been the main obstacle to development south of the Rio Grande.

Cultural-development theories emphasize the importance of religion, custom, and tradition in economic matters.

DEVELOPMENT AND INCOME DISTRIBUTION

How is economic development related to equality and inequality in income distribution? We shall give three different views on this question.

The Kuznets Hypothesis

Analyzing historical development and income distribution statistics for the present MDCs, the Nobel Prize-winning economist Simon Kuznets has noted a pattern of inequality over time. As development progresses, measured inequality has first risen and then fallen in most countries. At the same time, labor's share of income first fell and then rose.[5]

---

5. The "macroeconomic history" of *American Inequality,* by Jeffrey Williamson and Peter Lindert (1981), uses more data than was available to Kuznets himself.

Kuznets notes incidentally that the mid-nineteenth century, when Karl Marx was writing, marks the period of the greatest inequality in Great Britain, where Marx was living in exile. Could Marx have assumed, from what was happening in his lifetime, that the trend toward inequality would continue unchanged?

In the Kuznets model, three factors are interwoven to explain the pattern of rising and falling inequality. Part of the explanation is that capital accumulation first comes from profits and inequality, but later declines as the rate of return on capital falls because of its greater abundance relative to other inputs. Population and labor force growth also play a role. Population growth rates go up at first, increasing inequality, but go down later, raising wages and reducing inequality. Third, as time passes, highly paid skills are learned by a larger part of the work force, raising the proportion of high-paying jobs.

According to the Kuznets model, measured inequality first rises and then falls in most countries as development progresses.

What this theory means for the LDCs is presented in the following quote from the Canadian economist Harry G. Johnson:

> There is a conflict between economic efficiency and social justice. The importance of this conflict is likely to vary according to the state of economic development. The more advanced a country is, the more likely are its citizens to have consciences about the distribution of income, and the higher the level of income reached, the less serious will be any slowing down of the rate of growth brought about by redistribution policies. An advanced country can afford to sacrifice some growth for the sake of social justice. But the cost of greater equality may be great to any economy at a low level of economic development. It would therefore seem unwise for a country anxious to enjoy rapid growth to insist too strongly on policies aimed at ensuring economic equality.[6]

Development and Redistribution

Johnson's advice has not sat well with LDC political leaders, who either represent the political left in their countries or fear leftist revolution in the short run if they wait for the Kuznets turning point. They want *Redistribution with Growth*, which is the title of a joint study by economists at the World Bank and

6. Harry G. Johnson, *Money, Trade, and Economic Growth,* 2nd ed. (London: Unwin, 1964), p. 159.

the Institute of Development Studies in England. According to this study, redistribution can come about by "appropriate technology" and an "appropriate product mix," which substitutes labor, especially semiskilled labor, for capital goods and the more highly skilled specialties of the labor aristocracy. It can also come about by pouring capital into the LDCs either free of interest charges or on special terms from MDC governments or from international bodies. In either case, MDC taxpayers would eventually foot the bill.

Advocates of redistribution with growth say economic development can be achieved by substituting semiskilled labor for capital goods and by pouring MDC capital into LDCs.

Basic Human Needs

More extreme than "redistribution with growth" is the basic human needs strategy, already described. It aims directly at economic development, meaning by "development" first the reduction and finally the end of poverty and alienation. It is not concerned with measured rates of economic growth or with overall statistics in general. It is less popular in most LDC government circles than in MDC universities and in international organizations. (The LDC civil service is an important part of the country's urban labor aristocracy.)

Basic human needs strategy aims to achieve economic development by ending poverty. It is not concerned with measured rates of economic growth or with overall statistics.

DUALISM AND ENCLAVES

Imagine an MDC visitor returning to a Third World country after a lapse of five or ten years. The visitor will generally land at a major city airport, and spend the first few days in and around that city. Before leaving, the visitor will usually travel for some distance into the surrounding countryside.

What differences is he or she likely to find? Probably much of the capital or any other major city (aside from the slums) will seem more "modern" than it was during the earlier visit. There will be more pavement, more automobiles, more Western-style buildings, more neon signs, more billboards, and so on. But on a trip fifteen to twenty miles out into the farming areas, the banana trees or rice paddies will seem largely unchanged unless the traveler visits a model farm or commune.

This is the visual aspect of **economic dualism.** Dualism may be looked on as another distribution problem, a regional one, between the large cities and the rural areas. The cities, and particularly the areas where foreigners live and work, can easily become islands, or enclaves, of modernization and prosperity in otherwise stagnant and miserable LDCs.

To spread development from its original urban enclaves to the rural hinterland is the LDCs' great "second-generation" development problem. Some even call it a dilemma. It is in any case much more difficult than the spread of development from, say, Chicago to rural Illinois or from Montreal to rural Quebec.

Unless an export market suddenly opens up for a specialized item like cocoa in Ghana or cocaine in Colombia, the obvious path to rural development is by way of increasing farm prices. These prices may rise as a natural result of urban growth and development or from active agricultural policy. But the danger is the reaction of the urban poor, including former farmworkers who have migrated to the cities. A riot against increases in staple-food prices could topple most democratic, well-intentioned, pro-Western governments—especially, it seems, in Africa on either side of the Sahara.

But if no new crops emerge and farm prices remain stagnant, *rural* revolt may result, involving peasants and farmworkers and directed initially against landowners. Three examples are Mao Zedong's agrarian revolution within the communist revolution, Pancho Villa's career in Mexico, and more recently the Shining Path (*Sendero Luminoso*) in Peru.

Another distribution problem manifests itself as economic dualism, wherein Third World cities

---

become enclaves of prosperity in otherwise stagnant LDCs.

THE NORTH-SOUTH CONFRONTATION

We turn now to a fuller examination of the mutual-benefit issue in development theory, or rather, to the widespread rejection of this theory in the LDCs. The question can be phrased as follows: To what extent, if at all, do the interests of MDCs and LDCs—the "North" and "South," respectively—converge?[7] The neo-Marxian and *dependencia* theories imply that their interests do not converge at all, at least under capitalism. They say that there is a basic hostility between the MDCs and LDCs. From these theoretical bases, plus doses of MDC racism and condescension, LDC resentment and envy, and unconcern on each side with the other group's problems, has sprung today's North-South confrontation and conflict, culminating in the demand of the South for a New International Economic Order (NIEO).

From the ongoing hostility between the MDCs and LDCs has sprung the demand of the South for a New International Economic Order (NIEO).

A New International Economic Order?

Spokespersons and sloganeers for the South are more united in denouncing the existing international economic order (which they tend to equate with the freedom of trade) than in specifying what their proposed replacements might be. However, the following set of demands is fairly common:

---

7. The "North-South" geographic split should not be taken literally. The "North" includes MDCs from the Southern Hemisphere—Australia, New Zealand, and South Africa are examples. The "South" includes most of the tropical countries, whether in North America, South America, Africa, or Asia.

On LDC Trade

1. Preferential access of LDC-manufactured exports to MDC markets by general statutes of preference (GSPs), without reciprocal opening of LDC markets to MDC producers.

2. More remunerative and more stable world prices for LDC agricultural and mineral exports, with stockpiling financed by international agencies. These agencies are to be financed mainly by MDC taxpayers.

3. MDC acceptance of LDC cartels, modeled on OPEC, to raise the prices of LDC exports.

4. Eventual redeployment of industrial capacity to the LDCs, particularly light, labor-intensive industries like textiles. New capacity in such industries is to go mainly to LDCs.

On Debts, Aid, and Capital Movement

1. Renegotiation of LDC debts to MDC governments and banks including longer terms, lower interest rates, and new loans to finance the servicing of existing debts. This is the most pressing of the South's existing demands. It sometimes extends further, to outright cancellation of these debts. We shall soon deal separately with the debt problem.

2. Increased Official Development Assistance (ODA) from MDCs to LDCs, extending to 1 percent of MDC GNPs by the year 2000.[8] Such assistance, they say, is not charity but reparation payments for past sins of colonization and exploitation.

3. LDC access to international lending on concessional (preferential and below market) terms.

4. Use of International Monetary Fund (IMF) special drawing rights (SDRs or "paper gold") as a form of additional aid to LDCs.

On LDC Internal Economies

1. Low-cost transfer of technology to LDCs and, where such technologies do not yet exist or are not operational, development of appropriate technologies for LDCs by international bodies.

2. Acceptance by MDCs of full LDC control of the activities of multinational corporations (MNCs) within their borders.[9]

3. Eliminating conditionality in international lending to LDCs. IMF lending, in particular, has often been made conditional on highly unpopular austerity programs in the domestic LDC economy. When such programs are not carried out, the loans are discontinued.

On Essentially Political Issues

1. A larger share of LDC control of international financial institutions, especially the IMF and the World Bank.

2. Respect for LDC sovereignty. For example, LDCs want limitations on appeals to international tribunals of LDC domestic decisions on such matters as nationalization and confiscation of MNC property.

3. International control of natural resources in the open sea and its seabed to provide additional funding for LDC development.

4. MDC disarmament to free MDC resources for the purchase of LDC exports and for the provision of Official Development Assistance.

The South wants solutions for the problems of LDC trade, debts, aid, capital movement, internal economics, and various political issues.

What Can the South Do?

Among the countries of the North, Sweden and the Netherlands have gone farthest in making concessions to the South's demands, but these are relatively small countries. The largest industrial countries have made only token concessions,

---

8. This figure is suggested as a target or goal by the Brandt Report, *North-South: Program for Survival* (1980).

9. Both the political and economic activities of multinational corporations have been at times highly controversial, especially in situations where the economic resources of an MNC rival those of the governments that attempt to regulate it. MNC problems are taken up in advanced courses in both international and development economics. The best-known indictment of MNC activities in Third World countries is R. J. Barnet and R. E. Mueller, *Global Reach* (1974). For a more neutral view, see Raymond Vernon, *Sovereignty at Bay* (1971) and *Storm Over the Multinationals* (1977). Considerably more advanced and technical is Richard Caves, *Multinational Enterprise and Economic Analysis* (1982).

concessions only to their former colonies, concessions "subject to approval of Congress," or no concessions at all. Along the line of Stalin's "How many divisions does the pope have?" some have wondered, "Why should we pay any attention at all?"

It does appear that the South can do little to press its claims without injuring itself more than it hurts the North. Its most obvious weapon is repudiation or default on interest and/or principal payments on debts, which amounted to $1.2 trillion as of 1988. With that total, each 1 percent rise (fall) in the interest rate increases (decreases) the annual interest burden of the LDCs as a group by about $6 billion. Repudiation or default, advocated most stridently by Fidel Castro, might set off a financial crisis in the North and risk cutting the South off from future financial aid.

Some LDCs (Albania, Burma, Ethiopia, and North Korea) advocate (but do not always practice) "self-reliance." This more drastic tactic amounts to an economic boycott of the First World, while counting on other Third World countries plus the communist bloc for imports, for markets, for loans, and for aid in case of emergency. A historical precedent is the one ship a year that Japan allowed the Dutch, representing the entire Western world, to bring to Nagasaki, Japan's only open port, over a 250-year period ending in the mid-nineteenth century. There is no doubt that such a move would hurt the South, but some LDC politicians and ideologues claim that it would be the North that could not stand the strain. They argue that northern post-industrial growth has weakened its agricultural and industrial bases, while accustoming its people to affluent lifestyles. Perhaps neither capitalism nor the market economy could survive, if both require (as per *dependencia* theory) the exploitation of "peripheral" Third World countries. The more general Third World view, however, now seems to admit that it may be better to be "exploited" (even by MNCs) than not to be "exploited" at all, as would be the case if North-South economic relations were broken off completely.

There is little the South can do to force the North to accede to its demands. Strategies such as repudiation of debt and economic boycott would most likely end up hurting the South as well as the North.

THIRD WORLD DEBT

Third World debt is the most acute aspect of North-South confrontation and conflict. Table 3 indicates the size of the capital sums involved and also identifies the seventeen countries called by the World Bank "heavily indebted" relative to their GNPs and their export volumes.[10]

The table shows that "the poorest of the poor"—such low-income countries as the African Sahel—do *not* have heavy debts (Nigeria is an exception). Their creditworthiness is very small by anyone's standards. Twelve of the seventeen heavy debtors are in Latin America, including the Caribbean. The others are the Ivory Coast, Morocco, and Nigeria in Africa, the Philippines in Southeast Asia, and Yugoslavia in Europe. Thirteen of the seventeen are heavy oil importers, but four (Ecuador, Mexico, Nigeria, and Venezuela) are important oil exporters. Of these, all but Mexico are OPEC members.

Debt History

The great bulk of Third World debt dates from the initial oil shock of 1973–74. The Middle Eastern members of OPEC (Iran, Iraq, Kuwait, Qatar, Saudi Arabia, and the United Arab Emirates) rapidly accumulated large surpluses in convertible currency—more than they felt they needed for their own development. The funds were mainly held in American banks. In varying degrees, these countries were anti-American—alienated by what they considered a pro-Israel tilt in American Middle Eastern policy. The more radical of their leaders proposed withdrawing their balances from America, preferably in the form of gold. Such action might have produced a short-term financial panic

---

10. The World Bank apparently believes that private indebtedness is underreported by $200–$250 billion, since the total in the table is that much less than its own debt estimate.

TABLE 3
Debt in Developing Countries, 1987 (in billions of dollars)

Country or Countries	Long-Term Debt Public or Publicly Guaranteed	Total External Debt
Low-Income Countries (38)	216.1	263.3
(Nigeria)	(25.7)	(28.7)
Lower-Middle-Income Countries (34)	376.1	456.7
(Bolivia)	(4.6)	(5.5)
(Chile)	(15.5)	(21.2)
(Colombia)	(13.8)	(17.0)
(Costa Rica)	(3.6)	(4.7)
(Ecuador)	(9.0)	(10.4)
(Ivory Coast)	(8.5)	(13.6)
(Jamaica)	(3.5)	(4.4)
(Morocco)	(18.5)	(20.7)
(Mexico)	(82.8)	(107.9)
(Peru)	(12.5)	(18.1)
(Philippines)	(22.3)	(30.0)
Upper-Middle-Income Countries (15)	288.8	387.4
(Argentina)	(47.5)	(56.8)
(Brazil)	(91.7)	(123.9)
(Uruguay)	(3.0)	(4.2)
(Venezuela)	(25.2)	(36.5)
(Yugoslavia)	(14.4)	(23.5)
All Developing Countries	881.0	1,107.4
(17 Heavily Indebted Countries)	(402.1)	(527.1)

Note: Parentheses identify "heavily indebted" countries.
Source: The World Bank, *World Development Report 1989*, Table 21, pp. 204–205. New York: Oxford University Press, 1989. Used with permission.

on Wall Street—a bank run comparable to that of 1933. We can only guess how the Nixon administration in Washington, already embroiled in the Watergate crisis, might have reacted.

Third World debt is the most acute aspect of North-South confrontation. The great bulk of this debt dates from the oil shock of 1973–74.

The American financial community, anxious to avoid such a panic, proposed to offer the OPEC countries high interest rates for "recycling" their oil revenues, which meant keeping these revenues in the larger American banks. But how could they afford the interest rates that might be necessary to retain those mainly Moslem-owned "petrodollars?"[11] In the short run, this turned out to be no problem. Oil-importing countries, mainly in Latin America, had already embarked on ambitious development plans that depended on uninterrupted oil supplies. To secure these oil supplies at the high OPEC prices, the oil-importing countries needed dollars, and for the dollars, they were willing to pay the high interest rates requested by American banks. In many cases, it was the American lenders

11. An interesting sidelight is that, under the *Sharia* (Moslem religious law)—as under medieval Christian canon law—receipt of interest is strictly illegal! A lender must participate in the borrower's risk and uncertainty so that his income can pass as a profit, or he must prove "opportunities forgone" by the loan, which, under the law, do not include alternative opportunities to earn interest.

who took the initiative in negotiating the loan agreements. Large loans also were made to some non-Moslem oil-exporting LDCs, such as Mexico, avid to obtain funds to expand non-oil industries in advance of future oil revenues.

American lenders negotiated high-interest loans to oil-importing countries, mainly in Latin America, which these countries were subsequently unable to repay.

The loan agreements were drawn up and signed at high speed, without sufficient scrutiny by either side.[12] The oil importers were going to repay the dollar loans mainly from the proceeds of their new industries. Brazilian steel was an important example, and Brazil was the largest borrower. The oil exporters, most notably Mexico, had similar hopes, along with their plans for expanded oil outputs.[13] Both sides apparently assumed that the oil price would not fall or if it did, that Uncle Sam and the World Bank would between them bail out the banks if their loans soured. In these circumstances, "bailout" means paying off the banks' loans and themselves assuming the thankless creditor positions.

Sour the loans did, beginning with an unexpected Mexican default in the summer of 1982. OPEC could not enforce its quota limitations on oil production and exports. In addition, non-OPEC oil production increased—mainly from Mexico, the North Sea in Europe, and the North Slope in Alaska. The world demand for oil turned out to be more sensitive to price changes in the long run than in the short run. A Saudi attempt to use price cuts to force cooperation of non-OPEC members with OPEC rules was a failure. The trend of oil prices turned downward, although remaining above the pre-1973 level even in real terms. At the same time, borrowing countries and their rulers squandered much of the borrowed funds in corruption, capital flight, military budgets, and poorly planned projects.

Much of the borrowed money was squandered, even as oil prices turned downward.

The flamboyant Philippine president, Ferdinand Marcos, and his shoe-loving wife Imelda, became symbols of what went on, although they apparently concentrated their gains in American real estate and securities in preference to the Swiss bank accounts favored by LDC "malefactors of great wealth." Marcos was overthrown in 1986. Why should his successors, or the Filipino people as a whole, repay the bankers for the Marcos family's securities, real estate, and shoe collection—not to mention its mistakes and its corruption?[14] To protect new governments and their peoples, should there be some international equivalents of bankruptcy?[15]

Another part of the debt problem involves import restrictions set up by MDCs. We have mentioned Brazil's steel industry, which has indeed become one of the world's lowest-cost producers. Its expansion, however, has been crippled by a variety of barriers which limit its access to its potential output markets, which include the United States, western Europe, and Japan. And what is true for Brazilian steel is perhaps even more true for agricultural exports like sugar, coffee, and meat. U.S. bans on Argentine beef, except in cans, date back to the 1920s.

Would the suffering of the innocent be avoided by debt forgiveness all around, as suggested by Fidel Castro? When bank capital is so badly impaired that banks are required to close, or when large de-

---

12. Conventional "hard-nosed" commercial and investment banking practice refuses loans unless the borrower presents evidence of ability to earn more than the interest rate on the sum borrowed, over and above meeting the schedule of principal repayment.

13. Not being an OPEC member, Mexico was not contractually subject to that organization's restrictions and quotas on its members' oil production and exports. Although many OPEC members violated their obligations, Mexico refrained in practice from attempts to undermine OPEC.

14. The Aquino government of the Philippines sought to recycle the burden back to the American taxpayer by raising the rent for American military and naval bases there.

15. *Extra*legal equivalents are nothing new, as will be attested to by any holder of Confederate or czarist bonds! On the other hand, to quote President Coolidge on the 1917–1920 inter-allied war debts: "They borrowed the money, didn't they?" In 1931, Coolidge's successor, President Hoover, proposed a one-year moratorium on these debts and also on German reparations. The one-year moratorium then became permanent in practice.

positors withdraw their funds, the financial system comes under substantial strain.

If it is a government institution (rather than a privately owned bank) in a creditor country, or if it is the World Bank itself whose assets are impaired by debt cancellation, the result is an increase in national debts.[16] Directly or indirectly, the residents of creditor countries must pay assessed taxes or inflation taxes when what were to be loans to LDCs actually become grants-in-aid. In development economics as elsewhere, there is no such thing as a free lunch.

The Debt Impasse

The first Mexican debt crisis (1982) was followed by one or more debt crises a year, as one or another country got in trouble or as an earlier solution unraveled. The result looks like Ponzi finance—the carrying charges on debts are being paid, but the total volume of debt rises despite the repayments.[17] This is because new money has been lent to finance new programs as well as to finance old debts. The new loans are often conditional on "austerity"— higher taxes, lower public expenditures, reduced credit expansion and monetary growth, lower inflation rates, scrapping of price and wage controls, etc. When LDC legislatures, military, or trade-union movements reject or overturn some of these conditions, we call the result an unraveling of the previous solution and the outbreak of a new crisis.

The Mexican debt crisis of 1982 was followed by at least one LDC debt crisis a year for several years. The total volume of LDC debt keeps rising as new money is lent to finance both new programs and old debts.

Other provisions of debt renegotiations have been longer repayment periods, lower interest rates, and moratoria on principal repayments.[18] On the LDC side, there have been frequent attempts to form united fronts of debtor countries to demand still easier terms. None of these has as yet had great success. However, several plans for longer-term settlement have been suggested and to some extent put into effect. We mention four of these: the Baker plan, debt-equity swaps, the Camdessus plan, and the Miyazawa plan.

The Baker Plan James Baker was secretary of the United States Treasury in the second Reagan administration. His plan included generous renegotiations on a case-by-case basis, LDC austerity undertakings, and a substantial supply of new money by private banks on their own responsibilities (not involving American taxpayers). Many smaller lending banks, with little or no interest in the LDCs, refused to "send good money after bad" and did not cooperate. The Treasury Department made no serious attempt at administrative guidance or other forms of indirect pressure on the banks.

Debt-Equity Swaps Debt-equity swaps have become quite common, although on a relatively small scale. In a debt-equity swap, an LDC debt is written down by its creditor bank, which sells some part of that debt at a discount to a business firm. The firm then uses these (dollar) funds to buy LDC currency at a discount below the official rate and to erect facilities there, or it may choose to buy equity interests in existing LDC companies, either public or private. A serious problem arises when this device is used on a large scale or with regard to strategic companies. This is because MDC firms are not interested in minority stock ownership without effective control, while LDC governments and politicians worry about ceding too much control to foreigners, especially in public utilities and defense industries.

The Camdessus Plan Michel Camdessus, from the French Central Bank (Banque de France) and director-general of the International Monetary Fund, proposes new issues of Special Drawing Rights (SDRs, alias "paper gold"). His expectation

---

16. As for the World Bank, it raises most of its loan funds by the sale of its own securities on the open market, but its capital is subscribed by member governments. An impairment of its capital would therefore be a debt increase for all these member governments, even those of the LDCs.

17. Ponzi finance is a process of servicing old debts by disbursing "profits" out of the proceeds of new loans or contributions. It surely antedates Ponzi himself, an international swindler of 1919–20.

18. Many loan agreements call for interest rates a certain percentage above the London Inter-Bank Offered Rate (LIBOR). The LDCs prefer low rates independent of LIBOR.

is that LDC SDR allocations will be used to reduce their outstanding debts. The United States is skeptical about this approach, claiming that such increases in world liquidity are unnecessary and probably inflationary. For the same reason, the United States has opposed the large increases in IMF capital that would be required to put the plan into effect.

The Miyazawa Plan Kiichi Miyazawa, minister of finance in the first Takeshita cabinet in Japan, has suggested that his country lend money to LDC governments that are willing to cooperate. Japan would lend only to countries willing to carry out austerity and privatization programs under Japanese supervision, and the cooperating LDCs could repay part or all of their debts with the loan proceeds. The new Japanese loans would be guaranteed by the World Bank. Japan also looks with favor on the Camdessus (IMF) plan. The United States opposes the Japanese proposal as indirectly requiring taxpayers to guarantee loan repayments and as reducing the responsibilities of the lending banks.

Several plans for longer repayment periods have been suggested: the Baker plan (generous renegotiations, LDC austerity, loans by private banks), debt-equity swaps, the Camdessus plan (new issues of SDRs), and the Miyazawa plan (Japanese loans based on promises of austerity).

Effect on North-South Relations

Since 1982, the protest of the South has shifted at least temporarily from the grandiose NIEO package to the more prosaic matter of easing its own debt burden and considering a united front to present the North with a common set of debt-lightening demands. In the autumn of 1988, the IMF held an international conference in West Berlin. Radical partisans of the South picketed this meeting and conducted a four-day "people's tribunal" of the IMF and World Bank on the ground that the conditions they attach to financial aid to Third World countries amount to economic war against them.

Susan George, an American sociologist, attacked the North's position. She alleged that the debt obligations have become a means through which First World countries gain control over Third World countries. By insisting on austerity in the debtor countries, the IMF and World Bank assure that raw materials can be purchased at low prices, thereby maintaining the vitality of First World economies and keeping the debtor countries in dependency. In arrangements that swap debt for equity, creditors gain control of the infrastructures of these debtor countries, thereby gaining even greater control.[19]

---

19. Associated Press dispatch from Berlin (*Japan Times*, September 28, 1988). To George's remarks, George Wald, 1967 Nobel-laureate biologist, added: "The Third World debt is a marvelous instrument of control. And its advantage is, it's so large that it can never be paid back."

Economics in Focus

Debt-for-Nature Swaps

While economists worry about Third World debt, environmentalists have become alarmed about the destruction of tropical forests, the extinction of wildlife species, and other ecological damage in developing countries— damage that affects the entire globe, not just the nation in question. But Third World countries with huge debts have no extra funds for the environment, and they resent the suggestion that they should slow their development by setting aside critical lands and resources for conservation. Often they believe they must exploit every available resource to service their loans.

Recently some groups have tried to resolve the impasse with arrangements called debt-for-nature swaps. The details may vary, and they tend to be complex, but consider this hypothetical illustration. A U.S. environmental organization purchases $1 million of Costa Rica's debt from an American bank. Because the prospects of complete repayment are slim, the bank sells the debt for only $300,000. Next, the environmental group trades the debt (still worth $1 million at face value) to Costa Rica for new government bonds, also valued at $1 million but issued in Costa Rica's own currency. The U.S. organization then donates these bonds to a private Costa Rican environmental group that will use the proceeds for important conservation projects. Ideally, everyone benefits. Costa Rica has traded debt in hard-to-raise dollars, owed to foreigners, for debt in local currency that will be used for the nation's good. The environmental group has made a $1 million donation by spending less than a third of that amount. And the bank gets a tax deduction for its $700,000 paper loss, now dubbed a charitable contribution.

Debt-for-nature swaps have already taken place in Costa Rica, Bolivia, and Ecuador. In Costa Rica some of the funds have aided a massive effort to restore a dryland forest. In Ecuador the funds are being used to protect national parks. As of early 1989, further swaps were being negotiated for Peru, Mexico, the Philippines, and Jamaica, and environmental groups were trying to arrange similar deals for yet other nations that owed large sums to Western governments or international banks.

There are some drawbacks, however. These swaps can account for only a small portion of Third World debt. Thus, as larger-scale plans for handling the debt take hold, the swaps may seem less attractive to banks or to governments. Some analysts also worry that the exchanges aggravate inflation in the developing country by raising domestic spending.

Nevertheless, supporters believe the idea is worth pursuing. According to Alvaro Umaña, Costa Rica's minister of natural resources, "If you just do debt relief, you may be supporting an overvalued currency or faulty industrial policies. We would like to see debt relief support conservation instead—a policy that everybody agrees is good."

Sources: Clemens P. Work and Geri Smith, "Using Red Ink to Keep Tropical Forests Green," *U.S. News & World Report*, March 6, 1989, pp. 48–49; Thomas A. Lewis, "Nature Reaps a Cash Bonanza," *International Wildlife*, January-February 1989, p. 37; Thomas A. Sancton, "Hands Across the Sea," *Time*, January 2, 1989, pp. 62–63; "Banking on African Conservation," *Science News*, January 28, 1989, p. 62; Umaña quotation from Jason Zweig, "Capital Conservation," *Forbes*, April 17, 1989, p. 208.

SUMMARY

1. Economic development is different from economic growth. Economic development includes structural change, as progress is made toward some specific goal or set of goals that improve the welfare of the masses. (See page 454.)

2. Of the 129 countries reporting to the World Bank, close to 100 are regarded as LDCs belonging to the Third World. The First World comprises the essentially capitalist industrialized MDCs. (See page 455 and Table 1, page 455.)

3. There is no generally accepted theory of economic development. Hirschman classifies theories according to whether they assume that MDC analysis works well with LDCs (monoeconomics) and whether the theories assume that there is community of interest. (See page 458.)

4. Adam Smith was a development optimist. He believed that growth required little beyond "peace, easy taxes, and a tolerable administration of justice." (See page 458.)

5. Thomas Malthus was a development pessimist. He foresaw population increases overtaking food supplies and holding incomes to subsistence levels. (See page 459.)

6. Karl Marx and his followers—among them Lenin and Rosa Luxemburg—were pessimists about capitalist development. They saw development as leading to stagnation, imperialism, and war by a number of alternative routes. (See pages 459–460.)

7. *Dependencia* theory, pessimistic and influenced by Marxism, bases much of its argument on neomercantilism as well as capitalism generally. The division of labor between LDCs and MDCs, or between the mother country and her colonies, plays an important part in this theory. (See pages 460–461.)

8. The most striking feature of W. W. Rostow's "Non-Communist Manifesto" theory of economic development is its stress on a single-generation "takeoff" in which saving rates rise and "leading industries" increase sharply in both number and importance. (See page 462.)

9. The "vicious-cycle" theory states that unless helped from the outside, poor countries will remain poor because they cannot save and build the capital stock required to raise productivity, nor are they able to attract investment funds due to their low demand for most goods and services. (See pages 462–463.)

10. Cultural-development theories by social scientists outside of economics emphasize cultural factors such as religion, custom, and tradition. (See page 463.)

11. The development process in the present MDCs has been marked, according to the Kuznets hypothesis, by rising income inequality in its early stages—a trend that is later reversed. (See page 464.)

12. The World Bank seeks to correct the pattern of inequality in the present LDCs. The bank's efforts have stressed the basic human needs strategy and "appropriate technology" that keeps up the demand for semiskilled labor in meaningful jobs. (See page 464.)

13. Another distributive problem is the dualism between urban (industrial) and rural (agricultural) areas, as well as between modern and traditional industries, which usually accompanies growth. (See page 464–465.)

14. There is considerable hostility between the industrialized MDCs of the First World (the North) and the LDCs of the Third World (the South). LDC resentment and envy have brought about the South's demand for a New International Economic Order (NIEO) to replace the present system. Many LDCs consider the present system exploitative and blame it for their underdevelopment. (See page 465.)

15. LDCs' demands cover the areas of trade; debt, aid, and capital movements; internal economic policies; and political issues. (See pages 465–467.)

16. Third World debt is currently the greatest source of North-South confrontation and conflict. The World Bank has identified seventeen "heavy debtor" countries that have a combined external debt of about $527 billion. (See pages 467–468 and Table 3, page 468.)

17. Much of the outstanding Third World debt can be traced back to the desire of American banks to hold large sums of OPEC "petrodollars," for which high interest rates had to be paid, and the subsequent lending of these funds to oil-importing LDCs. (See pages 468–469.)

18. Debt crises have become commonplace as one LDC or another gets into financial difficulty or an earlier plan unravels. New loans, often to finance old debts, are frequently conditional on certain austerity behavior of the LDCs. (See page 469.)

19. We discuss four plans for longer-term Third World debt settlement that have been suggested and at least partially put into effect. These are the Baker plan, debt-equity swaps, the Camdessus plan, and the Miyazawa plan. (See pages 470–471.)

KEY TERMS

basic human needs (BHN): an approach to economic development that says a country is developing if and only if more and more of its people are gaining adequate diets, clean water, decent shelter, basic health care and education, and a peaceful means of making their views known to the government (page 454).

dependencia: neo-Marxist theories of underdevelopment that argue that the prosperity of the First World is dependent upon the poverty of the Third World, and the poverty of the Third World is dependent upon the prosperity of the First World (page 460).

economic development: economic progress that brings gains in welfare, making life better for the masses (page 454).

economic dualism: a regional distribution problem wherein LDC cities become enclaves of modernization and prosperity in otherwise stagnant countries (page 465).

First World: the advanced industrialized countries (page 455).

gross domestic product (GDP): the total value of production that takes place per year in a country (page 456).

monoeconomics: economic theories that assume that methods devised in MDCs to deal with

MDC problems also work well in LDCs (page 458).

Second World: countries with centrally planned economies (page 455).

social overhead capital: roads, harbors, schools, and public health facilities (page 462).

Third World: the developing countries (page 455).

DISCUSSION QUESTIONS

1. Describe two patterns of economic change in Faroffistan: (a) a process of growth without development, and (b) a process of development without growth.

2. To expand Adam Smith's prescription for development, what factors would you add to his "peace, easy taxes, and a tolerable administration of justice"?

3. Compare the Marxist-Leninist and the *dependencia* development theories.

4. Is there, in your opinion, a monoeconomics equally applicable to MDCs and LDCs?

5. Are the growth and development processes in the MDCs helpful or harmful to LDC aspirations?

6. What is the basic human needs approach to development theory?

7. Summarize the existing international economic order that the South is attacking. Are its free-trade or its protectionist features most under attack?

8. Do you agree that direct aid and concessional loans are owed by MDCs to LDCs as reparations for colonialism, imperialism, and/or MNC exploitation?

9. Some LDCs are oil exporters; most are oil importers. Nevertheless, the solidarity of the South was not broken after the rise of OPEC. How can this be explained?

10. Many Latin American countries consider the 1980s a "lost decade" or "dead decade" in economic development. Can you explain this?

Japanese-American Economic Warfare?

Japanese-American relations have taken a paradoxical turn in the last third of the twentieth century, as World War II (1941–1945, in the Pacific Theater) and the Allied Occupation of Japan (1945–1952) have faded into the mists of "ancient" history. The political and economic aspects of the two countries' relations have gone "out of sync" with each other. On the political front, a Japanese-American alliance has become a keystone of each country's diplomatic and defense policy in the entire Pacific basin. On the economic front, rivalry, hostility, and mutual recrimination have taken center stage, perhaps more in America than in Japan.[1] Doctrinaire economic "interpretationists" of political history assure us that in such cases economics will eventually dominate and politics will follow along. Most of the rest of us—Japanese, Americans, and citizens of other countries—hope that this will not occur. There is considerable historical support for our hopes.[2]

MACROECONOMIC ASPECTS—BEHIND THE HEADLINES

Let us review what has happened. The traditional surplus position of the peacetime American bilateral trade and current-account balances with Japan began to fall in the 1950s as a result of Japan's postwar recovery—the so-called "second economic miracle"—which raised production of both potential exports and import-competing goods. The American surplus fell to zero during the Vietnam War period of the mid-1960s. By the early 1980s, the bilateral balance—now negative for America and positive for Japan—had become the largest such balance between any two countries in the entire history of international trade. Amounting to approximately one-third of the total (multilateral) American trade deficit, this negative bilateral balance with Japan became, not surprisingly, the focus of American producer-interests' resentment. The erosion of America's trade position—both the relative decline of its exports and the absolute increase in its imports—presented a very threatening situation. The American trade problem became, in the public media, a "Japan" problem.

The changes in the American trade and current-account positions were, however, *multilateral,* not merely bilateral with Japan or any other single country. In fact, by the mid-1980s, the United States had negative bilateral balances with almost all of its principal First World trading partners.

The opposite was true for Japan. The Japanese bilateral trade and current-account balances turned positive, not only with the United States but also with nearly all of Japan's trading partners, capitalist and socialist, advanced and developing. Australia became the only large country combining bilateral trade surpluses with Japan and bilateral trade deficits with the United States.

---

1. Japanese pollsters periodically survey public opinion, including questions on which foreign countries the Japanese like best (or dislike least). The United States has continued to rank quite high in this popularity contest, especially as compared with the Soviet Union.

2. Anglo-American relations were similarly "out of sync" in the last third of the nineteenth century. Political friendship coexisted with economic hostility, at least on the American side. Britain, secure in her position as "workshop of the world," was a free-trade country "too proud to fight" and waited complacently for America's dominant Republican party to repent the errors of its anti-British protectionism. The rise of Hohenzollern Germany, culminating in World War I, brought on a triumph of political friendship over economic rivalry. More recently, American relations with the European Community (EC) have also come to follow the same out of sync path as American relations with Japan.

The multilateral character of the changes in both American and Japanese international balances suggests that they reflect economic phenomena affecting their entire economies rather than relations between the two countries themselves. To examine such macroeconomic matters, we can employ macroeconomic identities. For each country, as we have seen,[3]

$$(I - S) + (G - T_n) + (X - I_m) = 0$$

and also

$$(\Delta I - \Delta S) + (\Delta G - \Delta T_n) + (\Delta X - \Delta I_m) = 0$$

In the American case, $(I - S)$ has trended upward because of a declining trend of private saving as a fraction of GNP.[4] At the same time, $(G - T_n)$ has also trended upward as a consequence of tax cuts, military-budget increases, congressional attachment to social spending, and home-district "pork barrels." The combination of positive $(I - S)$ and $(G - T_n)$ requires negative $(X - I_m)$, the multilateral current-account deficit.[5]

The international macroeconomic identities, precisely because they are identities, do not by themselves imply that the decline in the U.S. saving rate and the increase in government purchases caused the current account deficit. This sequence simply appears more realistic than other sequences, which might, for example, interpret the falling American saving rate as the result of deficits in the current account and the public finances.

The Japanese case is slightly, but only slightly, more complex. In Japan, private saving has traditionally been a high percentage of the national income. Its absolute amount has therefore risen with income more rapidly than has private domestic investment, so that $(I - S)$ has turned negative. While retreating from the Occupation's disinflationary insistence on budgetary balance, Japanese macroeconomic policy has in most years remained restrictive, so that the deficit $(G - T_n)$, while positive, has been close enough to zero for the subtotal $[(I - S) + (G - T_n)]$ to remain negative. Japan's positive multilateral current-account balance $(X - I_m)$ could therefore be regarded as a result of domestic saving and fiscal policies.[6]

THE EXCHANGE RATE

Let us grant that American macroeconomic practice and policy have led to a negative multilateral balance of the American current account, while Japanese macroeconomic practice and policy have led to a positive balance. The question remains, to what extent are these multilateral divergences reflected in the bilateral balances between these countries themselves? Any full answer to this question in real terms must include the sizes of the two economies, and the dependence of each country on its imports from and exports to the other. We shall not attempt to answer these questions here. We concentrate instead on a monetary factor, namely the exchange rate between their two monies. The yen-dollar exchange rate was fixed at ¥360 to the dollar in 1949, by the Allied Occupation under the command of General Douglas MacArthur. It remained at that level until 1971. Since that date it has fluctuated sharply. For example, the dollar rose fairly steadily from ¥170 to ¥260 between 1980 and 1985, then fell steadily to ¥120 in 1988. What difference have these fluctuations made? Has the cheaper dollar banked or fed the flames of Japanese-American economic cold warfare? Neither the one nor the other, from the American side at least. The principal effect of the cheaper dollar has been some shift of hostilities from the *trade* to the *capital*

---

3. Recall that:

I	is investment	T_n	is net taxes
S	is savings	X	is exports
G	is government purchases	I_m	is imports

4. There is as yet no agreement among economists regarding the responsibility for this decline. Among the candidates are Madison Avenue and its advertising industry, the rise of "plastic money" as an engine of easy credit, the expansion of welfare-state institutions—particularly Social Security and private pensions—and a tax system allegedly biased in favor of consumption, not saving.

5. The "twin towers" explanation of the trade deficit as the result of the towering budgetary deficit is at best a half-truth because it ignores the $(I - S)$ balance of the private sector.

6. A more devious, not to say conspiratorial, causation pattern is occasionally alleged by Japan-bashers. Hungry to build up their foreign assets (by capital exports), the Japanese have required current-account surpluses to pay for them. Maintenance of current-account surpluses, combined with Japan's large private saving $(I - S)$ deficit, prevents the Japanese government from stimulating domestic demand by increasing spending (or cutting taxes) as much as foreign critics would like. There seems to be no historical evidence for this pattern.

front. In the following paragraphs, we examine the effects of the so-called "bargain-basement dollar" on the bilateral current and capital accounts.

Current-Account Effects An increasing American complaint against Japan, in the last dozen years of the ¥360 rate, was Japan's unwillingness to recognize and remedy the alleged undervaluation of the yen. As Japanese productivity rose, the ¥360 rate—fixed by the Occupation, not by the Japanese—made Japanese products "unfairly" cheap in America and American products "unfairly" expensive in Japan. A "level playing field," as surveyed in America, apparently required a stronger yen to avoid wage cuts and "speedups" for American workers. The converse of a stronger yen was, of course, a weaker dollar—a phrase taboo outside of economics classes!

After 1973 the yen floated—usually not quite freely. The subsequent record seemed to show the American trade and current-account balances with Japan becoming more negative as the dollar rose and less negative as the dollar fell, but only after a time lag of eighteen to twenty-four months, and only in smaller degree than the Americans had hoped.[7]

Capital-Account Effects The fluctuating dollar has capital-account effects as well, and in the opposite

7. The so-called Marshall-Lerner condition for exchange markets tells us, under a number of restrictive conditions, that cheapening of a country's currency will increase its current-account balance if the sum of two price elasticities exceeds unity. These elasticities are the country's demand for imports from its trading partner and the trading partner's demand for the country's exports. (This topic is discussed more fully in advanced courses in international economics.)

direction to the current-account effects. A strong yen—or, if you prefer, a weak dollar—makes American real estate, government bonds, corporate securities, and companies themselves cheaper for the Japanese. It also makes the corresponding Japanese assets expensive for Americans. The so-called "bargain-basement dollar" accordingly fostered a significant net passage of American assets into Japanese ownership—chiefly urban real estate and public and private securities but also "directly productive facilities," meaning operating business enterprises.[8] Three features of this transfer process arouse American apprehension, sometimes approaching paranoia.

1. Concentration in particular localities, especially the Hawaiian Islands, southern California, and Alaska. These regions, the Japan-bashers claim, are in danger of becoming Japanese economic enclaves, with the American "natives" reduced to the second-class status of the Polynesians of Hawaii or the Eskimos of Alaska.

2. Holdings of Treasury securities—the national debt. In the short run, of course, Japanese demand has the effect of lowering interest rates. In the longer run, it may give Japanese interests too much control over American macroeconomic policy, including the power to destabilize the economy by "dumping the debt" and driving up U.S. interest rates. This means either perpetual depression or runaway inflation, at the will of the Japanese "malefactors of great wealth."

3. Holdings by Japanese multinationals. The great bulk of Japanese investments in American private securities seems to be passive "portfolio" investment by individuals seeking dividends and capital gains. It is criticized, however, as though it would soon become direct investment, which also strives for partial or complete control. Moreover, widespread control of American firms by large Japanese multinational conglomerates like Mitsubishi or Sumitomo may, say the critics, have frightening consequences for American national defense, for the location of research and development, for the international movement of technology, and for the advancement of American workers, both blue collar and white collar.

All three of these concerns may be less than rational, both quantitatively and qualitatively. There is too much American ownership to be bought up so easily—America is not Luxembourg or Monaco. Foreign ownership is more European and Canadian than it is Japanese. Most Japanese owners are merely portfolio investors. Foreign firms in America, including Japanese-controlled ones, are no more likely to be oppressive or predatory than American-owned firms in Canada, in Europe, or in other advanced countries (including Japan itself).[9] Finally, the checkered historical record of foreign investment in American enterprises, notably European investment in canals, railroads, and real estate before World War I, features the victimization of the gullible European investors by the American "robber barons," not the reverse.

MICROECONOMIC ASPECTS—THE HEADLINES THEMSELVES

Headlines, cover stories, and TV programs about Japanese-American economic rivalry have been about specific industries, from rice to computers. The macroeconomic storms, like cold waves from Siberia, have moved from one area to another, making headlines as they went.

In the mid-1950s, rivalry began with textiles and clothing. The Japanese "dollar blouse" was a symbol. It then moved in two directions. The first was

8. This essay does not inquire *why* the dollar fluctuated as it did. However, in the important case of the 1979–1985 run-up of the dollar in Tokyo—in the face of a negative and falling American current-account balance with Japan—the rate seems to have responded chiefly to the rise of American interest rates, which cheapened American assets for Japanese buyers, plus liberalization of Japanese rules that previously restricted the holding of such assets by Japanese. Summary: capital-account considerations were in this case more important than current-account ones in governing exchange markets.

9. In the dear dead days of the ¥360 dollar, you may well ask, why did *Americans* not buy up *Japanese* assets and gain access to all that productive, low-cost Japanese labor, not to mention that pool of low-interest Japanese saving? Because the Japanese did in fact fear infusion of American capital with as much paranoia as the Americans would later display toward Japanese capital. Any such invasion plans were therefore warded off by the Japanese Ministry of International Trade and Industry, the "notorious MITI," using the device of exchange control. MITI did not permit large-scale purchase of yen by present or potential rivals of Japanese firms in key industries.

toward heavy industry and high technology: autos, steel, electronics, semiconductors, financial services. The second direction was agricultural: beef, citrus, and rice.

There have also been two patterns of conflict. Most obvious to Americans has been the Japanese entry into the American market—the most lucrative and most nearly open fraction of the world market. Most obvious to the Japanese have been the American attempts to expand their footholds in the newly important Japanese markets for farm products and a wide range of services (banking, insurance, construction).

No single microeconomic skirmish in either country means very much in terms of the underlying macroeconomic realities. Each skirmish in its turn, however, has been where the action is.

Popular economics in both America and Japan has been conditioned by mercantilistic stress on producer as against consumer interests, and also by historical experience hardened into something close to "natural law." The American economy of mass production and high wages was fostered by a protectionist tradition dating from Alexander Hamilton and Henry Clay. "Yankee ingenuity" and relative immunity from the costs of two world wars gave twentieth-century America, it was commonly believed, a natural right to a God-given position as the world's technological leader, creditor, and economic power, with the world's most durable trade surplus and the world's highest standard of living. "All power corrupts, and absolute power corrupts absolutely," in economics as in politics. Japanese folk economics is colored by Japan's lack of natural resources. Forced to import both raw materials for their manufactured exports and (in the twentieth century) a significant fraction of their staple food, the Japanese came to regard as unpatriotic additional imports of goods that could be produced at home, either in the present or in the near future. This mercantilism was hardened by a history of periodic negative balances and import shortages causing recession or depression, or leading to malnutrition and dependence on American aid. Was the post-1965 prosperity a new order of things, or just a dreamlike interlude?

Why has Japanese-American competition become so embittered? The answer is different in each industry, which makes it difficult to avoid passing on horror stories—true and false—on both sides of each key industry. The Americans blame the Japanese. The Japanese are unfair. They play "dirty tricks." Japanese rules keep changing and are enforced selectively against foreign exporters. They dump subsidized products overseas below cost to gain market share and drive out competition. Their home market is surreptitiously but systematically closed. Their policy is to sell without buying. And the Japanese blame the Americans. The Americans engage in Japan-bashing and complain to Washington instead of adapting to the new realities of Japanese postwar recovery. The Americans cling to wage rates, labor costs, and profit margins that are now uncompetitively high, and to productivity and quality standards that are now uncompetitively low. Perhaps for racist reasons, they refuse to adjust their export offerings to foreign tastes and foreign ignorance of English. The oversized American car with its steering wheel on the "wrong" side was for many years a symbol in this regard.

The new protectionism of quotas, administrative protection, "voluntary" export restrictions, and "orderly marketing arrangements" is different from the old protectionism of tariffs. The guiding genius of the new protectionism was probably the American-born German banker Hjalmar Schacht, who became Hitler's finance minister. Japan learned the new protectionism more quickly and accepted it more wholeheartedly than America. This may be because Japan's elitist higher civil service, including MITI, recruits a larger fraction of its country's top legal and economic brains than its American equivalent and is more confident of its own knowledge of its country's best interests. Also, the bureaucracy and business interests are closely allied in Japan, whereas in America, the bureaucracy includes elements that business considers to be neutral, if not downright hostile.

GRIEVANCES AND POLITICAL REPERCUSSIONS

"Beauty," we say, "is in the eye of the beholder." Fairness, likewise, is in the ethos of the judge—especially between competitors who claim to be playing different games under different rules. When Japanese and American negotiators, public and private, cannot agree upon the rules and how they should be enforced, the best we can hope for may be an agreed-upon grievance procedure patterned after the binding arbitration provisions of collective-bargaining contracts in domestic industrial relations.

They might, but need not, proceed most smoothly and expeditiously under the auspices of GATT (the General Agreement on Tariffs and Trade). Binding arbitration has its problems too, however, even with the most knowledgeable and impartial of arbitrators.

Will increasing numbers of microeconomic Japanese-American controversies simply be allowed to fester unresolved? Each one is of supreme importance to participants on either side, and sometimes also to localities such as metropolitan Detroit with its auto plants and Akron with its tire plants. The eventual consequences of accumulating unresolved disputes may be also highly unpleasant to politicians in one or both countries.

Consider the following scenario, which may become more plausible in the future than it is now:

Another American trade bill goes into effect, with harsher provisions than the 1988 legislation.

There is now to be automatic discrimination across the board against unspecified countries with large positive bilateral trade balances with the United States who close their markets to American exports or whose own imports sell in America at prices below their average costs of production (plus 8 percent profit) as estimated by the American government. This law is enforced in practice primarily against Japan. Contemporaneously with this intensified Japan-bashing, the Soviet Union reverses its anti-Japanese stand. The Soviets offer to return to Japan the four southern-most islands of the Kurile chain, which have been in dispute between the two countries since 1945,[10] as part of a treaty of peace and friend-

10. These islands were part of Hokkaido Prefecture before 1945 and had never been under Russian rule. Their present population, however, is believed to include only Soviet citizens, all Japanese having been repatriated.

ship officially ending the Pacific War. The treaty also increases and improves investment opportunities for Japanese companies in the development of Soviet Siberia. In exchange, Japan is asked to become neutral, or "nonaligned," like Sweden, Switzerland, or India. This would require ending the Japanese-American Security Treaty of 1960 and require American evacuation of military, naval, and air bases in Japan and Okinawa. This consequence of festering trade disputes would surely be bad news for the American Department of Defense, even though it would not move Japan behind the Iron Curtain.

POSTSCRIPT

Discussions similar to this one could also be directed toward American economic relations with the European Community or with the newly industrialized economies of East Asia such as Korea, Taiwan, Hong Kong, and Singapore. They could also be written about Japanese economic relations with the European Community and with the East Asian countries just mentioned. The Japanese-American relationship differs from the others primarily because of its larger size and longer duration.

Consumer Choice

Market Demand and Elasticity

Business Firm Choice

Market Supply and Elasticity

PART VII
THE BEHAVIOR OF CONSUMERS AND FIRMS

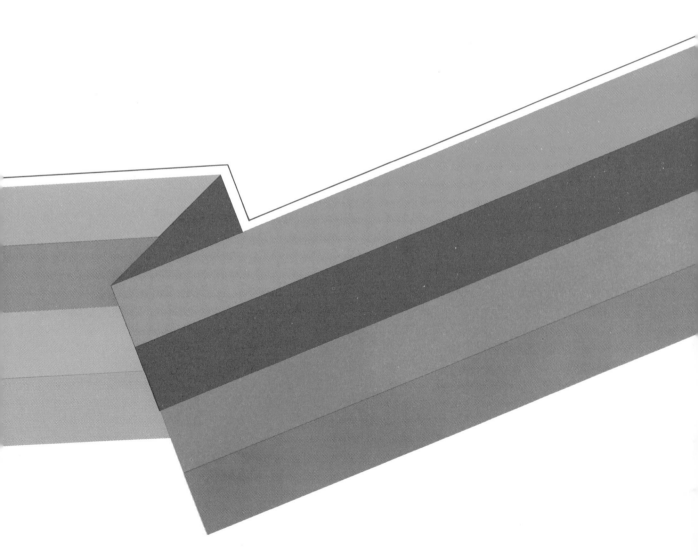

22
Consumer Choice

Preview In this chapter we begin the study of microeconomics, the part of economics that focuses on the behavior of particular decision makers within the economy. We start with the concept of the individual demander, which we introduced in Chapter 5.

Opening with a brief review of the demand curve, we then go on to present a more detailed explanation of why individual consumers spend their incomes the way they do. We look behind that curve at the underlying forces at work and show how the demand curve is derived. Economists have offered a number of theories of consumer behavior. Here we discuss the best-known one, which is called *utility analysis*. (The appendix to this chapter offers a second widely held approach, called *indifference curve analysis*.)

The explanation of utility analysis is followed by two extensions of this theory: *consumers' surplus* and the *paradox of value*. The first one explains why it is that consumers generally gain satisfaction from their market transactions. The second allows us to explain the apparent paradox, or contradiction, that consumers often pay higher prices for less useful goods than they do for more important ones.

REVIEW OF THE DEMAND CURVE

In Chapter 5 we suggested that it was reasonable to expect an inverse relationship between the quantity demanded and the price of a good or a service. Most students find it quite obvious, and also consistent with their own experience, that people demand greater quantities of goods and services at low prices and fewer at high prices. However, not wishing to rely on intuition alone, we offered in Chapter 5 an explanation consisting of two parts—the income effect and the substitution effect. The income effect is the effect that a price change has on a person's real income or purchasing power. The substitution effect is the effect that a change in price has on relative prices of substitutable goods. Together, the two effects suggest that people buy more of a good when its price is lower because the lower price causes them to be "richer" and because they now find that substitute goods have become relatively more expensive. On the other hand, they suggest that people will buy less of a good when its price is higher because the higher price causes them to be "poorer" and substitute goods to be relatively cheaper. Though this explanation may be adequate, further insight into the reasons behind consumer behavior will be helpful.

People demand greater quantities of goods and services at low prices and fewer at higher prices because of the income effect and the substitution effect.

UTILITY ANALYSIS

Utility analysis attempts to explain the underlying forces of consumer behavior. It dates back to the 1870s, when the British economist William Stanley Jevons, the Austrian economist Karl Menger, and the French economist Leon Walras introduced the theory to analyze why consumers buy what they do.

Assumptions of Utility Analysis

Utility analysis relies on the following key assumptions:

1. Consumers are rational.
2. Utility, meaning expected satisfaction, is for each consumer a measurable quantity.
3. Marginal utility (the additional utility gained from consuming one more unit of a product) decreases as the consumption rate of a particular product increases.
4. Total utility increases as the consumption rate of a particular product increases.
5. Consumers have limited income with which to buy the goods and services they want.
6. Consumers know the prices of all goods and services that they might buy.

These are the six main assumptions of utility analysis. You may remember from Chapter 3 that simplification and isolation are necessary in order to see and understand relationships between particular variables. Some of these assumptions may not fully describe reality, and some may not apply in all cases. But they are helpful in understanding the important relationships that are revealed in utility analysis theory. We shall take a closer look at each of these assumptions in the following paragraphs.

Utility analysis is a theory used to explain the underlying forces of consumer behavior. It assumes that consumers are rational, utility can be measured, marginal utility decreases as consumption increases, total utility increases as consumption increases, incomes are limited, and prices are known.

Consumer Rationality What economists mean by a **rational consumer** was briefly described in our discussion of rationality in Chapter 3. A consumer is assumed to be rational, meaning that he or she seeks to maximize his or her satisfaction. It is therefore rational to try to get the most out of one's income by selecting the mix of goods and services that promises to offer the greatest amount of personal satisfaction. For example, if a person is faced with the choice of buying a dollar's worth of bananas or a dollar's worth of ice cream, and if the person prefers the ice cream to the bananas, it would not be rational for him or her to purchase the bananas.

A rational consumer seeks to maximize his or her satisfaction.

Measurable Utility **Utility** is a measure or expression of an individual consumer's expected, or anticipated, satisfaction. As we have said, this may be either more or less than this person's actual satisfaction. Utility theory assumes that total and marginal utility are measurable. The measure of utility (unit of anticipated satisfaction) is often called a **util**. Try to imagine assigning a util value to things you are planning to consume. Of course, people do not assign these util values to goods and services in real life. However, the theory predicts that people act as if they do—as if they have roughly calculated utility schedules in their minds as they do their shopping. The theory also predicts that, at least in the long run, utility, measured in utils, has more power in determining consumption patterns than, say, the facts about a person's routine behavior.

Utility is a measure of an individual consumer's expected satisfaction. The unit of anticipated satisfaction is called a util.

Utility is subjective, or personal, in its meaning. The absolute number of utils assigned to a unit of a good or service by a person means nothing in itself. What is important is how that absolute number relates to the number that the person assigns to other units of the same good or service and to other available goods and services. For example, if an individual assigns 100 utils to the first potato at a meal, 50 utils to the second potato at this meal, and 1,000 utils to a steak at this same meal, it can be determined that this person likes the first potato twice as much as the second potato and the steak ten times as much as the first potato and twenty

times as much as the second potato. The individual could have expressed exactly the same tastes by assigning 2 utils to the first potato, 1 util to the second potato, and 20 utils to the steak. The second example simply uses a different scale, with the utility ratios left unchanged.

Modern economists who concern themselves with consumer welfare limit or qualify the measurability of utility in a very important way. They hold that utility comparisons can be legitimately made by a single individual, but that it is *not* valid to compare the satisfaction or utility that two different individuals receive from the same good or service. There is no comparable scale. Both an ascetic monk and a high-living playboy may assign 1,000 utils to a steak and 100 utils to a potato, so that they would both be expressing a 10 to 1 ratio. However, no one can be sure from this fact that the two receive the same satisfaction from the steak or the potato.

Economists realize that a person's expression of utility is not formed in a vacuum, but that it reflects one's social environment. Most of us have taboos against eating human flesh or buying slaves, but in other times or other societies we might feel differently. Orthodox Jews and Moslems will not eat pork, orthodox Hindus will not eat beef, and orthodox vegetarians will not eat meat of any kind or fish or sometimes eggs. People brought up in Italian households will seek carbohydrates largely from pasta in the form of spaghetti, ravioli, lasagna, and so on. People brought up in Oriental households will seek them largely from plain boiled rice. In the same way, people may value particular consumption patterns mainly to show how rich (or poor), how modern (or traditional), or how intellectual (or anti-intellectual) they are (or wish they were). The American economist Thorstein Veblen spoke of "conspicuous consumption," both of the rich showing off their wealth and of the poor pretending to be richer than they were. All such behavior may be entirely rational to the consumer who engages in it, whatever you, or we, or the rest of the world may think about it.

The absolute number of utils assigned to a unit of a good or service by a person means nothing

---

in itself. What is important is how that absolute number relates to the number the person assigns to other units of the same good or service and to other available goods and services.

Diminishing Marginal Utility Another essential ingredient in the theory of utility analysis is the assumption of **diminishing marginal utility**. This assumption is that over a certain time period a person's added satisfaction grows less as he or she consumes more and more units of the same good or service. It is another way of saying that additional units of the same good or service in a specified period of time satisfy less and less pressing wants. For example, diminishing marginal utility suggests that a person will gain more satisfaction from eating the first apple than the second apple, which in turn provides more satisfaction than the third apple, and so on—when all the apples are eaten at one sitting. Note that the consumption activity is defined over a certain period of time. It is *not* assumed that an apple eaten next week will not provide just as much satisfaction as one eaten today. Similarly, it suggests that a first lamp in a room will provide more satisfaction than the second lamp in that room and that under usual circumstances a second car wash during the period of a week provides less utility than does a first car wash.

In a world where individuals can choose among many different goods and services, diminishing marginal utility also expresses a philosophy of "variety as the spice of life." Most people prefer to have one or a few of a lot of different goods and services rather than a great many of only a few goods and services. For example, you may buy only two pounds of apples because you prefer also to buy some oranges, pears, and bananas, rather than more apples.

Exceptions to diminishing marginal utility are rarely observed. They can usually be classed as cases of addiction, compulsive buying, conspicuous consumption, or set completion. An example of addiction is an alcoholic, who, at one sitting, derives more satisfaction from a third drink than from a second drink and even more from a fourth drink

than from a third, and so on—for a while. Compulsive buying may be a form of addiction, where the individual gets "turned on" by the act of buying. Conspicuous consumption—consuming in order to impress others—may take the form of owning an unusually large quantity of some good: many rings on one's fingers or several poodles to strut around with. An illustration of set completion would be a stamp collector, whose satisfaction from additional stamps to complete a set (such as stamps portraying U.S. presidents) increases as he or she gets closer to completing the set. The theory of utility analysis recognizes these as exceptions. They are rare enough so that they may be neglected.

Let us illustrate diminishing marginal utility with a numerical example. Consider the case of Terry Smith, a college student, whose marginal-utility schedule for sweaters is presented in Table 1. The first sweater that she might consume during the year would give her 1,500 utils, but the second one gives only 1,200 utils, and the seventh sweater just 500 utils. Terry's marginal-utility curve is shown in Figure 1. The negative slope of the whole curve reflects diminishing marginal utility.

Diminishing marginal utility means that over a certain time period a person's added satisfaction diminishes as he or she consumes additional units of the same good or service.

Increasing Total Utility The **total utility** that a person gains from any good or service is the sum of all the marginal utilities that he or she gains from successive units consumed. For example, Terry Smith's total-utility schedule for sweaters in Table 2 is derived from the marginal-utility schedule in Table 1. As she consumes more and more sweaters, the total utility increases by the amount of the marginal utility that she gains from each additional one. The assumption of **increasing total utility** is expressed in the fact that each additional sweater provides her with additional utility—her marginal utility continues to be positive. Terry's total-utility curve is shown in Figure 2. It is positively sloped throughout its length (total utility increases with more sweaters). However, it rises at a decreasing

TABLE 1
Terry Smith's Marginal-Utility Schedule for
Consumption of Sweaters During the Next Year

Unit of Sweater	Marginal Utility (in utils)
First	1,500
Second	1,200
Third	1,000
Fourth	840
Fifth	720
Sixth	600
Seventh	500

The numbers are the arbitrary absolute values that a particular hypothetical person, Terry Smith, assigns to the extra satisfaction that she would receive from each additional sweater that she might consume during the year.

rate, reflecting Terry's diminishing marginal utility (total utility increases by less and less for each additional sweater).

The possibility of a negatively sloped segment of a total-utility curve does exist. The assumption of diminishing marginal utility does not rule out the possibility that marginal utility could become negative. You can certainly come to have a real dislike for additional units of something after a point. You can get quite "sick" of it. Taken to the extreme, diminishing marginal utility will likely become negative marginal utility sooner or later. A Swedish economist, Staffan Burenstam Linder, wrote *The Harried Leisure Class,* about the plight of people without time to enjoy all the goods they had accumulated. He suggested that their marginal utility not only was diminishing but also was negative, and thus that their total utility might be greater if they had fewer goods. As the Scottish historian and philosopher Thomas Carlyle put it, "Things are in the saddle and ride mankind." But since consumers generally have a very large number of goods and services from which to select their purchases, since these goods and services are not free, and since consumers have limited incomes, it is not likely that they will consume so much of any one good or service that negative marginal utility is actually reached. Moreover, extending consumption when marginal utility is negative violates our first assumption that the consumer is rationally seeking

to maximize satisfaction. The theory of utility analysis recognizes decreasing total utility as an exception, rare enough that it may be neglected.

The total utility that a person gains from any good or service is the sum of all the marginal utilities that he or she gains from successive units consumed. The assumption of increasing total utility is that a person will continue to derive satisfaction from consuming additional units of the same product.

Income So far our discussion has covered only consumer preferences. Two other important variables involved in utility analysis theory are income and the prices of goods and services.

Utility analysis assumes the income (here defined as the broader concept of buying power) of

FIGURE 1
Terry Smith's Marginal-Utility Curve for
Consumption of Sweaters During the Next Year

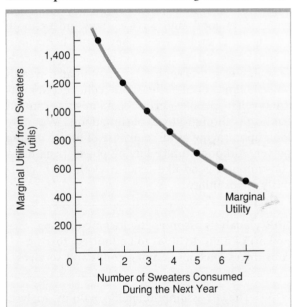

The numbers from Table 1 are plotted on the graph to establish the points along Terry Smith's marginal-utility curve. The curve conforms to the assumption of diminishing marginal utility—that during some specified time period an individual's added satisfaction diminishes as he or she consumes additional units of the same good.

TABLE 2
Terry Smith's Total-Utility Schedule for Consumption of Sweaters During the Next Year

Number of Sweaters	Total Utility (in utils)
1	1,500
2	2,700
3	3,700
4	4,540
5	5,260
6	5,860
7	6,360

The total-utility numbers are the arbitrary absolute values that a particular hypothetical person, Terry Smith, assigns to the total satisfaction that she receives from alternative quantities of sweaters that she might consume during the year. As she consumes successively more sweaters, her total utility increases by the amount of the marginal utility that she gains from each additional one.

an individual to be limited. It may be $10 a week or $1 million a week, but some income limit is assumed to exist. Individuals cannot buy unlimited amounts of goods and services; they must choose among goods and services. They must "live within their income," if we include in *income* the proceeds of selling or mortgaging their accumulated wealth and the limits on their lines of credit. (Economists know that people—even economists!—can go bankrupt through overconsumption.) We may look upon saving as the purchase of future buying power. Although future buying power is hardly a consumption good like food or clothing, it obviously yields utility.

Utility analysis assumes the income (buying power) of an individual to be limited, forcing consumers to choose among goods and services.

Price The last assumption made in utility analysis theory involves price. In order to make rational choices among products, individuals are assumed to know and to take account of the prices of all goods and services that they might buy. Frequently it is very easy to discover the price. Many goods are tagged. The price is stamped right on a container of milk or the price tag attached to a shirt or a belt.

For many services the price is announced "up front." The price of admission to a movie house is clearly displayed at the box office, and the price of a haircut can usually be found on a price board. Occasionally, however, prices may be more difficult to determine. What is the price of a rare stamp that was last sold at an auction in 1962? What is the price of the "price negotiable" skis advertised in the classified section of a local newspaper? Indeed, what is the price of a new car in the dealer's showroom that flaunts a *list price* of $16,807, but that you know you can buy for considerably less? The rare stamp, the skis, and the new car all have prices. The price of each will be determined jointly by the seller and buyer at the time of the actual transaction. The theory of utility analysis assumes that the individual either knows *transaction prices* or can estimate them closely.

Again we realize that this assumption is less than realistic. Many people actually are ignorant of

FIGURE 2
Terry Smith's Total-Utility Curve for Consumption of Sweaters During the Next Year

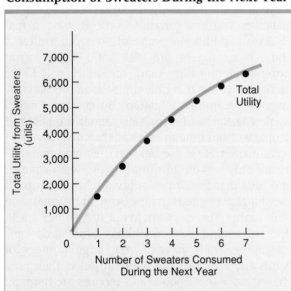

The numbers plotted from Table 2 establish the points along Terry Smith's total-utility curve. The curve conforms to the assumption of increasing total utility—that during some specified time period an individual's total satisfaction increases by diminishing amounts as he or she consumes greater total amounts of the same good.

many prices. But the theory of utility analysis sets this problem aside in order to penetrate as deeply as possible into the pure logic of choice.

In order to make rational choices among products, consumers must know and take account of the prices of all goods and services they might buy.

Utility and Demand

Having examined the six main assumptions of utility analysis, we are now ready to show how it can predict consumer demand. We bring together the variables of satisfaction (expressed in utils), income, and prices. In order to make rational choices among different mixes of goods and services, we must weigh prices against our expected utility. For example, Terry Smith, whose marginal-utility and total-utility schedules and curves appeared earlier, may be choosing among sweaters and shirts to replace her clothing destroyed in a fire. She may like a sweater (she assigns 600 utils to that unit) twice as much as a shirt (she assigns 300 utils to that unit). However, the sweater may be priced three times as high as the shirt ($24 compared to $8). In this case, Terry would buy the shirt because she can gain 300 utils by spending $8 as opposed to 600 utils by spending $24. She obtains 37.5 utils per dollar (300/$8) spent on the shirt compared to only 25 utils (600/$24) from each dollar spent on the sweater. In other words, in making this choice, she will decide in favor of the alternative that offers the greater amount of marginal utility per dollar of expenditure. Only when she maximizes the marginal utility that she gains from each dollar that she spends will she be able to maximize her total utility from her total expenditures.

In order to make rational choices among different mixes of goods and services, it is necessary to weigh prices against expected utility.

Only when a consumer maximizes the marginal utility that he or she gains from each dollar

---

spent, will that consumer be able to maximize total utility from total expenditures.

Consumer Equilibrium At this point we can combine the assumptions of utility analysis into a method of explaining consumer choice. The theory predicts that, in making each choice, the consumer will decide in favor of the alternative with the greatest marginal utility per dollar. When this is done, the assumption of diminishing marginal utility holds that the next unit of this good will offer less marginal utility per dollar than the one just purchased. Following this reasoning to its logical conclusion, we find that, in maximizing satisfaction, the consumer will purchase a mixture of goods and services such that their marginal utilities per dollar will be equal to one another.

If an individual at first fails to equate the marginal utility per dollar spent on one good or service with that of another, that person will later have the chance to increase his or her total utility by buying a little less of the good that is lower in marginal utility per dollar and a little more of the one that is higher. Only after a person has made all of his or her purchases, and finds that the marginal utility per dollar received from each good or service is the same, has that person achieved **consumer equilibrium**—the maximum possible utility or satisfaction.

If, for example, Larry finds that his marginal utility per dollar spent on food is higher than his marginal utility per dollar spent on entertainment, the theory predicts that he will change his consumption pattern so that the two marginal utilities per dollar will be equated. He will accomplish this by consuming somewhat more food at the expense of somewhat less entertainment. Consuming more units of food will decrease his marginal utility per dollar of food (he is sliding *down* and to the *right* on his negatively sloped marginal utility curve for food), and consuming less units of entertainment will increase his marginal utility per dollar of entertainment (he is moving *up* and to the *left* on his negatively sloped marginal utility curve for entertainment).

To state the consumer equilibrium rule more generally, where an individual buys goods and

TABLE 3
Terry Smith's Utility Schedules for Consumption of Sweaters and Shirts During the Next Year

	Utility for Sweaters (in utils)			Utility for Shirts (in utils)	
Unit	Marginal Utility	Total Utility	Unit	Marginal Utility	Total Utility
1	1,500	1,500	1	325	325
2	1,200	2,700	2	300	625
3	1,000	3,700	3	281	906
4	840	4,540	4	264	1,170
5	720	5,260	5	250	1,420
6	600	5,860	6	240	1,660
7	500	6,360	7	234	1,894
			8	228	2,122
			9	223	2,345
			10	218	2,563
			11	214	2,777
			12	210	2,987
			13	206	3,193
			14	203	3,396
			15	200	3,596

The marginal utilities and total utilities assigned by Terry Smith for sweaters are repeated from Tables 1 and 2. Similar information is provided for her with regard to shirts. Sweaters are priced at $24 each and shirts at $8 each.

services A through N, thereby exhausting his or her income, the person will maximize his or her satisfaction if

$$\frac{\text{marginal utility of good } A}{\text{price of good } A} =$$

$$\frac{\text{marginal utility of service } B}{\text{price of service } B} =$$

$$\cdots = \frac{\text{marginal utility of good } N}{\text{price of good } N}$$

or, simplified, if

$$\frac{MU_A}{P_A} = \frac{MU_B}{P_B} = \cdots = \frac{MU_N}{P_N}$$

Let us return to Terry Smith and her depleted wardrobe. Table 3 presents her marginal-utility and total-utility schedules for sweaters from Tables 1 and 2 and adds similar information about her utility schedules for shirts. We know that sweaters

are priced at $24 each and shirts at $8. With the added information that Terry can spend only $168 of her income for the year on these items, we can calculate her consumer equilibrium allocation between sweaters and shirts and be well on our way to predicting her actual buying behavior.

Suppose that she spent all of her $168 on 2 sweaters (2 × $24 = $48) and 15 shirts (15 × $8 = $120). Her marginal utility per dollar from sweaters (1,200/$24 = 50) would then exceed her marginal utility per dollar from shirts (200/$8 = 25). Her total utility would be 6,296 (2 units of sweaters yield 2,700 utils and 15 units of shirts yield 3,596 utils; 2,700 + 3,596 = 6,296). If, instead, Terry had bought 6 shirts (9 fewer) and 5 sweaters (3 more), her marginal utility per dollar from the two goods would have been equal (240/$8 = 720/$24). She would have lost 1,936 utils by buying 9 fewer shirts (3,596 − 1,660 = 1,936), but she would have gained 2,560 utils by buying 3 more sweaters (5,260 − 2,700 = 2,560). Since she was able to buy the 3 additional sweaters with the $72 that she gained from not buying the seventh through fifteenth shirts, she experiences a net gain of 624 utils (2,560 − 1,936). Thus, when Terry buys 5 sweaters and 6 shirts, equating her marginal utility per dollar between sweaters and shirts, her total utility will be 6,920. This is the greatest total utility that she can attain, given her utility schedules, the amount of money that she can spend on sweaters and shirts ($168), and the prices that she must pay ($8 per shirt and $24 per sweater).

A consumer reaches consumer equilibrium—the maximum possible utility or satisfaction—when he or she finds that the marginal utility per dollar received from each good or service is the same.

Derivation of the Demand Curve Since utility analysis enables us to predict that Terry Smith will demand 6 shirts at a price of $8 per shirt, it provides us with a point on her demand curve for shirts. This is illustrated as point *A* in Figure 3. It follows that additional points on Terry's demand curve for shirts—at different prices of shirts—can be derived in the same manner. At a lower price for shirts (and the same price for sweaters), Terry's marginal utility per dollar spent on shirts will increase while her marginal utility per dollar spent on sweaters will remain the same.

For example, if shirts went down in price to $6 per unit, her marginal utility per dollar spent on the sixth shirt would rise to 40 (240/$6 = 40), which would then be higher than her marginal utility per dollar spent on the fifth sweater (which remains at 30). Terry will therefore want to buy more shirts and fewer sweaters in order once again to equate her marginal utility per dollar spent on the two items. Specifically, she will want to buy 12 shirts (6 more than before the price decrease) and 4 sweaters (1 less than before). Her marginal utility per dollar spent on shirts will then be 35 (210/$6 = 35), which is equal to her marginal utility per dollar spent on sweaters (840/$24 = 35), and her $168 will again be entirely spent. This provides us with a second point on Terry's demand curve—at a price of $6 per shirt, she will demand 12 shirts (this is point *B* in Figure 3).

FIGURE 3
Terry Smith's Demand Curve for Shirts

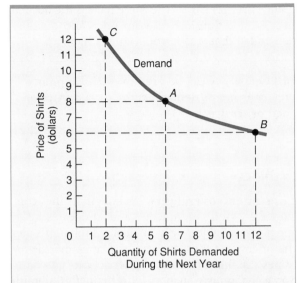

With her income and the prices of other products held constant, Terry's consumer equilibrium solutions occur where her marginal utility per dollar spent on shirts is equal to her marginal utility per dollar spent on every other product that she buys. These solutions establish the points along her demand curve. The resulting demand curve conforms to the normal negative relationship between price and quantity demanded.

At prices higher than the original $8 per shirt, Terry's marginal utility per dollar spent on shirts will decrease, while her marginal utility per dollar spent on sweaters will remain the same. For example, if shirts went up in price to $12 per unit, her marginal utility per dollar spent on the sixth shirt would fall to 20 (240/$12 = 20). Terry will therefore want to buy fewer shirts and more sweaters in order once again to equate her marginal utility per dollar spent on the two items. Specifically, she will want to buy 2 shirts (4 fewer than she bought at the original $8 price) and 6 sweaters (1 more than originally). Her marginal utility per dollar spent on the second shirt will then be 25 (300/$12 = 25), which is equal to her marginal utility per dollar spent on the sixth sweater (600/$24 = 25), and her $168 will again be entirely spent. This example provides us with a third point on Terry's demand curve—at a price of $12 per shirt, she will demand 2 shirts (point *C* in Figure 3).

In Figure 3 we have joined the three points that we derived in order to illustrate Terry's demand curve for shirts. The curve reflects the normal negative relationship between price and quantity demanded that was introduced in Chapter 5.

Utility analysis can be used to establish points on a consumer's demand curve for a particular good or service.

Is the Consumer Sovereign?

Consumer sovereignty means that the consumer is "king" or "queen" and so does as he or she pleases. Subject only to income limitations and the prices that must be paid, the consumer determines the mix of goods and services to purchase. Some economists, such as John Kenneth Galbraith in *The New Industrial State,* point out that consumers are uninformed or misinformed about the thousands of goods and services among which they choose, and can be easily pressured by salesmanship and advertising. You may have heard the definition of the American consumer as a person who "buys goods he does not really want for prices he cannot really afford, because of advertising he does not really believe, to impress other people he does not really care about."

Consumer sovereignty means that the consumer determines the mix of goods and services to purchase, subject only to income limitations and the prices that must be paid.

The view that consumers are frequently manipulated by sellers probably arises because of the massive amount of advertising and promotion to which consumers are subjected in a market-capitalist system. Are consumers told what satisfies them most? Do they believe what they are told? If the answer is "yes," isn't the producer sovereign rather than the consumer? These are questions of fact (positive economics), and the evidence is mixed. Certainly some advertising campaigns are successful. We see them over and over in newspapers, magazines, and television. But many advertising campaigns fail. They soon disappear from the media. Do more campaigns succeed than fail? Would the answer to this question be decisive with respect to the "validity" of utility theory? Is the question whether utility analysis is "true or false," or are there degrees of acceptance for the theory? How much faith do you choose to place in utility analysis? As far as the theory itself is concerned, utility analysis merely accepts consumers' preferences, no matter how they are formed. How they are formed is a separate question.

Those who question the validity of utility analysis raise a very important set of questions. No doubt, there is much consumer ignorance. Consumers can only guess at the amount of satisfaction that they will derive from goods and services with which they have had little or no experience. However, utility analysis does not assert that consumers maximize their satisfaction under perfect conditions, but only that they act as though they are doing the best they can with the limited and biased information they possess. If they are disappointed after making one purchase, the theory predicts that they will alter their purchases the next time they shop.

The root of the issue is whether consumer choice should be in the driver's seat in determining what to produce with an economy's resources. The word *should* tells you that this involves a value judgment. It is in the realm of normative rather than positive economics. If consumers should not be given this power, to whom should it be given?

Some economists believe that consumer ignorance and/or manipulation by sellers invalidates utility analysis theory.

EXTENSIONS OF UTILITY ANALYSIS

Utility analysis provides a method for exploring some interesting and frequently puzzling observations about consumer behavior. At this point, we shall limit ourselves to only two. The first, called **consumers' surplus,** suggests that consumers are really very lucky because in most cases they gain in utility to the extent of receiving "more than they pay for," or even "something for nothing." The second and related observation is the so-called **paradox of value,** or the fact that consumers sometimes pay lower prices for goods and services that they consider to be essential than for goods and services that they consider luxuries and use in a frivolous manner.

Consumers' Surplus

Alfred Marshall (1842–1924), the British economist, described consumers' surplus as follows:

> . . . the price which a person pays for a thing can never exceed, and seldom comes up to that which he would be willing to pay rather than go without it: so that the satisfaction which he gets from its purchase generally exceeds that which he gives up . . . and he thus derives from the purchase a surplus of satisfaction. The excess of the price which he would be willing to pay rather than go without the thing, over that which he actually does pay, is the economic measure of this surplus satisfaction.[1]

Let us illustrate consumers' surplus by returning to Terry Smith and her shirt purchases. Figure 4 reproduces (from Figure 3) Terry Smith's demand curve for shirts that we derived by using utility analysis. Recall that at a price of $12 per shirt she was willing to buy 2 shirts. However, she would buy more than 2 if the price were lower—we found that at $8 she would buy 6 shirts. The extra satisfaction (marginal utility) that she gained from each of the 4 additional shirts was successively lower, but the price reduction made them worth the money. Terry's total satisfaction from the 4 additional shirts is the sum total of the marginal satisfaction that she receives from each of the third through sixth shirts. Her satisfaction from the 4 additional shirts is therefore pictured as the blue (both light and dark) area under her demand curve between the second and sixth shirts. But she pays only $8 per shirt, so that her expenditure for these 4 additional shirts is $32. This is pictured as the light blue rectangular area between the second and sixth shirts and below the horizontal line drawn at

1. Alfred Marshall, *Principles of Economics,* 8th ed. (New York: Macmillan, 1948), p. 124.

FIGURE 4
Terry Smith's Consumers' Surplus from Shirts 3 through 6

The figure reproduces Terry's demand curve for shirts from Figure 3. At a price of $12 she demands 2 shirts and at a price of $8 she demands 6 shirts. Her total satisfaction from the third, fourth, fifth, and sixth shirts is shown as the blue (both light and dark) area under her demand curve. She pays the market price of $8 for each of these shirts (the light blue area). The difference between these two areas—the satisfaction that she receives minus the amount that she paid for them—is her consumers' surplus from these 4 shirts, and is shown as the dark blue area.

the $8 market price. The blue color (both shades) indicates that satisfaction is being realized, and the light blue indicates that payment in full is being made for this portion of the marginal utility. From the additional shirts, she is gaining consumers' surplus represented by the dark blue area. This is the satisfaction that Terry receives from shirts 3 through 6, over and above the amount that she paid to obtain these additional shirts. Although it is not shaded in Figure 4, she received some consumers' surplus from shirts 1 and 2 before the price decrease and even more from them after the price decrease.

Consumers' surplus is value received for which the consumer does not have to pay.

Consumers' surplus is the result of two important facts of economics—one related to consumer behavior and the other related to markets. The first is that people are normally willing to buy more and more of a particular good or service only at lower and lower prices because additional units of the same good or service satisfy less and less pressing wants. This fact is expressed in the concept of diminishing marginal utility. The second fact of economics is that if a uniform price prevails in a market, the price consumers pay for each unit of a good or service represents the value they place on the last unit (the marginal unit) bought. This is because sellers set prices on the basis of the total amount of product that they hope to sell. Taking these two facts together, we see that, except for the last unit purchased, consumers receive satisfaction or utility from each unit bought that is greater than what they actually pay for it. Expressed in terms of utility analysis, consumers' utility per unit consumed decreases as they consume more units over some time period. But consumers pay only according to the utility they receive from the last unit bought. Therefore, they get an increase in utility that they need not pay for.

Because of diminishing marginal utility and the fact that sellers set prices on the basis of the total amount of product that they hope to sell, it is commonplace for consumers to receive consumers' surplus.

Paradox of Value

The other puzzling observation that utility analysis helps to explain is the *paradox of value*. Adam Smith expressed the paradox as follows:

> The things which have the greatest value in use have frequently little or no value in exchange; and on the contrary, those which have the greatest value in exchange have frequently little or no value in use. Nothing is more useful than water: but it will purchase scarce anything; scarce anything can be had in exchange for it. A diamond, on the contrary, has scarce any value in use; but a great quantity of other goods may frequently be had in exchange for it.[2]

FIGURE 5
Paradox of Value

Pictured here is a person's marginal-utility curve for water and, superimposed on it, the same person's marginal-utility curve for diamonds. The green (both light and dark) area under the marginal-utility curve for water represents the total utility the person gains from the 20,000 gallons of water consumed. The dark green area under the marginal-utility curve for diamonds represents the total utility the person gains from the 1/2 carat of diamonds consumed. Marginal utility is merely read off each curve at the point of quantity actually purchased. "Value in use" is shown by the total utility, and "value in exchange" by the marginal utility of the last unit purchased. Since the total utility for water is seen to be much greater than the total utility for diamonds, whereas the marginal utility of diamonds is seen to be greater than the marginal utility of water, the "paradox of value" is resolved.

What Adam Smith observed in the eighteenth century is just as readily seen today. Now, however, we have some economic concepts (including consumers' surplus) that allow us to explain this apparent paradox. **Value in use** is total satisfaction, while **value in exchange** is determined not by total satisfaction but rather by what people are willing to pay for the last unit they buy. Although we expect the total satisfaction from water to be much higher than that from diamonds, the addi-

2. Adam Smith, *The Wealth of Nations* (New York: The Modern Library, 1937), p. 28.

tional satisfaction gained from the last unit of water is expected to be very low compared with diamonds, since water is plentiful in most areas and the typical consumer buys so many more units of water than of diamonds. This fact may be observed in Figure 5, where two marginal-utility (satisfaction) curves are pictured for a typical consumer of both water and diamonds. For early units of water, which most consumers consider to be essential for their survival, marginal utility is very much higher than it is for diamonds. But the marginal utility for water declines as a large number of units are consumed, so that for most consumers at equilibrium the marginal utility for diamonds is actually much higher than the marginal utility for water. For example, note that the consumer pictured in Figure 5 may be reaching consumer equilibrium (equating marginal utility per dollar spent on diamonds and on water) when he or she is consuming $\frac{1}{2}$ carat of diamonds and 20,000 gallons of water. Since total utility (satisfaction) is the sum of the marginal utilities received from each unit bought, it can be read as the area under each marginal-utility curve up to the last unit bought. The very much larger area under the marginal-utility curve for water (colored green—both light and dark) than under the marginal-utility curve for diamonds (colored dark green) shows the difference in "value in use" be-

tween the two products. However, the marginal utility for the last unit of water is shown to be below that for the last unit of diamonds, explaining the higher "value in exchange" of diamonds. The relative abundance of water compared to diamonds explains why the price of the marginal unit of water is much less than the price of the marginal unit of diamonds. For each of these products, the difference between (a) the "value in use" (total utility) and (b) the "value in exchange" (marginal utility) times the number of units consumed, is consumers' surplus. It is very large for water, much smaller for diamonds.

According to the paradox of value, consumers often pay far lower prices for goods and services that are considered essential than they pay for goods and services considered relatively unimportant. This paradox can be explained by the concept of value in exchange, which is determined not by total satisfaction (value in use) but by what people are willing to pay for the last unit they buy.

The difference between (a) total utility and (b) marginal utility times the number of units consumed, is consumers' surplus.

Economics in Focus

The Sovereign Consumer and the Edsel

Large corporations spend extraordinary amounts of time and money to predict and influence consumer choice. Within this century market research has evolved from an art into a science. Consumers are probed, surveyed, analyzed, and converted into statistical data. Companies test the product, the name, the color, the packaging. Advertising uses sophisticated demographic and psychological techniques to pinpoint the audience and manipulate the consumer's desires. Yet for all of this razzle-dazzle, the result is sometimes a fizzle.

In 1955 the Ford Motor Company, known for its economical cars, decided to produce a brand-new vehicle for the medium-priced market. The middle price range already accounted for 60 percent of car sales, and research indicated that the next ten years would bring even greater demand as more American families moved into higher income brackets. To help executives focus the new car's "personality," Ford commissioned extensive consumer surveys. Mercuries sold to young hot-rodders, the researchers found; Oldsmobiles, Buicks, and Pontiacs appealed to more staid, middle-aged people. Therefore, Ford's new car should aim for an in-between market. It was designed as a perfect choice for "the younger executive or professional family on its way up." The advertising agency was selected with equal care, and the ad campaign built a sense of mystery, showing the car in vague, stylish images that would tickle the consumer's curiosity before the vehicles reached the showroom.

But in spite of all the preparation, the new car hit the market with a resounding crash. Its name—the Edsel—became a byword for a product failure, and it was discontinued only two years after it first appeared.

Many economists and business analysts have offered reasons for the debacle. First, the timing was terrible: 1958, the first model year, was a time of recession. Second, American consumers had already begun a shift toward smaller cars, a trend that Ford's research had completely missed. Third, the styling—a primary part of the all-important "personality"—was disturbing. Consumers thought the vertical grille looked like a "horse collar" or "an Oldsmobile sucking a lemon." Fourth, the car's name sounded silly to many people. (This, at least, was not the fault of marketing research; the executives at Ford had discarded outside suggestions and named the car after Henry Ford's son.) Finally, the sleek advertising campaign only increased the disappointment of consumers who rushed to the showrooms to see the new marvel. Summing up the fiasco, *Time* declared the Edsel "the wrong car for the wrong market at the wrong time."

Economists who believe in consumer sovereignty can point to the Edsel as a spectacular illustration of the concept. In that particular case, American consumers proved immune to state-of-the-art marketing and advertising techniques. They didn't like the product, and they didn't buy it.

Sources: "The $250 Million Flop," *Time*, November 30, 1959, pp. 87–88; "The Edsel: Requiem for a Flop," *New York Times*, September 4, 1982; "Agency Exec Explores Reasons New Products Fail," *Marketing News*, August 3, 1984, pp. 9, 16.

SUMMARY

1. Utility analysis is a theory used to explain why consumers choose as they do. It examines the forces behind the demand curve and how the demand curve is derived. (See page 476.)

2. Utility analysis relies on six key assumptions. These are that (a) consumers are rational, (b) utility can be measured, (c) marginal utility diminishes as consumption goes up, (d) total utility increases as consumption rises, (e) incomes are limited, and (f) prices are known. (See page 476.)

3. Consumer rationality means that consumers seek to maximize their satisfaction. (See page 476–477.)

4. Utility is defined to mean satisfaction, which is measured in terms of utils. Utility is subjective in nature, so that when a person assigns a certain amount of utility to a unit of a product it is meaningful only in terms of its relationship to that same person's assignments of utility to other units of that product or to other goods and services. (See page 480.)

5. Diminishing marginal utility means that during some specified time period an individual's added satisfaction diminishes as he or she consumes additional units of the same product. (See page 478.)

6. The meaning of increasing total utility is that a person will continue to attain positive satisfaction from consuming additional units of the same product—at least over the range of consumption that is consistent with the assumption of rationality. Because of the assumption of diminishing marginal utility, as the person consumes additional units of the same product over a specified period of time, he or she will find that utility will increase at a decreasing rate. (See pages 478–479.)

7. A consumer will maximize total utility or satisfaction (reach "consumer equilibrium") when his or her total purchasing power is spent so that marginal utility per dollar for each product is the same as for every other product purchased. (See page 481.)

8. An individual's consumer equilibrium position at any particular price for a product establishes a point on that individual's demand curve for that product. By joining a number of such points, an individual's demand curve for a product can be drawn. (See pages 481–482.)

9. Utility analysis explains that the consumer buys what he or she pleases. Some economists believe that consumer ignorance and consumer manipulation by sellers (through advertising) is so widespread that marginal-utility theory is largely irrelevant and useless in explaining consumer behavior. They reject the view that the consumer is truly "sovereign" in deciding what to buy. (See pages 484–485.)

10. Consumers in competitive markets receive consumers' surplus—value received for which they do not have to pay. This happens because of diminishing marginal utility and because consumers usually pay a uniform price for all units of the same good or service—a price representing the value that they place on the last unit bought. (See pages 485–486.)

11. Consumers often pay far lower prices for goods and services that are called essential than they pay for goods and services considered relatively unimportant. This phenomenon is referred to as the "paradox of value." The paradox is resolved when one understands that price, or "value in exchange," is based on marginal utility whereas the importance of a product, or its "value in use," is based on total utility. (See pages 486–487.)

KEY TERMS

budget line: a curve that shows all of the combinations of the goods and/or services measured on the axes of a graph that can be purchased by an individual who has a particular income and who faces particular prices for those goods and/or services (page 495).

consumer equilibrium: the maximum possible utility or satisfaction a consumer can achieve, given that person's income and the prices of the goods and services that he or she faces (page 481).

consumer sovereignty: the theory that the consumer determines the mix of goods and services that he or she purchases, subject only to income limitations and the prices that must be paid (page 484).

consumers' surplus: value received for which the consumer does not have to pay (page 484).

diminishing marginal utility: an assumption of the theory of utility analysis that over a certain time period a person's added satisfaction grows less and less as he or she consumes more and more units of the same good or service (page 478).

increasing total utility: an assumption of the theory of utility analysis that each additional unit of a good or service provides the consumer with additional utility (page 478).

indifference curve: a curve that shows all the combinations of goods and/or services measured on the axes that a particular individual finds will satisfy him or her equally well (page 492).

indifference curve analysis: a theory of consumer behavior that expresses the consumer's tastes in the form of indifference curves (page 492).

indifference map: a graph displaying some of the infinite number of indifference curves representing an individual's preferences (page 493).

paradox of value: the observation that consumers sometimes pay lower prices for goods and services that they consider essential than for goods and services that they consider relatively unimportant (page 485).

rational consumer: an assumption that consumers seek to maximize their satisfaction—to get the most out of their income by selecting the mix of goods and services that promises to offer the greatest amount of personal satisfaction (page 476).

total utility: the sum of all the marginal utilities a person gains from successive units consumed of any good or service over a particular period of time (page 478).

util: the unit of measure used to gauge a person's anticipated utility or satisfaction (page 477).

utility: a measure or expression of an individual consumer's expected or anticipated satisfaction (page 477).

utility analysis: a theory that attempts to explain the underlying forces of consumer behavior (page 476).

value in exchange: the value of a good or service as determined by what people are willing to pay for the last unit that they buy (page 486).

value in use: the value of a good or service as determined by the total satisfaction received from it (page 486).

DISCUSSION QUESTIONS

1. "Diminishing marginal utility is sufficient reason for a government program that takes from the rich and gives to the poor." Do you agree? Explain.

2. Discuss three instances in which you did not experience diminishing marginal utility. How important are such instances in your overall buying pattern? Do they involve a significant proportion of your total expenditures?

3. Bonnie spends her income according to the assumptions of the theory of utility analysis. How would her pattern of purchases be different if she did not experience diminishing marginal utility?

4. The utility analysis theory of consumer choice assumes that a person's total utility derived from a good or a service always increases with additional units of that good or service within a specified period of time. However, you can probably think of dozens of hypothetical examples that do not comply with this assumption. Give at least three. Why, then, does this assumption still allow us to make reasonably good predictions about consumer choice? Why is this not a particularly heroic assumption to make?

5. Carefully explain why Martin maximizes his satisfaction when, after he has made all of his purchases, the marginal utility per dollar spent is the same for all the goods and services he bought.

6. Assume that the following tables are Ms. Rational's utility schedules.

Clothing ($10 per Unit)

Units	Marginal Utility (in utils)	Total Utility (in utils)	Total Expenditure ($)
1	10,000	10,000	10
2	5,000	15,000	20
3	3,500	18,500	30
4	2,000	20,500	40

Clothing (continued)

Units	Marginal Utility (in utils)	Total Utility (in utils)	Total Expenditure ($)
5	1,000	21,500	50
6	500	22,000	60
7	300	22,300	70

Food ($1 per Unit)

Units	Marginal Utility (in utils)	Total Utility (in utils)	Total Expenditure ($)
1	10,000	10,000	1
2	8,000	18,000	2
3	5,000	23,000	3
4	2,000	25,000	4
5	800	25,800	5
6	400	26,200	6
7	250	26,450	7
8	200	26,650	8
9	150	26,800	9
10	100	26,900	10
11	75	26,975	11
12	50	27,025	12

Concerts ($5 per Unit)

Units	Marginal Utility (in utils)	Total Utility (in utils)	Total Expenditure ($)
1	1,200	1,200	5
2	1,000	2,200	10
3	500	2,700	15
4	400	3,100	20
5	200	3,300	25

Assume also that Ms. Rational has a disposable income of $75 per week and that she cannot buy partial units. How many units of clothing, food, and concerts will she buy in this world of just three goods and services?

7. How does the issue of consumer sovereignty affect the validity of the utility analysis theory of consumer choice?

8. Why are sellers so "kind" as to offer buyers the benefit of consumers' surplus?

9. Distinguish between "value in use" and "value in exchange." How are these two concepts related to total utility and marginal utility?

10. Devise a pricing scheme for selling shoes that does not permit the consumer to gain any consumers' surplus.

Appendix:
Indifference Curve Analysis

Indifference curve analysis is a theory of consumer behavior that expresses the consumer's tastes in the form of curves (indifference curves). Since it dates back to the 1930s, it is a newer approach to consumer behavior than utility analysis. It is based on less restrictive assumptions, but many students consider it more complex. Whereas utility analysis assumes that satisfaction can be measured, indifference analysis assumes only that it is possible to rank different combinations of goods in order of preference. For example, utility analysis assumes that each of us is able to measure our taste for goods X and Z by assigning a certain number of utils to each. Thus we may indicate that we derive 3.5 times as much satisfaction from X as from Z or that we like Z twice as much as X. In contrast, the indifference approach assumes only that we like one combination of X and Z more than we like another combination of them, or that we just don't care which of these two combinations we consume (are indifferent between them).

Indifference curve analysis is a theory of consumer behavior that does not require cardinal measurement of utility but only that it is possible to rank different combinations of goods and services in order of an individual's preferences.

THE INDIFFERENCE CURVE AND MAP

An indifference curve is made up of a very large number of points—an infinite number, since we draw it as a smooth line. Each point represents a different combination of goods and/or services that

a particular individual might consume. A single **indifference curve** includes all the combinations that will satisfy the individual equally well. That is to say, the individual is indifferent as to whether he or she consumes one or another combination of goods and/or services on the same indifference curve. Figure 6 pictures an indifference curve for Jim Gallo, who lives in the limited world of food and clothing. Looking at only three points on Jim's indifference curve (1, 2, and 3), we see that they represent different combinations of the two goods. (Point 1 is 110 units of food plus 40 units of clothing, point 2 is 50 units of food plus 80 units of clothing, and point 3 is the combination of 27 units

FIGURE 6
Jim Gallo's Indifference Curve

Pictured here is an indifference curve for Jim Gallo. He is equally well satisfied by each combination of food and clothing that is represented along this curve. He is indifferent among the three combinations that are marked and specified on this curve, as he is among all other combinations of food and clothing that can be read off this same indifference curve.

of food and 120 units of clothing.) Jim does not care which of these combinations he consumes or whether he consumes some other combination of food and clothing that can be read off the same indifference curve.

Each point on an indifference curve represents a different combination of goods and/or services a particular individual might consume. A single indifference curve includes all the combinations that will satisfy the individual equally well.

Indifference analysis assumes that many such indifference curves may be derived for an individual. An infinite number of indifference curves representing an individual's preferences is called an **indifference map.** Five indifference curves from Jim Gallo's indifference map appear in Figure 7. We can use this diagram to show that Jim would like to be on as high an indifference curve (farthest to the northeast) as he possibly can. That is, indifference analysis suggests that he prefers any combination on curve *B* to any combination on curve *A*, any combination on curve *C* to any on curves *A* or *B*, any on curve *D* to any on curves *A*, *B*, or *C*, and, finally, any combination on curve *E* to all the others. This follows if we assume that he prefers more of both goods to less of both goods. For example, it is easy to see that Jim prefers combination 4 on indifference curve *D* to combination 2 on indifference curve *C* because it entails more of both food and clothing. However, we can go further and conclude that Jim also prefers combination 4 to combination 3, even though combination 4 provides less clothing than does combination 3. Since Jim is indifferent between combination 2 and combination 3 (they are both on the same indifference curve *C*) and since he prefers combination 4 to combination 2, indifference-curve logic concludes that he also prefers combination 4 to 3.

An infinite number of indifference curves representing an individual's preferences is called an indifference map.

FIGURE 7
Five Indifference Curves on Jim Gallo's Indifference Map

Quantity of Food per Week

Quantity of Clothing Per Week

Shown here are five indifference curves from Jim Gallo's indifference map. The higher the curve he can reach (the farthest to the northeast), the better off he will be. Jim prefers any combination of food and clothing represented on curve *E* to any on curves *A*, *B*, *C*, or *D*. Similarly, he prefers a combination of food and clothing represented on curve *D* (such as the one marked 4) to any on curves *A*, *B*, or *C* (including such combinations as 1, 2, and 3 on curve *C*), and so on.

Relationships Among Indifference Curves

Does indifference-curve logic allow for the possibility of indifference curves to cross? In other words, is it possible for two different indifference curves on a single indifference map to have a common point? The answer is "no." Imagine that indifference curves *C* and *D* from Figure 7 intersect so as to make points 2 and 4 a single common point. (You may wish to draw them on a piece of paper.) In one direction from the intersection, curve *D* then lies above (to the northeast of) curve *C*, while curve *C* lies above curve *D* in the other direction. This situation denies indifference-curve logic. At the point of intersection in such a construct, Jim Gallo is indifferent between being on indifference curve *C* or *D*, since that point represents the same combination of food and clothing. Yet at all other points, he prefers being either on indifference curve D because it lies above indifference curve C or on indifference curve C because it lies above indifference curve D. Thus he would no longer be indifferent among all points along the same indifference curve.

The Shape of Indifference Curves

Jim Gallo's indifference curves were drawn on the basis of two assumptions that are characteristic of indifference analysis. First, his indifference curves are negatively sloped, and, second, they are bowed inward toward (are *convex* to) the origin.

A negatively sloped or downward-sloping indifference curve indicates that the individual considers the goods measured on the axes to indeed be good or desirable—more is always preferred to less. Some quantity of one good must be given up when some of the other good is added in order for the individual to remain equally well off. By contrast, let us briefly examine the meaning of positively sloped indifference curves, as it sometimes helps to see the results of other assumptions. A positively sloped or upward-sloping indifference curve would mean that the person was indifferent among combinations that included more of both things and less of both things. This sort of curve would make sense only if one of the things was a "bad" (something the individual wanted less of, such as garbage), and the other was a good. Each point on such an indifference curve would represent a particular combination of the "good" and the "bad," and the individual would be indifferent among all of these combinations.

An indifference curve that is a horizontal or a vertical straight line tells us that one axis measures a good and the other an "I don't care"—a product that neither adds to nor subtracts from the individual's well-being. A horizontal straight-line indifference curve indicates that the horizontal axis measures the "I don't care." The person cares only about how much he or she gets of the good on the vertical axis and is indifferent among the various amounts of the "I don't care" with which it is combined. Similarly, a vertical straight-line indifference curve shows that the "I don't care" is measured on the vertical axis. This time the person cares only about how much he or she gets of the good on the

horizontal axis and is indifferent among the various amounts of the "I don't care" with which it is combined.

A negatively sloped indifference curve indicates that the individual considers the goods measured on the axes to be desirable. A positively sloped indifference curve means that the person is indifferent among combinations that include more of both things and less of both things, that is, that one of the two is a "bad."

The second assumption of the theory is that indifference curves have the sort of curve pictured in Figures 6 and 7—convex to the origin. This convexity indicates that individuals desire variety. The theory predicts that if a consumer has, for example, a large quantity of food and a relatively small quantity of clothing, a large additional amount of food must be added if another unit of clothing is eliminated in order to allow him or her to maintain the same level of satisfaction. The same principle works if he or she has a lot of clothing in comparison to food.

Perhaps this convex-curve assumption reminds you of the diminishing-marginal-utility assumption used in utility analysis. There, utility diminished in terms of utils. Here, it appears as a changing "tradeoff" rate between goods. If an individual's indifference curves were bowed out instead of bowed inward to the origin, they would indicate the opposite. Such curves would show that added units of the good of which the person had a relatively large amount were valued more highly than added units of the good of which he or she has relatively little.

Finally, if the indifference curves had no curvature at all but were instead straight lines (but not vertical or horizontal ones), they would indicate that the goods measured on the axes were perfect substitutes for each other. The tradeoff rate between the goods would be the same no matter in what proportion the goods were held. Only the same good appearing on both axes would be a case of perfect substitutes, but near-perfect substitutes such as $5 bills and $10 bills exchanged on a two-for-one basis would come close.

An indifference curve drawn convex to the origin indicates that the individual desires variety, expressed as a mix of the goods and/or services measured on the axes.

THE BUDGET LINE

Indifference analysis involves consumer preferences, consumer income, and the prices of goods and services. So far, our discussion of the indifference approach to consumer behavior has dealt only with preferences (the indifference map). The income and price variables that act as constraints, or limits, on what the individual is able to buy can be expressed in the form of a budget line. The **budget line** shows the combinations of the goods and/or services measured on the axes that can be purchased by an individual who has a particular income and who faces particular prices for those goods and/or services.

We can construct a budget line for Jim Gallo, whose preferences we have previously mapped. Suppose that his income is $100 per week, that food sells for $5 per unit, and that the price of clothing is $10 per unit. The line in Figure 8 extends down from 20 units of food to 10 units of clothing. If Jim were to spend his entire $100 income on food, he could buy 20 units of food ($100/$5 = 20); on the other hand, if he were to spend his entire income on clothing, he could buy 10 units of clothing ($100/$10 = 10). In between these two extremes are many other combinations. Two such combinations, shown in Figure 8, are 15 units of food plus 2½ units of clothing and 10 units of food plus 5 units of clothing. Given his income and the prices of food and clothing, Jim can afford to buy any combination on his budget line or beneath it, but he cannot afford any combination outside his budget line.

The budget line shows the combinations of the goods and/or services measured on the axes that can be purchased by an individual who has a

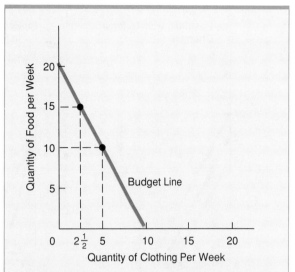

**FIGURE 8
Jim Gallo's Budget Line**

Jim Gallo's budget line pictures the constraints that are placed on his ability to purchase food and clothing by his income and the prices of food and clothing. His income is $100 and food sells for $5 per unit and clothing for $10 per unit. If he buys none of the other, he can buy 20 units of food or 10 units of clothing. Between these two extremes lie many alternative combinations that offer him positive amounts of both food and clothing. Two such alternative combinations are marked—15 units of food plus 2½ units of clothing and 10 units of food plus 5 units of clothing.

particular income and who faces particular prices for these goods and/or services.

The budget line will shift if either price or income changes. Panel (a) in Figure 9 illustrates budget-line shifts that occur if income changes while prices remain the same. If Jim's income decreases to $80 per week, the budget line will shift to the left, so that it will extend from 16 units of food to 8 units of clothing. The new budget line is derived in the same way as the original one. If Jim spent his entire $80 of income on food, he could buy 16 units of food ($80/$5 = 16). On the other hand, if he spent all of his $80 income on clothing, he could buy 8 units of clothing ($80/$10 = 8).

Similarly, an increase in Jim's income to, say, $120 a week will shift his budget line to the right, so that it extends from 24 units of food to 12 units

FIGURE 9
Budget-Line Shifts

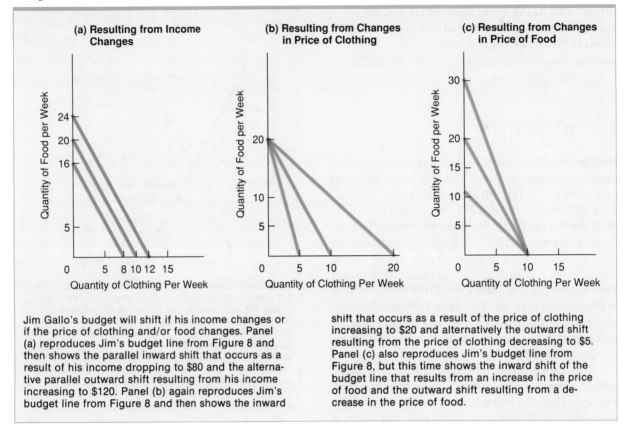

(a) Resulting from Income Changes

Quantity of Food per Week

Quantity of Clothing Per Week

(b) Resulting from Changes in Price of Clothing

Quantity of Food per Week

Quantity of Clothing Per Week

(c) Resulting from Changes in Price of Food

Quantity of Food per Week

Quantity of Clothing Per Week

Jim Gallo's budget will shift if his income changes or if the price of clothing and/or food changes. Panel (a) reproduces Jim's budget line from Figure 8 and then shows the parallel inward shift that occurs as a result of his income dropping to $80 and the alternative parallel outward shift resulting from his income increasing to $120. Panel (b) again reproduces Jim's budget line from Figure 8 and then shows the inward

shift that occurs as a result of the price of clothing increasing to $20 and alternatively the outward shift resulting from the price of clothing decreasing to $5. Panel (c) also reproduces Jim's budget line from Figure 8, but this time shows the inward shift of the budget line that results from an increase in the price of food and the outward shift resulting from a decrease in the price of food.

of clothing. If Jim spent all of his $120 of income on food, he could buy 24 units of food ($120/$5 = 24). On the other hand, if he spent his entire $120 of income on clothing, he could buy 12 units of clothing ($120/$10 = 12).

Panel (b) in Figure 9 shows budget lines at several different prices of clothing, assuming that the price of food and Jim's income both remain the same. If the price of clothing increases to $20 per unit, the budget line intersects the horizontal axis at 5 units. The most clothing that Jim's $100 income can now buy is 5 units ($100/$20 = 5). If, instead, the price decreases to $5, the budget line intersects the horizontal axis at 20 units. Jim's $100 income can now buy 20 units of clothing ($100/$5 = 20). Panel (c) in Figure 9 shows similar shifts of budget lines when the price of food changes while the price of clothing and Jim's income remain the same. The shift to the left reflects

an increase in the unit price of food, and the shift to the right reflects a decrease in the unit price of food.

The budget line will shift if either price or income changes.

CONSUMER EQUILIBRIUM

An individual's indifference map expresses what that person would *like* to consume, and an individual's budget line tells what that person is *able* to consume. When the two are put together, the consumption pattern that maximizes that individual's satisfaction can readily be determined. Superimpose the individual's budget line on his or her indifference map and seek the point where it is *tangent* to (where it just touches) an indifference curve. This point (the tangency solution) identifies the combination of goods and/or services that will maximize that person's satisfaction under the given income and price constraints.

Figure 10 shows the case of Jim Gallo. Recall that Jim's income is $100 per week and that food sells for $5 per unit and clothing for $10 per unit. If we superimpose his budget line (Figure 8) on his indifference map (Figure 7), we can find the point where it is tangent to an indifference curve. He would like to reach indifference curve *E*, but since it lies completely outside of his budget line (as do indifference curves *D* and *C*), he cannot. On the other hand, he can reach a number of points on indifference curve *A*, two of which will exhaust his income. (These combinations are 15 units of food

plus 2½ units of clothing and 4 units of food plus 8 units of clothing.) But by choosing a different combination, Jim is able to reach the higher indifference curve *B*. Indifference curve *B* is just tangent to his budget line, which means that he can reach no higher indifference curve. The combination of 8 units of food plus 6 units of clothing is a solution that uniquely maximizes satisfaction for Jim. He could have spent his $100 per week in any number of different combinations along his budget line, but his satisfaction is maximized *only* when he buys 8 units of food plus 6 units of clothing.

When an individual's indifference map and budget line are superimposed, one on the other, the point at which the budget line is tangent to an indifference curve identifies consumer equilibrium—the combination of goods and/or services that will maximize that individual's satisfaction under the given income and price constraints.

In summary, the indifference curve analysis approach to consumer behavior relies on three pieces of information to predict what an individual will demand: (1) the person's preferences, (2) the person's income, and (3) the prices of the goods and services that the person has to choose from. It makes the same assumptions as does utility analysis except that it does not assume that utility can be measured. Instead, it assumes that consumers can rank-order the desirability of different combinations of goods and/or services. Preferences are expressed by the indifference map; income and the prices determine the budget line. The point where the budget line is tangent to one of the indifference curves represents the consumption pattern that maximizes satisfaction. In other words, it represents "consumer equilibrium."

Indifference curve analysis relies on three pieces of information to predict what an individual will demand: (1) the person's preferences, (2) the person's income, and (3) the prices of the goods and services the person has to choose from.

FIGURE 10
Jim Gallo's Consumer Equilibrium Solution

Jim Gallo's budget line (from Figure 8) is superimposed on his indifference map (from Figure 7) to show his "consumer equilibrium"—the combination of food and clothing that, given his income and the prices of food and clothing, maximizes his satisfaction. Indifference curve *B* is the highest one that Jim can reach, since his budget line is just tangent to it. The combination of 8 units of food plus 6 units of clothing is the solution that uniquely maximizes satisfaction for Jim.

DERIVING A DEMAND CURVE

What you have learned about indifference curves and budget lines allows you to see that this theory of consumer behavior contains all the ingredients required to derive a demand curve. In fact, we have already determined one point on Jim Gallo's demand curve for food and one point on his demand curve for clothing. Let us concentrate on his demand for clothing.

Figure 10 shows that Jim demands 6 units of clothing when clothing is priced at $10 per unit, given that the only other product in the world, food, is priced at $5 per unit and that his income is $100 a week. The top panel of Figure 11 reproduces that equilibrium situation at point *I*. Jim's indifference curve *B* is tangent to his budget line, which reflects the $10 price of clothing, the $5 price of food, and Jim's $100 income. In the lower panel of Figure 11, we have plotted the point showing that Jim demands 6 units of clothing when clothing sells for $10 per unit.

Suppose now that the price of clothing falls to $5 per unit while the price of food and Jim's income remain the same. Jim's budget line, shown in the top panel of Figure 11, shifts to the right. (See the same case in Figure 9b.) A new consumer equilibrium is reached at *m*, where Jim's indifference curve *Z* is tangent to his new budget line. At $5 per unit of clothing, $5 per unit of food, and $100 per week income, Jim wants to buy 14 units of clothing. This case is reflected as a second point on Jim's demand curve in the lower panel of Figure 11. Other points on Jim's demand curve can be derived in a similar way for other prices of clothing.

Indifference curve analysis can be used to derive an individual's demand curve for a particular good or service.

BEHAVIORAL PREDICTIONS

Not all economists accept the "rationality" assumptions that we have described. Among the "behavioral" opposition is the Nobel laureate econo-

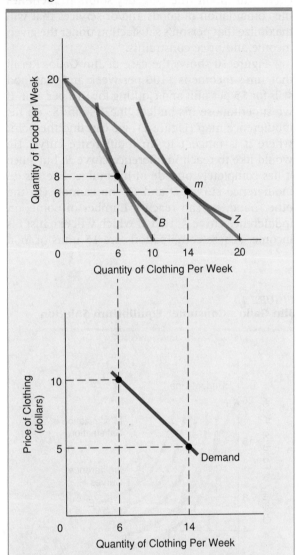

FIGURE 11
Derivation of Jim Gallo's Demand Curve for Clothing

The top panel shows a shift to the right of Jim Gallo's budget line in response to a decrease in the price of clothing. The original equilibrium point of *I* was maintained when the price of clothing was $10 per unit, given food at $5 per unit and Jim's income of $100 per week. The new equilibrium *m* is attained as a result of a decrease in the price of clothing to $5, the price of food and Jim's income remaining the same.

The lower panel shows the two points on Jim's demand curve for clothing that were derived in the upper panel. With no change in the price of food and no change in Jim's income, Jim demands 6 units of clothing when clothing sells for $10 per unit and 14 units of clothing when clothing sells for $5 per unit.

mist Herbert Simon. This opposition claims that a different explanation of consumer behavior fits the facts better, and that it too can be shown on an indifference map. Suppose that some indifference curve (crossed by the budget line) represents the consumer's "aspiration level." Once the consumer reaches that level, he or she is satisfied and does not care for anything more. Such a satisfied consumer, given his or her budget line, may choose *any* consumption pattern on this budget line that is not below his or her aspiration level. Most likely he or she will choose the point on the budget line that follows the pattern of the consumer's established routine—where he or she consumes the same proportions of the goods or services as in the past. The point of tangency has little or nothing to do with this choice, but rather it is the pre-established routine that influences consumer behavior.

DISCUSSION QUESTIONS

1. Using your knowledge of indifference curves, logically explain why Mary will probably be eager to reach a higher indifference curve than the one that she is currently on.

2. Draw each of the following indifference curves as described *and* tell what the indifference curve indicates about how the person views the products on the axes:

- *a.* a positively sloped indifference curve
- *b.* a vertical straight-line indifference curve
- *c.* a horizontal straight-line indifference curve
- *d.* a negatively sloped, straight-line indifference curve
- *e.* a negatively sloped, bowed-out (concave to the origin) indifference curve

3. Explain why Beatrice maximizes her satisfaction when she consumes that combination of goods represented at the point where her budget line is tangent to her indifference curve.

4. What may account for each of the following?

- *a.* a change in the shape of a person's indifference curves
- *b.* a parallel shift to the right of a person's budget line
- *c.* a parallel shift to the left of a person's budget line
- *d.* a person's tangency solution above and to the right of his or her previous tangency solution
- *e.* a shift to the right of all points on a person's budget line except for the point where he or she selects none of the good labeled on the horizontal axis

23
Market Demand and Elasticity

Preview   Chapter 5 introduced the concept of consumer demand. Consumers were seen to demand larger quantities of goods and services at lower prices and smaller quantities at higher prices. Both an individual consumer-demand curve and a market-demand curve were explained. Further insight into this negative relationship between quantity demanded and price was given in Chapter 22. There utility analysis was used to trace an individual consumer's demand schedule and curve for a good or a service.

In this chapter, we expand on the subject of market demand. We begin by explaining how the demands of individual consumers are added together to form a market-demand curve. Then we look at one important characteristic of market demand—elasticity, or the degree of responsiveness to changes in price or income. In studying the *price elasticity of demand,* you will discover why quantity demanded is much more responsive to price changes for some products (goods and services) than for others and what difference that fact makes to business decision makers. We also apply elasticity to changes in demand for one product caused by a change in price of a related product (called *cross elasticity of demand*). Finally, we apply elasticity to changes in the demand for a product caused by a change in income (called *income elasticity of demand*).

THE MARKET-DEMAND CURVE

Chapter 22 showed how economists explain the source of an individual consumer's demand schedule and curve. We move on now to show how these may be added together to form a **market-demand schedule and curve**. The market-demand schedule and curve sum up, or combine, all the individual consumers' demands for a particular product in a particular geographic area. This is what concerns sellers. Business firms want to know how much they can sell at alternative prices in various markets. Which consumer happens to buy their product doesn't really interest them very much except insofar as that knowledge might enable them to raise the total demand. Normally a business firm doesn't care whether more demand stems from John and Alice than from Mary and Jim or whether the reverse is true.

The market-demand schedule and curve combine all the individual consumers' demands for a particular product in a particular geographic area.

Summing Individual Quantities Demanded

Suppose that these four consumers—John, Alice, Mary, and Jim—constitute the entire market for fruit in a very small village. Their individual consumer-demand schedules are shown in Table 1 and then plotted and drawn as demand curves in Figure 1. The market-demand schedule and market-demand curve are then derived by horizontally adding them together. When fruit is offered at $0.25 per pound, for example, the quantity demanded by the four consumers adds up to 370 pounds per year (100 + 50 + 140 + 80 = 370), but when the price is $1.00 per pound, the market demand drops off to 140 pounds per year (40 + 10 + 60 + 30 = 140). The market demand at the four different prices is shown in the far right column of the demand schedules in Table 1 and plotted as the market-demand curve in Figure 1.

Market-Demand Shifts

It is not surprising that the market-demand curve shows the same negative relationship between price and quantity demanded as do individual-demand curves. As we explained in Chapter 5, individual demand in the schedule sense relates the quantity demanded for a product to the price of that product, while keeping constant other influencing variables—in particular, preferences, income, and the prices of related goods and services. When variables other than the price of this product are allowed to change, shifts in individual-demand curves may occur. The same must, of course, hold for market demand since it is merely the sum of individual demands. If, as a total for all these consumers, preferences for the product increase, or if income goes up, or if the price of a good substitute product increases, or if the price of a complement decreases, the market-demand curve will shift to the right (*ceteris paribus*). On the other hand, if preferences decrease or income goes down for the total of these consumers, or if the price of a good substitute product decreases, or a complement's price increases, the market demand will shift to the left (*ceteris paribus*).

Market-demand curves show the same negative relationship between price and quantity demanded that individual-demand curves do and are affected by the same shift variables (preferences, income, and prices of related goods and services).

In dealing with market-demand curves, two more influencing variables must be considered. The first is that market demand may grow or decline with the numbers of consumers that it includes. Extending our example, Linda and Larry may move into the village where only John, Alice, Mary, and Jim lived before. Linda's and Larry's individual-demand schedules for fruit must then be added to the others, thus shifting the market-demand curve to the right. However, the market-demand curve would shift to the left if one of the inhabitants of the village died or moved away.

In considering market demand, the second

TABLE 1
Four Individual-Demand Schedules and the Market-Demand Schedule for Fruit

Price of Fruit (dollars per pound)	Individual Quantity Demanded (pounds of fruit per year)				Market Demand (pounds of fruit per year)
	John	*Alice*	*Mary*	*Jim*	
0.25	100	50	140	80	370
0.50	70	30	100	50	250
0.75	50	20	80	40	190
1.00	40	10	60	30	140

Shown here are four individual-demand schedules for fruit. Since these four people constitute the entire market, the horizontal sum of their demands is the market-demand schedule.

variable to be added is the distribution of income among consumers. The combined income of the four inhabitants of our village may remain the same, but the *distribution* of income among them may change. Suppose that John, Alice, Mary, and Jim all earned incomes of $25,000 per year. Then suppose that Alice receives a big promotion, raising her income to $85,000 and John, Mary, and Jim

lose their jobs, so that each of their incomes falls to only $5,000 (unemployment compensation). Even though their combined income is still $100,000, we can well imagine that the additional fruit demanded by Alice, who is now much richer, may be more than offset by the much lower amount demanded by the three other people, whose incomes were so severely reduced.

FIGURE 1
Four Individual-Demand Curves and the Market-Demand Curve for Fruit

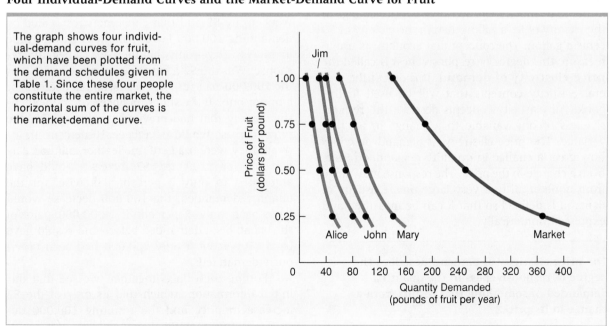

The graph shows four individual-demand curves for fruit, which have been plotted from the demand schedules given in Table 1. Since these four people constitute the entire market, the horizontal sum of the curves is the market-demand curve.

In addition to the shift variables that affect individual-demand curves, market-demand curves may also shift when there is a change in the number of consumers included in the market or in the distribution of their income.

PRICE ELASTICITY OF DEMAND

By now, you should feel comfortable with the idea that market-demand curves are negatively sloped—at lower prices consumers demand more, and at higher prices they demand less. Thus we can turn our attention to the *sensitivity* of that relationship. Just how sensitive or responsive is the quantity demanded to a change in price? We recognize that price sensitivity of demand may be greater for some goods or services than for others and that, even for the same product, this sensitivity may be greater at some price levels than at others. For example, the demand for cars may be more responsive to price than is the demand for table salt. In the case of gasoline, the quantity demanded has been found to be much more sensitive to price change in the vicinity of $1 a gallon than in the vicinity of 50 cents a gallon. The concept that economists use to measure this degree of responsiveness is called the **price elasticity of demand**. It is one of the several elasticity concepts that will be used in this book. All elasticity concepts describe the responsiveness of one variable to a change in another variable. The price elasticity of demand describes how great a change in quantity demanded results from a change in the price. The response may range from none at all to a very large one. Elasticity of demand is defined so that it can be measured and expressed numerically.

The price elasticity of demand describes the degree of responsiveness in the quantity demanded of something that results from a change in its price.

The Relationship Between Relatives

The price elasticity of demand (E_D) may be expressed in the following form:

$$E_D = \frac{\text{the percentage change in the quantity demanded}}{\text{the percentage change in the price that caused it}}$$

Notice that the concept shows a relationship between relative amounts—a ratio between percentage changes—and *not* between absolute numbers. Recall from Chapter 3 the discussion of "slope"—the concept that related the *absolute* change in one variable to an associated *absolute* change in another variable. Slope is not the same thing as elasticity. In trying to establish the price elasticity of demand, we are *not* asking how the absolute quantity demanded responds to the absolute change in price or, for example, how many fewer pairs of shoes consumers will demand when the price is $2 higher. Instead, the price elasticity of demand relates the *percentage* changes. It answers the question "By what percentage will the quantity of shoes demanded change in response to a certain percentage change in price?" Knowing that the price of shoes went up by $2 and that consumers responded by demanding 100,000 fewer pairs tells us very little about elasticity—only that there was a negative response. Was the $2 a big price change or not? Was the 100,000-pair response a substantial decrease or a minor one? If the shoes had been of an inexpensive variety that had previously sold for $20, the price increase would have been 10 percent. If, instead, they were made of fine leather and had earlier sold for $100, the $2 increase would have amounted to only 2 percent. Likewise, for the quantity demanded, the 100,000 decrease would have been only 5 percent if 2,000,000 pairs of shoes had been demanded before, but would have been 50 percent if only 200,000 had been previously demanded.

Putting these facts together, we see that our initial information, which told us only of the $2 increase in price and the resulting 100,000 decrease in the quantity demanded, did not reveal much about the demand response. However, as we learn about percentage changes, the picture becomes clearer. A 5 percent decrease in the quantity demanded (from 2,000,000 to 1,900,000) in response to a 10 percent price increase (from $20 to $22) would have been a meager response compared with a 50 percent decrease in the quantity demanded (from 200,000 to 100,000) in response to a 2 percent price increase (from $100 to $102).

Price elasticity of demand relates percentage changes—the percentage change in the quantity of a product demanded in response to a percentage change in the price of that product.

The fact that elasticity relates percentage changes means that it is independent of the unit of measurement used. The elasticity of a product measured in tons can be compared with one measured in ounces, as can goods priced in dollars be compared with others that are priced in pennies or for that matter in German marks or Japanese yen. If, in our previous example, we had chosen to price shoes in pennies instead of dollars or if the quantities demanded had been measured in dozens of pairs of shoes instead of single pairs, we would still have gotten the same answer using elasticity. However, if we had compared absolute changes—if we had used slope instead of elasticity—and had changed the price unit from dollars to pennies, the ratio of the absolute change in quantity demanded to the absolute price change would have become 100 times smaller.

Elasticity is independent of the unit of measurement used.

The Numerical Value of Elasticity

We have defined price elasticity of demand as the percentage change in quantity demanded divided by the percentage change in the price that caused it. This relationship can be shown in formula form as follows:

$$E_D = \frac{\Delta Q_D / \overline{Q}_D}{\Delta P / \overline{P}}$$

Here ΔQ_D is the change in quantity demanded, $\overline{Q}_D$ is the average quantity demanded, ΔP is the change in price, and $\overline{P}$ is the average price. The numerators of the two fractions, ΔQ_D and ΔP, are quite easy to understand, since they are figured simply by subtracting the original quantity demanded from the new quantity demanded and the original price from the new price. The denominators of the two fractions, $\overline{Q}_D$ and $\overline{P}$, need to be explained further. We choose to use average price and average quantity (the sum of the original price and the new price divided by 2, and the sum of the original quantity and the new quantity divided by 2). This method is much better than using either the original price and quantity or the new price and quantity in the denominators because the use of original or new prices and quantities will make the whole expression confusing. In other words, we would get one percentage change using the original price (or quantity) and a different percentage change using the new price (or quantity). If we stick to averages in the denominators, our elasticity measure will be the same for rising prices (and resulting quantity decreases) as for falling prices (and resulting quantity increases). So let's say that Q_{D_1} is the original quantity demanded and Q_{D_2} is the new quantity demanded and that P_1 is the original price and P_2 is the new price. The formula for computing elasticity would then appear as follows:

$$E_D = \frac{\dfrac{Q_{D_2} - Q_{D_1}}{(Q_{D_1} + Q_{D_2})/2}}{\dfrac{P_2 - P_1}{(P_1 + P_2)/2}}$$

When the twos cancel out, it would be:

$$E_D = \frac{\dfrac{Q_{D_2} - Q_{D_1}}{Q_{D_1} + Q_{D_2}}}{\dfrac{P_2 - P_1}{P_1 + P_2}}$$

Table 2 gives three examples of how the numerical value of elasticity is calculated. Four prices, with the corresponding quantity demanded at each, are shown on a market-demand schedule for

TABLE 2
Elasticity Coefficients Calculated from a Market-Demand Schedule for Sweaters

Price (dollars per sweater)	Market Demand (millions of sweaters per year)	Price Elasticity of Demand Calculation
$20	150	
		$\dfrac{\dfrac{125-150}{150+125}}{\dfrac{30-20}{20+30}} = \dfrac{\dfrac{-25}{275}}{\dfrac{10}{50}} = \dfrac{\dfrac{-1}{11}}{\dfrac{1}{5}} = \dfrac{-1}{11} \times \dfrac{5}{1} = -\dfrac{5}{11}$ or -0.45 or the absolute value of -0.45, which is 0.45
$30	125	
		$\dfrac{\dfrac{75-125}{125+75}}{\dfrac{40-30}{30+40}} = \dfrac{\dfrac{-50}{200}}{\dfrac{10}{70}} = \dfrac{\dfrac{-1}{4}}{\dfrac{1}{7}} = \dfrac{-1}{4} \times \dfrac{7}{1} = -\dfrac{7}{4}$ or -1.75 or the absolute value of -1.75, which is 1.75
$40	75	
		$\dfrac{\dfrac{20-75}{75+20}}{\dfrac{60-40}{40+60}} = \dfrac{\dfrac{-55}{95}}{\dfrac{20}{100}} = \dfrac{\dfrac{-11}{19}}{\dfrac{1}{5}} = \dfrac{-11}{19} \times \dfrac{5}{1} = -\dfrac{55}{19}$ or -2.89 or the absolute value of -2.89, which is 2.89
$60	20	

sweaters. Calculated is the elasticity between $20 and $30, between $30 and $40, and between $40 and $60. The numerical value, or the *elasticity coefficient*, may be expressed in fraction or decimal form. Since the relationship between price and quantity demanded is negative, the price elasticity of demand coefficients will be negative. However, by convention, economists usually use the absolute values of the coefficients, which means that the signs are ignored.

Let us work through the first of the three examples in Table 2. At the original price of $20, 150 million sweaters are demanded. At the higher price of $30, only 125 million sweaters are demanded. Plugging the quantities into the top half of the elasticity formula, as shown in the table, we subtract 150 million (Q_{D_1}) from 125 million (Q_{D_2}) and divide by the sum of these quantities (275 million, which is $Q_{D_1} + Q_{D_2}$). In the lower half of the elasticity formula we subtract $20 ($P_1$) from $30 ($P_2$) and divide by the sum of the prices ($50, which is $P_1 + P_2$). Dividing through by the least common denom-

inator, we get $\frac{-1}{11} / \frac{1}{5}$. By inverting the denominator fraction and then multiplying, we get an elasticity coefficient of $-\frac{5}{11}$ or -0.45, or the absolute value of -0.45, which is 0.45.

Elasticity Categories

How should we interpret price elasticities of demand such as those shown in Table 2? An elasticity coefficient of 0.45 means that for every 1 percent increase in price, the quantity demanded decreases by somewhat less than one-half percent (0.45 of 1 percent). Similarly, the elasticity coefficient of 1.75 means that for every 1 percent increase in price, the quantity demanded falls by 1¾ percent. You can immediately see a major difference between these two cases. In the first case the percentage response in the quantity demanded was less than the percentage change in the price that caused it. In the second case (and also in the third case) in the table the percentage response in quantity demanded was greater than the percentage change in price.

To describe such different degrees of elasticity, economists have grouped all possible cases into five categories. We have already taken note of the two most important ones. Whenever the percentage response in the quantity demanded is less than the percentage change in the price that caused it, with both expressed in absolute values, demand is said to be **inelastic**. That is, the elasticity coefficient is less than 1 in absolute value. And whenever the percentage response in the quantity demanded is greater than the percentage change in the price that caused it, in absolute values, demand is said to be **elastic**. Here the elasticity coefficient is greater than 1 in absolute value. The third category is the case that is just on the borderline between inelastic and elastic. Called **unitary elasticity**, it is where, in absolute value, the percentage response in the quantity demanded is exactly equal to the percentage change in price that caused it. Here the elasticity coefficient is 1 in absolute value. Such a case would be a 10 percent decrease in price leading to a 10 percent rise in the quantity demanded. The last two categories are the extreme cases of inelastic and of elastic demand. The extreme case of inelasticity, called **perfectly inelastic**, is when a price change causes no quantity response at all. The elasticity coefficient is zero. Finally, the extreme case of elasticity, called **infinitely elastic** (or **perfectly elastic**), is when a price change causes an infinite—greater than we can ever count—response in the quantity demanded.

Table 3 sums up the five elasticity categories and gives an example showing what the demand curve might look like for each. The inelastic demand curve is shown to be much steeper than the elastic demand curve. Over the same price range, this relationship will always hold as long as the axes are scaled in the same way. The unitary elastic demand curve is drawn so that the price times the quantity demanded is equal for all points on the curve. (Mathematicians call the shape a "rectangular hyperbola.") The perfectly inelastic demand curve is always parallel to the vertical axis, since the same quantity (80 in our case) will be demanded regardless of the price. The infinitely elastic demand curve is always parallel to the horizontal axis, since at any price above the current price ($10 in our case) the quantity demanded will be

zero and at the current price the maximum quantity demanded will be infinite.

Whenever the percentage response in the quantity demanded is less than the percentage change in the price that caused it, demand is said to be inelastic. Whenever the percentage response in the quantity demanded is greater than the percentage change in the price that caused it, demand is said to be elastic.

Demand is unitary elastic when the percentage response in the quantity demanded is exactly equal to the percentage change in the price that caused it.

Demand is perfectly inelastic when a price change causes no quantity response at all and perfectly elastic (infinitely elastic) when a price change causes an infinite response in the quantity demanded.

Determinants of Price Elasticity of Demand

Price elasticity of demand varies greatly among different products and also for the same product at different prices and for different periods of time. What do you think will be important in determining a product's price elasticity of demand? If you were asked to decide whether the demand for a good enclosed in a large black box—you have no idea what is inside—is relatively elastic or relatively inelastic, what sort of information would you look for? Of course, data on both price and quantity demanded would be best, but if that were not available, you might seek answers to the following questions:

1. Are consumers generally able to find close substitutes for this good?

2. What proportion of consumers' incomes is normally spent on this good?

3. Is this good generally considered a necessity or a luxury?

4. How much time are consumers generally given to adjust to a new price for this good?

TABLE 3
Price Elasticity of Demand Categories

Elasticity Category	Relationship Between Price and Quantity Demanded	Elasticity Coefficient	Numerical Example	Diagram of Demand Curve for This Example
Inelastic	In absolute values the percentage change in the quantity demanded is smaller than the percentage change in the price that caused it.	less than one (in absolute value)	A price increase from $10 to $20 causes quantity demanded to decrease from 60 to 40.	
Elastic	In absolute values the percentage change in the quantity demanded is greater than the percentage change in the price that caused it.	greater than one (in absolute value)	A price increase from $10 to $20 causes quantity demanded to decrease from 120 to 20.	
Unitary elastic	In absolute values the percentage change in the quantity demanded is exactly equal to the percentage change in the price that caused it.	one (in absolute value)	A price increase from $10 to $20 causes quantity demanded to decrease from 80 to 40.	
Perfectly inelastic	Any change in the price causes no response at all in the quantity demanded.	zero	A price increase from $10 to $20 causes no change in the quantity demanded.	
Infinitely elastic	Any change in the price causes a limitless (infinite) response in the quantity demanded.	∞ (infinity)	At any price above $10, the quantity demanded will be zero, and at the $10 price, quantity demanded is indefinitely small or large.	

The closer the substitutes available to consumers, the more elastic will be the demand for a product, *ceteris paribus*. If a good or service increases in price, the availability of close substitutes enables a consumer to switch to another one that is now relatively cheaper. Similarly, when a person uses a variety of products that are good substitutes for each other and one of them decreases in price, he or she will have a tendency to demand proportionately more of that product because it is now relatively cheaper. Table 4 lists a number of products along with estimates of their price elasticities of demand. The demand for restaurant meals is the most elastic short-term price elasticity of demand among those shown in Table 4, probably because most consumers believe that home meals are close substitutes for restaurant meals. By contrast, most people find only few and poor substitutes for household consumption of electricity and gas. The same appears to be true for legal services, medical care, and telephone service. Notice the rather inelastic coefficients for these products in Table 4.

The closer the substitutes available to consumers, the more elastic will be the demand for a product, *ceteris paribus*.

TABLE 4
Selected Short-Term Price Elasticities of Demand

Product	Elasticity
China, glassware, tableware	1.54
Electricity (household)	0.13
Furniture	1.01
Legal services	0.37
Medical care	0.31
Natural gas (household)	0.15
Restaurant meals	2.27
Shoe cleaning and repairing	1.31
Stationery	0.47
Telephone	0.30
Tobacco products	0.46
TV repair	0.47

Source: H. S. Houthakker and Lester D. Taylor, *Consumer Demand in the United States: Analysis and Projections,* 2nd ed. (Cambridge, Mass.: Harvard University Press, 1970), pp. 66–128. Used by permission.

A second determinant of price elasticity of demand appears to be the percentage of household income spent on a product. Price elasticity tends to be low when the portion of income spent for it is low, and high when the portion of income is high. The slightly elastic short-term demand elasticity of 1.01 for furniture (see Table 4) would probably be much more inelastic if the average piece of furniture were not priced so high, making it a large proportion of most households' incomes. By contrast, take the classic example of table salt. Even if the price of table salt rose by 50 percent, the increase might amount to only as little as 10¢ a month for the average household. Ten cents is surely a small portion of the income of most households. Because they would not be forced to cut back their purchases of salt very much, we would expect the price elasticity of demand to be very low (very inelastic).

Price elasticity tends to be low when the portion of income spent for it is low and high when the portion of income is high.

The third determinant of demand elasticity is whether people consider a product to be a necessity or a luxury. A product that is felt to be a "necessity" tends to be more inelastic, whereas a product considered to be a "luxury" tends to be more elastic. Household consumption of electricity and natural gas, legal services, medical care, and telephone serve as good examples of necessities. Table 4 shows their elasticity coefficients to be very low. Restaurant meals and china, glassware, and tableware, though not the best examples of luxuries, fit that description better than the other products in Table 4. Note that their elasticity coefficients are the highest among the twelve selected products.

The demand for a product that is felt to be a necessity tends to be more inelastic, whereas the demand for a product considered to be a luxury tends to be more elastic.

Finally, the time allowed for consumers to adjust to a new price is an important determinant of the price elasticity of demand. The longer the time interval, the more elastic will be the demand. If there is very little time for adjustment—not enough time to break the habit or to use up enough of a complementary durable good—demand is likely to be relatively inelastic. Although we saw in Table 4 that the short-term elasticity coefficient for tobacco products is 0.46, the same study estimates it at 1.9 in the "long run." The habit of smoking is usually not broken overnight. In fact, it takes some time for most people to cut down. The elasticity coefficient for gasoline has been estimated to be about three to four times higher in the "long run" than in the short term. This difference is explained by the fact that people who own drivable gas-guzzlers find that it pays to hold on to those cars, even in the face of sharply increasing gasoline prices. Once the gas-guzzlers break down, people will generally buy fuel-efficient cars to replace them.

The longer the time consumers are given to adjust to a new price, the more elastic will be the demand. If there is very little time for adjustment, demand is likely to be relatively inelastic.

We have explained four determinants of the price elasticity of demand. Actual products will have several or all of these characteristics, and they may be either contradictory or reinforcing. It is much harder to predict the elasticity for, say, vacation trips than for table salt. There are few close substitutes for a vacation trip, but it usually takes a large proportion of a person's income and it is generally not considered a necessity. On the other hand, table salt has no good substitutes, it is a small proportion of most people's incomes, and it is considered a necessity by most people.

Price Elasticity of Demand and Total Revenue

Business firms are keenly aware of elasticity. Why shouldn't they be? The price elasticity of demand will determine whether a price change of a product that they sell will lead to an increase or a decrease in their total revenue stemming from the product. **Total revenue**—the *total receipts* that a firm re-

ceives from selling its product or the *total outlay* that buyers spend on that firm's product—is figured by multiplying the quantity demanded of the product by the price per unit.

$$TR = P \times Q_D$$

where *TR* is total revenue, *P* is the unit price of the product, and Q_D is the quantity demanded of the product.

Total revenue is the total receipts that a firm receives from selling its product or the total outlay buyers spend on that firm's product. It is calculated by multiplying the quantity demanded of the product by the price per unit.

From your earlier study of demand, you know that when a company changes the price of a product that it sells, it can be pretty sure that the quantity demanded will move in the opposite direction. But will the price change increase or decrease total revenue? A price rise does not necessarily mean a higher total revenue. Neither does a price cut necessarily mean that total revenue will go down. The impact on total revenue depends upon the degree to which the quantity demanded responds to the price change that caused it—in other words, upon the price elasticity of demand. For this reason, the following relationships will hold:

Price Elasticity of Demand	Direction of Change in Total Revenue When Price Falls	Direction of Change in Total Revenue When Price Rises
elastic	increase	decrease
inelastic	decrease	increase
unitary elastic	constant	constant

When demand is elastic, the percentage change in quantity demanded is greater in absolute value than the percentage change in price. So if price falls, the increase in quantity demanded will more than offset the decrease in price, and total revenue will go up. When price rises, total revenue will go down because the decrease in quantity demanded will more than offset the rise in price. In the case of inelastic demand, in absolute values the percentage change in quantity demanded is less than the percentage change in price. A decrease in price will more than offset the increase in quantity demanded, and total revenue will drop. When price rises, total revenue will rise because the increase in price more than offsets the decrease in quantity demanded.

Finally, when demand is unitary elastic, the percentage changes in price and quantity demanded are exactly equal in absolute values. For this reason the two forces will cancel each other out, and total revenue will not change. Sometimes it is easier to see the relationships that we have been describing by looking at numerical examples. In Table 5 you can see what happens to total revenue when the price rises (read down) or the price falls (read up) under elastic, inelastic, and unitary elastic conditions.

When demand is elastic (coefficient of 1.5 in our case) and price rises from $5 to $10, the quantity demanded falls from 300 to 100, so that total revenue (price times quantity demanded) drops from $1,500 to $1,000. Under the same conditions, a drop in price from $10 to $5 will cause total revenue to rise from $1,000 to $1,500.

When demand is inelastic (coefficient of 0.6 in our case) and price rises from $5 to $10, the quantity demanded falls from 300 to 200, so that total revenue rises from $1,500 to $2,000. Under the same conditions a drop in price from $10 to $5 will cause total revenue to fall from $2,000 to $1,500.

When demand is unitary elastic (coefficient of 1.0), a price change in either direction will cause an equal percentage response in quantity demanded in the opposite direction, so that total revenue will remain at $2,000.

The impact of a price change on total revenue depends upon the price elasticity of demand.

CROSS ELASTICITY OF DEMAND

So far, we have been dealing only with the relationship between the quantity demanded for a

TABLE 5
Relationship Between Price Elasticity of Demand and Total Revenue

Price Elasticity of Demand	Price (dollars per unit)	Quantity Demanded (units per time period)	Total Revenue (in dollars)
Elastic (1.5)	5	300	1,500
	10	100	1,000
Inelastic (0.6)	5	300	1,500
	10	200	2,000
Unitary elastic (1.0)	5	400	2,000
	10	200	2,000

product and the price of the *same* product. **Cross demand** relates the quantity demanded for a product to the price of a *different* product. This functional relationship may be expressed as

$$Q_{D_A} = f(P_B), \textit{ceteris paribus}$$

where Q_{D_A} is the quantity demanded of good A, f is the symbol for function (which may be read "depends on"), P_B is the price of good B, and *ceteris paribus* means that all other variables are held constant.

It follows from the concept of cross demand that the **cross elasticity of demand** relates the percentage change in the quantity demanded for *one* product to the percentage change in the price of a *different* product, with other variables held constant. The cross elasticity of demand (E_C) may therefore be expressed as follows:

$$E_C = \frac{\text{the percentage change in the quantity demanded for one product}}{\text{the percentage change in the price of a different product that caused it}}$$

For goods A and B the formula for figuring cross elasticity is

$$E_C = \frac{\dfrac{Q_{D_{A_2}} - Q_{D_{A_1}}}{(Q_{D_{A_1}} + Q_{D_{A_2}})/2}}{\dfrac{P_{B_2} - P_{B_1}}{(P_{B_1} + P_{B_2})/2}}$$

After the twos cancel out, it is

$$E_C = \frac{\dfrac{Q_{D_{A_2}} - Q_{D_{A_1}}}{Q_{D_{A_1}} + Q_{D_{A_2}}}}{\dfrac{P_{B_2} - P_{B_1}}{P_{B_1} + P_{B_2}}}$$

Here $Q_{D_{A_1}}$ is the original quantity demanded for good A, $Q_{D_{A_2}}$ is the new quantity demanded for good A, P_{B_1} is the original price of good B, and P_{B_2} is the new price of good B.

Cross elasticity of demand relates the percentage change in the quantity demanded for one product to the percentage change in the price of a different product.

Recall from Chapter 5 that the demand curve of a product shifts as the result of a change in the price of a related product and that economists have described two kinds of relationships—substitutes and complements. When two products are **substitutes**—readily interchangeable—the cross elasticity of demand will be positive.[1] A rise in the price of one will increase the demand for the other, and a drop in the price of one will lead to less demand for the other. For example, when the price of beer goes up, the demand for ale will go up. In other words, at higher prices of beer many people will switch over to buying ale. Likewise, when the price of beer goes down, the demand for ale goes down as people switch from ale to beer. A high positive cross elasticity between two products means that they are close substitutes, whereas a low one means that not much substitution takes place when one product changes in price. A 10 percent rise in the price of beer may bring about a 30 percent increase in the demand for ale (cross elasticity coefficient of 3.0). Yet a 10 percent rise in the price of beer may cause only a 1 percent increase in the demand for brandy (cross elasticity coefficient of 0.1).

When two products are substitutes, the cross elasticity of demand will be positive: a rise in

---

the price of one will increase the demand for the other, while a drop in the price of one will lead to less demand for the other. A high positive cross elasticity between two products means that they are close substitutes.

When two products are **complements**—used along with each other—the cross elasticity will be negative. A rise in the price of one will decrease the demand for the other, and a drop in the price of one will increase the demand for the other. When the price of typewriters goes up, the demand for typewriter ribbons will go down. This happens because at higher prices of typewriters, the price of the combination made up of typewriter and ribbon rises, so that the quantity demanded for typewriters goes down and the demand for ribbons goes down. When the price of typewriters *decreases*, the demand for typewriter ribbons will go up, since the combination of the two complementary goods goes down in price. A large negative cross elasticity between two products means that they are close complements, whereas a small one means that the complementary relationship is weak. A 10 percent decrease in the price of typewriters may lead to a 20 percent rise in the demand for typewriter ribbons (cross elasticity coefficient of −2.0). Yet a 10 percent drop in the price of writing paper may cause only a one-half percent increase in the demand for pens (cross elasticity coefficient of −0.05).

When two products are complements, the cross elasticity will be negative: a rise in the price of one will decrease the demand for the other, and a drop in the price of one will increase the demand for the other. A large negative cross elasticity between two products means that they are close complements.

Some actual estimates of cross elasticities of demand have been made by Herman Wold and Lars Jureen. They appear in Table 6. Note that, while all three pairs of products were found to be substitutes, margarine for butter was found to be a much better substitute than beef for pork.

---

1. Be sure to recognize that the convention of ignoring the sign for price elasticity of demand coefficients *cannot* be carried over to cross elasticity of demand coefficients.

TABLE 6
Cross Elasticities of Demand for Three Pairs of Products

Product Pairs	Cross Elasticity Coefficient
The price of butter and the demand for margarine	0.81
The price of pork and the demand for beef	0.28
The price of animal fats and the demand for flour	0.56

Source: Herman Wold and Lars Jureen, *Demand Analysis: A Study in Econometrics* (New York: John Wiley & Sons, Inc., 1953). Copyright © 1953 by John Wiley and Sons, Inc. Reprinted by Greenwood Press, Westport, Connecticut, 1982. Used with permission.

Cross elasticity of demand was used in a very important antitrust case, to which we shall refer again in a later chapter. In 1956 the Supreme Court of the United States found the Du Pont Company innocent of monopolizing cellophane production on the grounds that the cross elasticity of demand between cellophane and other flexible packaging materials such as polyethylene, aluminum foil, and waxed paper was positive and very high.[2] The Du Pont Company had been accused of illegally monopolizing the production of cellophane because it produced about 75 percent of the cellophane sold in the United States. The Du Pont Company's defense was that the cross elasticity of demand between cellophane and the other flexible packaging materials was so high (they were such good substitutes) that the relevant industry was not cellophane, but rather flexible packaging materials, of which Du Pont held less than 20 percent of the market.

INCOME ELASTICITY OF DEMAND

So far, we have been dealing with the relationship between the quantity demanded for a product and

2. *U.S.* v. *E. I. Du Pont de Nemours and Co.*, 351 U.S. 377 (1956).

the price of either the same product or a different product. **Income demand** relates the quantity demanded for a product to the income level of the consumers or potential consumers of that product. This functional relationship may be expressed as

$$Q_{D_x} = f(Y), \text{ ceteris paribus}$$

where Q_{D_x} is the quantity demanded of good X, f is the symbol for function, Y is the symbol for the income level of consumers and potential consumers of X, and *ceteris paribus* means that all other variables are held constant.

It follows from the concept of income demand that the **income elasticity of demand** relates the percentage change in the quantity demanded for a product to the percentage change in the income level of the consumers or potential consumers of the good or service, with all other variables unchanged. Therefore, the income elasticity of demand (E_Y) may be expressed as follows:

$$E_Y = \frac{\text{the percentage change in the quantity demanded for a product}}{\text{the percentage change in the level of income}}$$

The formula for figuring income elasticity of demand is

$$E_Y = \frac{\dfrac{Q_{D_2} - Q_{D_1}}{(Q_{D_1} + Q_{D_2})/2}}{\dfrac{Y_2 - Y_1}{(Y_1 + Y_2)/2}}$$

After the twos cancel out, we have

$$E_Y = \frac{\dfrac{Q_{D_2} - Q_{D_1}}{Q_{D_1} + Q_{D_2}}}{\dfrac{Y_2 - Y_1}{Y_1 + Y_2}}$$

Here Q_{D_1} is the original quantity demanded for the product, Q_{D_2} is the new quantity demanded, Y_1 is the original income level, and Y_2 is the new income level.

Income demand relates the quantity demanded for a product to the income level of the consumers or potential consumers of that

---

product. Income elasticity of demand relates the percentage change in the quantity demanded for a product to the percentage change in the income level of the consumers or potential consumers of the good or service.

Again recall from Chapter 5 that the demand curve of a product shifts as a result of a change in the level of income. For most products we expect this relationship to be positive, because people demand more of a product when they can afford more. Where there is a positive relationship between the demand for a product and income, economists call that product **normal.**[3] As you know, students are likely to buy more automobiles, more dinners at a restaurant, and more clothing when their income is higher. A high positive income elasticity of demand for a product means that a change in the level of income will bring about a strong demand response in the same direction. A 10 percent increase in a college student's income may cause him or her to buy 50 percent more restaurant dinners (income elasticity coefficient of 5.0).

When there is a positive relationship between the demand for a product and income, economists call that product normal. A high positive income elasticity of demand for a product means that a change in the level of income will bring about a strong demand response in the same direction.

Goods and services differ widely in their income elasticities of demand. In general, goods and services considered to be luxuries, such as jewelry and furs, tend to have high income elasticities, and those considered to be necessities, such as salt and detergent, tend to have low income elasticities. Table 7 lists several products, along with estimates of their income elasticities of demand. The first five products are found to be normal. Automobiles were found to be quite income elastic (a 1 percent

TABLE 7
Income Elasticities of Demand for Selected Products

Product	Income Elasticity Coefficient
Automobiles	3.00
Beer	0.93
Fruits and berries	0.70
Cigarettes	0.50
Coffee	0.29
Margarine	−0.20
Flour	−0.36

Sources: Gregory C. Chow, *Demand for Automobiles in the United States* (Amsterdam: North Holland Publishing Company, 1957); T. F. Hogarty and K. G. Elzinga, "The Demand for Beer," *Review of Economics and Statistics*, May 1972; Herman Wold and C. E. V. Leser, "Commodity Group Expenditures Functions for the United Kingdom, 1948–1957," *Econometrica*, January 1961; S. M. Sackrin, "Factors Affecting the Demand for Cigarettes," *Agricultural Economics Research*, July 1962; John J. Hughes, "Note on the U.S. Demand for Coffee," *American Journal of Agricultural Economics*, November 1969.

increase in income causes a 3 percent increase in the demand for automobiles). On the other hand, coffee was found not to be very income elastic.

In some rare cases people demand more of a product when their income is low and less of the product when they have a higher income. Where such a negative relationship between demand and income exists, economists call the product **inferior.** For example, people may buy fewer potatoes and fewer bus tickets when their income is higher, since at higher income levels they may substitute some meat for some potatoes and an automobile for the bus. A 25 percent increase in a person's income may cause him or her to buy an automobile and thus buy 95 percent fewer bus tickets (income elasticity coefficient of −3.8).

Looking back at Table 7 once more, we see that Wold and Leser estimated negative income elasticities for both margarine and flour in mid-twentieth-century Britain.

When there is a negative relationship between the demand for a product and income, economists call the product inferior.

3. The income elasticity of demand coefficient is positive for normal goods and services. Even though most goods and services are normal, the sign may not be ignored.

Economics in Focus

The Price of Vanity

A few years ago, three economists—Neil Alper, Robert Archibald, and Eric Jensen—decided to investigate the price of vanity: that is, the fee charged for obtaining vanity license plates for a motor vehicle. Vanity plates display a personalized name or slogan of the owner's choice. For example, a driver named Barbara Jones might select license plates that read "B Jones"; or she might proclaim herself "BOSS #1"; or she could identify her chief hobby with "I SKI."

Most states make vanity plates available for an extra fee, and the sales can be an important source of state revenue. In Virginia, for instance, about 460,000 vehicles carry vanity plates—one-tenth of all the cars and trucks registered in the state. But the three economists noticed that the popularity of vanity plates varied greatly from state to state, and they wondered about this phenomenon. Upon investigation, they discovered that a number of factors, including income and age distribution, influenced the purchase of vanity plates. But the most important demand factor was price; in fact, the economists found a classic relationship among price, price elasticity of demand, and total revenue generated.

Prices for the vanity plates ranged from $2 a year in Georgia to $60 in Ohio. The price elasticity of demand also showed a large variation. In Ohio, with its high price level, the price elasticity coefficient was 2.6. This meant that demand was very elastic; in percentage terms, a relatively small change in price would produce a relatively large change in quantity demanded. The implication for state revenues was clear: Ohio could increase its revenue from vanity plates by lowering the price. At a lower price, many more people would buy the plates; though each sale would bring in less money, the total from all sales would rise.

Some states, in contrast, showed inelastic demand—an elasticity coefficient lower than 1.0. Montana, for example, had an elasticity of 0.34. In such states, a relatively large percentage change in price produced a relatively small percentage change in quantity demanded. In these cases the best strategy for maximizing revenues was to *raise* the price. At a higher price the decline in buyers would be more than offset by the higher revenue from each sale.

In most states the researchers found that unitary elasticity (an elasticity coefficient of 1.0) would be reached with prices in the neighborhood of $20–27. That was the point at which revenues from the vanity plates would reach their maximum. The precise figure depended on the other demand factors at work in each particular state; no two sets of conditions were exactly alike. But the three economists demonstrated that by ignoring price elasticity, many states were wasting an excellent chance to obtain more revenue—and obtaining revenue, after all, was the chief purpose of issuing vanity plates.

Sources: Adapted from Timothy Tregarthen, "The Demand for Vanity," *The Margin,* October 1987, p. 11. Colorado Springs: University of Colorado, 1987. © 1987 *The Margin.* Used by permission. Also, John Bohn, "New Vanity Car Tags Offer 'a Moving Billboard for Colleges,'" *Washington Post: Virginia Weekly,* March 23, 1989.

SUMMARY

1. A market-demand schedule and curve are derived by horizontally adding together all of the individual consumer-demand schedules and curves in a market that is clearly defined on the basis of both product and geography. (See page 502.)

2. Shifts in market-demand curves occur for the same reasons that cause individual consumer-demand curves to shift. (These reasons are changes in preferences, changes in income, and changes in prices of related goods and services.) In addition, market-demand curves may shift because of changes in the number of consumers that are included in the market and the distribution of income among the consumers. (See pages 502–503.)

3. Elasticity is a concept used to describe the responsiveness of one variable to a change in another variable. The changes are measured in percentages, and not in absolute numbers. This means that elasticity is independent of the unit of measure that is used. (See page 504.)

4. Price elasticity of demand measures the percentage change in the quantity demanded of a product in response to a percentage change in the price of that product. (See pages 504–505.)

5. There are five categories of elasticity. Demand is *elastic* when in absolute values the percentage change in the quantity demanded is greater than the percentage change in the price that led to it. Demand is *inelastic* when in absolute values the percentage change in the quantity demanded is less than the percentage change in the price that caused it. Demand is *unitary elastic* when in absolute values the percentage response in the quantity demanded is exactly equal to the percentage change in price that generated it. Demand is *perfectly inelastic* when a price change causes no quantity response at all. Demand is *infinitely elastic* when a price change causes an infinite response in the quantity demanded. (See pages 506–507 and Table 3, page 508.)

6. The price elasticity of demand of a product depends upon: (a) whether there are good substitutes available for it, (b) the proportion of consumer incomes spent on it, (c) whether the product is a luxury or a necessity, and (d) the amount of time that consumers have to adjust to the price change. (See pages 507–508.)

7. Whether a firm's total revenue from sales of a product will increase, decrease, or remain the same when the price of the product changes will depend upon the price elasticity of demand for that product. (See page 510.)

8. Cross elasticity of demand relates the percentage change in the quantity demanded for a product to the percentage change in the price of another product. It is positive for substitute products and negative for complements. (See pages 511–512.)

9. Income elasticity of demand relates the percentage change in the quantity demanded for a product to the percentage change in consumer income. It is positive for normal products and negative for inferior products. (See pages 513–514.)

KEY TERMS

complements: two products that are used along with each other (page 512).

cross demand: the relationship between the quantity demanded for a product and the price of a different product (page 511).

cross elasticity of demand: the percentage change in the quantity demanded for one product divided by the percentage change in the price of a different product that caused it (page 511).

elastic demand: a condition existing whenever the percentage response in the quantity demanded is greater than the percentage change in the price that caused it (page 507).

income demand: the relationship between the quantity demanded for a product and the income level of the consumers or potential consumers of that product (page 513).

income elasticity of demand: the percentage change in the quantity demanded for a product divided by the percentage change in the income level of the consumers or potential consumers of that product (page 513).

inelastic demand: a condition existing whenever the percentage response in the quantity demanded is less than the percentage change in the price that caused it (page 507).

inferior product: a product that people demand more of when their income is low and less of when they have a higher income (page 514).

infinitely elastic demand: a condition existing when a price change causes an infinite response in the quantity demanded (page 507).

market demand: the sum of all the individual consumers' demands for a particular product in a particular geographic area (page 502).

normal product: a product for which there is a positive relationship between quantity demanded and income level (page 514).

perfectly elastic demand: *see* **infinitely elastic demand.**

perfectly inelastic demand: a condition existing when a price change causes no response in quantity demanded (page 507).

price elasticity of demand: the concept that economists use to measure the responsiveness of the quantity demanded to a change in price; the percentage change in the quantity demanded of a product divided by the percentage change in its price (page 504).

substitutes: two products that are readily interchangeable (page 512).

total revenue: the total receipts that a firm receives from selling its product or the total outlay that buyers spend on that firm's product (page 510).

unitary elastic demand: a condition existing when the percentage response in quantity demanded is exactly equal to the percentage change in the price that caused it (page 507).

DISCUSSION QUESTIONS

1. A market-demand curve may shift to the left or to the right for a number of different reasons. List and briefly explain the five reasons that were discussed in the chapter. Which of these reasons also apply to individual-demand curves, and which are unique to market-demand curves?

2. Using the formula provided in the chapter, calculate the price elasticity of demand for each of the following cases:

a. The price of a certain cough syrup increases from $5 to $10 a bottle, which causes the quantity demanded for this cough syrup to decrease from 1,000 bottles per day to 700 bottles per day.

b. The price of a certain type of shirt increases from $18 to $19, which causes the quantity demanded for these shirts to decrease from 100,000 units per month to 75,000 units per month.

c. The price of a certain computer game decreases from $40 to $32, which causes the quantity demanded for this game to increase from 3,000 units per year to 5,000 per year.

3. Referring to the three cases given in the previous question, determine whether the demand for each product is elastic, inelastic, or unitary elastic.

4. Provide a numerical illustration of a case in which demand is unitary elastic. What is the elasticity coefficient?

5. Provide a numerical illustration of a case in which demand is perfectly inelastic. What is the elasticity coefficient?

6. Explain how each of the following characteristics or circumstances relating to a particular good or service is expected to affect its price elasticity of demand:

a. A small portion of most consumers' incomes is spent on it.

b. Most consumers consider it a necessity.

c. Most consumers find that rather close substitutes are available for it.

d. The change in the quantity demanded is measured only a few hours after its price changed.

e. Most consumers consider it a luxury.

f. It is a big-ticket product, so that most consumers find its price to be large relative to their annual income.

g. The change in the quantity demanded is measured five years after its price changed.

7. If you know whether the price of a good has gone up or down and if you know whether its price elasticity of demand is elastic, inelastic, or unitary elastic, you can determine whether the seller's total revenue has gone up, down, or remained the same. Provide numerical illustrations to show this statement to be accurate.

8. Discuss the difference between the concepts of price elasticity and cross elasticity of demand.

9. From your own experience, give five examples of pairs of products that you consider to be good substitutes. Provide five more examples of pairs of products that you consider to be complements. Of these ten examples, which do you suppose would have the highest positive cross elastic-

ity of demand coefficient? Which do you suppose would have the highest negative cross elasticity of demand coefficient?

10. If you know that Linda's consumption of potatoes fell from 200 pounds a year to 150 pounds a year when her income went up from $15,000 a year to $24,000 a year, you are able to calculate Linda's income elasticity of demand for potatoes. What is it? What do economists call this kind of a good?

24
Business Firm Choice

Preview   In the last two chapters we examined the demand side of product markets—the principles of consumer choice that economists use to predict what products will be demanded and in what quantities. In this and the next chapter we look at the supply side of product markets. This means that our interest turns to business firms, which concern themselves with production decisions. We shall therefore focus on the principles of business firm choice that economists use to predict what products will be supplied and in what quantities.

You may not be able to "wear the shoes" of the businessman or businesswoman quite as comfortably as those of the consumer. After all, each of us is a consumer, but only a small fraction of the population is likely to be engaged in making business decisions. However, it will be helpful for you to keep in mind the rationality assumption that economists make about business firms—namely, that they seek to maximize profits.

In this chapter you will study the fundamentals of production. Business firms seek an efficient way of combining inputs to produce certain outputs. The production function describes that relationship in terms of actual inputs and outputs. It cannot change during what economists call the short-run and long-run time periods. It is, however, subject to change in the very long run. You will see that business firm decision makers must be concerned with all three of these time periods at once.

Next you will learn a general theory of production in the short run. You will see what happens to output (goods or services produced) as a business firm adds more and more units of a variable input (such as the number of workers) to some other inputs that the firm cannot change (such as the size of a factory building). Then you will study the same case from the cost side. A whole family of business-cost concepts—seven in all—are defined, and the relationships between them are explained.

We then go on to discuss production in the long run. Economies and diseconomies of scale, as well as the important relationship between short-run and long-run average total cost, are explained.

Finally, we discuss production in the very long run, where inventions and innovations give rise to technological changes. Here we introduce the concept of *productivity* and explain the major determinants of productivity changes.

An appendix to the chapter, using a tool much like that used in the appendix to Chapter 22, shows one way of finding a firm's best input combination in the long run.

PRODUCTION

Production is the transformation of inputs into outputs. The **inputs** are the resources that we described in Chapter 4: labor, natural resources, and capital. These factors of production may appear in their original state, such as unskilled human labor or raw materials, or they may be the result of an earlier production process, as is the case with skilled labor, machines or semifinished goods. The **outputs** are the economic goods and services that business firms produce for sale to consumers, other business firms, and governments. For example, a company that manufactures shoes may transform such inputs as labor, shoemaking machinery, leather, nails, and laces into a variety of shoe outputs that are sold to individuals, to shoe stores, or to the U.S. Navy.

Production is the transformation of labor, natural resources, and capital (inputs) into the economic goods and services that business firms produce for sale to consumers, other business firms, and governments (outputs).

Technical Efficiency

Since economically rational business firms engage in production in order to obtain profits, they do not wish to use production methods that waste resources. Therefore, the first step in analyzing the behavior of firms in production is to understand what is meant by **technically efficient** methods of production. No waste of resources occurs when a technically efficient method of production is used. This means that no other method of production will yield the same output by using a lower quantity of any input without using a higher quantity of some other input. Combinations that are not technically efficient use more of at least one input and the same amounts of other inputs to yield the same output as another method of production. Table 1 illustrates this point. Five different production methods are shown (A through E), all of which yield 10 dozen pairs of shoes per day. Only production method E is technically efficient. Production methods A and B use more workers and more machines than does E, and so are technically inefficient. Production method C uses the same number of machines as E but requires two more workers. Production method D uses the same number of workers, but one more machine. Hence, both C and D are also technically inefficient.

Once the technically inefficient production methods have been weeded out, the way is clear to understand a basic economic concept about the behavior of firms—the production function.

A technically efficient method of production does not waste resources. That is, no other method of production will yield the same output by using a lower quantity of any input without using a higher quantity of some other input.

The Production Function The relationship between the physical units of inputs and outputs in the production process is expressed in a firm's production function. A **production function** shows the maximum output that can be obtained from given amounts of inputs as of a specified point in time. The word *maximum* shows that it includes only technically efficient input combinations. The production function can also describe the minimum amount of inputs needed to support a certain level of output. It tells us what is possible at the present level of technological development. For ex-

TABLE 1
Input Combinations Resulting from Different Methods of Production for Producing Ten Dozen Pairs of Shoes per Day

Production Method	Quantity of Shoes Produced per Day (in dozens)	Number of Shoe Workers (in 8-hour days)	Number of Shoemaking Machines (in 8-hour days)
A	10	30	10
B	10	25	7
C	10	22	5
D	10	20	6
E	10	20	5

ample, the production function may show that a certain quantity of shoes can be produced each day, given any one of a number of combinations of shoe workers and shoemaking machinery.

A production function shows the maximum output that can be obtained from given amounts of inputs as of a specified point in time. It also describes the minimum amount of inputs needed to support a certain level of output.

A general statement of a production function for a good or service is as follows:

$$X = f(A, B, C, \ldots N)$$

Here X is the quantity of output per unit of time, and A, B, C, all the way to N, are the quantities of different inputs used to produce the output. It is convenient to simplify the general statement of the production function by grouping all of the different inputs that are actually used under just two headings: labor and capital. (Natural resources are here assumed to be part of capital.) We can then write the following:

$$X = f(L, K)$$

Here again X is the quantity of output per unit of time, L is the quantity of labor used to produce X, and K is the quantity of capital used to produce X.

A production function for a good or service that groups all of the different inputs under two

headings can be written $X = f(L, K)$, where X is the quantity of output per unit of time, L is the quantity of labor used to produce X, and K is the quantity of capital used to produce X.

To illustrate this concept, we return to the case of shoe manufacturing. Suppose that shoes can be produced by using only combinations of shoe workers (L_s) and shoemaking machinery (K_s) as inputs and that, using only technically efficient combinations, the exact relationship between them and the quantity of shoes produced (S) is as follows:

$$S = \sqrt{L_s \times K_s}$$

Shoe output will be measured in dozens of pairs of shoes per day and the inputs on the basis of a standard eight-hour day. This production function may then be read as follows: The maximum quantity of shoes produced per day is equal to the square root of the number of shoe workers working an eight-hour day multiplied by the number of shoemaking machines operating for eight hours.[1]

If a certain shoe manufacturer wishes to produce 10 dozen pairs of shoes per day, the production function would indicate the following relationship:

$$10 = \sqrt{L_s \times K_s}$$

1. Recall that the square of a number is that number multiplied by itself. The square root of a number is merely the reverse of that calculation. As in the example we shall use here, the square of 10 is 100 and the square root of 100 is 10.

TABLE 2
Minimum Input Combinations for Producing Ten Dozen Pairs of Shoes per Day

Quantity of Shoes Produced per Day (in dozens)	Number of Shoe Workers (in 8-hour days)	Number of Shoemaking Machines (in 8-hour days)
10	100	1
10	50	2
10	25	4
10	20	5
10	10	10
10	5	20
10	4	25
10	2	50
10	1	100

It shows the way in which a firm can substitute one input for another without changing its total output. Note that $L_s \times K_s$ must always be equal to 100, so that the square root is always equal to 10. Alternative labor-capital combinations for our hypothetical shoe manufacturer are presented in Table 2. Given its production function, the firm cannot produce 10 dozen pairs of shoes per day with fewer inputs than those shown in Table 2. We are assuming that no fractional units of either workers or machines can be employed. (In other words, we assume that the firm cannot hire part-time workers or rent machines for part of a day.) The table shows nine different technically efficient ways of producing 10 dozen pairs of shoes per day. Comparing two of the alternatives from Table 2, we see that this firm can use a fairly high ratio of shoe workers to shoemaking machinery such as 25 workers and 4 machines $(10 = \sqrt{25 \times 4})$ or a low ratio of shoe workers to shoemaking machinery such as 2 workers and 50 machines $(10 = \sqrt{2 \times 50})$.

The preceding discussion makes the implicit assumption that business firms "know" their production functions. In reality, they often do not. Not enough information may be available, and business firms may not be willing to spend what it costs to find out about all of the possible input-output relationships. Just the same, we shall continue to make this simplifying assumption on the grounds

that firms do have a pretty good idea about many of their most immediate tradeoffs.

Economic Efficiency

The production function shows the various technically efficient input combinations that can be used to produce a given quantity of output. But which of these technically efficient alternatives should a firm adopt? The production function cannot answer this question. Rather, the answer is based on **economic efficiency**—the technically efficient method with the lowest cost to the firm. We continue our shoe example to make this point clear. Table 3, besides repeating the nine technically efficient combinations shown in Table 2, gives a cost figure for each of them. We arrive at these cost figures simply by adding together the cost of workers and the cost of machines for each combination. For example, the firm can employ 5 workers at a rate of $60 per worker per day, or $300, and use 20 machines at a cost of $50 each per day, or $1,000, so that the combination of 5 workers and 20 machines costs the firm $1,300. We assume that the small firm in our example does not influence input prices, so that the cost of shoe workers is $60 per day and the cost of shoemaking machines is $50 per day for all quantities shown in Table 3. The total-cost figures allow us to determine which

TABLE 3
*Minimum Input (Technically Efficient) Combinations and Total Cost for
Producing Ten Dozen Pairs of Shoes per Day*

Quantity of Shoes Produced per Day (in dozens)	Number of Shoe Workers (in 8-hour days at $60 a day)	Number of Shoemaking Machines (in 8-hour days at $50 a day)	Total Cost per Day (in dollars)
10	100	1	6,050
10	50	2	3,100
10	25	4	1,700
10	20	5	1,450
10	10	10	1,100
10	5	20	1,300
10	4	25	1,490
10	2	50	2,620
10	1	100	5,060

combination is economically efficient. The answer is, of course, 10 workers and 10 machines, since the total cost of $1,100 for that combination is less than for any other.

**An input combination is economically efficient
if it is the technically efficient method with the
lowest cost to the firm.**

THREE TIME SPANS FOR DECISION MAKING

When a business firm enters an industry, it comes in at a certain size or capacity to produce. It has already made a number of commitments that reduce its immediate flexibility. Besides having built a certain size plant, it may have contracted to buy a minimum amount of some material inputs for a certain length of time or hired some workers or leased some land for a number of years. For example, automobile firms commonly enter into long-term agreements to purchase steel and tires from suppliers, and professional ball clubs enter into em-

ployment contracts with some of their players covering several years.

At any given time, a firm is expected to be less than perfectly flexible, since it faces some fixed obligations. The **short run** is defined as the period of time during which at least one of the firm's inputs cannot be varied.[2] It would be ideal if we could say exactly how long the short run generally lasts. But we cannot. For a small housepainting firm that wishes to expand, the short run may be only the two days that it takes to hire one more painter and buy the equipment that he or she needs. By contrast, a steelmaking firm may find that the short run lasts four years, since that is how long it takes to get delivery on a new basic oxygen furnace and to put up a building around it. In other words, the steel firm has a commitment to its present plant for four more years.

**The short run is the period of time during
which at least one of the firm's inputs cannot
be varied.**

---

2. Some economists also like to recognize the *very short run,* a time period so short that the firm is unable to vary any of its inputs. We choose not to include the very short run in our discussion since it adds little to the analysis of business firm choice.

The second time span in which business decisions are made is called the **long run**. It is a period of time long enough to make all the changes that a firm wants to make within the limits of its existing production function. That is, the level of technological development does not change, even though all of the inputs that are recognized in the firm's production function are variable. In the long run, for example, a firm would be able either to double its capacity by building another plant and training additional workers or to produce only a third as much as it could before by selling off enough of its machines and letting go enough of its workers.

The long run is a period of time long enough to make all the changes that a firms wants to make within the limits of its existing production function.

Business decisions also involve what economists refer to as the **very long run**. This is a period of time long enough so that a whole new technology can be introduced and the production function itself can be changed. The shoe manufacturer in our earlier example would no longer be bound by the alternatives offered in Table 2, since a new shoemaking machine or a new organizational system may now enable only 15 shoe workers and 4 shoemaking machines to produce 10 dozen pairs of shoes per day.

The very long run is a period of time long enough so that a whole new technology can be introduced and the production function itself changed.

Business firms do *not* make short-run decisions in the short run, long-run decisions in the long run, and very-long-run decisions in the very long run. Instead, they make decisions in all three at the same time. A business decision maker decides the quantity and mix of products to produce and the prices to charge for them in the relatively inflexible environment of the short run. But at the same time the businessperson must also plan for the long run. If more steelmaking capacity is

wanted in four years, the order for the furnace must be placed right now. Furthermore, firms must coordinate their short-run and long-run decisions with their very-long-run decisions. A firm must determine how much of its resources will be devoted to research, development, and adaptation.

PRODUCTION IN THE SHORT RUN

The short run is a time period during which a business firm is not perfectly flexible because at least one of its inputs cannot be varied. Important production decisions must be made in the short run. Economists have formulated some useful theories that allow us to make some generalizations about short-run production.

Suppose that a shoe manufacturing firm can vary the number of shoe workers that it employs, but it cannot change the number of its shoemaking machines. (Even though we are again using an example in which shoe workers and shoe machines are the only inputs necessary to produce shoes, it is not the same example that we used earlier in the chapter in our discussion of technical efficiency. For the sake of simplicity, we have switched to fewer workers and machines producing single pairs instead of dozens of pairs of shoes.) The numbers in Table 4 are strictly hypothetical, but the relationships are what economists predict about short-run production. Column 1 shows that the firm has fixed inputs (those it cannot change) of 3 units. It cannot in the short run increase or decrease the number of shoemaking machines. Column 2 gives the number of workers hired to produce shoes. This is a variable input—that is, this number can be changed in the short run. Column 3 shows the **total product**—the number of pairs of shoes per day that are produced when a certain number of shoe workers is employed to work with the 3 shoemaking machines. No shoes are produced when no workers are hired. The firm produces 3 pairs per day when 1 worker is employed, 7 pairs per day with 2 workers, and so on. Column 4 shows the **marginal product**—that is, the number of additional pairs of shoes per day that are produced as a

TABLE 4
Short-Run Production in a Hypothetical Shoe Firm

(1) Quantity of Fixed Input (machines used for 8 hours per day)	(2) Quantity of Variable Input (workers working 8-hour days)	(3) Total Product (pairs of shoes per day)	(4) Marginal Product (pairs of shoes per day)	(5) Average Product (pairs of shoes per day) (3) ÷ (2)
3	0	0		0
3	1	3	3	3
3	2	7	4	3½
3	3	10	3	3⅓
3	4	12	2	3
3	5	13	1	2⅖
3	6	12	−1	2

result of employing one more worker. The first worker adds 3 pairs of shoes per day to the firm's output (3 − 0). The second worker adds 4 pairs per day (7 − 3), the third worker adds 3 pairs per day (10 − 7), and so on. Be sure to recognize the fact that the marginal product of a worker—say, the third worker—is not the output produced by the third worker but rather the addition to the total output as a result of employing the third worker. The last column shows **average product**—the total number of pairs of shoes produced per day divided by the number of workers employed (column 3 divided by column 2). Average product is 3 when 1 worker is employed (3 ÷ 1), it is 3½ when 2 workers are employed (7 ÷ 2), and so on.

Total product is the total quantity of output produced by a firm during a period of time.

Marginal product is the amount of extra output that results from the addition of one more unit of a variable input to one or more fixed inputs.

Average product is the total product that a firm produces in a given time period divided by the quantity of a variable input that it uses to produce it.

All of these measures—total product, marginal product, and average product—are related to one another in simple mathematical ways. They are alternative ways of describing relationships between inputs and outputs. The patterns shown in the table represent those that economists predict will exist in the short-run time period. Let us describe these patterns further.

Total product, marginal product, and average product are alternative ways of describing relationships between inputs and outputs.

Increasing, Diminishing, and Negative Returns

Short-run production theory predicts that when a firm adds successive units of a variable input to certain fixed inputs, it may first result in increasing marginal product, then will result in diminishing marginal product, and eventually in negative marginal product. There are sound, logical reasons for these expectations.

According to short-run production theory, when a firm adds successive units of a variable input to certain fixed inputs, it results first in increasing returns, then in diminishing returns, and eventually in negative returns.

The best illustration of **increasing returns** is our example of the second worker adding more product (4 pairs of shoes per day) than was added by the first worker, who added only 3 pairs of shoes per day to the firm's output. There are several ways to explain why increasing returns occur. The higher marginal product may be gained by specialization. One worker operating a number of different machines may be a "jack of all trades, but a master of none," whereas performing fewer different tasks may cause a worker to become expert and thereby to increase the rate of output. Also, one worker handling three machines may spend a great deal of time moving from machine to machine, whereas two workers may greatly reduce this time loss. A third way to explain this pattern is to imagine that one worker alone is not able to take full advantage of the capabilities of three machines. Some machines may have "down time" while the worker is busy with another machine. Adding the second worker allows more effective use of the machines' potential. Even though it may seem a bit unfair to the machines, we attribute the production increase to the additional worker. This explanation makes sense in the short run. Since the firm cannot change the number of machines, its decisions are made in terms of the variable input.

Increasing returns (rising marginal product) means that each successive variable input adds more product to a firm's output than was added by the preceding variable input.

Diminishing returns occur when the marginal product is falling—that is, when the marginal product of each additional worker is smaller than the marginal product of the worker hired just before. It is an essential feature of short-run production that, after some point, each successive addition to a firm's variable input will result in a smaller addition to the firm's output. As shown in Table 4, diminishing returns set in with the hiring of the third worker, who adds only 3 pairs of shoes per day to the total product, as compared with 4 pairs per day added by the second worker. The total product increases. But in our example the gain

(marginal product) from the third worker is not as great as the gain from the second worker. Diminishing returns have set in.

In these examples, we are assuming that there is no difference in the quality, diligence, or skill of these workers. The third worker is just as "good" as the second worker. The only thing that is changing is the ratio or mixture between workers and machines. As we add successive units of the variable input to the fixed amount of some other input, the mixture changes. It is the changing mixture that is responsible for the changing levels of the marginal product.

Diminishing returns (falling marginal product) occur when the marginal product of each additional unit of the variable input is smaller than the marginal product of the variable input unit added just before. According to short-run production theory, after some point, each successive addition to a firm's variable input will result in a smaller addition to the firm's output.

There are **negative returns** when the marginal product of a unit of variable input is negative—that is, when the total product is less when using this additional unit of input than it was before it was used. In our example, negative returns set in with the hiring of the sixth worker. The total product falls from 13 pairs of shoes per week to 12 pairs. The sixth worker is "excess baggage" and gets in the way of the others when there are only three machines available. We doubt that a profit-seeking firm would ever intentionally expand its operations to hire this worker, but mistakes do happen.

Negative returns (falling total product and negative marginal product) occur when the marginal product of a unit of variable input is negative—when the total product is less when using this additional unit of input than it was before it was used.

The Stages of Production

In Figure 1 we have plotted the data from Table 4. The horizontal axis of each graph in this figure shows quantities of the variable input—shoe workers in our shoemaking example. The vertical axes represent different measures of production. The total product is shown on the vertical axis of the upper graph. The average product and marginal product are shown on the vertical axis of the lower graph.

The horizontal axes in these graphs are divided to show three stages of production. In Stage I the average product is increasing, and the marginal product is above it. In Stage II the average product is decreasing, but the marginal product is still positive. In Stage III the marginal product is negative. Another way to see these stages is to note that the peak of the average product curve, separates Stage I from Stage II and that the peak of the total product curve, separates Stage II from Stage III. A third approach notes that average and marginal product are equal at the separation between Stage I and Stage II and that marginal product becomes negative at the separation between Stage II and Stage III. Finally, note that these relationships all arise because total product is rising at an increasing rate in much of Stage I, rising at a decreasing rate in Stage II, and falling in Stage III. Division of the production function into three stages will help you to understand the behavior of the firm in the short run.

Short-run production has three stages: in Stage I the average product is increasing but is less than marginal product; in Stage II the average product is decreasing and greater than marginal product, which nevertheless is still positive; in Stage III the marginal product is negative.

These different relationships should not be surprising once you know that all these curves (total, average, and marginal) are mathematically derived from the same set of data—the production function as applied in short-run production theory. Once you understand the mathematical relationships, it is not hard to recognize the characteristics of each stage. However, the relationship between the marginal product and the average product deserves a closer look.

Whenever marginal product is *higher* than average product—whether marginal product is rising or falling—average product must be rising. Likewise, whenever marginal product is *below* average product—whether marginal product is rising or falling—average product must be falling. Therefore, when marginal product is neither higher than nor lower than average product—that is, when they are equal to each other—average product is no longer rising, nor has it yet begun to fall, so it is at its peak. This relationship always holds. It is a mathematical relation. In a sense, the marginal product "causes" the average product to rise or fall, or remain the same. The relationship is easily understood if we think in terms of sports averages such as in bowling or baseball. Suppose that a baseball player is carrying a .250 batting average in 45 games as a result of 50 hits in 200 times at bat. The player's average will increase or decrease or remain the same depending on his or her success in getting hits in the forty-sixth (the marginal) game. If the player's marginal performance is above .250, his or her average will increase. For example, 2 hits in 4 times at bat—a marginal performance of .500—will cause the player's average to climb to .255 (52 ÷ 204). On the other hand, a marginal performance below .250 will decrease the player's average. No hits in 4 times at bat during the forty-sixth game—a marginal performance of zero—will cause the player's average to decline to .245 (50 ÷ 204). Of course, his or her marginal performance could exactly equal .250—1 hit in 4 times at bat—so that the player's average would remain unchanged at .250 (51 ÷ 204).[3]

---

3. For those of you who are not sports enthusiasts and are therefore unfamiliar with the intricacies of baseball batting averages, try examining the relationship between your overall grade point average (GPA) and your grade in a marginal course. For example, if you receive an "A" (4 point) in this class, as you will no doubt do, it will raise your GPA, which, let us say, was somewhat below a 4 point.

FIGURE 1
Total Product, Average Product, Marginal Product, and the Stages of Production

The numbers plotted from Table 4 establish the points along the three curves. The total-product and average-product points are plotted at the end points of the units of the variable input, while the marginal-product points are plotted as midpoints. The upper graph shows the total-product curve, first increasing at an increasing rate (where marginal product is increasing), then increasing at a decreasing rate (where marginal product is decreasing yet remains positive), and then decreasing (where marginal product is negative). The lower graph shows average product rising where marginal product is above it and average product falling where marginal product is below it.

Stage I is shown to be the range in which average product is increasing. Average product is at its peak (after 2 workers are employed) at the borderline between Stages I and II. In Stage II average product is falling, but marginal product remains positive. Total product is at its peak (after 5 workers are employed) at the borderline between Stages II and III. Stage III is shown to be the range in which total product decreases and marginal product is negative.

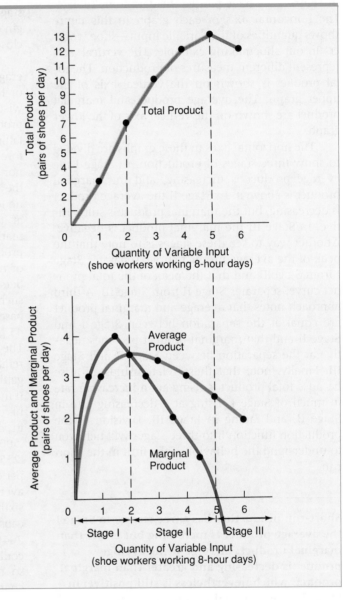

Whenever marginal product is higher than average product, average product must be rising. Whenever marginal product is below average product, average product must be falling. When marginal product equals average product, average product is at its peak.

COSTS IN THE SHORT RUN

So far we have presented a general theory about the relationships between a business firm's physical inputs and outputs in the short run. Of course, a firm's inputs cost the firm something. Since we assume that business firms want to make the highest possible profit, it follows that they want to produce the output of their choice at the lowest possible cost. Therefore we must bring cost into our discussion.

Economists view cost in terms of what is given up to attain something else. (See the discussion of opportunity cost in Chapter 4.) From the point of view of society, cost is the value of all the resources (labor, capital, and natural resources) that are used in production. From the point of view of a business firm, cost is a narrower concept. It is merely what the firm itself gives up to hire inputs that it uses in producing outputs. When a firm uses resources but does not itself incur that cost (as when a firm pollutes a river by dumping waste products into it and is not required to clean it up or pay for it in any way), it is considered a cost to society but *not* to the firm.[4] Since this chapter deals with business firm choice, the costs to society that are not costs to business firms will not be considered.

In the theory of the firm, the term *cost* refers to what a business firm gives up to hire inputs that it uses to produce output.

Transaction and Information Costs

When you think of the costs that a firm incurs to produce its product, you naturally think of costs such as wages (including fringe benefits) of production workers, sales personnel, and managers; payments for plant, equipment, and training; and payments for the raw and semifinished material inputs that the firm requires. Within such examples of cost lie certain categories of costs that are not always readily recognized. We refer to *transaction costs* and *information costs*.

Transaction costs are the costs associated with facilitating the workings of a market by enabling potential buyers and sellers to interact. Such costs are usually not borne by either the buyer or the seller alone, but are shared in some way. For example, in a typical stock-market transaction both the buyer and the seller pay a commission to a

"middleman" called a stockbroker. Business firms experience many types of transaction costs. Much of the working time of highly paid corporate executives, lawyers, and consultants is spent on negotiation aimed at facilitating exchange. Examples include the writing and enforcing of contracts, the gathering and keeping of accurate records, and a good deal of the promotion and advertising effort.

Information costs, often considered a part of transaction costs, are the costs of acquiring information that decreases the uncertainty of making transactions. Business firms hire experts who possess specialized information or whose job it is to obtain such information about the availability and characteristics of productive inputs or the whereabouts and nature of customers. A business firm with perfect information would not face uncertainty. That is, of course, unrealistic, but to the extent that it pays for a firm to reduce uncertainty, the firm will be willing to incur the costs of obtaining information.

Transaction costs are the costs associated with facilitating the workings of a market by enabling potential buyers and sellers to interact. Information costs, often considered a part of transaction costs, are the costs of acquiring information that decreases the uncertainty of making transactions.

Explicit and Implicit Costs

Some costs incurred by business firms are more easily identified than others. It is important, however, that *all* costs to firms be recognized and included in their decision-making calculations. For example, a couple that owns a small independent grocery store incur many different costs. Among these costs are payments for the groceries they buy as stock, the salary they pay a clerk, the gas and electric bill, and the rent for the shop. Economists call these **explicit costs**—money payments for the use of inputs. Other costs are incurred for inputs for which no such obvious payment is made. These **implicit costs** also divert resources from other uses, but money payment is not actually made. The husband (Papa) works, let us say, sev-

---

4. This point will be more fully explained in our discussion of externalities in a later chapter.

enty hours a week but never collects a salary check. His wife (Mama) works only "part-time"—forty hours a week—but she doesn't receive a salary check either. Also, the couple may have $50,000 tied up in store capital (shelving, refrigerator and freezer cases, and a stock of groceries), for which they receive no obvious return. At the end of each week the owners take out of the cash register the amount of money not needed to pay their current bills (explicit costs). They probably call it "profit." Actually, it goes largely to help cover implicit costs. The grocery store owners could probably be employed in a nearby supermarket for $6.50 per hour, and the $50,000 investment in the store could be deposited in a bank, where it would earn 10 percent interest. Therefore, the implicit cost of their labor is $37,180 per year (5,720 hours × $6.50 per hour), and the implicit cost of the store capital is $5,000 per year (0.10 × $50,000). Papa and Mama may be under the impression that they are making $50,000 profit this year. An economist might be ornery enough to point out that their implicit cost, which they disregarded, is $42,180 ($37,180 + $5,000 = $42,180), so that their profit is only $7,820 ($50,000 − $42,180 = $7,820).

Explicit costs are money payments for the use of inputs. Implicit costs are those incurred for inputs for which no obvious payment is made since no transaction takes place.

Total Costs of Production

In the short run, a firm's total cost may be broken down into total fixed cost and total variable cost.

Total Fixed Cost (TFC)   The **total fixed cost (TFC)** is the cost that does not vary with the quantity of output that a firm produces. It will be the same whether a firm produces 5 units per day or 5,000 units per day or even zero units per day. For the hypothetical shoe manufacturer in our previous example, fixed input consisted of three shoe-making machines (see Table 4). Each machine costs $50 per eight-hour day, so that *TFC* is $150 per day. Table 5 gives the cost figures for this firm. Column 3 shows *TFC* to be $150 for the whole range of output from zero production to an output

TABLE 5
Costs for a Hypothetical Shoe Firm

(1) Variable Input (number of shoe workers)	(2) Total Output (pairs of shoes produced per day)	(3) Total Fixed Cost (TFC) per Day	(4) Total Variable Cost (TVC) per Day	(5) Total Cost (TC) per Day	(6) Marginal Cost (MC) per Day	(7) Average Fixed Cost (AFC) per Day	(8) Average Variable Cost (AVC) per Day	(9) Average Total Cost (ATC) per Day
0	0	$150.00	$ 0	$150.00		—	—	—
					$20.00			
1	3	150.00	60.00	210.00		$50.00	$20.00	$70.00
					15.00			
2	7	150.00	120.00	270.00		21.43	17.14	38.57
					20.00			
3	10	150.00	180.00	330.00		15.00	18.00	33.00
					30.00			
4	12	150.00	240.00	390.00		12.50	20.00	32.50
					60.00			
5	13	150.00	300.00	450.00		11.54	23.08	34.62

FIGURE 2
Total-Cost Curves for a Hypothetical Shoe Firm

The numbers plotted from Table 5 establish the points along the three total-cost curves that are drawn for our hypothetical shoe firm. *TFC* is shown as a horizontal straight line, since *TFC* does not vary with output. The curve *TVC* is positively related to output and increases at a decreasing rate over the range of output (0–7 pairs) where the firm's marginal product increases and after that (7–13 pairs) increases at an increasing rate, since diminishing returns have set in. The curve *TC* is the vertical sum of the *TFC* and *TVC* curves. It has the same shape as the *TVC* curve because a constant ($150) is added to *TVC* at every level of output.

of 13 pairs of shoes per day. Figure 2 shows a total-fixed-cost curve for this example. Note that it is a horizontal straight line at $150.

Total fixed cost (*TFC*) is the cost that does not vary with the quantity of output that a firm produces.

Total Variable Cost (TVC) Those costs that are not fixed are called variable costs. The **total variable cost (*TVC*)** is the cost that varies with the quantity of output that a firm produces—the higher the level of output, the higher the total variable cost, and vice versa. (Most labor and material input costs are in this category.) But while the relationship between a firm's output and its *TVC* is positive, it is not expected to be proportional. In fact, it would be inconsistent with short-run production theory if we now found that, say, each time a firm doubled its output it would also double its *TVC*. What did we learn in our discussion of production in the short run? At very low levels of output, a firm is expected to experience increasing returns,

so that its marginal product rises. At a somewhat higher level of output (but still in Stage I), diminishing returns set in, so that the firm's marginal product falls. Therefore *TVC*—the cost of the inputs needed to produce the additional output—will rise with output at a *decreasing rate* until diminishing returns set in. We can illustrate this point by looking at the second and fourth columns in Table 5. The *TVC* for producing 3 pairs of shoes is $60, but a doubling of *TVC* to $120 will more than double the number of shoes—from 3 pairs to 7 pairs—that can be produced. For this range of output, *TVC* related to the output of shoes has increased at a decreasing rate, since the firm is experiencing increasing returns. The *TVC* for producing 7 pairs of shoes is $120, but a doubling of *TVC* to $240 will less than double the number of shoes—from 7 pairs to 12 pairs—that can be produced. For this range of output (and beyond) *TVC* related to the output of shoes has increased at an *increasing rate*, since the firm is experiencing diminishing returns. Figure 2 shows a *TVC* curve for this example. Note that it is not a straight line, but rather that it is bowed up (increasing at a decreasing rate) in the range of increasing returns and bowed down (increasing at an increasing rate) afterward, when diminishing returns prevail.

Total variable cost (*TVC*) is the cost that varies with the quantity of output that a firm produces. The higher the level of output, the higher the total variable cost, and vice versa.

TVC will rise with output at a decreasing rate until diminishing returns set in; after that point, *TVC* rises with output at an increasing rate.

Total Cost (TC) The last of the family of total-cost curves is the total cost itself. **Total cost (*TC*)** is the sum of *TFC* and *TVC*. For our shoe firm, *TC* is presented in column 5 of Table 5. Each cost figure in that column is derived by adding together the costs in columns 3 and 4. Figure 2 pictures the total-cost curve for our example. Note that it has exactly the same shape as the total variable-cost curve, except that it is higher by the amount of *TFC*. At every level of output (including zero) the vertical distance between the total-variable-cost curve and the total-cost curve is $150.

Total cost (*TC*) is the sum of total fixed cost (*TFC*) and total variable cost (*TVC*).

Average Costs of Production

Besides the total-cost concepts, economists are often interested in costs per unit. The unit cost is found by dividing the same three cost concepts just discussed by the output level.

Average Fixed Cost (AFC) **Average fixed cost (*AFC*)** is the total fixed cost divided by the quantity level of output. For our shoe firm, *AFC* is given in column 7 of Table 5. The figures are derived by dividing column 3 by column 2. For zero output, *AFC* is not defined, since we cannot divide a number by zero. For an output of 3 pairs of shoes, *AFC* is $150 divided by 3, or $50. As output increases, *TFC* ($150) is spread over larger and larger levels of output, so that *AFC* continuously declines. Yet, as long as there is still some *TFC*, *AFC* cannot be zero.

An average-fixed-cost curve conforming to our example is shown in Figure 3. Note that it continuously slopes downward but will never reach the horizontal axis because it will always be positive.

Average fixed cost (*AFC*) is the total fixed cost divided by the quantity level of output.

Average Variable Cost (AVC) **Average variable cost (*AVC*)** is the total variable cost divided by the quantity level of output. For our shoe firm, *AVC* is shown in column 8 of Table 5 and is the result of dividing column 4 by column 2. Average variable cost falls during early levels of production and increases after that. Just as we explained *TVC* by recalling our discussion of *marginal* product, we can explain *AVC* by remembering what we learned about *average* product. In Stage I, where the hiring of successive units of a variable input (at a fixed price of, say, $60 per day as in our example) results in an increase in average product, *AVC*—the variable cost per unit of output—must be falling. In Stage II the opposite happens. The hiring of successive units of the variable input (assuming its price does not change) results in a decline in average product and therefore a rise in *AVC*. An average-variable-cost curve for our example is pictured in Figure 3. Note that it is U-shaped.

Average variable cost (*AVC*) is the total variable cost divided by the quantity level of output. *AVC* falls in Stage I production and rises after that.

Average Total Cost (ATC) **Average total cost (*ATC*)** is the total cost divided by the quantity level of output. It is the sum of *AFC* and *AVC*. For our shoe firm, *ATC* may be found in column 9 of Table 5 and can be figured either by dividing each figure in column 5 (*TC*) by the corresponding quantity in column 2 (Total Output) or by adding together columns 7 (*AFC*) and 8 (*AVC*). Average total cost decreases over a greater range of output than *AVC*, but eventually, when the rise in *AVC* is greater than the fall in *AFC*, *ATC* will rise. Figure 3 shows the average-total-cost curve for our example, which is

FIGURE 3

Average-Cost Curves for a Hypothetical Shoe Firm

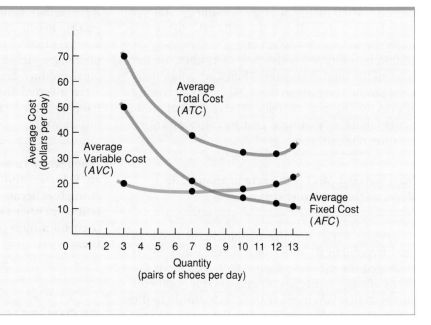

The numbers plotted from Table 5 establish the points along the three average-cost curves that are drawn for our hypothetical shoe firm. The curve *AFC* continuously declines since, as output increases, *TFC* must be divided by larger and larger quantities. The curve *AFC* remains positive—does not touch the horizontal axis—because *TFC* is positive. The curve *AVC* is U-shaped, since it decreases when the firm's average product increases and increases when its average product decreases. The curve *ATC* is the sum of the *AFC* and *AVC* curves. It is also U-shaped. At early levels of output, it is far above *AVC* because *AFC* is high. At high levels of output, *ATC* is much closer to *AVC* since *AFC* is low.

U-shaped. Note that the average-total-cost curve is far above the average-variable-cost curve at early levels of output—where *AFC* is high. Also note that the average-total-cost curve and the average-variable-cost curve are relatively close together at higher output levels, where *AFC* is low. Of course, they will never actually meet, since *AFC*, which is the difference between *AVC* and *ATC*, will always be positive in the short run.

Average total cost (*ATC*) is the total cost divided by the quantity level of output. It is the sum of average fixed cost (*AFC*) and average variable cost (*AVC*).

Marginal Cost of Production

The last short-run cost concept to be explained is marginal cost. **Marginal cost (*MC*)** is the addition to total cost when one more unit of output is produced. Column 6 of Table 5 presents *MC* for our hypothetical shoe firm. Notice that the figures in column 6 are not placed on the same horizontal

lines as all the other numbers in the table, but are read between those lines. Also, since successively adding variable inputs (in column 1) does not increase output (in column 2) by single units, we *cannot* find *MC* merely by subtracting (in column 5) one total-cost figure from the next. Instead, *MC* is found by dividing the additional cost of hiring another unit of the variable input by the additional output that it helps to produce. For example, in Table 5, the *MC* of $15 associated with hiring the second shoe worker is found by dividing the additional cost of hiring the second worker ($60) by the increase in output (4 pairs of shoes) gained by hiring that worker. Another way to calculate marginal cost in Table 5 is to divide the increase in total cost (column 5) by the associated increase in output (column 2).

Marginal cost (*MC*) is the addition to total cost when one more unit of output is produced.

Marginal cost decreases over early production levels and rises afterward. Earlier in this chapter, when we discussed the shape of the total-cost curve, we explained that when marginal *product* is rising, total *cost* must be increasing at a decreasing rate and when marginal *product* is falling, total *cost* must be increasing at an increasing rate. Since *MC* is the rise in total cost when output increases by an additional unit, *MC* is the rate of change, or the *slope*, of the total-cost curve. Therefore, when marginal product is rising so that total cost is increasing at a decreasing rate, *MC* falls. When marginal product is falling so that total cost increases at an increasing rate, *MC* rises.

Marginal cost (*MC*) is the rate of change, or slope, of the total-cost curve.

Figure 4 pictures the marginal-cost curve of our hypothetical shoe firm. Note that it is U-shaped. In the same figure we have drawn the firm's average-variable-cost and average-total-cost curves so that you may see their relationship to the marginal-cost curve. Notice that the marginal-cost curve intersects both the average-variable-cost curve and the average-total-cost curve at their lowest points. When *MC* is below *AVC* and *ATC*, it causes them to fall. When *MC* is above *AVC* and *ATC*, it causes them to rise. Only when *MC* is equal

to *AVC* is *AVC* neither falling nor rising (and at its lowest point), and only when *MC* is equal to *ATC* is *ATC* neither falling nor rising (and at its lowest point). Recall the comparison to baseball batting averages that we used earlier in this chapter in explaining a similar relationship between the marginal-product and average-product curves. Those were inverted U-shaped curves, whereas here we have U-shaped curves, but the relationship holds just as well.

Whenever *ATC* and *AVC* are falling it is because *MC* is lower, and whenever *ATC* and *AVC* are rising it is because *MC* is higher. *ATC* and *AVC* will be neither falling nor rising and will be at their minimum points when *MC* is equal to them.

PRODUCTION IN THE LONG RUN

In the long run, business firms can vary any and all of their inputs. For this reason, even though they are still subject to the same production function, they face no fixed costs. There is no longer—as

FIGURE 4
Marginal-, Average-Variable-, and Average-Total-Cost Curves for a Hypothetical Shoe Firm

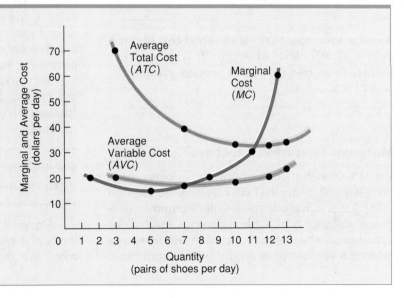

The numbers plotted from Table 5 establish the points along the three curves that are drawn for our hypothetical shoe firm. The curves *ATC* and *AVC* are the same as drawn in Figure 3. The curve *MC* is U-shaped. It decreases when the firm's marginal product is increasing and then increases when its marginal product declines. The curve *MC* intersects the minimum points of the *ATC* and *AVC* curves, since it must be below them when they are falling and above them when they are rising.

there was in the short run—a need to be concerned about adjusting variable inputs to fixed inputs. Firms simply seek out their lowest-cost methods of producing their desired levels of outputs. Our shoe firm, for example, was able to raise its output in the short run only by adding workers, since the number of shoemaking machines was fixed. But in the long run, it can add (or eliminate) as many shoe-making machines as it wants. It can also build a new factory building that uses a method of production better suited to its planned output level. Or it can sell off some of its production facilities and change its method of production to suit its smaller operation.

Total costs in the long run are made up entirely of variable costs. Therefore, of the seven cost concepts that we explained in our discussion of the short run (*TFC, TVC, TC, AFC, AVC, ATC, MC*), only three remain in the long run. These are long-run total cost, long-run average cost, and long-run marginal cost.

In the long run, business firms can vary any and all of their inputs. Therefore, they face no fixed costs, and total costs are made up entirely of variable costs.

Long-run total cost (*LRTC*) is the total cost of producing a certain level of output when a firm is able to vary all of its inputs. For example, when the Boeing Company plans for the production of a new-generation aircraft, it does not allow itself to be restricted by its present resources. Long-run planning may be for the beginning of production ten years from now, which gives Boeing the opportunity to make all of the facility and work force changes that it wishes.

Long-run total cost (*LRTC*) is the total cost of producing a certain level of output when a firm is able to vary all of its inputs.

Long-run average cost (*LRAC*) is the long-run total cost divided by the quantity level of output. **Long-run marginal cost (*LRMC*)** is the addition to *LRTC* when one more unit of output is produced. The mathematical relationships among total, average, and marginal values are the same for long-run costs as for short-run costs. However, we must explore long-run cost and production theory in order to understand how these costs vary with output.

Long-run average cost (*LRAC*) is the long-run total cost (*LRTC*) divided by the quantity level of output.

Long-run marginal cost (*LRMC*) is the addition to long-run total cost (*LRTC*) when one more unit of output is produced.

Effects of Plant Size on Long-Run Average Cost

Economic theory suggests that there are predictable results from changing the size of a firm's plant. According to the theory, plants that are set up to produce a low volume of output are not able to use certain known methods of production. They cannot effectively use an assembly-line method, for example. But a firm that sets up a plant to produce a greater volume may find that it does pay to use an assembly line in production. In fact, the larger-volume plant offers a wider range of choice about methods of production. If some of these added choices allow the firm to produce goods at a lower average total cost than would be possible in the small-volume plant, economies of scale exist. Economic theory predicts that this advantage will not last forever. At some point, constant returns set in, and larger plant size will no longer bring about lower average total cost. Economic theory even predicts that plants can be too large. Muscle-bound giants could experience higher average total cost than smaller plants. Thus, even diseconomies of scale are possible. Let us carefully define and illustrate the economists' concepts of economies, constant returns, and diseconomies of scale.

Economies of Scale Long-run increasing returns are called **economies of scale.** They occur when a firm has a more-than-proportionate rise in its output because of increasing its inputs. For example, if a firm were to double total inputs, and if its output more than doubled as a result, economies of scale would exist. The importance of economies of scale over a fairly extensive range of output may be seen

FIGURE 5
Cost Curves with Economies of Scale

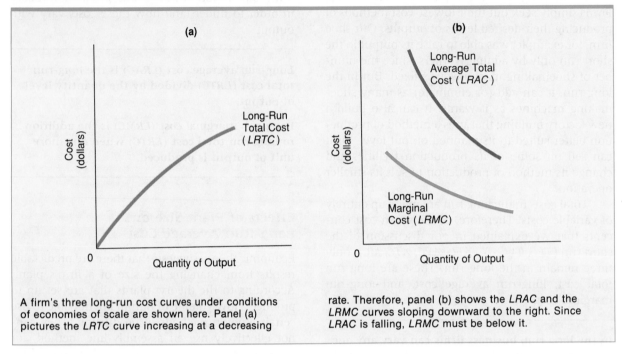

(a)

Cost (dollars)

Long-Run Total Cost (*LRTC*)

0 — Quantity of Output

A firm's three long-run cost curves under conditions of economies of scale are shown here. Panel (a) pictures the *LRTC* curve increasing at a decreasing

(b)

Cost (dollars)

Long-Run Average Total Cost (*LRAC*)

Long-Run Marginal Cost (*LRMC*)

0 — Quantity of Output

rate. Therefore, panel (b) shows the *LRAC* and the *LRMC* curves sloping downward to the right. Since *LRAC* is falling, *LRMC* must be below it.

---

in the example of General Motors' stamping operations. Some years ago General Motors used a single die set, valued at about $500 million, in the manufacture of car bodies for many different car lines both within the same division, such as Chevrolet or Buick, and across divisional lines. The company maintained that if it had used specialized dies to stamp out panels such as hoods, doors, fenders, deck lids, underbodies, and roofs for each individual car model, its average total cost would have been substantially higher.[5]

Figure 5 pictures a firm's three long-run cost curves under conditions of economies of scale. Panel (a) shows its *LRTC* curve. It increases at a decreasing rate, showing that when input prices remain constant and output doubles, total cost will less than double. Panel (b) shows the *LRAC* curve and the *LRMC* curve for the same firm. These curves slope downward to the right because *LRTC* rises at a slower rate than output. The *LRMC* curve lies below the *LRAC* curve for the usual reason.

5. General Motors Corporation, *Competition and the Motor Vehicle Industry*, April 1974.

When marginal cost is below average cost, average cost must be falling.

Economies of scale are long-run increasing returns—an increase in a firm's inputs results in a more-than-proportionate increase in its output.

Constant Returns to Scale Long-run returns with an increase in output is exactly proportionate to the increase in inputs are called **constant returns to scale.** For example, a firm finds that doubling total inputs causes its output also to double. Figure 6 pictures a firm's three long-run cost curves under conditions of constant returns to scale. Panel (a) shows its *LRTC* curve as a straight line coming out of the origin. When input prices remain constant and output doubles, total cost will also double. Panel (b) shows that the *LRAC* curve and the *LRMC* are both constant (the same at each level of output) and are equal to each other. (Recall that when average total cost is neither rising nor falling, marginal cost must be equal to it.)

FIGURE 6
Cost Curves with Constant Returns to Scale

(a)

Long-Run
Total Cost
(*LRTC*)

Cost
(dollars)

0   Quantity of Output

(b)

Long-Run
Average Total
Cost (*LRAC*)
and
Long-Run
Marginal
Cost (*LRMC*)

Cost
(dollars)

0   Quantity of Output

A firm's three long-run cost curves under conditions of constant returns to scale are shown here. Panel (a) pictures the *LRTC* curve increasing at a constant rate. Therefore, panel (b) shows the *LRAC* and the

LRMC curves as the same horizontal straight line. The curves *LRAC* and *LRMC* are the same at each level of output and are equal to each other.

Constant returns to scale are long-run returns when an increase in output is exactly proportionate to the increase in inputs.

Diseconomies of Scale   The opposite of economies of scale—**diseconomies of scale**—are long-run decreasing returns. They occur when a firm has a less-than-proportionate increase in its output as a result of increasing its inputs. For example, a firm finds that doubling its inputs causes its output to less than double. Scaled-up process vessels and machines may become difficult for workers to handle or require special facilities to house them. As an instance, cement kilns experience unstable internal aerodynamics above a capacity of 7 million barrels a year.[6] Figure 7 shows a firm's three long-run cost curves under diseconomies of scale. Again, panel (a) pictures its *LRTC* curve. It is rising at an increasing rate, showing that at constant input prices when output doubles, total cost will more than double. The companion graph, in panel (b), again shows the same firm's *LRAC* and *LRMC* curves. This

time they are increasing, since *LRTC* rises at a faster rate than does output. The *LRMC* curve lies above the *LRAC* curve. Remember that when *ATC* is rising, *MC* must be above it, or when *MC* is above *ATC*, *ATC* must be rising. Now look back at Figures 5, 6, and 7 and compare the *LRTC*, *LRAC*, and *LRMC* curves in each figure.

Diseconomies of scale are long-run decreasing returns—an increase in a firm's inputs results in a less-than-proportionate increase in its output.

The Causes of Economies and Diseconomies of Scale   Economies and diseconomies of scale stem from changes in the relationship among a firm's inputs within a plant. (A *plant* is a factory or other production facility in a particular geographic location. A firm may operate only one plant or a number of plants.) When a firm uses a different size

6. F. M. Scherer, *Industrial Market Structure and Economic Performance*, 2nd ed. (Chicago: Rand McNally, 1980), p. 84.

plant, it often adopts a different method of production or technology—the one that is expected to offer a lower average total cost. Large plants typically use a significantly different mode of production than do small plants in the same industry. Though it pays to use very specialized machines and workers in a very large operation, it does not pay in a relatively small one. The cost advantages gained through such specialization largely explain economies of scale. For example, a plant designed to produce cars at a rate of 100 per year would use a very simple technology—a few highly versatile workers and a few fairly simple machines. By contrast, a plant designed to produce 400,000 cars per year would use an assembly-line method, which calls for very specialized workers, sophisticated machines, and an elaborate organization. In between the 100-per-year and the 400,000-per-year plants are many plants of different sizes in which a firm might wish to produce in the long run. As the output level becomes larger, it calls for a somewhat different technology and, presumably, a lower cost in terms of inputs per unit of output. It is reasonable to expect that such gains from specialization will come to an end at some level of output. After that point, there might be a range of output over which the firm can realize only constant returns to scale. Finally, at a very large plant size, diseconomies of scale will set in. As in the case of economies of scale, these are caused by a change in input relationships. For example, when an automobile plant gets so large, say, above the 800,000-cars-per-year level, that it requires several layers of management—managers of managers who manage other managers—the increased ratio of managers to production workers may bring about diseconomies of scale.

Figure 8 illustrates the *LRAC* curve for the hypothetical car firm example. For the output range up to 400,000 cars, the firm experiences economies of scale, so that the *LRAC* curve is like the one drawn in Figure 5. Plant sizes between 400,000 and 800,000 cars per year offer constant returns to scale; this range of the *LRAC* curve resembles the one drawn in Figure 6. Finally, plants that produce more than 800,000 cars per year experience dis-

FIGURE 7
Cost Curves with Diseconomies of Scale

A firm's three long-run cost curves under conditions of diseconomies of scale are shown here. Panel (a) pictures the *LRTC* curve increasing at an increasing rate. Therefore, panel (b) shows the *LRAC* and the *LRMC* curves sloping upward from left to right. Since *LRAC* is rising, *LRMC* must be above it.

FIGURE 8
Economies, Constant Returns, and Diseconomies of Scale for a Hypothetical Automobile Firm

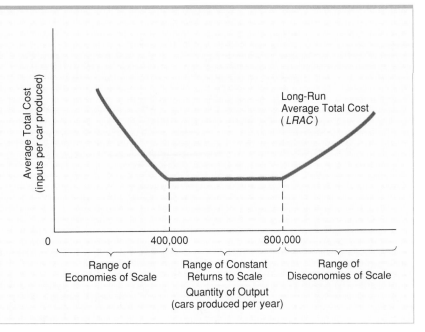

The *LRAC* curve shown here is that of a hypothetical automobile firm. Larger and larger plants up to the one used to produce 400,000 cars per year bring lower *LRAC*. Plants that produce between 400,000 and 800,000 cars per year experience the same *LRAC*. Even larger plants bring higher and higher *LRAC*.

economies of scale, so that portion of the *LRAC* curve resembles the one we drew in Figure 7.[7]

Economies and diseconomies of scale stem from changes in the relationship among a firm's inputs within a plant. As a firm changes the size of a plant, it often adopts a different method of production or technology.

The Relationship Between Long-Run and Short-Run Average Total Costs

The long-run nature of economies, constant returns, and diseconomies of scale is clearly illustrated by the relationship to short-run cost curves. The long-run average-cost curve is made up of points from all the short-run average-total-cost

7. All along we have been assuming a single underlying production function. However, no single mathematical production function will give rise to the three distinct portions of the long-run average-cost curve shown in Figure 8.

curves. At every possible output level, there is a point on some short-run average-total-cost curve that indicates the lowest average cost at which that quantity of output can be produced. All such points taken together over the whole range of possible outputs define the long-run average-cost curve. Figure 9 shows the same *LRAC* curve that we drew for our hypothetical automobile firm in Figure 8. It also shows six short-run *ATC* curves. These short-run *ATC* curves indicate the presence of some fixed inputs—a certain plant size—so that each describes operations within a plant of a particular size. Every point on the *LRAC* curve shows the lowest cost per unit of output at which a certain quantity level of output may be produced.

For example, ATC_1 represents a plant that can produce 150,000 cars per year at the lowest possible average total cost in the long run. This is the output level at which ATC_1 is tangent to (just touches so that they have a point in common) the *LRAC* curve. Likewise, ATC_6 represents a plant that can produce 1,150,000 cars per year at the lowest possible average total cost for a single plant in the long run. In between we show four more short-run

FIGURE 9
Relationship Between Long-Run and Short-Run Average-Total-Cost Curves for a Hypothetical Automobile Firm

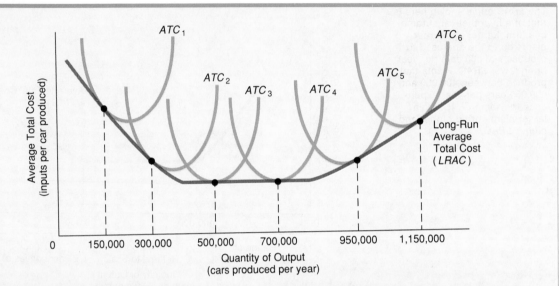

The *LRAC* curve and the six short-run *ATC* curves belong to the same hypothetical automobile firm shown in Figure 8. Each of the six short-run *ATC* curves describes operations within a certain-sized plant, and the *LRAC* curve shows the lowest cost per unit at which any level of output may be produced. Along the economies-of-scale portion of the *LRAC* curve, short-run *ATC* curves such as ATC_1 and ATC_2 are tangent at a level of output that is less than the one associated with minimum average total cost of production in that plant. Along the diseconomies-of-scale portion of the *LRAC* curve, short-run *ATC* curves such as ATC_5 and ATC_6 are tangent at a level of output that is greater than the one associated with minimum average total cost of production in that plant. Only along the constant-returns-to-scale portion does minimum short-run *ATC* coincide with minimum *LRAC*.

average-total-cost curves (ATC_2, ATC_3, ATC_4, and ATC_5) representing plants of four other sizes out of the huge number that could be drawn.

Figure 9 reveals that the U-shaped, short-run average-total-cost curves that are tangent to the constant-returns-to-scale part of the *LRAC* curve, such as ATC_3 and ATC_4, are tangent at their lowest points. (That is, no other level of production in those plants would yield lower cost per unit.) By contrast, ATC_1 and ATC_2, which are tangent along the economies-of-scale part of the *LRAC* curve, are tangent at a level of output that is less than the one associated with lowest average total cost of production in that plant. Likewise, ATC_5 and ATC_6, which are tangent along the diseconomies-of-scale part of the *LRAC* curve, are tangent at a level of output that is greater than the one associated with lowest-average-total-cost production in that plant.

These facts may suggest that in the short run a firm will wish to expand output in plants with curves such as ATC_1 and ATC_2 and to contract output in plants with curves such as ATC_5 and ATC_6 in order to produce at the lowest point of its short-run *ATC* curve. However, in the long run—when a firm is able to change the size of its plant—it hopes to produce along the constant-returns-to-scale part of its *LRAC* curve in a plant with a curve like ATC_3 or ATC_4.

The relationships in Figure 9 provide interesting food for thought. In the economies-of-scale part of the *LRAC* curve, short-run efficiency implies that the plant is a bit too large. That is, the lowest-cost way to produce a given output in the long run is to have a plant that is a little too large and to leave some of this capacity unused (wasted). This situation implies that the economies of scale made possible by the extra plant size more than make up for the ''waste'' of operating at less than capacity. An opposite set of possibilities can be seen in the diseconomies part of the *LRAC* curve.

A firm's long-run average-cost curve is made up of points from all of its short-run average-total-cost curves. But with the exception of the short-run *ATC* curve(s) that is (are) tangent to the minimum point(s) of the *LRAC* curve, the minimum points of the short-run *ATC* curves are not the ones that make up the points of the *LRAC* curve.

PRODUCTION IN THE VERY LONG RUN

Besides the short-run and long-run decisions that are subject to its production function, a business firm also makes decisions that have the potential of changing its production function. These decisions are classified as being very long run in nature. They deal with such activities as research, development, invention, and innovation. The firm's purpose is to increase its profits through the discovery of new and better products for consumers and new, lower-cost production methods that raise its productivity.

Invention and Innovation

Invention is the discovery of a new product or a new technical tool or process. A large percentage of the products and processes that we use and take for granted in the United States today were not even imagined, say, one hundred years ago. Among these are television sets, computers, penicillin, and synthetic materials. Some inventions are the work of private persons, but more and more often they are the product of company or university research.

Innovation is the development of an invention from the original idea to a practical use. Innovation, even more than invention, stems from a firm's decision to use its resources for research and development (R&D). For example, Chester Carlson invented xerography in 1938. However, the first Xerox photocopying machine was not introduced

to the market until 1959. During those twenty-one years, the Battelle Development Company and then the Haloid Corporation (later called the Xerox Corporation) worked to make a useful machine from Carlson's invention. They took the basic idea of xerography and overcame some important physics and engineering problems to develop a single-unit copier that outperformed all other copying machines available at the time.

Very-long-run decisions have the potential of changing a firm's production function. They involve activities such as research, development, invention, and innovation.

Productivity and Business Decisions

Very-long-run business decisions will have an effect on productivity. **Productivity** is the amount of output produced by a unit of resource input during a given span of time. Generally, productivity is expressed in terms of product output per hour of labor input. Of course, labor uses capital and natural resources to produce output, so this measure also captures changes in how these other inputs are used and combined.

Productivity is the amount of output produced by a unit of resource input during a given span of time. It is usually expressed in terms of product output per hour of labor input.

Over the past two to three hundred years, impressive productivity gains have been made in most of the industrialized countries of the world. Their standards of living—measured by the amount of goods and services consumed by the average citizen—have dramatically increased. How can we explain these changes? The most important reasons for these productivity increases come under two fairly broad headings: (1) input substitution and (2) increasing quality of inputs.

Input Substitution   Input substitution means using a more productive input in place of one that is less productive. Recall from our earlier discussion that some such substitution takes place in the long run when one known technology replaces another as the scale of operation is changed. Input substitution becomes very long run when the change is brought on by **technological progress**—an advance in knowledge of the industrial arts and/or improved techniques of organizing production. In the very long run, input substitution may be limited to a single resource class (one machine for another, or one kind of skilled worker for another) or may be between different resource classes such as capital for labor. In fact, important productivity gains have been made by substituting capital for labor. One construction worker running a power shovel may be more productive than ten workers using hand shovels. One farmer with a combine may outproduce fifty farmers using only hand tools. One manager using a computer may be able to coordinate a firm's productive activity with greater precision than could an army of managers without that tool.

Productivity may increase because of input substitution—using a more productive input in place of one that is less productive. Input substitution becomes very long run when the change is brought on by technological progress.

Quality of Inputs The second reason why productivity may increase is that the quality of many of the inputs improves. As you have already seen, technological progress may improve the quality of capital. Education and training enhance the quality of labor. Firms may also discover higher grades of raw materials or be able to purchase better-quality semifinished inputs. The upgrading of some inputs without others may, however, do little to raise productivity. Higher productivity often calls for a balanced improvement in the quality of inputs. For example, a modern plant with the latest capital equipment will likely yield a low quantity and quality of output if it is operated by poorly trained and undereducated workers. Can the quality of inputs decrease? If high-quality mineral resources are used up, so that lower-quality ones must be used, productivity may go down.

Productivity may increase if the quality of many of the inputs improves.

Productivity in the United States

Throughout most of its history the record of productivity growth in the United States has been impressive. U.S. productivity today is the highest in the world, but over the period of the last two decades its growth has trailed such countries as Japan and Germany. From 1948 to 1968, U.S. productivity rose at an average annual rate of 3.2 percent. From 1968 to 1973 the annual increase was just under 2 percent, and the remainder of the 1970s saw an average annual increase between 0.5 and 1 percent. The 1980s saw a reversal of this declining trend, but the productivity increases of the 1980s were still less than half the rates of the twenty-five-year period after World War II. Why did the decline in the U.S. productivity increases take place? Some blame government, arguing that government regulations hinder productivity growth, that tax policies do not offer enough incentives for firms to spend large amounts on R&D, and that there is not enough direct government R&D support. Some blame labor unions, claiming that they prevent firms from making changes that may lead to greater efficiency. During the 1970s many blamed soaring energy prices fueled by the OPEC cartel. Others argue that faltering productivity growth has been due largely to the huge rise in employment in the service industries, where productivity is more difficult to increase. Finally, there are those who contend that U.S. business managers have lost their entrepreneurial spirit and are simply no longer willing to make risky very-long-run commitments. Probably, the answer is some combination of these reasons. Our theory suggests that very-long-run decisions are based on expectations of payoffs. If firms see a likelihood that R&D spending will lead to profitable new products and/or processes, there will be a tendency for productivity to increase.

The impressive productivity growth of the United States has slowed in recent decades.

Economics in Focus

How Short Is the Very-Long Run?

The rapid change of our high-tech society has made business innovation more important than ever. Today, new technologies arise every year; products arrive, succeed in the marketplace, and then disappear with a speed that would have astonished the business managers of a generation ago. Consumers, moreover, have tuned into this ever-changing parade of products; if they see a higher-tech mousetrap, they will probably buy it, with little reverence for the tried and true mousetraps of the past.

In this environment large companies need to spend huge amounts on research and development (R&D) in order to stay competitive. At General Electric R&D expenses climbed 54 percent between 1982 and 1987, reaching a total of $1.2 billion a year. At Johnson & Johnson the R&D costs quintupled in ten years; the 1987 figure of $617 million represented about 8 percent of sales revenues. The results of such large expenditures can be equally stunning: at 3M in 1987 more than a quarter of the company's worldwide sales derived from products that had been on the market less than five years.

To illustrate the rapid pace of innovation in today's industry, we can look at a product that nearly everyone has experienced at close range: diapers. In the 1960s Procter & Gamble introduced Pampers, a disposable variety of this very basic product. Pampers were enormously successful; American parents were quick to abandon cloth diapers that had to be washed in favor of the new products that could be tossed in a trash can. With Pampers and a premium brand called Luvs, Procter & Gamble dominated the market during the early years despite competition from other manufacturers. But in the 1980s Kimberly-Clark introduced important design changes in the Huggies brand, and suddenly Pampers were in decline. Then researchers at Procter & Gamble found a way to reduce diaper rashes and create a slimmer, neater-looking diaper using superabsorbent polymers. Procter & Gamble developed this discovery into new product lines, Ultra Pampers and Ultra Pampers Plus, and by the late 1980s the company's market share looked healthy again. Thus Procter & Gamble succeeded not by a single innovation alone, but by constant research and continued innovation.

At the national level, the United States has long been considered the paragon of business inventiveness, but economic analysts now worry that Americans are losing their edge. In 1987 almost half of new U.S. patents were granted to foreign inventors. Even for advances that originated in the United States, foreign companies are frequently quicker to adapt the technology to the needs of the marketplace. According to innovation experts, many large U.S. corporations are "risk averse"; their corporate culture rewards safe and plodding behavior rather than the taking of chances. This is a matter for long-term concern, for in today's economic environment it is often unhealthy to play it safe.

Sources: Kenneth Labich, "The Innovators," *Fortune,* June 6, 1988, pp. 49–64; B. R. Inman, "Why We're Slipping—and What's to Be Done," *Washington Post,* October 3, 1988, p. A11; "More Young Millionaires, Please," *The Economist,* February 4, 1989, p. 13.

SUMMARY

1. Business firms engage in production, which is the transformation of inputs into outputs. (See page 520.)

2. Technically efficient input combinations are those that cannot be improved upon. That is, the equivalent output cannot be obtained by using less of some input without using more of some other input. (See page 520.)

3. Technically efficient relationships between a firm's physical units of inputs and outputs are expressed in its production function. It presents the maximum output that can be obtained from given amounts of inputs at a given level of technological development or the different technically efficient combinations of inputs that can produce a given output. (See pages 520–521.)

4. An input combination is economically efficient if it produces a given output at the lowest possible cost. (See page 521.)

5. Firms make decisions for three different time spans: the short run, the long run, and the very long run. The short run allows a firm the least amount of flexibility because at least one of its inputs cannot be varied. The long run allows complete flexibility within the firm's production function. In the very long run, a firm's production function can be altered through technological change. (See pages 523–524.)

6. The theory of production in the short run predicts that when a firm adds successive units of a variable input to some fixed inputs, it will first result in increasing returns (rising marginal product), then diminishing returns (falling marginal product), and eventually in negative returns (falling total product and negative marginal product). (See pages 524–525.)

7. The theory of production in the short run separates production into three stages. In Stage I total product rises, average product rises, and marginal product first rises and then falls. In Stage II total product rises at a decreasing rate, marginal product falls, and average product falls. In Stage III total product falls, marginal product is negative, and average product continues to fall. (See page 527.)

8. The economic theories of increasing and diminishing returns explain the shape of a firm's short-run cost curves. (see pages 525–526.)

9. Business firms are assumed to want to maximize their profits and therefore to want to minimize the costs of what they choose to produce. Economists separate a firm's costs into seven short-run cost concepts. These are: *TC, TFC, TVC, ATC, AFC, AVC,* and *MC.* They are related in the following ways:

$$TC = TFC + TVC$$
$$ATC = TC \div \text{quantity level of output}$$
$$ATC = AFC + AVC$$
$$AFC = TFC \div \text{quantity level of output}$$
$$AVC = TVC \div \text{quantity level of output}$$
$$MC = \text{the change in } TC \text{ when output changes by one unit.}$$

(See pages 530–534.)

10. In the long run, there are three cost concepts: *LRTC, LRAC,* and *LRMC.* When *LRTC* increases at a decreasing rate, *LRMC* will be below *LRAC,* which is falling. Such long-run increasing returns are called economies of scale. When *LRTC* increases at a constant rate, *LRMC* and *LRAC* will be constant and equal. This condition is called constant returns to scale. When *LRTC* rises at an increasing rate, *LRMC* will be above *LRAC,* which is rising. Such long-run decreasing returns are called diseconomies of scale. (See pages 534–535.)

11. With plants designed for increasingly higher levels of output, *LRAC* is expected first to decrease, then to level off, and finally to increase. Each larger and larger plant size calls for the adoption of a somewhat different method of production. At first there are gains from specialization, but eventually these fade out, and finally wasteful bureaucracy is expected to set in. (See page 535.)

12. The *LRAC* curve is made up of points from all the short-run *ATC* curves. Each short-run *ATC* curve represents a certain-sized plant. In the long run, economists predict that a firm will choose a plant or plants that offer minimum *ATC* at the level of output it wishes to produce. Only in the constant-returns-to-scale range of plant size will a firm achieve both minimum short-run and minimum long-run *ATC.* In the output ranges of economies and diseconomies of scale, short-run minimum *ATC* will not coincide with long-run minimum *ATC.* (See pages 535–536.)

13. Very-long-run business decisions involve invention and innovation. Invention is the discovery of a new product or process, and innovation brings it to practical use. (See page 541.)

14. Very-long-run business decisions affect productivity. Productivity—usually measured in terms of product output per hour of labor input—can be changed by input substitution and by changing the quality of inputs. Productivity increases have slowed significantly in the United States over recent decades. (See pages 541–542.)

KEY TERMS

average fixed cost (*AFC*): the total fixed cost divided by the quantity level of output (page 532).

average product: the total product that a firm produces in a given time period divided by the quantity of a variable input that it uses to produce it (page 525).

average total cost (*ATC*): the total cost divided by the quantity level of output (page 532).

average variable cost (*AVC*): the total variable cost divided by the quantity level of output (page 532).

constant returns to scale: long-run returns when an increase in output is exactly proportionate to the increase in inputs (page 536).

diminishing returns: a condition that occurs in the short run when the marginal product is falling—that is, when the product of each additional unit of a variable input is smaller than the product of the unit of the variable input added just before (page 526).

diseconomies of scale: long-run decreasing returns (page 535).

economic efficiency: the technically efficient input combination with the lowest cost to the firm (page 524).

economies of scale: long-run increasing returns (page 535).

explicit costs: money payments for the use of inputs (page 529).

implicit costs: costs incurred for inputs for which no obvious payment is made because no transaction takes place (page 529).

increasing returns: the condition that occurs in the short run when each successive unit of a variable input adds more product to a firm's output than was added by the preceding unit of the variable input (page 526).

information costs: the costs of acquiring information that decreases the uncertainty of making transactions (page 529).

innovation: the development of an invention from the original idea to a practical use (page 541).

inputs: labor, natural resources, and capital. Also called resources or factors of production. (page 520).

invention: the discovery of a new product or a new technical tool or process (page 541).

isocost line: a curve made up of points showing alternative combinations of the inputs on the axes that a firm can buy for a given cost outlay (page 549).

isoquant: a curve based on a firm's production function that shows all of the technically efficient input combinations for producing a certain quantity of output (page 548).

isoquant map: a graph showing several out of an infinite number of isoquants, one for every quantity of output that a firm could possibly produce (page 549).

long run: a period of time long enough to make all the changes that a firm wants to make within the limits of its existing production function (page 524).

long-run average cost (*LRAC*): the long-run total cost divided by the quantity level of output (page 535).

long-run marginal cost (*LRMC*): the addition to long-run total cost when one more unit of output is produced (page 535).

long-run total cost (*LRTC*): the total cost of producing a certain level of output when a firm is able to vary all of its inputs (page 535).

marginal cost (*MC*): the addition to total cost when one more unit of output is produced (page 533).

marginal product: the additional product produced per time period when one more unit of a variable input is added (page 524).

negative returns: the condition that results when the marginal product of a unit of variable input is negative (page 526).

outputs: the economic goods and services that business firms produce for sale to consumers, other business firms, and governments (page 520).

production: the transformation of inputs into outputs (page 520).

production function: a relationship that shows the maximum output that can be obtained from given amounts of inputs as of a specified point in time (page 520).

productivity: the amount of output produced by a unit of resource input during a given span of time (page 541).

short run: the period of time during which at least one of a business firm's inputs cannot be varied (page 523).

technically efficient: a method of production that does not waste resources (page 518).

technological progress: an advance in knowledge of the industrial arts and/or improved techniques of organizing production (page 541).

total cost (*TC*): the entire cost incurred by a firm producing a certain level of output. In the short run it is the sum of total fixed costs and total variable costs (page 532).

total fixed cost (*TFC*): the cost that does not vary with the quantity of output that a firm produces (page 530).

total product: the amount of product that a firm produces per time period with a certain number of fixed (in the short run) and variable inputs (page 524).

total variable cost (*TVC*): the cost that varies with the quantity of output that a firm produces (page 532).

transaction costs: the costs associated with facilitating the workings of a market by enabling potential buyers and sellers to interact (page 529).

very long run: a period of time long enough so that a firm can introduce a whole new technology and change its production function (page 524).

DISCUSSION QUESTIONS

1. The production function describes a set of alternative input combinations that are all technically efficient. What is meant by technical efficiency? Distinguish between technical efficiency and economic efficiency. Are all economically efficient methods of production technically efficient as well?

2. Distinguish among the three time perspectives for decision making—short run, long run, and very long run. Suppose that you are a high-level decision maker for a firm that manufactures and sells tires. Give two examples of short-run decisions you might have to make, two examples of long-run decisions, and two examples of very-long-run decisions.

3. Distinguish between diminishing returns and negative returns. Which do you expect firms to experience more frequently? Why?

4. "The theory of diminishing returns has a rather bleak prediction to offer. As time goes on, we shall get lower and lower returns." Do you agree? Why or why not?

5. Without looking at Figure 1, draw a total-product curve on a set of axes that measures total product along the vertical axis and the quantity of a variable input along the horizontal axis. Compare your diagram with Figure 1 to be sure you have it right. Using the concept of marginal product, explain why the theory of production suggests that the total-product curve looks this way in the short run.

6. Discuss the relationship between the marginal-product and the average-product curves in the short run. Specifically, explain their relationship:

   a. in Stage I

   b. in Stage II

   c. at the borderline between Stage I and Stage II

7. Without looking at Figures 2 and 3, on a single set of axes draw a total-cost curve, a total-fixed-cost curve, and an average-fixed-cost curve as you would expect them to look for a particular firm in the short run. Compare your diagram with Figures 2 and 3 to be sure you drew the curves correctly. Using what you learned about increasing and diminishing returns, carefully explain why the total-cost curve is shaped as it is. Then explain the relationship between the total-fixed-cost curve and the average-fixed-cost curve. When will the average-fixed-cost curve reach the horizontal axis?

8. Without looking at Figure 4, draw an average-variable-cost curve, an average-total-cost curve, and a marginal-cost curve on a single set of axes, as you would expect them to look for a particular firm in the short run. Compare your diagram with Figure 4 to be sure you have it right. Explain why the marginal-cost curve intersects the average-variable-cost curve and the average-total-cost curve at their minimum points. Why is average total cost far more in excess of average variable cost at low quantity levels of output than at high quantity levels of output?

9. Economists use seven different cost concepts to analyze a firm's production decisions in the short run, but only three in the long run. True or false? Explain.

10. Why is a firm's long-run average-cost curve expected to be U-shaped? (What accounts for the negatively sloped and then the positively sloped segments?)

11. "A firm would be foolish not to increase its level of output as long as it is operating on the negatively sloping portion of its long-run average-cost curve." True or false? Explain.

12. Distinguish between invention and innovation. Explain how either may affect productivity through input substitution and through increasing the quality of inputs.

Appendix:
A Firm's Best Input Combination

How can a firm find the combination of inputs that allows it in the long run to produce the output that it wants at the lowest possible cost? To answer this question, we use a tool not very different from the one we used in the appendix to Chapter 22. If you understand the indifference-analysis approach to the theory of consumer behavior, you will probably find the material in this appendix quite easy to follow. In order to find the right combination, a company must know both the technically efficient combinations of inputs that can be used to produce different levels of output and the prices of these inputs. Remember that the technically efficient combinations are shown by a firm's production function. By using input prices, it is possible to discover the combination that is economically efficient—the least-cost input combination.

To show how the best input combination may be found, we shall first present graphically the combinations of inputs offered by a company's production function and then picture their input prices. Finally, we shall combine the two.

A firm must know both the technically efficient combinations of inputs that can be used to produce different levels of output and the prices of these inputs to be able, over the long run, to produce the output that it wants at the lowest possible cost.

ISOQUANTS

The word **isoquant** means "same quantity." Economists use this term to describe a curve (based on a firm's production function) that shows all of the technically efficient input combinations for producing a certain quantity of output. Each point on an isoquant shows a different combination of inputs that can be used to produce a specified quantity of output. Table 6 presents a number of labor–capital combinations for three different quantities of output that a shoe company might produce. We have used the same two-input (shoe workers and shoemaking machines) production function that we used earlier in this chapter. Table 6 shows nine different combinations for producing 10 dozen pairs of shoes per day, ranging from using 100 workers plus 1 machine to using 1 worker plus 100 machines. Also shown are several different combinations for producing 8 dozen and 6 dozen pairs of shoes per day.

An isoquant is a curve that shows all of the technically efficient input combinations that a firm can use to produce a certain quantity of output.

The alternative combinations for each of the three quantities of output shown in Table 6 have been plotted in Figure 10. A smooth line drawn through the alternative combinations for each of the output levels enables us to read off a large number of additional combinations of the two input levels for each of the three quantities of output. For example, besides the points plotted from the two left-hand columns of Table 6, we can see that 13 workers and 7.9 machines will also produce 10 dozen pairs of shoes per day (assuming that machines can be rented on a part-time basis).

Isoquants have been drawn for 10 dozen, 8 dozen, and 6 dozen pairs of shoes per day. The figure does not show the isoquant for 2 dozen, for 76 dozen, or for 300 dozen. But there is an isoquant for every quantity of output that a firm could

TABLE 6
Technically Efficient Combinations for Producing Ten Dozen, Eight Dozen, and Six Dozen Pairs of Shoes per Day

10 Dozen Pairs of Shoes per Day		8 Dozen Pairs of Shoes per Day		6 Dozen Pairs of Shoes per Day	
Number of Shoe Workers (in 8-hour days)	Number of Shoemaking Machines (in 8-hour days)	Number of Shoe Workers (in 8-hour days)	Number of Shoemaking Machines (in 8-hour days)	Number of Shoe Workers (in 8-hour days)	Number of Shoemaking Machines (in 8-hour days)
100	1	64	1	36	1
50	2	32	2	18	2
25	4	16	4	12	3
20	5	8	8	9	4
10	10	4	16	6	6
5	20	2	32	4	9
4	25	1	64	3	12
2	50			2	18
1	100			1	36

possibly produce. All of these isoquants—an infinite number—on a single graph are called an **isoquant map**. Since each one refers to a different output, no two isoquants on an isoquant map can ever touch each other. After all, each one is made up of all of the technically efficient possibilities for producing a particular quantity. If two touched, the common point would represent the minimum quantities of all inputs for two different quantities of output. For example, if the isoquant for 6 dozen pairs of shoes touched the isoquant for 8 dozen pairs of shoes, it would indicate that both quantities could be produced with the same combination of the inputs. That is to say, it would take no more inputs to produce 8 dozen than to produce 6 dozen. But since it is clear that 6 dozen can be produced with fewer inputs than 8 dozen, a given input combination cannot be on the isoquant for both 6 dozen and 8 dozen pairs of shoes.

There is an isoquant for every quantity of output that a firm could possibly produce. All or several of these isoquants on a single graph make up an isoquant map.

ISOCOST LINES

The isoquant map graphically illustrates a firm's production function for all possible quantities of output it may wish to produce. But in order to be able to decide on the best input combination for a firm, input costs must also be brought into the picture. Shoe workers receive a wage, and shoemaking machinery must be bought or rented. These costs are expressed in the form of isocost lines. An **isocost line** (meaning ''same cost'') shows the combinations of inputs a firm can buy for a given cost outlay. For every possible cost outlay there is an isocost line. The slope of the isocost line is the price of the input on the horizontal axis relative to the price of the input on the vertical axis. The line becomes steeper or flatter as the cost of one of the inputs increases in relation to the cost of the other.

Our example of the shoe manufacturer can also be used to illustrate isocost lines. If we know that a shoe worker receives a wage of $60 per day and that a shoemaking machine costs $50 per day (based on purchase price or rental fees, maintenance, and the fuel required to run it), we can draw some isocost lines for several different cost outlays (see Figure 11). In the case of the $1,500 cost outlay, if the firm were to spend it all on work-

FIGURE 10
Three Alternative Isoquants

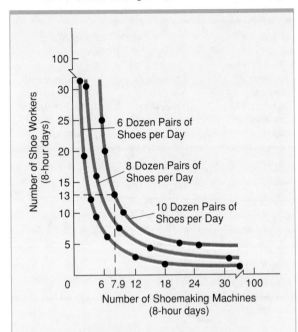

The numbers plotted from Table 6 establish the points along the three isoquants for a hypothetical shoe firm. Each isoquant shows all of the technically efficient combinations of workers and machines that will enable this firm to produce the quantity of shoes specified for that isoquant. For example, 10 dozen pairs of shoes per day can be produced by employing 20 shoe workers and 5 shoemaking machines or by employing only 13 workers but using 7.9 of the machines (7 for the full 8-hour day and an eighth machine for nine-tenths of the day).

ers, 25 workers could be hired ($1,500/$60 = 25). Or the firm could have 30 machines ($1,500/$50 = 30) if it were to spend all $1,500 on machines. In between these two extremes there are many other combinations. One such combination, as shown in Figure 11, is 20 shoe workers and 6 shoemaking machines. The other two isocost lines are constructed in the same way. With a cost outlay of $900, the most workers that the firm could hire is 15 ($900/$60 = 15), or the most machines it could have is 18 ($900/$50 = 18). The two extreme alternatives when the cost outlay is $600 are 10 workers ($600/$60 = 10) and 12 machines ($600/$50 = 12).

An isocost line shows the alternative combinations of inputs a firm can buy for a given cost outlay. The slope of the isocost line is the price of the input on the horizontal axis relative to the price of the input on the vertical axis.

FINDING THE BEST INPUT COMBINATION

A firm's isoquant map expresses its production function at different levels of output. Its isocost lines show input combinations possible at different total-cost outlays. When the two are put together, the best input combination for any given level of

FIGURE 11
Three Alternative Isocost Lines

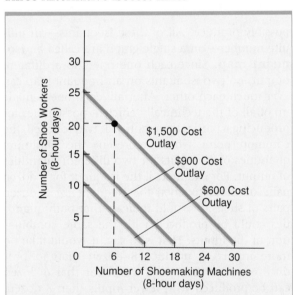

Three isocost lines for our hypothetical shoe firm are drawn. Each isocost line shows all of the different combinations of shoe workers and shoemaking machines that the firm can buy for a specified cost outlay. For example, the firm can spend $1,500 on 25 shoe workers or on 30 shoemaking machines, or on 20 workers plus 6 machines. The slope of the isocost line is the ratio of the price of shoemaking machines to the wage rate of shoe workers—$50 to $60.

FIGURE 12
Looking for the Best Input Combination to Produce Ten Dozen Pairs of Shoes per Day

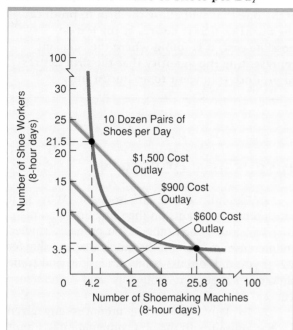

The isoquant for 10 dozen pairs of shoes per day has been added from Figure 10 to the set of isocost lines that were shown in Figure 11. If this shoe firm wishes to produce 10 dozen pairs of shoes per day, it is evident that neither the $600 nor the $900 cost outlay is enough. (At every point, the 10-dozen isoquant lies above the $600 and the $900 isocost lines.) We see that $1,500 is enough. The $1,500 isocost line is twice intersected by the 10-dozen isoquant. Ten dozen pairs of shoes per day can be produced with 21.5 workers plus 4.2 machines or with 3.5 workers plus 25.8 machines. However, neither of these combinations represents the lowest-cost method of producing 10 dozen pairs of shoes. There are surely isocost lines (not drawn here) between the $900 one and the $1,500 one that will allow the firm to produce 10 dozen pairs of shoes per day. The isocost line that represents the lowest cost outlay that will enable the firm to produce 10 dozen pairs of shoes per day is shown in Figure 13.

output for the firm can be readily determined. It is the one that will allow the firm to produce the desired quantity at the lowest possible cost. In the case of our shoe firm, we begin in Figure 12 by drawing the isoquant that corresponds to the quantity the firm wishes to produce. Suppose that, on the basis of its expected sales, the firm decides to

produce 10 dozen pairs of shoes per day. Thus, in Figure 12, we have added the firm's isocost lines developed in Figure 11 to the 10-dozen isoquant from Figure 10. Figure 12 shows that both the $600 and the $900 isocost lines do not represent enough cost outlay to produce 10 dozen pairs of shoes. Both are shown to be below the 10-dozen isoquant and are only enough for a lower level of output. The remaining isocost line ($1,500 cost) is enough. It intersects the isoquant at two places. Ten dozen pairs of shoes per day can be produced with 21.5 workers plus 4.2 machines or with 3.5 workers plus 25.8 machines, at a cost of $1,500 per day in each case. Could the firm do better? Could it produce the 10 dozen pairs of shoes per day at a lower cost? The answer is "yes." Any isocost line

FIGURE 13
Best Input Combination to Produce Ten Dozen Pairs of Shoes per Day

If our hypothetical shoe firm wishes to produce 10 dozen pairs of shoes per day, its best input combination will be 10 shoe workers plus 10 shoemaking machines. Given the assumed wage rate for shoe workers and price for shoemaking machines, the $1,100 isocost line represents the lowest possible cost of producing 10 dozen pairs of shoes per day since it is just tangent to the 10-dozen isoquant.

that lies below the $1,500 line but is high enough to reach the 10-dozen isoquant will enable the firm to produce 10 dozen pairs of shoes per day at a lower cost than $1,500 per day. The isocost line that corresponds to the lowest possible cost is the one just tangent to the isoquant. This isocost line is illustrated in Figure 13, and it turns out to be the one at $1,100. This isocost line is drawn parallel to the others (has the same steepness) and thus shows that the ratio of $60 to $50 between the input prices has been maintained. The point of tangency—the only point at which 10 dozen pairs of shoes per day can be produced for $1,100 per day—shows that the firm will use the input combination of 10 shoe workers and 10 shoemaking machines. This combination is the only solution that minimizes the cost of producing 10 dozen pairs of shoes per day.

In summary, given the facts that the firm wishes to produce 10 dozen pairs of shoes per day, that shoe workers cost $60 per day, and that shoemaking machines cost $50 per day, employing 10 shoe workers and operating 10 shoemaking machines is the best input combination for the firm.

When a firm's isoquant map is superimposed on its isocost lines, the best input combination for any given level of output for the firm can be readily determined. **The best input combination is the one that will allow the firm to produce the quantity that it desires at the lowest possible cost; it is found where the isoquant representing the quantity that the firm desires to produce is tangent to an isocost line.**

DISCUSSION QUESTIONS

1. Carefully define an isoquant. Why is it that no two isoquants on the same firm's isoquant map can touch each other? You probably studied indifference curves in the appendix to Chapter 22. If you did, discuss some similarities and some differences between isoquants and indifference curves.

2. Explain why a firm produces any given level of output with the best combination of inputs where one of its isoquants is tangent to an isocost line.

3. A profit-maximizing firm will always try to reach the highest isoquant that it can on its isoquant map. True or false? Explain.

25
Market Supply and Elasticity

Preview In this chapter we continue our discussion of the supply side of product markets. The last chapter presented the fundamentals of production theory. With this background, you are ready to learn how business firms determine the supply of products that they will offer. We assume that firms act in a rational way, which means that they will supply products according to the principles of profit maximization and loss minimization. In other words, they want to make as high a profit or as low a loss as possible. But the term *profit* and the term *loss* are used differently in different fields. You will see that the economist's definition is not the same as the one used by the accountant.

In this chapter you also will study the logic that is used by economists to arrive at predictions about the quantity of output that firms will actually supply. This reasoning involves both the revenue side and the cost side of firms' operations. We use the concepts of total revenue and total cost as well as marginal revenue and marginal cost to explain equilibrium-supply solutions.

We shall also ask the age-old question, "To supply or not to supply?" You will see that the answer may be different in the short run than in the long run. The short-run question is: When will a rational business firm decide to shut down? The long-run question is: When will a rational business firm decide to exit from an industry?

Finally, we describe the price elasticity of supply. It is the same elasticity concept that we applied earlier to demand. Here you will learn why the quantity supplied is much more responsive to price changes for some products than it is for others.

RATIONAL BUSINESS FIRMS

Recall from Chapter 3 that economists often assume that business firms act rationally—that they try to maximize their profit and minimize their loss. Important theories of the firm make this assumption in order to simplify what is really a very complex set of motives that influence business firm decision makers.

How realistic an assumption is profit maximization? Does it allow economists to make fairly reliable predictions? It is hard for us to give a simple answer. We realize that firms have goals other than making the maximum profit and that even when firms aim for maximum profit, they may be frustrated and fail to achieve it. But probably there is no other simple assumption, at least for the long run, that allows economists to make better predictions.

Economists often assume that business firms act rationally—they try to maximize their profit and minimize their loss.

We know that firms must make their decisions in a world of uncertainty. They do not know what will happen tomorrow. They can only guess about the input and output prices that they must pay and receive in the future. They can only guess about their future sales and future cost. The best they can do is to assign probabilities to particular outcomes. Suppose, for example, that a builder who is trying to decide whether or not to build another house this month assigns probabilities to two different selling prices. If the builder assigns a probability of .8 to successfully selling the house at a profitable price and .2 to having to sell it at a loss, the builder may decide to go ahead and build the house. If, instead, the probabilities were reversed (.8 that the house would be sold at a loss), the builder would probably not build the house. But how reliable are a builder's predictions? Can we expect the builder to assign the correct probabilities? It is hard to say. Some business people have more information about business conditions than do others. Also, it is important to recognize that predictions depend on the time period over which business people attempt to maximize profits. How many years into the future are being considered?

Another problem with the profit maximization assumption is that large and complex companies have so many layers of decision making that even if the top management wants to maximize profits, it may not be able to do so. The sales department is often more interested in maximizing sales than profit. The marketing department usually wants to maximize sales per dollar spent on advertising. In the accounting department the aim may be to maximize cash flow. And the research and development department may be more interested in making an exciting new discovery than in just how much this discovery will contribute to company profits. Therefore, directives from top management may be compromised, so that profit is lower than it would be if a strict profit-maximization policy were followed.

A final reason why the profit-maximization assumption may not lead to entirely reliable predictions is that top management itself has goals that are not always consistent with profit maximization. Herbert Simon, a Nobel Prize–winning economist, suggests that many managers **satisfice**—that is, seek satisfactory profit instead of maximum profit. Satisfactory profit for a firm may be an amount of profit that leaves the firm's stockholders and members of the board of directors satisfied with the firm's performance. Thus, top management may be more interested in showing a steady growth of profit than higher but fluctuating profit. Besides satisficing, top managers are concerned with the security of the firm. They want to make sure that it will still be around in twenty-five years, fifty years, or more. For this reason they are often willing to trade off some profit for greater diversification or a better public image, both of which may add to the security of the firm. Top managers may have personal goals that are not entirely consistent with maximum profit for the firm. Since the money they earn is at least as closely related to the size of the firm (measured in sales or assets) as to its profitability, managers may lean toward maximizing growth rather than profit. They are also concerned with the security of their positions. Profit improvement and steady year-after-year profit may make their jobs safer than a very high profit in one year but a much lower one in another year. Of course, managers are motivated by more than money and security. They seek prestige, power, and glory, too. Being written up in *Fortune* magazine or in *Business*

Week and being recognized when approaching the first hole at the country club may be more readily achieved through the firm's growth than through the firm's profitability.

Many managers satisfice—seek satisfactory profit instead of maximum profit—because they may be more interested in steady growth or security and prestige than in spectacular profits.

Where does our discussion of business goals leave us? We hope a bit wiser and more tolerant of how hard it is to predict in a world of uncertainty and multiple goals. We find that we do not make better predictions when we redefine a rational business decision maker as one who tries to maximize sales or security or any of the just-mentioned personal goals of managers. Therefore, even though we know it does not capture all of a firm's goals, profit maximization remains as the best single simple assumption about how business firms behave.

The assumption of rationality allows economists to make predictions about business decisions, but they recognize that business firms operate in a world of uncertainty, that large companies may have difficulty maximizing profits because of competing interests within their bureaucracies, and that top management may have goals of its own that are not always consistent with profit maximization.

THE MEANINGS OF PROFIT

A wise old trader (who never had a course in principles of economics) once advised, "Buy sheep and sell deer." The play on words, of course, refers to making a profit when one can buy "cheap" and sell "dear." This advice recognizes that **profit** is the difference between cost and revenue, or the difference between what a firm gives up to produce a product and what the firm takes in from the sale of that product. When revenue is greater than cost, the firm is said to have made profit. When cost is

greater than revenue, it has experienced negative profit, or loss.

Profit is the difference between cost and revenue—the difference between what a firm gives up to produce a product and what the firm takes in from the sale of that product. When revenue is greater than cost, the firm has made a profit.

Unfortunately, these commonly understood definitions are complicated by accountants and economists not always defining cost in the same way. Remember from Chapter 24 (see 529–530) Mama and Papa, who own a grocery store and who "forget" to pay themselves wages for the hours that they work and interest for the money that they have tied up in store capital and inventory. We called such items "implicit costs" and argued that they are just as much a part of a firm's costs as are those that are transacted ("explicit costs") such as a clerk's wages and the utility bill.

Accountants, who are most interested in the funds that flow to and from a business firm, often do not include some of the implicit costs. It is customary for accountants to include depreciation of plant and equipment and the rental value of property. But wages not paid to owners and the return on money that owners have in their businesses are usually omitted. Thus, accountants may overstate the amount of profit that is earned by a firm. Economists, who use the concept of opportunity cost, include implicit costs and so give a more realistic picture of a firm's profit.

Accountants and economists do not always define cost in the same way. Accountants often do not include some of the implicit costs and thus they may overstate the amount of profit that is earned by a firm.

It follows that an amount of profit that is considered to be "normal" for a firm to earn is recognized by economists as a cost of doing business. Therefore, if it takes $42,180 a year of "accounting profit" to keep Mama and Papa operating their grocery business, that is the amount of *normal profit* in this example. Accounting profit greater than

$42,180 in this example is called *greater-than-normal profit,* or **economic profit**. Accounting profit of less than $42,180 in this example is called *less-than-normal profit,* or **economic loss**. If economic loss persists, the firm will likely go out of business.[1]

The minimum amount that a firm has to earn in order for it to be willing to continue in its present business activity is called normal profit; profit in excess of this amount is called economic profit. Less than normal profit is called economic loss.

In summary, profit is simply the difference between total revenue and total cost. But we must be sure that just as all of a firm's receipts are included in its total revenue, all of its costs, explicit and implicit, are included in its total cost. **Normal profit**—the return to enterprise that the firm must receive in order for it to be willing to continue in its present business—is treated as a cost by economists. Firms try to earn an economic profit and will go out of business in the long run if they earn an economic loss. Just how to determine the amount of profit a firm is able to earn is discussed in the next section.

Normal profit is treated as a cost by economists. It is the return to enterprise that the firm must receive in order for it to be willing to continue in its present business.

IDENTIFYING THE PROFIT-MAXIMIZING LEVEL OF OUTPUT

An economist who wishes to predict the quantity of output that a firm will supply must examine the

---

1. In the short run, a firm earning less-than-normal profit or economic loss may remain in business since its revenue may exceed its variable cost and thus reimburse the firm for part of its fixed cost. If the firm shut down its operation, it would lose all of its fixed cost. We shall elaborate on this point later in this chapter.

costs and the revenues that are associated with alternative output levels of that firm. Only then can the amount of profit or loss be determined. The logic of the profit-maximizing solution may be seen in two different ways: one using total cost and total revenue and another using marginal cost and marginal revenue.

Total Cost and Total Revenue

Total cost, as you have seen, includes all the costs—explicit and implicit—that a firm incurs in production. **Total revenue** is the total amount of receipts or income that a firm obtains from selling what it produces. Over any period of time, the difference between a firm's total revenue and its total cost is its profit or loss. Suppose that we have reliable total-cost and total-revenue data for a firm that produces yachts. Table 1 shows this information along with the profit or loss that would be realized for different numbers of yachts that this firm could produce. Total revenue is seen to increase with increases in the number of yachts sold each year. However, the amount of the increase goes down as more units are sold. This happens because we assume a normal downward-sloping demand curve, which means that in order to sell more units, the firm has to lower its price. Thus, total revenue is $300,000 when the firm sells 1 yacht, but $575,000 when it sells 2 at a price of $287,500 each, $825,000 when it sells 3 at a price of $275,000 each, and so on. Ten yachts a year cannot be sold for more than $187,500 each.

Total cost also goes up with increases in sales. You learned in the previous chapter that cost and output are positively related, but that during early levels of output we may expect increasing returns (total cost rising at a decreasing rate) and that at higher output levels diminishing returns will set in (total cost rising at an increasing rate). In our example, increasing returns occur over the output range of zero to 3 yachts. After that, diminishing returns set in.

When the firm sells no yachts, it loses $50,000, the amount of fixed costs that it incurs. When the company sells 1 yacht, it loses $100,000, since the total cost of producing that unit is $400,000, though it can sell the yacht for only $300,000. At 2 units of output the firm breaks even, since the total

TABLE 1
Total Revenue, Total Cost, and Profit Data for a Hypothetical Yacht Firm

Output of Yachts (per year)	Total Revenue (in thousands of dollars)	Total Cost (in thousands of dollars)	Profit or Loss (in thousands of dollars)
0	0	50	−50
1	300	400	−100
2	575	575	0
3	825	700	125
4	1,050	835	215
5	1,250	985	265
6	1,425	1,160	265
7	1,575	1,370	205
8	1,700	1,700	0
9	1,800	2,180	−380
10	1,875	2,860	−985

cost is equal to the total revenue. (Remember that "breaking even" means that the firm does earn "normal profit" but that "economic profit" is zero.) Producing 3 yachts is profitable ($125,000), 4-unit production brings a higher profit ($215,000), and producing 5 or 6 yachts a year is even more profitable ($265,000). Over the range from zero to 5 units, the total revenue rises faster than the total cost, so that loss falls or profit rises. At output levels higher than 6, profit drops because the total cost rises faster than the total revenue. At 8 units the firm again breaks even, and above that amount, it has a loss.

It is clear from the data in Table 1 that the company—which is assumed to be a profit-maximizing firm—will not produce less than 5 yachts or more than 6 yachts a year. However, we cannot predict whether the firm will produce 5 units or 6 units. Because the company produces and sells very few yachts, the data are quite "lumpy." Somewhere between producing 5 and 6 yachts there may be a unique point where profit would theoretically be at a maximum. But that point may be at 5½ units, and we all know that half a yacht would sink. When the good can be more easily divided, or when we allow the firm to have inventory to carry over to the next year, we approach a single profit-maximizing level of output.

Of course, we could predict whether our firm will produce 5 or 6 yachts by bringing more vari-

ables into our theory. For example, we may reason that the firm's size is positively related to its security and to the individual managers' goals such as compensation, job security, and prestige. On that basis we might predict that this company will produce 6 yachts a year, and not 5. However, we might alternatively reason that the firm's size is positively related to more work, responsibility, and hassles for managers. On that basis we might predict that the company will produce 5 yachts a year, and not 6. We see, then, that additional variables may be relevant but do not give economists the simple generalization that is offered by the profit-maximization assumption. Also, there is generally no need for predictions to be narrowed down to a single level of output. The cost and revenue data are usually not so reliable that one can reasonably expect to gain very much greater precision from doing so. Based on the assumption of profit maximization alone, we are left with our prediction that this firm will produce 5 or 6 yachts a year.

Total cost includes all the costs (explicit and implicit) that a firm incurs in production. Total revenue is the total amount of receipts that a firm obtains from selling what it produces.

The difference between a firm's total revenue and its total cost is its profit or loss.

Marginal Cost and Marginal Revenue

A second way to see the logic that leads us to the profit-maximizing level of output is to use the concepts of marginal cost and marginal revenue. We have seen that marginal cost is the addition to a firm's total cost that comes from producing one more unit of output. Likewise, marginal revenue is the addition to a firm's total revenue that comes from selling one more unit of output.

Marginal cost is the addition to a firm's total cost that comes from producing one more unit of output. Marginal revenue is the addition to a firm's total revenue that comes from selling one more unit of output.

Let us return to our example of the yacht firm. Table 2 repeats the data in Table 1 but adds columns for marginal revenue and marginal cost. (The amounts in these two new columns are printed on lines lying between units to show that they refer to the *changes* that take place in total revenue and in total cost each time one more yacht is added to the firm's level of total output.) Notice that since the company must lower its price in order to sell more, marginal revenue falls as more yachts are produced and sold. Marginal cost goes down as increasing returns are experienced for up to 3 yachts. But after that point marginal cost goes up as diminishing returns set in. Under these conditions, marginal-cost and marginal-revenue data allow us to find the level of output that will maximize a company's profit. The rule is as follows: A firm will maximize its profit when it produces that level of output at which marginal revenue equals marginal cost, as long as marginal revenue is greater than marginal cost at somewhat lower levels of output and marginal cost is greater than marginal revenue at somewhat higher levels of output.

Why this rule will always hold can be seen by studying the data in Table 2. We shall not concern ourselves with the zero-to-1 range of output, since it is excluded by the profit-maximization rule. (Marginal cost is higher than marginal revenue for the first unit of output.) Marginal revenue is equal to marginal cost between 5 and 6 units of output.

To see that this must be the profit-maximizing level of output, we shall look at the alternatives of producing less than 5 units and producing more than 6 units. At a production level of 3 yachts, the firm is encouraged to raise output, since producing the fourth yacht adds more to revenue than it does to cost. Because the marginal revenue is $225,000 and the marginal cost is $135,000, producing 4 yachts a year instead of 3 raises the firm's profit by $90,000. The same reasoning explains why the firm would rather produce 5 yachts than 4. Because the marginal revenue of $200,000 is greater than the marginal cost of $150,000, the company would give up $50,000 of profit if it did not produce the fifth yacht. When the firm considers whether or not to produce 6 yachts, it finds that marginal cost is equal to marginal revenue (both $175,000). Revenue rises just as much as cost does, so that profit is not changed. As we found in our earlier discussion about total revenue and total cost, if we wish to predict on the basis of profit maximization alone, we are not able to say whether the firm will produce the sixth yacht or not, since there is neither a profit incentive nor a profit penalty for doing so.

In raising production from 6 to 7 units, the firm's marginal cost of $210,000 is greater than its marginal revenue of $150,000. This means that the company adds more to total cost than to total revenue when it produces the seventh unit. Profit will be $60,000 less than it would have been if the company had produced only 6 yachts. Producing more than 7 yachts a year lowers profit even more. An output level of 8 yachts a year lowers profit to the breakeven point. (Remember that "breaking even" means that the company does earn "normal profit" but that "economic profit" is zero.) The eighth yacht adds $125,000 of revenue for the firm, but it also means that it has added costs of $330,000. The difference between the marginal revenue and the marginal cost ($205,000) is a drop in profit that the company can avoid by not producing the eighth yacht.

A firm will maximize its profit when it produces that level of output at which marginal revenue equals marginal cost, as long as marginal

---

TABLE 2
Revenue, Cost, and Profit Data for a Hypothetical Yacht Firm

Output of Yachts (per year)	Total Revenue (in thousands of dollars)	Marginal Revenue (in thousands of dollars)	Total Cost (in thousands of dollars)	Marginal Cost (in thousands of dollars)	Profit or Loss (in thousands of dollars)
0	0		50		−50
		300		350	
1	300		400		−100
		275		175	
2	575		575		0
		250		125	
3	825		700		125
		225		135	
4	1,050		835		215
		200		150	
5	1,250		985		265
		175		175	
6	1,425		1,160		265
		150		210	
7	1,575		1,370		205
		125		330	
8	1,700		1,700		0
		100		480	
9	1,800		2,180		−380
		75		680	
10	1,875		2,860		−985

revenue is greater than marginal cost at somewhat lower levels of output and marginal cost is greater than marginal revenue at somewhat higher levels of output.

In summary, a profit-maximizing firm will not produce less output than the amount at which a rising marginal cost is equal to marginal revenue. As long as marginal revenue is greater than marginal cost, more output will add more to revenue than to cost, and a company would be giving up profit by not producing more. Likewise, a profit-maximizing firm will not produce more output than the amount at which a rising marginal cost is equal to marginal revenue. If marginal cost is greater than marginal revenue, more output will add more to cost than to revenue, and each added unit of output will lower profits.

A profit-maximizing firm will not produce more or less output than the amount at which a rising marginal cost is equal to marginal revenue.

Graphic Presentation of Profit Maximization

To show the profit-maximizing solution as a diagram, we have plotted the data from Table 2 on two sets of axes on Figure 1. Total revenue and total cost are shown in the top part and marginal revenue and marginal cost in the lower part.

As shown in the top panel, total revenue rises by decreasing amounts over the whole range of output levels. Total cost rises by decreasing amounts up to 3 yachts and then by increasing amounts over the remaining range. Total cost is higher than total revenue for fewer than 2 yachts

FIGURE 1
Profit Maximization for a Hypothetical Yacht Firm

The top panel shows the yacht firm's total-cost and total-revenue curves. At production levels of less than 2 yachts a year or more than 8 yachts a year, total cost exceeds total revenue and thus a loss is incurred. The firm just breaks even if it produces either 2 or 8 yachts a year. The firm realizes a profit if it produces more than 2 but less than 8 yachts per year. Within this profit range, total revenue lies above total cost by the greatest amount when the firm produces 5 or 6 yachts a year. This dual profit-maximization solution is shown as the gold area between the curves.

The lower panel shows the same firm's marginal-cost and marginal-revenue curves. We analyze only the range from one breakeven point to the other. Between the output levels of 2 and 5½ yachts a year, marginal revenue exceeds marginal cost. This is shown as the green (both light and dark) area. Between the output levels of 5½ and 8 yachts a year, marginal cost exceeds marginal revenue. This is shown as the red (both light and dark) area. Profit maximization takes place at the level of output where the firm's marginal-cost curve intersects its marginal-revenue curve from below. This is at 5½ yachts a year. Since half of a yacht cannot be sold, the firm maximizes its profit when it produces either 5 or 6 yachts a year. The dark red and dark green areas to the right and to the left of the intersection represent equal amounts of marginal profit that is sacrificed because of the need to produce whole units.

per year, and so the company has a loss (less-than-normal profit, or economic loss) over that very low range of output. At a production level of 2 yachts a year, total cost is equal to total revenue (the curves intersect). In this case the company is just breaking even (only normal profit is earned). The firm makes a profit (greater-than-normal profit, or eco-nomic profit) over the range of output between 2 and 8 yachts per year. Total revenue is above total cost over that range. Producing 8 yachts a year again finds the company just breaking even (the curves intersect). At levels above 8 yachts a year, the total-cost curve is above the total-revenue curve, so that the firm shows a loss (less-than-normal profit or economic loss). Within the profit range, where total revenue is above total cost, the greatest vertical distance between total revenue and total cost appears at the level of output between 5 and 6 yachts. This is, of course, the same solution that we described earlier. Since the data are lumpy, rather than continuous, the solution appears as a range on the figure (the gold portion between the total-revenue and total-cost curves) rather than as a single point.

The lower panel of Figure 1 pictures the marginal-revenue and marginal-cost curves of our yacht-producing firm. Each level of output along the horizontal scale corresponds to the level in the upper panel, though the vertical scale is stretched out so that you can see the details more clearly. Note that the marginal-revenue curve slopes downward over the whole range of output levels. This corresponds to the total-revenue curve, which increases by decreasing amounts (upper panel), from which it is derived. The marginal-cost curve falls at early levels of output and rises afterward. It decreases over the output range where total cost rises by decreasing amounts and then increases when total cost rises by increasing amounts.

Because of our lumpy data, we shall begin our analysis in the lower panel of the figure at the breakeven output of 2 yachts a year. At that point we see that marginal revenue is higher than marginal cost. It remains higher up to the production level of 5½ yachts. This means that, within that output range, the production of every additional yacht causes revenue to rise more than cost, so profit goes up. At output levels beyond 5½ yachts, marginal cost lies above marginal revenue, so that the firm adds more to cost than to revenue and profit goes down. Producing 8 yachts a year will again allow the company only to break even. We see then that the green (both light and dark) area to the left of the intersection at 5½ yachts (the excess of marginal revenue over marginal cost between the output levels of 2 and 5½) is exactly equal to the red (both light and dark) area to the right of the intersection (the amount of marginal cost in excess of marginal revenue between the output levels of 5½ and 8). At production levels greater than 8 yachts a year, the company suffers a loss (earns less-than-normal profit or economic loss).

Where marginal cost intersects marginal revenue from below is the profit-maximizing level of output. At that volume of production, the company takes advantage of all units of output at which marginal revenue is greater than marginal cost, yet does not produce so much that marginal cost is higher than marginal revenue. Of course, we still have the problem caused by the lumpy data. We cannot predict that the company will produce 5½ yachts (remember that half a yacht will not float). For this reason, the company is said to maximize its profit when it produces either 5 or 6 yachts a year. In the lower panel of Figure 1 the small dark green area to the left of the intersection of marginal cost and marginal revenue is equal to the small dark red area to the right of that intersection. Each of these dark colored areas shows the amount of marginal profit that is lost because of the need to produce whole units.

To Supply or Not to Supply?

So far we have taken it for granted that all firms will supply a product. The question was only how much. In fact, a firm may choose not to supply anything at all. The decision to produce nothing at all may come in two different ways. One involves a long-run decision and the other involves a short-run decision.

Long Run: Exit   Recall that the long run is a period of time long enough for a firm to make all the adjustments in production that it wishes. There is no fixed cost in the long run. If, in this case, a firm supplying its profit-maximizing quantity level of output cannot earn at least a normal profit, economists predict that it will leave (exit) the industry. Since economists consider normal profit to be a cost of doing business, the company would find that its opportunity cost of staying in this business is simply too great. Total revenue would not cover total cost. The rational business firm—one that will minimize its losses—will exit. No loss at all is better than even a small loss.

If the firm supplying its profit-maximizing quantity level of output cannot earn at least a normal profit in the long run, economists predict that it will exit the industry because total revenue will not cover total cost.

TABLE 3
Four Alternative Short-Run Cases for the Verbo Company

	Case 1	Case 2	Case 3	Case 4
Variable cost	$ 5,000	$ 5,000	$ 5,000	$ 5,000
Fixed cost	10,000	10,000	10,000	10,000
Total cost	15,000	15,000	15,000	15,000
Total revenue	16,000	11,000	9,000	4,000
Profit (+) or loss (−) if Verbo operates	+1,000	−4,000	−6,000	−11,000
Profit (+) or loss (−) if Verbo shuts down	−10,000	−10,000	−10,000	−10,000
Expected decision by Verbo	Operate	Operate	Operate	Shut down

Short Run: Shut Down In the short run, however, there is a good reason why a rational firm may continue to operate even though it does have a loss. That reason is the presence of fixed cost. In the short run, a firm's total cost is made up of both fixed cost and variable cost. Fixed cost cannot be shed, even by shutting down.[2] For this reason, if a firm supplying its profit-maximizing quantity of output can earn enough to recover all of its variable cost and at least some of its fixed cost, it will pay for it to operate. In other words, according to the principle of loss minimization, it is better for a firm to lose only some of its fixed cost rather than to lose all of it. On the other hand, economists predict that if a company producing its profit-maximizing quantity of output in the short run is not even able to recover its variable cost, then it will shut down.

Let us predict the short-run decision that a rational business firm, the Verbo Company, would be expected to make under each of four alternative sets of conditions. Table 3 shows these four cases. We assume that the cost conditions—$5,000 of variable cost, $10,000 of fixed cost, and therefore $15,000 of total cost—are the same in all four cases. However, total revenue is different in each of the cases: $16,000 in case 1, $11,000 in case 2, $9,000 in case 3, and only $4,000 in case 4.

In case 1, Verbo earns $1,000 of profit by operating the business. Shutting down would cause it

to have a loss of $10,000, the amount of the fixed cost, since variable cost and total revenue would become zero. This would make Verbo $11,000 worse off. We would therefore expect Verbo to operate.

In case 2, Verbo suffers a loss of $4,000 by operating the business. Our first inclination might be to think that it would want to shut down. But would it be better off by shutting down in the short run? The answer is "no," because Verbo's total revenue exceeds its variable cost by $6,000, so that by operating it will lose $6,000 less than if it shut down. If it were to shut down, it would lose its entire fixed cost of $10,000, whereas by operating it can cut its losses to $4,000.

In case 3, Verbo suffers a loss of $6,000 by operating the business. In this case, it still pays for Verbo to produce. Its total revenue of $9,000 is more than enough to offset its variable cost of $5,000. It will lose $4,000 less than if it shut down. Notice that the rational decision to produce even though the firm incurs a loss does not require revenue sufficient to cover fixed cost. The shut-down decision is made on the basis of the relationship between revenue and variable cost.

In case 4, Verbo suffers a loss of $11,000 by operating the business. In this case, it will want to shut down because that will enable it to cut its losses to $10,000. Its total revenue of $4,000 is not enough to offset its variable cost of $5,000. By shutting down, it can bring both total revenue and variable cost to zero and thus suffer only the loss of the $10,000 of fixed cost.

---

2. We use the term *shut down* instead of the term *exit* because a firm still incurs fixed cost in the short run and therefore cannot exit.

In the short run, if a firm supplying its profit-maximizing quantity level of output can earn enough to recover even slightly more than its variable cost, it will pay for it to operate. According to the principle of loss minimization, it is better for a firm to lose only some of its fixed cost rather than to lose all of it.

If a company producing its profit-maximizing quantity level of output in the short run is not able to recover its variable cost, then it will shut down.

ELASTICITY OF SUPPLY

The concept of elasticity was presented in Chapter 23. There we applied it to demand. Here you will learn about the elasticity of supply. The basic idea is the same—the degree of responsiveness—but of course it takes on a different meaning when applied to supply.

The supply curve that we constructed in Chapter 5 was defined in the schedule sense. It related certain quantities of supply to a number of different prices. We saw that it was positively sloped, since sellers, whose input prices were held constant, found it profitable to supply more at higher prices and less at lower prices. The degree of that response, or the sensitivity of that quantity-price relationship, is numerically measured by the elasticity concept.

The **price elasticity of supply (E_S)** may be stated in the following form:

$$E_S = \frac{\text{the percentage change in the quantity supplied}}{\text{the percentage change in the price that caused it}}$$

This is a ratio of percentage changes and so is independent of the units of measure (pounds, pairs, inches, dollars, and so forth) that may be used. In formula form it may be expressed as follows:

$$E_S = \frac{\Delta Q_S / \overline{Q}_S}{\Delta P / \overline{P}}$$

Here ΔQ_S is the change in quantity supplied, $\overline{Q}_S$ is the average quantity supplied, ΔP is the change in price, and $\overline{P}$ is the average price. The formula used in the computation can also be stated as follows:

$$E_S = \frac{\dfrac{Q_{S_2} - Q_{S_1}}{(Q_{S_1} + Q_{S_2})/2}}{\dfrac{P_2 - P_1}{(P_1 + P_2)/2}}$$

or since the twos cancel out, as

$$E_S = \frac{\dfrac{Q_{S_2} - Q_{S_1}}{Q_{S_1} + Q_{S_2}}}{\dfrac{P_2 - P_1}{P_1 + P_2}}$$

Here Q_{S_1} is the original quantity supplied, Q_{S_2} is the new quantity supplied, P_1 is the original price, and P_2 is the new price.

Table 4 gives three examples of how the numerical value of elasticity, or the elasticity coefficient, is figured. We have used the same good (sweaters) and the same four prices that we did for demand in Table 2 in Chapter 23. Of course, the supply responses are positive, whereas the demand responses in Table 2 in Chapter 23 were negative. Again, by convention, we do not use the sign.

The price elasticity of supply (E_S) is the percentage change in quantity supplied divided by the percentage change in the price that caused it. It is independent of the unit of measure that is used.

Elasticity Categories

Price elasticity of supply categories are the same as those used for demand (see Chapter 23, pages 506–507). In Table 4, the elasticity coefficient of 0.56 is inelastic (smaller than 1.0) and means that for every 1 percent rise in price, the quantity supplied increased by a bit more than $\frac{1}{2}$ percent (0.56 of 1 percent). The other two examples in Table 4 show elastic (larger than 1.0) supply, since for every 1 percent rise in price, the quantity supplied increases by more than 1 percent (1.17 percent and 1.96 percent).

TABLE 4
Elasticity Coefficients Calculated from a Market-Supply Schedule for Sweaters

Price (dollars per sweater)	Market Supply (millions of sweaters per year)	Price Elasticity of Supply Calculation
$20	100	
		$\dfrac{\dfrac{125-100}{100+125}}{\dfrac{30-20}{20+30}} = \dfrac{\dfrac{25}{225}}{\dfrac{10}{50}} = \dfrac{\dfrac{1}{9}}{\dfrac{1}{5}} = \dfrac{1}{9} \cdot \dfrac{5}{1} = \dfrac{5}{9}$ or 0.56
$30	125	
		$\dfrac{\dfrac{175-125}{125+175}}{\dfrac{40-30}{30+40}} = \dfrac{\dfrac{50}{300}}{\dfrac{10}{70}} = \dfrac{\dfrac{1}{6}}{\dfrac{1}{7}} = \dfrac{1}{6} \cdot \dfrac{7}{1} = \dfrac{7}{6}$ or 1.17
$40	175	
		$\dfrac{\dfrac{400-175}{175+400}}{\dfrac{60-40}{40+60}} = \dfrac{\dfrac{225}{575}}{\dfrac{20}{100}} = \dfrac{\dfrac{9}{23}}{\dfrac{1}{5}} = \dfrac{9}{23} \cdot \dfrac{5}{1} = \dfrac{45}{23}$ or 1.96
$60	400	

Table 5 presents all five categories for supply elasticity, as did Table 3 in Chapter 23 for demand elasticity. Notice that the definitions and examples are alike. The inelastic supply curve is steeper than the elastic one, and the perfectly inelastic supply curve is a vertical straight line, whereas the infinitely or perfectly elastic supply curve is a horizontal straight line. The only elasticity category in which the supply curve is not similar (although sloping in the opposite direction) to the demand curve in the same category is unitary elasticity. The demand curve of unitary elasticity is a rectangular hyperbola, but the supply curve of unitary elasticity is a straight line drawn through the origin. The amount supplied changes in fixed proportion with the price. For example, a 12 percent rise in the price of basketballs causes sellers to increase the supply of basketballs by 12 percent.

There are five categories of price elasticity for supply, just as there are for demand: elastic, inelastic, unitary elastic, perfectly inelastic, and infinitely elastic.

Determinants of Price Elasticity of Supply

Actual elasticities of supply vary greatly among goods and services. Elasticity of supply is determined largely by two factors: (1) the change in average total cost that is incurred by a firm when it changes the quantity of its output, and (2) the time that it takes a company to raise or to lower its level of output. These two factors are like those for the elasticity of demand, which we described earlier.

Elasticity of supply is determined largely by (1) the change in *ATC* incurred by a firm when it changes the quantity of its output, and (2) the time it takes a company to raise or lower its level of output.

Changes in Average Total Cost Remember that the availability of good substitutes was one of the factors influencing demand elasticity. For supply elasticity the corresponding influences come from the changes in average total cost to a company

TABLE 5
Price Elasticity of Supply Categories

Elasticity Category	Relationship Between Price and Quantity Supplied	Elasticity Coefficient	Numerical Example	Diagram of Supply Curve for This Example
Inelastic	The percentage change in the quantity supplied is smaller than the percentage change in the price that caused it.	less than one	A price increase from $10 to $20 causes quantity supplied to increase from 40 to 60.	
Elastic	The percentage change in the quantity supplied is greater than the percentage change in the price that caused it.	greater than one	A price increase from $10 to $20 causes quantity supplied to increase from 20 to 120.	
Unitary elastic	The percentage change in the quantity supplied is exactly equal to the percentage change in the price that caused it.	one	A price increase from $10 to $20 causes quantity supplied to increase from 40 to 80.	
Perfectly inelastic	Any change in the price causes no response at all in the quantity supplied.	zero	A price increase from $10 to $20 causes no change in the quantity supplied.	
Infinitely elastic	Any change in the price causes a limitless (infinite) response in the quantity supplied.	∞ (infinity)	At any price below $10, the quantity supplied will be zero, and at the $10 price, quantity supplied is indefinitely small or large.	

when it raises or lowers output in response to price changes.

When labor, capital, and natural resources flow easily from the production of one good or service to the production of another, we say that they are readily substitutable. This means that resources can easily be switched from producing one product to producing another. In this situation, we expect the supply of such goods and services to be relatively elastic. This may be illustrated by what happens to a firm's average total cost when the level of output is changed. Let us suppose that the price of women's skirts goes up 10 percent. The garment workers who make dresses, blouses, robes, and other clothing, as well as the cutting and sewing machines that they use, can easily be switched to skirts without paying the higher wages that might be needed to train new people or the extra money needed to buy new machines. It follows, then, that average total cost will be bid up only slightly, if at all, as the level of output increases, and that skirt production will become more profitable. We would expect that the 10 percent price rise together with no important rise in average total cost would cause companies to respond with an output increase of greater than 10 percent. If, on the other hand, increases in output could be managed only by bidding up the prices of inputs or by using only relatively poor (high-cost) substitute inputs, we would expect relatively inelastic supply. This would happen if key resources are very specialized and thus are very hard or even impossible to switch to another use. For example, the supply of works of art by a well-known contemporary painter would be very inelastic since no one else is able to produce that artist's paintings. If the price of such works doubled, he or she might produce only 5 or 10 percent more paintings, so that supply elasticity would be very low. The limit case is that of a dead artist, where supply elasticity would be zero (perfectly inelastic), since no matter how much the price goes up, no more of this artist's paintings can be produced.

When labor, capital, and natural resources flow easily from the production of one good or service to the production of another, that is,

when they are readily substitutable, resources can easily be switched from producing one product to producing another and supply is relatively elastic.

Adjustment Time The second determinant of the price elasticity of supply of a product is the length of time needed for adjustment. This same time variable was explained in the demand elasticity discussion. A price change may cause only a very small response in the quantity supplied after a short time, but, as time passes, that response may increase. For example, suppose that the price of steel increases by 20 percent. Steel firms might quickly respond by hiring more labor and buying more iron ore and other material inputs. Still, they might find that they can raise output by only 10 percent, representing a supply elasticity of 0.5. Production increases are limited by the number of furnaces that they have. Of course, furnaces are major pieces of capital equipment for steel companies. They must be ordered in advance, factories must be built to house them, and their operation must be well timed with the operations of the existing furnaces. This process may take several years to complete. If the steel companies decide that the 20 percent price rise will be permanent, they will probably increase their productive capacity. Then, over the next five years, production may, for example, rise by 40 percent, representing a supply elasticity of 2.0. Instead of the supply being inelastic (0.5), as it was when measured shortly after the price rise, it would be quite elastic (2.0) when measured after five years. In general, then, price elasticity of supply is likely to be higher for long time periods than for short time periods.

Adjustment time is more important in determining elasticity of supply in some industries than it is in others. Some industries, including steel, call for large capital inputs. Other industries, like airlines, employ highly skilled workers—pilots—who require long training periods. Both of these industries are most likely to have larger supply elasticities for long periods than for short periods. By contrast, an industry like window cleaning uses only minor capital goods—a pail, a squeegee, and a

TABLE 6

Estimated Short-Run and Long-Run Price Elasticities of Supply for Selected U.S. Fresh Vegetable Markets, 1919–1955

Fresh Vegetable Market	Short-Run Price Elasticity of Supply	Long-Run Price Elasticity of Supply	Ratio of Long-Run to Short-Run
Beets	0.13	1.0	7.7
Cabbage	0.36	1.2	3.3
Carrots	0.14	0.9	6.4
Celery	0.14	1.0	7.1
Cucumbers	0.29	2.2	7.6
Cauliflower	0.14	1.1	7.9
Eggplant	0.16	0.3	1.9
Green lima beans	0.10	1.7	17.0
Green peas	0.31	4.4	14.2
Green peppers	0.07	0.3	4.3
Lettuce	0.03	0.2	6.7
Onions	0.34	1.0	2.9
Spinach	0.20	4.7	23.5
Tomatoes	0.16	0.9	5.6
Watermelons	0.23	0.5	2.2

Source: Marc Nerlove and William Addison, "Statistical Estimation of Long-Run Elasticities of Supply and Demand," *The Journal of Farm Economics,* November 1958, pp. 861–880. Used by permission of the American Agricultural Economics Association.

strong belt—and it employs low-skilled workers. It should have only a slightly larger elasticity of supply for long time periods than for short time periods.

Unfortunately, there are not many studies available that compare carefully measured short-run versus long-run supply elasticities. However, one such study by Nerlove and Addison provides some interesting results for a number of U.S. fresh vegetable markets. Table 6 lists estimates of short-run and long-run price elasticities of supply. Notice that the short-run elasticities are significantly lower than the long-run equivalents. Prices and supplies

were studied over a thirty-five-year period, and the short run was taken as one production period. The column farthest to the right shows the ratios between the long-run and short-run elasticities. They range from a close to doubling for eggplant to a multiple of over 23 for spinach.

In most instances the elasticity of supply for a product is directly related to the amount of adjustment time that a firm has to change its quantity supplied following a change in price.

Economics in Focus

Supply in the Oil Industry: Drilling, Spilling, and Price Fluctuations

In the oil industry, supply in the long run depends on exploration—drilling in search of new oil fields. If companies do not invest in exploration, worldwide supply eventually will dry up. Decisions about exploration are made in every budget period, and they are affected by fluctuating market conditions.

During the 1970s and early 1980s, buoyed by high prices, the Western oil industry poured a great deal of money into exploration for new oil. This was the era when major new oil fields were tapped in Mexico and the North Sea; the Alaska pipeline was built, and the general outlook for "upstream" operations (exploration and production) was rosy.

Prices were high largely because of OPEC, the Organization of Petroleum Exporting Countries, a cartel that sets quotas on its members' production. But as the 1980s progressed, dissension within OPEC led some members to exceed their quotas. Meanwhile, production by non-OPEC countries was also rising, from 15 million barrels a day in 1977 to 24 million in 1985; and at the same time energy-conservation measures were cutting into demand. The result was a general drop in oil prices throughout the 1980s, with especially big dips in 1986 and 1988.

Though Western oil companies were glad to see OPEC's dominance reduced, they had to adjust their strategies to cope with the decline in prices. Suddenly investments in exploration no longer looked so attractive. Moreover, the attitude among oil company executives seemed to be changing as managers put more emphasis on current profits. "We want to replace reserves," said ARCO chairman Lodwrick Cook in 1989, "but only in the context of profitability."

By the end of the 1980s a new factor was added: a heightened public awareness of environmental dangers. In March 1989 the supertanker *Exxon Valdez* struck a reef in Alaska's Prince William Sound, spilling more than 10 million gallons of crude oil into the waters. The monumental disaster sparked a public outcry, and both state and federal governments began to impose costly new restrictions on the oil industry. Simultaneously there was a movement to produce motor vehicles that would run on cleaner fuels raising doubts about the long-range demand for oil.

In this context many experts predicted that Western oil companies would cut back their exploration efforts and concentrate instead on increasing profits in their refineries. In 1989 major shifts in that direction were already visible. These ups and downs in the oil industry demonstrate the uncertain environment in which business firms must operate. Long-run decisions about oil exploration must constantly be made and remade, even though no one can predict exactly what the future will bring.

Sources: "Oil on Troubled Waters," *The Economist,* May 6, 1989, pp. 59–64; Todd Vogel with John Rossant and Sarah Miller, "Oil's Rude Awakening," *Business Week,* September 26, 1988, pp. 44–45; Toni Mack, "Refined Profits," *Forbes,* May 15, 1989, pp. 110–111; Edgar K. Browning and Jacquelene M. Browning, *Microeconomic Theory and Applications,* 3rd edition (Glenview, Ill.: Scott, Foresman, 1989), pp. 373–375; Cook quotation from Richard W. Stevenson, "Why Exxon's Woes Worry ARCO," *New York Times,* May 14, 1989.

SUMMARY

1. For many important theories of the firm, economists assume that business firms are rational. Rational business firm behavior is defined as attempting to maximize profits and minimize losses. (See page 554.)

2. Economists recognize that firms will not strictly maximize profits. They must make their decisions in the face of uncertainty. Also, firms are often so complex that top management directives aimed at maximizing profits may be compromised. Moreover, firms' top management often pursues goals that are not completely consistent with profit maximization. (See pages 555–556.)

3. Economists and accountants do not define profit in the same way. Accountants concentrate on the funds that flow to and from a firm and tend to ignore implicit costs. What is considered "normal" for a firm to earn, or the minimum that a firm has to earn in order for it to be willing to continue in its present business activity, is considered part of "profit" by accountants, but is recognized as "cost" by economists. Such cost is called "normal profit." Profit in excess of this amount is called "greater-than-normal profit," or "economic profit." "Less-than-normal profit," or "economic loss," will cause a firm to go out of business in the long run. (See pages 555–556.)

4. The level of output at which a firm will maximize its profit or minimize its loss may be identified by examining its total cost and total revenue or its marginal cost and marginal revenue. A firm will maximize its profit at the level of output at which its total revenue exceeds its total cost by the greatest amount. Similarly, a firm will maximize its profit at the level of output at which its marginal cost is equal to its marginal revenue, as long as marginal revenue is greater than marginal cost at somewhat lower levels of output and marginal cost is greater than marginal revenue at somewhat higher levels of output. (See pages 558–559.)

5. In the long run, a firm will go out of business (exit from its industry) if it cannot earn at least normal profit. In the short run, when some of a firm's cost is fixed, it will operate if it can earn enough to recover all of its variable cost and at least some of its fixed cost. If, however, it cannot recover all of its variable cost, the firm will shut down. (See pages 561–562.)

6. Price elasticity of supply measures the percentage change in the quantity of a product supplied in response to a percentage change in the price of that product. This is analogous to the price elasticity of demand concept discussed in Chapter 23. (See page 563.)

7. There are five categories of elasticity. Supply is elastic when the percentage change in the quantity supplied is greater than the percentage change in the price that generated it. Supply is inelastic when the percentage change in the quantity supplied is less than the percentage change in the price that generated it. Supply is unitary elastic when the percentage change in the quantity supplied is exactly equal to the percentage change in the price that generated it. Supply is perfectly inelastic when a change in price causes no response at all in the quantity supplied. Supply is infinitely elastic when a change in price causes an infinite response in the quantity supplied. (See pages 563–564 and Table 5, page 565.)

8. The price elasticity of supply of a product depends on (a) the change in average total cost that is incurred by a firm when it alters the quantity level of its output and (b) the time that it takes a firm to expand or to contract its output level in response to a change in the price of the product. (See pages 565–567.)

KEY TERMS

economic loss: less than normal economic profit (page 556).

economic profit: greater than normal economic profit (page 556).

normal profit: the minimum return a firm must receive in order for it to be willing to continue in its present business (page 556).

price elasticity of supply (E_S): the percentage change in the quantity of a product supplied divided by the percentage change in the price of that product that caused it (page 563).

profit: the difference between revenue and cost—the difference between what the firm takes in from the sale of a product and what it gives up to produce a product (page 555).

satisfice: the seeking of satisfactory profit instead of maximum profit (page 554).

total cost: all the costs, implicit and explicit, that a firm incurs in production (page 556).

total revenue: the total amount of receipts or income that a firm obtains from selling what it produces (page 556).

DISCUSSION QUESTIONS

1. The theory of the firm relies heavily on the assumption that business firms act in a rational manner. Economists define a rational firm as one that tries to maximize its profit. Discuss three reasons why this rationality assumption may not lead to entirely reliable predictions concerning what firms will and will not do.

2. Carefully distinguish between the accountant's concept of profit and the economist's concept of profit. In your answer be sure to show how the economist's terms of normal profit, economic profit, and economic loss fit in. Does zero economic profit mean that the firm earns no accounting profit? Under what conditions might a firm's economic loss be an accounting profit?

3. You learned that a firm will maximize its profit when it produces the level of output at which its total revenue exceeds its total cost by the greatest amount and that this is also where its marginal revenue is equal to its marginal cost. Explain why this is so.

4. Without looking at Figure 1, draw a firm's negatively sloped marginal-revenue curve and its U-shaped marginal-cost curve so that the latter intersects the former at two different levels of output. Compare your diagram with Figure 1 to be sure you have it right. Which output level is the one at which this firm maximizes its profit? Why? Why is the other not a profit-maximizing output?

5. "Economics makes a big deal out of a very simple point. Everyone knows that a firm wants to have its marginal revenue exceed its marginal cost by the greatest possible amount." Do you agree? Explain.

6. "A company makes a long-run decision to go out of business. It necessarily follows that this firm is unable to earn either economic profit or normal profit." True or false? Explain.

7. "A company makes a short-run decision to operate instead of shutting down. It necessarily follows that this firm is able to earn either economic profit or normal profit." True or false? Explain.

8. Would you expect a firm that has fixed cost of $100,000 a day, variable cost of $300,000 a day, and total revenue of $360,000 a day to operate in the short run? Why or why not? Under the same total cost and revenue conditions, do you expect it to stay in business in the long run? Why or why not?

9. Using the formula provided in the chapter, calculate the price elasticity of supply for each of the following cases:

a. The price of certain shoes decreases from $50 to $42 a pair, which causes the quantity supplied of these shoes to decrease from 500,000 pairs a month to 450,000 pairs a month.

b. The price of a certain kind of calculator increases from $8 to $12, which causes the quantity supplied of these calculators to increase from 20,000 a week to 40,000 a week.

c. The price of a certain kind of vacuum cleaner increases from $95 to $100, which causes the quantity supplied of these vacuum cleaners to increase from 900,000 a year to 920,000 a year.

In each of these three cases, determine whether the supply is elastic or inelastic.

10. Why is it that elasticity of supply measurements are independent of the unit of measurement? Does that increase or decrease the usefulness of this concept?

11. Without looking at the diagrams in Table 5, draw a perfectly inelastic supply curve for a product. Compare your diagram with the perfectly inelastic supply-curve diagram in Table 5 to be sure you have it right. Give two examples of products that might logically have perfectly inelastic supply curves.

12. Actual elasticities of supply vary greatly among goods and services. Discuss two important determinants of the price elasticity of supply.

Neoclassical Economics: The Complacent Science

We have spoken of classical economics as the dismal science, a nickname that best described certain theories of Malthus and Ricardo.[1] Malthus, as you will recall, saw population pressure holding wages at or near a bare subsistence level as the economy grew. Ricardo believed that the gains of progress would go mainly to the idle landowning classes, as land rent rose steadily under the pressure of population. At the same time, profits would decline because the accumulation of capital was subject to diminishing returns. Ricardo also saw growth ending in a stagnant state after profits had fallen to the point where capitalists would save no more than would make up for the consumption of raw materials and the depreciation of capital.

These dire predictions did not all come true. In fact, real wages began to rise sometime during the middle of the nineteenth century, and the stationary state seemed to have been pushed ever further into the future.

DISSENT FROM THE CLASSICAL THEORY

Dissent from the classical views took many forms. The greatest of the dissenters was Karl Marx (1818–1883), whose theories we discuss in Chapter 40. However, many early opponents of classical economics wanted to get away from all abstract or deductive theory. These people wanted to substitute what we would now call economic history, economic sociology, or "institutional economics." But begin-

ning in the 1870s,[2] a new kind of economic theory took over, which was later called "neoclassical economics." Outside the English-speaking world, its main center was in Austria. In fact, today's "Austrian school" is purely neoclassical. This new theory was based on demand rather than supply, on utility rather than cost, and on marginal quantities rather than average ones. Its rapid rise to prominence has been called the "utility revolution" or the "marginalist revolution" in economic thought.

Why did the neoclassical ideas win out when they did? Because the first volume of Karl Marx's *Capital* appeared in 1867, some saw the popularity of neoclassical economics as an evasion of the conclusions that Marx had drawn from the labor theory of value.[3] Another explanation was the use by some neoclassical writers of mathematical methods and physical analogies at a time when the natural sciences and mathematics were riding high.

THE COMPLACENT REVOLUTIONARIES

In calling the neoclassical economists and their followers "complacent," what do we mean? For one thing, we mean that they were not dismal. Like many Western Europeans and North Americans of the generation that ended in 1914, they looked back on a century of progress and expected another prosperous century to follow. (Alas, posterity was to disappoint them!) They were not utopians, but some may have been optimistic enough to hope that a better world might be only a century or so away "in the natural course of things."

Few were rigid in their beliefs. Most would be considered today people of good will and liberal re-

1. Even though other important classical economists like Adam Smith and John Stuart Mill were much less dismal than Malthus and Ricardo, one good epithet is often worth a hundred facts.

2. However, these ideas were really much older. For example, J. B. Say, of "Say's Identity" fame, had proposed a utility theory of value and price early in the century.

3. The labor theory of value is explained in Chapter 40.

formers—some very stuffy, others quite erratic. However, most were not very active politically, and none shed blood at any barricade. In fact, most of them were professional economists, who taught at well-known universities for much of their later lives. Coming mainly from the middle classes, they passed most of their time surrounded by cultured upper-middle-class people. Many devoted themselves to the interests of the poor, as seen from "the other side of the tracks." However, as Robert Heilbroner put it in his *Worldly Philosophers,* they saw the world as composed of sheep without wolves. Reasonable optimism plus their reasonably comfortable and quiet lives made them complacent.

Who were the most important of these "revolutionists"? In the first generation of the 1870s, they were William Stanley Jevons of England, Carl Menger of Austria, and Léon Walras of France. These men were all professional economists, who wrote independently of each other. But all concentrated on the problems of microeconomics—the allocation of scarce resources among alternative uses—rather than on growth and development. In the next generation, the English leaders were Alfred Marshall, F. Y. Edgeworth, and A. C. Pigou. In America, they were J. B. Clark, Irving Fisher, and F. W. Taussig. The European leaders were Eugen von Böhm-Bawerk of Austria, Vilfredo Pareto of Italy, and Knut Wicksell of Sweden. Of this whole group, the most influential in English-speaking countries, and by a wide margin, has been Alfred Marshall. Marshall's *Principles of Economics,* first published in 1890, went through eight editions during its author's life. It replaced Mill's *Principles of Political Economy* as the standard advanced text for its subject in its generation.

CONTRIBUTIONS OF THE NEOCLASSICAL ECONOMISTS

Neoclassical economics became less popular after 1914 because it failed to speak "with one voice" on the great problems of the day: the war economy of World War I, the postwar adjustment in the early 1920s, and finally the Great Depression. Individuals, of course, talked very good sense on particular aspects of all these problems. In the case of the depression, it has been argued that the strongly neoclassical University of Chicago economics faculty as a group had an excellent record throughout the crisis. But one swallow does not make a summer, and Chicago was only one campus among many.

Alfred Marshall (1842–1924)

If they couldn't handle the postwar readjustment, the Great Depression, or other major problems of their day, why bother with these economists' ideas at all? We are interested in them mainly because so many of our contemporary ideas, especially our microeconomic ideas, spring from these writers' works. Let us note them briefly.

One of their ideas was that economics could and should aspire to the status of a pure science. These economists felt that the subject should rise above the debating-tool status that was implied by its older name, political economy.

Another of the neoclassical ideas, as mentioned earlier, was that economics should concentrate on problems of the allocation of resources under given conditions. That is, it can best proceed by examining conditions as though they changed only by small marginal increments and only one at a time, other things being equal. Their principles were most concerned with the "special case" of the more developed countries that had market systems.

In the neoclassical view, demand is determined by the marginal utilities of various goods to individual people. It is at least as important a determinant of value and price as are cost and supply. Marshall speaks of demand and supply as the two blades of a pair of scissors, neither one capable of cutting by itself. More extreme writers try to reduce "cost" further to the utility of alternative products, and to the utility of leisure as opposed to work.

Marginal productivity analysis, often with ethical implications, was worked out mainly by J. B. Clark. The first welfare economists were Edgeworth, Pareto, and Pigou. They derived conditions under which a policy change could be objectively called socially superior or inferior.

Most of the "apparatus" of microeconomics today comes from Marshall's work. The standard diagrams showing supply and demand, elasticity, and the distinction between the short-run and long-run periods were all developed, though not necessarily originated, by Marshall. The use of economic models to determine unknowns in a general equilibrium system comes from Walras. Among those who developed real (nonmonetary) interest theory were Böhm-Bawerk, Fisher, Clark, and their followers.

The term *macroeconomics* was unknown in the heyday of neoclassical economics. However, the neoclassical writers made important contributions to some macroeconomic concepts. On the monetary side, equations of exchange relating to money, incomes, and prices were developed by Fisher in the United States and by Pigou in Britain. Fisher went on to develop the quantity theory of money—really a quantity-of-money theory of the price level—more fully than had ever been done before. He also worked on schemes of price-level stabilization. In monetary interest theory, too, Fisher's name is important, though it was Wicksell who provided the most useful steppingstone to contemporary thinking.

In his *Structure of Scientific Revolutions,* the philosopher and historian of science Thomas Kuhn distinguishes normal from revolutionary science. Normal science solves more or less routine problems. Revolutionary science concentrates on discovering anomalies in the earlier theory and on developing new or modified theories for the normal science of the next era.

When we apply these ideas to economics, neoclassical economics, like many other kinds, is mainly normal science or "puzzle-solving." Its problem may be that, since about 1914, it has come to contain so little beyond this level, and to pay so little attention to the real-world anomalies that have developed.

Pure Competition

Monopoly

Monopolistic Competition and Oligopoly

Oligopoly: The Real World

PART VIII

MARKET STRUCTURES AND ECONOMIC PERFORMANCE

PART VIII

26
Pure Competition

Preview The last two chapters have helped you to understand some of the most important concepts that economists use to predict the actions of business firms. Because all firms are assumed to be rational, what each will supply depends upon its costs and revenues.

In this and the next several chapters, we view firms in the context of their markets. Every business firm operates in one or more markets, and not always on the same side of the market. For example, General Motors Corporation is a buyer in the steel market and a seller in the automobile market. You will learn that the way in which markets are organized has an important effect on consumer welfare. A large number of buyers may be exploited by a single seller, whereas those buyers might get a much better deal if the market were composed of several or a great many sellers.

In this chapter we shall briefly introduce four sellers' market structures—pure competition, pure monopoly, monopolistic competition, and oligopoly—and then focus on the first of these. Monopoly will be presented in Chapter 27, monopolistic competition in Chapter 28, and oligopoly in both Chapters 28 and 29.

In this chapter, after carefully defining pure competition, we explain the model. Alternative short-run equilibria, as well as long-run equilibrium, are described. You will see that, although some industries come quite close to it, the pure competition model is an abstract idea and not exactly representative of any real-world industry.

Pure competition is sometimes held out to be the "best of all possible worlds"—the ideal market structure—if only it could be attained. We shall examine the basis of such arguments and end by presenting some arguments in opposition to this point of view.

FOUR SELLERS' MARKET STRUCTURES

Classification is a tricky business and often involves a number of arbitrary distinctions. However, most economists feel comfortable with the idea of four different sellers' market structures: (1) pure competition, (2) pure monopoly, (3) monopolistic competition, and (4) oligopoly. There are three important bases for distinguishing among these types. The first is the number of firms that sell in the market. The second is whether or not the product is differentiated. That is, do all firms in the market sell the same standardized product, or do buyers believe there are differences among the products sold by the different firms? The third is how easy it is for new firms to enter the market.

In **pure competition** there are a large number of firms in the market. All the firms sell a standardized product. Entry to the market is perfectly easy. At the opposite pole is a **pure monopoly** market, with only a single seller. No product differentiation or entry into the market is possible. In fact, there is no other product offered in the market, and entry is completely blocked. **Monopolistic competition**, like pure competition, is a market type in which there are many sellers and entry into the market is easy. Unlike pure competition, however, each firm sells a somewhat different product. Buyers are not indifferent among the products sold by the many firms that sell in a monopolistically competitive market. Finally, **oligopoly** is a market type in which there are few sellers. The degree of product differentiation among the firms ranges from very little in some markets to a great deal in others. The ease of entry also differs from market to market, but generally it is not very easy to enter an oligopoly market.

Table 1 summarizes the characteristics of the four different sellers' market structures based on the three distinguishing features of markets.

There are four different sellers' market structures: pure competition, pure monopoly, monopolistic competition, and oligopoly. These market types are distinguished from one another by the number of firms selling in the market, product differentiation, and ease of entry into the market.

These different market structures, which will be much more fully explained in this chapter and the next three, give rise to different patterns of behavior by firms. For example, firms in pure competition can readily ignore their rivals in the market, but those in an oligopoly market must pay a great deal of attention to what their rivals do and might do. In turn, how firms conduct their rivalry in a market strongly affects the economic performance of that market. Consumers may pay lower prices for better products when buying from a monopolistically competitive firm than when buying from a pure monopolist.

The different market structures give rise to different patterns of behavior by the firms that operate in them.

TABLE 1
Structural Characteristics of Four Different Sellers' Market Types

Market Type	Distinguishing Structural Criteria		
	Number of Firms	Product Differentiation	Ease of Entry
Pure competition	many	none	easy
Pure monopoly	one	none	impossible
Monopolistic competition	many	some	easy
Oligopoly	few	varying amounts	varying degrees of difficulty

PURE COMPETITION

The term **competition** is used in two different senses in economics. First, it may be used to describe *rivalry* among sellers or buyers. One firm may be said to "compete" with another for a certain buyer's business, or one buyer may "compete" with another to obtain certain products from a seller. Adam Smith recognized competition in this "rivalry" sense more than two hundred years ago in his *Wealth of Nations*. That is still a common way to use the term. Most business people today think of competition as meaning the striving among a number of rivals in a contest aimed at obtaining the purchase or the sale of a particular product. The second sense in which the term *competition* is used in economics is as a label for the specific market type that we are about to discuss: the market structure called *pure competition*. It is important not to confuse the two meanings. Competition in the rivalry sense may be used in referring to *any* market in which there are rivals. However, pure competition refers *only* to the specific market structure that bears this name.

Pure competition describes a market in which there are so many firms that each acts as though it can exert no control over price. In pure competition, each individual firm sells such a tiny part of the total market supply that it assumes its actions have no effect on the market price. Because a small wheat farm is just one of over a million farms in the same market, it is very unlikely to produce less wheat this year in an attempt to raise the price of wheat. Likewise, an owner of 100 shares of General Motors stock is not likely to hold off selling 50 of them on the ground that this would depress the price of his or her remaining 50 shares. About 613 million shares of General Motors stock are outstanding, and tens of thousands are generally traded every day. Thus, the owner feels that the additional supply of 50 shares is quite insignificant.

The term *competition* can be used to describe rivalry in a market, or it can refer specifically to one kind of market structure—pure competition—which is a market in which there are so many firms that each acts as though it can exert no control over price.

Of course, the equilibrium price really *is* affected by a change in a seller's supply. However, the price change may be so small (for example, one ten-thousandth of a cent) that it is not even noticed. The important characteristic of pure competition is that each firm *believes* that it cannot change the price. For this reason, it assumes the role of a **price taker**, one that accepts the price as given and therefore does not adjust its own sales so as to try to influence that price.

In a purely competitive market, each firm believes that it cannot change the price, therefore, it acts as a price taker—one that accepts the price as given.

Conditions for Pure Competition

A purely competitive market requires: (1) many sellers, (2) standardized product, (3) no artificial restrictions placed upon price or quantity, and (4) easy entry and exit to and from the market. Each of these conditions bears a relationship to our definition of pure competition.

Many Sellers We are not able to say whether the minimum requirement of "many firms" means 1,000 or 50,000 firms. We can only say that the number of firms must be large enough so that each firm (because it is such a small part of the market) believes that it cannot affect the market price by selling more or less.

Standardized Product The product of the various firms in the market must be so standardized (so much like one another) that customers do not prefer one seller's product over another's. Since buyers do not care which seller's product they purchase, any firm that raised its price above the price charged by its competitors ("rivals") would lose all of its sales. If the products of the various firms were differentiated so that customers would not be indifferent among the products sold by the rival firms, then a company could affect the price by changing the quantity that it offers for sale. In such a case, we would *not* have pure competition.

No Artificial Restrictions   Any artificial restriction on the free movement of prices or on the quantity of output keeps a market from being purely competitive. Pure competition cannot exist under government price setting (such as price freezes) or agreements among competitors as to prices or the quantities to be sold (such as a collusive deal that involves price fixing). Any action of this sort prevents the free market forces from determining the market price. The firms would no longer be price takers since either through effective lobbying they persuade the government to set the price or through effective collusion the price is set by the sellers themselves.

Easy Entry and Exit   Sellers must be free to enter and to leave a purely competitive market, and a newly entered firm must be able to sell its product as easily as a long-established firm. Any barriers to entry into a market would be inconsistent with the pure competition model.

A purely competitive market requires many sellers, standardized product, no artificial restrictions placed on price or quantity, and easy entry and exit to and from the market.

Perfect Competition

Pure competition may be taken one step further to what economists call **perfect competition**. Besides the pure competition conditions that we just described, buyers and sellers in a perfectly competitive market also have complete and continuous knowledge of all bids and offers made in the market and the full mobility to take immediate action. In a strongly competitive setting, this perfect knowledge or complete information, combined with the full mobility to take advantage of it, results in a market in which there is only one price prevailing at any given time. To explain this condition, we shall use the case of a large trading village where farmers and merchants meet once a week in the village square to sell and buy corn. Suppose that in one part of the square farmers were selling—and merchants were buying—large amounts of corn for $3 a bushel. If a farmer knew about those transactions and was able to get over to that part of the square, he or she would not be willing to sell corn anywhere else in the square for less than $3 a bushel. Likewise, a knowledgeable, mobile, and competitive merchant would not be willing to buy corn anywhere else in the square for more than $3 a bushel. That single price of $3 would be the only one that could prevail at that particular time and place.

In perfect competition, all the pure competition conditions exist, plus buyers and sellers have complete and continuous knowledge or information of all bids and offers made in the market and the full mobility to take immediate action.

THE PURE COMPETITION MODEL

So far you have learned that individual firms in a purely competitive market are powerless price takers. The only decision that each needs to make is whether to produce and, if so, how much. The pure competition model that you will learn next clearly shows the outcome of this decision, for both the short run and the long run.

The Firm versus the Market

In dealing with the pure competition model, it is essential to keep separate the concept of the individual economic enterprise, which we call the *firm*, and the group of competing firms or the industry, which constitutes the *market*.

The market-demand curve (the demand that faces the whole industry) is expected to be a normal downward-sloping curve. The product of this industry competes with the products of other industries. Because of the substitution effect, a larger quantity is demanded at lower prices and a smaller quantity is demanded at higher prices. When this is combined with the income effect, which explains that buyers can afford more at lower prices and less at higher prices, the result is a normal, negatively sloped demand curve. Such a market-demand curve is pictured in panel (a) of Figure 1.

FIGURE 1
Market and Firm in Pure Competition

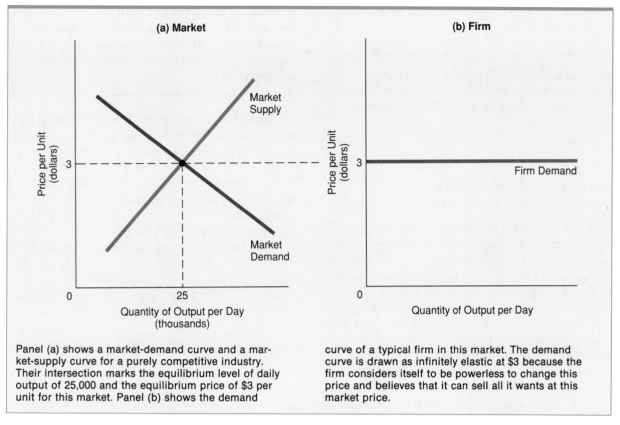

(a) Market

(b) Firm

Panel (a) shows a market-demand curve and a market-supply curve for a purely competitive industry. Their intersection marks the equilibrium level of daily output of 25,000 and the equilibrium price of $3 per unit for this market. Panel (b) shows the demand

curve of a typical firm in this market. The demand curve is drawn as infinitely elastic at $3 because the firm considers itself to be powerless to change this price and believes that it can sell all it wants at this market price.

The market-supply curve (the total supply that is offered by all the firms in the industry) is expected to be a normal upward-sloping curve. As explained in Chapter 5, profit-minded companies are willing to supply more at higher prices and less at lower prices, other things being equal. Such a market-supply curve is also pictured in panel (a) of Figure 1.

In the pure competition model, the market-demand curve (the demand that faces the whole industry) is expected to be a normal downward-sloping curve and the market-supply curve (the total supply offered by all the firms in the industry) is expected to be a normal upward-sloping curve.

At the intersection of the market-demand and market-supply curves is the equilibrium market output and price. Panel (a) of Figure 1 shows that 25,000 units are bought and sold each day at a price of $3 per unit.

At the intersection of the market-demand and market-supply curves is the equilibrium market output and price.

As explained earlier, each pure competitor firm takes this price ($3) as a set fact. So from the firm's viewpoint, it faces a perfectly flat or infinitely elastic demand curve, as shown in panel (b) of Figure 1. The firm believes that it can sell all it wants to at the market price of $3. It also is aware that it can sell none of its standardized product at a higher-than-market price, say $3.01, and that it would be foolish to offer any at a lower-than-market price, say $2.99, since it can sell all it wants to at the $3.00 market price.

Because purely competitive firms are price takers, each individual firm faces a perfectly flat (horizontal straight line) or infinitely elastic demand curve.

Demand and Revenue for the Firm in Pure Competition

A firm's demand schedule and curve allow us to find its various revenue schedules and curves. The price that a firm charges multiplied by the quantity of output that it sells is the **total revenue** that the firm receives. Table 2 shows five different quantities of output that a pure competitor firm might sell. Suppose that market price is $3 per unit. If it decides to sell 5 units a day, it receives total revenue of $15. Total revenue is $18 for 6 units, $21 for 7 units, and so on. Each time the firm raises its output by one unit, total revenue increases by a constant amount equal to the market price. Figure 2 shows the total-revenue curve for the company whose data appear in Table 2. For a pure competitor, this curve is always a straight line drawn with a positive slope out of the origin.

TABLE 2
Revenue for a Purely Competitive Firm

(1) Market Price	(2) Quantity Sold	(3) Total Revenue	(4) Average Revenue	(5) Marginal Revenue
$3	5	$15	$3	
				$3
3	6	18	3	
				3
3	7	21	3	
				3
3	8	24	3	
				3
3	9	27	3	

The price that a firm charges multiplied by the quantity of output that it sells is the total revenue that the firm receives. Each time the firm raises its output by one unit, total revenue increases by a constant amount equal to the market price.

Average revenue is total revenue divided by the quantity of goods sold. In Table 2, column 3 divided by column 2 equals column 4. Average revenue is the price per unit as a buyer looks at it and the revenue per unit from the firm's point of view. Therefore, an average-revenue curve is just another name for a demand curve. Figure 2 shows that they are one and the same.

We demonstrate the relationships as follows:

$$TR = P \times Q$$

$$AR = \frac{TR}{Q}$$

$$AR = \frac{P \times Q}{Q}$$

$$AR = P$$

where TR is total revenue, AR is average revenue, P is the price per unit of the product, and Q is the quantity of units of the product sold.

Average revenue is total revenue divided by the quantity of goods sold. It is the price per unit from the buyer's standpoint and the revenue per unit from the firm's standpoint. Thus, the average revenue curve and the demand curve are the same.

Marginal revenue, as you will remember from the last chapter, is the extra revenue that a firm receives when it sells another unit of output. Since a pure competitor firm can sell all it wants to at the market price, it is the market price that the firm receives when it sells an additional unit. In pure competition, marginal revenue will always be equal to price. Table 2 shows that whenever the firm decides to sell one more unit of output, its marginal revenue—its addition to total revenue—

FIGURE 2
Revenue for a Firm in Pure Competition

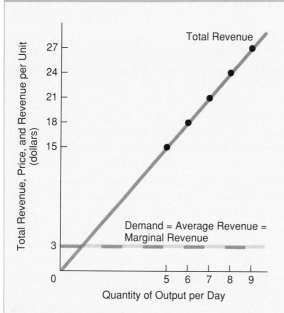

The linear curve drawn out of the origin is a purely competitive firm's total-revenue curve. It takes this shape because total revenue is price times quantity, and in pure competition, price remains the same as quantity is varied. In this example, the market price is $3, so that as the firm increases its level of output by one, total revenue increases by $3.

The horizontal curve drawn at $3 is this firm's demand curve (as in panel (b) of Figure 1, but graphically lower down because the scaling is less stretched out here) and is also its average-revenue curve and its marginal-revenue curve. Average revenue is the price per unit or the revenue per unit and is therefore just another name for a demand curve. Marginal revenue—the extra revenue that a firm receives when it sells an additional unit of output—is equal to the market price in pure competition.

will be the market price of $3. Figure 2 shows that the pure competitor firm's demand (average-revenue) curve is also its marginal-revenue curve.

Marginal revenue is the extra revenue a firm receives when it sells another unit of output. In pure competition, marginal revenue will always be equal to price. Thus, the marginal revenue curve and the demand (average-revenue) curve are always the same.

To summarize, in the case of pure competition, a firm's infinitely elastic demand curve, which is drawn at the market price, is not only its average-revenue curve but also its marginal-revenue curve.

Supply and Cost for the Firm in Pure Competition

We have described a purely competitive market as one in which firms believe that they can sell all they want to at the market price. In order to determine just how much each firm wants to sell—how much supply each firm will offer—we will use the concepts that you learned in Chapter 25. There you learned that rational firms—those that maximize profit or minimize loss—will seek to supply the level of output at which their total revenue exceeds their total cost by the maximum amount and so where their marginal revenue is equal to their marginal cost.

To illustrate this point, in Figure 3 (page 578) we have redrawn the pure competitor's total-revenue curve from Figure 2 and, beneath it, its marginal-revenue curve, also from Figure 2. In the lower graph, the vertical scaling has been stretched out (as in Figure 1) so that you can see it better. We have added the firm's short-run total-cost curve in the upper diagram and its short-run marginal-cost curve in the lower one. These data are taken from Table 3 (page 579), which also repeats the total-revenue and marginal-revenue data from Table 2. Profit maximization takes place at between 7 and 8 units. At this level of output, the pure competitor's marginal cost of $3 is equal to its marginal revenue of $3, which is the prevailing market price. Given the requirement of having to produce whole units, producing either 7 or 8 units is an equilibrium situation because the firm is obtaining maximum profit.

Rational firms seek to supply the level of output at which their total revenue exceeds their total cost by the maximum amount (where marginal revenue is equal to marginal cost).

With this reasoning—and with what you learned in the previous chapter about when a firm will shut down rather than produce in the short run—we are able to show that a pure competitor's

FIGURE 3
**Equilibrium Output of
a Purely Competitive Firm**

The level of output at which this purely competitive firm maximizes its profit is 7 or 8 units. This is shown in the upper diagram by where the firm's total-revenue curve exceeds its short-run total-cost curve by the greatest amount and in the lower diagram by where its short-run marginal-cost curve intersects its marginal-revenue curve from below.

marginal-cost curve (above its average variable cost) is also its short-run supply curve. You can see this by examining the three diagrams in Figure 4 (page 580). Panel (a) pictures five alternative market equilibria. Each change in market price and output (such as from $3 and 25,000 units to $4 and 35,000 units) is brought about by a change in market demand (a shift in the market demand curve). Panel (b) pictures the effect on a typical firm—the firm that we studied earlier in this chapter—in this purely competitive market. The firm's five alternative horizontal demand curves correspond to five different market equilibria. Each is labeled to show that it is also the firm's average-revenue and marginal-revenue curve. In order to determine how much this firm will supply at each price, we examine its marginal-cost and average-variable-cost curves. Supply takes place where the firm's marginal cost is equal to its marginal revenue (the price). For example, at a price of $3, the firm will supply between 7 and 8 units per day, and at $5 it will supply between 9 and 10 units per day. Recall from the last chapter that the only exception to this rule is when, in the short run, a firm's revenue is not enough to cover its variable cost. In that case— when it stands to lose more than its fixed cost—the firm will minimize its loss by shutting down. In the short run, the firm will produce no output as long as its average revenue cannot at least cover its average variable cost. Therefore, that part of a pure competitor firm's marginal-cost curve that lies below its average-variable-cost curve is not part of its supply curve. In our example, the part of the marginal-cost curve that lies below $1 is not part of the firm's supply curve since the firm would not supply any output at prices under $1. Finally, panel (c) shows what we have now demonstrated—that the pure competitor's short-run supply curve is the part of its marginal-cost curve that lies above its average variable cost.

A pure competitor's marginal-cost curve (above its average variable cost) is also its short-run supply curve.

Once we have found a typical firm's short-run supply curve, it takes only simple summation to derive the short-run market-supply curve. A mar-

TABLE 3
Revenue and Cost for a Purely Competitive Firm

(1) Market Price	(2) Quantity Sold	(3) Total Revenue	(4) Marginal Revenue	(5) Total Cost	(6) Marginal Cost
$3	5	$15		$12	
			$3		$1
3	6	18		13	
			3		2
3	7	21		15	
			3		3
3	8	24		18	
			3		4
3	9	27		22	

ket-supply curve is the sum of the supply curves of all the individual firms in that market.[1] If marginal cost for firms changes, market supply will change. Of course, since in pure competition each individual firm's supply represents only a very small part of market supply, any change in marginal cost for only one or a few companies will not affect market supply very much.

A market-supply curve is the sum of the supply curves of all the individual firms in a market. If marginal cost for firms changes, market supply will change.

Profitability of Firms in Pure Competition

How profitable are purely competitive firms? The answer depends upon whether we are dealing with the short run or the long run. Before presenting these cases, let us quickly review what you learned in Chapter 25 about how economists define profit. Normal profit (an amount of profit that is equal to a firm's opportunity cost of remaining in its market) is considered a cost. Economic profit, then, is a return that is greater than opportunity cost. A re-

1. We assume that the market is not so significant as to have supply changes affect resource prices.

turn less than opportunity cost is an economic loss. With these definitions in mind, we shall look at short-run and long-run equilibrium in pure competition.

Economic profit is a return that is greater than opportunity cost (greater than normal profit). A return less than opportunity cost (less than normal profit) is an economic loss.

Short-Run Equilibrium In the short run, firms in pure competition may have an economic profit, an economic loss, or just a normal profit. Figure 5 pictures the three possible short-run equilibrium positions. (These are not a continuation of our previous example. We have chosen to use a less lumpy example for the remainder of this chapter so that we shall no longer be bothered with dual solutions for our equilibrium output level.) Each of the three diagrams shows a company's profit-maximization position when it faces a market price of $10. Its marginal-cost curve (*MC*) intersects its marginal-revenue curve ($D = AR = MR$) from below at an output level of 20,000 units a day. To enable us to see whether the firm is earning economic profit, normal profit, or suffering economic loss, we show an average-total-cost curve (*ATC*) in each of the three diagrams. Note that average total cost (cost per unit of output) at the equilibrium level of output is different in each of the three cases shown. At

FIGURE 4
Derivation of a Purely Competitive Firm's Short-Run Supply Curve

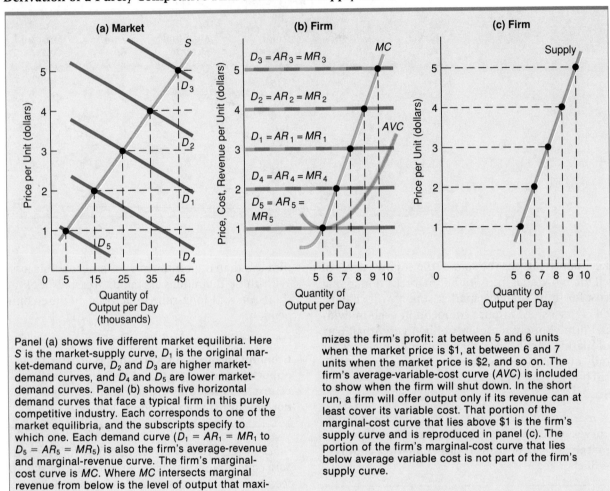

Panel (a) shows five different market equilibria. Here S is the market-supply curve, D_1 is the original market-demand curve, D_2 and D_3 are higher market-demand curves, and D_4 and D_5 are lower market-demand curves. Panel (b) shows five horizontal demand curves that face a typical firm in this purely competitive industry. Each corresponds to one of the market equilibria, and the subscripts specify to which one. Each demand curve ($D_1 = AR_1 = MR_1$ to $D_5 = AR_5 = MR_5$) is also the firm's average-revenue and marginal-revenue curve. The firm's marginal-cost curve is MC. Where MC intersects marginal revenue from below is the level of output that maxi-

mizes the firm's profit: at between 5 and 6 units when the market price is $1, at between 6 and 7 units when the market price is $2, and so on. The firm's average-variable-cost curve (AVC) is included to show when the firm will shut down. In the short run, a firm will offer output only if its revenue can at least cover its variable cost. That portion of the marginal-cost curve that lies above $1 is the firm's supply curve and is reproduced in panel (c). The portion of the firm's marginal-cost curve that lies below average variable cost is not part of the firm's supply curve.

the equilibrium point in each panel, the vertical distance (if any) between average total cost and average revenue (price) shows the deviation from normal profit per unit of output. In panel (a), the company is earning an economic profit. At equilibrium, average revenue is $3 higher than average total cost ($10 − $7 = $3). The firm in panel (b) is experiencing an economic loss. At equilibrium, average total cost is $2 higher than average revenue ($12 − $10 = $2). Since it sells 20,000 units per day, the firm suffers a total economic loss of $40,000 a day ($2 × 20,000 = $40,000). In this diagram we have included the firm's average-vari-

able-cost curve (AVC) to show that it will indeed supply the 20,000 units, since at that level of output its average revenue is greater than its average variable cost. If average variable cost had been greater than average revenue at equilibrium, the firm would of course have shut down. In panel (c), the firm has neither an economic profit nor an economic loss, as it is earning just a normal profit. At equilibrium, its ATC curve is tangent to its AR curve so that its average revenue ($10) is equal to its average total cost ($10).

Will the three alternative equilibrium positions pictured in Figure 5 persist? Yes, they will, in the

FIGURE 5
Three Alternative Short-Run Equilibrium Profit Positions for Firms in Pure Competition

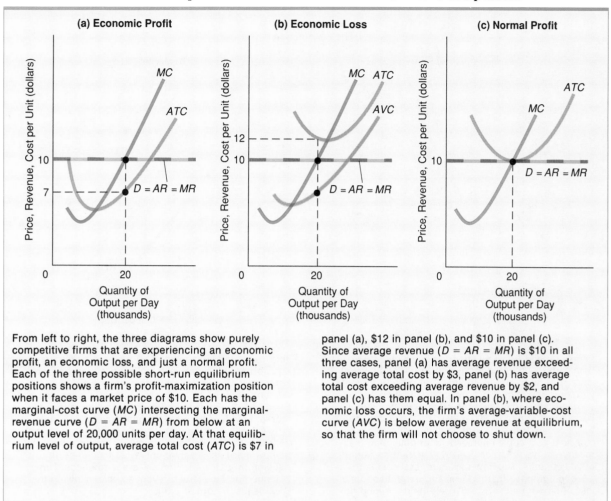

From left to right, the three diagrams show purely competitive firms that are experiencing an economic profit, an economic loss, and just a normal profit. Each of the three possible short-run equilibrium positions shows a firm's profit-maximization position when it faces a market price of $10. Each has the marginal-cost curve (*MC*) intersecting the marginal-revenue curve (*D = AR = MR*) from below at an output level of 20,000 units per day. At that equilibrium level of output, average total cost (*ATC*) is $7 in panel (a), $12 in panel (b), and $10 in panel (c). Since average revenue (*D = AR = MR*) is $10 in all three cases, panel (a) has average revenue exceeding average total cost by $3, panel (b) has average total cost exceeding average revenue by $2, and panel (c) has them equal. In panel (b), where economic loss occurs, the firm's average-variable-cost curve (*AVC*) is below average revenue at equilibrium, so that the firm will not choose to shut down.

short run. Remember that the short run is defined as a period of time that is not long enough for firms to make all the adjustments that they would like to make. There is always some fixed cost in the short run. When the companies in the market suffer an economic loss, they would like to exit from the market, but the short run does not allow enough time for them to liquidate their assets and leave. By contrast, when the companies in the market earn an economic profit, it is likely that firms in other markets or entirely new firms would like to enter this market. Again, the short run does not allow enough time for these changes to take place.

In the short run, firms in pure competition may have an economic profit, an economic loss, or just a normal profit.

Long-Run Equilibrium In the long run, there is enough time for firms to adjust their previously fixed inputs so that they can leave or enter a market. In fact, "easy" exit and entry is a condition of the pure competition model. Whenever firms suffer an economic loss, the model dictates that in the long run they will exit from the market, and when-

FIGURE 6
Achieving Long-Run Equilibrium Through Exit or Entry in Pure Competition

The Case of Exit

(a) Firm

(b) Market

Panels (a) and (b) show a market in which an economic loss is suffered in the short run and how exit eliminates such loss in the long run. Short-run equilibrium in the market occurs where the market-demand curve intersects the original market-supply curve at an output of 200 million units and a price of $10. For the firm, short-run equilibrium is where its marginal-cost curve intersects its original marginal-revenue curve (original $D = AR = MR$) at an output of 20,000 units. The firm's average total cost is $14 at equilibrium, so that the firm suffers an economic loss of $4 per unit ($14 − $10 = $4). In the long run, firms will exit, so that the market-supply curve will

shift to the left, as shown in panel (b). A new market equilibrium (long-run) is established where the market-supply-after-exit curve intersects the market-demand curve at an output level of 150 million and a price of $12. The typical firm that remains in the market now faces a new demand curve at $12 (new $D = AR = MR$). It adjusts its daily level of output to 25,000 units (where its marginal-cost curve intersects its new marginal-revenue curve). At this long-run equilibrium point, the firm's average-total-cost curve is tangent to its average-revenue curve, showing that it earns just a normal profit.

ever firms earn economic profit, the model dictates that in the long run new firms will enter the market. As you will see, under conditions of economic loss, the exit of some firms allows the remaining companies to earn normal profit. Similarly, under conditions of economic profit, the entry of new firms eats away the economic profit and leaves all the companies with normal profit. Thus, no matter whether firms had an economic loss, an economic profit, or just a normal profit in the short run, all will earn just normal profit in long-run equilibrium. These facts are illustrated in Figure 6. The top half shows the effect that exit has on market supply

and so also on the equilibrium market price upon which firms act. The bottom half shows the effect that entry has on market supply and on the equilibrium price.

In Figure 6 (panels a and b) we begin by showing a firm with an economic loss in the short run (as in Figure 5b) and the market that it is in. The market is in short-run equilibrium when it supplies 200 million units of output per day at a price of $10 per unit. The firm is suffering an economic loss of $4 per unit (at equilibrium output of 20,000 units per day its average total cost is $14 while its average revenue is $10). In the long run, firms will

The Case of Entry

(c) Firm

(d) Market

Panels (c) and (d) show a market in which economic profit is earned in the short run and how entry eliminates such profit in the long run. Short-run equilibrium in the market occurs where the market-demand curve intersects the original market-supply curve at an output of 200 million units and a price of $10. For the firm, short-run equilibrium is where its marginal-cost curve intersects its original marginal-revenue curve (original $D = AR = MR$) at an output of 20,000 units. The firm's average total cost is $9 at equilibrium, so that the firm enjoys an economic profit of $1 per unit ($10 − $9 = $1). In the long run, firms will enter, so that the market-

supply curve will shift to the right, as shown in panel (d). A new market equilibrium (long-run) is established where the market-supply-after-entry curve intersects the market-demand curve at an output level of 250 million and a price of $8. The typical firm now faces a new demand curve at $8 (new $D = AR = MR$). It adjusts its daily level of output to 15,000 units (where its marginal-cost curve intersects its new marginal-revenue curve). At this long-run equilibrium point, the firm's average-total-cost curve is tangent to its average-revenue curve, showing that it earns just a normal profit.

begin to exit. As firms leave the market, the short-run market-supply curve shifts to the left (panel b) because it is now composed of the marginal-cost curves of fewer firms. Long-run equilibrium occurs at the lower level of market output of 150 million units and at the higher price of $12 per unit. The companies that remain in the market earn just a normal profit. The typical surviving firm pictured in our example is in long-run equilibrium when it now produces 25,000 units per day at a price of $12 per unit.

In panels (c) and (d), we begin by showing a firm with an economic profit in the short run (as in

Figure 5a) and the market that it is in. The market is in short-run equilibrium when it supplies 200 million units of output a day at a price of $10 a unit. The firm is earning an economic profit of $1 a unit (at equilibrium output of 20,000 units a day its average revenue is $10 and its average total cost is $9). In the long run, firms will enter this market. As firms enter, the short-run market-supply curve shifts to the right (panel d) because it is now composed of the marginal-cost curves of more firms. Long-run equilibrium occurs at the higher market output of 250 million units and at the lower price of $8 per unit. The firms in the market earn normal profit. The typical firm pictured in our example is in long-run equilibrium when it produces 15,000 units a day at $8 a unit.

In the long run, firms can adjust their previously fixed inputs so that they can leave or enter a market. Economic profit encourages new firms to enter, and economic loss encourages firms to exit. Thus, no matter whether firms had an economic loss, an economic profit, or just a normal profit in the short run, all will earn just a normal profit in long-run equilibrium.

Long-Run Market Supply

You have learned that the short-run market supply curve in a purely competitive market is the sum of the marginal-cost curves of the firms in that market. As firms leave or enter the market, the supply curve shifts to the left or right. Now we must examine the long-run supply curve—that is, the curve that includes the effects of entry and exit in response to changes in market price. The shape of the long-run market-supply curve is caused by *shifts* in the cost curves of the individual firms that come with expansion and contraction of total output in the market. This adds a new aspect to the explanation of cost and price in the long run.

FIGURE 7
Long-Run Market Supply in Pure Competition—The Case of Constant Cost

This purely competitive market is in long-run equilibrium where the short-run market-supply curve (S_1) intersects the market-demand curve (D_1) so that the daily output is 200 million units, which sell at $10 each. The typical firm shown produces 20,000 units per day.

This long-run equilibrium is disrupted by a shift to the right of the market-demand curve (D_1 to D_2). A short-run equilibrium is reached where the new demand curve (D_2) intersects the supply curve (S_1) at an output of 280 million units per day, sold at $16 per unit. The firm's new demand curve is $D_2 = AR_2 = MR_2$. The firm is in short-run equilibrium when it

adjusts its output to 28,000 units per day so as to earn $4 a unit economic profit. In the long run, firms will enter this market. This entry is reflected in the market diagram as a shift to the right of the short-run market-supply curve (S_1 to S_2). A new long-run market equilibrium is attained where S_2 intersects D_2 so that the market now sells 360 million units at the original price of $10 each. The firm reverts to its original long-run equilibrium position. It again produces 20,000 units per day. The increase in market production from 200 million to 360 million per day did not affect average total cost. The long-run supply curve is perfectly or infinitely elastic.

The long-run supply curve in a purely competitive market shows the cost effects of entry and exit in response to changes in market price.

We shall discuss three possible cases: (1) long-run supply in a constant-cost market, (2) long-run supply in an increasing-cost market, and (3) long-run supply in a decreasing-cost market. In each case we shall begin with the market in long-run equilibrium so that each firm earns just a normal profit. Then we shall assume a rise in market demand and price that will allow firms to earn an economic profit in the short run.[2] Then in the long run, when other firms enter the market, you will learn how the new market equilibrium is formed: at the same price in the constant-cost case, at a higher price in the increasing-cost case, and at a lower price in the decreasing-cost case.

The Constant-Cost Case In the constant-cost case, long-run changes in the level of market output do not affect the average total cost of producing the output, so that long-run prices remain the same. The presence of more or fewer firms in the market does not affect the cost to individual firms. Each firm's average total cost curve remains the same from one long-run equilibrium to the next.

As the market expands, there is greater demand for the types of labor, capital, and natural resources that are used by the firms producing the product exchanged in this market. If these inputs are in abundant supply, if they are unspecialized, or if the market uses only a very small part of their available supply, the increased demand will bring no significant change in the prices of these inputs. Therefore, the average- and marginal-cost curves of the firms in the market will not shift because of the market's expansion. After new firms enter, the average total costs of the companies in the market will be the same as they were before the expansion

of the market. In the long run, costs are constant. Let us examine the case of constant cost in graphic form.

We begin in Figure 7b with a purely competitive market in long-run equilibrium. The market short-run supply curve (S_1) intersects the market-demand curve (D_1) at a level of output of 200 million units a day and at a price of $10 a unit. The firm diagram in Figure 7a pictures a typical firm in that market. It accepts the market price of $10 and maximizes its profit by producing 20,000 units per day. At this level of output the firm's marginal-cost curve (MC) intersects its marginal-revenue curve ($D_1 = AR_1 = MR_1$) from below. We know that it is in long-run equilibrium since its average-total-cost curve (ATC) is tangent to its average-revenue curve ($D_1 = AR_1 = MR_1$), showing that it is earning just normal profit.

Now suppose that this long-run equilibrium is upset by a rise in the demand for the output produced by the firms in this market. This change is shown in panel (b) as a shift to the right of the market-demand curve from D_1 to D_2. The market price rises to $16 and daily market output to 280 million units. The typical firm reacts to the higher market price by supplying 28,000 units a day, as shown where its marginal cost (MC) intersects its new marginal-revenue curve ($D_2 = AR_2 = MR_2$). This short-run equilibrium allows the firm to earn economic profit of $4 a unit (average revenue is $16 and average total cost is $12). We know that, in the long run, economic profit will draw more firms into the market. Their entry is shown in panel (b) as a shift to the right of the market short-run supply curve, from S_1 to S_2. A new long-run market equilibrium is reached at an output level of 360 million units and, once again, at a price of $10. The typical firm again sells at $10 a unit, so that its previous long-run equilibrium is restored. It once again produces 20,000 units a day. This is true because there has been no shift of its cost curves.

This example helps us to identify two points on this market's long-run supply curve: the original point at 200 million units and the new one at 360 million units. Notice that both appear on the same horizontal straight line. Because the rise in market production from 200 million to 360 million did not affect firms' costs, the long-run equilibrium price remained at $10. Whenever average total cost does

2. We could, of course, alternatively assume a decrease in market demand and price, which would cause firms to earn an economic loss or even shut down in the short run. But since it turns out to be nothing more than the same cases backward, we have decided to economize on space and ask you to work out those cases on your own.

not change with a change in the level of output produced in a market, the market's long-run supply curve will be infinitely elastic.

In a constant-cost market, long-run changes in the level of market output do not affect the average total cost of producing the output, so price remains the same in the long run.

Whenever average total cost does not change with a change in the level of output produced in a market, the market's long-run supply curve will be infinitely elastic.

The Increasing-Cost Case In the increasing-cost case, long-run increases in the level of market output raise the average total cost of producing the output, so that the price rises in the long-run adjustment to the larger volume. Each firm's average total cost increases as the market reaches higher and higher long-run equilibrium levels of output. This will occur in markets that are large enough so that the resources they use represent a significant part of the total demand for those resources. For example, when output is increased in an industry (market) that accounts for as much as, say, 25 percent of the demand for polymer chemicals, or for platinum, or for basic oxygen furnaces, we would expect the prices of these fairly specialized inputs to be bid up quite a bit. Let us examine the case of increasing cost in graphic form.

In an increasing-cost market, long-run increases in the level of market output raise the average total cost of producing the output, so that the price rises in the long-run adjustment to the larger volume. This will occur in markets that are large enough so that the resources they use represent a significant part of the total demand for those resources.

As in the constant-cost case, we begin with a purely competitive market in long-run equilibrium. The market diagram in Figure 8b shows the market short-run supply curve (S_1) intersecting the market-demand curve (D_1) at a level of output of 200 million units a day and at a price of $10 a unit.

And the firm diagram in Figure 8a shows a typical company in that market maximizing its profit by producing 20,000 units a day at the $10 price. Since it is in long-run equilibrium, it is earning just a normal profit.

Now suppose, as we did in the constant-cost case, that this long-run equilibrium is upset by a rise in the demand for the goods or services produced by the firms in this market. This is shown in panel (b) as a shift to the right of the market-demand curve, from D_1 to D_2. The market price rises to $16 and daily market output to 280 million units. As in the constant-cost case, the typical firm reacts to the higher market price by increasing its level of output to 28,000 units a day. It earns an economic profit of $4 a unit in this short-run equilibrium position. In the long run, new firms are attracted into the market. Their entry is shown in panel (b) by a shift to the right of the market short-run supply curve, from S_1 to S_2. A new long-run market equilibrium is reached but, unlike the constant-cost case, at a price above the earlier long-run equilibrium price (at $14 a unit instead of $10 a unit). Why? Because the firms that entered the market bid up resource prices so that average total cost increased for all the firms in the market. This can be seen in Figure 8a. The typical firm's average-total-cost curve shifted up from ATC_1 to ATC_2 and its marginal-cost curve shifted up from MC_1 to MC_2. The firm, now facing a $14 market price, is once again in long-run equilibrium—this time, at the point where its new marginal-cost curve (MC_2) intersects its new marginal-revenue curve ($D_3 = AR_3 = MR_3$) from below. Its new average-total-cost curve (ATC_2) is tangent to its new average-revenue curve ($D_3 = AR_3 = MR_3$), so that it is earning just a normal profit.

This example allows us again to identify two points on this market's long-run supply curve: the original point at 200 million units and the new one at 310 million units. Notice that the curve drawn through these two points—the long-run market-supply curve—is positively sloped. Along with the rise in market production from 200 million to 310 million, there was a $4 increase in average total cost and thus a $4 increase in price. Whenever average total cost rises with the level of output produced in a market, that market's long-run supply curve will be positively sloped.

If long-run equilibrium in an increasing-cost market is upset by a rise in demand for the goods or services produced by the firms in this market, a typical firm reacts to the higher market price by increasing its level of output. New firms are attracted to the market, and their entry causes resource prices to rise for all the firms in the market.

Whenever average total cost rises with the level of output produced in a market, that market's long-run supply curve will be positively sloped.

The Decreasing-Cost Case   In the decreasing-cost case, long-run increases in the level of market output lower the average total cost of producing the output, so that prices decrease in the long-run ad-

FIGURE 8
Long-Run Market Supply in Pure Competition—The Case of Increasing Cost

This purely competitive market is in long-run equilibrium where the short-run market-supply curve (S_1) intersects the market-demand curve (D_1), so that the daily output is 200 million units, which sell at $10 each. The typical firm shown produces 20,000 units per day.

This long-run equilibrium is disrupted by a shift to the right of the market-demand curve (D_1 to D_2). A short-run equilibrium is reached where the new demand curve (D_2) intersects the supply curve (S_1) at an output of 280 million units per day, sold at $16 per unit. The firm's new demand curve is $D_2 = AR_2 = MR_2$. The firm is in short-run equilibrium when it adjusts its output to 28,000 units per day. The firm earns an economic profit of $4 per unit. In the long run, firms will enter this market. This fact is reflected in panel (b) as a shift to the right of the short-run market-supply curve (S_1 to S_2). The new firms bid up resource prices so that the new long-run market

equilibrium—where S_2 intersects D_2—takes place at a higher price ($14) than the previous long-run equilibrium price. The new long-run equilibrium market level of output is 310 million. The higher resource prices are reflected in the upward shifts of the typical firm's average-total-cost curve (from ATC_1 to ATC_2) and marginal-cost curve (MC_1 to MC_2). The new long-run equilibrium for the firm is where its new marginal-cost curve (MC_2) intersects its new marginal-revenue curve ($D_3 = AR_3 = MR_3$). The firm again produces a daily level of output of 20,000 units at the new market price of $14.

The market diagram (panel b) shows the long-run market-supply curve as a positively sloped curve. The increase in market output (from 200 million to 310 million) raises firms' average total cost by $4 and thus the market price by the same amount (from $10 to $14).

justment to greater demand. Because more firms are present in the market, the cost to individual firms goes down. Each firm's average total cost decreases as the market reaches higher and higher long-run equilibrium levels of output. Cases of decreasing cost are expected to be found far less often than either increasing- or constant-cost cases. In order to have a case of decreasing cost, the presence of new firms in a market must bring about lower average total cost for all the firms in that market. For example, let us assume that the coal-mining firms supplying a certain market are located in a single huge coal mining area. A major problem facing them is the water that builds up in their mine shafts and that has to be pumped out. Suppose now that there is a sharp rise in the demand for coal from this area. In the short run, the firms earn an economic profit, but in the long run, this profit falls as new firms enter the market. But the additional pumping by the new firms means that

FIGURE 9
Long-Run Market Supply in Pure Competition—The Case of Decreasing Cost

This purely competitive market is in long-run equilibrium where the short-run market-supply curve (S_1) intersects the market-demand curve (D_1), so that the daily output is 200 million units, which sell at $10 each. The typical firm shown produces 20,000 units per day.

This long-run equilibrium is disrupted by a shift to the right of the market-demand curve (D_1 to D_2). A short-run equilibrium is reached where the new demand curve (D_2) intersects the supply curve (S_1) at an output level of 280 million units per day, sold at $16 per unit. The firm's new demand curve is $D_2 = AR_2 = MR_2$. The firm is in short-run equilibrium when it adjusts its output to 28,000 units per day. The firm earns an economic profit of $4 per unit. In the long run, firms will enter this market. Their entry is reflected in panel (b) as a shift to the right of the short-run market-supply curve (S_1 to S_2). The addi-

tional firms cause average total cost to decrease so that the new long-run market equilibrium—where S_2 intersects D_2—takes place at a lower price ($6) than the previous long-run equilibrium price. The new long-run equilibrium market level of output is 420 million. The lower cost is reflected in the downward shifts of the typical firm's average-total-cost curve (from ATC_1 to ATC_2) and marginal-cost curve (MC_1 to MC_2). The new long-run equilibrium for the firm is where its new marginal-cost curve (MC_2) intersects its new marginal-revenue curve ($D_3 = AR_3 = MR_3$). The firm again produces a daily level of output of 20,000 units at the new market price of $6 (panel a).

Panel (b) shows the long-run market-supply curve as a negatively sloped curve. The rise in market output (from 200 million to 420 million) decreased firms' average total cost by $4 and thus the market price by the same amount (from $10 to $6).

there is less water to be pumped out by the original firms. As a result, all firms have lower average total cost since each is required to pump out less water. Let us examine the case of decreasing cost in graphic form.

As in the two earlier cases, we begin with a purely competitive market in long-run equilibrium. The market diagram in Figure 9b shows the market short-run supply curve (S_1) intersecting the market-demand curve (D_1) at a level of output of 200 million units a day and at a price of $10 a unit. The firm diagram in Figure 9a shows a typical company in that market maximizing its profit by producing 20,000 units a day at the $10 price. Its average-total-cost curve (ATC_1) is tangent to its average-revenue curve ($D_1 = AR_1 = MR_1$), so that it earns just a normal profit.

Now suppose, as we did in the previous two cases, that this long-run equilibrium is upset by a rise in the demand for the output produced by the firms in this market. This is shown in Figure 9b as a shift to the right of the market-demand curve, from D_1 to D_2. The market price rises to $16 and daily market output to 280 million units. As in the other cases, the typical firm reacts to the higher market price by increasing its level of output to 28,000 units a day. It earns an economic profit of $4 per unit in this short-run equilibrium position. In the long run, new firms are attracted into the market. This is shown in panel (b) by a shift to the right of the market short-run supply curve, from S_1 to S_2. A new long-run market equilibrium is reached, but unlike the other two cases, at a price below the original long-run equilibrium price (at $6 a unit instead of at $10 a unit). Why? Because the firms that entered the market caused a reduction in average total cost for all the firms in the market. This effect can be seen in panel (a) of Figure 9. Our typical firm's average-total-cost curve shifted down from ATC_1 to ATC_2, and its marginal-cost curve shifted down from MC_1 to MC_2. The firm, now facing a $6 market price, is once again in long-run equilibrium—this time, at the point where its new marginal-cost curve (MC_2) intersects its new marginal-revenue curve ($D_3 = AR_3 = MR_3$) from below. Its new average-total-cost curve (ATC_2) is tangent to its new average-revenue curve ($D_3 = AR_3 = MR_3$), so that it is earning just a normal profit.

Again we have identified two points on a long-run market-supply curve: the original point at 200 million units and the new one at 420 million units. In this case, the curve drawn through these two points—the long-run market-supply curve—is negatively sloped. Along with the rise in market production from 200 million to 420 million was a $4 decrease in average total cost and thus a $4 decrease in price. Whenever average total cost decreases with an increase in the level of output produced in a market, that market's long-run supply curve will be negatively sloped.

In a decreasing-cost market, long-run increases in the level of market output lower the average total cost of producing the output, so prices decrease in the long-run adjustment to greater demand. Because more firms are present in the market, the cost to individual firms goes down.

Whenever average total cost decreases with an increase in the level of output produced in a market, that market's long-run supply curve will be negatively sloped.

EVALUATION OF PURE COMPETITION

Though some actual industries approach the pure competition situation, the model is an abstract idea, not exactly representative of any real-world industry. Why in the world, then, have we used so much of our scarce space in this book to explain this model and asked you to spend your scarce time to read and study it? Did we practice good economics? We believe that the answer is "yes." First, the pure competition model gives us a yardstick for comparing actual characteristics of industries. Discovering how close a firm or industry comes to meeting the conditions of pure competition may help in predicting the actions of firms and the market equilibrium that will result.

Second, even though the pure competition model is an extreme case, some real-world industries do in fact come quite close to it. Therefore the model allows us to do a better job in analyzing these industries. Many small wheat farms, corn farms, and poultry farms in the United States are price takers. So are most sellers of shares of stock in the New York Stock Exchange. And relatively small coal-mining, silver-mining, and gold-mining firms are price takers as well. All of these and many others operate in markets with many sellers, and what they sell is quite standardized. However, they are not perfect examples of pure competition. To the extent that there is cooperative organization, such as a regional wheat sellers' cooperative, or government intervention, such as the U.S. government deciding to sell a large amount of silver out of a stockpile, the examples do not conform to the model. Also, these examples suffer from the fact that there are generally some exit and entry barriers that prevent free movement of resources out of and into these markets. For example, some farmers have decided to stay on their farms in the face of economic loss because they prefer to live there. They have decided to support their farming business with earnings from extra jobs.

Finally, the pure competition model involves relationships among variables that are also relevant in markets other than pure competition. Therefore, understanding this model helps in learning other models. Its usefulness will become clear in the next two chapters, where we explain the other market types.

Discovering how close a firm or industry comes to meeting the conditions of pure competition may help in predicting the actions of firms and the market equilibrium that will result.

The Virtues of Pure Competition

Would pure competition be desirable for our society, or would we be better off with markets containing at least some elements of monopoly? The answer must involve a value judgment. Those who favor pure competition argue that it would result in the "best of all possible worlds." Such arguments may be separated into political and economic ones.

Political Arguments   A purely competitive society will have no big business, no big labor, and no big government. All the actors on the economic scene are powerless, one against the other. There is no centralized power that can dictate behavior. All

power rests in the hands of the impersonal market forces of supply and demand, and, as Adam Smith explained in his *Wealth of Nations,* those hands are invisible.

Each of the many firms that make up a market simply adjusts its level of output according to market conditions. Labor has no reason to bargain for wage increases because gaining higher wages from companies that earn just a normal profit can result only in the loss of jobs. Likewise, there is no reason for government to intervene in the market process.[3] Any temporary excess demand or excess supply will be quickly eliminated by the market.

Furthermore, pure competition offers freedom of opportunity or "free enterprise." Anyone desiring to enter a business is free to do so. There are no barriers placed in the way. If you want to establish a new pizzeria in your town, you need no Department of Health certificate. If you want to open a bar, you need no liquor license. And if you want to own and drive a taxicab in New York City, you need no medallion.

Advocates of pure competition argue that since there is no centralized power to dictate behavior, all power rests in the invisible hands of the impersonal market forces of supply and demand. Pure competition also offers freedom of opportunity.

Economic Arguments   There are a number of persuasive economic arguments in favor of pure competition. Three of them become clear when you look at the pure competition long-run equilibrium firm diagram (Figure 10). You can see that at equilibrium (1) the price charged is equal to the firm's marginal cost, (2) the firm earns just a normal profit, and (3) the firm produces at the minimum point of its average-total-cost curve. Let us see how each of these results benefits society.

When a firm charges a price that is equal to marginal cost, that is, when $P = MC$, any consumer who is willing and able to pay what it costs the firm

3. Of course, government may do things that affect the demands or costs with which the markets operate. Government may force firms to pay the pollution costs that they impose on the rest of society. Also, it may force a redistribution of income and wealth.

to produce one more unit will be able to buy and consume it. This happens *only* in the case of pure competition. In the next two chapters, you will see that firms in all other market types charge a price that is higher than their marginal cost.

When a firm earns just a normal profit, its earnings are exactly equal to its opportunity cost. If it earned any less, it would leave the industry, but it takes no more than what it is earning to keep it in this business. In the next two chapters, you will see that the reason why firms in other market structures are able to earn an economic profit in the long run is that resources are somehow prevented from flowing in. Those outside the industry who would like to share in the economic profit and whose resources would be more productive in this industry than where they are currently used are not able to enter. Too many resources are then devoted to other markets and not enough to the one that the firms would like to enter, which is poor resource allocation.

Finally, when a firm produces at the minimum point of its average-total-cost curve, the least amount of resources are being used to produce that level of output. Firms that produce at any higher average total cost suffer an economic loss and are forced out of the industry. Only those that waste no resources remain.

These three favorable aspects of pure competition can be seen on a diagram such as our Figure 10, but there are two others that are not readily visible on a diagram. The first is that none of the economy's scarce resources are devoted to advertising or promotion. Although a great deal of advertising is useful insofar as it provides important information to consumers, economists generally agree that much advertising is wasteful. Ads that say, "My product is better—buy it" are simply canceled out by rival ads that offer a similar message. Advertising is inconsistent with the pure competition model. Why should a firm add to its cost when the product that it sells is so standardized that it cannot be distinguished from the output of other firms? Furthermore, why should a firm advertise when it can already sell all that it wants to at the going market price? Advertising just doesn't make any sense in a pure competition context.

Another way in which pure competition might benefit society is that purely competitive firms are pushed to adopt quickly any new and better prod-

FIGURE 10
A Purely Competitive Firm in Long-Run Equilibrium

This purely competitive firm is in long-run equilibrium. It faces an infinitely elastic demand curve at a price of $10. Its marginal-cost curve (*MC*) intersects its marginal-revenue curve (*D = AR = MR*) from below at a daily level of output of 20,000 units. This profit-maximizing position earns normal profit for this firm since its average-total-cost curve (*ATC*) is tangent to its average-revenue curve (*D = AR = MR*).

uct or new and cost-saving technological process. Any pure competitor who lags behind its rivals will have an economic loss and be forced to leave the industry. In other market types, firms that believe it doesn't pay for them to introduce a new product or process right away may be able to "sit on it" for a while, so that it is the consumer who loses in this case.

Economic arguments in favor of pure competition are that: (1) the price charged is equal to a firm's marginal cost, (2) the firm earns just a normal profit, (3) the firm produces at the minimum point of its average-total-cost curve, (4) no resources are wasted on advertising, and (5) firms are pushed to adopt quickly any new and better product or technological process.

The Failings of Pure Competition

By now you are likely to be in favor of pure competition. But before you join the "Pure Competition Movement," it is only fair to point out some failings of this "ideal" market. There are at least three reasons why we might not want all industries to be purely competitive.

First, standardized products may not be what consumers want, and variety may well be worth a somewhat higher price. Imagine that the sweater industry were purely competitive. This would mean that wherever you shopped, you would be offered only a few standardized varieties of sweaters—perhaps only one. You could not choose among different colors, stitches, designs, fiber content, and brand. Would you miss that? Most people would. A much lower price may be enough to make up for a lack of variety, but that requires a value judgment that we can only make for ourselves.

Second, the incentive of economic profit may be necessary to persuade companies to carry on progressive research and development programs. If a purely competitive firm makes an important product discovery, it will not be able to take advantage of it alone very long. Since pure competition does not allow restrictions such as patent laws, all the firms in the industry will be able to take advantage of the discovery as soon as it is made. Similarly, if a purely competitive firm makes an important cost-saving process discovery, it will not be able to exploit it for very long. After all, in the long run, only normal profit can be earned. Firms that are aware of these facts will not be willing to risk their money in research and development. Coupled with this lack of incentive is a possible lack of money available for this purpose. Because pure competitors earn only a normal profit, they do not have opportunities to finance research and development from long-run economic profit.

Finally, in many industries a few large firms are able to produce the demanded level of output at lower average total cost (taking advantage of economies of scale) than are many small producers. In many industries there is simply not enough demand in the market to accommodate a large number of firms big enough to take advantage of all the economies of scale that exist. Even if each purely competitive firm produces at the minimum point along its average-total-cost curve, its average total cost may be higher than the average total cost at which much larger firms are able to produce. For example, suppose that we broke up the existing auto manufacturing firms in the United States into 100,000 separate companies. Each firm becomes a price taker, so that for all practical purposes pure competition is achieved. Each of these 100,000 firms might plan to sell about 100 cars a year. Their production method would probably make use of far more labor and unsophisticated capital than big auto firms actually use. As a result, each firm's minimum average total cost might be, say, $50,000, which in pure competition is also the price that is charged. By contrast, three or four firms can use a mass-production method that captures important economies of scale and can sell cars at around $10,000.

Taken together, these three failings of pure competition help to explain why most economists would not be in favor of having all of our industries conform to the pure competition model.

The flaws of pure competition are that: (1) there is no variety, given that products are standardized, (2) without the incentive of economic profit, companies may not carry on research and development programs, and (3) in many markets there is insufficient demand to support a large number of firms each of which is big enough to achieve important economies of scale.

Economics in Focus

Competition in the Egg Business

One industry that approaches the conditions of pure competition is the egg business. Traditionally there are plenty of sellers—farmers who sell at wholesale prices to distributors. These farmers are price takers, forced to accept the going market rate. Their product is standardized (most people cannot tell one hen's egg from another's); the market has few artificial restrictions; and entry and exit are generally easy.

In recent decades the egg business has faced two major problems. First, the price of chicken feed began to rise sharply in the 1970s. As farmers had to pay more to feed their chickens, the cost of producing eggs rose. The industry supply curve shifted to the left and egg prices increased, but many firms could not achieve normal profit. In order to reduce those costs, producers had to change their production methods. They did so, in effect, by making their chickens work harder with fewer vacations, and they lowered the average amount of grain required to produce a dozen eggs from 7.9 pounds in 1976 to 6.0 pounds in 1980.

Producers were still adapting to the cost problem when a second major difficulty arose. American consumers, scared by cholesterol warnings, began to eat fewer eggs; in fact, per capita consumption dropped to under 250 eggs per year by the late 1980s. (By comparison, the per capita figure had been 390 after World War II.) As the demand curve shifted to the left, prices plunged; the wholesale egg price dropped from 72 cents per dozen in 1984 to 68 cents in 1986 to under 50 cents in 1988.

Under conditions of pure competition less than normal profit would bring about mass exit of suppliers in the long run. Interestingly, though, many of the adaptations that producers made were attempts to escape the purely competitive market. In New England egg producers mounted an advertising campaign asserting that local eggs were fresher than those imported from outside the region. In other areas of the country producers cut their volume and concentrated on local markets, where they could offer faster, more dependable service than national suppliers. Still other producers switched to a new type of egg that was touted as being lower in cholesterol. In all these cases the producers were trying to establish differentiation between their product (or service) and their competitors'; in this way they might escape the condition of being price takers.

Nevertheless, many producers followed the route that economists would have predicted: between 1980 and 1989 almost half of the big egg producers left the business. Many small producers gave up as well. Economist Timothy Tregarthen studied the monks of St. Benedict's, a monastery in Colorado. The monks had entered the egg business in 1967, struggled through the era of rising costs, coped with unproductive hens and the national change in eating habits. But when Tregarthen returned to the monastery in 1988 he found that the chickens were gone. Instead of eggs, the monks were selling cookies—a field with much less competition!

Sources: Timmothy Tregarten, "The Monks of St. Benedict's: Getting Out of the Egg Business," *The Margin,* September/October 1988, pp. 14–15; Jack Willoughby, "Eggshells Everywhere," *Forbes,* May 29, 1989, pp. 254–262; David Snyder, "The Egg Man," *Forbes,* February 22, 1988, p. 120.

SUMMARY

1. Economists classify sellers' markets into four different structures or types. These are: (a) pure competition, (b) pure monopoly, (c) monopolistic competition, and (d) oligopoly. The structural criteria used to classify them are the number of sellers, the existence of product differentiation, and the ease of entry. A market's structure affects the behavior of firms, which in turn affects the market's economic performance. (See page 572 and Table 1, page 572.)

2. The term *competition* may be used in the sense of rivalry or in the sense of the pure competition market type. Pure competition describes a market in which there are so many firms selling a standardized product that each one acts as a price taker. Besides the conditions of many sellers and a standardized product, pure competition requires that no artificial restrictions be placed upon price or quantity and that easy entry and exit are available. Perfect competition requires all of the conditions of pure competition plus complete knowledge or information and full mobility. (See page 573.)

3. The pure competition model describes how the market sets equilibrium price and quantity and then how each typical firm adjusts its output to that market price. (See pages 573–574.)

4. The market-demand curve is negatively sloped, but since each firm believes that it is powerless to affect the price, an individual firm's demand curve is infinitely elastic. A firm's total-revenue curve will therefore be a positive linear curve drawn out of the origin. Average revenue is the price per unit and so is just another name for the demand curve. Since a firm does not have to lower its price in order to sell more, its marginal-revenue curve is the same as its demand curve. (See pages 574–575.)

5. Since firms maximize their profit when they produce the level of output that equates their marginal cost and marginal revenue, a purely competitive firm's marginal-cost curve, above its average variable cost, is also its short-run supply curve. A short-run market-supply curve is the sum of all the individual firm-supply curves in a market. (See pages 576–577.)

6. In the short run, firms in pure competition may experience an economic profit, an economic loss, or a normal profit. In the long run, economic profit invites entry, and economic loss causes firms to exit, so that in the long run all purely competitive firms earn just a normal profit. (See pages 579–581.)

7. A purely competitive market's long-run supply curve may reflect constant cost, increasing cost, or decreasing cost. In a constant-cost industry, long-run changes in the level of market output do not affect firms' average total costs, so that price is not increased as a result of greater volume in the market. In an increasing-cost industry, long-run increases in the level of market output increase firms' average total costs, so that price increases as a result of greater volume. In a decreasing-cost industry, long-run increases in the level of market output decrease firms' average total costs, so that price decreases as a result of greater volume. (See pages 581–589 and Figures 7, 8, and 9.)

8. The pure competition model is an abstract idea, and not exactly representative of any real industry. However, it provides a norm or yardstick against which actual industries can be compared. Some industries approach this norm. Also the model involves important relationships that are relevant to other market types. (See page 589.)

9. Pure competition is often held up as an ideal market situation. Its virtues may be divided into political arguments and economic arguments. Among the political arguments are: (a) that power is decentralized, (b) that the impersonal market forces of supply and demand determine results, and (c) that it provides freedom of opportunity. Among the economic arguments are: (a) that each firm charges a price equal to its marginal cost, (b) that each firm earns only normal profit in the long run, (c) that each firm produces at the minimum point of its average-total-cost curve, (d) that no resources are wasted on unproductive advertising or promotion, and (e) that firms are pushed to quickly adopt new and better products and new and cost-saving technological processes. (See pages 589–591.)

10. Pure competition may not be all that it is cracked up to be. The failings of pure competition are: (a) that consumers are denied variety, (b) that there is a lack of incentive for firms to carry on research and development, and (c) that average total cost may be high because of firms' inability to take advantage of important economies of scale. (See page 592.)

KEY TERMS

average revenue: total revenue divided by the quantity of goods sold (page 576).

competition: rivalry among sellers or buyers; also, a label for a specific market type (page 573).

marginal revenue: the extra revenue that a firm receives when it sells another unit of output (page 576).

monopolistic competition: a market type in which there are many sellers, entry is easy, and each firm sells a somewhat different product (page 572).

oligopoly: a market characterized by few sellers (page 572).

perfect competition: a market characterized by the same features as pure competition plus the added attributes that buyers and sellers have complete and continuous information or knowledge of all bids and offers made in the market and the full mobility to take immediate action (page 574).

price taker: a firm that accepts the equilibrium market price as given and does not adjust its own sales so as to try to influence that price. It is the distinguishing characteristic of a firm in a purely competitive market (page 573).

pure competition: a market characterized by a large number of firms, a standardized product, and easy entry so that each firm acts as a price taker (page 572).

pure monopoly: a market characterized by a single seller, no product differentiation, and blocked entry (page 572).

total revenue: the price a firm charges multiplied by the quantity of output that it sells (page 576).

DISCUSSION QUESTIONS

1. Firm X and firm Z sell in the same market. Firm X and firm Z compete with each other for the sale of their products to buyers. From this information alone, can you determine whether or not firms X and Z are pure competitors? Explain.

2. Purely competitive firms are price takers. Carefully explain what it means for a firm to be a price taker. What conditions must be present in order for a firm to be a price taker?

3. In the market structure of pure competition, the market-demand curve is shown as a negatively sloped function. However, each individual purely competitive firm's demand curve appears as a horizontal straight line. Explain this seeming inconsistency.

4. Explain each of the following statements as it pertains to the purely competitive market model:

a. An individual firm's demand curve is the same as its marginal-revenue curve.

b. An individual firm's demand curve is the same as its average-revenue curve.

c. The portion of an individual firm's marginal-cost curve that lies above its average variable cost is the same as its supply curve.

5. In the short run, a purely competitive firm may earn an economic profit, a normal profit, or an economic loss. Without looking back at Figure 5, draw a diagram showing each of the three situations below:

a. a short-run equilibrium for a purely competitive firm that is earning economic profit.

b. a short-run equilibrium for a purely competitive firm that is earning normal profit.

c. a short-run equilibrium for a purely competitive firm that is earning economic loss.

Compare your diagrams with the ones in Figure 5 to be sure you have them right. In each of these three cases, what will happen in the long run? (Discuss the process through which the change, if any, will take place.)

6. Why is it that an increase in the market demand for a product produced in a purely competitive industry will sometimes cause the equilibrium price for that product to increase in the long run? You may wish to explain this both verbally and by using a diagram.

7. "It is really a waste of time studying pure competition since economists are very hard pressed to find actual industries that conform to all the conditions of the pure competition model." Do you agree? Why or why not?

8. Discuss the arguments for and against using the long-run pure competition equilibrium solution as an ideal to which all of our actual industries should conform.

27
Monopoly

Preview   One down, three to go. In the last chapter we took a close look at pure competition, the first of the economist's four market structures or types. In this chapter we examine the second one, pure monopoly. Then in the next two chapters we cover the remaining two, monopolistic competition and oligopoly.

As with the term *competition*, economists use the term *monopoly* in various ways. In order to avoid confusion, we begin the chapter by discussing the differences between pure monopoly, actual monopoly, and monopoly control. You will learn why many actual monopolies exist and how they are able to keep their monopoly positions. Some will be described as "natural" monopolies, and these may or may not be "government-enforced." Other actual monopolies may be created by government even though they are not natural monopolies. We shall introduce government regulation of monopolies here, but wait until Chapter 35 to explain the reasons behind such regulation and the degree and variety of government regulations.

Pure monopoly, like pure competition, is a useful, yet unrealistic, model. In some important ways, it can be seen as an extreme opposite of pure competition. A pure competition market is made up of a large number of firms, and a pure monopoly market is composed of a single firm. And whereas purely competitive firms are price takers, the pure monopolist is a price maker.

After presenting both short-run and long-run equilibrium positions for a pure monopolist, we evaluate them in light of what we know about pure competition. We then point out the inefficient nature of pure monopoly as compared to pure competition, but add words of caution about the meaning of such conclusions.

Finally, we explain how monopolists may increase their profits by engaging in price discrimination. We look at the requirements for successful price discrimination and evaluate its effects.

PURE MONOPOLY, ACTUAL MONOPOLY, AND MONOPOLY CONTROL

In the last chapter you studied a pure form of competition. Here we begin with a pure type of monopoly and then consider several more realistic forms.

Pure Monopoly

Pure monopoly, like pure competition, is an extreme market type and does not exist in the real world. Pure monopoly describes a market in which there is only a single seller. The firm and the market are one and the same. No acceptable substitutes are available for the product that the pure monopolist offers for sale. It is a market in which there is no competition—now or in the future—because entry into the industry is effectively barred. For this reason, the pure monopolist does not significantly affect other firms by such actions as price changes or advertising campaigns. Similarly, the actions of other firms do not significantly affect the pure monopolist. This substantial amount of isolation and lack of concern about rivals or would-be rivals is what puts the "pure" in pure monopoly.

Pure monopoly describes a market in which there is only a single seller; there are no acceptable substitutes and no potential competition because entry into the industry is effectively barred. The firm and the market are one and the same.

Actual Monopoly

No firm that we can actually identify—be it the only seller of natural gas in a region, the only seller of bus service in a city, or the only seller of a certain drug in the whole country—is an "island unto itself." Although in all three of these examples we are correct in applying the "monopoly" label, none is an example of a pure monopolist. We choose to call them **actual monopolies**. Each is the only seller in its market. However, sellers in other markets offer more-or-less good substitutes, potential competition cannot be ruled out, and the government protection that some of them enjoy may be taken away or altered.

An actual monopoly market is one in which there is only a single seller, but sellers in other markets offer substitutes, potential competition exists, and the seller may be subject to more or less government regulation.

Government-Enforced Monopoly Actual monopolies are often "government-enforced" monopolies. They are common in *public utility* industries such as natural gas, electric power, telecommunication, and local public transportation. Generally, they are confined to a particular geographic area and regulated by one or more government agencies. Let's return to our example of the only seller of bus service in a certain city. Such a firm most likely has an exclusive franchise to offer bus service in that city, so that it does not face competing bus lines. However, it does face other kinds of competition. There are private cars, bicycles, taxis, and possibly a subway available as substitute transportation. Even walking may offer a practical alternative for covering a short distance. The bus monopolist affects other firms by its actions—for example, a large bus-fare decrease may hurt the taxicab companies. Similarly, actions of other firms affect the seller of bus service. For example, the introduction of beautiful new subway trains may cause people to switch from bus travel to subway travel.

Our example of the natural gas firm that has a monopoly in a certain region may be a somewhat stronger (closer to pure monopoly) case of actual monopoly. Of course, consumers of gas are able to substitute oil, electricity, or even coal, wood, or solar energy to heat their homes. But if they already own gas furnaces, they might feel compelled to buy gas from the monopolist, at least for a while, even after the price goes up much higher.

In both the bus and natural gas cases, the future position of the firm as a monopoly is not safe. Besides the prospects of lower prices and better service by competing and potentially competing firms in similar markets, the government that granted the exclusive franchise might decide to make it less exclusive or simply take it away. Government-enforced monopolies of this sort are discussed further in Chapter 35.

Actual monopolies, which are common in public utility industries, are often government-enforced and regulated by one or more government agencies.

Another kind of government-enforced actual monopoly arises from the government granting a patent to a firm. A **patent** is a right of temporary limited monopoly over a new product or process granted to its inventor or to a company that purchases the right from the inventor. In the United States a patent is valid for seventeen years. The reason most often put forward for granting them to companies is that it is fair to compensate a firm for the time, effort, and money usually spent in the invention (research and development) process. However, the main reason why most countries have a patent system is to stimulate invention. It is believed to be a strong incentive that encourages firms to risk large sums of money in research.

Earlier we used an example of the only seller of a certain drug in the whole country. Such a monopoly most likely depends on a patent. No other firm may sell that drug until the patent expires. Even during this seventeen-year period, however, the firm is not a pure monopolist. In most such cases, rival companies sell other drugs that have slightly different chemical structures but still offer about the same medicinal value for the illness to be treated. Most likely these rivals also have patents on their drugs, so that competition takes place among several actual monopolists. If, indeed, a drug firm were the only one to hold a patent on a certain kind of drug and if the volume of expected sales and profit were high enough, other companies would try to develop and obtain a patent on an acceptable substitute as quickly as possible. Even if they failed, the actual monopolist's patent which was probably obtained years before the drug was first offered for sale, would run out before very long.

A patent is a right of temporary limited monopoly over a new product or process granted to its inventor or to a company that purchases the right from an inventor. In the United States, a patent is valid for seventeen years.

Monopoly Without Government Enforcement Some actual monopolies do not rely on government at all. They may exist simply because it doesn't pay for more than one firm to operate in a certain market or industry. Examples of actual monopolies that exist without government enforcement are found in many small-town service industries. The only obstetrician in a small town is an actual monopolist, as he or she doesn't compete very much with the local general practitioners or with other obstetricians who are some distance away. The same may be said for the only divorce lawyer, the only funeral director, the only commercial real estate broker, and the only fancy restaurant in town. Other firms offering such services are not prevented from entering the market. The license that they might need is not a big problem. The reason why firms do not enter this market is that they believe that it would not pay for them to do so. The small amount of business in the market does not justify starting a second firm. The actual monopoly's fixed cost is in place, and demand is not great enough for it to operate at or near full capacity. Therefore, the marginal cost of providing the service is less than the average total cost. If, instead of one firm, two firms were to compete in such a market, each would find that its marginal cost would be below its average total cost. Competition for customers would persuade each firm to charge a price below its average total cost. In the long run, after some period of fierce competition resulting in an economic loss, the weaker of the two firms would go out of business. Suppose, for example, that there are two dentists in a small town that offered only enough patients to keep one dentist busy. If each had total cost of $3,000 a week (for an office, equipment, personnel, and the like), each had ten patients a week (average total cost of $300), and each found marginal cost to be $25, the competition for patients might very well drive the price down to just over $25. Even at $30 per patient, each of these dentists suffers an economic loss of $2,700 a week ($30 × 10 = $300, $3,000 − $300 = $2,700). After a while, one of them will head for greener pastures. The remaining one becomes an actual monopolist.

Some actual monopolies exist without government enforcement because it does not pay for more than a single firm to operate in some markets. Many examples can be found in small-town service industries.

Natural Monopoly   Some actual monopolies are natural monopolies. These may be government enforced, as our example of the natural gas firm, or exist without government enforcement, as our example of the dental monopoly in a small town.

A **natural monopoly** refers to a market in which a single seller is required for efficient production. In such a market, economies of scale—the decrease in long-run average total cost as the level of output is expanded—are so important in relation to demand that only a single firm can take full advantage of them. Natural monopolies usually involve services that are provided to specific geographical markets. Later, in Chapter 35, we shall discuss government regulation of natural monopolies.

A natural monopoly refers to a market in which a single seller is required for efficient production. In such a market, economies of scale are so important in relation to demand that only a single firm can take full advantage of them.

Monopoly Control

Monopoly control (or **monopoly power**) refers to the degree of control or power that a firm has over the price of the product that it sells. Monopoly

control does *not*, as the words unfortunately seem to imply, refer only to monopolists. In fact, all firms, except those in purely competitive industries, have some degree of monopoly control. In pure competition, all firms are price takers, so that each can exert no power over price. (Remember from the last chapter that a purely competitive firm cannot sell any output at a price even slightly above the price set in the market.)

Monopoly control (monopoly power) refers to the degree of control or power that a firm has over the price of the product that it sells. All firms, except those in purely competitive industries, have some degree of monopoly control.

A pure monopolist has more power over price than other types of firms, but this fact does not mean that such a firm faces a perfectly inelastic demand curve. When a pure monopolist raises the price of its product, it will sell less. The higher price causes consumers' real incomes to fall (the income effect) and the quantity demanded of that product to fall. The substitution effect would be very weak since no acceptable substitutes are available for a pure monopolist's product. For example, if a pure monopolist of parachutes raised the price of all parachutes, very few people would find another product to substitute for a parachute.[1]

In a pure monopoly, the substitution effect is very weak, since no acceptable substitutes are available for a pure monopolist's product.

Actual monopolists have less monopoly control than do pure monopolists. Somewhat better substitutes are available, and there is the threat of other companies entering the market. As you will see, firms that operate in oligopolistic markets have less monopoly control than do monopolists, and those in monopolistic competition have even less.

---

1. This example does not hold for all uses of parachutes. For example, some sports parachutists might switch to another sport. But remember, pure monopoly does not exist in the real world.

The particular degree of monopoly control varies from industry to industry and from firm to firm.

Actual monopolists have less monopoly control than do pure monopolists.

THE PURE MONOPOLY MODEL

At this point you should have a clear understanding of pure monopoly as a market structure in which a single firm sells a product for which there is no acceptable substitute. We now turn our attention to the pure monopoly model, which will allow us to predict the level of output that such a company would offer and the price that it would charge.

In the pure competition model in the last chapter, we drew separate diagrams for the market and for a typical firm in that market. In pure monopoly only one diagram needs to be drawn, since the firm and the market (industry) are one and the same.

Demand and Marginal Revenue

The pure monopolist faces the demand curve for the whole market. Its negative slope is explained by a normal income effect and a normal (but weak) substitution effect. Consumers can afford to buy more at lower prices and less at higher prices. Changes in relative prices will cause them to make some switches from or to products in other markets. Figure 1 illustrates a pure monopolist's demand curve. As we explained in our discussion of pure competition, the demand curve facing a firm is also its average-revenue curve (the price per unit of output that the firm receives at each different level of output). We have labeled it accordingly.

The pure monopolist's demand curve is negatively sloped. In a pure monopoly, as in pure competition, the demand curve faced by a firm is also its average-revenue curve.

FIGURE 1
Demand and Revenue for a Pure Monopolist

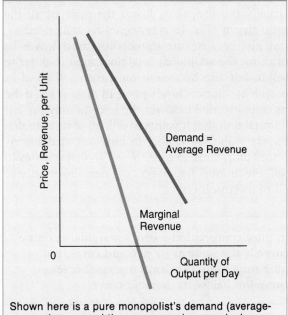

Shown here is a pure monopolist's demand (average-revenue) curve and the accompanying marginal-revenue curve. The marginal-revenue curve lies beneath the demand curve because the monopolist must lower its price in order to sell more, and in most instances, the new lower price must be charged for all units of output to all of the monopolist's customers.

In Figure 1 we have also drawn this pure monopolist's marginal-revenue curve, which shows the addition to its total revenue each time it raises its level of output by one more unit. The relation between the demand (average-revenue) curve and the marginal-revenue curve that we see in Figure 1 appears very different from the relation between these curves that we saw in the pure competition model. In pure competition a firm's marginal-revenue curve is the same as its demand curve, but in pure monopoly the firm's marginal-revenue curve lies below its demand curve. Here we can recognize the basic difference between the two market types. In pure competition a firm does not have to lower its price in order to sell a larger quantity of output. But in the case of the pure monopolist—in fact, in any market where an individual firm faces a demand curve that is negatively sloped over the range of the firm's possible output—price must be lowered in order to sell more. In most cases, lowering the price does not mean that the monopolist is able to lower the price of only the last unit to be sold. Usually the firm must lower the price of all the units that it sells. Thus marginal revenue declines, not just because the monopolist must lower its price for the additional (marginal) unit in order to sell it, but also because it must then sell all of its output at this new lower price. In most cases, if the monopolist tried to lower the price of only the additional unit that it wants to sell, all of its potential buyers would be willing to buy only that lower-priced unit. Thus, in order to sell all that it wants to sell, the monopolist charges the new lower price to all of its customers.

In pure competition a firm's marginal-revenue curve is the same as its demand curve, but in pure monopoly the firm's marginal-revenue curve lies below its demand curve.

As an illustration of this important difference between pure monopoly and pure competition, let us look at the example shown in Table 1. Over the range of four different levels of output (column 1), the left side of the table (columns 2–6) provides data for a purely competitive firm and the right side (columns 7–11) for a pure monopolist. The purely

competitive firm is a price taker at the market price of $10 shown in column 2. It can sell any of the levels of output at $10 a unit and does not have to lower its price in order to sell more. Its total revenue (price times quantity) is given in column 3. Column 4 shows its gain from selling an additional unit, which is the $10 price. Nothing is subtracted in column 5 (loss due to price reductions on the previous volume of sales) because the firm does not have to lower its price to make an additional sale. Finally, column 6 shows the firm's marginal revenue. As you already know, this is the change in the firm's total revenue when it sells one more unit. More important for our purpose here, however, marginal revenue is also the firm's gain (column 4) minus its loss (column 5).

Figure 2 shows the situation in graphic form. Panel (a) pictures the purely competitive firm's marginal revenue and is keyed to the case in which its level of output changes from 3 to 4 units per day. Its demand curve ($D = AR = MR$) is infinitely elastic at the $10 market price. Its marginal revenue between selling 3 and 4 units is shown as the gold vertical rectangle ($1 \times \$10 = \$10$).

Let us return to Table 1 and this time concentrate on the situation of the pure monopolist firm which faces a negatively sloped demand curve and decreasing marginal revenue. In our example in Table 1, we again begin with a price of $10, at which the firm can sell 3 units. But, as shown in

TABLE 1
Derivation of Marginal Revenue in Pure Competition and in Pure Monopoly

(1) Quantity of Output (per day)	Pure Competition						Pure Monopoly				
	(2) Price ($)	(3) Total Revenue ($)	(4) Gain ($)	(5) Loss ($)	(6) Marginal Revenue ($)		(7) Price ($)	(8) Total Revenue ($)	(9) Gain ($)	(10) Loss ($)	(11) Marginal Revenue ($)
3	10	30					10	30			
			10	0	10				9	3	6
4	10	40					9	36			
			10	0	10				8	4	4
5	10	50					8	40			
			10	0	10				7	5	2
6	10	60					7	42			

FIGURE 2
Derivation of Marginal Revenue in Pure Competition and in Pure Monopoly

Panel (a) shows a firm in pure competition and panel (b) a firm in pure monopoly. Originally, both sell 3 units of output per day at a price of $10 per unit. Both wish to increase their level of output to 4 units per day. In (a), the firm in pure competition merely produces one more unit and sells it at the $10 market price. Its marginal revenue is the price of $10, which is represented by the gold vertical rectangle. In (b), the pure monopolist must lower its price to $9

in order to sell 4 units per day. The gain of $9 from selling the fourth unit is shown as the gold vertical rectangle. But the monopolist must now sell all of its output at $9 per unit (not just the fourth unit), so that it loses $3, which is shown as the red horizontal rectangle. The pure monopolist's marginal revenue is derived by subtracting the horizontal (loss) rectangle from the vertical (gain) rectangle—$6 ($9 − $3 = $6) in this case.

column 7, the monopolist can sell more only by lowering its price. It can sell 4 units at $9 per unit, 5 at $8, and 6 at $7. This causes total revenue (price times quantity, which is shown in column 8) to increase by decreasing amounts. The gain from selling another unit (column 9) is partially offset by the loss (column 10) that results from having to sell the previous quantity of output at a lower price. For example, lowering the price from $10 to $9, so that 4 units can be sold instead of only 3, offers a gain of $9, which is the price received for the fourth unit. But the price decrease also causes a loss of $3, stemming from the $1 lower price received for each of the first 3 units. Marginal revenue (column 11) can then be calculated either by subtracting the

previous total revenue from the new one or by subtracting the loss (column 10) from the gain (column 9).

Panel (b) of Figure 2 pictures the loss and the gain that this pure monopolist experiences when it decreases its price from $10 to $9 in order to increase its sales from 3 to 4 units per day. It gains $9, which is shown by the gold vertical rectangle (1 × $9 = $9). However, as it must now sell all of its output at $9 per unit, it also loses $3, which is shown by the red horizontal rectangle (3 × $1 = $3). The monopolist's marginal revenue is then derived by subtracting the horizontal (loss) rectangle from the vertical (gain) rectangle. In this example, marginal revenue is $6 ($9 − $3 = $6).

In pure competition a firm does not have to lower its price to sell a larger quantity of output. But in pure monopoly, price must be lowered to sell more, and all of a firm's output must be sold at this new lower price.

Marginal revenue may be positive (as in our example), it may be negative (when the revenue loss exceeds the revenue gain), or it may be zero (when the revenue loss just equals the revenue gain). But in all three cases the marginal revenue is less than the price charged by the monopolist. For this reason, the marginal-revenue curve lies below the demand curve in Figure 1. At greater and greater outputs, marginal revenue is less and less. Eventually it becomes zero and then negative.

Marginal revenue for a monopolist can be positive, negative, or zero, but it is always less than price.

Relationship to Elasticity

In Chapter 23 (see pages 510–511) you learned how the price elasticity of demand affects a company's marginal and total revenue. We showed that when the demand is price elastic, a decrease in the price causes the company's marginal revenue to be positive and its total revenue to go up. The reasoning offered was that the percentage rise in the quantity demanded more than offset the percentage decrease in the price. Also, when demand is price inelastic, a drop in price lowers the company's total revenue and causes its marginal revenue to be negative. This time the percentage rise in the quantity demanded is not enough to offset the percentage decrease in price. Finally, with unitary elastic demand, marginal revenue is zero, and total revenue does not change. The percentage changes in the quantity demanded and in the price are equal but opposite, so that they cancel each other.

We review these relationships in Figure 3. The top part shows a straight-line demand and average-revenue curve and the related marginal-revenue curve for a pure monopolist. The bottom part shows the same company's total-revenue curve.

FIGURE 3
Elasticity of Demand and Revenue for a Pure Monopolist

Shown here are three revenue curves for a pure monopolist—average revenue (demand) and marginal revenue in the top panel and total revenue in the bottom panel. The relationship between them and the price elasticity of demand for the product that this monopolist produces can be observed. Over the output range from 0 to *B*, demand is elastic, marginal revenue is positive, and total revenue increases. At the output level of *B*, demand is unitary elastic (since this is a straight-line demand curve, it is at the midpoint of the demand curve), marginal revenue is zero, and total revenue is at its peak. Over the output range from *B* to *T*, demand is inelastic, marginal revenue is negative, and total revenue decreases.

(At any level of output, total revenue is found either by adding together all the marginal revenue up to that output or by multiplying the price by the level of output.) Over the range of output from 0 to B, the demand is elastic, the marginal revenue is positive, and the total revenue rises. At the output level of B, the demand is unitary elastic, the marginal revenue is zero, and the total revenue is at its maximum. Over the range from B to T, the demand is inelastic, the marginal revenue is negative, and the total revenue falls.

When demand is elastic, the marginal revenue is positive and the total revenue rises. When demand is unitary elastic, the marginal revenue is zero and the total revenue is at its maximum. When demand is inelastic, the marginal revenue is negative and the total revenue falls.

Equilibrium Output and Price

In pure competition, the firm is a price taker and simply adjusts its output to the level at which it maximizes its profit. By contrast, in pure monopoly, the firm is a **price maker** and chooses the combination of output and price that maximizes its profit. The price taker versus the price maker distinction is the key to your understanding of the essential difference between pure competition and pure monopoly. However, the term *price maker*, which implies the possession of full information and the ability to act upon it in every case, should be strictly limited to pure monopoly. Actual monopolists and firms with varying degrees of monopoly control might be better labeled *price searchers*. A **price searcher** is a firm that is able to choose the price for its product, but because it lacks full information, it must search for its profit-maximizing price.

In pure monopoly, the firm is a price maker and chooses the combination of output and price that maximizes its profit. Actual monopolists and firms with varying degrees of monopoly control are price searchers because they lack full information.

In Chapter 25 (see pages 556–561) you learned the logic and techniques used to find the equilibrium output of a firm that faces a negatively sloped demand curve. We showed how a hypothetical yacht firm maximized its profit when it produced the level of output at which its total revenue exceeded its total cost by the greatest amount and at which its marginal revenue equaled its marginal cost. We use the same logic and techniques to find the equilibrium level of output for a pure monopolist. In Figure 4, the top part shows a pure monopolist's total-cost and total-revenue curves, and the bottom part shows the corresponding marginal cost and marginal-revenue curves. Profit is maximized when the company produces Q units a day. In this example, Q units a day is the equilibrium level of output. What is the equilibrium price? Logically, it is the highest price that the monopolist will be able to get from buyers for this level of output. How much that is will be determined by the demand curve that the monopolist faces. In the bottom part of Figure 4 we show this pure monopolist's demand curve. Like any other demand curve, it indicates the maximum price that buyers are willing and able to pay for each different level of output. We see that the monopolist in our example is able to charge a price of P. (This equilibrium price is always determined by finding where the vertical perpendicular drawn from the equilibrium quantity intersects the demand curve and then drawing a horizontal perpendicular from that point of intersection to the price axis.)

The equilibrium level of output for a monopolist is where its total revenue exceeds its total cost by the maximum amount and at which its marginal revenue is equal to its marginal cost. The equilibrium price for a monopolist is determined by its demand curve that shows the highest price that consumers are willing to pay for the equilibrium level of output.

Short-Run and Long-Run Profit

A pure monopolist, like any other firm, may have an economic profit, an economic loss, or just a nor-

FIGURE 4
Equilibrium Output and Price for a Pure Monopolist

The top panel shows this pure monopolist's equilibrium output at Q. This is where its total revenue exceeds its total cost by the maximum amount. The same equilibrium is observed in the bottom panel. At output Q the monopolist's marginal-cost curve intersects its marginal-revenue curve from below. The firm will charge a price of P, since the demand curve indicates that this is the highest price that consumers are willing to pay for output Q.

mal profit in the short run. And like any other company, a pure monopolist will shut down if its revenue is not high enough to cover its variable cost in the short run, and it will leave the industry (causing the industry to disappear) if it cannot earn at least a normal profit in the long run. Unlike firms in pure competition, a pure monopolist may, however, earn an economic profit in the long run.

In the long run, a pure monopoly firm may earn an economic profit, unlike firms in pure competition.

The Short Run Figure 5 pictures four different short-run profit (or loss) situations for a pure monopolist. Panel (a) presents the case most often associated with pure monopoly. Here the company is earning an economic profit. The equilibrium level of output is Q, since this is where the company's marginal-cost curve (MC) crosses its marginal-revenue curve (MR) from below. The equilibrium price is P, since the vertical perpendicular drawn from Q hits the demand curve (D = AR) at point A. If, as in this case, the price or average revenue exceeds the average total cost for some positive volume of output, the firm earns an economic profit. The amount by which average revenue (point A) exceeds average total cost (point B) is the firm's average (per unit of output) economic profit. Its total economic profit (AB × 0Q) is shown as the gold rectangle (P-AC-B-A).

If a monopoly firm's price or average revenue exceeds its average total cost for some positive volume of output, it will earn an economic profit. The amount by which its average revenue exceeds its average total cost is its average economic profit.

Panel (b) shows a pure monopolist that is earning just a normal profit. We show its equilibrium output level of Q and price P. At equilibrium output, the company's average total cost is exactly equal to its average revenue (the average-total-cost curve is tangent to the average-revenue curve at point A), so that no economic profit is earned.

FIGURE 5
Four Alternative Short-Run Profit (or Loss) Situations for a Pure Monopolist

Shown here are four possible short-run profit or loss situations for a pure monopolist. In the first three panels the firm's marginal-cost curve intersects its marginal-revenue curve at output Q, and the demand curve that it faces indicates that it should charge a price of P. Panel (a) shows the firm's average revenue above its average total cost at equilibrium, so that it is earning an economic profit, represented by the gold area. Panel (b) shows the firm's average total cost equal to its average revenue (point A) at equilibrium, so that it is earning just a normal profit.

Panel (c) shows the firm's average total cost above its average revenue at equilibrium, so that it is suffering an economic loss, represented by the red area. The firm will not want to shut down, because its average revenue (point A) exceeds its average variable cost (point C). Panel (d) shows that both the firm's average total cost and average variable cost exceed its average revenue at the output level where its marginal cost is equal to its marginal revenue, so that it will want to shut down and produce nothing.

The other two panels show situations that you might not expect. However, even pure monopolists may run into trouble. They may find that they have a monopoly on a product that is quite costly to produce, and the world is not breaking down any doors to get to it. In other words, the equilibrium price for the product is below the average total cost of producing it. Panel (c) shows a monopolist suffering an average (per unit of output) economic loss, represented by the vertical distance from point A to point B and a total economic loss represented by the red rectangle P-AC-B-A. This is the very best that this monopolist can do in the short run. It minimizes its economic loss by producing the output level of Q and charging the price of P. Furthermore, it pays for this firm to keep operating rather than to shut down, since at equilibrium its average revenue (point A) is above its average variable cost (point C). If it shut down, its total economic loss would grow by an amount represented by the rectangle VC-P-A-C.

If a monopolist is earning a normal profit, its average total cost is exactly equal to its average revenue. If, however, its equilibrium price for the product is below its average total cost of producing it, the monopolist will suffer an economic loss.

Finally, panel (d) shows the case of a monopolist that finds itself in a situation where it is better to shut down than to operate at all. At the level of output that equates the firm's marginal cost and marginal revenue, its average variable cost (point C) is greater than its average revenue (point A). The firm minimizes its economic loss by shutting down (Q = 0), so that it will lose only its fixed cost but will avoid the further loss represented by the rectangle P-VC-C-A.

If a monopolist finds that at the level of output that equates its marginal cost with its marginal revenue, its average variable cost is greater than its average revenue, it will minimize its economic loss by shutting down.

The Long Run Recall that in the long run all costs are variable. There is enough time to allow firms to make any and all adjustments that they wish to make. Such adjustments could possibly turn things around for a pure monopolist that had been suffering an economic loss in the short run. It might now be able to modernize or change the size of its plant enough to earn at least a normal profit. If that can be done, the firm will remain in the industry. On the other hand, if that cannot be done, the monopolist leaves the industry in search of more profitable ventures.

If, in the long run, a pure monopolist that had been suffering an economic loss can modernize or change the size of its plant enough to earn at least a normal profit, the firm will remain in the industry. If that cannot be done, the monopolist will leave the industry.

Monopolists that earned normal or economic profit in the short run may be able to do even better in the long run. Long-run adjustments may help a firm that was earning just normal profit in the short run to make an economic profit in the long run. And since the pure monopoly model assumes that firms would rather earn more than less economic profit, a company already earning an economic profit in the short run may improve upon it in the long run.

Notice that the effects of long-run adjustments are very different in the pure monopoly than in the pure competition model. In the pure competition model, short-run economic profit automatically brought new firms into the industry, so that all the pure competitors earned just a normal profit in the long run. In pure monopoly, no other firm can enter the market. Firms in other industries or completely new firms that would love to share in the economic profit enjoyed by the pure monopolist are denied entry. Thus a pure monopolist may earn an economic profit in the long run, now and presumably forever, safe in the knowledge that no one can break its hold on an exclusive and rewarding market.

Long-run adjustments may help a firm that was earning just a normal profit in the short run to make an economic profit in the long run. In the pure competition model, all pure competitors earn just a normal profit in the long run, but in pure monopoly no other firm can enter the market, so a pure monopolist can earn an economic profit in the long run.

EVALUATION OF PURE MONOPOLY

Would you like to be a pure monopolist? If you are as greedy as most of us, your honest answer is probably "yes." Would you like to live in a country in which many important markets are monopolized? The consumer in you probably says "no." From the two market-structure models that you have studied—pure competition and pure monopoly—you have already learned enough to figure out that you would most likely pay higher prices for goods and services bought from monopolists, and so would be able to afford less of them. To help you review what you have learned, Figure 6 compares the two long-run equilibrium positions. Since the figure pictures one specific market, it is assumed that the market demand is the same whether the structure of this market is that of pure monopoly or pure competition. We also assume that marginal cost is the same no matter which of these market structures exists. Thus, the demand curve drawn in Figure 6 applies to both pure monopoly and pure competition. The positively sloped curve in the figure is both the market-supply curve in pure competition (the sum of the firms' marginal costs) and the marginal-cost curve of the pure monopolist. If the industry were purely competitive, the equilibrium price and the level of market output would be found at the intersection of the market-supply and market-demand curves: Q_{PC} level of output and P_{PC} price. If, instead, the industry were purely monopolistic, the equilibrium level of output would be limited to Q_{PM} and the equilibrium price would be the much higher P_{PM}.

Price, Marginal Cost, and Resource Allocation

It is clear from looking at Figure 6 that in pure competition consumers are able to buy products at a price equal to the seller's marginal cost, but that in pure monopoly they must pay a price that exceeds the seller's marginal cost. This difference in price results from the fact that pure monopolists face negatively sloped demand curves instead of the horizontal ones faced by individual firms in

FIGURE 6
Comparison of Long-Run Equilibrium Positions in Pure Competition and Pure Monopoly

The market-demand curve is assumed to be the same for pure competition and pure monopoly (PC and PM market demand). The market-supply curve in pure competition, which is the sum of the firms' marginal-cost curves, is assumed to be the same as the pure monopolist's marginal cost (PC market supply, PM marginal cost). The equilibrium price and level of market output in pure competition are P_{PC} and Q_{PC}, respectively. The equilibrium level of output in pure monopoly is Q_{PM}, and the price is P_{PM}.

In pure monopoly, as compared with pure competition, consumers who demand the product at prices within the range from just above P_{PC} to just below P_{PM} will be denied the opportunity to buy it. So consumers not only pay a higher price, but must make do with less of the product. This additional welfare loss is shown by the red triangle, called the welfare-loss triangle.

pure competition. What an additional sale is worth to a pure monopolist (its marginal revenue) is less than what it is worth to a consumer (the price or average revenue). But what an additional sale is worth to a pure competitor (its marginal revenue) is equal to what it is worth to a consumer (the price or average revenue).

In pure competition consumers are able to buy products at a price equal to the seller's marginal cost. In pure monopoly consumers must pay a price that exceeds the seller's marginal cost.

In pure monopoly, consumers are denied output equal to the difference between Q_{PM} and Q_{PC} in Figure 6. Consumers who demand the product at prices within the range from just above P_{PC} to just below P_{PM} will be denied the chance to buy it. So besides having to pay a higher price for the product that they buy, they must make do with less of the product. This additional welfare loss is shown by the red triangle in Figure 6. This **welfare-loss triangle** represents the amount of economic welfare that is lost to consumers of this product because it is produced and sold by a monopolist instead of by purely competitive firms.

In pure monopoly consumers not only have to pay a higher price for a product, they also have to make do with less of it. The welfare-loss triangle on a graph represents the amount of economic welfare lost to consumers of a product because it is produced and sold by a monopolist.

We can restate this point about welfare in terms of resource allocation. The pure competition market structure offers greater welfare to society than does pure monopoly because it allows impersonal market forces to determine the flow of resources. In pure competition, resources are devoted to producing additional units of a product as long as the price that buyers are willing and able to pay for another unit is greater than the additional cost of producing that unit. When price equals marginal cost, the equilibrium level of output is reached. By contrast, pure monopoly limits output and blocks entry to the market, so that fewer resources are devoted to producing the product. Equilibrium takes place at a lower output level and at a price that is greater than the additional cost of producing further units of the product.

Resource Transfer

We can see how monopoly prevents socially desirable resource allocation by examining the change in the value of output that results from a transfer of resources from a purely competitive market to a monopolized one. If, indeed, monopoly keeps resources from flowing to their most desirable social use, then a government action forcing a transfer of resources from a purely competitive market to a pure monopoly market would be expected to result in a higher value of what the two markets produce. A hypothetical example is set forth in Figure 7. We picture a purely competitive market that sells product X and a pure monopoly market that sells product Z. They are both in long-run equilibrium. Panel (a) shows that the purely competitive firms in this market have a combined daily level of output of 200 million units of X, each selling at a price of $10. Panel (b) shows a pure monopolist selling 4 million units of Z at a price of $18 each. Now suppose that the government forces a transfer of $100 worth of resources from the industry that produces X to the industry that produces Z. What effect will this transfer have on the value of output produced by these two industries? Since the marginal cost of producing X is $10 (marginal cost is equal to price in pure competition), 10 fewer units will be produced by the purely competitive industry. The value of output produced by that industry has been reduced by just over $100. (The market-supply curve shifts ever so slightly to the left, so that the equilibrium price rises by an insignificant amount.) The $100 worth of resources are then transferred to the pure monopoly market. The marginal cost of producing Z is also $10, so that 10 more units of Z can be produced. Since the price of Z is $18, the value of output by this industry is increased by almost $180. (The slightly higher level of output lowers the equilibrium price by an insignificant amount.) The transfer of $100 worth of resources from a purely competitive market to a pure mo-

FIGURE 7
Resource Transfer from Pure Competition to Pure Monopoly

(a) Pure Competition

Price per Unit of X (dollars)

Market Supply

Market Demand

10

0 200

Quantity of X per day (millions)

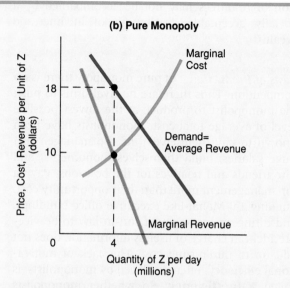

(b) Pure Monopoly

Price, Cost, Revenue per Unit of Z (dollars)

Marginal Cost

18

Demand= Average Revenue

10

Marginal Revenue

0 4

Quantity of Z per day (millions)

That monopoly prevents socially desirable resource allocation is shown by the results of a transfer of $100 worth of resources from a purely competitive industry (panel a) to a pure monopolist (panel b). At the time of the transfer, both the purely competitive market for X (selling 200 million units of X per day at a price of $10 per unit) and the monopoly market for Z (selling 4 million units of Z per day at a price of $18 per unit) are in long-run equilibrium. Transferring $100 worth of resources from the purely com-

petitive industry means that 10 fewer units of X will be produced (price is equal to marginal cost), thus reducing the value of output by $100. Since the marginal cost of producing Z is also $10, the transfer of the $100 worth of resources to the pure monopolist causes it to produce 10 additional units of Z, valued at $180 (10 × $18 = $180). The forced transfer thus increased the combined value produced by these two industries by $80.

nopoly market caused the combined value of these industries' outputs to increase by almost $80 ($180 gain in value of Z less $100 loss in value of X). Put in national terms, the real gross national product increased by almost $80. In our example, the transfer forced a flow of resources that would not otherwise have happened. If the forcing of resources into pure monopoly markets results in a higher total value of goods and services for society, then we have illustrated our argument that the restriction of output in pure monopoly causes an undesirable allocation of society's resources.

Monopoly prevents socially desirable resource allocation. More efficient resource allocation is provided by purely competitive firms.

Beyond Resource Allocation

So far our evaluation of pure monopoly has centered on comparing the long-run equilibrium of this model with that of the model for pure competition. We concluded that pure competition offers a more efficient way of allocating resources. But that is not the end of the story. Much was swept under the rug in the process of that limited analysis. Let us focus now on a few of those sweepings. First, we accepted the firms' costs as given by the existing resource prices and the state of technology. However, there is reason to expect that costs will not be alike in these two very different types of markets. Second, we did not look beyond the long run to what we called, in Chapter 24, the very long run. The prospects for progress differ greatly between these two market types. Finally, we did not address the question of equity. The most efficient allocation of resources may not be accompanied by a socially acceptable distribution of income and wealth.

Costs of Production   In pure monopoly there is no competition. Thus there are no rival firms to push the monopolist to produce at the lowest possible level of average total cost. Monopolists have been known to pay themselves (the top management) huge salaries, build themselves monuments, and hire friends and relatives for the best jobs. Paying top management more than their opportunity cost, building Taj Mahal-like executive office buildings, and hiring an incompetent son-in-law to be vice-president in charge of useless information does not add up to minimizing cost. This lack of motivational efficiency, often displayed by monopolists, is called **X-inefficiency**. So whether monopolists operate at the minimum point on their average-total-cost curves (and they probably will not) may be less important than whether they are likely to operate on the lowest average-total-cost curve available to them. To the extent that monopolists are X-inefficient—engage in high-cost internal practices—they operate on higher average-total-cost curves than do pure competitors.

An argument that leads to the opposite conclusion is that a monopolist may be more able to take advantage of economies of scale than a pure competitor. In many industries, there is not enough demand to accommodate a large number of firms, each large enough to take advantage of the most important economies of scale.

X-inefficiency (high-cost internal practices) results from the lack of motivational efficiency and leads to the failure of a monopoly firm to produce on the lowest possible average-total-cost curve. However, monopolists may be better able to take advantage of economies of scale than pure competitors.

Progress   Progress in industry refers to the discovery and production of new and better products as well as the discovery and putting to use of new cost-saving technology. In Chapter 24, where we introduced the economist's time-period language, we spoke of such discoveries as coming in the very long run. Should we expect a pure monopolist to be progressive? Would pure monopoly or pure competition be more likely to lower (shift down) the average-total-cost curve in the very long run? We have no clear answers.

On the one hand, as we said in the last section on cost, monopolists are not pushed by competition. Will a monopolist bother to pursue a really effective research and development program? Quite possibly not. Monopolists "have it made in the shade" and may just take a good snooze while collecting their profits. For example, U.S. Steel (now USX), which had substantial monopoly control in the American steel industry before the appearance of serious foreign competition, had been accused of such behavior. Whether it was guilty is a matter on which there is no agreement.

On the other hand, although a monopolist is not pushed by competition, it may very well be pushed by good sense and greed. Management may realize that while it has complete control over a product now, in the future some other company may discover a new product that consumers prefer. The monopolist may also realize that it can take advantage of any improvement in the product and any cost-saving gained through technological advances.

Thus, because of this incentive and the likelihood that the monopolist has earned an economic profit and so has the money to fund research and development, we have a pretty strong case for expecting substantial progress in monopoly markets. By contrast, recall from Chapter 26 the discussion of progress in pure competition industries. We suggested that because there was little incentive and money available, progressive research and development programs would probably not take place.

Some monopolists do not pursue an effective research and development program because they are not pushed by competition. Some monopolists do, however, motivated by both greed and good sense.

Equity for Consumers Monopolists are not generally thought of in a very kindly way. They are believed to milk consumers for all they can get, and since they have no competitors, they are thought to get plenty. Well-known examples of monopolists are the Rockefellers, the Du Ponts, the Mellons, and other great "robber barons" of the late nineteenth and early twentieth centuries in the United States. Was it fair for them to amass great monopoly fortunes while most Americans had modest incomes? Is monopoly consistent with justice? Many people answer such questions out of both sides of their mouths. "No," they say, John D. Rockefeller's monopolization of the U.S. oil industry in the late nineteenth century was not fair. "Yes," they say, the monopolies based on patents held by Xerox and Polaroid in the 1960s and 1970s were fair since their stockholders came from all walks of life and even included widows and orphans. Immediately we see that value judgments creep in. Not wishing to impose our values on you, what can we objectively conclude about equity? The conclusions must be drawn from the pure competition and pure monopoly models. No matter whether monopoly profits go into the pockets of robber barons or widows and orphans, sellers have the advantage over buyers. By limiting output and raising price, monopolists can become better off at the expense of consumers. Glancing back at Figure 6, which compares the long-run equilibrium solutions of pure competition and pure monopoly, you can see that monopoly not only decreases the welfare of consumers of their product by the red amount of the welfare-loss triangle but also transfers welfare from buyers to the monopolist. The concept of consumers' surplus—the amount that consumers are willing to pay for a unit of output in excess of what they have to pay to obtain it—was explained in Chapter 22 (see pages 485–486). The amount of consumers' surplus that would be received by consumers of the product in pure competition, but that is transferred to the seller in pure monopoly, is shown in Figure 6 by the rectangle P_{PC}-P_{PM}-f-g, which is formed by the price difference between the two market structures ($P_{PM} - P_{PC}$) multiplied by the amount that is sold by the monopolist (Q_{PM}). This consumers' surplus (plus the consumers' surplus represented by the welfare-loss triangle) is denied to them in pure monopoly.

> Many people believe that monopolies are responsible for inequities. By limiting output and raising price, monopolists can become better off at the expense of consumers.

PRICE DISCRIMINATION

Earlier in this chapter we assumed that a pure monopolist will charge the same price to all of its customers. The assumption was based on the reasoning that if a monopolist tried to increase its sales by offering a lower price to some customers, its other customers would not be willing to pay any more than this new lower price. We now relax this assumption and introduce the possibility of price discrimination. When a monopoly firm finds it possible to practice price discrimination, it is able to improve its profit beyond the amount provided by the usual "marginal cost equals marginal revenue" profit-maximization solution. Before we show how price discrimination is practiced, let us define and set out the requirements for price discrimination.

> When a monopoly firm finds it possible to practice price discrimination, it is provided with an opportunity to improve its profit relative to the amount that it would earn if it were to charge the same price to all of its customers.

Price Differentials and Price Discrimination

How many times have you noticed different prices for what appeared to be the same good or service? Most likely your answer runs into the hundreds. One example might be the price of prescription drugs for senior citizens versus the price for the rest of the public. Others are the admission price to musical, theatrical, or sports events for students versus that for the rest of the public, and the airplane, train, or bus fares for children versus the fares for adults. You could also point out the different prices of certain automobiles sold in Detroit and those sold in San Francisco. These, and thousands more, are cases of **price differentials**, but not necessarily price discrimination. A price differential exists whenever a firm follows the practice of selling the same product at the same time to different buyers at different prices. **Price discrimination** takes place only when a price differential is not justified by a difference in cost to the seller. Our prescription drugs, admissions, and transportation fares examples are cases of price discrimination. The drug costs the same to the seller whether it is sold to a twenty-year-old person or to an eighty-year-old person. A student takes up a seat in a theater or a stadium just as a nonstudent does. And children (but not babies) take up an airplane, train, or bus seat as do older people. By contrast, the automobile example turns out to be a case of a price differential, not of price discrimination. To explain why, let us assume that the automobile in our example is produced in Detroit and, when sold to a nearby dealer, is sold for $10,000. But a San Francisco dealer must pay a delivered price of $10,800. If the $800 difference in price simply reflects the difference in transportation cost (say, the cost of shipping an auto within the Detroit area is $100, but shipment to the West Coast is $900), it is not a case of price discrimination. Logically, the definition of price discrimination may be extended to include price equality for the same product sold at the same time to different buyers despite cost differences incurred by the seller. So if the Detroit-based auto manufacturer charges both its Detroit and San Francisco dealers the same delivered price, disregarding the $800 difference in transportation cost, it would be a case of price discrimination.

A price differential exists whenever a firm sells the same product at the same time to different buyers at different prices. Price discrimination takes place only when a price differential is not justified by a difference in cost to the seller.

Prerequisites for Price Discrimination

Price discrimination is possible only if certain conditions or prerequisites are present. These are that: (1) the seller has monopoly control, (2) the seller is able to separate buyers into different markets with different price elasticities of demand, and (3) the seller is able to prevent low-price buyers from reselling the product to high-price buyers.

Monopoly Control   In order to practice price discrimination, the seller must either be a monopolist or at least have a substantial amount of monopoly control. In other words, the seller must be able to have some control over price. One group of buyers would be willing to pay a higher price than another group only when they had no reasonable alternative. If they were able to buy a like product at a lower price from a different seller, they would do so, and no price discrimination would take place. Adults would not be willing to pay more than children for a seat on an airplane if they could fly to the same destination on another airline that charged children's prices to people of all ages. But when only one airline flies this route or the airlines that fly this route charge the same discriminating prices, adult passengers face monopoly control and must grin and bear it.

Different Elasticities   The second prerequisite for price discrimination is the ability of the monopolist to divide buyers into two or more groups whose demand curves have different price elasticities over a given price range. Recall that the price elasticity of demand (see pages 504–510) refers to the degree of responsiveness of the quantity demanded to a change in price. Buyers who have no good alternatives may respond to a substantial price rise by buying almost as much as before. Buyers who have good substitutes available will purchase far less in reaction to a price hike. An electric power firm, for example, might separate its industrial customers from its residential customers. If the price charged by the power firm were very high, industrial users might decide to generate their own power. Households, however, with no good substitutes available, might be a little more careful about turning off the lights and lowering the thermostat at night, but otherwise they would continue to demand the service.

Prevention of Resale   The final condition necessary for price discrimination is the ability to prevent arbitrage. **Arbitrage** is the purchase of a product in one market for the purpose of immediately reselling it in another market in order to take advantage of a price difference. A price-discriminating monopolist must be able to prevent the customers who buy the product at the lower price from reselling it to those customers who are faced with the higher price. For example, if a shirt manufacturer charges $12 per shirt to one group of retailers and $9 per shirt to another group of retailers, this price discrimination cannot be maintained if those retailers who buy at $9 resell shirts to the other group at less than $12. However, reselling is often prevented by a lack of information leading to a lack of communication among buyers or because of the nature of the good or service. Services, for example, are almost impossible to resell. How do you resell an appendectomy or a haircut? Also, airlines and movie theaters can quite easily enforce the rule that children are not allowed to resell their tickets to adults. Some goods such as certain fruits and vegetables or daily newspapers are difficult to resell because they are perishable or soon out of date. An extraordinary attempt at maintaining price discrimination is a case where two sellers, Rohm & Haas and Du Pont, sold a plastic molding powder to industrial users for $0.85 per pound and to denture manufacturers for $22.00 per pound. When the industrial buyers began to recognize the chance for arbitrage, Rohm & Haas, in its effort to maintain the profitable price discrimination, allegedly planted a rumor that the powder sold to industrial users contained a bit of arsenic.[2]

Three conditions must be present for price discrimination to occur: the seller must have monopoly control, be able to separate buyers into different markets with different price elasticities of demand, and be able to prevent low-price buyers from reselling the product to high-price buyers.

Arbitrage is the purchase of a product in one market for the purpose of immediately reselling it in another market in order to take advantage of a price difference.

---

2. G. W. Stocking and M. W. Watkins, *Cartels in Action* (New York: Twentieth Century Fund, 1946), pp. 402–404.

Another example of price discrimination that is generally quite easy to maintain is found in international trade. Firms may sell their products at a lower price to buyers in a foreign country than to buyers in their own country. This international price discrimination is called **dumping**. Firms may choose to engage in dumping because they have excess capacity, yet don't want to lower their prices to all of their customers. Or dumping might be part of a government's trade policy, in which case the sellers would be subsidized in some way. In several cases, Japanese steel firms have been accused of dumping steel products in the U.S. market with help from their government. And it is said that the U.S. government has often dumped farm products in foreign markets.

International price discrimination is called dumping. Firms may sell their products at a lower price to buyers in a foreign country than to buyers in their own country.

Profit Improvement Through Price Discrimination

You have learned that a nondiscriminating monopolist will maximize its profit when it produces the level of output at which its marginal-cost curve intersects its marginal-revenue curve from below and when it charges the price indicated by its demand curve at that quantity of output. You will see how a price-discriminating monopolist can do better than that.

Price discrimination calls for a monopolist to separate customers into two or more groups with different price elasticities of demand and, of course, with no chance of reselling the product to each other. Let us imagine that a power company separates its customers into two groups— residential and industrial. Figure 8 pictures this case. Panel (a) shows the demand curve and the accompanying marginal-revenue curve facing the firm from its industrial customers. Panel (b) shows the same curves with regard to residential customers. Notice that the demand curve of the residential group is much less elastic (the quantity demanded is less responsive to price changes) than the demand curve of the industrial customers. In panel (c) we

FIGURE 8
Price Discrimination Among Industrial and Residential Customers by a Hypothetical Power Company

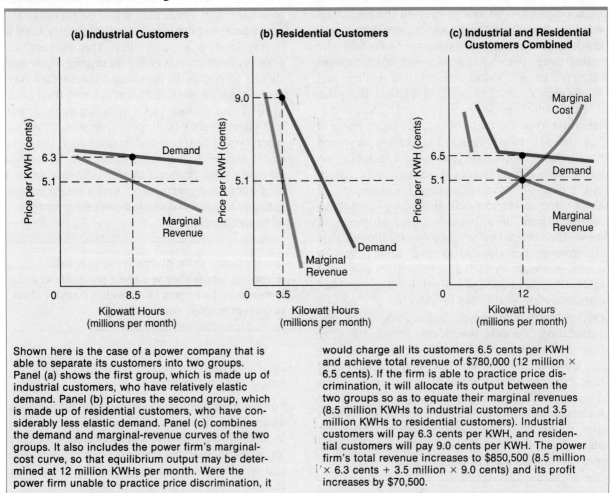

Shown here is the case of a power company that is able to separate its customers into two groups. Panel (a) shows the first group, which is made up of industrial customers, who have relatively elastic demand. Panel (b) pictures the second group, which is made up of residential customers, who have considerably less elastic demand. Panel (c) combines the demand and marginal-revenue curves of the two groups. It also includes the power firm's marginal-cost curve, so that equilibrium output may be determined at 12 million KWHs per month. Were the power firm unable to practice price discrimination, it would charge all its customers 6.5 cents per KWH and achieve total revenue of $780,000 (12 million × 6.5 cents). If the firm is able to practice price discrimination, it will allocate its output between the two groups so as to equate their marginal revenues (8.5 million KWHs to industrial customers and 3.5 million KWHs to residential customers). Industrial customers will pay 6.3 cents per KWH, and residential customers will pay 9.0 cents per KWH. The power firm's total revenue increases to $850,500 (8.5 million × 6.3 cents + 3.5 million × 9.0 cents) and its profit increases by $70,500.

have added together the demand and marginal-revenue curves for the two groups. Assuming that the firm incurs no cost differences in serving the two groups, we have drawn a single marginal-cost curve for the combined output for industrial and residential customers. We can now predict how much output—measured in kilowatt hours (KWHs)—the monopolist will want to produce. Its marginal cost and marginal revenue of a KWH are both 5.1 cents when it produces 12 million KWHs per month.

If the firm were a nondiscriminating monopolist, it would charge all its customers 6.5 cents per

KWH and find that its marginal revenue received from industrial customers greatly exceeds its marginal revenue from residential customers.[3] By practicing price discrimination, the company can raise

3. In order not to complicate the main points in Figure 8, we have not shown the marginal revenues from the industrial customers versus the residential customers that the power firm would receive if it were not practicing price discrimination. To see that marginal revenue from the industrial customers would be much higher than from the residential customers, just extend the horizontal perpendicular drawn at 6.5 cents to the left. Where it intersects each group's demand curve, draw a vertical perpendicular down to that group's marginal-revenue curve. That will enable you to read off marginal revenue of 5.6 cents for industrial customers and 0.2 cents for residential customers.

its profit. Output can be allocated between the two groups so that the marginal revenue from each is the same. Industrial customers will therefore be assigned 8.5 million KWHs and residential customers 3.5 million KWHs. Their respective demand curves show that industrial customers are willing to pay 6.3 cents per KWH for the 8.5 million units and that residential customers will pay 9.0 cents for each of the 3.5 million KWHs. As a nondiscriminating monopolist, the firm in this case would receive total revenue of $780,000 per month (12 million × 6.5 cents), but as a price discriminator its total revenue would be $850,500 (8.5 million × 6.3 cents + 3.5 million × 9.0 cents). Since the monopolist's cost is the same in either case, price discrimination improves its profit by $70,500 per month ($850,500 − $780,000).

Price discrimination calls for a monopolist to separate customers into two or more groups with different price elasticities of demand.

Evaluation of Price Discrimination

Price discrimination is a controversial subject. It can either promote or reduce consumer welfare.

Harmful Price Discrimination The practice of price discrimination reduces consumer welfare by making it possible for monopolists to siphon off consumers' surplus. Price discrimination enables monopolists to "charge what the traffic will bear" so that each buyer or group of buyers will be forced to give up some or all of their consumers' surplus.

Price discrimination can seriously hurt competition by helping to increase the degree of monopoly control held by one or a few firms in an industry that they already dominate. A large and powerful firm may purchase some of its inputs at prices much lower than those paid by its smaller rivals, if it is able to pressure its suppliers into practicing price discrimination in its favor.[4] The resulting competitive advantage may help such a firm to force its rivals into submission so that it emerges

---

4. In Part IX of the book we shall refer to such power or control by a firm on the buying side as "monopsonistic."

with a still larger share of the market. For example, suppose that in a certain city there are ten retail stores that sell garden tractors. Further, suppose that one of these retailers sells about half of the tractors, far more than any other single store in town. This retailer might try to use its relative success to gain a price advantage from each of the several manufacturing firms that sell the tractors to the retailers. Each tractor producer might agree to practice price discrimination in order to keep this large retailer's business. Such price discrimination would allow the large retailer to gain an even larger share of the market, since it could afford to undercut its competitors' prices. Of course, the benefit to consumers would be short-lived if competing retailers were forced to leave the market. Quite possibly the retailer that benefited from the tractor manufacturers' price discrimination would become a monopolist, free to raise the price substantially above competitive levels.

Price discrimination reduces consumer welfare by making it possible for monopolists to siphon off consumers' surplus. In addition, it may hurt competition by helping to increase the degree of monopoly control held by one or a few firms in an industry that it or they already dominate.

Price discrimination may also be harmful when it eliminates socially desirable price competition. An industry agreement calling for each firm, no matter where it is located, to charge the same price for delivered goods is a form of pricing that discriminates against buyers who receive goods from nearby suppliers. This kind of price discrimination is known as a **basing-point system.** Probably the most famous case of basing-point pricing is the "Pittsburgh Plus" system used by the American steel industry from 1900 to 1924. It ensured that the same prices would be charged for all steel mill products to all buyers in a particular area. When a steel mill far away from Pittsburgh sold steel products to a buyer in its home town, it would charge a standard mill price plus the freight charges for shipping steel from the Pittsburgh area. Such a freight charge was made even though the product was not actually shipped over that distance. In the case where a steel producer based outside Pittsburgh shipped steel to a customer based in the Pittsburgh area, the seller had to absorb the freight charges. Whether a producer charged artificial freight costs or absorbed real freight costs, the result was always the same—the same delivered price in any particular area.

Price discrimination may also be harmful when it eliminates socially desirable price competition. This takes place in basing-point pricing systems.

Beneficial Price Discrimination   Price discrimination may also offer some benefits for society. Few people are upset when doctors or lawyers charge lower fees to poor persons than to higher-income people. Prohibiting this sort of price discrimination may raise prices for the poor without reducing prices very much for those with higher incomes.

Price discrimination may also lead to greater consumer welfare when it is practiced in an experimental and independent way. When price discrimination is used to experiment with lower prices and to compete more forcefully with rivals, the consumer may emerge as the winner. In an industry where a few firms have substantial monopoly control and charge the same price for a product, price concessions by one of these firms to a few customers may be just what is needed to stir things up. Other firms may then meet or even undercut the lower price, and before long the new competitive climate may have lowered the price to all customers.

Price discrimination may offer some benefits to society by providing greater equity and consumer welfare.

Economics in Focus

Patent Protection for U.S. Business

Today a new premium is being placed on getting—and enforcing—patent protection. Patents have always been important for industries such as pharmaceuticals, which require a lengthy research-and-development process to create new products. But for companies in rapidly changing, high-tech fields such as computers and biotechnology, patents are even more vital because innovation is the name of the game.

Not surprisingly, corporations are showing a greater willingness to file suit in order to stop infringement on their rights. This is true for all forms of "intellectual property"—copyrights, trade secrets, and trademarks as well as patents. The strategy has been successful because U.S. courts have radically altered their attitude toward intellectual property. Even for cases settled out of court, the new judicial atmosphere allows corporations to gain better settlements. Licensing fees and royalties—the prices charged by companies for use of their rights—are also on the rise.

But much of the recent poaching on U.S. inventiveness has come from overseas competitors, especially Asian firms that are quick to replicate new products and sell them at a lower price. The U.S. International Trade Commission (ITC) has placed a $61 billion annual price tag on foreign piracy. Some foreign governments refuse to protect U.S. products because they wish to encourage their own industries. Others are more willing to help, but their legal structures are inadequate.

U.S. companies have resorted to several methods of counterattack. Some have used the courts, but often a better and quicker option is to file a complaint with the ITC, which has the power to halt imports of offending foreign products. Some large corporations have hired staffs of detectives to ferret out and expose foreign infringements. Increasingly, too, U.S. companies have been vocal about their predicament, using the power of publicity to embarrass their overseas rivals and pressure Congress for better protection. The federal government has responded with a number of recent actions. A 1988 trade bill increased the government's power to retaliate against patent-infringing imports, and in the same year U.S. negotiators hammered out an agreement on basic copyright and patent protection with representatives from Japan and Europe.

In high-tech industries the matter is often complicated by the fact that products do not fit neatly into established legal categories. Is a computer software package entitled to protection because of its technical coding, its logic and sequence, its "look and feel"—or all of these? Moreover, can the maker reasonably claim monopolistic ownership, however temporary, in an era when any home computer user could make a copy? Generally the courts and Congress have been sympathetic to the business view that intellectual property should be protected, but many problems remain to be addressed before the issue is resolved.

Sources: Norm Alster, "New Profits from Patents," *Fortune,* April 25, 1988, pp. 185–190; Anne W. Branscomb, "Who Owns Creativity? Property Rights in the Information Age," *Technology Review,* May/June 1988, pp. 39–45; Clemens P. Work and Don L. Boroughs with Mike Tharp and Nanci Magoun, "Whose Property Is This Anyway?" *U.S. News & World Report,* November 14, 1988, pp. 50–52; Steven J. Dryden and Neil Gross, "The U.S. and Japan Look for a Patent Medicine," *Business Week,* September 5, 1988, pp. 28–29.

SUMMARY

1. Pure monopoly is an extreme market type in which there is only a single seller. No acceptable substitutes are available, and entry into the market is barred. The pure monopolist and the industry are one and the same. (See page 598.)

2. Actual monopoly is a real-world form of monopoly. An actual monopolist is the only seller in its market, yet it competes with rivals in other markets, recognizes potential competition, and may be subject to more or less government regulation. (See page 598.)

3. Actual monopolies may or may not be "government-enforced." Government-enforced monopolies may be firms that have received an exclusive franchise from the government or that have been granted a government patent. Actual monopolies may or may not be "natural monopolies." Natural monopolies are those that owe their monopoly status to the particular cost conditions in their industries. Economies of scale are so important in relation to demand in such markets that only a single firm can take full advantage of them. (See pages 598–599.)

4. Monopoly control refers to the degree of control or power that a firm possesses over the price of the product that it sells. All firms except those that are in purely competitive industries possess some degree of monopoly control. (See page 600.)

5. A pure monopolist is expected to face a negatively sloped demand curve. Its marginal-revenue curve slopes beneath its demand curve because price must be lowered in order to sell more and because the new lower price must be charged for all units of output to all of the monopolist's customers. (See pages 601–604.)

6. When demand is elastic, marginal revenue is positive, and total revenue is rising. When demand is unitary elastic, marginal revenue is zero, and total revenue is at its maximum. When demand is inelastic, marginal revenue is negative, and total revenue is falling. (See page 604 and Figure 3, page 604.)

7. A pure monopolist will maximize its profit at the level of output at which its total revenue exceeds its total cost by the maximum amount,

which is also where its marginal cost and marginal revenue are equated. The price it will charge is determined by the demand curve that it faces. (See page 605 and Figure 4, page 606.)

8. In the short run, a pure monopolist may experience an economic profit, just a normal profit, or an economic loss. If its revenue is not enough to cover its variable cost, it will shut down. In the long run, a pure monopolist may experience an economic profit or just a normal profit. (See pages 606–608 and Figure 5, page 607.)

9. Given a certain market demand for a product and a certain cost to produce it, pure monopoly as compared with pure competition offers its consumers less output and higher prices. Purely competitive firms offer consumers greater welfare than does pure monopoly since the purely competitive firm charges a price that is equal to marginal cost, whereas the monopolist charges a price in excess of marginal cost. (See pages 609–610.)

10. More efficient resource allocation is provided by purely competitive firms as compared with pure monopoly. This fact is demonstrated by forcing a transfer of resources from a purely competitive industry in long-run equilibrium to a pure monopoly market also in long-run equilibrium. Because price is equal to marginal cost in pure competition and price is higher than marginal cost in pure monopoly, a given dollar value of resource transfer will increase the combined value of output produced by the two industries. (See pages 610–611 and Figure 7, page 611.)

11. Pure monopolists may operate on higher average-total-cost curves than do their counterparts in pure competition because they are not pushed by competitors to produce at the lowest cost possible. However, a monopolist may produce at lower average total cost than its counterparts in pure competition because it is large enough to capture economies of scale not available to smaller pure competitors. (See page 612.)

12. Through effective research and development, the average-total-cost curve may be shifted downward in the very long run. There is no clear answer as to whether or not monopoly will foster such progressive actions. On the one hand, a monopolist is not pushed by competitors and may simply not bother, but on the other hand, monopolists have the incentive of long-run economic profit and probably the money to carry out research. (See page 612.)

13. Pure monopoly may or may not be consistent with equity. Monopolies owned largely by a few individuals or families promote an unequal distribution of income and wealth. But when the stock of monopolies is widely held and includes large numbers of widows and orphans, they cannot be condemned on the basis of equity. (See page 613.)

14. When a firm sells the same product at the same time to different customers at different prices, there is a price differential. Price discrimination takes place when a price differential is not justified by a difference in cost to the seller. In order to practice price discrimination, the seller must possess monopoly control, must be able to separate buyers into different markets with different price elasticities of demand, and must be able to prevent low-price buyers from reselling the product to high-price buyers. (See pages 613–615.)

15. By practicing price discrimination, a monopolist may be able to improve its profit position. It may be able to earn more profit than it would if it were simply equating its marginal cost and marginal revenue and charging a single price determined by its demand curve. (See pages 615–617.)

16. The practice of price discrimination sometimes is detrimental to society's welfare and at other times is quite beneficial. Price discrimination may serve as a vehicle for an already powerful firm to gain even greater monopoly control and may also be used as a way to eliminate price competition in markets where such competition is socially desirable. On the other hand, price discrimination may be used to provide greater equity and also to lessen monopoly control. (See pages 617–618.)

KEY TERMS

actual monopoly: a firm that is the only seller in its market, but that faces sellers in other markets offering acceptable substitutes. In addition actual monopolists face potential competition and uncertain government regulation (page 598).

arbitrage: the purchase of a product in one market for the purpose of immediately reselling it in another market in order to take advantage of a price difference (page 614).

basing-point system: a type of price discrimination wherein each firm in an industry, no matter where it is located, charges a delivered price that includes transportation charges based on the presumption that the product was shipped from a common origin (page 617).

dumping: a form of international price discrimination wherein firms sell their products at a lower price to buyers in a foreign country than to buyers in their own country (page 615).

monopoly control (monopoly power): the degree of control or power that a firm has over the price of the product that it sells (page 600).

natural monopoly: a market in which a single seller is required for efficient production (page 600).

patent: a right of temporary limited monopoly over a new product or process granted to its inventor or to a firm that purchases the right from an inventor (page 599).

price differential: a price difference that exists whenever a firm follows the practice of selling the same product at the same time to different buyers at different prices (page 614).

price discrimination: a price differential that is not justified by a difference in cost to the seller (page 614).

price maker: a firm with monopoly power that chooses the combination of output and price that maximizes its profit (page 605).

price searcher: a firm that, because it lacks full information, searches for rather than chooses the price for its product (page 606).

pure monopoly: a market in which there is only a single seller, no acceptable substitutes are available, and there is no potential competition because entry is barred (page 598).

welfare-loss triangle: the amount of economic welfare lost to consumers because a product is produced and sold by a monopolist instead of by purely competitive firms (page 598).

X-inefficiency: producing with high-cost internal practices because of a lack of motivational efficiency (page 612).

DISCUSSION QUESTIONS

1. Carefully distinguish between pure monopoly and actual monopoly. Why is your local telephone company not a good example of a pure monopolist?

2. Actual monopolies may or may not be government enforced. Those that are government enforced may or may not be natural monopolies. Explain these two statements by carefully defining each of the four situations and providing an example for each.

3. "Only monopolists possess monopoly control." True or false? Explain.

4. A purely competitive firm's demand curve is equal to its marginal-revenue curve. Carefully explain why this is not the case for a pure monopolist's demand curve. What is the relationship between a pure monopolist's average revenue and marginal revenue?

5. Explain the relationship between the total-revenue, average-revenue, and marginal-revenue curves for a monopolist. Why is price elasticity of demand unitary when marginal revenue is zero?

6. Without looking at Figure 5, draw a diagram showing a pure monopolist earning an economic profit in the short run. Compare your diagram with panel (a) in Figure 5 to be sure you have it right. What long-run adjustments do you expect?

7. An outstanding difference between the long-run equilibrium conditions for pure competition and pure monopoly is that in pure competition price is equal to marginal cost, whereas in pure monopoly price is greater than marginal cost. What is the explanation for this difference? What important welfare implication can be drawn from this difference?

8. Make a case for each of the following:

a. X-inefficiency is more likely to occur in a monopoly structure than in other market structures.

b. The opportunity for taking advantage of existing economies of scale is more likely in monopoly than in other market structures.

c. Progress stemming from research and development is less likely to occur in a monopoly market structure than in other market structures.

d. A monopolist is likely to conduct more research and development than a pure competitor.

e. Monopolists take unfair advantage of consumers.

9. Distinguish between a price differential and price discrimination. Give an example of a price differential that is not price discrimination. In your example, what change would have to occur to make it price discrimination?

10. From the point of view of the seller, carefully explain the preconditions that are necessary in an industry before price discrimination can be successful.

11. A monopolist that sells its output to customers in different markets may find that charging the same price to all of its customers in all of the different markets results in a much higher marginal revenue from sales to some markets than to others. Given that this monopolist is able to practice price discrimination, will price discrimination enable it to increase its profit? Why or why not?

12. Price discrimination may be used to eliminate price competition among the firms in an industry. Explain how a basing-point system may accomplish this end.

28

Monopolistic Competition and Oligopoly

Preview   In Chapter 26, when we began our study of sellers' market structures, we introduced four different types—pure competition, pure monopoly, monopolistic competition, and oligopoly. So far we have explained the first two. That leaves monopolistic competition and oligopoly yet to be covered.

The first part of this chapter deals with monopolistic competition. After defining its meaning, we discuss its origins and explain its major characteristics. Monopolistic competitors vie with one another on both price and nonprice bases. That gives us the chance to discuss the role of advertising in competition and to explain some of its advantages and disadvantages for society. We then introduce the monopolistic competition model and, as we did with pure competition and pure monopoly, we carefully examine the short-run and long-run equilibria. That leads us to an evaluation of this market structure, both on its own and as compared with pure competition and pure monopoly. Here we point out certain important similarities and differences among these market types.

The second part of this chapter deals with oligopoly. We define oligopoly and explain its most important characteristic—interdependence. You will see that, of the four market structures, oligopoly comes the closest to industries as we know them.

Of the four market models, however, oligopoly turns out to be the most complicated and hardest to understand. We shall explain why we are not able to determine short-run and long-run equilibria *in the same way* that we did for the other three market types. But we shall not leave you high and dry. You will learn about several oligopoly theories that predict certain price and level-of-output equilibria. These are based on such ideas as reaction, the kinked demand curve, game theory, collusive agreements, price leadership, and rules of thumb. Finally, we shall evaluate oligopoly and compare it with the other market types.

MONOPOLISTIC COMPETITION

The models for pure competition and pure monopoly market structures date back one hundred years. Alfred Marshall explained them in his *Principles of Economics,* published in 1890. For the next forty years, these were the only models that economists could use to analyze firm and industry behavior. In the early 1930s, however, two economists, Joan Robinson of Cambridge University in England and Edward Chamberlin of Harvard University in the United States, introduced a third market model. They worked independently, but published their results at about the same time. Their model of market organization is what we refer to as monopolistic competition.

Robinson and Chamberlin were disturbed about the separation of the ideas of competition and monopoly and suggested that the two be blended. They pointed out that nonidentical sellers offer nonidentical products, so that every seller is really a monopolist of its own good or service. Yet they understood that these monopolists compete against each other in certain fairly distinct markets or industries. Their logical conclusion was that most firms are really competing monopolists operating in a type of market that may be called **monopolistic competition.**[1]

Robinson and Chamberlin argued that most firms are really competing monopolists operating in a monopolistically competitive market.

Conditions for Monopolistic Competition

A monopolistically competitive market requires: (1) a large number of independent sellers, (2) product differentiation, and (3) fairly easy entry and exit. We shall take a look at each of these conditions next.

---

1. Actually, the term *monopolistic competition* is Chamberlin's. His book is titled *The Theory of Monopolistic Competition,* and Robinson's book is *The Theory of Imperfect Competition.* Both were published in October 1932.

The monopolistically competitive model requires: (1) a large number of independent sellers, (2) product differentiation, and (3) fairly easy entry and exit.

Large Number of Sellers   The condition of a large number of sellers may remind you of our "many sellers" condition in pure competition. However, it turns out to be not quite so extreme. You learned that pure competition required so many firms that each one believed it could not affect the price. Monopolistic competition requires only a large enough number of firms so that each one believes that the other firms in the market will ignore its actions. Each independently operated firm in the industry must have a small enough market share so that it believes its actions will bring no reactions from competitors. For example, suppose there is an industry made up of 100 firms, each selling 1,000 units of output per day. Now, if one of these firms decides to lower its price by 10 percent, so that its sales rise by, say, 20 percent (assuming price elasticity of demand of 2), this firm would take away only 200 units of sales from its 99 competitors, or about 2 from each. Since this firm believes that each of its rivals' sales will drop only from 1,000 to 998 (a rather small percentage), it will expect its rivals hardly to notice it and not to react at all.

Monopolistic competition requires a large enough number of firms so that each one believes the other firms in the market will ignore its actions.

Product Differentiation   The condition of product differentiation is the most important distinction between monopolistic competition and pure competition. **Product differentiation** means that basically similar products are changed in some way to create some differences among them in the eyes of consumers. Recall that in pure competition there is no product differentiation. In pure competition the product is completely standardized, and consumers couldn't care less whether they buy from one firm or another in the same industry. Of course, product differentiation is also inconsistent with pure monopoly. In that market structure, consumers find no acceptable substitute for what the monopolist sells.

The term *product differentiation* covers a lot of ground. In the words of Edward Chamberlin, "it may be real or fancied." It does not matter which, as long as the difference is important to buyers and therefore influences consumer preference. For example, identical peaches that come from the same orchard and are processed in the same way are seen as different products when some are canned under the label of one firm and others carry a different firm's brand name. Some consumers are willing to pay a few cents more per can for Del Monte brand peaches, and other consumers are willing to pay more for the Libby brand.

In other cases, the product differentiation may take the form of a minor technical product difference, such as embossed versus clear plastic wrap or swivel versus stationary two-track razors. Or it may go beyond the basic character of the product and include such features as packaging, color, and size. The location of the firm may be crucial as well. The grocery store around the corner is able to sell at somewhat higher prices than the supermarket in a shopping center several miles away. Finally, certain characteristics of the seller rather than of the product itself may play a major role in product differentiation. The reputation of a certain company in terms of its outstanding efficiency, courteousness, or trustworthiness differentiates it from other companies that are not held in as high regard by consumers. Monopolistic competition recognizes that all of these characteristics are "purchased" when a customer buys the product.

Product differentiation means that basically similar products are changed in some way to create differences among them in the eyes of consumers. The difference may be real or imagined.

Fairly Easy Entry and Exit The final condition required for monopolistic competition is that firms outside the industry find it fairly easy to enter and that firms established in the industry find it fairly easy to exit. Entry and exit are not free, as they are in pure competition. The presence of product differentiation means that new firms would not be

likely to gain immediately the level of consumer acceptance attained by long-established firms. But no great barriers exist, since new firms need to add only a small percentage of the industry's level of output. Likewise, exit is somewhat more costly than in pure competition. When a monopolistically competitive firm leaves its industry, it loses the consumer acceptance that it had built up.

Real-World Markets?

Some actual markets come close to being monopolistically competitive. Retail markets in fairly large cities, such as gas stations in Milwaukee, men's clothing stores in Boston, and Chinese restaurants in San Francisco, are reasonably good examples. Each of these markets is made up of a fairly large number of firms that sell products that are somewhat differentiated from each other. But while each of the many firms has a small share of the total market, they do not completely ignore one another. Generally, the owner or the manager of a gas station does keep an eye on the price charged at other gas stations in the neighborhood, the clothing store operator makes it his or her business to know other retailers' prices for certain items, and restaurant owners or managers are aware of the menus (including prices) of at least some of their major competitors. To the extent that firms do look over their shoulders to see what competitors are doing, the important characteristic of independent action is missing, and the industry only approaches the monopolistic competition market structure.

Some actual markets, such as certain retail markets in fairly large cities, come close to being monopolistically competitive. However, these firms generally do not completely ignore one another, so that the important characteristic of independent action is usually missing.

Advertising

Advertising plays a part in the product differentiation condition of monopolistic competition. However, it is a controversial area in economics. Among the major arguments are those concerning: (1) the effect of advertising on economic freedom, (2) the effect of advertising on the efficiency of providing information to consumers, (3) the effect of advertising on competition, and (4) the effect of advertising on the cost of production.

Advertising and Economic Freedom Advertising is said to be a hallmark of a free-enterprise economy. Free-enterprise capitalism depends on the ability of firms and individuals to engage in any business that they wish and to tell people that they are ready, willing, and able to provide the good or service that they seek to sell. The most common means of doing so are to use billboards and a sign above the place of business, radio and television commercials, and advertisements in newspapers and magazines. What is so controversial about doing these things? Why is there a question of economic freedom? Who would deny business people the "right" to communicate their message? A number of people would.

There are many complaints about the nuisance caused by a great deal of advertising—heavy magazines and newspapers in which there is little to read, ugly billboards along roads, and commercials interrupting one's favorite television and radio programs. There are also attacks on serious philosophical and economic grounds. It is argued that advertising threatens "consumer sovereignty"—that what consumers want should dictate what business firms produce, and not the other way around. A great deal has been written about how business firms use psychology, prey on the consumer's subconscious mind, and in other ways persuade people to buy products that they really didn't want in the first place.

Vance Packard, a popular writer in the 1950s, recognized this threat to consumer sovereignty. In *The Hidden Persuaders,* Packard writes about the motivation research that goes into preparing many advertising campaigns. He quotes the head of a major Chicago research firm, who explains that "motivation research is the type of research that seeks to learn what motivates people in making choices. It employs techniques designed to reach the unconscious or subconscious mind because preferences generally are determined by factors of which the individual is not conscious. . . . Actually in the buying situation the consumer generally acts emotionally and compulsively, unconsciously reacting to the images and designs which in the subcon-

scious are associated with the product."[2] Packard argues that to be successful in selling a product, business firms sell "emotional security," "reassurance of worth," "ego gratification," "creative outlets," "love objects," "sense of power," "sense of roots," and "immortality."[3]

Since most advertising is done by private business firms, a companion argument is that advertising causes too large a percentage of a country's resources to be used for producing private rather than public goods and services. The hidden persuaders force an extra car into your garage rather than good streets to drive on and a nice park to drive it to.

Advertising and Information Advertising is said to provide useful information to consumers. Consumers cannot possibly know everything there is to know about every product at every moment in time. At which grocery store can you get the best buy on frozen pizza today? Where can you get the best deal on a bicycle? And how can you best satisfy your sweet tooth today? Firms recognize that, by providing information, they can attract more sales. Telling people about the characteristics of products, their prices, and where to buy them often translates into sales. The A&P Company reasons that if consumers know that the company is offering Whamo Italian pepperoni fourteen-inch pizzas at $2.87 today, they will jam the aisles to buy them. Likewise, the Brach Candy Company believes that if consumers see a picture of their delicious-looking chocolate kisses, they will recognize their ability to satisfy the craving that they have for sweets. Their view is that advertising provides mutual benefits—consumers receive information, and business firms make sales. In fact, proponents of advertising go even one step further. They argue that advertising is a very efficient way of providing information because once consumers "learn" that the best buys are at A&P or that Brach candies are delicious, the store or brand loyalty built up through advertising saves them the trouble of searching for better products in the future.

But to what degree is advertising actually informational? Critics of advertising see little infor-

2. Vance Packard, *The Hidden Persuaders* (New York: Pocket Books, 1957), p. 5.
3. Ibid., pp. 61–70.

mation given in the soft drink ad that pictures a beautiful woman and a handsome man enjoying a certain brand of soft drink together at the beach, or the many cigarette, beer, and automobile ads that carry no message other than "Buy mine, it's best." Such advertisements are largely self-canceling, leaving consumers no better informed than they were in the first place.

Advertising uses scarce resources. About 2½ percent of U.S. national income (about $125 billion) is devoted to advertising. Are consumers getting $125 billion worth of information? As we have indicated, some advertisements provide little information and are clearly wasteful. But it would be foolish to condemn advertising in general. Just leaf through a trade magazine and read the ads for industrial products. They are usually chockfull of details about the product, how it can be used, and other useful information.

Advertising is a controversial area in economics. Some complain that it is a nuisance, that it threatens consumer sovereignty, and that it wastes resources.

Proponents of advertising say that it serves the function of providing consumers with useful information.

Advertising and Competition   Advertising is at the heart of what economists call *nonprice competition*. Along with price competition, it is a means by which firms compete with each other. Does it follow, then, that advertising causes an industry to be more competitive? The answer is "no." In fact, successful advertising accomplishes the opposite. Besides trying to shift customers' demand curves for their products to the right (to sell more at any particular price), firms also advertise in order to make their demand curves less elastic. Firms hope to gain greater control over price by making their competitors' products appear to be poorer substitutes. For example, suppose that a firm faced the flatter (more elastic) demand-curve segment shown in Figure 1 and that at equilibrium it sold 40,000 units per day at a price of $7 per unit. The firm does not advertise and has relatively little control over price. It is not a pure competitor that has

no control over its price, but at somewhat higher prices it will lose a lot of its sales. Its demand curve before advertising indicates that if it decided to raise its price to $9, its sales would drop by half to 20,000 units a day. Now suppose, instead, that the company did advertise so that its demand curve for prices above $7 is much steeper (less elastic). The advertising has the effect of making rivals' products appear to be poorer substitutes. Many customers are now so convinced that this product is better that they are willing to keep on buying it in spite of a somewhat higher price. If the firm is again at equilibrium when it sells 40,000 units at $7 each, the same $2 rise in price to $9 will cause its level of sales to drop by only 10,000 units to 30,000. Advertising has made poorer substitutes of its competitors' products, allowing it to gain monopoly control.

FIGURE 1
The Effect of Advertising on the Elasticity of Demand

The flatter demand-curve segment (labeled "demand before advertising") is faced by a firm that sells 40,000 units per day at $7 per unit without doing any advertising. At the higher price of $9, it would lose half of its sales. The steeper demand-curve segment (labeled "demand after advertising") is faced by the same firm after it has made its competitors' products appear to be poorer substitutes through advertising. At the higher price of $9, it would now lose only a quarter of its sales.

> **Advertising is a form of nonprice competition between firms. Besides trying to shift customers' demand curves for their products to the right, firms also advertise in order to make their demand curves less elastic.**

Another way in which advertising has an impact on competition in an industry is through its influence on entry by new firms. Successful advertising by established firms in an industry may create an important entry barrier. If established firms have gained great consumer acceptance through advertising—making their brand names household words—a new company with an unknown name may find it very hard to compete effectively. For example, we find few companies interested in entering the toothpaste, detergent, or beer industries, perhaps because of the large amount of consumer acceptance that firms in those industries have gained through their advertising. Some economists are so concerned about the lack of interest in entering such industries that they favor a complete ban on advertising. But would that work? Perhaps it would just solidify the monopoly control of the established firms. It would mean that no new company could enter and communicate with consumers. The few companies that successfully enter industries in which consumers are brand conscious are those that enter with a very large dose of advertising. This allows them to gain consumer acceptance and some respectable market share. If advertising were banned in such industries, almost no possibility of entering would exist, and that important aspect of competition would disappear.

FIGURE 2
Four Alternative Effects of Advertising on Long-Run Average Total Cost

(a) Large Change In Output due to Advertising
(b) Small Change In Output due to Advertising

Each of the four diagrams shows two long-run average-total-cost curves, one without advertising and one with advertising. Since advertising uses resources, the latter is always above the former. In all four diagrams, the horizontal distance (A to B or A to C) measures the demand response to advertising and the vertical distance (T to S) the change in average total cost that results from the combination of the demand response to advertising and the economies of scale. Economies of scale are illustrated by the slope of the average-total-cost curves.

In panels (a) and (b), the slopes of the cost curves are the same, but the demand response to advertising is much greater in panel (a). In that case,

Successful advertising by established firms in an industry may create an important entry barrier.

Advertising and Production Cost   Another controversy about advertising centers on whether advertising raises or lowers the cost of producing goods and services and, in turn, the prices paid by consumers. We have already pointed out that advertising uses resources; so of course advertising costs are part of the total cost that firms spend on production. But, it is argued, advertising shifts demand curves to the right. Since many firms operate on the negatively sloping part of their long-run average-total-cost curves, advocates of advertising say that the economies of scale that result from advertising more than compensate for the advertis-

ing costs. It is impossible to generalize on this important point. Advertising may or may not shift a product's demand curve to the right. If it does, it may shift it a little or a great deal. In industries where advertising is largely self-canceling, firms' demand curves may not shift at all. Companies may advertise only for defensive reasons. They recognize that if demand for one firm's product rises, it may be at the expense of a competitor's product. Individual firms may be trying to keep their demand curves from shifting to the left. Also, firms may or may not be operating on the negatively sloping part of their long-run average-total-cost curves. If they are on the decreasing part, the curve may be sloping either steeply or very gradually.

Figure 2 pictures four different cases. In panels (a) and (b), the long-run average-total-cost curves (both with and without advertising cost included)

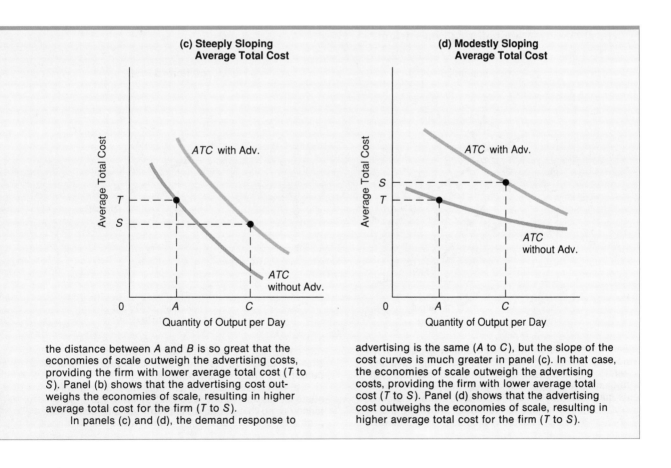

the distance between *A* and *B* is so great that the economies of scale outweigh the advertising costs, providing the firm with lower average total cost (*T* to *S*). Panel (b) shows that the advertising cost outweighs the economies of scale, resulting in higher average total cost for the firm (*T* to *S*).

In panels (c) and (d), the demand response to

advertising is the same (*A* to *C*), but the slope of the cost curves is much greater in panel (c). In that case, the economies of scale outweigh the advertising costs, providing the firm with lower average total cost (*T* to *S*). Panel (d) shows that the advertising cost outweighs the economies of scale, resulting in higher average total cost for the firm (*T* to *S*).

are the same. But, the change in sales (output) due to advertising (the horizontal distance between quantity *A* and quantity *B*) is much greater in panel (a) than in (b). In panel (a), the sales (output) response is so great that average total cost with advertising is lower than average total cost without advertising (*S* is below *T*). In panel (b), the sales (output) response to advertising is so small that average total cost with advertising is higher than average total cost without it (*S* is above *T*).

In panels (c) and (d) of Figure 2, the sales (output) responses to advertising (the horizontal distances between quantities *A* and *C*) are the same. However, the slopes of the long-run average-total-cost curves (with and without advertising cost included) are much steeper in panel (c) than in panel (d). In panel (c), average total cost falls so quickly as output rises (economies of scale are great) that average total cost with advertising is

lower than average total cost without advertising (*S* is below *T*). In panel (d), the decline in average total cost that goes with increases in the level of output is much less (economies of scale are relatively small). As a result, average total cost with advertising is greater than average total cost without advertising (*S* is above *T*).

Another controversy about advertising centers on whether it raises or lowers the cost of producing goods and services.

The Monopolistic Competition Model

We are now ready to explain the monopolistic competition model. In some respects it is like the pure competition model. Economic profit, eco-

---

FIGURE 3
Four Alternative Short-Run Equilibrium Profit (or Loss) Situations for a Typical Firm in Monopolistic Competition

Each diagram shows a possible short-run equilibrium point for a firm in a monopolistically competitive market. Each pictures the firm's demand or average-revenue curve (*D = AR*), its marginal-revenue curve (*MR*), its marginal-cost curve (*MC*), and its average-total-cost curve (*ATC*). Profit maximization occurs where the firm's marginal-cost curve intersects its marginal-reve-

nue curve from below. In all but the shut-down case shown in panel (d), the firm wishes to produce a level of output of *Q* and charge a price of *P*.

In panel (a), at equilibrium the firm's average revenue exceeds its average total cost by the vertical distance *PC*, so that the gold area represents its economic profit. In panel (b), at equilibrium the firm's nomic loss, or normal profit may be earned by monopolistically competitive firms in the short run. In the long run, entry or exit plays a major role to ensure that each firm earns only normal profit. An important difference between monopolistic competition and pure competition is that monopolistically competitive firms may be making changes in their advertising expenditures, which affect their costs.

In monopolistic competition, unlike pure competition, firms may make changes in their advertising expenditures, which affect their costs.

Short-Run Pricing and Output Figure 3 pictures four alternative short-run equilibrium profit (or loss) positions for a typical firm in monopolistic competition. Notice that the demand, or average-revenue curve ($D = AR$), in each of the diagrams has a negative slope. This slope shows that even though the companies have many competitors that sell fairly close substitutes, each firm has some control over price—that is, some monopoly control. It means that a monopolistically competitive firm will not lose all of its customers when it raises price a bit, and that in order to sell a higher level of output, it must lower its price. Lying below each demand curve is the firm's marginal-revenue curve (MR). As we said in the discussion of pure monopoly (see pages 601–604), the marginal-revenue curve always lies below a negatively sloped demand curve. Also pictured in each of the four diagrams is this typical firm's average-total-cost curve (ATC) and marginal-cost curve (MC). These curves are drawn in the usual way, with the marginal-cost curve intersecting the minimum point of the average-total-cost curve. However, they include not only the cost

average total cost is equal to its average revenue (the ATC curve is tangent to the $D = AR$ curve), so that it earns a normal profit. In panel (c), at equilibrium the firm's average total cost exceeds its average revenue by the vertical distance CP, so that the red area represents its economic loss. The firm will

want to operate because its average revenue (point P) exceeds its average variable cost (point V). In panel (d), at equilibrium both the firm's average total cost and its average variable cost exceeds its average revenue so that it will want to shut down and produce nothing ($Q = 0$).

incurred in making the product—as in pure competition—but also the cost incurred in trying to differentiate the company's product. Thus, advertising and promotional costs are included in the cost curves.

The demand or average-revenue curve faced by a monopolistically competitive firm always slopes downward. Therefore the marginal-revenue curve always lies below the demand curve.

Advertising and promotional costs are included in the cost curves for monopolistically competitive firms.

Profit maximization occurs where the firm's marginal-cost curve crosses its marginal-revenue curve from below, so that in all but the shut-down case shown in panel (d), the firm wishes to produce Q units of output a day and sell this output at price P. In panel (a), the firm is earning economic profit. At equilibrium output Q, its average revenue exceeds its average total cost by the vertical distance PC. The gold area ($PC \times Q$) represents its economic profit. Panel (b) shows a case of normal profit. At equilibrium output Q, the average-total-cost curve is tangent to the average-revenue curve. In panel (c), the firm is suffering an economic loss represented by the red rectangle. In the short run it minimizes its economic loss by producing the output level of Q and charging the price of P. It pays for the firm to continue to operate rather than to shut down since at equilibrium its average revenue (point P) is above its average variable cost (point V). Finally, panel (d) shows the case of a monopolistic competitor that finds itself in a situation where it is better to shut down than to operate at all. At equilibrium, its average variable cost is greater than its average revenue.

In monopolistic competition, as in pure competition, firms may earn an economic profit, just normal profit, or suffer economic losses in the short run.

Long-Run Pricing and Output What will happen in the long run? The answer is the same as for pure competition. Each firm will earn only a normal profit. Some companies will enter if there is short-run economic profit. Some will exit if there is short-run economic loss. In the case of short-run economic profit (Figure 3a), the entry in the long run will shift the typical firm's demand curve to the left because the market demand is now divided among more companies. The economic profit begins to decline. Likewise, in the case of short-run economic loss (Figure 3c and d), as firms leave the industry, the remaining firms' demand curves shift to the right. This happens because the market demand is now divided among fewer firms. In this case, the economic loss begins to decline.

Demand shifts brought on by entry or exit may not entirely explain why economic profits and losses decline in the long run. Two other factors may be at work. First, as we explained in our discussion of pure competition, industries may be characterized by rising or falling cost as firms enter or leave the industry, so that the average-total-cost and marginal-cost curves of firms in these industries may shift in the long run. Second, monopolistically competitive firms' average-total-cost and marginal-cost curves also may shift because of changes in the amounts that firms spend on advertising. They may try to raise or protect their profit by spending more on advertising. If one company or only a few of them do this, we might expect that their efforts would be rewarded. However, since the "typical" firm (the one we are describing) represents the actions of the many firms in a monopolistically competitive industry, the sales gains attempted through this advertising will not be realized, as all the advertising will largely cancel itself out. Instead of large sales increases, the typical company will have higher cost but little, if any, change in output.

Monopolistically competitive firms' average-total-cost and marginal-cost curves may shift because of changes in the amount they spend on advertising. Since all the competitors advertise, an increase in advertising expenditure may mean that a significant sales gain will not be realized, and that each firm will experience higher cost but little, if any, increase in output.

FIGURE 4
Long-Run Equilibrium for a Typical Firm in Monopolistic Competition

Shown here is a monopolistically competitive firm in long-run equilibrium. Its marginal-cost curve (*MC*) intersects its marginal-revenue curve (*MR*) from below at a daily level of output of 13 units, and its demand or average-revenue curve (*D = AR*) shows that it can sell this output at $13 per unit. At equilibrium its average total cost (*ATC*) equals its average revenue (the *ATC* curve is tangent to the *D = AR* curve), showing that the firm earns only a normal profit.

Figure 4 shows a typical monopolistically competitive firm in long-run equilibrium. Whether that equilibrium was reached through entry or exit, through shifts of cost curves, or through some combination of the two, it offers the typical company only a normal profit.

In the long run, just as in pure competition, monopolistically competitive firms earn only a normal profit.

Evaluation of Monopolistic Competition

In evaluating monopolistic competition, we first ask about the realism of the model. How well does the monopolistic competition model explain what happens between the rather unrealistic extremes of pure competition and pure monopoly? Next, we compare it with pure competition and give the arguments on both sides as to which is the more appropriate "ideal."

How Realistic is Monopolistic Competition? We first presented monopolistic competition as a market structure that is realistic and for this reason appropriate to use in analyzing many existing industries. It is a model that recognizes that firms have negatively sloping demand curves but are not pure monopolists, and that they compete with each other but are not pure competitors. The model also covers both price and nonprice competition, so that the effects of advertising can be analyzed. Just the same, after more than fifty years of familiarity with the monopolistic competition model, economists generally agree that its direct application to the real world is quite limited.

The problem is that monopolistic competition describes a market in which sellers are not interested in their rivals' responses. All actions are assumed to take place at the same time rather than in response to one another. Thus, impersonal market forces—as in the case of pure competition—determine what firms do and ensure that only a normal profit is earned in the long run. But in the real world, it is usual for companies to react to one another and to expect rival firms to act and react in certain ways. For this reason, critics say that the model does not give a "realistic" view of the world.

The key weakness of the monopolistic competition model is that it describes a market in which sellers act as if they are not interested in their rivals' responses. In the real world, of course, companies do react to one another.

Comparison of Monopolistic Competition with Pure Competition Even though the monopolistic competition model does not describe real-world markets very much better than the pure competition model does, the question of deciding which is the more appropriate "ideal" still remains. If it were in effect, which of these two market structures would offer greater consumer welfare?

Those who would vote for pure competition ask us to compare the long-run equilibrium position of a typical firm in pure competition with the long-run equilibrium position of a typical firm in monopolistic competition. Figure 5 allows us to do so. We have combined Figure 10 from Chapter 26 (showing a purely competitive firm in long-run equilibrium) and Figure 4 (showing a monopolistically competitive firm in long-run equilibrium). To distinguish between them, the pure competitor's curves are drawn in purple and the monopolistic competitor's in orange. Notice that the purely competitive firm's demand curve is infinitely elastic and the same as its marginal-revenue curve. However,

as you can see, the monopolistically competitive firm faces a negatively sloped demand curve with its marginal-revenue curve lying beneath it. Also notice that the average-total-cost and marginal-cost curves are higher for the monopolistic competitor, reflecting the amounts it spends on advertising. In this case, we find that the firm in pure competition will sell 20 units a day at a price of $10 and the firm in monopolistic competition sells 13 units a day at a price of $13.

Economists who believe that pure competition is the ideal will quickly point out that purely competitive firms will sell more goods or services at a lower price. This will always happen because price is equal to marginal revenue and to marginal cost in pure competition, but price is above marginal revenue and marginal cost in monopolistic competition. Figure 5 also shows that monopolistic competitors produce on higher average-total-cost curves than pure competitors do and that they do not produce at the lowest point of their average-total-cost curves, as pure competitors do. The monopolistically competitive company in this figure has a price and average total cost of $13, which is $3 above the price and average total cost of the pure competitor. About $2 of that cost difference is explained by the amount spent on advertising, and about $1 by the monopolistically competitive company producing on the downward-sloping part of its average-total-cost curve rather than at the lowest point, where its marginal-cost curve crosses its average-total-cost curve.

Those who favor monopolistic competition admit to all these points. However, they still say that monopolistic competition is the more attractive ideal. They base their argument on the view that it is worth paying somewhat higher prices for a lower level of output in order to gain product differentiation. They argue that in pure competition the gains in consumer welfare stemming from greater efficiency are outweighed by the loss in consumer welfare resulting from having only standardized products available in the marketplace.

Who is right? That is difficult to say, since the answer is based on value judgments. The tradeoff between the greater efficiency offered by the pure competition model and the product differentiation offered by the monopolistic competition model cannot be measured in any objective way.

FIGURE 5
Comparison of Monopolistic Competition with Pure Competition

The diagram showing a monopolistically competitive firm in long-run equilibrium, which was drawn in Figure 4, has been printed in orange along with the diagram showing a purely competitive firm in long-run equilibrium (from Figure 10 in Chapter 26), which has been drawn in purple. The monopolistically competitive firm has higher costs brought on by advertising and other selling expenses incurred to achieve product differentiation. Output is restricted, and the price is higher than in pure competition.

Economists who believe that pure competition is the ideal point out that purely competitive firms sell more goods and services at lower prices. Those who favor monopolistic competition say that it is worth paying somewhat higher prices for a lower level of output to gain product differentiation.

OLIGOPOLY

At the beginning of Chapter 26, we introduced **oligopoly** as a sellers' market that is made up of a few firms producing anywhere from rather standardized to quite differentiated products and that may be fairly easy or quite difficult to enter. The key to understanding this market type is to get a good grasp on what the economist means by "few firms."

An oligopoly is a sellers' market made up of a few firms producing anywhere from rather standardized to quite differentiated products. It may be fairly easy or quite difficult to enter.

Fewness

It was quite clear when we told you that a pure monopoly is made up of a single firm. It was less clear when we observed that pure competition and monopolistic competition require many firms. We had to explain what is meant by "many." In pure competition it means the presence of so large a number of firms that each one acts as a price taker. In monopolistic competition it means that there are so many firms that each one can safely ignore the others. Now we state that in oligopoly there are few firms. So we must explain what is meant by "few." Again the definition depends on how the firms in a market behave in relation to each other. It cannot be easily defined in numerical terms. Instead, it must be interpreted operationally. Fewness means **interdependence** among firms. It means that firms will worry about each other. They will

consider their rival firms' potential reactions to any action that they are thinking of taking. For example, an oligopolist would not change the price of its product, the quality of its product, or its advertising outlay without at least taking into consideration what the response of its rivals might be. Three or four firms in an industry are surely "few firms," but thirty-five or fifty-five may or may not be. Where the line is drawn depends upon the maximum number of firms an industry can accommodate before they ignore each other and it becomes a "many firms" monopolistically competitive industry.

Fewness means interdependence, and interdependence among oligopolists is expressed in how they make important economic decisions. What one of these firms will do depends upon what it believes that its rivals will do in response, and each rival in the industry makes decisions in the same way.

Fewness means interdependence among firms—they consider their rivals' potential reactions to any action they are thinking of taking.

The Real World

Real-world industries are more often characterized by oligopoly than by any of the other three market types. In other words, "fewness" or interdependence is a common industry trait. It is found over a very wide range of industries. No one is surprised to find interdependence among four or five giant firms that dominate an industry. Surely the cereal breakfast foods industry, the computer hardware industry, the passenger car industry, and the cigarette industry are examples of oligopolies. More surprisingly, interdependence is also found in many industries made up of relatively small firms. The half-dozen gas stations in your neighborhood make up an oligopoly industry. So do the "better" men's clothing stores in town, the scrap metal dealers within a twenty-mile radius, and television repair shops in a town or a neighborhood within a large city. Between the giant and the small are countless medium-sized firms grouped in oligopoly industries. Ready-mixed-concrete firms in a metropolitan area, women's and misses' dress manufacturers in various price categories, and bottlers of soft drinks in certain regions are examples. In fact, you probably realize that it is a great deal easier to think of examples of oligopoly industries than to think of examples of any of the other three market types. Interdependence among firms in an industry is the *usual* case, not the exception. Except for the monopoly (a single firm), an industry is made up of a group of competing firms, and that group usually conforms to "fewness." There are many thousands of gas stations in the United States, just as there are many thousands of "better" men's clothing stores and television repair shops, but there is no nationwide gas station, "better" men's clothing store, or TV repair shop industry. To find appropriate industry definitions, product categories must be geographically broken down. A person living in Paw Paw, Michigan, is quite unlikely to have his or her TV set repaired in Bangor, Maine. Nor will you ordinarily gas up at a station twenty-five miles away from your home, school, or place of work. We shall say more about industry boundaries in the next chapter. Our primary aim here is to show you how common the oligopoly structure is.

Real-world industries are more often characterized by oligopoly than by any of the other three market types. Interdependence, then, is a common industry trait.

Oligopoly Models

The difference between oligopoly and the other three market structures becomes very clear when we discuss oligopoly models. Oligopolists do not determine their level of output and their prices by examining only consumer demands and production costs. In contrast to the other three market types, oligopolists also consider the effects of rivals' expected responses. This means that the demand curve faced by an oligopolist is not derived simply from consumer data but also includes what rivals are likely to do in reaction to any output level and price change. For example, an oligopolist in an industry with nine other firms may estimate that, at a price of $10, consumers will buy 1,000 units a day

from the whole industry. The oligopolist may further estimate that, if all ten firms charge $10, it can sell 150 units a day. But if it lowers its price to $9 and the other firms keep their price at $10, it can sell 700 a day. However, it may reason and know from experience that the $9 price would cause its rivals to cut their prices as well. Depending upon the price elasticity of demand for the product, the oligopolist would then expect its sales to rise to, say, 160 a day. It is even quite possible that the cutthroat nature of the industry would cause rival firms not just to follow but actually to undercut the $9 price. If others charged $8, the company in our example might lose all but a few very loyal customers.

Oligopolists do not determine their levels of output and their prices by examining only consumer demands and production costs. They also consider the effects of rivals' expected responses.

This simple example shows how much more complicated it is to determine demand curves for oligopolists than for firms in the other three market types. However, it is not impossible. It just means that in order to determine an oligopolist's demand curve, other variables beyond the usual ones must be taken into account. These are called **experience variables**—the oligopolist's knowledge of previous rival reactions to price changes in the industry, the personality traits of key managers of rival firms, and the political effects of the rivals' reactions. It is difficult but essential for the economist to evaluate this kind of material when dealing with an oligopolistic market.

Determining demand curves for oligopolists involves taking experience variables into account—the oligopolist's knowledge of previous reactions by rivals to price changes in the industry, the personality traits of key managers in rival firms, and the political effects of rivals' reactions.

A fairly large number of different oligopoly models have been offered by economists. We shall describe the most important of these: (1) early duopoly models, (2) the kinked-demand-curve model, (3) game theory, and (4) oligopoly coordination models.

Early Duopoly Models The first attempt at explaining oligopoly came from Augustin Cournot in 1838. Cournot's model introduced the concept of rival firms reacting to each other. His model described a **duopoly,** an industry made up of two sellers. He assumed that with a fixed price for a standardized product each firm would produce a level of output that, together with its rival's output, would bring it the maximum profit. The key assumption made by Cournot was that each company always believes that the other will keep on producing the same level of output as it presently does.

A duopoly is an industry made up of two sellers who react to each other.

Later economists refined the Cournot model using price rather than output as the key decision variable. However, the assumption that each company expects the other to keep on doing what it is doing was retained. This unreasonable assumption, which implies that firms are not able to learn and to anticipate each other's moves, leads to less-than-very-useful predictions. Even so, the contribution made by Cournot and his followers was an important one. It introduced *reaction* into industry models.

The Kinked Demand Curve In the late 1930s several economists introduced a theory of pricing in oligopolistic industries that relies on the idea of a kinked demand curve. A **kinked demand curve** is made up of two segments of a firm's demand curve, which are divided at the industrywide price that has been established. The demand segment relating to lower prices is less elastic than the demand segment relating to higher prices. The reason is that rival firms are expected to match price reductions quickly and fully, since they want to keep their market share. But they are expected to follow price rises only slowly and partially since they would like to increase their market share. Figure 6 shows a kinked demand curve as it might appear to a firm in an oligopolistic industry. The firm, which pres-

FIGURE 6
A Kinked Demand Curve

Shown here is a kinked demand curve for an oligopolistic firm that is presently producing 9,000 units of output per day and selling them at the industrywide price of $10 per unit. The demand segment for prices higher than $10 is much more elastic than the segment for prices below $10. If the firm increases its price by $2 to $12, its sales will decline by 7,000 to 2,000 units. But if it lowers its price by $2 to $8, its sales will only increase by 1,000 to 10,000 units.

ently charges the industrywide price of $10, expects that if it raises the price to $12, it will cause a large decrease in the quantity demanded—from 9,000 down to 2,000 units—because few competitors will match the increase. By contrast, the firm expects that if it decreases the price to $8, this cut will be matched by almost all of the firm's rivals, so that it will sell only 1,000 more units. The theory states that usually oligopolists will not find either prospect very attractive and so will have a tendency not to change the price at all. Fairly rigid prices are consistent with what is generally found in actual oligopoly industries.

A kinked demand curve is made up of two segments of a firm's demand curve. The demand segment relating to prices below the present price is less elastic than the demand segment relating to prices above the present price.

Another explanation for the rigidity of prices in oligopoly industries is offered by the unusual shape of an oligopolist's marginal-revenue curve when it faces a kinked demand curve. Figure 7 shows a hypothetical firm's kinked demand curve and its marginal-revenue and marginal-cost curves. Pay special attention to the marginal-revenue curve and understand why it has a vertical segment at the established quantity level of output. The dark orange portion of the marginal-revenue curve is derived from the more elastic portion of the demand curve (at quantity levels below 9,000), and the light orange portion of the marginal revenue curve is derived from the less elastic portion of the demand curve (at quantity levels above 9,000). Thus a discontinuity, which we draw as a vertical segment of the marginal revenue curve, appears at the established quantity level (9,000 in our example) where the kink in the demand curve appears. Notice that the marginal-cost curve intersects the marginal-revenue curve from below at point A, indicating that this firm will maximize its profit by producing 9,000 units at the industrywide price of $10. If now its marginal cost would increase a bit (shift somewhat to the left) or decrease a bit (shift somewhat to the right), but in either case still intersect the vertical segment of the marginal-revenue curve, the firm's profit-maximizing position would not change—it would still offer 9,000 units per day at a $10 price.

A fundamental objection to the theory of the kinked-demand-curve is that it does not explain how the industrywide price was established in the first place.

According to kinked-demand-curve theory, competitors have a greater tendency to match price cuts than price increases. Oligopolists tend to have rather rigid prices.

Game Theory A third approach that economists use to analyze oligopoly was developed by John von Neumann and Oskar Morgenstern in their classic book, *Theory of Games and Economic Behavior*, published in 1944. **Game theory** allows economists to liken the relationship between competing oligopolists to a game of cards (especially poker) or chess, and even to war. It helps to identify the con-

FIGURE 7
Equilibrium Output and Price with a Kinked Demand Curve

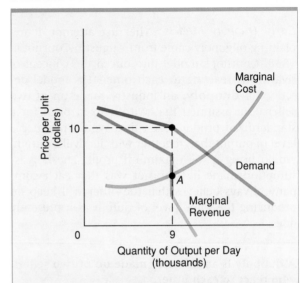

Shown is the kinked demand curve for an oligopolistic firm along with its marginal-revenue and marginal-cost curves. The dark orange portion of the marginal revenue curve is derived from the more elastic portion of the demand curve, which corresponds to quantity levels below 9,000, and the light orange portion of the marginal-revenue curve is derived from the less elastic portion of the demand curve, which corresponds to quantity levels above 9,000. The vertical segment of the marginal-revenue curve appears at the kink, which is at the established price ($10) and quantity level (9,000). Since slight shifts in marginal cost will still intersect the vertical portion of this firm's marginal-revenue curve (at points somewhat above or below point A), such shifts will not alter this firm's equilibrium price or quantity level.

flict relationship among oligopolists and the incentive that they have for cooperation.

Table 1 illustrates a "payoff matrix," which shows the results of various strategies that can be adopted by rival duopolists A and B. We assume that each has only two alternative price strategies, charging $6 per unit or $5 per unit. The dollar figures in the boxes are the profit payoffs that the firms receive as a result of the combination of strategies represented by that box. The first number that appears (to the left of the comma) is Firm B's payoff, and the second number is Firm A's payoff. Reading across the table, you can see that by charging a price of $6, Firm B can earn either $200 or

$100 (depending upon what Firm A charges), or by charging $5, it can earn either $250 or $150 (depending upon what Firm A charges). Similarly, reading down the table, you can see that by charging a price of $6, Firm A can earn either $200 or $100 (depending upon what Firm B charges), or by charging $5, it can earn either $250 or $150 (depending upon what Firm B charges). Which strategy will the firms choose, and what will be the outcome? The answer depends upon what you assume. One popular game-theory assumption is that each firm will try to avoid the worst possible outcome. In our example this would mean that both firms would charge a price of $5, since this allows them to avoid the risk of earning only $100. The solution is found in the lower-right box—each firm earns $150. Each would have liked the other to charge $6, so that it could earn $250 instead of $150. That is likely to be impossible to achieve, since it would mean that the other firm would earn only $100. However, the solution of $150 profit for each is lower for both of them than it needs to be. If each charged $6, they could be in the upper-left box, where each would earn $200. But given the assumption that each will act so as to avoid the worst possible outcome, they would have to cooperate with each other to reach the more favorable solution.

TABLE 1
Game-Theory Payoff Matrix for Duopoly

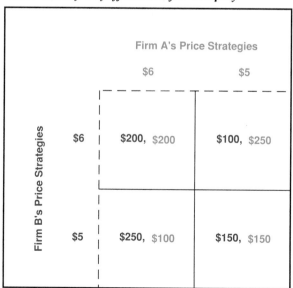

The game in our example is one of many that can be used to analyze oligopoly markets. Depending upon the rules of the game, a specific solution can be found for each set of assumed behaviors.

Game theory helps identify the conflict relationships among oligopolists and the incentive they have for cooperation.

Oligopolistic Coordination   Under the heading of oligopolistic coordination there are three practices found in oligopolistic industries that can help us make better predictions of the equilibrium level of output produced by firms and the equilibrium price charged by firms. These are: (1) collusive agreement, (2) price leadership, and (3) rules of thumb.

Collusive Agreement   **Collusion** takes place when firms in an industry agree among themselves to take actions that will improve their mutual well-being. It is a cooperative effort to gain monopoly control in order to gain a high economic profit. The smaller the number of companies in an industry, the easier it is to collude. Of course, collusion is inconsistent with the pure competition and monopolistic competition models, but it is likely to happen in oligopoly. In oligopoly there is a tendency for the firms in an industry to maximize their joint profit and to divide that profit in some prearranged way. We shall go no further here than to point out this tendency. There are both natural and legal reasons why collusion does not usually take place. In Chapter 35 we shall deal with collusion more fully in our discussion of government antitrust policy.

Collusion takes place when firms in an industry agree among themselves to take actions that will improve their mutual well-being. Collusion is more likely to happen in oligopoly than in other market types because there is a tendency for the firms in an oligopoly industry to maximize their joint profit and to divide that profit in some way. However, there are natural and legal reasons why collusion is not that common.

Price Leadership   In an oligopolistic industry, firms that are prevented from colluding may still find it fairly easy to coordinate their pricing behavior by means of **price leadership**. This is a practice that allows oligopolists to coordinate their price adjustments to changes in demand or cost conditions without engaging in collusion. As the term implies, price leadership means that one firm announces a price change, and all the other firms quickly follow the price leader's action. Price leadership can be explained best by asking and answering the question: Why do firms follow a particular firm in their industry when it raises or lowers its price? Economists give three different answers: (1) One firm in the industry (the leader) is so dominant that the others do not have much choice but to follow. (2) The price leader is seen as a barometer of market conditions, so that the other firms will want to imitate this respected firm. (3) By following the price change of any major firm, it is possible to avoid price competition. Let us look more closely at each of these answers.

Price leadership means that one firm announces a price change and all the other firms quickly follow the price leader's action.

Dominant-firm price leadership describes the condition of a firm so powerful compared with the other firms in the industry that the other firms accept its price as the one prevailing throughout the industry. This is something like the condition of a firm in pure competition which is convinced that it cannot affect price and so accepts the price set by the industry. In other words, dominant-firm price leadership takes place when small and relatively weak firms believe that they will not be able to sell at a higher price than that charged by the dominant firm and that they can sell all they want to at the "going" price.

Dominant-firm price leadership may take place when small and relatively weak firms believe that they cannot sell at a higher price than that charged by the dominant firm in the industry. They act very much like pure competitors.

Barometric-firm price leadership takes place when the firms in an industry consider one firm's price changes to be a good barometer of the market climate. The barometric price leader is usually a large and important firm in the industry. But, more important, it is a firm that historically has been proved to be "correct" in its evaluation of changing market conditions and in its price changes in reaction to them. The firms want to follow the price of the barometric price leader. They are neither forced to follow, as in the dominant-firm case, nor trying to avoid price competition, as in the case we are about to discuss.

Barometric-firm price leadership may take place when the firms in an industry consider one firm's price changes to be a good barometer of the market climate.

Price leadership to avoid price competition may occur when collusion is considered undesirable or impossible. It is based on the realization by the firms in an oligopolistic industry that they will be more profitable if they charge the same price than if they engage in price competition. If one of several large and important firms in such an industry changes its price, all the other firms will follow in order to eliminate price competition.

Price leadership to avoid price competition is based on the realization by the firms in an oligopolistic industry that they will be more profitable if they charge the same price than if they engage in price competition.

Rules of Thumb   Another means of coordinating the firms in an oligopoly industry is for them to follow some rules of thumb, or industry "conventions," that have been developed over some period of time. These rules of thumb may involve variables such as the nature of the product, advertising, research and development, and, most important, price. Interdependence among firms, the hallmark of oligopoly, causes oligopolists to keep a very close watch on each other. Companies discover from their rivals' responses just what actions are considered acceptable or unacceptable. Certain actions by firms may cause hardly any response, and certain other actions may bring strong retaliation by rivals. When these responses become known and accepted, they appear as rules of thumb.

In the important matter of pricing, the rule of thumb may be a **cost-plus price principle** such as the retailers in a certain industry adding 25 percent to the cost of the products that they purchase from the manufacturers. If all the retailers in that industry purchase at the same unit price from the same manufacturers, the 25 percent rule will assure all the firms that their prices will not be undercut by their competitors.

Rules of thumb may also surface in the particular dollars-and-cents price that is charged by firms. At retail, jeans are customarily sold at $19.95 or $22.95 or $29.95, but not at $19.40 or $22.31 or $29.00. Therefore, if retailers are selling certain jeans at, say, $21.95 and manufacturers raise the price to them by 40 cents, it is likely that the rule of thumb followed for pricing jeans will bring all the competing retailers' prices up to $22.95. Again, without collusion or leadership, each oligopolist will be able to predict easily what rival firms will charge.

Oligopoly firms discover from their rivals' responses just what actions are considered acceptable or unacceptable. When these responses become known and adopted, they appear as rules of thumb.

Short-Run and Long-Run Pricing and Output
Keeping in mind that oligopolists do not determine their level of output and their prices by examining only consumer demands and production costs but that they are also influenced by experience variables, we can now picture different possible oligopoly short-run and long-run profit (or loss) situations.

The Short Run Figure 8 (page 642) pictures four different short-run profit (or loss) situations for an oligopolist.[4] Panel (a) presents the most

---

4. So as not to complicate the diagrams, we will assume that the demand curves are not kinked and therefore that the corresponding marginal-revenue curves do not have discontinuous segments.

likely case. Here the oligopolist is earning an economic profit. The equilibrium level of output is Q, since this is where the firm's marginal-cost curve (MC) intersects the marginal-revenue curve (MR) from below. The equilibrium price is P, since the vertical perpendicular drawn from Q hits the demand curve ($D = AR$) at point A. In this case the oligopolist's average revenue exceeds its average total cost (point A is higher than point B), showing that it earns an economic profit. Its total economic profit ($AB \times 0Q$) is shown as the gold rectangle (P-AC-B-A).

Panel (b) shows an oligopolist that is earning just normal profit. We show its equilibrium output level of Q and price of P. At equilibrium output, the firm's average total cost is exactly equal to its average revenue (ATC is tangent to AR at point A), so that this company neither earns an economic profit nor suffers an economic loss.

The remaining two panels show situations where an oligopoly firm has run into trouble. The equilibrium price for the product is below the average total cost of producing it. Just as in the other market structures that we have examined, the oligopolist's short-run decision to produce or to shut down will depend on the relationship between its average variable cost and its average revenue at its equilibrium level of output. Panel (c) shows the case of an oligopolist suffering an economic loss represented by the red rectangle P-AC-B-A. It minimizes the economic loss by producing the output level of Q and charging the price of P. If it shut down, its total economic loss would grow by an amount represented by the rectangle VC-P-A-C.

Finally, panel (d) shows the case of an oligopolist that finds itself in a situation where it is better to shut down than to operate at all. At the level of output that equates the firm's marginal cost and marginal revenue, its average variable cost (point C) is greater than its average revenue (point A). The oligopolist minimizes its economic loss by shutting down ($Q = 0$), so that it will lose only its fixed cost and will avoid the further loss represented by the rectangle P-VC-C-A.

The Long Run Recall that in the long run there are no fixed costs. Within the limits of a firm's production function there is enough time to allow it to make any and all adjustments that it wishes to make. Such adjustments could possibly turn things

FIGURE 8
Four Alternative Short-Run Profit (or Loss) Situations for an Oligopolist

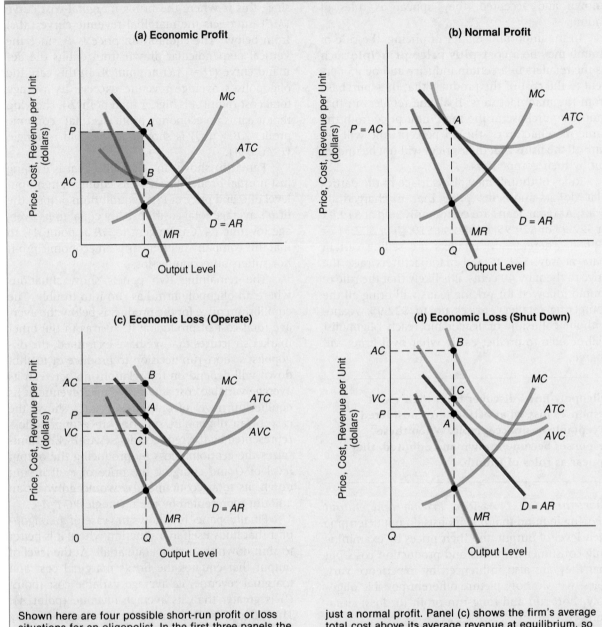

Shown here are four possible short-run profit or loss situations for an oligopolist. In the first three panels the firm's marginal-cost curve intersects its marginal-revenue curve at output Q and the demand curve that it faces indicates that it should charge a price of P. Panel (a) shows the firm's average revenue above its average total cost at equilibrium, so that it is earning an economic profit, represented by the gold area. Panel (b) shows the firm's average total cost equal to its average revenue (point A) at equilibrium, so that it is earning

just a normal profit. Panel (c) shows the firm's average total cost above its average revenue at equilibrium, so that it is suffering an economic loss, represented by the red area. The firm will not want to shut down, because its average revenue (point A) exceeds its average variable cost (point C). Panel (d) shows that both the firm's average total cost and average variable cost exceed its average revenue at the output level where its marginal cost is equal to its marginal revenue, so that it will want to shut down and produce nothing.

around for an oligopolist that had been suffering an economic loss in the short run. Some might be able to modernize or change the size of their plants enough to lower substantially their average total costs. Also, competitor firms who believe that they cannot turn things around may decide to exit the industry, leaving more business (shifting the demand curves facing the remaining firms to the right) to the remaining firms. It is likely, then, that some oligopoly firms that were suffering economic loss in the short run will earn at least normal profit in the long run.

Oligopolists that earned normal profit in the short run may be able to earn economic profit in the long run. Likewise, oligopolists that earned some economic profit in the short run may be able to earn greater economic profit in the long run. On the other hand, entry by new firms may occur in the long run, which may offset the increased economic profit potential of firms' long-run adjustments. The ease or difficulty of entering oligopoly industries varies greatly. Some will attract entrants when profits are only slightly above normal, while others experience no entry at even quite high rates of economic profit. In the next chapter we will discuss the conditions of entry and why some industries are so much more difficult to enter than are others.

In the long run, an oligopolist that had been suffering an economic loss in the short run might be able to modernize or make other changes to lower its average total cost. It is likely, then, that some oligopoly firms that were suffering economic loss in the short run will earn at least normal profit in the long run.

Notice that the effects of long-run adjustments are different in oligopoly than in the other models that you studied. In the pure competition and monopolistic competition models, short-run economic profit automatically caused firms to enter, so that all the firms earned just a normal profit in the long run. In the pure monopoly model no new firms could enter the market. Oligopoly is somewhere in between. Entry is not automatic when oligopoly firms earn economic profit, yet entry is not entirely

foreclosed so that oligopolists can just ignore potential competitors. Although some oligopolists may earn only normal profit in the long run, oligopolists can and do earn varying amounts of economic profit in the long run.

The effects of long-run adjustments are different in oligopoly than in other market structures. Entry is neither automatic nor entirely foreclosed when oligopoly firms earn economic profit. Oligopolists earn either economic profit or just normal profit in the long run.

Evaluation of Oligopoly

We are now ready to evaluate oligopoly. With certain qualifications and changes, many of the pros and cons of oligopoly are like those that we offered for pure monopoly and, to a lesser extent, for monopolistic competition.

Figure 9 pictures an oligopolist earning an economic profit in the long run. It sells 100 units a day at $18 a unit and earns an economic profit of $300 a day ($18 − $15 = $3; $3 × 100 = $300). The figure looks like the long-run equilibrium for a monopolist earning an economic profit. Of course, we realize that the monopolist's demand curve was based on consumer data alone, whereas the demand curve in Figure 9 includes, in addition, this oligopolist's expectations of what its rivals will charge at each possible price. As in pure monopoly and monopolistic competition, the oligopolist charges a price that is higher than marginal cost (Figure 9 shows the price to be $8 above marginal cost). The demand curve is expected to be somewhat more elastic than in pure monopoly and somewhat less elastic than in monopolistic competition. However, the particular elasticity of demand at equilibrium varies greatly from one oligopolistic industry to another.

At any given cost structure, the price that is charged in oligopoly will be much higher than pure competitors would charge and probably somewhat higher than what a typical firm in monopolistic competition would charge. But an oligopolist's

FIGURE 9
Oligopolist in Long-Run Equilibrium

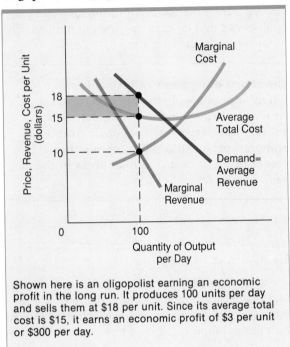

Shown here is an oligopolist earning an economic profit in the long run. It produces 100 units per day and sells them at $18 per unit. Since its average total cost is $15, it earns an economic profit of $3 per unit or $300 per day.

price is not expected to be quite as high as what a pure monopolist would charge. It follows that the level of output offered in oligopoly will be lower than in pure competition and monopolistic competition but higher than in pure monopoly. As in pure monopoly, but to a lesser extent, oligopolists restrict output. They also make it less than inviting to firms that might like to enter the industry. The results are again resource misallocation and a loss of welfare for society. Let us look a little closer at the extent to which prices, costs, and progress in oligopoly differ from those in the other three market types.

Compared to monopoly, oligopolists are expected to charge a somewhat lower price and restrict output somewhat less.

Price Rigidity in Oligopoly   One major difference between oligopolists and firms in the other three

market types is that oligopolists are much slower to change their prices. In the three market structures in which firms act independently of each other, the smallest change in demand or cost will cause firms to set a new profit-maximizing price. However, in oligopoly, prices tend to be sticky or rigid because of the discontinuity of the firm's marginal revenue curve when it faces a kinked demand curve (see our discussion earlier in this chapter) and because oligopolistic firms are never quite sure of the boundaries of acceptable action. They realize that the effects of being misinterpreted by rivals might be very severe—as in the initiation of a price war. For this reason, price rigidity appears as a normal oligopolistic price strategy. Firms take a "leave well enough alone" attitude and normally change the price only when it is safe to do so according to industry convention. Oligopolists commonly resort to various forms of nonprice competition, such as advertising and product changes, sometimes because these are believed to be more effective than price changes, but often as a "safer" way of achieving the same result.

Oligopolists are slower than firms in the other three market types to change their prices. Oligopolists commonly resort to various forms of nonprice competition instead.

Costs in Oligopoly   In our evaluation of pure monopoly in Chapter 27, we said that monopolists might not be pushed to produce on the lowest average-total-cost curve available to them. However, we also said that they might achieve quite a low average total cost since they are likely to be large enough to take advantage of economies of scale. The first point may or may not hold for oligopoly. If there is quite a bit of competition among the firms in an oligopolistic industry, each would be pushed to produce on its lowest available average-total-cost curve. But if there is effective collusion among the firms, if the industry is difficult to enter, or if there are conventions that discourage active competition, the result may not be very different from that in pure monopoly.

If there is quite a bit of competition among the firms in an oligopolistic industry, each would be pushed to produce on its lowest available average-total-cost curve. However, if there is collusion or if the industry is difficult to enter, the result might not be very different from that in pure monopoly.

The second point—the ability to take advantage of economies of scale—probably applies to oligopoly almost as well as to monopoly. The number of firms in an oligopolistic industry is likely to be related to the number of efficient firms that the industry is able to accommodate. There may be fewer, but seldom more. For example, given today's technology for producing automobiles, the demand for automobiles in the United States may only be great enough to accommodate five to ten efficient firms. If fifty fairly equal-sized auto firms produced for the U.S. market, they would surely incur a very high average total cost. They would not be able to take advantage of important economies of scale.

The number of firms in an oligopolistic industry is likely to be related to the number of efficient firms that the industry is able to accommodate.

Progress in Oligopoly Remember that progress occurs in the very long run and refers to the discovery and production of new and better products and the discovery and putting to use of new cost-saving technology. Would you expect oligopolists to be progressive? Again our answer is not very different from the one we gave in the last chapter regarding the progressiveness of pure monopolists. We suggested that, on the one hand, monopolists "have it made in the shade" and so might not bother to do much effective research and development. On the other hand, they probably have the incentive and the means to do a great deal of both.

The expression "having it made in the shade" is much less descriptive of oligopolists than of monopolists. With the exception of outright collusion, oligopolists cannot generally afford to be as complacent as monopolists. Generally, but not always, oligopolists face enough competition or potential competition to cause them to "bother" about carrying on research and development. In fact, most privately financed research and development is done by oligopolists. Whether more competition would raise or lower the amount spent on research and development is a matter of opinion.

The incentive to carry on research and development and the means to pay for it are on the average almost as great for oligopolists as for monopolists. Oligopolists often have a great deal of monopoly control, and many receive long-run economic profit. Joseph Schumpeter, a noted economist who taught at Harvard University during the 1930s and 1940s, argued that research and development was the backbone of competition in capitalist countries. He wrote that "the fundamental impulse that sets and keeps the capitalist engine in motion comes from the new consumers' goods, the new methods of production or transportation, the new markets, and the new forms of industrial organization the capitalist enterprise creates."[5] The capitalist businesses that Schumpeter writes about are the oligopolies that make up most of the industries in the United States as well as in the other industrial countries.

Most privately financed research and development is done by oligopolists.

5. Joseph A. Schumpeter, *Capitalism, Socialism, and Democracy* (New York: Harper & Brothers, 1950), p. 83.

Economics in Focus

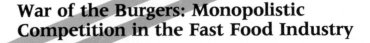

War of the Burgers: Monopolistic Competition in the Fast Food Industry

Fast food may no longer be the industry for a fast profit. Industry-wide sales growth, adjusted for inflation, declined from 4 percent in 1987 to 3.5 percent in 1988 and an estimated 2.5 percent in 1989. Wendy's opened 450 new restaurants in 1985 but fewer than 100 in 1987. Burger King's profits dropped 59 percent between 1987 and 1989. Some chains are still doing very well—McDonald's, for example, increases its per-store sales by 5 percent annually—and the industry overall remains strong; but the days of incredible expansion seem to be over.

Why this change? In the first place, the nutrition- and weight-conscious American public has cooled its passion for hamburgers and other high-calorie (high-cholesterol) meals; thus sales growth for the traditional menu items has slowed. On the cost side, the lower number of workers willing to supply their labor at minimum wage rates has forced employers to offer higher wage rates plus expensive new incentives, such as day-care programs.

But a primary reason for the changing economic climate in fast food is increased competition. In many areas the market is virtually saturated; also, acceptable building sites are hard to find. Furthermore, there are few "new" customers to be found; for Burger King to add customers, it must win them away from McDonald's or Wendy's or Hardee's.

The fast-food industry closely approximates monopolistic competition. Although the major chains are few in number, they operate many separate restaurants, so in most geographic areas the sellers are plentiful. The products are differentiated by taste, packaging, restaurant location, company reputation, and other factors; and entry to and exit from the industry are fairly easy. In such a situation, economists expect that success of the early entrants will prompt more firms to enter the market; but these new competitors will cause the demand curve that is faced by each individual firm to shift to the left, and in the long run the typical firm will earn no economic profit. This is essentially what is happening in fast food.

Other characteristics of the industry also match what we would expect in monopolistic competition: the stress on advertising, for instance. Advertising plays a major role in establishing product differentiation, which leads to a preference for one restaurant over another. The drive to add new menu items also serves to differentiate the products.

But like most other businesses in the real world, the fast-food industry fails to fit the monopolistic competition model in one key respect: the rivals do not ignore each other. Wendy's is keenly aware of menu and pricing moves by Burger King, and Burger King knows that Wendy's is watching. In fact, each successful change soon spawns imitators. Thus the economic environment becomes more complicated and interactive than the monopolistic competition model would suggest.

Sources: Timothy and Suzanne Tregarthen, "Hard Times for Fast Food," *The Margin,* November/December 1988, pp. 13–15; Pete Engardio with Brian Bremner, "Can a New CEO Pull Burger King Out of the Fire?" *Business Week,* May 22, 1989, p. 40; Scott Hume, "Fast-Food Menu: More Discounts," *Advertising Age,* December 19, 1988, pp. 2, 45.

SUMMARY

1. In the early 1930s a third market structure model—monopolistic competition—was introduced. Monopolistic competition describes a market in which there are many sellers, each selling a somewhat differentiated product. (See page 624.)

2. Just as in pure competition and pure monopoly, monopolistically competitive firms make all of their decisions independently of each other. Each firm believes that any action on its part will not cause a reaction on the part of its competitors. (See page 624.)

3. Some actual industries come close to being monopolistically competitive. However, upon closer inspection, it is usually found that the firms do not completely ignore each other, and so the crucial market characteristic of independent action is not met. (See page 624.)

4. The product differentiation characteristic of monopolistic competition is related to the controversial subject of advertising. Advertising is claimed to be, on the one hand, a pillar that supports free enterprise and, on the other, an obstacle to economic freedom since it threatens consumer sovereignty. Advertising can be valuable by providing information, but it can also be wasteful when it provides very little information. Because advertising is an important form of nonprice competition, it encourages more vigorous competition among firms. Yet if successful, it can result in less competition, since it can cause the demand for a firm's product to become less elastic. Advertising uses scarce resources, and so it adds to the cost of producing products. But it may also stimulate sales so that firms are able to take advantage of economies of scale. (See pages 624–630.)

5. Similar to pure competition, monopolistically competitive firms may earn an economic profit, an economic loss, or a normal profit in the short run, but may earn only a normal profit in the long run. Long-run equilibrium is assured by a combination of entry and exit and changes in the amount that firms spend on advertising. (See pages 630–633.)

6. Though neither pure competition nor monopolistic competition characterizes most real-world industries, economists debate about which one would provide greater consumer welfare and thus about which model should be considered the more appropriate ideal. Those who favor pure competition point out that purely competitive firms produce more output and charge a lower price. Their opponents argue that some sacrifice in output and price is not too much to pay for the differentiation of products provided by monopolistically competitive firms. (See pages 633–634 and Figure 5, page 634.)

7. Oligopoly describes a market in which there are few firms. "Fewness" here means interdependence. An industry is said to be oligopolistic when it is made up of few enough firms to have each one consider its rivals' reactions before taking any action itself. (See page 635.)

8. Real-world industries are more often oligopolies than any other market type. Interdependence among firms in an industry is the usual case, not the exception. In a large country like the United States, even when thousands of different firms sell the same product, they are often broken down into hundreds of different, geographically separated, oligopolistic industries. (See page 635–636.)

9. Oligopolists do not determine the amounts that they produce and the prices that they charge by examining only consumer demands and production costs. Oligopolists also consider what their rivals are likely to do in reaction to the output levels and prices that they choose. Thus, in order to determine oligopolists' demand curves, "experience variables" such as the toughness of rival managers must also be considered. (See page 637.)

10. Early duopoly models introduced the concept of rival firms reacting to each other. The earliest was an output reaction model presented by Augustin Cournot. These models were not directly applicable to real-world oligopolies, however, since they assumed that firms were unable to learn from experience and to anticipate each other's reactions. (See page 637.)

11. The kinked-demand-curve theory of oligopoly pricing is based on the expectation that rival firms are more likely to match price reductions than price increases. This causes the demand segment above the existing price to be more elastic than the demand segment below the existing price. Since neither prospect is attractive to oligopolists,

the theory predicts fairly rigid prices. (See page 637 and Figure 6, page 637.)

12. Game theory helps to identify the conflict relationship among competing oligopolists and the incentive that they have to cooperate. Depending upon the rules of the game (assumptions about behavior), a specific solution can be determined. (See pages 638–639.)

13. Oligopolistic coordination models (including collusive agreement, price leadership, and rules of thumb) are helpful in predicting price and output equilibria in oligopolies. Collusion is a cooperative effort by competing oligopolists to gain monopoly control. Price leadership is the oligopolistic practice of having one firm in an industry announce a price change, and all the other firms quickly following the price leader's action. Price leadership may be of the dominant-firm, barometric-firm, or avoidance-of-price-competition variety. Rules of thumb are industry conventions such as cost-plus pricing or a certain pattern of pricing that has the effect of keeping rivals in the same mold. (See pages 639–641.)

14. In the short run oligopolists may earn economic profit, just normal profit, or suffer economic losses. They may be able to improve their profit situation in the long run. Firms that in the short run earned economic profit may now earn greater economic profit, those that earned normal profit may now earn economic profit, and firms that suffered economic losses in the short run might be able to earn normal or even economic profit. Of course, as in all markets, firms that cannot at least earn normal profit in the long run, will exit from the industry. (See page 641.)

15. Oligopolists may earn a normal profit or an economic profit in the long run. They will restrict output and charge a price in excess of marginal cost. Prices in oligopoly tend to be more rigid than in any other market structure. Average total cost in oligopoly may or may not be high, depending on the amount of competition among rivals. Given the degree of competitiveness, oligopoly firms are usually large enough to take advantage of economies of scale. Oligopolies are expected to be quite progressive, since they usually face some competition or potential competition and have the means to engage actively in research and development. (See pages 641–645.)

KEY TERMS

barometric-firm price leadership: price leadership that takes place when the firms in an industry consider one firm's price changes to be a good barometer of the market climate (page 640).

collusion: an agreement among firms in an industry to take actions that will improve their mutual well-being; a cooperative effort to gain monopoly control (page 639).

cost-plus price principle: a rule of thumb practiced in some oligopoly industries in which firms determine their selling price by adding a uniform percentage to certain elements of average total cost (page 641).

dominant-firm price leadership: price leadership that takes place when small and relatively weak firms in an industry accept the price of one powerful firm as the prevailing price (page 640).

duopoly: an industry made up of two sellers (page 637).

experience variables: variables that oligopolists take into account in addition to consumer demand and cost such as the oligopolist's knowledge of previous rival reactions to price changes, the personality traits of key managers of rival firms, and the political effects of rivals' reactions (page 636).

game theory: an approach to analyzing oligopoly that allows economists to liken the relationship between competing oligopolists to a game of cards or chess (page 638).

interdependence: the recognition by oligopoly firms that actions they might take will bring reactions by their rivals (page 635).

kinked demand curve: a demand curve made up of two segments, divided at the industrywide price that has been established, where the segment relating to higher prices is considerably more elastic than the segment related to lower prices (page 637).

monopolistic competition: a market characterized by a large number of independent sellers, product differentiation, and fairly easy entry and exit (page 624).

oligopoly: a sellers' market made up of a few firms who recognize their interdependence and who produce anywhere from rather standardized to quite differentiated products; it may be fairly easy or quite difficult to enter (page 635).

price leadership: a practice that allows oligopolists to coordinate their price adjustments to changes in demand or cost conditions without engaging in collusion (page 640).

price leadership to avoid price competition: price leadership that may occur when collusion is considered undesirable or impossible (page 640).

product differentiation: basically similar products are changed in some way to create some differences among them in the eyes of consumers (page 624).

DISCUSSION QUESTIONS

1. Explain the "competing monopolists" concept that characterizes the monopolistic competition market structure.

2. Actual markets only approach the monopolistic competition market structure. What important condition of the monopolistic competition model is missing in most real-world industries? Give three examples of actual industries (but not the same ones as in the chapter) that conform to all but this one condition of monopolistic competition.

3. In your opinion, does advertising infringe upon consumer sovereignty? In your own case, do you buy what you really want, or are you very much affected by advertising? Why should we be concerned about this issue?

4. Larry says to Linda, "I would like to have firms compete more vigorously than they now do. Therefore I would like to see them increase the amount of advertising that they do." Linda replies, "I am also in favor of more competition, but I favor less advertising. Advertising is used by firms in an attempt to limit or decrease competition." Who is right? Why?

5. Without looking at Figure 3, draw a diagram showing a monopolistically competitive firm that is earning economic profit in the short run. Compare your diagram with panel (a) in Figure 3 to be sure you have it right. What will happen in the long run? (In addition to the change, if any, discuss the process that will take place.)

6. Some economists argue that pure competition is the ideal market type since it offers the greatest amount of consumer welfare. Others disagree and make the case that monopolistic competition is the more appropriate ideal market structure because it actually offers greater consumer welfare than does pure competition. First taking the side that pure competition is ideal and then taking the side that monopolistic competition is the ideal, on what differences between the two market types would you base your arguments?

7. Of the four market types that economists use to analyze industries, only oligopoly is characterized by fewness. What is meant by "few firms" in a market? What difference does it make whether an industry is composed of "few" or "many" firms?

8. "Oligopoly is the market type that accurately describes most industries in the United States." Do you agree? Why or why not?

9. A theory of pricing in oligopoly markets assumes that oligopolies face kinked demand curves. What is a kinked demand curve? What causes the kink in a kinked demand curve? What explanation does this theory offer for the way that an industry-wide price at the point of the kink is established in the first place?

10. Given the following payoff matrix for rival duopolists X and Z and the game-theory assumption that each of the firms will try to avoid the

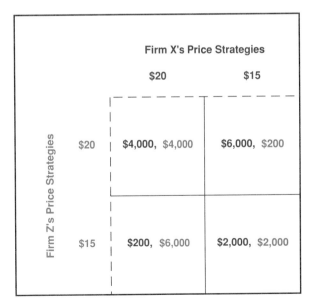

worst possible outcome, which strategy (prices) will the firms choose, and what will the outcome be?

11. Oligopolistic coordination may take place through price leadership. Describe what economists mean by the practice of price leadership. Distinguish among the three types of price leadership: dominant-firm price leadership, barometric-firm price leadership, and price leadership to avoid price competition.

12. In Figure 9 we drew a diagram of an oligopolist in long-run equilibrium. The diagram looks very much like one of the diagrams we drew for a monopolist in long-run equilibrium. Is there an important "hidden" difference? If so, what is it?

13. Applying what you have learned about the oligopoly market structure, explain each of the following statements:

a. Oligopolists are often reluctant to lower the price of a good that they sell and may be likely to resort to nonprice competition.

b. The degree of rivalry among the firms in an oligopoly industry helps to determine whether the firms in that industry produce on their lowest available average-total-cost curves.

c. Firms in oligopoly industries are expected to be quite progressive.

29

Oligopoly: The Real World

Preview   As you have learned, few industries come very close to the market structure of pure competition, pure monopoly, or monopolistic competition. In fact, most of our industries can best be described as oligopolies. An important social welfare question that must be asked, then, is whether or not an oligopolistic market is able to allocate resources well enough to meet people's wants. In other words, can a primarily capitalist economy such as the United States depend on oligopolistic companies to behave competitively enough to do what is best for society? This is a hard question to answer, partly because it is normative. Also, the answer may be very different for one industry than it is for another.

This chapter deals with how oligopolistic industries are organized and how, from the point of view of society, that kind of organization influences their economic performance. Competition among oligopolistic firms should be vigorous enough to cause them to operate efficiently, to offer a good variety of products, to invent and innovate better processes and products, and to pass productivity gains on to the consumer through lower real prices.

Here we introduce some concepts that economists use to determine the degree of competition in an economy and in specific industries. We begin with the idea of *economic concentration*, which measures the number and size distribution of firms. We show how this measure is used, the problems that surround it, its level, and its recent trends. Next we explain that firms grow either from within through building or from without through *merger*. Three kinds of mergers—horizontal, vertical, and conglomerate—are described, and their relationships to economic concentration and competition are assessed. The "urge to merge" has been strong. So we shall offer some reasons that help to explain why.

We also present another important economic idea that affects competition in oligopolies—the *condition of entry*. Potential entry depends upon whether certain "entry barriers" are present and to what degree they work in keeping companies from entering an industry. Four barriers that we describe are capital requirements, product differentiation, absolute cost differences, and the minimum optimal scale effect.

ECONOMIC CONCENTRATION

Economic concentration measures the control of economic activity in an industry, in a major part of an economy, in a whole economy, or in a region of the world. It may be measured by a **concentration ratio**, which expresses the percentage share of some key variable such as sales or assets accounted for by the largest firms. For example, of the 139 companies in the greeting card industry in the United States, the 4 largest accounted for 84 percent of the sales and the 8 largest for 89 percent of the sales in 1982. These figures are an example of *market* concentration ratios. *Aggregate* concentration ratios, however, cover a much wider area of economic activity. Out of about 200,000 manufacturing corporations in the United States in 1984, the 200 largest held about 61 percent of the country's manufacturing assets.

Economic concentration, the control of economic activity in an industry, sector, or economy, may be measured by a concentration ratio, which expresses the percentage share of some key variable accounted for by the largest firms.

Economic concentration ratios are gathered as a quantitative measure of potential monopoly control. The presumption is that there is a high level of monopoly control—and for this reason too little competition—in an economy where only a handful of giant companies control a very high percentage of the assets, sales, or profits in important sectors such as manufacturing, transportation, finance, or retailing. The same presumption applies in individual markets or industries. So the greeting card publishing industry just mentioned is presumed more likely to suffer from too little competition than is the women's and misses' dresses industry, where the 4 largest of the 5,489 firms operating in that industry accounted for only 6 percent of the sales in 1982.

Economic concentration ratios are gathered as a quantitative measure of potential monopoly control.

Aggregate Economic Concentration

Aggregate economic concentration relates to the share of economic activity undertaken by the largest firms in a region of the world, in an economy, or in some major sector beyond traditional market or industry lines. Each year *Fortune* magazine publishes data on the largest U.S. and foreign firms. The data cover the 500 largest U.S. manufacturing and mining firms (the *Fortune* 500), the 500 largest U.S. nonindustrial firms (the *Fortune* Service 500), the 500 largest foreign manufacturing and mining firms (the *Fortune* International 500), and the 100 largest foreign commercial banks.

Aggregate economic concentration measures shares of economic activity in a region, an economy, or in some major sector beyond traditional market or industry lines.

The Largest U.S. Firms   Table 1 gives a sample of 1988 *Fortune* data that throws some light on U.S. aggregate economic concentration. Part I lists the sales of the 10 largest industrial firms in the United States and their cumulative percentage of the sales of the 500 largest U.S. industrial firms. Note that General Motors (one-fifth of 1 percent of the 500 largest firms) accounted for 6 percent of their sales. One percent of these firms (the top 5) accounted for nearly 20 percent of the sales of the top 500, and 2 percent (the 10 firms listed) accounted for nearly 29 percent of their sales.

Table 1 also gives aggregate concentration data for three nonindustrial sectors of the U.S. econ-

TABLE 1
U.S. Aggregate Economic Concentration: A Sample of **Fortune** *Magazine's Data for 1988*

I. U.S. Industrial Sector

Rank (by sales)	Company	Sales (in millions of dollars)	Cumulative Percentage of 500 Largest
1.	General Motors	121,085	6.0
2.	Ford Motor	92,446	10.6
3.	Exxon	79,557	14.5
4.	I.B.M.	59,681	17.4
5.	General Electric	49,414	19.9
6.	Mobil	48,198	22.3
7.	Chrysler	35,473	24.0
8.	Texaco	33,544	25.7
9.	E.I. Du Pont de Nemours	32,514	27.3
10.	Philip Morris	25,860	28.6

II. U.S. Commercial Banking Sector

Rank (by assets)	Company	Assets (in millions of dollars)	Cumulative Percentage of 100 Largest
1.	Citicorp	207,666	9.6
2.	Chase Manhattan Corp.	97,455	14.1
3.	BankAmerica Corp.	94,647	18.5
4.	J. P. Morgan & Co.	83,923	22.4
5.	Security Pacific Corp.	77,870	26.0

III. U.S. Retailing Sector

Rank (by sales)	Company	Sales (in millions of dollars)	Cumulative Percentage of 50 Largest
1.	Sears Roebuck	50,251	14.1
2.	K Mart	27,301	21.8
3.	Wal-Mart Stores	20,649	27.6
4.	Kroger	19,053	33.0
5.	American Stores	18,478	38.2

IV. U.S. Transportation Sector

Rank (by sales)	Company	Sales (in millions of dollars)	Cumulative Percentage of 50 Largest
1.	United Parcel Service	11,032	8.5
2.	UAL	9,015	15.4
3.	AMR	8,824	22.2
4.	CSX	8,668	28.9
5.	Texas Air	8,573	35.5

Source: Fortune, April 24, 1989 and June 5, 1989. © 1989 Time Inc. All rights reserved. Used with permission.

omy. The commercial banking sector's aggregate concentration, as measured in assets, is quite high. The 5 firms listed (5 percent of the largest 100 firms) accounted for 26 percent of their total assets. In retailing, sales of the 5 largest firms account for over 38 percent of the largest 50 firms' sales. Finally, in the transportation sector, the largest 5 firms account for somewhat over 35 percent of the sales of the 50 largest.

The Largest Foreign Firms   Table 2 provides aggregate concentration data for industrial firms outside the United States. However, it is not comparable to Table 1 since what it shows is not for a single country, but rather for a large number of foreign countries combined. On a country-by-country basis, aggregate concentration may be higher, lower, or about the same as in the United States. Also, the *Fortune* data do not include Soviet bloc or communist Chinese firms. Our purpose in presenting Table 2 is to help you recognize the names of major foreign firms and to show you that, although they are giant firms, they are on average somewhat smaller than the ten largest U.S. industrial firms.

To give you further background on non-U.S. aggregate concentration, Table 3 presents a break-down by country of the largest 500 foreign industrial firms in 1988. Notice that Japan boasts by far the most large firms, with Great Britain and West Germany in second and third place, respectively. Together those three countries account for more than half of the total (286 of 500 firms). If Canada, France, and Sweden are included, about 75 percent (373 of 500 firms) are accounted for.

Aggregate concentration data focus, not on competing firms, but merely on firms in the same region of the world, or in the same economy, or in the same sector within a region or economy. Exxon, which produces petroleum, does not compete with General Motors, which is in the automobile and truck industry. Sears, Roebuck and Co., a general merchandise retailer, competes only marginally with Kroger, which sells primarily food products. In the international arena, there is very little competition among a petroleum firm such as Royal Dutch/Shell Group, an auto manufacturer such as Toyota Motor, and an electronics firm like Siemens. But the power that can stem from sheer size is of great concern to some economists. They argue that the economic and political advantages gained through size alone may enable a firm to control particular markets in which it is involved.

TABLE 2
Foreign Aggregate Concentration: **Fortune** *Magazine's Ten Largest Industrial Firms Outside the United States, 1988*

Rank (by sales)	Company	Country	Sales (in millions of dollars)	Cumulative Percentage of 500 Largest Firms
1.	Royal Dutch/Shell Group	Neth.-Britain	78,381	2.7
2.	Toyota Motor	Japan	50,790	4.4
3.	British Petroleum	Britain	46,174	6.0
4.	IRI*	Italy	45,522	7.5
5.	Daimler-Benz	W. Germany	41,818	9.0
6.	Hitachi	Japan	41,331	10.4
7.	Siemens	W. Germany	34,129	11.5
8.	Fiat	Italy	34,039	12.7
9.	Matsushita	Japan	33,923	13.9
10.	Volkswagen	W. Germany	33,696	15.0

* Government-owned.

Source: The 500 Largest Industrial Companies Outside the U.S., *Fortune*, July 31, 1989, © 1989 Time, Inc. All rights reserved. Used with permission.

TABLE 3
Fortune *Magazine's 500 Largest Foreign Industrial Firms:*
Rank Breakdown by Country, 1988

Country	Rank Breakdown					
	1–100	*101–200*	*201–300*	*301–400*	*401–500*	*Total*
Argentina	0	1	0	0	0	1
Australia	1	3	1	5	3	13
Austria	0	0	2	0	0	2
Belgium	1	2	0	0	1	4
Brazil	1	1	0	2	1	5
Britain	11	14	20	17	12	74
Britain/Netherlands	2	0	0	0	0	2
Canada	4	4	7	7	6	28
Chile	0	0	1	0	0	1
Colombia	0	0	0	0	1	1
Denmark	0	0	0	0	2	2
Finland	0	2	0	6	3	11
France	11	9	7	4	8	39
India	1	0	3	2	1	7
Indonesia	0	0	0	0	1	1
Ireland	0	0	0	0	1	1
Israel	0	0	0	1	0	1
Italy	4	1	0	1	0	6
Italy/Switzerland	0	1	0	0	0	1
Japan	31	31	34	31	32	159
Kuwait	1	0	0	0	0	1
Luxembourg	0	1	0	0	0	1
Malaysia	0	0	1	0	0	1
Mexico	1	0	0	0	1	2
Netherlands	2	1	2	3	1	9
Netherlands Antilles	0	1	0	0	0	1
New Zealand	0	1	0	0	0	1
Norway	1	1	0	0	1	3
Panama	0	0	0	1	0	1
Saudi Arabia	0	0	0	1	0	1
South Africa	1	1	0	1	3	6
South Korea	3	3	3	1	1	11
Spain	2	0	3	1	2	8
Sweden	2	3	7	5	3	20
Switzerland	3	4	3	0	3	13
Taiwan	0	1	0	0	3	4
Turkey	0	3	0	0	0	3
Venezuela	1	0	0	0	0	1
W. Germany	16	11	6	10	10	53
Zambia	0	0	0	1	0	1

TABLE 4

Aggregate Economic Concentration in U.S. Manufacturing from 1947 to 1982, Share of Total Value Added[a] by Manufacture—Accounted for by Largest U.S. Manufacturing Companies

Company Rank Group	Percentage of Total Value Added by Manufacture							
	1947	1954	1958	1963	1967	1972	1977	1982
Largest 50 companies	17	23	23	25.0	24.6	24.5	24.4	23.9
Largest 100 companies	23	30	30	32.7	32.8	33.1	33.4	32.8
Largest 150 companies	27	34	35	37.4	37.9	38.8	39.5	38.7
Largest 200 companies	30	37	38	40.9	41.7	43.1	43.8	43.2

a. Value added is the difference between the value of materials that a firm buys and the value of what it sells.

Source: Bureau of the Census, U.S. Department of Commerce, *1982 Census of Manufacturers,* Concentration Ratios in Manufacturing, Subject Series, MC 82-S-7, April 1986.

Aggregate concentration data focus on firms in the same region of the world or in the same economy or sector of a region or economy. They do not focus on competing firms.

Changes in the U.S. Economy Since the Civil War
Great changes have taken place in the U.S. economy since the Civil War (1861–1865). At that time, the United States was accurately described as an agricultural country, because manufacturing was confined to small-scale plants, largely in the New England and Middle Atlantic states. Economic concentration was then at a very low level. Since that time, however, technological and organizational changes have completely altered the character of the economy. The large corporation has become the dominant form of business, and the level of economic concentration has increased greatly.

In 1932, economists Adolf Berle and Gardner Means called attention to this growing aggregate concentration. They reported that during the period from 1909 to 1929 the 200 largest nonfinancial corporations in the United States were growing at a much higher rate than were all other U.S. nonfinancial corporations. They projected these growth rates into the future and concluded that, if no obstacles were placed in the way, the top 200 U.S. firms would control all U.S. business by the early 1970s. Of course this has not happened. But aggregate concentration—at least in manufactur-ing—has continued to increase in the United States. Table 4 gives some indication of this fact in terms of the value added. (The **value added** is the difference between the value of materials that a firm buys and the value of what it sells.) The table compares the largest 50, 100, 150, and 200 manufacturing corporations in the United States for selected years from 1947 to 1982. Though economic concentration was greater in 1982 than in 1947, the increase has been moderate since 1954. Most economists believe that the big jump from 1947 to 1954 should not be given great importance since it was primarily due to adjustments after World War II. For the years 1963 to 1982 we have added a decimal place to the percentages in the table, because the changes have been so slight that rounding off would distort these figures. During those years the percentage of total value added in manufacturing accounted for by the 50 largest U.S. manufacturing firms actually fell by over a percentage point. The percentage of total value added in manufacturing accounted for by the 100 largest U.S. manufacturing firms was the same in 1982 as in 1967 and the 150 and 200 largest firms decreased their shares from 1977 to 1982.

Since the Civil War, the large corporation has become the dominant form of business in the United States, and the level of economic concentration has increased greatly.

Market Concentration

We return to **market concentration**—the number and size distribution of firms in a specific industry or market. Examples of concentration ratios among groups of firms competing in particular markets, such as the greeting card publishing or women's and misses' dresses industry, were given earlier. But industries are not as easy to define as it may appear. If concentration ratios are to be used as indicators of competition, the definition of an industry must correctly describe a readily identifiable group of competing firms. However, most firms produce many different things and may sell them in widely separated geographic areas. For this reason, a workable classification system is required.

Market concentration is the number and size distribution of firms in a specific industry or market.

SIC Product Codes Industry definitions used by the U.S. Bureau of the Census in taking the Census of Manufacturers for the United States are set forth in the **Standard Industrial Classification (SIC) system**. Table 5 shows how this system is set up. The outputs of firms are divided into industry and product groupings, which are coded with numbers having from two to seven digits. Each time that another digit is added, the groups become narrower. Table 5 gives one example. The food and kindred products group shown in this table is one of 20 two-digit "major industry groups" in the manufacturing sector. Some others are textile-mill products and petroleum and coal products. These 20 major groups are further divided into 143 three-digit "industry groups," one of which (under food and kindred products) is meat products. The classification is then further narrowed to 452 four-digit "industries," such as meatpacking in our example. These in turn are separated into over 1,400 five-digit "product classes," an example of which in this sequence is fresh beef. To leave room for possible future expansion, there is no six-digit coding. Finally, all of manufacturing is divided into about 11,000 different seven-digit "products." Whole-carcass beef is one product in the sequence that we followed.

Definitions of industries are set forth in the Standard Industrial Classification (SIC) system.

Difficulty of Overstatement and Understatement How well does the SIC work? Can we confidently use the concentration ratios published by the Bureau of the Census in its Census of Manufacturers? Our answer is twofold: "yes," the data taken from questionnaires filled out by firms are reliable, but "no," they do not always lend themselves to the kind of analysis of markets that economists would like to do. However, if we recognize their limitations, we can make certain adjustments. Only then can we avoid seriously overstating or understating the concentration in actual markets.

Broad and Narrow Definitions The most widely used SIC category is the four-digit "indus-

TABLE 5
Standard Industrial Classification: An Example

Standard Industrial Classification Code	Designation	Name
20	Major industry group	Food and kindred products
201	Industry group	Meat products
2011	Industry	Meatpacking
20111	Product class	Fresh beef
2011112	Product	Whole-carcass beef

try." However, it may not properly define the market—that is, the group of competing firms. If the four-digit definition is too broad, it will understate the actual concentration; if it is too narrow, it will overstate the actual concentration.

In Table 6 we have listed a few of the over 450 four-digit SIC "industries." The number of firms in the industry and the 4-firm and 8-firm concentration ratios based on value of shipment (sales) in 1982 are given for each. The 4-firm concentration ratio presents the percentage share of that industry accounted for by the largest 4 firms in that industry, and the 8-firm concentration ratio presents the percentage share of that industry accounted for by the largest 8 firms in that industry. To make this clear, let us see what information is presented in the first line of Table 6. First, it tells us that in 1982 there were 19 firms producing cane sugar in the United States. Second, the 4 largest among them accounted for 65 percent of the total amount of cane sugar sold by these 19 firms. Third, the 8 largest firms accounted for 91 percent of industry sales. Thus, we can infer, that the remaining 11 firms accounted for only 9 percent of the total sales of the cane sugar industry.

Pharmaceutical preparations (2834), farm machinery and equipment (3523), and aircraft (3721) are generally regarded as too broad in their definitions and so understate economic concentration. The pharmaceutical firm that specializes in antibiotics competes very little with one that specializes in birth control pills. In that "industry," concentration ratios based on five-digit product classes or on seven-digit products may offer a better picture of the state of competition. A similar, but possibly weaker, case may be made for the farm machinery and equipment and the aircraft industries. Tractors are not good substitutes for combines, and small private planes do not compete with large commercial planes.

On the other hand, some industries are defined too narrowly in the SIC system so that concentration ratios overstate the concentration. Table 6 lists the cane sugar industry (2062) and the beet sugar industry (2063) as separate four-digit industries, but the difference in their products is hardly noticeable to consumers. Also, wood office furniture (2521) and metal office furniture (2522) are good substitutes in consumption, as are glass containers (3221) and metal cans (3411).

TABLE 6
Some 4-Firm and 8-Firm Concentration Ratios Based on Value of Shipments, 1982

SIC Code	Industry	Number of Firms	4-Firm Ratio	8-Firm Ratio
2062	Cane sugar	19	65	91
2063	Beet sugar	14	67	95
2371	Fur goods	503	12	19
2521	Wood office furniture	430	22	32
2522	Metal office furniture	224	45	59
2652	Setup paperboard boxes	241	15	26
2711	Newspapers	7,520	22	34
2834	Pharmaceutical preparations	584	26	42
3221	Glass containers	41	50	73
3273	Ready-mixed concrete	4,161	6	9
3334	Primary aluminum	15	64	88
3411	Metal cans	168	50	68
3523	Farm machinery and equipment	1,787	53	62
3711	Motor vehicles and car bodies	289	92	97
3721	Aircraft	139	64	81

Source: Bureau of the Census, U.S. Department of Commerce, *1982 Census of Manufacturers,* Concentration Ratios in Manufacturing, Subject Series, MC82-S-7, April 1986.

The SIC definition of an industry may be too narrow or too broad to define the market properly.

Omission of Foreign Competition The concentration data that are offered by the Bureau of the Census cover only U.S. production and omit imports from foreign countries. Omitting this foreign competition leads to significantly overstating economic concentration in some U.S. markets. For example, Table 6 shows that the 4-firm concentration ratio for motor vehicles and car bodies (3711) is 92 percent. Surely this figure is misleading, since U.S. auto firms strongly compete with the imported autos of such firms as Toyota Motor, Nissan Motors, Volkswagenwerk, and Daimler-Benz, to name just a few.

The concentration data supplied by the Bureau of the Census cover only U.S. production and omit imports from foreign countries, which leads to significant overstatement of economic concentration in some U.S. markets.

Regional Markets U.S. concentration ratios are calculated on a national basis, when, in fact, actual markets often cover only a region or just a small local area. This may cause a serious understatement of economic concentration. In Table 6 are three good examples: setup paperboard boxes (2652), newspapers (2711), and ready-mixed concrete (3273). The 4-firm concentration ratio for setup paperboard boxes is 15 percent. However, the actual markets for setup paperboard boxes are regional rather than national and are estimated to have an average 4-firm market concentration of about 75 percent.[1] Likewise, the 4-firm concentration ratio of 22 percent for newspapers tells us little about competition in that line of business. Most of the cities in the United States have only one major daily newspaper. These newspapers may compete with those of other cities (such as the *New York Times* or the *Washington Post*) to some extent, but for printed local news they are monopolists with a

---

1. United States Senate, *Hearings on Economic Concentration*, Part 8, Frank J. Kottke, 1970, p. 5388.

concentration ratio of 100 percent. Finally, 6 percent is a very misleading 4-firm concentration ratio for ready-mixed concrete. Because of the very high shipping cost, the actual markets are generally no wider than the size of a metropolitan area, and concentration ratios are quite high.

U.S. concentration ratios are calculated on a national basis when actual markets often cover only a region or local area, causing an understatement of economic concentration.

The Herfindahl-Hirshman Index An alternative measure of market concentration is the **Herfindahl-Hirshman Index (HHI)**. Market concentration ratios focus on only some of the firms in a market (the 4 or 8 largest) and they do not account for the distribution of the market shares among the firms included in the ratios (a market with a 52 percent 4-firm concentration ratio may be made up of one firm with 46 percent and each of the other firms with 2 percent or it may be made up of four equal-size firms, each with a 13 percent market share). These shortcomings are eliminated by the HHI, which includes all of the firms in a market and gives proportionately greater weight to the market shares of the larger firms in the market.

The HHI is calculated by summing the squares of the individual market shares of all the firms in the market. For example, a market consisting of six firms with market shares of 40 percent, 30 percent, 10 percent, 10 percent, 5 percent, and 5 percent has an HHI of 2,750 ($40^2 + 30^2 + 10^2 + 10^2 + 5^2 + 5^2 = 2,750$). The HHI ranges from 10,000 in the case of a monopoly to a number approaching zero in the case of an industry made up of a huge number of firms.

The Herfindahl-Hirshman Index (HHI) is an alternative measure of market concentration. It includes all of the firms in a market and gives proportionately greater weight to the market shares of the larger firms in the market.

Evaluation of Market Concentration In spite of the difficulties that we noted, concentration can be very revealing about the power that a few firms hold in oligopoly markets. Agreement among companies to limit or eliminate competition is much more likely among a few giant firms that control a large share of a market than it is among a larger number of small firms. Pricing and product decisions made in a collusive atmosphere come close to monopoly pricing and can harm consumers in the same way.

At least, studying concentration is a good starting point for analyzing an industry. If an industry is defined correctly—not too broadly, either in terms of product or geography—it is very likely that there will be some competition among the firms when the level of concentration is fairly low. But among industries with quite high levels of concentration there are very great differences in the amount of competition that exists. To be able to judge the amounts of competition more fully in oligopolies, we must study other characteristics such as the degree of product differentiation among the firms in the industry, cost structures of the firms, and the ease of entry into the industry.

Concentration is surely not the only indicator of the competitive climate in an industry. But, concentration is one of the few quantitative measures in an area of economics where analysis is often based on fairly qualitative evidence. It is tempting to depend too heavily on such a measure. For this reason, we must be careful not to assume that a high degree of concentration always indicates a lack of competition.

Concentration data can be very revealing about the power that a few firms hold in oligopoly markets and about the competitive climate in an industry. But one should also examine other characteristics and not rely solely on this quantitative measure.

MERGER

How did the United States and other industrial countries arrive at the high levels of aggregate and market concentration that they have today? The answer is that they reached their present levels in two ways—through internal growth and through external growth of firms. *Internal growth* is growth by building, which means adding to firms' productive capacities. *External growth* is growth by **merger**, or acquiring other companies. Both forms of growth are commonplace. Though many firms have grown mostly through internal means, others have combined internal growth with merger.

The United States and other industrial countries arrived at their current high levels of aggregate and market concentration through internal growth (adding to firms' productive capacities) and by external growth (merger with other companies).

Most economists argue that internal growth is better than merger for society because firms that grow in the face of competition must meet and pass the test of the market. Growth by merger does not offer the same assurance of competitive success. Any firm that can swing a deal using cash, bonds, or stock in an amount acceptable to the owners of the company being acquired can grow by merger.

Whether internal growth leads to higher aggregate or market concentration depends upon whether it is the larger or the smaller firms that are doing most of the growing. On the other hand, merger may or may not change the market concentration, depending on the kind of merger, but it will mean fewer and larger firms in the economy and so must lead to a higher degree of aggregate concentration.

Most economists believe that internal growth is better for society than merger because firms that grow in the face of competition show their ability to compete successfully.

Types of Mergers

Mergers are of three kinds: horizontal, vertical, and conglomerate. In a **horizontal merger**, a firm merges with another firm engaged in the same activity, operating on the same level, and serving the same geographic market. For example, the merging of two small supermarket chains that operate in

Chicago, Illinois, would be a horizontal merger. They both sell groceries, so they are engaged in the same activity. Because they both sell at retail, they are on the same level. And because they both sell to the people of Chicago, they serve the same geographic market.

Vertical merger occurs between companies at different levels of a particular business activity. That is, a firm merges with another firm that has served or could have served either as its supplier or as its customer. Examples are an automobile manufacturer acquiring a company that produces spark plugs, or a shoe manufacturer merging with a chain of retail shoe stores.

Conglomerate merger takes place when a firm acquires another firm engaged in a different industry. Conglomerate mergers are further divided into product extension, geographic market extension, and relatively pure conglomeration.

A **product extension conglomerate merger** occurs when a firm acquires another firm in an allied industry—a company whose product is functionally associated with that of the acquirer. When Procter & Gamble, a major detergent and soap producer, acquired Clorox, a major liquid bleach producer, a product extension conglomerate merger took place.[2] Detergent and liquid bleach are complements. That is, consumers use them together to wash their clothes. Also, they are found close to each other on grocery store shelves and can be advertised together.

A **geographic market extension conglomerate merger** takes place when a firm acquires another firm that is in the same business activity and on the same level, but is serving a different geographic market. Suppose that the supermarket chain in Chicago referred to earlier acquired a chain of supermarkets located in San Diego, California. This would be a case of market extension. They are both in the same line of business, but they are not in the same industry or market since they serve two different populations.

Finally, interindustry mergers that are neither product extension nor market extension may be described as **relatively pure conglomerate mergers**. In an absolutely pure conglomerate merger, there would be no relationship at all between

2. This merger was later disallowed in *Federal Trade Commission* v. *The Procter & Gamble Company,* 87 S. Ct. 1224 (1967).

the companies' activities. Cases of this sort are almost impossible to find. "Relatively pure" is the real-world equivalent. Here the acquiring and the acquired companies are engaged in quite different lines of business, yet there may be some slight relationship between them. Textron, a company that was originally in the textile industry, made a large number of relatively pure conglomerate mergers. During a period of about ten years, Textron acquired companies producing aircraft and parts, electronic equipment, optical instruments, bathroom fixtures, broadcasting equipment, glue, paints, plywood, chain saws, underwater exploration equipment, shoes, storm doors, golf carts, watch bracelets, poultry, and tourist travel. It probably seems to you that there is absolutely no relationship among several of these lines of business. True, the relationships are fairly remote, but not necessarily zero. The research scientist working on a better paint may also have ideas about better glue. The accounting department, as well as the advertising department, may provide equally good service to all the divisions. In particular, top management may be expected to provide its skills across the board.

In a horizontal merger, a firm merges with another firm engaged in the same activity, operating on the same level, and serving the same geographic market. Vertical merger occurs between companies at different levels of a particular business activity. Conglomerate merger takes place when a firm acquires another firm engaged in a different industry.

Merger Movements

There have been four fairly distinct merger movements in the United States. The first was around the turn of the century. It took place in reaction to the great technological changes in communications, manufacturing, and transportation of that period. The mergers were largely horizontal and formed dominant new companies. This was the time when Du Pont, General Electric, Eastman Kodak, International Paper, U.S. Steel (changed to USX Corporation in July 1986), American Can, Standard Oil (later to become Exxon, Mobil, and

Standard Oil of California, Indiana, and Ohio), and many others were formed through merger. Competition took a back seat to substantial monopoly control by these newly created giants. For good or for ill, the United States would never be the same again.

A second wave of mergers occurred during the decade after World War I. Most of these were horizontal, but more vertical and conglomerate mergers took place than at any time before. The horizontal mergers did not shape the giant "number one" firms as they did in the earlier merger wave. Instead, large "number two" firms were created, such as Continental Can and Bethlehem Steel. Economist Jesse W. Markham estimates that about 12,000 American firms disappeared through mergers between 1919 and 1930.[3]

The third wave of mergers took place from 1967 to 1970. What sharply distinguished this merger wave from the earlier ones was that it was made up largely of conglomerate mergers. According to the Federal Trade Commission, conglomerate mergers accounted for about 85 percent of all manufacturing mergers during those four years.

The fourth merger wave began in the mid-1970s and continues, stronger than ever, into the very late 1980s and early 1990s. It is composed largely of conglomerate and horizontal mergers. It is recognized as a merger wave more because of the huge size of the transactions than because of the number of mergers taking place. The annual dollar value of acquired assets increased about sixfold from 1972 to 1979, and the years 1980 to 1988 saw still more dramatic increases. In 1981 about $70 billion of assets were acquired, including acquisitions by Du Pont of Conoco Oil and by U.S. Steel of Marathon Oil, which together amounted to almost $14 billion of acquired assets. In 1984 over $122 billion of assets were acquired, close to $30 billion of which were involved in just three petroleum industry transactions—Texaco's takeover of Getty Oil ($10.2 billion), Mobil's of Superior Oil ($5.7 billion), and Chevron's of Gulf Oil ($13.3 billion). In 1987, acquisitions valued at about $163 billion were completed. This was again dwarfed in 1988, when acquisitions valued at almost $246 billion were reported.

Until about a decade ago, data classified by type of merger were prepared by the Federal Trade Commission (FTC), a government agency charged with the responsibility of maintaining competition in U.S. markets. The FTC has estimated that of the 2,023 large mergers in the manufacturing and mining sectors during the thirty-two-year period of 1948 to 1979, almost three-quarters of them were conglomerate. Table 7 presents the FTC findings for that period.

There have been four fairly distinct merger movements in the United States since the turn of the century. The first wave formed giant companies that have dominated the U.S. economy ever since. The fourth wave, which is still ongoing, is characterized by the huge size of the merger transactions.

Why the Urge to Merge?

Why do firms have such a strong urge to merge? Why do they so often prefer external growth to internal growth? There are a large number of clear advantages for the management of the acquiring firm in growth through merger. We shall briefly discuss six of them.

First, if there is excess demand for a firm's products and more plant capacity is desired, the quickest way to get it may be through acquisition. Expansion of the firm's own facilities may take so long that good will can be lost because customers become dissatisfied.

The second advantage for managers is that merger may be "cost effective" (the lowest-cost way), both in terms of the price paid for the acquired facilities and in terms of financing the expansion. The price paid for the acquired firm may be well below the "book value" (accounting value) of its assets. It is fairly common to find firms' stock prices to be severely undervalued during a poor stock market period. An offer by a would-be acquirer of a price somewhere between the current stock price and the "book value" may please the

3. Jesse W. Markham, "Survey of the Evidence and Findings on Mergers," in National Bureau of Economic Research, *Business Concentration and Price Policy: A Conference of the Universities—National Bureau Committee for Economic Research* (Princeton, N.J.: Princeton University Press, 1955), pp. 168–169.

TABLE 7
Large Acquisitionsᵃ in Manufacturing and Mining by Type of Merger, United States, 1948–1979

Type of Merger	Number	Percent
Horizontal	331	16.4
Vertical	201	9.9
Conglomerate	1,491	73.7
Total	2,023	100.0

Type of Conglomerate Merger	Number	Percent of Conglomerate
Product Extension	870	58.4
Geographic Market Extension	78	5.2
Relatively Pure	543	36.4
Total	1,491	100.0

a. The Federal Trade Commission defines a large acquisition as one in which the acquired firm has assets of $10 million or more.

Source: Bureau of Economics, Federal Trade Commission, *July 1981 Statistical Report on Mergers and Acquisitions,* 1979, Table 19, p. 109.

stockholders and yet be a bargain for the acquiring firm. As to financing, if the firm built its own plant, it might have some difficulty either in borrowing the required funds or in selling its not very well recognized stock to investors in a public distribution. However, in all but relatively pure conglomerate mergers, the sellers might very well know and respect the acquiring company's management and so would be more willing to accept payment in the form of the acquirer's stock.

A third reason is that a firm wishing to diversify into a new product or geographic market (conglomerate) or to use a new process in its present industry may find it advantageous to do so through merger. It would likely be easier, quicker, and less risky than starting from scratch. Merger allows the firm to gain instant experience and not make the mistakes of a newcomer.

A fourth motive for mergers—illustrated by the tremendous surge during the late 1960s—is the expectation of speculative gain. Consider the so-called "go-go" conglomerates of that period. The investing public was sold the idea that some firms had spectacular growth potential. So they merited an unusually high "price-earnings ratio" (the ratio between the price of a share of a firm's stock and the earnings per share of that firm). A growth firm

might be said to "merit" a 50-to-1 price-earnings ratio. For example, if it then acquired an ordinary firm that Wall Street had given only a 10-to-1 stock price-earnings ratio, the stock price of the growth firm would increase by $50 for every $1 of earnings provided by the acquired firm. The growth firm could therefore make an offer to the owners of the ordinary firm that would allow both sets of owners to make more money. The owners of the growth firm might offer the owners of the ordinary firm $20 for each $1 of the ordinary firm's earnings (double the value as determined by the 10-to-1 stock price-earnings ratio). But when each $1 of earnings from the ordinary firm is added to the earnings of the growth firm, it adds $50 to the value of the stock of the growth firm. The magic show is complete; the stockholders of both the acquired and the acquiring firm have made large gains.

Some growth firms of the late 1960s became specialists in merger. It did not matter very much what business the acquired firm was in, as long as the stock price-earnings ratio was low. Since the growth of go-go conglomerates depended on merger, they had to make acquisitions continuously to maintain their growth status. Once the investing public reacted to nagging doubts about the go-go conglomerates, the bubble burst. The stock price-earnings ratios of the growth firms fell, making it harder for these companies to find acquisition candidates with very much lower stock price-earnings ratios. This drop in the ratio added to the investing public's doubts and had a snowballing effect. Following such a pattern, one of the "hottest" go-go conglomerates, Ling-Temco-Vought, sold for $169.50 per share of stock in 1967 and for $7.12 per share in 1970.

The 1980s witnessed other forms of speculation. Mergers are not always "friendly" or welcomed by the managements of potentially acquired firms. *Hostile takeovers,* in which acquiring firms are able to consummate mergers by virtue of buying controlling quantities of stock, constitute a threat to the managements of potentially acquired firms. *Raiders* such as T. Boone Pickens, Carl Icahn, Irwin Jacobs, and Sir James Goldsmith have made huge speculative gains. A raider may quietly buy up large blocks of stock to obtain enough to threaten a takeover of the company. The merger may actually take place or the raider may extract *greenmail*—selling the stock to the company at a premium price offered by the defending management.

Hostile takeovers, in which acquiring firms are able to effect mergers by buying controlling quantities of stock, constitute a threat to the managements of potentially acquired firms.

During the late 1980s the form of speculation through acquisition known as the **leveraged buy-out (LBO)** became very much in vogue. In a leveraged buy-out investors (often including a firm's own management) rely almost entirely on debt financing to acquire a company. Successful buy-outs of "undervalued" firms have the potential of yielding huge profits for such speculators. The LBO concept itself is nothing new, as acquiring firms normally issue some bonds and borrow some money from banks in order to raise the necessary funds for making an acquisition. What was different about the LBO binge of the late 1980s was its magnitude and the fact that the acquirers were not firms who sought to acquire other firms through merger but instead were primarily financial speculators who sought speculative gain.

The late 1980s saw leveraged buy-outs of a larger number of major firms such as Fruehauf Corp., Trans World Airlines, Motel 6, Allied Stores Corp., Southland Corp., and Tiffany and Co. However, these were all overshadowed by the largest acquisition ever recorded—the leveraged buy-out of RJR Nabisco, a late 1988 takeover valued at over $25 billion. The buy-out was initiated by RJR Nabisco's chief executive officer, Ross Johnson, who headed a group of investors who were finally outbid by the investment firm of Kohlberg Kravis Roberts & Co. The food and tobacco firm's stock traded in the mid-$50s during the summer of 1988 before takeover bidding began and in the $90s by year's end. Substantial speculative profits were realized.

Leveraged buy-outs are speculative acquisitions of undervalued firms that rely almost entirely on debt financing and have the potential of yielding huge profits.

A fifth reason for merger is managerial pursuit of growth. Merger is often the quickest and most likely way for top managers to boost sales and asset growth and in this way to gain personal prestige, better pay, and job security.

Many studies conducted during the past twenty-five years or so have shown, however, that mergers are not very profitable for the long-term owners of the acquiring firms.[4] So growth through merger is pursued by managers, rather than by owners who are not merely speculators. On the average, firms that have grown through merger have not been more profitable than comparable firms that have grown mostly from within.

Finally, a sixth motive for merger—one that directly affects the public interest—is the desire to get rid of a competitor and in this way to give the company more monopoly power. A horizontal merger will, by definition, eliminate a competitor. Often a firm finds it attractive to expand by growing in absolute size and at the same time ridding itself of a major competitor. Potential competition may be reduced through conglomerate merger when a company seeking to diversify into a new

---

4. For a good survey of merger studies, see Dennis C. Mueller, "The Effects of Conglomerate Mergers: A Survey of the Empirical Evidence," *Journal of Banking and Finance* (1977), pp. 315–347.

product or geographic market immediately takes over the acquired firm's market and so need not compete with it.

Firms often prefer external growth (merger) to internal growth because (1) it may be the quickest way to expand plant capacity, (2) it may be the lowest-cost way to grow, (3) it may be the least risky way to diversify, (4) it may be a way to achieve speculative gain, (5) it may enable top managers to boost sales and asset growth, and (6) it may eliminate a competitor and thus increase a firm's monopoly power.

Merger, Concentration, and Competition

Are mergers harmful to society? Do they raise economic concentration and in turn decrease competition? The relationships between merger, economic concentration, and competition are far too complicated to permit simple "yes" or "no" answers to such questions. The answer in terms of a certain sector or market depends on the kind of merger, the size and power of the acquiring and the acquired firms, and the competitiveness of the involved sector or market before the merger.

Horizontal mergers are the most suspect. They increase concentration by decreasing the number of competitors in an industry. It does not always follow, however, that competition in the industry will lessen. Surely, if the largest and most powerful firm in an industry takes over a rival firm, competition will suffer. But in an industry in which the two or three largest companies have a good deal of monopoly control, a merger between, say, the fifth- and seventh-largest companies in that industry may in fact lead to greater competition.

Vertical mergers generally will not affect market concentration since the acquiring and the acquired companies do not operate on the same level of business activity. A firm acquiring a supplier or customer firm will lessen competition only if that merger hurts its competitors. Sometimes a company is able to gain a sure flow of an important input by acquiring a key supplier while its rivals remain threatened with interruptions in the supply of that input. In such cases the vertical merger may mean less competition in that industry.

Conglomerate mergers are the hardest to judge. They will raise aggregate concentration in a sector or an economy but, by definition, will be neutral in terms of market concentration. The acquisition of Marathon Oil by U.S. Steel (now USX) had no immediate effect on concentration in either the oil or the steel industries. The effect that conglomerate mergers have on competition (as distinct from concentration) has been hotly debated by economists for the past twenty-five years or so. Those who argue that conglomerate mergers do not threaten competition point out that competition takes place in markets and that these mergers do not affect a company's monopoly control in any market. Those on the other side feel strongly that such mergers do, however, affect a firm's economic control or power, which is a result of its size and its conglomeration. They say that conglomerates have "deep pockets," full of monopoly control profits gained in other markets, which can now be temporarily emptied into their newly gained subsidiaries enabling them to spend more (such as advertise more) and charge an unfairly low price. A companion attack on conglomerate mergers has to do with the chances that they offer for reciprocal selling. These "I'll buy from you and you buy from me" deals with other companies shut off sales to those who would like to compete, but are not conglomerate enough to be able to offer equal reciprocal buying opportunities.

Finally, conglomerate mergers may often take the place of internal conglomerate growth. The reasoning is that if the conglomerate merger were not allowed, the would-be acquirer would enter the industry anyhow. If the industry in question is highly concentrated and not very competitive, such entry would increase competition. However, entry by conglomerate merger would fail to take advantage of the chance to increase competition.

Horizontal mergers increase concentration by decreasing the number of competitors in an industry. Vertical mergers generally do not affect market concentration. Conglomerate mergers raise aggregate concentration in a sector or an economy but are neutral in terms of market concentration.

POTENTIAL ENTRY

The performance of an oligopoly depends very much on the amount of monopoly control held by the established firms in that industry. The less monopoly control or the more competition there is among the firms in an industry, the better we expect that industry to perform for society. So far in our discussion of oligopoly we have limited our attention to the relationship among the companies that make up an oligopoly. Now we look beyond the established firms in such an industry. We know that a further important determinant of the amount of monopoly control in an industry is the likelihood of entry into that industry.

This likelihood, or condition of **potential entry,** will importantly affect what established firms in an industry can and will do. The established firms in an industry that is fairly easy to enter may be very slow to raise their prices for fear that such an action would invite new competitors. In contrast, the established firms in an industry that is rather hard to enter are more apt to raise their prices, since the entry of new companies is not so likely.

An important determinant of the amount of monopoly control in an industry is the likelihood of entry into that industry. Established firms in an industry that is easy to enter may be slow to raise their prices for fear that such an action would encourage new competitors.

The Entry Concept in Economics

Entry is the act of coming into an industry by a new firm, which adds capacity to that industry. It takes place when a company that has not been producing in an industry joins that industry. The entering company may be one that did not exist before, or it may be an established firm in another industry that has decided to change industries or to expand into another industry. Economists see entry as taking place only if a new company in an industry adds to the capacity of that industry. When an established firm in one industry just acquires a firm's capacity in another industry but

does not add to it, no real entry has taken place. Nor is it entry if an already established company in an industry simply increases its own capacity to produce. So entry calls for adding to an industry's capacity as well as adding a new firm to the industry.

Entry is the act of coming into an industry by a new firm. Entry takes place only if that new firm adds to the capacity of the industry.

The idea of entry has for a long time been used by economists as an important part of economic theory. In pure competition, as explained by the well-known economist Alfred Marshall (1842–1924), entry and exit bring about the long-run equilibrium of an industry (see Chapter 26). Similarly, entry is relied upon to a considerable extent to attain the long-run equilibrium state in monopolistic competition. Yet entry was for some time a rather neglected part of oligopoly theory. When the amount of competition was studied in an industry, the emphasis was on the established competition and not on potential, or possible, competition. For example, a study seeking to discover the amount of monopoly control in the casualty insurance industry might have been limited to looking at the state of competition that already existed among established casualty firms. However, since companies in the life insurance industry were potential entrants, the chances of their entering the casualty business should also have been explored. Without these possible entrants, the casualty companies might have acted very differently. They might, we suppose, have charged higher prices and made higher profits.

A clear statement that potential competition strongly affects the actions of the established firms in an industry did not appear until Joe Bain of the University of California at Berkeley wrote *Barriers to New Competition* in 1956. Bain's work extended the theory of oligopoly beyond dealing only with the relationship among established firms to dealing with the relationship between established firms and potential entrants. Bain noted that interdependence, the main feature of oligopoly, includes the interdependence between established companies and potential entrants.

TABLE 8
An Evaluation of the Condition of Entry for Eighteen U.S. Manufacturing Industries

Standard Industrial Classification (SIC)	Industry	Condition of Entry
2094	Animal and marine fats and oils	Fairly easy
3498	Fabricated pipe and fittings	Fairly easy
3111	Leather tanning and finishing	Fairly easy
2013	Meat processing	Fairly easy
2311	Men's and boys' suits and coats	Fairly easy
2328	Work clothing	Fairly easy
3351	Copper rolling and drawing	Medium
2515	Mattresses and bedsprings	Medium
3652	Phonograph records	Medium
3576	Scales and balances	Medium
3317	Steel pipe and tube	Medium
2822	Synthetic rubber	Medium
3624	Carbon and graphite products	Fairly difficult
2073	Chewing gum	Fairly difficult
2111	Cigarettes	Fairly difficult
3641	Electric lamps	Fairly difficult
3717	Motor vehicles and car bodies	Fairly difficult
3612	Transformers	Fairly difficult

Source: P. David Qualls, "Market Structure and Price Behavior in U.S. Manufacturing, 1967–1972," Federal Trade Commission Working Paper No. 6, March 1977.

Potential competition strongly affects the actions of the established firms in an industry. Interdependence, the main feature of oligopoly, includes the interdependence between established companies and potential entrants.

The Condition of Entry

Not all oligopolistic industries are equally easy to enter. Sometimes a potential entrant has an advantage over the established firms in an industry. A company may hold a patent on a process that, after entry, allows it to produce at lower average total cost than can the established companies. On the other hand, sometimes entry into an industry is completely blocked. This might be a case where the government gives a company an exclusive franchise such as for telephone service or natural gas service within a certain geographic area. However,

most cases are somewhere in between these two. Established firms have some important advantages over possible entrants but are not able to keep them out without making some major sacrifices. A measure of the **condition of entry**, as Bain calls it, is found in the "extent to which established sellers can persistently raise their prices above a competitive level without attracting new firms to enter the industry."[5] In some industries the established firms can sell their output at a price much higher than the lowest average total cost at which it can be produced and yet keep new companies from entering. In others they can bar entrants only by keeping their price within a narrow range above their lowest average total cost. A few of the American four-digit SIC manufacturing industries that are believed by authorities to be fairly easy to enter, fairly difficult to enter, and of medium difficulty to enter are listed in Table 8. We have chosen six in

5. Joe S. Bain, *Barriers to New Competition* (Cambridge, Mass.: Harvard University Press, 1956), p. 3.

each of these categories from a much longer list prepared by P. David Qualls, formerly with the Federal Trade Commission.

A measure of the condition of entry is the extent to which established firms can raise prices above the competitive level without attracting new firms into the industry.

The Barriers to Entry

Why is it that the condition of entry varies so much from one industry to another? Why is it, for example, that manufacturers of fabricated pipes and fittings cannot raise their prices very much above their lowest average total cost before new companies are attracted into the industry, whereas cigarette or chewing gum manufacturers can? The answer lies in the type and height of entry barriers faced by potential entrants. We shall describe four kinds of barriers: (1) capital requirements, (2) product differentiation, (3) absolute-cost differences, and (4) minimum optimal scale effect.

Capital Requirements The **capital requirement** entry barrier refers to the amount of money that a new firm requires in order to compete adequately with the established firms in an industry. For example, a company may need much more than a billion dollars to enter the capital-intensive automobile industry in such a way as to compete with the established U.S., Asian, and European auto manufacturers. On the other hand, with a few simple tools and a pickup truck one can go into the business of building single-family homes. Given equal risk, the higher the capital requirement, the higher the entry barrier. (The amount of risk cannot be overlooked because it may be easier to raise large sums of money to enter a "sure bet" industry than smaller sums to enter an industry in which there have recently been many failures.)

Product Differentiation A second entry barrier involves the extent to which companies differentiate their products. The greater the degree of **product differentiation** (see Chapter 28, p. 624)—and the resulting consumer acceptance of established firms' products—the higher is this bar-

rier to entry. For example, a new firm selling a standard grade of bituminous coal might find almost no product differentiation disadvantage in relation to companies that have been in the bituminous coal business for many years. However, a new firm might find it very hard to sell its new brand of headache pills, razor blades, toothpaste, or detergent. The reason for this difficulty is that customers have generally accepted certain brands of these household products and are slow to try a new, unknown one. To overcome this high degree of consumer acceptance, new companies have sometimes had to hand out free samples or temporarily cut the price. But this approach can be very costly. Hence, product differentiation can be an important barrier to entry. In his study of twenty manufacturing industries, Bain found that product differentiation advantages of established firms "loom larger than any other source of barriers to entry."

Absolute-Cost Differences A third entry barrier is measured by the **absolute amount of cost difference** (per unit of output) existing between established firms in an industry and potential entrants. The established companies may have lower average total costs over the whole range of output that could possibly be supplied. Figure 1 pictures an average-total-cost curve facing an established company and one that would be faced by a potential entrant to a certain industry. What might account for such a cost difference? For one thing, the established firms may have exclusive access to the highest-grade and most favorably located raw materials needed in production. They may own the best and closest timberland or mines or farmland. A new company may be able to overcome the established firms' control only by paying higher production and transportation costs than those of established firms. The established companies may also hold patents on the best production techniques, which are either unavailable to potential entrants or available only through the payment of royalty fees. In either case the entering company would be at a cost disadvantage—in the first case because it would have to use a higher-cost production technique and in the second case because it would have to pay a fee to one or more of the established companies.

Another source of an absolute-cost advantage for the established firms is that potential entrants

FIGURE 1
**Absolute-Cost Differences Between
Established Firms and a Potential Entrant**

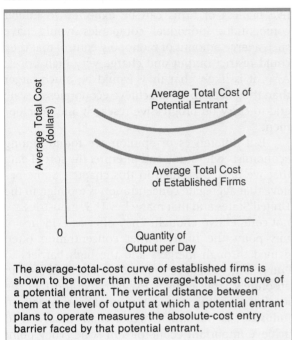

The average-total-cost curve of established firms is shown to be lower than the average-total-cost curve of a potential entrant. The vertical distance between them at the level of output at which a potential entrant plans to operate measures the absolute-cost entry barrier faced by that potential entrant.

may not be able to hire key inputs or to raise money on terms as favorable as those available to the established firms. A new company may have to pay much higher salaries to attract top managers and technical workers. Also, the established companies may be operating with long-term funds that were borrowed earlier at very low interest rates compared with those that new companies have to pay when they enter the industry. In the 1950s, businesses were able to sell forty-year bonds that paid about 4 percent interest. However, they had to pay about four times that much in the early 1980s.

Minimum Optimal Scale Effect   The last in our list of entry barriers is the **minimum optimal scale effect** barrier. This is the effect on the price of the product that cannot be avoided when a new company successfully enters the industry. The size of the unavoidable change in price is determined by the smallest possible addition to the output of the industry that the new firm must make if it is to survive in the industry. If the entering company has to produce a very large percentage of the total industry output in order to keep its average total

cost low enough to be competitive, it will add greatly to the supply of the industry. With a given demand curve, this added supply would cause the equilibrium price to fall sharply. This would amount to an important entry barrier, since the lower price after entry would be faced not only by the established companies but also by the new one. A potential entrant, which would be attracted by the price and profit in an industry before entry, would have to anticipate the degree to which price and profit would be forced down because of its own entry.

The minimum optimal scale effect is measured by the minimum optimal output of an entrant as a percentage of the existing total output of the industry. Sometimes an entering company adds only a very small percentage to industry output while reaching competitively low average-total-cost production. In such a case, the added supply might easily be absorbed in the market, so that this barrier would not be very important.

Figure 2 pictures a case in which the minimum optimal scale is 100 units of output a day. The industry in this case is made up of four companies that together produce 600 units a day (130, 140, 160, and 170). A potential entrant must produce at least 100 units a day to have a low enough average total cost to be competitive. The ratio of 100 to 600 (16.7 percent) expresses the potential for downward impact on price. This shows the minimum optimal scale effect. If the minimum optimal scale had been 50 units a day instead of 100, or if the industry daily output had been 1,200 instead of 600, the ratio would be only 1 to 12 (8.3 percent) and the entry barrier only one-half as high. Since price elasticity of demand (see Chapter 23) may be different in some industries than in others, the percentage gives only a rough idea of the real effect.

Four types of barriers to entry into an industry are: (1) the capital requirement, or the amount of money that is needed, (2) the degree of product differentiation, (3) the absolute cost difference per unit of output between established firms and potential entrants, and (4) the minimum optimal scale effect, or the degree of downward pressure on market price that is caused by an entrant's added supply.

FIGURE 2
Minimum Optimal Scale Effect

Shown is the long-run average-total-cost curve faced by the firms in a certain industry. Firms in this industry experience economies of scale up to the production level of 100 units per day, which is the minimum level of output at which a potential entrant would be able to attain low enough average total cost to be competitive. The output levels of the four established firms that now comprise the industry are marked on the horizontal axis (130, 140, 160, 170). The minimum optimal scale effect entry barrier depends upon how much an entrant adding 100 units to the industry supply of 600 units will depress the equilibrium price in this industry.

OLIGOPOLY AND SOCIAL WELFARE

In the preview to this chapter we asked whether or not oligopolistic industries can be expected to perform well enough to meet people's wants. We warned you that this is a hard question to answer because it is normative and because it is difficult to generalize for all oligopolistic industries. To help in answering this question, we developed the concepts of economic concentration, merger, and the condition of entry. It is doubtful that an economy with high aggregate concentration, high market concentration, rampant mergers, and high entry barriers would perform very well for society. We

suspect that the oligopolies, unchecked by government in such an economy, would not be very efficient or very progressive. Both absolute and relative bigness of firms can be expected to inhibit competition. Individual companies would have such a large amount of monopoly control that they could restrict output and charge very high prices. Also, it is likely that they would be much larger than they need to be to achieve economies of scale and to carry on progressive research and development.

But differences of opinion are found among economists who study and interpret the sort of data that we have presented in this chapter. Some believe that aggregate concentration is too high in the United States and that many key U.S. industries are not competitive enough. They offer as evidence of this point the high market concentration often gained through mergers and the high barriers to entry. Others believe that the power attributed to absolutely large firms is exaggerated and that the level of economic concentration of most American industries is not much higher than is needed to achieve important economies of scale. They point out that since the great majority of mergers in the United States are conglomerate, they do not have a bad effect on competition, and that the entrance of foreign companies into U.S. markets shows that the entry barriers to many U.S. industries are not very high.

Who is right? Both sides make valid points. Certain oligopolistic industries are quite competitive in the rivalry sense and perform very well for society. Yet other oligopolistic industries are not competitive enough, causing social welfare to suffer. In Chapter 35 we take a look at the U.S. record and see what role the government can play in regulating oligopolies.

Some economists believe that both aggregate and market concentration in the United States are too high, and that many industries are not competitive enough. Others believe that the level of economic concentration of most American industries is not much higher than is needed to achieve important economies of scale.

Economics in Focus

Is Big Business in Decline?

Despite the merger wave of the 1970s and 1980s, there are signs that the glory days of the huge American corporation may be ending. Even while mergers continue, executives have hastened to "downsize," cut costs and reduce labor forces, and generally streamline their businesses in order to meet intense foreign competition. Moreover, a survey conducted for *Fortune* in 1988 revealed that many executives see a decline in power and influence for America's largest corporations.

This survey sampled the opinions of the chief executive officers (CEOs) of two hundred large American companies. Thirty-three percent of the respondents indicated that the power of the large U.S. corporation was decreasing, as opposed to only 16 percent who thought it was increasing. Those who saw a waning of power offered a number of reasons. Some said that hostile takeovers, bankruptcies, and product liability suits have made even the behemoths of U.S. industry vulnerable. Many CEOs also claimed that their influence in Washington and among the general public had dwindled.

While many big firms are deliberately shrinking to make themselves "lean and mean," the last decade has brought a surge in small businesses. Average real GNP per firm (that is, total real GNP divided by the total number of firms) dropped more than 14 percent between 1980 and 1987, indicating a lesser degree of concentration in American industry. Firms with fewer than 500 workers raised their share of employment from 51 percent in 1976 to 53 percent in 1984. The proportion of American nonfarm workers who were self-employed rose from 6.9 percent in 1975 to 7.4 percent in 1986.

Why are small businesses on the rise? Some experts believe that computers and other high-tech systems have reduced or eliminated economies of scale, so that a small company with up-to-date equipment can be just as efficient as a large one. In *Fortune*'s survey over a third of the CEOs felt that economies of scale were disappearing. Instead of large size, many executives now value adaptability—what some refer to as being "light on one's feet." Because of rapid changes in technology, competition, and consumer preferences, firms that are too ponderous to change their habits will suffer. The Small Business Administration has also suggested, as the result of a 1985 study, that small businesses are more innovative than large ones. As we say in Chapter 24, innovation is a key to success in today's economy.

These arguments do not imply that large corporations will soon be extinct—nothing could be further from the truth. But in the long run the conditions that produce giant firms in close-knit oligopoly industries in many sectors of the U.S. economy may gradually be changing. Smaller firms may have a better chance to penetrate certain markets and wage battle with the giants.

Sources: Carrie Gottlieb, "And You Thought You Had It Tough," *Fortune,* April 25, 1988, pp. 83–84; "The Rise and Rise of America's Small Firms," *The Economist,* January 21, 1989, pp. 67–68; Stephen W. Quickel, "Companies in Crisis," *Business Month,* January 1989, pp. 46–47.

SUMMARY

1. Economic concentration measures the control that the largest firms have of a particular economic activity in a region of the world, an economy, a sector of an economy, or an industry. The presumption is that competition and concentration are negatively related. (See page 652.)

2. Aggregate economic concentration measures concentration beyond traditional industry lines. It is most often used to measure the share of economic activity undertaken by the largest firms in a major sector of an economy, but sometimes it is used in the context of a whole economy or even a region of the world. (See pages 652–654.)

3. Aggregate economic concentration does not focus on competing firms. The interest in aggregate concentration stems from the belief that the economic and political advantages gained through size alone may enable a firm to control those particular industries in which it is involved. (See page 654.)

4. Market concentration measures the control by the leading firms within a group of competing firms. (See page 657.)

5. To help solve the problem of defining industries or markets (the group of competing firms), the U.S. government has designed an elaborate classification system called the Standard Industrial Classification (SIC). This system divides the outputs of firms into groups beginning with a small number of broad, two-digit major industry groups and ending with a large number of narrow, seven-digit products. (See page 657.)

6. Market concentration levels may be measured by traditional 4-firm and 8-firm concentration ratios or by calculating Herfindahl-Hirshman Indexes (HHIs), which take account of all the firms in a market and the distribution of their market shares. (See pages 657–658.)

7. The U.S. concentration ratios that are published by the Bureau of the Census may be quite revealing, but should be viewed with caution as they may contain some serious overstatements and understatements of concentration in actual industries. These may result from: (1) too broad or narrow a definition of the industry product, (2) the omission of foreign competition, and (3) the use of national rather than regional or local geographic scope. (See pages 659–660.)

8. High levels of economic concentration may be reached by firms growing either internally through building or externally through merger. Economists usually favor internal growth because it must be accomplished in the face of competition. (See page 660.)

9. Mergers are of three different types: horizontal, vertical, and conglomerate. In a horizontal merger a firm acquires another firm engaged in the same activity, existing on the same level, and serving the same geographic market. In a vertical merger a firm acquires another firm that is either in a buyer or a seller relationship to it. In a conglomerate merger a firm acquires another firm engaged in a different industry. Conglomerate mergers are further broken down into product extension, geographic market extension, and relatively pure conglomeration. (See pages 660–661.)

10. There have been four fairly distinct merger movements in the United States. The first took place around the turn of the century and was largely horizontal. The second came just after World War I and was again primarily horizontal, though some vertical and conglomerate mergers also took place. The third merger wave came in the late 1960s and was predominantly conglomerate in nature. The latest merger movement began in the mid-1970s and continued into the very late 1980s. It is composed primarily of conglomerate and horizontal mergers. (See pages 661–662.)

11. Firms often prefer merger to internal growth for the following reasons: (a) It may be the quickest way to expand plant capacity. (b) It may be the lowest-cost way to grow or the easiest to finance. (c) It may be the lowest-risk way to diversify. (d) It may be a way to capture speculative gains. (e) It may best suit the personal goals of managers as distinct from owners of the firm. (f) It may increase a firm's monopoly control by eliminating a competitor or a potential competitor. (See pages 662–665.)

12. An important determinant of the degree of monopoly control in an industry is the likelihood of entry into that industry. Entry, as defined in economics, requires an addition to industrial capacity plus the addition of a new firm to an industry. Just as interdependence exists between the established firms in an oligopolistic industry, interdependence also exists between those established firms and potential entrants. (See pages 666–667.)

13. Some industries are harder to enter than others. A measure of the ''condition of entry'' is the extent to which established firms are able to charge high prices and earn economic profit without attracting new firms into their industry. (See page 667.)

14. An industry's condition of entry depends on the type and height of the barriers to entry in that industry. There are four kinds of barriers: (a) capital requirements, (b) product differentiation, (c) absolute-cost differences, and (d) minimum optimal scale effect. (See page 667.)

15. The capital-requirement barrier is determined by the amount of money that an entrant must have in order to acquire the plant, equipment, and other things that it needs to compete with established firms. The product-differentiation barrier is caused by established firms' ability to differentiate their products and thus gain consumer acceptance, which is difficult for an entrant to overcome. The absolute-cost barrier exists when established firms in an industry experience lower average total cost than an entrant can achieve. Finally, the minimum optimal scale effect barrier relates to how much an industry's price will be depressed by the additional output supplied by an entrant operating at minimum optimal scale. (See pages 668–669.)

KEY TERMS

absolute amount of cost difference entry barrier: an entry barrier based upon the disadvantage faced by a potential entrant firm with a higher absolute cost per unit of output than that of established firms (page 668).

aggregate economic concentration: a measure of the share of economic activity undertaken by the largest firms in a region of the world, in an economy, or in some major sector beyond traditional market or industry lines (page 652).

capital requirement entry barrier: an entry barrier based upon the amount of money needed by a potential entrant firm in order to compete adequately with the established firms in an industry (page 668).

concentration ratio: a measure that expresses the percentage share of some key variables such as

sales or assets accounted for by the largest firms (page 652).

condition of entry: the extent to which established firms in an industry are able to raise prices and earn economic profit without attracting new firms into that industry (page 667).

conglomerate merger: a merger that takes place when a firm acquires another firm engaged in a different industry (page 661).

economic concentration: a measure of the control of economic activity in an industry, in a major part of an economy, in a whole economy, or in a region of the world (page 652).

entry: the act of coming into an industry by a new firm, which adds capacity to that industry (page 666.)

geographic market extension conglomerate merger: a merger that takes place when a firm acquires another firm that is in the same business activity and on the same level but is serving a different geographic market (page 661).

Herfindahl-Hirshman Index (HHI): a measure of market concentration that includes all of the firms in a market and gives proportionately greater weight to the market shares of the larger firms in the market (page 659).

horizontal merger: a merger in which a firm acquires another firm engaged in the same activity, operating on the same level, and serving the same geographic market (page 660).

leveraged buy-out (LBO): a form of speculation through acquisition in which investors rely almost entirely on debt financing to acquire a company (page 664).

market concentration: the number and size distribution of firms in a specific industry or market (page 657).

merger: the acquisition of another company (page 600).

minimum optimal scale effect entry barrier: an entry barrier based upon the degree of downward pressure on market price that would be caused by the additional output supplied by an entrant operating at minimum optimal scale (page 669).

potential entry: the likelihood of entry into an industry (page 666).

product differentiation entry barrier: an entry barrier based upon the degree to which established firms in an industry have successfully differentiated their products (page 661).

product extension conglomerate merger: a merger that occurs when a firm acquires another firm in an allied industry (page 661).

relatively pure conglomerate merger: an interindustry merger that is neither product extension nor market extension (page 661).

Standard Industrial Classification (SIC) system: industry definitions used by the U.S. Bureau of the Census that use numerical codes to group industries and products (page 657).

value added: the difference between the value of materials that a firm buys and the value of what it sells (page 656).

vertical merger: a merger that occurs between companies at different levels of a particular business activity (page 661).

DISCUSSION QUESTIONS

1. Distinguish between aggregate economic concentration and market economic concentration. Give an example of each. Which do you think is more important to study if you wish to analyze the competitiveness of an economy?

2. "The economic concentration data that appear each year in *Fortune* magazine are aggregate concentration data." True or false? Explain.

3. Define what is meant by "value added." Using "value added" as the measuring variable, describe the change in aggregate economic concentration in the U.S. manufacturing sector from the mid-1950s to the early 1980s. (Before answering, look at Table 4.)

4. Explain the Standard Industrial Classification (SIC) system that is used in the United States to report market concentration data. Why might

you want to use a four-digit classification to describe a certain industry and a five-digit classification to describe a different industry?

5. Joe says to Alex, "The government ought to go in there and break up some of the big corporations in the XYZ industry—after all, the four-firm concentration ratio is 73 percent." "Wait a minute," Alex replies. "There are a lot of difficulties surrounding those figures. There are certain things that I would want to find out about before I'd be ready to make such a recommendation." What might Alex have in mind?

6. Distinguish between internal and external growth of companies. Why would most economists prefer to see firms that are already large grow through internal means rather than through external means?

7. Distinguish among the three categories of mergers that economists use. Give a hypothetical example of each. How do you suppose each affects economic concentration?

8. Economists divide conglomerate mergers into three categories. Distinguish among them and provide a hypothetical example for each. What effect would each of these have on market economic concentration?

9. Growth through merger has been rather common in the United States. Discuss several reasons why firms choose to grow this way.

10. An industry's "condition of entry" depends upon the extent to which four barriers to entry exist in that industry. Briefly explain each of these barriers.

11. In addition to the amount of money necessary to enter an industry in which the minimum optimal scale is very large in relation to total output, what other conditions would keep firms from entering such an industry?

12. "Economists are of a single mind. They readily agree that oligopolistic industries are a detriment to public welfare and, whenever possible, should be done away with." Are these statements true or false? Explain.

Living with Oligopoly

Everyone knows that the "competition" he or she observes among sellers—retailers or professional people—is somehow different from the "pure" competition of economics books. (By the way, pure unregulated monopoly is at least as rare as pure competition!)

Something similar is true of the buying side of other markets, such as employers or the "middlemen" buyers of the farmer's crops or the manufacturer's output. The question is not whether the so-called imperfections of competition exist—they certainly do—but of their importance, especially their long-run importance. Two prominent subquestions under this head are:

1. What are the more obvious symptoms of the grosser departures from pure competition, which on the supply side of the market are called monopolistic competition, oligopoly,* and monopoly, and on the demand side are called oligopsony (buyers' oligopoly) or monopoly?

2. What principal defenses does the market system itself provide for those who feel themselves victims of oligopolistic behavior? And what additional economic and political defenses are open to their victims, short of overthrowing the market system altogether?

The main body of this essay is divided into two parts, one part dealing with each of these questions.

NOT SIZE BUT PRICE BEHAVIOR

The danger sign of oligopoly in action—the smoking gun at the murder scene or the sugar content of the diabetic's blood and urine—is *not* size but *price be-*

* Note that when we use the term "oligopoly" in this essay (including the title) we do not refer to all markets classified as oligopolies, but only to those that possess a high degree of monopoly control or market power.

havior, which includes a wide range of specifics. For an organization, or union, or cartel of a town's or a county's "independent" grocers, or druggists, or gasoline station proprietors can and often does exercise a higher degree of monopoly-type control within its own bailiwick than do the local branches of the regional or national chains it claims to combat under the label of "antimonopoly."

Here are three specific price behaviors that should lead the watchful consumer to suspect oligopoly at work:

1. Confining competition to "quality" and "service," so that price is 95 or 98 percent excluded. Dogged refusal to cut prices *openly,* for *all* purchasers, and for *indefinite* periods. ("This week only" and "One to a customer" are the common substitutes, not to mention "Just for you, and don't tell anyone.")

2. Along with this, pressure to keep competitors from cutting *their* prices below cost plus a reasonable markup. This may be done by legislation or administrative decree on particular products; milk is a frequent example. For branded goods, the standard device is to connive with manufacturers on resale price maintenance, under the excuse of orderly marketing.

3. Advertising and slogans like "Costs more—worth it" and "New and improved," encouraging the gullible to judge quality by price. (If this year's model is "new and improved," precisely *what* is "new," *wherein* lies the "improvement," and *how large* is the price increase not mentioned in the advertising?) Occasionally this trick extends to not only concealing one's own prices (till the bill is presented) but forbidding competitors to advertise or display their (lower) ones, or indeed to mention price at all in their displays or publicity.

A second smoking gun, less smoky than the first, is *parallel action.* A worker is fired by Company A in City X. There is no job for him or her in other firms in A's industry or X's trading area. This looks like blacklisting. It can be applied as readily to the family farmer or small manufacturer who has trouble with a large corporate buyer as to the worker who has trouble with his or her bosses. Again, if you are not judged creditworthy by the Impregnable National Bank, you may somehow find that no "competing" bank in town will lend to you either. Or, after your life or health or auto insurance application with Oversize Mutual has been rated with extra premiums or exclusions, no competing insurance company will offer better terms. All such cases may of course be coincidental. Or they may be the "scientific" results of the application of "scientific" standards. But don't bet against some element of communication and collusion between ostensible competitors!

INSTITUTIONAL DEFENSES

The real-world person in the real-world street is, however, far from helpless against real-world oligopoly. Some of his or her defenses are institutional, built into the market system itself. Others require supplementing the market system by organization, legal action, or legislative lobbying. (The market, like Benjamin Franklin's God, helps those who help themselves.) More drastic action requires partial or complete replacement of the market system by regulation, socialization, or even violent revolution.

Let us concentrate first on the institutional defenses, which vary from one oligopolistic industry to the next. We divide them into eight sorts.

1. Inter-industry Competition At the turn of the century, the Pacific Southwestern (modeled on the Southern Pacific Railroad) was "The Octopus" of Frank Norris's muckraking novels, and every big city had one or more streetcar and gas-company tycoons. Three generations later, the railroads are in trouble, the streetcars are dying, and the gas companies (often regulated) are fighting for their lives against electric and fuel-oil competition. Steel competes with lighter metals like aluminum—sometimes even with plastics. Tin is (practically) gone from the old tin can, which itself competes with glass, cardboard, plastics, and with freeze-drying processes. And what would an oligopoly position in the stagecoach, buggy-whip, or livery-stable industry be worth today?

2. Consumer Mobility At the turn of the century, every Main Street or crossroads merchant, in his bank, his general store, or his ice-coal-hay-grain-and-feed establishment, had a considerable measure of local oligopoly, which he sometimes exercised to the full. Three generations later, the potential customer has the choice of a dozen or more shopping centers within driving radius, perhaps an entire metropolitan area. Mobility extends over still longer distances by phone, by mail, or in some cases by airplane.

3. International Competition "The tariff is the mother of the trusts," said Henry Havemeyer of the old Sugar Trust during the Taft administration just after the first decade of the twentieth century. He was right, if by "the tariff" he meant protection in general. And by the same token, "Free trade is the Lord High Executioner of the Trusts." Cheap foreign imports—frequently of bargain-basement quality, frequently products of cheap labor, and sometimes produced by "runaway" domestic companies—have become since World War II a major defense of American consumers against American oligopolists in both industry and the trade union movement.

In the years immediately after World War II, the prospect of antitrust action seems to have been for a time the main factor that kept the Big Three of the American automobile industry from becoming the "Big One"—General Motors (sometimes called *The* Corporation). But Volkswagen, from Germany, put in its appearance in 1949, followed by other contenders from Britain, France, Italy, Sweden, and Germany itself. By the late 1960s, Japanese competitors were entering too, and in the mid-1980s came new entrants from Korea and Yugoslavia. Detroit's Big Three, and also the United Auto Workers, were calling for help.

4. Consumer Surrogates A surrogate, or "attorney in fact," is an official or unofficial representative of people unable or unwilling to represent themselves. For the ordinary consumer this role is often played by a subset of firms called "price-cutters."

Whereas oligopolists compete mainly on quality and service, surrogate firms compete almost entirely on price. They are often mail-order houses, discount houses, or chain stores. When the oligopolists sell nationally advertised brands, the price-cutters concentrate on "off-brands," "store-brands," or unbranded "generics." To the oligopolists' "Costs more—worth it" they reply, "Just as good—for less." Unfortunately for the consumer, successful consumer surrogates tend to change strategy and go "up-market"—with higher prices, atmosphere, ambience, and all—to join the oligopoly club. Fortunately for the consumer, other surrogates often take their place. (In the auto industry, Ford, which charged $385 for a brand-new Model T "tin Lizzie," played the surrogate role in the 1920s, to be succeeded by the Volkswagen "beetle" of the next generation, and later still, by an international bevy of "econoboxes.")

5. Contestable Markets These are also called "potential competition." The basic idea is simple; firms are in business to make money and are not bound to any particular product line. The more venturesome they are, the more willing they are to try their hands at some other field in which other firms are making excess profits. (The Duke interests shifted from tobacco to electric power and nuclear energy; the Mellons, from real estate and banking to aluminum, coke, and petroleum; railroads have

Used cars, an alternative for the American consumer

branched into real estate, steel companies into petroleum refining, oil companies into department stores and entertainment.) In any oligopolistic business, a significant probability exists that exercising its powers to gouge the consumer will attract the lightning of both small newcomers and conglomerate competitors, just as "ripe" dead animals attract the scavenging efforts of vultures, hyenas, jackals, and bacteria. It is the contention of William J. Baumol and others that real-world oligopolistic markets are in fact sufficiently contestable so that real-world oligopolists cannot, if they are to maintain their positions, act much differently from pure competitors in similar situations.

Some writers, Joseph Schumpeter most particularly, stress contestability by innovation, meaning new products or new processes. This course of action he calls "creative destruction." We have already mentioned cases of this kind under other heads—the railroads, the gas companies, and so on.

6. New-Used Competition For durable goods—autos, trucks, tractors, and farm machinery are examples—an oligopolist's principal competitors include some of its own customers of the past few years. There are more used-car lots (not to mention private small-scale suppliers) than new-car dealers and manufacturers combined. If you can't afford this year's "new and improved" price increase, or this year's "lemon" probability, why not try last year's

model, with its price cut to compensate for both wear and tear and the loss of the intangible attribute called "newness." (If, that is, you can be reasonably sure of not sampling last year's bumper "lemon" crop!)

7. Do-It-Yourself Avoidance of market transactions is often possible by doing it yourself. Obvious examples of do-it-yourself include growing produce in suburban backyards, home laundering, barbering, tailoring, and medical practice. For the mechanically adept, the range is much greater; a wide range of home and vehicular maintenance and repair, furniture making (partial or complete), light trucking, and other hobbies expanded to save money. The extension to barter—"I'll fix your roof and plumbing if you care for my family's teeth"—are obvious. They can expand further to a network of avoidance and evasion, not only of oligopoly and cartel arrangements but also of taxation, licensing, trade union rules, and regulations of all kinds. Estimates of the size of the American second, or underground, economy run between 10 and 25 percent of the first, or above-ground, economy, but also cover large-scale criminal activities—drugs, prostitution, extortion, and racketeering not elsewhere classified.

8. Just Say No! Just say "no," not only to the drug pusher but to selling and advertising in general. Seldom being under any compulsion to buy is the consumer's major defense. The urgency is all the other way. In the typical retail transaction, especially for perishable goods and for services, a seller's need to sell and to sell quickly is more acute than the buyer's need to buy and buy quickly, although all of us can think of exceptions, such as medical services in a heart attack or similar emergency.

ACTIVE DEFENSES

Active defenses against oligopoly and cartels go further and faster than the passive institutional defenses we have discussed. Some such defenses are erected against buyers' oligopoly (oligopsony). One is the trade union movement with its direct action (strikes and slowdowns). Another is the farm movement with its indirect action (legislative lobbying and political pressure). Our question here is, rather, why is the American consumer movement so weak? Why isn't it, for example, a powerful force against protectionism in international trade? (Consumer movements are much stronger in northern and western Europe.)

One reason follows from the institutional defenses themselves. The market does much of the consumers' work for them; few oligopoly or cartel abuses are big enough or permanent enough to keep the ordinary consumer angry enough to do more than complain. OPEC, perhaps because it was foreign, was an exception in the decade after 1973.

Second, if consumers literally lived by bread alone, they would surely organize against any oligopoly or cartel of bakers or flour millers, just as the machinist or the dairy farmer, whose incomes depend on the prices, respectively, of machinists' labor and dairy products, organize against oligopsonists who hold those prices down. But the vast majority of real-world consumers scatter their resentments randomly over so many people and professions ("Rich man, poor man, beggarman, thief/ Doctor, lawyer, Indian chief") with no consensus about whom to deal with first. This is not to deny that consumer guides and testing services, like the magazines *Consumer Reports* and *Consumer Digest,* survive by catering to a minority of consumers.

A third reason is political. The representative consumer activist is antibusiness, and two aspects of being antibusiness are to be prolabor and profarmer. But where high union wages and high farm prices translate into high consumer prices, what is there to do but mutter vaguely about "middlemen" and "profiteers"? Also, many consumer activists are during working hours themselves employees of oligopolistic companies, members of oligopolistic unions, or practitioners of oligopolistically organized professions. (How is the cost of health care to be reduced, without reduction in the quality, if the services of doctors, nurses, hospital administrators, and hospital staffs are all sacrosanct?)

As a result, the American consumer has acquired a reputation as a fool, although consumers in other advanced countries may be little better. Thorstein Veblen mocked American "conspicuous consumption" and "conspicuous waste" in 1899. Wesley Mitchell described "the backward art of spending money" in 1912. Later, Herbert Marcuse denounced the "one-dimensional man," the consumer, as a narcotized addict, desperately searching for a long-term satisfaction that consumption—like heroin or cocaine—can never provide. And an anonymous American wag has ridiculed the consumer for buying goods he does not want, at prices he cannot afford, on the basis of advertising he does not believe, to impress neighbors he does not care about.

So the consumer—who is also a producer in business hours—goes his or her not-so-merry way, pacifying his or her conscience for contributing to oligopolistic or cartel activities in production by resenting similar activities as they bear on the consumer. Not an inspiring sight, perhaps, but surely preferable to the shortages, outages, malnutrition, and starvation that haunt so much of the remainder of our planet.

Resource Supply and Demand

Labor, Wages, and Collective Bargaining

Capital, Interest, and Investment

PART IX
RESOURCE MARKETS

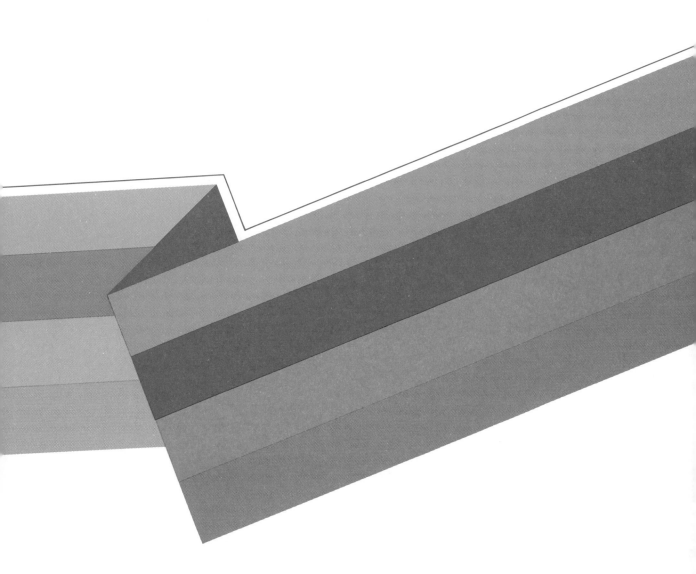

30

Resource Supply
and Demand

Preview In Parts VII and VIII you studied product, or output, markets. Part IX deals with resource, or input, markets. Supply and demand interact in resource or input markets in much the same way as they do in product or output markets. However, the supply of resources and the demand for them change the parts that the actors play on the economic stage. In the output markets, businesses supply and consumers demand; in the resource markets, the business firms are the demanders, while the people who own the labor, natural resources, and capital are the suppliers.

In a certain sense, this chapter offers you little that you haven't already learned. Your main challenge will be to apply some ideas that you learned earlier in a different context. You will have to keep reminding yourself that you are now studying demand from the viewpoint of a profit-maximizing firm and supply from the viewpoint of the owners of the factors of production (labor, natural resources, and capital).

We begin by reviewing the definitions of the resources. We recognize that enterprise or entrepreneurship should be separated out of the labor category. But where does labor end, and where does entrepreneurship begin? Why are certain labor skills or human capital sometimes classified as capital? And where do you draw the line between land that is a natural resource and land that should be classified as capital?

Next we discuss the supply of resources. We explain the difference between the supply of a resource for all the uses to which it can be put and the supply of a resource for a specific use. You will see that the supply curve for a resource is generally positive—as it is for products—but that it will vary in slope depending on the resource's opportunity cost. You will also learn about the price elasticity of resource supply and some of the more important determinants of supply elasticity.

Turning next to the demand side, we explain why the demand for resources is called a "derived demand." We also describe the price elasticity of resource demand and its main determinants. Then we present marginal productivity theory. Given certain simplifying assumptions, it explains the amounts of a specific resource that profit-maximizing companies will demand at different resource prices. Next, we combine supply and demand to discover the equilibrium level of resource quantity and price. The earnings that owners of resources receive are broken down into transfer earnings and economic earnings. Transfer earnings are the part that is equal to what a resource can earn in its next-best use, and economic earnings account for the rest. Finally, we deal with the economic and public policy implications of resource earnings made up only of transfer earnings, only of economic earnings, or of certain mixes of the two.

THE RESOURCES REVISITED

In Chapter 4 we explained that production brings together certain inputs, which we called the factors of production, or resources. At that point in the book, we separated them into three broad categories: (1) labor, (2) natural resources, and (3) capital. Here we make one change. We separate enterprise, or entrepreneurship, out of the labor category. So here we look at four kinds of resources and the payments, or returns, that each receives:

1. Labor resources, which receive wages
2. Entrepreneurial resources, which receive profit
3. Natural resources, which receive rent
4. Capital resources, which receive interest.

Labor Resources

Labor covers most forms of human work that are or can be directed toward production. It includes the labor of the assembly-line worker and of the computer programmer. The only kind of human work that we are not classifying as labor is the entrepreneur's effort. Entrepreneurship is different from management or administration. Managerial and administrative jobs are considered to be labor, but entrepreneurship is that special kind of human effort that sets the course that a company will take. An entrepreneur makes the key decisions about the use of labor, natural resources, and capital. Labor receives wages (in some cases called salaries) in return for its productive work. An entrepreneur does not. Instead, he or she receives a residual payment called profit or incurs a loss. Whatever is left over after labor, natural resources, and capital are paid goes to the entrepreneur.

Labor resources include most forms of human work that can be directed toward production. Labor receives wages in return for its productive work.

Entrepreneurial Resources

As leaders of business firms, **entrepreneurs** seek the best opportunities for production and coordinate all the other resources in order to carry them out. An entrepreneur is one who visualizes needs and takes the necessary actions to initiate the process by which they will be met. This often means taking risks and innovating. In the construction business, an entrepreneur might decide to build a new housing project. He or she decides where to build it, what kind of housing it will be, what materials to use, how much and what kind of labor and capital to employ, plus the million and one other questions that arise in leading such an enterprise. Of course, the entrepreneur can never be sure of the results of these decisions. Perhaps a different building site would have been better. Possibly mortgage rates will rise after the project is started. The technology that was chosen may turn out to be a mistake because of some change in a labor market that greatly reduces the cost of certain workers. Just the same, the entrepreneur must make decisions about all these things, and more, before the project gets under way.

Entrepreneurs seek the best opportunities for production and coordinate all the other

---

resources in order to carry them out. This normally involves the taking of risks and innovating. An entrepreneur makes the key decisions about the use of labor, natural resources, and capital and receives any profit from the enterprise.

Natural Resources

Natural resources are the "gifts of nature" that can be used to produce goods. Land in its natural state is an essential input for most production. Raw materials such as crude oil, iron ore, and water are also important natural resource inputs for much that is produced. Finally, vegetation that grows without anyone planting it and animals that are not domesticated are also natural resources. Payment for the use of natural resources is called rent.

Natural resources are the "gifts of nature" that can be used to produce goods. Payment for the use of natural resources is called rent.

Capital Resources

Capital is made up of goods and skills that are used as inputs for production. Factory buildings, tools, and equipment are examples of **capital goods,** and the abilities to heal the sick, operate a lathe, and program a computer are examples of capital skills, or **human capital.** Unlike the other resources, capital must first be produced itself before it is available for use in further production. Capital is produced, not for final consumer use, but rather for entrepreneurs to use, along with labor and natural resources, in producing goods and services for final consumption. Payment for the use of capital is called interest.

Capital is made up of the goods and skills that are used as inputs for production. Payment for the use of capital is called interest.

Resource Packages

Before we continue our discussion of the four categories of resources, you should understand that in the real world it is actually very difficult to know where one resource ends and another one begins. They are not as easy to separate as our classification implies. Very rarely do we find a productive resource that does not include some capital. In fact, capital is a part of almost all labor, entrepreneurship, and natural resources. Labor that is totally untrained and uneducated is little more than brute force and, with no tools or machines with which to work, will probably be very unproductive. The same may be said for entrepreneurship. An untrained and uneducated entrepreneur will probably lack the vision to see business opportunities as well as the ability to combine resources effectively in a business firm. Natural resources, too, are of little use without the knowledge and skills of people who are able to use them productively. Often capital goods are needed to turn a pure natural resource into a productive input.

You can see, then, that production usually requires the use of certain combinations of resources, or **resource packages,** that cannot be separated except in theory. For example, a company that is building a housing project must have the land leveled, holes dug in the ground for foundations, wood put together in certain ways, bricks cemented together, and so on. The entrepreneur has many choices to make, but these are choices among different resource packages, and not choices about whether or not to use labor or capital or natural resources. The houses must be built on land that is prepared by labor and capital. The foundations must be dug by more or less skilled labor using more or less sophisticated capital equipment. The carpentry and the brickwork also call for combinations of labor and capital. So it is clear that entrepreneurs must base their decisions on the productiveness of alternative resource packages at particular prices.

Production usually requires the use of certain combinations of resources—resource packages— that cannot be separated except in theory.

THE FUNCTIONAL DISTRIBUTION OF INCOME

Before we turn to the supply and demand for resources, let us examine their relative shares of U.S. national income. Table 1 shows these shares for selected years since 1929.

Several facts about the functional distribution, or relative resource shares, become clear from studying the table. Compensation of employees (labor's share) is the largest share by far and has increased over the past half-century. Proprietor's income (the net profits of unincorporated businesses) and rental income are relatively small shares of the total and have decreased. Corporate profits and interest also are relatively small shares, but have fluctuated over the years.

Certain problems arise in relating these statistics to our four-part classification of resources. Because proprietor's income is a mixture of wages, rent, interest, and profit, it combines some income from all the noncorporate categories. On the other hand, the rental income data do not include rental income received by proprietorships or corporations. Therefore, some caution should be used in interpreting changes in shares over time. To the extent that corporations have replaced large numbers of small unincorporated businesses, the share of income has shifted away from proprietor's income to all the other categories. The most important shift has been to compensation of employees. Suppose that the Ma and Pa grocery goes out of business when the new A&P grocery opens up, but that Ma and Pa are able to get jobs at the new A&P. In the statistics, compensation of employees has gone up and proprietor's income has gone down, but the actual growth in labor income is not as large as the statistics suggest. Much of the income of proprietors, like Ma and Pa, was probably labor income in the first place. Also, to the extent that title deeds to natural resources are sold by individuals to organized businesses, the rental income share will show a decrease, and corporate profits and proprietor's income will show a gain. In fact, rental income may be as great as ever.

The functional distribution of income refers to relative resource shares. Compensation of employees makes up almost three-fourths of the U.S. national income, with most of the remainder fairly equally accounted for by proprietors' income, corporate income, and interest.

TABLE 1
Functional Distribution of National Income in the United States, Selected Years, 1929–1988 (percentages)

Year	Compensation of Employees (Wages and Fringe Benefits)	Proprietors' Income	Rental Income	Corporate Profits	Interest
1929	60.5	17.1	5.8	11.4	5.6
1940	65.6	15.8	3.4	11.1	4.1
1945	67.9	17.3	2.8	10.8	1.2
1950	64.8	16.2	3.2	14.6	1.3
1955	67.2	13.5	3.6	14.0	1.7
1960	69.8	12.3	3.6	11.6	2.7
1965	68.3	11.1	3.1	13.9	3.6
1970	74.3	9.6	2.2	9.0	4.9
1975	73.6	9.7	1.0	9.1	6.5
1980	74.3	8.2	0.3	8.0	9.1
1985	73.2	7.9	0.3	8.7	9.9
1988	73.3	8.0	0.5	8.2	9.9

Note: For some years, percentages do not add up to 100 percent because of rounding.
Source: Economic Report of the President, 1989, Table B-24.

THE SUPPLY OF RESOURCES

At any time there are certain amounts of resources in existence. There are only so many people in the world or in a country, only a certain amount of recognized natural resources, and only a certain amount of capital goods and human capital. However, it would be nonsense to dismiss the supply side of resource markets on the ground that the total quantity of each resource is fixed. Supply explores the quantities that are *offered* at various prices. Every waking hour of every "working-age" person is a potential hour of labor, but that vast amount is only remotely related to the actual supply of labor. We expect that much more labor of any kind will be supplied at high wages than at low wages. The same positive relationship is expected for specific uses of labor, as well as for all uses of labor put together. It is also expected for the other resources. More natural resources will be offered at higher rents and less at lower rents. More capital will be produced and offered at higher interest payments and less at lower interest payments. In the same way, higher profit will attract more entrepreneurs, and economic loss may cause them to seek employment as workers.

The supply of resources focuses on the quantities offered at various prices. Higher payments will lead to more of a particular input being supplied.

It makes a considerable difference whether we are examining a supply response for *all uses* of a resource or for just *one specific use* of that resource. For example, we may want to know how much more labor will be offered after an across-the-board 10 percent wage increase for all workers in the United States. Or we may want to know only about the change in the quantity of hospital nursing labor that is supplied when the wages of hospital nurses are raised 10 percent, if all other wage rates remain the same. In the first case, the supply response will depend upon how many people who are already working will decide to work more hours than before the wage increase and on how many people who were not part of the labor force before will be persuaded to offer their services at the higher wage rate. In the specific-use case of hospital nursing, the supply response will not be limited to how many working hospital nurses will decide to offer more hours of work and how many trained nurses not in the labor force will decide to enter or re-enter hospital nursing. This response will also be affected by how many nonhospital nurses—such as nurses in doctors' offices, schools, factories, and nursing homes—will switch over to hospital nursing.

Supply for All Uses

The preceding discussion has probably convinced you of two important facts about the supply of resources. The first is that supply responses are normally positive—more of a resource is expected to be supplied at higher prices and less at lower prices. Second, the supply for all uses of a resource is normally less responsive to a change in the price of that resource (less elastic or more inelastic) than is the supply for a specific use.

In this section we shall focus our attention on the supply for all uses of a resource. We expect positive supply responses to price changes, and we expect elasticity to increase with the passage of time. As with all responses, the greater the length of time between a change in price and when the quantity response is measured, the more elastic the response will be.[1] For example, after one month a 10 percent increase in the price of a natural resource such as coal or silver may bring about only a 5 percent increase in the quantity supplied of that natural resource. But after two years, when established firms in the coal- or silver-mining business have had time to make many more adjustments and new firms have had time to enter these industries, the supply response to the original 10 percent price increase may be as high as 15 or 20 percent.[2]

The supply for all uses of a resource is normally less elastic than is the supply for a specific use.

---

1. Recall our discussions of price elasticity of demand on the output side in Chapter 23 and price elasticity of supply on the output side in Chapter 25.
2. For the moment we ignore the possibility that speculation about future prices of coal or silver might persuade owners to leave the resource in the ground.

Supply for All Uses of Labor At any particular price (wage rate), the quantity of labor that is supplied in a country depends upon many things. Some important variables include: (1) the size of the population, (2) the age distribution of the population, (3) the proportion of the population that chooses to participate in the labor force, (4) the portion of the year, week, or day that those participating in the labor force choose to work, and (5) the age when people normally enter the labor force and the age when they normally retire. Also, the country's customs, laws, and attitudes influence who should work, for how long each year, week, or day, and over what periods of their lives. In the next few pages, we take a closer look at these five major influences on the supply of labor for all uses.

Size of Population The size of the population and its rate of growth are important determinants of the supply of labor. Population growth varies for many reasons including ignorance about birth control, religious and moral beliefs, usefulness of children as workers, the security of having children to take care of aged parents, life expectancy, and so on. The size of some populations is kept down by extreme poverty, and the size of others is kept down by substantial wealth.

The size of the population of a country is affected not only by birth and death rates but also by immigration. It is common for people who live in poorer countries with few opportunities for work to emigrate to wealthier ones. In the United States, the history of the labor supply is closely tied to immigration, mainly from Europe in earlier years and from Mexico and other Latin American countries and Southeast Asia in more recent years. However, the supply of labor through immigration may not be permanent. During the past three decades, countries like Germany and Italy have had a large number of temporary immigrants from countries like Yugoslavia and Turkey. Generally these people work in the host country for ten years or so and, after saving some money, return to their own country.

Age Distribution Two countries with populations of about equal size may not have the same labor supplies, since their age distributions may be very different. One of the countries may have a smaller labor supply because its population includes a large percentage of old people above working age. The other country may have a much greater supply of labor since its age distribution is more concentrated around the working years. Of course, a country that hosts a large number of temporary immigrants who come for the purpose of finding better jobs will have a larger proportion of working-age people than the country from which the workers emigrate.

Labor Force Participation Rate Not every working-age person is willing or able to participate in the labor force. Because some people are physically or mentally handicapped, they cannot perform most kinds of work. "Housewives" or "househusbands" choose not to supply their labor to business firms or governments so that they can take care of their young children and their homes. Many people will decide to spend extra years in school or to retire earlier than is usual. Others who have inherited wealth or have income from property may simply decide to spend their time in ways other than working for wages. There are also some people who have such low living standards that welfare payments are sufficient to satisfy them.

Labor force participation rates go up or down depending upon a number of different variables. Changes in wage rates have both a substitution effect and an income effect on the amount of labor supplied. Clearly, higher wage rates, which mean a higher opportunity cost of not working, will attract people into the labor force and also keep other people from leaving the labor force. Lower wage rates, which mean a lower opportunity cost of not working, will often cause people to stay in school longer, retire earlier, stay at home to tend the garden, or stay at home to take care of the children. That is the substitution effect. However, the income effect is functioning at the same time, but in the opposite direction. Participation rates are expected to have a negative response to changes in real income. When real income rises, people may want to have more leisure time and so will supply less labor. And when real income falls, people may be willing to supply more labor.

Cultural changes may also bring about increases or decreases in the labor force participation rate. For example, before World War II relatively few American women worked in factories, and it was customary for women who did work to quit when they married or became pregnant. But the needs for labor were so great during the war that women flocked to the factories. Working side by side with men, like "Rosie the Riveter," they convinced American society that they could handle what traditionally were "men's" jobs. Many families found that a second income in a household was a desirable thing. Today about 57 percent of all working-age American women participate in the labor force.

A country's labor force participation rate is also affected by legislation. Laws prohibiting child labor or requiring attendance in school may decrease the labor force participation rate. By contrast, laws prohibiting forced early retirement and laws that are very strict about who may receive welfare payments tend to increase the labor force participation rate.

Work per Year, Week, or Day   The supply of labor is a function not only of how many people are available for work but also of how many hours per year, week, or day they are available for work. Before the American Civil War, most people worked twelve-hour days, six days a week, fifty-two weeks a year.[3] Vacations, holidays, a five- or even four-day workweek, and seven- to eight-hour workdays are relatively recent. As real wages increased, it took fewer hours of work to earn enough money to buy the necessities of life, so that some money was left over for luxuries. With the higher real wage, leisure time became not only more expensive but also more valuable. What good is it to earn enough to buy a sailboat, a sports car, and a house with a swimming pool, if one doesn't have time to sail, drive, or swim?

This point is a further application of the income effect and substitution effect. An increase in wages—the price of labor—has a tendency both to increase the number of hours people are willing to work (the substitution effect) and to decrease the number of hours they are willing to work (the income effect). Because the substitution effect of a

wage increase makes leisure time relatively more expensive, it makes people more willing to give up some leisure time in order to get the additional goods and services they can afford with a higher income. But the income effect of a wage increase works in the opposite direction. It makes people richer, causing them to buy more of what they want, and that includes leisure time. What the net result will be is not easy to predict. People often respond positively—that is, they are willing to work more hours—when they are given a chance to receive time-and-a-half or double-time pay for overtime. However, over the longer run, more leisure has been chosen and less labor has been supplied as wages have increased. In the very long run, productivity increases enable everyone to work fewer hours while simultaneously receiving higher real income.

Changes in wage rates have both a substitution effect and an income effect on the amount of labor supplied.

Working Age   So far we have used the term *working age* as though it had a fixed definition. It does not. The legal, socially accepted, or typical working age varies greatly from country to country and from time to time within the same country. Even though it is common today to see very young children working in the rural areas of developing countries, most industrial countries have strict laws that forbid young children to work. However, during the nineteenth century, particularly in the textile industries of England and America, young children worked long hours in sweatshops. Not until the 1930s were laws passed in the United States to prohibit child labor.[4]

The lower age limit for workers is also very much influenced by the society's attitudes about education, as reflected in its laws. The amount of taxpayer-supported public education affects how many years most people go to school. "Free" or

---

3. Harold F. Williamson, *The Growth of the American Economy* (New York: Prentice-Hall, 1951), p. 659.

4. The Walsh-Healey Act of 1936 and the Fair Labor Standards Act of 1938 established a minimum age of 16 for general employment and 18 for employment in hazardous occupations. For certain occupations, where work is performed outside of school hours, the minimum age was established at 14.

largely subsidized higher education gives people a strong incentive to withhold their labor until about age twenty-two (or older if they pursue graduate education).

The supply of labor also depends on the upper limit of the working age. There is no legal upper limit and since 1986, with few exemptions, employers may not force persons to retire.[5] However, incentives for early or late retirement may be provided by firms or by the government. For example, in the United States the retirement pension provided by the Social Security Act of 1935 can be claimed by a retired person at age 65 or a scaled-down version at age 62. From age 65 (or 62) until age 70, the Social Security recipient may earn only a small sum of money each year before having to pay back his or her Social Security benefits in the form of a 50 percent tax on "excess" earnings.[6]

Five variables that affect the supply for all uses of labor are (1) size of population, (2) age distribution of population, (3) proportion of population that chooses to participate in the labor force, (4) the amount of time that those participating choose to work, and (5) the age when people enter into and retire from the labor force.

Supply for All Uses of Entrepreneurship Much of our discussion about labor also applies to entrepreneurship. Of course, people may be willing and able to participate in the labor force, yet not willing and able to be entrepreneurs. Many do not like to take risks. Nor does everyone have the education, training, and other qualities to be able to visualize needs and take the necessary steps to initiate the process by which they will be met.

The laws, educational systems, and cultures in some countries offer more encouragement to entrepreneurs than in other countries. Just how the entrepreneurial "spirit" is best achieved and culti-

vated is not easy to determine and goes well beyond the subject matter of this book.[7]

Many of the same variables that affect labor also affect entrepreneurship. In addition, some countries offer more encouragement to entrepreneurs than other countries.

The business ventures of many entrepreneurs have a short life span. In general, small firms fail at a higher rate than larger businesses.[8] One study found that about one-half of the new businesses that were founded or acquired during the late 1940s and early 1950s were "disposed of" within two years, one-third lasted as long as four years, and only one-fifth were still in operation after ten years.[9] According to another study for the years 1959 to 1962, the number of U.S. businesses increased by about 172,000, because 1,291,000 new businesses were started and 1,119,000 businesses failed.[10] There are many reasons for the rapid turnover and instability of entrepreneurs' business ventures. Unexpectedly poor business conditions causing low sales and high inventories are often cited to explain the rash of business failures during recessions and depressions. But Dun and Bradstreet, the leading source of information on business failures in the United States, stresses managerial incompetence and lack of experience as the major reasons for business failure.

Small business ventures of entrepreneurs who lack know-how and experience are often doomed to fail.

The quantity supplied of entrepreneurs is believed to be positively related to the returns expected by would-be entrepreneurs. The higher the expected profit, the more likely it is that a person will become an entrepreneur and the greater the

---

5. Before the 1986 amendment to the Age Discrimination in Employment Act, a mandatory retirement age of seventy or higher was legal.

6. A person may earn $6,480 if under age 65 and $8,880 if between the ages of 65 and 70 in 1989. There is no limit on property or pension income.

7. See Douglass C. North, *Structure and Change in Economic History* (New York: Norton, 1981).

8. A. B. Cochran, "Small Business Mortality Rates: A Review of the Literature," *Journal of Small Business Management,* October 1981, p. 57.

9. Betty C. Churchill, "Age and Life Expectancy of Business Firms," *Survey of Current Business,* December 1955, pp. 15, 16.

10. Cochran, "Small Business Mortality Rates," pp. 56, 57.

quantity supplied of this resource will be. As you have learned from your study of market types in Part VIII, firms are more likely to make a high and lasting profit in less-competitive rather than more-competitive markets. It follows then that the more monopoly control a potential entrepreneur expects to gain, the more likely it is that he or she will become an entrepreneur. In other words, entrepreneurs will be more attracted to oligopolistic and monopolistic industries than to those that approach monopolistic competition or pure competition.

For this reason, government policies in the areas of patents, taxation, and antitrust can influence the supply of entrepreneurs. Remember from Chapter 27 that a patent is a temporary (seventeen years in the United States) government-enforced actual monopoly that may be given to inventors or to companies that purchase the rights of inventors. The easier it is to get patents, the longer they run, and the harder it is to infringe upon them, the greater will be the supply of entrepreneurs. Also, low corporate income tax rates, generous deductions for business expenses, and favorable ways of figuring the depreciation of capital result in higher net profits and so should attract more entrepreneurs. Of course, antitrust law and enforcement is a two-way street. On the one hand, the less strict a country's antitrust laws (see Chapter 35) and the less vigorous their enforcement, the freer companies will be to pursue monopoly control and presumably the greater the supply of entrepreneurs will be. On the other hand, the stricter the antitrust laws and the better they are enforced, the easier it may be for entrepreneurs to enter industries and to compete on a fair basis.

The quantity supplied of entrepreneurs is believed to be positively related to the returns expected. The higher the expected profit, the more likely it is that a person will become an entrepreneur.

Entrepreneurs find oligopoly and monopoly market structures more attractive than those that approach monopolistic competition or pure competition. In addition, a country's patent, antitrust, and tax laws have an effect on the supply of entrepreneurs.

Supply for All Uses of Natural Resources   At first blush, natural resources seem to be fixed or unchanging. In the early nineteenth century, the well-respected British economist David Ricardo defined land as the "original and indestructible power of the soil." Indeed, there are some naturally renewable and therefore "indestructible" resources. The water in a stream fed by melting snow from a mountain may be used over and over again. However, most natural resources are at least to some extent "exhaustible" and will not easily or quickly renew themselves. Once crude oil, natural gas, or iron ore is taken out of the ground, there is that much less left for future production. The soil can be depleted, or "farmed out," when farmers do not follow proper soil-maintenance practices. Waterways will no longer be productive if waste products are dumped into them.

If the price, or rent, of these resources is so low that it doesn't pay to bring them to market, their quantity supplied may dwindle. On the other hand, the quantity supplied of natural resources will be increased if their prices, or rents, are high enough to make it pay to bring them to market. Higher prices which encourage more extensive exploration for crude oil, natural gas, or iron ore may lead to discoveries that increase the quantity supplied. In recent years the response to OPEC price increases has included important new discoveries of oil in Alaska, the North Sea, and the Yucatán Peninsula in Mexico and of natural gas in Siberia. Advances in technological knowledge can also change the amount of usable natural resources and shift their supply curves. For example, in the early 1950s, when the rich red ore of the Mesabi iron range in northeastern Minnesota and the upper peninsula of Michigan was nearly used up, new techniques were discovered that allowed the economical mining of a lower-grade ore called taconite. Once again a thriving iron ore industry was created in that part of the country.

In a sense, land can also be increased. That is, it can be reclaimed from under water, and deserts can be irrigated. Northwestern University has built a lovely library as well as other buildings on land that once lay under Lake Michigan. In the southwestern United States and in many parts of Israel, desert land has been made fertile through irrigation. In a new section of Belgrade, Yugoslavia, swamps have been drained to allow the building of huge apartment complexes and shopping areas.[11]

You can see, then, that the quantity supplied of natural resources responds to rent just as the supply of labor responds to wages and the supply of entrepreneurs responds to profit. With few exceptions, the higher the rent of natural resources, the higher the quantity supplied, and vice versa.

One important exception, however, should be noted. If a natural resource is defined in terms of a certain location, supply cannot be increased beyond its natural limitation. For example, no more street-level land on the northeast corner of State and Randolph streets in Chicago can be created. No matter how high the rent is, that precisely defined natural resource's supply is fixed. Its supply is perfectly inelastic, and its supply curve appears as a vertical straight line.

Supply for All Uses of Capital Recall that capital is divided between capital goods and capital skills, called human capital. The stock of capital goods is the quantity of factory buildings, tools, and equipment that exists at a particular time. In the production process, this stock of capital is continuously being reduced. That is, it is used up or depreciated when it is producing consumer goods or other capital goods. But at the same time, it is usual to produce capital goods to replace the ones that are used up and possibly to increase the stock of capital

goods. Whether and to what degree capital goods are added or drawn down depends on the return or expected return to capital, which is called an interest payment.

Since capital goods are themselves outputs produced by firms, the quantity supplied responds to price in the same way as other outputs. More will be supplied at a high price than at a low price, other things being equal. In considering the supply of capital for all uses, the choice is between using resources to produce capital goods or using them to produce consumption goods. In this context, the price of capital takes the form of an interest payment. When the interest payment for capital is high relative to the price of consumer goods, firms will use more resources to produce capital goods and less to produce consumption goods.

Human capital may be treated in much the same way as capital goods. However, it is more complicated because it is mixed with labor. The return to the labor–human capital package is a mixture of wages and interest. How much of your economics professor's paycheck is a return for his or her sweat, blood, and tears expended in teaching you the subject, and how much is a return for the many years of education and training in which he or she invested?

The quantity supplied of human capital depends on the return or expected return to human capital. The quantity supplied of human capital is positively related to that return. At higher returns from an education, we expect more people to go to school, and vice versa.

11. These are, of course, examples of resource packages. Capital, entrepreneurship, and labor are embodied in this additional land.

Supply for Specific Uses

As you may remember, we separated our discussion of the supply of resources into the supply for all uses and the supply for specific uses. The second is a subset of the first, so that everything we explained about the supply for all uses also applies to the supply for a specific use. Other things being the same, the greater the supply is for all uses, the greater will be the supply for each specific use, and likewise, the lower the supply is for all uses, the lower will be the supply for any specific use.

However, as we have already pointed out, the supply response to a change in the price of a resource defined in terms of a specific use is greater than when that resource is defined for all uses. In the case of resource supply for all uses, a higher price has to attract a greater total quantity of that resource. However, in the case of resource supply for a specific use, no more of that resource needs to be attracted, since it need only switch from one use to another. As we said, it may take a 10 percent wage hike to increase the quantity supplied of nurses by 5 percent; but a 10 percent wage increase for only those nurses working in hospitals is likely to swell the quantity supplied of hospital nurses by much more than 5 percent, since nurses working in doctors' offices, schools, factories, and nursing homes will want to take advantage of the relatively higher wage.

In the case of resource supply for all uses, a higher price has to attract a greater total quantity of that resource. In the case of resource supply for a specific use, no more of that resource needs to be attracted, since it need only switch from one use to another.

Resources have many different uses. If all uses of a certain resource are equally attractive to the owners of that resource, they will seek out the use that offers the highest price and, as the markets for the different resource uses reach equilibrium, all suppliers of that resource will be paid the same price. If, for some reason, there was a slight increase in the price for one use, much more would be supplied for that use and correspondingly less for other uses. This would mean that bids being made for the other uses would have to be higher,

so that the price would once again be the same for all uses.

Actually, not all uses are equally attractive to owners of resources. Most nurses find it more pleasant to work in a doctor's office than in a hospital. This is probably the reason why hospital nurses earn higher wages than nurses in doctors' offices do. Similarly, real wages for certain labor resources vary according to the climate, the scenery, the environmental pollution, the cultural and recreational amenities, and the population density of a place.

If all uses of a certain resource are equally attractive to the owners of that resource, they will seek out the use that offers the highest price.

Price Elasticity of Resource Supply

Recall from our discussion of supply in Chapter 25 that the concept of price elasticity of supply relates the percentage change in the quantity of something that is supplied to the percentage change in the price that brought about the change:

$$\frac{\text{percentage change in quantity supplied of X}}{\text{percentage change in price of X}}$$

In that earlier discussion, X was some output such as shoes or hamburgers. Now that we are discussing inputs for specific uses, X may be the nurses working in doctors' offices or land for growing wheat or die presses used to produce lawn mowers.

There are important differences in the price elasticities of supply for different resources. Some resources are very *mobile*—that is, they can easily change from one activity to another—and so may have high price elasticities of supply for any specific use. Others are relatively immobile, and so may have much lower elasticities. Unspecialized labor is generally more mobile among occupations than labor which has invested in training for a particular occupation. Flat, fertile land in the midwestern United States is much more mobile, in the sense that it can be used for many more different purposes, than the sharply sloped and rocky land in Albania. The rocky land might be productive only for raising goats, whereas the flat, fertile land may be suited to many different agricultural uses. For example, a 2 percent increase in the expected price of wheat may cause so many farmers to switch their planting from corn, barley, or soybeans to wheat that 20 percent more wheat land is supplied (price elasticity of supply equals 10). A drill press may be quite mobile, as it can be used to drill holes in many different metal products, but a die press used to stamp out lawn-mower parts is more specialized and less easily shifted to another use. It would therefore take a great decrease in its earnings (interest payments) to cause its owner to convert it to another use.

Some resources are very mobile among uses and so may have high price elasticities of supply for any specific use. Others are relatively immobile among uses and so have much lower elasticities.

As with all applications of the elasticity concept, the time variable is very important. Nearly all resources are quite inelastic when measured over a very short period of time and become much more elastic over a longer period of time. A farmer isn't likely to switch from corn to wheat after the corn is already planted and before it is harvested, but at the next planting the change is easily made. Likewise, it takes time for people to learn about job opportunities in other parts of a country, and it takes even more time to make the move. If a new skill is required, it takes time to train or retrain. Sometimes the change is made in the next generation. For example, a farmer may see great opportunities in engineering or computer programming, but often the best he or she can do is support a child's education so that the child can later work as an engineer or computer programmer.

The quantity supplied of nearly all resources are quite price-inelastic when measured over a very short period of time and become much more price-elastic over a longer period of time.

THE DEMAND FOR RESOURCES

As you learned in Chapter 22, consumer demand for a certain product depends on how much satisfaction consumers expect to receive from that product as compared with other products that they could buy for the same expenditure. If we substitute the word *profit* for the word *satisfaction*, the statement also applies to business firm demand for resources. In this context the statement now reads: Business firm demand for a certain resource depends on how much profit business firms expect to receive from that resource as compared with other resources they could acquire for the same expenditure.

Just changing that one word, and also the economic context, amounts to a very important change in the statement's meaning. Consumers demand goods and services because they like them—because they taste good, sound good, look good, or feel good. That is *not* the case with business firms. They are not likely to demand a worker's services simply because he or she is a nice person. Generally they will not demand a certain machine because of its exquisite design or beautiful shining metal. Nor will they usually demand a piece of land just because of its scenic beauty. These characteristics are not important unless they contribute to the reason why they will demand or not demand the resource: the firm's expected profit. Certainly, if a company is hiring a salesperson, it will prefer a "nice" person because he or she is expected to sell better. Similarly, the exquisitely designed machine may perform better, and the scenic piece of land may be just what is required for a resort hotel. But, a bouncer for a bar should be intimidating, a very ugly machine may outperform all others, and the best farmland is often flat and dull. As has been our assumption in all of the economic theory of the firm, which you studied earlier, firms are in business to maximize their profit. Resources, whether human or nonhuman, are simply inputs needed to produce the outputs that business firms believe they can sell most profitably.

Business firm demand for a certain resource depends on how much profit firms expect to receive from that resource compared with other resources they could acquire for the same expenditure.

Derived Demand

The recognition that business firms do not demand resources as ends in themselves is expressed in the concept of derived demand. The demand for a resource is a **derived demand** because it is derived from the demand for the products that this resource helps to produce. The demand for automobile workers depends on the demand for automobiles, and the demand for buggy-whip makers depends on the demand for buggy whips. In the early twentieth century, when automobiles began to replace horse-drawn buggies, more automobile workers and fewer buggy-whip makers were demanded.

Important lessons can be learned from this simple concept. Derived demand tells labor that it doesn't matter how "skillful" people are in some abstract sense. What matters is that they are skilled at performing particular tasks that are important inputs to the production of those goods or services for which there is great demand. During the 1980s, college students who majored in accounting, engineering, or computer science and otherwise prepared themselves for these careers found good jobs when they graduated. Other equally capable students who majored in sociology, history, or English found fewer jobs in their chosen fields. There was little demand for their labor because there was little demand for the services they were trained for.

Another lesson learned through the understanding of derived demand involved agricultural land values in early nineteenth-century England. The concept of derived demand, which tells us that the demand for land depends on the demand for the goods and services produced on it, was not well understood at that time. Most people blamed the high price of wheat in England on the high rent that had to be paid for land. However, the leading British economist, David Ricardo, disagreed with many of his contemporaries. He argued that the high price for the use of land to grow wheat on was a result of the high price of wheat. England had a quite inelastic supply of rural land, so that rents on this land were largely determined by the demand for land on which crops might be grown or sheep grazed. Since growing wheat was very profitable at prevailing prices, farmers who wanted more wheat land would bid up the price (rent) for the land.

The demand for a resource is a derived demand because it is derived from the demand for the products this resource helps to produce.

Price Elasticity of Resource Demand

At this point in your economics course, you will not be surprised to learn that the quantity demanded for specific resources is negatively related to their prices. For example, more automobile workers are demanded at lower wage rates for automobile workers, and fewer are demanded when their wage rates are higher. Why is this so? Remember that the demand for automobile workers is a derived demand and that automobile firms are not interested in hiring these workers as an end in themselves. The answer lies in a series of relationships. Since automobile workers' wages are a large part of the total cost of producing automobiles, lower wages paid to automobile workers will result in much lower production costs for automobile firms. If there is enough competition in the automobile industry, the lower cost will be passed on to consumers in the form of lower automobile prices. Since the quantity demanded for automobiles is negatively related to the price of automobiles, more automobiles will be demanded. The greater quantity demanded for automobiles means greater quantity demanded for automobile workers.

We call this response the **price elasticity of resource demand**—meaning the degree of responsiveness of the quantity demanded of a resource to a change in its price. The strength of the response depends upon a number of factors as shown in our automobile workers example.

First, the larger the proportion of the total production cost that is accounted for by a certain resource, the more price elastic is the demand for that resource. So if automobile workers' wages account for 50 percent of the total cost of producing automobiles, and their wages go down by 20 percent, the total cost decreases by 10 percent. But if, instead, workers' wages account for only 25 percent of the total cost, then a 20 percent decline in wages causes total cost to decrease by only 5 percent.

Second, the greater the price elasticity of demand of the final product (in this case, the automobile), the more price elastic is the demand for that resource. If the demand for automobiles is unitary elastic, a 10 percent decrease in the price of automobiles will be matched by a 10 percent increase in sales, which might mean a 10 percent rise in the demand for automobile workers. But if, instead, the price elasticity of demand of automobiles is 2, the same 10 percent decrease in the price of automobiles brings about a 20 percent rise in sales and presumably a 20 percent increase in the demand for automobile workers.

Third, the more competition there is in an industry, the more likely it is that changes in resource prices (costs) will be passed on to consumers, and so the more price elastic will be the demand for the resources used by the firms in that industry. If the automobile industry were a monopoly, most of the decrease in the wages of automobile workers might be retained by the monopolist in the form of higher profit. But if the industry were fairly competitive, most of the wage decrease would be passed on in the form of lower prices to consumers.

Finally, the price elasticity of resource demand depends on how easy or difficult it is to substitute one resource for another. The easier it is for a firm to respond to a rise in the price of a resource by substituting other resources for it and the easier it is for a firm to respond to a decrease in the price of a resource by substituting it for other resources, the more price elastic the demand for the resource. For example, in recent years the price elasticity of demand for certain automobile workers has increased because of the development of robots that can perform their tasks.

The price elasticity of resource demand is the degree of responsiveness of the quantity demanded for a resource to a change in its price. The strength of the response depends on (1) the proportion of the total cost of producing a product that is accounted for by that resource, (2) the price elasticity of demand for the product that the resource helps to produce, (3) the amount of competition in the industry in which the resource is being used, and (4) the ease of substitution of one input for another.

Resource Demand and Marginal Productivity

As you know, the demand for resources is a derived demand. Of course, business firms demand resources in order to produce goods and services that they can sell at a profit. Since companies are

assumed to be in business to earn as much profit as they can, we can predict just how much of any resource a firm will demand. We use much the same reasoning that we used in Chapter 25 when we predicted how much output a firm will produce. Resource demand depends on two variables: (1) the contribution that a resource makes to the value of the product it helps to produce, and (2) the price of that resource.

The contribution that a resource makes to the value of output is actually very hard to determine. As we noted earlier, there is much interdependence among resources in production. "Packages" of resources produce firms' outputs. But in order to present the logic of the theory of resource demand in a fairly simple way, we shall assume that we are able to add or subtract units of particular resources and evaluate their precise contributions to production one at a time.

The other variable used in predicting a firm's demand for a resource—the price of the resource—may also be complicated. Firms often find that by buying more or less of a resource they can affect the price that they have to pay for it. But again to simplify our explanation, we shall assume that resources are sold in a pure competition setting, so that their prices will not change, no matter how little or how much a firm buys.

Resource demand depends on (1) the contribution a resource makes to the value of the product it helps to produce, and (2) the price of that resource.

Given these assumptions about the contribution of a resource to a firm's production and the price at which that firm buys the resource, we can predict how much of that resource the firm will demand. The theory of resource demand is based on the logic that a firm will want to keep on buying additional units of a resource as long as it will add more to its revenue than to its cost. The extra cost to the firm is what it has to pay to add another unit of the resource or factor of production. We call this the **marginal factor cost (MFC)**. The extra revenue to the firm is the amount of money it receives as a result of selling the additional quantity of output that one more unit of the resource input (all other resources remaining the same) allow it to

TABLE 2
Derivation of Marginal Revenue Product of Pertadium for the Buildem Company, Which Produces Corterboard

(1) Quantity of Pertadium Used in Production (per day)	*(2)* Total Product (quantity of Corterboard produced per day)	*(3)* Marginal Physical Product (additional quantity of Corterboard produced per day)	*(4)* Price per Unit of Corterboard (in dollars)	*(5)* Total Revenue (dollar receipts from Corterboard per day)	*(6)* Marginal Revenue Product (additional dollar receipts from Corterboard per day)
0	0		$10	$ 0	
		30			$300
1	30		10	300	
		35			350
2	65		10	650	
		30			300
3	95		10	950	
		26			260
4	121		10	1,210	
		23			230
5	144		10	1,440	
		20			200
6	164		10	1,640	

produce. This is called the **marginal revenue product (MRP)**.[12] As long as a company's *MRP* is greater than its *MFC,* with regard to any specific resource, it will continue to demand more units of that resource. It will stop demanding more units of the resource when its *MFC* is greater than its *MRP.* Therefore, a firm will be in equilibrium with regard to any specific resource when its *MFC* is equal to its *MRP.*

Let us review this conclusion by using a hypothetical case. Suppose that a building products firm, the Buildem Company, produces a building material called Corterboard and that Corterboard is made by combining a number of different resources, including a certain natural resource called pertadium. Our problem is to predict how many units of pertadium the Buildem Company will demand per day. As before, we assume that we can separate ''packages'' of resources so that pertadium is not tied to other resources and that the Buildem

Company buys pertadium in a purely competitive market so that it faces the same pertadium price no matter how little or how much it buys.[13] Let us also make the simplifying assumption that Buildem is operating in a purely competitive product market so that it does not have to lower its price for Corterboard in order to sell more of it.[14] Finally, since we are interested only in the demand for pertadium, we are keeping all the other resources that Buildem uses to produce Corterboard at a constant level. This means that diminishing returns (decreasing marginal product) will set in and that the marginal revenue product will at some point have to diminish.[15]

Table 2 provides the data needed for deriving Buildem's marginal revenue product when it uses different amounts of pertadium. To derive *MRP,* we

12. Note that the terms *marginal factor cost* (*MFC*) and *marginal revenue product* (*MRP*) are variants of the terms *marginal cost* (*MC*) and *marginal revenue* (*MR*), which are used to express similar logic about the quantity of output that a firm wishes to produce and sell.

13. The assumption about the purely competitive market will be relaxed in the next chapter when we show the case of labor employed in a monopsonistic labor market.

14. This assumption will also be relaxed in the next chapter when we show the case of labor helping to produce a product that is sold in a monopolistic market.

15. See Chapter 24, especially pp. 525–528

follow two steps. First, we calculate the marginal product, or more precisely, the **marginal physical product (*MPP*)**—meaning the additional output produced by an extra unit of the variable resource. Second, we multiply the *MPP* by the price of the product. For example, using the first unit of pertadium causes total product (the quantity of Corterboard that is produced each day) to increase from zero to 30 units, so that the *MPP* will be 30. Multiplying the *MPP* of 30 by the $10 price of Corterboard gives us *MRP* of $300. Note that increasing returns to pertadium occur when a second unit is added (the *MPP* rises from 30 to 35, and the *MRP* rises from $300 to $350). After that point, diminishing returns set in, so that additional units of pertadium bring decreasing *MPP* and *MRP*.

Another way to calculate *MRP* is first to determine total revenue, as we have done in column 5 of Table 2. Then for each additional unit of the variable input, *MRP* is figured by subtracting the previous total revenue from the new one. For example, notice that in Table 2, by adding a fourth unit of pertadium we increase total revenue from $950 to $1,210, so that *MRP* is $260 ($1,210 − $950 = $260).

Given the information provided in Table 2, we need only know the price that Buildem must pay for pertadium to determine its demand for this input. Table 3 provides that additional information. It repeats columns 1 and 6 from Table 2 and adds three columns showing three alternative prices of pertadium. We follow the profit-maximizing logic that a firm will demand a resource up to the point where its *MRP* equals its *MFC*. In this way, we can predict that Buildem will demand a bit more than 6 units when pertadium is at a price of $190 per unit, just over 5 units at a price of $220 per unit, and between 3 and 4 units when pertadium costs $270 per unit. This is shown in Figure 1. We have drawn Buildem's *MRP* curve for pertadium by plotting amounts from column 2 of Table 3 and then joining the plotted points. The negatively sloping part of the *MRP* curve is Buildem's demand curve for pertadium. (Each possible price of pertadium is Buildem's *MFC* at that price, and it will demand that quantity where its *MFC* equals its *MRP*.) Also shown in the figure are *MFC* curves at the three alternative prices of pertadium—$190, $220, and $270—taken from columns 3, 4, and 5 of Table 3. Where each of these *MFC* curves intersects the *MRP*

TABLE 3
Marginal Revenue Product and Marginal Factor Cost of Pertadium for the Buildem Company at Three Alternative Prices of Pertadium

(1)	*(2)*	*(3)*	*(4)*	*(5)*
		Marginal Factor Cost (additional dollar cost for additional units of pertadium) When Price of Pertadium Is:		
Quantity of Pertadium Used in Production (per day)	*Marginal Revenue Product (additional dollar receipts from Corterboard per day)*	*$190*	*$220*	*$270*
0				
	$300	$190	$220	$270
1				
	350	190	220	270
2				
	300	190	220	270
3				
	260	190	220	270
4				
	230	190	220	270
5				
	200	190	220	270
6				

FIGURE 1
Three Alternative Demand Levels for Pertadium by the Buildem Company

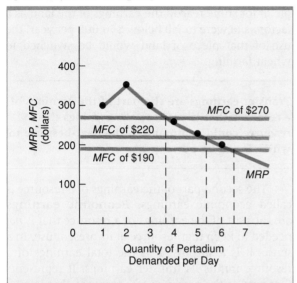

Pictured here is the marginal-revenue-product (*MRP*) curve for the natural resource pertadium used by the Buildem Company to produce Corterboard. It is plotted from column 2 in Table 3. Also shown are the three alternative marginal-factor-cost (*MFC*) curves plotted from columns 3, 4, and 5 in Table 3. Buildem's equilibrium level of quantity demanded is where its marginal revenue product (*MRP*) equals its appropriate marginal factor cost (*MFC*)—somewhat more than 6 units at the price of $190, slightly more than 5 units at the price of $220, and between 3 and 4 units at the price of $270.

curve is Buildem's quantity demanded at that price—a little more than 6 units at $190, a bit more than 5 units at $220, and between 3 and 4 units at $270.

The theory of resource demand is based on the logic that a firm will want to keep on buying additional units of a resource as long as it will add more to its revenue than to its cost.

The marginal factor cost (*MFC*) is what a firm has to pay to add another unit of a resource, or factor of production. The marginal revenue product (*MRP*) is what the firm receives as a result of selling the additional quantity of

output that one more unit of the resource (input) allows it to produce.

A firm is in equilibrium with regard to any specific resource when its *MFC* is equal to its *MRP*.

THE INTERACTION OF SUPPLY AND DEMAND IN A RESOURCE MARKET

We have separately introduced you to the supply of resources and to the demand for resources. You are now ready to learn how they interact to determine equilibrium price and quantity of resources in a market. Our explanation of resource supply led us to expect positively sloped supply curves, and our explanation of the demand for resources led us to expect negatively sloped demand curves, so that we are on familiar ground. The interaction between supply and demand in resource markets is much the same as the interaction between supply and demand in product markets. Figure 2 pictures a supply curve and a demand curve for a resource called X. The supply curve pictures the total supply of X, and the demand curve is the sum of all the individual firms' demand curves for X. It doesn't matter whether X is a certain kind of skilled labor, agricultural entrepreneurs in a certain part of the United States, a certain natural resource like pertadium, or some sort of capital equipment. If the curves in Figure 2 reflect the market supply and demand functions for resource X, equilibrium takes place at price *P*, where quantity level *Q* is supplied and quantity level *Q* is demanded.

The interaction between supply and demand in resource markets is much the same as the interaction between supply and demand in product markets. Equilibrium price and quantity are found where a positively sloped supply curve intersects a negatively sloped demand curve.

FIGURE 2
The Market Supply of and the Market Demand for Resource X

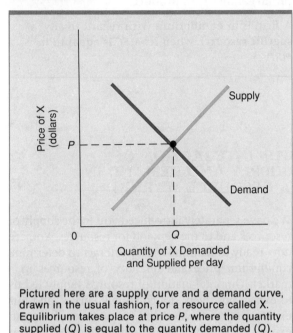

Pictured here are a supply curve and a demand curve, drawn in the usual fashion, for a resource called X. Equilibrium takes place at price *P*, where the quantity supplied (*Q*) is equal to the quantity demanded (*Q*).

Transfer Earnings and Economic Earnings

The equilibrium earnings of a resource may be thought of as being composed of transfer earnings and economic earnings.[16] **Transfer earnings** are the part of the earnings of a resource that is equal to the earnings that this resource could command in the next-best use to which it can be put.[17] For example, the earnings of a certain piece of land that is presently being used as a site for a factory complex might be $1 million per year. Its next-best use might be as a wheat farm, in which it could earn only $50,000 per year. The $50,000 are the transfer earnings of this piece of land. Transfer earnings

16. Because this analysis grew out of an early nineteenth-century concern about land values, much of the literature uses the term *economic rent* instead of *economic earnings*. Since we are applying this term not just to land or other natural resources but to all resources, the more neutral term *economic earnings* will be used.

17. Do not confuse transfer "earnings" with transfer "payments." *Transfer payments* are defined as payments that are *not* made in exchange for currently provided goods or services.

may also be thought of as that part of the earnings of a resource which it must earn to keep it from being transferred to its next-best use. In our example, if for some reason the earnings of the land as a factory site were to fall below $50,000 per year, the use of that piece of land would be switched to wheat farming.

Transfer earnings are the part of the earnings of a resource that is equal to the earnings this resource could command in the next-best use to which it can be put.

The second part of the earnings of a resource is called economic earnings. **Economic earnings** are the part of the earnings of a resource that is *not* needed to keep that resource at its present use. In a sense, it is a surplus. It is the total earnings of a resource minus its transfer earnings. It represents that part of the earnings of a resource that is over and above what it would earn in its next-best use. In our case, where the earnings of a piece of land are $1 million per year and the transfer earnings are $50,000 per year, economic earnings are $950,000 per year.

Economic earnings are the part of the earnings of a resource that is not needed to keep that resource at its present use; it is the total earnings of a resource minus its transfer earnings.

Just as a piece of land generally has a next-best use in production, so do people have a next-best use for their production efforts. For example, a college professor who is employed at $32,000 a year may find that her next-best employment possibility is as a sales representative earning $28,000 a year. Her transfer earnings are $28,000, and her economic earnings are $4,000. If all other variables surrounding these two jobs—including relative satisfaction received, working conditions, and fringe benefits—were equal and held constant, the woman in our example would change jobs if her teaching salary were cut by more than $4,000 a year or if the earnings available as a sales representative were increased by more than $4,000.

Dramatic examples of persons receiving a huge amount of economic earnings can be found among athletes and entertainers. A very large part of the salaries of big-time athletes, actors, actresses, and musical groups consists of economic earnings. A seven-foot center on a major professional basketball team may earn $1 million a year. His transfer earnings might be the $20,000 a year he could earn as a medical technician, for which he trained during college. His economic earnings are $980,000 a year. Of course, the demand for his services is a derived demand. It is only because there is great competition among basketball club owners for the services of the few available seven-foot basketball players who are able to spark fans' interest and bring in large television and gate revenue that the athlete in our example is able to attract his high salary.

The breakdown of a resource's earnings into transfer earnings and economic earnings has important implications for resource allocation. The greater transfer earnings are in relation to economic earnings, the more likely it is that a resource will be transferred to another use. The lower the proportion of transfer earnings is to economic earnings, the less likely it is a resource will be transferred to another use. You may understand this idea better after studying three different cases: two extremes and one case in between.

The greater transfer earnings are in relation to economic earnings, the more likely it is that a resource will be transferred to another use.

Case I: All Economic Earnings   When a resource has only a single use, its transfer earnings are zero, and the price of the resource is made up entirely of economic earnings. Panel (a) of Figure 3 (page 694) pictures such a case. Shown are a supply curve and a demand curve for land on a certain mountain in Vermont. The land is used as a ski slope and cannot be economically used for anything else. The mountain is in a fixed location, and we assume that a usable ski slope requires exactly these 800 acres. Its supply is perfectly inelastic. The demand for skiing on that mountain will determine its price, $100 an acre in this case. Transfer earn-

ings are zero, and so the whole payment for the 800 acres—$80,000, represented by the gold area—is economic earnings. If the demand curve shifted to the left, the price would be lowered, but no land would be transferred to another use. If the demand curve shifted to the right, the price would be raised, but there would be no increase in quantity supplied.

When a resource has only a single use, its transfer earnings are zero, and the price of the resource is made up entirely of economic earnings.

Case II: All Transfer Earnings   When a resource is put to a use for which it commands a price just barely above what it can command for its next-best use, its economic earnings are almost zero. Such a case is shown in panel (b) of Figure 3. You will recognize this case as the exact opposite of the previous one. In panel (a) the supply curve is a vertical straight line, whereas in this case it is a horizontal straight line. This might be a case of farmland used to produce beans. At $100 an acre, almost unlimited amounts of farmland are available to grow beans. The supply is virtually infinitely elastic. If the price were lowered by as little as a penny an acre, all 800 acres would switch over to their next-best use—say, the growing of peas. Thus, practically the whole payment for the 800 acres ($80,000, represented by the green area) is transfer earnings.

When a resource is put to a use for which it commands a price just barely above what it can command for its next-best use, its economic earnings are almost zero.

Case III: Mix of Transfer Earnings and Economic Earnings   When a resource has more than a single use, and when a slightly lower price will not cause all of it to switch to its next-best use, its earnings are a mix of transfer earnings and economic earnings. This is a common situation. Panel (c) in Figure 3 pictures such a case, where the supply of a resource for a particular use is neither fixed

FIGURE 3
Three Alternative Cases: All Economic Earnings, All Transfer Earnings, and a Mix of Economic Earnings and Transfer Earnings

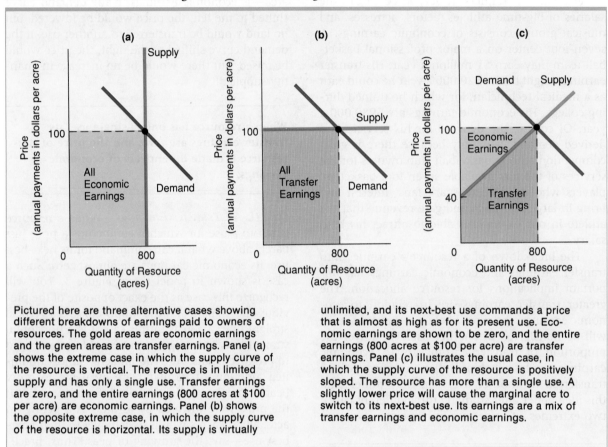

Pictured here are three alternative cases showing different breakdowns of earnings paid to owners of resources. The gold areas are economic earnings and the green areas are transfer earnings. Panel (a) shows the extreme case in which the supply curve of the resource is vertical. The resource is in limited supply and has only a single use. Transfer earnings are zero, and the entire earnings (800 acres at $100 per acre) are economic earnings. Panel (b) shows the opposite extreme case, in which the supply curve of the resource is horizontal. Its supply is virtually unlimited, and its next-best use commands a price that is almost as high as for its present use. Economic earnings are shown to be zero, and the entire earnings (800 acres at $100 per acre) are transfer earnings. Panel (c) illustrates the usual case, in which the supply curve of the resource is positively sloped. The resource has more than a single use. A slightly lower price will cause the marginal acre to switch to its next-best use. Its earnings are a mix of transfer earnings and economic earnings.

nor infinitely responsive to changes in price. Here the supply curve is positively sloped. This might be a case of farmland used to produce corn. As in the other two panels, the payment for the 800 acres is $80,000, but this time it is made up partly of transfer earnings (the green area below the supply curve) and partly of economic earnings (the gold area above the supply curve). If the demand curve shifts to the left ever so slightly, so that the price is lowered by a very small amount, one acre (the eight-hundredth acre) would be transferred to another use such as growing wheat or soybeans. At successively lower prices, more and more of this land would switch out of corn production and into

other uses. However, some acreage will remain in corn until the price falls to just below $40 an acre. At prices below $40, all 800 acres will have been transferred out of corn into other uses. (This is just like the transfer that takes place at a price just below $100 in case II, shown in panel (b).)

When a resource has more than a single use, and when a slightly lower price will not cause all of it to switch to its next-best use, its earnings are a mix of transfer earnings and economic earnings.

Taxing Economic Earnings

By now you probably realize that the concept of economic earnings explained in this chapter has already been dealt with in this book. Recall that the concept of economic profit was first introduced in Chapter 25 and used in later chapters dealing with different market structures. Economic profit is just one kind of economic earnings—the one that entrepreneurs may receive. In addition, economic earnings may take the form of economic wages to labor, economic rent to natural resources, and economic interest payments to capital.

What do all these economic earnings have in common? They are all payments for the use of resources that are above what has to be paid to their owners in order to keep them in their present use. In Chapters 26 and 28 we praised the long-run equilibrium solutions of pure competition and monopolistic competition, in part because only normal profit (not economic profit) is earned. Yet later on we recognized that oligopolistic and monopolistic firms might spend some or all of their economic profit on socially desirable things such as research and development of new products and processes. What about the other resources? Will the seven-foot basketball player in our example spend his economic wage of $980,000 a year in a socially desirable manner? Will owners of capital and natural resources spend their economic interest and economic rent in socially desirable ways? The answer to all of these questions has to be "maybe." We really don't know. All that our theory tells us is that as long as the owners of resources receive earnings equal to or greater than their transfer earnings, the allocation of resources will remain the same.

Economic earnings may take the form of economic profit to entrepreneurs, economic wages to labor, economic rent to natural resources, and economic interest payments to capital. These are all payments for the use of resources that are above what has to be paid to their owners to keep them in their present use.

Henry George, an American social reformer in the late nineteenth century, understood this principle. In fact, he was nearly elected the mayor of New York City in 1886 on this issue alone. He proposed that all existing taxes be abolished and that they be replaced by a single tax on the economic earnings of urban land (but not buildings or improvements on the land). George believed that economic earnings on natural resources and particularly land were probably greater than for any other resource. He argued that a tax on economic rent is the best tax to impose for two reasons. The first was that rents go up because of population increases and not because of the services performed by landowners. Second, the tax would not cause landowners to shift the use of their land. He believed that there would be no need for any other taxes to meet the expenditures of government.

Whatever we may think of Henry George's theory, landowners are not the only ones who benefit from economic earnings. Taxes on land are of course commonplace in the United States, as well as in most other countries, today. But there is little justification for placing the whole tax burden on landowners while letting the owners of the other resources go without paying any taxes on their economic earnings.

As long as the owners of resources receive earnings equal to or greater than their transfer earnings, the allocation of resources will remain the same. Therefore the taxing of economic earnings only will not affect resource allocation.

Economics in Focus

The Shortage of Nurses

The last two decades have brought repeated shortages of trained nurses. Usually, when the quantity of nurses demanded by hospitals, nursing homes, and other facilities outstrips the number who offer their services, wage levels rise. The higher wages then lead more students to enroll in nursing programs, entice some unemployed nurses back to work, and encourage others to work longer hours. In this way the shortage is eventually resolved by an increase in quantity supplied, and a new equilibrium develops. However an unusual pattern has emerged from the most recent shortage: though quantity demanded is rising, quantity supplied is falling.

The increase in demand stems from several causes. Since the U.S. population is aging, the need for health care continues to grow. Although the price of medical care has skyrocketed, insurance coverage is more widely available—hence more people have the means to pay for the care they need or want. Furthermore, the 1983 change in Medicare has forced hospitals to discharge patients quickly, and they now receive a greater proportion of care in alternative settings such as community clinics. Even more than hospitals, clinics rely on trained nurses. Home-care nurses are also in greater demand as more patients recuperate in their own homes.

In spite of the rising demand, enrollments in registered-nursing programs fell 13 percent between 1983 and 1987. How could this happen? For one reason, women have always made up the vast majority of nurses, and women now have many more career options than they used to have. For instance, it is perfectly reasonable today for a woman to become a doctor instead of a nurse, and many are choosing that route. Others are opting for business careers in which they expect to earn higher salaries.

Another reason for the falling supply lies in the demographics of the U.S. population. The number of 18- to 24-year-olds—the primary group of candidates for nursing or any other profession—has dwindled. Moreover, nursing jobs often involve high levels of stress and burnout, and the shortage of trained personnel increases the stress on those now working. Many nurses complain, too, that they have relatively little status in the medical community. Others say that the traditionally low salaries have not risen enough despite the recurrent labor shortages. For these and similar reasons, some potential candidates are reluctant to enter the field, and many experienced nurses move on to greener pastures.

This combination of rising demand and falling supply is proving difficult to change. Already hospitals are offering special incentives for new nurses: bonuses, tuition reimbursement, flexible schedules, four-day work weeks, and so on. But throughout the American economy skilled workers are becoming more scarce. In the nursing profession the quantity supplied may not approach the quantity demanded until nurses themselves get what they seek: not only higher wages and benefits, but also more respect and an improved working environment.

Sources: Timothy Tregarthen, "Critical Condition: Supply of Nurses Wearing Thin," *The Margin,* October 1987, pp. 12–13; "Nursing Shortage Poll Report," *Nursing88,* February 1988, pp. 33–41.

SUMMARY

1. In the study of input markets we separate resources, or factors of production, into four categories: (a) labor, which includes all forms of human work efforts except entrepreneurship and which receives wages as payment; (b) entrepreneurship, which visualizes needs and takes the necessary actions to initiate the process by which they will be met and which receives profit as payment; (c) natural resources, which are "gifts of nature" and which receive rent as payment; and (d) capital, which is made up of goods and skills used to further production and which receives interest payments. (See pages 676–677.)

2. Resources are actually not as easy to separate as the four-part classification implies. Production usually calls for certain combinations of resources, or "resource packages." Capital is embodied in most usable resources. (See page 677.)

3. The supply of resources focuses not on the amount of resources in existence but rather on the quantity that is offered at various prices. Normally there is a positive relationship between the price of a resource and the quantity of it that is supplied. The supply of a resource defined in terms of a specific use is generally more price elastic than is the supply for all uses of a resource. (See page 679.)

4. The supply for all uses of labor depends on (a) population size, (b) age distribution, (c) labor force participation rate, (d) hours worked, and (e) working age. All of these factors are, in turn, more or less influenced by laws and customs. (See pages 679–682.)

5. The supply for all uses of entrepreneurship is to some degree dependent on the same variables that influence the supply of labor. However, some countries encourage entrepreneurship more than others do. The quantity supplied of entrepreneurship is influenced by expected profit, which is related to a country's patent, taxation, and antitrust policies. (See pages 682–683.)

6. Except for those natural resources that are defined in terms of particular locations, the supply for all uses of natural resources varies just as supplies of the other resource categories do. Many natural resources will not renew themselves. Others will, if properly cared for. At low rents there is a tendency for the quantity supplied to dwindle. At high rents natural resources are cared for, exploration is encouraged, and technology is put to work to find new supplies of natural resources. (See pages 683–684.)

7. The supply of capital is divided between capital goods and human capital. Since capital goods are themselves outputs of firms, the quantity supplied is expected to be greater at a high price than at a lower price, other things being equal. The supply for all uses of human capital is more complicated because human capital cannot be divorced from labor. The supply of the labor–human capital package depends on all the variables that influence labor plus those that influence society, firms, or individuals to invest in education and training. Higher expected earnings (interest payments) are expected to increase the quantity of human capital supplied. (See page 684.)

8. Resources have many alternative uses. If owners of a resource find all uses for that resource equally attractive, all owners of that resource will receive the same price. But, in fact, owners of resources do not find all uses equally attractive. (See page 685.)

9. The price elasticity of supply of a resource depends on its mobility and the time it takes to switch from one use to another. The less specialized a resource, the more mobile it is and the greater its price elasticity of supply will be. The more time that is allowed for a resource to switch from one use to another in response to a price change, the more elastic its supply will be. (See pages 685–686.)

10. Consumers demand mixes of products that allow them to use their limited incomes to maximize their satisfaction. In contrast, because firms are profit maximizers, they demand mixes of resources that let them produce their chosen outputs at the lowest possible cost. It follows, then, that the demand for resources is a derived demand—the demand for a resource is derived from the demand for the products that this resource helps to produce. (See pages 686–687.)

11. The price elasticity of demand for a resource is positively related to: (a) the proportion of the total cost of producing a product that is accounted for by that resource; (b) the price elasticity of demand for the product that it helps to produce;

(c) the amount of competition in the product's industry; and (d) how easy it is to substitute it for other resources and to substitute other resources for it. (See pages 687–688.)

12. The quantity of a resource that a firm demands depends on the contribution made by that resource to the value of the firm's output and on the cost that the firm must pay for that resource. A firm will want to continue to buy additional units of a certain resource as long as they will add more to its revenue (marginal revenue product, *MRP*) than to its cost (marginal factor cost, *MFC*). A firm is in equilibrium in its purchasing of a resource when its marginal revenue product is equal to its marginal factor cost. (See pages 688–691.)

13. The interaction between resource supply and demand is much the same as the interaction between product supply and demand. Equilibrium price and equilibrium quantity are found where a positively sloped supply curve intersects a negatively sloped demand curve. (See page 691.)

14. The earnings of a resource may be divided into two parts: transfer earnings and economic earnings. Transfer earnings are what a resource can earn in its next-best use, and economic earnings are the rest. (See pages 692–693.)

15. In the extreme case where a resource has only a single use, its earnings are entirely economic since its transfer earnings are zero. In such a case, the supply curve of the resource is vertical. In the opposite extreme case where a resource has more than a single use and it earns an amount just barely above what it can earn in its next-best use, its economic earnings are almost zero, and practically all of its earnings are transfer earnings. In such a case, the supply curve of the resource for that specific use is horizontal. A slightly lower price causes all of the resource to switch to its next-best use. (See page 693 and Figure 3, page 694.)

16. In the normal case, where a resource has more than a single use but where a slightly lower price will not cause all of it to switch to its next-best use, its earnings are a mix of transfer earnings and economic earnings. In such a case, the supply curve of the resource is positively sloped. At lower prices some, but not all, of the resource would switch to its next-best use. (See pages 693–694 and Figure 3, page 694)

17. Resource allocation does not change according to the amount of economic earnings that owners of resources receive. For that reason some people have found economic earnings to be an excellent target for taxation. (See page 695.)

KEY TERMS

capital: goods and skills used as inputs for production (page 677).

capital goods: factory buildings, tools, and equipment used as inputs for production (page 677).

derived demand: the demand for a resource depends on the demand for the end products that the resource helps to produce (page 687).

economic earnings: the part of the earnings of a resource that is not needed to keep that resource at its present use (page 692).

entrepreneur: a person who seeks the best opportunities for production and coordinates all the other resources in order to carry them out (page 676).

human capital: the skills that human beings provide as an input in the production of goods and services (page 677).

labor: human work that is, or can be, directed toward production (page 676).

marginal factor cost (*MFC*): what a firm has to pay to add another unit of a resource, or factor of production (page 688).

marginal physical product (*MPP*): the additional output produced by an extra unit of a resource (input) (page 690).

marginal revenue product (*MRP*): the revenue (amount of money) a firm receives as a result of selling the additional quantity of output that one more unit of a resource (input) allows it to produce (page 689).

natural resources: the ''gifts of nature'' that can be used to produce goods (page 677).

price elasticity of resource demand: the degree of responsiveness of the quantity demanded of a resource to a change in its price (page 687).

resource packages: combinations of resources required to produce goods and services (page 677).

transfer earnings: the part of the earnings of a resource that is equal to the earnings that this resource could command in the next-best use to which it can be put (page 692).

DISCUSSION QUESTIONS

1. Earlier in the book we separated resources into three broad categories: labor, natural resources, and capital. In this chapter we separated entrepreneurship out of the labor category. How is entrepreneurship different from labor?

2. Why is it more realistic to discuss inputs in terms of "resource packages," rather than in terms of individual resources?

3. The functional distribution of income in the United States during the past fifty years indicates a substantial increase in the labor share as shown by the percentage of total national income accounted for by the "compensation of employees." How would you explain this change?

4. We expect the quantity supplied of resources to respond to the price of resources just as the quantity supplied of output responds to the price of output. However, it makes a great deal of difference whether we are referring to the response for all uses of a resource or for just one specific use of that resource. Explain this difference in general terms and then give an example for each of the resource categories.

5. What is the relationship between the "mobility" of resource use and the price elasticity of supply of resources? Give an example of a case in which you would expect the supply curve to be highly elastic and one in which you would expect it to be quite inelastic.

6. How does the concept of derived demand help you to analyze the demand for resources? How can you use the concept of derived demand to help you to determine what to major and minor in at your college or university?

7. Why is a firm said to be in equilibrium with regard to any specific resource that it uses in production when marginal factor cost is equal to marginal revenue product?

8. Carefully define each of the following concepts and explain how they relate to one another: (1) the earnings of a parcel of land, (2) the transfer earnings of that parcel, and (3) the economic earnings of that parcel. Give a numerical example to illustrate the relationships involved.

9. Larry says to Linda, "The price of wheat is so high because the price of farmland is so high." Linda says to Larry, "The price of farmland to grow wheat on is so high because the price of wheat is so high." Who is right? Discuss.

10. What makes it particularly appealing from an economic theory point of view to tax at least some of the economic wages of a rock star? The economic interest payment for a capital good? The economic rent for some natural resource? The economic profit of an entrepreneur?

31
Labor, Wages, and Collective Bargaining

Preview In the last chapter we introduced you in a fairly general way to all of the input markets. Here we focus on just one—the labor markets. As you may remember, labor accounts for more than three-quarters of U.S. national income, by far the most of any of the resources.

We begin with the supply and demand for labor. After reviewing the analysis that was presented in Chapter 30 as it pertains to labor, we extend it beyond pure competition. We compare the case of a firm that hires workers in a purely competitive labor market and sells its output in a purely competitive product market with the case of a firm that hires workers in a purely competitive labor market but sells its output in a monopolistic product market. We then turn to monopsonistic labor markets, in which individual firms hire a large enough percentage of workers to influence their wage rates. The case of a firm that is a monopsonist in the labor market and sells its output in a purely competitive product market is compared with the case of a firm that is a monopsonist in the labor market but sells its output in a monopolistic product market.

To help you understand the part that labor unions and collective bargaining play in our economy, we present a few highlights from the history of the labor movement in the United States. We show how hard it was in the early days for the unions to get started because the laws reflected a strong resentment of unions by the general public. During the Great Depression of the 1930s many of these negative attitudes were turned around, though some persist even to the present time. The important events that gave rise to American unionism, the major labor laws passed by Congress, and some recent statistics on American organized labor are outlined here. We also discuss the main issues in collective bargaining—the conditions of employment and the relationship between union and management—as well as the process of collective bargaining and its possible results.

The last two parts of the chapter deal with how unions and government can and do affect workers' wage rates and general welfare. Having studied earlier the theory of wage rates in the absence of unions and government, you will learn here how much influence these two important forces have on the welfare of workers.

We first ask what unions can do to raise the wage rates of their members when they are working in a purely competitive labor market. Three possible answers are studied: (1) restricting the supply of labor, (2) bargaining for a higher-than-equilibrium wage rate and (3) raising the demand for labor. Then we ask the same question for a union facing employers who have enough control in the labor market to be able to influence the wage rate that they pay (monopsonistic employers).

Next we turn to the part that the government plays through (1) the laws that strengthen or weaken unions, (2) tax policies, and (3) the direct setting of a minimum wage rate. We look at the effects of a minimum wage rate under conditions of a purely competitive labor market and of a monopsonistic labor market.

LABOR SUPPLY AND DEMAND

In the last chapter you learned about marginal productivity theory. We explained why a profit-maximizing company is expected to demand the amount of a resource that equates its marginal revenue product (MRP) with its marginal factor cost (MFC).

With this important background in mind, we are now ready to apply the theory to labor markets. In Chapter 30 we limited our attention to purely competitive product and resource markets, but here we move on to study monopolistic and monopsonistic cases as well. As you learned in Part VIII, a monopolistic product market is one in which individual companies can use their control over market supply to influence the price of the product. A **monopsonistic resource market** is one in which individual companies can use their

control over the purchase of a resource to influence the resource price. Just as the companies that are monopolistic in product markets (monopolistic competition, oligopoly, or monopoly) face negatively sloped demand curves for their outputs, the companies that are monopsonistic in resource markets (monopsonistic competition, oligopsony, or monopsony) face positively sloped supply curves for their inputs.

A monopsonistic resource market is one in which individual companies can use their control over the purchase of a resource to influence the resource price. Companies that are monopsonistic in resource markets face positively sloped supply curves for their inputs.

Hiring in a Purely Competitive Labor Market

Let us quickly review from the last chapter the case of a company that is a pure competitor in both resource and product markets. Then we can show how much difference it makes when that company is a monopolist in its product market.

Our hypothetical case will deal with the bagel industry. We shall suppose it to be first purely competitive and later monopolistic. The variable labor resource in our case will be people who know how to prepare dough, boil, and bake the bagels. Let us turn our attention to a single company within the bagel industry, which we shall call the Big O Bagel Company.

Selling in a Purely Competitive Bagel Market Table 1 presents the data for the Big O Bagel Company when it is assumed to be a purely competitive seller in the bagel market and a purely competitive employer of bagel makers in the labor market. No matter how many or how few bagels Big O produces, it is able to sell them at $2.00 a dozen. Similarly, no matter how many bagel makers Big O hires, it is able to hire them at $125 a day. Remember that marginal revenue product (MRP) is found by either multiplying marginal physical product (MPP) by the price (in pure competition) or subtracting the total revenue without the additional

TABLE 1
Marginal Revenue Product and Marginal Factor Cost for the Big O Bagel Company: The Case of Pure Competition in Both the Bagel and Bagel Maker Markets

(1) Quantity of Bagel Makers (per day)	(2) Total Product (in dozens of bagels per day)	(3) Marginal Physical Product (in dozens of bagels per day)	(4) Price of Bagels (dollars per dozen)	(5) Total Revenue (dollars)	(6) Marginal Revenue Product (dollars)	(7) Wage of Bagel Makers (dollars per day)	(8) Total Cost of Bagel Makers (dollars per day)	(9) Marginal Factor Cost (dollars)
3	800		$2.00	$1,600		$125	$ 375	
		200			$400			$125
4	1,000		2.00	2,000		125	500	
		150			300			125
5	1,150		2.00	2,300		125	625	
		125			250			125
6	1,275		2.00	2,550		125	750	
		100			200			125
7	1,375		2.00	2,750		125	875	
		75			150			125
8	1,450		2.00	2,900		125	1,000	
		50			100			125
9	1,500		2.00	3,000		125	1,125	
		25			50			125
10	1,525		2.00	3,050		125	1,250	

resource unit from the total revenue with the additional resource unit. Also recall that marginal factor cost (*MFC*) is equal to the wage (in pure competition) or to the change in total cost spent on that resource when one more unit of the resource is hired.

Figure 1 pictures the Big O Bagel Company's *MRP* and *MFC* curves taken from columns 6 and 9 in Table 1. The quantity of bagel makers demanded by Big O is shown at the intersection of its *MFC* curve and its *MRP* curve. In this case the wage is $125 a day. So it pays for Big O to hire the eighth bagel maker (*MRP* is $150, which is greater than *MFC*, which is $125), but not the ninth (*MRP* is $100, which is less than *MFC*, which is $125). The *MRP* curve is Big O's demand curve for bagel makers. The quantity demanded is found in the same way for all other wage rates.

Selling in a Monopolistic Bagel Market In this case, Big O is again a pure competitor in the market

for bagel makers, but this time it is a monopolistic seller in the bagel industry. Table 2 presents new data for the Big O Bagel Company. Except for columns 4, 5, and 6, it is the same as Table 1. As a monopolistic seller in the bagel market, Big O can now change the equilibrium price of bagels by changing the quantity of bagels that it produces and sells. Column 4 shows that Big O could still sell bagels at $2.00 a dozen if it hired 8 bagel makers and produced 1,450 dozen bagels a day. But now that Big O is a monopolistic seller of bagels, it must estimate the change in the price of bagels that would result from a change in its level of output. These price changes are also shown in column 4. Column 5 shows the total revenue corresponding to the different number of bagel makers that Big O might hire, and column 6 shows the marginal revenue product for each successive bagel maker. We see that Big O's marginal revenue product from bagel makers is $400 a day for the fourth bagel maker, but that the marginal revenue product from

TABLE 2
Marginal Revenue Product and Marginal Factor Cost for the Big O Bagel Company: The Case of a Monopolistic Bagel Market and a Purely Competitive Bagel Maker Market

(1) Quantity of Bagel Makers (per day)	(2) Total Product (in dozens of bagels per day)	(3) Marginal Physical Product (in dozens of bagels per day)	(4) Price of Bagels (dollars per dozen)	(5) Total Revenue (dollars)	(6) Marginal Revenue Product (dollars)	(7) Wage of Bagel Makers (dollars per day)	(8) Total Cost for Bagel Makers (dollars per day)	(9) Marginal Factor Cost (dollars)
3	800		$2.50	$2,000.00		$125	$ 375	
		200			$400.00			$125
4	1,000		2.40	2,400.00		125	500	
		150			245.00			125
5	1,150		2.30	2,645.00		125	625	
		125			160.00			125
6	1,275		2.20	2,805.00		125	750	
		100			82.50			125
7	1,375		2.10	2,887.50		125	875	
		75			12.50			125
8	1,450		2.00	2,900.00		125	1,000	
		50			−50.00			125
9	1,500		1.90	2,850.00		125	1,125	
		25			−105.00			125
10	1,525		1.80	2,745.00		125	1,250	

bagel makers drops more rapidly when Big O is a monopolistic seller than when it is a purely competitive seller. This is because both the marginal physical product and the price of bagels drop as output increases for the firm that has monopoly power in the product market. For a firm that is a purely competitive seller, only declining marginal physical product contributes to the decline in the marginal revenue product of an input.

Figure 2 pictures the Big O Bagel Company's MRP curve taken from column 6 in Table 2 and its MFC curve taken from column 9. In this figure the MRP curve reflects the monopolistic bagel market and so is steeper than MRP in the purely competitive case shown in Figure 1. In Figure 2 the MRP curve intersects the MFC curve at a point somewhere between 6 and 7 workers. It pays for Big O to hire the sixth bagel maker (MRP is $160, which is greater than MFC, which is $125), but not the seventh (MRP is $82.50, which is less than MFC, which is $125). The quantity demanded is found in

the same way for all other wage rates. Thus, the MRP curve is Big O's demand curve for bagel makers.

In which of the two bagel markets are bagel makers better off? If you were a bagel maker, would you prefer the bagel industry to be monopolistic or purely competitive? You would recognize that, while the work and wages ($125 a day) are the same, your chances of getting a job are better in the competitive industry. That is, Big O hires 8 bagel makers when the bagel market is purely competitive and only 6 when it is monopolistic. This restriction in hiring is a reflection of the monopolistic firm's output restriction, which we studied in Chapter 27.[1]

---

1. We realize that the market for bagel-making labor could not actually be purely competitive if there were only one employer of bagel makers. But our illustration is important anyway, since it shows the effect of monopoly in the product market, without any additional complication from monopsonistic elements in the labor market.

Both the marginal physical product and the price of the product drop as output increases for the firm that has monopoly power in the product market. For a firm that is a purely competitive seller, only declining marginal physical product contributes to a decline in the marginal revenue product of an input.

Labor Supply of an Individual You have seen how, under certain conditions, we can derive an individual firm's demand curve for a certain type of worker. Let us now switch to the supply side and see how we can derive a supply curve for this type of labor. Table 3 (see top of page 707) provides information concerning the supply of labor offered by an individual named Nancy. Nancy is willing to supply different amounts of her labor according to

FIGURE 1
Big O Bagel Company's Marginal-Revenue-Product and Marginal-Factor-Cost Curves When the Market for Bagel Makers Is Purely Competitive and the Market for Bagels Is Purely Competitive

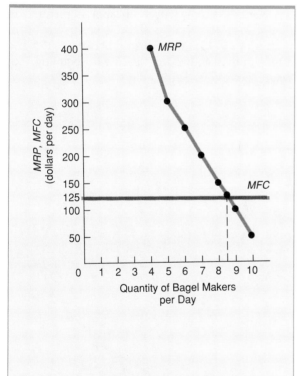

Shown here are the Big O Bagel Company's marginal-revenue-product (*MRP*) and marginal-factor-cost (*MFC*) curves plotted from columns 6 and 9 in Table 1. Big O is assumed to hire bagel makers in a purely competitive labor market and to sell bagels in a purely competitive product market. It can hire all the bagel makers it wishes at $125 per day. It will want to hire 8 bagel makers because its *MRP* exceeds its *MFC* when it hires 8, but its *MFC* exceeds its *MRP* when it hires 9.

FIGURE 2
Big O Bagel Company's Marginal-Revenue-Product and Marginal-Factor-Cost Curves When the Market for Bagel Makers Is Purely Competitive and the Market for Bagels Is Monopolistic

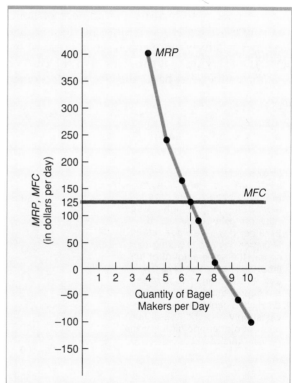

Shown here are the Big O Bagel Company's marginal-revenue-product (*MRP*) and marginal-factor-cost (*MFC*) curves plotted from columns 6 and 9 in Table 2. Big O is assumed to hire bagel makers in a purely competitive labor market and to sell bagels in a monopolistic product market. It can hire all the bagel makers it wishes at $125 per day. It will want to hire 6 bagel makers because its *MRP* exceeds its *MFC* when it hires 6, but its *MFC* exceeds its *MRP* when it hires 7.

the wage rate paid. At $25 a day she is willing to work for only 100 days a year, but at $175 a day she is willing to work three times as many days. At this point in your study of economics, you will not be surprised to find a positive supply relationship—the higher the wage rate, the greater the supply of labor, and vice versa. However, you may be a bit surprised to find that Nancy is not willing to work more days when the wage rate is $200 a day than when it is $175 a day and that she is actually willing to supply less of her labor at even higher wage rates. Why? The reason involves the tradeoff between work and leisure, which we introduced in the last chapter. At higher wage rates Nancy's leisure time becomes more expensive, but also more valuable.

The substitution effect of a higher wage rate has a tendency to increase the number of hours that she is willing to work, since her leisure time becomes relatively more expensive in terms of the goods and services that she gives up if she chooses leisure. On the other hand, the income effect of the wage increase causes her to demand more leisure. At wage rates from $25 to $175 a day, the substitution effect outweighs the income effect. Between the wage rates of $175 and $200 a day, the substitution effect and income effect exactly compensate for each other. At wage rates higher than that, the income effect outweighs the substitution effect.

Compare Nancy's situation when the wage rate is $250 a day instead of $200 a day. At $250 a day she chooses to work 30 days less, yet she earns $7,500 more ($67,500 − $60,000). Had she chosen to work 300 days, she would have earned $75,000. However, the extra 30 days of leisure were more important to Nancy than the goods and services she could have bought with the extra $7,500 ($75,000 − $67,500 = $7,500) she would have earned from working the additional 30 days.

Nancy's supply curve of labor is pictured in Figure 3. Notice that its slope is positive at wage rates up to $175 a day, vertical between $175 and $200, and negative, or "backward-bending," at wage rates above $200 a day.

FIGURE 3
Nancy's Supply of Labor

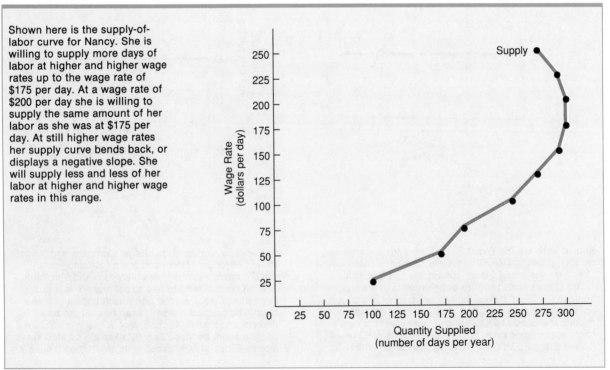

Shown here is the supply-of-labor curve for Nancy. She is willing to supply more days of labor at higher and higher wage rates up to the wage rate of $175 per day. At a wage rate of $200 per day she is willing to supply the same amount of her labor as she was at $175 per day. At still higher wage rates her supply curve bends back, or displays a negative slope. She will supply less and less of her labor at higher and higher wage rates in this range.

TABLE 3
Nancy's Supply of Labor and Her Annual Income

Wage Rate (per day)	Supply of Labor (number of days per year)	Annual Income
$ 25	100	$ 2,500
50	170	8,500
75	190	14,250
100	240	24,000
125	270	33,750
150	290	43,500
175	300	52,500
200	300	60,000
225	290	65,250
250	270	67,500

The substitution effect of a higher wage rate has a tendency to increase the number of hours a worker is willing to work, since leisure time becomes relatively more expensive in terms of the goods and services given up if the worker chooses leisure. However, the income effect of the wage rate increases causes greater demand for leisure. Once the wage rate becomes high enough, the income effect is expected to outweigh the substitution effect.

An individual's supply curve of labor first slopes upward, then turns vertical, then becomes negative, or backward-bending.

Market Demand and Market Supply You have seen that an individual firm's demand curve for labor in a purely competitive labor market is its *MRP* curve. Let us derive the market-demand curve for labor now by adding together the *MRP* curves of all the firms that demand this type of labor. Figure 4 shows the market-demand curve for bagel makers in our hypothetical example. It is based on the assumption that the bagel industry is made up of a large number of bagel firms similar to the one in Figure 1.

Deriving the market-supply curve of bagel makers follows a somewhat different route. We

have examined Nancy's supply curve of labor. If we were to add together the supply curves of all the people in an economy, we could derive a labor-supply curve for that economy. It would look something like Nancy's, but the backward-bending feature would probably disappear. This is because some people will experience the backward-bending (income) effect sooner than Nancy and some will experience it later.

A labor-supply curve for an economy can be derived by adding together the individual supply curves for all the people in that economy. However, the backward-bending feature usually disappears.

Moreover, analyzing Nancy's labor-supply curve does not tell us whether Nancy will work as a bagel maker, or as a bricklayer, or as a schoolteacher. Similarly, the labor-supply curve for the economy or the labor market in general does not

FIGURE 4
Market-Demand Curve for Bagel Makers

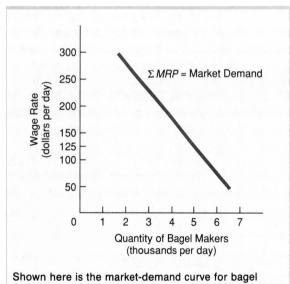

Shown here is the market-demand curve for bagel makers for our hypothetical purely competitive bagel industry. "Σ" is a summation sign, which indicates here that the market-demand curve for bagel makers is merely the horizontal summation of all the individual bagel firms' marginal-revenue-product (*MRP*) curves with regard to bagel makers.

tell us how many workers will be offering their services as bagel makers or as bricklayers or as schoolteachers. Given enough time to learn skills, Nancy will offer to work in whatever job offers the highest wage rate, assuming that other aspects of the jobs are alike. If bagel-making wage rates rise in relation to other wage rates, she and thousands of others will offer their services as bagel makers. If the relative wage of bagel makers falls, she and many other workers will give up bagel making and turn to the jobs that are now more attractive. Figure 5 shows a supply curve for bagel makers that reflects this reasoning. If the wage rate for bagel makers is $125 a day, 5,000 people will offer their services as bagel makers. If the wage rate is $200 a day, over 6,000 bagel makers will be supplied, and so on.

If wage rates for a particular occupation rise relative to other occupations, more and more people offer their services to that occupation.

Market Equilibrium We are now ready to put demand and supply together and in this way to find the equilibrium wage rate and the equilibrium quantity. In panel (a) of Figure 6 we have redrawn the two market curves from Figures 4 and 5. The quantity demanded for bagel makers in this market is equal to the quantity supplied of bagel makers in this market when 5,000 bagel makers are hired at $125 a day. Since the market for bagel makers is assumed to be purely competitive, each bagel firm accepts the equilibrium wage for bagel makers as given and faces a horizontal supply curve. In panel (b) of Figure 6 we once again show the Big O Bagel Company. As shown in Figure 1, Big O will hire 8 bagel makers since its *MRP* is greater than the $125 wage rate (its *MFC*) up to that point, but its *MRP* from a ninth bagel maker is less than $125.

Hiring in a Monopsonistic Labor Market

Our discussion of the supply of labor and the demand for labor has assumed that workers are hired in a purely competitive labor market. Market supply and demand determined the equilibrium market wage, which was accepted as given by each

company. Since there were so many companies employing the same kind of worker, the number of workers hired by each individual company was assumed to have no effect on the wage rate of those workers. We now abandon this assumption and go on to see what difference it makes when individual firms have some monopsonistic control. Recall from earlier in the chapter that a monopsonistic market is made up of firms that each hire a large enough percentage of workers to influence the wage rate. Any one of them will bid up the wage rate when it hires more workers and cause the wage rate to fall when it hires fewer. Now, if Big O wishes to hire more bagel makers, it must raise the wage rate in order to attract them. In other words, it faces a positively sloped supply curve.

In a monopsonistic labor market, a firm that hires more workers will bid up the wage rate.

FIGURE 5
Market-Supply Curve for Bagel Makers

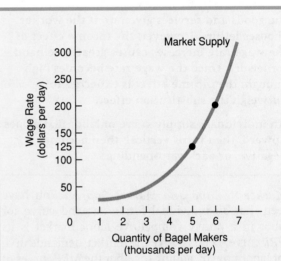

Shown here is the market-supply curve for bagel makers relating to our hypothetical bagel industry. As the wage rate for bagel makers rises in relation to the wage rates for other occupations, more and more people will offer their services as bagel makers. At a wage rate of $125 a day, 5,000 people will offer their services as bagel makers. At a wage rate of $200 a day, over 6,000 bagel makers will be supplied per day, and so on.

FIGURE 6
**Equilibrium Wage and Quantity of Bagel Makers When Hiring in a
Purely Competitive Labor Market**

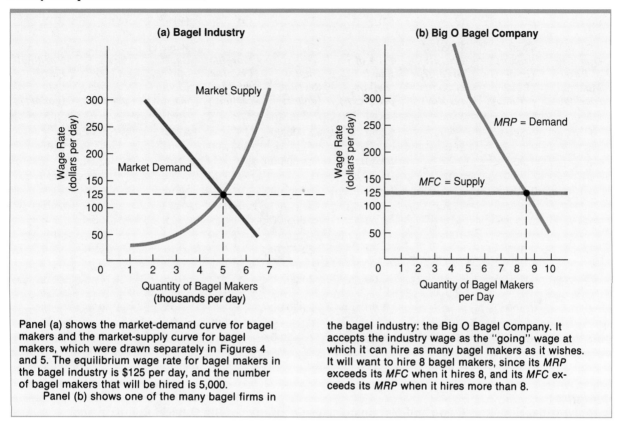

(a) Bagel Industry

(b) Big O Bagel Company

Panel (a) shows the market-demand curve for bagel makers and the market-supply curve for bagel makers, which were drawn separately in Figures 4 and 5. The equilibrium wage rate for bagel makers in the bagel industry is $125 per day, and the number of bagel makers that will be hired is 5,000.

Panel (b) shows one of the many bagel firms in the bagel industry: the Big O Bagel Company. It accepts the industry wage as the "going" wage at which it can hire as many bagel makers as it wishes. It will want to hire 8 bagel makers, since its *MRP* exceeds its *MFC* when it hires 8, and its *MFC* exceeds its *MRP* when it hires more than 8.

Table 4 repeats columns 1 through 6 from Table 2, showing that Big O sells bagels in a monopolistic market, but reflects in columns 7, 8, and 9 that Big O is hiring bagel makers in a monopsonistic market. Column 7 shows that Big O must offer a higher and higher wage rate in order to attract more and more bagel makers or can pay a lower wage rate if it hires fewer bagel makers. For example, Big O is able to hire 6 bagel makers at $125 a day, but if it wishes to hire 7, each must be paid $135 a day. Big O cannot get away with paying $125 to the first 6 workers and paying $135 only to the seventh worker, since each of the 6 workers receiving $125 a day would have good reason to quit and become the marginal worker who is paid $135 a day. Columns 8 and 9 in Table 4 show that Big O's total cost for 7 bagel makers is $945 and that this is $195 more than it has to pay for 6

workers. The *MFC* of $195 is made up of the extra $135 paid to the seventh bagel maker plus the extra $10 paid to each of the first 6 workers ($135 + 6($10) = $195). As you can see, then, in a monopsonistic labor market the extra cost of hiring an additional worker (*MFC*) is greater than the wage that he or she receives. This is shown in Figure 7. Here the supply curve of bagel makers (the varying quantity of bagel makers' labor that is forthcoming at different wage rates) that is faced by Big O is drawn from column 7 in Table 4. With it is drawn Big O's *MFC* curve from column 9 of the table.

In a monopsonistic labor market, the extra cost of hiring an additional worker (*MFC*) is greater than the wage rate that is paid to that worker.

TABLE 4
Marginal Revenue Product and Marginal Factor Cost for the Big O Bagel Company: The Case of a Monopolistic Bagel Market and a Monopsonistic Bagel-Maker Market

(1) Quantity of Bagel Makers (per day)	(2) Total Product (in dozens of bagels per day)	(3) Marginal Physical Product (in dozens of bagels per day)	(4) Price of Bagels (dollars per dozen)	(5) Total Revenue (dollars)	(6) Marginal Revenue Product (dollars)	(7) Wage of Bagel Makers (dollars per day)	(8) Total Cost for Bagel Makers (dollars per day)	(9) Marginal Factor Cost (dollars)
3	800		$2.50	$2,000.00		$ 95	$ 285	
		200			$400.00			$135
4	1,000		2.40	2,400.00		105	420	
		150			245.00			155
5	1,150		2.30	2,645.00		115	575	
		125			160.00			175
6	1,275		2.20	2,805.00		125	750	
		100			82.50			195
7	1,375		2.10	2,887.50		135	945	
		75			12.50			215
8	1,450		2.00	2,900.00		145	1,160	
		50			−50.00			235
9	1,500		1.90	2,850.00		155	1,395	
		25			−105.00			255
10	1,525		1.80	2,745.00		165	1,650	

FIGURE 7
Supply-of-Bagel-Makers Curve and Marginal-Factor-Cost Curve of Big O Bagel Company in a Monopsonistic Bagel-Maker Market

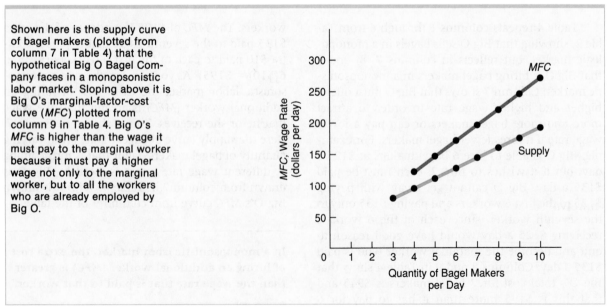

Shown here is the supply curve of bagel makers (plotted from column 7 in Table 4) that the hypothetical Big O Bagel Company faces in a monopsonistic labor market. Sloping above it is Big O's marginal-factor-cost curve (MFC) plotted from column 9 in Table 4. Big O's MFC is higher than the wage it must pay to the marginal worker because it must pay a higher wage not only to the marginal worker, but to all the workers who are already employed by Big O.

FIGURE 8
Equilibrium Wage and Quantity of Bagel Makers When Hiring in a Monopsonistic Labor Market

Both diagrams show the equilibrium wage and quantity of workers hired in a monopsonistic labor market. In panel (a) the firm is selling its output in a purely competitive product market, and in panel (b) the firm is selling its output in a monopolistic product market. In both diagrams the equilibrium quantity of workers is determined by where the firm's *MFC* equals its *MRP*, and the equilibrium wage rate is found on the supply curve, which shows how high a wage rate must be paid to attract that number of workers.

Equilibrium   Having explained the *MFC* curve in a monopsonistic labor market, we are ready to determine the equilibrium quantity of labor that will be hired in such markets. The rule that we follow is the same as the one that we used in our discussion of competitive labor markets: a profit-maximizing firm will continue to hire more workers as long as its *MRP* exceeds its *MFC*.

Figure 8 pictures two equilibrium solutions. In both cases Big O is hiring bagel makers in a monopsonistic market. However, panel (a) assumes that Big O sells its bagels in a purely competitive market and panel (b) pictures the case where

Big O sells its bagels in a monopolistic market. Panel (a) repeats the supply and *MFC* curves from Figure 7 (taken from columns 7 and 9 in Table 4) and adds the *MRP* curve from Figure 1 (taken from column 6 in Table 1). The equilibrium quantity of bagel makers is 7. As you can see, *MRP* exceeds *MFC* for 7 workers, but not for 8 workers. The diagram also shows the equilibrium wage rate that Big O must pay in order to attract 7 bagel makers a day. This point is read off the supply curve, which tells us that 7 bagel makers are willing to work at a wage rate of $135 a day. In a monopsonistic labor market, *MFC* is higher than the wage rate, since the additional cost to a firm of hiring another worker is not only the higher wage paid to that worker but also the wage increase that has to be paid to all the workers who are already employed by the firm.

In a monopsonistic labor market, a profit-maximizing firm will continue to hire more workers as long as its *MRP* exceeds its *MFC*.

Panel (b) in Figure 8 combines the same supply and *MFC* curves with Big O's *MRP* curve from Figure 2 (taken from column 6 in Table 2 and Table 4). The only difference between the two diagrams in Figure 8 is that *MRP* drops more quickly in panel (b), because of the monopolistic character of the bagel market. In such a market the equilibrium quantity of bagel makers and the equilibrium wage rate will be lower. Because *MFC* intersects *MRP* somewhere between 5 and 6 workers, it will pay for Big O to hire 5 workers, but not 6. The supply curve tells us that Big O can hire 5 bagel makers per day for a wage rate of $115.

In a monopsonistic labor market, *MFC* is higher than the wage rate, since the additional cost to a firm of hiring another worker is not only the higher wage paid to that worker but also the wage increase that has to be paid to all the workers already employed by the firm.

Equilibrium Wage and Marginal Revenue Product
You have probably noticed from our example that workers in a monopsonistic labor market receive a wage rate that is lower than their *MRP* but that workers in a purely competitive labor market are paid a wage rate equal to their *MRP*. This difference will always be found because *MFC* is equal to the equilibrium wage rate in a purely competitive labor market whereas it is above the equilibrium wage rate in a monopsonistic labor market.

Workers in a monopsonistic labor market receive a wage rate that is lower than their marginal revenue product, while workers in a purely competitive labor market are paid a wage rate equal to their marginal revenue product.

LABOR UNIONS AND COLLECTIVE BARGAINING

In our example of bagel makers, we have assumed that workers compete among themselves in offering their services. In fact, this is not always the case. When labor unions bargain collectively for groups of workers, competition among workers is limited.

Labor unions are organizations whose major goals are to improve the wage rates and working conditions of their members. **Collective bargaining** is the approach used by labor unions to negotiate with employers or their representatives.

Labor unions are organizations whose major goals are to improve the wage rates and working conditions of their members. Labor unions bargain collectively for groups of workers.

Labor unions in the United States had a hard time at the beginning. Many people resented them as intruders that undermined the legitimate rights of firms and threatened the free-enterprise system. Even today some people view unions as monopolistic organizations that benefit their members at the expense of the rest of society. Others go so far as to argue that labor unions don't even benefit their own membership on the whole. Many, however, view unions as a positive social force. They find unions to be the only reasonable way in which most wage and salary workers are able to increase their share of the economic pie. Without unions, they argue, workers would be powerless in relation to their (monopsonistic) employers. Feelings run high on both sides of the union issue, and unfortunately objectivity often takes a back seat.

Highlights in the History of the Labor Movement

The union concept goes back to at least the medieval craft guilds of twelfth-century England. Our brief history, however, will deal only with the labor movement in the United States. We shall divide this history into three parts: (1) before the American Federation of Labor, (2) from the 1880s to the Great Depression, and (3) since World War II.

Before the American Federation of Labor   In colonial America, industry was largely in the handicraft stage. Master craftsmen, journeymen, and their apprentices carried on many trades such as carpentry, blacksmithing, milling, tanning, shoemaking, and bricklaying. They set up guilds, which at first were generally charitable and mutual-aid societies, but after a time many of them began to take part in certain activities that we now associate with unions. They often formed political action groups, working to rid themselves of unfavorable laws passed by colonial legislatures. Later on, they became more interested in internal craft matters, such as the use of apprentices and the level and structure of wage scales. For example, the Carpenters Society of Philadelphia, started in 1724, set up a secret wage scale for its members. Journeymen hatters, coopers, printers, and shoemakers also carried on wage negotiations.

After the American Revolution these organizations began to take on an even stronger resemblance to modern unions. The first wage earners to go on strike were the journeymen printers in Philadelphia in 1786. Then in 1799, the journeymen shoemakers in Philadelphia went on strike for nine weeks to oppose the cutting of their wages. However, these early unions faced many problems. They were challenged as illegal conspirators by employer associations and unfriendly courts. During recessions it was difficult for them to maintain membership. For these reasons, among others, most survived only a few years.

Before the 1820s, unions were almost exclusively of the craft type. **Craft unions** are organizations representing certain kinds of skilled workers such as carpenters, typographers, and plumbers. By the middle 1820s, the less-skilled workers in America's factories began to organize in industrial unions. **Industrial unions** represent all the workers in an industry, such as mine workers or clothing workers.

Craft unions are organizations representing certain kinds of skilled workers. Industrial unions represent all the workers in an industry.

Union gains were largely wiped out by the recession of the late 1820s, and frustrated workers turned to political action—that is, they formed the first American labor parties. During the early to middle 1830s unionism began to revive, and on the eve of the 1837 panic union membership had reached 300,000, nearly half of all people employed in manufacturing. However, most of these unions were not able to survive the long depression that lasted until 1843.

During the 1840s workers made a great attempt to escape from the hardships of industrialization. Many joined so-called "utopias" of communal working and living, inspired by such leaders as Robert Owen and Charles Fourier. However, these experiments failed. They were based on a desire to return to the "good old days" of preindustrial society, but the forward movement of the Industrial Revolution was much too powerful to be put in reverse.

When economic conditions improved, local unions again emerged, and by the 1850s the first national ones were formed. The National Typographical Union was established in 1852. Then followed the hat finishers, stonecutters, iron molders, cigar makers, and locomotive engineers.

Early unions faced many problems, and few survived for very long. The first national unions were formed in the 1850s.

The Civil War brought the worst inflation and labor shortages the country had ever experienced, but both actually helped the unions. The first federation of national unions was attempted by the National Labor Union in 1866. A more successful federation, the Noble Order of the Knights of Labor, followed in 1869. The Knights of Labor, which was a secret society in its early days, admitted all types and grades of labor except lawyers, bankers, and saloon-keepers. During the hard times of the 1870s, the unions had few successes. But for the first time they were not generally wiped out, as had been the case in earlier depressions. By 1886 the Knights of Labor claimed 730,000 members, but then declined rapidly because of some unsuccessful strikes, loose organization, and a strong new competitor, the American Federation of Labor.

From the 1880s to the Great Depression **The American Federation of Labor (AF of L)** was formed by trade unionists who were unhappy with the Knights of Labor. Seceding from the Knights in 1881, they organized the AF of L in 1886. Under the leadership of two cigar makers, Samuel Gompers and Adolf Strasser, the AF of L ushered in a new kind of unionism. These leaders decided, after many years of experience, that direct participation in politics and grandiose attempts to reform the whole economic system should be abandoned. Instead, they practiced **business unionism**, emphasizing that American trade unions must rely on their economic power to achieve their goals of higher real wages and better working conditions. During its first dozen years the AF of L grew slowly but steadily and then at the turn of the century took a great leap forward. By 1904 its membership had grown to about 1.7 million, which accounted for about 80 percent of all union membership.

The American Federation of Labor was organized in 1886. Rather than attempting reform of the entire economic system, the AF of L practiced business unionism and emphasized that American trade unions must rely on their economic power to achieve their goals of higher real wages and better working conditions.

The conservative business unionism approach of the AF of L was not to everybody's taste. In 1905 eastern socialist labor groups joined with some militant western metal-mining and logging unions to form the Industrial Workers of the World (IWW). This radical union, with its revolutionary goals and violent tactics, received a great deal of notoriety, but actually never attracted more than about 70,000 members. By the eve of World War I, the IWW had lost most of its influence.

During World War I, unions began to grow once again, particularly the craft unions that represented workers in the war-related industries, such as the shipbuilding, machinery, and the garment trades. Union membership doubled from about 2.5 million in 1914 to 5 million in 1920.

The Roaring Twenties, a time of great industrial prosperity in the United States, were not a roaring success for unions. In fact, many workers who had joined during the war decided to drop out. A number of unpopular strikes gave unions a bad press. Taking advantage of this atmosphere, employer groups, backed by courts that were unfriendly to the unions, intensified their campaigns against the unions. But probably the most important reason for the decline of unions during this period was the AF of L's continued emphasis on craft unionism at a time when the mechanization of factories gave semiskilled workers much greater importance in American industry. By 1929, union membership had dropped to about 3.6 million.

During the 1920s, the union movement declined, largely because of the AF of L's continued emphasis on craft unionism at a time when the mechanization of factories gave semiskilled workers much greater importance in American industry.

The Great Depression of the 1930s was a time of economic chaos for most Americans. Workers were no exception. But along with the suffering during the Great Depression came a change in attitudes that was to benefit unions for many years to come. One observer later wrote,

> For the first time in our history a national administration was to make the welfare of industrial workers a direct concern of the government and act on the principle that only organized labor could deal on equal terms with organized capital in bringing about a proper balance between those two rival forces in a capitalistic society.[2]

The first clear evidence of a more favorable union climate came with the passage of the **Norris-LaGuardia Act** of 1932. Before this act, unions had often been frustrated by the unfriendly

2. Foster D. Dulles, *Labor in America: A History* (New York: Crowell, 1955), p. 264.

treatment they received from the courts. Employers found it very easy to get restraining orders, called injunctions, from the courts to keep workers from starting a union, striking, or picketing. The courts also enforced the so-called **yellow-dog contract**—an agreement that a worker will not join a union—which was often made a condition of employment. The Norris-LaGuardia Act made a blanket statement that workers should have full freedom of association and self-organization. It also specifically limited the courts' power to issue injunctions in labor disputes and made the yellow-dog contract unenforceable.

The Great Depression brought a more favorable union climate. The Norris-LaGuardia Act of 1932 limited the courts' power to issue injunctions in labor disputes and made the yellow-dog contract unenforceable.

Three years later, Congress passed an even stronger law favoring unions. The **Wagner-Connery Act** of 1935, more formally called the National Labor Relations Act, is often referred to as the "Magna Carta of labor." Through this act it became U.S. public policy to encourage "the practice and procedure of collective bargaining." Congress outlined several unfair labor practices by employers and set up the National Labor Relations Board to prevent these practices. Among other things, employers could no longer keep workers from starting a union, or discriminate against union members, or refuse to bargain collectively with duly elected worker representatives. For the first time it became possible for workers to organize into unions and to bargain collectively without getting into trouble with the law.

The Wagner-Connery Act of 1935 (National Labor Relations Act) proclaimed that the practices and procedures of collective bargaining should be encouraged. It became official U.S. public policy to prohibit unfair labor practices of employers.

The year 1935 was also the year that an internal union conflict over craft versus industrial un-

ionism came to a head. The AF of L served the craft unions and was controlled by them. However, the greatest opportunities for union organizing were to be found among semiskilled workers in the newer mass-production industries such as steel, aluminum, electrical equipment, and automobiles. In 1935 several national unions connected with the AF of L formed a Committee for Industrial Organization to promote industrial unionism. Driven out of the AF of L in 1938, they formed a rival federation, the **Congress of Industrial Organizations (CIO)**. The CIO, which was led by John L. Lewis, the head of the United Mine Workers, was very successful and became a powerful competitor of the AF of L.

In 1938 several national unions formed the Congress of Industrial Organizations (CIO), which became a powerful competitor of the AF of L.

Since World War II Union membership had tripled from 1933 to the eve of World War II, when it reached about 9 million. By the end of the war in 1945, union membership had climbed to about 14 million. Among the reasons for this growth were the wartime labor shortages, rises in the cost of living, and a friendly government attitude toward unions as expressed by the War Labor Board's generous granting of fringe benefits.

The Taft-Hartley Act At the same time, however, unions declined somewhat in public favor. It was felt that some unions abused their newly gained power. And when an epidemic of strikes broke out just after the war, there was a growing popular demand for restraints on union power. As a result, the **Taft-Hartley Act,** more formally called the Labor-Management Relations Act, was passed in 1947. This law retains the key provisions of the Wagner-Connery Act, but added some unfair labor practices by unions. For example, unions are forbidden to interfere with the organization of employers, to refuse to bargain with employer representatives, or to enter into closed shop arrangements. (The **closed shop** arrangement requires a person to be a member of the union before he or she can be hired.) The act also has a provision that temporarily prevents workers from striking. That is, the president of the United States is given the power to order an eighty-day "cooling off" period when it is judged that a dispute "imperils the national health or safety." In addition, the act outlaws secondary boycotts and strikes, jurisdictional strikes, and featherbedding. A **secondary boycott or strike** is a boycott or a strike against an employer other than the one with which the union has a dispute. A **jurisdictional strike** is a strike concerning which union will represent a given group of workers. **Featherbedding** is the practice of forcing an employer to pay for services that workers do not actually perform.

In 1947 the Taft-Hartley Act (Labor-Management Relations Act) forbade unions to interfere with the organization of employers, to refuse to bargain with employer representatives, or to enter into closed shop arrangements.

The rate of union growth slowed considerably after 1947, but one should not jump to the conclusion that this slowdown was necessarily due to the Taft-Hartley Act. In fact, even though the Taft-Hartley Act was often denounced by union leaders as a "slave labor act," it did not have a strong negative impact on organized labor. For example, while closed shops were outlawed, **union shops** (which allow employers to hire nonunion employees but require that they join the union within thirty days) remained legal.[3] Also, featherbedding has been interpreted so narrowly by the courts that very few contracts have been canceled because they call for "unnecessary" work to be performed.

Merger of the AF of L and CIO   In 1955 the AF of L and the CIO merged. Over the years since the CIO was driven out of the AF of L in 1938, the AF of L itself had become much broader-based, with a large industrial union membership. Also, the struggle for the leadership of the merged federation was eased because the presidents of both the AF of L and the CIO had died in 1953.[4] The merger did not give rise to a great "labor monopoly" as some had feared. After all, the AFL-CIO is a federation of separate national unions. Its main functions are lobbying, public relations, and research.

In 1955, the AF of L and the CIO merged. The AFL-CIO is a federation of separate national unions. Its main functions are lobbying, public relations, and research.

Problems with Corruption   Soon after the merger, the AFL-CIO was faced with a major problem—corruption and racketeering in some of its member unions. The best known of these was the Teamsters Union, though several others, such as the Bakers, United Textile Workers, the Operating Engineers, and the Laundry Workers were also involved. For a year and a half, a committee of the U.S. Senate, chaired by Senator John L. McClellan, investigated and held public hearings on union corruption. Even though the AFL-CIO expelled the Teamsters as well as several other unions (which together had more than 1.5 million members), public outrage was great enough to cause Congress to pass the **Landrum-Griffin Act**, officially called the Labor-Management Reporting and Disclosure Act, in 1959. This act contains a detailed set of rules governing the relationship between union governments and their members. Besides offering a "bill of rights" for every union member, it sets forth rules for holding union elections, places limits on the control by national unions over local unions, and sets up strict penalties for any union official who is found guilty of mishandling union funds.

Corruption in some unions, most notably the Teamsters, led to their expulsion from the AFL-CIO and the passage of the Landrum-Griffin Act (Labor-Management Reporting and Disclosure Act) in 1959.

---

3. However, states that pass so-called "right-to-work" laws can outlaw union shops. About 40 percent of the states have chosen to enact such laws.

4. President William Green of the AF of L and President Philip Murray of the CIO both died in November 1953. George Meany of the Plumbers' Union became president of the AFL-CIO and remained in that position until 1979.

The Civil Rights Act In the early 1960s many unions became interested in the issue of racial discrimination. A number of the more industrial unions that had a large proportion of black members were strongly committed to the goal of racial equality. Along with the other civil rights groups, they worked hard to get the **Civil Rights Act** passed in 1964. Title VII of that act prohibits discrimination in hiring, firing, or promotions based on race, color, religion, sex, or national origin.

The Civil Rights Act carried a strong message, but its effects have been hard to measure. Lines 5 through 12 in Table 5 present labor force participation rates for certain classes of workers over the years 1960 to 1986. Whether any of these changes were affected by the Civil Rights Act and, if so, to what extent, is not known. What is quite clear from these numbers is that the proportion of males of all races in the labor force has fallen while the proportion of females of all races participating in the labor force has risen.

Many unions fought for the passage of the 1964 Civil Rights Act, which prohibits discrimination in hiring, firing, or promotions based on race, color, religion, sex, or national origin.

Changes in Union Membership Union membership increased during the 1960s, held fairly constant during the 1970s, and fell dramatically in the 1980s. Line 4 in Table 5 shows the totals. As a percentage of the noninstitutional population, sixteen years of age and older (line 2 of Table 5), union membership has actually fallen from 15.1

TABLE 5
Changes in the U.S. Population and Civilian Labor Force, 1960–1986

	1960	1965	1970	1975	1980	1986
	(millions of people)					
1. Total population	181	194	205	216	228	242
2. Noninstitutional population, 16 years of age and older	119	128	139	155	169	182
3. Civilian labor force	70	74	83	94	107	118
4. Union membership	18	19	21	22	22	17
	(percentages)					
5. Percentage of males in civilian labor force	84	82	80	78	77	76
6. Percentage of females in civilian labor force	38	39	43	46	52	55
7. Percentage of white males in civilian labor force	83	81	80	79	78	77
8. Percentage of black males in civilian labor force	83	80	77	71	71	71
9. Percentage of Hispanic males in civilian labor force	n.a.	n.a.	n.a.	n.a.	81	81
10. Percentage of white females in civilian labor force	37	38	43	46	51	55
11. Percentage of black females in civilian labor force	48	49	50	49	53	57
12. Percentage of Hispanic females in civilian labor force	n.a.	n.a.	n.a.	n.a.	47	50

Source: Statistics from the U.S. Department of Commerce, U.S. Bureau of the Census, *Statistical Abstract of the United States: 1981 and 1988,* Tables 13, 605, 608, 667.

TABLE 6

Membership in Large U.S. Unions Affiliated with the AFL-CIO, 1987
(in thousands of people)

Union	Membership	Union	Membership
Auto Workers	998	Laborers	371
Bakery	109	Letter Carriers	200
Boilermakers	90	Machinists	509
Carpenters	609	Musicians	60
Clothing & Textile	195	Painters	128
Communications	515	Paperworkers	221
Electrical	765	Plumbers	220
Electronic	185	Postal Workers	230
Engineers	330	Retail, Wholesale	140
Firefighters	142	Rubber	97
Food & Commercial	1,000	Service Employees	762
Garment	173	State, County (AFSCME)	1,032
Government (AFGE)	157	Steelworkers	494
Hotel & Restaurant	293	Teachers (AFT)	499
Iron Workers	122	Transit	85

Source: U.S. Department of Commerce, U.S. Bureau of the Census, *Statistical Abstract of the United States,* 1988, Table 665.

percent in 1960 to 9.3 percent in 1986. The concentration of union membership is shown in Table 6, which lists 1987 membership figures for thirty large American unions that are affiliated with the AFL-CIO.

A dramatic development in unions since the early 1960s is the falling percentage of private employees who are union members and the rising percentage of government employees who belong to unions. One explanation is that the greatest growth in private employment during this period was in jobs and regions of the country that have generally attracted the fewest union members, while the greatest declines were in jobs and regions that are more likely to organize. For example, young people, women, and white-collar workers became a larger percentage of the labor force, but blue-collar males decreased in relative importance. Many jobs were lost in the automobile and steel industries, which are highly unionized. Also, the industrial states of New York, New Jersey, Pennsylvania, Ohio, Michigan, and Illinois, where unionism made its greatest early gains, grew more slowly than the states in the southern and southwestern United States.

Union membership increased in the 1960s, held constant in the 1970s, and fell dramatically in the 1980s. However, a rising percentage of government employees joined unions during this period.

Before 1960 relatively few people who were working for the federal, state, or local governments were unionized. Only the state of Wisconsin allowed bargaining by public employees. But in 1962 President John Kennedy issued an executive order stating that federal employees have the right to organize and bargain collectively. This executive order was strengthened by another one issued by President Richard Nixon in 1969. Not only did these executive orders pave the way for large-scale unionization at the federal level, but they also led to more unionization among state and local government workers. Many professional public employees joined together in "associations" rather than "unions." But while there may be some philosophical differences, association activities are hard to distinguish from union activities. A case in point is the National Education Association, which had nearly 2 million members in 1989. Lloyd Reynolds, a well-known labor economist, recently wrote: "If we include bargaining associations which function much like unions, . . . then about half of all federal employees are organized, as are 40 percent of state employees and 55 percent of local government employees."[5] Though public employees got a late start in American unionism, they are now about twice as heavily unionized as employees in the private sector.

In 1962, President Kennedy issued an executive order stating that federal employees have the right to organize and bargain collectively. President Nixon issued a similar order in 1969. These executive orders paved the way for large-scale unionization at the federal level and also led to more unionization among state and local government workers.

Confrontation and Cooperation in Contemporary Labor-Management Relations Organized labor's bargaining clout was seriously eroded in the 1980s. As the 1990s unfold, union leaders are struggling to halt the draining away of their rank and file. The 1980s saw unions surrendering on many fronts to employer demands for concessions. General wage concessions were sometimes won by companies that threatened plant shutdowns or moves to the less-unionized Sunbelt or to foreign countries. Some firms went even so far as to file for bankruptcy in order to void labor contracts.

One compromise solution that has developed takes the form of two-tier contracts that place new hires on a lower pay scale than previously hired workers. Contracts of this type have been agreed upon in the U.S. Postal Service and in the food wholesaling, food retailing, trucking, aerospace, and airlines industries. Unions claim that these concessions have had a devastating effect on worker morale.

Confrontation has appeared alongside a movement toward greater cooperation in relations between unions and employers. Worker concern

about job security and income maintenance and employer realization that high productivity depends on satisfied workers with good attitudes about job performance have spawned a revolution of labor-management partnership. Following the Japanese model, this frequently involves profit sharing, long-term job security, bonuses linked to productivity increases, and the surrender by workers of hard-won systems of rigid work rules and job classifications. The most outstanding example thus far is the 1985 United Auto Workers (UAW) agreement with General Motors Corporation for the $5 billion Saturn project, which is to start producing small cars in the early 1990s. Consensus is required for action. UAW representatives sit in on planning and operating committees. Work teams operate without foremen. Workers participate in job assignment and are salaried, just like management, rather than paid by the hour. Under the agreement, wages are about 80 percent of UAW scale, but workers receive bonuses based on performance as measured by productivity and profitability.

In 1989, the United Auto Workers failed in an attempt to organize workers in the Japanese-owned Nissan plant in Tennessee. The firm's good relationship with the workers forestalled the union's effort to gain a role in the plant.

Worker concern about job security and income maintenance and employer realization that high productivity depends on satisfied workers with good attitudes about job performance have spawned a revolution in labor-management cooperation.

Collective Bargaining

The goal of collective bargaining is to find terms satisfactory to both employees and management on many important issues. Once agreed on, these terms are carefully set down in the form of a labor contract.

Issues in Collective Bargaining The issues in collective bargaining fall into two very broad categories: (1) the conditions of employment and (2) the relationship between the union and management.

---

5. Lloyd G. Reynolds, *Labor Economics and Labor Relations,* 8th ed. (Englewood Cliffs, N.J.: Prentice-Hall, 1982), p. 337.

The conditions of employment include wage rates, fringe benefits, work standards, and job security. Among the wage issues are the basic rate for each job category and the pay steps for advancing within each category. **Fringe benefits** are forms of compensation other than wages, such as pensions, life insurance, health plans, child-care benefits, severance pay, maternity/paternity leaves, as well as paid vacations, holidays, birthdays, and even coffee breaks and cleanup time. **Work standards** specify the amount of work to be performed. For example, they state the size of the crew to be employed to do a standard job or the number of units to be handled on an assembly line. Finally, **job security** has to do with the conditions for job continuance and the handling of grievances. Generally, job continuance is determined by **seniority rules**. For example, the worker who has been on the job the longest is the last to be laid off and the first to be called back when the firm hires again.

Union and management must also agree on their own relationship over the life of the contract. They have to decide how to define the **bargaining unit**, which identifies the workers for whom the union is bargaining and so to whom the labor contract applies. They must also agree on the privileges given to **shop stewards**, elected to represent the union on the job. For example, stewards may be allowed to confer with workers and supervisors during working hours. Union and management may also agree on the checkoff of union dues. The **checkoff** is a form of union security that calls for the employer to deduct or withhold union dues from workers' paychecks and to pay those dues directly to the union. In many cases, labor contracts have provisions for **arbitration**, a procedure for settling union-management differences by having a neutral outside party make a decision that will be binding on both sides. Finally, the union and management must agree on when the contract begins and ends and how it may be renewed.

Collective bargaining issues include: (1) the conditions of employment, such as wage rates, fringe benefits, and job security, and (2) the relationship between the union and management.

The Bargaining Process and Some Possible Results

In general, the union wants the bargaining process to lead to as favorable a "benefits package" of wages, fringes, and working conditions as possible, consistent with the firm's being able to remain in business at its existing scale. Likewise, management wants as low a "cost package" of wages, fringes, and expenses related to working conditions as possible, consistent with being able to attract a sufficient number of workers. Somewhere between these two positions, a settlement will eventually take place.

In the bargaining process the union and management each want the other to think that a settlement cannot be reached unless the other gives in to most of its demands. So each side must put on a great show of strength. For example, the union may reveal a large strike fund, and management may build up its inventory of finished goods. Each side tries to learn how far the other will really go before giving in, while concealing its own position.

At some point both parties usually will give up their extreme positions and reach a compromise. If negotiations break down, the employer may begin a lockout or, more commonly, the union may call a strike. A **lockout** is a work stoppage in which the company closes the plant to its workers. As you know, a **strike** is a stoppage in which the workers refuse to work. The strike is the ultimate weapon of a union. It is often supported by other weapons such as picketing and boycotts. **Picketing** refers to the parading of striking workers before the entrance to their plant or other work place in the hope of convincing other workers, customers, or suppliers not to enter. A **boycott** is an attempt to block the distribution and sale of the employer's products. It can be only a refusal by striking workers themselves to buy the products, but it may include a request that others also refuse to buy from the firm.

The longer a strike or a lockout continues, the easier it generally becomes to reach an agreement. Even though tensions may rise, over time both parties suffer more and more. As the union's strike fund dwindles and the company's losses grow, a compromise solution begins to look better and better.

Both union and management put on a show of strength during the bargaining process. If negotiations break down, the employer may begin a lockout, or the union may call a strike, supported by picketing and boycotts.

THE IMPACT OF UNIONS ON WAGE RATES

As you learned earlier, a union's major goal is to improve the working conditions of its members. Management and unions usually recognize that there are important tradeoffs among different types of working conditions, such as wage rates, fringe benefits, work standards, and job security. Sometimes management will prefer to offer a more generous future pension instead of a higher present wage rate. Or it may be willing to hire larger work crews for certain jobs instead of paying a higher wage rate. Or it may even be willing to trade off some control over its work force for a lower wage rate. Since most changes in working conditions cost the employer something and may be translated into an equivalent amount of wages, our discussion will use wage rates to cover all working conditions.

Do unions have an impact on the level of wage rates? All the evidence at hand points to an answer of "yes," but it is hard to tell just how much impact they have. The average wage in unionized industries is estimated to be from 15 to 20 percent higher than the average wage in nonunionized industries. But these figures may overstate the impact of unions because these industries also hire workers with a higher-than-average skill level. On the other hand, nonunion workers may be paid higher wages as a direct result of union successes. Sometimes nonunion workers are given higher wages in order to keep out the union. When unions are successful in raising wages, some nonunion employers who are afraid to lose valuable employees will match those wage increases.

How do unions go about raising wage rates? We shall answer this question, assuming first that a union faces a purely competitive labor market. Later we shall assume that firms are monopsonistic buyers of labor.

Unions appear to have an impact on the level of wage rates, although the higher average wage rate in unionized industries may be due as much to higher skill levels as to the presence of unions.

Bargaining in a Purely Competitive Labor Market

As you learned earlier, we describe a labor market as purely competitive when the individual firms in an industry made up of a large number of firms have no influence on the wage rate. Each firm faces a horizontal supply curve of labor and hires the number of workers shown by the point where its demand curve for these workers intersects that horizontal supply curve. Figure 9 shows such a case. (It is much like our bagel-makers case in Figure 6.) In panel (a) are shown the market-supply and market-demand curves for a certain kind of worker. The equilibrium wage rate is $80 a day, and the equilibrium number of workers employed is 60,000. Panel (b) shows the supply and demand curves for one of the many companies that hire this kind of worker. The negatively sloped demand curve is that firm's *MRP* curve. The supply curve facing the company is horizontal, since it hires only a very small percentage of the total number of these workers and so has no influence on their wage rate. At the equilibrium wage rate of $80 a day, this company will hire six workers.

Under these conditions, what can a union do to raise wage rates? There are three approaches. First, it may raise the equilibrium wage rate by shifting the market-supply curve to the left. Second, it may bargain for a wage rate above the competitive market equilibrium wage rate. Third, it may raise the equilibrium wage rate by shifting the market-demand curve to the right.

FIGURE 9
Equilibrium Wage Rate and Quantity of Workers Hired in a Purely Competitive Labor Market: The Case of No Union

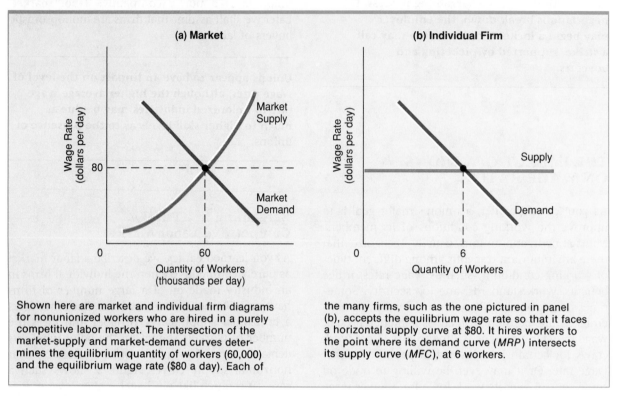

Shown here are market and individual firm diagrams for nonunionized workers who are hired in a purely competitive labor market. The intersection of the market-supply and market-demand curves determines the equilibrium quantity of workers (60,000) and the equilibrium wage rate ($80 a day). Each of the many firms, such as the one pictured in panel (b), accepts the equilibrium wage rate so that it faces a horizontal supply curve at $80. It hires workers to the point where its demand curve (*MRP*) intersects its supply curve (*MFC*), at 6 workers.

Restricting the Supply of Labor A union can raise the equilibrium wage rate of its workers by restricting their supply—that is, by shifting the market-supply curve to the left. Craft unions have often used this approach. They have in the past tried to force companies to hire only union members. By restricting the number of people who can join their unions, they gain a great deal of control over the supply. Among their methods are high initiation fees, long periods of apprenticeship, and limits on the size of the union. Restricting supply may also be helpful for industrial unions. Both craft and industrial unions pressure employers for shorter workdays or workweeks, early retirement, and longer vacations. They pressure Congress for stricter child labor, mandatory retirement, and immigration laws. All of these methods aim at reducing the supply of workers. In other words, raising the age below which a child is not allowed to work, lowering the age above which a person may be forced to retire, and keeping foreigners from entering the country all reduce the supply of labor.

In recent years unions, or associations of workers in certain occupations that act like unions, have stepped up their efforts to have states pass laws requiring a license or certificate in order to practice their trade. Licensing and certification standards are generally determined by state boards, which are customarily packed with members of the occupations with which they deal. All states require licenses for doctors, dentists, lawyers, and teachers. But many states also require certification for auto mechanics, plumbers, barbers, beauticians, dog trainers, and hundreds of other occupations. What do the practitioners of all these occupations have in common? They all have a desire to control their supply in order to bring about and maintain higher wage rates. Each time a state board raises the standards—for the stated purpose of protecting the public from frauds and cheats—it lowers the supply of workers and raises their equilibrium wage rate.

Figure 10 pictures a union's successful effort in restricting supply and in this way raising the equilibrium wage rate paid to its members. As you can see, the original equilibrium is a market wage rate of $80 a day, total employment of 60,000 workers, and employment of 6 workers by the individual firm shown. This is the same as the no-union case pictured in Figure 9. However, in Figure 10 the monopoly power of the union is used to cause the market-supply curve to shift to the left. The equilibrium market wage rate is then raised to $120 a day and the employment in the market reduced to 42,000 workers. The individual firm that hired 6 workers at $80 a day now hires only 4 workers at $120 a day. Most likely, the workers who are still employed are very pleased with the union's effort,

which raised their wage rate by 50 percent. However, the 18,000 persons who would be working in this occupation if the union had not become involved are probably worse off.

A union can raise the equilibrium wage rate of its workers by restricting their supply. This approach often costs some workers their jobs.

Above-Equilibrium Wage Agreement A second approach that a union may take to raise the wage rate of its members is to bargain for a higher-than-competitive market equilibrium wage rate. The effect of a higher-than-competitive wage agreement is shown in Figure 11. The equilibrium solution is the same as in the no-union case pictured in Figure

FIGURE 10
Equilibrium Wage Rate and Quantity of Workers Hired in a Purely Competitive Labor Market: The Case of a Union Restricting Supply

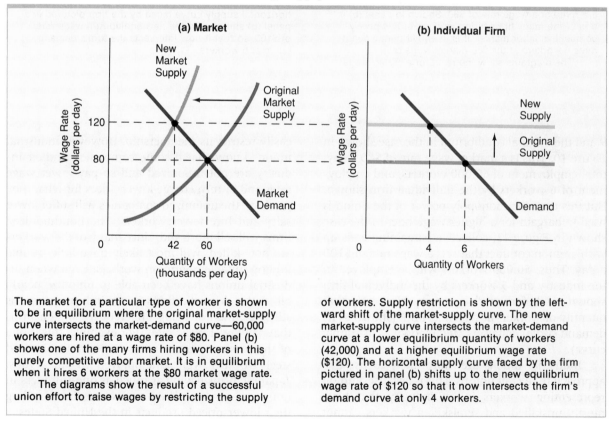

The market for a particular type of worker is shown to be in equilibrium where the original market-supply curve intersects the market-demand curve—60,000 workers are hired at a wage rate of $80. Panel (b) shows one of the many firms hiring workers in this purely competitive labor market. It is in equilibrium when it hires 6 workers at the $80 market wage rate.

The diagrams show the result of a successful union effort to raise wages by restricting the supply

of workers. Supply restriction is shown by the leftward shift of the market-supply curve. The new market-supply curve intersects the market-demand curve at a lower equilibrium quantity of workers (42,000) and at a higher equilibrium wage rate ($120). The horizontal supply curve faced by the firm pictured in panel (b) shifts up to the new equilibrium wage rate of $120 so that it now intersects the firm's demand curve at only 4 workers.

FIGURE 11
Wage Rate and Quantity of Workers Hired in a Purely Competitive Labor Market: The Case of Setting an Above-Equilibrium Wage Agreement

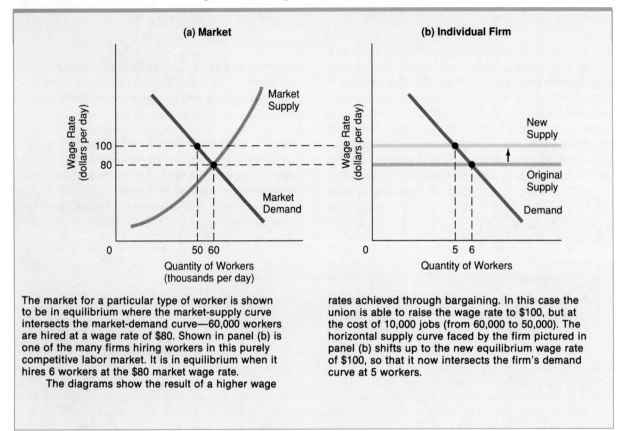

(a) Market

(b) Individual Firm

The market for a particular type of worker is shown to be in equilibrium where the market-supply curve intersects the market-demand curve—60,000 workers are hired at a wage rate of $80. Shown in panel (b) is one of the many firms hiring workers in this purely competitive labor market. It is in equilibrium when it hires 6 workers at the $80 market wage rate.

The diagrams show the result of a higher wage

rates achieved through bargaining. In this case the union is able to raise the wage rate to $100, but at the cost of 10,000 jobs (from 60,000 to 50,000). The horizontal supply curve faced by the firm pictured in panel (b) shifts up to the new equilibrium wage rate of $100, so that it now intersects the firm's demand curve at 5 workers.

9 and the original equilibrium in the case shown in Figure 10. This is a market wage rate of $80 a day, total employment of 60,000 workers, and employment of 6 workers by the individual firm shown. But this time the monopoly power of the union is used to bargain for a higher wage rate. In the case shown in Figure 11, collective bargaining ends up with a union contract that sets a wage rate of $100 a day. Thus, 50,000 workers will be employed in the industry and 5 workers by the individual firm shown. As before, each company hires only that quantity of workers at which its *MRP* (shown as its demand curve) equals its *MFC* (shown as its supply curve).

Industrial unions are more likely to use this approach than craft unions. This is because a union representing workers in an industry that hires mostly unskilled and semiskilled workers cannot

easily restrict its membership. However, industrial unions know that if some companies in their industry are not unionized and so pay lower wage rates and in turn charge lower prices for what they produce, the unionized companies will suffer lower sales and hire fewer workers. The nonunionized firms will sell more and, since many of the workers are not skilled, will most likely have little trouble finding suitable nonunion workers. Even when industrial unions have been able to unionize nearly all of the domestic firms in an industry, there is still the threat of being undercut by foreign firms that pay lower wage rates. For example, this is one of the reasons why so many American unionized steel workers were unemployed in the 1980s. Japanese firms paying as much as one-third less in hourly wages have been very successful in selling their lower-priced products in the United States.

FIGURE 12
Equilibrium Wage Rate and Quantity of Workers Hired in a Purely Competitive Labor Market: The Case of a Union Raising Demand

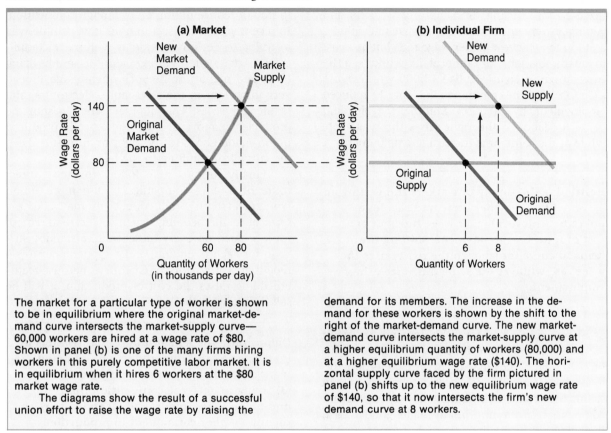

The market for a particular type of worker is shown to be in equilibrium where the original market-demand curve intersects the market-supply curve—60,000 workers are hired at a wage rate of $80. Shown in panel (b) is one of the many firms hiring workers in this purely competitive labor market. It is in equilibrium when it hires 6 workers at the $80 market wage rate.

The diagrams show the result of a successful union effort to raise the wage rate by raising the demand for its members. The increase in the demand for these workers is shown by the shift to the right of the market-demand curve. The new market-demand curve intersects the market-supply curve at a higher equilibrium quantity of workers (80,000) and at a higher equilibrium wage rate ($140). The horizontal supply curve faced by the firm pictured in panel (b) shifts up to the new equilibrium wage rate of $140, so that it now intersects the firm's new demand curve at 8 workers.

A union may also raise the wage rate of its members by bargaining for a higher-than-competitive market equilibrium wage rate. Industrial unions are more likely to use this approach than craft unions. This approach also costs some workers their jobs.

Even when industrial unions have been able to unionize nearly all of the domestic firms in an industry, there is still the threat of being undercut by foreign firms that pay lower wage rates to their workers.

Raising the Demand for Labor The demand for labor is a derived demand. When a union is able to increase the demand for the products that its workers produce, the union can shift the demand curve

for its workers to the right. Figure 12 shows such a case. The original equilibrium is the same as Figures 9, 10, and 11, with a market wage rate of $80 a day, total employment of 60,000 workers, and employment of 6 workers by the individual firm shown. The union causes the market demand curve for its workers to shift to the right, so that the new market equilibrium wage rate becomes $140 a day for 80,000 workers. (The individual firm's new *MRP*, or demand curve, then intersects its new *MFC*, or supply curve, at 8 workers.)

The demand for labor is a derived demand. When a union is able to increase the demand for the products that its workers produce, the union can shift the demand curve for its workers to the right.

In contrast to the first two approaches that we have described, this one, if successful, allows the union to "have its cake and eat it too." We recognized that restricting the supply of workers and getting an agreement on a higher wage rate enables a union to achieve a higher wage rate, but at a cost of unemployment for some of its workers. (The case shown in Figure 10 had 18,000 workers lose their jobs, and the case shown in Figure 11 reduced employment by 10,000.) Shifting the demand curve for labor to the right raises the wage rate while at the same time increasing employment.

Restricting the supply of workers and getting an agreement on a higher wage rate enables a union to achieve a higher wage rate, but at a cost of reducing employment. Shifting the demand curve for labor to the right raises the wage rate while at the same time increasing employment.

How can unions raise the demand for union workers? Unions have followed four general approaches. First, they may try to raise the productivity of the union workers. Second, they may help in selling the product. Third, they may try to decrease competition from non-union-made goods. Last, they may try to raise the union-labor component in production.

To the extent that unions are able to influence the sort of technology and resource mix that companies use in producing their products, unions can affect the companies' productivity. A lower unit cost of production is generally reflected in lower product prices, which increase the amount of product demanded (a downward movement along the product-demand curve) and, in turn, the amount of labor demanded.

A second approach that unions may take is to try to get their members to buy union-made goods and to ask family and friends to do the same. The union label that shows a product is union made is sometimes used in such a program. In a few cases, unions will go even further. The International Ladies Garment Workers Union actually gave financial aid to employers so that they could do much more advertising of their union-made goods.

The aim of this approach is to shift the product-demand curve to the right.

A third approach that unions may take is to try to stop or reduce nonunion or foreign competition. In recent years American unions have led the way in trying to get import quotas, voluntary compliance pacts, better enforcement of antidumping laws, and higher tariffs. Such attempts have been very important in the steel, auto, electronics, and textile industries. This approach tries to shift the product-demand curve for domestically produced union-made goods to the right or at least to keep the curve from shifting to the left.

Finally, unions may follow the most direct route of forcing companies to use more union workers in their production. This may take the form of featherbedding,[6] such as the requirement for a fireman on every diesel train, a standby surgeon for each operation, and a typographer to set type that won't be used. Of course, because featherbedding raises the cost of production, it will be self-defeating in the long run.

Unions raise the demand for union workers by: (1) trying to raise the productivity of union workers, (2) helping to sell the product, (3) trying to decrease competition from non-union-made goods, and (4) trying to raise the union-labor component in production.

Bargaining in a Monopsonistic Labor Market

Unions are monopolistic sellers of labor. So far we have assumed that they face firms that are pure competitors in their labor markets. We now relax that assumption to see what happens when a union bargains with monopsonistic buyers of labor. In such cases *both* the union and the firm or firms with which it bargains have monopoly power and so can influence the wage rate. The extreme case in which a union represents all of the workers in an industry and in which only a single firm hires these workers is called **bilateral monopoly**. This might be the case of a union representing workers

---

6. Recall the definition on page 716.

FIGURE 13
**Union-Management Bargaining in a
Monopsonistic Labor Market**

Shown here is a diagram much like the ones in Figure 8, where the firm is a monopsonist in the labor market. In the absence of a union, 7,000 workers would be hired (where *MFC* = *MRP*) at a wage rate of $44. Here we suppose that a union represents these workers. It will probably argue for a much higher wage rate. It might, for example, argue for $90, which according to the demand, or *MRP*, curve is the highest wage at which 7,000 workers would be hired. Without knowing about the relative power and bargaining skills of the union and management, it is not possible to determine just where they will settle. One possible settlement—at the competitive level—is shown at $60, where 10,000 workers are hired.

The firm would like to hire 7,000 workers, since this is where its *MFC* curve intersects its *MRP* curve. It would like to pay them a wage rate of $44, since the supply curve indicates that 7,000 workers could not be hired at a lower wage than that. However, the union (the monopolistic seller of these workers) will probably argue for a much higher wage rate. It will recognize, of course, that there is a tradeoff between the number of members that will be employed and the wage rate that they will receive. It might, for example, desire to have no fewer than 7,000 members employed and therefore argue for a wage of $90. At wage rates higher than $90, the firm's demand curve (*MRP*) indicates that it would not be willing to hire as many as 7,000 workers.

This is as far as economic theory takes us. Without knowing about the relative power of the union and management, their respective bargaining skills, and the policies that they adopt, we cannot predict just where the wage settlement will take place. Our model suggests that the supply curve will have a horizontal segment at whichever wage rate actually is determined and that this will determine the number of workers who will be employed. For example, as shown in Figure 13, if they settle at the competitive wage of $60 a day, 10,000 workers will be hired. Another kind of result will be described later in connection with the setting of a minimum wage rate.

In a monopsonistic labor market, both the union and the firm with which it bargains have monopoly power and so can influence the wage rate.

---

in a one-company town. Workers have to move into the town if they are hired by the company and move away from the town if they lose their jobs. More common, however, are cases in which unions face a few firms that have monopsonistic power. Examples are auto firms in the Detroit area, steel firms in the Gary, Indiana area, and aerospace firms in the Houston area.

As you learned earlier, a monopsonistic firm faces a positively sloped supply curve of labor, and its marginal-factor-cost (*MFC*) curve lies above this supply curve. Figure 13 shows such a case. You may find that it looks familiar, since the diagram is much like the ones in Figure 8. The demand curve for labor is the monopsonistic firm's *MRP* curve.

THE EFFECT OF GOVERNMENT ON WAGE RATES

Wage rates and the quantity of workers employed are not determined only by labor and management. Government often also plays an important part. In our short history of the American labor movement, we described some of the labor laws that greatly strengthened union power as well as some that held union power in check.

Taxing Employees and Employers

Whenever the government levies a tax either on employees or on employers, it affects wage rates and employment. An added tax on employees' wages effectively decreases their disposable income. This has a substitution effect in that it discourages them from working as much as before and encourages them to buy more leisure time. It also has an income effect, which works in the opposite direction. If, as is very likely, the substitution effect outweighs the income effect, the result is an increase in before-tax wage rates and a decrease in employment.

A tax on employers is even more likely to decrease the number of workers who will be employed. A tax on employers that raises their marginal factor cost of hiring workers causes them to want to hire fewer workers. Given a firm's *MRP* for certain workers, fewer will be hired when the firm's *MFC* shifts upward. For example, if government raises the payroll tax (Social Security contribution by employers), it raises the cost of hiring workers, causing firms to hire fewer people. In such a case it is hard to say whether wages were increased or not. Employers pay more for labor, but employees who keep their jobs may or may not receive more. If a higher payroll tax means higher Social Security benefits for workers, then we may say that wages have increased.

When the government levies a tax on employees or employers, it affects wage rates and employment. An added tax on employees' wages decreases their disposable income and will likely decrease employment. A tax on employers is even more likely to decrease the number of workers who will be employed.

Setting Minimum Wage Rates

Finally, the government can affect wage rates and employment by setting a lower limit on the wage rate that firms are allowed to pay. This is called a **minimum wage.** Massachusetts set a minimum wage for women and children in 1912. The first federal minimum wage law in the United States, the Davis-Bacon Act of 1931, applied only to workers on federal construction projects. It was not until the Fair Labor Standards Act of 1938 that wider coverage was provided. It set the minimum wage at 25 cents an hour for millions of workers. Since then coverage has been widely extended, and the federal minimum wage has been increased to $3.35 an hour.[7]

Minimum wage legislation does not affect all industries and all labor markets equally. Obviously it affects those industries and labor markets in which workers could otherwise be hired below the minimum wage. If workers in an industry earn between $5.50 and $24.50 an hour, a $3.35-an-hour minimum wage has no direct effect on them. However, if workers in an industry are paid less than the minimum wage, they will probably be affected.

Government can also affect wage rates and employment by setting a minimum wage (a lower limit on the wage rate firms are allowed to pay).

Competitive Labor Markets Firms in industries affected by minimum wage laws are generally in fairly competitive labor markets. Examples are found in much of retailing and especially in fast-food retailing industries. The workers are often teenagers and part-time help. Thus the competitive model is usually the most appropriate one to use in analyzing the effects of a minimum wage. Repeated in Figure 14 is the competitive-labor-market diagram that we have used several times before. We begin with an equilibrium wage of $2.00 an hour, at which 100,000 workers are demanded and supplied. When a minimum wage is set at $3.35 an hour, some "bittersweet" results can be seen. It sweetens the wage rate for 43,000 workers from $2.00 to $3.35 an hour. Forty-three thousand workers (not necessarily the same people who held the jobs originally) will be demanded at $3.35 an

---

7. At the time of this writing, in mid-1989, there are strong indications that the federal minimum wage will be raised—the question is by how much. When you read this there is a high likelihood that the federal minimum wage is closer to $4.00 per hour than to $3.35. But since we cannot foretell the future, we will use $3.35 here and in the analysis surrounding Figures 14 and 15.

FIGURE 14
The Imposition of a Minimum Wage in a Purely Competitive Labor Market

Shown here are a market-demand curve and a market-supply curve in a purely competitive labor market. In the absence of any government intervention 100,000 workers are hired at $2 an hour. When a minimum wage is imposed at $3.35 an hour, only 43,000 workers are hired, so that 57,000 workers who would otherwise have been employed in this market are not. Moreover, 42,000 additional workers who were not willing to work in this market at a $2 wage rate are willing to work at $3.35 an hour.

Monopsonistic Labor Markets Even though low-wage labor markets are generally competitive, an interesting exception to the conclusion that a minimum wage reduces employment is found in the rare case of a low-wage monopsonistic labor market. Figure 15 repeats the monopsonistic-labor-market diagram that we have used several times earlier. Equilibrium occurs where the monopsonis-

FIGURE 15
The Imposition of a Minimum Wage in a Monopsonistic Labor Market

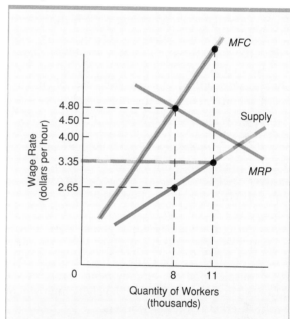

Shown here is the case in which a firm is a monopsonist in the labor market. In the absence of a union and of government intervention, 8,000 workers are hired at $2.65 an hour. When a minimum wage is set at $3.35 an hour, not only is the wage rate increased, but more workers are hired. The minimum wage causes the monopsonistic firm to face a horizontal supply curve (drawn in light blue and light purple) for the 11,000 workers willing to work for the minimum wage. Additional workers are attracted according to the remainder of the supply curve (drawn in dark blue and light blue). When the supply curve is horizontal, it also represents the firm's MFC. But for the range of employment greater than 11,000, MFC is the segment of the former MFC curve that is drawn in light purple.

The equilibrium level of employment in this case is 11,000 workers. The firm's MRP is greater than its MFC for all levels of employment below 11,000 and its MFC is greater than its MRP for all employment levels greater than 11,000.

hour. However, the bitter result of unemployment falls on the 57,000 workers who were demanded at a wage rate of $2.00, but are no longer demanded at $3.35 an hour. Furthermore, Figure 14 shows that an additional 42,000 workers who were not willing to work at $2.00 an hour are willing to work at $3.35 an hour. So the excess supply of labor created by the minimum wage is shown as 99,000 workers—the 57,000 who would have worked at $2.00 an hour plus the 42,000 who have been persuaded to offer their labor at $3.35 an hour.

When the minimum wage rate is raised above the equilibrium rate that would otherwise exist in a competitive labor market, it creates an excess supply of labor.

tic firm's *MFC* curve intersects its *MRP* curve. A wage of $2.65 an hour is paid to 8,000 workers. Now suppose that a minimum wage is set at $3.35 an hour. The minimum wage causes the monopsonistic firm to face a horizontal supply (and *MFC*) curve for the quantity of labor willing to work at the minimum wage—11,000 workers in our example. To attract more than 11,000 workers, the firm must, as before, pay higher wage rates. The supply curve is therefore kinked at that point. (In Figure 15, where the minimum wage has been set at $3.35 an hour, we have drawn the supply curve as a light blue and light purple continuous line.) Over the range of employment for which the supply curve is horizontal, so is the *MFC* curve, but when the supply curve resumes its upward slope, the *MFC* curve does the same. At 11,000 workers there is a discontinuity. Up to that level of employment the *MFC* curve is the horizontal part of the supply curve, but afterward it is that part of the former *MFC* curve that we have drawn in light purple.

Given a minimum wage of $3.35 an hour, what is the equilibrium level of employment? The answer is determined as before—where *MFC* is equal to *MRP*. Figure 15 shows that *MRP* is greater than *MFC* (the horizontal line drawn in light blue and light purple) for all employment levels below 11,000 and that *MRP* is less than *MFC* (the positively sloped part of the former *MFC* curve drawn in light purple) for all employment levels above 11,000. Thus, the equilibrium level of employment in this market is 11,000 workers.

Had the minimum wage been set at a little higher level, say at $3.50 or $4.00 an hour, equilibrium employment would be even higher. The largest number of workers are employed when the minimum wage is set at the level where supply intersects demand (*MRP*). At minimum wage levels higher than that, say at $4.50 an hour, the equilibrium level of employment is lower again. Finally, if it were set at $4.80 an hour, the same number of workers would be hired as when no minimum wage was set and the equilibrium wage rate was $2.65 an hour.

In a low-wage monopsonistic market, a raise in the minimum wage rate may cause an increase in employment.

Policymakers are intrigued by this economic analysis. What can be better than creating higher wage rates that also bring about higher levels of employment? That scenario is surely better than the competitive one, in which jobs must be traded off for higher wage rates. Unions entering monopsonistic markets may be able to raise *both* wage rates and employment. But for governments legislating minimum wage laws the problem is that low-wage labor markets (those in which the minimum wage is greater than the equilibrium wage) are generally competitive and not monopsonistic. Studies have found that minimum wage laws do raise wage rates at the expense of some jobs.[8]

WAGE DIFFERENTIALS

Up to this point in our discussion we have explained the general theory of wage determination. You have learned that, in any particular labor market, an equilibrium wage rate is determined by the interaction of the forces of supply and demand. But that general proposition does not deal specifically with a great many variables that operate to produce wage differentials. We read in our newspapers that certain actors, athletes, and chief executive officers of giant corporations receive annual salaries in the range of $1 million or more, while the help-wanted ads in those same newspapers offer a baker's helper $9,600 a year and a fast-food clerk $7,700 a year. So as not to dwell on extreme cases, Table 7 presents the average weekly earnings of workers in ten major U.S. industries in December 1988. A quick glance reveals that the wage differentials are quite great. Of course, within each of these industries there is a diversity of jobs paying widely different wage rates.

What explains wage differentials among individual workers? The answer to this question may be separated into three parts: (1) the qualifications of the workers, (2) the desirability of the job, and (3) the institutions that surround the labor market.

8. Two very telling studies are: John Peterson, "Employment Effects of Minimum Wage Laws, 1938 to 1950," *Journal of Political Economy*, October 1957, pp. 412–430; and Finis Welch, "The Rising Impact of the Minimum Wage," *Regulation*, November/December 1978, pp. 28–37.

TABLE 7
Average Weekly Earnings in Selected
U.S. Industries, December 1988

Industry	Average Weekly Earnings
Petroleum and coal	668
Motor vehicles	657
Chemicals	557
Primary metals	541
Fabricated metals	446
Food	379
Lumber and wood	356
Furniture and fixtures	326
Textile mill products	312
Apparel	234

Source: Employment and Earnings, U.S. Department of Labor, Bureau of Labor Statistics, January 1989, Table C-2, pp. 122–137.

Wage differentials are caused by: (1) worker qualification, (2) job desirability, and (3) labor market institutions.

Worker Qualifications

Workers are not all alike. They have different abilities to get a job done. In the sense of having a higher marginal product, some workers are more "productive" than others because of innate characteristics. Some people are born with greater intelligence than others. If they have sufficient money to spend on education and enough motivation, they can become nuclear physicists, neurosurgeons, or high-level computer programmers. Others are born with superior physical characteristics that make them particularly productive in certain occupations. The seven-foot-four-inch basketball player, the big, strong football player, the small, agile jockey, the jet fighter pilot with perfect vision, and the exceptionally attractive model are all examples. Yet others are born with special talents that, with proper training and motivation, allow them to become successful painters, dancers, singers, or concert pianists.

The productiveness of workers may also depend on their socioeconomic background. The

child who grows up in a home where education and good work habits are highly valued and where he or she has good role models is likely to develop the kind of personal characteristics that are appreciated in the work place.

Finally, how productive a worker will be depends greatly on his or her education and training. Intellect alone will not enable one to become a neurosurgeon or even a college professor. It takes an investment in human capital, which not everyone is willing or able to make. Since human capital comes from capital investment, we shall postpone our discussion of this important subject until the next chapter.

These differences in worker qualifications are part of the reason for wage differentials. Workers with desirable qualifications usually will receive higher wage rates than workers who do not have them.

Worker qualifications such as intelligence, physical characteristics, education and training, and personal characteristics help explain wage differentials.

Job Desirability

All jobs are not equally desirable. Even though people have different tastes and preferences for jobs, some jobs are generally considered to be more attractive than others. Most people prefer a clean job to one that is dirty. Most prefer a quiet office to a noisy factory. Safe working conditions are preferred to a dangerous work setting. Most people would rather have a challenging job with a varied pace than a boring job with a fixed pace of work. Finally, people generally have preferences about where they will work. Some parts of the country have a favorable climate or offer a relatively low cost of living, and most people would rather not have to commute.

If there were no wage differentials among jobs, most people would apply for the desirable jobs and few for the unattractive jobs. However, in a free market, employers who are swamped with applications for desirable jobs offer lower wage rates, and employers who can't fill their relatively undesirable jobs offer higher rates. In other words, people who accept unattractive jobs are paid a *compensating wage differential*. This helps to explain the relatively high wage rates paid to coal miners, construction workers on high-rise projects, and oil drillers in northern Alaska. It also helps one to understand the 1,500 commercial deep-sea divers in the United States who "are exposed to the dangers of drowning, the rigors of construction work with cumbersome gear, a lonely and hostile work environment, . . . who earned $20,000 to $45,000 per year in the mid-1970s, or about 20 percent to 170 percent more than the average high-school graduate."[9]

In a free market, people who accept unattractive jobs are paid a compensatory wage differential—relatively higher rates for relatively unattractive jobs.

Labor Market Institutions

Each labor market is surrounded by somewhat different institutions. None is perfectly free. But the sources of imperfection differ from one labor market to another. We have already discussed unions, governments, and monopsonistic employers as sources of imperfection. A union that is able to limit entry into its ranks and thereby restrict the supply of labor is able to raise wage rates for its members. Similarly, a government that sets a minimum wage for some workers or requires a license for workers to practice a craft, such as auto mechanics or hairdressing, restricts supply and raises wage rates for the affected workers. Monopsonistic employers can reduce both wage rates and employment below competitive levels.

The lack of geographic labor mobility is another source of market imperfection. For similar jobs, the wage rate may be higher in one part of the country than in another. People are often reluctant to move very far away for an only slightly better-paying job. Most reason that it doesn't pay to leave house and home and neighbors for 50 cents or a dollar more an hour. Anyway, in a year or two that wage might be lowered or the job itself lost. Furthermore, those workers who might be willing to relocate for higher-paying jobs often don't know that these jobs exist. Of course, such information is often available and if workers have the initiative to search for it, they may be able to find it. In 1982, when the industrial midwestern United States was hit very hard by recession, Texas newspapers full of help-wanted ads were readily available at newsstands in Michigan and Ohio. However, that was an extreme situation. Usually workers employed in one part of the country have limited information about jobs and wage rates in faraway places.

Finally, most labor markets suffer from some discrimination, which shows up as wage differentials. Labor market *discrimination* means that different economic opportunities are offered to persons on the basis of their personal characteristics (especially their race or sex). The Civil Rights Act of 1964 declared it illegal for firms to discriminate in hiring or promoting persons on the basis of race, religion, sex, age, or national origin and created the Equal Employment Opportunities Commission (EEOC) to oversee compliance with the law. Through court orders the EEOC can force employers to compensate workers who have been held back or underpaid because of discrimination. Also, under the law, employers are not allowed to end wage discrimination by lowering the pay of those employees who have not suffered from discrimination. Even though the United States has laws against discrimination, it is often practiced in subtle ways that are hard to detect. The actual numbers seem to indicate that enforcement is not completely effective. It is clear that some part of the wage differentials that continue to exist between whites and blacks, between whites and other minorities, and between men and women are due to discrimination. In Chapter 34 we shall present some further data.

Wage differentials are caused by such labor market institutions as unions, governments, and monopsonistic employers. Lack of geographic mobility and discrimination also cause wage differentials.

---

9. Ronald G. Ehrenberg and Robert S. Smith, *Modern Labor Economics: Theory and Public Policy* (Glenview, Illinois: Scott, Foresman and Company, 1988), p. 252.

Economics in Focus

The Share Economy

In 1984 MIT economist Martin Weitzman published a book called *The Share Economy*, in which he argued that major improvements could be made in the U.S. economy by changing the method used to compensate workers. He recommended that wages be at least partially indexed to some measure of the firm's performance or well-being—in short, that American industry adopt profit sharing or revenue sharing.

In the traditional wage system, a firm in equilibrium conditions has no incentive to hire an additional worker because the marginal factor cost of hiring that worker equals the marginal revenue product that the extra worker can produce. In the share system, on the other hand, the marginal factor cost of an additional worker is tied to the additional revenue that the worker contributes. Weitzman uses the example of a hypothetical General Motors contract that pays each worker a two-thirds share of the company's average revenue per worker. As long as each additional worker produces *some* additional revenue, it will be to GM's benefit to continue hiring workers. Thus, Weitzman argues, the economy will drive toward a higher level of employment.

In Weitzman's scenario firms have a powerful incentive *not* to raise prices. Each price increase also becomes a cost increase, because the extra revenue from the higher prices is shared with the workers. Therefore, firms would tend to meet economic stresses by lowering prices and increasing output—exactly the opposite of what most companies do now. Government would also be freer to apply monetary controls to stem inflation, since policy makers would not have to worry about causing unemployment.

With employment near its maximum, inflation under control, and output rising, there would be less poverty and more economic security. Workers would be treated better because each would be a valuable commodity. Weitzman even supposes that racial and other forms of discrimination would decrease because of the strong competition for labor.

This is indeed a rosy scenario, but some sharp criticisms have been made. For instance, in Weitzman's own GM example, hiring additional workers would reduce the company's average revenue per worker (at least in the short run) and therefore lower each worker's pay. Would established workers tolerate this? Or would they make life difficult for the new arrivals? Also, if capitalists must share all gains with the workers, will they be as willing to invest as much as they are in a wage economy?

Despite the reservations, the response to Weitzman's proposals has been enthusiastic; some have called his ideas the best since Keynes. Rather than tugging at the knotty connection between unemployment and inflation, the share economy tries to sever the knot with one bold stroke. Economists are still debating whether the blade is sharp enough.

Sources: Martin L. Weitzman, *The Share Economy: Conquering Stagflation* (Cambridge, Mass.: Harvard University Press, 1984); "The 'Share Economy': Can It Solve Our Economic Ills?" (interview with Martin Weitzman), *U.S. News & World Report,* August 26, 1985; Alan S. Blinder, "On the Share Economy: A Bottle Half Full," *Challenge,* November/December 1986; Lawrence H. Summers, "On the Share Economy: Prospects and Problems," *Challenge,* November/December 1986.

SUMMARY

1. Economists study the supply and demand for labor under different sets of conditions. Companies may hire workers in competitive or monopsonistic labor markets, and they may sell their output in competitive or monopolistic product markets. An individual company in a purely competitive product market cannot affect the price of the goods or services that it sells, nor can an individual company in a purely competitive labor market affect the wage rate that it pays to its workers. However, an individual company that is a monopolist in the product market does affect the price of the goods or services that it sells, and an individual company that is a monopsonist in the labor market affects the wage rate that it pays. (See page 702.)

2. A company that hires workers in a purely competitive labor market faces a horizontal supply and *MFC* curve. It will want to hire more workers if it sells its goods or services competitively than if it is a monopolist in the product market. This is the case because in a monopolistic product market a company's *MRP* curve is steeper than in a purely competitive one and so will intersect its *MFC* curve at a lower level of employment. (See pages 702–704.)

3. An individual worker's supply curve of labor is expected to be positively sloped at most, but not necessarily all, wage rates. At very high wage rates it may "bend back," or become negative, as the worker's income effect outweighs his or her substitution effect. (See pages 705–706.)

4. A market-supply curve of labor slopes upward because as the wage rate for that particular occupation rises in relation to the wage rates for other occupations, more and more people will offer their services for that occupation. A market-demand curve for labor is derived by aggregating all of the individual firms' *MRP* curves. The equilibrium wage rate and quantity of workers employed in a labor market is identified by the intersection of the market-supply curve with the market-demand curve. In a purely competitive labor market, that wage rate will be accepted as the going wage, and each individual firm will be able to hire as many or as few workers as it wishes to hire at that wage. (See pages 707–708.)

5. Individual firms that are monopsonists in the labor market face positively sloped supply curves of labor. This means that in order to attract more workers, they have to pay higher wage rates. Their *MFC* of hiring an additional worker is, however, higher than the wage rate paid to that additional worker, since all of the workers hired earlier must also be paid the higher wage rate. As in competitive labor markets, the equilibrium number of workers that a monopsonist will hire is found at the point where the monopsonist's *MFC* curve intersects its *MRP* curve. But, whereas for a purely competitive employer, *MFC* is equal to the equilibrium wage rate, for a monopsonistic employer, *MFC* is above the equilibrium wage rate. (See pages 708–712.)

6. Labor unions are collective organizations whose primary goals are to improve the wages and working conditions of their employee members. It was difficult for them to become established in the United States. At first many people resented them and considered them a threat to the American free-enterprise system. (See page 712.)

7. Before the formation of the AF of L in 1886, American unions were fairly local and were often involved in political actions. In a sense, they were on a roller coaster, doing well during prosperous times but being all but wiped out during recessions. With the founding of the AF of L came the beginning of business unionism. (See pages 713–714.)

8. It was not until the Great Depression of the 1930s that public opinion swung over to support the union cause. This change of heart led to the passage of two important pro-union laws, the Norris-LaGuardia Act and the Wagner-Connery Act. After World War II, Congress passed a somewhat compensating pro-employer labor law, called the Taft-Hartley Act. (See pages 715–716.)

9. An internal union struggle between craft unions, representing particular types of skilled workers, and industrial unions, representing all the workers in an industry, had been festering during the first three decades of the twentieth century. This struggle came to a head in 1938 when the AF of L expelled the CIO from its ranks. It was not until 1955 that the two finally merged. (See pages 716–717.)

10. The problem of corruption and racketeering in some unions led to the passage of the Landrum-Griffin Act in 1959. The problem of racial discrimination was a major concern of many

unions in the early 1960s. Unions supported the efforts to pass the Civil Rights Act of 1964. (See page 717.)

11. Union membership increased during the 1960s, held fairly constant during the 1970s, and fell dramatically in the 1980s. The 1960s and 1970s saw a great change in the composition of union membership. The percentage of private firm employees who were union members declined, whereas the percentage of public employees who were unionized rose. (See pages 717–719.)

12. Collective bargaining is the approach used by labor unions to negotiate with employers or their representatives. The issues in collective bargaining fall into two broad categories: (a) the conditions of employment, such as wage issues, fringe benefits, and work standards, and (b) the relationship between the union and management. The process of collective bargaining often calls for a great show of strength on both sides. The ultimate weapon of a union is the strike, which may be supplemented by picketing and boycotts. (See pages 719–720.)

13. Unions have an impact on wage rates. Just how much they are able to raise wage rates is difficult to determine. When bargaining takes place in purely competitive labor markets, unions may achieve higher wage rates through restricting the supply of labor, bargaining for an above-equilibrium wage rate, or raising the demand for labor. When bargaining takes place in a monopsonistic labor market, we cannot predict just how high the equilibrium wage rate will be. The relative power of the union and management along with the policies that they follow will dictate the result of the bargaining. (See pages 721–727.)

14. Government also has an impact on wage rates. Labor laws have strengthened unions and in turn have tended to raise wages. Whenever the government increases or decreases taxes that employees or employers must pay, it has an effect on both employment and wage rates. (See pages 727–728.)

15. Government affects some wage rates when it sets a minimum wage, or a lower limit on the wage rate that firms are allowed to pay. Generally, firms in industries affected by minimum-wage legislation are in fairly competitive labor markets, so that although the legislation increases the wage rates of some low-wage employees, it also reduces employment. In monopsonistic labor markets, the result of a minimum wage may be not only to increase the wage rate of low-wage employees but also to bring about a higher level of employment. (See pages 728–730.)

16. The general proposition that an equilibrium wage rate in a labor market is determined by the interaction of the forces of supply and demand hides a great many variables that operate to produce wage differentials. These variables may be placed in three categories: (a) the qualifications of the workers, (b) the desirability of the job, and (c) the institutions that surround the labor market. In most cases, workers who possess desirable qualifications will receive higher wages than workers who do not possess them. Workers who accept undesirable jobs are usually paid a compensating wage differential. Labor market institutions that stem from union action, government action, geographic labor immobility, and discrimination affect the degree of imperfection in a labor market and, in turn, wage rates. (See pages 730–732.)

KEY TERMS

American Federation of Labor (AF of L): a federation of national unions formed in 1886 (page 714).

arbitration: a procedure of settling union-management differences by having a neutral outside party make a binding decision (page 720).

bargaining unit: the workers for whom the union is bargaining and to whom the labor contract applies (page 720).

bilateral monopoly: when a union represents all the workers in an industry and only a single firm hires these workers (page 726).

boycott: an attempt by union members to block the distribution and sale of the products of the employer with whom they are having a labor dispute (page 720).

business unionism: an emphasis by trade unions on their economic power as a means of achieving higher real wages and better working conditions (page 714).

checkoff: a form of union security that calls for the employer to deduct or withhold union dues from workers' paychecks and to pay those dues directly to the union (page 720).

Civil Rights Act: a U.S. law passed in 1964 that prohibits discrimination in hiring, firing, or promotions based on race, color, religion, sex, or national origin (page 717).

closed shop: an arrangement that requires a person to be a member of a specific union before he or she can be hired (page 715).

collective bargaining: the approach used by labor unions to bargain for groups of workers (page 712).

Congress of Industrial Organizations (CIO): a federation of industrial unions formed in 1938 to rival the AF of L (page 715).

craft unions: Organizations representing certain kinds of skilled workers (page 713).

featherbedding: the practice of forcing an employer to pay for services that workers do not actually perform (page 716).

fringe benefits: forms of compensation other than wages (page 720).

industrial unions: unions that represent all the workers in an industry (page 713).

job security: the conditions for job continuance and the handling of grievances (page 720).

jurisdictional strike: a strike concerning which union will represent a given group of workers (page 716).

labor unions: organizations whose major goals are to improve the wage rates and working conditions of their members (page 712).

Landrum-Griffin Act: a U.S. law passed in 1959 that regulates the relationship between union governments and their members (page 716).

lockout: a work stoppage in which the company closes a plant to its workers (page 720).

minimum wage: a wage rate set by government as the lowest that firms are allowed to pay (see page 728).

monopsonistic resource market: a market in which individual companies can use their control over the purchase of a resource to influence the resource price (page 702).

Norris-LaGuardia Act: a U.S. law passed in 1932 granting workers full freedom of association and self-organization; it also limited the courts' power to issue injunctions and made the yellow-dog contract unenforceable (page 714).

picketing: the parading of striking workers before the entrance to their work place in the hope of convincing other workers, customers, or suppliers not to enter (page 720).

secondary boycott or strike: a boycott or strike against an employer other than the one with which the union has a dispute (page 716).

seniority rule: the worker who has been on the job the longest is the last to be laid off and the first to be rehired (page 720).

shop steward: a worker elected to represent the union on the job (page 720).

strike: a work stoppage in which workers refuse to work (page 720).

Taft-Hartley Act: a U.S. law passed in 1947 that forbade unions to interfere with the organization of employers, to refuse to bargain with employer representatives, or to enter into closed shop agreements (page 715).

union shop: an arrangement that allows employers to hire nonunion employees, who are then required to join the union within thirty days (page 716).

Wagner-Connery Act: a U.S. law passed in 1935 that made collective bargaining part of U.S. public policy and named several unfair employer labor practices (page 715).

work standards: rules that specify the amount of work to be performed (page 720).

yellow-dog contract: an agreement entered into by a worker that, as a condition of employment, he or she will not join a union (page 715).

DISCUSSION QUESTIONS

1. How is a firm's demand curve for labor affected by whether it sells its output in a purely competitive product market or in a monopolistic product market? Assuming that the firm hires workers in a purely competitive labor market, explain how the number of workers hired will depend on the type of product market in which the firm sells its output.

2. Explain why an individual worker's supply-of-labor curve may be backward-bending. In terms of the relationship between the substitution effect and the income effect, explain what is occurring when an individual worker's supply curve for labor is:

a. positively sloped
b. a vertical straight line
c. negatively sloped

3. Distinguish between a purely competitive labor market and a monopsonistic labor market. Why is it that the marginal-factor-cost curve for labor is equal to the supply curve of labor for a firm that is a pure competitor in the labor market whereas this marginal-factor-cost curve lies above the supply curve for a firm that is a monopsonist in the labor market?

4. What role did each of the following play in the development of the labor movement in the United States?

a. guilds
b. Knights of Labor
c. American Federation of Labor
d. Industrial Workers of the World
e. Congress of Industrial Organizations

5. Briefly discuss each of the four major pieces of labor legislation enacted in the United States during the years 1932 through 1959.

6. Briefly identify each of the following:

a. yellow-dog contract
b. business unionism

c. craft unions
d. jurisdictional strike
e. a closed shop
f. featherbedding
g. industrial unions
h. a union shop
i. a lockout

7. "Labor unions made a lot of sense during the nineteenth century and the first few decades of the twentieth century, but they seem to have outlived their usefulness." Do you agree or disagree? Why?

8. Given the case of a purely competitive labor market, discuss the three approaches that a union may take to raise the wage rates of its members. Putting yourself in the place of each of the following persons, tell which approach you would prefer and why you would prefer it:

a. a top-level official of this union
b. a working member of this union who has substantial seniority
c. a working member of this union who was recently hired

9. Without looking at Figure 14, draw a diagram showing what happens when a government imposes a minimum wage rate in a purely competitive labor market. Turn to Figure 14 to see if you have it right. What are the pros and cons of government taking such an action?

10. Discuss the most important explanations for the existence of wage differentials. Discuss five different actions that a government could take to decrease wage differentials.

32

Capital, Interest, and Investment

Preview In Chapter 30 we introduced you to the different kinds of resources and also to the theory of marginal productivity, which explains why companies demand certain amounts of these resources. Chapter 31 applied that theory to labor resources. In this chapter we apply it to capital resources—both physical capital and human capital. In analyzing capital resources, we must take account of a number of variables that usually do not concern us when we study the use of other types of resources. They stem from the fact that capital generally lasts a long time and is expected to bring a return for many years after it is created.

We begin by reviewing the characteristics of capital resources. In explaining why they are created, we present the idea of "roundabout" production of consumer goods. We also explain what determines the amount of new capital created during any particular time period. Economists refer to the creation of new capital as "investment," and we analyze what is called the "investment decision."

The investment decision relates the cost of capital to the return that is expected to be generated from the use of capital. Since the return to capital often takes place over a long period of time, a rational investment decision calls for figuring the present value of future receipts, through a process known as discounting. Discounting recognizes the opportunity cost of the invested funds and also the risks and uncertainties inherent in investment decisions. In explaining discounting, we give an example that shows how a company may find the present value of its future investment returns. Since investment returns must be discounted by using a specific interest rate, we then describe how interest rates are determined in a free market for loanable funds.

In the last part of the chapter, we compare investment decisions that involve physical capital with those that involve human capital. Human capital is different from physical capital because skills cannot be separated from the persons who possess them, and because human beings can no longer be bought and sold as slaves. Also, the returns to physical capital are mostly monetary, whereas psychic returns and consumption value are important in human capital investment decisions.

We separate the returns from human capital investment into private returns and social returns. Even though persons and companies invest in human capital in order to gain private returns, there may also be social returns. Governments invest in human capital to gain social benefits, but in doing so, they offer many private benefits as well.

Finally, we present some findings from studies done by economists who have tried to measure private and social rates of return from investing in education.

PHYSICAL CAPITAL

Recall from Chapters 4 and 30 that capital is used by business firms as an input—together with labor (including entrepreneurship) and natural resources—for the production of consumer goods and services or other capital goods. **Physical capital** such as factory buildings, machines, and equipment make it possible for companies to produce more efficiently than they can without them. Textile firms use mechanical looms, for example, because a worker can produce much more cloth with such a machine than he or she can produce by hand-weaving. Even when the cost of producing the loom is counted, cloth is still produced at a far lower cost with the loom than without it.

Capital is an input, used by business firms together with labor and natural resources to produce consumer goods and services or other capital goods. Physical capital, such as factory buildings, machines, and equipment, make it possible for companies to produce more efficiently.

Physical capital is also used by governments. Such *social capital* helps to produce the many goods and services that governments provide. Some obvious examples are government office buildings, courthouses, school buildings, and roads.

Physical capital used by governments is called social capital.

Roundabout Production

The use of capital in production was first described as **roundabout production** by the Austrian economist Eugen von Böhm-Bawerk (1851–1914). He suggested that firms have a choice between using labor and natural resources for the direct production of consumer goods and using these resources first to produce capital, which in turn is used to produce consumer goods. Choosing roundabout production means that some resources are diverted from the direct production of consumer goods. At first, some amount of consumer goods must be given up in order to produce capital goods. But once the capital goods are available for the production of consumer goods, the greater efficiency that they offer may more than compensate for the initial reduction in consumer goods. In a successful business, the expanded production that is gained through the use of capital can finance the replacement of the capital goods as they wear out and may justify adding even more capital as more and more consumer goods are being produced. And in fact, the record of the so-called "industrial revolution" of the past two hundred years shows that roundabout production works.

Roundabout production refers to the process of producing consumer goods by first using resources to produce the capital goods that will allow more efficient production of the consumer goods.

The Investment Decision

Capital goods are created by purposeful human effort. They are produced with the use of other resources. To create capital, there must be a conscious decision on the part of a business firm. When a company decides to provide money for the resources that are needed to create new capital, it has made an investment decision. The **investment decision**—whether to provide for the creation of new capital and, if so, how much—is much like the decisions that business firms make with regard to other resources. The principle of equating marginal revenue product (*MRP*) and marginal factor cost (*MFC*) presented in Chapter 30 and applied to the labor resource in Chapter 31 governs the investment decision as well. For example, a company that manufactures shoes must decide how many shoe-making machines to use. For each added machine, the company must determine how many more pairs of shoes will be produced each year and how much more revenue will be received from shoe sales, assuming no change in any other inputs by the company. This additional revenue is the marginal revenue product from the added machine. Following the principle of diminishing marginal productivity, we expect the marginal revenue product to grow smaller as more machines are added.

When a company decides whether to provide money for the resources needed to create new capital, it makes an investment decision.

Marginal factor cost is the addition to total costs that comes from adding one more machine. The company is expected to keep adding more machines as long as the marginal revenue product from an additional machine is greater than its marginal factor cost. Productivity theory predicts that when the marginal revenue product is falling and becomes equal to the marginal factor cost, investment in more machines will stop.

Productivity theory predicts that a business firm will invest in capital as long as the marginal revenue product remains greater than the marginal factor cost. Once *MRP* falls and becomes equal to *MFC*, investment will stop.

The Risks and Uncertainty of Investment The theory behind the investment decision is the same

as for decisions about other business inputs. However, there are certain points that are especially important in their application to investment. Three major problems faced in the investment decision are (1) the time problem, (2) the obsolescence problem, and (3) the derived-demand problem.

The Time Problem Investment decisions usually must be made well in advance of receiving all or even a major part of the return from that investment. Labor is paid *after* its work is performed, and raw materials are paid for *after* they are delivered. However, capital goods usually must be purchased *before* they are used in production. For this reason, there is a time lag between the time the investment is made and when the new equipment actually starts operating on the production line. Also, capital goods tend to be rather durable. Factory buildings, blast furnaces, auto body presses, tractors, computers, and mechanical looms are produced and bought with the expectation that they will last for a fairly long time. These considerations combine to make time an especially important element in the investment decision. During all of the time that a firm has invested its funds but has received only part of its return on that investment, it suffers an opportunity cost. For example, a company that decides to expand its capacity by building a new factory will not receive any return from it for the years it takes to construct the building and ready it for production. Once in production, the payoff will not come all at once but may be spread over a period of fifty years. The opportunity cost of having funds tied up in its new factory instead of in, say, stocks, bonds, or the bank must not be forgotten.

Investment decisions usually must be made well in advance of receiving all or even a major part of the return from that investment.

During all of the time that a firm has invested its funds but has received only part of its return on that investment, it suffers an opportunity cost.

The Obsolescence Problem The term **obsolescence** means that something becomes no longer useful or economically suited for its intended purpose, even though it may still be in good working order. Since capital goods are usually expected to last for many years, one cannot be sure that they will not become obsolete at some point. For example, a computer that a firm plans to use for twenty years or more may actually become obsolete after only two years because a new generation of much more efficient computers is invented and readied for commercial use.

The Derived-Demand Problem A third problem in the investment decision arises from the fact that the demand for capital goods depends on the demand for the end products that these capital goods help to produce. That is, the demand for capital goods is a **derived demand**. For this reason, the expected return from an investment is linked to a firm's expectations about the price of its end products. Since the expected return from an investment extends over a long period of time there is plenty of opportunity for the price of its end product to change. If the price of the end product is lower than expected, the firm may have a much lower than expected return from the investment. For example, the expected return from a machine used in the manufacture of video cassettes depends on the price of video cassettes. If more companies decide to produce video cassettes, or if the demand for them declines, their price will fall, and the expected return from the investment in the video cassette-making machine will have been too high.

Investment is risky because capital goods may become obsolescent, or outdated. Also, the end product that the capital goods are used to produce may decrease in price.

Discounting Future Returns The time, obsolescence, and derived-demand problems help explain why investment decisions involve more risk and uncertainty than do most decisions about other production inputs. Economists attempt to handle these problems through the process of discounting.

Recall from the last chapter that when economists predict the amount of labor that a firm will hire, their approach is to compare that firm's marginal revenue product from labor with its marginal factor cost for labor. In the simplest explanation of that process, time is not taken into account. It is assumed that the extra revenue contributed by an added worker flows into the firm during the same time period as the worker is paid for his or her labor. But time is an important element in the investment decision and must not be ignored. When making an investment decision, a firm must figure the present value of the marginal revenue product that it expects over a period of time. Then this expected present value is compared with the marginal factor cost, most or all of which is incurred at the start of the process.

Present value is the value at the present time of a sum of money to be received in the future. To get a clearer understanding of present value, imagine that someone offers you a very pleasant choice. You may choose between receiving $1,000 right now or an iron-clad guarantee that $1,000 will be paid to you one year from today. Which would you choose? If your answer is that you would take the $1,000 right now, you are making the economically correct choice. The $1,000 paid to you now is worth more than the assurance that $1,000 will be paid to you in one year. Why is that so? Because money can earn money. By merely placing the $1,000 in your neighborhood bank or savings and loan association, you may very well receive $1,060 one year from now (assuming that you are paid a 6 percent annual rate of interest). In that case, a rephrasing of our original question would be as follows: "Would you prefer $1,000 to be paid to you one year from now or $1,060 to be paid to you one year from now?" When the question is put this way, the answer is even more obvious than before. A certain sum of money received now has greater value than that same sum of money to be received in the future. Turning this sentence around and using the economist's language we can say, "The present value of a certain sum of money to be received in the future is less than the value of that same sum of money were it received now." The difference between the two values is determined by how far in the future the money will be received and by the interest rate used to discount the future payment. The rules that govern these relationships are as follows:

1. At any given interest rate, the further into the future a sum of money will be received, the lower is its present value.

2. The higher the interest rate used to discount the future payment, the lower is the present value of that future payment.

Present value is the value at the present time of a sum of money to be received in the future. At any given interest rate, the further into the future a sum of money will be received, the lower is its present value. Given the time period between the present and when the return will be received, the higher the interest rate used to discount the future payment, the lower is the present value.

Discounting is the process of calculating the present value of payments that are to be received in the future. To begin with the simplest case, let us suppose that the payment will be made one year from now. The formula is as follows:

$$PV = \frac{X}{1 + i}$$

Here PV is the present value, X is the payment to be received in one year, and i is the annual rate of interest that could be earned on alternative uses of money that face the same amount of risk. This is so because in one year $PV(1 + i) = X$. For example, if the appropriate rate of interest is 8 percent and $1,000 is the payment to be received in one year, the present value is $925.93.

$$PV = \frac{\$1,000}{1.08} = \$925.93$$

And this is the same as $925.93 (1.08) = $1,000.

Discounting is the process of calculating the present value of payments that are to be received in the future. The higher the interest rate used to discount the future payment, the lower the present value of that payment.

We use a slightly more complicated formula to derive the discounted present value of a sum of money that is to be received further into the future.

$$PV = \frac{X}{(1 + i)^t}$$

Here t is the number of years between the present time and the time that the payment will be received.

The t in the above formula reflects the fact that interest usually is compoundable. This means that each year after the first year, interest is earned not only on the principal amount of money but also on the interest paid earlier. So if $100.00 is placed in a savings account at 5 percent interest, it will be worth $110.25 after two years. The $110.25 is made up of the original $100.00 placed in the bank plus $5.00 interest earned on the $100.00 during the first year plus $5.00 interest earned on the $100.00 during the second year plus $0.25 interest earned during the second year on the $5.00 interest earned during the first year.

Interest is usually compoundable—each year after the first year, interest is earned not only on the principal amount of money but also on the interest paid earlier.

To see the importance of compounding, let us calculate the present value of $1,000 that is received after four years rather than after only one year. At 8 percent interest, the PV of $1,000 in four years is as follows:

$$PV = \frac{\$1,000}{(1.08)^4} = \frac{\$1,000}{(1.08)(1.08)(1.08)(1.08)}$$

$$= \frac{\$1,000}{1.3605} = \$735.02$$

This example may be read as follows: At 8 percent interest, $735.02 would have to be "invested" today in order to receive $1,000.00 four years from today. Another way of reading it, which is more relevant to our discussion, is this: At 8 percent interest, $1,000 to be received four years from today is presently worth $735.02.

At lower rates of interest the present value is higher. At 4 percent interest, for example, the PV of $1,000.00 in four years is $854.80. Similarly, the further away the payment date, the lower is the PV. For example, at 4 percent interest, the PV of $1,000.00 in twelve years is $624.60.

The discounting formula allows us to take care of the opportunity cost part of the problem that arises because the investment decision deals with returns that extend over a period of time. The obsolescence and end-product-price problems are more difficult to handle. In the discounting formula, higher discount rates should be used for investments that involve greater amounts of risk and uncertainty, and lower rates should be used for investments that are less risky and uncertain. But no simple formula can deal with these problems; that is, none can tell us the probability of obsolescence or of change in future end-product price. Success in making investment decisions requires wisdom, experience, and a generous helping of luck. In some ways, investment decision making is an art as well as a science.

At lower rates of interest, the present value is higher. The further away the payment date, the lower the present value.

Capital Costs and Returns For a firm to make an investment decision, such as whether or not to purchase a particular machine, both the marginal factor cost (*MFC*) of that machine and the marginal revenue product (*MRP*) expected from it must be calculated.

The *MFC* of capital is very easy to determine. It is merely the price of a capital good at the time of its purchase. The difficult problem is to estimate the *MRP* (the return to capital) in a way that is comparable. Two requirements must be kept in mind. First, the *MRP* that is to be counted must be net of all operating costs. For a machine, the *MRP* would be what this machine adds to the firm's total revenue minus the cost of labor required to operate it, the cost of energy to run it, and the cost incurred for maintenance. Second, as we have explained, the firm must discount future returns to their present values.

A firm making an investment decision must calculate both the *MFC* and *MRP* of a capital good. The *MFC* is the price of a capital good at the time of its purchase.

The *MRP* is the present value a capital good adds to the firm's total revenue minus the cost of labor, energy, and maintenance required to run it.

Suppose that a business firm is trying to decide whether to invest in a certain machine. The firm knows that its *MFC* for this machine is $35,000. Furthermore, it estimates that its *MRP* (net of all operating costs) from this machine will be $40,000 received in an income stream of $10,000 per year for four years.[1] Should the firm make this investment? To find the answer, let us calculate the present value of the *MRP* (the $40,000 income stream). If the appropriate interest rate to use for discounting the *MRP* were 2 percent, the following calculation would provide an answer of "yes."

$$PV = \frac{\$10,000}{1.02} + \frac{\$10,000}{(1.02)^2} + \frac{\$10,000}{(1.02)^3} + \frac{\$10,000}{(1.02)^4}$$

$$= \frac{\$10,000}{1.02} + \frac{\$10,000}{1.0404} + \frac{\$10,000}{1.0612} + \frac{\$10,000}{1.0824}$$

$$= \$9,803.92 + \$9,611.69 + \$9,423.29$$

$$+ \$9,238.73 = \$38,077.63$$

The present value of the *MRP* from the machine is $38,077.63, which exceeds the cost of the machine (*MFC*), which is $35,000.

If, however, the correct interest rate to use for discounting the *MRP* in this case were 8 percent, the firm would be expected to give a clear-cut answer of "no." As the following calculation shows, the present value of the *MRP* would be $33,121.29, which is less than the *MFC* of the machine ($35,000).

$$PV = \frac{\$10,000}{1.08} + \frac{\$10,000}{(1.08)^2} + \frac{\$10,000}{(1.08)^3} + \frac{\$10,000}{(1.08)^4}$$

$$= \frac{\$10,000}{1.08} + \frac{\$10,000}{1.1664} + \frac{\$10,000}{1.2597} + \frac{\$10,000}{1.3605}$$

$$= \$9,259.26 + \$8,573.39 + \$7,938.40$$

$$+ \$7,350.24 = \$33,121.29$$

Here we can see clearly why successful investment decision making calls for skill, experience, and good luck. Estimating the amount of risk and uncertainty in a given investment project is a very important part of the investment decision. Underestimating the amount of risk and for this reason

---

1. We have chosen an unrealistically short income stream in our example in order to save on space.

using too low a discount rate will cause a company to make investments that turn out to be unprofitable. On the other hand, overestimating risk and using too high a discount rate will cause the company to turn down investment opportunities that would have been profitable.

Estimating the amount of risk and uncertainty in a given investment project is a very important part of the investment decision.

INTEREST-RATE DETERMINATION

Now that you understand the important part that the interest rate plays in investment decision making, we must look deeper to discover what determines interest rates in the economy. To start this analysis, it is helpful to recognize that, in economic theorizing, the interest rate is like the wage rate paid to hire labor or the rental rate paid to obtain the use of natural resources. Just as wages pay for the use of someone's time and skill, and just as rent pays for the use of someone's natural resources, interest pays for the use of someone's money. Also, just as wage rates are determined in a labor market or rent rates are determined in a natural resource market, interest rates are determined in a **loanable funds market**. This market consists of arrangements and procedures to carry out transactions between people who want to borrow money and people who want to lend money.

Interest pays for the use of someone's money. Interest rates are determined in a loanable funds market, which consists of arrangements and procedures to carry out transactions between people who want to borrow money and people who want to lend money.

Figure 1 pictures supply and demand in a loanable funds market. On the horizontal axis are quantities of money demanded and supplied for loans (called **loanable funds**). On the vertical axis

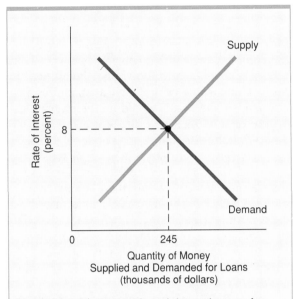

FIGURE 1
Market for Loanable Funds

Shown here are the supply and demand curves for loanable funds. The curves show that at higher rates of interest more loanable funds will be supplied and less will be demanded and at lower rates of interest less loanable funds will be supplied and more will be demanded. In the case shown, the equilibrium rate of interest is 8 percent, at which $245,000 is supplied and demanded.

are rates of interest, which act as prices in bringing equilibrium between quantities of loanable funds demanded and supplied. The supply curve shows how lenders respond to interest-rate changes (if other things remain unchanged). The demand curve shows how borrowers respond to interest rate changes (if other things remain unchanged). In this case, the equilibrium rate of interest, which balances the quantity demanded and the quantity supplied, is 8 percent.

At higher rates of interest, more loanable funds will be supplied and less will be demanded, and at lower rates of interest, less loanable funds will be supplied and more will be demanded. At equilibrium, the quantity of loanable funds supplied equals the quantity demanded.

The Investment Demand for Loanable Funds

The $35,000 machine in the earlier example is just one of many capital goods that might be bought by that company or by other companies in the economy. We have already shown that investment in this machine would be profitable at an interest rate of 2 percent and that it would not be profitable at an interest rate of 8 percent. From this, we can reason that there is some interest rate, higher than 2 percent but lower than 8 percent, at which the company would just break even from investing in this machine. In other words, there is some interest rate at which the present value of the future net income from the machine (*MRP*) is exactly equal to the $35,000 cost of the machine (*MFC*). By trial and error, we estimate that this interest rate is 5½ percent. This is known as the *internal rate of return* on this investment.

Figure 2 shows where the machine in our example fits into the investment-demand curve for loanable funds. As shown by the green area, this machine involves the money between $315,000 and $350,000 along the horizontal axis of this figure. If the interest rate were 5½ percent, this investment would have been exactly at the margin of profitable undertakings.

The demand curve for investment loans in Figure 2 combines the demand for the machine in our case with the demands for many other possible investments. Those investments that promise to pay off at a higher rate (have a higher internal rate of return) are located to the left of our machine along higher reaches of the demand curve. Those that pay off at a lower rate (have a lower internal rate of return) are located to the right along the lower reaches of the demand curve. Thus, the investment-demand curve for loanable funds shows a range of many possible investments, arranged in descending order of their expected returns.

As you learned in Chapter 5, a demand curve may *shift* because of a change in some variable other than the one shown on the vertical axis of a graph. Shifts in the investment demand for loanable funds can come from a change in any variable other than the interest rate. You were introduced to some of these other variables when we discussed business expectations about the likelihood of obso-

FIGURE 2
Investment Demand for Loanable Funds

This graph shows the investment-demand curve for a loanable funds market. The green area represents the annual interest payment at a 5½ percent rate of interest for the $35,000 machine under consideration for investment by the firm in our example. Its 5½ percent interest rate (internal rate of return) determines its position along the demand curve compared with other potential investments. Investments with higher internal rates of return make up the demand for investment loans at higher rates of interest. Those with lower internal rates of return make up the demand at lower rates of interest.

lescence for the machine or the likelihood that the price of the end product would rise or fall. We know that all these matters involve risk and uncertainty, but the borrower nevertheless must make his or her best estimate. When the best estimates about these matters change, the investment-demand curve for loanable funds shifts. Changes that promise greater returns shift the curve to the right, and changes that promise smaller returns shift the curve to the left.

The internal rate of return on an investment is that interest rate at which the present value of the future net income from the investment is exactly equal to the cost of the investment.

Other Demands for Loanable Funds

In this chapter, we have been most interested in investments made by business firms for such production inputs as machinery and equipment. We have noted, however, that there are other demands for loanable funds. Households sometimes want to borrow money to finance consumption purchases. This happens when members of households want to have consumption goods and services now and do not want to wait until they have saved enough money to buy them. If the desire for present consumption is strong enough, the household may be willing to pay the interest needed in order to buy now and save later.

Governments are responsible for another component of the demand for loanable funds. Like households, governments may also want to buy more today than can be financed from their current income (tax receipts). This means that there is a budget deficit. When this happens, governments enter the market as demanders for loanable funds.

The household and the government demands for loanable funds are also expected to be inversely related to the rate of interest. In other words, as the interest rate goes up, the quantity demanded for loans goes down, and vice versa. For this reason, the combined demand curve for all sources (firms, households, and governments) will have a negative slope. Shifts in household and government demand for loanable funds can arise from many non-interest-rate variables. For example, if households become more optimistic about the future, their demand for loans may increase, since they expect to have no trouble in repaying the loans. Government demand for loanable funds, on the other hand, would be expected to shift to the right if the economy goes into recession and government receives less money in taxes.

There are other demands for loanable funds besides business firm investment: households and governments also borrow money. Household and government demands for loanable funds are inversely related to the rate of interest: as the interest rate goes up, the quantity demanded for loans goes down, and vice versa.

The Supply of Loanable Funds

What about the supply side of the loanable funds market? Here we must focus on households, firms, and governments that are saving, rather than spending, money. They are receiving more income than they wish to spend today. Their preferences between purchasing things today and postponing purchases until sometime in the future are just the opposite of the preferences of those on the demand side of this market. We are quite sure that this supply curve will slope upward to the right, as we have shown in the earlier figures. At low interest rates, these potential lenders are not nearly as eager to make loans as they are at high rates of interest.

The supply curve for loanable funds can shift in response to changes in variables other than the interest rate. Much depends on the outlook and attitudes of the people who are lenders or potential lenders. If their attitudes change so that they want to use their wealth today and not postpone using it until later (that is, if their time preference changes in favor of more present consumption), the supply curve will shift to the left and interest rates will rise, if other things remain unchanged. Of course, if their time preference changes in the other direction, the supply curve will shift to the right and interest rates will fall, if other things remain unchanged. During much of the 1980s, an important part of the supply of loanable funds came from foreigners who found returns better in the U.S. loanable funds market than in the loanable funds markets in their home countries.

In Figure 1 the demand and supply for loanable funds are in equilibrium at $245,000 a year when the interest rate is 8 percent. At lower interest rates, more would be demanded than supplied, pushing the interest rate upward. At higher interest rates, more would be supplied than demanded, pushing interest rates down. The equilibrium interest rate itself may move up or down because of shifts in the demand curve, supply curve, or both.

The supply of loanable funds comes from households, firms, and governments that are saving money. At low interest rates these potential lenders are not as eager to make loans as they are at high rates of interest.

Many Different Interest Rates

In beginning this section on interest-rate determination, we said that the interest rate is like the wage rate paid to hire labor or the rental rate paid to obtain the use of natural resources. Now we must add that, just as there are different wage rates for different kinds of labor and different rental rates for different kinds and locations of natural resources, so also are there different interest rates for different kinds of loans. The main reason for interest-rate differences is that some loans involve more risk than others. A higher interest rate will be charged on high-risk loans than on low-risk loans because the lenders insist on receiving enough interest from loans that are paid off to make up for the losses they will suffer on loans that are not paid off. At any given time, there are different kinds of loans involving many different degrees of risk. So it is not surprising that many different interest rates exist, all at the same time.

Interest-rate differences occur primarily because some loans involve more risk than others. A higher interest rate is charged on high-risk than on low-risk loans.

HUMAN CAPITAL

In Chapter 4, when we first presented the categories of resources, or factors of production, you learned that the skills that people use in combination with their labor effort are a kind of capital, called human capital. **Human capital** is that part of the productive power of individuals that has been developed through earlier expenditures for education, job training, and health care. The term recognizes that the capital concept can be applied to human beings as well as to physical capital. Economists speak of "investing in people" just as they do of "investing in machines."

Human beings have different degrees of productive capability. Just how good a "producer" a person is will depend on several important variables. One is how intelligent a person is. People are born with different kinds and degrees of intellec-

tual ability, which can have an effect on their productive capability. Another variable is a person's socioeconomic background. The value system within which a person grows up affects his or her outlook on life including the attitude toward work. How productive a person is will also depend on his or her physical and mental health and the type and amount of education and on-the-job training he or she has received.

Human capital is that part of an individual's productive power that has been developed through earlier expenditures for education, job training, and health care. Productive capability varies from individual to individual depending on such variables as intelligence, socioeconomic background, physical and mental health, education, and training.

Investing in human capital—making people healthier, better educated, and more highly trained—may be thought of as capital creation. As with all capital creation, this form of investment uses the resources of the economy. Achieving a healthier population takes medical facilities, the services of physicians and other medical personnel, nutritious food, and healthful living and working conditions. To educate people requires school buildings, trained teachers, books, and time for people to attend classes and to study. Developing job skills takes instructors and time away from the routine work tasks. Whether or not to allocate these scarce resources to human improvement, and if so, to what extent, is the human capital investment decision.

Investing in human capital may be thought of as capital creation.

The Human Capital Investment Decision

The economic theory of the investment decision pertaining to human capital is like that involving physical capital. That is, investment in human capital is predicted to take place when the expected return from an investment exceeds its cost. However, there are some added complications, which differ depending on who is making the human capital investment decision. Business firms, for example, are expected to be most interested in the contribution that the investment will make to profits. That is, they are looking for monetary returns. Individuals, however, are expected to take into account more than the expected monetary returns when they decide whether or not to invest in their own or someone else's education. They will most likely consider that decision as involving not only investment but also consumption. Returns to investment in human capital by government also entail more than the monetary returns. A government may invest in its citizens' education in order to help them become better-informed voters or to bring about a more equal distribution of income.

Since the kinds of returns to investment in human capital differ so much, we shall treat individuals, firms, and governments separately.

Individuals Investing in Human Capital You, and probably your parents (or other benefactors), are investing in your higher education. How did you and they make that decision? Most likely in a more casual way than we describe in this chapter. It may have been taken for granted that you would go to college. But why? Why does it "obviously" pay to make this investment in you? In economic language, the answer is based on the results that are obtained from comparing the costs of this investment with the expected return from it.

Costs of the Investment As in the case of physical capital, the cost is somewhat easier to identify and measure than is the return. For example, you may estimate that the out-of-pocket cost to you and your family of a four-year college education is $12,000 tuition, $6,000 for added living expenses away from home, and $2,000 for books and supplies. To this total you might add $60,000 in lost wages—the difference between what you might earn if you were not going to college and what you expect to earn at part-time summer jobs while attending college. The total cost comes to $80,000.

Returns from the Investment The estimates of the returns call for more guessing. You may dis-

cuss the present and expected salary ranges in the field of your choice with counselors, placement officers, and friends of the family whom you trust, and on that basis estimate your differential income stream for the years of your working life. You may estimate, for example, that your monetary income will be $8,000 a year higher with a college degree than without one and that your expected working life after college is thirty years. Your $80,000 cost is incurred during your college years. However, your monetary return from the college education is not the whole $240,000 (30 × $8,000 = $240,000) of additional salary, but only the present value of that additional income stream. Using the present-value formula presented earlier in this chapter, we would have to discount each $8,000 annual return by an appropriate interest rate over the number of years between college graduation and the time when you expect to receive it. The sum of the thirty separate present-value calculations would yield the present value of the entire monetary return from your college education. If, let us say, you choose 8 percent as the appropriate rate of interest by which to discount, then the present value of the $240,000 monetary return is $90,048.[2] So the present value of your monetary return is more than $10,000 higher than your cost. On that basis alone, you and your family may decide to invest in your college education.

Let us now suppose that the present value of your monetary return from investing in your college education were below your cost. This could be the case when you estimate a lower monetary return, a shorter working career, or use a higher interest rate by which to discount the return. For example, had you estimated that your income would only be $7,000 a year higher with a college degree than without one, the present value of your income stream over thirty years at 8 percent interest would be $78,792. Similarly, if the appropriate interest rate to discount the return were 10 percent, the present value of $8,000 a year over thirty years would be $75,416. Does that mean that you would not attend college? Only you can answer that question. Possibly you and your family would still decide to invest in your college education. In that

2. To save time, use a present-value table. These are found in the back of most basic mathematics books.

case, you and they may be expecting more than just a monetary return.

Economists refer to the nonmonetary returns from investing in human capital as **psychic returns**. Psychic returns from investing in your college education might come to you in the form of a higher social position, a better-educated marriage partner, pleasing your family, self-satisfaction, or the opportunity to obtain more enjoyable work in a more desirable location. Some of these returns may come to your parents in the form of pride in a son or a daughter with a college education and in knowing that they had a part in making that possible.

Psychic returns are the nonmonetary returns from investing in human capital.

Besides the monetary and psychic returns that we have discussed so far, an individual's decision to add to his or her own human capital may be in part a *consumption* decision. Most students consider the college years to be fun and therefore worth paying for. You may be less sure of that right before an important exam, but most students agree that going to school "beats working."

Besides the monetary and psychic returns, an individual's decision to add to his or her own human capital may be in part a consumption decision.

It is very difficult to separate the investment and consumption components in an individual's human capital investment–consumption decisions. It is also difficult to translate psychic returns into monetary returns. But there is little doubt that consumption and psychic returns are important considerations. A high school graduate may want very much to become an accountant and to associate with people who have attended college. He or she may also expect the college years to be enjoyable ones. Such a person will probably spend the money for a college education even if the expected present value of the monetary return is below the expected cost of going to college.

Firms Investing in Human Capital Individuals are not the only ones to invest in human capital. Firms may invest in human capital as a strategy for gaining higher profits. Sometimes firms provide their employees with free medical checkups, nutritious lunches, and various kinds of safety equipment. These expenditures may be fringe benefits and part of total employee compensation (along with wages), but they may also be profitable investments in the firms' employees. Similarly, firms that offer training programs for their employees probably do so partly because they believe that such investments in human capital will be profitable to themselves. For example, the present value of the return from an investment of $1,000,000 in a training program for young managers may be significantly greater than $1,000,000. The return will depend on how much more productive the managers become as a result of the training that they receive and also on how long the trainees decide to remain with the company.

The fact that employees can leave their employer is unique to the human capital investment decision. When a firm invests in physical capital, it has a clear property right to the machine or building. Since firms do not have a property right in people—slavery being illegal—a firm cannot be sure that an employee trained at company expense will not soon resign. In fact, the U.S. labor force is quite mobile. Employees frequently "job hop" to improve themselves. For this reason, U.S. firms are generally reluctant to invest very much in human capital.

By contrast, in Japan it is common for workers to be employed by the same firm for their entire working lives. It follows, then, that Japanese companies are much more willing to invest in human capital than are American companies.

In the United States, human capital investment by employers is found to a more limited extent. As an investment it is most justified in fields such as professional sports and the armed forces, where courts have been willing to uphold certain work contracts. In some professional sports leagues, players are not permitted to change employment from one team to another for a specified number of years. The military offers specialized training only to persons who are willing to sign up for a certain number of years.

Firms invest in human capital as a strategy for gaining higher profits. Because the U.S. labor force is very mobile, U.S. firms are generally reluctant to invest as much as they would otherwise in human capital.

Government Investing in Human Capital So far we have dealt only with private investment in human capital—private individuals and business firms seeking private returns. But, governments may also invest in human capital. Public investment in human capital is aimed at providing returns that benefit society as a whole.

There is a good deal of overlapping between government and private decisions. On the one hand, government investments can bring about both private and social returns. On the other hand, private decisions also can bring about both kinds of return. For example, a private investment in education not only offers a higher earning potential to those persons receiving the education but also produces better-informed citizens. An expansion of the frontiers of knowledge that is financed privately can increase both an individual's income and the well-being of the society as a whole. In a similar way, public investment results not only in social returns but also in private returns, such as higher earning potential for those citizens who are direct recipients of government-sponsored training programs or education grants.

In most countries the government is an important investor in human capital. The justification for this investment is that the social returns are substantial. Better-informed citizens are very important for the satisfactory functioning of a democratic country. The society as a whole depends on educated people to carry on the research and development leading to the discovery of the new products and new processes that raise the nation's standard of living. How productive people are and how much they earn affects a society's distribution of income and even its unemployment rate. Serious underinvestment in human capital might occur if the investment decision were left entirely to the private sector. To understand this point, suppose for a moment that education in the United States were not supported by the government. Would

nearly all children attend primary school? Would the vast majority complete high school, and about half attend college? Would our citizens' health suffer if we had no programs for food stamps, subsidized housing, and hot school lunches? It is not easy to answer such questions in a precise way. But to the extent that the returns to investment in human beings are social rather than private, economists predict that the free market acting alone would devote fewer of our resources to such human capital investments.

Government (public) investment in human capital is aimed at providing returns that benefit society as a whole. Government investments can also bring about private returns.

Some Findings on the Returns from Education

Several economists have studied the economics of human capital and have tried to calculate the costs and monetary returns, both private and public. These studies have generally been limited to investment in formal education. For example, the 1979 Nobel Prize winner Theodore W. Schultz, a pioneer in this field, calculated that in 1949 the social rate of return on an investment in a grade school education was about 35 percent.[3] Another economist, Gary S. Becker, calculated that the private rates of return from a high school education were 16 percent in 1939, 20 percent in 1949, 25 percent in 1956, and 28 percent in 1958. He found private rates of return from investing in a college education to be much lower but still very high in relation to rates of return possible from other forms of investment. Specifically, he calculated that the private rate of return from investing in a college education ranged from 12 percent to 15 percent for the years 1939 to 1961.[4] The lowest calculated rates of return have been for investment in graduate studies. Orley Ashenfelter and Joseph D. Mooney found that in 1960 private returns to investing in an M.A.

3. Theodore W. Schultz, *The Economic Value of Education* (New York: Columbia University Press, 1963).
4. Gary S. Becker, *Human Capital,* 2nd ed. (New York: National Bureau of Economic Research, 1975).

FIGURE 3
A Comparison of the Median Income of College-Educated Men and Women and High School-Educated Men and Women (in thousands of dollars)

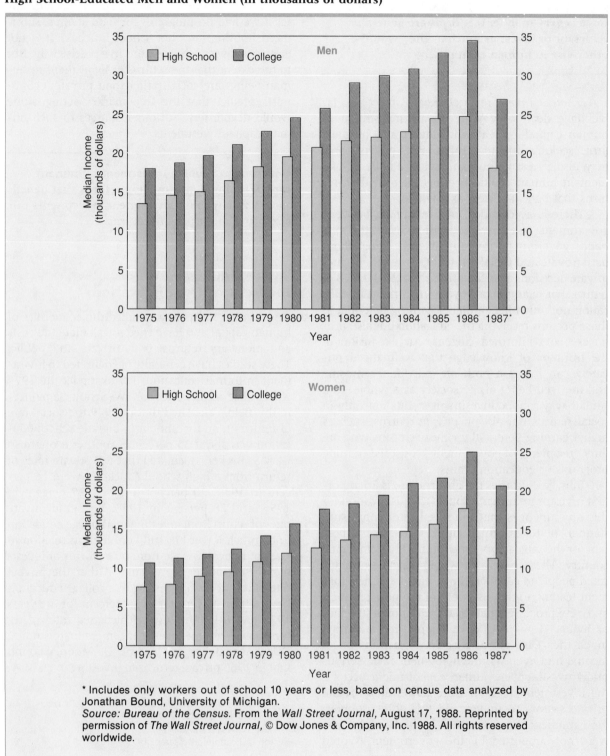

* Includes only workers out of school 10 years or less, based on census data analyzed by Jonathan Bound, University of Michigan.
Source: Bureau of the Census. From the *Wall Street Journal*, August 17, 1988. Reprinted by permission of *The Wall Street Journal*, © Dow Jones & Company, Inc. 1988. All rights reserved worldwide.

degree were under 8 percent and that returns to the Ph.D. degree ranged between 7 percent and 11 percent.[5]

Data from the 1960s by G. Hanoch, showing private monetary rates of return to formal education, are summarized in Table 1.[6] Notice that completing the eighth year of schooling (the last year of junior high school) provides a private monetary return of 22 percent, the twelfth year of schooling (the last year of high school) provides a 16 percent return, the sixteenth year of schooling (the last year of college) provides a 12 percent return, and the seventeenth or higher year (master's, doctoral, or professional school) provides a private monetary return of 7 percent.

Some more recent findings indicate that the private rate of return to higher education in the United States dropped in the 1970s and then sharply rebounded in the 1980s. According to U.S. Census Bureau reports, male college graduates in the work force earned 23.8 percent more than high school graduates in 1979 and 39.2 percent more in 1986. Likewise, female college graduates increased their differential from 27.9 percent to 40.5 percent between the same two years.

Figure 3 compares the median income of college-educated men and women versus high school-educated men and women. The difference—the "college edge"—is substantial. The greater relative advantage of college graduates appears to have arisen because pay gains for high school graduates slowed in the 1980s. Increasingly high technology in the work place operates to the disadvantage of workers with only a high school education. (Note that the 1987 data include only workers out of school for ten years or less and therefore are not comparable to the data for earlier years.)

It is important to recognize that these data re-

TABLE 1
Estimated Rates of Return to Investment in Human Capital: Private Rates of Monetary Return to Investment in Additional Years of Formal Schooling

Additional Year of Schooling	Private Rate of Monetary Return (percent)
8th	22
9th	16
10th	16
11th	16
12th	16
13th	7
14th	7
15th	7
16th	12
17th or more	7

Source: G. Hanoch, "An Economic Analysis of Earnings and Schooling," *The Journal of Human Resources,* 2, 1967, pp. 310–329 (data reprinted by permission of The University of Wisconsin Press); summarized by John T. Addison and W. Stanley Siebert, *The Market for Labor: An Analytical Treatment* (Santa Monica, California: Goodyear Publishing Co., 1979), p. 158. Used by permission.

fer to all college degrees, whereas the returns differ greatly depending on a student's major. There is no market for college-educated workers, but rather there are many markets, each for a different type of college-educated specialist. In recent years degrees in computer science, engineering, chemistry, and mathematics have offered much higher monetary returns than degrees in the humanities and social sciences such as philosophy, history, and sociology. Finally, remember that these data completely neglect psychic returns and the consumption value of attending college.

5. Orley Ashenfelter and Joseph D. Mooney, "Graduate Education, Ability, and Earnings," *Review of Economics and Statistics,* February 1968, Vol. 50, pp. 78–86.

6. G. Hanoch, "An Economic Analysis of Earnings and Schooling," *Journal of Human Resources,* 2, 1967, pp. 310–329.

Economics in Focus

Investing in Education

In 1987 New York Telephone Company administered a simple test on basic math, reading, and reasoning skills to 57,000 job applicants. Of these, 54,900 flunked the test. Similarly, when Chemical Bank wants to hire a teller trainee, it must interview about 40 applicants before finding one who can handle the job.

Those who study the U.S. educational system are not surprised by such statistics. The 1980s were a decade of rising alarm about the state of American education. The functional literacy rate is down to roughly 80 percent, compared to 95 percent in Japan. A third of the nation's recent high school graduates cannot figure out how much change they should receive when they order two items from a lunch menu and hand the cashier $3.00. Many experts contend that poor education of the work force dooms the United States to the status of a second-rate economy unless the trend is quickly reversed. Indeed, the landmark educational report *A Nation at Risk,* issued in 1983 by the National Commission on Excellence in Education, contained this dire conclusion:

> If an unfriendly foreign power had attempted to impose on America the mediocre educational performance that exists today, we might well have viewed it as an act of war.

To regain its competitive edge, the United States needs a massive investment program in human capital—in the education and training of the young people who will form the work force of the future.

A host of educational reports have offered recommendations. Most of the analysts want to improve the salaries and status of teachers in order to attract more qualified people to the schools. Others recommend that the school year be lengthened: on average, American students spend only 180 days in school each year, compared to 220 days for French and West German students and 240 days for Japanese. The educational reports also outline a myriad of potential reforms in teaching methods, teacher training, school organization, and curriculum.

The problem is aggravated by the changing nature of the jobs available in today's economy. As business grows increasingly high-tech, the skills demanded become more complex. Even blue-collar jobs require vastly more sophistication than they did a few decades ago.

Throughout the 1980s state governments acted to raise performance standards for both students and teachers. Some corporations have begun to assist by making cooperative arrangements with local schools, offering funds, equipment, or help with the curriculum. But many analysts say that the steps taken so far are not nearly enough. They believe that the United States must do more to develop our human capital.

Sources: "Needed: Human Capital," Special Report, *Business Week,* September 19, 1988, p. 100ff.; David Whitman et al., "The Forgotten Half," *U.S. News & World Report,* June 26, 1989, pp. 44–53; Dan Subotnik, "Productivity's Little Secret: Hard Work," *New York Times,* May 14, 1989; Allan C. Ornstein and Daniel U. Levine, *Foundations of Education,* 4th ed. (Boston: Houghton Mifflin, 1989), pp. 32–35, 578–579, 605–606, 613–614; National Commission on Excellence in Education, *A Nation at Risk: The Imperative for Educational Reform* (Washington, D.C.: U.S. Department of Education, 1983), p. 14.

SUMMARY

1. Capital is a resource, or factor of production, used in combination with other resources to produce consumer goods and services or other capital goods. Capital may be either physical capital, such as factory buildings and machines, or human capital, such as education and training. (See page 740.)

2. The use of capital in production is sometimes described as "roundabout production." That term recognizes that producers often have a choice between using labor and natural resources directly to produce consumer goods and services or first using these noncapital resources to produce capital, which is in turn used to produce the consumer products. Long-term efficiency is often increased by following the roundabout production method. (See page 740.)

3. The creation of capital is called investment. Whether to provide for the creation of new capital, and if so, how much, is called the investment decision. Because a business firm will invest in order to make a profit, it is expected to invest up to the point where the marginal revenue product of capital is equal to its marginal factor cost. (See pages 740–741.)

4. When making the investment decision, firms face problems related to the fact that the cost of capital is usually incurred well before the returns to capital are received. Capital is durable and generally provides returns in the form of an income stream over a considerable period of time. Not only do firms suffer an opportunity cost (the time problem), but they also must contend with the risks and uncertainties of obsolescence and the possible decrease in end-product prices (the derived-demand problem). (See pages 741–743.)

5. The concept of present value recognizes that the value of a certain sum of money to be received in the future is less than the value of that same sum of money if it were received now. At any particular interest rate, the further into the future that a sum of money will be received, the lower is its present value. The higher the interest rate used to discount the future payment, the lower is the present value of that future payment. (See pages 742–743.)

6. Discounting is the method used to deter-

mine the present value of returns that will be received in the future. Future returns from capital goods must be discounted to their present values to make the marginal revenue product of capital comparable to its marginal factor cost, most or all of which is incurred at the time the investment is made. Only the present value (*PV*) of the marginal revenue product should be used to compare with the marginal factor cost. (See page 743.)

7. Interest is payment for the use of someone's money. Interest rates are determined in markets for loanable funds. The equilibrium rate of interest is the interest rate at which the quantity demanded of loanable funds is just equal to the quantity that lenders are willing to supply. If a firm finds that the internal rate of return for a particular investment is below the equilibrium market rate of interest, then it will not undertake this investment. (See page 745.)

8. The demand for loanable funds comes from business firms, households, and governments. Business firms seek profits through investment. Because households want to buy consumer goods, they are often willing to pay the interest that will enable them to buy them now rather than later. Governments may also want to spend more than they can finance from their current tax receipts. The demand curve for loanable funds is expected to be negatively sloped, since high interest rates will discourage borrowing and low interest rates will encourage borrowing. (See pages 746–747.)

9. The supply of loanable funds comes from savers. At times, business firms, households, and governments don't want to spend all of their income right away. The supply curve for loanable funds is expected to be positively sloped, since high interest rates will usually encourage saving and lending, and low interest rates will usually discourage saving and lending. (See page 747.)

10. Human capital is that part of the productive power of individuals that has been developed through earlier expenditures for education, job training, and health care. How good a "producer" a person is will depend partly on the amount that has been invested in him or her. Whether or not to allocate scarce resources to human capital, and if so, in what amount, comprises the human capital investment decision. (See page 748.)

11. Individuals invest in human capital for

both monetary and psychic returns. They may also consider their expenditures for something like higher education to be partly consumption. Therefore, in analyzing an individual's "human capital investment decision," all three returns—monetary, psychic, and consumption—must be weighed against his or her cost. (See pages 748–749.)

12. Firms invest in human capital in order to gain higher profit. They do not have a property right to people as they do to physical capital. Therefore, in countries like the United States, where labor is quite mobile, firms are more reluctant to invest in training their employees than in a country like Japan, where employees are more likely to remain with the same firm. (See page 750.)

13. Governments invest in human capital in order to benefit society as a whole. Their aim may be to have better-informed citizens or to expand the frontiers of knowledge. But just as private investment in human capital yields some social returns, government investment in human capital results in some private returns. (See page 751.)

KEY TERMS

derived demand: the demand for capital goods depends on the demand for the end products that these capital goods help to produce (page 742).

discounting: the process of calculating the present value of payments that are to be received in the future (page 743).

human capital: that part of the productive capability of individuals that has been developed through earlier expenditures for education, job training, and health care (page 748).

investment decision: a decision a firm makes about whether to provide for the creation of new capital and, if so, how much (page 741).

loanable funds: the money demanded and supplied for loans (page 745).

loanable funds market: the arrangements and procedures needed to carry out transactions between people who want to borrow money and people who want to lend money (page 745).

obsolescence: the condition of becoming less useful in production (page 741).

physical capital: the factory buildings, machines, and equipment that make it possible for companies to produce more efficiently (page 740).

present value: the value at the present time of a sum of money to be received in the future (page 742).

psychic returns: nonmonetary returns from investing in human capital (page 750).

roundabout production: using natural resources and labor to first produce capital, which in turn is used to produce consumer goods (page 740).

DISCUSSION QUESTIONS

1. What is meant by roundabout production? Under what circumstances would roundabout production add to an economy's efficiency? Give an example of roundabout production.

2. An investment decision by a firm involves three major problems:
   a. the time problem
   b. the obsolescence problem
   c. the derived-demand problem
Briefly explain the nature of each of these three problems.

3. When calculating the return to capital, why should a firm use the present-value technique?

4. Explain the relationship between the present value of the return to an investment and:
   a. the discount rate
   b. the number of years between the present and the time that the return will be received
   c. the number of payments of a given size that constitute the return in the form of an income stream

5. Would you expect a firm to invest in a certain machine under the following conditions?
   a. The cost of the machine is $10,000.
   b. Using a 5 percent discount rate, the present value of the firm's net return from this machine is $12,000.
   c. Using an 11 percent discount rate, the present value of the firm's net return from this machine is $9,300.

d. The equilibrium rate of interest in the relevant loanable funds market is 12 percent. Why or why not?

6. Distinguish between physical capital and human capital. Give three examples of each. Discuss the differences and the similarities in analyzing a possible investment in physical versus human capital.

7. John learns that it will cost him $50,000 in out-of-pocket expenses and $50,000 in forgone income to attend a professional school. He estimates that the degree he will attain will add $5,000 per year to his income for twenty-five years. The relevant rate of interest is 8 percent. Suppose that John is having some difficulty in deciding whether or not to attend the school and that he comes to you for advice. Carefully analyze his situation for him. (What questions would you ask him? What answers would you give him?)

8. Explain why business firms are usually more hesitant to invest in human capital than in physical capital.

9. Distinguish between private returns and social returns to investment in human capital. Give two examples of each. Is it correct to assume that investment in human capital by individuals and business firms will yield only private returns and that government investment in human capital will yield only social returns? Explain.

"Fairness" in Industrial Relations—and Beyond

Samuel Gompers was the guiding genius and long-time president of the American Federation of Labor (AF of L). To him is due an official AF of L slogan, "A Fair Day's Wage for a Fair Day's Work." (Gompers was strongly antisocialist.) But when journalists asked him about labor's aims, Gompers had a short and informal answer—"More!" Are these answers mutually consistent? Not necessarily.

Part of the problem is that "fair" outcomes may also be impossible. There is nothing unfair about putting 100 percent of the workers in the top 10 percent of the income distribution. Such an outcome may be devoutly to be wished, and certain politicians seem to base careers on such proposals, aptly disguised. The laudable aim just happens to be both algebraically and economically impossible.

THIRTY QUESTIONS

Here is a list of thirty "fairness" questions in the area of labor and industrial relations. With a little more time and much more space, the number could be extended indefinitely. In your opinion, which of the following is "fair"?

1. A wage below the poverty line (for a four-person family).
2. A wage so high that the supply of competent workers exceeds the demand for their services.
3. Property incomes based on the productivity of what one owns rather than of one's own efforts.
4. Profit sharing in profitable companies and loss sharing in unprofitable ones.
5. Out-sourcing of components and services from high-wage to low-wage firms.[1]
6. A closed shop contract with an effectively closed union.[2]
7. A yellow-dog contract with unorganized workers. A statewide right-to-work law.[3]
8. Compulsory co-determination in large companies.[4]
9. Use of bankruptcy laws to void existing labor contracts.
10. Founding and financing of company unions.
11. Blacklisting workers by groups of employers. Of companies by federations of unions.[5]
12. Compulsory arbitration of labor disputes with all strikes and lockouts illegal.
13. Mass picketing, sit-down strikes, sympathy strikes, political strikes.[6]
14. Recruiting of strikebreakers and transporting them at company expense.

1. *Out-sourcing* means the purchase of goods and services, previously provided by company employees, from lower-paid outside sources.

2. A *closed shop* limits employment to members of a particular union; a *closed union* restricts its membership unreasonably.

3. A *yellow-dog contract* makes a worker agree not to join a union as a condition of employment; a *right-to-work law* bans the closed and union shop.

4. *Co-determination* gives employees approximately equal representation with shareholders on board of directors.

5. *Blacklisting* of a worker prevents the worker from being employed by any of the group of employers; blacklisting of a company by a union bans the handling or transporting of the products of particular companies.

6. *Mass picketing* blocks entry into a struck plant, often by violence; in *sit-down strikes* workers occupy a plant to prevent operation by management or by strikebreakers; in a *sympathy strike* one group of workers strikes in support of the demands of another group; a *political strike* is for a purpose not related directly to the plant being struck.

Samuel Gompers

15. Primary boycotts, secondary boycotts.[7]

16. Provision of public relief for strikers and their families, or for workers dismissed for cause.

17. Affirmative action in employment and promotion, in favor of women, the aged, and certain minorities.

18. Reverse discrimination against white males of prime working ages.

19. Plant closing without notice to workers.

20. Government intervention to prevent plants from being closed.

21. The runaway shop—domestic or international.[8]

7. A *primary boycott* is against products of a firm involved in a labor dispute; a *secondary boycott* is against firms that sell the products of a company involved in a labor dispute.

8. A *runaway shop* is one that has been moved to a different state or a different country in order to avoid health, safety, or environmental regulations or to hire labor at lower wage rates.

22. Basing layoffs and promotions primarily on seniority of employment or on loyalty to the company.

23. Forbidding layoffs of "regular" employees in depressed periods, as long as the company remains in business.

24. Preference shown in hiring to family members of present employees.

25. Basing pension rights exclusively on employment within a single company.

26. Use of lie detectors in employment or firing decisions.

27. Hiring on a piecework basis for work done in the worker's home. Payment in goods rather than in cash.

28. Separate facilities (dining rooms, washrooms, etc.) for executives and ordinary employees.

29. Selective enforcement of company work rules against tardiness, absenteeism, etc., and against militant workers.

30. Speed-ups and featherbedding.

Certain of these practices are entirely legal in some or all American states. The question is, should they be banned? Others are illegal in the United States but have at times been legal in other countries. Should they be legalized more generally?

IT DEPENDS ON WHAT?

Two extreme positions give easy answers to many of these "fairness" questions. One extreme is a pro-employer position sometimes called in the law "the greater includes the lesser." If the employer is doing a favor to the employee by going into business and providing a job—neither of which the employer is obligated to do—the employer is entitled to hire and fire the employee as he sees fit, including purely arbitrarily, provided only that neither force nor fraud is involved. This is the "managerial prerogative" position. The other extreme is the Marxist-Leninist one, which makes the class struggle itself the basis for morality and ethics. Whatever aids the proletariat—or organized labor, or minorities and women—is fair; whatever opposes these interests is unfair. "Bleeding-heart" liberalism approximates this view, but stops short of revolution.

A common intermediate view is "It depends," or "Tell us more." The answers to questions like those just listed are neither categorically "yes" or "no."

Rather, they depend on the very historical, economic, and even quantitative considerations that "fairness" is supposed to transcend. What, for example, is the present or recent-past state of industrial and race relations in the firm we are talking about, in its industry, or in the larger society? What are the specifics of the conflict—what, for example, are the wage proposals of the two sides? What difference will it make to outsiders—to consumers, for example—which side wins or which compromise is reached? Can the bureaucracy, the courts, or the church be treated as an informed and impartial arbitrator of the issues involved?

Our next question: Why do people hold widely different versions of what is fair and what is not? To some extent, of course, "fair" is what people are used to For example, in public finance, "an old tax is a good tax." But beyond use and custom, we suggest that differences in ethical judgment reflect differences in ethnicity, nationality, religious philosophy, and economic class, as these impinge on the conflicts at issue. Middle-class English and Irish may discuss industrial relations on common ground as long as "the Irish question" is not involved. And patriotic Americans from middle- and working-class backgrounds can do the same, except for a few red flags, like further limits on managerial prerogatives to hire, fire, and relocate, or further restrictions on "the God-given right to strike" and to picket.

So we see that the contribution of "fairness" to conflict resolution in labor and industrial relations—or indeed of ethics and morality more broadly conceived—is less than many of us wish it were. The applicability of "fairness" must await the establishment of a higher degree of commonality about the applicable fundamentals of ethical philosophy itself. This is equally true, we think, in other branches of economic policy, such as problems of international trade and finance, of the regulation of monopolies and near-monopolies, and of the tax system. The potential contributions of fairness considerations to the solution of economic problems in all these fields are quite large—but only among participants whose ethical systems are in general agreement in their applicability to concrete situations.

THE (FAIR?) GAME OF ECONOMIC ACTIVITY

In the early 1920s, Frank H. Knight, philosophical economist at the University of Iowa and the University of Chicago, wrote an influential essay entitled "The Ethics of Competition." In this essay, Knight likened economic activity to a gigantic game of each against all, and inquired if the game was a fair one. We can apply his argument and perhaps expand it a little.

Eastern Strikers

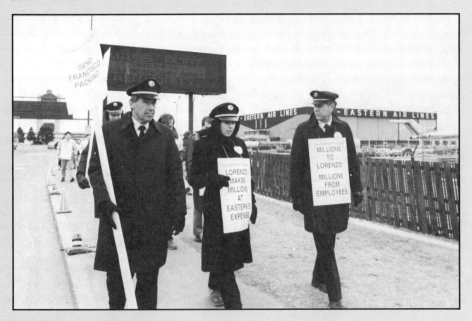

Knight felt that competitive economics was a fundamentally unfair game because—like chess or checkers between opponents of approximately equal skill—any initial or temporary advantage tends to cumulate. (A folk proverb puts it this way: "It takes money to make money.") Suppose that A and B begin economic play at age twenty, with A having a slight advantage in genetic endowment, family environment, investment in his or her human capital, or "pull" or "connections." Knight argued that this advantage, assuming other things equal, would usually grow over time, both absolutely and proportionately. It would probably be greater at age forty than it was at age twenty, and so on, until A's chance of retiring at sixty or seventy as a wealthy rentier is far greater than that of B. Compare the economic game with athletic contests, where "It ain't over till it's over," or until the "last man is out in the bottom of the ninth inning," and where the second game of a double-header is entirely independent of the outcome of the first.

What other considerations may make economic competition something less than a fair game? Let us suggest three:

1. It is extraordinarily difficult for losers to withdraw, short of death or bankruptcy. One can leave a gambling table after losing a preassigned amount—although compulsive gamblers sometimes have difficulty accepting this option. In economics there are no equally adequate safety nets. The loser in one casino—such as the labor market for his or her services as, let us say, an ethical philosopher—can only turn to another casino—say, as a trader in commodities or securities—with the extra handicap of prior failure. Perhaps, indeed, he or she cannot change casinos at all. Withdrawing from the economy means subsistence agriculture or reliance on private charity, neither of which is an acceptable alternative for most of us. Cases of rising to the top after repeated failures—like Abraham Lincoln's rise from backwoods farmer to failed storekeeper to mediocre country lawyer to one-term congressman to failed senatorial candidate to Civil War president of the United States—are inspirational precisely because of their rarity.

2. It is extraordinarily difficult, if not impossible, to avoid participation in the economic game in the first place, even if one is not talented at it or feels no desire to play. Refusal can be costly if not ruinous. A common withdrawal is by marriage, but it is dangerous if one chooses the wrong (or an unlucky) spouse. Some can live on the income of inherited property, with or without the advice of such agents as investment counselors, trustees, and astrologers. However, such people are few in number and have been the prime victims of inflation. The groves of academe, the civil and military services, and the clerical life are often viewed, with a certain condescension, as refuges from the "real world" of business and industry, but such withdrawals are only partial and halfhearted. From the economic point of view, withdrawal into these fields is usually costly in monetary terms, although the loss can be repaid in quality of life and longer life expectancy.

3. In a fair game, or at least in some people's idea of a fair game, victory is to the admirable as well as to the strong or swift. Durocher's Law—"nice guys (and gals) finish last"—in particular, does not hold. But in the real world the financial wizard, like the champion athlete, entertainer, or bathing beauty, may not qualify as what the Victorians called a "scholar and gentleman." Is it the economy that is out of joint, or is it rather traditional notions of "scholarship and gentility"?

A FAIR ECONOMY IN AN UNFAIR WORLD?

"Life is unfair," we are often told. What does this mean in industrial relations or, for that matter, in the whole economy? It implies that the Holy Grail of complete fairness or equity—whether by your criteria or by ours—is unattainable. It may be a mistake to squander too much of one's physical or psychic resources either in searching for it at some rainbow's end or in striving for it here and now. At the same time, it does not imply that fairness be ignored entirely in favor of efficiency, the revolution, or even the quiet life of personalization and privatization.

Insofar as enough of us can agree as to its nature over a sufficient period of time, fairness or equity is an economic good like any other. Perhaps, as in John Rawls's philosophy, it is even *the* supreme economic good. But as between people and parties with fundamental disagreements about the content of fairness, fairness itself is likely to furnish false leads in economic and social policy—including industrial and labor relations. A hard-line stand for *Fiat justicia ruat caelum*—let justice be done though the heavens fall—is more likely in practice to mean the falling of the sky than the building of Jerusalem on anyone's green and pleasant land. Jurists, ethical philosophers, and labor arbitrators, of course, remain free to propound higher degrees of optimality.

Government and Taxation

Poverty and Income Distribution

Government Antitrust and Regulation Policy

International Microeconomics:
Free Trade versus Protection

Agriculture, Food, and Hunger

Natural Resources and the Environment

PART X
APPLIED
MICROECONOMICS

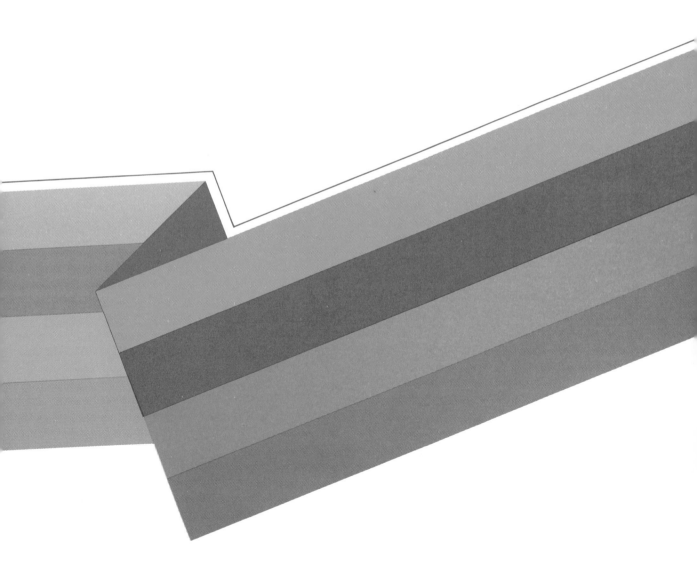

33
Government and Taxation

Preview   This is the first of a group of chapters on applied microeconomics. Their purpose is to explain how the tools of microeconomic analysis, which you have just studied, can help in understanding certain real-world situations and in solving some of the problems that face contemporary societies.

We begin with a chapter on government and taxation. As you learned in Chapter 2, government is one of the "actors on the economic stage." We start this chapter with an overview of United States government finance. This is followed by an analysis of why government is needed for efficient resource use in a market-capitalist economic system. Then we examine government expenditures and the major revenue sources of governments in the United States—the individual income tax, Social Security taxes, the corporation income tax, sales and excise taxes, motor fuels taxes, and property taxes. We focus on using microeconomic tools of analysis to understand the effects of these taxes.

In the final part of the chapter, we explain the theory of public choice, which explores how the tools of economics can help in understanding how voters in a democracy try to tell the government what they want it to do. This includes a theory about how responsibilities might be divided between the national, state, and local levels of government in a federal system such as that in the United States.

This chapter does not cover the macroeconomic aspects of government—activities relating to the control of business cycles, inflation, macroeconomic unemployment, and economic growth—which are considered in depth in macroeconomics.

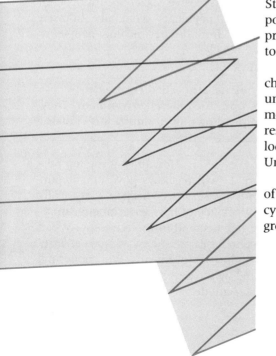

AN OVERVIEW OF GOVERNMENT FINANCE IN THE UNITED STATES

We begin our analysis of government and taxation with a brief overview of the expenditures and receipts of governments in the United States. Taken together, expenditures and receipts make up the fiscal, or budgetary, aspects of government. There are many levels of government in the United States, including townships, school districts, cities (municipalities), counties, states, and the federal government in Washington, D.C. In order to provide an overall picture of government in the United States, our overview combines data about all these levels of government.

Government Expenditures

Government expenditures in the United States, combining all levels of government from your local school district all the way up to the federal government in Washington, amounted to around $6,728 per person in 1988. If you have a father and a mother and one brother or sister, government expenditure amounted to around $26,912 for your family of four that year.

There are two basic categories of government expenditure. Some, called transfer payments, simply pass money to citizens. Other expenditures purchase goods and services for the use of the government itself. The difference between these types of expenditure merits a closer look.

There are two basic categories of government expenditure: transfer payments and government purchases.

Transfer Payments   Figure 1 pictures government expenditures in the United States for 1986. Look first at the red area at the bottom of the chart, which shows transfer payments. **Transfer payments** are payments that are not in exchange for any good produced or service rendered during the year in question. They include Social Security benefits, other retirement payments, unemployment insurance, and welfare payments. Interest on the public debt is another large expenditure recorded as transfer payment. Altogether, transfer payments

amount to more than 40 percent of total government expenditures. Your own family may receive some of the money. These payments, which are often called "entitlements," have grown greatly in recent years.

Transfer payments are payments, such as Social Security benefits, unemployment insurance, welfare payments, and interest on the public debt, that are not given in exchange for any currently produced good or service. They amount to about 40 percent of total government expenditures.

Among the different levels of government in the United States, the federal government is responsible for most of the transfer payments. About 85 percent of all transfers come directly from the federal government, and much of the rest, though administered by state and local government, is actually financed through grants from the federal government. State and local governments have some freedom to design their own transfer payment programs, but most of the direction is set by laws passed in Washington.

The purpose of most transfer payments is to redistribute spending power among individuals. For example, Social Security benefits transfer spending power from people who are currently working and paying Social Security taxes to others who are retired and receive Social Security benefit checks. Welfare payments generally transfer spending power from higher-income people to lower-income people.

Transfer payments, also called entitlements, come mostly from the federal government. They redistribute spending power among individuals.

Government Purchases   Now look at the top portion of Figure 1, which shows government purchases of goods and services. This part is especially important in the study of how government can influence aggregate demand in the economy. When government purchases are increased, jobs are created in the industries producing the goods and services desired by the government; when government purchases are decreased, jobs are lost.

FIGURE 1
Expenditures by National, State, and Local
Governments in the United States, 1986 (percentage distribution)

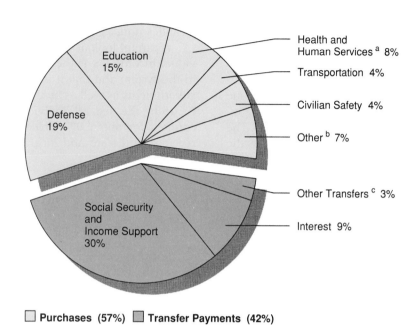

□ **Purchases (57%)** ■ **Transfer Payments (42%)**

Over 40 percent of the total expenditures of governments in the United States are transfer payments, under which people receive money from the government without rendering service to the government that year. Nearly 60 percent of annual expenditures are for purchases of goods and services, directly generating demand for goods and services produced in the economy. This chart shows the breakdown of government expenditures by function.
a. Health and human services include goods and services purchases for veterans, health and hospital services, and housing and community services, recreation, culture, labor training, and income support.

b. Other goods and services purchases include energy, natural resources, space, development and regulation, postal services, agriculture, and miscellaneous unallocable purchases.
c. Other transfer payments include international payments and miscellaneous unallocable expenditures.
Note: Amounts do not add to 100 percent because of rounding.
Source: Survey of Current Business, 68, No. 7, July 1988, Tables 3.15 and 3.16, pp. 64 and 66. Washington, D.C.: United States Dept. of Commerce/Bureau of Economic Analysis, 1988.

Education and national defense are the two largest functional areas for government purchases of goods and services. They are also good illustrations of how, under a federal system, different functions are assigned to different levels of government. Defense is entirely funded by the federal government. Most of the funds for education come from state and local governments even though some federal government money is sent as grants to help the states, cities, and school districts to finance education.

Government influences aggregate demand in the economy. When government purchases are increased, jobs are created in the industries producing the goods and services desired by the government; when government purchases are decreased, jobs are lost.

The other government purchases are scattered over a wide variety of functions, and financial responsibility is often shared by national, state, and local governments. Under a complicated system of **grants-in-aid**, money from a larger government, such as the federal government or a state government, is handed over to a smaller government, such as a state or local one. Some of these grants are "conditional," meaning that the smaller government can receive the money only if it spends it according to rules set down by the granting government. Other grants-in-aid, such as revenue sharing, are "unconditional," so the receiving government can use the money any way it wants. The grant-in-aid system has expanded greatly in the United States since the 1930s.

An important fact about government expenditures that does not show up in Figure 1 is that state and local governments spend much more on currently produced goods and services than the federal government does. The major state and local spending areas are education, health and human services, transportation, civilian safety, and housing. Even though federal grants help in many of these areas, state and local purchases would exceed federal purchases even if grant-in-aid funding were counted as federal purchases. Public finance theories suggest that grants-in-aid are useful when no single government has complete responsibility for a service.

Through the grants-in-aid system, money collected by a larger government is handed over to a smaller government. Grants-in-aid are useful when no single government has complete responsibility for a service.

Education and national defense are the two largest functional areas for government purchases of goods and services. Defense is entirely funded by the federal government; the major state and local spending areas are education, health and human services, transportation, safety, and housing.

Government Receipts

The major sources of government receipts in the United States are shown in Figure 2. Again the circle is divided into two main parts. This time the bottom part, over one-third of the total, shows

revenue collected by state and local governments. The top part of the circle shows revenue sources of the federal government. Even though the federal government collects almost two-thirds of the total, some of the money is turned back to the states and localities under grant-in-aid programs.

A careful look at Figure 2 shows that the individual income tax is the largest revenue producer in the system and that it is used by state and local governments as well as by the federal government. In 1986 the federal individual income tax accounted for about 27 percent of all government receipts, and state and local income taxes added another 6 percent.

The individual income tax is the largest revenue producer for government.

Social Security and corporation income taxes also are based on income. As indicated in Figure 2, Social Security taxes amounted to 22 percent of total government tax receipts in 1986. Federal, state and local corporation taxes added another 7 percent. Thus, by combining individual income taxes, Social Security taxes, and corporation income taxes, taxes based on income amounted to 62 percent to government tax receipts. The United States relies more heavily on income-based taxes than do most other countries. Whether this is good or bad depends on the criteria used in evaluating revenue systems. Many believe that income is the best way to compare the abilities of different taxpayers and that it also is directly linked to the distribution function of government. Others believe that taxing income imposes a penalty on success and reduces incentives to work and save, thus lowering output and economic growth.

As you can see from Figure 2, the remaining 38 percent of government revenue comes from a variety of taxes, imposed primarily at the state and local levels. Property taxes and sales taxes are important revenue producers for state and local governments, as are various fees and charges for services rendered by these governments. Figure 2 does not show borrowing as a revenue source, although budget deficits have become routine at the federal level. The reason for not including borrowing as a revenue source is the presumption that funds that are borrowed must eventually be paid back. This

FIGURE 2
Receipts of National, State, and Local
Governments in the United States, 1986 (percentage distribution)

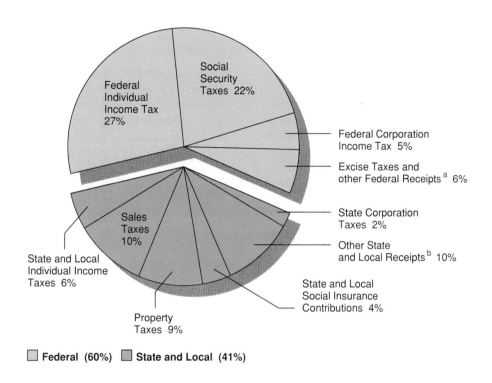

The federal government collects about 60 percent of total government receipts (as shown in the upper part of the circle), and state and local governments collect about 40 percent (as shown in the lower part). Individual income taxes and Social Security taxes are both assessed on individual earnings and total more than half of total government receipts. Some federal receipts are sent as grants-in-aid to state and local governments. Though they are not specifically shown on this chart, they amount to about 8 percent of total government receipts.

a. Other federal receipts include estate and gift taxes, customs duties, and miscellaneous receipts.

b. Other state and local receipts include fees and charges for services and miscellaneous nontax receipts.

Note: Amounts do not add to 100 percent because of rounding.

Source: Economic Report of the President, 1989, Table B-77, p. 399, and Tables B-82 and B-83, pp. 404–405.

presumption is reasonable for state and local government borrowing, but it may be less reasonable for federal government borrowing, since federal borrowing is part of the modern system of money creation—a power granted to the federal government by the U.S. Constitution.[1]

1. The relation between government borrowing and money creation involves monetary policy, which is explained in macroeconomics.

Taxes based on income (individual income taxes, Social Security taxes, and corporation income taxes) amount to about 60 percent of government receipts. The rest of government revenue comes primarily from state and local taxes, especially property and sales taxes.

EXTERNALITIES AND MARKET FAILURE

In a market-capitalist economy, most economic questions are expected to be resolved through the market system, without a large amount of government intervention. Consistent with this principle, it is an important responsibility of government to help ensure an economic environment suitable for the functioning of markets. For example, governments in market-capitalist economies are expected to provide legal systems for the protection of property and the enforcement of contracts. This is because market systems function more effectively when people can enter into contracts and be assured that they actually will be carried out. Along the same line, it is government's responsibility to help protect property. Business firms are much more willing to invest in capital goods such as factory buildings and machines when they have assurance that their property is safe from theft and destruction.

In market-capitalist economies, government is expected to ensure an economic environment suitable for the functioning of markets.

In addition to market-support activities such as these, governments are expected to carry out several specific functions related to **market failure** situations—situations in which markets are unable to perform satisfactorily. These functions of government were outlined in Chapter 2, where government's role as an actor on the economic stage was discussed. The three market failure functions, as we saw in Chapter 2, are:

1. the **allocation function** of helping the economy to provide the assortment of goods and services most desired by the people.
2. the **distribution function** of altering the distribution of income, as necessary, to obtain the degree of income equality considered appropriate.
3. the **stabilization function** of moderating fluctuations in the volume of aggregate economic activity and assuring reasonable levels of employment, price stability, and economic growth.

The stabilization function is an important part of the study of macroeconomics. The allocation and distribution functions, on the other hand, are microeconomic topics. This chapter examines the allocation function of government. The following chapter looks at poverty and income distribution.

When markets fail to provide satisfactory outcomes, governments' functions include resource allocation, income distribution, and stabilization of the economy.

Externalities

An **externality** is an economic effect (either beneficial or harmful) experienced by a person who had no control, through the market system, over the action that led to the effect. For example, suppose a person contracts lung cancer from breathing smoke and fumes from the smokestacks of a steel mill. Suppose this person does not work at the steel mill and that his or her purchases of steel or steel-made products are an insignificant part of the mill's total demand. Since the victim had no power through the market system to influence the production methods used or to force the mill to stop the discharge of the harmful smoke and fumes, the lung cancer is a negative (harmful) external effect of the operation of the mill. The effect is called "external" because it is outside the control mechanism of the market system.

Some externalities are positive (beneficial). For example, education (especially elementary and secondary education) is generally believed to provide benefits to the whole community as well as benefits to the children who attend school and to their families. Voters will be better informed, productivity will be higher, literature and the arts will advance, and so on. If schools were financed entirely by tuition payments, families would demand education service primarily for the private enjoyment and benefit of the family itself. These benefits would be internal to the market system of providing education services. Any benefits to others in the community would be external benefits, since others in the community would not be effective demanders of education services.

An externality is an economic effect experienced by a person who has no control, through the market system, over the action that led to the effect. Some externalities are beneficial, and some are harmful.

Negative Externalities and Misallocation of Resources

Figure 3 illustrates market failure in the case of a good or service that generates negative externalities. Our earlier illustration of a negative externality was lung cancer caused by smoke from the smokestack of a steel mill. Steel production is shown on the horizontal axis of Figure 3 because the production of this product may generate these negative externalities. As you know from your study of microeconomics, the demand curve, D, illustrates how the quantity demanded depends on price. This curve represents the behavior of purchasers and reflects the benefits they expect to receive from consuming steel. The market-supply curve, S_m in Figure 3, illustrates how the quantity of steel offered for sale depends on its price. As you learned in microeconomics, the supply curve represents the behavior of those supplying the good or service. In this market, the equilibrium price is P_m and the quantity demanded and supplied is Q_m.

If negative external effects are generated by this good or service, some costs are being experienced by people not represented by either the market-demand curve or the market-supply curve. In other words, when negative externalities are generated, the market fails to record some costs associated with this product. Since costs normally are represented by the supply curve, we can say that the presence of negative externalities means that the market-supply curve, S_m, is too far to the right. A supply curve representing both the costs incurred by suppliers and also the costs experienced by those who suffer from externalities would lie upward and to the left of supply curve S_m. The social-supply curve, S_s in Figure 3, is constructed to represent the full **social costs** of the good or service. These social costs include both the costs incurred by the producers of the good or service (called **private costs**) and also the **external costs**, that is, the costs experienced by those suffering negative

FIGURE 3
Negative Externalities and Market Failure

The demand curve, D, represents the behavior of purchasers of steel. The market-supply curve, S_m, represents the behavior of the suppliers. Only private costs are reflected in this curve. The social-supply curve, S_s, reflects both private costs and external costs (negative externalities). External costs are represented by the vertical distance between S_m and S_s. At equilibrium point A, the market provides an inefficiently large quantity (Q_m). The socially efficient equilibrium is at B, with quantity Q_s and price P_s.

externalities. For each successive unit of the good or service, the amount of external cost is represented by the vertical distance between the S_s curve and the S_m curve.

The social costs of a good or service include both the costs incurred by the producers of the good or service (private costs) and the costs experienced by those suffering negative externalities (external costs).

In negative externality situations, market failure results in the market providing an inefficiently large quantity of the good or service. This failure arises because the producers and consumers of the good or service (steel in our illustration) do not have to pay some of the costs of the product, in this case, the suffering from cancer and the costs of treating it. If all the social costs were recognized by the market, the equilibrium price and quantity would be P_s and Q_s, as indicated in Figure 3 by the intersection at point B of the demand curve, D, with the social-supply curve, S_s. By comparing this socially efficient equilibrium with the equilibrium shown by the market-demand curve and the market-supply curve, we can observe how market failure leads to a misallocation of resources. Unless some correction is applied, the market solution will result in too low a price to consumers (P_m) and too large a quantity demanded and supplied (Q_m). We may state it as a general rule that market failure takes the form of an excessive quantity produced and consumed when harmful externalities exist and no corrective action is taken.

In negative externality situations, market failure results in the market providing an inefficiently large quantity of the good or service.

Government Corrections for Negative Externalities

The economic way of thinking that you have developed from your study of microeconomics suggests that market failures due to externalities can be corrected by making market-demand and market-supply curves reflect the full social costs and benefits of the goods or services being demanded and supplied. In the case of negative externalities, as illustrated in Figure 3, the effort to correct the market failure would take the form of shifting the market-supply curve (S_m) to the left until it matches the social-supply curve (S_s). After this correction was made, the market would provide the socially efficient quantity of the good or service. Resources would be efficiently allocated.

Market failures due to externalities can be corrected by making market-demand and market-supply curves reflect the full social costs and benefits of the good or service being demanded and supplied.

Governments have many powers that enable them to cause shifts in market-supply curves. For example, to correct for negative externalities from smoke and fumes coming from chimneys and smokestacks, government regulations might require the installation of filters or scrubbers that remove harmful materials from the emissions. To correct for negative externalities coming from automobile emissions, government may require cars to be equipped with exhaust systems that remove or deactivate harmful substances. The costs of these filters, scrubbers, and exhaust systems would have to be paid initially by those who operate the chimneys or smokestacks and by those who manufacture autos and auto exhaust systems. This would shift the market-supply curve to the left. In this way, these costs would be passed on to the consumers who purchase products produced in factories and to motorists who purchase cars equipped with the improved exhaust systems. So, appropriate use of government's regulatory powers could bring the desired shift in the market-supply curve and could correct for market failure due to negative externalities.

Taxation is another government power that can be used to correct for market failure due to negative externalities. For example, a tax could be imposed on smoke and fumes coming from chimneys and smokestacks or on automobile emissions that are believed to cause negative external effects. The tax would have to be paid by the persons responsible for the harmful emissions—the firms or households operating the chimneys or smokestacks or the motorists operating the automobiles. Microeconomic analysis leads to the conclusion that these people would quickly start looking for ways to save taxes by reducing the amount of the taxable (i.e., harmful) substances coming from their chimneys, smokestacks, autos, etc. In other words, government need not require specific filters, scrubbers, or auto exhaust systems. Instead, it could count on the self-interest (economic rationality) of firms and households to discover and install effective devices on their own initiative and at their own expense.

Government has the power to cause shifts in market-supply curves through regulation and taxation.

Would the government raise much money from a tax designed to correct for market failures? The answer is that the government would not collect much money from the tax if the tax actually did its job of persuading people to stop doing the things that generated negative externalities. As better and better filters, scrubbers, and auto exhaust systems are invented and installed, less and less of the harmful substances will be generated and the tax will yield less and less money for the government. In other words, the purpose of the tax is not to raise money for the government but to persuade people to change their behavior and thereby avoid the tax. The main advantage of the tax approach over the regulatory approach is that the tax provides incentives that encourage people to discover better and less expensive ways to reduce the quantities of the substance being taxed.

The tax approach to correcting negative externalities has an advantage over the regulatory approach because it provides incentives that encourage people to discover better and less expensive ways of reducing the quantities of the substance being taxed.

Positive Externalities and Resource Misallocation

Positive (beneficial) externalities also lead to market failure and resource misallocation. In this situation, the market failure takes the form of an inefficiently small quantity being demanded and supplied. Figure 4 illustrates market failure through positive externalities such as those generated by elementary and secondary education. In this figure, the supply curve, S, represents the costs of supplying education services while the market-demand curve, D_m, represents the willingness to pay for these services as recorded by market transactions. In other words, the market-demand curve, D_m, represents only the willingness of families to purchase education services for their own children. This market-demand curve reflects only the **private benefits** and fails to include the **external benefits** received by others in the community. In terms of the microeconomic tools of analysis, the market-demand curve, D_m, is located too far to the left on the graph. The social-demand curve, D_s in Figure 4, includes both the private benefits and the

FIGURE 4
Positive Externalities and Market Failure

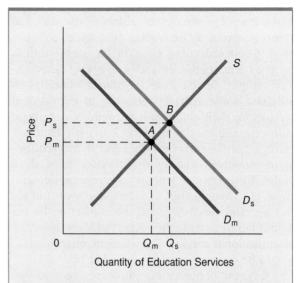

The supply curve, S, represents the behaviors of suppliers of education services. The demand curve, D_m, represents the behavior of purchasers. Only private benefits are reflected in this curve. The social-demand curve, D_s, reflects both private benefits and external benefits (positive externalities). External benefits are represented by the vertical distance between D_m and D_s. At equilibrium point A, the market provides an inefficiently small quantity (Q_m). The socially efficient equilibrium is at B, with quantity Q_s and price P_s.

external benefits of education services. It is located to the right of the market-demand curve, D_m. The vertical distance between the market-demand curve (D_m) and the social-demand curve (D_s) shows the amount of external benefit for each successive unit of education services. The socially efficient quantity is Q_s, as indicated by the intersection between the supply curve (S) and the social-demand curve (D_s). By comparing this socially efficient equilibrium with the market equilibrium, it is clear that the market failure that arises from positive externalities takes the form of a price (P_m) that is too low to bring about the socially efficient quantity supplied.

Positive externalities lead to market failure in the form of an inefficiently small quantity being demanded and supplied.

Government Corrections for Positive Externalities

In the case of positive externalities, as illustrated in Figure 4, a remedy for market failure is to shift the market-demand curve (D_m) to the right until it matches the social-demand curve (D_s). Government might, for example, require all families to purchase some specified quantity of educational services for their children. If this requirement were enforced, the market-demand curve in Figure 4 could be shifted to the right, and if the requirements involved exactly the services needed to match the external benefits, the market-demand curve (D_m) would shift to correspond with the social-demand curve (D_s) and the market no longer would fail to provide the socially efficient quantity of educational service. The efficient quantity (Q_s) would be demanded and supplied at price P_s.

A system of mandatory purchases, such as that described above, undoubtedly would run into difficulty because some consumers would not have the money to pay for the services they would be required to purchase. Moreover, why should any of the recipients of the private benefits, whether they are rich or poor, be required to pay for the benefits enjoyed by the external beneficiaries? Instead, the external beneficiaries—the community in general in the education illustration—should pay for services that generate the external benefits if we follow the ethical notion that people who benefit should pay for what they get. Therefore, government programs to correct for market failures caused by external benefits are likely to pay a **subsidy** to encourage the desired increase in production and consumption. A subsidy is a payment by someone other than the buyer that helps to cover all or some of the cost of a good or service. It may be used either along with or entirely separate from mandatory purchase requirements.

A subsidy is a payment by someone other than the buyer that helps to cover the cost of a good or service.

In our education example, the government might give to each child a certificate (sometimes called a "voucher") redeemable at an approved school to help pay the tuition bill for required education services. The money to finance the certificates would come from taxpayers so that the community in general, which receives the external benefits, would pay its share of the cost of the service. The market failure would be corrected, and the socially efficient quantity of education service would be demanded and supplied.

Government can correct positive-externality market failure by regulation or subsidies, which shift the market-demand curve.

Subsidies Paid Directly to Suppliers

The number of firms that supply a good or a service usually is much smaller than the number of people who purchase it. Therefore, for goods and services generating beneficial externalities, it often is easier for the government to provide a subsidy through suppliers than to pay it to the purchasers. Figure 5 illustrates how subsidies paid to suppliers can correct for market failures related to beneficial externalities. In this figure, in the absence of government subsidy, the market demand is D_m and the market supply is S_m. At equilibrium (point A), the market provides an inefficiently small quantity of the good or service (Q_m).

In order to correct for the market failure, the government pays to the supplier a subsidy that covers part of the cost of supplying the good or service, thus shifting the market-supply curve to the right to S_s. The amount of the subsidy, per unit of the good or service, is shown by the vertical distance between the supply curves S_m and S_s. If the subsidy has been correctly calculated, this distance corresponds to the value of the external benefits enjoyed by the community. After the shift of the supply curve, equilibrium is at point B and the socially efficient quantity (Q_s) of the good or service is supplied. Consumers pay price P_c, indicated by point B on the demand curve, but suppliers receive price P_s, indicated by point C on the presubsidy supply curve (S_m). Thus, suppliers receive the price needed to call forth the socially efficient quantity of the good or service. Only the part of this price that

FIGURE 5
Subsidy Paid to Suppliers

Market equilibrium is at *A*, where the market-demand curve, D_m, intersects the market-supply curve, S_m. Quantity Q_m would be demanded and supplied. A subsidy paid to suppliers shifts the supply curve to the right to S_s. The new equilibrium is at *B*, with the socially efficient quantity, Q_s, demanded and supplied. At this equilibrium, consumers pay price P_c and suppliers receive price P_s. The amount of the subsidy for the marginal unit of the good or service is shown by the distance from *B* to *C*.

corresponds to marginal private benefit is paid by private consumers. The part that corresponds to marginal external benefit is paid by the government with money collected from taxpayers.

To correct for market failure it usually is easier for government to provide a subsidy to suppliers than to provide a subsidy to the purchasers.

The actual system of education finance in the United States does not match the theoretical models just explained. In practice, public elementary and secondary schools in the United States do not charge any tuition at all. In these schools, the subsidy pays all of the costs of supplying education services. Thus, the subsidies pay for some services that would have been financed privately if the gov-

ernment had not entered the picture. A more extensive analysis of the economics of education would extend beyond the subject of beneficial externalities that we are considering here.

COLLECTIVE GOODS AND SERVICES

Collective goods and services are those that are consumed by the community as a group (i.e., "collectively"). Markets typically fail to provide them in efficient quantities. The reasons for this market failure provide another economic explanation for government spending and taxation in a market-capitalist economic system.

Collective goods and services are those consumed by the community as a group. Markets typically fail to provide them in efficient quantities.

Nonexclusion and Free Riders

One characteristic of a collective good or service is **nonexcludability**, which means that, once it has been produced, it is either not possible or extremely expensive to deny any person in the community the opportunity to consume it. For example, once weapons have been produced and service men and women have been hired to operate them, defense protection cannot be provided to one person in a community while being denied to another member of that community. All must be protected together, as a group. If New York City is protected from enemy attack, all the people in that city are protected. This is the meaning of the nonexcludability feature of a collective good or service.

Nonexcludability means that, once a good or service has been produced, it is either not possible or extremely expensive to deny any person in the community the opportunity to consume it.

Nonexcludability clearly distinguishes collective goods and services from private goods and services, which have excludability as a hallmark characteristic. Common exclusion devices include checkout counters, ticket takers, shoplifting alarm systems, bars on windows, locks on doors, and so on. Without exclusion devices, business firms would not be able to collect money in exchange for the goods and services that they supply. Without revenue from sales, these firms would have no incentive to engage in business and would not be able to finance the production of goods and services. In short, the market system will not provide goods and services unless exclusion devices operate.

Unlike collective goods and services, private goods and services are excludable. In fact, the market system will not provide goods and services unless exclusion devices operate.

For collective goods and services, the absence of exclusion devices opens the door to the **free-rider problem**. A person is a free rider if he or she obtains a good or service at the expense of others. When exclusion devices are not available, many people will refuse (or understate their willingness) to pay for a good or service because they hope that they will be able to obtain it without charge after others have paid for it. According to the free-rider logic, for example, you will refuse to pay for defense services, or understate your willingness to pay for them, hoping that others will come up with enough money to pay for the service, after which you will receive its benefits without paying or without paying your full share.

The seriousness of the free-rider problem depends on the number of people in the group that collectively consumes the good or service. The problem is not serious for small groups, such as the family. In small groups, people recognize that their own refusal to pay may mean that the good or service will not be provided at all. Knowing this, it is likely that all members will pay more or less their fair share. But in large groups, where formal governments operate, each person feels that his or her own payment has little effect on the quantity of the good or service that actually will be provided.

Thus, the tendency to be a free rider becomes very widespread, perhaps almost universal. Because of nonexcludability and free riding, an efficient quantity of collective goods and services is not likely to be provided through a voluntary payment system such as the market, even when benefits clearly exceed costs.

A person is a free rider when he or she obtains a good or service at the expense of others. The tendency to become a free rider becomes widespread in large groups, where individuals may feel that their payments have little effect on the quantity of the good or service that will be provided.

As you probably have guessed, taxation is a cure for the free-rider problem. Taxes are not voluntary, unless you consider fines and imprisonment to be reasonable alternatives. By forcing people to pay, taxes make it impossible to have a free ride. Taxes enable governments to finance goods and services that people want and are willing to pay for, but which they could not obtain adequately through the voluntary payments procedures of the market system.

Taxes make it impossible to have a free ride and enable governments to finance goods and services that people could not obtain adequately through the voluntary payments procedures of the market system.

Nonrivalry in Consumption

A second characteristic of collective goods is **nonrival consumption**. There is nonrival consumption of a good or service if one person can benefit from it without causing any significant reduction in the benefits that others receive from it. The clearest example of a service that is nonrival in consumption is national defense. The fact that you are benefited by this service does not increase or decrease the benefit that others receive from it. If you die or move away, the benefit that others receive from national defense is not increased, nor does an increase in the population significantly reduce their benefit. Of course, all persons may not benefit equally or feel that the protection is equally valuable, but that does not change the fact that consumption of the service is nonrival.

The nonrival characteristic of a collective good or service is important in the economics of government because it means that people need not object to having their tax money pooled or combined to pay for the good or service. For example, if each of the 250 million people in the United States felt that he or she received $1,000 worth of benefit from the defense system, the government could collect this amount of tax from each person and spend $250 billion for defense. It could pool each person's payment of $1,000 into a common fund to finance national defense services. Unfortunately, calculating the efficient quantity of a collective good to provide is not as simple as this illustration implies. But the nonrival characteristic determines that funds can be pooled, no matter how tax payments themselves have been distributed.

Nonrival consumption of a good or service means that one person can benefit from it without causing any significant reduction in the benefits others receive from it. Because of the nonrival characteristic of a collective good or service, people need not object to having their tax money pooled to pay for the good or service.

THE ECONOMICS OF TAXATION

Taxes are payments or contributions that a government requires from persons within its jurisdiction or from property or transactions located in its jurisdiction. We have already noted two uses of taxation. One was in situations where negative externalities exist, where taxes may be used to discourage activities giving rise to the externalities. This is referred to as **corrective taxation**. The second use of taxation was connected with the free-rider phenomenon, where taxes are used to require payments from those who benefit from

public goods and services but who might otherwise try to obtain these goods and services without payment. As we shall see when we explore theories of public choice, taxes also may encourage people to vote in elections and to reveal their preferences for public goods and services. This can be called the **preference revelation** use of taxation. Taxation may also be used to divide the costs of government in such a way as to alter the after-tax amount of income or wealth inequality among people in the society. This is an **income redistribution** use of taxation. From the economist's perspective, taxes also have the purpose of taking spending power away from private households and businesses so that resources that might otherwise have been employed to satisfy private demands can, instead, be employed to provide public goods and services. This is the basic **resource allocation** use of taxation.

Taxation has a number of uses: (1) discouraging activities that cause harmful externalities, (2) discouraging free riding, (3) encouraging people to reveal their preference by voting in elections, (4) redistributing income and wealth among people in the society, and (5) reducing private spending power in order to make resources available for government use.

No major tax in the United States is used exclusively for any one of these purposes. To some degree, each major tax operates in all of these applications. The economics of taxation is an important and complicated subject. We will briefly note the basic features of the major tax revenue sources used in the United States.

Individual Income Taxes

As noted earlier, individual income taxes are very important for government finance in the United States. The federal government relies heavily on its individual income tax. For state governments, individual income taxes roughly parallel sales taxes in the amounts of revenue raised. Local governments make only limited use of individual income taxation. We shall limit our discussion of individual

TABLE 1
1988 Tax Rate Schedules

Schedule X—Use if your filing status is **Single**

If the amount on Form 1040, line 37, is: Over—	But not over—	Enter on Form 1040, line 38	of the amount over—
$0	$17,850	------ 15%	$0
17,850	43,150	$2,677.50 + 28%	17,850
43,150	89,560	9,761.50 + 33%	43,150
89,560	------	Use **Worksheet** to figure your tax.	

Schedule Z—Use if your filing status is **Head of household**

If the amount on Form 1040, line 37, is: Over—	But not over—	Enter on Form 1040, line 38	of the amount over—
$0	$23,900	------ 15%	$0
23,900	61,650	$3,585 + 28%	23,900
61,650	123,790	14,155 + 33%	61,650
123,790	------	Use **Worksheet** to figure your tax.	

Schedule Y-1—Use if your filing status is **Married filing jointly or Qualifying widow(er)**

If the amount on Form 1040, line 37, is: Over—	But not over—	Enter on Form 1040, line 38	of the amount over—
$0	$29,750	------ 15%	$0
29,750	71,900	$4,462.50 + 28%	29,750
71,900	149,250	16,264.50 + 33%	71,900
149,250	------	Use **Worksheet** to figure your tax.	

Schedule Y-2—Use if your filing status is **Married filing separately**

If the amount on Form 1040, line 37, is: Over—	But not over—	Enter on Form 1040, line 38	of the amount over—
$0	$14,875	------ 15%	$0
14,875	35,950	$2,231.25 + 28%	14,875
35,950	113,300	8,132.25 + 33%	35,950
113,300	------	Use **Worksheet** to figure your tax.	

This table shows the U.S. Individual Income Tax Rate Schedules applicable to income reported for the 1988 tax year.

income taxation to the tax imposed by the federal government.

The federal government relies heavily on the individual income tax as a major source of its revenue.

To understand how the United States individual income tax is applied, it is helpful to think of a person's income as consisting of successive layers, starting from zero and moving upward. The first layer of income is free of tax as a **personal exemption**. In 1989, for example, each taxpayer was entitled to a personal exemption of $2,000 for himself or herself plus $2,000 for each dependent.

The second layer of income is also tax free. This layer consists of expenditures that are allowed as **personal deductions** such as extraordinary medical expenses, charitable contributions, certain interest payments, certain state and local taxes, and casualty losses. For some taxpayers, these deductions are replaced by an allowance called the **standard deduction**, which is a deduction that applies if people choose not to itemize the specific personal deduction amounts.

Although the details of filing an individual income tax return are extremely complex, the basic organization of the tax is quite straightforward. Each person or married couple with income above a specified minimum is required to file a return reporting the amount of income (as defined by the tax laws) received during the tax year. Next, the amounts allowed as deductions from income and as personal exemptions are subtracted from income. The amount remaining is called "net income subject to tax." The amount of tax to be paid is determined by applying the appropriate tax rate schedule to the net income subject to tax.

A proportion of each person's income is tax free due to personal exemptions and personal (or standard) deductions. The amount of income remaining is the net income subject to tax.

Table 1 shows the several tax rate schedules applicable to income received in 1988—Schedule X for single persons, Schedule Y-1 for married persons filing jointly or for qualifying widows or widowers, Schedule Y-2 for married persons filing separately, and Schedule Z for persons who are the head of a household but who have no spouse with whom to file a joint return. Each of these tax rate schedules illustrates the basic **tax bracket** system used to assure that taxpayers with differing incomes pay differing *rates* (as well as amounts) of tax. For 1988, income in the lowest rate bracket was taxed at a rate of 15 percent, income in the second tax rate bracket was taxed at the rate of 28 percent, and additional income in what amounted to a third tax rate bracket was taxed at a rate of 33 percent. The 33 percent tax rate bracket only extended over an amount of marginal income that would cause high income taxpayers to pay 28 percent on all of their taxable income. Once this 28 percent average tax rate had been achieved, the marginal tax rate returned to 28 percent.

The tax bracket system assures that taxpayers with differing incomes pay differing rates, as well as differing amounts, of tax.

The system of exemptions, deductions, and tax brackets makes income taxation a very flexible instrument for government policy. Deductions can tailor the tax to suit special circumstances (such as extraordinary medical expenses) and can encourage certain private expenditures (such as charitable contributions). At the same time, the personal exemptions and tax-rate brackets make it possible for the tax to be **progressive**, meaning that persons with higher incomes pay a higher percentage of their income in tax than do persons with lower incomes. Progression is achieved because each higher layer of income pays a higher tax rate. (Note that once U.S. taxpayers pay an average rate of 28 percent, there is no further progression.) The **marginal tax rate** for each taxpayer is the rate applicable to the next dollar of income that might be received by that individual.

The personal exemptions and tax-rate brackets allow the individual income tax to be progres-

---

sive—people with higher incomes pay a higher percentage of their income in tax than people with lower incomes.

Unfortunately, the features that give the income tax its flexibility—exemptions, deductions, and rate brackets—have also generated serious problems for the tax. The flexibility offered by exemptions and deductions has encouraged special-interest provisions that lower taxes for some while forcing tax rates up for most taxpayers. Each special exemption or deduction may make sense in itself, but their cumulative effect makes the tax extremely complicated and raises questions about its basic fairness. In the Tax Reform Act of 1986, Congress eliminated or reduced many special provisions and lowered tax rates substantially.

Unfortunately, the flexibility offered by exemptions and deductions has encouraged special-interest provisions that lower taxes for some but force tax rates up for most other taxpayers.

Indexing the Income Tax During the 1970s and early 1980s, a period of exceptionally high inflation, many taxpayers experienced **bracket creep** as inflation pushed them into higher and higher tax-rate brackets. This happened because the dollar amount of their income, along with their cost of living, went up with the inflation. As they moved into higher brackets in the income tax, taxpayers faced higher and higher marginal tax rates, even when they were not better off in real terms. The net result of bracket creep was that average tax rates increased throughout the economy. Inflation was yielding a tax revenue bonus for the government without any new legislation to authorize the increase.

To put a stop to bracket creep, indexing was built into the federal individual income tax starting in 1985. **Indexing** is a system that automatically makes adjustments for changes in the general price level. When the price level increases, the personal exemption and certain limits on personal deduction amounts are increased accordingly. In addition, each tax bracket is widened so that bracket

creep caused by inflation is not a serious problem.[2] A taxpayer does not move into a higher bracket unless his or her income increases proportionately more than the general price level.

To put a stop to bracket creep—inflation pushing taxpayers into higher tax-rate brackets and personal exemptions and limits on deductions changing in real terms—a system of indexing was instituted in 1985. Indexing automatically makes adjustments for changes in the general price level.

Tax Simplification and the "Flat Tax" As just noted, the flexibility of the income tax has encouraged Congress to grant many special allowances to help particular interest groups or to promote politically popular causes. Income set aside for retirement can be "sheltered" from taxation, employer payments for employee health insurance are excluded from taxation, and so on. Over the years, increasing amounts of money flowed into these favored areas and off the tax rolls, reducing the **tax base**, which is the amount of income actually subjected to the tax. As a result, in order to maintain government revenues, higher tax rates were necessary.

The Tax Reform Act of 1986 was the result of a concerted effort to reverse this erosion of the tax base. By eliminating many special deductions and exclusions, tax rates could be reduced while maintaining revenue neutrality—that is, not changing total tax revenue. In addition, the 1986 legislation reduced the number of tax-rate brackets. In this respect, the ultimate simplification would be a **flat tax**, which would have only one tax-rate bracket.

Special deductions increasingly ate into the tax base (the amount of income subjected to taxation) until the Tax Reform Act of 1986,

---

2. Inflation still causes problems in taxing business profits and gains and losses on sales of assets. This is because indexing has not been applied to determining the costs of assets. Without such an adjustment, the dollar amount of gain on the sale of an asset overstates the real (price-level-adjusted) amount of that gain when inflation has taken place.

which eliminated or reduced many deductions and exclusions.

In the years preceding the 1986 tax reform, flat-tax and tax-simplification proposals were offered by each major political party and by the U.S. Treasury as well. The major advantage of flat-rate tax systems is that they avoid many complications that arise when tax rates increase as the amount of reported income increases. Perhaps the most prominent example of this problem is the so-called "marriage tax"—the increase in tax that arises when two individuals, each with their own income, marry. Once married, they must combine their incomes on a joint return and face the higher marginal tax rates specified for the higher total income.[3]

A flat-rate tax system would eliminate this problem. A flat-rate tax system would also eliminate the penalty that graduated tax-rate systems impose on incomes that fluctuate widely from year to year. For the same reason, under a flat-rate tax, there would be little incentive for taxpayers to try to artificially shift income from one tax year to another or to divide income among several family members in order to minimize tax liability. Strange as it may seem, a flat-rate tax could still be progressive if personal exemptions were retained. This is because the exemption would be a larger fraction of a low income than of a high income, so that the average tax rate on total income would be higher for high incomes than for low incomes.

The major advantage of flat-rate tax systems is that they avoid many complications that arise when tax rates increase as the amount of reported income increases.

Social Security Taxes

Social Security taxes are another large revenue producer for government in the United States. Because there are two Social Security taxes, one of

3. Actually, they have the option of filing separately and paying tax according to Schedule Y-2. However, the rates on this schedule do not entirely eliminate the marriage penalty.

which is almost completely hidden from the taxpayer, many people do not realize how much money is actually paid. One of the Social Security taxes is taken directly out of the worker's paycheck. Most taxpayers are aware of this tax. For 1989, this tax was 7.51 percent of pay up to total pay of $48,000 (with no tax on pay over this amount). The second tax, of an equal amount, is paid by the employer, so that the total tax rate in 1989 was 15.02 percent on pay covered by the law.

The Social Security taxes have no deductions for individual circumstances and the only exemption is for pay in excess of the annual maximum. Therefore, for persons who earned less than $48,000 in 1989, it was a **proportional tax**, that is, the average tax rate was the same regardless of the amount of income. But average tax rates go down for people who earn more than the annual maximum base income, since no tax is paid on amounts over this maximum. Therefore, considering the entire range of individual incomes, the Social Security tax is a **regressive tax**, that is, the average rate of tax is lower for those with high income than it is for those with lower income.

There are two Social Security taxes, one paid by the worker and one paid by the employer. The Social Security tax is regressive because the average rate of tax is lower for those with an income higher than the maximum base as compared with those with income below the maximum tax base.

The money collected from Social Security taxes goes into a special trust fund that is used to pay benefits to retired people and others entitled to receive benefits under the law. In other words, Social Security benefits are part of the transfer payments component of government expenditure. However, amounts received in benefits are not exactly proportional to the amounts paid in taxes. Instead, the benefit system is tilted to favor low-income persons.

Labor Market Effects Your knowledge of microeconomics can help you recognize some of the economic effects of the Social Security system. Since the employer pays tax on labor inputs but not on machinery inputs, the tax raises the relative cost of labor and encourages firms to substitute machines in place of workers in the production process. This is illustrated in Figure 6. In this figure, the horizontal axis shows quantities of labor demanded and supplied, and the vertical axis shows market wage rates that might be agreed to between workers and employers. The supply curve, S, shows the amounts of labor that will be offered at various possible wage rates and the demand curve, D_1, shows the quantities that would be demanded by employers if they did not have to pay the Social Security payroll tax. Equilibrium would be at A, with wage rate W_1 and Q_1 quantity of labor demanded and supplied. If the tax causes firms to use machines instead of labor, the payroll tax shifts the demand curve to the left to D_2, and equilibrium will move to B, with wage rate W_2 and Q_2 quantity of labor demanded and supplied. Other things being equal, the wage rate will be lower and the quantity of labor demanded and supplied will be less because of this payroll tax. This is especially likely for unskilled workers, who are most likely to be displaced by machines.

The Social Security payroll tax raises the relative cost of labor and encourages firms to substitute machines for workers, especially unskilled workers.

The economic effect of the part of the tax that is taken out of the worker's paycheck is more difficult to analyze because much depends on whether workers believe that this tax payment (and the matching employer payment) is buying retirement income that would otherwise not be received. Let us assume that the supply curve in Figure 6 is based on workers believing that Social Security tax payments lead to higher retirement income. As long as workers hold this belief, equilibrium will be as described above. But if workers come to believe that the tax payments have no effect on the amount of retirement income they will receive, the amount of labor they will be willing to offer at any given market wage rate will be smaller, and the supply curve will shift to the left. Market wage rates would move up from W_2, and employment would be less than Q_2.

FIGURE 6
Payroll Tax and the Demand for Labor

The supply curve, S, shows the quantities of labor supplied at various wage rates. The demand curve, D_1, shows quantities demanded at various wage rates if there is no tax on the payroll of the employer. A payroll tax, such as is imposed for Social Security, shifts the demand curve for labor to D_2. At the new equilibrium, B, the wage rate is lower, and less labor is demanded and supplied than at the original equilibrium at A.

Effects on Saving Another exercise in microeconomics arises from the benefit side of Social Security. Since government insurance is a substitute for private insurance, covered individuals may buy less retirement insurance from private insurance companies. Thus, voluntary saving for retirement is displaced, to some extent, by the Social Security system. This leads to one of the most controversial aspects of Social Security. Private insurance companies must, by law, build up reserves to guarantee the future payment of benefits. The companies loan these reserve funds to business firms to finance investment in machines and other forms of capital. But the Social Security system is not required to build up such reserves. Instead, the system allows for today's tax receipts to be used to pay benefits to today's retirees. By reducing the supply of loanable funds, the Social Security system may raise interest rates and reduce the equilibrium quantity of investment in the economy. This could lead to a slower rate of economic growth for the economy.

Voluntary saving for retirement is displaced, to some extent, by the Social Security system. Since the Social Security system is not required to build up reserves, it may reduce total saving and slow economic growth.

Corporation Income Tax

The corporation income tax is another powerful revenue producer for government, though the amounts collected are much smaller than individual income and Social Security taxes. Like the individual income tax, the corporation income tax is used by both the federal government and state governments, with the federal government getting more money from the tax than do state governments.

Corporation income taxes are based on the net income (accounting profits) of corporations. For 1988 the highest bracket rate for the federal tax was 34 percent, and because the brackets are small, most corporate income falls in the highest bracket. Corporations are quick to react to changes that the government may make in defining income subject to the tax. For example, changes in ways of figuring depreciation or in credits allowed for investments can have powerful effects on the behavior of corporations.

Corporation income taxes, another major source of revenue for federal and state governments, are based on the net income of corporations.

Economists are not sure exactly who bears the major burden of corporation income taxes. To see why this is so, think back to your study of market types. Suppose that an income tax is imposed on a corporation that operates in a purely competitive or monopolistically competitive market. At long-run equilibrium, this firm will have some accounting profit and some tax liability, but it will have zero economic profit. Therefore, the tax will force the firm out of business unless it can engage in **tax shifting** by transferring the burden of the tax either forward in the form of higher prices to consumers or backward in the form of lower wages for labor or lower prices for other inputs. Whether the tax can be shifted forward to consumers depends on whether competing firms also are subject to the tax and on whether there are good substitutes for the product. Similarly, whether or not labor and other resource suppliers can be forced to accept lower prices depends on conditions in their factor (resource) markets. The tax may be shifted partly forward and partly backward. Since individual firms and markets differ greatly from one another, it is not possible to make a general statement about who bears the burden of the tax.

If the corporation is an actual monopoly or an oligopoly, microeconomic analysis suggests that it may receive some economic profit in the long run. In this situation, some of the tax may be paid from the economic profit. The owners of the corporation (the shareholders) might bear some of the burden of the tax through lower dividends and lower stock values. But there still may be forward shifting to consumers and backward shifting to labor and other resource suppliers. The part that is borne by shareholders may have a progressive effect, since most (but not all) corporate shares are owned by high-income people, but the part passed to consumers and the part passed to resource suppliers may have regressive effects.

The corporation income tax may be shifted either forward in the form of higher prices to consumers or backward in the form of lower wages for labor or lower prices for other inputs.

Sales Taxes and Excise Taxes

A **sales tax** is imposed on the sale of a product whereas an **excise tax** may be imposed on either the sale or the manufacture of a product. Their economic effects are much the same. States and some local governments have general sales taxes, which apply across the board to most sales, as well as selective sales taxes on particular products, such as gasoline, cigarettes, and alcoholic beverages. The federal government imposes excise taxes on gasoline, motor oil, and a number of other products. Consumers are likely to bear most of the burden of sales or excise taxes. However, some of the tax may be passed back to workers as well as other owners of resources used to produce the product. A simple supply-and-demand exercise shows how this can happen.

Figure 7 shows the demand curve for a product and two supply curves, one (S_1) showing supply without a tax and the other (S_2) showing supply after an excise tax is imposed. Without the tax, the equilibrium is at A, with quantity Q_1 demanded and supplied at price P_1. The tax is put into the model as an added cost of supplying the product. Thus, the supply curve is shifted to the left and the new supply curve is S_2. The new equilibrium is at B, with quantity Q_2 and price P_2. Because the price has risen from P_1 to P_2, consumers bear some of the burden of the tax. But the price increase is less than the full amount of the tax per unit, which is shown as the vertical distance from B to C. The per unit amount received by suppliers is P_3, which is less than they received before the tax was imposed. Therefore, part of the burden of the tax falls on people other than consumers of the product. Since the quantity of the product supplied has fallen because of the tax, labor and other resources have been forced to accept lower wages or change jobs (or both), and some firms may have gone out of business. These workers, business people, and resource owners bear some of the burden of the tax.

A sales tax is imposed on the sale of a product; an excise tax may be imposed on either the sale or the manufacture of a product. Consumers are likely to pay higher prices for products that are subject to sales or excise taxes and some of the tax may be shifted backward to suppliers of resources used in producing the taxed products.

Excise Burden There is also an **excess burden** from this type of tax, as there is from most types of tax. That is, the total burden is greater than the amount of money collected by the government from the tax. The money collected by the government is shown by the green rectangle in Figure 7. The vertical dimension of this rectangle (BC) is the amount of tax collected per unit of the product,

FIGURE 7
Effects of an Excise Tax

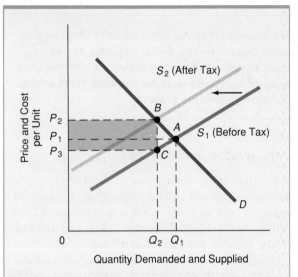

Quantity Demanded and Supplied

The supply curve for this product is S_1 when no tax is imposed on its manufacture. Equilibrium is at A, with quantity Q_1 demanded and supplied at price P_1. An excise tax is shown as an added cost of supplying the product. After the tax, the supply curve is S_2, and equilibrium is at B, with price P_2 and quantity Q_2. P_3 is the amount received per unit by suppliers after the tax is imposed. The green area shows tax revenue collected by the government, since the vertical dimension of this rectangle, BC, shows the amount of tax per unit, and the horizontal dimension shows the number of units on which the tax is collected. The triangular area ABC shows excess burden—that is, the net gain from those units of the product that were produced when there was no tax but that are not produced after the tax is imposed.

and the horizontal dimension shows the number of units on which the tax is collected. The excess burden is shown by the triangle ABC. This triangle shows net welfare gains from units of the product that were produced when there was no tax, but which are not produced after the tax is imposed. Net welfare gains existed because the amounts that consumers were willing and able to pay (shown by the demand curve) were greater than the amounts that suppliers needed to receive to persuade them to supply the product (shown by the supply curve).

A sales tax has much the same effect as an excise tax. At equilibrium under a sales tax, consumers pay more per unit of the product than they did before the tax, and less will be purchased, other

FIGURE 8
Price Elasticity of Demand and the Effect of an Excise Tax

(a) Price-Inelastic Demand

(b) Price-Elastic Demand

In each panel, supply curve *S* represents the relationship between price and quantity supplied in the absence of an excise tax. Equilibrium exists where price is $1.00 and quantity is 50,000. Purchasers spend $50,000 a day for the good or service. In each of these panels, supply curve S_1 shows amounts offered for sale at various possible prices after an excise tax is imposed. The amount of the tax is the same in each panel. In panel (a), the demand curve, *D*, is price inelastic over this price range. After the tax, equilibrium is at a price of $1.50 and a quantity of 40,000 units a day. Purchasers spend $60,000 a day. In panel (b), the demand curve, *D*, is price elastic over this price range. After the tax, equilibrium is at a price of $1.20 and a quantity of 30,000 units a day. Purchasers spend $36,000 a day.

things being equal. Suppliers receive less per unit than before the tax. Thus, some burden is imposed on consumers and some is shifted to suppliers of resources used in producing the taxed goods and services.

Like other taxes, sales and excise taxes create an excess burden—the total burden on consumers, workers, business people, and other resource owners is greater in value than the amount of money collected by the government from the tax.

Price Elasticity Effects The economic analysis of excise and sales taxes offers a convenient review of your understanding of the concept of price elasticity. For example, if the demand for the taxed good or service is price inelastic over the range of its price increase due to the tax, the total amount of money spent by purchasers will be greater after the tax

than it was before the tax. The supply shift caused by the tax will bring a large price increase but little reduction in the quantity demanded. Most of the tax burden will be borne by consumers and little will be shifted back to suppliers of resources.

This is illustrated in panel (a) of Figure 8. The supply curve shifts from *S* to S_1 because of the tax. As a result, the equilibrium price rises from $1.00 to $1.50, and the equilibrium quantity falls from 50,000 to 40,000 per day. The proportionate change in quantity demanded is less than the proportionate change in the price. The coefficient of price elasticity is 0.556.[4] The total amount spent by purchasers increases from $50,000 to $60,000 a day.

4. The formula for calculating price elasticity of demand is

$$E_D = \frac{\dfrac{Q_{D_2} - Q_{D_1}}{Q_{D_1} + Q_{D_2}}}{\dfrac{P_2 - P_1}{P_1 + P_2}}$$

On the other hand, if demand is price elastic over the price range involved, the supply-curve shift will bring a smaller price increase to consumers, and there will be a larger reduction in the equilibrium quantity demanded and supplied. This is shown in panel (b) of Figure 8. In this panel, the two supply curves are identical to those in panel (a); that is, the original supply curve and the amount of the tax per unit of the product are the same. However, because demand is price elastic, the equilibrium quantity falls all the way to 30,000 units per day, and the price rises only to $1.20. The proportionate change in quantity is larger than the proportionate change in the price. Price elasticity of demand is 2.75. The total amount spent by purchasers falls from $50,000 to $36,000 a day. Consumers will spend less for this good or service after the tax than they did before, and most of the burden of the tax will fall on resource owners rather than on consumers. Also, the government will collect less tax if demand is price elastic than if it is price inelastic, other things being equal. Therefore, economic analysis leads us to expect that both government and resource owners will prefer to have sales and excise taxes placed on goods and services for which demand is price inelastic. Taxes on cigarettes and alcoholic beverages, for example, are powerful revenue raisers and do relatively little to reduce quantities produced and consumed. These taxes do more to raise revenue than they do to reduce consumption.

Motor Fuels Taxes

The motor fuels tax ("gas tax") is a selective sales tax that is especially interesting because the money collected is put into a special fund and used to construct and maintain highways. This adds a new dimension to microeconomic analysis because highways are complementary in consumption with motor fuels. The tax will shift the supply curve for motor fuels to the left, but the new or better highways will shift the demand curve for motor fuels to the right. It is quite possible that the shift of the demand curve for motor fuels could more than make up for the reduction in the quantity demanded caused by the tax. More gasoline may be sold with the tax than would have been sold without it!

When motor fuel tax money is used for highway construction and maintenance, it is good microeconomic logic to see the government as a supplier of highway services and to see the motor fuels tax as a **user charge**, that is, as a price that the government charges to cover the costs of this service. Actually, highways are just one of many semi-commercial activities carried on by government. Parking meters collect user charges for parking services, the postal service sells stamps for delivering mail, water departments charge fees for water service, and so on. For highway finance, the gasoline pump becomes a device (like a highway tollbooth) to collect a price for the use of the highway.

Property Taxes

A **property tax** is a tax that is imposed on the market value of property (mainly land and buildings) and collected annually from the owners of the taxed properties. In the United States, most property taxes are collected by local governments. They are especially important for school districts.

The system for collecting property taxes is different from the system used for income, profits, sales, or excise taxes, where some kind of transaction must take place before any tax is due. Property taxes are collected each year, whether or not there has been any transaction involving the property. An assessor estimates how much the property would sell for if an actual transaction were to take place, and this value is multiplied by the tax rate to determine the amount of tax to be paid. The payment is made by the person or business that holds legal title to the property. If the tax is not paid, the property may be taken by the government and sold for the amount of the taxes.

A property tax is an annual tax imposed on the market value of property. Most property taxes in the United States are collected by local governments. They are important in financing elementary and secondary education.

Another unique feature of the property tax is that the tax rate (often called **millage**—one mil being one-tenth of 1 percent) is set after, rather than before, the government's expenditure budget is determined. Government expenditure is determined and then the tax rate is set to bring in exactly the amount of money needed. This differs from the procedure for most taxes, where tax rates are set first and actual collections determine how much money will be available to spend. Economists sometimes contend that the property tax gives citizens more control over local governments than they have over state and national governments that do not depend on the property tax.

The property tax rate is set after the government's expenditure budget is determined.

Property Taxes and Housing Property taxes offer many opportunities to apply microeconomic tools of analysis. For example, consider how the tax may affect the market for housing or the markets for factories or office buildings. If the tax is considered part of the cost of supplying housing, or factories, or office buildings, increases in the tax will shift the supply curves to the left. Other things being equal, this will result in higher prices for houses, factories, or office buildings compared with the prices of other things that are not taxed under the property tax. The higher relative prices will, economists predict, reduce the quantities of housing, factories, or office buildings compared with the quantities of goods and services not subject to the tax.

Property Taxes and Education The largest use of property-tax revenues is to finance elementary and secondary schools. Because school districts involve relatively small geographic areas, it often happens that the property value per pupil is much greater in some school districts than in others. This, in turn, means that, in order to provide equal educational services per pupil, the low-property-value district would have to charge a higher tax rate ("millage") than the high-property-value school district. Alternatively, the low-property-value school district may simply spend less money per pupil, which may mean that pupils in these districts will be less well educated than pupils in high-property-value districts.

To apply microeconomic analysis to this situation, go back to the concepts of externalities and collective goods that you studied earlier in this chapter. The services of schools have important external and collective aspects, since students from one district often meet and work with people from other school districts. These externality and collective-consumption features, plus ethical considerations of human rights and income redistribution, have led states to set up grant-in-aid systems under which money from the state or the federal government is used to even out the services rendered by different school districts.

PUBLIC CHOICE

Public choice is an area of study that combines economics and political science in an effort to understand how decisions are made in group situations. It is an important, exciting, and relatively new field of study. Since our focus is on the U.S. economy, we will examine public choice analysis as it applies economic concepts to decision making in a democracy with free and frequent elections. As you can easily imagine, different public choice models apply in different governmental systems.

Public choice is an area of study that attempts to understand decision making in group situations.

Taxation and Voting

In democratic public choice models, a key role of taxation is to provide information to voters about how the costs of government services will be shared among citizens. For example, suppose that a proposal is made that the government should provide a new defense program or a new medical research program. According to public choice analysis, in a democracy each voter should be able to estimate how much he or she would have to pay in order to finance each new program. For example, if the government were financed entirely by an individual income tax and if the government proposed to finance a new program with a 1 percentage point increase in the tax rate, each citizen should be able to figure his or her share of the cost. If your taxable income were $30,000, you would have a tax increase of $300 if the program were carried out. If your taxable income were $40,000, your share would be $400, and so on.

In the public choice model, the second step in democratic decision making is to give the citizens an opportunity to vote on whether or not each new program should be provided. Each voter is expected to estimate the benefit he or she would get from the program, to compare this benefit against his or her share of its cost, and to vote accordingly. If benefits exceed costs, they will vote "yes." They will vote "no" if their cost exceeds their estimate of benefit. In other words, voters are expected to vote according to their self-interest. In this approach, government is the servant of the people, providing those goods and services that citizens want and are willing to pay for.

In the public choice model, a key role of taxation is to provide information to voters about how the costs of government services will be shared among citizens. Each citizen then votes, according to self-interest, on whether his or her benefit from the proposed service will outweigh the tax that he or she would have to pay to finance it.

The illustration above is a very simplified explanation of the basic idea of taxing and voting in public choice theory. Because we are offering only an overview of public choice theory, we will just note some of the many additional factors that go into this decision-making process. For example, is a simple majority vote really enough to make sure that the proposed system is worth its cost, or would a two-thirds vote be better? Is the individual income tax the best way to divide costs among citizens, or would it be better to use some other tax, such as a sales tax or a property tax, which might come closer to matching the different amounts of benefit received by different citizens? These are important questions in the study of public choice.

The view that voters are motivated by self-interest illustrates the **benefits-received principle** of taxation, which says that the amount of tax that a person should pay for the marginal unit of a good or service should equal the money equivalent of the benefit that he or she expects to receive from it. It is quite different from the **ability-to-pay principle** of taxation, which says that higher tax rates should be paid by those who can afford to pay more, even if their benefit is equal to or less than the benefits received by others. The ability-to-pay approach often is used to support **progressive taxation**, that is, taxation designed to redistribute after-tax incomes in the direction of greater equality. Both the benefits-received and the ability-to-pay principles are *normative* statements about how the tax liabilities of different individuals *should* be determined. However, much of the research of public choice economists suggests that benefits received is a *positive* statement about voter behavior.

The benefits-received principle of taxation says that the amount of tax a person should pay for

---

the marginal unit of a good or service should equal the money equivalent of the benefit he or she expects to receive from it. The ability-to-pay principle says that higher tax rates should be paid by those who can afford to pay more.

Elected Officials

Public choice theory offers economic models to explain the behavior of elected officials. According to these models, the candidate for elective office assembles a package of proposals that he or she hopes will appeal to the voters. Candidates who do a good job of sensing the desires of the voters and of designing proposals to cater to these desires will be the ones who win elections and hold office. In this sense, political candidates have certain similarities to business entrepreneurs. The successful political entrepreneurs win elective offices. This means, however, that instead of choosing one item at a time as they usually can in a market, citizens need to vote for and appear to back the whole set of positions associated with some candidate for office, even though they differ from the candidate on some of these positions. All of us who have voted have experienced this frustration. Seldom is there a candidate who offers exactly the set of views that we favor. Therefore, messages from citizens to government are less than perfectly transmitted. Additional problems arise from the rather short time horizons that are forced on elected officials because they must seek re-election every few years. These officials are encouraged to take a biased view of government programs when the timing of benefits is different from the timing of costs. Since benefits help them to win votes and costs (to be paid from taxes) make them lose votes, the elected official favors programs that offer quick benefits but put off the costs.

According to public choice theory, candidates who do a good job of sensing the desires of the voters and of designing proposals to cater to those desires will be the ones who win elections.

Since benefits help elected officials win votes, and costs make them lose votes, elected officials favor programs that offer quick benefits but put off the costs.

Once elected, the officeholder starts working and planning for the next election. In part, this means trying to carry out the promises made to the voters in the past election. This may involve trading a vote on one issue in exchange for the vote of another officeholder on an issue that is more important to the officeholder's re-election. Vote-trading and compromises, which are important in public choice theory, have obvious economic overtones.

It is generally recognized that people are more careful about spending their own money than they are about spending someone else's money. Undoubtedly this problem exists in large corporations as well as in governments. But governments not only spend someone else's money; they spend it through appropriations out of a "general fund." One of the theories of public choice economics is that general fund spending is often both unwise and excessive.

The potential waste and excessive spending under the general fund system is illustrated by the following hypothetical case. Suppose that the people in your congressional district develop a proposal that asks for $250 million of federal money to build a flood-control dam in your district. A program of this size will help a lot of people in your district, and your local representative will make every effort to pass the legislation. Since $250 million amounts to an average of only one dollar from each citizen of the country, most voters and taxpayers who pay into the general fund may not even notice the proposal, much less organize any campaign against it. Moreover, if your local representative is enterprising, he or she may promise to vote for harbor improvements or urban renewal projects for other districts if their representatives will vote for your flood-control measure. The net effect of all this political activity is that many local-interest projects may be undertaken that are wasteful or inefficient. Local benefits may exceed local costs, but only because most of the cost is borne by people elsewhere in the country and the amounts that these outsiders pay are so small for each individual that no effective political opposition is organized. Therefore, for many of these programs the total benefits are less than the total costs.

According to public choice economics, general fund spending is often both unwise and excessive.

A similar public choice model provides an economic explanation of the power of special-interest groups. Some government actions affect millions of people, but have so little effect on each individual that no one takes time off to go to Washington or the state capitol and lobby for or against the action. On the other hand, other government actions may affect only a few people, but if each of these individuals faces large gain or loss, most of them will appear at the capitol to influence the result. Because of this political fact of life, the influence of lobbies and pressure groups on government decisions is out of proportion to the overall importance of their positions or the number of people involved.

Bureaucracies and Budgets

Government bureaus and agencies provide another important dimension of public choice theory. They are composed of people employed by the government to implement existing legislation and to collect information related to possible new legislation. Typically, these bureaus and agencies are keyed to particular interest groups. The best known are the government departments, such as the Department of Agriculture, for the interests of farmers, the Department of Labor for workers, the Department of Commerce for business, and so on.

In public choice theory, government bureaucracies are perceived as motivated by self-interest. Individuals working in these bureaucracies seek higher pay, security, prestige, and power. In each bureau and agency, these self-interest goals translate into an agency goal of obtaining as much money as possible from the Congress. Thus, the theory suggests that, in the government budget process, vigorous rivalries develop among agencies and bureaus. In order to get as much as it can, each

agency or bureau is always looking for new programs and ideas, and is always trying to persuade voters and officeholders of the merits of agency proposals. They generate a strong pressure for ever larger budgets and ever more government spending.

According to public choice theory, government bureaucracies are perceived as motivated by self-interest. They try to obtain as much money as possible from Congress by constantly proposing new programs, generating pressure for ever larger budgets.

Benefit-Cost Analysis   **Benefit-cost analysis** is a procedure sometimes used by government agencies to decide whether or not a proposed project should be undertaken. As its name implies, the procedure involves estimating the money equivalent of the benefits of the project and comparing these benefit estimates with the costs of providing the good or service. The cost estimates are similar to calculations done by business firms in making an investment decision. Also, since benefits usually are realized long after most costs have been incurred, discounting procedures must be used.[5] But, because of the nonrival and nonexcludable features of collective goods, benefit-cost analysis by government agencies faces problems that are different from those faced by business firms. Since prices cannot be charged, it is especially difficult to obtain reliable estimates of the willingness of benefit receivers to pay for the proposed services. Nevertheless, good benefit-cost analysis can help government agencies forecast whether legislators and voters will support their proposed projects. Therefore, benefit-cost analysis plays an important role when an agency prepares its proposals to present to the Congress.

Benefit-cost analysis is a procedure sometimes used by government agencies to decide whether or not a proposed project should be

---

5. For an explanation of the investment decision and discounting, see Chapter 32.

undertaken. It involves estimating the money equivalent of the benefits of a project and comparing these benefits with the costs of that project.

The Budget Process Actual spending decisions are made through the budget process. Initial budget requests are prepared by the government departments (Agriculture, Defense, Interior, Education, and so on) and are assembled by the Office of Management and Budget into the official budget document that is presented by the president to the Congress in January or February each year. Congressional committees then consider separate parts of this budget request and make recommendations to the houses of Congress for action. During the spring and summer the Congress passes some dozen or fifteen appropriations bills, which, taken together, constitute the government's official budget. Tax legislation is separate from expenditure legislation. Even though the basic tax laws are not enacted anew for each budget year, a considerable amount of congressional action is usually taking place about proposals to alter tax rates or particular features of the tax laws.

A bias in the direction of deficit spending has been apparent for a long time to both public choice economists and to the general public. The basic source of the bias probably lies with the voters themselves, who give less support to legislators who raise taxes than they give to legislators who raise expenditures. Over the years, many attempts have been made to devise a budget process to counteract this bias toward deficits. In the 1960s, for example, Congress attempted to discipline itself through the **Planning-Programming Budget System (PPBS)**, which required agencies to specify the different programs that they wished to carry out and to plan expenditure needs for several years in advance. In the 1970s, budget reform required the Congress to set spending targets for itself early in its deliberations and then to see that actual appropriations came close to the targets. However, not a single one of these measures has succeeded in preventing budget deficits.

The **Gramm-Rudman-Hollings Act**, passed in 1985, is another experiment in reforming the budget process. The act establishes year-by-year deficit-reduction targets. Each year, estimates are to be made of the amount of revenue that will be raised by the tax system and of the amount of expenditure that would take place under prevailing legislation. If these estimates reveal impending deficits that are too large, a process is set in motion to bring about expenditure reductions.

In an effort to combat a bias in the direction of deficit spending, Congress has attempted several budget reforms in the past thirty years. The latest effort to reform the budget process is the 1985 Gramm-Rudman-Hollings Act, which establishes year-by-year deficit-reduction targets.

The Federal System

Another branch of public choice theory focuses on relationships among different levels of government. The United States has a **federal system** of government, that is, one formed through the union of several separate states. The U.S. federal government has powers that are either specified or implied in the Constitution, while governmental powers not specified or implied in the Constitution are reserved to the separate states that make up the federal union, or to their local governments, which have powers delegated to them by their state governments or constitutions. Thus, the United States has a multilevel system of government decision making—federal, state, and local.

In the part of public choice theory called **fiscal federalism**, the importance of a multilevel system of government lies in the opportunities that it offers for dividing up the responsibilities of government, placing each in the hands of the level that is able to do the job best. For example, responsibilities for police and fire protection are placed at the local level. Highways and higher education responsibilities are mainly at the state level, while national defense is a responsibility of the federal government. The theories of externalities and collective goods and services, which you studied earlier, provide models for how these governmental activities may be shared. The key idea is to assign each service responsibility to the level of government that comes closest to matching the geographic area over which collective benefits or external effects are important. For example, local governments are expected to do the best job with police and fire protection because the area of collective consumption is local and because local citizens have the most at stake in these operations. They can be counted on to see that effective service is provided at lowest possible cost. Similarly, national defense, which generates collective benefits nationwide, can be handled best by the federal government. When the areas of benefit do not exactly match the areas of government jurisdiction, intergovernmental cooperation is needed. Often, areas of responsibility shift as public demands change.

According to fiscal federalism, the multilevel system of government places each responsibility of government in the hands of the level best able to do the job. The key idea is to assign each service responsibility to the level that comes closest to matching the geographic area over which the collective benefits are important.

Economics in Focus

Taxes Unsimplified

The Tax Reform Act of 1986 was designed to simplify the income tax code, close loopholes, and make the system fairer. But as the filing deadline for 1987 returns approached, the act had prompted 2,704 changes in the tax code, 65 announcements from the Internal Revenue Service (IRS), 42 extra regulations, 32 revenue rulings, and 48 new tax forms.

Some ordinary calculations became extraordinarily complicated. A home mortgage interest deduction, for example, originally occupied a single line on the 1040 tax return, but after the reform it required two pages of calculations based on four pages of instructions. The procedures for determining inventory cost grew so involved that Ford Motor Company revised its entire system of inventory accounting. Worse, experts noted more than 300 ambiguities in the 1986 law, and Congress delayed passage of a corrective act to deal with them.

The result was widespread bewilderment, even some panic. Although the IRS opened 50 new walk-in offices, added staff, and set up toll-free hotlines, many individuals who had always prepared their own returns now flocked to accountants and other professional tax-preparers for help. Accountants themselves found the revised rules confusing, and they signed up by the score for special courses in the new tax code.

How did a supposed simplification become so unsimplified? First, the tax reformers had to compromise on certain key issues in order to push the bill through Congress. Some loopholes and deductions were not eliminated but only reduced, so the procedures for using them became more complicated. Second, many experts contended that change itself was the main problem: the tax rules had been altered so frequently that no one could keep up with the endless variations.

The Tax Reform Act certainly had its virtues. It eliminated some two million low-income citizens from the tax rolls. The new system of fewer brackets and lower rates combined with fewer tax shelters was, arguably, a fairer one. It also allowed a greater number of people to use a short tax-return form rather than the long form. It seemed to have a good effect on tax compliance as well: on individual returns the tax gap (the amount owed to the government but not voluntarily paid) dropped from $79 billion in 1986 to $63 billion in 1987. The overall tax gap, however, was still higher than it had been in 1982.

Everyone agrees in the abstract that taxes should be simple, fair, and easy to collect. The saga of the 1986 Tax Reform Act shows how difficult it is to achieve that goal in a modern economy. Perhaps the most ironic reports came from the General Accounting Office, which conducted surveys to determine the reliability of the advice that the IRS provided to taxpayers over the telephone. According to these surveys, the IRS's own experts gave wrong answers to questions 20 to 40 percent of the time.

Sources: "Pity the Taxman," *The Economist,* April 15, 1989, pp. 29–30; Annetta Miller et al., "The Tax Nightmare," *Newsweek,* February 29, 1988, pp. 40–41; Bill Powell and Rich Thomas, "Don't Roll Back Tax Reform," *Newsweek,* February 29, 1988, p. 47; Annetta Miller et al., "Get Ready for the 1040 Blues," *Newsweek,* January 18, 1988, pp. 50–51; Daniel Benjamin, "Caught in a Brier Patch of Changes," *Time,* March 21, 1988, pp. 52–53.

SUMMARY

1. Government expenditures include both transfer payments, which distribute money to citizens, and purchases of goods and services, which are part of aggregate demand in the economy. About 57 percent of government expenditures are for purchases, and the remainder are for transfers. (See pages 760–762 and Figure 1, page 761.)

2. About 60 percent of government receipts are from taxes imposed by the federal government, and the remainder are from taxes imposed by state and local governments. Through grants-in-aid, money collected by one level of government may be used to pay for goods and services provided by another level of government. (See pages 762–763 and Figure 2, page 763.)

3. Microeconomic analysis suggests that, in a market-capitalist system, government may be able to improve resource allocation by providing market-support services and by correcting for market failures, such as those that arise from externalities. (See page 764.)

4. Markets provide excessive quantities of goods or services that generate negative externalities. Government may correct negative-externality market failure by shifting the supply curve to the left through regulations or through taxes. (See pages 765–766.)

5. Positive externalities cause markets to provide quantities that are less than the socially efficient quantity. Government may correct positive-externality market failure by shifting the demand curve to the right through regulations or through subsidies to purchasers. However, it usually is easier to provide subsidies to suppliers, thereby shifting the supply curve to the right. (See page 767.)

6. Because of nonexcludability, markets encounter the free-rider problem and fail to provide efficient quantities of goods and services that are consumed collectively. Government can overcome the free-rider problem by imposing taxes to finance collective goods and services. Because of non-rivalry in consumption, tax money can be pooled into a common fund to finance the provision of a collective good or service. (See pages 769–770.)

7. Tax payments have several purposes: market correction, discouraging free riding, preference revelation, income redistribution, and resource allocation. Individual income taxes are the largest source of government revenue in the United States. Through personal exemptions and tax-rate brackets, individual income taxes are progressive. Average tax rates are higher as income rises. Indexing has been installed in income taxes to prevent inflation from causing bracket creep. The Tax Reform Act of 1986 eliminated or reduced many deductions and exclusions so that tax rates could be lowered. However, the tax is still very complicated. Flat-tax proposals advocate having only one tax bracket and only one tax rate. (See pages 771–775.)

8. Two taxes are used to finance Social Security—one on the worker's pay and one on the employer's payroll. Microeconomic analysis indicates that the payroll tax reduces the demand for labor and lowers employment and wage rates. The Social Security system may reduce saving if it leads workers to reduce private saving to finance retirement. (See pages 775–777).

9. Corporation income taxes are imposed on the accounting profits of corporations. These taxes may be shifted forward to consumers or backward to labor and other suppliers of resources. Dividends and other returns to stockholders also may be reduced by the tax. The actual burden of these taxes is uncertain. (See page 777.)

10. Sales and excise taxes also may be shifted. Price-inelastic demand tends to place more burden on purchasers of the good or service, whereas price-elastic demand tends to place more of the burden on resource owners. Government collects more revenue if demand is price inelastic than if it is price elastic, other things being equal. Excess burden will arise from these taxes if reduced quantities involve units of the good or service on which benefits exceeded costs. (See pages 777–780.)

11. Motor fuels taxes may be classed as user charges when the money collected from the tax is used to finance construction and maintenance of highways. A user charge is similar to a price charged for a good or service. (See page 780.)

12. Property taxes are annual taxes on the value of property, mainly land and buildings. They tend to reduce the supply and increase the market price of housing. Property taxes are used mainly by local governments and are especially important in financing elementary and secondary education. (See pages 780–781.)

13. Public choice theory applies economic concepts to decision making in group situations. Taxpayers, voters, elected officials, and government employees are assumed to base their actions on self-interest. Taxation is based on benefits-received rather than on ability-to-pay principles. Government agencies often use benefit-cost analysis in designing programs. Fiscal federalism studies the assignment of responsibilities to different levels of government in a multilevel system of government. (See pages 781–786.)

KEY TERMS

ability-to-pay principle: a principle of taxation that states that higher tax rates should be paid by those who can afford to pay more, even if their benefit is equal to or less than the benefits received by others (page 782).

allocation function: the responsibility of government to help the economy provide the assortment of goods and services most desired by the people (page 764).

benefit-cost analysis: a procedure sometimes used by government agencies to decide whether or not a proposed project should be undertaken (page 784).

benefits-received principle: a principle of taxation that states that the amount of tax a person should pay for the marginal unit of a good or service should equal the money equivalent of the benefit that he or she expects to receive from it (page 782).

bracket creep: when inflation pushes taxpayers into higher tax-rate brackets (page 774).

collective goods and services: those goods and services that are consumed by the community as a group (page 769).

corporation income taxes: taxes based on the net income (accounting profits) of corporations (page 777).

corrective taxation: taxes used to discourage activities giving rise to negative externalities (page 771).

distribution function: the responsibility of government to alter the distribution of income, as necessary, to obtain the degree of income equality considered appropriate (page 764).

excess burden: when the total burden of a tax is greater in value than the amount of money collected by the government from the tax (page 778).

excise tax: a tax imposed on either the sale or the manufacture of a product (page 777).

external benefits: beneficial effects of an action over which the person receiving the benefit has no control (page 767).

external costs: harmful effects of an action over which the person suffering the harm has no control (page 765).

externality: an economic effect (either beneficial or harmful) experienced by a person who has no control, through the market system, over the action that led to the effect (page 764).

federal system: a system of government consisting of several distinct levels of government such as the national, state, and local governments in the United States (page 785).

fiscal federalism: a system of government in which the responsibilities of government are divided up, each placed in the hands of the level best able to do the job (page 785).

flat tax: a tax with only one tax-rate bracket (page 774).

free-rider problem: the public finance problem that arises because people seek to obtain collective goods or services at the expense of others (page 770).

Gramm-Rudman-Hollings Act: a 1985 U.S. act that attempts to bring about balanced budgets by establishing year-by-year deficit-reduction targets (page 785).

grants-in-aid: programs under which money from a higher level of government is handed over to a lower level of government (page 762).

income redistribution: an attempt to alter the amount of income or wealth inequality among people in a society (page 771).

indexing: a system that automatically makes adjustments for changes in the general price level (page 774).

marginal tax rate: the tax rate applicable to the next dollar of income that might be received by a taxpayer (page 775).

market failure: a situation in which the market is unable to perform satisfactorily (page 764).

millage: a term used in reference to tax rates in property taxation; a mil is 1/10th of a percent (page 781).

nonexcludability: a characteristic of a good or service that makes it impossible or extremely expensive to deny any person in the community the opportunity to consume the good or service once it has been produced (page 769).

nonrival consumption: a characteristic of a good or service that means that one person can benefit from it without causing any significant reduction in the benefits others receive from it (page 770).

personal deductions: expenditures such as extraordinary medical expenses, charitable contributions, certain interest payments, certain state and local taxes, and casualty losses that can be subtracted from income in determining net income subject to tax (page 773).

personal exemption: the amount that can be deducted for the taxpayer(s) and each dependent in calculating income subject to tax (page 773).

Planning-Programming Budget System (PPBS): a budget process employed in the United States during the 1960s that was designed to counteract a bias in the direction of deficit spending; this system required agencies to specify the different programs they wished to carry out and to plan expenditure needs for several years in advance (page 785).

preference revelation: the indication or pronouncement of an individual's desire for public goods and services (page 771).

private benefits: benefits received by an individual directly participating in a transaction, as distinguished from benefits received by others (page 767).

private costs: the costs incurred by persons participating in a transaction, as distinguished from costs experienced by others (page 765).

progressive tax: a tax structured so that persons with higher incomes pay a higher percentage of their income in tax than do persons with lower incomes (page 773).

progressive taxation: taxation designed to redistribute after-tax incomes in the direction of greater equality (page 782).

property tax: a tax imposed on the market value of property and collected annually from the owners of the taxed properties (page 780).

proportional tax: a tax structured so that persons with higher incomes pay exactly the same percentage of their income in tax as do persons with lower incomes (page 775).

public choice: an area of study that combines economics and political science in an effort to understand how decisions are made in group situations (page 781).

regressive tax: a tax structured so that the average rate of tax is lower for those with high income than it is for those with lower income (page 775).

resource allocation: the division of resources among alternative uses (page 771).

sales tax: a tax imposed on the sale of a product (page 777).

social cost: the total value of opportunities forgone because of the production and consumption of a product. It includes both private cost and external cost (page 765).

stabilization function: the responsibility of government to moderate fluctuations in the volume of aggregate economic activity and assure reasonable levels of employment, price stability, and economic growth (page 764).

standard deduction: a deduction in calculating income taxes that applies if people choose not to itemize specific personal deduction amounts (page 773).

subsidy: a payment by someone other than the buyer that helps to cover the cost of a good or service (page 768).

tax base: the amount actually subjected to a tax (page 774).

tax bracket: a range of income over which a specified tax rate is applicable (page 773).

taxes: payments or contributions that a government requires from persons within its jurisdiction or from property or transactions located in its jurisdiction (page 771).

tax shifting: a process of transferring the burden of a tax either forward in the from of higher prices to consumers or backward in the form of lower wages for labor or lower prices for other inputs (page 777).

transfer payments: payments that are not in exchange for any good produced or service rendered during the year in question (page 760).

user charge: a price the government charges as a condition for the use of a service (page 780).

DISCUSSION QUESTIONS

1. Explain the difference between transfer payments and government purchases. Which is part of aggregate demand? Why is the other part not part of aggregate demand? Name the three leading areas of government purchases. Check Figure 1 to make sure you are correct.

2. Do you believe that cigarette smoking results in negative externalities? Are taxes on cigarettes an effective means of reducing such externalities? What use do you believe should be made of the money that the government collects from taxes on cigarettes? Draw a graph to illustrate how negative externalities lead to market failure.

3. Do you believe that especially good students generate positive externalities in your college or university? If so, construct a graph to illustrate the market for good students and explain how merit scholarships can improve resource allocation.

Should tuition for ordinary students be increased to finance merit scholarships?

4. Explain how the free-rider problem may affect the amount of money raised by fund-raising activities (such as the United Way) in your local community. In what sense do the services financed by these contributions produce nonrival consumption benefits?

5. What is the difference between personal exemptions and personal deductions in the individual income tax? Considering the bracket system of tax rates, explain why an individual's marginal tax rate is expected to be higher than his or her average tax rate if the system is progressive.

6. Distinguish between the two taxes used to finance Social Security. Why does the payroll tax lower both employment and market wage rates? Explain how the Social Security tax system is regressive. Compare this with how a flat-rate income tax with personal exemptions would be progressive.

7. Illustrate graphically how an excise tax on a good or service may be shifted partly to consumers and partly to resource owners. How does price elasticity of demand influence these shifts? With a second graph, illustrate how price elasticity of supply affects forward and backward shifting.

8. Illustrate graphically how a property tax on houses can be expected to change the equilibrium price and quantity of housing, other things being equal. What features should be added to this graph if the money collected from the property tax is used to finance a fire station located four blocks away?

9. Discuss how benefit-cost analysis might be applied in deciding whether or not to obtain a college education. For which benefits is discounting likely to be important in your calculations? What are the major costs?

34

Poverty and Income Distribution

Preview This chapter is about poverty and income inequality—problems that arise because the economy neither insures the whole population against poverty nor provides an income distribution that everyone considers fair and just. It also outlines some of the measures that may help to solve these problems.

First we deal with poverty. After discussing poverty concepts and statistical poverty lines, we describe the incidence of poverty among different groups in the population. Then we consider some of the methods for dealing with it. Particular attention is paid to what critics call the "welfare mess" and to proposals for negative income taxes and their impact on the labor supply. The concept of intractable poverty, or the poverty underclass, is discussed, along with the growing visibility of the homeless and the panhandlers.

In the second part of the chapter, we turn to the subject of income distribution and its inequality. We discuss the statistical problems of measuring income inequality and the weaknesses of published figures—such as their omission of nonmoney incomes from home-grown food or subsidized housing. We shall be especially interested in the *personal* income distribution—that is, the distribution among individuals by income-size groups or brackets—but we shall also review the *functional* distribution, as between labor income and property income. In looking at the history of the personal income distribution in the United States, we find that its connection with the functional distribution is surprisingly imprecise.

Finally we examine the question of whether the measured degree of income inequality constitutes *maldistribution,* that is, an unacceptable amount of equality or inequality. We present some arguments that it does and some that it doesn't. The chapter ends by considering several methods of redistributing income.

POVERTY

"For ye have the poor always with you," said Jesus (Matt. 26:11), and Abraham Lincoln asserted that "God must love the poor—he made so many of them." Both Jesus and Lincoln left to lesser successors the jobs of deciding who was poor, who was not, and why.

Before considering some alternative poverty concepts, let us distinguish between poverty and income distribution. Even though poverty and income distribution are related matters, they are different and separate. For example, poverty exists when the real income or living standard of some members of the society is lower than is considered acceptable in that society. Income distribution, on the other hand, simply refers to income equality or inequality, the latter meaning that some people have a different amount of real income than others. Income inequality can exist without anyone's income being below the poverty level. However, in some countries today, complete equality would mean that *all* would be living in poverty, at least according to the standards of most other parts of the world.

Poverty exists when the real income of some members of a society is lower than is considered acceptable in that society. Income distribution refers to income equality or inequality.

Poverty Concepts and Poverty Lines

Over the years, four poverty concepts or criteria have arisen. We shall call them the amenity, proportionality, budgetary, and public-opinion criteria. The *amenity* criterion is the most optimistic in its implications. An amenity is a component of some "decent" level of consumption, such as a certain calorie level in a person's diet, a certain number of square feet of living space per person in a family, or the availability of inside plumbing or running hot water. A person or a family is regarded as living in poverty if it has less than a certain level of such key amenities. This concept of poverty is optimistic because, under its terms, it is conceivable that poverty could be completely eliminated. By the amenity standards of the middle and late nineteenth century, poverty has today been almost eliminated in both Western Europe and North America, but not in the Third World countries, where a great majority of the world's population lives.

According to the amenity criterion, a person is considered to be living in poverty if he or she has less than a certain level of such key variables as a particular calorie level in the diet, a certain number of square feet of living space, or inside plumbing or hot water.

The *proportionality* criterion is the most pessimistic in its implications. According to this concept, people in the lowest-income 10 (or 15, or 20) percent of the population generally feel psychologically alienated, or separated, from society and believe they are victims of discrimination or unfairly treated, whatever their income levels happen to be. "One feels poor with only a Rolls-Royce and a private plane when the neighbors own spaceships." By this criterion, there is no solution for the poverty problem short of something close to absolute equality of income and wealth.

According to the proportionality criterion of poverty, people in the lowest-income segment of the population always feel they are unfairly treated, no matter what their levels of income.

The *budgetary* criterion is the most widely used in practice. The first step in developing this is to determine the cost of a set of standard food budgets providing nutritive diets for families of different sizes, ages, and environments (rural, urban, and so on). As applied in the United States, this food budget is multiplied by 3, since surveys suggest that poor American workers spend about one-third of their income on food. When the basic food budgets are multiplied by 3, the result is a series of **poverty lines**, or income levels below which poverty is said to exist. In lower-income countries, the multiplier in computing poverty lines should be less than 3, since more than one-third of workers' income is spent on food.

TABLE 1
1987 U.S. Poverty Lines by Family Size, Age, and Number of Children (in thousands of 1987 dollars)

Size of Family Unit	Number of Related Children Under 18					
	0	1	2	3	4	8+
One person						
Under 65	5.9					
65 and over	5.4					
Two persons						
Householder under 65	7.6	7.8				
Householder 65 and over	6.9	7.8				
Three persons	8.8	9.1	9.2			
Four persons	11.7	11.9	11.5	11.6		
Five persons	14.1	16.3	16.0	13.6	13.3	
Nine persons or more	25.2	25.3	25.0	24.7	24.2	22.0

Note: Figure in box is considered "the" poverty line for 1987.

Source: U.S. Bureau of the Census, *Poverty in the U.S., 1987* (Series P-60, No. 163, February 1989, Table A-2, p. 157).

The budgetary criterion defines poverty by applying a poverty-line measurement—an income level below which poverty is said to exist. This criterion is the one that is most widely used.

The *public opinion* (or survey research) criterion is the most recent concept of poverty. Under this system, a sample of people are asked how much income a family of standard size (usually four, including two children) needs to "get by" (whatever that means) in a particular city. It is interesting that the answers seem to cluster in a range between 45 and 50 percent of the average family income for the area where the survey is made.

The public opinion criterion surveys a sample of people to determine the income they feel is necessary to "get by" in a geographic area.

Poverty Profiles in the United States Table 1 shows official poverty lines for the United States for 1987. Tables 2 and 3 show profiles of American poverty as measured by these official poverty lines. Table 2 covers the 29-year period from 1959 to 1987, and Table 3 provides detailed information for 1987. Several patterns emerge from these tables. Some popular notions are confirmed, but others are not. The following list identifies some of patterns that emerge from these tables.

1. Poverty as officially defined has *not* been eliminated. In 1987, 13.5 percent of the population and 20.6 percent of the children under 18 lived below the poverty line. These poverty ratios, which were 22.4 and 27.3 percent in 1959, fell during the so-called War on Poverty and then rose again.

2. Poverty is *not* exclusively a minority problem even though the poverty ratio for blacks and Hispanics is considerably higher than the white ratio.

3. Poverty is *not* entirely an urban problem. The central-city ratios are higher than the metropolitan area ones, and the ratio for the farm population is about the same as the ratio for the metropolitan areas.

4. Poverty is *not* concentrated either in the northeast "snowbelt" or the southern "Appalachia." The "golden west" ratio is almost the same

TABLE 2
**U.S. Poverty Profiles by Family Status and Type, Age, and Race
(Selected Years, 1959–1987)**

	All Persons (%)	Age 65 and Over (%)	Female Households No Husbands (%)	Unrelated Individuals (%)	Children Under 18 (%)
All races					
1959	22.4	35.2	49.4	46.1	27.3
1969	12.1	25.3	38.2	34.0	14.0
1979	11.7	15.2	34.9	21.9	16.4
1987	13.5	12.2	38.3	20.8	20.6
White					
1959	18.1	33.1	40.2	44.1	n.a.
1969	9.5	23.3	29.1	32.1	n.a.
1979	9.0	13.3	25.2	19.7	11.8
1987	10.5	10.1	29.5	18.2	15.6
Black					
1959	55.1	62.5	70.6	57.0	n.a.
1969	32.2	50.2	58.2	46.7	n.a.
1979	31.0	36.2	53.1	39.3	41.2
1987	33.1	33.9	54.8	38.3	45.8
Hispanic					
1959	n.a.	n.a.	n.a.	n.a.	n.a.
1969	n.a.	n.a.	n.a.	n.a.	n.a.
1979	21.8	26.8	37.2	28.8	28.0
1987	28.2	27.4	55.0	30.5	39.8

Note: Figures are percentages of each group with incomes below the poverty line.

Source: U.S. Bureau of the Census, *Poverty in the U.S., 1987* (Series P-60, No. 163. February 1989, Tables 1–2, pp. 7–10).

as the midwest one, and higher than the northeastern one.

5. Over time, the most marked alleviation of poverty (a falling poverty ratio) has been among the elderly (65 and over).

6. Poverty has "a female face," meaning that poverty ratios are especially high for female family heads (no husband present).

7. The highest figures for any age group relate to children under eighteen. Senator Daniel Patrick Moynihan (D-NY) uses such figures to speak of the entire family system and the younger generation as being "at risk." The figures are especially high for children who live in female-headed single-parent families and for children in what are called "unrelated subfamilies," a polite term comprising foster homes, orphanages, reformatories, hospitals, etc.

Poverty ratios are especially high for blacks, Hispanics, and children who live in female-headed single-parent families.

All of these estimates, however, are criticized as too high because they are based entirely on money income, neglecting entirely any income in kind— from an owned home, a garden, food stamps, Medicaid, public housing, etc. Several studies suggest that allowing for these omissions would cut the census estimates (of percentages below the poverty line) by one-half or three-quarters.[1]

1. Milton and Rose Friedman, *Free to Choose* (New York: Harcourt Brace Jovanovich, 1980), p. 108. The studies that the Friedmans mention are summarized in Martin Anderson, *Welfare* (Stanford, Calif.: Hoover Institution Press, 1978).

TABLE 3
Characteristics Related to U.S. Poverty, 1987

Characteristic	Percent of Population Below Poverty Levels
Age 0–17	20.6
18–64	10.8
Over 65	12.2
Sex Male	12.0
Female	15.0
Family Type	
Married-couple families	6.0
Male-headed families, no wife present	12.5
Female-headed families, no husband present	34.3
Families with related children under 18	16.2
Residence	
Farm	12.6
Nonfarm	13.5
Metropolitan areas	12.5
Inside central cities	18.6
Region	
Northeast	11.0
Midwest	12.7
West	12.6
South	16.1

Source: U.S. Bureau of the Census, *Poverty in the United States, 1987,* Series P-60, No. 163, February 1989, Tables 2, 3, 5, 6, 7, pp. 7–29.

The Islands and the Cases   What sorts of Americans are most likely to be classified as living in poverty for part or all of their lifetimes? In his book *The Affluent Society,* J. K. Galbraith asserts that there are "islands" of poverty—economic backwaters with poor schools and poor opportunities for acquiring marketable skills. People who live their early lives in these areas are more likely to be poor. Among these areas are mountain Appalachia and the rural South, as well as black and Hispanic ghettos of the so-called "inner cities."[2] Also, there is "case" poverty, which relates to particular individuals and to characteristics that appear to be associated with poverty. Here are eight categories of such cases:

1. Nonwhites (especially blacks and Indians).

2. The young (under 20) and the elderly (over 65) living alone. However, poverty among the elderly is most likely to be exaggerated by official

2. J. K. Galbraith, *The Affluent Society* (Boston: Houghton Mifflin Company, 1958).

statistics since many low-income elderly people own their homes and cultivate small vegetable gardens.

3. Those handicapped by reason of present or recent-past deficiency, injury, or illness, either physical or psychological.

4. The unemployed and the intermittently employed.

5. Members of households headed by women—widows, divorcees, or unmarried mothers—who are employable only as unskilled laborers.

6. Those with less than a high school education, or the functionally illiterate in the English language.

7. Those with records of criminal behavior (frequently associated with illegal drugs) or prolonged unemployment.

8. Victims of racial, religious, and sexual discrimination. (These include many people in classes 1–7 above.)

These possible handicaps are cumulative. That is, combinations of them help explain why the incidence of poverty for, say, nonwhite single persons is greater than for either all nonwhites or for all single persons.

Certain characteristics appear to be associated with poverty, such as race (nonwhite, especially blacks and Indians), age (under 20), handicaps, unemployment, female-headed households, lack of education, criminal records, and racial, religious, and sexual discrimination.

Antipoverty Policies

In rich countries, the poor become objects of either private charity (aid from friends and relatives or organizations such as churches and settlement houses) or public charity (generally called welfare or relief). In poor countries, they turn mainly to begging or worse. In all countries, the life expectancies of the poor are lower than those of the nonpoor of the same ages.

U.S. Welfare Programs In the United States, much of the expansion of public welfare programs followed the publication, in 1962, of Michael Harrington's *The Other America*.[3] This book became the *Uncle Tom's Cabin* of antipoverty policy and the inspiration for the Johnson administration's War on Poverty. Among the major welfare programs are Aid for Families with Dependent Children (AFDC), food stamps (which allow people to buy food below market prices), subsidies for rent and medical care, and a guaranteed minimum Social Security payment for low-income persons who may not have qualified for that amount of benefit under the regular Social Security rules.

Of course, Social Security is not primarily an antipoverty program. The great majority of people receiving Social Security payments have qualified by reason of age, disability, or the death of a parent or spouse. They have incomes above the poverty line and have contributed to the cost of their benefits through taxes paid while they were employed.

Public assistance programs in the United States are both expensive and controversial. The ''welfare mess'' view points out that there is a great deal of cheating by recipients as well as harshness in the administration of welfare, and that administrative costs are high. If the whole welfare appropriation could go directly to the poor, the welfare family of four would be receiving an income above the U.S. median. The programs also have been described as ''regulating the poor.'' This point of view asserts that welfare programs expand when the poor threaten to revolt and then systematically dehumanize the recipients when the threat dies down.[4] A more supportive view of these programs is the following:

> There may be great inefficiencies in our welfare programs, the level of fraud may be very high, the quality of management may be terrible, the programs may overlap, inequities may abound, and the financial incentive to work may be virtually nonexistent. But if we judge by two basic criteria—the completeness of coverage for those who really need help and the adequacy of the help they do receive—the picture changes dramatically. Judged by these standards, our welfare system has been a brilliant success.[5]

Among the major welfare programs in the United States are Aid for Families with Dependent Children, food stamps, subsidies for rent, and guaranteed minimum Social Security payments. There programs are both expensive and controversial.

Welfare Reform Proposals for welfare reform abound on both the political left and right. Many persons have proposed ideas that combine the following three ingredients of welfare reform: (1) adequate payments to the poor, (2) greater motivation for the poor to exchange welfare payments for the wages of low-paying jobs, and (3) lower administrative costs, even though this means throwing many social workers, accountants, lawyers, and others out of work. In this imperfect world, however, welfare reformers also must pay attention to the political effects of their proposals. They must take care that their proposals will neither lower the living standards of any important group of present welfare clients nor reduce the political

---

3. Michael Harrington, *The Other America* (Baltimore: Penguin Books, 1962).

4. Richard Cloward and Frances Fox Piven, *Regulating the Poor* (New York: Random House, 1971).

5. Anderson, *Welfare*, running quote from p. 135.

power of the "welfare constituency" of any member of Congress or other legislator who must depend on that group for votes in the next election. Violations of these rules have torpedoed many a nobly intentioned proposal.

The main tenets of most welfare-reform proposals are: (1) adequate payments to the poor, (2) greater motivation for the poor to obtain jobs, and (3) lower administrative costs.

Negative Income Tax

Under a **negative income tax,** persons who receive less than a specified amount of income receive payments from the government (a "negative tax"), and persons who receive more than that amount of income pay money to the government (a "positive tax"). Thus, the idea of a negative income tax is really an extension of existing progressive income taxation.

Under a negative income tax, persons who receive less than a specified amount of income receive payments from the government.

Several widely discussed reform suggestions fit under the general heading of negative income taxes. We shall describe the simplest of these, presented by Milton Friedman.[6] Friedman would like to replace the whole public welfare system (including AFDC, food stamps, Medicaid, rent subsidies, and the welfare part of Social Security) with a single welfare payment in money, equal to half of the difference between a family's income and its personal exemptions under the federal income tax. These exemptions would be increased from their present level so that an amount equal to half of them would constitute a generous poverty line.

We shall illustrate the negative income tax with the help of Figure 1. The horizontal axis shows the family's income *before* these taxes. For simplicity, we shall call this income the family's earnings. The vertical axis is a family's income *after* income taxes, both positive and negative. The 45-degree line from the origin of the graph shows

6. Milton Friedman, *Capitalism and Freedom* (Chicago: The University of Chicago Press, 1962).

FIGURE 1
Negative Income Tax

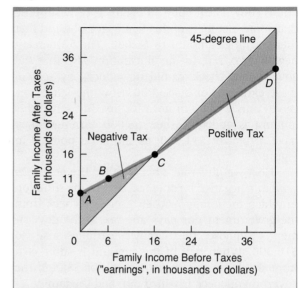

If this family had no earnings at all, it would receive a government check (negative income tax payment) for $8,000, which would place it at the poverty line, so that the family's income after taxes would be at point A. With a 50 percent negative tax rate, if the family earned $6,000 for working, its negative tax payment check would be reduced by half of these earnings ($3,000), and the family's after-tax income would be $11,000 ($6,000 earnings plus a $5,000 negative tax receipt). This situation is shown at point B. The breakeven point is at C, where the family earns $16,000 and receives no transfer payment. With earnings above $16,000, the family pays positive taxes, so that its after-tax income follows line CD. The 45-degree line shows combinations where there are no negative and no positive income taxes.

combinations where earnings are exactly equal to income after taxes. That is, it illustrates the relationship that would exist if there were no income taxes, either positive or negative. In Figure 1 we illustrate a system in which the poverty line is $8,000, personal exemptions under the income tax amount to $16,000, and in which, following Friedman, the negative tax takes up half of the difference between the family's earnings and its exemptions under the income tax. This means that the rate of negative tax is 50 percent.[7]

Let us begin with a family that has no earnings at all. This family would receive a negative tax pay-

7. Today's higher price level would require higher figures than in Friedman's illustration.

ment from the government in the amount of $8,000, just equal to the poverty line. Such a situation is shown as point A in Figure 1. Now suppose that some members of this family get jobs and that their earnings amount to $6,000. The 50 percent negative tax rate in our illustration says that the government check would be reduced by half of these earnings, or by $3,000. Now the family receives only $5,000 in negative tax. But when this amount is added to their $6,000 earnings, they have a total of $11,000, as shown at point B in Figure 1.

Next we illustrate what is called the *breakeven point* in a negative income tax, that is, the situation in which the family neither receives a check from the government nor pays any tax to the government. Suppose the family's earnings rise to $16,000. When half of this amount is subtracted from the basic government check of $8,000, the government check is wiped out, and the family receives nothing in negative tax from the government. This breakeven point is shown at C in Figure 1. Following Friedman's system, personal exemptions under the income tax would amount to $16,000 to make this system operational. Of course, if the family earned more than $16,000, it would become a payer of positive taxes along the line from C to D in Figure 1. We have drawn the line CD somewhat steeper than the line ABC because we assume that the tax rate for positive income taxes would be something less than 50 percent.

Incentive Effects   One of the basic appeals of the negative income tax is that a family will always have a higher after-tax money income from working than it will from not working. In our illustration, the family would retain 50 cents from every dollar earned by working. Although this tax rate is high compared with those now imposed on incomes above the breakeven point, the negative income tax may provide more incentive to work than the present welfare system does. Under present regulations, if enforced strictly, most of the income earned from working would be deducted from the family's welfare check, and the family would not retain very much of its income from work. For this reason, the system very likely discourages people from working.

One of the basic appeals of the negative income tax is that a family will always have a higher after-tax money income from working than it will from not working.

A number of costly experiments have been carried out in attempts to measure the incentive effects of the negative income tax. Negative income tax payments have actually been given to samples of families drawn from the "working poor"—that is, those slightly above present poverty lines—in the hope of determining the effects of the system on labor force participation. Unfortunately, the results are not very clear because the subjects received their payments only for short periods and not as a way of life. The results suggest, however, that not many principal breadwinners would quit work or reduce their working hours if a negative income tax plan were available. However, quite a few secondary workers in multiple-earner families (mainly wives and teenagers) would reduce the number of hours they work in order to care for children or get further education and training. This may of course be socially desirable in the long run at the same time that it acts as a short-run disincentive to work.

Conflicts among Objectives   As you may have observed already, there are three key features in a negative income tax system: (1) the poverty line or guaranteed minimum after-tax income, (2) the rate of negative tax, and (3) the breakeven income level. Because each of these features reflects a different policy objective in the system, conflicts arise among them. The poverty line represents the goal of eliminating poverty. The rate of negative tax reflects the work incentive feature of the system, with greater work incentives presumably coming from lower tax rates. Finally, the location of the breakeven point greatly influences the overall cost of the program. This cost increases rapidly as the breakeven level rises, since each upward move takes people out of the positive tax-paying group and adds them to the negative tax-receiving group. The resulting problems can easily be imagined. For example, lowering the rate of negative tax to offer stronger work incentives must either lower the poverty line or raise the breakeven level or do both things at the same time.[8] Or, an attempt to lower the cost of the program by lowering the breakeven level would require either a lower poverty line or a higher rate of negative tax. Raising the poverty line would increase the cost of the program unless the rate of negative tax were also raised, possibly damaging work incentives.

There are three key features in a negative income tax system: (1) the guaranteed minimum after-tax income, (2) the rate of negative tax, and (3) the breakeven income level.

Administrative and Political Problems A negative income tax can also lead to certain administrative and political problems. Administrative problems arise in handling income from the short-term jobs that many poor people keep getting and losing. It is also alleged that the poor themselves would rather deal with social workers than with revenue agents. A major political problem is that many individual families would lose by a change from the present welfare system to a negative income tax, even if welfare recipients would gain in the aggregate. Among the possible losers are those who do little or no work and whose current welfare entitlements (food stamps, rent subsidies, and so on) are large, as indeed they are in many cities with high living costs. A change in political balances could arise if these people reacted to a negative income tax by moving back to the lower-cost small towns and rural areas from which many of them originally came. Any such dispersion of the "welfare vote" would surely lower the political power of welfare clients as a group and of legislators who depend largely on their votes.

Compulsory Labor

Should able-bodied welfare recipients be required to perform suitable work on public projects or receive compulsory job-related training? One object

of compulsory-labor plans is to reduce welfare costs. But if the recipients receive union wage rates and if new training programs must be added to the budget, such savings may be disappointing.

Objections to compulsory labor come from civil service employees and from welfare rights advocates. Civil service workers and their unions fear reductions in the number of jobs opening up for themselves, even when they are secure against direct displacement. The welfare rights advocates reject "slavefare" on principle, especially when the wages and other benefits are below union scales. They are also concerned with the definitions of "able-bodied" and "suitable" in the plans, and with the provision of care for the children of parents required to work or to be trained. They are, of course, aware that perfunctory or low-level care provided by incompetent people may be worse than no care at all when we consider the dangers of child abuse, child neglect, and exposure to illness or to injury.

The issue of requiring able-bodied welfare recipients to perform suitable work is controversial. Objections to compulsory labor come from civil service employees and welfare rights advocates.

The Poverty Underclass

Perhaps the most difficult and intractable aspect of poverty is presented by the so-called "underclass," which appears to exist in most countries. For the United States it is estimated by the Urban Institute of Washington to number 8 million people, perhaps 25 percent of America's poor and 3 percent of America's population.

What is an underclass? We have no precise definition, and therefore the numbers in the last paragraph are subject to question. But it is safe to call an underclass those poor persons whose ancestors have lived in poverty for more than one generation and whose descendants are, for whatever reasons, unlikely to escape the poverty trap. We can clarify the notion to some extent with the help of Table 4.

---

8. The rate of negative tax is equal to the poverty line or guaranteed minimum income, divided by the breakeven income level, provided a flat-rate tax is used.

TABLE 4
Mobility among Wealth Categories (In Probability Terms: Certainty = 100)

		Period 2				Period 2	
	Wealthy	Middle Class	Poor		Wealthy	Middle Class	Poor
Period 1 Wealthy	60	30	10	**Period 1** Wealthy	50	50	0
Middle class	20	60	20	Middle class	50	50	0
Poor	20	20	60	Poor	0	0	100

The figures in each half of the table show probabilities that a person who, in time period 1, is in the economic class indicated at the left, will, in time period 2, be in the economic class indicated at the top. In each half of the table, the figures add horizontally to 100 percent. The left side of the table reveals some mobility among economic classes. The right side reveals no mobility into or out of the poor class. Thus, the right side illustrates the existence of an economic underclass.

An underclass consists of those poor persons whose ancestors have lived in poverty for more than one generation and whose descendants are unlikely to escape from poverty.

Suppose a society is divided, as in this table, into three economic classes: the wealthy, the middle class, and the poor. These economic classes need not be equal in size. The figures in the two parts of this table—all hypothetical, all percentages, and adding horizontally to 100 percent—are probabilities of an individual or a family, in one economic class in Period 1, being in each of the three economic classes in Period 2. In the left-hand part, people in (say) the middle class in Period 1 have a 20 percent probability of moving upward and a 20 percent probability of moving downward. We need not inquire whether this represents a high or a low economic mobility, but we should note that it is pretty much the same for each of the three classes.

In the right-hand part, however, there is complete mobility between the wealthy and the middle class, but the entire poor population constitutes an underclass. Nobody from this class has any chance of rising to either of the other classes, and nobody from the other classes has any danger of becoming poor. The underclass problem is obviously more serious in the right-hand half of this table, although we cannot claim that it is entirely absent in the left-hand half.

In practice, the Urban Institute defines the underclass, at least for the United States, on the basis of *residence*. It is composed of families and single persons "living in neighborhoods where welfare dependency, female-headed families, male joblessness, and dropping out of high school are all common occurrences."[9] It is not a racial or racist definition: less than 6 percent of the black population, and less than 20 percent of the black poverty population live in such areas. But the size of the underclass, so defined, grew from 0.75 million to 2.5 million (a 167 percent increase) between 1970 and 1980, when the general population grew by only 8 percent.

Part of the problem of dealing with the underclass and its special needs is the public ambivalence toward its members. When the typical poor person was a well-behaved elderly invalid widow of majority racial stock, it was easy for society to act compassionately, and providing income was a sufficient solution. However, when the typical underclass member is an unwed mother of minority racial stock, in an inner-city area where crime, drugs, teenage pregnancy, and multiple-generation welfare dependency are all common, there is a stronger temptation to leave her alone—"After all, it's her own fault." A major challenge will be to integrate underclass members—including this un-

9. The source of this quotation, and of the figures which follow, is Isabel Sawhill's chapter in the Urban Institute's 1988 volume, *Challenge to Leadership*, digested in her essay "What About America's Underclass?" *Challenge* (May–June 1988), pp. 27–29.

wed mother, her babies, and their several fathers—into the mainstream of society. It will take more than the dole to do this. It will require strengthening family responsibility, providing better jobs, and adapting elementary education to break the intergenerational cycle of poverty, which is a polite name for the underclass phenomenon.

Part of the problem of dealing with the underclass is the public ambivalence toward its members. The solution to breaking the intergenerational cycle of poverty lies in integrating underclass members into the mainstream of society.

Homelessness and Panhandling

The 1980s were a period of general prosperity in America. At the same time, in its large cities both poverty and near-poverty became more visible than they had been since the Great Depression. Two types of poor people, the homeless and the panhandlers (beggars), appeared in increasing numbers in respectable middle-class and upper-class neighborhoods—not merely passing through but also living on the street. Often they were the same people: the homeless supported themselves by begging, and the beggars appeared to be homeless. Although most of the homeless and the panhandlers were also members of the poverty population, most of the poverty population were neither homeless nor panhandlers.

What had happened to cause the twin epidemics of homelessness and panhandling? We do not really know, but it is helpful to divide the problem into three subproblems: What happened to the existing stock of low-cost housing? What happened to the supply of new low-cost housing? What happened to the demand for low-cost housing?

Two types of poor people, the homeless and the panhandlers, appeared in increasing numbers in the 1980s. Often they were the same people.

Destruction of Housing Stock The *stock* of low-cost housing was the victim of urban renewal, plus

(in some cities) rent control and racial conflict. Urban renewal was a post-1945 movement to beautify and modernize the blighted areas of inner cities by tearing down blocks of outmoded, substandard slum housing and replacing it with commercial buildings, public buildings, schools and hospitals, parks and playgrounds, town houses, luxury apartments, and even vacant lots (when the money ran out). When any housing at all was built for the poor, it was in huge, fortresslike blocks, impressive from the air but taken over on the ground by criminal gangs and eventually abandoned or demolished in their turn. The Pruitt-Igoe development in St. Louis was a horrible example. It was said at the time, "Urban renewal is Negro removal." To this might be added, "Homelessness is the illegitimate child of urban renewal" when the poor, black and white, do not leave town. The surprise is that homelessness took so long to grow up.

Urban renewal destroyed housing stock by tearing down substandard slum housing and replacing it with commercial buildings, public buildings, schools, parks, and luxury apartments.

Rent control destroys the housing stock when rents are fixed at such low levels that it does not pay "slumlords" to keep their buildings in repair. The buildings are allowed to depreciate and become uninhabitable, after which the raw land is supposedly more valuable for redevelopment—not necessarily urban renewal—than it was with money-losing apartments on it. The processes of decay and abandonment were often accelerated by fire, including arson. Either landlords or tenants may be guilty of arson in particular cases.

Rent control destroys the housing stock when rents are fixed at such low levels that it does not pay to keep the buildings in repair.

In the racial conflicts following the assassination of the Reverend Martin Luther King, Jr., in 1968, resentful blacks burned down large sections of their ghettos. The slogan "Burn, baby, burn!" predates that period as it stems from a 1965 riot in the Watts section of Los Angeles. Black resentment was certainly understandable, but it was also perverse. What, in fact, replaced the burnt-out black ghettos? All too often, nothing but vacant lots, with life worse in the 1980s than it had been a generation earlier.

Supply of New Low-Cost Housing For centuries, the *flow* of new construction, along with the conversion of obsolescent buildings erected for other purposes, had supplemented the country's stock of what is called "affordable housing."[10] At a time when the holdover housing stock was either falling or increasing at subnormal rates, why did not the flow of new construction expand to fill the gap? In fact, the flow slowed, except in the most rapidly expanding sections of the southern and southwestern sunbelts.

Numerous explanations can be offered, some of which we have already seen as contributing to the reduction or deterioration of the housing stock. We will mention six of them:

1. Rising urban land prices. As the population grew, the "baby boom" boomed, and people moved from rural areas to the cities and their suburbs.

2. Rising building-trades wages and (to a lesser extent) building-materials prices. Building-trades workers had in the past included a disproportionate number of recent immigrants, but the immigration of manual workers was now restricted.

3. Higher standards imposed on housing construction, directed against noise, fire, overcrowding, unsanitary conditions, inadequate heating, etc.

4. Rent controls, which usually did not apply to nonresidential and upper-income construction but were sometimes applied to lower-income construction. Where they were not, agitation by tenants' rights activists presented a constant danger that such application might be just around the corner.

5. Public disillusionment with large-scale public housing.

6. Working-class families, larger in size and with higher incomes than previously, becoming less willing than earlier generations had been to subdivide family units by taking in boarders.

The supply of affordable housing diminished because of higher land prices, higher construction costs, higher standards for construction, rent controls, disillusionment with public housing, and less willingness to subdivide existing dwelling units.

Demand for Low-Cost Housing What about the demand side of the equation? All might have gone smoothly, possibly even well, if the homeless and the panhandlers had drifted to the clean, green countryside—if, in economic jargon, their demand curves for affordable housing had shifted leftward and/or rotated toward higher price elasticity. But nothing of the sort happened—rather the reverse. As in Latin America and other Third World countries, migration to the cities and their suburban satellites included the poor, often in disproportionate numbers.

An especially noteworthy factor, whose quantitative importance remains open to question, operated to make the crisis more visible and therefore more acute. High-grade (near-normal) patients were released from public psychiatric hospitals into the community, partly to save money and partly to secure the benefits of association with normal people. The expected provision of halfway houses and similar sorts of outpatient care for the mentally and emotionally handicapped seldom developed.[11] In their stead, the cities were confronted by the spectacle of hundreds of muttering, chattering, unsanitary "bag ladies" and "winos" wandering the streets on their own resources, sometimes in advanced stages of semiconsciousness and senile de-

---

10. An arbitrary definition of affordable housing: a housing unit is affordable if it would rent, unfurnished, for a monthly rental of not more than 50 percent of the monthly wage of an unskilled worker, fully employed in that community, without imposing an economic loss on the landlord.

11. The original community-care proposals included such facilities. In addition to costing taxpayer money, however, these facilities might have lowered both property values and the quality of life in the neighborhoods where they would have been located. They aroused *nimby* ("not in my backyard") reactions in prospective neighbors, whose community activists prevented the facilities from being built in any adequate numbers.

mentia, with no one looking out for them on any regular basis.

The demand for affordable housing increased for two reasons. As in Third World countries, migration to the cities and their suburbs included the poor, often in disproportionate numbers. In addition, many near-normal patients were released from psychiatric hospitals into the community, with inadequate halfway housing to receive them.

There was also a "learning" factor at work—a form of learning by doing. This was the acceptance, usually reluctant, of homelessness-*cum*-panhandling as an alternative way of life and even as a counterculture in the traditions of the radical 1960s. A number of people came to realize how easily a marginal subsistence can, in a generally affluent society, be attained and maintained by panhandling. According to rumor, the New York area includes private schools that collect tuition and turn a profit by teaching the techniques of panhandling on the streets and in the subways.

INEQUALITY

As we said earlier, poverty and inequality are related but quite different things. We turn now to an examination of inequality. What are the facts about income inequality? Why does it arise? What can or should be done about it?

The Distribution of Income

Economists have always been interested in the distributions of income and wealth. There are many ways of organizing information on these matters, such as by countries at various stages of development, by gender, by race, by occupation, by region, and so on. But by far the most commonly considered distributions are the **functional** (between labor, property, and other sources of income) and **personal income distributions** (by income brackets or size classifications). Because you studied the functional distribution of income earlier in the book,[12] we shall simply review it briefly and then go on to discuss personal distribution.

Functional Income Distribution In Chapters 30, 31, and 32, we explained how resource markets help to determine how the various factors of production will be combined to produce the goods and services demanded in the economy. A functional distribution of income for the United States was presented in Table 1 in Chapter 30.[13] There you learned that wages, salaries, and fringe benefits amount to more than three-fourths of the total national income when most proprietors' income is considered labor income, as it should be. The remaining types of income—rental income, corporate profits, and interest—are property incomes and amount to less than one-fourth of the total. The labor share has grown over the sixty years since 1929 and the property income share has decreased.

Functional income distribution shows how income is distributed between labor, property, and other sources of income.

Personal Income Distribution When we examine the personal distribution of income, we want to know about the individual people who provide the factors of production, whose shares of national income are shown in the functional distribution.

The two parts of Table 5 show two different ways of describing the personal income distribution of American households. (A household may be either a family or a single individual.) Personal income includes transfer payments—public and private pensions, relief payments, unemployment compensation, and so on. It excludes nonmoney income, capital gains, and the undistributed profits of corporations. In part (a), the arrangement is by income brackets in 1986 dollars and shows the effects of both the rapid real income growth from 1970 to 1975 and the slowdown since that time. In part (b), the arrangement is by quintiles (fifths) of equal numbers of households for 1986 plus a display showing the top 5 percent—the top one-

12. See Chapters 2 and 30.
13. See page 678.

TABLE 5
Personal Income Distribution of Households in the United States

(a) By Income-Size Brackets in 1986 Dollars (selected years)

Income-Size Class (thousands of 1986 dollars)	Percentage of Households			
	1970	1975	1980	1986
Under 5	8.2	6.8	8.3	7.4
5–9.99	10.9	12.6	11.8	11.7
10–14.99	10.3	11.4	11.8	11.0
15–24.99	21.4	21.2	21.0	20.0
25–49.99	37.7	35.6	34.4	33.1
50 and over	11.5	12.3	12.7	16.8
Total	100.0	100.0	100.0	100.0
Median income ($)	24,666	24,039	23,565	24,897

(b) By Income Quintiles (families only, 1986)

Income Quintile	Percentage of Total	Lowest Income in Group (in thousands of dollars)
First (lowest)	4.6	—
Second	10.8	13.9
Third	16.8	24.0
Fourth	24.0	35.0
Fifth	43.7	50.4
(Top 5 percent)	(17.0)	(82.3)
Total	100	

Source: Statistical Abstract of the United States, 108th ed. (1988), (a): Table 690, p. 422, (b): Table 701, p. 428.

fourth of the top quintile. In the last column of this table, we can find the lowest income included in each income quintile.

In the lowest quintile are the poor and the near-poor. The second is mainly unskilled labor, both white-collar and blue-collar, sometimes called the working poor. The third (middle) quintile is mainly semiskilled labor (the assembly-line workers). In the fourth quintile are skilled labor and the lower "middle class" (clerical workers). The fifth (top) quintile includes both the upper middle class and the truly rich. Most tuition-paying college and university students do not think of themselves as rich, but in fact come from families mainly in the fifth or upper-fourth quintiles of the income distribution.

Personal income distribution shows how income is distributed among individual people. Personal income includes transfer payments but excludes nonmoney income, capital gains, and the undistributed profits of corporations.

Relations Between Functional and Personal Distributions The functional distribution of income by type and the personal distribution of income by size classes are of course related. Most "workers," who receive most of their incomes from wages and salaries, are poorer than most "capitalists," whose income is derived mainly from property and profits. It is natural to suppose that any increase in the labor share of the functional distribution also increases the equality of the personal distribution.

This is not, however, always true, especially when the level of *total* income changes at the same time. During the Great Depression of the 1930s, the labor share seems to have risen, but measured equality declined. The main reason why this happened was that the distribution of labor income itself became more unequal, depending on how the individual worker families were affected by unemployment and underemployment. Another reason was that profit income was distributed more equally, with fewer big windfall gains—and more big windfall losses—than during the "roaring" 1920s.

The functional distribution of income by type and the personal distribution of income by size classes are related, but the relationship is not precise—an increase in the labor share of the functional distribution does not necessarily increase the equality of the personal distribution.

Measuring Inequality

Of the many possible ways to measure inequality, we consider only two—the Lorenz curve and its associated Gini ratio, used in most countries of North America and Western Europe, and the quantile ratio, used in many socialist countries.

The Lorenz Curve and the Gini Ratio   The Lorenz curve and the Gini ratio are ways of illustrating and measuring income inequality. A **Lorenz curve** is an illustration of inequality that is constructed by plotting the percentage of total income received by successive percentages of the population, starting from the lowest-income persons or families and proceeding cumulatively upward. A Lorenz curve is shown in Figure 2. In this figure, the vertical axis shows the cumulative percentage of total income, and the horizontal axis shows the cumulative percentage of families. The curve itself is constructed by using the numbers in the "percentage of total" column of Table 5(b). The lowest 20 percent of the families got 4.6 percent of the total income. This is

FIGURE 2
Lorenz Curve, Family Personal Income in the United States, 1986

Point *a* shows the percentage of total income received by the lowest 20 percent of the families. Point *b* shows the percentage received by the lowest 40 percent of the families, and so on. The curved line connecting these plotted points is a Lorenz curve. The "line of equality" shows how the curve would look if incomes were distributed with perfect equality. The purple area is the area of inequality. The Gini ratio is computed by dividing the area of inequality by the entire right-triangular area 0AB of the lower right-hand half of the figure.

The figure is based on the data in Table 5(b).

plotted as point *a* in Figure 2. The lowest 40 percent of the families (the first and second quintiles combined) received 15.4 percent of the total income (4.6 + 10.8 = 15.4). This is plotted at point *b*. The bottom 60 percent of the families got 32.2 percent of the total income (4.6 + 10.8 + 16.8 = 32.2), which is plotted at point *c*, and so on. The curve drawn to connect the plotted points is called a Lorenz curve. If income were distributed with perfect equality, the Lorenz curve would be a straight line from one corner of the diagram to the other (45-degree line). This is called the "line of equality" in Figure 2. If income is not distributed with perfect equality, the Lorenz curve will lie below this perfect equality line, and an area of inequality will exist between the Lorenz curve and the line of equality. This is the purple area in Figure 2.

The Lorenz curve is an illustration of inequality that is constructed by plotting the percentage of total income received by successive percentages of the population, starting from the lowest-income persons or families and proceeding cumulatively upward.

The **Gini ratio** is a measure of inequality computed by dividing the area of inequality shown by a Lorenz curve by the whole right-triangle area (shown as $0AB$) in the Lorenz-curve diagram. If incomes are distributed with perfect equality, the Gini ratio is zero, because the area of inequality is zero. If incomes are distributed with perfect inequality, with all going to only one family, the ratio will be 1.00, since the area of inequality will be the same as the entire right triangle $0AB$.[14]

The Gini ratio is a measure of inequality computed by dividing the area of inequality shown by a Lorenz curve by the whole right-triangle area below the line of equality in the Lorenz-curve diagram. If incomes were distributed with perfect equality, the Lorenz curve would be a straight 45-degree line and the Gini ratio would be zero.

The Gini ratios for the United States in 1986 were .389 for families and .443 for unrelated single individuals. This is a high value for advanced industrial countries in which Gini ratios cluster around the range of .30 to .35. But it is lower than economists estimate for non-socialist developing countries. However, socialist countries prefer to publish Lorenz curves for wage rates, which exclude the effects of property income, multiple job-holding, and multiple income earners within families. A study by Williamson and Lindert estimates

that the Gini ratio was low in colonial America (outside the South) but that it rose steadily because of expanding black slavery and unrestricted immigration.[15] They estimate, however, that the ratio has been falling since about 1929. Since 1945, the income share of the lowest quintile has been rising and that of the highest has been falling, with income shares of the three middle quintiles remaining nearly constant. Williamson and Lindert do not explain these trends by changes in the functional distribution of income between labor and property. They claim the key factor is within the labor share, with a rise and then a fall in skilled labor wages in relation to unskilled labor wages. Their figures fit quite well with a theory about the distributional effects of economic development—that inequality increases in the early stages of development, but decreases later as physical capital accumulates and human capital becomes the key to further economic progress.

One theory of the distribution effects of economic development states that inequality increases in the early stages of development but decreases later as physical capital accumulates and human capital becomes the key to further economic progress.

Economic statisticians have pointed out a number of flaws in the Gini ratio as a measure of inequality. One criticism is that these ratios may be affected by changes in the population itself. Because both young and elderly people on the average have lower incomes than prime-age workers, changes in the age pattern of the population will change the Gini ratio. Similarly, blacks and other minorities receive on the average lower wages than whites, so that changes in the racial mix may alter the ratio. For the United States, a Gini ratio designed to adjust for changes in variables such as age and race would probably show a stronger trend toward equality than is shown by the unadjusted ratio.[16]

---

14. The Gini ratio is sometimes called the concentration ratio, and the Lorenz curve is sometimes called the Gini curve. The original research to develop these concepts was done independently by the American statistician Max Lorenz and the Italian statistician Corrado Gini in the first decade of the twentieth century.

15. Jeffrey Williamson and Peter Lindert, *American Inequality* (New York: Academic Press, 1980).

16. Morton Paglin, ''The Measurement and Trend of Inequality: A Basic Revision,'' *American Economic Review*, Vol. 65, No. 5 (September 1975), pp. 598–609.

Another criticism is that the statistics used to compute the ratio for the United States do not include government transfers in kind such as food stamps, subsidized housing, or subsidized medical care. These transfers rose during the 1970s and probably furthered the movement toward equality.

The Gini ratio may be affected by changes in population or racial mix. Also, the statistics used to compute the ratio do not include government transfers in kind.

Quantile Ratios Socialist countries do not use Lorenz curves and Gini ratios to measure inequality of income. Instead, they use a **quantile ratio**, which compares the percentage of total income received by the *highest k* percent of the population with the percentage of total income received by the *lowest k* percent. With the numbers from Table 5(b), we can illustrate this method as follows, where $k = 20$ and we are dealing with *quintile* ratios:

$$\frac{\text{percentage of income received by the highest 20 percent}}{\text{percentage of income received by the lowest 20 percent}} = \frac{43.7}{4.6} = 9.5$$

So for the United States in 1986, the quintile ratio was 9.5. A higher ratio would suggest more inequality, and a lower one would suggest less inequality. Changes among the middle-income ranges are ignored by this method. In practice, socialist countries generally compute these ratios by comparing top and bottom tenths (deciles) or even top and bottom twentieths (semideciles) of the population, focusing even more on the extremes of the distribution and producing even higher ratios. One criticism of the socialist countries' distribution statistics is that they tend to compare wage rates rather than family incomes. In this way they hide two important sources of inequality: multiple-job holdings by individual workers and multiple-wage earning within households.

Socialists countries measure inequality of income by means of a quantile ratio, which compares the percentage of total income received by the *highest k* percent of the population with the percentage of total income received by the *lowest k* percent. A higher ratio suggests more inequality, while a lower one suggests less inequality.

Why Inequality?

What are the major causes of inequality? A full answer to this question would require a long discussion of genetics, social conditions, and educational factors. Because our aim here is to give only a general understanding of why inequality persists, we shall simply list some of the major causes.

1. *Genetic endowments.* Some people are born with either better or worse bodies, minds, and nervous systems than other people. Environmental factors cannot be counted on to cancel out such differences. More often, perhaps, they reinforce them, as when bright students go on to college and less-bright ones drop out of high school.

2. *Environmental endowments.* Better or worse conditions and more or fewer facilities for health, safety, education, training, and socialization explain some income inequality. However, the child of rich, talented, and intelligent parents, brought up by a succession of expensive governesses, step-parents, tutors, and private schools under a cloud of unrealistic expectations, may get as poor a start in life as most children growing up in the slums.

3. *Inheritances.* Wealth can be inherited. So can opportunities for education, training, and entry to meaningful jobs and professions—not to mention membership in exclusive trade unions, country clubs, and college Greek-letter organizations. Some studies suggest that education, not wealth, is the most important mechanism of inheritance. Financial bequests are less closely correlated with heirs' economic status than are the number of years of education provided by parents.[17]

17. John Brittain, *The Inheritance of Economic Status* (Washington, D.C.: The Brookings Institution, 1978).

TABLE 6
*Median Money Income of U.S. Households, by Racial Origin of Householders,
for Selected Years, 1970–1986*

Year	Median Income (thousands of 1986 dollars)				Ratios	
	All Households	White	Black	Hispanic	Black/White	Hispanic/White
1970	24.7	25.7	15.6	n.a.	0.61	n.a.
1975	24.0	25.1	15.1	18.1	0.60	0.72
1980	23.6	24.9	14.3	18.2	0.57	0.73
1986	24.9	26.2	15.1	18.4	0.58	0.70

Note: "Hispanics" are persons of all races who consider their first or native language to be Spanish. The term includes persons of all degrees of English-language fluency.

Source: Statistical Abstract of the United States, 108th ed. (1988), Table 691, p. 422.

4. *Discrimination.* Inheritance can be a negative quantity. Just as some people inherit property and opportunity, others "inherit" the "wrong" race, gender, religion, or language. It is difficult to choose one's own parents. In the next section of the chapter, we shall have more to say about discrimination.

5. *Economic change.* Consider the workers on a Detroit assembly line. They "had it made" in the second, or possibly even the first, quintile of the personal income distribution in the late 1960s. Twenty-five years later, the demands for these workers' skills or human capital had been cut by three main factors: (1) automation and robotization, which have substituted machinery for the workers' skills within the factory; (2) OPEC, which for a decade reduced demand for automobiles, and especially for the heavy cars that the workers had been specially trained to make; (3) foreign competition, as more and more Asian workers acquired the same skills as American workers had, and in some cases more relevant ones.

6. *Luck.* There are elements of "pure blind luck" in every one of the preceding categories. But luck also enters in other ways as well. What if Shakespeare had never learned to read or write? And what if some super-Einstein capable of unifying all physics had not died at Auschwitz, Hiroshima, Stalingrad, Vietnam, or wherever he or she did die?

The major causes of inequality include: differences in genetic and environmental endowments and inheritances (including educational opportunities), discrimination, economic change, and luck.

Discrimination and Inequality

Discrimination means that different economic opportunities are offered to persons on the basis of personal characteristics unrelated to the jobs themselves. The causes that we have just listed tell us that some inequality would exist even if there were no discrimination on such bases as race, gender, religion, or ethnic background. But the inequality that would exist in the absence of discrimination would not be strongly associated with gender, race, religion, and so on. However, it is clear that discrimination does exist. Data on incomes clearly reveal differences that are difficult to explain by the personal factors listed in the preceding section. Table 6 compares median annual incomes for white, black, and Hispanic households in the United States in 1970, 1975, 1980, and 1986. The incomes of black and Hispanic households are significantly less than those of white households. There is no clear evidence that the substantial differences are falling over time. Persistent differences of this size are strong evidence that discrimination is a cause of inequality.

Discrimination means that different economic opportunities are offered to people on the basis of personal characteristics unrelated to the jobs themselves. Incomes of black and Hispanic households are significantly less than those of white households, evidence that discrimination is a continuing cause of inequality.

The four parts of Table 7 compare money incomes of males and females in the United States in 1986, with coverage limited to full-time workers and removing biases due to the greater prevalence of part-time work among married women. Part (a) shows that female incomes were approximately one-third less than male incomes, except for single-person households. These, Part (b) suggests, were mainly concentrated among the relatively young (ages 20–35). As indicated in Part (d) the differential is greater among whites than among blacks or Hispanics.

It is frequently maintained that much of the explanation for the significant and doubtless discriminatory inequality shown in Table 7 is the

TABLE 7
Male-Female Money Income Comparisons, United States, 1986
(year-round full-time workers)

	Thousands of Dollars		Ratio
	Male	*Female*	*Female/Male*
(a) By Family-Status Category			
Householder, spouse present	27.2	17.4	0.64
Householder, spouse absent	27.4	17.1	0.62
Individual	21.9	18.0	0.82
(b) By Age			
20–24	13.8	11.8	0.86
25–34	22.2	16.7	0.75
35–44	29.0	18.5	0.64
45–54	29.7	17.0	0.57
55–64	28.4	16.8	0.59
(c) By Major Occupation			
Executive-Administrator-Manager	33.5	20.6	0.61
Professional	32.8	21.8	0.66
Technical support	26.3	18.2	0.69
Sales	25.4	12.7	0.50
Clerical support	23.0	15.2	0.65
Precision production	23.3	15.1	0.65
Machine operation	24.8	12.2	0.49
Transport	20.6	12.6	0.61
Semiskilled labor	15.8	12.7	0.60
Services	16.8	10.2	0.63
Farming, forestry, fishery	10.4	6.8	0.65
(d) By Race			
White	25.7	16.5	0.64
Black	18.0	14.6	0.81
Hispanic	17.3	13.5	0.78

Source: U.S. Bureau of the Census, Consumers Income Series, P-60, No. 156 (August 1987), Table 27, p. 98.

near-exclusion of women from high-paying and more prestigious occupations. This may be true, as argued by the feminist agitation for **comparable worth** in the pay scales for these jobs, but it is not the whole story of the "gender gap" in income.

Comparable worth means the basing of pay in different occupations on these occupations' scores on "scientific" point systems that weight the arduousness of jobs, their education and experience requirements, and so on. Such scores allegedly permit comparisons, independent of labor markets, between the "worth" of truck drivers (predominantly male) and secretaries (predominantly female) or between medicine (male) and nursing (female). The underlying theory is that female workers have been concentrated in a "pink ghetto" of women's jobs whose pay is unfairly low.

Comparable worth systems, if adopted widely, would surely decrease employment in occupations that had been upgraded, and perhaps create labor shortages in those that had been downgraded. Similar systems, however, are practiced. Civil Service Commissions or personnel offices rate one job as Grade 10 and another as Grade 15, when one is a librarian and the other an electrician. When high school pay scales for teachers are set independently of teaching fields, should we be surprised to find shortages of science and math teachers coexisting with surpluses of English, foreign language, and history teachers?

Comparable worth means basing the pay in different occupations on their arduousness, their experience and educational requirements, etc. If adopted widely, comparable worth systems would tend to decrease employment in occupations that were upgraded and create labor shortages in those that were downgraded.

Part (c) of Table 7 shows median annual earnings in 1986 for a wide range of occupational categories. The ratio is approximately the same for all the occupational groups considered, except for salespersons and machine operators.

Race and gender differentials will probably shrink over time as women and nonwhites have more time to work their way up to higher levels in higher-status occupations. One cannot, however,

escape the conclusion that discrimination, past and present, partly explains the current inequality. As you learned earlier, the economic case against discrimination is strong. Discrimination is not a rational policy for a profit-maximizing firm. Not only is discrimination ethically unfair to individuals, who deserve to be treated on their own merits, but it is wasteful not to make the best possible use of their resources in the economy.

Maldistribution

Maldistribution means excessive inequality or equality of personal income or wealth. Generally it implies that too much inequality exists, although maldistribution can mean too much equality—with too little reward for hard work, risk-bearing, saving, and investment in physical and human capital. In these matters, equity and equality need not always move in the same direction.

Maldistribution may be individual, economic, or ethical. We shall consider each in turn.

Individual Maldistribution **Individual maldistribution** means dissatisfaction about the particular people at the upper and lower ends of the income or wealth distribution. It may indeed be true, for example, that "good guys (and gals) finish last" in business. As Jonathan Swift said, "Mankind may judge what Heaven thinks of riches by observing those upon whom it has been pleased to bestow them."

Economic Maldistribution **Economic maldistribution** theories raise the possibility that the market economic system may operate less well under some distributions than under others. One of the best known of these theories comes from John A. Hobson (1858–1940), an English economist whose doctrines influenced many, ranging from Lenin to Roosevelt, and whom Keynes recognized as a predecessor. Hobson believed that business depressions were caused by underconsumption (too little spending on consumer goods) and that this problem could be solved by redistributing income from the rich to the poor. However, the macroeconomics of Keynes says that government's taxing and spending policies and its control over banks and money can stabilize the economy and thus do the job that Hobson assigned to income redistribution. For this reason, interest in economic maldistribution has declined.

Ethical Maldistribution **Ethical maldistribution** means that the income or wealth distribution does not correspond to some standard based on what is believed to be just or fair. Consider, for example, the doctrine of "justice is fairness," outlined by John Rawls, which concludes that complete equality is the best distribution.[18] Essentially, Rawls asks what sort of income distribution would be chosen by a person who had absolutely no idea what position he or she would occupy in it. Rawls supposes that if we had no knowledge of the consequences of our own talents and circumstances, we would all choose equality in order to avoid the risk of poverty. In this construct, it is a person's *relative* income position that counts. It matters only whether you are better or worse off than those around you. It does not matter what the absolute size of your income is, as long as it is above the starvation level. In developing his theory, however, Rawls grants a case for some inequality. A higher income might be ethically justified for some person (presumably an inventor or innovator) who, in exchange for extra income for himself or herself, improves the absolute position of what Rawls calls "the poorest of the poor."

An entirely different ethical argument, this one presented by Robert Nozick, says that what matters in income distribution is the process by which it developed into whatever it is, rather than that end-state itself.[19] He argues that the present distribution is fair, no matter how nearly equal or unequal it may be, if the following conditions have been met: (1) An "original" distribution of abilities and property must have been fair, or at least no one can specify precisely to whom it was unfair and to what extent and who today represents those wronged by the unfairness. (2) All subsequent transactions must have been carried out without force or fraud.

To understand this argument better, consider the following story. Adams and Baker are about equal in income and wealth. By his own free choice, Adams saves and invests, leaving his son, Adams, Jr., a substantial income-yielding property and a degree from a college or university. In contrast, Baker, by his own free choice, enjoys the easy life and leaves his son, Baker, Jr., nothing at all. According to Nozick, the resulting distribution between Adams, Jr., and Baker, Jr., is entirely fair, no matter how unequal it is, because it resulted from the free choices of Adams, Sr., and Baker, Sr., without any force or fraud involved.

In the real world, you may wonder whether either condition 1 or condition 2 has been satisfied. Nevertheless, there is substance to Nozick's line of argument.

Another ethical argument is related quite directly to microeconomic analysis. John Bates Clark (1847–1938) was a leading American economist and one of the fathers of marginal analysis. Clark argued that, in an ethical sense, one deserves the marginal product of his or her labor and capital. Therefore, he said, whatever distribution results from the unrestricted operation of the marginal productivity principle is a correct one.

Again, objections arise. Is the owner of physical capital (machines and equipment) to be considered productive because his or her capital is? Does it matter whether this capital was inherited or accumulated by this person himself or herself? Or consider the income earned because of a professional education (human capital). Does it matter whether the education was financed by government or by gifts from alumni or educational foundations? Also consider the case of slavery. Southern masters often rented skilled and reliable slaves to other plantations and even to urban factories, collecting for themselves part or all of the wages paid the slaves.[20] Who was productive in these cases—the slave or the master? All of these objections relate to the institutions of private property in one form or another. Also, as you already know, wages may not be equal to marginal revenue product in monopsonistic labor markets.

Maldistribution means excessive inequality or equality of personal income or wealth. It may be individual, economic, or ethical.

---

18. John Rawls, *A Theory of Justice* (Cambridge, Mass.: Belknap Press of Harvard University Press, 1971).

19. Robert Nozick, *Anarchy, State, and Utopia* (New York: Basic Books, 1974).

20. Robert Fogel and Stanley Engerman, *Time on the Cross* (Boston: Little, Brown, 1974).

TABLE 8
Thurow's Proposed Personal Income Distribution and Actual U.S. Distribution

	Percent of Personal Income	
Quintile	Actual (1986)	Thurow Proposal[a]
Fifth (highest)	43.7	36.7
Fourth	24.0	23.5
Third (middle)	16.8	18.2
Second	10.8	13.9
First (lowest)	4.6	7.7

a. Percentage distribution of earnings of fully employed white males, United States, 1977.

Source: U.S. Bureau of the Census, *Current Population Reports.* Consumer Income 1977, Series P-60, no. 118 (March 1979), Table 33-4(b), p. 228. *Statistical Abstract of the United States,* 108th ed. (1988), Table 701, p. 428.

A Compromise Position Since none of the maldistribution arguments that we have offered is entirely convincing, the door is open to compromise. Lester Thurow, dean of the Sloan School at the Massachusetts Institute of Technology, has made the following suggestion: ". . . our general equity goal should be . . . a distribution of incomes for everyone that is no more unequal than that which now exists for the earnings of fully employed white males."[21] Thurow does not try to defend this proposition in ethical or operational terms but simply asserts that it would be better than the existing distribution or other suggestions.

Table 8 compares the Thurow distribution (presumably based on 1977 data) with the actual 1986 distribution. As you can see, his proposed distribution is closer to equality than the existing one for personal income in the United States.

The Parable of the Bamboo Flute Before leaving the subject of maldistribution, we present the "parable of the bamboo flute," devised by the Indian economist Amartya Kumar Sen.[22] Suppose that only one bamboo flute exists and that it is to be given to only one of four persons, each of whom

21. Lester Thurow, *Zero-Sum Society* (New York: Penguin Books, 1981), p. 201.
22. "Ethical Issues in Income Distribution," in A. K. Sen, *Resources, Values, and Development* (Oxford: Blackwell, 1984), p. 290f.

believes he or she deserves it. Table 9 describes these persons and their claims to the flute. One claims it because he or she made it, another because he or she has the most musical talent, a third because he or she is the poorest or has the greatest need, and a fourth because he or she will practice most. Which person should have the flute? In real life, there may also be a fifth claimant—the one who offers enough money to buy the claims of the others. (Sen finds no ethical merit in mere economic demand.)

To make the parable more interesting to you, we have added to Table 9 a parallel list of claims relating to medical school admissions. Suppose there is one last vacancy in next year's entering class. Should it go to the one who studied the hardest as a premedical student, the one with the highest aptitude for medicine, the one who has obtained education so far under the most severe handicaps, or the one who will be most industrious as a medical student? Or, we might add, should it go to the one who can pay the most tuition?

REDISTRIBUTION METHODS

With the extension of democratic institutions, spokespersons for the poor have entered the political mainstream of the leading market-economy countries. In this section, we shall discuss redistribution methods in an equalizing direction. We begin with some familiar reformist measures and close with a brief note on more radical and socialist ones.

Progressive Taxation

Progressive taxation means that taxes take a larger percentage of income from those with high incomes than from those with low incomes. In individual income taxation, this is attempted through both substantial personal exemptions and increasingly higher tax rates as income rises. It has long been the standard means of redistributing income.

However, increasing doubt surrounds the effectiveness and wisdom of this instrument as it has evolved in practice. In spite of the changes brought on by the Tax Reform Act of 1986, U.S. tax law still provides preferences and shelters which greatly reduce actual progressivity. The great expansion of the underground economy, caused partly by the desire to avoid taxes, also reduces its effectiveness. As measured by Gini ratios such as those described earlier in this chapter, income after tax in the United States is only slightly more equal than income before tax.

Progressive taxation—taxation that takes a larger percentage of income from those with high incomes than from those with low incomes—has long been a standard means of redistributing income. It appears not to be very effective.

Regressive Expenditures

Government social welfare expenditures are planned to provide goods and services that the poor could not otherwise purchase in private markets. Beginning with relief for the poor and elementary education for all, they have spread to higher education, social insurance, health care, and housing. These have become more powerful means of redistribution than the individual income tax. However, their net equalizing effect is reduced when higher-income people take advantage of these programs. It is often argued, for example, that state universities, when financed largely by sales taxes, are aimed at educating middle- and upper-class youth at the expense of taxpayers poorer than the students' families.

Government social welfare expenditures have become more powerful means of redistribution than the individual income tax.

Trade Unionism and Collective Bargaining

The trade-union movement is often thought of as an agent of income equalization. It probably increases the functional share of labor income in the total national income more by its political advocacy of restricted immigration than by its directly economic activities such as collective bargaining. Collective bargaining itself may make the personal distribution of labor income somewhat *less* equal, since its most successful practitioners have been the labor aristocrats of the skilled trades and the em-

TABLE 9
The Parable of the Bamboo Flute

| Claimant | Basis of Claim | |
	Bamboo Flute	Medical School Admission
A	Made the flute	Studied hardest as premedical student
B	Most musical talent	Highest aptitude for medicine
C	Poorest claimant: greatest need	Has obtained education under most severe handicaps
D	Will practice flute most assiduously	Will be most industrious medical student

ployees of industries with substantial market power. Their wage gains relegate other workers to less desirable jobs or to underemployment. In addition, their collective bargaining is collusive. That is, there is a tacit understanding that the wage gains of workers are to be passed on to the general public (including the poor) in price increases so that profit margins are not disturbed.

The trade union movement probably increases the functional share of labor income in the total national income more by its political advocacy of restricted immigration than by its directly economic activities which may make the distribution of labor income somewhat less equal.

Price Fixing and Rationing

Minimum wages, food stamps, floors under farm prices, and ceilings on retail prices receive some support from people who hope that they will redistribute income. However, as equalizing devices, all look better on paper than they eventually become in practice. Minimum wage laws, for example, raise the wages of those poor workers who remain employed, but they reduce the number employed, at least in private profit-seeking businesses. They do nothing for those unable to find work at legal minimum wages. Similarly, farm price supports do little for the poorest farmers, who are for the most part subsistence farmers with only tiny cash crops to sell at any price. Also, retail price ceilings, with or without rationing, do not guarantee that goods will be available at the legal prices, even to honor minimum rations. An extreme case occurred in Japan under American occupation in 1945–46. Extraordinary honesty and professional pride induced a Tokyo judge to limit his food to what he or his family could buy at controlled prices. He soon died of starvation or acute malnutrition.

Socialization of Wealth

Under socialist systems, most physical capital is taken over by the government or, if left in private hands, is taxed almost 100 percent ("socialization

of the flow"). Much of the sentiment that favors these measures comes from a belief in the equalizing effects that they are expected to have. Both income and wealth appear to be more evenly distributed in socialist countries than in capitalist ones, but in no case does the distribution approach anything like complete equality. Even though government is expected to use a large part of the income from capital for investments to promote economic growth, it is not clear that socialist economies expand their production possibilities any faster than, or even as fast as, capitalist economies. Thus, even if greater equality is achieved, there may be slower improvement in the real standards of living. Whether the poor are actually better off under socialism remains an open question. Moreover, equalization of income is not necessarily the primary goal in socialist systems. We should not forget that Soviet dictator Josef Stalin considered egalitarianism to be a "petty bourgeois heresy" and favored substantial inequality of Soviet wages and incomes.[23]

Since Stalin's death in 1953, and especially since Mikhail Gorbachev's accession to power, there has been a substantial retreat from Stalinism. This has included retreat from Stalin's hard-line anti-egalitarian position. The Soviet distribution of *labor* income remains unequal, but we must remember that the distribution of total income in capitalist countries is less equal than that of labor income alone. Also, we judge the Soviet distribution from published data on wage rates alone, not on family earnings. We can only guess at the distributional effects of multiple-job holding by individual Soviet citizens, and of multiple-wage-earner families in Soviet society. We believe that they result in greater inequality, because they do so in capitalist countries, but we cannot be certain.

Minimum wages, food stamps, farm price supports, retail price ceilings, and socialization of wealth all have advocates as instruments of income redistribution. However, in practice, none of these measures has proven effective as an equalizing device.

---

23. Abram Bergson, *The Structure of Soviet Wages* (Cambridge, Mass.: Harvard University Press, 1944), pp. 177–179.

Economics in Focus

Proposals for a Renewed War on Poverty

The stubborn nature of poverty in the United States has brought many proposals for new methods of attack. Some involve variations of a negative income tax or tax-credit scheme to provide a basic, livable income for all. Others are aimed specifically at groups that appear to need the most help—children and single parents, for example. Although we cannot survey all of the ideas that are being debated, we can look at a few of the more popular or innovative ones.

To help children escape poverty, many reformers have proposed improvements in public education, especially in the development of cognitive skills. Head Start could be expanded to reach more people at a younger age, before children from poverty backgrounds fall behind their wealthier counterparts. Better prenatal care for mothers would also help; many poor children start out with health deficits that are never fully overcome. Analysts have also suggested scrapping Aid for Families with Dependent Children (AFDC) and replacing it with a universal child-support program that would guarantee an acceptable living standard.

Economist Robert Haveman has offered a more radical concept for reducing the number of young adults in poverty. Give every eighteen-year-old, he suggests—rich and poor alike—a grant of perhaps $20,000 to spend on education or health care. Within certain guidelines, let the youths choose their own options. Such a program, Haveman believes, would not only expand opportunities for the poor but also allow them the dignity of planning their own lives rather than depending on government paternalism.

The question of jobs has received a good deal of attention. Some experts would like to see a large-scale government jobs program for the inner cities, something on the order of the Works Progress Administration of the 1930s. It would not be make-work, they contend, because there is much that needs doing; for instance, low-income workers hired under such a program could repair city infrastructures that are literally falling apart. Other analysts have proposed reviving the New Jobs Tax Credit of the late 1970s, a program that offered tax incentives to businesses that created new jobs for low-skilled workers. Haveman suggests coupling the jobs tax credit with a subsidy program by which the government would pay part of the wages of any new worker from a disadvantaged background. People below the poverty line would then have an advantage in the job market—and an encouraging reason to seek work.

Though it is hard to generalize about current antipoverty proposals, many of them incorporate a greater reliance on incentives than the programs of the 1960s. They envision the poor not as passive recipients of aid, but as active participants in their own economic betterment.

Sources: Robert H. Haveman, "New Policy for the New Poverty," *Challenge,* September–October 1988, pp. 27–36; Robert Haveman, *Starting Even: An Equal Opportunity Program to Combat the Nation's New Poverty* (New York: Simon and Schuster, 1988); Richard Stengel, "The Underclass: Breaking the Cycle," *Time,* October 10, 1988, pp. 41–42; Robert B. Reich, "As the World Turns," *The New Republic,* May 1, 1989, pp. 23–28; Charles G. Burck, "Toward Two Societies?" *Fortune,* October 10, 1988, pp. 48–49.

SUMMARY

1. The problems of poverty and inequality are related but not the same. Inequality can exist without anyone being poor, according to most definitions. (See page 794.)

2. Poverty lines are estimated by four principal criteria: amenities, proportionality, budgetary, and public opinion. The results and implications differ. The budgetary criterion is the one most widely used. (See pages 794–795.)

3. Certain characteristics of families and single individuals increase the probability of living below the poverty line. These characteristics include being nonwhite, very young, physically or mentally handicapped, having little formal education or training, records of criminal conduct or mental illness, no regular employment, being members of households headed by females, or having been reared in economic backwaters. In general, the more of these handicaps that apply, the more likely is the family or individual concerned to be poor. (See pages 797–798.)

4. Antipoverty policies received great attention in the United States starting in the 1960s. Major programs include Aid for Families with Dependent Children, food stamps, subsidies for housing and medical care, and guaranteed minimum Social Security payments. These programs are controversial because of abuse, high costs, and adverse effects on work incentives. (See page 798.)

5. Negative income tax proposals are among the reform suggestions for antipoverty programs. Three key elements in negative income taxes are a guaranteed minimum income to fight poverty, a rate of negative tax designed to preserve work incentives, and a breakeven income level that strongly influences the overall cost of the program. Conflicts exist among these elements. Besides these problems, there are political and administrative difficulties that might arise from negative income taxation. (See pages 799–801.)

6. Antipoverty programs that involve compulsory labor and/or training for aid recipients are controversial. Training programs may be expensive, while compulsory labor raises questions of the suitability of the work and the care of dependent children when the parent or parents must work. (See page 801.)

7. A poverty underclass exists when there is little mobility in or out of the poverty group, so that poverty extends over several generations of the same family. In this circumstance, a cultural gap tends to arise between the general population and the underclass. The gap increases the difficulty of resolving poverty problems. (See pages 801–802.)

8. Homelessness and panhandling are aspects of poverty that have increased in severity in part because of reduced availability of housing that is affordable to the poor. Factors contributing to the reduced availability of affordable housing for the poor include urban renewal, rent controls, and increasing construction costs. The release of near-normal persons from psychiatric hospitals has added to the demand for affordable housing for the poor. (See pages 803–805.)

9. Economists are interested in both the functional and the personal distributions of income, though there are many other ways of measuring inequality that apply to particular areas of study. The functional distribution is by income types, and the personal distribution is by income-size classes. (See page 805.)

10. In the functional distribution, labor income amounts to over 75 percent of American national income and property income amounts to less than 25 percent. In the personal distribution, over 40 percent of personal income goes to the top fifth of recipients, and less than 5 percent goes to the bottom fifth. (See page 805 and Table 5, page 806.)

11. Inequality of the personal income distribution is commonly measured in America and Western Europe by Gini ratios, based on Lorenz curves. In Eastern Europe, it is commonly measured by quantile ratios. (See pages 805–806 and Figure 2, page 807.)

12. Changes in American inequality over time seem to depend more on the difference between the wages of skilled and unskilled labor than on the size of the labor share of total income. (See pages 806–807.)

13. There are many factors that may explain the continued existence of income inequality. Among these are genetic endowments, environmental endowments, inheritances, discrimination, and pure blind luck. (See pages 809–810.)

14. Income statistics based on race and gender suggest that discrimination has contributed to

lower incomes for women, blacks, and Hispanics in the United States. (See pages 810–811 and Tables 6 and 7, pages 810 and 811.)

15. Comparable worth is the name given to systems that attempt to specify pay for various jobs based on their arduousness and their requirements for skills, education, and so on. If adopted, comparable worth systems probably would lead to labor shortages in those occupations that were downgraded and to labor surpluses in those that were upgraded. (See pages 812–813.)

16. Several varieties of maldistribution can be identified, including individual maldistribution, economic maldistribution, and ethical maldistribution. There are many theories about whether particular income distributions are ethically justified. (See pages 813–814.)

17. Among the instruments for redistributing income, progressive taxation and regressive government expenditures are the most widely practiced in the United States. Price fixing and rationing are sometimes suggested as redistributional devices, though they typically fail in practice to accomplish this objective. Socialization of wealth sometimes is advocated as a redistributive measure, but this may have adverse effects on real income growth and is not necessarily a major aim in socialist systems. (See pages 814–816.)

KEY TERMS

comparable worth: the name given to systems that attempt to specify pay for various jobs based on their arduousness, their requirements for skills, education, and so on (page 812).

discrimination: different economic opportunities being offered to persons on the basis of personal characteristics unrelated to the jobs themselves (page 810).

economic maldistribution: An income or wealth distribution that causes the economic system to function less well than it would under a different income distribution (page 812).

ethical maldistribution: an income or wealth distribution that does not correspond to some standard based on what is believed to be just or fair (page 813).

functional income distributions: how wealth and income are distributed between labor, property, and other sources of income (page 815).

Gini ratio: a measure of inequality computed by dividing the area of inequality shown by a Lorenz curve by the whole right-triangle area below the line of equality in the Lorenz-curve diagram (page 808).

individual maldistribution: dissatisfaction about the particular people at the upper and lower ends of the income or wealth distribution (page 812).

Lorenz curve: an illustration of inequality that is constructed by plotting the percentage of total income received by successive percentages of the population, starting from the lowest-income persons and proceeding cumulatively upward (page 807).

maldistribution: excessive inequality or equality of personal income or wealth (page 812).

negative income tax: a system whereby persons who receive less than a specified amount of income receive payments from the government, and persons who receive more than that amount of income pay money to the government (page 799).

personal income distribution: the distribution of income and wealth by income brackets or size classifications (page 805).

poverty lines: income levels below which poverty is said to exist (page 794).

progressive taxation: taxation that takes a larger percentage of income from those with high incomes than from those with low incomes (page 815).

quantile ratio: a measurement of income inequality that compares the percentage of total income received by the highest k percent of the population with the percentage of total income received by the lowest k percent (page 809).

DISCUSSION QUESTIONS

1. Explain the differences between the problems of poverty and maldistribution. Can either problem persist after the other is satisfactorily solved?

2. Explain the difference between "island" and "case" poverty in Galbraith's usage. Which variant do you think is more important in your community? In the United States as a whole?

3. What is the published poverty line? How well do you think it distinguishes the poor from the nonpoor? What if the American poverty line were applied to the population of Bangladesh or Haiti?

4. Developmental and child psychologists think the American standard of living leads to child neglect by forcing potentially poor parents to work full time to stay out of poverty. How important a social problem do you think this is?

5. Professor Robert J. Lampman (University of Wisconsin) distinguishes *income* poverty from other sorts of poverty, and from poverty in general. What other varieties of poverty might he have in mind?

6. Would a negative income tax be preferable to the present American "welfare mess"? Defend your answer.

7. Compare the Gini ratio and the quantile ratio as measures of income inequality. Which do you think is preferable? Defend your answer.

8. Distinguish "ethical" from "economic" maldistribution. Is "bad ethics" necessarily "bad economics" or vice versa?

9. It has often been proposed to replace or supplement the federal income tax by a consumption tax (which excludes certain sorts of saving from the tax base). How would this affect the redistributive effectiveness of the tax system?

10. Compare the "fairness" concepts of Rawls, Nozick, and Thurow.

11. Many working-class married women have worked outside the home for a long time. With the rise of the women's movement, more middle-class and upper-class married women have also joined the labor force. What are the consequences of this change on the measured distribution of family income? (In your answer, assume that most married couples come from roughly similar income classes.)

12. For many years, the American minimum wage was $3.35 per hour. It has been estimated that the productivity of the lower 10 percent of the labor force (with measured IQ under 85) did not justify employment at this wage rate. How do you think this problem should be handled? What is the distributional effect of doing nothing about it?

35
Government Antitrust and Regulation Policy

Preview   Competition in fairly free markets and government regulation in markets without competition can both work. Both can provide good results for society in terms of large levels of desired output at low prices. Consumer welfare is threatened, however, when companies find ways to limit competition and gain substantial monopoly control in markets where we depend on competition. Consumer welfare is also endangered when the government fails to regulate a market that is without competition or when it regulates it very poorly. It follows, then, that government has an important part to play in making sure that there is enough competition in those markets where competition is desirable and that regulation takes place and is effective in those markets where monopoly is desirable. This dual role of government is the subject of this chapter. In the first half we explain antitrust policy, and in the second half we deal with the regulation of certain actual monopolies.

In this chapter we examine the three major pieces of U.S. antitrust legislation—the Sherman Antitrust Act of 1890, the Clayton Act of 1914, and the Federal Trade Commission Act of 1914. Together they can be used to promote competition to almost any extent that is desired by the government.

We also trace the changing U.S. antitrust philosophy over the past one hundred years. By referring to a number of landmark court cases, we show how our antitrust laws have been used and interpreted. The discussion will be broken down into three parts: (1) monopolization, (2) mergers, and (3) price fixing.

We end the first half of the chapter with a discussion of international cartels, using the case of the Organization of Petroleum Exporting Countries (OPEC).

The second half of this chapter recognizes that competition may not be the best answer for all industries. Here we review the concept of natural monopoly and explain why the government sometimes gives certain companies public utility status.

Government regulation takes place on both the national and the state level. We mention some of the better-known federal regulatory commissions that are responsible for regulating certain industries. We also explain the theory of rate regulation.

During the eighty years following the establishment of the Interstate Commerce Commission in 1887, regulation in the United States continuously increased. By the mid-1970s the American public became concerned about the spread of regulation into a number of industries that seemed not to need it. We look at some of the problems of unneeded regulation and some of the efforts that have been made to reverse the trend. Deregulation, at first only a catchword, has to some degree become a reality. Finally, we recognize a contemporary concern that deregulation may have gone too far. Both at the conclusion of this chapter and in an essay on savings and loan associations in the United States at the end of this part, we examine the call for reregulation.

ANTITRUST POLICY

The United States and many other industrialized countries of the Western world have long depended on competition to provide the discipline that is needed for efficient allocation of scarce resources. When firms find ways to limit competition in such an environment, public welfare is in danger. Companies may restrict competition within their industries through certain practices such as agreements to limit output in order to be able to charge very high prices. Collusion among companies always aims at lessening or eliminating competition in their industry and at earning higher profits. Simply put, companies have a strong profit incentive to lessen or eliminate competition among themselves. In this way they act like monopolists. It stands to reason that this sort of behavior is more likely to occur in oligopolies, where there are "few" firms, than in industries that more closely resemble pure competition or monopolistic compe-

tition and that are made up of "many" companies. Also, oligopolies with rather high levels of economic concentration and with high entry barriers are more likely to act in a collusive way than are oligopolies with lower levels of economic concentration and with low barriers to entry.

Companies have a strong profit incentive to lessen or eliminate competition among themselves. Collusion is more likely in oligopolies than in other kinds of market structure.

For this reason, governments in the United States and other countries are on their guard against the dangers of anticompetitive practices. The government policy that deals with this threat to the public interest is called **antitrust policy**. It includes all of the executive, legislative, and judicial actions that aim at maintaining or restoring competition in markets where it is needed. Government may act directly to keep companies from colluding or from interfering with competition in other ways. Government may also use its antitrust powers indirectly by encouraging competitive market structures. For example, it may not allow a merger of two large firms in an industry that is already highly concentrated.

Government antitrust policy includes all of the executive, legislative, and judicial actions that aim at maintaining or restoring competition in markets where it is needed.

U.S. Antitrust Statutes

The policy in the United States has generally been to protect and foster competition. However, there are certain exceptions such as public utility pricing, which we explain later in this chapter, and some price freezes during times of war and rising inflation. The major laws that prohibit the restriction of competition are the Sherman Antitrust Act, the Clayton Act (including the Robinson-Patman Act and the Celler-Kefauver Antimerger Amendment), and the Federal Trade Commission Act (including the Wheeler-Lea Amendment).

U.S. policy has generally been to protect and foster competition. Several major laws prohibit the restriction of competition: the Sherman Antitrust Act, the Clayton Act, and the Federal Trade Commission Act.

The Sherman Antitrust Act   During the quarter-century after the Civil War, big business in the United States was getting bigger, and many small businesses were driven out in the process. The public was very upset about these changes because they appeared to bring high prices for consumers and high income to giant firms. Some companies were able to eliminate competition almost completely by forming a **trust**—a device used by supposedly competing firms that allowed a central board of trustees to vote all of their stock. During the 1880s and 1890s, for example, John D. Rockefeller organized more than forty oil companies into the Standard Oil Trust, which nearly monopolized the whole crude and refined oil market in the United States.

In the late nineteenth century, companies were able to eliminate competition by forming a trust—a device used by supposedly competing firms that allowed a central board of trustees to vote all of their stock.

In answer to what became a public clamor to do something about this "monopolization," both state and federal legislatures enacted antitrust laws. The U.S. Congress passed the first federal antitrust law, the **Sherman Antitrust Act**, in 1890. This law has two main parts. The first prohibits "every contract, combination in the form of a trust or otherwise, or conspiracy" that limits competition, and prescribes the penalties of imprisonment and/or fines for violators. The second part of the law prohibits monopolization or attempts to monopolize, again specifying the penalties for violators. Moreover, people or firms injured by a violation of the Sherman Act are allowed to sue for damages, and if successful, will be awarded an amount three times the actual damages suffered.

It soon became clear, however, that several problems had to be solved. One was that the Sher-

man Act was poorly enforced during its very early years. In fact, the government lost its cases against the whiskey and sugar trusts in the early 1890s. Besides the poor handling of cases, there was no government agency responsible for enforcing the act. Therefore, at the urging of president Theodore Roosevelt, the Antitrust Division of the Department of Justice was created in 1903. Then in 1914 the Federal Trade Commission Act added a second enforcement agency—the Federal Trade Commission. Another major problem was that the language of the Sherman Act was too general and failed to state clearly just what practices were anticompetitive. The solution to this definition problem was the passage of the Clayton Act of 1914.

The first federal antitrust law, the Sherman Antitrust Act, was enacted in 1890. It prohibited monopolization and combinations in restraint of trade. To help with enforcement, the Antitrust Division of the Department of Justice was created in 1903 and the Federal Trade Commission in 1914.

The Clayton Act   The well-publicized Standard Oil and American Tobacco cases of 1911 directed public attention to certain restrictive practices. The **Clayton Act** was passed in 1914 to deal with four types of potentially anticompetitive business practices. These are: (1) price discrimination, (2) mergers, (3) exclusive dealing and tying arrangements, and (4) interlocking directorates.

The Clayton Act was passed in 1914 to deal with four types of potentially anticompetitive business practices: price discrimination, mergers, exclusive dealing and tying arrangements, and interlocking directorates.

Price Discrimination   The practice of price discrimination by firms that have monopoly control ' was discussed at some length in Chapter 27 (see pp. 613–618). Recall that price discrimination is defined as a price differential that is not justified by a difference in cost to the seller. Section 2 of the Clayton Act prohibits such price discrimination when it "substantially lessens competition or tends to create a monopoly." The act makes it illegal for a firm to try to drive out competitors in one of its geographic markets by charging a lower price to its customers in that market than in its other geographic markets.

The Clayton Act makes it illegal for a firm to try to drive out competitors in one of its geographic markets by charging a lower price to its customers in that market than in its other geographic markets.

It turned out that the language used in Section 2 still left some big loopholes. In fact, in the twenty-two years from 1914 to 1936 only eight price-discrimination cases (after all appeals) were decided in favor of the government.[1] Also, the retailing sector in the United States was rapidly changing during the 1920s and 1930s. Chain stores such as the A&P were replacing small, independent retail stores. These independents and their supporters cried "foul" and argued that the large chain stores were winning in the competition against their smaller rivals mainly because they were able to get discriminatory price concessions from suppliers. Though the best explanation for the chains' success was actually their greater efficiency, the public outcry was politically powerful enough to cause Congress to amend Section 2. In 1936 the **Robinson-Patman Act** changed the language of Section 2 so that during the next thirty-five years over a thousand price-discrimination cases were decided in favor of the government.[2]

The Robinson-Patman Act is certainly the most controversial of all U.S. antitrust laws. Though in some cases it limits unfair pricing practices and so aids competition, in many other cases it simply protects competitors (keeps inefficient companies in business) and does not increase competition.

The Robinson-Patman Act of 1936 attempted to strengthen the Clayton Act by limiting unfair pricing practices, but in many cases it helps keep inefficient companies in business without increasing competition.

---

1. F. M. Scherer, *Industrial Market Structure and Economic Performance,* 2nd ed. (Chicago: Rand McNally, 1980), p. 572.
2. Ibid.

Mergers We discussed merger, or the acquisition of one firm by another, in Chapter 29 (see pp. 660–665). There we explained that whether or not a certain merger has anticompetitive effects depends on the kind of merger and the conditions in the industry involved. Section 7 of the Clayton Act prohibited a company from acquiring the stock of another company if the deal would result in much less competition between *those two firms*. For this reason, it applied only to horizontal mergers. Vertical and conglomerate mergers were not covered by the act. Also, since it dealt only with merger by stock acquisition, mergers in which a company acquired the assets of another company escaped the clutches of the act. No wonder that more vertical and conglomerate mergers took place and that the horizontal mergers that did occur were completed through asset acquisition. It was not until 1950 that these loopholes were closed.

In 1950, Section 7 of the Clayton Act was amended by the **Celler-Kefauver Antimerger Amendment**. This new law covered asset acquisitions and eliminated the wording that made the act applicable only to horizontal mergers. The Supreme Court has interpreted the amendment as covering vertical mergers.[3] However, the Court has never heard a case in which it could offer a clear statement on the inclusion of conglomerate mergers. During the early 1970s several very promising conglomerate merger cases, including three by International Telephone & Telegraph, were headed for the Supreme Court, but they were settled out of court between the companies and the Department of Justice under the Nixon administration. It is quite strange that we do not even know whether conglomerate mergers—the most numerous and important of all mergers—are covered by merger-control laws passed as long ago as 1950. Some legislators and antitrust practitioners have called for new legislation to deal directly with conglomerate mergers. Others believe that the 1950 amendment is sufficient.

In 1950, the Celler-Kefauver Antimerger Amendment eliminated the wording that made the Clayton Act applicable only to horizontal mergers.

---

3. *Brown Shoe Co.* v. *U.S.,* 370 U.S. 294 (1962).

Exclusive Dealing and Tying Arrangements
Section 3 of the Clayton Act prohibits exclusive dealing and tying arrangements that substantially lessen competition or tend to create a monopoly. An **exclusive dealing arrangement** exists when a firm obtains the product of a certain supplier on the condition that it will not buy the products of competing suppliers. Often the buying firm that enters into such an agreement will receive in return the exclusive right to handle the seller's product in a particular market. For example, an exclusive dealing arrangement may be entered into between an auto manufacturer and a local auto dealership. The agreement may be that only cars produced by that manufacturer will be sold by the dealer and that the manufacturer will not sell its cars to any other dealers in that town. If many wholesale or retail companies are bound in this way, potential competitors for sales to these distributors will be severely hampered. In such cases, if these agreements are found to lessen competition substantially, they are illegal.

Tying arrangements are more often found to be illegal than are exclusive dealings. A **tying arrangement** is one that forces a firm to buy certain products along with certain other products. For example, the International Salt Company owned patents on two important salt-handling machines. One machine dissolved rock salt, and the other injected salt tablets into canned products during the canning process. Firms leasing these machines were required to purchase all the rock salt and salt tablets used in the machines from International Salt Company. In 1947 the Supreme Court ruled that International Salt Company had violated the Clayton Act by preventing other firms from competing for the sale of salt to firms using International's machines.[4]

An exclusive dealing arrangement exists when a firm obtains the product of a certain supplier on the condition that it will not buy the products of competing suppliers. A tying arrangement forces a firm to buy certain products along with certain other products.

---

4. *International Salt Company* v. *U.S.*, 322 U.S. 392 (1947).

Interlocking Directorates   Section 8 of the Clayton Act prohibits certain **interlocking directorates**. This term refers to a person serving on the boards of directors of two or more competing firms. The reasoning behind this provision was that such a person would be in a good position to restrict competition among the firms in which he or she had a policy-making role. Such "direct" cases of interlocking directorates are fairly easy to spot, and once the government decided to enforce Section 8 vigorously in the late 1960s, most were quickly eliminated. However, so-called "indirect" interlocking directorates seem to be outside the scope of the Clayton Act. These cases occur when directors of a firm—generally a bank—are placed on the boards of directors of various competing companies that do business with the firm (bank). For example, suppose that two directors, Mr. Pea and Mr. Pod, of the Wholesome National Bank serve on other boards of directors as well. Mr. Pea is on the board of ABC Computers and Mr. Pod is on the board of XYZ Computers. Since both ABC and XYZ do business with Wholesome National Bank, it is likely that when Mr. Pea and Mr. Pod get together at the bank, they discuss more than just bank business. They might even see to it that ABC and XYZ have a good, wholesome relationship.

The Clayton Act also prohibits interlocking directorates—the practice of the same person serving on the boards of directors of two or more competing firms.

The Federal Trade Commission Act   The **Federal Trade Commission Act** was passed in 1914, the same year as the Clayton Act. It added a blanket statement outlawing "unfair methods of competition" to the illegal practices that had been listed in the Clayton Act. Among these "unfair methods" are corporate spying, boycotts, and bribing the employees of potential customers in order to get their business. The courts interpreted "unfair methods of competition" to refer only to the relationship among companies, and not to the relationship between firms and consumers. To fill this gap, the **Wheeler-Lea Amendment** to the act was passed in 1938. It covered "unfair or deceptive acts or practices" aimed at the consumer. These include false advertising claims and deceptive packaging.

The Federal Trade Commission Act, passed in 1914, outlawed unfair methods of competition such as corporate spying, boycotts, and bribery. In 1938, the Wheeler-Lea Amendment outlawed unfair or deceptive acts or practices aimed at consumers.

Possibly the most important provision of the Federal Trade Commission Act was its creation of the **Federal Trade Commission (FTC)** to enforce the law. The FTC supplemented the Antitrust Division of the Justice Department, as a second federal government antitrust agency. Its duty is to investigate and prosecute cases of unfair competition.

The Federal Trade Commission Act created the Federal Trade Commission to supplement the Antitrust Division of the Justice Department.

Antitrust Philosophy

How have these important U.S. antitrust laws been used and interpreted over the years? In answering this question, we shall discuss monopolization, mergers, and price fixing.

Monopolization　Recall that Section 2 of the Sherman Antitrust Act prohibits monopolization and attempts to monopolize. What does that mean? Does the act outlaw all cases of monopoly control (significant market power), or is it reserved only for those cases where a company abuses its monopoly control? The first answer to this question came from the Supreme Court in the 1911 Standard Oil case.[5] The Rockefeller brothers had gained a 90 percent market share of the important kerosene and lubricating oil markets of that time. They gained this control over a period of thirty or forty years, during which they acquired a large number of competing firms and engaged in **predatory price cutting** (price cutting aimed at forcing competitors out of business). The Supreme Court found Standard Oil guilty of violating Section 2 of the Sherman Act. However, the Court very clearly

stated that it did so not just because of its "monopoly position," but rather because of Standard Oil's intention to become a monopoly and its unreasonable practices in limiting competition. This focus on intent and conduct became known as the "rule of reason." The **rule of reason** means that substantial monopoly control alone is not against the law but that the intent to gain monopoly power and the abuse of it make it illegal. In the same year the Supreme Court found the American Tobacco Company also guilty of violating Section 2 of the Sherman Act, again stating its "rule of reason" philosophy.[6] The Court held that the company's guilt was based on its hundreds of horizontal acquisitions and its unreasonable business practices such as predatory pricing and preventing competitors from dealing with suppliers.

In the 1911 Standard Oil antimonopoly case the Supreme Court based its decision on the "rule of reason," which means that substantial monopoly control alone is not against the law, but the intent to gain monopoly power and the abuse of it make it illegal.

Although the Standard Oil and American Tobacco cases were decided in favor of the government and both trusts were later broken up,[7] in 1920 the Supreme Court invoked the "rule of reason" to find the huge and powerful U.S. Steel (now USX Corporation) trust not guilty of violating Section 2 of the Sherman Act.[8] U.S. Steel clearly controlled prices during that period, but it did not undercut competitors to try to drive them out of business. The Supreme Court ruled that mere size and the possession of monopoly power are not offenses. Only when companies use their size and power to harm competitors are they in violation of the Sherman Act.

---

5. *U.S.* v. *Standard Oil Co. of New Jersey*, 221 U.S. 1 (1911).

6. *U.S.* v. *American Tobacco Co.*, 221 U.S. 106 (1911).

7. Standard Oil was separated into thirty-three geographically determined subsidiaries, which later became Exxon, Standard Oil of California, Standard Oil of Indiana, Mobil Oil, and Standard Oil of Ohio. American Tobacco was separated into sixteen parts, including American Tobacco, Liggett & Myers, P. Lorillard, Reynolds, and a new American Tobacco.

8. *U.S.* v. *U.S. Steel Corp.*, 251 U.S. 4–17 (1920).

In the U.S. Steel case of 1920, the Supreme Court again invoked the "rule of reason" and ruled that mere size and the possession of monopoly power are not offenses. Only when companies use their size and power to harm competitors are they in violation of the Sherman Act.

The "rule of reason" guided the Court for another twenty-five years after the U.S. Steel decision. It was not until the Alcoa case of 1945 that the Supreme Court reversed itself. Alcoa, like U.S. Steel, had a huge market share but had not abused it. The findings in the case reinterpreted Section 2 of the Sherman Act, saying that it did not condone "good" trusts and condemn "bad" ones, but rather that it forbade all trusts. Size alone became an offense because the possession of power could not be separated from the abuse of that power. Alcoa's market share of 90 percent was "enough to constitute a monopoly."[9] The judge added that "it is doubtful whether 60 or 64 percent would be enough" and that "certainly 33 percent is not [enough]."[10]

In 1945, in the Alcoa case, the Supreme Court reversed itself, when it ruled that size alone is an offense on the grounds that the possession of power cannot be separated from the abuse of that power.

The Alcoa decision was upheld by the Supreme Court in several important cases in the late 1940s and early 1950s.[11] In one of these cases involving the motion picture industry, Justice William O. Douglas stated that "monopoly power, whether lawfully or unlawfully acquired, may itself constitute an evil and stand condemned under Section 2 even though it remains unexercised."[12] The rule of reason was found to be unreasonable.

9. *U.S.* v. *Aluminum Co. of America,* 148 F. 2d 416 (1945).
10. Ibid.
11. These include the American Tobacco case of 1946, the Griffith Amusement Company case of 1948, the A&P case of 1949, and the United Shoe Machinery case of 1953.
12. *U.S.* v. *Griffith Amusement Co.,* 334 U.S. 100 (1948).

By the mid-1950s some backtracking took place. In a case concerning the monopolization of the cellophane market, Du Pont was found not guilty on the basis of the Supreme Court's willingness to accept a broad definition of what constituted the packaging materials market.[13] A number of cases that involved firms having a fairly large amount of monopoly control were initiated in the 1960s and 1970s, but these were resolved out of court or were thrown out of court altogether. Important cases that were settled out of court affected such firms as Eastman Kodak, RCA, United Fruit, and General Motors. A case involving IBM that had been in court since 1969 was finally thrown out in 1982. An exception during this period was the 1982 AT&T settlement which, while a compromise that allowed AT&T to retain Western Electric, Bell Labs, and the long-distance division, did force it to divest itself of its local telephone business provided by its Bell System operating companies.

The dominant view during the 1980s—the Reagan administrations—was that antitrust action interferes with efficient and progressive business activities. Monopolization was not considered a great threat as low entry barriers, innovation, and foreign competition were relied on to maintain adequate competition and low prices for consumers.

American antitrust philosophy had come full circle, with a return to a rule of reason. The view that "big is bad" was at least temporarily out of fashion during the 1980s. At this writing it is too early to judge just how lenient an antitrust policy the Bush administration will pursue. We would suppose that the pendulum will swing back to some degree and that the Bush administration will be somewhat more concerned with monopolization than was the Reagan administration.

Mergers Closely related to monopolization is the practice of merger. It is the most common way for companies to gain monopoly control. As you know, Section 7 of the 1914 Clayton Act and the 1950 Celler-Kefauver Amendment of that act prohibit mergers that substantially lessen competition or tend to create a monopoly. How has this part of

13. *U.S.* v. *E. I. du Pont de Nemours and Co.,* 351 U.S. 377 (1956).

the law been interpreted by the courts? What has been the governing antitrust philosophy with regard to merger?

As we said earlier, the power of antitrust authorities was greatly increased by the passage of the Celler-Kefauver Antimerger Amendment in 1950. From 1950 to 1965 the Justice Department and the Federal Trade Commission initiated more than twice as many antimerger complaints as they had during the thirty-six-year life of the original Section 7 of the Clayton Act.[14] Furthermore, the government won many of these cases. In an important 1958 horizontal merger case, Bethlehem Steel Company, the nation's second-largest steel producer, was prevented from acquiring Youngstown Sheet & Tube Company, the sixth-largest steel firm.[15] In 1962 the Supreme Court ruled in favor of the government in a case that involved both a horizontal and a vertical merger. The Brown Shoe Company, which was primarily a manufacturer of shoes, acquired the G. R. Kinney Company, which also manufactured shoes, but was mainly in the retail shoe business. Although the two firms together accounted for only 4½ percent of shoe production in the United States and Kinney's market share at retail was only about 1½ percent, the Supreme Court did not allow the merger.[16] This decision was strengthened by a 1966 Supreme Court decision that ruled against the acquisition of Shopping Bag Food Stores by Von's Grocery Company. Von's accounted for less than 5 percent of the retail food market in the Los Angeles area, and the Shopping Bag Food Stores held less than a 3 percent share of the same market.[17] These and other 1960s cases made it clear that horizontal and vertical mergers of companies with as little as 5 to 10 percent of the market share would be challenged and probably denied by the courts.

But what about conglomerate mergers? In Chapter 29 we showed that these accounted for more than three-quarters of all the mergers in the 1960s and 1970s. Earlier in this chapter we complained that no clear statement on the legal status of conglomerates has ever been issued by the Supreme Court. Many so-called conglomerate merger cases did reach the Supreme Court during the 1960s, and most rulings went in favor of the government. However, the rulings were not that conglomerate mergers were illegal, but rather that the mergers in question contained anticompetitive horizontal or vertical aspects or, in other words, that they were not conglomerate enough. As the Court became more conservative in the mid-1970s, chances decreased for a precedent-setting case refusing to allow a conglomerate merger merely on the grounds that the acquiring firm would become too large and powerful.

In early 1979, the Justice Department, the Federal Trade Commission, and certain members of Congress led by Senator Edward Kennedy tried to secure new legislation aimed directly at preventing large firms from becoming even larger through conglomerate mergers. One bill would have prohibited almost any merger between companies whose combined sales were $2 billion or more. Another would have required that mergers between companies where each had sales of $2.5 billion could take place only if the acquiring firm at the same time rid itself of an equal amount of business.[18] None of these bills was passed by Congress, and by the time President Reagan was elected to his first term in 1980, the "big is bad" philosophy had all but disappeared from Washington, D.C.

Merger is the most common way for companies to gain monopoly control. In the 1950s and 1960s, the government won many of its horizontal and vertical merger cases, but there have been no rulings on the legal status of conglomerate mergers.

The 1980s were characterized by a much more friendly attitude toward merger. The concern had turned directly toward how a certain merger could be expected to affect efficiency and thus prices for consumers. Some predominantly horizontal mergers in highly concentrated markets were still questioned, but in most cases vertical and conglomerate mergers were allowed to go through unchallenged.

---

14. F. M. Scherer, *Industrial Market Structure and Economic Performance*, 2nd ed. (Chicago: Rand, McNally, 1980), p. 548.

15. *U.S.* v. *Bethlehem Steel Corp.*, 168 F. Supp. 576 (1958).

16. *Brown Shoe Co.* v. *U.S.*, 370 U.S. 294 (1962).

17. *U.S.* v. *Von's Grocery Co.*, 384 U.S. 270 (1966).

18. *The Wall Street Journal*, January 29, 1978, and January 17, 1979.

In 1981 Mobil, an oil company with $60 billion in sales, tried to acquire Conoco, another oil company with sales of $18 billion, and Marathon Oil Company with $8 billion in sales. In both cases, the Antitrust Division of the Justice Department announced that if the mergers went through, it would look into their effects on competition. In the meantime, du Pont acquired Conoco (a vertical merger), and U.S. Steel acquired Marathon (a conglomerate merger), both with the blessings of the Justice Department. But in 1984 the green light was given for Mobil to acquire Superior Oil, Texaco to acquire Getty, and Standard Oil of California (now Chevron) to acquire Gulf Oil. All three mergers contained a mixture of conglomerate, vertical, and horizontal aspects. In 1984 and 1985 mergers involving huge household brand-name firms were allowed to take place—Esmark by Beatrice Foods, Nabisco Foods by R. J. Reynolds, Carnation by Nestlé, General Foods by Philip Morris, and Richardson-Vicks by Procter & Gamble. In 1986 General Electric Corporation acquired RCA for about $6.5 billion. If we ignore leveraged buy-outs such as the 1988 $25 billion RJR Nabisco deal that we discussed in Chapter 29, this 1986 conglomerate and horizontal merger is the largest non-oil industry acquisition made to date.

The 1980s were characterized by a much friendlier attitude toward merger; in most cases, vertical and conglomerate mergers were allowed to go through unchallenged.

In 1982 the U.S. Department of Justice issued "Merger Guidelines" to update those that had been in effect since the late 1960s. The guidelines were further refined in 1984. The unifying theme of the new guidelines is that mergers generally play an important, positive role in the American economy, but that they should not be permitted in those cases where they create or enhance significant market power. The focus is on the postmerger concentration level of affected markets, as measured by the Herfindahl-Hirschman Index (HHI) of market concentration discussed in Chapter 29. Recall that the HHI is calculated by summing the squares of the individual market shares of all the firms in a market. A monopoly would have an HHI of 10,000

(100×100). The Department of Justice characterizes an industry with an HHI of below 1,000 as "unconcentrated," an HHI of between 1,000 and 1,800 as "moderately concentrated," and an HHI of over 1,800 as "highly concentrated."

The merger guidelines of the 1980s, issued by the Department of Justice, are based on the premise that mergers generally play a positive role in the American economy, but they should not be permitted if they create or enhance significant market power, as measured by the Herfindahl-Hirschman Index of market concentration.

Price Fixing The most steady and consistent part of the American antitrust policy has been with regard to price fixing. Agreements among competing firms to establish specific prices and to restrict output in order to maintain those prices have been prohibited in the United States ever since the passage of Section 1 of the Sherman Antitrust Act in 1890.

Price fixing—agreements among competing firms to establish specific prices and to restrict output in order to maintain those prices—has been illegal since 1890.

Early Price-Fixing Cases A precedent-setting case was decided by the Supreme Court in 1897. It involved a formal price (rate) agreement among eighteen western railroads that had engaged earlier in very damaging price wars.[19] The Court ruled that collusive agreements among competing firms to restrict output and fix prices was illegal *per se* (that is, illegal in any case, rather than just illegal in that particular case). That direct evidence of price fixing is enough to determine illegality was repeated by the Supreme Court in the 1927 Trenton Potteries case.[20] Remember that by this time the Court had adopted the "rule of reason" in monopolization cases, and there was concern that this rule might also be applied to price fixing. However, it was not.

19. *U.S.* v. *Trans-Missouri Freight Association,* 166 U.S. 290 (1897).
20. *U.S.* v. *Trenton Potteries Co.,* 273 U.S. 392 (1927).

Even though the price-fixing arrangement in this case was weak and possibly "reasonable," the Court again stated its *per se* illegality decision. Reasonable or not, price fixing is against the law. With the exception of one Great Depression case in 1933,[21] the Supreme Court's blanket condemnation of price fixing has been consistent.

Since 1897, the Supreme Court has consistently ruled that collusive agreements among competing firms to restrict output and fix prices are illegal *per se*—illegal in any case, not just some particular case.

The Great Electrical Conspiracy In spite of the Supreme Court's consistent action with regard to price fixing, each year many firms in many different industries are found guilty of this illegal practice. An outstanding case of price fixing in a highly concentrated industry is the "great electrical conspiracy" of the 1950s.

The case involved twenty-nine firms, including the two giants of the heavy electrical equipment industry—General Electric and Westinghouse. For a period of about seven years, the top electrical equipment executives from these companies met in hotel rooms, private homes, and resorts to fix prices, to share sales, and to rig bids on contracts involving some $7 billion worth of heavy electrical equipment. This practice began in the early 1950s, when the postwar demand had slackened and the industry had a great deal of excess capacity. The firms first resorted to price cutting to make use of their capacity and to sell their equipment, but this caused their profits to fall sharply. Getting together to discuss their mutual problems, they saw price fixing and market sharing as very tempting solutions. Clever ways of cutting down the number of meetings were worked out, such as "phase of the moon" pricing. This meant bidding high or low according to the moon's fullness.

The conspiracy did not come to light until a newspaper reporter noticed that several high bidders quoted exactly the same prices for transformers to be sold to the Tennessee Valley Authority. Before it was all over, seven executives were jailed, and fines totaling close to $2 million were levied.

Hundreds of millions of dollars in damages have since been paid by the firms.

The Cartel

Price fixing may be practiced in a more formal setting than that described in the "great electrical conspiracy." A collusive arrangement among sellers that affects the level of their joint output and thus the price that they charge is called a **cartel**. Cartels depend on companies' willingness to give up their independence in making their own decisions. For example, a group of companies that jointly controls all or most of the output of steel may decide that it pays for them to act together to limit their joint output so that they can sell it at a higher price. If, instead, each firm acted on its own, the whole industry's output would be much greater and the price much lower.

A collusive agreement among sellers that affects the level of their joint output and thus the price they charge is called a cartel. The success of a cartel depends on companies' willingness to give up their independence in making their own decisions.

National and International Cartels Many people have never heard of any cartel except OPEC (Organization of Petroleum Exporting Countries). Actually, cartels are not rare, nor are they a new development. In the 1890s the sale of coal in the Ruhr Valley of Germany was conducted under a cartel known as GEORG. It allocated orders among different coal companies when the demand was low and rationed supply among buyers when the demand was high. In this way it effectively shut out all price rivalry. In the United States, certain agricultural producers' cooperatives operate as cartels.

International cartels for steel, copper, wire and cable, tiles, silica, vacuum cleaners, and phonograph records have been operating for many years in several Western European countries. For example, in 1953 Switzerland was found to be taking part in over 130 national and international cartels.[22]

---

21. *Appalachian Coals, Inc.* v. *U.S.*, 288 U.S. 344 (1933).

22. Corwin D. Edwards, *Cartelization in Western Europe* (Washington, D.C.: U.S. Department of State), June 1964, p. 3.

The Instability of Cartels By joining a cartel, firms agree to reduce their output and to raise their price. Each firm is given a quota for production and sales that is lower than its sales volume before the cartel was formed. Once the members have all agreed to such changes, however, it will pay for any one firm in the cartel to break the rules set forth by the cartel. For example, a single firm may have been given a quota representing 10 percent of the total output that a cartel agrees to produce. The company will find it profitable to secretly produce and sell a little more than that amount. If it were to produce 10 percent more than its allotted output, only 1 percent would be added to the total output of the cartel. Such a small increase would not drive down the price very much. Because the company in our example would be selling 10 percent more output at a price that would be only slightly lower, it could earn a much higher profit. Of course, the success of the company that cheats will depend on how willing all other firms in the cartel are to abide by their quotas. If other firms in the cartel also produce more than their allotted quotas, the supply will rise enough to cause a large drop in price and finally to break up the cartel.

By its very nature, then, a cartel is unstable. If each firm in a cartel acts to maximize its own profit, the goals of the cartel cannot be met. Most successful cartels have been subject to the discipline of outside agencies, generally governments.

Each member of a cartel is given a quota for production and sales that is lower than its sales volume before the cartel was formed. However, it pays for any one firm in the cartel to break the rules, and if other firms cheat as well, the cartel falls apart.

The OPEC Cartel The cartel that has aroused the most attention in recent years is the international cartel known as OPEC (Organization of Petroleum Exporting Countries). It was formed in 1960 but was not very effective until the early 1970s. Among OPEC's members are Algeria, Ecuador, Gabon, Indonesia, Iran, Iraq, Kuwait, Libya, Nigeria, Qatar, Saudi Arabia, the United Arab Emirates, and Venezuela. In January 1971 the standard crude oil known as "Saudi Arabian Light" was selling for $1.10 a barrel. Two years later it was selling for

$1.62. In October 1973 its price had gone up to $3.15 a barrel, and by January 1974 it sold for $7.11. In September 1975 the price of this crude oil was $11.50 a barrel, an increase of more than 1,000 percent in less than five years. For the next three years the price of OPEC crude oil increased only moderately, but in 1978 it once again took off, reaching $32 a barrel by early 1980 and $34 by mid-1982.

How can these dramatic price increases be explained? World inflation, a decrease in the excess capacity of crude oil in the United States and Canada, wars and revolutions in the Middle East, and a rising demand for petroleum products partly explain some of the increases. However, by far the most important part of the explanation is the ability of the OPEC cartel to restrict supply. Before the Yom Kippur war between some of the Arab states and Israel in 1973, the cartel was fairly ineffective. In fact, some members refused to abide by the quotas assigned to them. After the war a new unity emerged among the Arab states, allowing them to restrict effectively the supply of crude oil. The fact that the arrangement worked so well for each of the members of the cartel further strengthened their determination. The Iranian revolution in 1978 reduced that country's previously large output to a trickle and brought a new wave of large price increases. Then came the war between Iran and Iraq, which further decreased supply and presented a new opportunity for increases in price.

What many economists had been predicting since the mid-1970s finally occurred in the 1980s. OPEC's monopoly prices reduced consumption, caused non-OPEC production to increase, and triggered cheating by OPEC members. World oil consumption decreased by almost 20 percent from 1979 to 1985 as consumers found ways to conserve oil and to use other fuels that were relatively cheaper. During that time period OPEC cut its production almost in half in an attempt to prop up prices. But that was not sufficient, since nonmembers of OPEC increased their combined production by at least one-third. Mexico tripled its output, Great Britain and Norway boosted North Sea output by about 60 percent, and other countries such as Angola, China, Colombia, Egypt, India, Malaysia, and the Soviet Union added new production as well. In 1973 OPEC accounted for 56 percent of world oil production, but by 1985 the same thirteen OPEC countries accounted for only about 30 percent. In 1983, for the first time in its history, OPEC reduced its official price from $34 to $29 per barrel. In January 1985 the price was further reduced to $28, but by that time the official OPEC price was no longer very important since at least 75 percent of its own members' oil sold at free-market prices.

Cheating has been a fact of life for OPEC from the start, but the progressively greater excess capacity that its members experienced increased the temptation. From the mid-1970s to the mid-1980s, when countries such as Nigeria, Ecuador, and Iran increased their production above their quotas, pleas for OPEC unity and Saudi Arabia's willingness to reduce its output below its quota kept prices from plummeting. In December 1985 OPEC announced that it would no longer attempt to prop up oil prices by restricting its production. In other words, it had collapsed. Since that time, OPEC has made several attempts to revive its influence. None have been very successful. During the late 1980s free market crude oil traded at prices as low as about $10 per barrel and as high as about $20 per barrel. What OPEC does matters, but as a cartel it no longer has great influence.

The best-known cartel in recent years has been OPEC, whose restrictions of petroleum supplies in the 1970s caused oil prices to rise dramatically. By the 1980s, however, OPEC's monopoly prices reduced consumption, caused non-OPEC production to increase, and triggered cheating by OPEC members.

REGULATION POLICY

The philosophy that underlies antitrust policy is that competitive markets serve society better than do markets that are substantially monopolized. This philosophy agrees with the economic theories of competition and monopoly presented in earlier chapters. However, as we have said in discussing actual monopoly (see pages 598–600), there are some important exceptions. In order to stimulate research, most governments offer temporary legal monopolies in the form of patents. They also accept so-called natural monopolies on the grounds that in certain markets it is not efficient to have more than a single firm.

In government-enforced monopoly, there arises the question of whether or not the government should regulate the monopolies that it has created. For patent monopolies, government regulation makes little sense since the temporary monopoly granted by a patent is itself the incentive designed to stimulate research. Government regulation that would keep a patent holder from taking advantage of the monopoly position would not be helpful. Where patents are not involved, however, the case for government regulation is much stronger. If, indeed, the hope of gaining greater efficiency leads the government to put a company in a monopoly position in a market, government regulation may be in keeping with that goal. The reason for regulating a monopoly is that if government gives monopoly status to a firm, it must also guard against abuse of that monopoly power.

In general, competitive markets serve society better than monopoly markets, but there are some important exceptions. Some industries are granted monopoly status by the government, which then guards against potential abuse of monopoly power by regulating them.

Nearly all American businesses are regulated by the government in some way. It is important, however, to point out the difference between social regulation and monopoly regulation. Most firms are subject to **social regulation**, such as environmental protection rules, food and drug rules, truth-in-packaging rules, and occupational health and safety rules. A much smaller number of companies, however, are subject to **monopoly regulation**, which covers a firm's level of output, its price, and the scope of its production. Firms in such fields as transportation, utilities (electric power and natural gas), and communications are sometimes granted a monopoly by government and then become subject to monopoly regulation. Such industries are called **regulated industries**, and they are governed not only by social regulation but also by monopoly regulation.

Monopoly regulation covers a firm's level of output, its price, and the scope of its production. Regulated industries, which are usually in such fields as transportation, utilities, and communications, are governed by monopoly regulation as well as social regulation.

Natural Monopoly

A common reason why government grants a firm a monopoly position is that it is a natural monopoly. As you learned in Chapter 27, a **natural monopoly** refers to a market in which a single seller is required for efficient production. Cost conditions are such that it doesn't pay for more than one com-

pany to operate in such a market. Economies of scale—or the decrease in long-run average total cost as the level of output rises—are so important, relative to the limited demand in such markets, that only a single firm can take full advantage of them.

A natural monopoly is a market in which a single seller is required for efficient production.

In most industries the minimum size at which a firm can be efficient is much smaller than the total demand in the market. For example, the market demand in the U.S. women's and misses' dresses industry can support thousands of efficient firms. Each firm's long-run average-total-cost curve may look like the one drawn in panel (a) of

FIGURE 1
Long-Run Average Total Cost: A Normal Industry and a Natural Monopoly

Panel (a) shows a long-run average-total-cost curve (*LRAC*) for a firm in an industry in which the minimum efficient scale is 100 units per day. This is one of a very large number of efficient firms that this industry is able to support since the market demand at the price being charged is far greater than 100 (700,000 units per day in the example on page 834).

Panel (b) shows a long-run average-total-cost curve (*LRAC*) for a firm in a natural monopoly indus-

try. Minimum optimal scale is 500 million units per day, but the total market demand at the price being charged is only 200 million units per day. This industry must be composed of a single firm in order to be efficient. A single firm has an average total cost of 4.2 cents. If, instead, two equal-sized firms shared the market, each would have an average total cost of 6.3 cents.

Figure 1. It shows that a firm in an industry such as women's and misses' dresses reaches minimum optimal scale at 100 units a day, while the market demand at the prices being charged is far greater—maybe 7,000 times that much. (Such a market is able to support 7,000 efficient firms.)

In some industries the minimum size at which a firm can be efficient is larger than the total quantity demanded in the market at the price being charged. An example may be a company running an electric transmission system. Panel (b) in Figure 1 pictures the long-run average-total-cost curve for such a firm. It shows minimum efficient scale at 500 million units, while at the price being charged the total market demand is only 200 million units. (At no price sufficient to cover long-run average total cost would the quantity demanded be high enough to come close to the minimum efficient scale of 500 million units.) In this way the firm is seen to be a natural monopolist since a single seller is required for producing as efficiently as possible. If two or more electric transmission firms shared this market, each would have a much higher long-run average total cost than if it were a monopoly. In our example a single firm has an average total cost of 4.2 cents, but if two equal-sized firms shared the market, each would have an average total cost of 6.3 cents.

Furthermore, if two or more firms shared this market, competition among them would most likely bring about a monopoly anyway. If the market is shared unequally, the largest of the firms—the one that benefits the most from economies of scale—is able to charge a price lower than the average total cost of its somewhat smaller rival or rivals. After a while, all but the largest firm will be forced to exit, and the industry will become a monopoly. If, instead, the market is equally shared, so that no one firm has an advantage over another, we would still expect only one firm to survive. This is because marginal cost is below declining average total cost. In a competitive situation the market price is expected to be bid down to a level just above marginal cost, which will not be high enough to cover average total cost. Firms then have an economic loss, and one by one they will leave the industry. The company that can hold out the longest will be the surviving monopolist.

In most industries, the minimum size at which a firm can be efficient is much smaller than the total demand in the market. In some industries, however, the minimum size at which a firm can be efficient is larger than the total quantity demanded in the market at the price being charged.

Government Intervention

Should government intervene in markets that are natural monopolies? Many economists believe that it should. In its role of protecting the public interest, the government might be able to prevent some of the problems often associated with natural monopolies. First, if firms were to compete actively, much waste of economic resources would take place. For example, four electric transmission firms might each lay a transmission line when one would be enough. Second, as already explained, severe price competition among the firms would eventually drive out all but one firm. Consumers would then suffer from the restricted output and high prices of an unregulated monopolist. Third, firms might anticipate ruinous competition and so enter into a collusive agreement to avoid price competition. The result would be a waste of resources stemming from unnecessary duplication of facilities along with restricted output and high monopoly prices. Finally, firms may not enter such industries at all. They may expect that collusion will fail and that they will only be involved in ruinous competition. If companies avoid such industries altogether, consumers would be without some essential services.

For these reasons the government often tries to recognize the industry as a natural monopoly before firms begin operation and the undesirable results occur. Sometimes the government itself will go into such a business, but more often it will give a special status to a private firm.

Government tries to prevent the problems associated with natural monopolies, such as waste of natural resources, restricted output and high prices, and collusion to avoid price competition by recognizing an industry as a natural monopoly before firms begin operation.

Public Enterprise   On the federal, state, and local level, government may decide to provide a **public enterprise** (a government monopoly). Among the many such enterprises run by the federal government are the U.S. Postal Service, the Tennessee Valley Authority (TVA), which provides electric power for residents in that region of the country, and Amtrak, which operates railroads in some parts of the United States. State governments generally monopolize lotteries, ports, and parks. Some states go even further. Nebraska, for example, is the only provider of electricity in the state. Finally, local governments often operate public enterprises for such utilities as water, sewage disposal, garbage disposal, some forms of transit, and such social services as libraries, museums, zoos, and cemeteries.

Some monopolies are provided by the government itself; these are called public enterprises, such as the U.S. Postal Service, the TVA, and Amtrak.

Regulated Public Utilities   More often in the United States, however, government chooses to regulate privately owned companies rather than to go into business itself. Certain firms are given **public utility** status. This means that the government provides them with monopoly positions—presumably because it has recognized those markets to be natural monopolies. Even if a certain market is not really a natural monopoly, the company that is chosen to become a public utility is given an exclusive franchise and is subjected to government regulation at all times. Whether this turns out to be in the public interest will depend upon whether or not the market really is a natural monopoly and, if it is, whether or not it is regulated well enough.

In the United States it is more common for government to regulate privately owned companies than to form public enterprises. The government will then grant public utility status.

Regulatory Commissions

Both state and federal governments regulate public utilities through regulatory commissions. Most of the states regulate local-retail electric, gas, and telephone service. Some of the states also regulate water, sewage, pipelines, and warehouses. State public utility commissions are generally made up of three to seven commissioners who set policy and from forty to a thousand engineers, lawyers, accountants, and economists who act as support staff.

On the federal level there are many regulatory bodies. These have authority over interstate markets. The best-known ones are the Interstate Commerce Commission (ICC), the Federal Communications Commission (FCC), the Federal Energy Regulatory Commission (FERC), and the Securities Exchange Commission (SEC). These commissions have from five to seven members and staffs of about eight hundred to two thousand people.

Regulation

Regulatory commissions become involved in almost all parts of a regulated company's business. However, the most important of their duties have to do with pricing or the setting of rates. They are interested in the level and the structure of these rates.

Both state and federal governments regulate public utilities through regulatory commissions, which are primarily concerned with the setting of rates.

The Level of Rates   When the government assures certain firms of a monopoly position, it has a duty to protect society from any harmful actions of the monopoly. But what rate level should regulated firms be allowed to charge? What return on invested capital should they be allowed to earn? In the language of regulators, the general answer is "a fair return on a fairly valued rate base." What this answer means in the language of economists is "normal profit on replacement cost of capital." **Normal profit**, you will recall, is the opportunity cost of a firm—the minimum amount that it must earn in its industry in order for it to remain in this business. **Replacement cost** refers to the method of determining the value of capital (the rate base) by estimating what it would cost to replace it.[23] Earning a normal profit on replacement cost of capital means that consumers will continue to receive the services provided by these firms, yet the minimum amount of resources needed for supplying these services will be used. It also means that regulated firms will have no difficulty in attracting further resources for necessary replacement and expansion, since the regulated firms are earning a rate of return that is equal to what they have to pay to borrow funds in financial markets.

One problem connected with rate regulation is that it may discourage cost efficiency. If commissions use a cost-plus-normal-profit formula, firms have no incentive to use lowest-cost methods, and their higher operating costs plus a normal profit will just be passed on to consumers. Regulatory commissions are aware of this problem and have tried to offer incentives to keep costs down. Also firms can sometimes gain a temporary benefit from cost cutting through **regulatory lag**. This term refers to the length of time it takes a regulatory commission to bring about a rate change that reflects a regulated company's change in average total cost. Regulatory lag works against the firms when average total costs are rising. During periods of high

23. Other methods of determining the value of capital are "original cost," which uses the amount that the firm originally paid for its capital minus depreciation, and "reproduction cost," which uses what it would cost the firm to literally replace its present capital. Economists find "replacement cost" to be the fairest valuation of a firm's rate base because inflation causes "original cost" to be unrealistically low, and technological change causes "reproduction cost" to be unrealistically high. Replacement cost allows for the fact that technological change may force the firm to replace its equipment with different (more productive, new-generation) equipment.

inflation, regulatory lag can place a heavy burden on public utilities. For example, during the double-digit inflation period of the late 1970s and early 1980s a number of states were so concerned about regulatory lag that they eliminated it by adopting rules that provided for automatic pass-through of higher utility-firm costs to consumers in the form of higher rates.

Regulators allow regulated firms to earn normal profit on replacement cost of capital, which means that consumers will continue to receive the services provided by these firms, yet the minimum amount of resources needed for supplying these services will be used. One problem connected with rate regulation is that it may discourage cost efficiency.

Regulatory lag is the length of time it takes a regulatory commission to bring about a rate change that reflects a regulated company's change in average total cost. Regulatory lag works against a firm when average total costs are rising.

The economic theory of the rate regulation of a natural monopoly is illustrated by the three different cases shown in Figure 2. Panel (a) shows an unregulated monopolist in a natural monopoly market. The company maximizes its profit (where its marginal-cost curve, MC, intersects its marginal-revenue curve, MR, from below) when it produces 22 units a day and sells them for $8 a unit. Notice that the price of $8 is well above the firm's marginal cost of $3. The loss of consumer welfare that stems from monopoly pricing was discussed in Chapter 27. In this case, some consumers who are willing to pay a price greater than marginal cost are denied the use of the product. The firm earns economic profit of $2.20 a unit, or $48.40 a day ($8.00 − $5.80 = $2.20; $2.20 × 22 = $48.40).

Panel (b) in Figure 2 shows the same firm, but under very different conditions. In this case the firm is regulated. Furthermore, the regulatory commission requires the firm to act like a pure competitor—that is, to equate its price to its marginal cost. The reasoning behind this policy is that it provides

FIGURE 2
Alternative Pricing by a Natural Monopolist

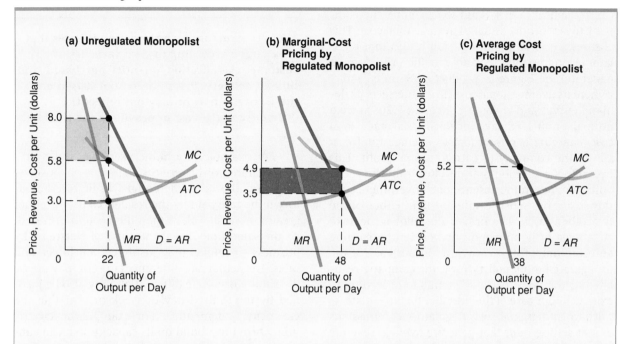

Shown are the demand or average-revenue (*D* = *AR*), marginal-revenue (*MR*), marginal-cost (*MC*), and average-total-cost (*ATC*) curves for a firm in a natural monopoly market under three different conditions. Panel (a) shows this firm's equilibrium position (a level of output of 22 units and a price of $8.00) when it is not regulated. Panel (b) shows this firm's equilibrium position (a level of output of 48 units and a price of $3.50) when it is required by a regulatory commission to set its price equal to its

marginal cost. Panel (c) shows this firm's equilibrium position (a level of output of 38 units and a price of $5.20) when it is required to set its price equal to its average total cost.

The case shown in panel (c) provides the firm with only normal profit, whereas the firm earns economic profit of $2.20 per unit of output ($8.00 − $5.80) in the case shown in panel (a) and economic loss of $1.40 per unit of output ($4.90 − $3.50) in the middle case.

the social optimum as it avoids restriction of output and monopoly pricing. Indeed, it does. This firm in our example produces 48 units a day (where its marginal-cost curve intersects its demand curve) and charges a price of $3.50. However, you will notice a problem. Since average total cost is falling, marginal cost is below it. This means that the firm will suffer an economic loss. In our example, average total cost is $4.90 while average revenue is $3.50, so that the firm has an economic loss of $1.40 a unit, or $67.20 a day ($1.40 × 48 = $67.20). Here we see the regulatory dilemma. Unless the government gives the firm a subsidy equal to the economic loss—so that it will earn a normal

profit—the firm will eventually leave the industry.[24] When this happens, the consumer will not receive the product, and welfare will be diminished.

Panel (c) shows the same firm under still different conditions. It is regulated as in the previous case, but this time the regulatory commission rec-

24. In order not to clutter the diagram, we have not included the firm's average-variable-cost curve. If we had, we could see whether or not the firm will shut down in the short run. It will shut down if its average variable cost is above $3.50. If its average variable cost is below $3.50, it will continue to produce in the short run. In either case, it will exit in the long run.

ognizes the regulatory dilemma—that without a government subsidy, marginal-cost pricing would cause the firm to exit—and so it requires the company to set its price equal to average total cost. This ensures a normal profit—the fair return that regulatory commissions seek to provide. The firm in panel (c) of Figure 2 produces 38 units a day (where its average-total-cost curve intersects its demand curve) and charges a price of $5.20. Since a normal profit is always included in average total cost, charging a price equal to average total cost allows the company to earn a normal profit. This case offers a solution that deviates from the social optimum, but in the absence of a government subsidy is a more sensible solution than either of the two other cases. The firm is not allowed to take advantage of its monopolistic position by earning an economic profit as was true in our case of the unregulated monopolist. Nor is the company regulated to the point of an economic loss (leading to exit) as in our case of the firm that had to equate its price to its marginal cost. Regulatory commissions aim at setting rates that generate average revenue equal to firms' average total costs. Of course, the question still remains as to whether or not this solution is better than a government-subsidized social optimum solution.

Regulatory commissions aim at setting rates that generate average revenue equal to firms' average total costs.

The Rate Structure Regulatory commissions are interested in more than just the level of rates set by firms. They are also interested in the **rate structure**, which refers to the variation in rates that are charged according to such variables as customer classification, quantity purchased, and time of delivery. Price differentials based on any of these criteria may or may not reflect the difference in the cost of providing the product. Remember from Chapter 27 (page 613) that a price differential that is not based on the difference in cost is price discrimination. Since public utilities are monopolists, they can sometimes keep different classes of customers separate, and often face different elasticities of demand among customer classes. These industries are likely areas for price discrimination to take place.

The rate structure is the variation in rates that are charged according to such variables as customer classification, quantity purchased, and time of delivery. Price differentials based on these criteria may or may not reflect the difference in the cost of providing the product.

For example, if a home user of electricity requires more costly services than does a business customer, the rate differential will be discriminatory if the rate paid by the residential user is either greater or smaller than the difference in unit cost. At the same time, the greater use of electricity by business customers may justify certain lower unit rates. The actual rate differences may or may not be discriminatory. Rate differentials may also be justified by the time of day or week or year that the electricity is demanded. For example, an electric utility firm must build up its capacity so it can supply enough electricity at the peak level of demand, as on the hottest days of the summer when air conditioners are on at full blast. Customers who use electricity mostly during off-peak times, when there is excess capacity in the system, can be served at a relatively low cost. Higher rates should be paid by peak-load users to finance the otherwise unneeded capacity. Most regulatory commissions encourage price differentials, but try to avoid price discrimination. They want prices to reflect costs so that greater efficiency may be gained.

Regulatory commissions encourage price differentials but try to avoid price discrimination.

Deregulation

Regulation has been a part of U.S. economic policy for over a hundred years. An 1887 landmark court case, *Munn* v. *Illinois*, set the general precedent that monopolies can be regulated to protect the public interest. Soon afterward the ICC was created to regulate railroads. After the turn of the century, regulation began to spread, but it became fully established only in the mid-1930s. For the next quarter of a century, regulation was little questioned. It was the way to control an ever-increasing number of American industries. Besides the traditional regulated industries such as railroads, telephone and telegraph service, and electric power, regulation also covered trucking, airlines, natural gas, television broadcasting, cable television, taxis, and others.

During the 1960s some economists suggested that certain regulated industries that had been natural monopolies when they were first regulated had over the years attracted actual and potential competition and should therefore be deregulated. For example, the wider use of trucks and more superhighways to drive them on meant actual and potential competition for railroads. A more recent example where technological change altered the status of an industry is long-distance telephone service. This industry was a natural monopoly when telephone lines had to be laid, but no longer is a natural monopoly because of the introduction of modern microwave transmission.

In the 1960s, some economists suggested that certain regulated industries that had been natural monopolies when they were first regulated had over the years attracted actual or potential competition and should therefore be deregulated.

In the early 1980s several economists suggested that even if a market is a natural monopoly, it may still not be a good candidate for regulation.[25] They say that in **contestable markets** (markets that are very easy to enter and leave) potential competition will keep a monopolist from charging high prices. For example, it may be efficient for only a single airline to provide passenger service between two specific cities. Yet this monopoly firm need not be regulated if other airlines have access to this market (route). If the airline flying between

these two cities charges a monopoly price, another airline can easily enter this route and be successful by offering somewhat lower prices.

Those who favor deregulation also point to economic studies showing that many public utilities invest in too much capital equipment in order to broaden their rate base. Others show that regulation has prevented new competitors and the introduction of new technologies, both of which would lead to better service and lower prices.

In the 1970s more voices joined the call for deregulation. Inflation, rising energy prices, and environmental protection issues all touched upon the performance of regulated industries. And perhaps just as important, economic education had spread the word that competition was a good thing. When deregulation was proposed, the regulated firms and their employees cried "foul." The public was shocked to learn that those who opposed deregulation the most were the regulated firms themselves. Contrary to what it had been led to believe, the public began to realize that the regulated firms were not shackled in chains by the commissions, but instead had to some degree captured their regulators. Many had developed a cozy relationship in which firms were all but guaranteed the "good life"—a good return on their investment and no trouble from competitors or would-be competitors.[26]

The first serious political rumblings in favor of deregulation were heard during the Nixon administration in the early 1970s. These views were picked up by President Ford in the mid-1970s, and this time attention was directed specifically at the airline and trucking industries. In 1977 President Carter continued the effort, which finally led to the Airline Deregulation Act of 1978 and the Motor Carrier Act of 1980. The Airline Deregulation Act called for a gradual decrease of the control of routes

---

25. William J. Baumol, John C. Panzar, and Robert D. Willig, *Contestable Markets and the Theory of Industry Structure* (San Diego: Harcourt Brace Jovanovich, 1982).

26. A few examples follow. A trucking firm was required to have a "certificate of public convenience and necessity" issued by the ICC in order to be allowed to haul certain goods over a particular interstate route. An airline had to be certified by the Civil Aeronautics Board (CAB) in order to fly passengers between two cities. In order to broadcast on the radio or on television, a license has to be obtained from the FCC. Before a new gas pipeline can be run, the FERC must approve it. Driving a taxi in some large cities requires a license in the form of a medallion.

and fares by the Civil Aeronautics Board (CAB) ending in its elimination in late 1984. New airlines entered the industry, and established airlines entered new routes. Air fares have been substantially reduced, and fewer empty seats are flying in the sky. One exception is the international portion of the airline industry, which had not been deregulated. Several hundred ex-CAB personnel are still busy regulating international routes and fares from their offices in the Department of Transportation.

The Motor Carrier Act diminished the regulatory powers of the Interstate Commerce Commission (ICC), which had been regulating almost every aspect of trucking since 1935. As a result, the 1980s witnessed the entry of thousands of new trucking firms, improved services (such as guaranteed delivery time), and substantial price competition. The latter has led to many business failures but also to considerably lower prices.

The movement toward deregulation grew in the 1970s. The Airline Deregulation Act of 1978 and the Motor Carrier Act of 1980 substantially reduced regulation in two key industries.

Deregulation has also occurred in other industries, including the railroad, taxicab, bus, petroleum, natural gas, telecommunications, broadcasting, cable TV, stockbrokerage, and banking industries. Deregulation has been in various degrees and has accomplished uneven results. It has brought massive restructuring in the railroad industry. The clearest success of deregulation in telecommunications has been in the equipment segment of that industry. Relatively little regulation is left in the broadcasting and cable TV industries. Some taxicab markets, such as Boston and New York City, are still highly regulated. Others, such as San Diego and Kansas City, have begun to deregulate. Deregulation in the stock-brokerage industry has significantly lowered the average price paid to make a stock market transaction. Finally, banking deregulation has eliminated interest-rate ceilings and has blurred the difference among the functions of varying financial institutions such as commercial banks, savings and loan associations, and credit unions.

Most economists agree that deregulation has been a good thing in most industries. It has allowed more competition, which has increased efficiency and lowered prices. However, deregulation is not a panacea and, in a few industries, there has been a call for reregulation. An outstanding example is the case of savings and loan associations. (See the essay at the end of this part, "Regulation, Deregulation, Reregulation: The S&L Case".)

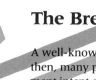

Economics in Focus

The Breakup of AT&T

A well-known adage advises us not to fix things that are not broken. Why then, many people demanded in the early 1980s, was the federal government intent on breaking up AT&T? Yes, AT&T held a near-monopoly over U.S. phone service, but that service was the best in the world. Who needs competition if monopoly works so well? The government and AT&T finally settled the antitrust action with a consent decree that called for the company to divest itself of its local telephone operations as of January 1984. Seven regional phone companies ("Baby Bells") took over local service, and critics predicted disastrous consequences.

Some of their predictions have come true. As everyone expected, local phone charges quickly began to rise. For years the earnings from long-distance service had subsidized local rates; by 1989, with that subsidy largely removed, 90 million residential customers and 18 million small businesses were paying almost 35 percent more for local phone calls. This was particularly hard for subscribers on fixed incomes—elderly people, for instance, who depend on their phones not only for casual calls but also for access to doctors, hospitals, and emergency services.

Confusion also reigned, at least in the beginning. Before the breakup, customers with telephone problems could simply notify the "phone company." Now, they often had to guess who was responsible: AT&T? the regional Bell company? the store that sold the telephone? Moreover, the sudden opening of the enormous American market led to an invasion by foreign phone manufacturers. Before the consent decree the United States had enjoyed a $275 million trade surplus in telecommunications equipment; by 1988 this became a $2.5 million deficit.

But the divestiture has also produced a number of benefits—more than the critics anticipated. As a result of increased competition, equipment costs have dropped; many telephone units now sell for less than the 1982 rental price. Long-distance rates, freed from the need to subsidize local operations, have also plunged as companies such as MCI and US Sprint provide vigorous competition for AT&T. Some large businesses find that their long-distance charges have been cut in half. Because of this price break, the number of long-distance calls has risen by 46 percent. In real terms (adjusted for inflation), Americans are now spending less on phone calls than they did in 1984.

Perhaps most important, the competition has produced a spurt in technology. Experts say that fiber optics, cellular phones, facsimile machines, voice mail, widespread data-transmission services, and other innovations would not have developed as quickly under the old monopoly. The average office worker now uses a sophisticated communications system that was scarcely imagined a decade ago. All things considered, it appears that the antitrust action against AT&T served the public well, even though the nation's telephones were in no obvious need of repair.

Sources: Kenneth Labich, "Was Breaking Up AT&T a Good Idea?" *Fortune,* January 2, 1989, pp. 82–87; Calvin Sims, "Long-Distance-Rate Drop Brings a Surge in Calling," *New York Times,* May 22, 1989; Robert W. Crandall, "Surprises from Telephone Deregulation and the AT&T Divestiture," *American Economic Review,* May 1988, pp. 323–327; Mark L. Goldstein, "Splicing the Wires—Again," *Industry Week,* March 9, 1987, p. 51.

SUMMARY

1. The firms in an oligopolistic industry, more so than in a purely competitive or a monopolistically competitive industry, are susceptible to collusion aimed at lessening or eliminating competition among them so that each can earn a higher profit. The government policy that deals with this threat to public interest is called antitrust policy. It includes all government action aimed at maintaining or restoring competition. (See page 822.)

2. In reaction to a large amount of monopolization during the quarter of a century after the Civil War, the first federal antitrust law, the Sherman Antitrust Act, was passed in 1890. It prohibited the restriction of competition, monopolization, and attempts to monopolize. (See page 823.)

3. In order to be more specific about firms' actions that are likely to restrict competition, Congress passed the Clayton Act in 1914. It dealt with four types of potentially anticompetitive business practices: (a) price discrimination, (b) mergers, (c) exclusive dealing and tying arrangements, and (d) interlocking directorates. Two of the sections of the act were beefed up in later amendments—the price-discrimination section in the Robinson-Patman Act of 1936 and the merger section in the Celler-Kefauver Antimerger Amendment of 1950. (See pages 823–826.)

4. The third major piece of antitrust legislation, the Federal Trade Commission Act, was also passed in 1914. It prohibited unfair methods of competition among firms, and after the Wheeler-Lea Amendment in 1938, it also covered unfair and deceptive practices toward consumers. In addition, the act set up a second enforcement agency. The Federal Trade Commission was added to the already established (1903) Antitrust Division of the Justice Department. (See page 826.)

5. The Sherman Antitrust Act prohibited monopolization or attempts to monopolize, but it was left to the courts to interpret just what that meant. From the time of the Standard Oil case in 1911 until the Alcoa case in 1945, the Supreme Court adopted a "rule of reason," which focused on intent and conduct rather than on the presence or absence of substantial monopoly control. The Alcoa case and several others that followed in the late 1940s and early 1950s overturned the "rule of rea-

son" and made monopolization itself illegal. Since then some backtracking toward a rule of reason has occurred. (See pages 826–827.)

6. Mergers that substantially lessen competition are illegal under the Clayton Act, but due to certain loopholes the act had limited power until the Celler-Kefauver Antimerger Amendment in 1950. During the 1950s and 1960s the government impressively won a number of horizontal and vertical merger cases. However, the Supreme Court was not given a good opportunity to make a definitive statement regarding conglomerate merger. Attempts in the 1970s to pass new legislation that would prevent huge firms from making acquisitions failed. In the first half of the 1980s the "big is bad" philosophy was pretty well discarded, and acquisitions by huge firms of other huge firms were given the government's blessings. (See pages 827–829.)

7. Ever since the passage of the Sherman Antitrust Act in 1890, the courts have ruled that price fixing—the agreement among competing firms to restrict output in order to maintain high prices—is illegal. The Supreme Court's blanket condemnation of price fixing has been consistent. (See pages 829–830.)

8. A cartel is a collusive arrangement among sellers to fix output and prices. Cartels are inherently unstable. It pays for individual members to cheat because they can sell additional output at monopoly prices. However, when cheating becomes widespread, the level of industry output increases so much that monopoly prices can no longer be maintained. The best-known cartel is OPEC. For the decade beginning with 1973 it was quite successful in restricting the supply of crude oil and raising its price. Since that time the combination of lower demand, lower market share, and cheating by various OPEC members has seriously eroded OPEC's ability to control the world oil market. (See pages 830–832.)

9. Some industries, called "regulated industries," are granted monopoly status by the government. In return they are regulated so that they are not able to take advantage of their monopoly power. Such "monopoly regulation" is in addition to the usual "social regulation," to which most firms are subject. (See page 832.)

10. Most regulated industries are diagnosed as natural monopolies. A natural monopoly is a market in which a single seller is required for efficient production. Economies of scale are so great in relation to the quantity demanded in the market that only one firm can take full advantage of them. If more than one firm operated in a natural monopoly market, price competition among them would cause all but the strongest firm to leave the market. (See pages 833–834.)

11. The government attempts to recognize an industry as a natural monopoly before firms begin operation and ruinous competition takes place. In such instances the government may establish a public enterprise, but more likely it will grant a private firm public utility status and then regulate it. Regulation takes place by both state and federal regulatory commissions. The four most prominent federal regulatory commissions are the ICC, FCC, SEC, and FERC. (See pages 834–835.)

12. Regulatory commissions concern themselves mainly with the prices that public utilities charge. They regulate both the level of rates and the structure of rates. They seek to set a rate level that gives public utility firms a fair return on a fairly valued rate base. This is usually interpreted as normal profit on the replacement cost of a firm's capital. Regarding the structure of rates, firms have an incentive to charge different rates according to the class of customer, the quantity purchased, and the time of delivery. Regulatory commissions encourage price differentials based on cost differences, but try to prevent price discrimination. (See pages 835–838.)

13. Until the 1960s few economists and government officials questioned the appropriateness of regulation. But in the 1960s and more so in the 1970s, suggestions to deregulate were frequently heard. Because of technological change, some industries no longer were natural monopolies. Some natural monopoly industries were recognized to be contestable markets, in which regulation actually prevented new firms from entering and offering better service and lower prices. The public also became more disenchanted with regulation because of high prices and a greater recognition that regulated firms had in many cases captured their regulators. Beginning in the late 1970s various degrees of deregulation occurred in many public utility industries, the outstanding example being the domestic airline industry. (See pages 838–840.)

KEY TERMS

antitrust policy: the government policy that deals with the maintenance or restoration of competition in markets (page 821).

cartel: a collusive arrangement among sellers that affects the level of their joint output and thus the price that they charge (page 830).

Celler-Kefauver Antimerger Amendment: a law passed in 1950 that covered asset acquisitions and eliminated the wording that made the Clayton Act applicable only to horizontal mergers (page 824).

Clayton Act: a law passed in 1914 to deal with four types of potentially anticompetitive business practices: price discrimination, mergers, exclusive dealing and tying arrangements, and interlocking directorates (page 823).

contestable markets: markets that are very easy to enter and leave so that potential competition can be relied upon to prevent monopoly pricing (page 839).

exclusive dealing arrangement: an anticompetitive situation that exists when a firm obtains the product of a certain supplier on the condition that it will not buy the products of competing suppliers (page 825).

Federal Trade Commission (FTC): a government antitrust agency established in 1914 by the Federal Trade Commission Act; its duty is to investigate and prosecute cases of unfair competition (page 826).

Federal Trade Commission Act: a law passed in 1914 that outlawed unfair methods of competition, such as corporate spying, boycotts, and bribery, and created the Federal Trade Commission to investigate and prosecute cases of unfair competition (page 825).

interlocking directorates: the potentially anticompetitive situation when the same person serves on the boards of directors of two or more competing firms or when two or more directors of one firm sit on the boards of competing firms (page 825).

monopoly regulation: regulation that covers a firm's level of output, its price, and the scope of its production (page 832).

natural monopoly: a market in which a single seller is required for efficient production (page 833).

normal profit: the opportunity cost of a firm; the minimum amount that it must earn in its industry in order for it to remain in that business (page 836).

predatory price cutting: price cutting aimed at forcing competitors out of business (page 826).

public enterprise: a government-owned business; often a monopoly (page 837).

public utility: a privately owned company that is provided by the government with a monopoly position in its market (page 835).

rate structure: the variation in rates that are charged according to such variables as customer classification, quantity purchased, and time of delivery (page 838).

regulated industries: firms that are granted monopoly status by government and then become subject to monopoly regulation (page 832).

regulatory lag: the length of time it takes a regulatory commission to bring about a rate change that reflects a regulated company's change in average total cost (page 836).

replacement cost: the method of determining the value of a firm's capital by estimating what it would cost to replace it (page 836).

Robinson-Patman Act: a law passed in 1936 that amended the section of the Clayton Act that deals with price discrimination (page 826).

rule of reason: a line of reasoning used by the Supreme Court that was based on the belief that substantial monopoly control alone is not against the law but that the intent to gain that control and the abuse of it make it illegal (page 826).

Sherman Antitrust Act: a law passed in 1890 that prohibits monopolization and combinations in restraint of trade (page 823).

social regulation: regulations most firms are subject to, such as environmental protection rules, food and drug rules, truth-in-packaging rules, and occupational health and safety rules (page 832).

trust: an arrangement whereby supposedly competing firms avoid competition through a central board of trustees that votes all their stock (page 823).

tying arrangement: a potentially anticompetitive practice that forces a firm to buy certain products along with certain other products (page 825).

Wheeler-Lea Amendment: an amendment to the Federal Trade Commission Act passed in 1938 that prohibited unfair or deceptive acts or practices aimed at the consumer (page 825).

DISCUSSION QUESTIONS

1. List and briefly describe each of the most important U.S. antitrust laws.

2. In retrospect, how reasonable was the U.S. Supreme Court's "rule of reason"?

3. What is meant by a cartel? Why are cartels said to be very unstable? Why, in your opinion, did the cartel known as OPEC remain relatively stable over most of the 1970s and early 1980s?

4. Suppose that you were hired to manage a cartel made up of the copper-producing companies of the world. How would you manage the cartel? What rules would you set and how would you justify them to your members?

5. What are the characteristics that enable economists to single out industries as "natural monopolies"? Give two examples of industries that are probably natural monopolies. Give one example of a regulated industry that is probably not a natural monopoly.

6. "Regulatory agencies are doing consumers a disservice when they compel natural monopolies to equate price to average total cost rather than to marginal cost." Do you agree or disagree? Explain.

7. "Government is really very inconsistent; the United States has a whole lot of antitrust laws designed to combat monopolization but at the same time it gives some firms an exclusive right to operate an entire industry." Do you agree or disagree? Explain.

8. Once government recognizes an industry to be a natural monopoly, it has a choice between providing a public enterprise or conferring public utility status on a private firm. Suppose that you were in a government position that called for you to make a recommendation on this matter. What would you recommend and why?

9. Under what condition does the theory of contestable markets argue against government regulation of natural monopoly industries?

36

International Microeconomics: Free Trade versus Protection

Preview The choice of free trade versus protection has been a key policy issue for generations and centuries. In the past, it was a conflict between market and planning principles. Those who favored free trade believed that competition among trading countries would lead to greater economic efficiency. Those favoring protection felt that a certain amount of protection of domestic industries from the effects of trade with other countries was necessary.

We begin with a simple case of a freely traded standardized product in a freely competitive world. We discuss gains and losses in both importing and exporting countries from trade in such a product. Then we turn to a second question: Which goods will a country export when free trade is opened up, and which goods will it import? This leads to the classical idea of "comparative advantage," and the various reasons or explanations for its existence. One explanation is based on differences in productive efficiency, and another on differences in "endowments" of resources or factors of production.

Next we examine the gains from trade between two or among several countries and the effects of trade on wage and interest rates in the trading countries. You will see that free trade has much the same effect as free immigration or free movement of capital in equalizing wage and interest rates between countries. This is called "factor price equalization."

So much for free trade. Next we define *protection* and consider some of protection's many forms: tariffs, quotas, antidumping duties, and administrative protection, including an important distinction between *nominal* and *effective* rates of protection. We present a number of arguments for protection. Some of these are economic, relating to such questions as "cheap foreign labor" and helping "infant industries." Others are noneconomic, such as those related to national defense and the dangers of boycott or blockade. These formal defenses of protection, however, may have little to do with its wide popularity. Many economists believe that its popularity is due largely to the activities of "intense minorities," otherwise known as "special interests."

The last major subjects that we cover are international negotiation and the shifting U.S. trade position. Trade treaties are discussed and then customs unions and free trade areas, which can be viewed as attempted compromises between free trade and protection. Finally we present the reasons why the United States experienced negative trade balances during the 1980s.

GAINS AND LOSSES FROM TRADE

The basic principles of international trade are among the best established in the whole field of economics. Economic arguments for free trade were prominent in the writings of the classical economists of England in the eighteenth and nineteenth centuries and fit in well with the trading interests of an island nation.

The basic case for free international trade is an extension of the case for free trade among individuals. For individuals, the freedom to engage in trade makes it feasible for each person to specialize in the tasks for which he or she is relatively well suited. As each person specializes, production goes up and the fruits of the greater output can be traded with others who, likewise, have specialized in the things they do relatively well. In other words, trading opens the door to specialization, specialization increases productivity, and higher productivity raises real living standards.

International free trade arguments simply observe that these same principles hold when the two parties to an exchange are of different nationalities. Even though most actual international trade is carried on between individuals or firms in one country and individuals or firms in another, it is usual to speak of countries trading with one another. Then it is noted that, just as individuals differ from one another in talent and endowments, countries differ in climate, soil conditions, the size and skill of their labor forces, the availability of capital, and so on.

Thus, the theory readily shows that free international trade can raise the per capita real income in all trading countries.[1] Once the advantages of free international trade have been demonstrated, debate then usually centers on the following two questions. First, given the level of aggregate input and output, which goods should a country produce for itself and which ones should it produce for export? And second, what other goods, if any, would it be cheaper to import?

Trading opens the door to specialization, specialization increases productivity, and higher productivity raises real living standards. Thus, free international trade can raise the per capita income in all trading countries.

Just as individuals differ from one another in talent and endowments, so do countries differ in resources, size and skill of labor forces, availability of capital, etc.

Unfortunately, for those who favor internationalism, even though free trade may raise the measured real production and income per capita in all trading countries, it is not true that all persons who are affected gain from such trade. For example, when a country increases its exports, domestic consumers of the exported goods face higher prices for those goods, and their living standards may go down. In the same way, when a country increases its imports, domestic producers of goods that compete against these imports may lose. These facts of life must be recognized in understanding the conflict between free trade and protection.

When a country increases its exports, domestic consumers of the exported goods face higher prices for those goods. Likewise, when a country increases its imports, domestic producers of goods that compete against these imports may lose.

---

1. The principles governing trade and payments between American states are the same as those between countries. If U.S. prosperity is attributed largely to its being the world's most important free trade area, why not extend the same principle to whole continents, to the capitalist world, or to the world as a whole?

FIGURE 1
Trade in a Single Commodity

(a) The United States

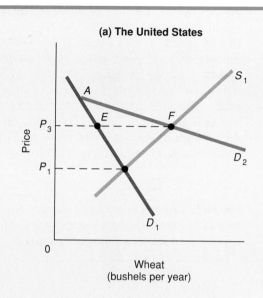

(b) The Rest of the World

Panel (a) represents the wheat market in the United States and panel (b) represents the wheat market in the rest of the world, treated as one country. In each panel, D_1 and S_1 represent demand and supply before there is any international trading in wheat. Excess supply exists in the United States at prices above P_1. In panel (b), the U.S. excess supply at each price is added to the domestic supply in the rest of the world to generate the supply curve S_2 for the rest of the world.

In the rest of the world, excess demand exists at any price below P_2. In panel (a), this excess demand at each price is added to domestic demand in the United States, generating the demand curve D_2. Equilibrium international trading occurs (ignoring shipping costs) at price P_3, with quantity EF exported by the United States and quantity JK (which is equal to EF) imported by the rest of the world. At equilibrium, there remains neither excess demand nor excess supply in either country.

Trade in a Single Commodity

We begin by describing the effects of trade in one commodity, such as wheat, which is produced in two countries. To keep our analysis simple, we shall consider trade between the United States and "the rest of the world," as if the rest of the world were all one country. Actually, the United States trades with many separate countries, involving many different situations.

Figure 1 shows the market for wheat in each of these two "countries." We use the same scale on the vertical (price) axis of both graphs. This means either that the two countries use the same money or that their monies exchange in a fixed ratio to each other.[2] In each graph, the demand curve D_1 shows only demand from domestic purchasers, and

2. The determination of exchange rates between monies is explained in Chapter 19.

the supply curve S_1 shows only the supply from domestic suppliers. In the absence of trade, wheat sells for P_1 per bushel in the United States and for P_2 in the rest of the world. These prices differ from each other because the two countries differ in their demands for wheat and in their endowments of resources used in producing it. Without trade, wheat would be more expensive in the rest of the world than in the United States.

We can illustrate the results of opening up trade between these countries by using the concepts of excess demand and excess supply. **Excess demand** is the amount by which the quantity demanded exceeds the quantity supplied at any specified price. In the absence of trade, excess demand would be zero in each country at the price at which domestic demand, D_1, intersects domestic supply, S_1. But a positive amount of excess demand would exist at any lower price. **Excess supply** is the amount by which the quantity supplied exceeds the quantity demanded at any specified price. In the absence of trade, excess supply would be zero at the price where the domestic demand and supply curves intersect, but would be positive at any higher price.

Excess demand is the amount by which the quantity demanded exceeds the quantity supplied at any specified price.

Excess supply is the amount by which the quantity supplied exceeds the quantity demanded at any specified price.

In Figure 1, the United States will export wheat because the U.S. price is lower than the price in the rest of the world. For an exporting country, the effect of trade is to add at each price the excess demand of other countries to its own domestic demand. The demand curve D_2 in the U.S. panel of Figure 1 shows the result of adding, at each price, excess demand from the rest of the world to the domestic demand, D_1, in the United States. Point A corresponds to the pretrade price for wheat in the rest of the world, so that excess demand in those countries is zero. In the United States, the horizontal distance between the demand curve (D_1) and the demand curve (D_2) is the same as the horizontal distance between S_1 and D_1 in the rest of the world at prices below P_2. At the world equilibrium price of P_3, the quantity exported by the United States (distance EF) is the same as the quantity imported by the rest of the world (JK).

For an exporting country, the effect of trade is to add at each price the excess demand of other countries to its own domestic demand.

The parallel situation for the rest of the world is illustrated by the supply curve S_2 in panel (b) of Figure 1. Point B corresponds to the price at which there is no excess supply in the United States. But at higher prices, excess supply exists in the United States, measured by the horizontal distance between its domestic demand and supply curves. The supply curve S_2 for the rest of the world is drawn by adding, at each price, excess supply from the

United States to the domestic supply curve (S_1) of the rest of the world. At the world equilibrium price of P_3, the quantity imported by the rest of the world (JK) is equal to the excess supply in the United States (EF). In Figure 1, the world equilibrium price is P_3. We show it as the same in both panels because we ignore the cost of shipping wheat between the countries. In practice, of course, the price in the importing country would be higher than the price in the exporting country by the amount of such shipping costs, and the quantity exchanged would be less than illustrated in Figure 1.

For an importing country, the effect of trade is to add at each price the excess supply of other countries to its own domestic supply.

Gains and Losses to Producers and Consumers

To analyze the gains and losses from trade to producers and consumers, we shall use Figure 2, which reproduces Figure 1, but adds further information. Let us first examine what happens in the exporting country (the United States). Before international trade, Q_1 bushels of wheat were sold at price P_1. After equilibrium is reached in international trade, Q_2 bushels of wheat per year were sold at price P_3. Total gain to wheat producers in the United States is shown by the gold (both light and dark) area in panel (a). For all outputs up to Q_2, their prices have risen more than their costs, which are represented by the supply curve. U.S. consumers of wheat lose, however. Before international trade, they consumed Q_1 bushels and paid price P_1, but after equilibrium is reached in international trade, they consume only Q_3 bushels per year and pay price P_3. The higher price, P_3, that they pay for the quantity that they purchase, Q_3, is clearly a loss to consumers. They also lose the **consumers' surplus** (the benefit to consumers from being able to buy at a uniform price rather than the sum of the amounts they might have been willing to pay for each unit separately) on the quantity of wheat between Q_1 and Q_3. Thus, the wheat consumers' loss is represented by the dark gold area that lies to the

FIGURE 2
Gains and Losses from Trade in a Single Commodity

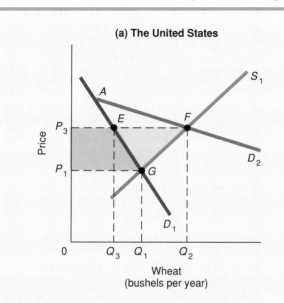

(a) The United States

(b) The Rest of the World

The demand and supply curves on these graphs are the same as those on the graphs in Figure 1. In the United States, export of wheat causes the price to rise to P_3 and the quantity supplied to increase to Q_2. Producers' gain is represented by the gold (both light and dark) area in this panel. But U.S. wheat consumers pay a higher price (P_3) and consume fewer bushels (Q_3). The consumer loss is the dark gold area to the left of the demand curve (D_1). The net gain in the United States is the light gold triangular area EFG.

In the rest of the world, importing causes the price to fall to P_3 and consumers increase their purchases to Q_2 bushels per year. Their gain is shown by the gold (both light and dark) area in panel (b). Wheat suppliers in the importing country lose because they sell less wheat at a lower price. Their losses are represented by the dark gold area to the left of the supply curve (S_1). The net gain from trading for the importing country is the light gold triangular area JKL.

left of the demand curve (D_1). The total of producers' gain is greater than the total consumers' loss in the exporting country by the area of the light gold triangle EFG in the U.S. panel of Figure 2. This shows the presumed net gain from export trade in wheat.

Panel (b) traces a similar argument for the rest of the world. Before international trade, consumers purchased Q_1 bushels of wheat per year and paid price P_2. After equilibrium is reached in international trade, these consumers purchase Q_2 bushels per year at price P_3. The combination of more wheat and the lower price expands their consumers' surplus by the amount represented by the gold (both light and dark) area in the rest-of-the-world panel. But wheat producers in the importing country lose from international trade. Before such trade, they sold Q_1 bushels at price P_2, but international trade causes both the price and the quantity that they sell to fall. Their loss is the dark gold area to the left of the supply curve S_1. But the gain to consumers in the importing country is greater than the loss to producers by the light gold triangular area JKL in panel (b).

Our analysis has demonstrated that both the exporting country and the importing country gain from free international trade. It does not necessarily follow, however, that the gains are evenly divided. The country that experiences the greatest price change for the traded commodity will gain more than the country that experiences a lesser change in price, other things unchanged. From this fact, we can reason that small countries may gain more from international trade than do large countries, which tend to dominate world trade and whose domestic prices may not change as much as a result of trade. This view is contrary to a popular one that the economic giants gain most from trade.

The country that experiences the greatest price change for the traded commodity, *ceteris paribus*, will gain more than the country that experiences a lesser change in price.

Other Economic Effects

Per capita real income gain, however, is not the whole story, because a gain to the country as a whole may still imply a loss to some and perhaps even to a majority of the country's citizens. Consider, for example, the cheap machine-made textiles exported to China from the West (primarily from England) in the half-century before World War I. The consumer gain to China, which economic theory suggests outweighed the loss to producers, went chiefly to those urban people (skilled workers, middle and upper classes) who bought them. The producers' loss was borne chiefly by poor peasants who had in the past spun and woven textiles to earn second incomes in the agricultural slack season. China was then an 80 percent peasant economy. So more individual Chinese lost than gained from the textile imports, and the distributional effects were in the direction of greater inequality. Moreover, the loss of a dollar of income probably meant more (in terms of utility, or anticipated satisfaction) to a rural peasant than to an urban white-collar worker. From this point of view, China may well have lost by the textile trade. As you can see, the presumption of net gains from trade is not a conclusive argument that trade is desirable.

The presumption of net gains from trade is not a conclusive argument that trade is desirable.

Another point is that not all products are traded between countries. Some, like real estate, are physically tied to one place. The more common problem, however, is that transportation costs are so high in relation to the prices of some goods that they are not exported or imported. Can producers and consumers of nontraded goods be left out when we try to assess the gains and losses from trade? The answer is "no" if these nontraded goods are complementary to or substitutes for either imports or exports in either production or consumption.[3] For example, consider the case of a Latin American country that exports a cash crop (such as coffee, sugar, or bananas) raised on land that might have been used for domestic food production (such as beans, rice, or other vegetables). In this case, producers of domestic food will lose from trade, because of the higher prices and rents they must pay for land and labor. The consumers of domestic food will also lose, because the price of domestic food will rise. Antitrade feeling results when the producers and/or consumers of domestic food are "the poor" and the majority of the population.

Another example is the importing of rice cookers into the United States. Invented in Japan, these cookers increased the American demand for American rice, by making it easier to cook and reducing the risk of cooking failures. (In this example, American rice plays the role of a nontraded good, though in fact much of it is exported.) Rice is complementary to rice cookers in consumption. The import of rice cookers, by raising the demand for rice, might be expected to raise its price—a good thing for rice producers but not for rice consumers.[4]

Producers and consumers of nontraded goods that are complementary to or substitutes for traded goods may gain or lose from trade.

COMPARATIVE ADVANTAGE

India and western Europe were almost completely cut off from each other for more than 500 years after the decline of the western Roman Empire.

---

3. Two goods are substitutes in production if they both use the same specialized inputs. Examples are corn and soybeans, which require the same type of land and climate. Two goods are complementary in production when they are joint products of a single production process, such as beef and hides, or when one is a raw material or an intermediate product in the making of another, as fish and fishing boats. Substitution and complementarity in consumption have been discussed in Chapter 23.

4. In fact, however, American agricultural policy both supported the domestic price of American rice above the world level and prevented the rice cooker from raising it further.

This period was the so-called Dark Ages. But despite high transportation costs and high risks, a trickle and then a stream of trade developed during and after the Crusades. What determined which goods would move in each direction? Similarly, what goods did Japan export and import when she was forced to open her doors to trade after 250 years of semi-isolation under the Tokugawa Shoguns?

Economists try to answer such questions by using the theories of comparative advantage. Here is the argument. When there is no trade or when it is restricted, a country will normally have a set of relative prices that is different from the set that exists in the rest of the world. For example, the price of apples may be twice the price of potatoes in one country, but may be three times the price of potatoes in the rest of the world. This is so because countries normally will have different combinations of resource endowments or will have developed special skills in different things. A good whose pretrade price or restricted-trade price is relatively lower in a country than in the rest of the world is likely to be exported by that country. On the other hand, a commodity whose pretrade or restricted-trade price is relatively higher in a country than in the rest of the world will likely be imported by that country. This is the well-known principle of **comparative advantage**.

According to the principle of comparative advantage, a good whose pretrade price or restricted-trade price is relatively lower in a country than in the rest of the world is likely to be exported by that country. A commodity whose pretrade or restricted-trade price is relatively higher in a country than in the rest of the world will likely be imported.

The following illustration, which comes from the English economist David Ricardo (1772–1823), is the classic demonstration of the principle of comparative advantage. Assume that one unit of English cloth requires 100 hours of English labor and that one unit of Portuguese wine requires 80 hours of Portuguese labor. Assume also that 120 hours of English labor would have been needed to produce a unit of wine in England. If, at equilib-

rium, one unit of cloth is exchanged for one unit of wine in international trade, England gains the product of 20 hours of labor by importing wine from Portugal in exchange for cloth. Ricardo does not tell us how many hours of Portuguese labor would be required to produce a unit of cloth. But any figure above 80 would give Portugal a gain from trade. If we suppose the figure to be 90, we would have the following costs for the two countries.

Country	Labor Cost per Unit Traded (in hours)	
	Cloth	Wine
England	100	120
Portugal	90	80

In terms of labor cost, Portugal has an **absolute advantage** in both cloth and wine since she can produce either one with less labor than would be required in England. Relative prices, however, would be 5:6 (100:120) in England and 9:8 (90:80) in Portugal. Cloth is relatively cheaper in England and wine is relatively cheaper in Portugal, giving England a *comparative* advantage in cloth and Portugal in wine. England would gain the product of 20 hours of English labor through trade and Portugal would gain the product of 10 hours of Portuguese labor. One partner's gain does not mean a loss to the other. However, one partner's gain may be larger than the other's. For example, were a unit of cloth in Portugal to cost 81 hours of Portuguese labor, the Portuguese gain would have been very small. Were a unit of wine in England to cost 101 hours of English labor, the major gain from trade would have gone to Portugal.

Another way to look at Ricardo's case is that Portugal is one-third better than England in wine production (40/120 = 1/3), but only one-tenth better in cloth production (10/100 = 1/10). Therefore, once we grant the existence of gains from trade, it is rational for England to export cloth and Portugal to export wine.

A later explanation of comparative advantage came from two Swedish economists, Eli Heckscher (1879–1952) and Bertil Ohlin (1899–1979). They explained comparative advantage as being due to differences between countries in their "endowments" of productive inputs, which affect the pretrade prices of goods traded. The United States, for example, has accumulated a great deal of capital equipment, but its labor has remained relatively scarce. This means that American real interest rates have been generally low, but American real wage rates generally high. For this reason, according to this theory, the United States should export capital-intensive goods and import labor-intensive ones, while the trade of Mexico or Guatemala should follow the opposite course.

Of course, there are complications and modifications. Countries produce many goods that can be traded. Comparative advantage cannot tell us exactly where the lines will be drawn between the potential exports, nontraded goods, and potential imports. Demand or supply may be so price inelastic that relative prices may change (and comparative advantage with them) when trade is freed. And trade may itself affect tastes and techniques so much and so permanently that the pretrade relative prices become entirely obsolete. But even with these and other qualifications, comparative advantage remains important in explaining trade patterns.

Comparative Advantage and Choosing a Career

A simple example of comparative advantage, outside the realm of international economics, is in students' choices of college majors and careers. Most economics teachers have had "star" students ask them about possible careers as economists. It is clear from their classroom performances that they have *absolute* advantages in economics. Absolute advantage simply means being more proficient than others in doing a given thing. However, *comparative* advantage is another matter. For all the economics teacher knows, the star student may be even more outstanding in history or mathematics, or even better suited to a career in law or medicine or engineering or journalism. So all the teacher can do for students is to estimate the size and the meaning of their *absolute* advantages in economics,

while advising them to estimate for themselves their *comparative* advantages in various fields before making up their minds.[5]

It is equally rational for a mediocre student to choose a major or a career in some field where his or her performance, while below average, is still better than in any other subject in terms of class ranking. Such a student's absolute disadvantage might be the least in economics, giving him or her a comparative advantage in that field as large or larger than that of the class's star student.

The Dynamics of Comparative Advantage

So far, we have presented comparative advantage as something static. That is, we might say, "A country *has* a comparative advantage in agriculture." To do so, however, is misleading in the light of economic history. As a country develops, its comparative advantages generally shift away from farming and handicrafts, first toward light industry and then toward heavy industry and later to service industries. These changes take place because land becomes more scarce, industrial capital accumulates, and labor increases in skill. In some cases, the process is only partial, as in Denmark or Iowa, which are developed areas that remain largely agricultural. In other cases, the process is nearly complete, as in the Ruhr Valley of West Germany or the "silicon valley" of California.

As a country develops, its comparative advantages generally shift away from farming and handicrafts, first toward light industry and then toward heavy industry and later toward service industries.

An especially interesting aspect of changes in comparative advantage over time is called the **product cycle**. At first, the comparative advan-

5. Of course, the relative incomes to be expected in different fields of endeavor are important too. One might hesitate to advise a student to become a tramp, a bum, or a hobo, however great that student's comparative advantage might be in such occupations.

tage in producing steel or automobiles is in developed high-wage countries that export to lower-wage developing ones. As the developing countries learn the manufacturing processes, and as these processes themselves become less skill-intensive, the less developed countries can first reduce their imports and then take up exporting on their own. After a time, the comparative advantage has shifted to newly industrialized developing countries, which come to dominate the world market. If the older developed country's import-competing industries survive, they do so largely because they are protected. The following "cycle" takes place in the developed country's industry. At first it is purely domestic. Next it becomes more and more of an export industry. Then, as lower-wage countries take over, it becomes more and more an import-competing industry.

In the product cycle, an industry that develops a product first produces for the domestic market, then adds production for export, but eventually becomes an import-competing industry as foreign producers, with lower input prices, learn how to produce the product.

Some high-wage countries and their labor movements fear that comparative-advantage dynamics will eliminate first their exports and then their domestic production of one manufactured good after another and thus "hollow out" their industrial sectors—first lower and then higher technology. Such countries could pay for imports in many ways—exports of farm products and of services, earnings on investments abroad, selling domestic assets (capital imports), or drawing down international reserves. Few or none of these are pleasant prospects, especially to the highest-paid elements of the industrial labor force. However, no country's industrial sector has actually become "hollowed out" and perhaps none ever will because, as one group of industries is lost, another may replace it. But the United States is a potential candidate for this sort of "hollowing out" under free trade and in the absence of factor price equalization—a feature of free trade to which we now turn.

FACTOR PRICE EQUALIZATION

Up to this point, we have explained that, except for transportation costs, freedom of trade equalizes the prices of traded goods and services across frontiers. However, what about the prices of nontraded inputs, such as wage rates for labor and interest rates for capital? The **factor price equalization theorem** states that free trade of goods and services across countries not only equalizes output prices but also input (or resource or factor of production) prices.

The factor price equalization theorem states that free trade of goods and services across countries not only equalizes output prices but also input prices, even when these inputs are not traded.

To illustrate this theorem, let us consider two countries (Mexico and the United States), two commodities (tractors and textiles), and two inputs (labor and machinery). Tractors and textiles are freely traded between the two countries. However, there is no migration of labor or trade in machinery between them, and in the short run neither the stock of labor nor the stock of machines in either country changes. We further assume that the quality of labor and of machines is identical between the two countries.

Suppose that, before trade, the price of textiles in relation to the price of tractors is higher in the United States than in Mexico and that the price of tractors in relation to the price of textiles is higher in Mexico than in the United States. Comparative advantage predicts that the United States will export tractors and that Mexico will export textiles. If the textile industry is labor intensive, its expansion in Mexico will cause Mexican wage rates to rise in real terms and also in relation to interest rates in Mexico. In the United States, where the capital-intensive tractor industry is expanding because of the export of tractors, the realignment of industry causes the return to machines (interest rates) to rise both in real terms and in relation to wage rates. So the real wage rate of Mexican workers should come closer to the real wage rate of American workers and would ultimately equal the American real wage rate if the volume of trade in textiles were large enough. Similarly, interest rates (the return to investments in machinery) in the United States should rise both in real terms and in relation to the U.S. wage rate as the American tractor industry expands. These interest rates will come closer to real interest rates in Mexico and would ultimately equal the Mexican real interest rates if the volume of trade were large enough. Thus, trade tends to equalize input prices, even when these inputs themselves were not traded.

In the real world, this theorem operates only as a general tendency. Free trade does tend to draw input prices closer together, but without leading to full factor price equality.[6] In practice, wage rates differ more than interest rates between countries, since capital moves more freely than labor migrates. However, even in its weakened real-world form, the factor price equalization theorem helps to explain why opposition often arises to free trade between countries with widely differing real wage and interest rates.

The factor price equalization theorem helps to explain why opposition often arises to free trade between countries with widely differing real wage and interest rates.

---

6. Why doesn't the equalizing process go all the way to bring about complete uniformity? Or to put the matter differently, what further conditions beyond freedom of trade are needed for our theorem to hold literally? Here are seven such conditions.
1. Conditions are stationary, with fixed amounts of each input in each country.
2. Transportation costs can be ignored.
3. Specialization is incomplete. Each country continues to produce some of each traded good under free trade.
4. Knowledge is uniform. Each country has access to the same set of production techniques, the same "book of blueprints."
5. Production takes place in both countries under purely competitive and increasing-cost conditions.
6. There are no factor-intensity "crossovers." If farming, let us say, is more labor-intensive than manufacturing when wage rates are low and interest rates are high, it will remain so even when wage rates are high and interest rates are low.
7. The number of separate outputs equals the number of inputs.

PROTECTION

The term **protection** makes most people think at once of **tariffs** (taxes on imports) and **quotas** (limitations on the quantity of imports) used to protect domestic import-competing industries. These are the most important forms of the old, or traditional, protection, but many other forms have arisen.

Tariffs are taxes on imports, and quotas are limitations on the quantities of imports. Tariffs and quotas are used to protect domestic industries from competition with imports.

The most important form of the so-called "new" protection is the wide variety of practices lumped together as **administrative protection**, perhaps developed most fully by the Japanese government's Ministry of International Trade and Industry (MITI). Under administrative protection, the right to import may be withdrawn, limited to public agencies, or awarded to the import-competing industries themselves. A more common method is to subject competitive imports to burdensome, idiosyncratic, costly, and time-consuming specifications or inspection procedures—ostensibly for reasons of safety and health. Germany has long banned beer with any preservatives whatever—or, more accurately, such beer can be imported but not sold as beer. Belgium has required that butter be packed in containers of different shapes from those used by the neighboring countries of France, Germany, and the Netherlands. The long-standing American ban on fresh beef from Argentina was imposed at a time when many Argentine cattle suffered from contagious hoof-and-mouth disease.

A more recent form of protection, called administrative protection, involves subjecting competitive imports to burdensome, idiosyncratic, costly, and time-consuming specifications or inspection procedures.

An export industry may be protected by an export bounty or a subsidy.[7] Or an import-competing industry may receive its own protection in bounty or subsidy form, in an effort to meet world prices. An American example has been shipbuilding.

Of more complex examples of protection, we need note only two. During the nineteenth and twentieth centuries, British duties on *exporting* wool were protective—for the rising British textile industry, to which the duties ensured cheap wool as raw material.[8] The OPEC countries collected large export duties on crude oil, which were intended to raise money and also to gain time for these countries to develop their agricultural and industrial economies before their oil resources were used up. (These policies became progressively less effective as non-OPEC countries increased their production and as oil-importing countries developed substitutes for petroleum products and otherwise economized on their use.) This is a form of protection for an economy as a whole rather than for any *specific* industry.

Nominal versus Effective Protection

The **nominal protection** given for an industry is simply the rate of the tariff imposed on the importation of foreign supplies of the industry's product. **Effective protection** involves two further variables. The first is whether protection also is given to goods that are raw materials or intermediate goods used in producing the protected good. Suppose that we want to estimate effective protection for the textile industry. If cotton is a raw material or intermediate good for the textile industry, and if cotton also is protected from foreign competition by a tariff, the effective protection for the textile industry is reduced. The reason is that the protection for cotton raises its price and so also raises the cost of producing the textiles. Foreign textile producers, who can buy cotton at lower (world) prices may be able to move into the "protected" market in spite of the tariff on imported textiles.

The second variable in estimating effective protection centers on the value added (mainly the profits earned and wages paid) by the protected industry. Owners and workers in protected industries are interested in how much protection they get as a percentage of their own earnings, that is, of the value added. Suppose that for every $100 of textiles produced, $50 is paid out for raw materials and other intermediate goods and that $50 goes for wages and profits. If there is no tariff on raw materials or intermediate goods but the tariff on textiles allows the price of textiles to rise to $110, the tariff has raised wages and profits by 20 percent, that is, by $10 from the original $50. Effective protection will almost always be greater than nominal protection, unless raw materials and intermediate goods are given substantial protection at the same time.[9]

Nominal protection is the rate of the tariff imposed on the importation of foreign supplies of an industry's product. Effective protection takes into account tariffs on the raw materials or intermediate goods used in producing the protected good and the value added by the protected industry.

---

7. If an industry that produces only for the domestic market is subsidized, bountied, or tax-relieved, it is not being protected in the international economic sense. But what of an industry that sells part of its output at home and part as exports? This is an important question in U.S.–Japanese economic relations because Japan uses general or production subsidies, without special favors for exports. The United States feels free to impose countervailing duties on goods benefiting from *specific* export subsidies, but what is the status of *production* subsidies, such as the Japanese, that extend also to domestic sales?

8. The U.S. Constitution (Article I, Section 9) bans export duties. This provision was a concession to southern agricultural interests. It is not clear whether this provision can also be extended to cover export bounties (negative export duties).

9. An equation for estimating effective protection is as follows: Let t_x be the tariff rate on imports that compete with an industry's output (such as textiles). Let t_y be the tariff rate on raw materials and intermediate goods (such as cotton), and let q be the share that raw materials and intermediate goods contribute to the value of final output. Then we have

$$T = \frac{t_x - qt_y}{1 - q}$$

where T is the rate of effective protection.

> Effective protection will almost always be greater than nominal protection, unless raw materials and intermediate goods are given substantial protection at the same time.

Disguised Forms of Protection

Besides these forms of more or less open protection, there are also three forms of hidden, or disguised, protection: (1) voluntary export restrictions, (2) orderly marketing agreements, and (3) the trigger price mechanism. Since World War II they have gained in popularity as substitutes for open protection in countries that, like the United States, have pressed other countries for greater freedom of trade.

Voluntary export restrictions are usually bilateral (between just two countries)[10] and seldom completely voluntary. Usually, an exporting country agrees to lower its exports to an importing country to a certain level or in accordance with a certain formula. For example, the United States has put pressure on Japan first to reduce and then not to increase too rapidly her exports of cars and trucks to the United States. **Orderly marketing agreements** are another form of disguised protection. They try to prevent "disorderly" price cutting in importing countries and are generally multilateral. That is to say, several exporting countries and/or several importing countries are usually involved. In most cases, the agreement is carried out under the threat of protective duties or quotas by one or more of the importing countries. A **trigger-price mechanism** need involve no agreement at all. An importing country, like the United States in the case of steel products, acting alone, may announce one or more "trigger prices" for different types of steel. Any imports below these prices are considered to be **dumping** (a sale below what authorities consider average total cost plus a fair markup) and subject to special "antidumping" duties.[11]

> Under voluntary export restrictions, an exporting country agrees to lower its exports to an importing country to a certain level or in accordance with a certain formula. Orderly marketing agreements try to prevent price cutting in importing countries.

> Imports below certain trigger prices are considered to be dumping—offering a good for sale at a price below average total cost plus a fair markup.

Protection Against Protection

In a number of trade acts since 1974, the United States established and strengthened the Office of the U.S. Trade Representative (USTR). The USTR, which now has a seat in the president's cabinet, was deliberately made independent of the old-line State, Treasury, and Commerce departments, whose economic viewpoints were allegedly diluted by political considerations and by the interests of consumers and importers. In its capacity as spokesperson for labor, business, and agricultural interests in export and import-competing branches of the American economy, the USTR has developed novel trade strategies.

USTR and its Advisory Committee for Trade Negotiations (ACTN) now proposes a **market-opening strategy** as protection against foreign protectionism. This strategy is directed especially against the new protectionism practiced by countries with positive bilateral balances in their trade with the United States and also against inbred foreign mercantilist prejudices against competitive imports. Market opening discriminates against a specific group of countries that reject competitive American exports at the same time that they run positive trade balances with the United States.

What is this strategy of market opening? It is a system of guaranteed minimum quotas for American goods in foreign markets—a quota system in

10. We usually treat the European Community (EC) as a single country.

11. The traditional international economic meaning of *dumping* has been the sale of some product abroad at a price lower than its domestic price (plus transportation costs). Dumping was regarded as a predatory tactic, designed to drive competitors out of business and then to exploit consumers. For this reason, coun-

tries impose antidumping duties, which are not usually considered strictly protective.

However, as goods have become less standardized and marketing tactics more complex, the term *dumping* has been redefined in the United States to mean any sale below what the American authorities consider "average total cost plus a fair markup," regardless of price in the exporting country.

reverse. In periodic bilateral negotiations with "Country X," the USTR insists that a certain amount or percentage of the X market in one or another group of goods be reserved for U.S. exports—the percentage being based on U.S. market penetration in other countries somewhat similar to Country X. Country X is left with the responsibility of selecting U.S. products of adequate quality and reasonable (world) prices. If Country X refuses to open its markets adequately or with sufficient speed (in USTR's opinion), USTR is to initiate retaliatory measures of penalty tariffs or quota restrictions against Country X's exports to the United States. For example, to increase its share of the internal Japanese semiconductor market, the United States has imposed restrictions on Japanese exports of electronic products to the United States—which indeed include semiconductor components.

Market-opening strategy, a system of guaranteed minimum quotas for American goods in foreign markets, is targeted toward countries that reject competitive American exports at the same time that they run positive trade balances with the United States.

USTR and its clients in business, labor, and agriculture claim that market opening, unlike standard protectionism, aims at increasing trade rather than decreasing it. In this strategy, trade contraction is a second-best alternative. How this will work in practice, we cannot yet say with confidence. Much depends on the reasonableness of rival negotiating positions and on the willingness of negotiating partners to compromise. The trade negotiations involving market-opening strategies have so far tended to be quite bitter in tone and have not increased international good will.

Unlike standard protectionism, market opening aims at increasing trade rather than decreasing trade.

Economic Arguments for Protection

"Free trade wins all the arguments, but protection wins all the votes." There is a great deal of truth in this statement. The historical record reveals the political effectiveness of "intense minorities" and "special interests."

Steel companies, their workers, and whole "steel communities" like Pittsburgh, Gary, and Birmingham *care* about that import-competing industry's prosperity, because steel is their livelihood. Steel consumers all over the United States may well lose more, in total, from steel protection than the steel industry gains. But each individual consumer's loss is minor, and consumers are spread over a wide area.

But over and above these political arguments, there are sound economic ones, which we should not forget. We shall briefly describe several of these arguments.

The Infant Industry Argument Perhaps the most important of the economic cases that favor protection is the **infant industry argument,** sometimes referred to as "learning-by-doing." We have already pointed out that comparative advantage is generally not a static but a changing concept. Why not speed up the changes if they seem desirable, or slow them down if they seem harmful?

The desire to speed up a change and the willingness to accept a loss in the present for the sake of the future were the base of the infant industry argument for protection, which Alexander Hamilton outlined in his *Report on Manufactures* during the late eighteenth century. The reason why American manufacturers were less efficient than their British or European counterparts, Hamilton believed, was that they lacked experience and on-the-job training. For this reason, Hamilton urged the country to protect American manufacturers temporarily while they were gaining experience. Then the next generation would be better off, particularly if manufacturing demanded higher skills and paid better wages than agriculture did.

The infant-industry argument is that an industry should be protected while it develops the skills and industrial techniques needed to compete effectively against foreign producers.

Sometimes we hear this argument in exaggerated form, to the effect that the latecomer's disadvantage simply *cannot* be overcome at all without some measure of protection. To see that this argument is often wrong, we might look at Japan in the last third of the nineteenth century. Manufacturing developed very rapidly, even though Japan had been forbidden, by "unequal treaties" with Western powers, from imposing tariffs on foreign goods at rates higher than 5 percent. Or consider a case of free trade within the United States—the southward migration of the cotton textile industry. Under free trade, the South eventually developed comparative advantage in textiles. However, trade might have shifted earlier had the Confederacy won the Civil War and imposed tariffs on the New England textiles. One can compare the infant industry argument to a request for a loan at zero interest from today's consumers, who pay higher prices, to tomorrow's workers and consumers, who may, as a result, have higher incomes.

Since there are senile as well as infant industries, there is also a "senile industry" argument for protection. It is quite different from the infant industry argument, however. Consumers are asked to pay more for certain goods to keep specialized workers in dying industries employed and off the relief rolls. This is an act of charity—which also saves taxes.

The High Wage Rate Argument

The *high wage rate* or "cheap foreign labor" argument for protection is very popular in high-wage-rate countries. A high-wage-rate country tries to limit imports of a low-wage-rate country's goods to check or slow down the working of the factor price equalization theorem, to raise real wage rates even higher, or, perhaps also to make income distribution in the high-wage-rate country more nearly equal. Most workers in a high-wage-rate country feel that it is "unfair" that they should have to compete with goods from low-wage-rate countries. American textile workers, for example, complain about competition from Taiwan and South Korea. Workers in Taiwan or South Korea might complain about unfair competition between people and the "cheap American machinery," which replaces labor in America. Essentially, the cheap foreign labor argument is an outright rejection of the theory of comparative advantage. Less developed countries rightfully complain that this form of protection impedes their development.

The high-wage-rate argument for protection is a rejection of the basic comparative-advantage theory of international trade.

The Terms of Trade Argument

A country's **terms of trade** are measured by an average of its export prices divided by an average of its import prices. The terms of trade improve when the average price of the country's exports rises or the average price of its imports falls, both being computed net of tariffs. Higher terms of trade with a given trade volume are considered beneficial. However, a rise in the terms of trade may not be favorable if the trade volume decreases. Lower terms of trade, similarly, are considered disadvantageous unless the trade volume rises.

Terms of trade arguments for protection make use of any monopoly or monopsony (buyers' monopoly) power that a country may have to drive up its own terms of trade ratio and to drive down the terms of trade ratio of its trading partners. If a country has monopsony power, it can impose a tariff that would raise the price of an imported good to consumers and lead them to reduce the quantity demanded. The foreign producers then face the uncomfortable choice of either (a) lowering their prices to cancel the effect of the tariff or (b) accepting a lower volume of sales, which may mean unemployment and hardship. Countries that depend on the monopsonist's market often will lower their price, and part of the tariff is actually shifted to the resource owners in the producing country. A country with monopoly power can accomplish the same result by imposing export duties, as OPEC tried to do. These duties are borne mostly by customers in consuming countries.

The terms of trade argument for protection makes use of a country's monopoly or monopsony power to force up the price of its exports or force down the price of its imports.

The Home Market Argument

In the nineteenth century, the protectionist "American System of Political Economy" had two major parts. One was the Hamilton infant industry argument, stated previously, which was addressed mainly to urban people. The other part, addressed to farmers, was the "home market" argument associated with Henry Clay, the "great compromiser" who would "rather be right than be president."[12] Clay's view was that some farm income should be sacrificed in favor of greater stability and certainty. The more U.S. agriculture remained dependent on the European market for its exported staples (cotton, corn, tobacco, and wheat), the more subject it would remain to disruption from European warfare, revolution, and depression—and also from European protection. Tariffs on European manufactured goods would reduce farm sales to Europe, but these tariffs would bring prosperity to American manufacturing and expand the home market for U.S. farm products. Farm prices would remain high and uncertainty would be reduced. The general idea involved is *risk aversion*, or at least a preference for one bundle of risks over another. It remains important even though Henry Clay's "American system" has been largely forgotten.

The home-market argument for protection asked American farmers to accept tariffs on manufactured goods in order to face less instability in the demand for their farm products.

The Capital-Attraction or Tariff Factory Argument The capital-attraction, or **tariff factory**, argument states that, if a country's market is important, tariffs and quotas set to keep out foreign goods will induce foreign capitalists to invest in that country and employ that country's labor in order to avoid the tariff. Canada has applied this approach effectively against the United States. American visitors to Canada may be surprised at the number of "American" brand names attached to products of "XYZ Company, Canada," with headquarters in Toronto, as distinguished from "XYZ Company" itself, with headquarters in New York. During the 1950s and the early 1960s, the European Community (EC) caused many Ameri-

can firms to establish European branches not only by setting up high Community-wide tariffs against U.S. goods but also by eliminating tariffs between member countries. This last change meant that a single American tariff factory in, say, Belgium, could service the whole EC. Thus there would no longer be any need to set up separate factories in each member country, a costly and often uneconomical procedure.

The tariff factory argument for protection says that tariffs will persuade foreigners to build factories in the tariff-imposing economy and hire workers there.

The Retaliation or Bargaining Argument The *retaliation* or *bargaining* argument for protection, like the infant industry one, involves "time preference." A retaliatory tariff or quota has the same harmful short-run welfare effects as any other tariff or quota. But, according to this argument for protection, in the long run it may cause foreigners to lower their duties or ease their quotas against one's exports. The historical record, however, suggests that retaliatory tariffs seem rather to lead to further retaliation and feed on themselves, growing more and more restrictive over time. Interest groups that gain from the retaliatory tariff gain strength the longer it remains effective. As time passes, it becomes increasingly difficult to oppose the political strength of these groups.

The bargaining argument for protection claims that foreigners will give up their tariffs in order to obtain the removal of the tariffs erected for bargaining purposes.

Macroeconomic Arguments We may lump together a number of economic arguments for protection that aim at relieving macroeconomic ills. For example, if a country has widespread unemployment, a tariff may be used to keep foreign goods out in order to open up more jobs for that country's own people. Or if the government's budget is in deficit, an argument can be made that tariffs should be used to raise revenue, rather than

---

12. It is quite a feat in any field to be at once a great compromiser and always right!

lowering public spending or taxing the people directly. Or if a country's total value of imports is exceeding the total value of its exports so that it is running a balance of payments deficit, tariffs may be used to reduce these imports and the deficit.[13]

Political Arguments for Protection

The political arguments for protection have been even more effective than the economic ones. Some of these are described below.

The National Defense Argument The national defense argument was persuasive for Adam Smith himself. In a famous passage from *The Wealth of Nations*, defending the Navigation Acts[14] against which the Thirteen Colonies were then protesting, Smith admitted that "defense is of much more importance than opulence." So he joined the chorus in favor of protecting potential defense industries.

The aim of the British Navigation Acts was to maintain ships and sailors for the Royal Navy. In the same way, Imperial German tariffs on grain were justified by the argument that country boys from the farm made better soldiers than city boys from the factory. However, the most common national defense arguments today are based on the need for tariffs and quotas on the importation of such "defense goods" as steel and ships. The country, it is said, should not become dependent on unreliable foreign sources for important defense needs.

The "Critical Minimum" Argument Allied to the national defense argument is protection aimed at supporting a *critical minimum* of production in some basic industry. An example today is from Ja-

pan, which imports a larger proportion of its staple foods (rice and wheat) than any other country in recorded history—larger even than Great Britain, which suffered under German submarine blockades in two world wars. It is therefore necessary for Japan—so runs the argument—with its dense population and its small post-1945 "maritime self-defense force," to protect its agriculture from low-price American and other import competition. At the very least, it must keep its dependence on foreign food from increasing any further.

The Predatory Foreigner Argument The *predatory foreigner* argument assumes that foreign suppliers have hostile intentions. According to this argument, it is especially dangerous to let one's country become dependent on unfriendly countries, which may cut off one's supplies of some critical commodity for political reasons or form cartels and raise prices. Even previously friendly countries can become hostile. If the United States had listened to free traders and become completely dependent on imported oil, the Arab boycott of 1973–74 would have caused even more harm than it did. The United States is fortunate, or so runs the argument, to have protected its high-cost domestic oil industry during the years before the boycott.

Special Interests The most effective way of getting protection, year in and year out, has been *intense minority* or *special interest* pressure. The beneficiaries of protection, however few they may be, put their hearts and their money into their cause. They also tend to be concentrated in particular areas. On the other hand, the injuries from protection are spread too thinly, both geographically and economically, for the victims to be mobilized year after year for commodity after commodity.

Political arguments for protection include: (1) protection of national defense industries, (2) support of a critical minimum of production in certain basic industries, and (3) protection against hostile foreign suppliers. The political influence of special interest groups is very effective in obtaining protective legislation.

---

13. Macroeconomic arguments for tariffs and quotas are discussed more fully in Chapter 19.

14. During the seventeenth and eighteenth centuries these acts limited British and colonial coastwise trade, as well as trade between Britain and its colonies, to British and colonial ships with British and colonial crews. They also prohibited import trade in ships other than those of Britain, its colonies, and the exporting country—a move aimed at French and Dutch competition in the "carrying trade" between third countries. Present American law bans only coastwise trade to foreign shipping, but requires that the bulk of American aid goods be carried in American ships.

COMMERCIAL TREATIES, FREE TRADE AREAS, AND CUSTOMS UNIONS

Trade between countries is governed by commercial treaties and other forms of international negotiation. We shall outline some of the important principles of these treaties, including those that involve customs unions and free trade areas.

Commercial Treaties

A **commercial treaty** is an agreement between countries dealing with economic and trade relations. Since World War II, most such treaties have been reasonably reciprocal. For example, under a treaty, the rights and duties of American citizens in Yugoslavia would be much the same as those of Yugoslav citizens in America, with certain allowances for such facts as America being a capitalist and Yugoslavia a socialist country.

However, many, if not most, nineteenth-century commercial treaties between more developed countries (MDCs) and less developed countries (LDCs) were very unequal. Some gave westerners in LDCs what was called "extraterritorial" rights to civil and criminal trial under MDC law in MDC courts attached to MDC embassies or consulates, without giving the same rights to Turks (or Persians or Chinese) living in the West. One reason for such laws was the practice of some LDC legal systems of getting evidence from people by torture and imposing "cruel and unusual punishment" for minor offenses. Other provisions of unequal treaties gave westerners rights to seize LDC customs receipts for payment of debts owed to MDC governments, restricted LDC rights to put tariffs on MDC goods, set aside areas in LDC cities where only MDC citizens could live, and so on. In all these cases, there were no reciprocal rights for LDCs. None of these unequal treaties survived World War II.

Commercial treaties are generally in force for a term of years, after which either party may reject the treaty and perhaps propose a new one more favorable to its interests. But even while the treaty is in force, the legal standing of its provisions varies between countries. No U.S. Congress can bind those that follow it. In fact, many Congresses have felt free to amend or to make laws in violation of commercial treaties that earlier Congresses had approved. For this reason, many countries feel that the United States is not a very reliable partner for a commercial treaty.

A commercial treaty is an agreement between countries dealing with economic and trade relations.

Free Trade Areas and Customs Unions

Commercial treaties may raise the degree of economic integration among the contracting parties, rather than simply legalizing and regulating the existing situation. Recent economic integrations have taken the forms of free trade areas and customs unions. In both cases, trade between the members is made free, either immediately or after periods of adjustment, by one or more commercial treaties. Differences exist, however, in how they deal with outsiders.

In a **free trade area,**[15] there are no tariffs or other trade restrictions for member countries, but each member country has its own set of tariffs, quotas, and so forth, for nonmember countries. In a **customs union**, there is also free trade for members, but a common tariff, generally based on an average of the member countries' previous tariffs, which nonmembers must face. (Each country, however, may keep its separate quota arrangements.) So an American exporter faces different tariffs in Norway and Sweden, both members of the European Free Trade Association (EFTA), but the same tariff in France and West Germany, both members of the European Community (a customs union).

15. A free trade area should be distinguished from a *free port*. In a free port like Hong Kong or Singapore, there is a special restricted area where raw materials or goods in process are landed duty free, processed further by local labor and materials, and then re-exported without entering the general Hong Kong or Singapore market.

In a free trade area, there are no tariffs or other trade restrictions for member countries, but each member country has its own set of tariffs for nonmember countries. In a customs union, there is free trade for members and a common tariff for nonmembers.

Today the most important experiment in economic integration is the European Community (EC). It developed in the 1950s from a number of multilateral agreements about (a) the division of Marshall Plan aid from the United States for rebuilding after World War II and (b) the reorganization of European production of such commodities as coal, steel, and atomic energy. Its founders and supporters, including many Americans, hoped that it might become a strong economic and financial community with a common circulating currency, and a political community as well. Another early hope, especially in the United States, was that the EC would be satisfied with a low common tariff, and that countries like the United States, Canada, and several former British dominions would join with it economically. In this way, the EC would not be simply a Western European power but would become a non-Communist world economic power as well.

These things have not happened. The British, who favored low tariffs, refused to join unless allowed to continue to import cheap food from the dominions. Representatives of high-cost European agriculture would not make this concession. Without the British, the EC became a high-tariff organization, especially after the strongly nationalist General Charles de Gaulle took power in France and a "farm bloc" of French and German agricultural interests gained political power. It has remained a high-tariff organization even after Great Britain, Ireland, and several other countries later joined.

Today the most important experiment in economic integration is the European Community.

Because the free trade area and customs union appear to be movements away from economic nationalism and protectionism, they seem to be steps toward freedom of trade. We might expect many internationalists and free-trade economists to welcome them wholeheartedly as steps in what they believe to be the right direction. In fact, their enthusiasm has been lukewarm at best. How can this be?

The problem is that a free trade area, a customs union, or any other experiment in partial economic integration has a dual effect on trade. Within the free trade area or the customs union itself, it *creates* trade between the individual member countries, which might not have developed if each country had kept its own tariff wall. At the same time, the free trade area or customs union *diverts* trade from nonmember to member countries, and in this case is usually a step away from freedom of trade.

If a highly isolationist self-sufficient country like North Korea today were to join a free trade area or customs union, the trade-creation effect would dominate the trade-diversion effect. If a free trade country like pre-1914 Britain were to join the same free trade area or customs union, the trade-diversion effect would dominate.

An example of trade diversion might be American automobiles in Denmark. Before Denmark joined the EC, U.S. automobiles competed there on equal terms with automobiles from Britain, France, Germany, and Italy. (Denmark itself has no automobile industry.) After Denmark joined the EC, competition for the Danish automobile market shifted favorably to Denmark's new EC partners, and away from outsiders like the United States and Japan. This move was against freedom of trade, even though Ford and General Motors continued to sell in Denmark the products of their European subsidiaries.

Free trade areas and customs unions create trade between member countries but divert trade from nonmember to member countries.

The EC in 1992 and Thereafter Trade-creation and trade-diversion issues will take on greater significance if the EC carries out its plans to achieve full economic unification by the end of 1992. Will the resulting New Europe be a trade-diverting "Fortress Europe" from which American and Japanese products, in particular, are effectively excluded by tariff walls, quotas, and the myriad "dirty tricks" of administrative protection?[16] Or will such outside producers be able to profit by expanded trade created by the integration of what is already the world's largest economic bloc—25 percent of total world trade?

ITO and GATT

After World War II, the "free world" members of the United Nations proposed that the world economy return to freer and less-discriminatory trade than had prevailed in the 1930s and that a new international code of conduct be set up to regulate quotas and other forms of nontariff protection. Their representatives drew up a charter for an **International Trade Organization (ITO).** The proposed charter, however, included a number of safeguards and escape clauses, which the U.S. Senate considered discriminatory against the United States. The Senate refused to ratify the proposed charter, and the ITO never came into being.

To replace the aborted ITO, a number of countries, mainly the industrial countries of North America and Western Europe, framed a less-formal **General Agreement on Tariffs and Trade (GATT).** GATT established its own bureaucracy, and representatives of GATT countries have held several "rounds" of meetings. It seeks to carry out gradually and by stages what ITO hoped to accomplish more quickly. GATT, however, has become something of an exclusive club for the wealthier nations, in the view of many LDCs. These countries, preferring a New International Economic Order (NIEO) to trade liberalization, have hesitated to cooperate with GATT. But within the so-called First World, GATT remains an active and often successful organization.

The General Agreement on Tariffs and Trade (GATT) seeks to reduce the general level of tariff and nontariff protection among its members, who are mostly First World nations.

---

16. American and Japanese *companies* will be able to compete in Europe through European subsidiaries or through joint ventures with European firms. Such subsidiaries, however, must be more than "screwdriver" assembly plants, and their outputs can only qualify as "European" if a sufficiently large percentage of its value is added in Europe.

THE SHIFTING U.S. TRADE POSITION

The U.S. balance of merchandise trade (as distinguished from services), which had been in surplus since the 1890s, went into deficit about 1970. In 1987, the trade deficit was about $160 billion—8 percent with Canada and 35 percent with Japan, America's most important trading partners in recent years. Preliminary statistics for 1988 show a 12 percent drop in the trade deficit and forecasts for 1989 are for another decline of at least that magnitude.[17]

Table 1 suggests the wide range of products involved. For nonfarm products—especially in those industries employing skilled and high-paid labor—the deficits reflect mainly rises in imports. In agriculture, which remains in surplus, exports have risen only slowly. The change also involves the great majority of U.S. trading partners, as can be seen from the data in Table 2.

The combined effect of these changes has been consternation in the United States, where a positive balance of trade had come to be regarded as part of the natural order of events. The present deficit situation has been called the "export of good jobs" and is blamed for making the nation "an economy of hamburger stands." It has been blamed on unfair tactics overseas—low wage rates, export subsidies, administrative protection, market closing, and "dirty tricks" in general. While most of these are practiced by the United States as well, the shift to a trade deficit has given rise in the United States to demands for increased trade restrictions more rigorously enforced, for negotiated opening of trading partners' "closed markets," and for an industrial policy of government planning and subsidies for industry and the management of trade relations.

The shift to a trade deficit in the United States has given rise to demands for increased trade restrictions more rigorously enforced, for opening of closed markets, and for an industrial policy.

---

17. The last previous decline was in 1980, as compared with 1979. It did not last.

TABLE 1
U.S. Trade Balances by Commodity Groups, 1970 and 1987 (billions of dollars)

	Agricultural Products	Petroleum	Industrial Materials	Capital Goods[a]	Automotive Goods	All Others[b]	Total
1970							
Exports	7.4	n.a.	12.3	14.7	3.9	4.2	42.5
Imports	5.8	2.9	12.3	4.0	5.7	9.2	39.9
Balance	1.6	−2.9	0.0	10.7	−1.8	−5.0	2.6
1987							
Exports	29.5	n.a.	62.8	88.1	26.3	42.9	249.6
Imports	20.4	42.9	71.2	84.8	85.2	105.4	409.9
Balance	9.1	−42.9	−8.4	3.3	−58.9	−62.5	−160.3
Net Change							
Exports	22.1	n.a.	50.5	73.4	22.4	38.7	207.1
Imports	14.6	40.0	58.9	80.8	79.5	96.2	370.0
Balance	7.5	−40.0	−8.4	−7.4	−57.1	−57.5	−162.9

a. Except automotive.
b. Mainly consumer goods other than automotive.
Source: Economic Report of the President, 1989, Tables B-100 and B-103, pp. 422 and 426.

In the early 1980s, the shift in the U.S. trade balance was blamed largely on an allegedly overvalued dollar. The overvaluation itself had been brought on by the combination of budget deficits and disinflationary monetary policies, which raised interest rates and increased the foreign demand for dollars. This is clearly wrong. The depreciation of the dollar relative to the Japanese yen—from ¥260 in 1985 to less than ¥130 in 1988–89—has not reduced either the overall American trade deficit or the bilateral American deficit with Japan. Nor should the American deficit be blamed on the OPEC cartel and the oil shocks of the 1970s. Both of these macroeconomic factors—the dear dollar and the shocks to aggregate supply—played significant roles in the history of the American trade balances. However, as Table 3 shows, the decline in this balance was already under way at the time of the first oil shock (1973–74), and it continued through the period of the falling and allegedly *under*valued dollar of the Carter administration (1977–1981). A significant macroeconomic factor—discussed in Chapter 19—has been the long declines in the saving rates of both the private and the public sectors of the U.S. economy.

The shift toward deficit in U.S. international trade began well before the OPEC oil embargos of the 1970s and the high value of the dollar in the early 1980s.

The Passing of the "Dollar-Shortage" Era

A full history of the U.S. trade balance must go back to the end of World War II and to the half-generation (1945 to 1966 approximately) that followed. During that period, North America (the United States and Canada) was the paramount source of both agricultural and manufactured goods for the entire world outside the Soviet bloc,[18] which, after 1949, included China. Because of America's dominant position, these twenty-one

18. Under the Marshall Plan in 1947, the United States offered to extend economic assistance to Soviet bloc countries. But the Soviet Union rejected the American offer and required its allies to do likewise—even after Czechoslovakia and Poland had already accepted. This rejection was due to Stalin's fear that economic dependency on the United States would lead to economic and political subordination.

years, particularly the first ten, were times of "dollar shortage"—since foreign countries had little to exchange for American goods. The leading American firms in a number of industries and American growers of a number of farm products found themselves in a position to obtain higher profits from their monopoly control. In turn, these high returns were reflected in the wages of specialized labor in those industries, the prices of agricultural land, and even in the sizes of welfare programs in the public sector.

Roughly midway in what was described as America's "soaring sixties," foreign recovery, accelerated by American aid, gradually brought this euphoric period to a close.

TABLE 2
U.S. Trade Balances by Area, 1979 and 1987
(billions of dollars)

	1979	1987	Change
Total Exports	184.5	249.6	65.1
Industrial Countries	115.9	164.9	49.0
Canada	38.7	61.1	22.4
Japan	17.6	27.6	10.0
Western Europe	54.2	68.8	14.6
Other Countries[a]	68.5	84.7	16.2
OPEC	14.6	10.7	-3.9
Eastern Europe	5.9	2.2	-3.7
Total Imports	212.0	409.8	197.8
Industrial Countries	112.8	259.8	147.0
Canada	39.2	73.6	34.4
Japan	26.3	84.5	58.2
Western Europe	41.8	96.2	54.4
Other Countries[a]	99.2	150.1	50.9
OPEC	45.0	24.4	-20.6
Eastern Europe	1.9	1.9	0.0
Overall Balances	-27.5	-160.3	-132.8
Industrial Countries	3.1	-94.9	-98.0
Canada	-0.5	-12.6	-12.1
Japan	-8.6	-56.9	-48.3
Western Europe	12.4	-27.5	-39.9
Other Countries[a]	-30.7	-65.4	-34.7
OPEC	-30.5	-13.7	16.8
Eastern Europe	4.0	0.3	-3.7

a. Includes transactions with international organizations and "unallocated." (Figures may not add to total because of rounding.)

Source: Economic Report of the President, 1989, Table B-104, p. 427.

TABLE 3
The Falling U.S. Trade Balance Since World War II, Five-Year Intervals, 1947–1987 (billions of dollars)

Year	Exports	Imports	Balance
1947	16.1	6.0	10.1
1952	13.4	10.8	2.6
1957	19.6	13.3	6.3
1962	20.8	16.3	4.5
1967	30.7	26.9	3.8
1972	49.4	55.8	-6.4
1977	120.8	151.9	-31.1
1982	211.2	247.6	-36.4
1987	249.6	409.8	-160.3

Source: Economic Report of the President, 1989, Table B-102, p. 424.

The special demands and inflationary financing of the Vietnam War postponed public awareness of this development, which emerged as something of a shock when hostilities died down in the early 1970s. Hindsight makes it clear that many segments of the American economy have been unwilling or politically unable to adapt to the new situation by appropriate or sufficient combinations of lower real wage rates, lower profit margins, lower tax burdens, higher productivity growth rates, and improved product quality. The net result of this refusal or inability is called declining American international "competitiveness." It is blamed on labor (by business), on management (by labor), on government waste (by taxpayers), and so on. No group has been willing to accept any substantial share of the blame. The universal path of least resistance has been to blame the foreigner—particularly the Asian foreigner—and to push for bigger and better protection, while leaving unquestioned the comfortable, if outmoded, relics of the dollar-shortage period.

Many segments of the U.S. economy have been unwilling or politically unable to adapt to the country's reduced international competitiveness by appropriate or sufficient combinations of lower real wage rates, lower profit margins, lower tax burdens, higher productivity growth rates, and improved product quality.

Changing Factor Endowments

An additional element in the new U.S. trade position has arisen from changes in rival countries' factor endowments, especially their endowments of human capital. The American view of Oriental labor remained, for entirely too long, that of illiterate coolies producing, with little mechanical aid, bottom-quality merchandise for the bottom fourth of the world's income distribution, while subsisting on "a fishhead and a handful of rice a day." However incorrect this picture might already have become before World War II, it became much more inaccurate thereafter. Oriental labor acquired training and skills, and Oriental wage rates became a larger fraction of American wage rates. It paid Oriental employers to increase labor productivity with better and newer machines of various kinds. In short, Asian labor could enter advanced industries formerly thought to be reserved for the West in general and for America in particular.

An Accelerated Product Cycle

Another element in the changing U.S. trade position has been an acceleration of the product cycle. We have already mentioned this cycle by which an economic innovation in a high-wage-rate country moves by stages from a domestic industry in that country to an export industry and then to an export industry in some lower-wage-rate country with the product imported into the country where the innovation originally took place. The automobile, radio, television, and computer industries in the United States are examples of this. We did not inquire then how long such a product cycle might take.

For the mass-produced automobile, forty years seem to have been required for the Ford Model T and its American successors (Chevrolet, Plymouth, and later Ford models) to be threatened seriously in their home market. When the threat came, it was initially from relatively high-wage-rate European companies—Volkswagen of Germany, Renault of France, Fiat of Italy, and Austin and Morris of Great Britain. An additional ten to fifteen years were required for Japanese competitors to enter the American domestic market to any serious extent. But the product cycle took much less time (only five or ten years) for the television set (first black and white and then color), the computer (whether hand-held, mainframe, or personal), the videocassette recorder, the air conditioner and heat pump, or the recreational vehicle and motorcycle developments of the automobile itself. Pity the American television set or computer manufacturer counting on a full generation's profits on its technological lead before foreign competitors would invade not only its export market but even its domestic market!

The acceleration of the product cycle by the up-market moves of competitors in lower-wage-rate countries is an economic aspect of the more general phenomenon popularized by the sociologist Alvin Toffler as *Future Shock*—except that the shocks are not future ones, but present and recent-past ones. The moral is that one cannot safely rest on one's laurels as many traditional American export industries have sought to do. Together, the passing of the "dollar-shortage" era, changing factor endowments, and the accelerated product cycle surely have been more important causes of the change in America's international trade position than the popular "dirty tricks," "subsidies," or "market closure" explanations so often given.

The changes in the U.S. trade position have resulted, in part, from changes in rival countries' factor endowments, an acceleration of the product cycle and the unwillingness or potential inability of many segments of the U.S. economy to adapt to the new situation.

Economics in Focus

The New Economic Nationalism

To many Americans, it seems unfair that Japanese companies can reap huge revenues by selling cars to the United States but Americans cannot sell rice to Japan. Furloughed autoworkers are especially indignant, and situations of this sort—combined with concern about bulging U.S. trade deficits—have led to the rise of a new economic nationalism, a general demand that the United States stop being mild-mannered toward foreign competitors and begin a more aggressive pursuit of America's "own interests." Political leaders, especially those from areas hard-hit by foreign competition, have spoken out for a new toughness in foreign trade. The 1988 Trade Act, which gave the federal government increased powers to combat unfair trading policies, was actually a compromise; Congress considered other measures that were even more protectionist.

By 1988 U.S. trade restrictions had already been expanding for some time. Although President Reagan was philosophically committed to free trade, his two terms in office witnessed the greatest rise in protectionism since before the Great Depression. According to one estimate, about 25 percent of U.S. imports were subject to protectionist policies by the end of Reagan's tenure. A change has also occurred within the economics profession: more and more economists are speaking out for economic nationalism. Questioning the time-honored principle of comparative advantage, they advocate one or another form of "managed trade." Some even argue that nationalistic principles, if pursued correctly, can benefit not only the country that adopts them but other countries as well.

In this climate public sentiment can easily swing too far. We can start thinking of foreign industries as enemies of the American worker, guilty of undermining our way of life. We can convince ourselves that an autoworker's job in Detroit is more deeply significant than the fate of a Japanese worker. Doing so, we can build up a great deal of moral fervor, but this may ultimately obscure our vision.

Analyzed objectively, some of the recent forays into protectionism seem dubious. The "voluntary" restrictions on Japan's auto exports to the United States probably hurt Americans more than Japanese. Japan's automakers, forced to ship fewer cars, raised their prices and moved toward the upscale end of the market; as a result they may have become stronger competitors. When domestic automakers boosted their prices too, American consumers paid royally for the jobs that had been saved.

On the other hand, many experts believe the government missed early opportunities to protect U.S. interests in semiconductors and high-definition television, two key technological fields. Economic nationalism needs to rely on reason more than on indignation or the desire to retaliate. Policymakers need a better understanding of the likely gains and losses from particular protectionist actions. Perhaps help will come from the economists who are casting a fresh glance at the question.

Sources: Rahul Jacob, "Export Barriers the U.S. Hates Most," *Fortune,* February 27, 1989, pp. 88–89; Robert Kuttner, "Economic Nationalism," *The New Republic,* November 21, 1988, pp. 19–22; David R. Henderson, "The Ugly Truth About Trade," *Fortune,* June 5, 1989, p. 330; Karen Pennar, "The Gospel of Free Trade Is Losing Apostles," *Business Week,* February 27, 1989, p. 89; "Talking Loudly and Carrying a Crowbar," *The Economist,* April 29, 1989, pp. 23–24; Samuel Bowles, "Economic Justice—For Us and Them," *Harper's Magazine,* December 1988, pp. 29–32 (reprinted from *Tikkun,* September/October 1988).

SUMMARY

1. Trade makes it feasible for people to specialize in jobs for which they have special talents. Specialization increases productivity. Therefore trade can play a role in raising real production and income. (See page 846.)

2. Because countries differ from one another in resources and special talents, trade between countries can be shown, under competitive conditions, to benefit both the exporting country and the importing country. (See pages 847–848.)

3. Nevertheless, particular groups lose from trade. Consumers of exportable goods lose from export trade under competitive conditions. Producers of importable or import-competing goods lose from import trade under the same conditions. Producers and/or consumers of nontraded goods may also lose from trade if the particular nontraded goods they produce or consume are complementary to or competitive with imports or exports in consumption or in production. (See pages 848–850.)

4. A country is said to have a comparative advantage in the production of one good and a comparative disadvantage in the production of another good if its pretrade or restricted-trade relative price of the first good is lower, and its relative price of the second good is higher, than those of its actual or potential trading partners or in the rest of the world. (See pages 850–851.)

5. Comparative advantages and disadvantages, when they exist, may be due to a number of different causes. The classical (Ricardian) theory stresses differences in productivity for different goods and services. The later Heckscher-Ohlin theory puts the most stress on differences in "factor endowments," meaning supplies of the several productive inputs. (See pages 851–852.)

6. Comparative advantage is not a static concept, but varies over time. The so-called product cycle is a case in point, as applied to advanced industrial products. (See page 852.)

7. Fears that free trade and an accelerated product cycle could wipe out the industrial sector of an economy ("hollow out" the economy) may be unfounded because new industries typically develop to replace those lost to foreign producers. (See page 853.)

8. Free trade also tends to equalize input resource prices between trading countries in the same manner as migration. (See pages 853–854.)

9. We cannot define protection rigorously. However, it includes a wide variety of aids to a country's import-competing goods and to its exports. It extends well beyond the traditional import tariffs and quotas to a wide range of bounties, tax preferences, and types of administrative protection. Administrative protection subjects competitive imports to burdensome, idiosyncratic, costly, and time-consuming specifications or inspection procedures. (See pages 854–855.)

10. The effective rate of protection is usually different from the nominal rate. The effective rate takes account of the protection given to the raw materials and components that go into a product in addition to the nominal rate on the product itself. Protection given to raw materials lessens the effect on that given to final products. (See page 855.)

11. To counteract administrative protection and mercantilistic public attitudes abroad, the Office of the U.S. Trade Representative (USTR) has adopted a strategy of market opening in countries with large positive trade balances with the U.S. According to this strategy, such countries must either guarantee U.S. exporters a reasonable share of their markets or face discriminatory penalties against their own exports to the U.S. (See pages 856–857.)

12. Among economic arguments for protection, the most effective have been the infant industry (learning-by-doing) and the high-wage-rate (cheap foreign labor) arguments. Others have been: the terms of trade argument; avoidance of risks by developing the home market; the attraction of foreign capital, and sometimes also of skilled labor, to "tariff factories"; the response or bargaining reaction to foreign protection; and the solution of problems connected with the country's employment level, payments balance, or government budget. (See pages 857–860.)

13. Among the political (and social) arguments for protection are: the national defense argument; the critical minimum of basic goods argument; resistance to possible predatory activities by foreign interests; and, most important, the political influence of "intense minorities," otherwise known as "special interests." (See page 860.)

14. Commercial treaties regulate trade and commerce among nations. Multinational treaties can be used to form free trade areas and customs unions, which are important means of economic integration. They differ mainly in that the members of a free trade area retain their separate tariffs against nonmember countries, while a customs union has a common tariff structure. (See page 861.)

15. The European Community is the most important move toward economic integration today. It is a customs union. There is also a European Free Trade Association. (See pages 861–862.)

16. Free trade areas and customs unions both create and divert trade. The trade-creation effects are welcomed by internationalists as moves toward greater freedom of trade; the trade-diversion effects work in the opposite direction. (See page 862.)

17. After World War II, a proposed International Trade Organization (ITO), affiliated with the United Nations, never came into being because of United States opposition. The various First World countries, however, are seeking to reduce the general level of tariff and nontariff protection among themselves, using for this purpose a General Agreement on Tariffs and Trade (GATT). (See page 863.)

18. After a long period of positive balances, the U.S. balance of trade has been increasingly negative since about 1970. America's reduced international competitiveness is attributed to an inability or unwillingness to adjust to increased productivity in the rest of the world. Factor endowments in foreign countries have improved, and the product cycle has accelerated. (See pages 863–866.)

KEY TERMS

absolute advantage: being more proficient than others in doing a given thing (page 851).

administrative protection: a form of protection that subjects competitive imports to burdensome, idiosyncratic, costly, and time-consuming specifications or inspection procedures (page 854).

commercial treaty: an agreement between countries dealing with economic and trade relations (page 861).

comparative advantage: the principle that states that a product whose pretrade or restricted-trade price is relatively higher in a country than in the rest of the world will likely be imported by that country and that a product whose pretrade or restricted-trade price is relatively lower will likely be

exported (page 851).

consumers' surplus: the benefit to consumers from being able to buy at a uniform price rather than at the sum of the amounts they would have been willing to pay for each unit separately (page 848).

customs union: a form of economic integration in which there is free trade among members and a common tariff for nonmembers (page 861).

dumping: the sale of a product below what authorities consider average total cost plus a fair markup (page 856).

effective protection: the net tariff advantage to a producer taking account not only of the tariff on the final product but also any tariffs on inputs used in producing the product (page 855).

excess demand: the amount by which the quantity demanded exceeds the quantity supplied at a specified price (page 846).

excess supply: the amount by which the quantity supplied exceeds the quantity demanded at a specified price (page 846).

factor price equalization theorem: a theorem that states that free trade of goods and services across countries not only tends to equalize output prices but also input prices (page 853).

free trade area: a form of economic integration in which there are no tariffs or other trade restrictions among member countries but each member country has its own set of tariffs, quotas, etc. for nonmember countries (page 861).

General Agreement on Tariffs and Trade (GATT): an organization of First World nations that attempts to regulate tariffs, quotas, and other forms of nontariff protection (page 863).

infant industry argument: an argument for protection based on the proposition that an industry should be sheltered from foreign competition while it develops needed skills and production techniques (page 857).

International Trade Organization (ITO): a proposed organization to regulate quotas and other forms of nontariff protection; the forerunner of GATT (page 863).

market-opening strategies: a system of guaranteed minimum quotas for American goods in foreign markets, intended to counteract foreign protectionism (page 856).

nominal protection: the rate of the tariff imposed on the importation of foreign supplies of an industry's product (page 855).

orderly marketing agreements: multilateral agreements that try to prevent price cutting in importing countries (page 856).

product cycle: the sequence of situations beginning with production for the domestic market and then for the export market, but ultimately becoming an import-competing industry (page 852).

protection: the general term applied to efforts to shelter domestic producers from foreign competition (page 854).

quotas: limitations on the quantity of imports (page 854).

tariff factory: an argument for protection that states that, if a country's market is important, tariffs and quotas set to keep out foreign goods will induce foreign capitalists to invest in that country and employ that country's labor to avoid the tariff (page 859).

tariffs: taxes on imports (page 854).

terms of trade: an average of a country's export prices divided by an average of its import prices (page 858).

trigger-price mechanism: a price assigned to a given import below which the product is considered to be dumped (page 856).

voluntary export restrictions: bilateral arrangements under which an exporting country agrees to lower its exports to an importing country to a certain level or in accordance with a certain formula (page 856).

DISCUSSION QUESTIONS

1. To remedy famine and malnutrition in poor countries, it has been suggested that they raise "food first" and consume it locally, rather than raising cash crops for export (tobacco, coffee, cotton, rubber, etc.). Can such suggestions be reconciled with the theory of comparative advantage?

2. Students often complain that many good teachers prefer to do their own research, leaving the teaching to ineffective teachers. To meet this complaint, one college president suggested that students grade their teachers, and that teachers

graded lowest by the students be assigned exclusively to research. Would this suggestion make "comparative advantage" sense?

3. The theory of factor price equalization has not been borne out by historical experience. Why do you think this is so, and does the experience invalidate the theory?

4. What do you think is meant by the term *dumping?* Do you think antidumping duties are justified? What about duties against goods whose production has been subsidized? What about duties against goods whose export has been subsidized?

5. Should high-wage-rate domestic industries be protected from the products of lower-wage-rate foreign labor? Should labor-intensive industries be protected from the products of automated or robotized foreign plants, which use less labor or none at all?

6. Do you think most American industries enjoy higher or lower effective protection than is suggested by nominal tariff rates? Explain.

7. Why has protection shifted away from tariffs to quotas, voluntary export agreements, orderly marketing arrangements, and other forms of administrative protection?

8. What is the difference between a customs union and a free trade area? How would you characterize the arrangements between the fifty American states?

9. It is generally agreed that American prosperity has been enhanced by the regional specialization permitted by the absence of interstate tariffs and other forms of protection. Should this result be applied to the world as a whole?

10. Can you find examples of product cycles in the histories of such American industries as shoes, steel, or automobiles? Explain.

11. Why has the American "industrial crisis of the 1980s" developed? Is it a real crisis? What, if anything, should be done about it?

12. Country X exports goods to the U.S. in exchange for U.S. assets (securities and real estate). The Xians are not interested in buying U.S. exports, which they consider both overpriced and of inferior workmanship. The USTR proposes to negotiate agreements with Country X to open its markets. This would force Xians to accept U.S. goods instead of U.S. assets, on penalty of reducing Country X's own exports to the U.S. Is this sound microeconomics?

37

Agriculture, Food, and Hunger

Preview When peasants are slaves, or serfs, or peons, what they claim to want is freedom. But when free peasants must rent their land from the lord of the manor or the absentee landlord in the city, or when they are hired hands on a plantation or a collective farm, what they say they want is a farm of their own. Therefore, readers of ancient and medieval agricultural history might think that the farmers' complaints would be muted in countries such as the United States that are dominated by the tradition of family farming. But this has not been the case. Agricultural unrest has been a recurring theme in American life. Indeed, most countries have had farm problems of one kind or another at various times in their histories. We will discuss the economics that surrounds these problems.

The first part of this chapter focuses on the problems faced by American farmers and their reactions to these problems. Their reactions have included the economic one of leaving the farm for other occupations and the political one of agitating for government help in controlling prices and quantities in the markets for major farm products. They also have formed cooperatives in efforts to help themselves.

The second part of the chapter examines the government programs that have arisen in the United States as a result of farm political action. These include price support programs and controls on the amount that farmers can produce. We take a look at how subsidies for farm output offer an alternative to the present system of price controls.

The last part of the chapter addresses the fear of increasing food shortages and malnutrition. Except for a few agricultural giants like the United States and Canada, the danger of shortages and hunger for most of the world has been increasing as soil is depleted and as what has been farmland is diverted to nonagricultural uses. We discuss several proposed solutions for the problems arising from the increase in world population and the heating of the planet due to the "greenhouse effect." The proposals include further increases in agricultural productivity per acre and per worker, falling rates of population growth mainly through lower birthrates, and shifting agricultural output to staple foods like grain and vegetables and away from luxury foods like meat and sugar or nonfood products like tobacco and flowers. We close with a discussion of the Food First proposals for resolving world food problems.

AMERICAN FARMERS AND FARM PROBLEMS

American agriculture is the envy of most of the world. Fertile soil, advanced technology, and highly skilled farmers produce outputs per hour of labor that were undreamed of only a generation or two ago. Nonetheless, the "farm problem" has been a recurring theme in American life. We begin by noting a few highlights of American agricultural history. We follow this overview by exploring the farmers' complaints and some of the responses farmers have made to their problems.

The farm problem has been a recurring theme in American life.

Historical Patterns and Highlights

Our brief review of agriculture problems in U.S. history begins with a farmers' rebellion not long after the country won its independence. Then, as background for the rest of the chapter, we trace the events and the protests that followed the Civil War and the two world wars.

The Whiskey Rebellion Before the building of canals or turnpikes, the cost of transportation meant that grain could not be marketed profitably by the farmers of western Pennsylvania. But the high value and small bulk of whiskey was a different matter. To sell their grain on the Atlantic seaboard, it was first distilled into whiskey. Thus, whiskey was an important farm crop in western Pennsylvania in the years shortly after the American revolution. During Washington's administration, the new federal government imposed a tax on distilled liquor. When serious attempts were made to collect the tax, the farmers rebelled. President Washington feared that the rebellion might become a real revolution and threaten the new government. He raised a force of 13,000 soldiers and put down the rebellion with a large show of force.

Populism The Civil War was financed by inflationary means. The country abandoned the gold standard and printed paper money—"greenbacks" that were not convertible into gold. Both prices and nominal interest rates rose, and in both the North and the South, farmers were encouraged to clear land, enlarge their farms, and expand production. To finance this expansion, farmers borrowed money secured by mortgages on their homes and land. After the war ended in 1865, deflationary policies were adopted by the government, and both farm prices and nominal interest rates fell. Farmers who had borrowed money during and right after the war found that interest charges and principal repayments at the old high rates were too high in terms of bushels of wheat or pounds of other produce at the new lower prices. Moreover, they were competing against farmers who had borrowed money later and were paying lower interest rates.

During the recessions that followed financial panics in 1873, 1890, and 1893, many farmers could not keep up their payments and lost their lands and homes. The resulting protest movement, called **Populism**, swept both the West and the South. It was the basis for two political parties, the People's Party and the Greenback Party, which wanted the government to increase the money supply by printing more greenbacks. The populist movement provided substantial support for William Jennings Bryan in his almost successful run for the presidency in 1896. About the same time, however, gold was discovered in the Yukon and in South Africa, and a new method of extracting precious metals from low-grade ore was found. Under the gold standard, which had been re-established in 1879, this new supply of gold brought an increase in farm prices and eased the plight of the farmer. The rise in farm prices is credited with killing Populism as a major political force and bringing on a "golden age of agriculture" during the years just before World War I.

During the recessions that followed financial panics in 1873, 1890, and 1893, many farmers could not keep up with their payments and lost their lands and homes. The resulting protest movement, called Populism, became the basis for two political parties that wanted the government to increase the money supply by printing more greenbacks.

War Prosperity and Postwar Recession The story was similar after both World War I and World War II. During and right after each war, farmers were encouraged by patriotism and high farm prices to borrow money and expand production. But after each war, when normal peacetime conditions returned to the countries that were devastated by the war, "overproduction" from American farmers hastened a fall in world prices for farm products. In the 1930s, the Roosevelt New Deal caused farm prices to increase again. However, these were years of drought, soil erosion, the Dust Bowl, and the "tractoring off" of tenant farmers by landlords who wanted to substitute machinery for labor. In the late 1930s, the great migration of the "Okies" and the "Arkies" to California seems to have been due more to tractoring off than to either dust-bowl drought conditions or foreclosures on farm mortgages. After World War II, the Roosevelt program remained in effect, but farmers called for more and more support to keep up with postwar advances in both agricultural productivity and urban incomes.

After both world wars, overproduction by American farmers hastened a fall in world prices for farm products. After World War II, farmers called for more and more support to keep up with postwar advances in both agricultural productivity and urban incomes.

The U.S. experience can be paralleled to some extent in other agricultural-exporting countries like Canada, Australia, and Argentina. But agricultural problems are different in countries and regions like the African Sahel (the southern edge of the Sahara Desert). Malnutrition and famine are serious problems because their agricultural productivity is low and because they do not have friendly or dependable sources for the import of basic foodstuffs.

The Farmers' Complaints

Why are so many farmers so sure that the economic cards are stacked against them, even when they own their own land? Basically, there are two types of complaints—one about the market structures in which farmers buy and sell and the other about the inelasticity of demand for farm products.

Competitors in a Monopolistic World In economists' language, the farmers' most common complaint is that they are very close to being pure competitors at the mercy of monopolistic sellers and monopsonistic buyers. Individual farmers see themselves as pure competitors or price takers in the markets for the goods they buy, including such inputs as agricultural machinery, fertilizers, insecticides, and credit. In addition, they see themselves as price takers in selling their output at harvest time. On the other hand, those who sell inputs to farms and buy farm products seem to be either local monopolists or agents of national monopolies. For these reasons, farmers believe they are exploited.

The list of alleged exploiters is a long one and varies from time to time and from place to place. It has included the following:

1. Local money lenders, such as bankers or other suppliers of credit. Rural towns are small, and owners of small farms have no access to larger market areas. For this reason, collusion between local money lenders is often easy to maintain, and farmers get little benefit from competition in the world outside.

2. Railroad or trucking companies, which transport farm goods to market.

3. Local grain elevators, warehouses, or other storage companies that hold farm goods for shipment.

4. Processing plants (flour mills, cotton gins, canneries, or creameries), which may be owned by a national or regional chain or a nationwide conglomerate.

5. Local agricultural implement dealers, who may be agents of national companies.

6. Local general stores or specialized merchants who sell seeds and fertilizers, fencing materials, work clothes, bagging, and even staple foods. These too may be local monopolies or owned by a national or regional chain.

7. Speculators on the commodity exchanges in Chicago and elsewhere who allegedly push the prices of the farmers' crops down just at harvest time when they have to sell it.

Farmers believe they are exploited because they are very close to being pure competitors who are at the mercy of monopolistic sellers and monopsonistic buyers. The list of alleged exploiters includes money lenders, railroad and trucking companies, local grain elevators and warehouses, processing plants, agricultural implement dealers, local general stores, and speculators on the commodity exchanges.

Regarding farmland, there are complaints on both sides of the market. Partly because of demand for nonfarm purposes like housing and partly because of demand by nonfarmers for investments and inflation hedges, the price of farm acreage is "too high" in relation to crop prices. A young couple may be unable to establish a family farm of economic size unless they have inherited such a farm. But at the same time, land prices are "too low" to justify the property, capital gains, and estate taxes levied on farm owners and their heirs. Moreover, farmland is a very nonliquid asset and must often be sold at a sacrifice in an emergency (by both the land-rich and the land-poor) to raise cash for the payment of debts or taxes or to permit the farmer to retire quickly under pressure of age or ill health.

Inelasticity of Demand   The second set of farmers' complaints usually is more impersonal. It centers around the low price and income elasticities of de-

mand for most basic farm products. The low *price* elasticity of demand for a farm product such as the whole American output of red winter wheat means that, in a free market, a large crop often brings farmers less income than a small crop. This is true even though the price elasticity of demand for the output of any individual farm is almost infinite.[1]

The low *income* elasticity of demand for a farm product means that, as consumers' per capita income rises, the percentage that they spend for this product falls. This applies not only to particular commodities but to food products as a whole. It causes farm incomes to lag behind nonfarm incomes and has prompted migration from the farm to the cities and to nonfarm occupations. The tendency for the percentage of a family's budget spent for food to decline as income rises sometimes is called **Engels' Law.**

Some specialized and large-scale farmers, like the citrus and raisin growers of the South and Southwest, have been able to take advantage of the low price elasticity of demand for their crops and keep their incomes high without government aid. To do this, they form organizations to "manage" their outputs—that is, to reduce output and sometimes to destroy "surpluses." But for major crops with more producers, there have been enough rugged individualists and free riders to break down such cartel arrangements despite urgings to "raise less corn and more Hell."

Farmers complain about the low price and income elasticities of demand for most basic farm products. Low price elasticity means that a large crop may bring farmers less income than a small crop. Low income elasticity means that as consumers' per capita income rises, the percentage they spend for farm products falls.

The Farmers' Responses

Farmers have reacted to unfavorable conditions in several ways. As individuals, they, and more importantly their children, have reacted both by supplementing farm income with income from non-

---

1. See Chapter 23 for an explanation of price and income elasticity of demand.

farm employment and by leaving the farm for nonfarm jobs in rural areas or by moving to the cities. They also have reacted by forming farm organizations and by striving, either directly or by political means, to change the rules of the economic game in their own favor, both within and beyond the limits of the ordinary market system.

Agricultural Fundamentalism   When an economic group feels systematically disadvantaged, it usually tries to prove that its interest is also the interest of the whole country. Farmers are no exception. The special doctrine that supports their claims has been called **agricultural fundamentalism.** The argument is that, since food is necessary to life, farmers should be at least as well off as any other group. Moreover, not only is farm produce fundamental in itself, but the agricultural countryside is an important market for the manufactured products of the city. The agricultural fundamentalists say that business depressions are "farm led and farm fed" because when farm income falls below a certain proportion of nonfarm national income, the farmers cannot purchase the products of the cities. From the failure of farm purchasing power comes urban overproduction and depression, say the agricultural fundamentalists. The Great Depression of the 1930s was often cited as a case in point because agriculture had been in a depressed state for several years before the Wall Street crash of 1929.

Agricultural fundamentalism has declined in the United States as the farm market has become less important as an outlet for the sale of manufactured goods. As part A of Table 1 (page 876) shows, at the turn of the century, nonfarm production in the United States was a little over three times as great as farm production. But part B of the table shows that, by 1987, nonfarm production was almost 50 times as great. This decline in the relative importance of farm production is reflected in the smaller proportion of Americans now living on farms, a trend that we shall examine next.

The doctrine of agricultural fundamentalism claims that since food is necessary to life, farmers should be at least as well off as any

---

other group. Agricultural fundamentalism has declined in the United States as the farm market has become less important as an outlet for the sale of manufactured goods.

Farmers Leave the Farm   Quantitatively speaking, the farmer's most important reaction has been to leave the farm—as one might expect from conventional economic theory. Over 40 percent of all Americans lived on farms in 1900. The percentage had fallen to 2 percent by 1987, as shown in Table 2. During World War II, farmers left the farm to take defense jobs; many never returned to farming. In peacetime, they often sell their farms when they retire and go to live in town. Sometimes, of course, landlords who wish to increase the size of their own farms force their tenant farmers off the land, or mortgage holders evict farmers who cannot meet mortgage payments. Forcing farmers off the land to allow landlords to increase the size of their farms is parallel, in some respects, to the "enclosure movements" in the late Middle Ages when sheep and cattle raising, which required little labor per acre, were substituted for grain farming, which required much more. In the 1950s, the development of the mechanical cotton picker displaced the sharecropper from much of the cotton-growing South.

The farmer's most important reaction to unfavorable conditions has been to leave the farm.

Farmers' Cooperatives   As Benjamin Franklin said, "God helps those who help themselves." Accordingly, farmers have tried to help themselves by organizing cooperatives to give themselves the market power required to counteract their several "exploiters." These co-ops, as they are called, have been of two general types, *producers' co-ops* and *marketing co-ops*; some co-ops combine both functions. Producers' co-ops concentrate on bulk buying of farm equipment and supplies. While they ordinarily sell at market prices, the profits are distributed to farmers in proportion to their purchases, and increase their incomes. Several types of farmers may belong to one producers' co-op. Marketing co-ops concentrate on bulk sales of particular products and are usually limited in the range of products they sell. The most powerful ones have attained some degree of monopoly control in dealing with wholesalers and chain stores in dairy products, citrus fruits, and dried fruit. They have formed powerful organizations, which operate stores, grain elevators, and processing plants.

Both types of co-op aim at securing part or all of "the middleman's profit" for farmers themselves, and both have had difficulties in hiring and retaining good managers. Both types have also been active politically. Some, dominated by the richer owners of the larger farms, have been conservative. Others have turned collectivist and sought public ownership of banks, railroads, and public utilities. The left-wing collectivist cooperative movement reached its peak in the Non-Partisan League of North Dakota, the Farmer-Labor Party of Minnesota, and the Progressive Labor Party of Wisconsin during and shortly after World War I.

Farmers have tried to help themselves by organizing cooperatives to give themselves greater market power. Producers' co-ops concentrate on bulk buying of farm equipment and supplies. Marketing co-ops concentrate on bulk sales of particular products.

TABLE 1
U.S. Farm and Nonfarm Production, 1897–1987

A. Gross Domestic Private Product (in billions of dollars, 1929 prices)

Years	Farm Product	Nonfarm Product	Nonfarm/Farm Product Ratio
1897–1901 (average)	8.4	27.4	3.26
1902–1906 (average)	8.9	6.3	4.08
1907–1911 (average)	9.2	43.7	4.75
1912–1916 (average)	10.1	49.8	4.93
1917–1921 (average)	9.7	57.3	5.90
1924	9.7	74.3	7.66
1929	10.7	88.6	8.28

B. Gross Domestic Business Product (in billions of dollars, current prices)

Year	Farm Product	Nonfarm Product	Nonfarm/Farm Product Ratio
1929	9.7	84.8	8.74
1939	6.3	73.0	11.59
1949	18.8	213.3	11.35
1959	19.0	417.9	21.99
1969	25.2	798.8	31.70
1979	71.8	2,054.5	28.61
1985	75.4	3,342.2	44.33
1986	75.4	3,547.1	47.04
1987	75.9	3,787.8	49.91

Note: Private product (A) excludes only government agencies, whereas business product (B) excludes also nonprofit agencies such as private hospitals and universities.

Sources: (A) Ben J. Wattenberg, ed., *Statistical History of the United States,* Bureau of the Census, Series F 125–129; (B) *Economic Report of the President, 1989,* Table B-8, p. 318.

TABLE 2
U.S. Farm Population, Employment, and Acreage, 1933–1987

| Year | Farm Population | | Farm Employment (millions) | Crops Harvested (millions of acres) |
	Millions	Percentage of U.S. Total		
1933	32.4	25.8	12.7	340
1940	30.5	23.1	11.0	341
1945	24.4	17.5	10.0	354
1950	23.0	15.2	9.9	345
1955	19.1	11.5	8.4	340
1960	15.6	8.7	7.1	324
1965	12.4	6.4	5.6	298
1970	9.7	4.7	4.5	293
1975	8.9	4.1	4.3	336
1980	6.1	2.7	3.7	352
1985	5.4	2.2	2.9	342
1987	5.0	2.0	2.7	302

Note: Farm population data starting with 1980 are based on a new definition of a farm.

Source: Economic Report of the President, 1986, Table B-95, p. 362, and Ibid., 1989, Table B-98, p. 420.

Political Pressure by Farmers Because farmers tend to be law-abiding property owners whose farms are scattered over wide areas, they have not been able to organize as successfully as many other groups. Farm organizations also have been less likely to strike or to take similar forms of direct action than have labor unions.[2] Instead they have depended on their voting power, which is a much smaller share of the total than in the past. They use this power to lower the prices and improve the quality of the things they buy, but their main effort has been to try to raise and maintain the prices of the crops they sell.

GOVERNMENT AGRICULTURAL PROGRAMS

When people speak of the American "farm program" without further specification, they usually

mean the programs for six basic commodities (wheat, corn, rice, cotton, tobacco, and peanuts) and major storable commodities such as oats, hay, milk, wool, and soybeans. Altogether, these amount to 14 out of a total of 116 farm products on which the U.S. Department of Agriculture keeps records, and they are raised by approximately one-third of the country's 2 million farmers.

The primary purpose of these programs has been to close the gap between the income of the average farmer and that of the average city dweller. In 1985, the national average family income was $28,716 while the average net income per farm family was $21,853. Because of the larger size of farm families, the per capita income of the farm population was even further below the national average.[3]

A second purpose of American farm programs has been to preserve family farming as a way of life. Until the time of the Civil War, an absolute majority of the American population lived on farms. The percentage was 44 in the first Census Bureau offi-

2. Exceptions to this generalization are not hard to find, particularly when farmers live close together in villages or small farms. The "Farmers' Holiday" movement of the 1930s, for example, stopped farm trucks and dumped milk on the roads. During the same period, farmers disrupted foreclosure sales of farms, permitting the mortgagor to buy his or her mortgaged farm free and clear for a fraction of its value by keeping outsiders from bidding on the property. Similar disruptions of farm sales occurred again on a smaller scale in the 1980s.

3. Comparisons between agricultural and nonagricultural incomes are treacherous for at least three reasons: (1) there are wide variations around the average in each group, (2) approximately seven-eighths of the "farm families" in the United States (concentrated in the lower income brackets) receive less than half of their incomes from farming, and (3) farm families typically are larger than nonfarm families.

cial estimate in 1880, and 26 at the time of the first government price support programs in 1933. The government programs have not prevented further declines in the farm population, as shown in Table 2, but they may have slowed them down.[4]

The primary purpose of farm programs such as price supports and income supplements has been to close the gap between the income of the average farmer and that of the average city dweller. A second purpose has been to preserve family farming as a way of life.

It may seem strange for farmers to combat reductions in the number of their own competitors. The paradox is explained partly by a widespread belief in the innate naturalness and superiority of rural over urban and suburban living, and partly by the desire to maintain farmers' traditional political clout at all levels of government. In addition, farmers seldom regard their neighbors as competitors—a sentiment that rarely extends to farmers in other regions, let alone to farmers in foreign countries. The noncompetitor attitude stems from the realization that all of the farmers in one township or county can exercise only infinitesimal influence over farm product prices and that nobody is lowering anyone else's income by raising his own output.

The American system, or rather systems, of farm price supports and income supplements has developed over more than a half-century, starting as a temporary program in 1933, part of the initial Roosevelt New Deal. It has since spread, with modifications, to other countries including the European Community (EC) and Japan. It has been characterized, somewhat unfairly, as "the government showing you how to grow two ears of corn where one grew before and then paying you not to harvest either one."

The programs have become an important, and perhaps basically immovable, aspect of the American economy, resulting from generations of politi-

cal compromise among farmers, taxpayers, and consumer interest groups. We should not be surprised to find separate programs for different farm products and to find them imperfectly consistent with each other. After all, the buyers of such farm products as cotton, wheat, and tobacco are business firms rather than final consumers. Moreover, in the case of feed grains, farmers producing meat, eggs, or dairy products purchase the products of other farmers.

Farm Parity

Parity means equality or equivalence. In general, **farm parity** now means parity of farm incomes rather than of prices of particular products. It refers to the relationship between the purchasing power or real incomes of farmers compared with the purchasing power or real incomes of others in the economy. If farmers had the same purchasing power or real income as others in the economy, they would have 100 percent of parity.

Farm parity means equality of farm incomes rather than of prices of particular products. It refers to the relationship between the purchasing power or real incomes of farmers compared with the purchasing power or real income of others in the economy.

In government farm programs, the parity concept is applied to the prices of individual farm products. For example, the **parity price** of wheat of a standard grade is the price that bears the same relation to some index of the farm production costs that it did in some past period. In these programs, the time period chosen as a reference or base in calculating parity prices usually has been a time of special prosperity for farmers, such as the "golden age of agriculture" in the years before World War I. However, farm prices usually are not supported at 100 percent of parity. Government programs simply prevent prices of supported farm products from falling below some politically determined relationship (percent of parity) to the prices of goods and services that farmers buy. Nothing prevents the market prices of these products from rising above 100 percent of parity in periods of high demand or low supply.

---

4. The actual decline may be larger than the numbers indicate because the opportunity to shelter other income from taxation by "tax losses" on "farm operations" keeps a certain number of individuals registered as living on "farms" that are such in name only.

Government programs prevent prices of supported farm products from falling below some politically determined relationship (percent of parity) to the prices of goods and services that farmers buy.

Market Prices, Support Prices, and Target Prices

To understand the price control aspects of the programs for major crops, it is helpful to identify three different prices for each product. These are (1) the **market price**, which is the price that would prevail in the absence of the government price support programs and which would involve only negligible surpluses resulting from speculation on "higher prices next year," (2) the **support price**, which is the price at which government agencies buy and store crop surpluses that accumulate at these higher prices,[5] and (3) the **target price**, which is still higher than the support price and which is the basis for calculating "deficiency payments" to farmers, as will be explained shortly. The target-price system did not exist in America until 1973, but had been used earlier in Japan and in the European Community.

It is useful to consider three different types of prices for major farm products: a market price, a support price, and a target price.

Figure 1 illustrates the three-tier system of prices for a crop covered by these government programs. The horizontal axis shows quantities of the crop (wheat, for example) demanded and supplied. The vertical axis shows price per bushel. The market price for this crop (P_m) is indicated by the intersection of the demand curve (D) and the supply curve (S) at point E. At this price, the market is cleared and there is no surplus or unsold output. The quantity demanded and supplied is Q_1 and to-

5. Sometimes the government holdings of crops are called **buffer stocks** or an **ever-normal granary** being kept as reserves against periods of bad weather or other disasters at home or abroad. However, these stocks often have been larger than necessary for these purposes.

FIGURE 1
Market Price, Support Price, and Target Price for a Farm Crop

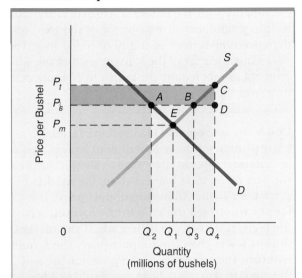

In the absence of government price and production controls, the market would clear at the equilibrium point E, with market price P_m and quantity Q_1 demanded and supplied. If the price is supported at P_s, quantity supplied will be Q_3, as indicated by point B on the supply curve, but consumers will purchase only quantity Q_2, as indicated by point A on the demand curve. Government must purchase quantity Q_2Q_3. Under a target-price system, with a target price of P_t, farmers will supply quantity Q_4. Consumers will again buy quantity Q_2 at the support price of P_s. The government will buy the remainder, quantity Q_2Q_4, at the support price, P_s. In addition, farmers will receive deficiency payments in the amount of $P_t - P_s$ per unit of output. Total deficiency payments are represented by the red area of the rectangle P_sP_tCD.

tal farm receipts from this crop are represented by the rectangle $0P_mEQ_1$. If Congress decides that this is not enough to attract or hold the farm vote, it may decide to raise the price to a higher and more attractive percentage of parity. Accordingly, Congress may decide to provide a support price of P_s.

Price Supports The support price (P_s) is implemented by the government through a system of **no-recourse loans**. Under the no-recourse loan system, farmers borrow money from a government agency and, as collateral for the loan, pledge their crop evaluated at the support price (P_s). If, at harvest time, the market price were higher than the support price, the farmer would sell the crop in the market, repay the government loan, and keep the difference. However, if the market price is below the support price, the farmer will turn over the crop to the government in repayment of the loan and the government must bear any resulting loss. The no-recourse feature of the loan means that the government cannot require the farmer to do more than turn over the crop.

Under the no-recourse loan system, farmers borrow money from a government agency and, as collateral, pledge their crop evaluated at the support price. If, at harvest time, the market price were higher than the support price, the farmer would sell the crop in the market, repay the loan, and keep the difference. If the market price is lower than the support price, the farmer will turn the crop over to the government and the government must bear any resulting loss.

At the support price P_s in Figure 1, quantity Q_2 will be demanded in the market, but quantity Q_3 will be supplied, leaving an unsold or "surplus" quantity of Q_2Q_3, shown by the horizontal distance from point A (on the demand curve at price P_s) to point B (on the supply curve at price P_s). This surplus is purchased, stored, and held off the market, mainly by government agencies but partly by individual farmers and other speculators. Some of it is given away in aid programs or sold under such programs at prices below the world price, which we suppose is close to the market price of P_m.

Under the support-price system, the total receipts of farmers are represented by the blue (both light and dark) rectangle $0P_sBQ_3$, which is considerably greater than the amount received at the equilibrium market price. Of these higher farm receipts, purchasers in the market (i.e., consumers) pay the amount represented by the dark blue rectangle $0P_sAQ_2$, and the government (i.e., taxpayers) pays the amount represented by the light blue rectangle Q_2ABQ_3. If the demand curve is price inelastic over the price range from P_m to P_s, which is usually the case, consumers' payments for this crop will be greater than before (even though they are buying less) so that they contribute to the farmers' gains. But most of the increase in farm receipts is paid by taxpayers. Taxpayers may recoup some

money from sales of the surplus (as just noted) but they also have to pay for storing the crop after it has been transferred to the government.

Target Prices   The price-support system described above prevailed for the forty years from 1933 to 1973, with some departures during the years of U.S. participation in World War II (1941–1945) and its immediate aftermath. But the farmers eventually wanted more. Partly because of consumer resistance to higher food prices and partly because of problems in storing large quantities of surplus crops, the government responded to the new farm demands with the target-price system rather than with higher support prices.

Under the target-price system, for each crop in the program, the government selects a price, such as P_t in Figure 1, which is above the support price. At this price, farmers will supply quantity Q_4, as shown by point C on the supply curve for this crop. Since the support price remains unchanged at P_s, the quantity purchased by consumers is unchanged at Q_2 and the entire increase in output (from Q_3 to Q_4) is purchased by the government along with the previously purchased quantity of Q_2Q_3.

The distinctive feature about the target-price system is that the farmer receives a **deficiency payment** directly from the government for each bushel produced and sold. The deficiency payment is equal to the difference between the target price and the support price so that, in Figure 1, the total of deficiency payments received by farmers is represented by the red rectangle P_sP_tCD. Thus, the target-pricing system means no additional cost to consumers but a substantial increase in cost to taxpayers, who finance not only the deficiency payments but also the purchase and storage of the increases in crop surpluses generated by the target price. The addition of the target-price feature accounts for much of the rise in the cost of government farm programs since 1973. Since 1985, Congress has reduced the loan rate to increase the competitiveness of U.S. farm exports, and target prices, where they existed, were reduced in 1988 and 1989.

Under the target-price system the farmer receives a deficiency payment from the govern-

ment for each bushel produced and sold. The deficiency payment per unit of output is equal to the difference between the target price and the support price.

The target-pricing system accounts for much of the rise in the cost of government farm programs since 1973.

Production Controls

To reduce the cost to taxpayers (and also to reduce soil erosion), many American farm programs include production controls. These may be voluntary, as in "soil bank" programs, with payments for participants in exchange for removing acreage from production, or they may be compulsory, as in the case of tobacco. In the tobacco program, each farmer proposing to grow this crop must first receive or purchase an allotment for the number of acres he or she may plant. It is illegal to grow tobacco, even for the farmer's own use, on acres not covered by an allotment. The right to grow tobacco on an acre of land was based, originally, on the use of land for tobacco-growing in 1933, but these rights could be sold apart from the land and transferred to other land owned by the buyer, provided that this land was in the same county. In tobacco-growing states today, rights to grow tobacco are worth more than the raw land without such rights. Once possessed of the right to grow tobacco on a given acre, the farmer may increase its yield and raise its quality to whatever extent that he or she considers worthwhile by piling on more labor, machinery, fertilizer, pesticide, and so on. As a result, tobacco production has decreased less than originally anticipated.

Figure 2 illustrates how a production-control program operates along with price support and target price programs. The demand curve (D), and the three prices (P_m, P_s, and P_t) are the same as in Figure 1. The supply curve from Figure 1 has been relabeled as supply curve S_1 in Figure 2. In addition, there is a new supply curve (S_2) that shows the results of the production-control program. The production-control program shifts the supply curve to the left. This reduces surpluses and government purchases under a price-support-only program to

FIGURE 2

Production Controls Combined with Support and Target Prices

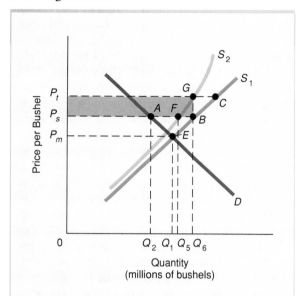

The demand curve, D, and the prices P_m, P_s, and P_t are the same as in Figure 1. The supply curve from Figure 1 appears here as supply curve S_1. Production controls shift the supply curve to the left, from S_1 to S_2. They reduce the quantity purchased by the government under a price-support-only program to quantity Q_2Q_5, as indicated by point F on supply curve S_2. They reduce the quantity purchased by the government under the support-plus-target-price system to Q_2Q_6, as indicated by point G on supply curve S_2.

the quantity Q_2Q_5, as shown by point F on the new supply curve. Under the system involving both price supports and target prices, the supply shift reduces the surplus purchased by the government to Q_2Q_6, as shown by point G. This saves money for taxpayers, although they still must finance the payments that are made, under voluntary programs, to induce farmers to remove land from production. As long as the support price, P_s, is above the market price that would exist without controls (P_m), the cost to consumers is not affected by the production controls.

Production controls are employed to maintain the price of farm products while reducing the taxpayer cost of price support programs.

Costs and Benefits

Over the more than half-century since their inception in 1933, the American farm price and income support systems are estimated to have cost taxpayers some $200 billion. Even adjusting for inflation, it now costs more than thirty times what it did in the era of Franklin Roosevelt. The systems are entrenched and heavily depended on. Were the system to be dismantled, the Department of Agriculture estimates that American farm income would fall by some 40 percent.

Table 3 shows that U.S. government expenditure on farm programs totaled $12.5 billion for the fiscal year 1988. An even greater amount was spent to maintain or increase consumer demand for farm products. In that category the largest domestic programs for "supplementary purchases of farm products" were for food stamps and school lunches. In addition, there were various international forms of food aid financed by U.S. taxpayers. The primary beneficiaries of this aid were poor and near-poor victims of unemployment, poverty, crop failures, or famine. But farmers in America were also beneficiaries.

In view of the great expansion of benefits, one may well wonder why so many people continue to leave the farm. The answer is not difficult. The key statistics can be seen in Table 4, which shows the distribution of farm support payments for 1987. Over 73 percent of the farms received only 19 percent of the direct government support payments. In contrast, over 55 percent of the payments went to only 13.7 percent of the farms. The farmers who have been abandoning agriculture have been overwhelmingly those with small farms. They have lit-

TABLE 3
U.S. Government Expenditure on Farm Programs, Fiscal Year 1988 (billions of dollars)

Program	Cost
Export enhancement program	1.0
Producers' storage payments	0.7
No-recourse loans	4.6
Deficiency payments under target price systems	4.0
Processing, storage, and transportation	1.1
Other	1.1
Total	12.5

Source: Agricultural Outlook, March 1989. Washington, D.C.: United States Dept. of Agriculture/Economic Research Service, 1989.

tle to sell. Another group leaving agriculture are those who have been producing unsupported crops, primarily fruits, vegetables, and other garden truck.

Since payments under most government programs are based mainly on what farmers sell, most gains go to the larger farms with large capital investments in land, machinery, and equipment. The operators of these farms rarely consider changing their occupation. True, there is a cap of $50,000 per year in target-price deficiency payments to a single farm, but this can be avoided by subdividing properties among family members.

People continue to leave agriculture in spite of large government expenditures because most of the government money goes to relatively large

---

TABLE 4
Farm Support Payments and Numbers of Farms, by Farm Size Class, 1987

Farm Size (annual sales in thousands of dollars)	Percent of Farms	Percent of Direct Government Support Payments
Under 40	73.1	19.0
40–100	13.2	25.5
100–250	9.2	31.4
250–500	3.2	16.2
500 and over	1.3	7.9

Source: Economic Indicators of the Farm Sector, National Financial Summary, 1987. Washington, D.C.: United States Department of Agriculture/Economic Research Service, October 1988.

TABLE 5
Losses and Gains from Farm Income Support Programs—Mid-1980s
(annual costs in billions of dollars)

Commodity	Consumer Loss	Taxpayer Cost	Producer Gain	Total Loss
Sugar	2.5 to 2.9		1.6 to 1.8	0.9 to 1.1
Milk	1.7 to 3.7	1.9	1.8 to 3.9	1.7 to 1.8
Wheat	0.1	3.2	2.1	1.2
Corn	0.5 to 0.6	3.0 to 4.1	2.1 to 2.5	1.5 to 2.1
Cotton		1.5	1.1	0.4
Rice	0.09	0.71	0.58	0.22
Peanuts	0.184		0.180	0.004
Oranges[a]	0.047 to 0.059		0.026 to 0.043	0.016 to 0.021
Total	5.12 to 7.63	10.31 to 11.41	9.49 to 12.20	5.94 to 6.85

a. California and Arizona navel oranges.
Source: Economic Report of the President, 1986, Table 4-4, p. 156.

---

farms whose operators rarely consider a different occupation. Farmers who operate small farms receive comparably small amounts of government money.

The analysis provided here can be usefully supplemented by intensive studies for particular crops and for smaller areas.[6] For eight important commodities, the Council of Economic Advisers (CEA) assembled and prepared estimates of gains and losses from farm programs as of the mid-1980s. We reproduce the CEA results as Table 5. In every case, the losses to consumers and/or taxpayers exceeded the gains to producers. When the beneficiaries of a policy (here, the farmers) gain less than the rest of society loses (here, consumers and taxpayers), economists speak of a "deadweight loss."

The CEA went on to present two proposals to reduce the losses to consumers and taxpayers, while maintaining benefits to farmers. Their basic idea was to break the link between benefits and production either by freezing benefits per acre or by basing them on past rather than on future produc-

6. A model study for Minnesota appeared in a Minneapolis newspaper and was attacked vigorously by representatives of farm organizations in the Minnesota countryside! See Mike Meyers, et al., "Propping Up the Farm," *Minneapolis Star and Tribune*, August 11–12, 1985.

tion. This reform was intended to reduce farmers' incentives to overproduction, while permitting prices to fall to free-market levels. Students with special interests in agricultural economics can profit by considering these proposals further.

In the 1980s, the losses to consumers and/or taxpayers from farm programs exceeded the gains to producers.

International Involvements

Other countries have farm programs of their own, all different from the American ones. Some, like the Common Agricultural Policy of the European Community (EC) are extremely complex, because of the desire to preserve "equity" among farmers in the different member countries. Because the agricultural exports of different countries compete on the world market and therefore sometimes influence each other's internal markets, trade conflicts are common even between political allies. Thus the major U.S. agricultural customer is Japan—which completely bans the import of rice and puts import restrictions on beef and citrus products. (Other Japanese rules discriminate by season; cherries, for example, are banned until July 1 of each year, to aid the earlier marketing of the domestic crop.) American-Canadian agricultural trade disagreements have centered on grains, potatoes, dairy products, and sugar.

In recent years, the main American agricultural-trade conflicts have been with the European Community. Because EC production controls must be allocated between and among so many countries in widely differing agricultural circumstances—some high-cost and some low-cost, some net exporters and others net importers—such controls are fewer than in the United States. Production goes flat out, and surpluses are proportionately much larger—"butter mountains," "wine lakes," and so on. The costs of accumulating and maintaining these mountains and lakes must also be allocated among member governments and their taxpayers. The temptation is greater than in the United States both to exclude competitive imports "unfairly" and to engage in export subsidies that force down world prices. (The United States claims it avoids export subsidies and takes world prices as given.) In 1985–86 the EC restricted imports of American grain and canned fruit. U.S. retaliations included penalties on the import of Italian *pasta* (allegedly made from export-subsidized wheat). This sort of sniping is nothing new, and it seems certain to continue. In 1988–89, another round was set off by an EC ban of hormone-treated U.S. beef exports, imposed ostensibly for reasons of health.

Because the agricultural exports of different countries compete on the world market and therefore sometimes influence each other's internal markets, trade conflicts are common even among political allies.

THE FARM DEBT PROBLEM

If you turn back to Table 2, you will see that U.S. farm acreage of crops harvested rose from 293 million in 1970 to 352 million in 1980. This was a 20 percent increase. The bulk of this increase was set off by a great expansion of U.S. agricultural exports to the Third World and the U.S.S.R. The expansion was encouraged by the U.S. government, which expected export demand to continue growing and hoped to avoid rises in domestic food prices. Encouragement took the form not only of propaganda but of easy credit in the inflation following the first oil shock (1973).

Farmers rushed to mortgage their land and houses, using the money to bring more land into cultivation. They also bought farm buildings, farm machinery, and livestock to increase their production per acre. When the export boom in fact subsided—partly because rival exporters also increased their outputs, and partly because the exchange value of the U.S. dollar rose in international markets—many of these borrowing farmers found themselves overextended and could not meet their obligations. Having followed the government "line" in getting into debt, resentful farmers naturally expected the government to bail them out after its forecasts had turned sour— which is to say, after farm prices turned down.

The farm debt crisis of the 1980s had its roots in the expansion of U.S. agricultural exports to the Third World and the U.S.S.R. in the 1970s. Farmers borrowed heavily to increase their production and when the export boom subsided, many found themselves overextended and could not meet their obligations.

Making matters worse for the farm debtors, the end of the export boom coincided with a shift to disinflation (falling inflation rates) in domestic monetary policy. This hurt farmers by decreasing the market value of the real-estate collateral for their loans. Land prices fell because so much of the demand for rural real estate had been for an inflation hedge related only indirectly to real agricultural productivity.

Total farm debt in 1985 was estimated at $188 billion—more than the international debts of Brazil and Mexico combined at that time. Preliminary data for 1988 showed a reduction to $160 billion, after a period of "wringing-out" through mortgage foreclosures and write-offs of uncollectible obligations. The seriousness of the problem to the debtor farmers was summarized by the Council of Economic Advisers as follows:

A succinct indicator of U.S. agriculture's financial problem is its debt/asset ratio. This ratio fell in the early 1970s, but in 1974 [it] again started to rise. In the 1980s [it] jumped to levels unseen since the Great Depression. A major reason was the erosion of land and machinery values. Land values fell an average of 19 percent between 1981 and 1985.

Financial problems are concentrated in the regions with the largest land-value declines; i.e., the Corn Belt, the Lake States, and the Northern Plains. Roughly 60 percent of farms classified as financially distressed by the U.S. Department of Agriculture (USDA) was in these regions; a farm is considered financially distressed if its debt/asset ratio exceeds 40 percent and it cannot generate enough cash income to pay its bills. About 12½ percent of all farms were in this category on January 1, 1985.[7]

In terms of farm size (as measured by crop value), financial distress was concentrated in the $40,000 to $250,000 categories. These medium-large farms accounted for 25 percent of the total number, produced 41 percent of gross farm income, and included 51 percent of the financially distressed farms, as shown in Table 6. The smaller farms were in most cases unwilling or unable to overborrow; the largest ones were more nearly able to finance their debt burdens.

Under these circumstances it was natural to argue that any reform in the existing price-support systems would endanger those farmers who were under the greatest financial stress—those in danger of being forced off the farm entirely or reduced to tenancy status on their own farms. The existing support systems were not well adapted to meeting the debt crisis, since the largest support payments went to the farms that produce the most. As Table 6 shows, these were in a less difficult position than somewhat smaller farms. Another way of looking at the situation is that farms in financial distress (as defined by USDA) received only 24 percent of direct government payments. Of these, the most distressed received slightly less than half (11 percent). The great bulk of government payments went to American farms that were not in a distressed position.

7. Running quotation from *Economic Report of the President, 1986*, pp. 132–133.

TABLE 6
Financially Distressed Farms by Sales Class, January 1985

Farm Sales Class (in thousands of dollars)	Percentage of Farms in Financial Distress
Less than 10	15
10–20	9
20–40	15
40–100	29
100–250	22
250–500	7
Over 500	3

Source: Economic Report of the President, 1986, Chart 4-1, p. 134.

The price-support system was not well adapted to meeting the debt crisis of the 1980s since the largest support payments went to the farms that produced the most.

THE AMERICAN AGRICULTURAL FUTURE

Farming in America has long been the butt of economic humor. Because land values have often been rising while farm incomes are low, it has been said that "farming is a way to live poor and die rich" or that farming is "a losing proposition financed by the profits from land speculation." Conventional views about the future of American agriculture include the following extensions of historical trends: (1) that the number of farms and farmers will continue to fall, (2) that the average size of farms will continue to rise, (3) that the proportion of farm families who rent part or all of their land from others will continue to rise, and (4) that the average measured income of farmers will continue to lag behind the measured income of nonfarmers. All of these conventional views may be correct, but they are often misinterpreted. Many demographic, technical, and economic factors work to modify them.

Conventional predictions about the future of American agriculture include: (1) the number of farms and farmers will continue to fall; (2) the average size of farms will continue to rise; (3) the proportion of farm families who rent part or all of their land from others will continue to rise; and (4) the average measured income of farmers will continue to lag behind that of nonfarmers. These trends, however, may be modified by other demographic, technological, and economic factors.

Misinterpreting Trends

Lower relative farm incomes need not mean lower relative incomes for families living on farms, because the multiple-earner family has come to the country. The farm husband, or wife, or young adult child, or semiretired parent can now commute for part-time or full-time work off the farm, as factory and office jobs move away from urban centers. More than most other kinds of work, farming can become and is becoming a part-time or part-family business, and farm families remain larger than nonfarm families.

Larger farms, higher land prices (if the 1945–1980 trend resumes), and more farm tenancy need not doom the family farm, lead to "corporate farming," or turn the farmer into a peasant. It is true that corporate farms and farm management companies are no longer novelties and will remain with us. This trend will become even stronger if nonfarmers continue to use investment in farmland as a hedge against inflation and if the "urban sprawl" of growing suburbs raises the price of land near cities. But there is little reason to expect corporate farming and farm management companies to replace the family farm. What is more likely is that the representative head of the farm family will be both wealthier and more highly trained than his or her parents or grandparents were. As to farm tenancy, many tenant farmers are young people in the process of buying some or all of the land they work, and many farm landlords are retired farmers.

More than most other kinds of occupations, farming is becoming a part-time or part-family business. It is likely that the representative head of a farm family will be both wealthier and more highly trained than his or her parents or grandparents.

Demographic, Technological, and Economic Factors

In the generation following the end of World War II, the so-called "population explosion," especially in developing countries, sharply raised world demand for American grains and other farm products. It is hard to predict how fast world population will grow in the future and to what extent that growth will mean increases in the commercial demand for American farm products. Since so many of these countries and people are poor, much of their demand has, in the past, been met on a relief rather than a commercial basis.

Technological advances in grain production (such as the Green Revolution, which we shall discuss later in this chapter) may continue to raise the capability of the growing populations in tropical and semitropical countries to feed themselves or even to export grain in competition with American farmers. Other technological revolutions, from the cotton picker to oleomargarine and the "square tomato," may affect other crops. An example is the hydroponic raising of vegetables on chemicals and water (without soil). This technology has been known for at least a generation and is becoming increasingly feasible economically.

Finally, the amount of freedom present in international trade will affect the size of the market for U.S. farm products. But here the picture depends on which farm crop we are talking about. On the one hand, Soviet purchases of American grain are important. So American farmers objected strongly to the export limitation imposed in protest against the Soviet invasion of Afghanistan in 1979. On the other hand freer trade would hurt American dairy farmers, potato farmers, producers of cane and beet sugar, and cattle ranchers. It would mean that more Canadian dairy products and potatoes, more Latin American and Philippine sugar, and more Argentine and Australian meat and wool would be supplied to the American market, causing downward pressure on their prices.

Technological changes and shifting world trade patterns will increase the demand for some American farm products, but will reduce the demand for others.

FOOD AND POVERTY

For the rest of this chapter, we move from the American to the world economy and from relative prosperity to threatening poverty. To mark this change, our section heading is part of the title of a pessimistic study of the world food problem by the Indian economist Radha Prasad Sinha.[8]

We have never had, and still do not have, any accurate count of world population, let alone an accurate forecast of its future course. (Imagine sending census takers into the middle of the Sahara Desert or into the Amazon jungles or up the Himalayas!) But reasonable estimates, such as those presented in Table 7, suggest that world population has increased rapidly so far in the twentieth century and that it is expected to increase still more rapidly in the remaining years before 2000. It is now estimated that the increase in world population during the first 85 years of this century was some 70 percent greater than all the previous increase from the beginning of the human race to the year 1900. World population in 1985 was almost three times greater than in 1900. Despite the apparent spread of various forms of birth control, the world population growth rate seems to be accelerating, thanks mainly to falling infant mortality rates and adult death rates from communicable and

8. Radha Prasad Sinha, *Food and Poverty: The Political Economy of Confrontation* (London: Croom Helm, 1976).

TABLE 7
World Population Estimates and Forecasts for the Twentieth Century

World population, 1900	1,620 million
World population, 1985	4,837 million
World population, 2000	6,121 million
Annual increase rate, 1900–1985	1.30 percent
Annual increase rate, 1985–2000	1.58 percent
Annual increase rate, 1900–2000	1.34 percent

Source: David Barrett, ed., *World Christian Encyclopedia* (Nairobi, Kenya: Oxford University Press, 1982). Used by permission. United Nations Educational, Scientific and Cultural Organization, *Statistical Yearbook 1988* (Paris: UNESCO, 1988), Tables 1.1 and 1.2.

epidemic diseases. These bald figures, estimates, and forecasts raise very important questions. How can all these people be fed? What will happen if they are not fed? The major contemporary danger is concentrated in the twenty-odd countries of sub-Saharan Africa, particularly those of East Africa.

In his famous *Essay on Population*, which appeared in 1798, the British economist Thomas Malthus predicted that limitations on the food supply would operate to limit population growth. He wrote of "positive checks," such as war, famine, and pestilence, as placing natural limits on population growth. Indeed, it does appear that such checks may have slowed the growth of world population, at least until the start of this century.

The world population growth rate seems to be accelerating, leading to concern about providing adequate food.

The Greenhouse Effect

In the spring, summer, and early fall of 1988, the United States experienced its worst drought in a generation. Nature struck back after decades of concern about allegedly chronic farm surpluses in North America. The drought of 1988 in the United States and Canada coincided with droughts in China and Western Europe and with severe flooding in South Asia—notably Bangladesh. These episodes show that, after more than two centuries of advances in technology, observation, and forecasting, agriculture remains fundamentally dependent on nature and vulnerable to its supply shocks. These shocks may be more than random, as we shall see.

The poor American yields of grain and livestock in 1988 caused increases in American food prices in 1988 and 1989, despite the overhang of surpluses from prior years. They did not, however, cause important increases in American malnutrition, let alone famine. On those farms whose yields were lowered severely, sometimes to zero, the drought would, in the absence of government relief, often have meant financial ruin. However, since some farm prices were rising to target levels, government spending for the aid of distressed farmers could be financed partially from lower expenditures on price-support programs—a small silver lining on a large black cloud. But a multiyear drought like that of the mid-1930s in the United States —the "dust bowl years"—could again be a major disaster both to consumers and to farmers, and possibly a disaster of worldwide proportions.

Under the head of the **greenhouse effect,** just such a longer-term worldwide disaster is anticipated for the twenty-first century by many climatologists and other earth scientists. If they are right, many or even most years of that century will be like 1988, with some even worse as the century progresses.

The greenhouse effect is a continuation or acceleration of a long-term heating of the earth's atmosphere. This heating trend may have been going on imperceptibly for as long as 100 or 150 years. Its principal cause is supposedly the increasing emission of such gases as carbon dioxide and methane. These emissions arise from the burning of fossil fuels such as coal and petroleum. They trap or absorb solar heat to a greater extent than natural nitrogen and oxygen compounds do, while reflecting less heat back into space. A second cause of the greenhouse phenomenon may be the wholesale cutting of the world's forests, first in temperate zones like Europe and North America and more recently in the tropical zones of the Third World. The dense foliage of these forests recycles carbon dioxide back into oxygen by the biochemical process of photosynthesis to a greater extent than garden vegetables, lawns, or field crops do—to say nothing of houses, factories, and office buildings.

Agricultural production is threatened by the predicted consequences of the greenhouse effect—the long-term heating of the earth's atmosphere brought on by emissions of such gases as carbon dioxide and methane and the destruction of the world's forests.

The greenhouse effect, if it is indeed occurring, is also melting the fringes of the two polar ice caps. This melting increases the volume of water in the ocean and threatens seacoast cities. It also promotes greater rainfall. How such effects will balance the dehydration caused by the heating trend is a question whose answer varies from one area to the next. Earth scientists use computer models to estimate what these balances may be. Most such models suggest increasingly unfavorable effects for both North America and the planet as a whole. That is, they forecast desertification of part of the American and Canadian breadbaskets, outweighing any conversion of bogs and marshes into fertile agricultural areas anywhere in the world.

Earth scientists forecast desertification of part of the American and Canadian breadbaskets, leading to the prospect of worldwide famine.

Is all this unduly alarmist? Economists lack competence, let alone expertise, in the earth sciences. They can do little more than explore the implications of the earth scientists' findings, without attempting to referee or arbitrate differences of opinion among these specialists. They can, of course, point out that the greenhouse effect is still a theory, and a theory accepted less universally than, say, the theory of eventual cooling of the sun itself over the much more distant future. While awaiting a possible resolution of the disagreements between greenhousers and antigreenhousers, what can economists do?

Even though economics has been called "the

dismal science," most economists continue to hope that the grimmer forecasts of global famine, based on both population explosion and greenhouse effects, are overdone. We shall describe four scenarios that offer hope that such famine can be postponed for at least another century, if not indefinitely.

Biotechnology

One scenario points to continuing or accelerated advances in agricultural productivity—in other words, technological "fixes" of many kinds, large and small, which Julian Simon and other writers trace largely to population growth itself.[9] Simon believes that the more people there are, the greater is the long-term likelihood of technological innovations and advances, even in the absence of higher education in any formal sense. So far, these advances have kept total food production per person rising steadily in spite of the twentieth-century population explosion. Some of the technological fixes may be new products, from chemical "food pills" to edible algae or bacteria. More likely are better methods of growing present crops or improving varieties of our present crops. More multiple cropping or better blight resistance, for example, could lead to larger farm yields, and new means of controlling weather, rodents, and insects during harvests or in storage could lead to smaller losses.

Expanded populations may act as a stimulus to advances in technology that ease food shortages.

The Green Revolution

To date, the most ambitious technological fix to make the desert blossom like the farms of Iowa has been called the **Green Revolution.** This consists of the development and propagation of high-yielding dwarf and hybrid varieties of both wheat and rice. Though it has not yet fulfilled the high hopes

9. Julian Simon, *The Ultimate Resource* (Princeton, N.J.: Princeton University Press, 1981).

generated for it in the 1960s, it may not yet have received a fair test.

The new varieties of crops are greatly dependent on modern inputs, mainly chemical fertilizers and pesticides. These in turn are feasible only in areas with both assured water supplies and little danger of flooding. Even in such areas, there is concern about the possible environmental effects of these chemicals in the long run. Also, successfully raising the new crops calls for increases in agricultural credit, which in many less developed countries is available at reasonable rates only to the large farms.

"As a result," says Professor Sinha with reference to Indian conditions, "the main advantage of the new technology accrued to the rich farmers or to regions which already had adequate factor endowments. . . . Undoubtedly, it was the large and medium farmers who were the main beneficiaries of the 'Green Revolution' in India. Some of these farms bought tractors and other agricultural machinery, which may have had some labour-displacing effect."[10]

To put matters more bluntly, the Green Revolution had the unintended side effect of turning many owners of small farms and tenants into landless laborers, since they could not obtain the credit they needed to use the new techniques and therefore sold their rights to their richer neighbors. Some, indeed, seem to have left the land entirely, or been driven from it like the Okies and Arkies in *The Grapes of Wrath*.

The Green Revolution consists of the development and propagation of high-yielding dwarf and hybrid varieties of wheat and rice.

Family Planning

Drastic reductions in world birthrates offer another possible way to solve the problems of food and poverty. In addressing the United Nations on October 4, 1965, Pope Paul VI said, "You must strive to multiply bread so that it suffices for the tables of mankind." After calling for this multiplication of

10. Sinha, p. 32.

bread, the Pope restated the traditional view of the Roman Catholic Church, opposing any "artificial control of birth, which would be irrational, in order to diminish the number of guests at the banquet of life." So far, much of the world seems to be following his advice. However, resistance to family planning is due only in part to the influence of Catholicism and other natalist religions. Certain social and economic considerations also play an important part.

In poor countries with traditionally high infant mortality rates, poor educational systems, and few facilities for the care of needy older people, children are their parents' social security; the more, the better. Children can work from early ages, either for their own families or for outside employers. There is little or no opportunity for a tradeoff between having many "low-quality" (unskilled, uneducated, and undernourished) children and fewer "higher-quality" (skilled, educated, and healthy) ones. Supporting these economic facts of life are social attitudes. A man who has fathered more children is believed to be sexually superior to a man who has fathered fewer children, and a woman who has borne more children is similarly thought to be superior to a woman who has borne fewer children.

But when economic growth does take place, birthrates soon fall, whether or not the people adhere to natalist religions or philosophies. The demographic records of the Western world, of Japan, and more recently of Taiwan and South Korea, show that both birthrates and (with a lag) population growth rates generally fall as medical and public health techniques improve and as per capita income rises, especially when modernization also includes mass education and social security institutions. The People's Republic of China is another, much larger example, but the Chinese government has used unusually harsh methods—the so-called "one-child policy"—to bring this about. The lag in the population figures is due to the rising life expectancy of adults and the gradual aging of the population as a whole. However, doubt remains as to whether economic growth will in fact take place in enough less developed countries to lower the population growth rates in time to keep the Third World malnutrition rate from rising as rapidly as the pessimists fear.

Demographic records show that birth rates and population growth rates gradually fall as per capita incomes rise, especially when accompanied by mass education and social security institutions.

Income Redistribution

A middle-class American today consumes nearly twice as many nutrients per day as the average person in a less developed country. Average energy and protein supplies are shown in Table 8. Redistribution of income would mean that less land would be used for raising luxury foods, particularly meat, and nonfood "crops" like flowers and tobacco, lawns, and golf courses. More land would be used for raising grains, vegetables, fruit, eggs, and dairy products.

Food First is the title of a book by two American writers, Frances Moore Lappé and Joseph Collins.[11] This book calls for both income redistribution and a restructuring of productive activity in the direction of food for the world's poor. It makes the following main arguments:

1. A concentration of land use and agricultural production on a basically vegetarian diet along with eggs, dairy products, and some fish, would allow "Spaceship Earth" to support 10 billion people free from famine and major malnutrition. This number would be nearly twice the present world population.

2. Given the present international distributions of income and wealth, neither technological fixes nor population restriction will prevent a future wave of malnutrition for the world's poor.

3. The redistribution needed for a "Food First" policy can come about only after a major revolution or similar confrontation between rich and poor people and between rich and poor nations. (The Sinha study comes to similar conclusions.)

Certain clear but insoluble *normative* questions are raised in connection with any Food First program. One might ask, for example, how important

11. Frances Moore Lappé and Joseph Collins, *Food First: Beyond the Myth of Scarcity* (New York: Ballantine Books, 1979).

TABLE 8
Average Energy and Protein Supply, by Region

Region	Energy (calories per person per day)	Protein (grams per person per day)
World	2,480	69.0
Developed countries	3,150	96.4
(North America)	(3,320)	(105.2)
(Western Europe)	(3,130)	(93.7)
Developing countries	2,200	57.4
(Latin America)	(2,530)	(65.0)
(Africa)	(2,190)	(58.4)
(Far East)	(2,080)	(50.7)

Source: Radha Prasad Sinha, *Food and Poverty: The Political Economy of Confrontation* (London: Croom Helm, 1976), Table 2. Used with permission.

the goal of alleviating hunger among the world's poor is, compared with the prospective living standards of the world's rich and middle classes.[12] Also, one may ask about the effect (perhaps positive) on consumers, both rich and poor, of shifting land to the Food First system and having less of certain industrial products, like rubber and wool, which are now produced on these lands. Remember that the consumer does not live by bread alone.

However, the three Food First propositions are stated in a positive rather than a normative way. For the sake of discussion, let us assume that the first and the third are true—that many more people could be supported at a poor person's living level than at a rich person's living level (given the amount and quality of the world's agricultural land) and that a major redistribution would require confrontation if not actual revolution. The second statement, however, needs further explanation. Why can't technological fixes and lower birthrates solve food problems and bring down real food prices as readily as redistribution and Food First?

In answering this question, the main point is that both technical fixes and lower birthrates act slowly and differentially. That is, they benefit some people much more immediately and completely than they benefit the mass of the population. As

12. During World War II, Secretary of Agriculture Henry A. Wallace was ridiculed for "globaloney" and "milk for Hottentots" even though his food-sharing proposals were mild compared with those in the Food First program.

you may recall, higher- and middle-income Indian farmers benefited more immediately than the rest of the Indian people in the Green Revolution case. This may mean that beneficiary groups will react by enlarging and improving their diets in the direction of the diets presently followed by high-income people and high-income countries. That is, they may eat more meat, fish, eggs, and sugar. As the ill-fated Marie Antoinette suggested, they may eat cake, pie, or pastry instead of bread, rice, or potatoes. They may also consume more coffee, tea, cola, tobacco, and alcohol. Not that there is anything immoral about luxuries, but their production may shift land at the margin away from the staples eaten by the poor. These marginal substitution processes may be so rapid and strong as to outweigh the expected effects of technical fixes and lower population growth rates themselves on the diets of the remaining poor. The poor may become a somewhat smaller proportion of the population and they may become fewer in number, but their misery, alienation, and susceptibility to violence would be no less.

The "food first" proposal advocates a worldwide redistribution of income and a change from luxury foods and sundries to a basic diet of vegetables, eggs, dairy products, and some fish.

Economics in Focus

Food Security

Although the General Agreement on Tariffs and Trade (GATT) was established in 1947, it was not until 1988 that the delegates directly faced the delicate issue of farm-support policies. In the interests of free trade, the United States boldly proposed a ten-year phaseout of agricultural supports worldwide. The Cairns Group (a coalition led by Canada, Australia, and New Zealand) offered a similar program. But these reforms were blocked by bitter opposition from the European Community.

One common argument for farm subsidies invokes national security. Can a country feel safe if it depends on basic food imports from other nations? The Japanese, for example, exclude foreign rice on the principle that Japan should remain self-sufficient in that staple. Japanese officials remember the 1973 U.S. embargo on soybean exports, and they do not want to be caught in a similar bind with rice. Even though the ban on rice imports costs Japanese consumers an estimated $28 billion annually, officials believe the gain in food security is worth the price.

In some cases domestic food production also helps to sustain a nation's self-image or sense of character. Again, rice in Japan serves as an example. Many Japanese feel that if their country did not grow its own rice, a critical part of the national spirit would be lost.

Opponents of agricultural supports begin by pointing out the huge price tag for consumers. They go on to demonstrate that the benefits of farm subsidies most often accrue to those who least need them—large rather than small growers. In addition, the critics argue, farm supports reduce crop diversification. In the United States the rational farmer tends to grow supported commodities such as wheat and soybeans rather than the hundred other crops that do not receive government support. Thus large numbers of farmers produce an excess of a few crops.

According to many experts, subsidies also encourage a quick-profit mentality that results in poor soil-conservation practices, wasteful use of limited water supplies, and widespread pollution from pesticides and other chemicals. Finally, farm-support critics note the ironic fact that the Soviet Union has been a principal beneficiary of Western farm subsidies. The Soviets can buy Western grain so cheaply that they donate it to poorer nations, winning the moral credit for themselves. Does this, skeptics ask, bolster our national security?

The remedy proposed at the 1988 GATT talks involved "decoupling" farm-income supports from production. In other words, needy farmers would be given direct aid unrelated to the crops they grew. The aid could be linked with programs to improve the rural environment. Despite their traditional aversion to welfare concepts, many U.S. farmers support this new approach.

Sources: "False Security," *The Economist*, December 17, 1988, p. 71; Barbara Rudolph, "Bitter Standoff in Montreal," *Time*, December 19, 1988, p. 58; Carlisle Ford Runge, "The Assault on Agricultural Protectionism," *Foreign Affairs*, Fall 1988, pp. 133–150; Robert J. Shapiro, "A Battle Royal over Food," *U.S. News & World Report*, May 23, 1988, pp. 56–57; James Bovard, "The Agricultural Swamp," *National Review*, February 10, 1989, pp. 46–48; Rahul Jacob, "Export Barriers the U.S. Hates Most," *Fortune*, February 27, 1989, pp. 88–89; Robert Kuttner, "Economic Nationalism," *The New Republic*, November 21, 1988, pp. 19–22.

SUMMARY

1. Farm discontent is a recurring theme in U.S. history. An especially widespread protest movement, called Populism, arose during the period between the American Civil War and the turn of the century. (See pages 872–873.)

2. Part of the farmers' dissatisfaction arises from the belief that they must sell their produce for what it will bring on competitive markets, while the prices of many goods and services that farmers buy are monopolized, cartelized, or otherwise controlled by nonfarm people who have the ability to exploit their positions. (See page 873.)

3. Among the "exploiters" cited by farmers in their protest movements have been the suppliers of credit (bankers), the railroads and truck lines, the operators of grain elevators and other storage facilities, the sellers of agricultural implements and fertilizer, and general merchants in rural towns. (See pages 873–874.)

4. Another set of problems for farmers arises from the price and income inelasticities of demand for their products. Price inelasticity means that large crops may mean low income. Income inelasticity means that the quantity of farm products demanded does not keep up with other products when consumers' incomes rise. (See page 874.)

5. Farmers also complain that farmland prices are too high to permit a young person to establish a family farm early in life, and at the same time that these prices are too low to justify the property and estate taxes on farm owners and their families. (See page 874.)

6. One response from farmers has been agricultural fundamentalism, the doctrine that, since food is essential to life, farmers should be at least as well off as others in the population. Depressions are allegedy "farm led and farm fed." (See page 875.)

7. Farmers have reacted to their grievances, and to technological changes that made them more acute, by leaving the farm, by political agitation, and by forming farmers' cooperatives. (See pages 875–876).

8. The principal benefit gained by political agitation in the United States is a system of farm price supports, based on a concept of parity for farm prices and incomes. The price-support system uses the device of the no-recourse loan to permit farmers to hold crops off the market while awaiting higher prices, without market risk if prices fall. (See pages 877–878).

9. The American price-support system usually involves government purchase of surpluses or buffer stocks and raises prices and gross incomes of farmers at the expense of both consumers and taxpayers. When price supports are combined with production restrictions, the burden on taxpayers is less than it would otherwise be. (See pages 879–880.)

10. Under the target-price system, farmers are compensated at taxpayer expense by the receipt of deficiency payments per unit of farm output. (See page 880.)

11. It is estimated that the cost of U.S. farm income support programs to consumers and taxpayers far exceeds the gains to producers. (See pages 882–883.)

12. Government farm support programs result in conflict with other countries when these programs lower the prices of products exchanged in international trade. (See pages 883–884.)

13. Indebtedness of U.S. farmers reached unprecedentedly high levels in the 1980s because of declines in farm exports and farm real estate values. Farm income-support programs were poorly suited to meeting this problem. (See pages 884–885.)

14. The future of American agriculture depends on a variety of demographic, technological, and economic factors. Much depends on the freedom of international trade and on population trends in the world. (See pages 885–887.)

15. The two main causes of pessimism about the future of world agriculture and the world nutrition level have been the population explosion and the greenhouse effect. The first of these is a continuance or acceleration of world population growth. The second is a gradual heating of the planet brought on by emissions of gases into the atmosphere and the clearing of forested areas. (See pages 887–889.)

16. The main remedies proposed for the threat of world malnutrition have been continued or accelerated technological improvements in agriculture, declining population growth, and the redistribution of world income and wealth. The Green

Revolution in the production of wheat and rice has been a promising technological development in world agriculture. (See pages 887–889.)

17. Many countries, including both developed countries and newly industrializing ones, have in fact lowered their reproduction and population growth rates. (See pages 889–890.)

18. The planet could support a much larger population than the present one if agricultural land were shifted from its present uses to the growing of staple foods. (See page 890.)

19. Worldwide income and wealth redistribution may reduce malnutrition and the threat of famine in the world. However, it could be at the expense of a considerable decline in the living standards of people who are not poor. Therefore, any significant redistribution or equalization of world income and wealth might require revolution or similar confrontation. (See pages 890–981.)

KEY TERMS

agricultural fundamentalism: the doctrine that, since food is necessary to life, farmers should be at least as well off as any other group (page 875).

buffer stocks: *see* **ever-normal granary.**

deficiency payment: a payment received by a farmer from the government for each unit of output produced and sold; it is based on the difference between a target price and the support price (page 880).

Engels' Law: the tendency for the percentage of a family's budget spent for food to decline as income rises (page 874).

ever-normal granary: government holdings of crops as reserves against periods of bad weather or other disasters at home or abroad (page 879).

farm parity: the relationship between the income of farmers and the income of others in the society (page 878).

greenhouse effect: an acceleration of a long-term heating of the earth's atmosphere caused primarily by the burning of fossil fuels and the wholesale cutting of the world's forests (page 888).

Green Revolution: the development and propagation of high-yielding dwarf and hybrid varieties of wheat and rice (page 889).

market price: the price that would prevail in the absence of government programs and that would involve only negligible surpluses resulting from speculation on next year's higher prices (page 879).

no-recourse loans: a system whereby farmers borrow from a government agency and, as collateral for the loan, pledge their crop evaluated at the support price. The lending agency has no claim beyond the pledged crop (page 879).

parity price: a price that bears the same relation to some index of farm production costs that it did in some past period (page 878).

Populism: a late-nineteenth-century protest movement that became the basis for two political parties that wanted the government to increase the money supply by printing more greenbacks (page 872).

support price: the price at which government agencies buy and store crop surpluses (page 879).

target price: a price higher than the support price that is the basis for calculating deficiency payments to farmers (page 879).

DISCUSSION QUESTIONS

1. What was "Populism"? Briefly describe how government monetary policies played a role in this movement. Why have farmers often prospered during wartimes but suffered hard times after the war was over?

2. Explain how both price and income inelasticities of demand for farm products have caused problems for farmers. How does price inelasticity of demand play a role in making government price support programs attractive for farmers? How do consumers fare under these programs?

3. Discuss the belief that American recessions and depressions are "farm led and farm fed."

4. Farm prices are systematically lower at harvest time than six or eight months later, other things being equal. Does the differential indicate exploitation of farmers by speculators on the commodity exchanges? Explain your answer.

5. Explain how the target-price system differs from the procedures under price-support plans.

6. Do you believe that farmers who faced a debt crisis in the 1980s were entitled to help from the government? Why or why not? In what way were existing farm income-support programs poorly suited to helping farmers facing a debt crisis?

7. In your opinion, is the world facing a major food crisis? Why or why not?

8. What is the greenhouse effect? How may it affect the future of American agriculture and the world level of nutrition?

9. Church, campus, and other socially conscious groups stage campaigns during which participants either fast or limit themselves to the diets of Asian or African peasants. Money saved by this frugality is sent to poor countries for food purchases. What good, if any, do you think is done by these campaigns?

10. It is forecasted that meat will become a much less important element in our diets during future years. What is the argument in back of such forecasts? Do you agree?

11. Should controls be enacted to limit the use of farmland for housing, factories, or other nonagricultural uses? Defend your answer.

12. Should American agriculture shift from nonfood cash crops to a Food First policy? Why or why not? Should Mexican agriculture make this shift? Why or why not?

38

Natural Resources and the Environment

Preview Your training in microeconomics can be helpful in understanding many issues relating to the conservation of natural resources and care of the environment. This chapter considers three such issues—the conservation of exhaustible resources such as petroleum or mineral deposits, the management of renewable resources such as wildlife or forests, and the protection of the environment from excessive pollution.

The first section of the chapter, on exhaustible resources, shows how the market system contains certain built-in features that control the depletion of these resources. It shows how production costs and interest rates help determine how rapidly known deposits of these resources are used. It also explains how markets may fail to control the use of these resources efficiently and thus invite intervention by government.

The second part of the chapter focuses on renewable resources, such as wildlife and trees in the forest. Microeconomic analysis provides useful guidelines for the efficient use and propagation of these resources. It also explains how treating these resources as common property can result in an inefficiently small amount for future generations.

The last section of the chapter applies economic analysis to the relationship between the quality of the environment and the disposal of waste generated by production and consumption. It explains how pricing mechanisms can be used to prevent excessive generation and dumping of waste. It also notes some of the problems that arise in using these pricing mechanisms and discusses how government controls may be used or misused in regulating environmental quality.

EXHAUSTIBLE NATURAL RESOURCES

Exhaustible natural resources are those whose stock cannot be replenished. What was used by past generations is not available today and what is used today will not be available to future generations. Crude petroleum is an exhaustible natural resource. The petroleum that exists today is the result of eons of time in the earth's evolution, during which the earth received energy from the sun and various forms of life grew, died, and decayed. In this sense, even now oil pools and new coalfields are being formed. Realistically, however, the time required for these changes to take place is so great that the process is irrelevant from the human point of view. For the people living today, or even for all of humanity, past, present, and, presumably, future, the stock of exhaustible natural resources cannot be increased.

Exhaustible natural resources should be clearly distinguished from **nonexhaustible natural resources,** such as energy from the sun, from winds, or from tides. Since the earth receives a continuing flow of these resources from the sun and from gravitational forces, there is no conservation problem. The economic questions for exhaustible resources are fundamentally different from those for nonexhaustible resources. For exhaustible resources, the overriding economic question is how rapidly the existing stock of these resources should be used.

Exhaustible natural resources are those whose stock cannot be replenished. The overriding question for exhaustible resources, unlike nonexhaustible resources, such as energy from the sun, the winds, or the tides, is how rapidly the existing stock of these resources should be used.

In the market system, there are certain mechanisms that regulate the rate at which exhaustible resources are used. This should not be surprising if you remember that the rate of use, per unit of time, is the variable that customarily appears on the horizontal axis of supply and demand graphs. The very first graph that you studied (in Chapter 3) showed,

on the horizontal axis, the number of hours that coal miners worked *per week*. That is a rate of use per unit of time. In Chapter 5 you studied the quantity of jeans demanded and supplied *per year*, and so on. These flows per unit of time are an easy starting place for our study of conservation. Figure 1 shows supply and demand for an exhaustible natural resource. Moving to the right along the horizontal axis means that the rate of use is increased and that the quantity of the resource that remains for future generations is diminishing rapidly. Moving to the left along this axis means that the rate of use is decreased so that the quantity remaining for future generations is diminishing less rapidly. As you know, these moves along the quantity axis take place because of shifts in demand and/or supply curves, which change the equilibrium point identified by their intersection.

In the market system there are certain mechanisms that regulate the rate at which exhaustible resources are used.

The Supply Curve of Exhaustible Resources

The supply curve shows the willingness of resource owners to extract the resource from its natural state and offer it for sale. For this reason, we are especially interested in forces that can shift the supply curve. In Figure 1, supply curves show how the quantity extracted from the earth and offered for sale depends on the market price of the natural resource. Extracting and selling the resource is more profitable at higher prices than at lower prices, other things being equal. Therefore, economic analysis leads us to expect that firms will respond to higher prices by increasing the rate of extraction of the resource.

The supply curve shows the willingness of resource owners to extract the resource from its natural state and offer it for sale.

As you have learned from your study of microeconomics, the supply curve may shift when the

FIGURE 1
Shifting the Supply Curve of an Exhaustible Natural Resource

Supply curve S_1 reflects the cost of extracting a resource when easily accessible deposits are being used. Equilibrium is at A, with price P_1 and quantity Q_1. As easily accessible deposits of the resource are used up, so that supply must come from more expensive sources, the supply curve shifts to S_2. Equilibrium is now at B, with price P_2 and quantity Q_2. As more and more of the relatively accessible deposits of the resource are used up, supply continues to shift to the left, and, other things being equal, equilibrium quantities extracted decrease.

ceteris paribus assumption is relaxed and some variable other than the price of the product or resource changes. In analyzing the supply of an exhaustible natural resource, the *accessibility* of deposits of the resource is a very important variable that can cause a shift of the supply curve. In terms of accessibility, firms engaged in mining coal or iron ore or in pumping crude oil usually start by extracting the deposits that are the easiest to get, since, at any given price, extracting and selling them generally brings the largest profit. In fact, if a firm holds title to a deposit that is difficult or costly to extract, it may simply be unprofitable to extract and sell the coal or oil in competition with supplies from firms that are using deposits that are easier and cheaper to extract. In such cases, the going price in the market will not be high enough to cover the costs of extracting the less-accessible deposit. So these

deposits will not be brought to the market until the more-accessible ones have been used up or until new technologies lower the cost of extraction.

The accessibility of deposits of an exhaustible resource is a very important variable that can cause a shift of the supply curve.

As easily accessible deposits of a resource are exhausted and supply must come from more expensive sources, the market-supply curve will shift to the left. Figure 1 shows what happens in this case. The supply curve S_1 reflects the costs of extracting the resource when easily accessible deposits are being used. It slopes upward because, even with easily available deposits, suppliers are willing to supply more at higher prices than at lower prices. While easily accessible deposits are available, equilibrium is at point A, with price P_1 and quantity Q_1 demanded and supplied per year. But as the easily accessible deposits are used up, so that supply must come from more costly sources, the supply curve shifts to S_2 and equilibrium is at point B, with price P_2 and quantity Q_2 demanded and supplied each year. As more and more of the relatively accessible deposits of the resource are used up, other things being equal, the supply curve shifts still farther to the left. The price climbs and the amount of the resource that is used each year falls. The market system of conservation is acting to prevent sudden exhaustion of the resource.

As easily accessible deposits of a resource are exhausted and supply must come from more expensive sources, the market-supply curve will shift to the left.

As more and more of the relatively accessible deposits of the resource are used up, the supply curve shifts still farther to the left. The price climbs and the amount of resource that is used each year falls. The market system of conservation is acting to prevent sudden exhaustion of the resource.

The accessibility of deposits of an exhaustible natural resource is not the only variable that can shift the supply curve in Figure 1. Changes in the technology of extracting the resource can have powerful effects on the location of the curve. Technological advances that lower costs of extraction shift the supply curve to the right. In this case, the price to consumers may not rise as the more accessible deposits are used up. The rate of use of the resource may not decrease. It is possible that the effect of technological advances in extracting the resource can exceed the price-increasing tendency of the exhaustion of easily accessible deposits. Therefore, we should not conclude that the market price of an exhaustible resource will necessarily increase just because the more accessible deposits have been used up. Sometimes, advances in technology lead to the discovery of previously unknown deposits of the resource itself. This also can shift the supply curve to the right and lower the price of the resource.

Other variables besides accessibility can shift the supply curve of an exhaustible resource. The effect of technological advances may even exceed the price-increasing tendency of the exhaustion of the readily accessible deposits.

The Mystery of "Proven Reserves"

Over the years, a great deal of confusion has arisen from published statistics on the amounts of "proven reserves" that exist for such exhaustible natural resources as oil, natural gas, iron ore, and coal. These statistics report the number of barrels of oil, or tons of coal, or cubic feet of natural gas that are known to remain. Confusion has arisen because the amount remaining often appears to *increase* at the same time that increasing amounts are extracted and used. To have more of the resource available when the rate of use rises seems to contradict the whole idea that resources are exhaustible. Fortunately, your understanding of economics can help you unravel this apparent contradiction.

The search for deposits of exhaustible resources is a more or less continuous process. Exploration companies are looking for new deposits at the same time that production companies are

drawing down deposits already known. The *expected future price* of the resource greatly influences the explorations that are undertaken. If the price of the resource is expected to rise, searches become more frequent and more intensive, since discoveries promise to be more profitable. Firms will be willing to spend more on exploration and on extraction of both old and new deposits. For example, at any given time, petroleum geologists know of many areas where oil is likely to be found. They also know that the cost of extracting the oil from many of these places would make production unprofitable. For this reason, they do not go to the expense of actually proving the presence of these deposits. But when price rises are predicted, it pays to explore and prove the existence of these previously suspected deposits. In this way, "proven reserves" may indeed increase at the same time that current production rises.

The expected future price of a resource greatly influences the explorations undertaken for new deposits of the resource. For this reason, "proven reserves" may increase as current production rises.

Geologists who estimate the total quantities of various natural resources find that impressively large amounts of most of them exist in small or inaccessible quantities scattered here and there throughout the world. It is not likely that we shall literally "run out" of any of them. However, for economic reasons, we may stop using some of them as their cost rises in relation to the cost of alternative resources.

The Importance of Price Elasticity of Demand

It can be seen from Figure 1 that the price elasticity of demand plays an important part in the market's method of conserving exhaustible natural resources. Shifting the supply curve to the left brings a much greater reduction in annual equilibrium quantities if the demand is elastic than if it is inelastic over that range. This is because an elastic demand generally means that there are good substitutes, so that consumers switch to them as the price of the exhaustible resource rises. Conservation is easier and quicker when good substitutes are available than when they are not. Indeed, the whole problem of resource conservation melts away if good substitutes can easily be found.

Shifting the supply curve to the left brings a much greater reduction in annual equilibrium quantities if the demand is elastic than if it is inelastic over that range, because an elastic demand usually means that there are good substitutes that consumers can switch to as the price of the exhaustible resource rises.

Our story cannot end, of course, with the confusing statement that conservation is both easier and less critical when demand is price elastic than when it is price inelastic. One of the most appealing features of the method that the market system uses to conserve resources comes from the likelihood that price elasticity itself increases as time passes. As you learned in Chapter 23, if only a very short time period is considered, consumers have little opportunity to discover substitute goods or services and to adjust their lifestyles to make use of these substitutes. Demand for an item that is presently being used may be quite price inelastic. But as time passes and consumers keep searching for ways to avoid the higher price of an increasingly scarce natural resource, new products are developed to take the place of those that have become more expensive, and people change their lifestyles so they can use these new substitutes. The demand curve becomes more price elastic as time passes, and the market system's conservation process becomes more and more effective.

The response of the American consumer to rising prices of oil during the 1970s is an excellent example of how the passage of time affects price elasticity of demand. At first, after oil prices shot upward in 1973–74 and again in 1979, consumers could only make (or were only willing to make) small adjustments in their earlier patterns of consumption. Vacation trips could be shortened somewhat and home heating temperatures could be reduced a bit (and more sweaters worn), but these measures offered only limited opportunity to reduce the amount of oil demanded. But as time

passed, consumers were able (willing) to change their lifestyles by joining car pools, taking fewer drives in the country, and so on. Also, small cars that use less gasoline per mile were introduced, better insulation was put into homes, and a host of energy-saving devices were developed to help consumers use less oil. The price elasticity of demand for oil was much greater when viewed over a five- or ten-year period than when viewed over a one-year period.

As time passes and consumers keep searching for ways to avoid the higher price of an increasingly scarce natural resource, and as new products are developed to take the place of those that have become more expensive, and as people change their lifestyles so they can use these new substitutes, price elasticity of demand becomes greater.

The Interest Rate and Conservation

The rate of interest has an important effect on the conservation of exhaustible natural resources. In our study of the role of interest rates, we shall first see how they are related to the price of exhaustible natural resources and then we shall see how they provide a connection between conservation and other values in the economy.

How Interest Rates Affect Natural Resource Prices To understand the role of interest rates on the price of exhaustible natural resources, imagine that you own an oil well, that you know exactly how much oil is in the ground, and that you expect the cost of extracting the oil to be a constant fraction of its selling price. All you need to decide is how much of the oil to extract this year and how much to leave for future years. Here is how the rate of interest affects your decision.

Suppose that the present price of the oil allows you to earn $10 a barrel profit after all costs of extraction have been paid. If the present rate of interest on securities of equivalent risk is 10 percent, you could extract a barrel of the oil, receive $10, and buy securities that would provide $11 one year from now. In other words, you could invest (in the financial sense) the $10 at 10 percent interest and realize $11 one year from now ($10 × 1.1 = $11). Is it a wise move for you to extract the oil today? The answer depends on how much profit you expect to earn on the oil one year from now. This will depend on what you expect the price of the oil and the cost of extraction to be one year from now. If the price one year from now yields a profit of $12 a barrel, leaving a $10 barrel in the ground would earn a return of 20 percent ($12/$10 = 1.2, that is, a gain in one year of $2 on an initial sum of $10 is a 20 percent gain). Your best choice would be to leave the oil in the ground. On the other hand, if the profit on the oil one year from now is only $10.50, your return per barrel left in the ground will be only 5 percent ($10.50/$10.00 = 1.05, that is, a $0.50 gain on an initial sum of $10.00 is a gain of 5 percent). In this case, your best move is to extract the oil and buy securities. Only if the profit one year from now is $11 a barrel are you exactly on the margin of whether or not to extract the resource.

The economic aspects of this little exercise arise from the effects that your decision has on the present and future prices of the resource. If you and thousands of others like you decide to leave the resource in the ground (as in the case of the $12 expected future profit), the supply curve for the resource in the *current* market will shift to the left, and the current price will rise to yield more than $10 profit per barrel. At the same time, the increased likelihood that a greater amount of the resource will be extracted one year from now will shift the supply curve in the *future* market to the right and lower the expected future price so that the expected future profit will be less than $12. Thus, the decision to leave the resource in the ground will tend to lower the rate of return from this strategy to less than the original 20 percent. The reasoning applies equally well in reverse. If you and thousands like you decide to go ahead and extract the resource and sell it in *today's* market (as in the case of the $10.50 expected future profit), the current price will fall to yield less than $10 profit, and the expected future profit will rise above $10.50. The rate of return from keeping the resource in the ground will rise above 5 percent.

As suppliers and potential suppliers routinely make calculations like these, an equilibrium will arise in which the year-to-year rate of increase in the price of the resource will approximate the rate of interest on alternative investments that are exposed to the same degree of risk. If this rate of interest is 10 percent, the resource price will rise at a rate of about 10 percent a year, other things being equal. The spread between present and future prices will be greater if the interest rate is higher and will be smaller if the rate of interest is lower, if other things remain unchanged. In effect, the expected future price of the resource, discounted to its present value with the appropriate interest rate, fixes a **reservation price**—that is, a price below which the resource will be reserved for future use by its owner.

The spread between present and future prices will be greater if the interest rate is higher and smaller if the interest rate is lower.

The expected future price of a resource, discounted to its present value with the appropriate interest rate, fixes a reservation price—a price below which the resource will be reserved for future use by its owner.

Conservation and Other Economic Values The exercise that we have just carried out leads to some interesting ideas about the relationship between interest rates, conservation, and other values in the economy. To help you understand these relationships, we must review some of the key principles about interest rates that we presented earlier.

When you studied interest rates in Chapter 32, you learned that there are two major forces operating on them. One is the willingness of people to put off immediate consumption in exchange for greater future consumption, called "time preference." The other is the ability of machines and other capital equipment to raise output through roundabout methods of production, called "the productivity of capital." Those ideas are presented here in Figure 2. The supply curve incorporates the time preferences of suppliers of money for loans. Under any given set of time preferences, higher interest rates call forth a larger flow of funds to be loaned. When time preferences change, the supply curve shifts.

FIGURE 2
Supply and Demand for Loanable Funds

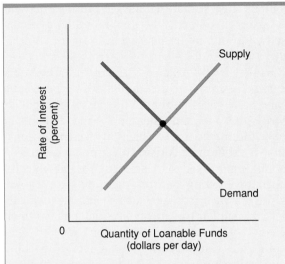

In the market for loanable funds, the supply curve incorporates the time preferences of suppliers of these funds. Under any given set of time preferences, higher interest rates call forth a larger flow of loanable funds, other things being equal. When time preferences change, the supply curve shifts. The demand curve incorporates the productivity of capital. Under given productivity conditions, the quantity demanded is greater at lower interest rates than at high interest rates. When the productivity of capital changes, the demand curve shifts. The interaction between suppliers and demanders of loanable funds tends to establish an equilibrium rate of interest.

The demand curve incorporates the productivity of capital. Under given productivity conditions, the quantity of loanable funds demanded will be greater at low interest rates than at high interest rates, other things being equal. When the productivity of capital changes, the demand curve shifts. The interaction between suppliers and demanders of loanable funds tends to establish an equilibrium rate of interest that balances the quantity demanded with the quantity supplied.

Falling Interest Rates To see how interest rates relate conservation of exhaustible natural resources to other economic values, suppose that something happens to change the time preferences of potential suppliers of loanable funds. To be specific, suppose that their time preferences change so that current consumption becomes less important and consumption in the future becomes more important. This might happen, for example, if war or the fear of war decreases, making people feel safer in planning for the future. This change in time preference would shift the supply curve in Figure 2 to the right and would bring a drop in interest rates, if other things remain unchanged.

As you learned earlier, lower interest rates narrow the spread between the present prices of exhaustible natural resources and their future prices. In this case, the narrowing takes place because resource owners find that the percentage return on other uses (financial investments) for their wealth has become less attractive. With less incentive to obtain funds for other uses, less of the resource is extracted, reducing the supply in the current market and raising its price.[1] In this way, the market responds to a shift in time preferences. When the preference for future consumption rises in relation to current consumption, interest rates fall and the rate of extraction of exhaustible natural resources also goes down. Thus, the pattern of use of the resource is consistent with time preference.

When the preference for future consumption rises in relation to current consumption, interest rates fall and the rate of extraction of exhaustible natural resources also goes down.

Rising Interest Rates Let us next take a case where interest rates rise because of a shift in the demand for loanable funds. Suppose there is a technological breakthrough that increases the productivity of machines and equipment. In order to finance the construction of these machines, firms borrow money—that is, they demand loanable funds. The demand curve for loanable funds shifts to the right, and interest rates rise. Our analysis of how interest rates affect the rate of extraction of exhaustible natural resources says that the spread between today's resource price and tomorrow's re-

1. We assume that the demand curve for the resource does not shift or at least that any shift in it will be quite small. We do so because the suppliers of loanable funds, whose time preferences have changed, are only a part of the total group of consumers of this resource and because this resource is only one of many items for current production.

source price will widen. This change takes place in the following way. With higher returns for alternative uses of their wealth, resource owners raise the rate at which they extract the resource in order to obtain the funds to take advantage of these new opportunities. The supply curve of the resource shifts to the right, and if other things remain unchanged, its current price falls, bringing a rise in the quantity demanded to match the rise in current extraction. The higher interest rate has encouraged more rapid use of the resource.[2]

Higher interest rates encourage more rapid use of a resource as owners raise the rate at which they extract the resource in order to obtain the funds to take advantage of the higher returns for alternative uses of their wealth.

These exercises show how rising and falling interest rates are signals of changes in preferences for present and future consumption and of changes in the productivity of machines and equipment. In this way, the price system integrates resource use rates with other aspects of the economic system. We do not mean to suggest, however, that high or low interest rates are either good or bad or that conservation of exhaustible resources is necessarily good or bad. Nor do we imply that the welfare of one generation of people is necessarily more or less important than that of another generation. We are simply showing you that the price system, when working smoothly, helps to answer the question of how rapidly these resources will be used.

How Markets May Fail

Markets sometimes fail to regulate the use of exhaustible natural resources as neatly as was implied in the model we just presented. We shall give several reasons why they may fail. We shall also

---

2. Of course, interest is also one of the costs of extracting the natural resource, since machines are used in these operations. This will moderate, but probably not eliminate, the changes just described. Also, it is important to distinguish this microeconomic exercise from macroeconomic models showing that higher interest rates reduce the volume of planned investment. This reduction does not take place in our model because it started with a technological breakthrough that increased demand for machines used in production.

explain how government regulations and monopoly can influence conservation. All of these observations suggest that markets, in practice, may not work quite so "perfectly" (or smoothly) as we assumed in our earlier discussion.

Government Influences on Interest Rates   In discussing interest-rate determination, we noted only time preferences and the productivity of capital as forces that can shift the supply and demand for loanable funds. There are, however, other forces that can shift these curves. Government tax policies about funds saved for retirement, for example, can encourage saving and shift the supply curve to the right or can discourage saving and shift it to the left. In a similar way, tax policies giving investment credits or favorable depreciation allowances to companies can affect the profitability of machines and equipment and shift the demand curve for funds to be loaned. In macroeconomics it is agreed that government budget deficits and surpluses and central bank policies also can raise or lower real interest rates, at least in the short run. Interest rates may also be raised or lowered by changes in the desire to hold cash and to speculate on future price changes. For these and other reasons, one cannot be sure that owners of resources dance to an interest-rate tune that will always lead to the "right" rate of extraction for exhaustible natural resources.

Markets do not always regulate the use of exhaustible natural resources as smoothly as the model implies. For example, government tax policies can affect the supply and demand for loanable funds and can raise or lower real interest rates, thus affecting the rate of extraction for exhaustible natural resources.

Monopoly and Conservation   Both our cost-of-extraction and our interest-rate models for exhaustible natural resource extraction assumed competitive markets. In fact, many deposits of exhaustible resources are owned by companies that have some monopoly control. Also, much of the demand for these resources comes from firms that are monopolistic. Economic theory is quite clear that monopolistic firms generally hold down output in order to get higher prices and earn larger profits. Producing less means using fewer exhaustible natural resources and other raw materials. For this reason, monopolistic firms may, in fact, aid conservation. The case of OPEC is well known. In trying to maximize profits, OPEC attempts to limit the number of barrels of oil that are pumped.

Monopolistic firms may aid conservation by holding down output in order to get higher prices and earn larger profits.

Of course, OPEC is not the first or the only monopolistic organization in the exhaustible natural resource area. High levels of concentration exist in other parts of the petroleum industry as well. As it happened, however, this monopolistic situation may have speeded up rather than slowed down the extraction of U.S. oil deposits. Major discoveries of oil in the Middle East and North Africa in the 1950s put a downward pressure on oil prices that threatened the profitability of oil companies depending mainly on higher-cost fields in the United States. These companies reacted by obtaining government restrictions on the amount of oil that could be imported into the United States and tax concessions (such as very generous depletion allowances) that amounted to a large subsidy for extracting oil from wells in the United States. The result was that market prices for oil remained relatively low; consumption was high, and auto makers, highway builders, and many others enjoyed prosperous times. But U.S. deposits of crude oil were pumped down at a rapid rate. For this reason, we must conclude that monopoly may promote conservation, but that much depends on the specific case, on the policies of the firms themselves, and on what protection and tax breaks they are able to get from government.

Nonmarket Systems and Conservation

Since the market system does not necessarily result in the best possible rate of use for exhaustible natural resources, other conservation arrangements can be considered. We have already noted how import restrictions in the 1950s and 1960s hastened the use of oil deposits in the United States while helping to conserve those located in foreign areas. Now we shall take a look at several other government policies that have had an important impact on the rate of extraction of exhaustible natural resources in the United States.

Preferential Tax Treatment Several features of U.S. income taxation encourage the exploration for and the extraction of exhaustible natural resources. Depletion allowances are the best known of these features. Under **depletion allowances,** part of the value of a resource that is removed from the earth is not counted as income to the owner of that resource. The reasoning behind this tax-free extraction is that the taxpayer already owns the oil or other resource that is in the ground, so that extracting and selling it does not really amount to any net improvement in his or her economic condition; that is, no income is received. In this sense, the allowance is like a deduction for the depreciation (wearing out) of a machine used in production. Actual income should be recognized only after the owner has gotten back all of his or her initial investment in the resource.

The details of depletion allowances are complicated. For our brief discussion, we shall note only two points. First, the value that can be recovered tax-free has not been, in fact, limited to the taxpayer's original investment in the resource. Therefore, finding and extracting exhaustible natural resources may be more profitable, after tax, than other economic undertakings. Second, the taxpayer can cash in on this extra advantage only by actually extracting the resource. The combination tends to speed up the discovery and extraction of resources eligible for depletion allowances.

A related tax feature that hastens exploration and extraction is a provision that allows an immediate tax deduction for the expenses of unsuccessful explorations, such as dry holes in oil exploration. The combination of an immediate tax deduction for unsuccessful searches plus overdeduction for the cost of successful searches has greatly speeded up the use of these resources in the United States.

Under depletion allowances, part of the value of a resource that is removed from the earth is not

---

counted as income to the owner of that resource. U.S. income taxation allows depletion in excess of the owner's original investment. This tax feature tends to speed up the discovery and extraction of resources.

Price Controls   Price controls are generally associated with wartime and with the fight against inflation. However, price controls in energy resources markets have been used in the United States in times of peace as well. These controls have influenced the conservation of energy resources.

Price Controls on Natural Gas

Price controls in the natural gas market became effective after the Supreme Court ruled in 1954 that regulation of natural gas prices paid by households and companies in consuming areas called for the regulation of the prices of gas in the natural gas fields themselves. It had long been recognized that companies selling gas in consumer areas were natural monopolies and therefore should be granted public utility status and be subject to regulation.[3] Also, as they developed, pipeline companies carrying gas from production areas were seen as natural monopolies. In the gas-producing areas, however, there are often many companies, since gas production is not a natural monopoly. But, in most cases, only one pipeline company serves a given production area and can have *monopsonistic* influence over price. For this reason, the Supreme Court ruled that the Federal Power Commission (later the Federal Energy Regulatory Commission) should fix natural gas prices at the well itself in order to protect consumers at the other end of the line.

Once regulation was in effect, natural gas prices were held below the equilibrium price that otherwise would have prevailed. The results of below-equilibrium prices are well known. As pictured in Figure 3, without regulation the interaction of supply and demand would result in equilibrium at *A* with price P_1 and quantity Q_1. If the regulated price is set below this equilibrium, say, at P_2, natural gas suppliers lower the quantity of gas supplied (a movement along the supply

3. See Chapter 35 for a discussion of monopoly regulation.

FIGURE 3
Regulated Natural Gas Prices Below Market Equilibrium

Without regulation, the interaction of supply and demand would result in equilibrium at *A*, with price P_1 and quantity Q_1. If the regulated price is below this equilibrium, as at P_2, natural gas suppliers reduce the quantity supplied, moving along the supply curve from *A* to *B*, and consumers increase the quantity demanded, moving along the demand curve from *A* to *C*. A shortage of natural gas appears, as illustrated by the horizontal distance from *B* to *C*. Actual production and consumption are at Q_2. Price controls can reduce usage of natural gas.

curve from *A* to *B*), and consumers raise the quantity demanded (a movement along the demand curve from *A* to *C*). As these responses take place, a shortage of natural gas appears, as shown by the distance from *B* to *C*. Part of the shortage comes from the greater quantity demanded, and part comes from the lower quantity supplied.

Actual U.S. experience with natural gas price controls has generally followed this simple economic model. However, because of the nature of the industry the consequences were slow to appear. Exploration and discovery of new gas reserves slowed down, and the drawing down of proven reserves set the stage for shortages. In the early 1970s, the *relative* price of natural gas went even lower after the OPEC embargo and the large price rises for oil. Many consuming industries switched from oil to gas. Others switched to natural gas from coal because of the environmental restrictions on coal burning. In the winter of 1976–77, serious natural gas shortages developed and gas was actually unavailable in some areas for some users.

Price controls in the natural gas market came into effect after a 1954 Supreme Court ruling; once in effect, natural gas prices were held below the equilibrium price that otherwise would have prevailed, leading to gas shortages after the 1973 OPEC embargo.

Regulators were, of course, aware of the economic problems. Even before the emergencies of the winter of 1976–77, prices of natural gas from certain sources were allowed to rise in order to provide incentives to explore for new gas reserves. Low prices were continued for gas from "old" wells (those in operation before January 1, 1973), but higher prices were allowed for gas from "new" wells (those drilled or completed after that date). In response to these higher prices, the number of new gas wells completed rose rapidly. Legislation in 1978 set down a schedule for ending all price controls on newly developed gas resources. In 1984 an attempt was made to reintroduce some more stringent price controls, but President Reagan refused to support that effort. By the time that President Bush took office in 1989 only about one-third of all natural gas was still subject to control, some at high prices and some at low prices. In 1989 legislation was passed that would remove all remaining price controls from natural gas at the well head by January 1, 1993.

Our brief historical survey of natural gas price controls suggests that regulatory measures may have had an impact on the rate of extraction of this exhaustible natural resource. However, many additional relationships would have to be examined before a conclusion could be reached. For example, government subsidies in the form of income tax depletion allowances (noted previously in relation to oil production) may have speeded up the use (or the "burning off") of the natural gas resource. Moreover, oil and natural gas often are found in the same areas and in the same exploration and drilling operations. This close production relationship between natural gas and oil suggests that restrictions on imports of petroleum may have increased the extraction of natural gas from domestic fields. It is not clear, therefore, whether actual regulation, combined with the other events of the period, resulted in much net conservation of gas in the United States.

Price Controls on Oil The story of price controls on oil is slightly different from the one about price controls on natural gas, though the economics of the two is alike. Except for wartime, price controls on oil were not applied in the United States until the crisis of the OPEC embargo in 1973 and the rapid increases in oil prices that followed. As the price of imported oil rose, huge profits were expected from the discovery and extraction of oil in the United States. The government faced a policy dilemma. Even though policymakers were eager for larger supplies of domestic oil, they did not want the owners of existing oil reserves to reap what they believed would be excessive profits. Price controls were imposed and, as in the natural gas case, a higher price was allowed for oil from "new" wells than was allowed for oil from "old" wells. Neither of these prices, however, was allowed to reach the level of the imported oil.

With oil from different sources (new domestic, old domestic, and imported) commanding different prices, a very complicated situation arose. Since oil from U.S. sources was priced below imported oil, one might have expected the quantity demanded from foreign sources to fall. However, this expectation was upset by a system of **entitlements,** certificates that refiners were required to obtain in order to purchase domestic oil at low controlled prices. In an attempt to make the multiple-price system fair among refineries, those that bought low-priced domestic oil had to purchase entitlements to bring their costs up. On the other hand, refineries that bought high-priced imported oil received entitlements, which they could sell to lower their cost of crude oil. The aim was to have all refineries pay the same average price for crude oil. Several results followed. Even though foreign oil was no longer more costly for the refineries than domestic oil, the domestic oil producers still received prices below the world (and the expected domestic) price for oil.

For this reason, they had an incentive to postpone production. Imports increased. At the same time, petroleum products were priced to consumers according to *average* total cost rather than *marginal* cost, which was the price of imported oil. The price to consumers was *below* marginal cost. From an economic efficiency point of view, prices to consumers were too low, and consumption was too high.

Entitlements are certificates that oil refiners were required to obtain in order to purchase domestic oil at low controlled prices.

As in the case of natural gas controls, price controls over oil tended to keep prices to U.S. producers below market equilibrium levels and to slow down the extraction of oil. They may have contributed to some conservation, but caused great uncertainty, confusion, and frustration.

In the face of high payments to foreign producers and complaints from domestic producers, President Carter, in 1980, launched a program to remove price controls on crude oil. President Reagan speeded up the decontrol process. With controls removed, domestic oil production increased. Oil production also increased from discoveries in Mexico, the North Sea, and Alaska. Oil shortages were replaced by downward pressures on price. Beginning in 1985, the OPEC cartel proved less able to continue its restrictions on oil production, and the price of crude oil fell dramatically before leveling off. Recent OPEC efforts to reassert its control over oil production have as yet (1989) achieved only limited results while the response by U.S. firms has been to lower their output level.

RENEWABLE RESOURCES

Renewable resources are different from exhaustible resources. As noted earlier, wildlife such as migratory birds, wild game, whales, and fish are renewable natural resources. Similarly, forests can renew themselves. Under normal conditions, nature can replace these resources rather quickly. From the economist's point of view, the problem is to work with nature to maintain adequate reproduction and restoration of these resources.

Environmental Constraints

We humans generally regard ourselves as one of the more successful species of animal life on the earth. Our numbers have risen greatly over the years, claiming ever-widening rule over other species. As human activities spread more widely over the earth, the space left undisturbed for other species contracts. Foraging areas for wild animals become smaller. Breeding areas for migratory birds are taken over by humans or so fouled by unwanted by-products of human consumption that they are no longer able to maintain the bird population. Marshlands are drained for farms or homes. River estuaries are contaminated or changed so much by sedimentation or the needs of commerce that they are not suited for fish spawning. Even the oceans, covering two-thirds of the earth's surface, feel the impact of human activity as oil spills and other pollutants contaminate the water.

Our claims on nature are a constraint, or limit, on the supply of fish, birds, and wild game and other renewable natural resources. Have we spread our influence too far and reduced the supply of renewable natural resources too much? Even by our very egocentric calculation, using only our own values, the answer is probably "yes." Externalities, which you studied in Chapter 33, provide the main basis for this conclusion. When we consider expanding our human domain by draining a swamp or building a housing development or damming a stream, benefits in most cases are clearly recognized because property rights to these benefits have been established. Farmers will gain from draining the swamp. Developers will gain from the land they build on. Electric utilities, irrigation projects, or recreational entrepreneurs will gain from damming the stream. On the other hand, many costs of the expansion may be unrecognized. Who is poorer when the quantity of wild game decreases? Who will speak for the migratory birds whose breeding grounds are gone? Who are the hunters that are denied the game or the fishermen who are denied the fish? In many cases, the costs of human intrusion, though real, are widely scattered and not clearly recognized.

When costs and/or benefits are not recognized,

market failures arise. As you recall from Chapter 33, negative externalities exist when costs are imposed on persons whose interests are not reflected in the market. In all likelihood, this is the case when swamps are drained for farmland or development projects, when streams are dammed, and so on. Thus, microeconomic analysis leads us to suspect that too many swamps may be drained and that too many streams may be dammed, since some of the costs of these enterprises probably are not reflected in market-supply curves.

In many cases the costs of human intrusion on the supply of renewable resources are not recognized. When costs and/or benefits are not recognized, market failures arise.

For renewable natural resources, market failure arises, in part at least, because no one has *property rights* to the wildlife that will be destroyed when extensions of human habitation shrink the habitat of the wildlife. If clear property rights existed, markets would more fully reflect the costs of actions that lead to reductions in wildlife living areas. Unfortunately, behind the problem of fixing authority over resources lie the even more basic problems of defining and measuring those resources. For example, is the oxygen content of the water in a flowing stream a separate kind of property? Are we able to identify and measure it so that rights over its use can be exercised by government or private individuals? What about the salt content of water in fish breeding areas or the water level in the Everglades? Can property rights be identified and enforced for whales in the ocean? Or for a certain kind of whale?

The economist's way of thinking suggests that efficiency in the extent of human intrusion in nature's domain is not likely to be achieved when the gains on one side of the bargain are clearly recognized by specific property rights, but the costs on the other side are vague and not imposed on anyone in particular. Laser beams, sonar, computers, and satellites can expand our ability to identify and measure things in nature and so can help set the stage for wise decisions about the balance between our development projects and those of nature. But the problems and conflicts are serious, and progress is likely to be slow.

For renewable natural resources, market failure arises, in part at least, because no one has property rights to the wildlife that will be destroyed when extensions of human habitation shrink the habitat of the wildlife.

Harvesting Constraints

The second economic problem for conserving renewable resources is control over harvesting— that is, control of the number of fish, birds, deer, or other wildlife that can be taken each year for human use. In this matter, the size of the parent population is a key variable. If the yearly catch is so great that it lowers the parent population, the species may be on its way to extinction. Let us look at the problem first from the biological point of view and then from the economic point of view.

Sustainable Annual Yield The biological aspect of the harvesting of a renewable natural resource is pictured in Figure 4. Shown on the horizontal axis is the population of some renewable natural resource, such as fish, deer, or wild geese. Shown on the vertical axis is the annual natural increase in this population. The graph tells a story of what happens when the habitat for the species is fixed in terms of land and water area, rainfall, temperature, and so forth. The only relationship that we show is between the size of the population and its own natural annual increase, with all other variables fixed.

At the origin of the graph, there is no population and no annual natural increase. The species does not exist! To the right of the origin, there is some parent population, and reproduction takes place. As we move to the right along the horizontal axis, there are more births than deaths, so the population rises. At population A, births exceed deaths by the greatest possible amount, and the annual population increase is at a maximum, as shown by the peak of the curve, at E. As population exceeds quantity A, the environmental constraints become effective—crowding becomes worse, the food supply becomes less abundant, and the death rate rises so that births exceed deaths by less than before. This lowers the annual natural population increase, and the curve slopes downward. At popula-

FIGURE 4
The Sustainable-Annual-Yield Curve

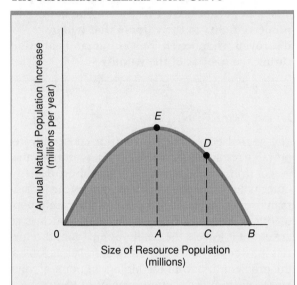

The sustainable-annual-yield curve shows the quantity of a renewable natural resource that could be harvested each year for an indefinite period. At the origin of the graph, there is zero population. The species does not exist. Moving to the right along the horizontal axis, births exceed deaths and the population increases. At A, births exceed deaths by a maximum amount, and the quantity that could be harvested annually (AE) is at a maximum. As population exceeds A, environmental constraints raise the death rate so that births exceed deaths by less than before. At B, the death rate equals the reproduction rate. At any given population, such as A or C, humans could harvest the natural annual increase, which is shown by AE and CD, without upsetting the stability of the population at that level.

every year and the population would remain stable at C. The easiest way to understand this idea is to imagine that we harvest from the parent population after their offspring for the year have been born. In the year ahead, the offspring replace their parents and the species carries on with the stable population.[4]

The sustainable-annual-yield curve shows the quantity of a renewable natural resource that could be taken each year and still leave a large enough parent population to sustain the species.

Figure 4 suggests several interesting features about harvesting nature's renewable resources. One is that, moving to the left from point B, harvesting can increase all the way to the yearly amount of AE without endangering the species itself. In a sense, harvesting reduces crowding and other environmental pressures on the species and permits a larger annual natural population increase. But a conservation problem arises from annual harvesting greater than AE because this will lower the parent population and cause a smaller natural population increase in the next reproduction cycle. If excessive harvesting continues, the population may be driven to zero and the species to extinction. Clearly, efficient conservation requires that the population be maintained at A and that harvesting not be allowed to exceed the quantity represented by the vertical distance AE, the maximum sustainable annual yield.

Economics and Harvest Control The economic aspects of harvest control do not focus just on preventing the extinction of a species of wild animal, bird, or fish. In fact, because the cost of finding and harvesting is likely to rise as the resource population declines, harvesting alone might not by itself lead to the extinction of the species. From an economic point of view, the aim of harvest control should be to prevent any entry into the "danger zone" where the population of the species is less

tion B, the environmental constraint has increased the death rate until it matches the reproduction rate and the annual natural population increase is zero. The population has reached a natural equilibrium.

Suppose that we or some other predator enters the picture and begins to kill off the population. How many fish, birds, deer, or other members of the population can be taken and still leave a large enough parent population to sustain the species? The answer is shown by the sustainable-annual-yield curve. Consider, for example, the annual population increase at population C, as shown by the vertical line from C on the horizontal axis to D on the sustainable-annual-yield curve. This number of fish or deer or wild geese could be harvested

---

4. Wildlife management specialists know that much depends on when hunting and fishing are allowed and on which members of the population are actually taken. Distinctions are made between male and female members of the species and their ages. Different guidelines apply for different species.

than *A* (in Figure 4). The next step is to work out practical ways of moving toward this result.

Common Property One way that does *not* work well is the system of **common property,** under which everyone has a legal right to harvest the resource. The problem is that no one has an incentive to limit his or her harvest on the basis of what that harvest may do to future supplies of the resource. Instead, each individual reasons that his or her harvesting will not make any difference, first because it is a very small part of the total, and second because if they do not catch the fish or shoot the bird, someone else will and the resource will be depleted anyway. In this variation of the *free-rider problem,* each individual harvests without effective constraint. People behave in much the same way when they litter parks and roadsides with bottle caps and empty containers. As you can see, the common property system opens the way for people to impose the costs of their consumption on others. In other words, it is a variety of the *externalities* problem.

The common property system, under which everyone has a legal right to harvest a resource, is a variation of the free-rider problem: each individual reasons that his or her harvesting will not make any difference because it is a very small part of the total.

The common property system opens the way for people to impose the costs of their consumption on others; it is a variety of the externalities problem.

Property Rights and Reservation Prices Property rights provide owners with an incentive to take account of the effects that present use will have on future production. Property owners build the future into their current supply decisions by means of **reservation prices,** as explained earlier in connection with decisions about whether or not to extract exhaustible natural resources. The reservation price is the present value of the future production that would be sacrificed if the resource were harvested today. To apply the reservation-price concept to decisions about harvesting renewable natural resources, the owner first estimates the

changes in future harvests that would take place as a consequence of current harvesting. Will current harvesting reduce future harvests (that is, put the population of the resource in the left-hand part of the sustainable-yield curve)? If so, the owner estimates the profit that would be lost if this future production were sacrificed, at whatever prices and production costs he or she expects will prevail in the future. Next, this future profit is discounted to determine its present value, using whatever interest rate the owner believes to be correct in view of the amount of risk involved. This discounted amount is the reservation price of the resource. It becomes part of the cost of harvesting the resource. In this way, the reservation price provides an operational recognition of future interests and a guide for conservation.

Examples of the property rights system of harvest control exist in many areas. Foresters know how long trees should be allowed to grow for maximum yield, and oystermen make similar calculations before harvesting oysters. Perhaps modern technology will lead to new kinds of property rights and new ways of applying economic principles to the conservation of renewable natural resources.

Property rights provide owners with an incentive to take account of the effects that present use will have on future production. Property owners build the future into their current supply decisions by means of reservation prices.

Government Regulation As you learned in Chapter 33, the existence of externalities is one of the reasons for government intervention in the economy. When externalities arise from common property in renewable natural resources, government may step in and place limits on common property rights. Hunting and fishing may be restricted to certain times of the year, licenses may be required, and limits may be placed on the number of fish or birds or animals each person can take. Many governments have programs of this sort, which, in effect, raise the cost that a person must bear in order to harvest some of the resource. These costs (both money cost and time-and-convenience costs) reduce the quantity harvested. Ideally, this quantity could be brought in line with the maximum sustainable yield.[5]

Difficulties for government regulation arise when the habitat of a renewable resource extends across the borders of several states or countries. Sometimes agreements between governments can be reached, such as migratory bird agreements between states in the United States and among the United States, Canada, and Mexico. More serious problems arise when resources are found in areas where no government has jurisdiction, such as the oceans, the atmosphere, or outer space. Many governments have extended their territorial waters outward from the old twelve-mile limit to two hundred or more miles. These extensions, often taken without consulting other countries, can increase international tensions. Even so, they fail to solve the problems for resources farther out in the oceans. Establishing government jurisdictions in the atmosphere and outer space pose similar difficulties. These problems are not new, of course. Over the centuries, as population has grown and new technologies have developed, countries have time and again faced such challenges. Sometimes they have led to wars and conflict. Can we hope that international cooperation will result in better-reasoned solutions in the future?

When externalities arise from common property in renewable natural resources, government may step in and place limits on common property rights. Serious problems can arise when resources are found in areas where no government has jurisdiction, such as the oceans, the atmosphere, or outer space.

THE ENVIRONMENT

In this section, we shall examine how the techniques of economic analysis can help in understanding some important aspects of humanity's

relationship with the environment. We deal specifically with pollution that may arise from the dumping of waste materials into the environment. In this analysis, a key idea is to recognize that nature's ability to recycle many waste materials is a natural resource that should be utilized efficiently.

Nature's ability to recycle waste materials is a natural resource that should be utilized efficiently.

The Laws of Conservation of Energy and Matter

Until the space age, it was generally believed that what goes up must come down. A similar law (with similar space age exception) applies to the unwanted by-products of human occupation of the earth. The law of the conservation of matter states that the mass of waste material is approximately equal to the mass of raw materials used in production. This means that production and consumption simply rearrange materials to put them into forms that provide the services desired by humans. There is no change in the mass of these materials themselves, and at some point all that is used becomes waste. In a parallel way, the law of the conservation of energy suggests that humans can redirect but cannot destroy the energy that the earth receives or has received from the sun.

The mass of waste material is approximately equal to the mass of raw material used in production. At some point, all that is used becomes waste.

Two important ideas that follow from the laws of conservation of matter and energy should be emphasized in our study of environmental pollution. First, any action that increases the mass of material taken out of the earth or the amount of energy diverted from its usual path increases the amount of waste that must finally be put back into the earth or its atmosphere. On this basis, one can argue that, in connection with economic growth and higher living standards, public policy should discourage increases in material goods and should,

5. You may find it interesting that governments sometimes offer cash payments (bounties) to encourage people to increase their hunting of species that are increasing too rapidly and making inroads on farm crops or other, more desired, species of game. This is just the reverse of the system of requiring licenses and paying fees for hunting.

instead, stress increases in services and other non-material satisfactions.

Any action that increases the mass of material taken out of the earth or the amount of energy diverted from its usual path increases the amount of waste that eventually goes back into the earth or its atmosphere.

The second message from these laws is that waste treatment cannot reduce the mass or the energy aspects of waste. Instead, waste treatment can only move the waste to more acceptable places or process it into more acceptable forms before putting it back into the earth or the atmosphere. Therefore, two questions require attention in analyzing the environmental impact of the unwanted by-products of human activity. The first is "How much waste should be generated?" The second is "What are the most acceptable forms and locations for waste?" Are they the forms and locations that cause the least trouble for people today? Or are they the ones that will yield the best environment for our children and grandchildren?

Waste treatment cannot reduce the mass or the energy aspects of waste; it can only move the waste to more acceptable places or process it into more acceptable forms.

The Efficient Quantity of Waste

Figure 5 illustrates an economic model that will help to analyze the question of the efficient quantity of waste that should be generated and disposed of in the environment. To use this graph, think of "Mother Nature" as providing waste-disposal services—a dumping ground for the unwanted by-products of human consumption. The horizontal axis of the graph shows the quantities of this service demanded and supplied, the tons or cubic yards of waste discharged into the environment. The vertical axis shows the price and the cost of this service. The cost represents the dollar equivalent of the damages and disruptions that come from waste disposal.

The demand curve on this graph shows the

FIGURE 5
The Efficient Quantity of Waste-Disposal Service

Wastes are unwanted by-products from the production and/or consumption of goods. The demand curve, D, is derived from the demand for goods that generate the waste. Consumers will be willing to pay a high price to dispose of waste generated by final goods that they value highly and a low price to dispose of waste from final goods of low value. The MC_s curve illustrates the marginal cost to society that arises when waste disposal disrupts nature's existing ecological systems. The efficient quantity of waste-disposal service is Q_1, identified by the intersection of the demand curve for waste-disposal service with the MC_s curve. If nature supplies waste-disposal services at zero price, the equilibrium quantity will be Q_2. An effluent charge of P per unit would result in the supply curve S and equilibrium at the efficient quantity of waste-disposal service, Q_1.

quantities of waste-disposal service demanded at various prices. To understand this curve, we must recognize that wastes are unwanted by-products generated in the production and consumption of goods.[6] How much we are willing to pay for the disposal of unwanted by-products depends on how much we value the good that comes along with this by-product. For goods that we value very highly, we are willing to pay a large amount for disposal of the wastes generated. The willingness to pay for disposal of these wastes is represented along the upper-left part of the demand curve for waste-dis-

6. Unlike goods, the production and consumption of services usually do not generate unwanted by-products of the sort that involve waste-disposal problems.

posal service. We are willing to pay less for disposal of the unwanted by-products of goods that are themselves less valuable to us. Therefore, the willingness to pay for their disposal appears farther down along the demand curve for Mother Nature's waste-disposal service. We can view nature's waste-disposal service as a natural resource and the demand for this resource as being like the demand for other resources. Thus, the demand for nature's waste-disposal service is a **derived demand,** much as the demands for other resources or factors of production are derived demands (see Chapter 30).

How much we are willing to pay for the disposal of unwanted by-products depends on how much we value the good that comes along with this by-product.

The demand for nature's waste-disposal service is a derived demand.

Cost of Waste Disposal   Now look at the curve in Figure 5 labeled MC_s, which represents the marginal cost to society of disposing of waste. The first part of this curve lies along the horizontal axis itself, meaning that marginal cost is zero over this range of waste-disposal service. This reflects the assumption that a certain volume of waste can be handled without damage to nature's existing ecological system. Within this range, humans disposing of unwanted by-products of their consumption are in the same class as squirrels disposing of acorn shells. Nature has come to terms with this volume of waste, and the process that takes care of the waste is viewed as "natural."

As the volume of waste (per year, for example) increases beyond this zero-marginal-cost range, nature's ecological systems are changed. Water from certain sources or air in certain areas may become dangerous to the health of existing life, possibly even yours. The change in the ecology harms some life forms, and we record this harm as a social cost of nature's waste-disposal service. In Figure 5 the MC_s curve becomes steeper and steeper as the volume of waste per year increases. This is because it appears that ecological disruption has more than a simple arithmetic relation to the volume of waste. That is, the more waste generated

per unit of time, the higher is the cost of disposing of each additional unit of waste.

The curve showing the marginal cost of waste disposal is drawn as increasing at an increasing rate. This is based on the expectation that the more waste generated per unit of time, the higher the cost of disposing of each additional unit of waste.

Balancing Cost and Benefit   All waste must be disposed of through nature's waste-disposal service. In Figure 5, the efficient volume of waste is shown by the intersection of the demand curve and the MC_s curve. The efficient quantity is Q_1. Each unit of waste-disposal service up to this point generates benefits (as shown by the demand curve) that are greater than its cost (as shown by the MC_s curve). On the other hand, a volume of waste-disposal service in excess of Q_1 is inefficient because the costs from these units are greater than their benefits.

Although some people are uncomfortable with the idea that any volume of waste that changes nature's established ecological systems can be called efficient or optimal, the concept of an efficient quantity of waste and an efficient amount of environmental degradation is clear. Difficulties arise only in the practical application of the concept, most often in determining the location of the MC_s curve. If we underestimate the effects of wastes and place the MC_s curve too far to the right, our model will justify too much use of nature's waste-disposal service. On the other hand, if we overestimate the effects, the MC_s curve will be too far to the left, and society will not make full use of available natural resources.

The Supply of Nature's Waste-Disposal Service The MC_s curve in Figure 5 is *not* a supply curve. A supply curve, as you know, shows the quantities of a good or service that will be offered at various possible prices. Economists say that the quantity supplied depends on the price. But nature is not in a position to charge a price as a precondition for the use of her waste-disposal service. Instead, her service is given at zero price to anyone who chooses to use it. In terms of Figure 5, if nature supplies waste-disposal service at zero price, the supply curve is on the horizontal axis of the graph, and the equilibrium quantity of nature's waste disposal service is Q_2, where the demand curve meets the horizontal axis. The economic model indicates that an inefficiently large amount of waste will be generated and dumped if the price for nature's disposal service is zero.

Since Q_2 is greater than the efficient quantity, Q_1, social policy for efficient resource use may try to find a way to lower the volume of waste. Economic analysis suggests that one way to do so is to charge a price to those who use nature's disposal system. As the price rises from Mother Nature's zero-price offer, the intersection of the supply and demand curves will move to the left along the demand curve. The efficient quantity would be generated if the price were P, resulting in the supply curve shown in the figure and an equilibrium quantity of Q_1.

The economic model of nature's waste-disposal service indicates that an inefficiently large amount of waste will be generated and dumped if the price for this service is zero. One way to lower the volume of waste, then, is to charge a price to those who use nature's disposal system.

Excess Waste as an Externalities Problem The dumping of excessive waste into nature's disposal system can be explained as market failure coming from negative externalities.[7] For example, consider the nonreturnable soft-drink container. If you throw it along the roadside, your private cost for disposing of the container is very low. But you know that your private cost is not the whole story. Others must suffer the unsightliness of the discarded container or else pick it up and dispose of it properly. Thus, the social cost of disposing of the nonreturnable container includes both your effort in throwing it away and the discomfort and exertion of others in dealing with it later. The costs imposed on others are external costs or negative externalities.

The dumping of excessive waste into nature's disposal system can be explained as a market failure coming from negative externalities.

---

7. Negative externalities were discussed in Chapter 33.

As you learned in Chapter 33, the market-supply curve is located too far to the right when negative externalities exist. This is precisely the situation that was illustrated in Figure 5. When nature charges a zero price for waste disposal, virtually all of the costs of each act of waste generation and disposal are imposed on some person other than the one generating the waste. Moreover, people often reason that their own small amount of waste is insignificant compared with the total amount generated. Since the environment will be polluted in any event, they conclude that their small amount of waste will not make any perceptible difference. In other words, the individual not only sees little private cost from dumping but also sees that little will be gained by not adding his or her bit to the total. With nature's service at zero price, economists predict that waste generation will greatly exceed the socially efficient quantity.

When nature charges a zero price for waste disposal, virtually all the costs for each act of waste generation and disposal are imposed on some person other than the one generating the waste.

Pricing to Internalize Externalities

In Figure 5, the price P can represent an **effluent charge,** or price for the use of nature's waste-disposal service.[8] A firm might be required, for example, to pay a specific amount for each cubic yard of refuse deposited in a landfill, for each gallon of sewage sent to a disposal system, and so on. When this price is charged, the supply curve S in Figure 5 becomes effective and the efficient amount of waste would be generated.

Advantages of Effluent Charges The main advantage of effluent charges is that they put self-interest to work to reduce the generation of wastes. The reason why this charge is so effective is that, in

---

8. An *effluent* is "something that flows out . . . an outflow of a sewer, storage tank, irrigation canal or other channel." *The American Heritage Dictionary of the English Language, New College Edition.* © 1976 by Houghton Mifflin Company.

a competitive system, consumers themselves end up paying the charges imposed on the unwanted by-products of goods that they consume. Wastes that are generated in manufacturing processes will be paid for at first by the firms that produce these goods, but then the costs will be passed on to consumers in higher prices. For the leftovers from consumption, such as empty cartons and garbage, consumers pay the effluent charge directly to the local waste disposal service.

Self-interest provides powerful incentives to reduce waste in the least-costly way. For example, firms that discover new production processes or new products that generate less waste will be able to sell at a lower price and gain customers and profits at the expense of firms that have not found ways to reduce waste. Also, consumers have an incentive to use fewer disposable containers when they must pay the local garbage service to dispose of them. Probably the greatest reduction in waste comes through the change in the product mix, as consumers change their consumption patterns to goods that cause less waste.

An effluent charge is the price for the use of nature's waste-disposal service. Effluent charges are effective because they put self-interest to work to reduce the generation of wastes.

An interesting aspect of effluent charges is that the revenue collected from these charges may be more than enough to cover the costs of waste disposal and the cost of administering the charge itself. If all disposers of waste pay price P, the money paid in effluent charges is represented by the green area in Figure 5. Since the total social cost of disposing of these wastes is only the part of this area lying beneath the MC_s curve, surplus money would be available to use for other purposes. In other words, providing efficient use of natural resources could generate a surplus and add to the financial power of the public sector. The meaning of this model, then, is not so different from the meaning of Henry George's idea of a single tax on land values (see Chapter 30). In fact, there is plenty of precedent for gaining public-sector revenue from natural resources. In oil- and gas-rich areas, governments

that have retained title to mineral rights enjoy abundant revenue.

Problems with Effluent Charges The greatest technical problem with effluent charges is discovering the actual location of the MC_s curve in Figure 5. Our model greatly oversimplified this task. For example, we implied that there is only one sort of waste and only one MC_s curve that must be estimated when, in fact, there are many different kinds of waste and many different MC_s curves. Solid waste is not the same as chemical waste or the disposal of heat. Waste released into the air from a smokestack or your car is not the same as waste dumped into the ocean, lakes, or flowing streams or buried in the ground. Effective action against one kind of waste or one method of waste disposal may simply lead to a shift to some other kind of waste or method of disposal. If the second type or method is more harmful than the first, effective action may do more harm than good. A great deal of information and analysis is needed to plan a wholly constructive program of effluent charges.

To identify the efficient quantity of nature's waste-disposal service, we must also discover the location of the demand curve for these services. There are several ways this might be done. If we use a trial-and-error approach, a series of different prices might be charged, eventually leading to some knowledge of the demand curve. Another method is to advertise for bids for waste-disposal permits. The bids could be arranged from the highest to the lowest, and the demand curve could be constructed by adding up the cumulative total amount of waste-disposal service requested, starting from the top down. If the cost curve had already been estimated, the equilibrium quantity could be determined and the bids accepted, from the highest down, until the efficient quantity had been authorized. This method would allow the government to operate like a discriminating monopolist (see Chapter 27) and gain revenue corresponding to the whole area under the demand curve up to quantity Q_1 in Figure 5.

To identify the efficient quantity of nature's waste-disposal service, we must discover the

---

location of the marginal cost curves for all the different wastes and the demand curve for nature's waste-disposal services.

Textbook exercises such as this, however, cannot solve a remaining, and perhaps the key, problem with effluent charges. This is the problem of enforcement. Under a waste-disposal permit or effluent charge system, dumping waste without a permit or without paying the charge would be illegal. To carry out the program effectively would require fines and penalties as well as allocation of other resources for detecting, apprehending, and prosecuting those who break the law. All of these things are expensive and are upsetting to many Americans, who cherish the image of the frontier, where nature's services could be treated as a zero-price resource.

The key problem with effluent charges is the difficulty of enforcing them.

Government Standards

As an alternative to effluent charges, the government may establish rules governing methods of production, the ingredients in products, and waste-treatment procedures in order to control various types of waste. For example, government regulations may prohibit the use of certain chemicals, or require filters on smokestacks, or specify that all autos be equipped with emission-control devices. Even though these standards and controls do not raise any money for the government, they usually are more appealing than effluent charges, which are thought of as taxes by the public and their representatives. Moreover, laws setting standards enable elected officials to point to specific and supposedly constructive actions that have been taken. The requirements will raise the price of the product to the consumer almost as certainly as a tax on that product would. But a tax that would bring about an equal reduction in the quantity of that product is almost certain to be more unpopular than standards and controls.

Government regulations may be one alternative to effluent charges. These standards and controls would raise the price of the product to the consumer just as a tax would but would probably be less unpopular than a tax.

Although government standards and controls are a politically popular approach to problems of waste disposal and environmental pollution, economic analysis brings to light some serious shortcomings in them. Standards and controls tend to lock methods of production or of waste disposal into the technology specified in the laws. Two separate problems arise. The first is the problem of too much uniformity. Production methods that are the best for large firms may not be the best for small firms, and methods that are the best for firms in one part of the country may not be the best for those in another part of the country. Requiring all to use the same technology means that some companies must use less than the best technology for their particular size and situation. For example, air-quality problems in the Los Angeles basin are different from those at the "four corners," where New Mexico, Arizona, Colorado, and Utah come together. Applying the same standards to both areas can prevent the full use of natural resources. An especially glaring case of too much uniformity arises when all the businesses in an area (along a given river system, for example) are required to lower their waste discharges by the same percentage. Since marginal cost for this reduction may be much more for some than for others, the costs of cleaning the river are much too high for the amount of cleaning accomplished. Moreover, those who had reduced emissions before the law was passed are penalized for their socially constructive action.

The second problem with standards and controls is that they may slow the search for better methods of waste treatment or for new production methods that cause less waste. This problem is probably more serious than the uniformity problem because new products and techniques for production and waste treatment probably offer the most promising routes to reducing harmful externalities. As just noted, effluent charges offer profit incentives for companies to find better methods.

Those that succeed will be able to lower the charges that they have to pay and in this way raise their net profits. To most economists, the incentive effect is the strongest argument for effluent charges as well as the greatest weakness of standards and controls.

Although government standards and controls are a politically popular approach to the problems of waste disposal and pollution, they have serious shortcomings: they tend to lock methods of production or of waste disposal into the technology specified in the laws, which may not always be appropriate for a specific firm, and they may slow the search for better methods of production or waste treatment.

To most economists, the incentive effect is the strongest argument for effluent charges as well as the greatest weakness of standards and controls.

Subsidies for Waste Treatment

During the 1960s and 1970s, many cities and towns built new sewage-treatment plants, partly with federal money and partly with local money. The local money for these facilities usually was raised by selling bonds, which would be paid off from charges collected from the households and firms that would dispose of sewage through the facility. Thus, the local funding illustrated the use of effluent charges. The federal money was a subsidy paid by taxpayers.

From the perspective of economic analysis, there is a fundamental difference between subsidies for waste treatment on the one hand and effluent charges and government standards on the other. Both effluent charges and government standards raise the price of goods that generate waste, thus activating economic incentives to encourage con-sumers and firms to reduce the amount of waste generated. But subsidies for waste treatment operate in the opposite direction. They lower the cost of producing goods that generate waste and lower the price to consumers. Thus, subsidies for waste treatment tend to *increase* the total amount of waste actually generated. When taxpayers pay part of the bill for waste treatment, the private cost to producers and consumers of goods that generate waste are reduced and the quantity demanded rises. For this reason, economists are critical of this procedure.

Both effluent charges and government standards raise the price of goods that generate waste, thus activating economic incentives to encourage consumers and firms to reduce the amount of waste generated. But subsidies for waste treatment lower the cost of producing goods that generate waste and lower the price to consumers, thus tending to increase the amount of waste generated.

Much of the appeal of waste-treatment subsidies is political rather than economic. Government spending programs that concentrate benefits in local areas but spread tax costs in small amounts over millions of taxpayers are attractive vehicles for legislative vote trading.[9] For citizens of the district on the receiving end, benefits are far greater than tax costs. Even though many people realize that their taxes also pay for thousands of projects in other districts, most are not willing to drop out of the game, fearing that their own project will simply be carried out in some other district. Of course, the idea of treating waste before it is released into the environment is quite sound, since this treatment can lower the social costs of waste. The problem with treatment subsidies is not with the facilities, as such, but with the financing method, which increases the quantity of waste itself.

---

9. See Chapter 33 for a discussion of vote trading.

Economics in Focus

Saving the Environment: Activism and Incentives

For two months a chemist prowled around the American Cyanamid plant in Linden, New Jersey, gathering samples. He examined data on plant effluents and secretly interviewed employees. After he made his discoveries public, the state attorney general filed charges against the company, and in 1987 American Cyanamid pleaded guilty to 37 counts of pollution. The company was fined $900,000, and in many quarters the guerrilla chemist was hailed as a hero.

In the past several years a new wave of environmental concern has swept the United States, prompted by a series of ecological disasters, disturbing natural events, and dire scientific warnings. Oil spills, headlined by the wreck of the tanker *Exxon Valdez* in March 1989, have killed wildlife and stained shorelines. Droughts and high temperatures have brought fears that the world is already experiencing a "greenhouse effect"—global warming from increased atmospheric concentrations of carbon dioxide and other heat-absorbing gases. At the same time, tropical forests, which remove carbon dioxide from the air, are being cut down at a rate equivalent to one football field a second. Beach users encounter untreated sewage and medical wastes, including used hypodermic needles. Scientists believe the atmosphere's ozone layer, which helps to protect us from ultraviolet radiation, is eroding because of careless use of chlorofluorocarbons (CFCs).

The list of environmental problems goes on and on, and governments at all levels—federal, state, and local—have begun to respond to public concern. Some recent measures and proposals use a carrot rather than a stick—in other words, incentives not to pollute, rather than merely bans, regulations, and penalties. For example, Seattle bases its trash-collection charges on the amount of trash a household produces; but for those who want to reduce their bills, the city offers free collections of recyclable wastes such as bottles and newspapers. Thus residents have a financial incentive to participate in the recycling process. One proposal to curb emissions of noxious gases is to tax cars that emit such gases and give rebates for vehicles that do not. Similarly, companies could be taxed for activities that generate carbon dioxide, and they could be given credits for planting trees. Perhaps cash incentives could also be offered for turning in worn-out refrigerators and air conditioners, whose CFCs could then be reused instead of released into the atmosphere.

Not all of these ideas may be politically practical, but the new environmentalism has shown a willingness to try different approaches. Incentives like those in Seattle's recycling program are being combined with old-fashioned crackdowns such as New Jersey's prosecution of the Linden chemical plant. Environmentalists hope to spread the idea that conserving the environment is in everyone's best interest.

Sources: "Planet of the Year" (special report), *Time*, January 2, 1989, pp. 24–73; Jeremy Main, "Here Comes the Big New Cleanup," *Fortune*, November 21, 1988, pp. 102–118; Michael Satchell, "The Toxic Avenger Strikes at Corporate Polluters," *U.S. News & World Report*, June 26, 1989, p. 28; Eliot Marshall, "Clean Air? Don't Hold Your Breath," *Science*, May 5, 1989, pp. 517–520.

SUMMARY

1. Customary supply and demand graphs show how rapidly a good is being consumed. For exhaustible natural resources, conservation takes place when the quantity on the horizontal axis moves to the left. Conservation can be achieved by shifting the supply curve on such a graph to the left. (See page 898 and Figure 1, page 899.)

2. The cost of extracting a resource is one of the forces affecting the location of the supply curve. Easily accessible deposits, with low extraction costs, are generally used first. So, other things being unchanged, as more and more of the resource is used, the supply curve for an exhaustible resource tends to shift to the left and encourages conservation. (See pages 898–899.)

3. As exhaustible natural resource prices rise, it pays firms and individuals to search more vigorously for new deposits of the resource. For this reason, "proven reserves" often increase as prices rise. (See page 900.)

4. The conservation effect of shifting the supply curve to the left is greater when the price elasticity of demand for the resource is high, and it is smaller when price elasticity is low. Since price elasticity of demand is usually greater as the length of time increases, conservation effects of supply-curve shifts increase with the passage of time. (See pages 900–901.)

5. Low interest rates encourage the conservation of exhaustible natural resources, and high interest rates discourage conservation, other things being equal. This is so because high interest rates mean, for resource owners, that alternative uses of their wealth are more attractive than leaving that wealth in its natural state as a resource. (See pages 901–902.)

6. Because interest rates reflect time preferences and the productivity of capital goods, they provide a connection between resource conservation and other aspects of an economic system. Conservation of exhaustible natural resources is just one aspect of the many different choices between the present and the future. (See pages 902–903.)

7. Interest rates may fail to provide appropriate guidelines for conservation. Central bank poli-

cies, government budget surpluses or deficits, and tax policies relating to saving and investing all can influence the real interest rate in the economy. (See page 903.)

8. Monopoly power exists in some natural resource markets. Since monopolistic firms tend to restrict output in order to increase profits, they may help to conserve exhaustible natural resources. However, much depends on the specific circumstances and policies followed by these monopolistic enterprises. (See pages 904–905.)

9. Government tax policies and price controls can affect the conservation of exhaustible natural resources. U.S. preferential tax treatment for natural resource extraction may have speeded up the use of some resources. However, price controls on natural gas and on oil may have slowed down the use of these resources. (See page 905.)

10. For renewable resources, conservation calls for attention to the economic factors that determine the conditions for the reproduction and growth of such resources. Because property rights are not clearly defined in some areas, human activities may have reduced renewable resource habitats too much and worked against the conservation of these resources. (See pages 908–909.)

11. Conservation of renewable resources also may require some limitations on the annual harvesting of these resources. The sustainable-annual-yield curve shows the quantities that may be harvested without causing a change in the population of the species. To conserve the species, harvesting should not be allowed to exceed the sustainable yield. (See pages 909–910 and Figure 4, page 910.)

12. The common property system sometimes fails to ensure that harvesting of renewable resources does not exceed the sustainable yield. Government regulations may be used to limit harvesting in common property areas. Extending the scope of private property rights is another way to control harvesting. The concept of a reservation price shows how property rights build future interests into present decisions about resource use. (See pages 911–916.)

13. The laws of the conservation of energy and matter suggest that waste treatment cannot reduce the total amount of waste but can change the

forms and locations of waste dispositions. (See pages 912–913.)

14. The demand for nature's waste-disposal services is derived from the demand for the goods and services that produce the waste. Waste disposal generates social costs through its disruption of natural ecological systems. In economic terms, the efficient quantity of nature's waste-disposal service is achieved when the value of the marginal unit of waste-disposal service, as indicated by the demand curve, is equal to the social cost of that unit. (See pages 913–914 and Figure 5, page 913.)

15. Waste-disposal charges (effluent charges) can make up for nature's inability to charge a price as a condition for disposing of waste. Correct effluent charges can establish a supply curve and bring about the efficient quantity of waste-disposal service. (See page 914.)

16. Externality problems arise in waste disposal because property rights are not well established or enforced for waste disposal into public areas. Government can improve the efficiency of waste disposal by exercising property rights in areas where private property rights are not established. (See pages 915–916.)

17. Effluent charges lead to price rises to producers and consumers for goods and services that generate harmful externalities. In this way they provide incentives for consumers to switch to other goods and services and for producers to find methods of production that cause less waste. These are attractive features of effluent charges. Developing reliable estimates of the actual demand and costs of waste is the main problem with these charges. (See pages 916–917.)

18. Standards and controls are a means of limiting waste by specifying product characteristics and methods of production and waste treatment. These methods of controlling the volume of waste are attractive politically. However, economists are critical of standards and controls because they tend to lock production and treatment methods into current technologies and to offer little incentive for developing better technologies. (See pages 917–918.)

19. Subsidies for waste treatment are criticized by economists because they tend to lower costs to producers and prices to consumers of goods that generate waste and in this way tend to increase the total volume of waste. (See page 918.)

KEY TERMS

common property: a system under which everyone has a legal right to harvest a resource (page 911).

depletion allowance: a feature of U.S. income taxation whereby part of the value of a resource that is removed from the earth is not counted as income to the owner of that resource (page 905).

derived demand: the demand for a resource that arises because of the demand for a good or service that the resource helps to produce (page 914).

effluent charge: the price charged for permission to dispose of waste (page 915).

entitlements: certificates that U.S. oil refiners were required to obtain in the 1970s in order to purchase domestic oil at low controlled prices (page 907).

exhaustible natural resources: those resources whose stock cannot be replenished (page 898).

nonexhaustible natural resources: resources such as energy from the sun, from winds, or from tides for which there is no conservation problem since the earth receives a continuing flow of them (page 898).

reservation price: a price below which a resource will be reserved for future use by its owner (page 911).

DISCUSSION QUESTIONS

1. Why is the supply curve for an exhaustible natural resource expected to shift to the left as more and more of the stock of that resource is used up? How can technological changes slow down or even reverse this shift?

2. "The market's method of conserving exhaustible natural resources operates more effectively when demand is price elastic than when it is price inelastic and more effectively when long time periods are considered than when short time periods are considered." Explain and illustrate with graphs.

3. "Proven reserves of crude oil always go up when the price of oil rises and go down when the price falls. This proves that these numbers have no basis in fact but are simply made up by oil companies for propaganda purposes." Do you agree or disagree? Explain.

4. If you owned an oil well and had to decide whether to pump oil or to cap the well, how would the interest rate influence your decision? Use the interest-rate connection to illustrate what would tend to happen to the extraction rate of exhaustible natural resources if people change their time preferences toward more current consumption.

5. Construct a supply and demand graph to illustrate a regulated price for energy set below the free-market equilibrium price. Compare your graph with Figure 3. Will this regulated price increase or decrease the rate at which deposits of the natural resource are used? Explain.

6. The "entitlements" oil-pricing system in the United States in the 1970s led to oil being priced to consumers below its actual marginal cost and increased both consumption and oil imports. How might a refinery operate at its profit-maximizing output and still sell at a price below the actual marginal cost? How did the system lead to increased imports?

7. How has the difficulty of establishing property rights tended to reduce the habitat of renewable resources such as wild game below the economically efficient level? Explain how this problem involves the concept of externalities. Does government have a role to play?

8. Construct a graph of the sustainable-yield curve for a renewable natural resource. Compare your graph with Figure 4. How does this help explain why the threat of extinction appears quite suddenly, even though harvesting has increased for many years with no apparent problem?

9. Explain how a reservation price limits the current harvesting of a renewable resource. How is this similar to the way interest rates influence extraction of nonrenewable resources? Why does a common property system fail to install the reservation-price constraint on current harvesting?

10. Explain how the demand for waste-disposal service is a derived demand stemming from the demand for goods that satisfy wants. Construct a graph illustrating the economically efficient quantity of waste disposal. Why will this efficient quantity usually not be obtained unless effluent charges are established?

11. It is sometimes argued that it is a waste of time to make firms pay for the waste they deposit in nature or for the environmental damage caused by their production processes because they simply pass the cost on to the people who buy their product and then continue to pollute as before. Do you agree or disagree with this position? Why or why not?

12. Excessive uniformity and failure to use the profit motive effectively are weaknesses of the standards and controls approach to limiting harmful externalities. Explain the basis for each of these criticisms.

13. What is the economist's basic criticism of government subsidies that help pay the costs of waste-treatment facilities? Does it follow that economists believe that waste-treatment facilities are not useful? Why or why not?

Regulation, Deregulation, Reregulation: The S&L Case

EASY ANSWERS, RIGHT AND LEFT

We say it boldly and baldly: No regulation system has ever worked perfectly. Some regulatees get away with murder; others are quibbled to "the death of a thousand cuts." Some vital decisions are made too hastily before "the facts" are in; others are postponed until "after the horse is stolen" . . . or never made at all. In one puddle rules King Log, doing nothing; in the next puddle rules King Stork, feeding on the frogs who selected him. Some regulators are fools; some are crooks; some are both. From all such cases, the Absolutist on the Right draws an easy moral: "Deregulate! Trust the market! Rational expectations! Invisible hands! Supply and demand!"

We say it equally boldly and equally baldly: No market has ever worked perfectly. Monopoly, monopsony, collusion, and cartelization have long half-lives. Social costs and benefits diverge from private ones in every direction. Information is all on one side. Dollar votes are not the same as people votes. Durocher's Law holds, and "Nice guys finish last."[1] The whole charade starts from unfair distributions of income, wealth, status, and power. From all such cases, the Absolutist on the Left draws an easy moral: "Regulate! Pass a law—or quicker, issue an order! Me for dictator! Market failure! Planning! *Nullum crimen sine poena*—no crime without punishment!"

1. Gilbert and Sullivan said it in verse, before "Leo the Lip" was born:

> Thus do the Fates their gifts allot.
>   While A is happy, B is not,
> Yet B is worthy, I dare say,
>   Of more prosperity than A!

Still more boldly and still more baldly: Both Absolutes are wrong. But who is right? The Poet has indeed said:

> Of forms of government let fools contest;
> That which is best administered is best.

Can the Economist do any better than the Poet (in this case, Alexander Pope)? Do the choices of rules to be administered, and methods of administration, really make no difference?

METHODOLOGICAL DIGRESSION

Mainstream economic analysis, including most of this book, assumes certain basic noneconomic factors as given, or as variable only one at a time: population, tastes, technology, resources, and the rules of the economic game. Institutional economics, on the other hand, concentrates on those rules themselves: How have they developed? What alternatives might be considered? How are they likely to develop? How might they be improved? The present essay is an exercise in institutional economics thus conceived. We trace the checkered history of "the rules" in one (financial) industry, and wonder whether we may be drifting.

THE SAVINGS AND LOAN INDUSTRY: AN INTRODUCTION

Savings and loan associations (S&Ls, also called *thrifts*) are a branch of the financial intermediation industry. This is among the more closely regulated industries in most countries, because many outsiders are both ignorant of "high finance" and suspicious of its professional practitioners. This regulation usually includes an artificial division of financial intermediation (brokerage between savers and investors) into several different industries. In each of these industries one sort of institution is given certain advantages, but there is usually plenty of room for interindustry competition. The principal competitors of the S&Ls are the commercial banks, the credit unions, and the securities dealers (stockbrokers).

America's S&Ls, numbering 4,200 at the beginning of the 1980s, traditionally received deposits from individual savers and made loans to purchasers and builders of residential housing. They were regulated by the Federal Home Loan Banks and also by regulatory bodies in the individual states in which they operated. Deposits in S&Ls were almost always insured by the Federal Savings and Loan Insurance Corporation (FSLIC), which imposed a further layer of regulation. S&Ls were permitted to pay higher interest rates than commercial banks on savings deposits, but depositors could not write checks against S&L deposits. S&Ls were not permitted to lend money for purposes other than residential housing within a 50-mile radius, although commercial banks could also make housing loans.

The typical S&L loan was a long-term first mortgage,[2] secured by a piece of residential real estate. To provide liquidity for such paper, there were nationwide markets in mortgages, supported by semipublic national mortgage associations for different sorts of mortgages, the best known of these being "Fannie Mae" (the Federal National Mortgage Association).

Regulators were expected to assure themselves and the public that the S&L limitation to residential housing loans was enforced, that loans were not suspiciously concentrated to S&L officers or other favored borrowers, that mortgage values were a sufficiently small percentage of actual property values, that a sufficient proportion of outstanding mortgages were "performing," and that sufficient reserves were kept against the "sour apples" in the institution's portfolio. If regulators were not satisfied on such points, or if an S&L's capital (less reserves) was too small a fraction of its deposits, they could close the institution and force its liquidation, or refuse to continue insuring its deposits (which had much the same effect).[3] In the late 1950s, community and minority activists also began to exercise unofficial regulation, denouncing S&Ls that did not lend to women or minorities or that refused loans on property located in ghetto or minority neighborhoods—a practice called *red-lining*.

DEREGULATION

Despite multiple regulation by suspicious regulators and despite competition for deposits from commercial banks and securities dealers, the S&L business was on the whole genteel, placid, and even somewhat sleepy as American business goes. Some of their senior officers even felt themselves free to operate routinely by a "3-6-3 rule": pay 3 percent on deposits, lend funds on 6 percent mortgages, and be on the golf course by 3 P.M. What ended this idyllic existence?

The primary culprit was inflation, the secondary culprit was disintermediation, and the third was deregulation of the commercial banks. Because inflation had raised nominal interest rates (unadjusted for inflation), depositors began withdrawing their savings from commercial banks and S&Ls with their low rate ceilings—actually negative in real terms. (When a depositor removes funds from a financial intermediary and invests them himself or herself in either debt or equity securities, the process is called *disintermediation*.) Among the more favored high-yield substitutes for bank and S&L deposits were the so-called money-market funds. These were to the bond markets what investment trusts were to the stock market, namely, vehicles for the small investor to diversify his or her holdings. Like the investment trusts, they were initially managed primarily by securities dealers and investment counselors.

The commercial banking industry, larger and more vocal than the S&Ls, was the principal loser from the diversification of small investor holdings and the rise of the money-market funds. In self-defense against the securities dealers, the bankers lobbied Congress successfully, in the late 1970s and early 1980s, for the repeal of a complex body of regulations that limited the rates they could pay on checking and savings deposits. They also secured the right to manage money-market funds themselves, but failed to extend deposit insurance to deposits in these funds.

These developments left the S&Ls at a severe

---

2. In case of default by the borrower, holders of a first mortgage must be paid off before any payment is made to holders of a second mortgage. The holder of the first mortgage has the prior claim.

3. These are balance-sheet concepts not related directly to the income statement. Thus the income statements of a closed S&L might be showing a strong profit position. On the other hand, an S&L might have many years of losses without being subject to liquidation.

competitive disadvantage. How could an S&L pay a competitive rate to its depositors when its assets were tied up in long-term 6 percent mortgages? To make matters worse, the differential-rate cushion (over the commercial banks) on rates paid depositors disappeared with the elimination of ceilings on the rates commercial banks could pay. It was the S&L's turn to lobby in Congress, and lobby they did. In 1980–81 they secured relief from the low ceilings they could charge on mortgages—first on fixed-rate mortgages of the traditional sort and then on new variable-rate mortgages (VRMs), which they were permitted to issue for the first time.[4] The bulk of their assets, however, continued to be in fixed-rate mortgages at lower rates; such was the disadvantage of holding a long-term money-denominated asset in inflationary times. The S&Ls felt they needed additional relief, since 85 percent of them were losing money in 1981.

Deregulation was what the S&Ls won from Congress in 1982. The Thrift Institutions Restructuring Act of 1982 applied especially to them. It featured the right to make loans on business and commercial as well as residential property and opened up much lucrative turf for competition with the banks and credit unions. In some states, the S&Ls also won the right to grant their depositors checking privileges and to manage money-market funds in competition with the banks.

The S&Ls also won a purely unofficial victory over the powers of regulation—as important, perhaps, as the official victory in explaining the events of the subsequent years. Extension of S&L activities beyond residential housing increased both the quantitative burden on their regulators and the range of competence required for performance of their functions. In other circumstances, the expected response of the regulatory system might have been increases in staff and upgrading of jobs. But in the "Reaganomic" climate of antiregulation, not to mention budgetary deficit, neither reaction was feasible, and neither one occurred. At the state level, the situation was at least as bad. In some states, including Texas and California, the S&Ls were practically per-

4. The interest rate on a VRM is revised at intervals, usually annually or semiannually, to follow other interest rates, often with a lag.

mitted to "run wild."[5] The deposits remained safe; depositors earned higher interest rates; some S&Ls profited beyond the wildest dreams of their rule-of-thumb predecessors. Again we ask: What went wrong?

REREGULATION

"What went wrong" in half a decade of economic freedom—first in Maryland and Ohio, later mainly in Texas and California—was an outbreak of incompetence and fraud, plus the collapse of an oil boom. These events have left over 500 of the 3,150 remaining federally insured S&Ls—approximately 20 percent of the total number of firms in the industry—technically insolvent as of early 1989. They also threatened the United States with a bill, variously estimated at as much as $200 billion over ten years, half of it payable directly by taxpayers. Paying this bill would permit FSLIC, the deposit-insurance agency, to finance repayment of deposits in those S&Ls that will eventually be liquidated and to re-establish the rest of the "over 500" on a firmer footing. (No insured depositor has yet lost a penny of his or her deposits, however, and five-sixths of the surviving S&Ls are in no apparent danger.)

More can be said about incompetence and fraud. The "feel" of the hometown residential housing market was itself not easy to acquire or maintain, when the "hometown" was a city growing in some directions and not in others. Expanding one's expertise to include skyscrapers, shopping centers, and resort hotels thousands of miles away was an added strain. But the stakes were high, and the new climate of deregulation was mild and gentle. A good many S&L managements raised their sights accordingly, without adequate notice to the depositors. Other owners and managements, more cautious, were bought out on profitable terms (at least on paper) by new owners and managements more willing to gamble with other people's money. Many of the risk-lovers succeeded—but many failed.

The situation was worst in the "oil-patch" states, particularly Texas. OPEC had forced a rise in the world price of crude oil, from which Texas profited along with Kuwait, Iran, and Saudi Arabia. The boom had naturally expanded from oil fields to oil towns and oil-related real estate. Houston was America's Kuwait, Riyadh, Teheran, and Abu Dhabi rolled into one. The price rises of oil and Texas realty were expected to last indefinitely. However, when the oil

5. Barbara Rudolph, "Finally, the Bill Has Come Due," *Time* (February 20, 1989).

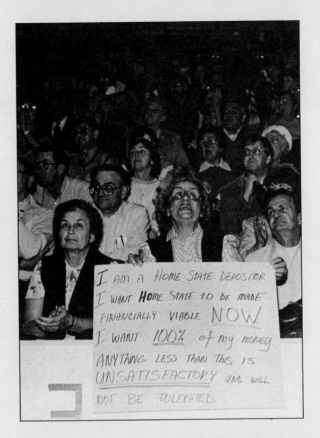

price peaked and fell in the mid-1980s, the real estate boom collapsed with it. Houston was found, by 20-20 hindsight, to have overbuilt tremendously in anticipation of a future that had been postponed. Numerous S&Ls, not all of them in Texas, collapsed with Texas real estate. Some collapsed into outright liquidation, but others into a limbo called technical insolvency. (The FSLIC would have had insufficient funds to pay off depositors if too many had closed their doors.[6])

Serious illegality, if not outright fraud, complicated the problem in perhaps one case in four. Certain S&L owners and managers, previously no more dishonest than other persons, yielded to the temptations of big money and slack regulation to lend S&L money to themselves, their friends, their relatives, and their business associates, with occasional disastrous results. Many S&Ls passed from the control of the stodgy to the control of the high fliers, who were more willing to cut regulatory corners and to live

6. A number of S&Ls were allegedly kept open longer than they should have been, losing money in the process and increasing the eventual burden on the FSLIC. (More 20-20 hindsight!) To stay open when regulators proposed liquidation, these S&Ls appealed to Congress to pressure the Home Loan Bank Board on their behalf.

high on the hog while cutting them. (Private planes, palatial estates, and jet-setting—as celebrated by the popular television serial "Dallas.") As for the funds involved, they appear to have been dissipated in high living or laundered at home and abroad in advance of exposure.

The total amount of deposits at risk was well beyond the resources of the FSLIC. To save face and keep the FSLIC afloat, the Home Loan Bank Board approved sales of weak S&Ls to stronger ones, using the sales proceeds to pay off depositors in those S&Ls that were actually liquidated. It was a buyer's market in shaky S&Ls, and many acquired them at much less than critics believed to be their long-term values. The FSLIC and the Federal Home Loan Banks were accused of panicking and permitting "sweetheart" deals—even of collusion with the purchasers.

In the late 1980s, the federal government moved in the direction of more thoroughgoing reform and reregulation. The purpose was both to cut its losses and to prevent a recurrence of the apparent abuses of deregulation while continuing to protect S&L depositors. The Bush administration proposed weakening the discretion of the Home Loan Banks and scrapping their governing board—allegedly too friendly to the S&L industry—in favor of transferring final oversight to presumably higher-caliber regulators within the Treasury Department. Another proposal was to increase the deposit-insurance premiums paid by the S&Ls to the FSLIC.[7] These would in all probability be shifted to depositors in lower rates of return.[8]

THE LONGER RUN

We have left to the end the longer-run problem of the S&L industry, either deregulated or reregulated. For better or worse, financial developments in many countries, and even internationally, have included homogenization of the entire financial intermediation industry. Homogenization has left more types of institutions competing with one another over a broader range of services, if not across the board. In addition to the S&Ls, commercial banks, credit unions, and securities dealers, these institutions include investment banks, bond dealers, exchange dealers, insurance companies, and even the larger department stores and express companies. In this environment, there is some doubt whether S&Ls can survive in their traditional form, that is, without becoming banks or being taken over by banks. If S&Ls cannot survive competition, should regulation subsidize them in some fashion or insulate them again from competition?

These questions became acute in the late 1980s. The S&L industry as a whole seemed to be in decline. It reported losses of over $13 billion in 1988 and over $7 billion in the first half of 1989. As we have said, the number of S&Ls was 3,150 at the beginning of 1989, a decline of 1,000 in little more than a decade, and at least 500 of the survivors were "shaky." The industry held about one-third of U.S. home mortgages, down from 60 percent two decades previously. "The average homeowner can get a mortgage without stepping inside an S&L. Maybe the thrifts have outlived their usefulness."[9]

It is time to point the moral and adorn the tale. But what is the moral to be? Did the problems arise because of too much regulation before 1982 or because of too little regulation thereafter? What would have happened had the S&Ls not been regulated in the first place? If they had never been deregulated? We cannot be sure. Draw your own conclusions—or your own confusions, if confusions are more appropriate.

---

7. To equalize competition between S&Ls and commercial banks, this plan required the latter also to pay increased premiums to the Federal Deposit Insurance Corporation (FDIC). (The FDIC insures commercial bank deposits.) However, commercial bank premiums to FDIC could not be used by the FSLIC to pay off S&L depositors.

8. The original Bush administration proposal would have imposed fees directly on S&L and commercial bank depositors. This plan, seen as unfair and much too obvious for American public opinion, aroused a storm of opposition.

9. Quoted from Laurence Fink, partner in an investment firm, by Rudolph, "Finally, the Bill Has Come Due," p. 73.

Comparative Economic Systems—
More Planning or Less?

Radical Economics

PART XI
COMPARATIVE
ECONOMIC SYSTEMS

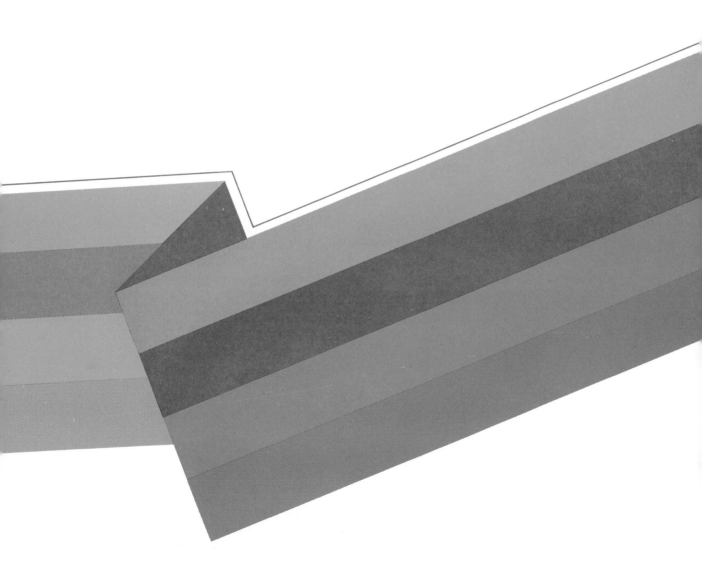

39

Comparative Economic Systems—More Planning or Less?

Preview As you learned earlier, societies manage their scarcity problems in different ways. In today's world, the most important of these are the impersonal *market* and deliberate *planning* by the public authorities, though in some places *traditional* economies survive.

You also know that no existing economy is *pure* and that all are *mixed*. The United States is primarily, but by no means exclusively, a market economy, since about 30 percent of the American gross national product now passes through the public sector and need not "meet the test of the market." Similarly, the Soviet Union is primarily but not exclusively a planned economy, since much of its agricultural output is raised and marketed by peasants from their private plots.

The question raised in this chapter is a normative one. Should we favor using "more planning" or "less planning" by public agencies in our economy? In other words, should we shift our economic "mix" toward greater reliance on public planning, greater reliance on the market, or leave it alone?

We begin by reviewing our criteria for judging economic systems. Next we discuss the relationship of planning to freedom and power, and distinguish among planning, collectivism, and the welfare state. Even though these three kinds of institutions are often found together, a country may have any one or two without the rest. Then, turning specifically to planning, we introduce several general planning types.

At this point, we discuss first the Soviet Union as a representative of collectivist (also socialist) planning, and then Japan and Sweden as two widely different examples of economic planning under capitalism. As examples of socialist collectivism that is combined with a largely market economy, we turn to the countries of Yugoslavia and China.

To illustrate some of the problems raised by the Russian experience in particular, we return to theory for the last part of the chapter. One theory that we present is the market socialist model of Oskar Lange and A. P. Lerner. The other is the forecast of Ludwig von Mises and Friedrich von Hayek that planning is incompatible with freedom and will lead eventually to what Hayek calls "serfdom."

SOCIAL GOALS

We take as given the goals suggested in Chapter 1, but not their relative importance. These goals are as follows:

1. High *present* standards of living

2. High growth rates, leading to high *prospective* standards of living

3. Equitable distribution of income and wealth

4. Security of the standard of living against short-term downward shocks from recessions and depressions, and also against long-term shocks from resource exhaustion and technological change

5. Compatibility of economic institutions with personal liberty and civil rights

6. Compatibility of economic institutions with physical and mental health

Even with agreement on these goals, the question of "more planning or less?" arouses violent and sometimes irrational emotions. Two stories illustrate this point.

The first story is about Hassan, an Egyptian student of one of the authors, who was describing the wonders that the Aswan Dam, built in the late 1950s, would bring to his country. The teacher recalled that the British, during their period of rule over Egypt, had also built an Aswan Dam and placed high hopes on it, with disappointing results. "But, Professor," said Hassan politely, "you don't understand. This Aswan Dam is *planned!*" Hassan knew that the British dam was also planned—engineering projects always are! He meant that the Egyptian dam was part of a comprehensive national plan for Egypt, whereas the British dam had been an isolated project. Confidence like Hassan's

that a plan will work just because it *is* a plan is what we call "magic wand" planning. Much of the appeal of some of the more grandiose kinds of planning is of the magic wand sort.

The second story is about a Polish friend of one of the authors. When the Nazis invaded Poland in 1939, this man fled to the Soviet Union. The U.S.S.R., then allied with the Nazis, sent him to a remote part of Siberia. There, after the Nazis had invaded the U.S.S.R., a peasant asked him if the Nazis were as bad as he had been told. The Polish refugee assured the Siberian peasant that the Nazis were indeed bad people who committed atrocities, but the peasant was not satisfied. "Do the Nazis have collective farms in Germany?" he asked. (Collective farms are the basis for Soviet agricultural planning.)

"No, there are no collective farms in Germany."

"Well, then, the Nazis cannot be so bad as you say," concluded the peasant.

The question of the amount of deliberate planning by public agencies needed to achieve economic goals is a controversial one.

PLANNING, FREEDOM, AND POWER

When economists speak of planned economies, the planning they have in mind is done by legislators, experts, and civil servants. But in any case, every individual, to some extent, plans for himself or herself. Every family plans for itself. Every organization—be it a corporation, a university, a club, or a government bureau—plans for itself. In economics **planning** means an institutional arrangement in which some individual or organization in a public position plans for another individual or organization, who or which has little say about the plan and whose economic freedom is restricted by the planning decision.

The relation between freedom and planning is by no means a simple matter. When I plan for myself today, my freedom is restricted by whatever long-term plans I may have made earlier. For example, I cannot buy a new car or take a trip to Europe because I carried out last year's plan to buy a house, and "my mortgage payments are killing me." Families and organizations present even more problems than individuals. Students have lost their best friends because their parents decided to move from one neighborhood to another, or from the Snow Belt to the Sun Belt. Workers have lost their jobs when their employer's home office decided to close their factory or office. Retailers have gone bankrupt when major suppliers or customers closed down or moved away—or when competitors opened up shop across the street. When City Hall, the State Capitol, or "Washington" carries out some plan we dislike, and which limits our economic freedom in some way, are we hurt any less because we can still vote for legislators who promise to change or repeal the plan, or because we can "vote with our feet" by moving to some other place? One point should be clear: public planning, when carried out through laws and regulations, may be either more or less restrictive of freedom than private planning, when carried out through market forces.

In economics, planning means an institutional arrangement in which some individual or organization in a public position plans for another individual or organization, whose economic freedom is restricted by the planning decision. The relationship between freedom and planning is complex.

Public planning, when carried out through laws and regulations, may be either more or less restrictive of freedom than private planning, when carried out through market forces.

Freedom should be distinguished from *power*. You are quite free to visit the moon, or Mars for that matter, but are powerless to exercise that freedom unless you are an astronaut, a cosmonaut, or a flying-saucerite from outer space. You have the power to abuse small children or drive while drunk, but your freedom does not extend to such illegal activities. Planners, too, often do not have the power to carry out plans they are free to make. The controversial architect and city planner Frank Lloyd Wright said that one American city "needs

another fire" and that another should be "torn down and started over," but no urban planner has the power to burn or tear down any city.

Freedom-versus-power problems arise whenever the protection of someone's freedom interferes with someone else's planning power, or whenever the protection or enhancement of someone's planning power interferes with someone else's freedom. Yet a more basic freedom-power problem is this one: Can a person be said to have freedom at all, when either natural forces or the actions of others—including their economic plans—deprive him or her of the power to exercise it effectively? Is your freedom of speech worth anything if you do not own a newspaper or a television station, have no pulpit or professorship, and cannot otherwise persuade people to listen to you? What is it worth to be free to air your views if you are shunned by your customers or lose your job because of them, even when you fear neither legal prosecution nor mob violence? And if your freedom of speech cannot be translated into the power to influence others, how much better off are you than someone else who must follow the "party line," keep his or her mouth shut, or else face "re-education" in prison, labor camp, or mental hospital?

Freedom should be distinguished from power. Can a person be said to have freedom at all when either natural forces or the actions of others deprive him or her of the power to exercise it effectively?

PLANNING, COLLECTIVISM, AND THE WELFARE STATE

We have already suggested that planning is related to both freedom and power. Now we consider how it is related to collectivism and to the so-called welfare state.

In **collectivist economies**, land and physical capital such as buildings and machinery are largely or completely owned by collective agencies, not by private individuals or business firms. Most planned economies are in fact collectivist, and most of them are socialistic. In **socialistic economies** these col-

FIGURE 1
Types of Economic Systems

Planned Collectivism	Market Capitalism
Planned Capitalism	Market Collectivism

Planned economies are indicated to the left of the center line, and market economies to the right. Collectivist economies are shown as red, and capitalist economies are shown as blue. Most collectivist economies are in fact socialistic.

lective agencies are governmental.[1] On the other hand, most but not all market economies are **capitalistic.** In these economies, land and physical capital are owned largely by private individuals or business firms. Aside from traditional economies, there are four distinct types of economic systems, as pictured in Figure 1. In this figure, planned economies are shown to the left of the center line and market economies to the right. Collectivist (usually socialist) economies are colored red, and the capitalist ones colored blue.

Just as many people confuse planning with socialism or communism, and the market with capitalism, they also associate planning with the welfare state, and the market with something less compassionate.

In collectivist economies, land and physical capital are largely or completely owned by collective agencies, not by individuals or business firms. In socialist economies, these collective agencies are governmental.

---

1. A **communist** is a socialist who believes that socialism on a world scale will lead to an economy of abundance, and who accepts violence, revolution, and dictatorship as a means to that end.

Most market economies are capitalistic—land and physical capital are owned largely by private individuals or business firms.

A **welfare state** is an economy that places an especially high value on our goals 3 and 4 among the objectives of the economy. The "equity" of its income and wealth distributions is a matter of first importance. "Equity," moreover, is treated as including a relatively high poverty line or "safety net," below which no person or family need remain for long, along with a high degree of distributional equality above this poverty line. Either a capitalist or a socialist economy, and likewise either a planned or a market economy, may be a welfare state. Any of these may also be something other than a welfare state.

Any economic system, whether capitalist, socialist, planned, or market, that places great value on a high poverty line and a high degree of distributional equality above this line may be called a welfare state.

TYPES OF PLANNING

You have learned that not all markets are alike. Monopoly, for example, is different from competition. In the same way, planning systems are not all alike. In the next few paragraphs we outline several of the major types of planning.

Imperative Planning

The most rigorous form of planning is **imperative planning.** It is imperative in that, to quote Josef Stalin, "A plan is a command." Failure to reach an important plan target is a criminal offense. In extreme cases those who fail may be punished by imprisonment or even death, as sometimes happened in Stalin's Russia. Imperative planning goes beyond the aggregate economy to include the "fine structure" of the economy as a whole and also of a country's regions.

Indicative Planning

A milder form of planning is **indicative planning.** It operates mainly by convincing plan participants that following the plan will help them economically, though in some cases they are threatened with the denial of privileges (or even with penalties) for not following "administrative guidance." Most peacetime capitalist planning is of this kind. Indicative planning is generally also *consensual*, meaning that the planning authority includes representatives of various interest groups as well as civil servants and planning technicians. Among the groups represented may be some or all of the following: the financial community, the military, organized business, organized labor, organized agriculture, organized taxpayers, organized consumers, and spokespersons from the different regions of the country.

Most peacetime capitalist planning is indicative: it operates mainly by convincing participants that following the plan will help them economically. Indicative planning is generally consensual.

Public Sector Planning

Public sector planning covers only the public sector. The many different organs of central and local government, while producing a small percentage of the total national income and product, often dominate the economy's "commanding heights," or key industries, in mixed systems. To treat them as a single enterprise, therefore, goes a long way toward controlling the whole economy. However, it is also hard to do so, because of jealousy between different branches of the government—between "national defense" and "social services," between the central and local governments, and between the more and less advanced parts of the country. The private sector is also affected by public sector planning because private companies sell to or buy from public agencies, and because the plan gives the public sector priority over strategic and especially over imported resources. This kind of planning has been used most widely in India.

Macroeconomic Planning

Macroeconomic planning is less ambitious than any of the three kinds of planning covered so far. Planned or target quantities generally include standard aggregate measures such as gross national product, the division between consumption, investment, and government sectors, the supplies of money and credit, the government surplus or deficit, international balances, and interest rates. The fine structure of the aggregates is left to the market.

Macroeconomic planning generally includes the simple forecasting or projection of present policies or the results of certain changes that have been proposed. This is technically not planning at all. Indeed, it is sometimes done entirely by computer simulation, with little aid from human hands or brains. It often precedes real planning, but is treated as planning by the mass media.

Magic Wand Planning

We have already noted **"magic wand" planning.** A magic wand plan is built around a collection of projects and/or an appealing slogan. The projects or the slogan are expected to produce all kinds of good things by some unspecified processes, including the mystical power of the word *planning*. One example is the "fourth national plan" proposed for Japan in Herman Kahn's *Japanese Challenge*. This plan proposed to produce an industrialized environmentalist utopia, called "the machine in the garden." Another is the Humphrey-Hawkins bill in the United States. In its original form, it called for targets of low inflation and low unemployment that were to have been reached in 1983, but indicated only in the vaguest language how this was to have been done.

In the next few parts of this chapter, we shall present case studies of actual economies illustrating planned collectivism, planned capitalism, and market socialism. (Most of this book has assumed a market-capitalist economy, and so we see no need to illustrate such an economy again here.)

The several major types of planning include imperative planning, indicative planning, public

---

sector planning, macroeconomic planning, and magic wand planning.

A PLANNED COLLECTIVIST ECONOMY: THE SOVIET UNION

We begin with the Soviet model of imperative planning. Its vision of the economy is a huge factory, producing not only the country's final products, or consumer goods, but also its own intermediate products. As his model for Russia, Vladimir Lenin (1870–1924) may have used the Ford works in and around Detroit, which were the industrial marvels of his time. Ford produced not only automobiles, trucks, and tractors, but also many of their parts, and raw materials like coal and steel. Another vision was one that the Soviets shared with many other hostile critics of capitalism: that business administration can be reduced to the clerical routine of "office management," if the firm only had the information that a plan could provide and if it need not be concerned with competition. In this way, Lenin hoped that a national plan, maximizing welfare for the whole society much as a business firm plans to maximize profits, could be made simple and clear enough so that the average worker, without formal training in economics or statistics, could understand it and criticize it intelligently.

The Soviet model of imperative planning views the economy as a huge factory, producing not only the country's consumer goods but also its intermediate products.

Stalin and the Growth of Gosplan

The Russian revolutions of 1917 were followed by civil war, foreign intervention, and famine. With all these troubles, the planning process floundered over the years from 1917 to 1928. After Lenin died

in 1924, the "Soviet" planning model developed under the leadership of Josef Stalin (1880–1953). This model was both imperative and highly centralized in a single agency, called **Gosplan,** which has since grown to huge proportions. Gosplan is subdivided along both industrial and regional lines, with consultation extending down to and up from the individual factory. That is, the manager of a factory or a collective farm is informed of his or her role in the plan: what outputs should be produced, and what inputs should be used to produce them. The manager may suggest changes, but final authority rests with Gosplan in Moscow.

The plans are usually but not necessarily for five-year periods. The actual length of time is a practical compromise. Shorter periods may not allow completion of many planned projects, and could overtax Gosplan facilities. Longer periods might result in many plants being out of date by the time they were built.

Every part of the plan must be coordinated with other parts, since in economics nearly everything depends on nearly everything else. Every output has to be expanded as fast as its inputs, and no faster than its own demand. To coordinate the parts of the plan, the Soviets have used two specialized techniques—materials balancing and input-output analysis.

Materials Balancing The simpler of the two seems to be **materials balancing.** For every one of the thousands of final and intermediate products, potential supplies and demands are estimated for each year of the plan, allowing for both domestic production and international trade. The problem with this method is the difficulty of tracing the results of changes from the last plan, of technological progress, or of economic growth. For example, how much will a rise in the output of heavy trucks, including their engines and tires and fuel, eventually increase the demand for coal? And by how much will these trucks increase the supply of coal?

Input-Output Analysis To solve problems of this last sort, **input-output analysis** was developed (outside the U.S.S.R.) by the Russian-born Nobel Prize–winning economist Wassily Leontief (1906–   ).

TABLE 1
An Input-Output Table (in dollars)

Supplying Industry	Using Industry				
	Agriculture and Fisheries (1)	Food and Kindred Products (2)	Tobacco Manufactures (3)	Textile Mill Products (4)	Apparel (5)
(1) Agriculture and Fisheries	.2609	.4041	.2941	.2139	.0015
(2) Food and Kindred Products	.0572	.1319	.0055	.0062	.0007
(3) Tobacco Manufactures	0	0	.3110	0	0
(4) Textile Mill Products	.0015	0	0	.1341	.2955
(5) Apparel	.0011	.0055	0	0	.1494

This is a portion of the American input-output table for 1947, published by the Bureau of Labor Statistics and condensed in Robert Dorfman's book, *The Price System* (Englewood Cliffs, N.J.: Prentice-Hall, 1964); used with permission.

We focus our attention on the highlighted number .2955. It says that to produce a dollar's worth of its own output, a using industry (apparel) bought $.2955 worth of products from a supplying industry (textiles).

For a complete input-output table, each column and each row would add up to 1.00 (one dollar), since "industries" can be included for "households," "foreign trade," or any other source or use of output.

Input-output analysis is based on matrix algebra, which is studied in more advanced economics as well as mathematics courses. We can illustrate the basic features of the process with the help of Table 1, which is part of an input-output table. The first step in setting up the system is to divide the economy into separate industries for which data can be collected. The table illustrates five such industries—agriculture and fisheries, food and kindred products, tobacco manufactures, textile mill products, and apparel. Each of these industries is listed twice in the table, once as a supplying industry at the left end of a row, and again as a using industry at the head of a column in the table. In the body of the table, each number shows the value of goods from a supplying industry that is used to produce a dollar's worth of goods from a using industry.

For example, the highlighted number in the table tells us that $.2955 worth (or 29.55 cents' worth) of supplies from the textile mill products industry is used by the apparel industry for each dollar's worth of apparel produced. In the complete system, the whole column for the apparel industry would add up to 1.00 (one dollar). Similarly, the whole row of values for the textile mill products industry would add up to 1.00, since all of its out- put supplied will be used somewhere in the economy. One of the "industries" is "households," so that consumption is recognized. Another "industry" can be foreign trade, to account for exports and imports, and so on.

For the planning specialists at Gosplan, the problem is to estimate accurately what the actual input-output relationships are for the economy. If their estimates do not correspond to what happens in the actual execution of the plan, shortages and surpluses will develop, and the goals of the plan will not be met. As you can easily imagine, the method becomes unwieldy when the classification of the outputs and inputs approaches the fineness of materials balancing. One needs not only to have enough steel for rails but also to have it in the form of rails as distinguished from girders, stainless steel, or armor plate. Nevertheless, progress in planning has been marked by a rise in the relative importance of input-output techniques.

Under Stalin, the imperative planning process was highly centralized in a single agency, called Gosplan, which uses the techniques of materials balancing and input-output analysis.

Problems of Soviet Planning

Far from being clear enough for Lenin's "ordinary worker" to understand, Soviet planning is a highly complex system that has not worked very well. Before the day of the computer, Soviet writers feared "drowning in an ocean of paper" by the year 1980, in the effort to record, digest, and apply the information needed in forming and revising plans. Even though the computer provided a breathing space, the danger of "drowning in computer output" remains for the planners.

In practice, the key problems of Soviet planning can be reduced to three. The first is disappointingly low productivity, particularly for labor on collective farms. (Peasants do much better, it appears, on their private plots.) Second, since planning is done in terms of physical quantities or weights of goods, quality is often skimped or products are too heavy for use, particularly toward the ends of planning periods. Third, the plans are too rigid. They do not allow for unavoidable shortfalls, so that they have seldom, if ever, been carried out in full. For this reason, the plans include a **leading links** system. This means that when the whole plan cannot be carried out, certain leading links are completed in full, and the rest of the plan is postponed in part until the next planning period. The leading links are generally military hardware and capital goods; the postponements are generally in consumption goods. This is why each successive plan promised Western European living standards to the Soviet citizen, and why the promises have remained unfulfilled. However, the conditions of the Russian economy and the Russian consumer were so poor under the Czarist regime[2] that to the Soviet citizen these deficiencies of Soviet planning seemed minor when compared with the advances made over prerevolutionary Russia, and with the conditions of most LDCs of the present world.

The key problems of Soviet planning are: (1) disappointingly low productivity, (2) poor quality of goods, and (3) inflexibility.

---

2. Some economic historians, notably Alexander Gerschenkron, have argued that Czarist Russia was making rapid progress during the 1890–1913 generation, so that continuation of the 1890–1913 trend would have equaled actual Soviet performance had Czar Nicholas II and his ministers avoided the disastrous World War I. But this is conjecture.

Under the leading links system, when the whole plan cannot be carried out, certain parts (leading links—generally military hardware and capital goods) are completed in full, and the rest of the plan is postponed until the next planning period.

From Stalin to Gorbachev

Stalin died in 1953. Under his first few successors, Soviet planning became on balance somewhat less severe in the U.S.S.R., despite occasional Stalinist revivals under the leadership of Leonid Brezhnev. Change was actually more marked in the socialist countries of Eastern Europe and in China (after the death of Mao Zedong in 1976) than in the Soviet Union itself. After partial successes in Hungary and China, the pace of reform accelerated in the Soviet Union under General Secretary Mikhail Gorbachev, who came to power in 1985. The reforms are lumped together under the Russian title, **perestroika** (restructuring)—a term applied by Gorbachev and his economic adviser, Abel Agenbegyan.[3]

The principal components of *perestroika* appear to be as follows.

1. A much wider scope for an unplanned and private (but noncapitalist) "dual economy" alongside the planned socialist economy.[4] This aspect of *perestoika* is resisted strongly by Soviet conservatives in the Communist party, in the Gosplan, and in the other ministries charged with centralized planning of such sectors of the economy as agricul-

---

3. An earlier reform attempt, supported hesitantly and intermittently by General Secretary Nikita Khrushchev in the late 1950s and early 1960s, was called **Libermanism,** from the name of an early academic advocate, Yevsei Liberman. Libermanism did not long survive Khrushchev's fall from power in 1964.

4. How can a private economy be noncapitalist? In the first place, private firms do not own land or capital instruments. They hold land and capital only under lease from the state, which retains the legal title. In the second place, the private enterprises are family firms or producers' cooperatives (in Russian, *artels*). They do not employ more than a limited number of people in "commodity production," and their growth outside the service industries is strictly limited. Employment of workers for wages or fees as servants, doctors, lawyers, etc., is quite legal under socialist regimes because no salable goods are produced for private profit.

ture, construction, and heavy industries in general. These bureaucrats fear not only for their own power and prestige but consider themselves orthodox Marxist-Leninists ideologically opposed to "taking the capitalist road."

2. Much more slack in the plans themselves so that a bad harvest or a drought or a power failure can be absorbed without extensive plan revisions.

3. More leeway for plant managers to run their plants without the continuous supervision of functionaries from either the Soviet state or the Communist party bureaucracies. Indeed, if planned targets are met at planned prices, and if the state receives its planned rents from the land and capital goods the (socialist) firm uses, the firm may make a "profit." If it does, some or all of the profit may be kept within the firm and spent at the manager's discretion as bonuses for the work force, for improvements in housing and other facilities, or even for the manager's own use. For obvious reasons, this reform is viewed with alarm by state and party conservatives and bureaucrats.

The principal components of *perestroika* (restructuring) include: (1) a much wider scope for an unplanned private economy alongside the planned economy, (2) more flexible plans, and (3) more leeway for plant managers to run their plants.

To illustrate the three components of *perestroika,* let us consider a Hungarian bakery, run by a large family with many relatives or by a producers' cooperative. Hungary has moved further away from Stalinism than have other Eastern European countries. The bakery receives each week a planned amount of flour, from which it must produce planned amounts of bread, to be sold at planned prices. But the plan is incomplete, or "slack," so that the bakery is free to buy additional flour at higher prices on the open market and to sell cake and pastry to private customers for whatever prices the market will bear.

At the current stage of *perestroika,* Soviet managers are not free to change output prices, wage rates, or employment levels. It appears that existing Soviet outputs are priced too low and that existing Soviet payroll costs and rents are too high to encourage enough additional production to remedy widespread consumer shortages under existing production methods. At the same time, prices cannot be raised, wages cut, or excess workers fired without endangering (in the short run) the living standards of Soviet citizens, which are already low by comparison with the West and with Japan. Indeed, the representative Soviet firm appears to run at a loss under present prices, with the loss made up by grants or "loans" from the state, financed by monetary expansion. This, in turn, raises the money supply, which adds to aggregate demand and to the suppressed inflation, shortages, and outages that plague the Soviet economy.[5] It is not clear what the reallocation of administrative power within the firm—more to the manager, less to the regulators—would do about this situation. Some outside specialists, notably Marshall Goldman of Harvard and Wellesley, doubt that the malaise can be cured at all within the Soviet system. In this view, *perestroika* is little more than another slogan. What needs to be done is to get the prices right.

A more sanguine view makes the key factor not prices but productivity. Since payrolls are so largely fixed in the representative firm, Soviet marginal costs are extremely low. Expanded production, even at existing prices, could be profitable if some combination of carrots and sticks could increase productivity and reduce waste of materials. *Perestroika* apparently expects managers to use more carrots. Stalinist conservatives prefer bigger and better sticks. If neither carrots nor sticks work, the Soviet firm may be like the legendary businessperson who "takes a loss on every item but makes it up on volume."

It appears that existing Soviet output prices are too low and existing Soviet payroll costs and rents are too high to encourage enough additional production to remedy widespread consumer shortages under existing production methods.

---

5. The Soviet housewife's shopping bag is called an *avoska,* which translates as "perhaps." "Perhaps" something in short supply will be available today and she can snap it up.

The Chinese Variant

Under the Chinese variant of Stalinist economic planning, as propounded by Mao Zedong (Mao Tse-tung, 1892–1976), rural people lived and worked in large collective farms called *communes*. Many of them went far beyond Soviet models in drawing up their own plans to produce and consume not only farm products but also a wide variety of manufactured goods (including parts).[6]

Each commune presented to the authorities in its provincial capital—and indirectly to the capital in Beijing (Peking)—a list of its expected surpluses and deficits (production minus consumption). The planning authorities acted as a clearinghouse for the communal plans, trying to match the surpluses and deficits of the communes with the less thoroughly organized outputs of the cities and with planned imports and exports—always with minimal changes in prices.

When economic reform came to China after Chairman Mao's death, peasants were permitted to lease land for private plots, as indeed they could again do in the Soviet Union. On both private plots and on communal land, peasants could (within broad limits) grow or manufacture whatever they wished. Only the prices of basic foods remained fixed, and communes were required to make deliveries of specified minimum amounts at these prices. A result, which seems not to have been anticipated, was that peasants shifted production to high-priced luxuries—including rabbits, raised for meat and fur—and away from basic foodstuffs like wheat and rice. This side effect led to food shortages, black markets, and inflation in urban China.

Under the Chinese variant of imperative economic planning, rural people lived and worked in large collective farms called communes. After Chairman Mao's death, economic reforms were instituted that

---

6. In Russia, this system is called *argogorod*, or agricultural city. It was never tried on a large scale in the U.S.S.R. Even after its failure in China, President Nicolae Ceausescu attempted to implement it in Rumania, demolishing farm villages in the process and forcing peasants into urban-style apartment blocks. This large-scale forced movement of the rural population had seldom if ever been done in China.

permitted peasants to lease land for private plots on which they could grow whatever they wished.

PLANNING UNDER CAPITALISM: JAPAN AND SWEDEN

Business people and procapitalists desire planning chiefly under one or more of four sets of conditions: (1) a serious or prolonged depression; (2) a major war, including both its preparation and its aftermath; (3) a widespread desire to speed up economic growth beyond what the market has provided; (4) a desire to ensure that political power will be held by moderates more dedicated to planning than to socialization. (By going along with a limited amount of planning, one perhaps can avoid the socialization of one's business and have a voice in the planning process.)

The United States has not been immune to the desire for planning. A planning "boom," led by business people along with academics, was a feature of the Great Depression of the 1930s. One of the most widely discussed plans was outlined by Gerard Swope, then president of General Electric. The National Recovery Administration was a 1933 New Deal experiment that reflected the planning philosophy but accomplished little and was finally ruled unconstitutional by the Supreme Court. During the Great Stagflation of the 1970s, the desire for planning revived in the form of the Humphrey-Hawkins bill, which we have already mentioned. Calling for the reduction of both unemployment and inflation, it made the government the employer of last resort. (It was passed by Congress only in weakened form after Senator Hubert Humphrey's death as a tribute to his memory. In its weakened form, as we have said, it mandated nothing even though it expressed fond hopes.)

Because large-scale "capitalist planning" has had little success in the United States, we draw our examples from overseas. The Japanese plan, our first example, was inspired by the desire to move beyond mere recovery to rapid growth after the disaster of World War II. Carried out under conservative governments, it featured the doubling of the GNP in less than a decade. The Swedish plan, our next example, arose under the long rule of the Social Democratic party, partly as a defense against nationalization of the private sector. Because the two systems turned out so differently, we describe both. Other countries that we might have cited are France, the Netherlands, Norway, and India.

Proposals for more comprehensive planning in the United States were made during the Great Depression of the 1930s and the Great Stagflation of the 1970s. The two best examples of large-scale planning under capitalism, however, are Japan and Sweden.

Japan, Inc.?

In *Taking Japan Seriously*, the British sociologist and Japanologist Ronald Dore views Japan as a modernized version of a **corporate society**.[7] A corporate society is organized in accordance with principles advocated by nineteenth-century reformists—mainly ethicists and theologians—and formulated most influentially in papal encyclicals of Roman Catholicism. It preserves capitalist private ownership of the means of production but reserves large regulatory powers for the state. The state is expected to delegate these powers largely to such corporate bodies as trade associations, farm cooperatives, and trade unions, whose negotiations would determine "fair" prices, wages, and income distributions in accordance with the public interest, as itself determined by the state and its ruling party.

Japan, according to Ronald Dore, is a modern version of a corporate society; it preserves capitalist private ownership of the means of production but reserves large regulatory powers for the state, which delegates these powers to trade associations, farm cooperatives, and trade unions.

---

7. Ronald P. Dore, *Taking Japan Seriously: A Confucian Perspective on Leading Economic Issues* (Stanford: Stanford University Press, 1987).

Corporatism fell into disrepute in the mid-twentieth century. Its doctrines, taken over and distorted by nationalistic, militaristic, fascist movements in Italy and Germany, came to be associated with dictatorship, concentration camps, aggressive warfare, mass murder, and genocide. However, the contemporary Japanese variant of corporatism has none of these outgrowths. If it is fascist at all—which the Japanese vigorously deny—the Japanese corporate society is "Fascism with a Human Face."

The Japanese economy has been called "Japan, Inc." by critics who claim that it subordinates all other interests to those of big business. Other critics say it is run by its bureaucracy and by graduates of the Tokyo University Faculty of Law, with its chief power center in Japan's notorious MITI.[8]

Clearly, these charges cannot both be true. If there is an economic power elite in Japan, it must include both big business and the big bureaucracy. But it must also include, as guardians of the public interest, the Liberal Democratic party, which has ruled the country since 1948. And, many Japanologists add, one must include Big Agriculture, since the rural vote is disproportionately powerful in Japan's political structure and therefore also in its political economy. Workers and consumers, however, are "on the outside looking in," although they would be equal partners in the idealized corporatism of the papal encyclicals.

Planning—capitalist planning—there is. Perhaps for this reason, Japan is sometimes described as "in the neighborhood of capitalism" rather than as a capitalist economy. Japan's plans are drawn up not in MITI but in a small Economic Planning Agency (EPA) connected with the Finance Ministry (MOF). In drawing up its plans, EPA receives information and suggestions from other departments, including MITI and MOA, from business and agricultural organizations, and from anyone desirous of feeding his or her ideas into the hopper.

Japan's plans, both long-term and short-term, are purely indicative. In fact, Japan's plans are often imperfectly consistent with one another and

8. MITI is the acronym for the Ministry of International Trade and Industry in the Japanese government. Similarly, MOF is the Ministry of Finance, and MOA is the Ministry of Agriculture, Forestry, and Fisheries—two other important bureaucratic players in the political-economic game.

are often ignored. Nevertheless, the government is more likely to approve and assist projects consistent with these plans. As long as they operate within the plans and thus in accord with the public interest, the plans protect the larger Japanese companies against failure, forced cutbacks, or "excessive competition," especially competition from foreign companies and their Japanese affiliates.[9]

For companies planning overambitious expansion programs to increase their shares of Japanese and world markets, there may be "administrative guidance" against such rashness. If, on the other hand, supply shocks or world market conditions force a Japanese industry to cut back production, administrative guidance suggests the timing and allocation of the cuts with an eye to minimizing the pain and suffering involved and to preserving the competitive status quo among the leading firms of the industry. Administrative guidance has no legal force, but carries with it the veiled threat of unspecified government displeasure—selective enforcement of tax and antimonopoly laws, unfavorable consideration in government purchases, etc.—if it is violated too frequently or too brazenly. In some firms and on some issues, administrative guidance has the force of (unwritten) law. In other firms and other industries, it is a matter of little concern.

Japan's planning system is indicative. The plans serve mostly to protect the larger Japanese companies against failure, forced cutbacks, or excessive competition.

Productivity Another feature of the Japanese economy is its high and rising labor productivity. Even though the government plan allows for this high productivity, the planning for it is done only by individual companies, with the cooperation of the educational system, both public and private. Many male workers (but fewer females) are hired with the expectation that they will never be fired or laid off, but will be kept on until retirement or until the company goes out of business. For this reason, it pays the employer to invest heavily and continu-

ously in their on-the-job training and retraining. Neither workers nor their unions[10] object to technological progress. At the same time, "dead wood"—defined as people hard to train or to promote—is reduced by careful selection and training programs. The most successful companies limit their search to high-level graduates of "good" high schools and universities.[11] They investigate and interview even the brightest and most promising applicants in order to weed out troublemakers, deviants, militants, or even simple nonconformists. The successful candidates are then subjected to a period of "basic training," observation, and "socialization" by the company before they are accepted as permanent employees. Young men and women who do not make the grade may find work in less good firms, in a succession of temporary jobs, or in family businesses. As a result, unemployment has been a serious problem only for young people who have "dropped out" for a while, or for older workers whose employers have gone out of business.

Even though the government plan allows for Japan's high and rising labor productivity, the planning for it is done only by individual companies, with the cooperation of the educational system.

Reaction to Japan's Success The outstanding success of the Japanese economy and the high rate of measured Japanese growth since the end of the Korean War (1953) have inspired great interest in the West. At the same time, they have caused great envy and resentment, expressed in the form of restrictions on the export trade that Japan needs in order to buy both its food and nearly all of its industrial raw materials. Such restrictions have been strongest in the countries of the European Community. As anti-Japanese protectionism has spread to the United States and the Third World, Japan's

---

9. "Excessive competition" is an elastic term that appears to include any degree of competition that forces leading Japanese firms to cut their domestic prices, profit margins, scales of operation, or employment.

10. Japanese unions are enterprise and not craft unions. This means that a worker can be retrained in a different craft—a welder as a machinist, for example—without jurisdictional disputes between separate union locals.

11. Entrance examinations are required for Japanese high schools and universities, both public and private. A "good" high school or university is one whose entrance examinations are difficult, and which can reject a high percentage of applicants on academic grounds.

economy, its capitalism, and its indicative planning are all being severely tested. Japan remains a fragile economy, dependent on the good will of its suppliers and its customers.

The outstanding success of the Japanese economy since the end of the Korean War has inspired both interest and resentment in the West, and anti-Japanese protectionism has spread from the European Community to the United States and the Third World.

Sweden's Welfare State

Sweden is famous for its welfare-state institutions. The Social Democratic party has dominated Swedish politics since the Great Depression, and Sweden has had a flourishing consumer cooperative movement for many years. For these reasons, many non-Swedes believe Sweden to be a socialist country. It is not. The Swedish mixed economy remains largely capitalist, with certain features that are called "laboristic." That is, even though capital and land are privately owned, employees as well as stockholders must be represented on the boards of directors of large Swedish corporations, and corporate decisions are "co-determined" by labor and capital.[12] Swedish companies must share their profits with workers and are allowed to establish foreign branches or export capital to existing branches only with the consent of their workers in Sweden.

Elements of Swedish Planning Most of Sweden's plans are indicative and short term. In a changing world, and particularly in a small country like Sweden, dependent on both foreign imports and foreign markets, it seems impractical to draw up comprehensive five-year plans. One-year plans are the standard practice. However, there are some long-term public works and housing projects as well.

A Swedish corporation does not have to pay corporate income tax on the part of its profits that it places in a special investment reserve. As a rule,

---

12. This co-determination system is not peculiar to Sweden. It is most highly developed in West Germany, and is common in Northern Europe.

---

funds in this reserve cannot be invested free of tax during boom periods when labor is in short supply, but can be invested tax free whenever unemployment exists or is threatened. Moreover, these investment reserves can be invested tax free only in those parts of Sweden where there is underemployment and surplus labor—often in the cold northern half of the country. If the United States were to follow this Swedish policy, the government would be guiding capital to the Snow Belt by offering tax privileges, rather than letting Snow Belt workers find their own way to the Sun Belt, where investment has been concentrated in recent years.

Swedish planning is also *consensual*. That is to say, the indicative plan targets must be acceptable to representatives of large and small business, labor, agriculture, finance, the public sector, and so on. Such major macroeconomic variables as the growth rates of money, credit, employment, labor productivity, and wage and price levels must also be agreed on. The same is true of changes in taxes and spending, as well as the means of financing deficits and surpluses. Even changes in imports, exports, capital movements, and the balance of payments position must be approved by consensus.

Sweden has a largely capitalist mixed economy characterized by many welfare-state institutions. Most Swedish plans are indicative and short term, and labor plays a large role in corporate decisions.

Problems of Swedish Planning Two basic problems have developed in connection with Swedish planning and have given the economy an inflationary twist. The first has to do with forecasts. It is nearly always easier to reach a planning consensus under optimistic "first-best" assumptions, which let every interest group have most of what it wants, than under more cautious assumptions, whose results would disappoint some or all of the bargainers. For example, the forecast of a sharp rise in labor productivity plus ideal weather on the farms will permit larger wage increases, smaller price rises, and a more positive trade balance than will more realistic forecasts. In fact, "first-best" assumptions are very seldom justified. There may be droughts and floods, strikes and absenteeism,[13] oil shocks and foreign wars, tax evasions and welfare frauds. The public deficit, the volume of credit, and the money supply are the variables with most "give" when the first-best combination of circumstances does not come about, so that the inflation is generally greater than expected.

In mentioning strikes, we have already hinted at the second problem. Suppose that a general 5 percent rise in wage rates is accepted by the representative of the national labor federation. Further suppose that this rise keeps all wage differentials in place, in percentage terms. The problem is that no representative of any pressure group can speak for all the subgroups within it, particularly in the case of labor. It has happened that the workers with less skill or education or the workers in jobs hiring mainly the young, the elderly, or the female worker may demand that the traditional differentials be ended or reduced. However, if these demands are met and the differentials are reduced, the skilled workers and male family heads may press for the return of their advantage on grounds of custom, usage, and equity. This kind of whipsaw movement raises wage rates all around. The next step is a price rise. If consumers are not willing to pay higher prices, the government meets the resulting unemployment with unplanned transfer payments or unplanned public-service jobs financed by unplanned money and credit expansion along with higher-than-planned inflation rates, and so on.

Swedish planning has two basic flaws that lead to inflationary pressures: a bias in favor of "first-best" forecasts and a tendency toward inflation to deal with demands for higher wages.

The Meidner Plan The planned Swedish economy has remained largely capitalistic, but some elements of the socialist-dominated trade union movement and the Social Democratic party pro-

pose to turn it sharply in a collectivist direction. The labor economist Rudolf Meidner is author of a nonviolent but revolutionary proposal for bringing this change about.

The basic Meidner plan is simple. Corporate income taxation of large companies is increased. The revenues from the increased tax rates go to the trade unions.[14] The unions use these revenues to buy shares in Swedish corporations on the stock exchange. With this process repeated every year, the unions eventually own enough stock to control all the larger corporations of Sweden.[15] This result would be technically **syndicalist**, with the economy controlled by trade unions rather than by the government as under socialism. It is ordinarily called socialism, however.

The main arguments against the Meidner plan are the power it gives the trade-union leadership and the fear that union-controlled firms would try to maximize wage rates and employment, which might lead to featherbedding and low productivity. Such union-controlled companies may eventually need subsidies to keep going, may oppose labor-saving technological changes, and may fail in international competition with capitalist business. In addition, private saving is likely to fall, in which case investment would presumably be financed by still higher taxes, or by inflation.

To forestall such problems, the Meidner plan, at least the mild version adopted in 1984, shares control over the "workingman's funds" between union leaders and civil servants, the latter representing the interests of the nonunion public. Also, control is decentralized regionally, rather than being centralized in Stockholm.

The Meidner plan has brought some collectivist elements to Sweden's largely capitalist economy. The plan proposes gradually to bring the economy under the control of trade unions.

---

13. Swedish companies and unions have led the way in devising ingenious systems of job sharing and job rotation, aimed at motivating workers and reducing high absenteeism rates on Mondays and Fridays particularly. So far, these systems have not been notably successful.

14. *Not* to individual workers! Socialists fear that profit-sharing will turn workers into petty capitalists, and oppose it.

15. Were American unions to control pension funds, invest these funds in corporate stock, and vote that stock at stockholders' meetings, the United States too might become a country of "pension-fund socialism" (actually syndicalism).

MARKETS UNDER SOCIALISM: YUGOSLAVIA AND CHINA

The Yugoslav Case

Karl Marx's attempt to control the International Workingmen's Association (First International) was opposed by **anarchists**. Anarchists propose to abolish all forms of government compulsion. For example, they believe that compulsory collection of taxes is a form of robbery. Instead, they would like to have people join and contribute to small voluntary associations, which they could leave at any time, either to join some other group or to form new ones. These associations could themselves combine voluntarily to manage larger projects. The anarchists accused Marx and his followers of planning to substitute bureaucratic control for capitalistic ownership of the means of production. Such a change, they thought, was likely to make matters worse rather than to help the people.

Marshal Josip Broz Tito of Yugoslavia (1892–1980) was a Marxist and a communist, not an anarchist. Even while rebelling in 1948 against the spread of Soviet Stalinism to his own country, he kept his strong government under Yugoslav Communist party control. For the Yugoslav economy, however, Tito and his advisers downgraded central planning, substituting a system of *workers' self-management* that attracted a great deal of attention during Tito's lifetime but that has largely broken down since his death.

The Role of Workers' Collectives Yugoslavia is a socialist state where land and capital goods are publicly owned. However, many of these resources are leased to and operated by groups of workers at rentals set by the state. These workers' collectives or cooperatives decide their own inputs and outputs as well as their own membership of workers with various skills. They elect their own managers and set their own prices for the goods they produce. If they make any profits after taxes are paid, they may distribute them among their members as they wish (subject to the requirement that minimum "wages" be paid), or they may use them for such purposes as housing or environmental improvements. To a certain extent, they may even act as a bank and lend surplus funds to other groups.

Yugoslavia is a socialist state, but many of its resources are leased to and operated by groups of workers.

The Role of the Central Authorities Plenty is left for the central economic authorities of Yugoslavia to do, as well as for the authorities of the six republics that make up the country. They must enforce minimum income levels for participants in the co-operative firms. The authorities also make sure that new or younger people in these firms have equal shares in management and are not simply disguised employees of the older workers. They must judge the creditworthiness of the firms' requests for continued and expanded rentals of land and capital, and keep them from wasting these resources. When a new firm is either being set up "from scratch" or separating from an old one, the authorities must judge whether it should receive land and capital at all.

Failure of the Yugoslav System More than many other economic systems, the Yugoslav system developed disappointing weaknesses in practice, particularly after the death of Marshal Tito. It is now regarded as less a helpful model than a horrible example. We list seven of its principal weaknesses, many of which are more peculiar to Yugoslavia itself than to the Yugoslav economic experiment.

1. Yugoslavia is by no means the only socialist country beset by regional, linguistic, or religious conflicts. It is, however, one of the least successful in controlling them, especially after the passing of Marshal Tito's unifying influence. The Yugoslav (Southern Slav) state is a federation of six republics. Two of them, Croatia and Slovenia, were relatively developed under somewhat enlightened Austro-Hungarian rule well before World War I. The other four (Serbia, Montenegro, Macedonia, and Bosnia-Herzegovina) had suffered under Turkish rule during the long decay of the Ottoman Empire and had been involved in both civil and international warfare after Turkish rule ended. They were economically far behind the two leaders. Political power, however, was concentrated in Serbia, the most important of the economically backward republics. The Serbian-dominated central government, including its planning bureaucracy, concentrated resources on the backward areas even though these resources could have been used more productively in Croatia and Slovenia. The central government practiced regional redistribution in preference to economic growth, and achieved neither.

2. Marxian doctrine treats paper money as "fictitious capital." Consequently, many socialist governments pay little attention to its management. In Yugoslavia, the collectives managing the banks included representatives of the banks' debtors—collectives that had borrowed from the banks and that wanted more loans on easier terms in the future.[16] The banks' creditors—the depositors—did not have equal representation. Although Yugoslavia did not use inflation deliberately to ruin the rentier class, it soon had one of the highest inflation rates in Europe and has not been able to get it under control. In this respect, Yugoslavia is a claimant for the unenviable title of Europe's Brazil.

3. Labor-managed firms are sometimes run by a small minority of "labor aristocrats," usually skilled or white-collar workers, while the other members remain passive most of the time.

4. The Yugoslav Communist party has feared the creation, within the labor-managed firms, of an economic base for opposition political movements like the Polish Solidarity movement. The party has therefore encouraged its individual-enterprise "cells" to interfere in in-plant elections so as to win managements supportive of government policies. In such attempts, it has allegedly had the strong-arm support of the local and national police forces.

5. Once in place and flourishing, the more established Yugoslav firms have been able to use a good deal of political influence and monopolistic power to delay and limit the progress of rival firms and the opening up of Yugoslavia to foreign competition.

6. The labor-managed firm of the Yugoslav sort can be looked on as maximizing net income *per worker* rather than its total net income or profit. This puts the Yugoslav firm under pressure to use more capital and less labor than would a private company in a similar case. This is unfortunate in a country like Yugoslavia, which is capital-poor and labor-rich.[17]

7. Partly for the same reason—too much capital per worker—Yugoslavia seldom attains high employment in practice. To find jobs, Yugoslav workers have left the country in large numbers and become "guest workers" in other European countries.

The Yugoslav economic system developed several major weaknesses that have caused it largely to break down.

The Chinese Case

Mao Zedong, "Great Helmsman" of Chinese communism and author of a *Little Red Book* containing cryptic answers to all social problems, died in 1976. Chairman Mao's death set off a struggle between the so-called "Gang of Four," who were headed by his widow and faithful to his doctrines, and the so-called "Capitalist Roaders," headed by Deng Xiaoping (Deng-Hsiao-ping, 1904–   ), who proposed various "revisionist" reforms.

With almost no bloodshed, the capitalist roaders won, and Premier Deng proceeded with "four modernizations" of China's agriculture, economy, technology, and national defense. Progress since 1977 has been marked in the countryside—less so in the cities. To the foreign observer, the most interesting points include these four.

1. Drastic modification—which some call abolition—of Mao's communes. The state still owns all agricultural land, but now leases plots to indi-

---

16. The justification for such loan extensions is the **productive credit theory**—that if more credit to a firm (whether socialist or capitalist) is matched by a corresponding increase in the firm's output, the loan is not inflationary. This argument is fallacious, as is the theory on which it is based. If, after receiving more credit, the firm increases its output by bidding resources away from other firms, there is an output increase for the community only if the borrowing firm is more efficient than the other users of the resources. And even if the community output increases, the new money circulates more rapidly than the new goods, so that the net effect of the credit will be inflationary.

17. Maximizing company income per worker also leads to "wrong" reactions to product price changes—raising output when prices fall, and vice versa.

vidual families, which are no longer compelled to join collective farms or communes (although a great majority have chosen to remain members).

2. Breaking Mao's "iron rice bowl." Under Mao, full employment meant, in practice, the assignment of workers by batches of 50,000 or more to organizations that might or might not have any use for them. Also, managers and supervisors could not dismiss individual workers, so that laziness and absenteeism were prevalent. The worker's "rice bowl" (his or her income) was "iron," meaning it could not be broken or the worker dismissed. Workers are still assigned in batches and wages remain fixed, to the great disgust of foreign concerns used to "cherry-picking" individual workers by paying wages above the market level.

While full employment is still officially enforced, many young high school graduates spend months or even years waiting for their "work assignments." (Nobody is expected to look for a job in China.) To keep these people busy and out of trouble, they may be herded into "collectives," given some machinery and a little training, and let loose on society without wages or benefit guarantees. Some of the collectives, and their members, have been highly successful. Most, however, have not.

3. The one-child family. To reduce both present consumption and future "assignment problems," the Deng regime has imposed a stringent one-child policy on Chinese families. (Minority races are exempted, and pressure to conform seems to be looser in rural areas.) Families with two or more children are discriminated against in various ways, such as access to education and medical care. The program is allegedly voluntary, but there are many reports of compulsory abortion. Also, in a society that has traditionally undervalued its female members, the one-child family has led to neglect and even infanticides of sickly, defective, and girl babies to give the family another chance for a "good" (i.e., healthy male) child. The rigor of this policy is expected to be relaxed. It was adopted as a short-run expedient when the population of China ran to over a billion people.

4. Special economic zones. In a number of areas, many of them close to Hong Kong, foreign companies have been invited to set up shop and earn profits much as they would in a capitalist country. (Legal details are difficult to specify, however, since Communist China has neither a commercial code nor a governing body of case law.) The areas are expected to do two things: offer Chinese workers training in high technology and process both imported and Chinese raw materials for export. Initial reports indicate that production is mostly low-tech, that it is aimed at the Chinese internal market, and that the zones themselves threaten to become foci of "dangerous thoughts," "capitalist decadence," and other forms of sacrilege to the memory of the Great Helmsman.

"Special economic zones" have, at various times, been established in many Third World countries as aids to the country's international trade and financial position. A special financial zone has even been proposed for the United States, where participants might enjoy the protection of American law without the handicaps of American taxes and financial regulations. But nowhere else were "special economic zones" to play so large a part in the twentieth-century economic development of their host country.

Under Deng Xiaoping, China has made further reforms in its planned economy. Families are no longer compelled to join communes, changes are being made in the system of guaranteed full employment, a one-child policy has been adopted for the short term, and special economic zones for foreign industry have been established.

Aside from these special features, Chinese socialism appears to be evolving in ways less different from post-Stalin Soviet and European socialisms than is generally supposed. Like the U.S.S.R., but unlike Yugoslavia, China concentrates development in certain key areas—the Pacific Coast, the Yangtze Valley, and the Northeast (Manchuria)—leaving the rest of the country to catch up later. At the same time, the Chinese have achieved their first and greatest successes in agriculture, while the agricultural sector has remained thus far a weak spot in Gorbachev's *perestroika*. Like their European counterparts, the Chinese encountered serious inflation problems, which delayed the pace not only of price reform but of the entire reform process in the later 1980s. China's central bank, called the People's Bank of China, is assigned responsibility for the money supply and the price level, but its authority has not extended to the lavish credits granted by local governments and exports industries. The theory of *productive credit*, noted in our discussion of Yugoslavia, is popular in China, too. Were the People's Republic of China (P.R.C.) a small country instead of including nearly a quarter of the world's population—or were it still a Soviet dependency or satellite—Premier Deng's experiments would receive less attention than economists now accord them.

In mid-1989 there is much uncertainty concerning China's path or at least the speed with which she will continue to pursue economic reform. The 1989 student demonstrations for greater freedom and democracy, that ended in bloodshed and purges, have left questions concerning the ease with which past reforms can be carried out, new reforms instituted, and, possibly most important, the degree of willingness by foreign governments and firms (including U.S. firms) to do business with China.

THE THEORY OF MARKET SOCIALISM

Market socialism is an adaptation of the microeconomics of pure competition to a socialist system. Oskar Lange (1904–1965), born and educated in Poland, and Abba Lerner (1904–1982), born in Bessarabia and educated in Britain, were both socialists. After meeting in Britain in the 1930s, the two men continued their friendship in the United States.[18] Their views are not in complete agreement, but the term *market socialism* applies equally well to the work of either man.

Market socialism is an adaptation of the microeconomics of pure competition to a socialist system.

---

18. Lange, then a political refugee, later became Polish ambassador to the United States, Polish delegate to the United Nations, and finally vice president of Communist Poland after World War II—after disavowing many of the views that will concern us here.

How the System Works

The Lange-Lerner theory of market socialism reacts strongly against both the weakened capitalism of the Great Depression and the tough Stalinist planning methods of arbitrary pricing, imperative production quotas, and consumer rationing. Under the Lange-Lerner system, prices would be set by public authorities, but they would be changed when necessary to maintain approximate equilibrium between supply and demand for most products. Managers of firms would be civil servants, who need not depend on capitalists or on workers or on consumers. They would be required to operate industrial plants or large farms so as to keep the marginal cost of output about equal to output price at all times. Similarly, they would be required to keep the marginal revenue product of each input equal to the input price at all times. In the short run, profits would go to the state, with losses subsidized by the state (unless it was decided to shut the business down). In the long run, it was hoped that changes in the number and/or size of firms would reduce both profits and losses almost to zero.

Under the Lange-Lerner model of market socialism, prices would be set by public authorities, but they would be changed when necessary to maintain approximate equilibrium between supply and demand for most products. Managers of firms would be required to operate industrial plants and farms so as to keep the marginal cost of output about equal to output price at all times and to keep the marginal revenue product of each input equal to the input price at all times.

So far, this theory is just like that of pure competition, but with fuller and more reliable information available to both buyers and sellers of all goods and services. However, since the economy would be a socialist one, there would be no landlords and capitalists to claim the returns from land and capital, which would go instead to the state. The state would accept these returns in place of taxes and carry on the usual government activities including subsidies to businesses suffering losses. Whenever possible, the state would distribute what would otherwise be property income equally to all the people as a social dividend—so much for each person or for each family. If socialism could also sharply lower military spending, the social dividend would be far greater than transfer payments in any capitalist welfare state!

Of course, if the socialization process were undertaken within the rule of law, the socialist state would have a huge debt for buying the capitalists' properties. This burden might be expected to keep the social dividend very low over its first few generations.

Planning for the proportion of national income to be saved and invested would be left in the hands of a central planning agency. The agency could raise the investment rate, and most likely the rate of growth as well, by imposing higher taxes or lowering social dividend distributions, and using the extra funds for investment. Private saving and dissaving would be entirely legal, but at zero or very low rates of interest to keep a capitalist class from springing up.[19] Private investment in single-family housing would also be legal, with gains from resale or speculation taxed at high rates for the same reason: to keep capitalism from returning.

Criticisms of the Theory

Many questions about technique and procedure have been raised in criticism of the Lange-Lerner scheme of market socialism. How, in real life, would managers be chosen and assigned? What if they followed the rules but were lacking in "human relations" skills? How could one decide after the fact whether the rules had been followed without turning half the population into accountants, statisticians, or computer technologists?

Suppose, however, that it was determined that a manager had failed to equate marginal cost to output price, or marginal revenue product to input price. The problems would not be over. Was the differential avoidable, or had there been unforeseeable problems like machine breakdowns, worker illness, or delays in delivery of raw materials or parts? If the differential appeared both large and avoidable, was it a misdemeanor or a crime? Was it

just an honest mistake, or was it unlawful speculation that prices might change in the course of production? Was it an attempt to influence future prices by creating shortages or surpluses, after the fashion of a monopolistic firm or the members of a cartel?

Let us consider a hypothetical case from Lange-Lernerland. Sourpuss Smith and Jovial Jones are plant managers in Podunk. They are also rival candidates for promotion to a larger and more important plant in Megalopolis. Sourpuss Smith, a lightning calculator, has followed all the rules to the letter and the last decimal place. In doing so, he has come to be regarded as a holy terror by his subordinates. Morale and productivity in the Smith plant are low, and it is plagued by high labor turnover. Jovial Jones, on the other hand, plays fast and loose with the rules, some of which he is not smart enough to apply accurately. He hires "too many" workers, puts them into wage brackets that are "too high," turns out "too much" product, and fails to maximize returns. But productivity in the Jones plant is the pride of Podunk, so that costs are correspondingly low. Which manager should get the Megalopolis promotion?

This answer is easy by business standards under the rules of the capitalist game: Jones goes onward and upward to Megalopolis, and Smith goes back to Podunk or perhaps to a cost accountant's job. But it is not clear that this will happen under the Lange-Lerner rules.

From a socialist point of view, a more important social or philosophical question is raised by the whole process of market socialism, and by the Lange-Lerner variety in particular. Among other things, socialism aims at fostering the new socialist men and women, who subordinate their personal interests to the interests of the society as they have been taught to see them. Such persons demand fewer economic rewards, especially consumer goods and leisure time, than they would have demanded as individualists, and also supply more and better labor services. The Lange-Lerner men and women, however, remain essentially individualists in socialist clothing. To maximize their own utility, they demand what they want when they want it. They supply labor according to their own labor-leisure choices and are subject to dismissal if the value of their marginal revenue product falls below their wage rate. Such "selfish" individual-

19. At minimal interest rates, the demand for personal consumption loans (dissaving) might well exceed the supply (saving), creating a black market in consumer credit. As a control on such a market, loan contracts between private individuals could be made unenforceable at interest rates above the legal limit.

ism, relying on "economic" as against "moral" incentives, makes market socialism suspect in socialist eyes, particularly in the eyes of the advocates of socialist central planning.

Socialists distrust market socialism because it does not try to create men and women who subordinate their personal interests to the interests of society.

AUSTRIAN THEORY: PLANNING AS THE ROAD TO SERFDOM

Many writers take strong stands against planning, whether the planning is socialist or capitalist. They claim that pricing and resource allocation in a planned economy must be arbitrary and dictatorial, unless the planners adopt the international prices of the remaining market-economy countries. These writers argue that the processes of setting and enforcing arbitrary prices and wage rates lead to an increasingly serious loss of individual freedoms.

Many economists take strong stands against planning, whether socialist or capitalist. They argue that the processes of setting and enforcing arbitrary prices and wage rates lead to an increasingly serious loss of individual freedoms.

Three economists are well known for their views on this question—Friedrich von Hayek (1899–   ), Ludwig von Mises (1881–1973), and Joseph Schumpeter (1883–1950).[20] All three were born and educated in Austria, and their views are called "Austrian." None of the three ever lived under communist rule. However, it is interesting to note that many refugees from socialist or communist countries share the Austrian view of planning.

20. Schumpeter, unlike both Mises and Hayek, saw socialism and planning as inevitable consequences, like death and taxes, of capitalism and of the "treason" of intellectuals who have lost social status to business people. Schumpeter's vision of the socialist planned economy was also less grim than Hayek's serfdom or Mises' "planned chaos."

The Growth of Controls Under Planning

Four points, all made by Hayek, explain why he thinks planning leads to "serfdom." The first is that partial planning or control tends to grow in its extent and rigor, in order to keep people from dodging its rules. For example, one might ask: Why not simply control prices and wages in "essential" industries and jobs in order to check inflation and leave the rest of the economy free? The answer is that if the uncontrolled sectors are free to pay higher wages and make higher profits, labor and capital will move, unless restricted, away from essential to nonessential activities—from making work shirts to making sports shirts. One might also ask how civil liberties could be preserved while preventing capital from being taken out of a country where most of "the rich" distrust the economic plan. Hayek believes that people are clever about arranging "capital flights" by mail, by telephone, and by foreign travel, in underpriced exports, overpriced imports, and other fictitious deals. For this reason, mail and telephone censorship, as well as passport controls over people on "watch lists," would be essential to the enforcement of capital controls.

Arbitrary or Corrupt Bureaucracy

The second point that Hayek stresses is that, however detailed and comprehensive a plan may be, it cannot cover all the special cases that later arise under it. So a great deal of leeway must be left to administrative (bureaucratic) judgment. For example, if a Soviet citizen wants to repair or enlarge his or her house in a city where building materials are in short supply, the citizen must obtain two permits if the work is to be legally done. The person must convince one government official that his or her needs are great enough to obtain certain building materials. Once the materials are received, another official (possibly located at the other end of the city) must be convinced that he or she *has* these materials, and that they are adequate for the project. Such procedures allow plenty of opportunity for arbitrariness, which is our problem here, and also for corruption.

Propaganda and Suppression

According to Hayek's third point, morale is so important to the success of the plan that critics are often silenced. Official propaganda will of course sing the plan's praises and advertise its successes. The temptation is very great to suppress and punish any who spread pessimistic rumors about the plan and its feasibility, who forecast its failure in whole or in part, or who want the present plan scrapped in favor of another one—or in favor of the market. Under Soviet and Eastern European conditions, critics blame the plan's concentration on the "leading links" of heavy industry and military hardware for shortages of consumer goods and civilian housing. Prior to Gorbachev, at least, it was rare for such critics to be allowed open expression of their views, let alone access to the public, since the plan regulates the supply of paper, the programs of the schools, and the broadcast media, as well as the economy. Nevertheless, the misdeeds of particular incompetent, tyrannical, or corrupt bureaucrats or administrators are often exposed in official publications, and punished in official courts.

The Power Seekers

Finally, "the worst get on top," Hayek claims. This fourth and last point means that the would-be dictator, the corrupt grafter, and the envious or vindictive person is most likely to seek work in carrying out the daily and minor details of running and enforcing the plan. Such people are also very likely to call for extending the plan's authority over the remaining unplanned sectors of the economy.

The Austrian economist Friedrich von Hayek believes that partial planning tends to grow in extent and rigor in order to keep people from dodging its rules, that the system is prone to

---

arbitrariness and corruption, that criticism is stifled, and that the system tends to be run by corrupt, power-hungry, vindictive people. In short, planning leads to "serfdom."

Criticism of the Theory

Many criticisms of the Austrian theory have been voiced. The simplest is the claim that the benefits of planning are worth its costs, and that the critics of planning are reactionaries who are destined for "the dust-bin of history." This approach is most effective where the market economy is associated with recent-past colonialism, backwardness, or dependency, and where there has been no experience with successful liberal democracy. In more advanced countries, however, it is argued that existing liberal or democratic traditions will be strong enough to keep the citizens from traveling the road to serfdom despite the problems Hayek sees. Furthermore, as in Sweden, dependence on foreign trade with countries that have market economies will limit the spread and the impact of arbitrary planning. One can even rely on institutions based on merit, such as schools, colleges, and civil service examinations, to lower the likelihood that the worst will get on top.

Perhaps the most effective anti-Austrian argument is that serfdom does not have to be the end of the road. One can gain comfort from the experience of the U.S.S.R., Poland, Hungary, and Yugoslavia in backing away from the extremes of Stalinism after Stalin's death in 1953; and from the experience of the Chinese People's Republic in reversing the Maoist "cultural revolution" after Mao Zedong's death in 1976. But optimism must be tempered by experience. Gorbachev's liberalization efforts face stiff opposition. The Chinese government's bloody suppression of the prodemocracy movement may stifle criticism for a long time.

Economics in Focus

Private Business and *Perestroika*

Perestroika, Mikhail Gorbachev's program of economic restructuring, has permitted more private business in the Soviet Union. Known as "cooperatives," the new private companies are intended to improve consumer products and services, bring the underground economy above ground, and give budding entrepreneurs a chance to exercise their creativity. The Wheel cooperative in Michurinsk, for example, makes auto parts in a factory that was formerly notorious for its organized crime ring. After the plant was leased to the *kooperativshchiki,* output tripled and theft declined. Long-time observers of the Soviet economy considered this a minor miracle.

Between 1987 and June 1989, more than 100,000 cooperatives were founded, and their employment mushroomed to 2.7 million workers, over 2 percent of the Soviet labor pool. If the trend continues, the cooperatives will become a major force in the Soviet economy. Their areas of business include manufacturing, engineering, management consulting, and tourism. Not content with the domestic trade, some are pursuing foreign markets as avidly as Western capitalists.

Nevertheless, the Soviet Union's black market—which the cooperatives should supposedly replace—continues to flourish. Well over three-quarters of Soviet citizens use the black market when they cannot find the goods they need in state-run stores. For years Gorbachev's predecessors allowed the underground economy to prosper, and observers believe that hundreds of illegal factories dot the countryside. According to one estimate, as many as 20 million people worked in black-market activities in 1989, a number that dwarfed the infant cooperative movement. As consumers, Soviet citizens complain about high prices charged by cooperatives, but they freely buy at even higher prices from underground merchants.

In competing with the black market, cooperatives face a certain distrust simply because they bear the government's stamp of approval. Furthermore, rumors circulate about racketeering in the cooperatives: extortion, robbery, money laundering, and the like. In fact, since many cooperatives depend on the willingness of central planners to allocate raw materials and equipment, the potential for corruption is obvious. Some Soviets assert that in spite of Gorbachev's stern anticorruption campaign, the black marketers have bribed bureaucrats to keep goods away from the cooperatives. In such a climate of suspicion, many would rather deal with the old evil they know than the new evil they suspect.

In a country where blue jeans can sell for the equivalent of three weeks' pay, the free market's potential seems golden. Yet the change to free-market practices requires a revolution in industrial methods, in bureaucratic operations, and in the entire society's way of thinking. As the Soviets are well aware, revolutions do not come easily.

Sources: Peter Galuszka, "The Paradox of *Perestroika:* A Raging Black Market," *Business Week,* June 5, 1989, pp. 66, 70; Richard I. Kirkland, Jr., "Why Russia Is Still in the Red," *Fortune,* January 30, 1989, pp. 173–175; John Kohan and Yuri Shchekochikhin, "Tambov: *Perestroika* in the Provinces," *Time,* April 10, 1989, pp. 86–92.

SUMMARY

1. The controversy between advocates of market and planned economic systems is a heated one, even though all existing economies are mixed systems. The distinction between the two types of systems is a useful one. (See pages 923–924.)

2. Every person or organization plans for itself. However, we speak of an economy as being planned only when a central planning body (public, private, or mixed) makes plans that dominate those of the individual persons, firms, or industries that make up the economy. (See page 924.)

3. A market economy is more likely to be capitalist than is a planned one. A planned economy is more likely to be collectivist than an unplanned one. (See pages 924–925.)

4. Planning and collectivism are not the same thing, any more than capitalism and a market system are the same. Furthermore, neither planning nor collectivism should be confused with the welfare state. Any economic system that places high value on a high poverty line and on lowering inequality in the distribution of income and wealth may be called a welfare state. (See pages 925–926.)

5. Planning is of different sorts. We distinguish imperative, indicative, public sector, macroeconomic, and magic wand planning. We do not consider statistical projections of past trends to be plans at all, unless they are combined with measures to see that these trends continue. (See pages 926–927.)

6. The Soviet Union under Stalinist rule has been the most important example of imperative planning under socialist collectivism. Planning was highly centralized in a single agency called Gosplan, using the techniques of materials balancing and input-output analysis. Since 1985, General Secretary Mikhail Gorbachev has been engaged in a process called *perestroika,* aimed at decentralizing the planning process and increasing the scope of economic incentives in individual decision-making. (See pages 928–932.)

7. The United States has a large public sector and so has more public-sector planning than is generally realized. Proposals for more comprehensive planning in the United States were made during the years of the Great Depression (for example,

the National Recovery Administration), during both world wars, and more recently in the original Humphrey-Hawkins bill. (See page 932.)

8. Japan and Sweden are widely differing examples of economic planning within a capitalist framework. In the Japanese case, sometimes called ''Japan, Inc.,'' the principal planners come from big business, agriculture, and the public bureaucracy. In Sweden, labor also participates in the planning, and the government is dominated by the Social Democratic party. (See pages 933–936.)

9. Yugoslavia is a socialist country with a substantial degree of workers' management supplementing or even replacing its central plan. (See pages 937–938.)

10. China, under the leadership of Deng Xiaoping, has moved ever further from the Soviet planning model. Agricultural collectivization is now voluntary. The ''iron rice bowl'' variety of full employment is in the process of being eliminated. Foreign techniques and management methods are permitted to foreign firms in special economic zones. Prices and wages, however, remain fixed, and the government continues to own land and capital goods. (See pages 939–940.)

11. The Lange-Lerner scheme of market socialism attempts to combine the advantages of market and planned economies in a somewhat utopian socialist model. (See pages 940–942.)

12. A number of writers, chiefly Austrian, hold that planning, once undertaken under either capitalism or socialism, tends to increase in both importance and arbitrariness over time. They expect planning to end in a servile state, which Hayek has called ''serfdom,'' with few individual freedoms and civil rights remaining. Some writers of the ''Austrian school'' believe that there is little hope of preserving the market economy and avoiding ''serfdom,'' but others are more optimistic. (See pages 942–943.)

KEY TERMS

anarchist: one who proposes to abolish all forms of government compulsion (page 937).

capitalistic economies: economies in which land and physical capital are owned largely by private individuals or business firms (page 926).

collectivist economies: economies in which land and physical capital such as buildings and machinery are largely or completely owned by collective agencies (page 925).

communist: a socialist who believes that socialism on a world scale will lead to an economy of abundance and who accepts violence, revolution, and dictatorship as a means to that end (page 926).

corporate society: a society organized to preserve capitalist private ownership of the means of production but that reserves large regulatory powers for the state (page 933).

Gosplan: the Soviet agency in charge of planning the economy in the U.S.S.R. (page 928).

imperative planning: a form of economic planning that must be followed; failure to reach an important plan target is considered a criminal offense (page 926).

indicative planning: a form of economic planning that operates mainly by convincing plan participants that following the plan will help them economically (page 927).

input-output analysis: an integrated analysis for an entire economy focusing on organizing information about the relationships between resources used in production and the goods and services produced (page 928).

leading links: a feature of the Soviet planning system whereby, when the whole plan cannot be carried out, certain leading links (usually military hardware and capital goods) are completed in full, and the rest of the plan is postponed in part until the next planning period (page 930).

Libermanism: an early attempt to reform Soviet planning (page 930).

macroeconomic planning: a form of economic planning that covers gross national product, the division between consumption, investment, and government sectors, the supplies of money and credit, the government surplus or deficit, international balances, and interest rates (page 927).

"magic wand" planning: a form of economic planning built around a collection of projects and/or an appealing slogan (page 927).

market socialism: a theoretical adaptation of the microeconomics of pure competition to a socialist system (page 940).

materials balancing: a technique used to coordinate the Soviet planning system; for every one of the thousands of final and intermediate products, potential supplies and demands are estimated for each year of the plan, allowing for both domestic production and international trade (page 928).

perestroika: restructuring; reforms of the Soviet planning system that include a wider scope for an unplanned economy, more flexible plans, and more leeway for plant managers (page 928).

planning: an institutional arrangement in which some individual or organization in a public position plans for another individual or organization, who or which has little say about the plan and whose economic freedom is restricted by the planning decision (page 924).

productive credit theory: a theory that states that if more credit to a firm is matched by a corresponding increase in the firm's output, the loan is not inflationary (page 938).

public sector planning: economic planning that covers only the public sector (page 927).

socialist economies: economies in which government agencies own the land and physical capital (page 925).

syndicalist: an economy controlled by trade unions (page 936).

welfare state: an economy that places an especially high value on equitable distribution of income and wealth and security of living standards (page 926).

DISCUSSION QUESTIONS

1. Jonathan Swift (1667–1745) is best known as the author of *Gulliver's Travels* and is considered the greatest satirist in the English language. His works include a *Modest Proposal for Preventing the Children of Poor People from Being a Burden to Their Parents or the Country.* (They are to be fattened, and then sold for food to the rich.)

Suppose that one were to believe seriously—as Swift did not—in exporting fattened babies from overpopulated poor countries for food in rich countries as part of a development plan for the poor countries. Should such a person be allowed to propagate his or her "outrageous" opinions? Suppose that this person were an organic chemist; should he or she be permitted to teach organic chemistry? If his or her specialty were development economics, what would your answer be? Suppose that this person were already teaching development economics before being converted to cannibalism, should he or she be forbidden to continue teaching in this field? Finally, are your answers to the four preceding parts of this question logically consistent with one another?

2. The Swedish economist Knut Wicksell was prosecuted and imprisoned, at the turn of the century, for propagating certain radical ideas, including contraception and the disestablishment of the state church. (One of his major works, *Interest and Prices*, was finished in prison.) When his jail term was over, Wicksell returned to his teaching at the University of Lund. Some years later, the American economist Scott Nearing, a socialist and pacifist, advocated strict neutrality in World War I and opposed "preparedness." He was not prosecuted, but his contract (at the University of Pennsylvania) was not renewed, and he could obtain no other teaching post. Did the Swedish or American system impinge more harshly on freedom of expression?

3. Distinguish among collectivism, socialism, and communism.

4. Can a market-capitalist economy also be a welfare state? Explain.

5. Briefly distinguish among imperative planning, indicative planning, public sector planning, and macroeconomic planning. Which, if any, of these are used in the United States?

6. Distinguish between materials balancing and input-output analysis as tools for economic planning.

7. What is *perestroika?* Assess the chances of its success in raising the living standards of the Soviet people.

8. Describe the important features of the Japanese economic system that have contributed to Japanese economic growth. Do you believe that similar arrangements would be workable and desirable for the United States?

9. Briefly summarize the Meidner plan. Do you believe that it is a feasible alternative to socialist revolution? Explain.

10. Market-socialism proposals, such as those of Lange and Lerner, are usually proposed for societies in which all production processes are already known. How would an innovation (a new product or process) be introduced under market socialism? (In your answer, assume that there are no other economies from which to copy.)

40
Radical Economics

Preview This chapter goes beyond economics as usually conceived. It deals with questions that political scientists, sociologists, or psychologists handle more fully and expertly than economists do. We begin by discussing the dissatisfactions that many people (not only radicals) feel with market-capitalist institutions as they exist in North America. Rather than arguing about the justice of this indictment, we go on to outline the social theory that is used by the radical Left in advocating the overthrow of capitalism. Marxian economics is a very important part of this theory. As further ''background,'' we note certain characteristics that distinguish the radical from the reformist critic of market-capitalism.

In the second half of the chapter, we look at contemporary radical movements, primarily but not only on the political Left. First we take up the so-called New Left, which has itself become divided into a number of groups—some socialist, some anarchist, and some syndicalist. Then we consider the radical Right, which may be descended from what is called Social Darwinism—the doctrine of ''survival of the fittest'' among social groups and institutions.

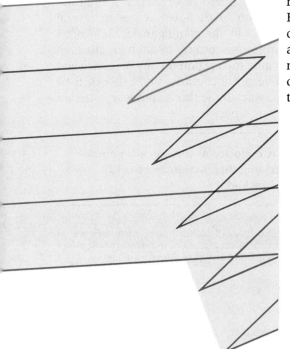

INDICTMENTS OF CAPITALISM

In the eyes of its critics, capitalism is "the root of all (social) evil." To many people, some of the indictments seem far-fetched, or related to industrialization under any economic system. Nevertheless, we offer a sweeping picture of the indictment, to show the scope and intensity of radical views. At the beginning of the book, we singled out six criteria for judging economic systems and for preferring one system to another.[1] In none of these does market-capitalism represent any utopian ideal.

With discontent about every point, we single out three criteria among our six, since they seem to have caused the greatest amount and intensity of discontent. These are:

1. The alleged maldistribution of income and wealth, both within and between individual countries.

2. The alleged insecurity of the standard of living already achieved against downward pressure, both short run and long run.

3. The alleged incompatibility of the system with full physical and mental health.

Criticism of capitalism centers around three points: (1) inequality of the distribution of income and wealth, (2) insecurity of the standard of living against downward pressure, and (3) incompatibility of the system with physical and mental health.

Maldistribution

It is no secret that the distribution of income is unequal both within and between individual countries, that people at the bottom of the income and wealth distributions are living in poverty, that "it takes money to make money," and that in many fields of economic activity "nice guys finish last." For the great majority of the world's population, upward mobility within the world economy is

1. See Chapter 1.

blocked, except by rules and on terms set by those already at the top. A low-wage country's rise to affluence may be blocked if it can no longer use the cheapness of its labor as a competitive advantage because the access of its goods to affluent markets is blocked by protectionism. When its workers cannot migrate to high-wage areas, the country's rise is limited to methods more acceptable to those who are already affluent. One route may be receiving aid on terms set by the givers. Others may include a more restrictive population policy, or more reliance than the low-wage country desires on unskilled hand labor in agriculture and mining.

Within a country like the United States, the question is the *terms* on which blacks or other minorities can rise. When black people's chances of becoming wealthy depend largely, as is alleged, on following white people's rules, the economically successful blacks are not, to put it mildly, objects of admiration within the black community itself. For this reason, their chances of advancement are much less in fact than they are in the statistics.[2]

To some extent, inequality is based on prejudice—race, gender, religion, language, and so forth. Capitalism and the capitalists are blamed for fostering such prejudices to keep workers or farmers disunited, reducing both their economic and their political power. When blacks came north or were brought north during and after World War I to break strikes or to forestall them, one result was an outbreak of race riots, and another was a weakening of organized labor. When a multinational corporation holds down wages in several countries at once by threatening major shifts of its operations from one country to another, critics of capitalism blame such action for any prejudice and hostility between the countries and between their populations, which those threats provoke, whether intentionally or otherwise.

For the great majority of the world's population, upward mobility within the world economy is blocked.

---

2. Anthropologists speak of "cultural rape" when members of one culture are either forced or bribed to conform to the mores and standards of another and quite different culture.

Insecurity

Under capitalism, mass living standards are supposedly under constant pressure, both from the short-term shocks associated with business-cycle declines and from the long-run shocks associated with chronic inflation, technological change, pollution, resource exhaustion, warfare, and so on. "Hoovervilles," which were shantytowns for the unemployed in flood plains and city dumps, are among the best-remembered pictures of the Great American Depression of the 1930s.

On the individual level, there are different kinds of threats to the living standards of certain people, especially the aged or otherwise immobile. One such threat is inflation, a device to which capitalism has often turned for recovery from recessions and depressions. Capitalism is also blamed for technical change, symbolized by automation and robotization, which throws some people out of work at the same time that it provides opportunities for others. Pollution is a third living standard threat blamed on capitalism and population growth. Pollution has turned fields and forests into lunar landscapes, and rivers and streams into open sewers. Also, its health effects may become apparent only after many years, often in the form of cancer. A fourth threat is resource exhaustion, which turns prosperous lumbering, mining, and oil-well communities into ghost towns, and fertile farmland into desert. And finally, there is war, the supreme pollutant, now associated with genocide, nuclear holocaust, and the possible extermination of humanity.

In all of these cases, capitalism is blamed for failure either to prevent the catastrophes or to provide adequate "safety nets" to those who are injured. In every case, market capitalism and the urge for short-term profits are blamed for causing or at least accelerating the catastrophe and for allowing too little time for adjustments to be made.

Capitalism is indicted on the grounds that mass living standards are under constant pressure, both from the short-term shocks associated with business-cycle declines and from the long-run shocks associated with chronic inflation, technological change, pollution, resource exhaustion, and warfare.

Alienation

The characteristic psychological ailment of capitalism—and also of any other social system in which one or another social class or group dominates or exploits the rest of the society—is called **alienation**. This ailment is most serious among the victimized classes, races, or other social groups. However, a "guilty conscience" can also lead to alienation in the upper classes.

When one feels always hostile or indifferent to someone or something that people in one's society generally consider attractive, one is said to be "alienated" from that person or thing. Alienation may appear in many different forms. The victim may actively hate himself or herself, or be bored to the point of disgust, not with "the real me," but with the self as "processed" by advertising, propaganda, television, or the school system. Or one's feelings of alienation may focus on a "dull" or "commonplace" family, a "meaningless" or "dehumanizing" job, a "hopeless" future, a "drab" community, a society "rotten to the core."

The sufferer from alienation may just become sleepy, lazy, and vaguely depressed. In more acute cases, he or she may take refuge in overeating or starving, in overconsumption or oversaving, in drink or drugs or sex, in "dropping out" of mainstream society, or even in suicide. Alienation may also lead to violent or criminal behavior, even to terrorism and mass murder.[3]

While admitting or even insisting that criminal behavior be punished, critics of capitalism believe that an exploitative society is, in the last analysis, responsible for the actions of those whom it alienates. They protest against "blaming the victim," meaning the criminal, whom they see as being hurt by the society.

3. The Jonestown colony of Guyana had both an alienated leader and an alienated population when it exploded in 1978. Many leaders and members of the Nazi party were alienated both by the Germany of the Weimar Republic, which followed World War I, and the whole "Jazz Age" civilization of the 1920s.

Here is a single extreme case:

CAMBRIDGE—A former Polaroid Corp. engineer who attacked his wife and child with an ice pick won a $1.9 million out-of-court settlement from Polaroid, claiming that the company was negligent in treating the depression that led to his assault.

Lawrence L. Okerblom, Jr., his wife and son, will receive the money in monthly payments for at least 25 years. Most of the money will go to the son, who was brain-damaged and lost much of his vision in the attack.

After attacking his family, Mr. Okerblom tried to kill himself. The family split up after the incident.

In the suit filed in 1974, Mr. Okerblom said that a Polaroid doctor and counselor were negligent in treating his anxiety. Mr. Okerblom was in a ''psychotic state'' because he feared Polaroid was about to fire him, his lawyer said. The Polaroid doctor and counselor didn't take Mr. Okerblom's symptoms seriously and didn't prescribe the proper treatment, the attorney said. Polaroid officials weren't available for comment.[4]

Both the ''insecurity'' and the ''alienation'' aspects of this case are obvious and interrelated. There is, of course, also a ''maldistribution'' aspect. Do you think the settlement was unreasonably high or low, given the circumstances? Was Polaroid exploiting Mr. Okerblom, or was Mr. Okerblom exploiting Polaroid? If similar cases had arisen among lower-ranking blue-collar workers, do you think they would have been handled in the same way?

Alienation—a feeling of continual hostility or indifference toward something or someone that people in one's society generally consider attractive—is the characteristic psychological ailment of capitalism.

---

4. Abridged from *The Wall Street Journal*, March 10, 1983. Reprinted by permission of *The Wall Street Journal*, © Dow Jones & Company, Inc. 1983. All rights reserved worldwide.

SOME MARXIAN PROPOSITIONS

In North America leftist critics of market capitalism may not think of themselves as Marxists, and have never read much of Marx's writings. Nevertheless, they have almost certainly been influenced indirectly by some of Marx's ideas.

Karl Marx (1818–1883), a German philosopher and economist of Jewish descent, lived the last thirty-five years of his life as a refugee in London. He was both capitalism's greatest critic and socialism's greatest prophet. He may also have been the greatest overall secular (nonreligious) social scientist who has yet lived. He made important contributions not only to economics but to the other social sciences as well, including history and philosophy.

It is an injustice to Marx, and likewise to his great coworker Friedrich Engels (1820–1895), to compress their whole system into a small set of propositions, which is all we can do here. These propositions are eight in number. Although we have tried to ensure that they are distilled accurately from the writings of Marx and Engels, none is a direct quotation.

1. Natural science and technology have advanced to the point where, in a well-run world, all basic goods and services can be made free to all, the economy of abundance can be realized, and the profession of economist can become obsolete.[5]

2. The history of past societies has shown that nearly all surplus production, above some minimal subsistence level, has been appropriated by the social class that owns strategic inputs or factors of production. At successive stages of history, these strategic inputs have been raw physical labor (in slave societies), farmland and mines (in feudal societies), and industrial plant and equipment (in capitalist societies). At every stage, membership in the ruling class has been largely hereditary.

5. In the late twentieth century this seems an extravagant conclusion to have drawn a century earlier. But Marx and Engels were both greatly impressed by the technical achievements of the Industrial Revolution in England, then in full swing—as well as with its seamy side, which inspired much of their anticapitalism.

3. The exclusion of the main body of a society from the bulk of that society's economic surplus is called **exploitation**. Because of their exploitation and their resentment of it, members of exploited classes often become alienated from the society, from their work, from each other, and even from themselves. That alienation leads to crime and other ills, which societies blame on the victims of alienation rather than on the exploiting institutions that have brought about the alienation.

4. The governmental, educational, religious, and other noneconomic institutions of society generally support and legalize the interests of its ruling class. At the same time, they seek to suppress the hostilities of the exploited and the alienated. Examples are "pie in the sky when you die" religion, relief systems that "regulate the poor," judicial systems too costly for the average person, representative governments with voters' choices limited to candidates who supply or attract large-scale campaign financing, and so on. The list is long and scandals under each head are, to the Marxist, more than just scandals. Rather, they are the way the system works.

5. What is important in history is the record of conflict between one exploiting class and its successor, or between the exploiters and the exploited. This is the meaning of the Marxist statement that "history is the record of class struggles." As in proposition 4, certain excesses and outrages on both sides are more than scandals. They are the way the system has worked, with war and violent revolution as integral parts of the whole process.

6. Whereas Adam Smith called the market-capitalist economy "the obvious and simple system of natural liberty," Marxists think of it as just another exploitative regime. True, it has accomplished great things—which Marx and Engels took great pains to recognize in their *Communist Manifesto* of 1848—but it harbors within itself class conflicts and "contradictions," which will lead ultimately to its collapse. The *economic* aspects of Marxism enter into the demonstration of this proposition. We shall outline them in the next part of this chapter.

7. The revolution that overthrows capitalism will involve the whole exploited underclass, the workers or **proletariat**. When the proletariat comes to power, it will own the means of production through a government that it controls. This is the regime of socialism, in which there will be no class left to be exploited because all the means of production will be owned by society as a whole.[6]

8. In a relatively few years after the firm establishment of socialism in the major countries of the world, there will emerge **New Socialist Man and Woman**. Such persons will willingly work harder and more skillfully than anyone in the past. As Leon Trotsky (1879–1940) put it, the average man or woman will rise to the level of "an Aristotle, a Hegel, or a Marx." At the same time, the New Socialist Man or Woman will demand less from society in terms of wealth or the consumption of luxuries. A few generations will be enough to bring on the economy of abundance and to overcome scarcity. With no scarcity or class conflict, the repressive political state can and will wither away.

The main tenets of Marxian thought include the propositions that members of exploited classes often become alienated, that this alienation leads to crime and other social ills, that the governmental, educational, and religious institutions of society generally support and legalize the interests of its ruling class, that a proletariat revolution will eventually overthrow capitalism, that all the means of production will then be owned by society as a whole, and that under socialism a new socialist man and woman will appear.

Marxian Economics: The Statics

Marxian economics is most easily explained in macroeconomic terms, though Marx himself set it out microeconomically. We shall begin with the statics of how the capitalist economy operates and

6. But *ownership* need not be *control,* and anti-Marxists see Marxian socialism as a regime controlled by a "new class" of military and civilian bureaucrats and administrators, with the rest of society exploited much as the proletariat is exploited under capitalism.

then go to the dynamics of how it changes through time. Remember that Marx was analyzing market capitalism as he saw it. (Marxian economic analysis deals with capitalism and not with socialism.)

The macroeconomic formulation of Marx's theory uses W to represent the national income, evaluated in hours of labor. This W is divided into three parts, also expressed in labor hours. These are constant capital (C), variable capital (V), and surplus value (S). Therefore,

$$W = C + V + S$$

Constant Capital Of total labor input (W per period), **constant capital** (C) is the number of labor hours embodied in (used to produce) raw materials and in the depreciation of machinery and other long-lived capital goods. Marxian constant capital is not the same as the ''fixed capital'' of conventional accounting.

Variable Capital Nor is V the ''variable capital'' of conventional accounting. **Variable capital** represents hours of direct labor—mainly blue-collar labor, but also the ''productive'' portions of white-collar labor[7]—but not all those hours! Suppose that you work a 40-hour week on an assembly line but that your week's wages will buy only 30 hours of others' labor as embodied in food, clothing, and other consumption goods. In that case, your 40 hours of labor will represent only 30 hours of variable capital, the Marxian V.

Surplus Value But what of the other 10 hours of your labor? Marx does not forget them, but calls them ''surplus'' labor. The value of the surplus labor is retained by the employer. Out of it is paid all kinds of property income—interest, rent, and profits—and also the ''unproductive'' portion of white-collar labor (including, for example, doctors, lawyers, soldiers, bureaucrats, and teachers as pre-

dominantly dependents, or hangers-on of the capitalist class). Surplus labor is, in the case of your work on the assembly line, your personal contribution to total **surplus value** or S.

How large is this surplus value, in relation to the total of variable capital? In this microeconomic case, it is $10/30$ or $1/3$. In an aggregate economy with $C = 5,000$, $V = 3,000$, $S = 1,000$, W would equal their sum, or 9,000, and the ratio S/V would again equal $1/3$. In many of the numerical illustrations in his *Capital*, Marx himself sets this ratio equal to one. However, Marxists believe that in the United States today it is actually above one and tending to rise over time, at least in periods of prosperity.

The ratio S/V or S' is called the **rate of surplus value**, or sometimes the **exploitation rate**. It represents the contribution of each hour of variable capital to the total of surplus value. It is important in Marxian economic analysis, as you will see.

S/V, the rate of surplus value (the exploitation rate), is the amount of labor-produced value retained by the employer divided by the amount of labor-produced value received by the worker. All value is labor-produced.

Profit The Marxian concept of profit comprises all surplus value, including the wages and salaries of unproductive labor. This concept of profit is clearly more inclusive than the ''net income'' of either conventional economics or conventional accounting.

The Marxian concept of profit comprises all surplus value, including the wages and salaries of unproductive labor.

To compute a rate of profit, which Marx calls P', we divide total surplus value S by total capital, defined as $C + V$. The result is: $P' = S/(C+V)$.

If we divide both numerator and denominator of this expression by variable capital V, the numerator becomes, by definition, the exploitation rate S/V, which Marx called S'. In the denominator, dividing by V gives us $C/V + V/V$ or $C/V + 1$. Marx used the term **organic composition of capital** for the

---

7. The distinction between ''productive'' and ''unproductive'' labor is very difficult in all economic theories that, like the Marxian, make such a distinction. For an elaborate explanation of the issues from a Marxian viewpoint and with careful attention to Marx's own statements, see David Laibman, ''Unproductive Labor: Critique of a Concept,'' in William L. Rowe, editor, *Studies in Labor Theory and Practice* (Minneapolis: Marxist International Press, 1982).

ratio between constant capital (raw materials plus depreciation) and variable capital (direct labor, as described above). Calling this ratio k, Marx's formula for profit becomes

$$P' = \frac{S'}{1 + k}$$

In terms of our figures for an aggregate economy if $C = 5,000$, $V = 3,000$, and $S = 1,000$, the organic composition of capital k becomes $5,000/3,000$ or $5/3$, and the exploitation rate S' is $1/3$. This makes the profit rate equal to

$$P' = \frac{1/3}{1 + 5/3} = \frac{1/3}{3/3 + 5/3} = \frac{1}{8}$$

The organic composition of capital is the ratio between constant capital (raw materials plus depreciation) and variable capital (direct labor).

Marxian Economics: The Dynamics

Then Marx goes on to investigate "the laws of motion of capitalism." The main purpose of all his apparatus was dynamic. As he moves from economic statics to economic dynamics, Marx uses the last equation. He argues that the organic composition of capital k (like the static capital-labor ratio) tends to rise over time. It rises because, in the absence of war or of natural catastrophe, the capital stock generally grows at a faster rate than does the labor force or employment, and also because innovations tend to be motivated to save direct labor costs more than to save capital costs. That is, they are more likely to be labor-saving than capital-saving.[8] As capitalism progresses and capital is accumulated, the rising trend of k means that the profit

rate P' must fall, that the exploitation rate S' must rise, or most commonly both.

Marx argued that the organic composition of capital tends to rise over time because the capital stock generally grows at a faster rate than does the labor force or employment and also because innovations tend to save direct labor costs more than capital costs.

Falling Rate of Profit At some point, however, either of the above developments will be disastrous for capitalism. If the rate of profit falls below a certain level, capitalists will no longer find it worthwhile to invest much more than the amount needed to replace fixed capital as it wears out. Marx thought that capitalists would not raise their consumption very much but would try to hoard money, real estate, "collectibles," or other goods not currently being produced. In this way, they would in turn lower the equilibrium level of national output and raise the unemployment rate. Increasing unemployment is one form of what Marxists call the "increasing misery" of the working class, which they see as the consequence of capitalism as it matures.

Marx predicted long-term stagnation for capitalism, with short business-cycle booms and long business-cycle depressions and with a rising rate of measured unemployment. In Marxian literature this is called a **liquidity crisis**. If wages were raised in relation to prices to maintain mass purchasing power, the liquidity crisis would only be intensified, since the rate of profit would fall even lower. Falling-rate-of-profit arguments are used by Marxists against liberal reformers and trade unionists who propose to save capitalism by income-redistribution measures.

Marx foresaw increasing unemployment as the consequence of maturing capitalism. He predicted a liquidity crisis—long-term stagnation, with short business-cycle booms and long business-cycle depressions, along with rising unemployment.

---

8. Notions of class warfare are not required to explain the tendency of innovations to be labor-saving rather than capital-saving. A sufficient explanation is that labor costs (primarily payrolls) are a larger part of production costs than are capital charges, so that a 1 percent saving of labor costs is worth more than a 1 percent saving of capital charges. In contemporary North America, a 1 percent saving of labor cost is worth approximately as much as a 2.5 percent saving of capital charges.

Tendency to Overproduction Suppose that capitalists form cartels to keep profit rates up or even raise them, in spite of the rising organic composition of the capital. Marxists answer that such moves cause prices to rise in relation to wages and cause the exploitation rate S' to rise, and that the capitalists will not find buyers for the goods produced. As the exploitation rate rises, a falling proportion of the labor force is needed to produce the output that the masses can still buy. Again there is rising unemployment and increasing misery, even though the profit rate remains high. Such a development is called a **realization crisis**. This argument is used by Marxists to answer the conservatives who would call for "self-government in business," as well as for wage cutting, union busting, and similar cures for business recessions and depressions.

As the exploitation rate rises, a falling proportion of the labor force is needed to produce the output the masses can still buy. This is called a realization crisis.

In closing this section, we make three final points. First, Marx's *Capital* is about capitalism, and it has little to say about how a socialist system would manage the problems that capitalism allegedly mismanages. Second, Marx's labor theory of value builds on the classical theories of Smith and Ricardo and does not deal with demand and utility as determinants of value. Finally, the Marxian analysis leaves no major role for government fiscal or monetary policy. In Marx's day, these instruments most likely played too small a part for them to make much difference. Could they today offer a way out of the Marxian dynamic-economic dilemma?

Marxian analysis is about capitalism; it has little to say about how a socialist system would manage these same problems. Also, Marx's labor theory does not deal with demand and utility as determinants of value, nor does it grant an important role to governmental fiscal or monetary policy.

ARE YOU A RADICAL?

In the dictionary, the term **radical** is defined as extreme, sweeping, or revolutionary. However, yesterday's radical ideas may be today's moderate, conservative, or reactionary ones, and today's radical ideas may be tomorrow's moderate, conservative, or reactionary ones. And what is true over time is equally true over space. The Soviet "conservative" is a Stalinist.

The conventional connotation of *radical* is unfavorable, at least in the United States. Its associations are with mob violence, terrorism, bomb-throwing, and assassination. What is overlooked is that radical ideas have sometimes been correct in the past and may be so again. Within the radical movement itself, on the other hand, the connotation of the term is favorable. Anything less than radicalism is cowardly, pussyfooting, compromise with "the Establishment" or with "the Great Satan." What the movement overlooks is that radical ideas can be and have been wrong. Neither radicalism nor its alternatives can insure anyone against making stupid mistakes.

Radicalism, including radical economics, may be of the political Left or the political Right. In the context of planning versus the market, the radical Left generally, but not always, calls for giant steps toward a purely planned economy, and the New Right proposes equally giant steps toward a purely market one.

The radical Left generally calls for a purely planned economy, while the radical Right favors a purely market economy.

It is a long way from Karl Marx developing "the laws of motion of capitalism" in the British Museum to the campus radical howling down some visiting speaker who he or she has been told is "reactionary." Marx himself, by the way, warned his audience that he was not a Marxist!

Here is a set of seven questions. If you answer "Yes" to most or all of them, you probably qualify as a true believer "under the radical sign."

1. Are you sure that piecemeal reforms (monetarism or fiscalism, demand side or supply side, more deregulation or less, freer trade or more protection) are like "rearranging of deck chairs on the *Titanic*"—too marginal to carry out the "radical restructuring" that society needs?

2. If some combination of such reforms (as in the last paragraph) were indeed massive enough and well enough thought out to do much good, would you oppose the reforms all the more? Do you want to see "the system" overthrown *rather than* improved, even when improvement is possible?

3. Do you believe "the Revolution" must take place very soon—in your own generation—if world war or world pollution or some similar catastrophe is to be avoided?

4. Do you favor mass demonstrations and "direct action,"[9] distrusting the electoral process and representative government because the electoral process is too slow, too heedless of intense-minority opinion, too easily thwarted by judges or bureaucrats, or "all of the above"?

5. Is the present system so bad that there is no real danger that its overthrow would lead to something worse? Is there no danger of jumping from the frying pan into the fire?

6. Do you have no clear idea of what the new system that would succeed the present one might look like, beyond such general ideas as "a planned society" or "public ownership of the means of production" or "more equality"? Are you willing to leave the everyday details to be worked out "in the course of the struggle"?

7. Do you believe the intellectual support for your position has already been worked out well enough by one or more great intellectual leaders to allow you to accept it as given, so that you can depend on nonrational ways of knowing—such as faith, intuition, song lyrics, or the authority of the leadership group of your particular movement?

Most radicals believe that society needs large-scale restructuring, which can be accomplished only by overthrowing the current system.

---

9. "Direct action" may range from individual kidnappings and assassinations to mass revolts and revolutions, which turn violent if resisted.

THE NEW LEFT

In most countries the main body of radical economists has been affiliated with the so-called **New Left**. However, most supporters of the New Left are neither economists nor radicals as we have described radicalism. A question then arises: If Marx and Engels may be taken to represent the Old Left at its best, why do we need a New Left?

In the first place, Marx's theories were not accepted by all the political Left of Marx's own day. Marxists struggled continually both with reformists and with anarchists for control of the First International—the International Workingmen's Association of which Marx was a founder and which was the center of his political activism for the last dozen years of his life. Today we would call the reformists liberals or social democrats.[10] We shall discuss the anarchists later in this chapter.

In the second place, within fifteen years after Marx's death, Marxists began to differ among themselves with increasing vehemence.[11]

In the third place, and most importantly, the victories of European fascism in the period between the two world wars were blamed on disagreement and disunity among members of the political Left. The story was especially tragic in Germany, where the Social Democratic party had been both strong and well organized, but had been unable to form any common front with the Communist party to check the rise of Hitler and his National Socialists (Nazis). The Social Democratic party collapsed after Hitler came to power in 1933.

The New Left hopes to avoid a similar fate by playing down intellectual hair-splitting and by maintaining a united front. The American New Left grew out of the conviction of both liberals and radicals that the "McCarthyism" of the 1950s was a

10. In most of the nineteenth century the term *liberal* meant a doctrinaire disciple of free enterprise and *laissez-faire*. Now it means an advocate of various economic and social reforms attached to a framework that includes private ownership of most of society's capital goods. A *social democrat* differs from a liberal in advocating public ownership of the means of production. But, like a liberal, the social democrat proposes to achieve change entirely by nonviolent means centering on free elections.

11. We discuss the evolution of Marxian ideas "from Karl Marx to the New Left" in the essay that concludes this part of the book.

real fascist threat, which the country had been lucky to avoid. Next came the formation of a university-based (not labor-based) organization called Students for a Democratic Society (SDS) at Port Huron, Michigan, in 1962. In the SDS "Port Huron Statement," doctrinal differences, both economic and political, were papered over with evangelical language. However, the SDS was overcome by some of these same differences—in particular, the role of violence—and broke up in 1968–69.

The American New Left grew out of the conviction that the McCarthyism of the 1950s was a real fascist threat that the country had been lucky to avoid. The main organization of the New Left, the Students for a Democratic Society (SDS), was prominent during the 1960s but broke up at the end of the decade.

SDS was founded before the upsurge of the civil rights movement and any extensive military involvement in Indochina. These issues became the focal points for agitation against the entire capitalist civilization, including the capitalist economy. As the civil rights movement and the Vietnam War retired from the front page, student interest shifted from reform or revolution to qualifying for good jobs in the world much as it was. The SDS, the New Left, and the racial and campus riots all retreated into ancient history, sometimes tinged with nostalgia. (Something similar happened in other countries, where direct involvement with American civil rights and Vietnam problems had been minimal but where pervasive anti-Americanism had become part and parcel of the political Left.)

Since 1970, there have been a number of efforts to revive the New Left coalition of the late 1960s, but around other issues. Some candidates for a unifying issue have been ecology and environmentalism, nuclear war, feminism, South African *apartheid,* and American policy in Central America. As of 1989, none of these issues had succeeded. Nevertheless, the "ancient history" label is premature for the New Left.

Branches of the New Left

The New Left is not and never has been an exclusively radical movement. It has always had and

continues to have a liberal and reformist following. Its radical vanguard, however, has been divided among anarchists, socialists, and syndicalists, who get along together well at some times, badly at others. All three are **collectivist,** since they all oppose individual or private ownership of the means of production. All of them want capital goods—including consumers' goods held in inventories—to be owned "collectively." But they mean quite different things by collective ownership. It may be helpful to classify the New Left radicals further into five groups. There seem to be two quite distinct anarchist groups, two different socialist (or communist) groups, and a single embryonic syndicalist group.

The subgroups of the New Left—two anarchist groups, two socialist groups, and a syndicalist group—are all collectivist, since they oppose private ownership of the means of production.

Anarchism I **Anarchists,** who fear the state as much as they fear the capitalist class, want control of capital goods to be by purely voluntary associations, which people may enter by negotiation and leave more or less as they please. These groups would have no power to levy taxes or to impose compulsory penalties on members except to suspend or expel them from membership.

What we shall call *Anarchism I* includes a great number of variations on a theme that calls itself "the counterculture." Their common feature is withdrawal from organized society into independent communes, whose members now and then go forth with food, medical aid, and political propaganda for people in the slums. These groups attempt to show the larger society the error of its ways. They hope that such demonstrations will lead to the reorganization of society as a network of larger communes.

Some communes are rural, with strong back-to-the-land, ecological, or primitivistic flavors, like the *kibbutzim* in Israel. Others are urban, sometimes using violent guerrilla tactics. They may center on economic, sexual, or psychedelic experimentation, religious revivalism, occultism, or simply "living cheap." More than any other radicals, these people often feel that economic issues are irrelevant. So, while most radicals call for massive redistribution of income and wealth, these folks would most likely accept the following view:

> Distribution is irrelevant because income is irrelevant. There is already too much consumption of the wrong kind: soul-less, artificial ''satisfaction'' encouraged by advertising, which robs people of their freedom, makes them empty and unhappy. Property is theft, and 'income distribution' fits in with it. We ought to abandon the whole rotten production and consumption structure of industrialism. We ought to live in communes, be directly supplied with simple, natural goods, and arrange distribution in direct consultation with one another.[12]

Terrorism and parasitism are among the charges that have been made against this radical group. However, those who believe in violence as a way of life are a rather small fraction. Most prefer to provoke the Establishment, by ridicule or violence, into dropping its liberal front and showing its true colors, which they consider repressive. Neither should they be considered parasites. Many traffic and barter with ''straight'' society, selling farm products and handicrafts to earn money for what they need to buy. Parasitism is dependence on handouts from parents, friends, passers-by, and the government relief system. This aspect of communal living also obviously exists, but only as an offshoot.

Counterculture anarchists withdraw from society into independent communes and would like to see society as a whole organized into a network of communes.

Anarchism II This group works within society but only to destroy it, either by violence (terror) or by ridicule.

In the United States of the late 1960s, the favorite weapon was ridicule, in the grand tradition of Till Eulenspiegel, Voltaire, and Bernard Shaw. Their ''revolution'' would be a day or week of merry pranks—fraternity initiations on a grand scale. It is hard to believe that their manifestos were meant to do more than shock people into serious thought about social issues—people such as:

12. Jan Pen, *Income Distribution: Facts, Theories, Policies* (London: Allen Lane, 1971), p. 293.

> And there's doctors and lawyers,
> And business executives,
> And they're all made out of ticky tacky
> And they all look just the same.[13]

Their high priest, Abbie Hoffman, produced the best known of these manifestos for the 1968 Democratic Party convention held in Chicago. Planks 7 and 8 dealt with economic matters:

7. The abolition of money, the abolition of pay housing, pay medicine, pay transportation, pay food, pay education, pay clothing, pay medical help, and pay toilets.

8. A society which works for and actively promotes the concept of full unemployment. A society in which people are free from the drudgery of work. Adoption of the concept ''Let the machines do it.''

''Machines'' were to produce everything we need, and repair each other in their spare time, whatever damages they may have suffered in the Revolution. The people, meanwhile, would dance and sing, write poetry, make love, and heighten their awareness through ''body chemistry.''[14]

New Left anarchists have subsequently stopped playing games and turned to terroristic violence. The Baeder-Meinhof gang in West Germany and the Red Brigades in Italy seem to be examples of terrorism with an anarchist accent. (The American Weathermen, the violent offshoot of the SDS, were, however, Trotskyist rather than anarchist.)

The Anarchism II group of the New Left turned to terroristic violence in its attempt to restructure society.

It is in general a great, though common, mistake to associate terrorism exclusively with anarchism, socialism, or any other form of radicalism, Old or New, Left or Right. Terrorism is a set of violent tactics that, when used by others than the uniformed armed forces and the police, is aimed at some sort of social change and is denounced by

13. Extract from the song ''Little Boxes.'' Words and music by Malvina Reynolds. © 1962 Schroder Music Company. Reprinted with permission.

14. ''Free'' [Abbie Hoffman], *Revolution for the Hell of It* (New York: Dial Press, 1968).

worldwide public opinion. But the American Ku Klux Klan, the Nazi Gestapo, the Irish Republican Army (IRA), the extremist factions of the Palestine Liberation Organization, and the shadowy overseas agencies of the Khadafy government of Libya are none of them either anarchist or primarily leftist in orientation. They aim at such diverse goals as white supremacy, anticommunism, a united Ireland, and the elimination of Israel from the Middle East. Some profess leftist sympathies and others profess antileftist ones, but the particular cause seems unrelated to the tactics. Terrorism, in short, is not an economic category.

Terrorism is a set of violent tactics aimed at social change. It should not be associated exclusively with radicalism of the Left or Right.

Socialism I   **Socialists** are both more numerous and more important than the anarchists within the New Left. Their tradition is also more rational and less emotional, as indicated by the importance attached to Marxian analysis. Socialists (and communists)[15] see ownership of land and capital by the political state and its agencies (themselves controlled by a political party representing the working class) as the only feasible short-run alternative to capitalism. When the world turns socialist, it may be sensible to speak of the eventual "withering away" of political states. At the present time, say the socialists, such talk is a harmful diversion.

Socialists see ownership of the land and capital by the political state and its agencies as the only feasible short-run alternative to capitalism.

What we shall call *Socialism I* embodies a neo-Stalinist approach, which its enemies call "Red

Fascism." The economy is to be planned on scientific principles, and planning is to be largely imperative—the Plan plus a machine gun or a firing squad. Dissent, including economic dissent, is tolerated only "repressively," if at all, meaning that the dissenters may let off steam harmlessly, short of action. Monopoly of the formal means of propaganda is imposed and reinforced if necessary by compulsory study and by criticism and self-criticism sessions. In such group therapy, orthodoxy is drummed into the members, who are expected to apply it to current practical problems. No one is allowed to remain silent, or to hide dissent behind a mask of ignorance. "I don't know" is not an escape hatch.

"Liberty," Lenin is supposed to have said, "is a commodity so precious that it must be rationed." Under the neo-Stalinists, civil rights are subordinated to the dictates of planning. The rule of law normally remains in effect, but the content of the law is shifted in favor of the state and against defendants in such "details" as the presumption of innocence, protection against self-incrimination, free choice of defense lawyer, double jeopardy, and the statutes of limitation.

One branch of socialism embodies a neo-Stalinist approach and advocates imperative planning coupled with monopoly of the formal means of propaganda and education, little toleration of dissent, and subordination of civil rights.

Socialism II   The camp we call *Socialism II* is often referred to as "Marxist humanism." Its inspiration comes from the younger Marx of the 1830s and 1840s, who was more concerned with "human values" and less with "class struggles" than he would become later on. Socialism II is less authori-

---

15. Communists go beyond socialists in three main ways, more political than economic.

First, they believe more firmly than other socialists that an economy of abundance would shortly follow the establishment of socialism on a world scale. In this way, they are closer to the teachings of Marx.

Second, orthodox communists (or Marxist-Leninists) accept violence as a necessary aspect of revolution, especially in less developed countries. They propose not only to use it in self-defense, but also to take the offensive when the time is right. As

a result, they want their political party to be limited to activists, and to be disciplined tightly like a military organization.

Third, orthodox communists also see a need for a dictatorship of the proletariat (and its "vanguard party") for a long period after the socialist revolution—again, especially in less developed countries.

They do not believe that any existing economy has actually gone beyond socialism to communism, though Mao Zedong hoped to attain communism for China in a "Great Leap Forward," which ended in failure in 1958–1962.

---

tarian than Socialism I, and seems less concerned with orthodoxy. However, the government monopoly of formal education and propaganda is as strong as under Socialism I. In practice, Socialism II may lead to the substitution of mob rule for bureaucracy, as in the Chinese Cultural Revolution of Mao Zedong's last decade (1966–1975).

Among the leading economic doctrines of Socialism II are the following: (1) there should be equality of income and wealth; (2) a wider range of goods and services should be made available completely free of charge; (3) "material incentives" should be replaced by "moral incentives" for economic activity; (4) there should be an end to the hierarchy and alienation of modern industrial society.

Marxist humanist socialists are less authoritarian and less concerned with orthodoxy than the neo-Stalinists, although government monopoly of formal education and propaganda remain strong. Marxist humanists advocate equality of wealth and income, a wide range of free goods and services, moral incentives for economic activity, and an end to the alienation of modern industrial society.

Isn't it likely that Socialism II would degenerate in practice to Socialism I? Without doubting the sincerity of Marxist humanists, one may indeed wonder if a society can go from the status quo to Marxist humanism without a longer or shorter period of "proletarian dictatorship." There is also the danger that a ruling bureaucracy under Socialism I would not permit the peaceful transition to Socialism II. One may also wonder if the degree of ideological control needed to make the New Socialist Man and Woman out of ordinary people can be combined with the Bill of Rights quite as easily as Socialist II followers expect or hope.

Syndicalism **Syndicalists** favor the separate ownership of each productive facility (which may be a single workshop, a factory, or a large industrial complex) by its own workers, who would elect representatives to a weak state, which would referee disputes between groups of workers and coordinate their economic plans. *Syndicalism* is an almost-forgotten word today. But California's "anti-Red" laws of World War I were anti-*syndicalist* rather than anti-*communist*, and a well-known economist chose the title "Reflections on Syndicalism" for his attack on the New Deal for strengthening the organized labor movement.[16]

Syndicalism is a system of economic and political rule by syndicates—a *syndicate* being another name for a guild or trade union. The syndicates are themselves above the law. Thus syndicalism could mean replacing Congress by a national assembly made up of trade unions. At one time, the Industrial Workers of the World (IWW) embodied the syndicalist threat in the United States.

An interesting feature of syndicalism is its strategy of the general strike rather than political revolution as the weapon of social change. Syndicalists hope not only to win strikes but also to prevent the workers' gains from being passed on to consumers in price rises. Starting with individual companies, syndicalism would spread to the whole economy as local strikes grew into general strikes, and as the issues turned from the purely economic to the openly political. The process of winning strikes, repeated over and over again, would both bring the value of the owners' equity down to zero and paralyze the economy. The unions could then buy out their employers for little or nothing.

It goes without saying that unions would be free to break all contracts and would not be subject to any lawsuits. Also, laws against striking or using the strike weapon for political ends would be ignored.

Many proposals and activities, not necessarily radical, have syndicalist implications. For example, in support for public employees' and welfare recipients' rights to strike and bargain collectively, the "syndicalist" feature is that their bargains are considered sacred. Elected legislatures may not refuse funding to carry them out. A case on the local level is a teachers' union (not consciously syndicalist) bargaining for higher pay and smaller classes, and in this way using the strike weapon to force hikes in property tax rates, which the people through their elected representatives may have refused. In other words, the elective machinery of government

---

16. Henry C. Simons, *Economic Policy for a Free Society* (Chicago: University of Chicago Press, 1948), Chapter 6.

is downgraded in relation to bargaining by employee unions, in terms of control of the taxpayer's dollar. If the legislature is limited to backing up the results of collective bargaining, the government's "power of the purse" is weakened.

Earlier versions of syndicalism were built around economic *blitzkrieg*, or lightning warfare. All workers were to lay down their tools at the same time, and that would be enough to paralyze the economy immediately. It was hoped that such a general strike might be spontaneous, so that the capitalists would be taken by surprise. There have in fact been general strikes. Some of them have succeeded, but the successful ones have been a part of or a trigger for political revolution, not substitutes for it.

Syndicalism is a system of economic and political rule by trade unions, which are free to break contracts and are not subject to lawsuits. Syndicalists favor the separate ownership of each productive facility by its own workers. They also advocate the general strike, rather than the political revolution, as the weapon of social change.

THE NEW RIGHT

From the New Left, we turn to the **New Right.** More than the New Left, it changes in character from one country to another. Moreover, it lacks any towering figure who corresponds to Karl Marx. The New Right is composed of people disgusted with things as they have become, but should not be confused with conservatism. Neither should it be confused with fascism, for its majority is composed of people bitterly opposed to authoritarian regimes. In the United States at least, the incidence of radicalism as we have defined it is less in the New Right than in the New Left. However, the truly radical New Right is a collection of paramilitary cells, which stage shoot-outs and bust-ups with people they call "commies" or racially inferior or which plot guerrilla warfare to follow nuclear attacks or communist takeovers. The Ku Klux Klan and the

Survivalists, respectively, exemplify these two strains.

Three intertwined branches compose the American New Right. Only one of these, the market-economy New Right, is primarily economic. The other two branches are ethical-religious and political. The ethical-religious branch wants the recognition of absolute ethics and morality. The political branch is strongly anti-Soviet, fearing Soviet plots for world domination and empire.

The Market-Economy New Right

The market-economy New Right glories in being reactionary, and proposes a return to the old-time religion of *laissez-faire*. On the macroeconomic side, it also calls for restoring the gold standard, the annually balanced budget, and sometimes Say's Identity (aided by downward wage rate flexibility) to ensure high employment. The New Right's god is Adam Smith, whose faith in free enterprise was much less fervent than their own.

The market-economy New Right can be subdivided into those for and those against trust-busting and similar controls. The **trust-busters** see a "decline of competition," which they would like to reverse. They fear that control by a big-business oligarchy will restrict output and employment, raise prices, and stifle the opportunity for new businesses to enter the prosperous mainstream of the American economy. Another of their fears is that a growing proportion of the people are being pushed into a relatively poor competitive segment of the economy.

The **laissez-faire** New Right is less impressed by the threat of economic segmentation into tightly knit oligopoly and competitive sectors. It depends not on antitrust laws or other controls but on technological change, which Joseph Schumpeter called "creative destruction," to overcome any tendencies toward segmentation. This group points, for example, to the displacement of the railroad "octopus" of the late nineteenth century by trucks, buses, planes, and automobiles less than fifty years later. It also points to a "product cycle" in international trade that leads to more foreign competition for companies like General Motors and Ford in automobiles, or like USX and Bethlehem Steel in the steel industry. To these people, monopoly and tightly knit oligopoly may indeed be diseases, uncomfortable where they strike and while they last, but more like the common cold than cancer. They believe that the struggle to gain and hold on to market positions in oligopolistic industries spurs both invention and innovation.

The market-economy New Right proposes a return to laissez-faire economic policies and calls for restoring the gold standard and the balanced budget. The "trust-buster" segment of the New Right wants to restore competition, which they feel is threatened by big business; the "laissez-faire" segment believes that technological change will overcome any tendencies toward long-term monopoly control.

The two groups within the market-economy New Right agree in general that the economy would do better with less regulation and greater reliance on law and equity. But how much less regulation? Less in what fields of economic activity? Which regulations should be lightened or scrapped first? We find disagreement on the specifics.

Similar disagreement on specifics plagues the New Right case against progressive taxation of income and wealth. But there is nearly unanimous New Right support for the view that such taxes be cut, that they should be simplified, and that their degree of progression should be reduced—possibly to zero.

Both groups within the New Right agree that the economy would do better with less regulation and greater reliance on law and equity.

The Libertarian Movement

The most radical branch of the economic New Right in its thinking, although decidedly not in its political tactics—is the **Libertarian** movement. There is no gospel common to all libertarians. Radical libertarians are like anarchists in their fear of the state as an engine of tyranny. However, they depart from collectivist anarchism by supporting private ownership of the means of production. Libertarians offer many proposals for changes in the rules of the economic game, intended to allow the market to govern and reduce the state (and therefore social planning) to zero. Money, defense, protection, streets, sewers, and the framing and administration of law would all be left to private firms and associations. Any person or voluntary group could found a new firm, or buy an existing one in any field (including the practice of law or medicine) without any formal certification of training or competence. All taxes would be replaced by payments for services and by voluntary dues to cooperative associations. People could move freely from place to place and from association to association, but no association would be forced to accept any particular new member or partner.

Libertarians believe the market should govern and the state should cease to exist.

Objectivism and Social Darwinism

Objectivism is the belief that each person's most objective view of "the good" is his or her knowledge of what is in his or her own (subjective) best interest. Another objectivist argument is that "altruism," "the general good," and "social equity" in practice are often self-interest arguments of various other people, who usually do not turn out to be in any way admirable. In the words of objectivist leader Ayn Rand (1905–1982), objectivism is "rational selfishness."[17]

To those who call themselves objectivists, the world and the economy are so interrelated that the Darwinian principle of "survival of the fittest"

17. Ayn Rand was Russian-born, and was (like Karl Marx) a philosopher by training. Disgusted with Soviet Russia after the Revolution, she emigrated to America in 1926. She became a Hollywood screenwriter, and later wrote a series of novels or "tracts for the times." Her ideas are expressed most clearly in the novel *Atlas Shrugged*, which deals with the disastrous things that would happen to society if the few superior individuals should all decide, like ordinary workers, to go on strike. Of her nonfiction works, a collection called *Capitalism: The Unknown Ideal* is the most explicitly economic. In it there is much that could pass as libertarian doctrine, but never a hint of anarchism.

should include survival of those who perform the best in the free market.

Objectivism is the belief that each person's most objective view of "the good" is his or her knowledge of what is in his or her own best interest.

The ideas of Rand and her followers are a revival of a philosophy called **Social Darwinism,** associated particularly with the English sociologist and philosopher Herbert Spencer (1820–1903). Social Darwinists believe that the survival and prosperity of individuals, families, nations, and races are determined, like those of animal species, by their biological and psychological fitness in perpetual struggle against each other and against the environment. It is dangerous in the long run for any family, nation, or race to thwart this struggle for survival, either by placing restrictions on its fittest members or by giving special aid to the least fit. It is not that "the fittest" are above the law, but if enforcement of the laws must be bent in any direction, it is better for society's future if the favored party is the superior person.

Social Darwinists believe that the survival and prosperity of individuals, families, nations, and races are determined by their biological and psychological fitness.

THE FUTURE OF RADICAL ECONOMICS

This final section of this final chapter returns to the radicalism of the Left, especially of the New Left. This is the only form of radical economics that can currently be regarded as a threat or menace to the established order, although it is now clearly in decline. Attempts to revive it—searches for moral equivalents of the Vietnam War in Central America, South Africa, the antinuclear movement, or saving the whales—have had little response or none at all. We observe four principal reasons for the decline.

1. For all of its bombastic manifestoes and its hopes for "the greening of America," the movement—or at least its rank and file—has been satisfied easily with minor victories. The most important of these, in the United States, were the phasing out of military conscription and the abandonment of the South Vietnamese regime to its fate.

2. During the Vietnam period, the domestic market for white-collar labor was unusually tight. The risk of long-term career damage from a police record, from draft-dodging in Canada, or from a year or two of "dropping out" in a counterculture commune seemed negligible. As American participation in Indochina wound down, and as Vietnam veterans rejoined the domestic labor market, this ceased to be true. At the same time, obvious and lucrative opportunity remained at hand for the conformist who "kept his nose clean and avoided dangerous thoughts." This middle way between labor shortage and mass unemployment provided the Establishment an optimal opportunity to discriminate against the unconventional, including of course the radical and the ex-radical. There seems to be no evidence, however, that the Establishment "planned it" that way.

3. The New Left, like the Old, helped dig its own grave by splitting into feuding factions, particularly over the desirability of violence and guerrilla warfare, and over the likelihood of race riots coalescing into a "black revolt." Such organizations as the Weathermen, the Black Panthers, and the Symbionese Liberation Army lost not only their skirmishes but their potential friends and allies as well. Lost them, moreover, for radicalism as a whole as well as for themselves.

4. As we saw in the last chapter, most socialist countries are apparently adopting reform programs that outside observers see as converging with reformist capitalism—however much the socialist leaders denounce any "convergence hypothesis" as backsliding from Marxian fundamentals. This means that radical splinter groups like the Revolutionary Communist party and the Communist Workers party in America, the Red Brigades in Italy, or the Shining Path guerrillas in Peru can no longer model themselves on idealized versions of

Soviet or Chinese reality. The unrealized or repudiated visions of a Leon Trotsky, or the "cultural revolution" of a superannuated Mao Zedong, seem to be inadequate substitutes.

But while radicalism may be hibernating, it is by no means dead. A serious depression or an exceptionally tight labor market would revive it in America, if the foregoing analysis is correct. A return to large-scale military conscription would be another path to radical revival. A third path might be intervention in foreign countries to support pro-American dictatorships or oligarchies. Fear of reigniting the New Left was probably one reason for governmental reluctance to oppose Leftist revolts and revolutions in Nicaragua and El Salvador or even to arm or support openly such movements as

the Contras against the Nicaraguan Sandinista government. Closing the book on radical economics is, in other words, a more difficult task than ending this chapter about it.

The New Left is currently in decline, partly because it split into feuding factions and partly because of current economic realities, but radicalism could easily be revived by a serious depression, a return to large-scale military conscription, or U.S. intervention in foreign countries to support pro-American dictatorships.

Economics in Focus

Toward a New Socialism

Even though socialism fell into eclipse in the 1980s as the New Left's energies dwindled, a number of theorists have tried to revive the movement by reexamining its goals and values. This is particularly true among the ranks of democratic socialists—those who insist on a firm commitment to democracy. Many of them believe that capitalism is approaching a crisis (probably a "slow" crisis) that will bring a new opportunity for socialism. Although the democratic socialists often disagree among themselves, they tend to unite on a few key proposals.

In the first place, they want to transform the nature of work through a radical type of economic democracy. Workers would be given a large degree of control over their factories and offices, either through ownership (as in worker cooperatives) or through democratic forms of self-management. Government tax policies and financial support would encourage such developments. Furthermore, the work week would be shortened, perhaps with government wage subsidies so that people could earn the same income for fewer hours of work without harming the company balance sheet. The shorter working hours would make jobs available for those who are currently unemployed, and workers would enjoy the higher quality of life that comes from greater leisure time. Both self-management and enhanced leisure would raise the creativity of the typical worker, the socialists argue, resulting in a rise in productivity.

There would also be direct measures to reduce inequality by redistributing income. The income tax would be revised in a progressive direction, and inheritance taxes may be changed to discourage the transmission of huge fortunes to single individuals. Government would guarantee a decent income and essential services to every member of society.

In most of their proposals the democratic socialists stress grass-roots participation. Planning, instead of being rigidly centralized, would begin at the local level: the community, the neighborhood, the shop floor. Since planning decisions in a technological society often require technical expertise, the government would support better education programs to make this kind of knowledge more widely available.

In this version of socialism, nationalization of industry is not necessarily a dominant feature. Some industries may be state-owned—health and education services, for example, as well as natural monopolies such as utilities—but others would not. The democratic socialists tend to distinguish "social" ownership and control from state ownership.

Finally, unlike orthodox Marxists, most of these theorists do not say that socialism is inevitable—only preferable. They envision the transition to socialism as a long, gradual process. But they insist that only socialism can bring a genuine realization of freedom and justice.

Sources: Michael Harrington, *Socialism: Past and Future* (New York: Arcade, 1989) and *The Next Left: The History of a Future* (New York: Henry Holt, 1987); "Voices from the Left: A Conversation Between Michael Harrington and Irving Howe," *New York Times Magazine,* June 17, 1984, p. 24ff.; Irving Howe, *Socialism and America* (San Diego: Harcourt Brace Jovanovich, 1985); Andrew Levine, *Arguing for Socialism: Theoretical Considerations* (Boston: Routledge & Kegan Paul, 1984); Stanley Aronowitz, "Are We Afraid to Be Radical?" *The Progressive,* September 1985, pp. 14–15; Peter Kellner, "When Democratic Socialists Must Come Off the Fence," *New Statesman,* November 28, 1986, p. 5; "New Ideas for the Left: Preserve the Goals, Rethink the Means," *The Economist,* September 26, 1987, pp. 25–28.

SUMMARY

1. Opposition to the capitalist-market economy centers on three problems: (a) inequality of the distributions of income and wealth; (b) insecurity of the standard of living against downward shocks, both cyclical and long term; and (c) incompatibility with physical and mental health. The major problem is psychological alienation. Alienation takes many forms and explains many forms of social pathology, ranging from boredom to violent crime. (See pages 950–951.)

2. Marxism is an integrated, unified system of social philosophy, including both economic statics and economic dynamics, and culminating in certain "laws of motion of capitalism." (See pages 952–953).

3. While admitting the accomplishments of the Industrial Revolution, Marxian economics uses a strict labor theory of value to develop certain "contradictions of capitalism." In its Marxian form this theory develops ideas about the exploitation of the worker and the receipt of surplus value by the capitalist class. (See pages 953–955.)

4. In the economic dynamics of Marx's theories, the contradictions of capitalism lead to "increasing misery" and to the eventual downfall of capitalism, either because a falling rate of profit leads to a *liquidity* crisis or because a tendency toward overproduction leads to a *realization* crisis. (See pages 955–956.)

5. Marxian analysis leaves no important role for monetary and fiscal policy. Also, the labor theory of value does not deal with demand and utility as determinants of value. (See page 956.)

6. Radicalism may be radical either because of what it proposes to accomplish, as in "a radical restructuring of society," or because of the tactics that it considers legitimate to accomplish these ends, which sometimes include illegality, violence, dictatorship, and the disregard of public opinion by a tightly organized political party. (See pages 956–957.)

7. The American New Left arose in the early 1960s as a search for unity on the political Left. Disunity of the Old Left was blamed for the rise of fascism in the period between World War I and World War II and McCarthyism in the 1950s. It is not an exclusively radical movement, but its leadership is for the most part radical. It has lost impor-tance since 1970, but keeps trying for revival using new issues in domestic and foreign policy. (See pages 957–958.)

8. The radical groups within the New Left are all *collectivist.* They favor collective ownership of the means of production. Subdivisions are *anarchist, socialist,* and *syndicalist.* (See page 958.)

9. The anarchist wing of the New Left can be subdivided into the "counterculture," which withdraws from the mainstream of society into communes, and the revolutionary wing, which proposes tearing down institutions and then possibly starting over. (See pages 958–959.)

10. Terrorism is a set of violent tactics, which can be used by partisans of a great variety of political, religious, racial, economic, or social positions, but it is not itself a category of economic thought. It is a great mistake to associate terrorism exclusively with any economic philosophy—radical or conservative, old or new, Right or Left. (See pages 959–960.)

11. Socialists favor state ownership of the means of production. The socialist wing of the New Left can be subdivided into neo-Stalinist imperative planners and "Marxist humanists," who emphasize equality, mass participation in decision making, and moral (rather than material) incentives. (See pages 960–961.)

12. Syndicalists favor ownership by trade unions of the workers. They believe that unions can bring down capitalism by winning strikes. Unions would be immune from lawsuits and could break all contracts. (See page 961–962.)

13. The economic New Right concentrates on achieving *laissez-faire*; the ethical-religious New Right, on re-establishing the old-time religion and morality, and the political New Right on thwarting alleged communist conspiracies to dominate the world. These three groups overlap to some extent, and only the first is relevant to our study of economics. It includes both libertarians and objectivists. (See pages 962–963.)

14. Libertarians are, ideologically speaking, the most radical branch of the economic New Right. They favor complete reliance on the free capitalist market and hope for the demise of the political state. They are distinguished from collectivist anarchists by their beliefs in private enterprise and private property. (See page 963.)

15. Objectivists believe that our most nearly

objective knowledge of the "good" and the "just" is our knowledge of what is good for ourselves. We should follow this knowledge rather than the urgings of ethical altruism, which is often a cover for dishonesty. (See page 963–964.)

16. Objectivists are impressed with the contribution to society of the few superior individuals. They fear that human evolution toward some ideal will be sidetracked if such people are restricted or if inferiors are helped to survive and reproduce. To this extent objectivists are Social Darwinists, applying the principle of "survival of the fittest" to social as well as biological relations. (See page 964.)

KEY TERMS

alienation: the characteristic psychological ailment of capitalism; hostility or indifference to something or someone generally considered attractive in society (page 951).

anarchists: people who believe that government should be abolished (page 958).

collectivist: a philosophy characterized by opposition to individual or private ownership of the means of production (page 958).

constant capital: in Marxian economics, the labor hours embodied in (used to produce) raw materials and in the depreciation of machinery and other long-lived capital goods (page 952).

exploitation: in the Marxist perspective, the exclusion of the main body of a society from the bulk of that society's economic surplus (page 953).

exploitation rate: *see* **rate of surplus value.**

laissez-faire: a branch of the market-economy New Right that believes that technological change will overcome any tendencies toward long-run monopoly in the economy (page 962).

Libertarian: a branch of the economic New Right that believes there should be private ownership of the means of production and that the market should govern and the state cease to exist (page 963).

liquidity crisis: according to Marxian thought, a long-term stagnation in a capitalist economy, with short business-cycle booms and long business-cycle depressions and a rising rate of unemployment brought on by a falling rate of profit (page 955).

New Left: contemporary groups that generally call for major changes away from the market economy (page 957).

New Right: contemporary groups that generally call for major steps toward a purely market economy (page 962).

New Socialist Man and Woman: people who will emerge after the establishment of socialism; they will work harder and more skillfully than workers in the past and will demand less from society in terms of wealth and material goods (page 953).

objectivism: the belief that each person's most objective view of "the good" is his or her knowledge of what is in his or her own best interest (page 963).

organic composition of capital: in Marxian economics, the ratio between constant capital (raw material plus depreciation) and variable capital (direct labor) (page 954).

proletariat: the workers (page 953).

radical: extreme, sweeping, revolutionary (page 956).

rate of surplus value: in Marxian economics, the ratio between the amount of labor-produced value taken from the worker and the amount that the worker is allowed to retain (page 952).

realization crisis: in Marxian thought, a crisis caused by a rising exploitation rate; as the exploitation rate rises, a falling proportion of the labor force is needed to produce the output that the masses can still buy (page 956).

Social Darwinism: a belief that the survival and prosperity of individuals, families, nations, and races are determined by their biological and psychological fitness in perpetual struggle against each other and the environment (page 964).

socialists: those who see ownership of land and capital by the political state and its agencies as the only feasible short-run alternative to capitalism (page 960).

surplus value: in Marxian economics, labor-produced value in excess of the amount that the worker is allowed to retain (page 954).

syndicalists: those who favor the separate ownership of each productive facility by its own workers (page 961).

trust-busters: a branch of the market-economy New Right that fears that control by a big-business oligarchy will restrict output and employment, raise prices, and stifle the opportunity for new businesses to enter the mainstream of the American economy (page 962).

variable capital: in Marxian economics, the purchasing power of the wage paid to labor, measured in labor hours embodied in consumption goods (page 954).

DISCUSSION QUESTIONS

1. Do you believe that the inequalities in the American distributions of income and wealth constitute "maldistribution"? Explain why or why not.

2. Does the market capitalist economy make adequate provision for a future in which the relative prices of natural resources and energy are both high and rising steadily? Would a socialist economy do better? Explain.

3. Is alienation the root cause of social pathology, as Karl Marx believed, or are those who engage in pathological behavior responsible for their own actions? Explain your answers.

4. What is meant by the Marxist "economic interpretation of history," "contradictions of capitalism," and "principle of increasing misery"?

5. Karl Marx states in the first chapter of *Capital* what he considers the chief theoretical problem of competitive capitalism. A capitalist buys labor power, raw materials, and intermediate goods at their values. He also sells his final product at its value, and still makes a profit. But where does this profit come from, and why has not competition eliminated it?

Marx then goes on to answer his own questions at some length. What, do you think, is the nature of Marx's solution?

6. Do you think that Marx would be satisfied with the economic performance of the contemporary United States? The contemporary Soviet Union? Contemporary Cuba or China? Explain why or why not in each case.

7. Distinguish between: (a) the Marxist and conventional concepts of profit and (b) the breakdowns of capital into "fixed and variable" (conventional) or "constant and variable" (Marxian).

8. To what extent is it reasonable to associate terrorism with the New Left or with any particular wing of the New Left, or with the New Left in general?

9. Distinguish libertarianism from both anarchism and objectivism.

10. What is Social Darwinism? How does it differ from ordinary (biological) Darwinism? Is it a racist doctrine? Explain why or why not.

11. Do you have an economic explanation for the relative decline of the American New Left after the end of the Vietnam War? Explain what economic circumstances, if any, might cause its revival.

From Karl Marx to the New Left

A prominent slogan of the New Left in the 1960s and early 1970s was "Marx, Mao, and Marcuse!" To this trio we add Lenin, whose importance is reflected in the fact that today Communist parties call themselves Marxist-*Leninist,* and not merely Marxist. Here we shall give a thumbnail sketch of the contributions of Lenin, Mao, Marcuse, and several other left-wing economists and social philosophers during the period between the deaths of Marx and Engels (late nineteenth century) and the rise of the American New Left, which we date from the SDS "Port Huron Statement" of 1962. Our account does not pretend to be a connected history of socialist thought.

Marx died in 1883. Engels, who lived until 1895, edited the last two volumes of Marx's *Capital.* At the same time, however, Engels's revolutionary zeal seemed to wane both with the passing of Marx and the failure of the Revolution to arrive "on schedule"[1] in any of the advanced countries of Europe and North America, where the evolution of capitalism had gone the furthest toward its expected downfall. In spite of several serious economic depressions in the 1870s and 1890s, the socialist revolution seemed much more remote when Engels died than it had seemed in the 1848 "year of revolution," when he and Marx had written their *Communist Manifesto.*

MARX'S FOLLOWERS

The first split in the Marxist ranks came in 1899, sixteen years after Marx's death and only four years

Karl Marx

after that of Engels. It came within the German Social Democratic party, then mainly Marxist and also the world's leading socialist party. The arch-heretic was Eduard Bernstein (1850–1932), who had been Engels's secretary. Bernstein wrote a book best known under its English title of *Evolutionary Socialism.* Bernstein's main points were the following:

1. Capitalism was *not* collapsing from internal contradictions. The middle class was *not* dying out, workers' living standards were *not* falling, and large-

---

1. Marx and Engels never drew up a timetable for the Revolution. They apparently expected it for 1848 or shortly thereafter. When it failed to occur, they wisely refrained from "rescheduling" it. But surely they would be disappointed to find capitalism still controlling major industrial countries in the late twentieth century.

scale agriculture was *not* replacing either the American family farm or its European equivalents.

2. Capitalism would not collapse, and therefore socialism must prove its own superiority and "fitness" in free competition in the marketplace of ideas.

3. Accordingly, socialists should stress reformist electoral and parliamentary paths, and give up the idea of violent revolution in the republics and constitutional monarchies of Europe and America.

Bernstein was answered by Karl Kautsky (1854–1938), "the Socialist Pope" and Engels's successor as editor of Marx's unpublished manuscripts. The German party, and other European Social Democratic parties,[2] officially accepted Kautsky's "orthodox" answer to Bernstein's economic heresies, but then quietly began to follow Bernstein's recommendations on political tactics.[3] For this reason, social democracy is regarded today as reformist rather than revolutionary.

The then much weaker and less important Russian Social Democratic party, operating largely underground and in exile, faced the same conflict. Its Menshevik (minority) faction favored positions close to Bernstein's. Its Bolshevik (majority) faction, which would later be led by Vladimir Ilich Lenin (1870–1924), also known as Nikolai Lenin, went beyond Kautsky in the vigor of its denunciations. In view of the later world leadership of the Russian party and of Lenin's remarkable success in combining theoretical and practical leadership, we move on to discuss the "Leninist" component of Marxism-Leninism.

Vladimir Ilich Lenin

LENIN

Lenin's major contributions to world socialism—as distinguished from his contributions to specifically Russian problems—are three in number, two of them ideological and the third tactical.

1. Lenin more than any other single Marxist writer is responsible for the "internationalization" of

the argument in Marx's *Capital*.[4] Lenin's explanation of capitalist survival was imperialism, the export of capital and capitalist domination to the less developed countries of the world. This extension kept the organic composition of capital—the k term in Marxian equations—low, thereby avoiding both the falling rate of profit and the "increasing misery" of at least the organized labor aristocracy of the capitalist countries. Lenin called such workers the "pampered palace slaves" of capitalism. But imperialism, with or without colonial rule, was not a permanent cure for capitalism's contradictions. On the one hand, it led to imperialist war between rival capitalist powers, for example, World War I. On the other hand, it led to warfare with the natives of the countries being "imperialized." In either form of warfare, the masses in

2. The American Socialist party was never a Marxist party, though many of its individual leaders were Marxists.

3. The test came with the outbreak of World War I in 1914. The Social Democratic party, demonstrating its patriotism, voted to support war credits (war loans). Kautsky went along with this decision. Social Democratic parties in other countries on both sides also expressed patriotic solidarity with their capitalist governments, though the pre-1914 party line had been to resist and sabotage international warfare and transform it into socialist revolution.

4. A number of Marxist writers made important contributions to this "internationalization" process, summarized in Anthony Brewer, *Marxist Theories of Imperialism* (London: Routledge and Kegan Paul, 1980). Chapter 2 deals explicitly with Lenin's *Imperialism, the Highest Stage of Capitalism*.

the capitalist countries must be armed and could be turned against their capitalist exploiters. "The road to London and Paris," Lenin once said, "runs through Peking and Calcutta."

2. It followed for Lenin that the worldwide socialist revolution against capitalist rule need not begin in those lands where capitalism had gone the furthest. It might just as well begin with a war of liberation in some colonial backwater, and spread from there. In fact, it might just as well begin in Czarist Russia, where misery and oppression were particularly bad, even though Russia was, economically speaking, only a backward outpost of European capitalism, and even though Russian capitalism was not well developed.

3. In a backward country like Russia, the workers were not ready for revolutionary activity "on their own." Marxists believed that trade unions could easily be sidetracked into "economism"—that is, concentrating on economic demands for small groups of labor aristocrats "within the system" and ignoring the need to overthrow the system as a whole. What was needed was a revolutionary "vanguard party" to represent the workers' true interests. Such a vanguard party must, Lenin felt, be revolutionary. It must not only be an elite group, unfettered by bourgeois law and morals, but must include an underground core organized in military fashion. This underground party must be prepared to seize full power in the revolutionary struggle, with no need for alliances with liberals and other reformists. Membership in the vanguard party should be limited to loyal activists who make the Revolution the main object of their lives. Also, once the vanguard party has seized power, it should hold on to its "proletarian dictatorship" until socialism is firmly established once and for all, ignoring the forms and machinery of electoral democracy. Of course, for Russia today, the vanguard party is the Communist party.[5]

LUXEMBURG

A middle position in these conflicts, both in Germany and Russia, was held by Rosa Luxemburg (1870–1919). Born in Poland, "Red Rosa" spoke German and Russian as well as Polish, and was active in the revolutionary Marxist politics of all three countries.[6] Her views have come to be respected since her death even more than during her rather short life.

Luxemburg too had a theory of imperialism. But whereas Lenin stressed the export of capital to prop up the domestic rate of profit and prevent *liquidity* crises, Luxemburg stressed the dumping of consumer goods in the less developed countries, when they could not be sold domestically at profitable prices. In terms of Marxist theory, the Luxemburg approach concentrates on avoiding *realization* crises by imperialist expansion.

Luxemburg was no Bernstein disciple or Menshevik reformist. Neither was she an "orthodox" follower of "Pope" Kautsky. She broke with him over the "war credits" issue in 1914, just as Lenin broke with the "patriotic" Mensheviks in Russia. Also, like Lenin, Luxemburg favored an activist, paramilitary vanguard party, ready to seize power in revolutionary struggles without waiting for the election returns. Unlike Lenin, however, she was always suspicious of party dictatorship. She took the "democracy" of the Social Democratic party label seriously in its conventional sense, which calls for the rule "of" and "by" the people as well as "for" them. Though welcoming the Bolshevik seizure of power in Russia in November 1917, she opposed the reign of terror by which the Bolsheviks held on to their power in the following years, beginning when they dissolved a constitutional convention in January 1918. These aspects of her thinking are highly respected by the "Marxist humanist" wing of the New Left.

FROM LENIN TO STALIN

Lenin died in 1924. In the Soviet Union his death signaled a long struggle for power among the subordinate Bolshevik leaders, ending in the dictatorship of Josef Stalin (1880–1953) and the execution of most of Stalin's rivals. This struggle too had important economic implications.

Faced with domestic economic disorganization and a major famine after the end of the Russian Civil

---

5. After the two Russian Revolutions of 1917, the Bolshevik wing of the former Social Democratic party called itself the Communist party. The Menshevik wing continued to call itself the Social Democratic party, but was largely liquidated in the Red Terror and Russian Civil War of 1918–1920.

6. She was assassinated in Berlin while under arrest as a leader of the "Spartacist" revolt. This was an attempt to duplicate in Germany the success of the Bolsheviks in Russia, in the chaos that followed the German defeat in World War I and the abdication of the last Hohenzollern Kaiser, Wilhelm II.

War, Lenin had modified his extremism[7] and accepted a "New Economic Policy" for the Soviet Union. Under this policy, private enterprise was allowed in small-scale industry, light industry, and agriculture, while heavy industry and finance remained in state hands. In the midst of economic revival, an agricultural crisis developed. Russia had lost perhaps 20 million people during World War I, the 1917 revolutions, and the Civil War. Because of the rapid industrialization of the New Economic Policy, many workers left the farms for jobs in the cities.[8] Farm prices began to rise, lowering workers' real wages and hampering industrialization by lowering the urban-rural income differential. But the pace of industrialization had to be maintained, both to prevent any future capitalist "encirclement" or economic "squeeze" and to provide an industrial working class that would support continued socialization. To the Marxist, the peasant was essentially a small capitalist, interested mainly in owning land and profiting by its produce. What was to be done?

In this crisis, the Communist Right Wing (later called *Right Deviation*) was led by an economist, Nikolai Bukharin (1888–1938).[9] Bukharin considered the rising trend of agricultural prices to be only temporary, since he expected that the higher farm prices would lead to more farm production. He saw no need to abandon the New Economic Policy or to put direct pressure on the peasants. The Left Wing (later called *Left Deviation*) was led by Leon Trotsky (1879–1940), whose lieutenant in economic matters was Yevgeny Preobrazhensky (1886–1937). Trotsky's position is not easy to understand. On the one hand, he favored the use of "persuasion" on the peasants to squeeze out more production at controlled prices while making them consume less and save more. But he also favored bringing the peasants into collective farms, along with their private holdings of land, machinery, farm animals, stored grain, and so on.

In the power struggle, Stalin at first sided with Bukharin against Trotsky and Preobrazhensky. Since that time, "Trotskyism" has remained a label attached in the Soviet Union to almost any Left deviation from the current party line. At the same time, Trotskyism became a flag under which dissidents from Stalinism rallied outside the Soviet sphere of influence.[10] Trotsky himself was sent to Siberia, exiled, and later murdered in Mexico. With Trotsky out of the way, Stalin adopted and intensified what had been the Left Wing economic platform. The New Economic Policy was followed by the Five Year Plans. The peasants were collectivized on harsher terms than had been recommended by the Left Wing. A quarter-century of Stalin's dictatorship ended only with his death in 1953.

MAO ZEDONG AND COMMUNIST CHINA

Our scene now shifts to China. To the historian of economic thought, the most important innovation of Mao Zedong (1894–1976) was his basing of the Chinese Communist revolution on discontented peasant farmers (for the most part tenants of richer farmers or absentee landlords), rather than on urban workers (the Marxian proletariat). In the late 1920s and early 1930s, urban-based attempts at revolution in China had failed despite Soviet support and advice, and the Soviets had been lukewarm in their backing of Chairman Mao's successful leadership in the late 1940s.[11]

Then, ten years after expelling the previous Chinese government to the island of Taiwan, Mao first led a "Great Leap Forward" (1958–1962) and then a "Great Cultural Revolution" (1966–1976). The Great Leap was intended to achieve the Communist goal of an economy of abundance through largely decentralized communes, combining agricultural and industrial production in "rural cities." The Cultural Revolution aimed at substituting moral incentives

---

7. Lenin's "extremism," shared by other Bolshevik economists at the time of the Bolshevik Revolution, had been based on an oversimplified planning system modeled after a concept of the country as "one big factory" and intuitively understandable to the average worker. Such a plan would, it was hoped, permit the Soviet Union to operate on a barter system, dispensing with the "bourgeois" social contrivance of money.

8. Technically, this drain of workers from the farms was largely a return flow. Urban workers and demobilized soldiers had gone to the country (where the food was) during the Civil War and the famine that followed it. With greater availability of food in the cities by the middle 1920s, many of these people were simply returning there.

9. Bukharin was the model for the hero Rubashov in Arthur Koestler's *Darkness at Noon*.

10. Trotsky lives on in literature as Emmanuel Goldstein in George Orwell's *Nineteen Eighty-Four*.

11. The Soviets have generally looked with disfavor on Communist party leaders in other countries who have assumed leadership positions without receiving their training in Russia and without the blessings of the Soviet leadership when other leaders having these advantages were available. Mao Zedong is the most important example.

for material ones, at equalizing income and wealth, and at preventing the rise of any bureaucratic "New Class" of white-collar elite workers within the Communist party, the government, or the People's Liberation Army.

Both of these innovations are now judged as failures. The Great Leap Forward, which planned to take over from the Soviet Union the world leadership of the communist movement, led instead to a near-famine in China and to a breakdown in the shaky alliance between the two leading Marxist countries. Such breakdowns were not dreamed of in Marx's philosophy. The Cultural Revolution degenerated into chaos and mob rule, which required military intervention to restore order and revive the economy. Before its failure, however, the Cultural Revolution had attracted worldwide New Left support for its "participatory democracy," its attacks on the Chinese bureaucracy, and its status as an egalitarian alternative to the Soviet system.[12]

12. Strangely enough, Mao Zedong found Stalinism less reprehensible than the somewhat milder regimes that were in power between Stalin's passing and his own death twenty-three years later.

MARCUSE AND THE NEW LEFT

Our account continues with Herbert Marcuse, the final member of the trio "Marx, Mao, and Marcuse." Marcuse (1898–1981) was a German sociologist of the so-called Frankfurt school. For much of his early life he was an academic, respected for his scholarship, but quite unknown to the general public. And before his death he had already been almost forgotten. But after fleeing to America to escape Hitler, he enjoyed more than a decade of fame, both in his native Europe and his adopted America, as a darling of the New Left. The slogan "Marx, Mao, and Marcuse" meant what it said. Marcuse was, for the time being, classed with Marx and Mao, despite the handicap of a difficult literary style.

Marcuse's main contributions were four in number. They ranged from his treatment of demand in economics to theories in the fields of sociology, psychology, and philosophy, with which Marcuse was more at home.

1. There has always been a libertine "free love" tradition in the political Left, which has had to exist along with the rival puritanical tradition, which equates sexual experimentation with "capitalist decadence." In *Eros and Civilization,* Marcuse combined ideas of Karl Marx and Sigmund Freud, and argued that true socialism means freedom for the human spirit. Such freedom, he said, must include sexual freedom—the liberation from "middle-class morality." This was what some members of the Left wanted to hear, and they welcomed it with enthusiasm.

2. "Work is a four-letter word," according to the hippies, and Marcuse "proved" it was quite unnecessary. In *One-Dimensional Man,* Marcuse argued that if we could only restrain our demands, we should easily be able to produce all we want by voluntary work, and could have the economy of abundance the minute after the Revolution. Also, we would be just as well off as we are now. Consumption—more goods, newer goods, new models, more *de luxe* frills—is simply narcotic and does *not* give more satisfaction. Marcuse argued that we are alienated from our society, as Marx had said, but we still expect fancier and more numerous consumer goods to cure our alienation, even though they have never done so in the past. So we become one-dimensional people—consumers of goods. It is better to forget about consumption and standards of living and to give up the rat race in favor of the natural life of play and song and love, all "on the cheap."

3. Marcuse said that the working class is hopelessly narcotized by consumerism and by advertising. It cannot be trusted to overthrow the system. Who then can overthrow it? Marcuse's answer is the student youth, not yet quite overcome by the pressure to consume, and possibly still able to resist the lure of one-dimensional "consumer fascism." As for allies, there are the underclasses at home and abroad—racial minorities, Third World peoples, domestic drifters, dropouts, junkies, hippies, migrants, even criminals—whom Marx himself had scored as *lumpenproletariat* (bums). The youth and the students, not the blue-collar working stiffs, will be the vanguard of the new society.

4. Nor did Marcuse believe in the need to tolerate the opposition. After all, he argued, Mussolini's Fascists and Hitler's Nazis got their start because of misplaced tolerance. They should not have been tolerated at all, but put down at once. Furthermore, today's Establishment uses toleration mainly to allow opponents to "let off steam" ineffectually. This tolerance simply conceals the repressive nature of society, which becomes apparent whenever the opposition becomes a real danger to "things as they are" or to the interests of the capitalist class. Such is the message of Marcuse's *Critique of Pure Tolerance.*

All this was heady stuff for student radicals, who were used to being patted on the head or told to go home and grow up. It went over big in the 1960s and the early 1970s. In fact, Marcuse's message was never refuted. Instead, the job market tightened after the Vietnam War, placing a greater value on "a smile and a shoeshine" and making potential troublemakers "think twice."[13] So the New Left and its heroes fell from fashion into nostalgia, with Marcuse a principal victim. Will New Left ideas and New Left tactics return to favor in the next period of high employment and labor shortage? We do not know, and we dare not forecast.

13. Unlike the situation of the Great Depression, unemployment was not a severe problem for the white students with the proper credentials and "nothing against them." Employers could and did engage in political discrimination. If the situation had deteriorated further, with no jobs for anyone, discrimination would have again been meaningless.

Appendix:
Suggested Outlines for One-Term Courses*

	Macro Emphasis	Micro Emphasis	Contemporary Problems Emphasis	Combined Macro-Micro
Chapter 1 **What Economics Is**	■	■	■	■
Chapter 2 **The Actors on the Economic Stage**	■	■	■	■
Chapter 3 **How Economists Approach Problems**	■	■	■	■
Chapter 4 **Scarcity: The Economic Problem**	■	■	■	■
Chapter 5 **Demand and Supply—or Supply and Demand**	■	■	■	■
Chapter 6 **The Circular Flow, Aggregate Demand, and Aggregate Supply**	■			■
Chapter 7 **National Income Accounting**	■			□
Chapter 8 **Inflation and Unemployment**	■		■	■
Chapter 9 **Economic Fluctuations**	■			□
Chapter 10 **The Keynesian Model of Income Determination**	■			■
Chapter 11 **Fiscal Policy**	■			■
Chapter 12 **Money and Depository Institutions**	■			□
Chapter 13 **The Federal Reserve System and Monetary Instruments**	■			□
Chapter 14 **Monetary Economics**	■			■

* Our assumption is that each of these would be a first course in economics

■ = recommended   □ = optional

(*continued*)

	Macro Emphasis	Micro Emphasis	Contemporary Problems Emphasis	Combined Macro-Micro
Chapter 15 **Aggregate Demand, Aggregate Supply, and Potential GNP**	■			■
Chapter 16 **The Phillips Curve, Adaptive Expectations, and Inflation Economics**	■		■	■
Chapter 17 **Rational Expectations and Contemporary Schools of Macroeconomic Thought**	■		■	■
Chapter 18 **Macroeconomics as a Branch of Knowledge**	■		■	■
Chapter 19 **Exchange Rates, International Balances, and International Finance**	■	□	■	■
Chapter 20 **Economic Growth**	■		■	
Chapter 21 **Economic Development**	■		■	
Chapter 22 **Consumer Choice**		■		■
Chapter 23 **Market Demand and Elasticity**		■		■
Chapter 24 **Business Firm Choice**		■		■
Chapter 25 **Market Supply and Elasticity**		■		■
Chapter 26 **Pure Competition**		■		■
Chapter 27 **Monopoly**		■		■
Chapter 28 **Monopolistic Competition and Oligopoly**		■		■
Chapter 29 **Oligopoly: The Real World**		■	■	
Chapter 30 **Resource Supply and Demand**		■		□
Chapter 31 **Labor, Wages, and Collective Bargaining**		■	■	□

(continued)

		Macro Emphasis	Micro Emphasis	Contemporary Problems Emphasis	Combined Macro-Micro
Chapter 32	**Capital, Interest, and Investment**		■	■	□
Chapter 33	**Government and Taxation**		■	■	
Chapter 34	**Poverty and Income Distribution**		■	■	
Chapter 35	**Government Antitrust and Regulation Policy**		■	■	
Chapter 36	**International Microeconomics: Free Trade Versus Protection**	□	■	■	■
Chapter 37	**Agriculture, Food, and Hunger**		■	■	
Chapter 38	**Natural Resources and the Environment**		■	■	
Chapter 39	**Comparative Economic Systems—More Planning or Less?**	□	□	■	■
Chapter 40	**Radical Economics**	□	□	■	□

Glossary

A

ability-to-pay principle a guide for taxation that advocates that tax liability should be a larger fraction of income (or wealth) for high-income (or high-wealth) receivers than for low-income (or low-wealth) receivers.

absolute advantage being more proficient than others in some branch of production.

absolute amount of cost difference (entry barrier) an entry barrier based upon the difference in average total costs existing between established firms in an industry and potential entrants.

accelerating inflation a situation in which the rate of inflation is increasing; if the acceleration is unexpected, money illusion and wage-cost lags continue to affect employment decisions, and unemployment remains below its natural rate.

accelerator effect the effect that a change in the rate of expansion or contraction in the economy has on the absolute volume of production and income in capital goods industries.

accommodation an action by monetary authorities shifting the money-supply curve so that shifts in the demand-for-money curve do not cause changes in the rate of interest; sometimes called *validation*.

accord, the an agreement reached in 1951 between the Federal Reserve System and the U.S. Treasury under which the Fed was freed from a wartime commitment to support the price of government securities.

acquisition See *merger*.

actual monopoly a real-world form of monopoly; a market in which there is a single seller, sellers in other markets may offer fairly good substitutes, potential competition cannot be ruled out, and the government protection that an actual monopoly may enjoy is not secure, as it may be taken away or altered.

adaptive expectations a proposition that states that the inflation rate that is being experienced during the present time period becomes the inflation rate that is anticipated for the future.

administrative protection a form of protection that subjects competitive imports to burdensome, idiosyncratic, costly, and time-consuming specifications or inspection procedures.

aggregate demand the total value of goods and services demanded in an economy, measured at some specified price level; the relationship between a change in the price level and the resulting change in the quantity of real GNP demanded.

aggregate-demand curve a graphic illustration of the relationship between a change in the price level and the quantity of real national income and product demanded.

aggregate economic concentration a measure of the share of economic activity undertaken by the largest firms in a region of the world, in an economy, or in some major sector beyond traditional industry lines.

aggregate quantity demanded the sum of total purchases, $C + I + G + X - Im$, of an economy during a specified time period at a certain price level.

aggregate quantity supplied the sum of all the goods and services that firms will produce and offer for sale in an economy during a specified time period at a certain price level.

aggregate supply the total value of all goods and services supplied in an economy, measured at some specified price level; the relationship between a change in the price level and the resulting change in the quantity of real GNP supplied.

aggregate-supply curve a graphic illustration of the relationship between the price level and the quantity of real national income and product supplied.

agricultural fundamentalism the doctrine or argument that since food is a necessity and since the countryside is the main market for the manufactured products of the city, farm revenue cannot fall below a certain percentage of national income or GNP without bringing on a depression; the doctrine that, since food is necessary to life, farmers should be at least as well off as any other group.

alienation a psychological ailment expressed in the feeling of hostility or indifference to someone or something in one's society that is generally considered attractive to others in that society.

allocation function the function or role of government involving influence upon the kinds and quantities of different goods and services produced in the economy.

American Federation of Labor (AF of L) a federation of national unions established in 1886 to practice business unionism and merged with the CIO in 1955 to form the AF of L–CIO.

anarchist one who opposes all forms of government compulsion and favors a society organized on the basis of voluntary associations, which individuals can leave at any time.

antitrust policy the course of action (by the government) aimed at maintaining or restoring competition in markets.

applied science an objective, factual, and systematic search for knowledge that includes practical utilizations along with theoretical inquires.

appreciation (in foreign exchange rates) an increase in the foreign exchange value of a nation's money.

arbitrage the purchase of a product in one market for the purpose of immediately reselling it in another market in order to take advantage of a price difference.

arbitration a procedure for settling union-management disputes by having a neutral outside party make a decision that is binding on both sides.

area of inequality the space between a Lorenz curve and the diagonal line of perfect equality on a Lorenz curve diagram.

assets valuable items that are owned; balance sheet entries recording the values of items that are owned.

assumption a statement that is accepted as being true in order to set forth the limits of the variables in a theory.

automatic (or built-in) stabilizers provisions of tax and spending laws that work automatically to moderate expansions and contractions of the economy.

automatic transfer service (ATS) a procedure through which balances can be changed automatically from one account to another in a financial institution.

autonomous consumption expenditure the amount of planned consumption expenditure that is independent of the level of disposable personal income.

average fixed cost (AFC) the total fixed cost of a firm divided by the quantity level of its output in that period. It is also the difference between a firm's average total cost and its average variable cost.

average product the total product that a firm produces in a given period divided by the quantity of a variable input that it uses to produce it.

average propensity to consume (APC) the amount of planned consumption expenditure (C) divided by the amount of disposable personal income (DPI).

average propensity to save (APS) the amount of planned saving (S) divided by the amount of disposable personal income (DPI).

average revenue the total revenue of a firm in a given period divided by the quantity level of output that it sells in that period.

average total cost (ATC) the total cost of a firm in a given period divided by the quantity level of its output in that period.

average variable cost (AVC) the total variable cost of a firm in a given period divided by the quantity level of its output in that period. A firm's average variable cost plus its average fixed cost equals its average total cost.

B

balanced-budget multiplier a change in the equilibrium level of national income and product divided by the size of the (equal) changes in government purchases and net taxes that brought it about.

balance of payments account a record of transactions affecting the international demand and supply for a nation's money.

balance of trade the amount by which the value of a country's exports of goods exceeds the value of its imports of goods. It may be negative.

balance on current account (current balance) the balance of payments account entry showing the extent to which credit items exceed debit items in a country's international transactions in goods, services, investment income, and unilateral transfers.

balance sheet an accounting report on the condition of a business firm or other organization as of the close of business on a particular date.

bank charter a document issued by a state or the federal government granting permission to engage in banking and specifying the terms and conditions of such permission.

bank examiner a government agent who investigates the condition and operation of a bank.

banking the business of accepting deposits and making loans including commercial loans.

bank note a certificate issued by a bank which promises to pay a specified sum to the bearer of the certificate.

bankruptcy a legal concept indicating a state of insolvency—of being unable to repay creditors.

bargaining unit the workers for whom a particular union is bargaining and to whom a particular labor contract applies.

barometric firm price leadership a condition in an oligopolistic industry in which one firm's price changes are followed by other firms in that industry because they respect the price leader and see its changes as being ''correct'' responses to market conditions.

barter the exchange of one good or service for another without the use of money as a medium of exchange.

base period the time period chosen as the reference period in constructing an index number.

basic balance of payments the international balance of payments concept that adds a country's long-term private capital imports and subtracts that country's long-term private capital exports from its balance on current account.

basic human needs amounts of food, clothing, shelter, education, health care, and access to public decision making considered to be necessary as a minimum before attention should be directed to conventional economic growth; a point of view that development is taking place only when a steadily falling percentage of the people of a country lacks good food, clean water, decent shelter, basic health care, elementary education, and a means of presenting their views to their government.

basing-point system an industry agreement calling for each firm, no matter where it is located, to charge a delivered price that includes transportation charges based on the presumption that the product was shipped from a common origin. It is a form of price discrimination.

beneficial externalities See *externalities.*

benefit-cost analysis a procedure for the systematic evaluation of the economic merits of a proposed undertaking.

benefit-received principle (of taxation) a guide for taxation that advocates that the tax payment made by an individual or a firm should be related to the value of goods and services provided by the government to the taxpayer.

bilateral monopoly a market situation in which a monopolist seller faces a monopsonist buyer.

black market an illegal market in which goods or services are sold above a legally set maximum price. See also *ceiling price.*

Board of Governors (of the Federal Reserve System) seven people, appointed by the President of the United States to establish policy for and supervise the operation of the Federal Reserve System.

bond a certificate of indebtedness promising to repay a principal sum and interest on specified dates.

borrowed reserves reserves borrowed by depository institutions at the discount window from district Federal Reserve Banks.

boycott refusal to engage in trade with another country or firm in specific goods of that country or firm; in labor-management relations, an attempt by employees (or a union) to block the distribution and sale of an employer's product.

bracket push (creep) the effect that inflation has of pushing taxpayers into higher tax rate brackets and increasing the proportion of income payable under progressive income tax systems that are not indexed.

break-even point in macroeconomics, the level of disposable personal income at which planned consumption expenditure equals disposable personal income and planned saving is zero; in microeconomics, a level of output at which a firm's total revenue is equal to its total cost.

Bretton Woods system the rules and institutions established at Bretton Woods, New Hampshire, in 1944, to regulate the international economic system. The principal Bretton Woods institutions are the World Bank and the International Monetary Fund.

budget deficit See *deficit.*

budget line in the indifference analysis theory of consumer behavior, a line showing the combinations of goods and/or services measured on the axes of a graph that can be purchased by an individual who has a particular income and who faces particular prices for these goods and/or services.

buffer stocks government holdings of farm products kept as reserves against periods of bad weather or other disasters to ensure an adequate supply. An ''ever-normal granary'' is a buffer stock of a basic grain such as wheat or rice.

building cycle   See *Kuznets cycle*.

built-in stabilizers   See *automatic stabilizers*.

bullionism   a seventeenth- and eighteenth-century school of economic thought that emphasized the accumulation of treasure.

burden (of a tax)   a reduction in real income resulting from a tax.

business cycles   expansions and contractions in the volume of aggregate economic activity that alternate with some regularity in an economy. Referred to as business "fluctuations" by those who wish to imply less regularity.

business unionism   a union philosophy that relies on economic power to achieve goals of higher real wages and better working conditions.

C

capital (or capital resources)   a factor of production or resource that is composed of goods and skills that are used as inputs for production. Unlike the other resources, it must first be produced itself before it is available for use in further production. See also *human capital*.

capital account   in balance of payments accounts, the record of international transactions in securities, long- and short-term loans, and deposits in financial institutions.

capital coefficient   the amount of additional capital required for a unit increase in the net national product.

capital consumption allowance   the national income accounting estimate of the value of capital goods (production equipment) used up in producing other goods. It is subtracted from gross national product to obtain net national product.

capital gain (or loss)   the gain (or loss) from a change in the market value of an asset that takes place while it is owned by a given individual.

capital goods   See *physical capital*.

capital resources   See *capital*.

capitalist system   an economic system in which most physical instruments of production are owned by private individuals and business firms.

capital/output ratio   the value of capital used in production divided by the value of output produced per time period.

capital requirement (entry barrier)   an entry barrier based upon the minimum amount of money needed to acquire the capital goods necessary for a new firm to compete adequately with the established firms in an industry.

capital resources   See *capital; physical capital*.

capital skills   See *human capital*.

cartel   an organization (a collusive arrangement) that coordinates and limits the outputs of producers for the purpose of raising the price of the product and the profits of the producers.

ceiling price   a maximum price at which a product can legally be sold. A meaningful ceiling price is set below the equilibrium price that would otherwise be established in that market.

Celler-Kefauver Antimerger Amendment   a 1950 amendment to the Clayton Act, which added coverage of asset acquisitions and eliminated the wording that made the Act applicable only to horizontal mergers.

ceteris paribus   a Latin phrase meaning "other things being equal," used in economic theorizing to hold constant all variables but those being considered.

checkable accounts   See *transactions accounts*.

checkoff   a form of union security that calls for the employer to deduct union dues from workers' paychecks and to pay those dues directly to the union.

circular flow equilibrium   when the sum of consumption purchases, investment purchases, government purchases, and net exports equals the amount paid out by firms for resources used in production plus expected profits: $C + I + G + X - Im = Y$.

circular flow model   a diagram illustrating the macroeconomic functioning of an economy as a system in which funds that flow from business firms to households constitute the national income and flows from households to business firms through various channels make up the national product.

Civil Rights Act   a law passed by the U.S. Congress in 1964. Title VII prohibits discrimination in hiring, firing, or promotions based on race, color, religion, sex, or national origin.

civilian employment rate   the number of civilians employed as a percent of the total civilian noninstitutional population age 16 years and over.

civilian labor force   the noninstitutional civilian population age 16 and over who are willing and able to work and who are either employed or actively seeking employment.

civilian labor force participation rate   the percentage of the civilian noninstitutional population age 16 or older that is working or looking for work.

civilian unemployment rate   the percentage of the civilian labor force that is unemployed according to official statistics.

classical economics   the school of economic thought, based on the ideas of Adam Smith (1723–1790), David Ricardo (1771–1823), and their successors, which was prominent in the first half of the nineteenth century.

Clayton Act   a law passed by the U.S. Congress in

1914 to control anticompetitive price discrimination, mergers, exclusive dealing and tying arrangements, and interlocking directorates. It also excluded trade union activities from the scope of the antitrust laws.

closed economy a country that severely restricts trade across its borders.

closed shop a form of union security arrangement requiring that a person must be a member of a certain union before he or she can be hired. It is illegal under the Taft-Hartley Act of 1947.

coincident indicators index numbers that move along with the total economy; they should be used to measure fluctuations.

collective bargaining the approach used by labor unions to negotiate with employers or their representatives.

collective goods and services goods and services which, by their nature, must be consumed in common by all people in an area.

collectivist a philosophy characterized by opposition to individual or private ownership of the means of production.

collectivist system an economic system in which land and physical instruments of production are owned by collective agencies, such as the government or labor organizations, not by private individuals or business firms.

collusion (or collusive agreement) an agreement among buyers, sellers, and/or outsiders upon a particular course of action. Firms may collude to gain monopoly control in order to achieve high economic profit. See also *price fixing.*

commercial bank a financial institution that provides a wide range of services including checking accounts.

commercial treaty an agreement between countries dealing with economic and trade relations.

commission a charge made by a stockbroker for services rendered in carrying out a transaction.

Common Market a term generally used in reference to the European Community, which is a customs union of nations in Europe.

common property a legal arrangement that gives everyone equal rights to particular resources.

commune a cooperative farm or other collectively organized unit.

communist a socialist who believes that after a few generations of near-worldwide socialism, socialist economies will reach a stage of communism where most or all important goods will be free and scarcity will be eliminated. Violence, revolution, and dictatorship are accepted means to that end.

comparable worth basing pay in different occupations on scores or point systems weighing, for example, the arduousness of the work, education requirements, and so on.

comparative advantage a principle of international trade that explains which commodities a given country is likely to import and export.

comparative statics the technique of studying variations in equilibrium positions that result from changes in the underlying variables.

competition used in two different senses in economics: (1) rivalry among sellers or buyers; striving among a number of rivals in a contest aimed at purchasing or selling a particular product; (2) the market structure resulting from pure competition.

competitive depreciation a situation in which countries contest with each other in trying to increase exports and reduce imports by lowering the foreign exchange value of their monies.

complements (or complementary goods) products that are used in conjunction with each other such as automobiles and gasoline or cameras and film.

concentration ratio a measure that expresses the percentage share of some key variable such as sales or assets accounted for by the largest firms. See also *economic concentration.*

concessional loan credit extended on terms that are more favorable to the borrower than are available in loanable funds markets; typically, long-term development loans to LDCs at interest rates well below international market rates.

condition of entry the "extent to which established sellers can persistently raise their prices above a competitive level without attracting new firms to enter the industry" (Bain, *Barriers to New Competition*).

conglomerate merger the acquisition by a firm of another firm engaged in a different industry.

Congress of Industrial Organizations (CIO) a federation of national industrial unions established in 1938 and merged with the AF of L in 1955.

conspicuous consumption the use of certain goods and services to display the owner's wealth and to gain prestige and the envy of others.

constant capital a Marxian concept describing the labor hours embodied in raw materials and in the depreciation of machinery and other long-lived capital goods.

constant dollars dollars adjusted by an index number to base year purchasing power.

constant returns to scale long-run returns when an increase in the level of output of a firm is exactly proportionate to the increase in that firm's inputs.

consumer equilibrium the condition existing when an individual has made all purchases and finds that the marginal utility per dollar spent for each good or service is the same. Maximum possible utility and satisfaction are realized. *Consumer equilibrium* (or *consumer equilibrium rule* in the theory of indifference analysis): the condition achieved when an individual consumes the combination of goods and services indicated at the point where his or her budget line is tangent to one of his or her indifference curves.

consumer price index (CPI) an index number representing a weighted average of the prices of all goods and services purchased by representative families in an economy; often called the cost-of-living index, used to measure changes in the cost of purchasing a group of basic consumer goods and services.

consumer rationality See *rational consumer*.

consumer sovereignty the theory that the consumer is free to determine the mix of goods and services that he or she will purchase, subject only to income limitations and prices to be paid.

consumers' surplus the difference between the amount that a consumer pays for purchases of a product and the total utility obtained from these products by that consumer; the benefit that consumers gain from being able to buy many units of a good or service at the price they are willing to pay for the last unit consumed.

consumption purchases (*C*) expenditure by households and individuals on goods and services; household use of goods and services.

consumption function the relationship between the level of disposable personal income and the amount of planned expenditures by households on currently produced consumer goods and services.

contestable markets markets that are very easy to enter and leave. Such markets may be actual monopolies, but the ease of potential entry makes them poor candidates for government regulation.

contractionary gap a gap between the equilibrium level and the target level of the national income and product that exists when the equilibrium level is less than the target level.

contraction phase the portion of a business cycle or fluctuation in which the volume of economic activity in an economy is steadily falling.

contractionary disequilibrium when the aggregate quantity supplied is greater than the aggregate quantity demanded so that output will be reduced and prices lowered.

controls See *price controls*.

corporate society a society organized to preserve capitalist private ownership of the means of production but that reserves large regulatory powers for the state.

corporation a business firm chartered by the government and established as a legal person separate from its owners and managers; common features are unlimited life for the corporation and limited liability for individual shareholders.

corporation income tax a tax based on the net income of corporations.

corrective tax a tax on a particular good or service imposed for the purpose of correcting for resource misallocations due to harmful externalities.

cost See *opportunity cost*.

cost of living adjustment (COLA) a provision in a labor contract specifying automatic changes in wage rates based on changes in an index number of prices.

cost of living index See *consumer price index*.

cost-plus pricing principle a rule of thumb practiced in some industries in which firms determine their selling price by adding a uniform percentage to certain elements of average total cost.

cost-push inflation a rise in the price level due to a leftward shift in the aggregate-supply curve.

Council of Economic Advisers three persons appointed by the President under the authority of the Employment Act of 1946, whose job is to conduct research and to advise the President on economic policy.

countertrade a fancy name for barter.

craft union a union representing a particular type of skilled worker such as carpenters, typographers, or plumbers.

credit an amount of money loaned; also, a positive accounting entry.

cross demand the relationship between the price of one product and the quantity demanded of another product.

cross elasticity of demand the percentage change in the quantity demanded of a product divided by the percentage change in the price of a different product that caused it.

crowding out the reduction in planned investment that takes place when real interest rates rise because of government borrowing to finance budget deficits; when some of the saving flowing through the financial markets is used to pay for government purchases rather than to finance investment purchases.

currency paper money usually issued by a government or central bank and given legal tender status.

current balance see balance on current account.

current dollars dollars with purchasing power based on the price level prevailing at the time when a purchase is made or income is received.

customs union a form of economic integration

among a group of countries that establishes a common tariff against nonmembers.

cycle theories theories that imply that a regular, predictable pattern exists to explain changes in the economy.

cycles See *business cycles.*

cyclical deficit the amount of government budget deficit that arises because the economy is operating below its target level of national income and product.

cyclical unemployment joblessness that arises because there are not enough job openings at current wage rates for all those qualified to fill them. See also *macroeconomic unemployment.*

D

debit a negative entry in an accounting system.

debt renegotiation changing the terms of existing loans, usually by extending or "stretching out" repayment dates without increases in nominal interest rates.

decelerating inflation a situation in which the rate of inflation is falling. See *disinflation.*

decision-making lag the time required to debate alternative remedies for economic problems and to choose among them.

deficiency payment In U.S. farm programs, a payment to a farmer from the government equal to the difference between the target price and the support price for quantities sold by the farmer.

deficit a state of budget imbalance in which expenditures exceed receipts; in balance of payments accounting, a condition in which negative or debit entries exceed positive or credit entries; government purchases greater than net taxes.

deficit financing funding those expenditures that are in excess of current receipts through borrowing, that is, through incurring debt.

deficit spending expenditures that are in excess of current receipts.

deflation a sustained decrease in the general level of prices, usually measured by the rate of change in some index number.

deflationist policy the plan to recover from a recession by allowing wage rates and other input prices to fall so that profit margins will expand and invite increases in output.

demand the willingness and ability to buy at certain prices. See also *individual consumer demand, market demand, quantity demanded.*

demand curve graph of a demand schedule; a curve illustrating the quantities of a good or service that are demanded at various possible prices.

demand deposits funds placed with a financial institution under terms that require the institution to pay out upon the demand of the depositor. A type of checkable account or transaction account.

demand for money the quantity of the monetary unit desired to be held as cash balances. See *precautionary, speculative,* and *transactions demands for money.*

demand-for-money curve the relationship between the rate of interest and the quantity of money demanded.

demand schedule a table showing the relationship between different prices of a good or service and the quantity demanded of that good or service at each of these prices.

demand-side economics an approach to macroeconomic analysis that emphasizes the aggregate-demand curve and includes both Keynesian and monetarist positions.

dependencia (theory of underdevelopment) the theory that countries with an early advantage in military technology used this power to impose domination over other countries and to prevent them from developing by taking their resources, denying them technological knowledge, and shifting the terms of trade against them.

dependent variable a variable that depends upon some other variable or variables in a functional relationship.

depletion allowance a provision of income taxation permitting resource owners to deduct from taxable income part of the value of resources that are extracted from the earth.

deposit-contraction process the sequence of events through which a withdrawal of funds from depository institutions leads to a contraction of the total amount of checkable account balances.

deposit-expansion factor the ratio between the amount of a change in total checkable account balances and the amount of a new deposit that caused that change. The factor is estimated to be approximately equal to the reciprocal of the reserve ratio.

deposit-expansion process the sequence of events through which a new deposit in the system of depository institutions leads to an increase in the amount of checkable account balances.

deposit insurance insurance issued by the Federal Deposit Insurance Corporation or other agencies to protect depositors from loss in the event of the failure of a financial institution.

depository institution an organization such as a bank, a savings and loan association, or a credit union that accepts deposits of funds and offers checking services.

Depository Institutions Deregulation and Monetary Control Act of 1980 legislation that, among other things, required the elimination, over a six-year-period, of upper limits on interest rates payable on deposits in depository institutions. See also *Monetary Control Act of 1980*.

depreciation the decline in the market value of a capital good as it wears out or becomes old-fashioned and out-of-date. In foreign exchange theory, a decline in the foreign exchange value of a nation's money.

depression severe contraction phase of a business cycle involving high rates of unemployment and a decline in national income.

deregulation the repeal of monopoly regulation.

derived demand a demand for a resource or factor of production that arises because of the demand for a product that it helps to produce.

desired excess reserves reserves held by depository institutions that are over and above those required by law so that they can avoid problems from unexpected withdrawals or be ready to accommodate customers who ask for loans.

devaluation the lowering of the foreign exchange value of a currency by reducing its official value, i.e., by lowering the amount of gold that will be exchanged for it.

diminishing marginal utility an assumption in the theory of utility analysis that during some specified time period an individual's added satisfaction grows less and less as he or she consumes more and more units of the same good or service.

diminishing returns decreases in marginal product that eventually set in when a variable input is successively added to one or more fixed inputs.

direct relationship (or positive relationship) a relationship in which the dependent and independent variables change in the same direction.

direct transmission mechanism the means whereby changes in the money supply affect the equilibrium level of national income and product through planned consumption expenditure with no necessary change in interest rates.

dirty float a situation in which official exchange rates among monies are not fixed but governments intervene in exchange markets from time to time to influence foreign exchange rates.

discounting the practice of purchasing securities or promissory notes for less than their maturity values; a procedure through which a Federal Reserve Bank makes loans to member institutions; also, the process of calculating the present value of payments to be received in the future.

discount rate the rate of interest that Federal Reserve Banks charge on loans to depository institutions.

discouraged workers people who have stopped searching for work because they believe there is little chance of finding a job; they are not counted in official measurements of the labor force.

discrimination the practice of treating persons differently on the basis of their personal characteristics, as in offering different economic opportunities on the basis of gender, race, or ethnic origin. See also *price discrimination*.

diseconomies of scale long-run decreasing returns resulting when an increase in the output level of a firm is less than proportionate to the increase in that firm's inputs; also called decreasing returns to scale or increasing long-run average total cost.

disembodied technical change technical change reflected incompletely or not at all in the quality of specific types of labor or machinery.

disequilibrium a state in which opposing forces are not in balance, so that there is a tendency for change to take place.

disinflation a reduction in the rate of increase in the price level; a lowering of the rate of inflation.

disintermediation the widespread withdrawal of funds from financial institutions that may occur when the limits on interest rates payable by these institutions are lower than rates of return that can be obtained elsewhere.

disinvestment a reduction in the stock of capital goods or inventories.

dismal science the label attached to economics in the nineteenth century because of forecasts of subsistence wages and diminishing returns.

displacement effect a change in one component of planned expenditure that arises because of and offsets an opposite change in some other component.

disposable personal income (DPI) the amount of personal income that remains after personal taxes and certain nontax items are subtracted. It is the amount available to households for either saving or consumption spending.

dissaving negative saving; financing current consumption by borrowing or by drawing from past savings.

distribution function the function or role of government involving changes in the amount of income or wealth inequality among people in the society.

dividends distributions of money or additional stock from a corporation to its shareholders.

division of labor labor specialization; the assignment of tasks among workers.

do-it-yourself production production without exchange, such as growing food in a family garden plot; often not included in official measures of national income and product.

dominant firm price leadership a condition in an oligopolistic industry where one firm is so powerful that small and relatively weak firms follow the price that it sets.

dumping the sale of some product abroad at an unfairly low price, as measured against its domestic price; the sale of a product below what authorities consider average total cost plus a fair markup.

duopoly an oligopoly made up of two firms.

dynamic analysis the description of the process of adjustment between equilibrium positions.

E

easy entry the absence of entry barriers in an industry.

econometrics an aspect of economics that combines theory, mathematics, and statistics to analyze economic questions.

economic concentration a measure of the control of a particular economic activity in an industry, in a sector of the economy, in an entire economy, or in a region of the world.

economic concentration ratio See *concentration ratio*.

economic development economic growth plus other changes that are judged to constitute progress or to make life better; progress in some sense that makes life better in an economy or society and brings gains in welfare for the people.

economic dualism a situation that arises in developing countries in which a relatively modern and prosperous economy, often urban, exists while most of the country, especially the rural areas, continues in age-old patterns of poverty.

economic earnings (also economic rent) the part of the earnings of a resource that is not required to keep that resource at its present use.

economic efficiency the lowest dollar cost of inputs that a firm requires to produce a certain amount of output.

economic growth increasing per capita real output in an economy.

economic loss an amount of accounting profit or loss that is less than normal profit.

economic maldistribution a division of income and wealth among individuals and groups that has an undesirable effect on the operation of the economic system.

economic profit an amount of accounting profit that is greater than normal profit.

economic rationality an assumption made in many economic theories that people can and will take actions that will make them better off or will prevent them from becoming worse off.

economic rent See *economic earnings*.

economics the social science concerned with using or administering scarce resources so as to attain the greatest or maximum fulfillment of society's wants; a method rather than a doctrine, an apparatus of the mind, a technique of thinking that helps its possessor to draw correct conclusions.

economic systems the combinations of institutions that different societies have developed to deal with economic problems.

economic theory See *model, theory*.

economies of scale long-run increasing returns occurring when an increase in the output level of a firm is more than proportionate to the increase in that firm's inputs; also called increasing returns to scale or decreasing long-run average total cost.

effective protection the tariff rate on a product, reduced by the tariffs on raw materials and intermediate products that go into it, with the result expressed as a percentage of the value added by the producers of that product.

efficiency See *economic efficiency, technical efficiency*.

effluent charge a price that is charged for depositing waste in the earth or its atmosphere.

elastic demand a condition existing whenever the percentage response in the quantity demanded is greater than the percentage change in the price that caused it.

elasticity a measure that relates the percentage change in quantity to the percentage change in price or income that caused it.

elasticity coefficient the numerical value of elasticity.

elasticity of demand See *cross elasticity of demand, income elasticity of demand, price elasticity of demand*.

elastic supply a condition existing whenever the percentage response in the quantity supplied is greater than the percentage change in the price that caused it.

elasticity of supply See *price elasticity of supply*.

employment labor engaged in regular work for pay.

Employment Act of 1946 landmark legislation through which the U.S. government announced its goals and established procedures to promote maximum employment, price stability, and economic growth.

employment rate See *civilian employment rate*.

Engels' Law the tendency for the percentage of a family's budget spent for food to decline as its income rises.

enterpriser (or entrepreneur) one of the factors of production or resources employed in production; a person who visualizes needs and takes the necessary action to initiate or change the process by which they will be met or the products used to meet them.

entitlements certificates used in the United States during the 1970s authorizing the purchase of oil from domestic producers at controlled prices, which were lower than the prices of oil from other sources; government transfer payments, the amount of which has been connected to events or circumstances in such a way that the recipients understand that the payment is assured once these conditions are met.

entrepreneur See *enterpriser*.

entry the act of coming into an industry by a new firm which adds capacity to that industry.

entry barriers See *absolute amount of cost difference entry barrier, capital requirement entry barrier, minimum optimal scale effect entry barrier, product differentiation entry barrier.*

equation of exchange the statement that the quantity of money in the economy multiplied by the number of times the average dollar is used each year to purchase newly produced final products must be equal to the quantity of these final products multiplied by their average price. The equation is $MV = PQ$.

equilibrium a state of balance in which the forces for change within a system offset each other so that there is no net tendency for change.

equilibrium price a price that equates the quantity demanded with the quantity supplied in a market.

equilibrium quantity a quantity of a good, service, or resource that equates the quantity supplied and the quantity demanded at a particular price in a market. The quantity supplied and demanded in a market when the equilibrium price prevails.

equity fairness and justice in the distribution of consumption, income, and wealth; also, ownership share in a corporation.

escalator clause See *cost-of-living adjustment.*

ethical maldistribution lack of correspondence between the actual income or wealth distribution and some standard of what is considered just or fair. See also *maldistribution.*

Eurocurrency deposits of one nation's money in banks of a different nation, which provide reserves for loans and which are free from regulations.

European Community (EC) a customs union among a number of nations in Europe.

European Currency Unit (ECU) the monetary unit of the European Currency Union; a money of account that does not exist in a physical sense; a weighted average of the value of the monies of member countries.

ever-normal granary See *buffer stocks.*

ex ante identifying a viewpoint of planned or anticipated activity as distinguished from an *ex post* viewpoint, relating to past activity.

excess burden (of a tax) the amount by which the burden or economic loss caused by a tax exceeds the amount of money received by the government from the tax.

excess demand the amount by which the quantity demanded of a good, service, or resource exceeds the quantity supplied at any specified price.

excess reserves official reserves held by depository institutions over and above the reserve requirement.

excess supply the amount by which the quantity supplied of a good, service, or resource exceeds the quantity demanded at any specified price.

exchange controls restrictions on the purchase or sale of foreign exchange, such as requiring licenses to engage in this trade and/or applying different exchange rates to different transactions.

exchange value (of a currency) See *foreign exchange value.*

excise tax a tax imposed on the manufacture or sale of a product.

exclusive dealing arrangement an agreement that gives a firm the exclusive opportunity to obtain a product from a supplier within a specified geographic area, usually on the condition that it will not buy the products of competing suppliers.

exhaustible natural resources gifts of nature usable in production, the supply of which could be eliminated by human use.

exit a firm leaving an industry as a result of its inability to earn at least normal profit in the long run. See also *normal profit.*

expansion a situation in the economy when real GNP is increasing and unemployment falling.

expansionary disequilibrium when the aggregate quantity demanded is greater than the aggregate quantity supplied so that output will be increased and/or prices raised.

expansionary gap a gap between the equilibrium and the target level of national income and product that exists when the equilibrium level is higher than the target level.

expansion phase the portion of a business cycle or fluctuation in which the volume of business activity in an economy is steadily increasing.

experience variables variables that oligopolists take into account in addition to consumer demand and cost variables. Examples include the previous reactions by rival firms to price changes in the industry, personality traits of key managers of rival firms, and the political consequences of the rivals' reactions.

explicit costs money payments by firms for the use of inputs to production.

exploitation restriction of some members of a society to an inferior income or welfare position; a wage rate that is less than the marginal revenue product; in the Marxist perspective, the exclusion of the main body of a society from the bulk of that society's economic surplus.

exploitation rate (or rate of surplus value) a ratio representing the proportion of each hour of labor contributed to surplus value in Marxian economics.

exporting unemployment efforts to create jobs in the domestic economy by expanding exports and reducing imports, usually by trade restrictions and manipulation of foreign exchange rates.

exports goods and services sold to foreigners.

ex post identifying past actions, as distinguished from an *ex ante* viewpoint, which deals with planned or anticipated events.

external benefit a benefit experienced by someone not a party to a transaction; a benefit experienced by one receiving a beneficial or positive externality.

external cost a cost experienced by someone not a party to a transaction; a cost experienced by one suffering a negative externality.

external growth See *merger.*

externalities costs or benefits from the consumption or production of a good or service affecting people other than the buyer and seller of the good or service; a source of market failure that may lead to government intervention.

F

factor price equilization theorem a proposition stating that free trade tends to equalize input prices among trading countries.

factors of production (or resources) inputs to production that are used to create goods and services (labor, entrepreneurship, capital, natural resources).

fallacy of composition the false notion that what is true for one part is necessarily true for the whole, or vice versa.

farm parity the relationship between the purchasing power or real income of farmers compared with the purchasing power or real income of others in the economy.

favorable balance (of trade) a positive, credit, or surplus balance in a country's international transactions in merchandise.

featherbedding the practice of forcing an employer to pay for services that workers do not actually perform.

Federal Deposit Insurance Corporation (FDIC) a U.S. government agency that insures deposits in certain financial institutions.

federal funds official reserve deposits of depository institutions with a Federal Reserve Bank.

federal funds rate the rate of interest charged when federal funds (reserve deposits at the Federal Reserve Bank) are loaned by one depository institution to another.

Federal Open Market Committee (FOMC) twelve people, including the seven members of the Board of Governors of the Federal Reserve System, who are responsible for directing the buying and selling of securities for the system.

Federal Reserve Banks the twelve district banks that together constitute the Federal Reserve System.

Federal Reserve Note currency issued by Federal Reserve Banks.

Federal Reserve System twelve district Federal Reserve Banks under the direction of policies set by its Board of Governors, appointed by the President of the United States, and fulfilling the functions of a central bank; the central bank of the United States.

federal system a system of government consisting of several distinct levels of government such as the national, state, and local governments in the United States.

Federal Trade Commission (FTC) a federal agency established in 1914 which enforces legislation aimed at deterring unfair methods of competition and restraint of trade.

Federal Trade Commission Act a law passed by the U.S. Congress in 1914 to prohibit unfair methods of competition among firms and establish the Federal Trade Commission.

financial intermediaries banks, credit unions, saving and loan associations, stock and bond brokers and other institutions that accept deposits of income saved and offer to loan these funds, in return for interest payments, to those who wish to borrow.

financial markets the organized interaction of buyers and sellers of financial assets.

fine tuning an approach to macroeconomic policy that calls for frequent adjustments in government spending, taxing, open market operations, and so forth, aimed at holding the economy near some target level of national income and product, employment, price level, foreign exchange rates, and interest rates.

firm   a business that combines factors of production or resources—natural resources, capital, labor, and entrepreneurship—to produce certain goods or services.

First World   the more-developed countries of Western Europe and North America plus Australia, Japan, and New Zealand.

fiscal   related to the taxing and spending operations of a government.

fiscal federalism   a system under which financing responsibilities are shared among different levels of government; the study of ways to allocate financial responsibilities among different levels of government.

fiscal instruments   taxing and spending devices used to influence the performance of the economy. Examples are tax rates and government purchases.

fiscal policy   a government's attempt to influence macroeconomic variables by changing the amount that it taxes or spends.

fixed cost   See *total fixed cost*.

fixed exchange rate   the exchange value at which a nation's money is held through government or international monetary agency buying and/or selling of official reserves in the foreign exchange market, or through the operation of a metallic standard.

flat tax   a tax without any graduation of rates; a tax with a single rate applicable to all amounts of the tax base.

flexible exchange rates   See *free exchange rates*.

floating exchange rates   See *free exchange rates*.

floor price (or support price)   a minimum price that is legally set for a product. A meaningful floor price is set above the equilibrium price that would otherwise be established in that market.

fluctuations   See *business cycles*.

foreign aid   a unilateral transfer from one nation to another, usually as an encouragement to economic development.

foreign exchange   the money of other countries.

foreign exchange markets   markets in which the monies of different countries are bought and sold.

foreign exchange value   the price of one nation's monetary unit in terms of the monetary units of another country or group of countries, or a weighted average of such monetary units.

45-degree line   a straight line drawn at a 45-degree angle from the origin of a diagram, such as the Keynesian cross.

Fourth World   those Third World countries that are the ''poorest of the poor.''

fractional reserves   See *partial reserves*.

free enterprise   freedom of opportunity to pursue any business venture; no legal restrictions to entry.

free (or floating or flexible) exchange rates   foreign exchange rates that can move up or down in response to shifts in demand and supply arising from international trading and finance and that are not purposefully influenced by governmental action.

free market   a market in which the economic forces of demand and supply have the full opportunity to alter the price.

free rider problem   the fact that people usually will not voluntarily pay for a good or service if they believe that they can consume it without paying.

free trade area   a form of economic integration among a group of countries that allows each member to maintain its own set of tariffs, quotas, etc., against nonmembers.

frictional unemployment   joblessness that arises because time is required to change from one job to another.

fringe benefit   a form of worker compensation other than wages, such as a pension, life insurance, health plan, vacation, and holidays.

full employment   a situation in which the volume of employment in an economy meets certain criteria of desirability. See *natural rate of unemployment* and *potential GNP*.

Full Employment and Balanced Growth Act (1978)   See *Humphrey-Hawkins Act*.

full-employment balanced-budget (rule)   a policy guideline under which Congress would decide on the amount of government purchases that voters would want at full employment, and would set tax rates and transfer payment systems so that net taxes would balance government purchases at full employment. Neither the tax rates nor programs would be changed because of business cycle conditions. Automatic stabilizers would moderate economic fluctuations.

function   the way in which one variable depends on some other variable or variables.

functional distribution of income   the division of income between different types of production inputs, such as labor and property.

G

game theory   an approach to analyzing competition in an oligopoly market that likens economic behavior to a game of cards (like poker) or chess, and even to war.

Garn–St. Germaine Depository Institutions Act (1982)   provided aid for depository institutions in distress and expanded the lending authority of thrift institutions.

General Agreement on Tariffs and Trade (GATT) an agreement, mainly between the industrial countries of North America, Western Europe, and Japan for the gradual liberalization of world trade.

general equilibrium analysis a method of analysis that takes into account all the different effects related to the specific variables that are being studied.

general fund a budget category denoting a source of financing available for a variety of expenditures.

generalized (macroeconomic) protection attempts by a country to deal with its international balance of payments problems by imposing a flat overall tax on all imports or by imposing restrictions on the export of capital.

general price level an average of all prices in the economy.

geographic market extension conglomerate merger the acquisition by a firm of another firm engaged in the same activity, existing on the same level, but serving a different geographic market.

Gini ratio a measure of income inequality computed by dividing the area between a Lorenz curve and the line of equality by the entire area under the line of equality on a Lorenz curve diagram. See also *Lorenz curve.*

Glass-Steagall Act (1932) legislation affecting the banking industry and permitting Federal Reserve Banks to use government securities as backing for Federal Reserve Notes.

GNP implicit price deflator an index number that shows the ratio between GNP measured at current prices and the amount that would have been required to purchase the same goods and services in a base year.

gold standard a monetary system featuring a constant price of gold in units of a country's money; for example, a system in which the monetary authorities of a country promise to exchange a specified amount of gold per unit of the country's money.

good a tangible product that is considered desirable or "good" by those who own it or could acquire it.

Gosplan the central planning agency of the Soviet Union.

government purchases currently produced goods and services bought by government.

Gramm-Rudman-Hollings Act legislation passed by the U.S. Congress in 1985 establishing deficit reduction targets and procedures to reach these targets.

grants-in-aid money given by a superior government, such as the federal or a state government, to a subordinate government, such as a state or local government.

Great Depression the period of severe unemployment, falling price level, and economic stagnation extending through the decade following the stock market crash of 1929.

Great Disinflation the period of time in the early and middle 1980s when the rate of inflation was greatly reduced.

greenbacks originally, inconvertible currency issued by the U.S. Treasury during the Civil War; sometimes used in reference to any U.S. currency.

greenhouse effect an acceleration of a long-term heating of the earth's atmosphere caused primarily by the burning of fossil fuels and the wholesale cutting of the world's forests.

Green Revolution the development and propagation of high-yielding dwarf and hybrid varieties of wheat and rice.

Gresham's Law the statement that the base (less valuable) money will always drive the dear (more valuable) money out of circulation and into hoards.

gross domestic product (GDP) the total value of production that takes place per year in a country.

gross national product (GNP) the total of all spending—by consumers, business firms, governments, and (net) foreigners—to purchase currently produced goods and services; the total market value of all currently produced goods and services.

growthmanship an overemphasis on measured economic growth.

guilds predecessors of modern unions; charitable and mutual-aid societies made up of workers in certain crafts who after a time took on certain activities that we now associate with unions, but including master craftsmen who employed journeymen and apprentices.

H

Herfindahl-Hirschman Index (HHI) a measure of market economic concentration derived by summing the squares of the individual market shares of all the firms in a market.

horizontal merger the acquisition by a firm of another firm engaged in the same activity, existing on the same level, and serving the same geographic market.

household a group living together and pooling major expenses in the same dwelling unit. Usually, members are related by blood, marriage, or adoption.

human capital (or capital skills) the portion of the productive power of individuals that has been developed through expenditures for education, job training, and health care.

Humphrey-Hawkins Act legislation, passed by the U.S. Congress in 1978, establishing goals in terms of price stability and low unemployment, but providing no enforcement mechanism.

hyperdeflation a situation in which the pessimism generated by unemployment and falling prices induces a leftward shift in the aggregate-demand curve, so that a recession feeds on itself, becomes worse, and is not alleviated by falling prices.

hyperinflation a situation in which the price level is rising rapidly, causing an increase in the velocity of circulation of money, and usually culminating in the breakdown of the monetary system.

I

identity an equation whose two sides are equal by definition.

immature creditor the international trade and finance situation of a country in the stage of its economic development in which its current balance is positive and its capital balance negative. Its exports of capital exceed return flows to it from investments abroad.

immature debtor the international trade and finance situation of a country in an early stage of its economic development in which its current balance is negative and its capital balance is positive.

imperative planning a rigorous form of planning under which failure to reach an important plan target may be treated as a criminal offense.

implementation lag the time required for programs to take effect, after they have been decided upon.

implicit costs costs incurred by firms for inputs for which no money payment is made and no transaction takes place; usually because the firms are using resources which they own themselves.

implicit price deflator for GNP an index number used to compare GNP measured in current dollars with the amount that would have been needed to purchase the same goods at the prices existing in some base year.

imports goods and services and resources purchased from foreign suppliers.

income the amount of money or its equivalent received in exchange for services rendered, or as net receipts over costs of a firm.

income and product budgets budgets that treat government transfer payments as negative taxes rather than as expenditures.

income effect the effect that a change in a person's real income (resulting from a change in the price of a good or service that the person buys) has on the quantity that this person demands of that good or service.

income demand the relationship between the quantity demanded for a product and the income level of consumers or potential consumers of that product.

income elasticity of demand the percentage change in the quantity demanded for a product divided by the percentage change in the income level of the consumers or potential consumers of that product.

income redistribution an attempt to alter the amount of income or wealth inequality among people in a society.

incomes policy an application of wage and price controls in a coordinated attempt to reach a set of macroeconomic goals.

income statement (or profit and loss statement) an accounting report of the operations of a business firm over some specified period of time.

inconvertible currency the money of a country that does not allow it to be freely exchanged for money of other countries.

increasing returns short run gains in marginal product that often occur over low levels of output when a variable input is successively added to one or more fixed inputs.

increasing returns to scale See *economies of scale*.

increasing total utility an assumption in utility analysis theory that during some specified time period an individual's total satisfaction increases as he or she consumes additional units of the same good or service.

independent variable the variable on which another variable depends in a functional relationship.

indexing a system that automatically builds an inflation or deflation adjustment into agreements for wage rates, savings accounts, taxes, interest rates, bond values, and other contracts in an economy.

index number a number that expresses a particular value in relation to some other value that has been specified as a base or reference value.

indicative planning a form of planning that operates primarily by convincing participants of a plan's economic benefits to them.

indifference curve analysis a theory of consumer behavior that expresses consumers' tastes in curves based on the ranking of combinations of goods and/or services in order of preference, but avoids the notion of measurable utility.

indifference curve a curve representing all of the combinations of goods and/or services measured on the axes that satisfy a consumer equally well.

indifference map a graph displaying some of the infinite number of indifference curves representing an individual's preferences.

indirect business taxes and subsidies an entry in the national product section that removes the tax and subsidy components of market prices; taxes imposed on and subsidies given to the production or sale of goods and services.

indirect transmission mechanism a process whereby the effects of a shift of the real money-supply curve are transmitted to the equilibrium level of real national income and product by affecting interest rates and the volume of planned investment.

individual consumer demand the amount of a good or service that an individual consumer wants and is able to purchase at a particular moment at each possible price that might be charged for that good or service.

individual firm supply the amount of a good or service that an individual business firm is willing and able to sell at a particular moment at each possible price that it might receive for that good or service.

individual maldistribution an unsatisfactory situation in respect to the particular people at the upper and lower ends of the income or wealth distribution.

induced expenditure in Keynesian analysis, a change in the volume of planned consumption, investment, government purchases, exports, or imports caused by a change in level of national income and illustrated as a movement along the $C + I + G + X - Im$ curve.

industrial union a union representing all the workers in an industry, such as auto workers, mine workers, or clothing workers.

industry a group of competing firms.

inelastic demand a condition existing whenever the percentage response in quantity demanded is less than the percentage change in the price that caused it.

inelastic supply a condition existing whenever the percentage response in the quantity supplied is less than the percentage change in the price that caused it.

infant industry (argument for protection) a proposal for temporarily protecting a country's new industries to give them time to develop skills comparable with more efficient foreign industries.

inferior good or service a good or service for which there is a negative relationship between quantity demanded and income level.

infinitely elastic See *perfectly elastic*.

infinitely elastic demand a condition existing when a price change causes an infinite response in the quantity demanded.

infinitely elastic supply a condition existing when a price change causes an infinite response in the quantity supplied.

inflation a significant and sustained increase in the general level of prices, usually measured by the rate of change in some price index number.

inflationary depression a situation in which an economy experiences a decrease in real GNP and also an increase in its general price level. See also *stagflation*.

inflationary expectations anticipations that the price level will rise in the near future.

inflation rate the rate of change in the index number that has been selected for measuring the general price level; a measurement of the change in the price level calculated by dividing the GNP deflator value for each year by the GNP deflator value for the previous year, subtracting 1.0, and multiplying the result by 100.

information costs the costs of acquiring information that decreases the uncertainty of making transactions.

infrastructure See *social overhead capital*.

injections planned expenditures other than consumption purchases, that is, planned investment (I), government purchases (G), and exports (X).

injunction a court order enjoining or prohibiting a person or firm from following a specific course of action.

innovation the development of an invention from the original discovery to a practical use.

innovator one who brings an invention out of the laboratory, makes it practical, and applies it to actual production.

input-output analysis a technique, developed by Wassily Leontief, that uses matrix algebra to solve production planning problems, including the relation between economic sectors.

inputs (or factors of production or resources) the labor, entrepreneurship, natural resources, and capital that are used in production.

interdependence a small enough number of firms in an industry to require that each considers its rivals' reactions to any action that it is thinking of taking; the most important characteristic of an oligopoly industry.

interest (or interest payment) the return or payment to capital in production.

interest rate the annual payment for the use of funds, expressed as a percentage of the funds used.

interest rate parity a condition in international capital account transactions when the domestic-money rate of return would be the same as the foreign-money rate of return after conversion to domestic money.

interest-rate theory the proposition that an increase in the price level, *ceteris paribus*, reduces the real money supply, increases the real rate of interest, and thereby reduces planned investment and the quantity of real GNP demanded. The theory works in the opposite direction for decreases in the price level; also called the *Keynes effect*.

interlocking directorates the potentially anticompetitive practice of having the same person serve on the boards of directors of two or more competing firms.

intermediate product an output which itself becomes an input in further production.

internal growth the growth of a firm through building from within as contrasted to acquiring other firms.

international fundamentalism an explanation for the Great Depression asserting that the U.S. economy was not able to support prosperity throughout the world and that recession elsewhere spread to the United States.

International Monetary Fund (IMF) an organization established in 1944 for the purpose of stabilizing exchange rates in international trade; a pool of gold and foreign exchange from which loans can be made to help countries stabilize foreign exchange rates. See also *Bretton Woods system*.

International Trade Organization (ITO) an organization proposed by "free world" members of the United Nations aimed at making world trade freer and less discriminatory. Never went into operation.

interstate banking when bank holding companies own banks in more than one state.

invention discovery of a new product or a new technical tool or process.

inventor one who discovers or devises a new or improved process or product.

inventory stocks of unsold goods and resources.

inventory cycle See *Kitchin cycle*.

inverse relationship (or negative relationship) a relationship in which the dependent and independent variables change in opposite directions.

investment (or investment purchases, I) the creation of capital; in national income accounting, the purchase of currently produced capital goods and additions to inventories.

investment decision a decision made by a firm as to whether to provide for the creation of new capital and, if so, how much.

investment income receipts from capital goods or from securities, usually in the form of dividends or interest.

iron law of wages the doctrine that population growth will push wages down to the subsistence level.

IS-LM system a model used in modern Keynesian economics; the *IS* curve incorporates the equilibrium requirements of the Keynesian total-planned-expenditure model, and the *LM* curve incorporates the requirements for equilibrium in the money market.

isocost line a line showing the alternative combinations of inputs that a firm can buy for a given cost outlay.

isoquant same quantity; a curve (derived from a firm's production function) that shows all of the technically efficient combinations of inputs for producing a particular quantity of output.

isoquant map a graph showing several out of an infinite number of isoquants, one for every quantity of output that a firm could possibly produce.

J

job security in collective bargaining agreements, conditions for hiring, job continuance, and the handling of grievances.

Joint Economic Committee a committee of the Congress established under the Employment Act of 1946 to conduct research and advise the Congress on economic policy.

Juglar cycle a business fluctuation that has a period of some seven to ten years and that has been a prominent feature in economic history.

jurisdictional strike a strike concerning which union shall represent a given group of workers.

K

Keynes effect the relationship between the price level and the quantity of real national income and product demanded that arises because of an induced change in real rates of interest.

Keynesian a person who accepts the teachings of John Maynard Keynes. One who believes that government purchases and tax collections are key instruments of macroeconomic policy.

Keynesian cross graphic representation of a relationship between the flow of planned expenditure and the level of national income and product.

Keynesian economics the school of economic thought based on the work of John Maynard Keynes (1883–1946), particularly *The General Theory of Employment, Interest and Money* (1936).

Keynesian-monetarist debate an extended discussion among macroeconomists concerning the best demand-side instruments to use in carrying out macroeconomic policy.

Keynesian theory the systematic body of knowledge associated with the work of the British economist John Maynard Keynes.

Keynesian transmission mechanism the means whereby changes in the real money supply affect the equilibrium level of national income and product through changes in interest rates and planned investment expenditure; an "indirect" transmission mechanism.

kinked demand curve a curve (characteristic of some oligopolistic industries) made up of two demand segments divided at the industrywide price that has been established with the segment related to lower prices less elastic than the segment related to higher prices.

Kitchin (inventory) cycle a business cycle that has a length of some three to five years and that is believed to be connected with the alternate buildup and depletion of business inventories; sometimes called the *inventory cycle*.

Kondratieff cycle a long wave or cycle of economic activity that has a length of 30 to 50 years and is sometimes thought to be associated with major technological innovations.

Knights of Labor, Noble Order of one of the first national federations of unions in the United States. Established in 1869, it was the forerunner of the AF of L.

Kuznets (building) cycle a business cycle that lasts between 15 and 25 years and appears based on the construction and replacement of buildings and transportation facilities; also called the *building cycle*.

L

L (money supply) M3 money supply plus near money (U.S. Savings Bonds, certain kinds of U.S. government securities, payment promises by large corporations, and other items that are potentially convertible into spendable money).

labor the resource or factor of production that includes most forms of human work effort directed toward production.

labor force See *civilian labor force*.

Labor-Management Relations Act See *Taft-Hartley Act*.

Labor-Management Reporting and Disclosure Act See *Landrum-Griffin Act*.

labor mobility the degree to which workers will move to available jobs or more attractive jobs.

labor resources See *labor*.

labor union (or trade union) a labor organization whose immediate objective is to improve the wage rates and the working conditions of its members.

Laffer curve a curve representing a relationship between average tax rates and the amount of govern-

ment net tax revenue collected, and suggesting that tax revenues will rise as average tax rates rise, but only up to a point. Beyond that point, higher tax rates will result in lower tax revenues.

lagging indicators index numbers that tend to change direction after changes in the volume of total economic activity.

laissez-faire a policy position favoring the market economy and opposing interference in the economy by the government; a branch of the market-economy New Right that believes that technological change will overcome any long run tendencies toward monopoly in the economy.

land the ground or the earth that makes up a large portion of the factor of production or resource called natural resources.

Landrum-Griffin Act (or Labor-Management Reporting and Disclosure Act) an act passed by the U.S. Congress in 1959 that set forth rules governing the relationship between union governments and their members.

Lange-Lerner theory a socialist plan that attempts to retain the advantages of competitive market economies.

leading indicators index numbers that tend to anticipate changes in the total economy.

leading links (system) a policy followed in Soviet planning that calls for the fulfillment of production plans for goods that the government considers most important even at the expense of other parts of the plan.

leakages uses of funds that take them out of the consumption path of the circular flow, such as net taxes, savings, or imports.

legal reserves See *official reserves*.

legal tender currency that, when offered in payment of an obligation, precludes the creditor from denying that payment was offered and from collecting further interest on the debt.

lender of last resort a responsibility of Federal Reserve Banks to make loans to member banks facing crisis situations.

less developed countries (LDCs) nations with levels of per capita income far below those in the industrialized or modern countries.

leveraged buy-out (LBO) a form of speculation through acquisition in which investors rely almost entirely on debt financing to acquire a company.

liabilities claims that outsiders have for payments from a business firm—usually the value of such claims as reported on a balance sheet.

Libermanism a policy position favoring a number of reforms aimed at introducing market-style decisions into Soviet-style planning; an early attempt at reform in the Soviet Union.

libertarian one who fears government control of the economy, supports private ownership of the means of production and, in extreme cases, private control of money, defense, police protection, streets, sewers, and law-making and administration; a branch of the economic New Right that believes there should be private ownership of the means of production and that the market should govern and the state cease to exist.

limited liability a characteristic of the corporate form of business that limits the responsibility of stockholders for losses suffered by the business.

limited life a condition in which a business firm does not continue to exist after the death or withdrawal of a proprietor or a partner.

linear relationship a relationship which, when plotted on a graph, will appear as a straight-line curve.

liquidity the ease with which an asset can be used in exchange or converted into a form that can be used in exchange.

liquidity crisis in Marxian terms, the long-term stagnation that results as capitalism matures. It is caused by the fall of the profit rate to a level that discourages investment and encourages hoarding.

liquidity trap a situation in which increases in the supply of money are absorbed into cash balances and do not lower the rate of interest or increase investment.

loanable funds money demanded and supplied for loans.

loanable funds market the arrangements and procedures for carrying out transactions between people who want to borrow money and people who want to lend money.

lockout a work stoppage in which the employer closes the plant to its workers.

locomotive theory the view that a large country, by expanding its economy and letting its inflation rate rise, can and should stimulate economic expansion in other countries.

long run in microeconomics, a period of time long enough to permit all changes that a firm wants to make within the limits of its existing production function; in macroeconomics, a period of time long enough to eliminate money illusion and wage-cost lags from price level changes.

long-run aggregate-supply the relationship between changes in the price level and changes in the quantity of real national income and product supplied that prevails as long as there is no change in physical production capability but when enough time has

passed for people to eliminate wage-cost lag and money illusion; also called potential GNP.

long-run average total cost (*LRAC*) the long-run total cost of a firm divided by the quantity level of its output.

long-run consumption function the relationship between disposable personal income and planned consumption expenditure when the level of disposable personal income has existed for a long enough period of time for consumers to adjust to it.

long-run marginal cost (*LRMC*) the addition to a firm's long-run total cost when it produces one more unit of output.

long-run total cost (*LRTC*) the total cost of producing a certain level of output when a firm is able to vary all of its inputs.

Lorenz curve a curve that illustrates income inequality by plotting the cumulative percentage of total income received by successive percentages of the population, starting from the lowest-income persons and proceeding cumulatively upward. See also *Gini ratio*.

lower turning point the point in a business cycle when a contraction phase ends and an expansion phase begins; also called the *trough*.

Lucas supply curve a curve that shows that unexpected changes in the price level lead to changes in the quantity of real GNP supplied.

M

M1 money supply concept coins, currency, and checkable account balances.

M2 money supply concept M1 plus such less liquid assets as small time deposits, money market mutual fund balances, noncheckable savings balances, repurchase agreements, and Eurodollars.

M3 money supply concept M1 and M2 plus large time deposit balances, long-term repurchase agreements, and certain other assets that are somewhat harder to convert into spendable money.

macro-dot a combination of the real rate of interest and the volume of real national income and product such that the flow of planned expenditure exactly matches real production in an economy and the demand for the country's stock of money is equal to its supply.

macroeconomic equilibrium the situation in which the real national income and product demanded at a given price level is equal to the real national income and product supplied at that price level; the condition existing at the intersection of an aggregate-demand curve and an aggregate-supply curve.

macroeconomic forecasting predicting the values of

economic variables through systematic analysis of empirically estimated relationships.

macroeconomic planning planning that includes target quantities only for macroeconomic measures (national income and product; the division between consumption, investment, and government sectors; the supplies of money and credit; the government surplus or deficit; international balances; and interest rates) but not the composition of the aggregates.

macroeconomic protection See *generalized protection.*

macroeconomics the branch of economics that focuses on aggregate or grand total economic activity. Unemployment and inflation are major problems considered in macroeconomics.

macroeconomic unemployment unemployment that exists throughout the whole economy or affects many parts of the economy at the same time and is not related to particular decisions about what or how to produce. See also *cyclical unemployment.*

"magic wand" planning a plan built around a collection of projects and/or an attractive slogan, which promises good things but does not specify adequately any processes for achieving them.

maldistribution excessive inequality or equality of personal income or wealth. See also *economic maldistribution, ethical maldistribution,* and *individual maldistribution.*

Malthusian theory of population the proposition that population increases according to a geometric progression until stabilized by death rates, which rise because of inadequate food supplies.

margin requirement the percentage of the value of a stock which the purchaser must finance from his or her own resources.

marginal additional or incremental.

marginal analysis a method used by economists for predicting or evaluating outcomes that is based on the last unit added or the next unit to be added.

marginal benefit the additional advantage gained when one more unit of a good or service is consumed.

marginal cost (*MC*) the addition to total cost when one more unit of output is produced.

marginal factor cost (*MFC*) the extra cost that a firm incurs for an additional unit of a resource or factor of production.

marginal physical product (*MPP*) the additional output that a firm can produce by using one more unit of a resource or factor of production.

marginal product, short run the amount of extra output that results from the addition of one more unit of a variable input to one or more fixed inputs.

marginal propensity to consume (*MPC*) the frac-

tion or percentage of a change in disposable personal income that appears as a change in planned consumption expenditure.

marginal propensity to save (*MPS*) the fraction or percentage of a change in disposable personal income that appears as a change in planned saving.

marginal revenue (*MR*) the extra revenue that a firm receives when it sells one more unit of output.

marginal revenue product (*MRP*) change in the total revenue of a firm resulting from the sale of the additional quantity of output that one more unit of a resource allows it to produce.

marginal tax rate the rate of income tax that applies to additional income received by an individual; the percentage of an additional dollar of income that would be payable in income tax.

marginal utility the additional utility gained from one more unit of a good or service.

margin requirements rules set down by the Federal Reserve Board specifying the minimum portion of the price of stock purchased that must be paid by the purchaser (not borrowed from the stockbroker).

market the organized action between potential buyers (market demand) and potential sellers (market supply) that permits trade.

market clearing the proposition that at the equilibrium price, no potential sellers who are willing and able to sell at that price are unable to carry out their desired transaction, and no buyers who are willing and able to buy at that price are unable to carry out their desired transaction.

market demand the sum of all the individual consumers' quantities demanded at particular prices for a particular product in a particular geographic area over some period of time.

market economic concentration the number and size distribution of firms in a specific market or industry. See also *Herfindahl-Hirschman Index.*

market economy an economic system in which the interaction of buyers and sellers is the main mechanism for making economic choices.

market failure a market outcome judged to be inadequate or unacceptable in relation to some goal of the society.

market-opening strategies a system of guaranteed minimum quotas for American goods in foreign markets, intended to counteract foreign protectionism.

market price the equilibrium price that tends to be established by the interaction of demand and supply for a specified product.

market socialism an adaptation of the microeconomics of pure competition to a socialist system.

market supply the sum of all of the individual firms'

quantities supplied at particular prices of a particular good or service in a particular geographic area over some period of time.

materials balancing a planning technique that requires estimating potential supplies of and demands for each of a number of final and intermediate products taken separately.

mature creditor the international economic situation of a country in an advanced stage of its economic development, in which its current balance is negative and its capital balance is positive. Returns from previous investment abroad are greater than current capital exports (net of repayments).

mature debtor the international trade and finance situation of a country in an intermediate stage of economic development, in which its current balance is positive and its capital balance is negative. The return flow of capital to foreigners (repayment of past debts) exceeds net capital inflows from them.

mechanism (basis for classifying economic systems) procedures used for making economic decisions—for example, markets, planning, and tradition.

medium of exchange a function of money that enables people to trade with one another more easily, since they do not need to match their specific wants with those of other people.

member bank a commercial bank that is a member of the Federal Reserve System.

menu costs costs entailed during a period of inflation by the need for frequent updating of price lists.

mercantilism an eighteenth-century school of economic thought that emphasized the achievement of economic power as a basis for military power. It emphasized high population and employment, low interest rates, accumulation of money, and strict regulation of trade, particularly international trade.

merger (or external growth or acquisition) the acquisition of one firm by another firm which adds to the acquiring firm's productive capacity.

microeconomics the branch of economics that focuses on the behavior of individual decision makers such as consumers, workers, business firms, and governments, assuming the major macroeconomic variables to be given. It focuses on how their behaviors affect the types of goods and services produced, the methods of production, and the distribution of income in the economy.

microeconomic unemployment unemployment that can be traced to decisions about what to produce or how to produce. It includes seasonal, frictional, and structural unemployment.

microfoundations the microeconomic behavior of individuals and firms that lie behind macroeconomic models.

millage the rate of tax applied under a property tax, with one mil equal to one-tenth of one percent.

minimum optimal scale effect (entry barrier) an entry barrier based upon the effect on the price of the product of an industry that results from adding the volume of output that a new firm of minimum optimal scale would supply if it enters that industry.

minimum wage a wage rate set by government as the lowest that firms are allowed to pay.

mixed economy an economic system combining significant elements of both planning and market modes of organization.

mobility See *labor mobility.*

model a formal statement of a theory.

monetarism the belief that the nominal money supply is usually more closely related to nominal national income and product than are nominal government expenditures and nominal investment expenditures; a school of economic thought that proposes that monetary policy make no attempt to deal with short-term fluctuations in economic activity but should instead establish a fixed rate of increase for the money supply and stay with this rate year in and year out.

monetarist a person who believes that control of the money supply is an important element in macroeconomic policy.

monetary base the total of official reserves and coins and currency in circulation in the economy.

Monetary Control Act of 1980 legislation that broadened the authority of the Board of Governors of the Federal Reserve System, including the authority to set required reserve ratios for all institutions offering checking account services. The full name of the legislation is the Depository Institutions Deregulation and Monetary Control Act of 1980.

monetary growth rule a policy guideline under which the money supply is increased at a constant rate without regard to cyclical fluctuations in the economy. The rate of money supply increase is to be approximately equal to the long-term growth trend in real productive capacity of the economy.

monetary instruments controls over financial markets and intermediaries used to influence the performance of the economy. The principal monetary instruments are reserve requirements, open market operations, and discount rates.

monetary policy a plan or a course of action governing the use of monetary instruments in an economy; a government's attempt to influence macroeconomic variables by changing the economy's money supply.

monetary-policy-target variable a variable used by the Federal Reserve System as a guide in implementing monetary policy.

monetized debt financial obligations that provide reserves to support money, as when loans provide a step in the expansion of bank deposits.

monetizing a public debt supporting the price of public debt instruments by monetary expansion if necessary.

money anything that is generally accepted in an economy as a medium of exchange, a unit of account, a store of purchasing power, and a standard for deferred payment.

money illusion the belief that nominal values are the same as real values; a belief that changes in nominal values brought on by a price-level change are also changes in real values; a theory implying that the aggregate-supply curve has a positive slope.

money income receipts measured in terms of the monetary unit and not adjusted for changes in the price level.

money market the interaction of the demand-for-money and the supply-of-money for use as a financial asset.

money multiplier the ratio between the amount of money (such as M1) in the economy and the size of the monetary base.

money supply (stock of money) the total quantity of money existing in an economy at a particular time (See *L*, *M1*, *M2*, and *M3* money supply concepts).

money supply curve the graphic representation of the relationship between the real rate of interest and the total quantity of money existing in an economy.

M1 (money supply concept) a money supply concept widely used by economists, consisting of coins and currency, demand deposits, and other checkable account balances.

M2 (money supply concept) the M1 money supply plus savings accounts, small time deposits, short-term repurchase agreements, money market mutual funds, and Eurodollars.

M3 (money supply concept) the M2 money supply plus fairly long-term repurchase agreements, large time deposits, and certain other assets.

monoeconomics economic theories that assume that methods devised in MDCs to deal with MDC problems also work well in LDCs.

monopolistic competition a market structure with a large number of sellers, some product differentiation, and fairly easy entry and exit.

monopoly a market in which there is only a single seller. See also *actual monopoly, pure monopoly*.

monopoly control (or monopoly power) the degree of control or power that a firm has over the price of the product it sells. Varying degrees are possessed by all but purely competitive firms.

monopoly regulation rules and laws that apply to firms granted monopoly status by the government and that involve the firm's level of output, its prices, and the scope of its production.

monopsonistic resource market (monopsony, oligopsony, monopsonistic competition) a market in which individual firms have some control over the quantity demanded of a resource and thus can influence the resource price.

monopsony a market in which there is only a single buyer.

moral suasion attempts by government and Federal Reserve System officials to persuade depository institutions and others in the economy to cooperate with their policy views or actions.

movement along a demand (supply) curve a change from one point on a demand (supply) curve to another point on the same curve due to a change in the price of the product.

multifactor productivity a weighted average of labor and capital productivity.

multinational (or transnational) corporation a corporation that has its headquarters in one country and carries on important business operations in several countries, including the home country.

multiplier the ratio of the change in the equilibrium level of national income and product to the change in planned expenditure that caused equilibrium to change. It is estimated to be equal to $1/(1 - MPC)$ when no changes are induced in net taxes or in expenditure streams other than consumption.

N

national banks banks whose charters are issued by the federal government.

national debt the total value of outstanding securities issued by a nation's government.

national income (NI) in national income accounting, the total amount earned by owners of resources used in producing goods and services during the accounting period.

national income and product accounts a set of reports on the volume and composition of economic activity in the United States over a specified time period; it consists of three major parts: the national product section, the national income section, and the personal income section.

national income gap   the difference between the target level of national income and the level that is predicted to prevail if the government undertakes no new action to change that level.

National Industrial Recovery Act (NIRA)   legislation enacted in 1933 containing a variety of emergency programs designed to help the economy recover from the Great Depression. Major portions of the act were ruled unconstitutional.

National Labor Relations Act   See *Wagner-Connery Act*.

national product   in national income accounting, the value of all goods and services produced in the economy during a given year, measured in terms of the prices prevailing at the time of production. See also *gross national product* and *net national product*.

natural monopoly   an industry in which only a single seller is required for efficient production.

natural rate of unemployment   the rate of unemployment that combines seasonal, frictional, and structural unemployment; believed by many economists to approximate full employment; the rate consistent with potential GNP.

natural resource   one of the factors of production or resources; a "gift of nature" that can be used in production, such as unimproved land or minerals in the ground.

near money   forms of wealth such as U.S. Savings Bonds, relatively liquid U.S. government securities, payment promises by large corporations, and so on, which can, with some delay, be converted into more liquid wealth forms, which would be counted as money.

negative income tax   a tax under which persons receiving less than a specified amount of income would also receive payments from the government.

negative relationship   See *inverse relationship*.

negative returns, short run   a decrease in total product (negative marginal product) that may occur after a great deal of a variable input has successively been added to one or more fixed inputs.

negative slope   an inverse relationship between variables, as shown on a graph.

negative taxes   transfer payments from the government.

negotiable order of withdrawal account (NOW)   a type of checkable account provided by savings and loan associations.

neoclassical economics   the school of economic thought based on the work of Alfred Marshall (1842–1924) and others, which dominated non-Marxian economic thought in the late nineteenth and early twentieth centuries.

neoclassical growth model   a model that describes a country's growth rate as the weighted sum of the changes in productivities of its productive inputs plus an additional term reflecting disembodied technical progress.

neocolonialism   domination by a more developed country over a less developed country, carried out without a military presence of the more developed country, and without any formal colonial relationship.

neo-Keynesian economics   a school of economic thought that preserves the basic Keynesian approach but includes monetary variables as well.

neo-Ricardian   an application of the rational-expectations theory that says that the method used to finance government expenditure does not matter.

net exports   the entry in the U.S. national income and product accounts showing the excess of exports over imports of currently produced goods and services. It may be negative.

net national product (NNP)   in national income accounting, the value of all currently produced goods and services (GNP) minus an estimated capital consumption (depreciation) allowance.

net taxes   the total amount of taxes paid minus transfer payments from the government.

net worth   the difference between the amount of total assets and the amount of total liabilities as reported on a balance sheet.

new classical   a school of economic thought that employs the theory of rational expectations and accepts the propositions that prices adjust quickly and that markets clear at equilibrium.

New Deal   a name used to refer to the economic programs of the first two administrations of President Franklin Roosevelt (1933–1941).

New International Economic Order (NIEO)   a pattern of international economic relations proposed by less developed countries as a replacement for the existing arrangements of international trade and aid; a set of demands from less developed countries for a restructuring of economic relations between developed and less developed countries.

New Left   contemporary radical groups that generally call for major steps away from a market economy.

New Right   contemporary radical groups that generally call for major steps toward a purely market economy.

New Socialist Man or Woman   a person, expected to emerge after socialism is firmly established, who will work harder than anyone in the past and will demand less in terms of wealth and luxurious consumption.

nominal protection   the statutory rate of a tariff on a product.

nominal value value that is stated or measured in terms of some monetary unit and that has not been adjusted for changes in the general price level.

nominal wage rate the amount of money a worker receives per hour (or other time unit) of work.

nonborrowed reserves total reserves in depository institutions minus amounts borrowed through discounting from Federal Reserve Banks.

nonexcludability the characteristic of public goods and services that makes it impossible or prohibitively expensive to prevent someone from consuming them, once they have been provided for others.

nonexhaustible natural resources gifts of nature usable in production, the supply of which cannot be eliminated by human use.

nonlinear relationship a relationship in which equal changes in the independent variable do not bring about the same responses in the dependent variable. When plotted on a graph, it will not appear as a straight line.

nonprice competition competition among firms by such nonprice means as advertising and product changes.

nonrenewable resources inputs for production that, once used, cannot be regenerated by natural processes within a time span that is relevant from the point of view of humans.

nonrival consumption consumption of a good or service by one person that does not prevent another person from consuming it.

no-recourse loan a government loan that a farmer may obtain on a crop at some percentage of its support price, and on which the government has no recourse against the debtor except the crop itself.

normal good or service a good or service for which there is a positive relationship between the income level and the quantity demanded.

normal profit the return to enterprise that is necessary for a firm to receive in order for it to be willing to continue its present business in the long run.

normative economics an approach to economics that is subjective and expresses an opinion or preference.

Norris-LaGuardia Act a U.S. law passed in 1932 granting workers full freedom of association and self-organization; it also limited the courts' power to issue injunctions and made the yellow-dog contract unenforceable.

O

objectivism the belief that each person's most objective view of the "good" is knowledge of what is in his or her own best interest.

obsolescence the process of becoming less or no longer useful or economically feasible for some intended purpose in production.

official reserves vault cash and deposits in Federal Reserve and other banks that are approved by the Federal Reserve System as meeting requirements.

official settlements balance the international balance of payments concept that combines all the entries in the capital account with all the entries in the current account and shows the net effect of all transactions except those in official government reserves.

oligopolistic coordination practices in oligopoly industries by which firms coordinate their output levels and pricing decisions. Practices include collusive agreement, price leadership, and rules of thumb.

oligopoly a sellers' market structure made up of a few interdependent firms.

oligopsony a market in which there are few buyers so that individual buyers can influence the price.

OPEC (Organization of Petroleum Exporting Countries) international petroleum cartel.

open economy a country that allows relatively unrestricted trade across its borders.

open market operations the buying and selling of government securities in the open market by the Federal Reserve System.

opportunity cost the true cost of choosing one alternative over another; that which is given up when a choice is made.

orderly marketing agreement an agreement among countries aimed at preventing price cutting in importing countries.

organic composition of capital the ratio between Marxian constant capital (raw materials plus depreciation) and variable capital (direct labor).

origin the point of intersection of the horizontal and vertical axes of a graph.

other things being equal See *ceteris paribus.*

outputs the economic goods and services that business firms produce for sale to consumers, other business firms, and governments.

overemployment working more hours than desired at a given wage rate.

owners' equity See *net worth.*

ownership (basis for classifying economic systems) the entities such as individuals, firms, collectives, or governments that are permitted to hold legal title to natural resources and capital goods.

P

paper gold See *special drawing rights.*

paradox of value the observation that consumers sometimes pay lower prices for goods and services that they consider essential than for goods and services that they consider relatively unimportant.

parity price (of a farm product) a price of an agricultural product that gives it a purchasing power, with respect to prices farmers pay, equivalent to what its price provided in some past period.

partial equilibrium analysis a method of analysis that deals with the effects of some disturbance on one set of economic variables, assuming that all other variables are unaffected.

partial (or fractional) reserves the situation in which cash or immediately available funds kept on hand by depository institutions are less than the total of the obligations to the people who have deposited money in the institutions.

participation rate See *civilian labor force participation rate.*

partnership a business firm created through an agreement in which two or more people share financial and managerial responsibilities as well as profits and losses.

patent a right of temporary limited monopoly over a new product or process granted to its inventor or to a firm that purchases the right from the inventor.

payments equilibrium in a balance of payments account, any situation in which a country's balance on current account is matched by an equal but opposite balance on its capital account.

PCE deflator an index number of prices for goods and services included in the personal consumption expenditures component of gross national product.

perestroika restructuring; reforms of the Soviet planning system that include a wider scope for an unplanned economy, more flexible plans, and more leeway for plant managers.

perfect competition a purely competitive market with the added feature that buyers and sellers have complete and continuous knowledge of all bids and offers in the market and the mobility to take immediate action on the basis of that knowledge.

perfectly elastic a condition existing when a price change causes an unlimited change in quantity.

perfectly elastic demand See *infinitely elastic demand.*

perfectly inelastic demand a condition existing when a price change causes no response in the quantity demanded.

perfectly inelastic supply a condition existing when a price change causes no change in the quantity supplied.

permanent income hypothesis the proposition that the level of a household's planned consumption expenditure is based on what it believes to be its long-run or ''permanent'' level of income.

perpendicular a straight line drawn from a point on a graph to form a right angle with the horizontal axis or the vertical axis on a graph.

personal deduction in individual income taxation, an allowance for certain expenditures that may be subtracted from income in determining the tax base.

personal exemption the amount that can be deducted for the taxpayer(s) and each dependent in calculating income subject to tax.

personal income (PI) the national income accounting concept equal to national income plus receipts not earned and minus earnings not received.

personal income distribution the division of income among individuals classified according to income size.

Phillips curve a relationship between an economy's unemployment rate and its inflation rate suggesting that trade-offs exist between these two rates such that policy makers can choose a preferred combination from among those that constitute the curve.

physical capital (or capital goods) resources or factors of production such as factory buildings, tools, and equipment that enable business firms to produce more efficiently.

physiocrats an eighteenth-century school of economic thought contending that economies operate according to certain natural laws and that government interference was useless and wasteful.

picketing the parading of striking workers before the entrance to their work place in the hope of convincing other workers, customers, or supplies not to enter.

Pigou effect the relationship between the price level and the quantity of real national income and product demanded that arises because of the effect of price-level change on the value of wealth holdings.

planned consumption in Keynesian analysis, the amount of expenditure on currently produced consumption goods and services that households intend to carry out in the time period under study.

planned economy an economic system in which the government coordinates decisions about what, how, and for whom to produce.

planned investment in Keynesian analysis, the amount of expenditure on currently produced capital goods and inventories that firms intend to carry out in the time period under study.

planned saving in Keynesian analysis, the amount of current disposable personal income that households intend to withhold from expenditure on consumption.

planning the directing of economic activity through prearranged priorities, and procedures, sometimes enforced by sanctions.

Planning-Programming Budget System (PPBS) a budgeting procedure that requires agencies to specify the programs they wish to carry out and to plan expenditure needs several years in advance.

plant a factory or other production facility in a particular geographic location that belongs to a firm, which may operate only this one plant or a number of different plants.

political economy the economic analysis of public policy questions.

populism a protest movement in the United States during the last decades of the nineteenth century that expressed farm dissatisfaction with the prices farmers paid and the prices they received, with interest and repayment requirements on farm loans, and with deflationary monetary policies.

positive economics the aspect of the discipline dealing with objective facts (what is) rather than value judgments and opinions (what ought to be).

positive relationship See *direct relationship*.

positive slope a direct relationship between variables, as shown in a graph.

post-Keynesians economists who use Keynesian and neo-Keynesian models, but emphasize institutional features of the economy, such as monopoly power and price rigidity, and often advocate incomes policy.

potential entry the likelihood that one or more firms will enter an industry or market.

potential GNP the quantity of real GNP when the economy is operating at its natural rate of unemployment; the economy's long-run aggregate supply.

poverty living at a standard or level below that considered adequate by the society.

poverty line an income level below which poverty is said to exist.

Prebisch thesis that the international economy has developed in a way that is unfair to agricultural and raw material producers because the producers of these goods are not able to restrict output and raise prices, as can be done by producers of manufactured goods.

precautionary demand for money a desire to hold money in order to be prepared for unexpected changes in the pattern of receipts or expenditures.

predatory price cutting reduction in price aimed at forcing competitors out of business.

preference revelation the indication or pronouncement of an individual's desire for public goods and services.

present value the discounted value at the present time of a sum of money to be received in the future. See also *discounting*.

present value formula the equation that illustrates the determination of the present value of an asset by the relation between the expected income flow and the rate of interest: PV = expected annual income flow/the rate of interest.

price the exchange value of a product or resource.

price controls the setting of maximum or minimum prices by the government. See also *ceiling price, floor price*.

price differential a difference between the prices charged to different buyers by a firm for the same product at the same time.

price discrimination the practice of charging a price differential that is not justified by a difference in cost to the seller.

price-earnings ratio the ratio between the price of a share of a firm's stock and the firm's earnings per share.

price elasticity of demand the degree of responsiveness of the quantity demanded of a good, service, or resource to a change in its price.

price elasticity of resource demand the degree of responsiveness of the quantity demanded of a resource to a change in its price.

price elasticity of supply the degree of responsiveness of the quantity supplied of a good, service, or resource to a change in its price.

price fixing agreement among the firms in an industry to establish specific prices. See also *collusion*.

price leadership a practice by firms in some oligopoly industries that coordinates their pricing behavior, where one or more firms announce a price change and other firms in the industry quickly follow it.

price leadership to avoid competition a practice in an oligopolistic industry based on voluntarily following the price changes of significant firms in that industry in order to avoid price competition harmful to industry profits; it is an alternative to collusion.

price level an average of all prices prevailing in an economy expressed as an index number based on the average prices that prevailed in a selected base year.

price maker a firm with sufficient monopoly power or control to be able to affect the price it can charge (or pay) by the level of output it chooses to produce (or the level of input it chooses to buy). See also *price searcher*.

price rigidity a tendency for prices to be sticky or rigid in oligopoly industries because of the interdependence among firms and their fear of being misinterpreted by rivals.

price searcher a firm that is able to choose the price for its product, but because it lacks full information, it must search for its profit-maximizing price.

price-specie flow the process of adjustment that the gold standard offered for countries with international balance of payments problems; the flow of gold to settle international payments imbalances and the resulting change in the price levels of trading partners.

price supports (in agriculture) government-operated programs that make sure the prices farmers receive for certain crops do not fall below specified levels. See also *floor price, parity (price)*.

price taker a firm that accepts prices set by the market as given and cannot influence them by changing its own sales or purchases. Characteristic of pure competition.

primary production agriculture, forestry, and fisheries.

primitive economy an economic system, usually traditional, that uses technologies significantly less advanced than those used elsewhere.

private benefit benefits that accrue to individuals and firms as distinguished from benefits that accrue to the society as a whole.

private cost the value of opportunities forgone by individuals and firms directly involved in the production and consumption of a good or service. It does not include external cost.

private returns benefits that accrue to certain individuals or firms as contrasted to society as a whole.

private sector the part of an economy directed by the decisions of individuals and firms.

producer price index a measure of the level of prices paid for inputs, expressed in terms of base year prices. See also *consumer price index*.

product the output of a firm; either goods or services or both.

product cycle a principle that explains changes over time among countries in their comparative advantage in producing a given product.

product differentiation changes in basically similar products in order to create some differences among them in the eyes of consumers.

product differentiation (entry barrier) an entry barrier determined by the extent to which established firms can differentiate their relatively well-known products from those of a newcomer.

product extension conglomerate merger the acquisition of a firm in an allied industry—one whose product is functionally associated with that of the acquirer.

production the transformation of inputs into outputs by firms.

production controls, agricultural legislation requiring farmers to limit their output of a supported crop.

production function a relationship that shows the maximum output that can be obtained from given amounts of inputs as of a specified point in time.

production possibilities boundary a curve that represents all of the alternative maximum combinations that can be produced during a given period of time with a given stock of resources and technological knowledge.

production possibility a concept describing the maximum quantity of goods and services that can be produced with a given stock of resources and technological knowledge during any given period of time.

productive credit theory a theory that states that if more credit to a firm is matched by a corresponding increase in the firm's output, the loan is not inflationary.

productivity the amount of output produced by a unit of resource input during a given span of time.

profit the return to the entrepreneurial resource or factor of production; also the difference between a firm's total revenue and total cost.

profit and loss statement See *income statement*.

profit maximization an assumption made in the theory of the firm that a firm will seek to produce a level of output and charge a price so that its total revenue exceeds its total cost by the greatest possible amount. A consequence is that its marginal cost equals its marginal revenue.

progressive tax a tax under which the percentage of income paid in tax increases as the amount of the taxpayer's total income increases.

proletariat a term used by Karl Marx to refer to the working class, which would come to power after the socialist revolution.

propensity to consume the inclination of households to spend a predicted portion of disposable personal income on goods and services for current consumption.

propensity to save the inclination of households to desist from spending a predicted portion of disposable personal income for consumption goods and services.

property rights the rights enjoyed by a property owner by reason of his or her ownership.

property tax a tax imposed on the estimated value of specified types of property, typically land and buildings.

proportional tax a tax under which the percentage of income paid in tax is the same without regard to the size of the taxpayer's income.

proprietorship a business firm owned and managed by one person.

prosperity a condition of an economy existing when living standards are relatively high and unemployment is relatively low; also, the expansion phase of a business cycle.

protection a system of tariffs and other measures aimed at defending a country's industries from foreign competition in its home market.

protectionism a policy position favoring aid to import-competing industries by tariffs, subsidies, quotas, other restrictions on imports, and sometimes also aid to export industries by direct or hidden subsidies.

proven reserves estimates of the amount of a natural resource that remains available for economically feasible extraction.

psychic returns nonmonetary returns such as prestige, excitement, and other personal feelings of satisfaction and enjoyment; may be earned from investing in human capital.

public choice an area of study that combines economics and political science ideas to gain a better understanding of how governments actually operate.

public-choice economists economists who specialize in the study of the decision making procedures and outcomes of governments.

public debt See *national debt.*

public enterprise a government commercial undertaking such as the U.S. Postal Service or Amtrak on the federal level; state lotteries or parks; local sewage disposal or libraries; often an actual monopoly.

public goods and services goods and services supplied either wholly or in large part through government because externality, nonrivalry, and nonexcludability features are so important that provision through market processes is seriously deficient.

public sector the part of an economy directed by government.

public sector planning planning that covers only the public sector of the economy.

public utility a private firm that is granted a monopoly position by the government and is regulated by the government.

pump-priming temporary injections of government money in an effort to build up business confidence and to raise planned investment; an economic policy model of the mid-1930s.

purchasing power of the dollar the reciprocal of the index number for the consumer price index, or the goods and services that a dollar will buy in a given year compared to what it would buy in the base year.

purchasing power parity a condition prevailing when the quantity of internationally traded goods and services that can be bought with a unit of a nation's money is the same in international trade as at home.

pure competition a type of market structure with a large number of sellers, a standardized product, no artificial restrictions on price or quantity, and easy entry and exit into and out of the industry, so that each firm is a price taker.

pure monopoly a market structure in which there is only a single seller, no acceptable substitutes are available for the product offered for sale, and no entry into the market is possible.

pure science an objective, factual, and systematic search for knowledge utilizing assumptions, principles and rules, but not engaging in practical applications.

pyramiding of reserves the arrangement in effect before the Federal Reserve System was established in 1913, under which reserves of country banks were held as deposits in city banks, which held their reserves in still larger banks in major cities (reserve cities).

Q

quadrant one of four sections of a graph formed by the intersection of horizontal and vertical axes. Each axis usually represents a variable with both positive and negative values.

quality bias the effect on a price index number of the failure to recognize that the quality of goods and services changes over time.

quantile ratio the percentage or fraction determined by dividing the percentage of total income received by the highest k percentage of the population with the percentage of the total received by the lowest k percentage. (k is a fraction. Commonly chosen values are .05, .10, and .20.)

quantitative economic forecasting the practice of using observed and/or estimated values for the variables in a macroeconomic model in order to predict future values for these variables.

quantity demanded the amount demanded per time period of a good, service, or resource at a certain price. See also *demand, individual consumer demand, market demand.*

quantity supplied the amount supplied per time period of a good, service, or resource at a certain price. See also *individual firm supply, market supply, supply.*

quantity theory of money the proposition, based on the equation of exchange, that changes in the quantity of money provide a useful way of predicting changes in nominal GNP; a theory that states that the velocity of money circulation is constant in the long run, so changes in the quantity of money provide a good way to predict changes in GNP.

quota a limitation on the quantity of imports.

R

radical extreme, sweeping, or revolutionary; a person whose beliefs are radical.

rate of economic growth the percentage change per year in an economy's potential GNP.

rate of return the proceeds or receipts from an undertaking expressed as a percentage of the amount put into it.

rate-of-return parity when the rate of return on a unit of money invested at home is the same as it would be if that money were converted into the money of a foreign country and invested there.

rate of surplus value See *exploitation rate*.

rate structure (for a public utility) pattern of prices charged according to such criteria as customer classification, quantity purchased, and time of delivery.

rational consumer an assumption that consumers seek to maximize their satisfaction—to get the most out of their income by selecting the mix of goods and services that promises to offer the greatest amount of personal satisfaction.

rational entrepreneur (business firm decision maker) a person who seeks to maximize profit and minimize loss over a certain period.

rational expectations the theory that, after sufficient experience with inflationary consequences of increases in aggregate demand, people will adjust their price-level expectations quickly when expansionary monetary or fiscal actions are taken, so that such actions have little effect on real output in the economy.

rationality See *economic rationality*.

rationing any method of restricting the demand for a good or a service. Government may formally invoke a system of rationing in order to deal "fairly" with what would otherwise be an excess demand situation.

Reaganomics the package of economic policy positions arising from the groups backing the Reagan administrations: anti-inflationists, anti-high-taxers, anti-high-interest-rate advocates, and those who favored more defense spending.

real balances wealth holdings adjusted for changes in the price level.

real balances theory the proposition that changes in the price level affect aggregate demand through changes in the real value of assets; called the Pigou effect.

real business cycle theories explanations of economic fluctuations based on patterns of changing labor productivity or labor supply.

real income the quantity of goods and services that can be purchased with the money received by a household; receipts adjusted for changes in the price level.

real interest rates interest rates that reflect actual purchasing-power values.

realization crisis in Marxian terms, the stage of capitalism where the profit rate remains high but less than full-employment output can be bought by workers and other consumers.

real values values stated or measured in terms of goods and services; numerical values that have been adjusted for price-level changes by applying an index number or deflator.

real wage rates wage rates adjusted for changes in the price level.

recession the contraction phase of a business cycle; a period of a relatively low volume of production and income in an economy.

recognition lag the time required for economists to recognize that there is trouble in the economy, to diagnose the trouble, and to prescribe remedies.

recovery the early part of the expansion phase of a business cycle; the phase immediately following the lower turning point of a business cycle.

reflation a rise in the price level toward a level that prevailed earlier.

regressive tax a tax under which the percentage of income paid in tax decreases as the amount of a taxpayer's total income increases.

regulated industries (or regulated firms) industries or firms whose prices (and sometimes other operations) are subject to monopoly regulation.

regulation See *monopoly regulation, social regulation*.

regulatory commissions federal and state agencies that regulate firms that have been given public utility status.

regulatory lag the length of time that it takes for a regulated firm's changes in costs to be reflected in rate changes.

relative price the market value of a good or service compared to the market value of certain other goods and services.

relatively pure conglomerate merger the acquisition by a firm of a firm whose activities have only remote relationships to those of the acquirer.

renewable resources inputs to production that, under normal conditions, can be replaced through natural processes.

rent the return or payment for the use of natural resources in production.

replacement cost the value of a firm's capital estimated by what it would cost to replace it.

required reserves See *reserve requirement*.

reservation price a price below which a resource will be held for future use or sale by its owner.

reservation wage rate the wage rate that a worker feels he or she must be offered before signing a contract of employment.

reserve ratio the total official (government-approved) reserves held by a depository institution divided by the amount of checking account liabilities of that institution.

reserve requirement the amount of official reserves that a depository institution must, by law, maintain in order to avoid legal penalities.

reserves vault cash and deposits with the Federal Reserve Bank, which may be used by a depository institution to fulfill official reserve requirements.

resource allocation the division of resources among alternative uses.

resource package a combination of two or more of the factors of production or resources necessary for production.

resources See *factors of production.*

revaluation changing the official exchange value of a country's money.

revenue See *total revenue.*

revenue sharing a system under which revenues collected by a superior government are transferred to subordinate governments in a federal system.

risk the probability that a harm or loss will be suffered.

rivalry competition among sellers or among buyers.

Robinson-Patman Act a 1936 amendment to the Clayton Act, which strengthened the government's control with respect to price discrimination.

roundabout production the diversion of resources from the direct production of consumer goods to the production of capital goods, which are then used in further production.

rule of reason a guiding principle adopted by the Supreme Court in 1911 that focused on intent and conduct rather than the presence or absence of substantial monopoly control.

rules of thumb conventions developed as a means of coordinating decisions among firms in an oligopoly industry.

run on a bank a situation in which many of a bank's depositors want to withdraw their deposits at the same time, and immediately.

S

sales tax a tax imposed on the sale of a product.

satisfice to seek satisfactory profit rather than maximum profit.

saving setting aside current income in order to increase wealth.

saving function the statement of a relationship between the level of disposable personal income and the volume of planned saving.

Say's Identity a proposition that states that the sum of all the wages, salaries, rents, interest, and profits in the economy must provide enough purchasing power to allow households to pay for all the goods and services produced at whatever price level was in effect when they were produced.

scaling the marks and numbers that indicate units of measure of the variables on the horizontal and vertical axes of a graph.

scarcity the circumstance in which the supply of something would not be sufficient to satisfy the demand for it if it were provided "free of charge."

school of economic thought a group of economists who employ the same or similar theories and who agree with one another much of the time about economic policy.

seasonal unemployment joblessness that arises because some occupations require workers during only part of each year.

SDRs See *special drawing rights.*

secondary boycott (or strike) a boycott (or strike) by a union against an employer other than the one with which the union has a dispute.

Second World countries with centrally planned economies.

secondary production manufacturing, mining, construction, and transport.

self-liquidating loans extensions of credit that are to be repaid from charges collected for goods or services financed by the credit.

seniority rule the requirement that the worker who has been on the job the longest shall receive preferential treatment in respect to layoff, rehiring, and other conditions of employment.

services intangible products.

share-draft account a checkable account in a credit union that permits the payment of interest.

shares of stock securities that represent ownership rights in a corporation.

Sherman Antitrust Act a law passed by the U.S. Congress in 1890 prohibiting the restriction of competition, monopolization, and attempts to monopolize.

shift of a demand (supply) curve a displacement of an entire demand (supply) curve to the right or left showing a change in demand (supply).

shoe-leather costs costs entailed during a period of inflation by the switching of assets from one form to another.

shop steward a worker elected to represent the union on the job.

shortage a disequilibrium market situation that results in excess demand; the extent to which the quantity demanded exceeds the quantity supplied at some specific price.

short run the period of time during which at least one of a firm's inputs cannot be varied; a period of time not long enough for entry into an industry or exit from an industry to take place.

short-run consumption function the relationship between disposable personal income and planned consumption expenditure during a limited time period after changes in disposable personal income.

shutdown decision the prediction in the theory of the firm that in the short run a firm will cease producing if its revenue is insufficient to at least cover its variable cost.

skill See *technological know-how*.

slope the change in the variable read on the vertical axis of a graph divided by the associated change in the variable read on the horizontal axis of that graph.

social cost the total value of opportunities forgone because of the production and consumption of a product. It includes both private cost and external cost.

Social Darwinism the belief that the survival and prosperity of individuals, families, nations, and races are determined, like those of animal species, by their biological and psychological fitness in the struggle not only against each other but also against the environment.

socialist system an economic system in which land and physical instruments of production are largely or completely owned by the state.

social overhead capital facilities such as roads, harbors, schools, and public health installations that provide public sector services needed by a society; also known as infrastructure.

social regulation rules and laws that protect the public against potentially harmful practices by business firms. Examples are environmental protection, food and drug, truth-in-packaging, and occupational health and safety rules.

social returns benefits that accrue to society as a whole as contrasted to individuals or firms.

Social Security Act (1935) legislation establishing a compulsory system of retirement and survivors' benefits financed by taxes from employers and employees. The system has since expanded to include certain disability, hospital, and medical care benefits.

special drawing rights (SDRs) or paper gold credit entries on the books of the International Monetary Fund given to particular countries, which can, in turn, uses them to meet their international obligations.

speculation taking action based on expectations of future changes in market values.

speculative demand for money a desire to hold money arising because of an expectation that the market values of nonmoney assets are going to fall in the future, or that interest rates will rise in the future.

stabilization function the function or role of government involving the direction of the aggregate economy in order to prevent serious depressions or inflations and to maintain high levels of employment and a reasonable rate of economic growth.

stable equilibrium a state of balance that tends to restore itself after disturbances.

stages of production (short-run theory of the firm) the division of a firm's input-output relationships into three categories when a firm adds successive units of a variable input to one or more fixed inputs. In Stage I average product increases. In Stage II average product decreases, but marginal product remains positive. In Stage III total product also decreases, and marginal product is negative.

stagflation a prolonged combination of inflation, substantial unemployment, and sluggish growth.

standard deduction in individual income taxation, an amount that can be subtracted from income provided that the taxpayer does not itemize personal deductions.

Standard Industrial Classification (SIC) system a classification system, used by the U.S. Bureau of the Census, that divides the outputs of firms into industry and product groupings.

standard for deferred payment a function of money used to specify amounts to be exchanged at some future date.

standardized product the product of different firms that is so much alike that customers do not prefer one seller's product over another's. Sometimes called a homogeneous product.

standard of living the well-being of people, usually expressed in terms of current income or consumption per person of real goods and services.

standards and controls rules governing such characteristics of goods as methods of production or methods of waste disposal.

static analysis the description of an equilibrium state.

statistical discrepancy in national income and product accounting, the difference between the estimate of national income and the estimate of net national product after allowing for indirect business taxes and subsidies.

stock a fixed quantity, such as the stock of money; also, a certificate denoting an ownership share in a corporation.

stockbroker an individual or firm which carries out transactions in corporate securities (stocks and bonds) on behalf of their buyers and sellers.

stock exchange an organization through which transactions in corporate stocks may be carried out.

stock phenomena the sums or quantities of economic variables as they exist at a specified time, as distinguished from flows of such quantities over a specified period of time.

store of purchasing power a function of money that enables people who have money to save some of it for use at a later time.

strike a work stoppage in which employees refuse to work until certain conditions are met.

structural deficit the total government budget deficit minus that portion arising because the economy is operating below its target level of national income and product.

structural unemployment unemployment that occurs when there is a mismatch between worker qualifications and job requirements; it often arises when changes occur in production methods and in the types of goods and services produced.

subsidy a grant or gift, often from a government, designed to give aid to and provide incentives for the recipient.

substitutes (substitute goods or services) goods or services that may be used instead of one another, such as beer and ale or pastel blue shirts and pastel green shirts.

substitution effect the effect that a change in relative prices of substitute goods or services (resulting from a change in the price of a good or service) has on the quantity that a person demands of that good or service.

supply the willingness and ability to offer for sale at certain prices. See also *individual firm supply, market supply, quantity supplied.*

supply curve graph of a supply schedule.

supply schedule a table showing different prices of a good or service and the quantity supplied of that good or service at each price.

supply shock an independent or exogenous event that shifts the aggregate-supply curve for an economy.

supply-side economics the approach to economics that is concerned with the forces that can shift the aggregate-supply curve of an economy.

support price See *floor price.*

surplus the excess supply that stems from a disequilibrium situation; in budgets, the excess of receipts over expenditures for the budget period.

surplus value a Marxian concept describing the value of labor that the employer retains to pay interest, rent, dividends, profits, and the unproductive portion of white-collar labor.

sustainable annual yield the quantity of a renewable natural resource that can be harvested each year consistent with maintaining a stable population of that resource.

syndicalism the ownership of individual capital facilities (such as workshops, factories, or industrial complexes) by their own workers, who would elect representatives to a weak government, which would act as a referee in disputes and as an economic plan coordinator.

T

Taft-Hartley Act (or Labor-Management Relations Act) a U.S. law passed in 1947 that forbade unions to interfere with the organization of employers, to refuse to bargain with employer representatives, or to enter into closed shop agreements.

target level of national income and product the level of national income and product that policy makers believe to be most desirable in terms of its effects on employment, prices, economic growth, and other goals of the economy.

target price a price for an American-grown farm product set by the U.S. Secretary of Agriculture under the Agriculture and Consumer Protection Act of 1973. Farmers who qualify under the terms of the legislation receive payments from the government if they sell their crop for less than the target price.

tariff a tax on imports.

tariff factory a plant set up by a foreign firm in order to avoid a tariff imposed by the country in which the plant is located.

tax a payment to government required by law.

tax base the amount of income or value on which tax liability is calculated.

tax brackets in individual income taxation, the layers or portions of income subject to different tax rates.

tax-change multiplier the ratio between a change in the level of equilibrium national income and product and the change in net tax collections that brought it about.

tax shifting transferring the burden of a tax to some person or group other than the one making the actual payment to government.

technical efficiency the least amount of inputs, measured in physical terms, required to produce a certain amount of output; a method of production that does not waste resources.

technological know-how the ability to combine resources in producing goods and services.

technological progress an advance in knowledge of the industrial arts and/or improved techniques of organizing production.

terms of trade the ratio of an index number of the prices of the goods and services that a country exports to an index number of the prices of the goods and services that it imports.

tertiary production trade, finance, government, education—the service industries.

theory a systematically organized body of knowledge that can be applied in a fairly wide range of circumstances and that provides a set of rules or assumptions for analyzing information and studying relationships.

Third World all countries not classified as in the First World or the Second World; characteristically, the less developed countries.

thrift institutions depository institutions such as savings and loan associations, mutual savings banks, and credit unions that accept deposits and make primarily consumer and mortgage loans.

Thrift Institutions Advisory Council a council set up in 1983 to provide a channel through which savings and loan associations, mutual savings banks, and credit unions can present their views to the Federal Reserve Board of Governors.

time deposit funds placed in a financial institution under terms that allow the institution to delay repayment for some period.

time lag the amount of time it takes for a change in an economic variable to have an effect.

total cost (TC) the entire cost incurred by a firm producing a certain level of output. In the short run it is the sum of total fixed costs and total variable costs; explicit and implicit costs that a firm incurs in production.

total fixed cost (TFC) short-run costs of a firm that do not vary with the quantity level of output that the firm produces.

total planned expenditure the sum of planned consumption expenditure, planned investment expenditure, government purchases, and exports minus imports.

total product the total quantity of output produced by a firm during a period of time.

total revenue the total income or receipts during a period of time that a business firm receives from selling what it produces.

total utility the sum of all the marginal utilities a person gains from successive units consumed of any good or service over a particular period of time.

total variable cost (TVC) the sum of those costs of a firm that vary with the quantity level of output that the firm produces. (In the long run, all costs are variable.)

tradeoff an exchange of one thing for another; especially, the quantity of one good or service that must be given up to gain a certain quantity of another good or service.

traditional economy an economic system in which decisions are made primarily on the basis of past practice.

transaction costs the costs associated with facilitating the workings of a market by enabling potential buyers and sellers to interact.

transactions accounts deposits in financial institutions that provide the depositor with checking-account privileges; also called *checkable accounts*.

transactions demand for money the desire to hold some wealth in the form of money because money is convenient for day-to-day buying and selling of goods and services.

transfer earnings the part of the earnings of a resource that is equal to the earnings that this resource could command in the next-best use to which it could be put.

transfer payments payments, such as Social Security benefits, unemployment compensation, or welfare, that are not compensation for any service rendered or product sold during the current accounting period; considered to be negative taxes.

transmission mechanism the means whereby changes in the money supply affect the level of national income and product. See *Keynesian transmission mechanism* and *direct transmission mechanism*.

transnational corporation See *multinational corporation*.

Treasury Bills a short-term debt instrument issued by the U.S. Treasury.

trend line of economic activity a pattern of growth taking place in the economy because of increases in the size and quality of labor, the quantity of capital, and better technology.

trigger-price mechanism a method of protection whereby an importing country unilaterally announces one or more prices, below which all sales are considered to be below cost and subject to antidumping duties.

trust a legal device through which supposedly competing firms allow a central board of trustees to vote all of their stock.

trust-buster an advocate of the market economy who fears control by big-business oligarchy and believes that the decline in competition should be reversed; a branch of the market-economy New Right.

turning point in business cycle measurement, the change from expansion to contraction or from contraction to expansion in the volume of economic activity.

tying arrangement a practice that forces a firm to buy certain products along with certain other products.

U

uncertainty the condition of not knowing the probability of the outcome of an event.

underemployment working fewer hours than desired at a given wage rate; working at a job that does not utilize all of the skill and training that the worker possesses.

underground economy income and production, both criminal and otherwise, that are not reported in official statistics, often because people want to evade regulations, union rules, or taxes.

undistributed profits tax a tax on the portion of corporation net income not distributed as dividend payments to stockholders.

unemployment in official statistics, a condition in which a person who desires and is able to work at the going wage rate is not able to find a job; in economic theory, a condition in which a person is spending more time for leisure than desired and less time for wage earning than desired at the going wage rate.

unemployment rate See *civilian unemployment rate.*

unfair labor practices practices by employers and by unions made illegal in the Wagner-Connery Act and the Taft-Hartley Act.

unfavorable balance (of trade) a negative, debit, or deficit balance in a country's international transactions in merchandise.

unilateral transfer in balance of payments accounting, a current account entry recording amounts of funds transmitted not in exchange for goods and services, such as gifts, donations, or foreign aid.

union (labor union/trade union) an organization of workers for the purpose of collective bargaining.

union shop a form of union security arrangement that allows employers to hire nonunion employees but requires that they join the union soon after employment.

unitary elasticity a condition existing where the percentage response in quantity is exactly equal to the percentage change in the price that caused it.

unitary elastic demand a condition existing when the percentage response in quantity demanded is exactly equal to the percentage change in the price that caused it.

unit of account a function of money that enables people to measure the values of different items.

unlimited liability an obligation that is not restricted or confined to a specified amount. For example, a proprietor's or a partner's responsibility for the obligations of a firm is not restricted to the amount of his or her financial investment in the firm.

unlimited life a condition in which the continued existence of a business firm is not restricted to the period of participation of any owner or manager; a characteristic of the corporate form of business organization.

unstable equilibrium a state of balance that has no tendency to restore itself if upset.

upper turning point the point in a business cycle when an expansion phase ends and a contraction phase begins; also called a *peak.*

user charge a price that government charges for services that it renders.

util a unit of anticipated satisfaction used to express an individual consumer's degree of pleasure derived from a unit of a product.

utility a measure or expression of an individual consumer's anticipated satisfaction to be derived from goods and services.

utility analysis a theory of consumer behavior based on assumptions of consumer rationality, the measurability of utility, decreasing marginal utility, increasing total utility, limited income, and knowledge of prices.

V

validation See *accommodation.*

value added the increase in the value of a good in each stage of its production; the difference between the value of materials that a firm buys and the value of what it sells.

value in exchange the transaction price of a good, service, or resource; the value of a good or service as determined by what people are willing to pay for the last unit that they buy.

value in use the value of a good or service as determined by the total satisfaction received from it; the total utility that is gained from a product.

value of output a method of measuring national income and product that makes no attempt to avoid double counting.

variable a quantity that can assume any of a set of values.

variable capital a Marxian concept of direct labor hours—not hours actually spent at work, but hours used to produce goods consumed by workers.

variable cost See *total variable cost.*

velocity (of circulation of money) the number of times a year, on the average, that a dollar of the money supply is spent in the purchase of currently produced goods and services. Velocity is usually measured by dividing the GNP by some measure of the money supply, such as M1.

vertical merger the acquisition by a firm of a firm that operates on a different level of a particular business activity, such as one that is a supplier or a customer of the acquirer.

very long run   the period of time long enough so that a new technology can be introduced and the production function itself can be altered.

voluntary export restriction   reduction of exports to a certain level or in accordance with a certain formula, undertaken by an exporting country.

W

wage and price controls   restrictions imposed by law on wage rates and prices of goods and services.

wage and price guidelines   suggested and voluntary constraints on changes in wage rates and prices of goods and services.

wage-cost lag theory   the proposition that changes in costs of production and wage rates lag behind changes in the general price level.

wage differentials   differences in wage rates usually due to different qualifications of workers, desirability of the job, and the institutions of the labor market.

wage rate   the payment to labor per unit of time worked.

wage-rate and cost "catch up"   the process through which wage rates and other input prices cease to lag behind the prices of final goods.

wages   the return or payment to labor in production.

Wagner-Connery Act (or National Labor Relations Act)   a pro-union act passed by the U.S. Congress in 1935. It proposed to guarantee rights of collective bargaining, outlawed various employer labor practices as unfair, and set up a National Labor Relations Board as its enforcement mechanism.

wealth   an accumulation of assets.

weighting bias   the failure of the CPI to recognize that consumer buying patterns tend to change when the price level changes.

welfare   the state of well-being or the quality of life; also, a term applied to government transfer payments designed to alleviate poverty.

welfare loss triangle   a graphic representation of the amount of economic well-being that is lost to consumers because a product is produced and sold by a monopolist instead of by purely competitive firms.

welfare state   an economic regime that places an especially high value on the equity of income and wealth distributions and on the provision of a floor or "safety net" below which income should not fall.

Wheeler-Lea Amendment   a 1938 amendment to the Federal Trade Commission Act that outlaws unfair or deceptive acts or practices aimed at the consumer.

wildcat banking   banking practices in which depositors were persuaded to entrust their savings to institutions that then made loans and issued bank notes until their obligations far exceeded their readily available assets.

worker's self-management   a system of production, most notably in Yugoslavia, in which workers' collectives operate and manage firms with capital leased from the state.

work standards   criteria determining the amount of work to be performed, such as the size of a work crew for a job or the number of units to be handled on an assembly line during a certain period of time.

X

X-inefficiency   waste of inputs due to a lack of motivation by management, which results in high-cost internal practices; often displayed by monopolists.

Y

yellow-dog contract   an agreement that a worker will not join a union, which was often made a condition of employment before the Norris-LaGuardia Act of 1932.

Index

Opportunity cost, 68–76
  in consumption, 69–70
  in health care, 77
  of leisure time, 155, 680
  marginal, 72–73
  in production, 70–77
  transactions and precautionary demands for money and, 307
Orderly marketing agreements, 856
Organic composition of capital, 954–955
Organization of Petroleum Exporting Countries (OPEC), 568
  history of, 831
  inflation and, 284, 359
  oil production and, 118–119, 184–185
  problems encountered by, 294, 831–832
  stagflation and, 350
  supply shock caused by, 341
  Third World debt and, 467–469
Origin, 47
"Original cost," 836n
Ornstein, Allan C., 754
Outputs, 520
  equilibrium, 605
  profit-maximizing level of, 556–563
  value of, 128
  see also Production
Overproduction, tendency to, 956
Overvaluation in foreign exchange rates, 409
Owen, Robert, 713
Owner, rational, 45
Ownership, direct and indirect, 20
Ownership basis, of economic systems, 8, 11

Packard, Vance, 626
Paglin, Morton, 808n
Panhandling, 803–805
Panzar, John C., 839n
Papandreou, George, 7, 454
Paper gold, see Special drawing rights
"Paper wealth," 151
Paradox of value, 484, 486–487
Parity price, 878
Park Chung Hee, 450
Partial equilibrium analysis, 54
Partial reserves, see Reserves, partial or fractional
Participation rate, see Labor force participation rate
Partnership, 27
Patent, 599
  U.S. business protection with, 619
Payments equilibrium, 428
"Payoff matrix," 638, 639 (table)
Peaks, see Upper turning points
Pen, Jan, 959n
Pennar, Karen, 343, 867
Penner, Rudolph G., 402
"Penny capitalism," 11
People's Bank of China, 940
People's Party, 872

Per capita income, international comparisons of, 455, 456
Percentage, graphs and, 50n
Perestroika, 15, 454, 930–931
Perfect competition, 574
Perfect elasticity, 507
Perfect inelasticity, 507
Permanent income hypothesis, 200
Perpendiculars, 48
Personal consumption spending, disposable personal income and, 132
Personal deduction, 773
Personal exemption, 773
Personal income (PI), 132
  disposable, 132, 201
  in national income accounting, 126, 132
  relationship to other national income measures, 132
Personal income distribution, 805–806
Personal saving, 132
Peru, 465, 472, 964; underground economy in, 137
Peterson, John, 730n
Peterson, Peter, 238
Phelps, Edmund, 351, 353–355
Philippines, 469, 472
Phillips, A. W. H., 348
Phillips curve, 348–355, 348 (fig.)
  adaptive expectations and, 353–354
  aggregate-supply curve and, 354–355
  macroeconomic policy and, 348–349
  unanticipated inflation and, 351–353
  U.S. experience with, 349–351
Physical capital, 740–745
  investment decision and, 740–745
  roundabout protection and, 740
PI, see Personal income
Pickens, T. Boone, 664
Picketing, 720
Pigou, A.C., 328
Pigou Effect, 328n
"Pittsburgh Plus" system, 617–618
Piven, Frances Fox, 798n
Planned economy, 10
Planned expenditures, see Expenditure(s): planned
Planned investment, see Investment: planned
Planned-investment-demand curve, slope of, 313–314
Planned-socialist economy, 9
Planning, 9–11, 924
  Austrian theory and, 942–943
  under capitalism, 932–936
  in China, 932, 938–940
  in collective economies, 925–926
  freedom and, 924–925
  imperative, 926
  indicative, 927
  in Japan, 932–935
  macroeconomic, 927
  magic wand, 927
  power and, 924–925
  in public sector, 927

under socialism, 937–940
  in Soviet Union, 928–931
  in Sweden, 935–936
  welfare state and, 926
  in Yugoslavia, 937–938
Planning-Programming Budget System (PPBS), 785
Plant capacity, as merger motive, 662
Plant size, effects on long-run average cost, 535
Plotting, 48
Poland, 943
  capitalism in, 15
  economy of, 12
  Solidarity, 938
Polaroid Corp., 343, 952
Policy(ies), see specific policies
Policy autonomy, international macroeconomics and, 427–428
Policy tradeoffs, 3–14
Political factors
  international trade and finance and, 406
  population trends and, 21
  in pure competition, 590
Political instability, inflation and, 152–153
Political pressure, by farmers, 877
Pollution, 135, 919
  economic growth and, 445–446
  see also Environment; Externalities; Market failure
Pollution control, 766–767
Ponzi finance, 470
Pope Paul VI, on birth control, 889–890
Population
  aging of, 446
  inaccuracy of counts of, 887
  size and age distribution of, 20–21
Population growth, agriculture and, 886
Population size, 20–21
  supply of labor and, 680
Populism, 872–873
Positive balance of payments, 427
Positive economics, 46
Positive slope, 48, 49 (fig.)
Post-Keynesian economists, 383–384
Potential entry, see Entry
Potential GNP, 338
  market clearing and, 375
  unexpected changes and, 372
Poverty, 794–805
  antipoverty policies and, 798–799
  compulsory labor, 801
  economic development and, 456–458
  food and, 887–891
  homelessness and panhandling and, 803–805
  islands of, 797–798
  negative income tax and, 799–801
  poverty concepts and poverty lines and, 794–798
  in share economy, 733
  as underclass, 801–803
  War on, 350, 414, 817
Powell, Bill, 787

	Population (millions)			Crude birth rate per thousand population 1987	Life expectancy at birth (years) 1987	Urban population as percentage of total population 1987	GNP per capita[a]		Average annual rate of inflation[a] (percent) 1980–87
	1987	2000[a]	2025[a]				Dollars 1987	Average annual growth rate (percent) 1965–87	
Low-income economies	2,824 t	3,625 t	5,161 t	31 w	61 w	30 w	290 w	3.1 w	8.6 w
Ethiopia	44	66	122	48	47	12	130	0.1	2.6
Bhutan	1	2	3	39	48	5	150	..	..
Chad	5	7	13	44	46	30	150	−2.0	5.3
Zaire	33	49	97	45	52	38	150	−2.4	53.5
Bangladesh	106	144	217	41	51	13	160	0.3	11.1
Malawi	8	12	29	53	46	13	160	1.4	12.4
Nepal	18	24	37	41	51	9	160	0.5	8.8
Lao PDR	4	5	8	42	48	17	170	..	46.5
Mozambique	15	22	42	45	48	23	170	..	26.9
Tanzania	24	37	75	50	53	29	180	−0.4	24.9
Burkina Faso	8	12	23	47	47	8	190	1.6	4.4
Madagascar	11	16	28	46	54	23	210	−1.8	17.4
Mali	8	11	24	51	47	19	210	..	4.2
Burundi	5	7	14	49	49	7	250	1.6	7.5
Zambia	7	11	23	50	53	53	250	−2.1	28.7
Niger	7	10	22	51	45	18	260	−2.2	4.1
Uganda	16	24	46	50	48	10	260	−2.7	95.2
China	1,069	1,269	1,528	21	69	38	290	5.2	4.2
Somalia	6	8	16	49	47	36	290	0.3	37.8
Togo	3	5	9	49	53	24	290	0.0	6.6
India	798	1,010	1,365	32	58	27	300	1.8	7.7
Rwanda	6	10	23	52	49	7	300	1.6	4.5
Sierra Leone	4	5	10	48	41	26	300	0.2	50.0
Benin	4	6	11	48	50	39	310	0.2	8.2
Central African Rep.	3	4	6	43	50	45	330	−0.3	7.9
Kenya	22	37	83	52	58	22	330	1.9	10.3
Sudan	23	33	56	44	50	21	330	−0.5	31.7
Pakistan	102	156	286	47	55	31	350	2.5	7.3
Haiti	6	8	11	34	55	29	360	0.5	7.9
Lesotho	2	2	4	41	56	19	370	4.7	12.3
Nigeria	107	157	286	47	51	33	370	1.1	10.1
Ghana	14	20	35	46	54	32	390	−1.6	48.3
Sri Lanka	16	19	23	23	70	21	400	3.0	11.8
Yemen, PDR	2	3	6	48	51	42	420	..	5.0
Mauritania	2	3	5	48	46	38	440	−0.4	9.8
Indonesia	171	214	279	29	60	27	450	4.5	8.5
Liberia	2	3	6	45	54	42	450	−1.6	1.5
Afghanistan	..	..	..	..	..	..	..	..	..
Burma	39	52	72	32	60	24	..	..	..
Guinea	6	9	16	47	42	24	..	..	..
Kampuchea, Dem.	..	..	..	..	..	..	..	..	..
Viet Nam	65	88	127	34	66	21	..	..	..
Middle-income economies	1,038 t	1,329 t	1,862 t	30 w	65 w	57 w	1,810 w	2.5 w	62.3 w
Senegal	7	10	20	46	48	37	520	−0.6	9.1
Bolivia	7	10	16	43	53	50	580	−0.5	601.8
Zimbabwe	9	13	22	44	58	26	580	0.9	12.4
Philippines	58	74	101	30	63	41	590	1.7	16.7
Yemen Arab Rep.	8	13	23	48	51	23	590	..	11.4
Morocco	23	32	47	35	61	47	610	1.8	7.3
Egypt, Arab Rep.	50	67	99	36	61	48	680	3.5	9.2
Papua New Guinea	4	5	8	39	54	15	700	0.8	4.4
Dominican Rep.	7	9	11	31	66	58	730	2.3	16.3
Côte d'Ivoire	11	18	36	51	52	44	740	1.0	4.4
Honduras	5	7	11	40	64	42	810	0.7	4.9
Nicaragua	4	5	9	41	63	58	830	−2.5	86.6
Thailand	54	65	82	25	64	21	850	3.9	2.8
El Salvador	5	6	10	36	62	44	860	−0.4	16.5
Congo, People's Rep.	2	3	7	47	59	41	870	4.2	1.8
Jamaica	2	3	3	26	74	51	940	−1.5	19.4
Guatemala	8	12	20	41	62	33	950	1.2	12.7
Cameroon	11	16	33	45	56	46	970	3.8	8.1
Paraguay	4	6	9	35	67	46	990	3.4	21.0
Ecuador	10	13	19	33	65	55	1,040	3.2	29.5
Botswana	1	2	2	35	59	21	1,050	8.9	8.4
Tunisia	8	10	14	30	65	54	1,180	3.6	8.2
Turkey	53	67	90	30	64	47	1,210	2.6	37.4
Colombia	29	36	48	26	66	69	1,240	2.7	23.7
Chile	13	15	19	24	72	85	1,310	0.2	20.6